LEGACIES

Fiction • Poetry • Drama • Nonfiction

SECOND EDITION

LEGACIES

Fiction • Poetry • Drama • Nonfiction

SECOND EDITION

Carley Rees Bogarad
SUNY New Paltz

Jan Zlotnik Schmidt
SUNY New Paltz

THOMSON
HEINLE

Australia Canada Mexico Singapore Spain United Kingdom United States

THOMSON
HEINLE

Legacies
Second Edition
Carley Rees Bogarad and Jan Zlotnik Schmidt

Publisher: *Earl McPeek*
Acquisitions Editor: *Bill Hoffman*
Marketing Strategist: *John Meyers*
Developmental Editor: *Michell Phifer*
Project Editor: *Elizabeth Cruce Alvarez*
Art Director: *Susan Journey*
Production Manager: *Lois West*

Cover Image: Giraudon/Art Resource, NY. *The Juggler* by Marc Chagall (1943). © 2001 Artists Rights Society (ARS), New York/ADAGP, Paris

Printed in Canada
3 4 5 6 7 8 9 10   07 06 05 04 03 02

For more information contact Heinle, 25 Thomson Place, Boston, MA 02210 USA, or you can visit our Internet site at http://www.heinle.com

ISBN: 0-1550-6953-5

Library of Congress Catalog Card Number: 2001090200

In Memoriam

Dr. Carley Rees Bogarad

An Inspirational Teacher
and Colleague

PREFACE

Legacies challenges students to enter the world of the new millennium, a culturally diverse place in which peoples' fates are crucially interconnected. It also introduces students to analysis of literature and to critical thinking. The readings—fiction, poetry, drama, and nonfiction—represent complex and exciting traditions from 500 B.C. to the final decade of the twentieth century. They include both global masterpieces and contemporary works from Lao-tzu to Luisa Valenzuela, from Sophocles to Rita Dove, from Rabindranath Tagore to Ernest Hemingway. As a thematic exploration of the individual in social, political, and cultural contexts, *Legacies* engages us in intellectual inquiry and provides the personal pleasures associated with the arts.

By reading and responding to fiction, poetry, drama, and nonfiction, we discover more about ourselves and others; we expand our thinking as conscious human beings. We develop moral imagination so that we can envision the views, experiences, and beliefs of others. Reading and writing about literature involves us in a process of critical analysis no different from the faculties we use in our everyday lives, but the process becomes directed, focused, and intensified. Interpretation of literary works encourages us to question, to observe keenly, to probe, and to critique—habits of mind central to liberal education.

Because we agree with Wittgenstein's statement that "the limits of [our] language mean the limits of [our] world," we have written and edited this textbook with excellence and expansiveness as guiding principles. We have divided the book into three major sections and two appendixes. In Part One, Acts of Interpretation, the first chapter defines types of critical thinking and then connects these ideas to the analysis of literature. Chapter 2 contains a discussion of critical reading and of reader response. Chapter 3 presents the process of writing about literary works and the forms of the essay. Part Two, the Thematic Anthology, features readings organized by genre around five themes that progress from exploration of the self to larger issues: Initiation and Identity, Family, Love, War and Injustice, and The Global Village. We hope that each work will open and illuminate the others in order to inspire dynamic and complex inquiry and insight in every reader. Part Three, Reading and Writing about the Genres, introduces forms and elements of the four genres of fiction, poetry, drama, and nonfiction. The appendixes include a full description of the research process and MLA documentation and an overview of contemporary approaches to literary criticism.

In each anthology chapter of Part Two, an introduction articulates provocative ideas about the theme, selections, and connections among the texts. We intend our comments not as definitive interpretations but as starting points for discussion. The Thematic Previews in the chapters combine works from different genres to offer various possibilities for analysis. Biographical headnotes precede all selections; and exploratory questions, suggestions for essays, and ideas for reader response and formal writing activities follow the texts. Extensive, process-oriented writing assignments appear at the end of each chapter.

New to this edition are:

- Expanded treatment of the critical thinking and reader response process, including more writing activities
- Expanded discussion of the research process, including use and evaluation of online sources
- Addition of more authors from the traditional canon (such as Shakespeare, Nathaniel Hawthorne, and Flannery O'Conner) as well as new pieces by multicultural authors (such as Sherman Alexie, Junot Diaz, and Edwidge Danticat)
- More innovative thematic pairings of selections, including essays that provide contexts for the readings
- Expanded and updated appendix on critical approaches to literature

Legacies engages students in the indivisible activities of reading and writing and enlarges their capacities to develop ideas and to appreciate the richness and depth of responding to literature through the following important features:

- **Emphasis on Critical Thinking and on the Reading and Writing Processes.** Chapters 1 to 3 present numerous examples of student responses, formal writing, and a profile of one student's writing process: notes and initial and final drafts of an essay on Gloria Anzaldúa's "horse."
- **A Wide Variety of Readings from Traditional and Nontraditional Canons.** Selections represent the best of new voices and of classic writers. These diverse readings, which prompt us to consider issues of gender, ethnicity, class, and sexual orientation, embody our heritage, our literary legacies. Note the number of Nobel Prize laureates.
- **Juxtapositions of Readings within Themes.** In each chapter, readings are organized by genre, but they can also be studied by juxtaposing a number of works, according to subtopics of the major theme, gender, new and traditional voices, or regions of the world, to name only a few possibilities. This process leads naturally to contrastive analysis, to questioning, and to examination of issues from multiple perspectives.
- **Thematic Previews: Combining the Genres.** These sets of suggested readings from each genre introduce each anthology chapter and exemplify the principle of juxtaposition. In each preview, the poem may serve, for example, as motivation for discussion; the essay may provide

a framework for analysis; and the fiction and/or drama may play against or complement each other. Together, these works can stimulate a dynamic process of critical inquiry.

- **Extensive Questions for Explorations of the Text.** These questions may be used for individual study, for guided class discussion, for lesson plans, or for collaborative (group) work. The questions begin with issues intrinsic to a given work (both textual and interpretive) and then consider thematic connections with other works. Questions have been field-tested: the number and nature of the exploratory questions represent the suggestions of students in classes.
- **Variety of Writing Activities.** Possibilities for reader response and ideas for writing follow each reading. They provide opportunities for personal reaction, creative expression, practice in various modes of exposition and argument, analysis, and interpretation of literature, and consideration of formal elements of the genres.
- **Sample Student Essays.** Each anthology chapter offers a model student writing, illustrating a different form of the essay about literature, such as thematic analysis, comparison/contrast, critical analysis, explication, and argument.
- **Interesting and Ample Writing Assignments.** At the end of each anthology chapter, many of the assignments require a number of stages that encourage thorough exploration of topics; many others are traditional, and some contain directed research topics.
- **Extensive Treatment of the Forms and Features of Each Genre.** Chapters 9 to 12 feature comprehensive discussions of the genres with lively examples. The models of student writing in each chapter offer a wide range of approaches to all aspects of the reading and writing processes: reader response, explication, critical analysis, and evaluation.
- **Research, MLA Documentation, and Student Essay with Editorial Comments (Appendix A).** This appendix introduces a complete study of the research process and documentation, all major forms of MLA citation, and an example of a student paper with comments. No handbook should be necessary for the research process.
- **Critical Theory (Appendix B).** *Legacies* presents a concise explanation of current approaches to literature and demonstrates these theories through multiple interpretations of Kate Chopin's "The Story of an Hour."
- **Extensive Definitions of Literary Terms.** Definitions of terms appear in the text as well as in the Glossary. Terms are printed in boldface type when they first appear in the text.
- **Comprehensive Instructor's Manual.** Our Instructor's Manual, based on materials tested and developed in the classroom, includes sample syllabi (with readings organized by theme or genre), answers to

the "Explorations of the Text" for each selection, suggested further works and films to complement the readings in each chapter, lesson plans, and a brief bibliography of books helpful to teachers of writing.

Eduardo Galeano suggests that "one writes out of a need to communicate and to commune with others. . . . One assumes that literature transmits knowledge and affects the behavior and language of those who read, thus helping us to know ourselves better and to save ourselves collectively." We hope that this book will prompt readers to "communicate and to commune." In large measure, we have based this volume on what our students have told us that they want to "know." It reflects their choices of texts and presents examples of their thoughts and writing. It is their book, their legacy.

ACKNOWLEDGMENTS

Thanks must go to everyone who contributed to *Legacies*. First, Fiona Paton and John Langan have contributed significantly to the authorship of this volume. Without their research, their writing, and their collaboration, this anthology would not exist. Second, we thank our students for their cooperation and contributions to this project. We also acknowledge colleagues who contributed their insights, suggestions, and proofreading skills. At the State University of New York New Paltz, Donna Baumler-Ceriale, Mark Bellomo, Dorrit Berg, Eudora Chikwendu, Lynne Crockett, Mary Fakler, Barry Henck, Joan Perisse, Rachel Rigolino, Abigail Robin, Jenica Shapiro, Robert Singleton, and Chris Tanis. Professor Thomas G. Olsen was particularly helpful in providing scholarly perspectives and discussion questions on *The Tempest* as well as excerpts from an online discussion from his introductory Shakespeare course.

Colleagues at Berea College, who helped in the research for and production of this manuscript, include Stephanie Browner, Phil English, Libby Faulk Jones, Dorothy Schnare, and Barbara Wade. Particular thanks must go to Luciana Davis, who provided invaluable assistance in the production of the manuscript, and Cassondra Chambers, who created the tear sheets for the volume. At Berea College, the students in Stories, U.S. Traditions, and Introduction to the Arts also provided invaluable feedback that helped in the selection of works for this new edition. At the State University of New York New Paltz, thanks also must go to students in the Composition Program who also commented insightfully on readings in the first edition of the anthology. In addition, the teaching assistants in the graduate program in the English department provided invaluable comments and suggestions. Finally, and most importantly, Harold A. Zlotnik—a consummate teacher, poet, and mentor—contributed his insights, proofreading and editing skills, and research on and writing activities for *The Tempest*. He provides a model of excellence in teaching that continues to inspire.

For her work on *Legacies*, for her commitment and dedication to this project, Vika Shock deserves extraordinary praise. This volume could not have come to fruition without her dedicated efforts.

We also are grateful for the many productive suggestions and comments from the following reviewers, though, of course, any remaining shortcomings of the volume are our responsibility alone: Sue Beebe, Southwest Texas State University; Doritt Berg, SUNY New Paltz; Jennie Dauterman, Miami University of Ohio; Ren Draya, Blackburn College; Mary Fakler, SUNY New Paltz; William Foster, Naugatuck Valley Community College; Charles Garard, Morris Brown College; Kip Hartvigson, Ricks College; William Lawlor, University of Wisconsin–Steven's Point; Jeremy Mach, Morton College; Corinne Miller, Miami University of Ohio; Zack Miller, Brookhaven Community College; Bob Mundhenk, Northampton Community College; Sean Nighbert, Southwest Texas State University; Joan Perisse, SUNY New Paltz: Lillian Ruiz, Greenfield Community College; Tija Spitsberg, University of Michigan; Andrew Tomko, Bergen Community College; Nancy Trautmann, Northampton Community College; Fred van Hartesveldt, Grand Rapids Community College; and John Venne, Ball State University.

We also thank Bill Hoffman, our acquisitions editor at Harcourt, for believing in this book, and Michell Phifer, an excellent developmental editor. Also of Harcourt we thank Beth Alvarez, project editor, Susan Journey, art director, and Lois West, production manager.

Finally, we acknowledge friends and family who contributed their suggestions, insights, proofreading skills, and most importantly, their support: Barbara and Michael Adams, Arthur Cash, Pam Corley, Jane Di Teresa, Judith Dorney, Phyllis R. Freeman, Mary Gordon, Daniel Kempton, Carole Levin, Maria Lichtmann, Patricia Phillips, Peggy Rivage-Seul, Deborah Roth, H. R. Stoneback, Keila and John Thomas, Pauline Uchmanowicz, and Robert and Katherine Waugh. Most of all, we thank our families—Leonard and Cynthia Bogarad; Catherine and Julie Banks; Marilyn Zlotnik, Peter Hultberg, Samantha and Gabriel; Adrienne and George Todd, Jared, Dylan, and Mechelle; Gayle, Segev, and Yotam Guistizia; Philip and Reed Schmidt; and Mae and Harold Zlotnik—for their unending encouragement and unwavering love. They have been our best readers. We dedicate this book to them and to our students.

BRIEF CONTENTS

CONTENTS

ALTERNATE CONTENTS

Fiction

Poetry

Drama

Nonfiction

Part One

Acts of Interpretation

CHAPTER 1

Critical Thinking and Critical Analysis of Literature

THE CRITICAL THINKING PROCESS

As human beings, we constantly seek meaning from and impose meaning upon experience. In our desire to comprehend, we reflect on our perceptions, feelings, experiences, and ideas; and, in the process, we create interpretations of our world. We consider critical thinking, then, to be these capacities to observe, to respond, to reflect, and to create patterns of meaning.

THE CRITICAL THINKING/CRITICAL READING CONNECTION

The acts by which we create meaning in daily life and the acts by which we read, write, and analyze literature and nonfiction are similar, although they take different forms. In critical analysis of literature, certain aspects of the thinking process that we use in daily life are heightened and intensified—analysis, interpretation, evaluation, and judgment. We observe and ask ourselves about the meaning and the effect of the words on the page. We look beneath the surface of the words to find implied meanings. We consider the ideas that are implicit in the words. In this process we ask ourselves the following questions:

1. What is stated?
2. What exists beyond the surface level? (What is implied?)
3. What information do we need to make inferences?
4. What are our biases? How does our perspective shape our view?
5. What conclusions do we form as to meaning?

We form conclusions about our inferences and develop patterns of meaning. These patterns of meaning constitute interpretations of a work.

We read a work to explore and to examine meaning—our interpretations of the work. We may ask how we respond to the world of the reading. For example, if we are reacting to a short story, we may analyze our responses to setting, to character, and to the plot; and we may ask ourselves if we are involved in the world of the reading; if the characters' experiences resonate with our own; if we come to realizations as a result of our reading; if our own experiences are illumined by the ideas represented in the literary work; or if we come to comprehend another world, culture, or time in history. We assess the impact of the work upon our inner lives and determine if the author's vision is going to enlarge or to change our views of self and of the world.

We also read to discern if the ideas presented in a work are of value. We evaluate the language of the text, assess words for evidence of a writer's bias and assumptions, and draw conclusions about a writer's attitude toward his or her subject and his or her beliefs. We may compare the author's stance with our own beliefs. We may criticize, argue with, and debate the meanings and views of a text—accept or reject its ideas and embrace or disdain its author's point of view.

We also may judge the language to determine its worth. If the text is an argument, we may ask if the writer is persuasive. If it is a descriptive piece, we may examine our involvement in the world of the reading. If it is a political speech, we may ask how the politician wants us to respond. We may wonder if we are being manipulated by the words of the speech; we may analyze the slant of the speaker, the use of evidence, and the logic of the approach. To determine the effectiveness of a literary work, we may focus intensively on a study of language and explore the effects of words: the **denotations** (dictionary definitions) and **connotations** (associations, suggested and implied meanings) of the words; the author's **tone** (attitude) and **point of view** (perspective) toward his or her subject; the **structure** (organization) of the work; **style** (detail, imagery, word choice); and the nature of the themes presented. Finally, we may ask ourselves if the work seems effective and worthwhile and determine its merits according to our standards of judgment.

Consider students' responses during a class discussion of Lorna Dee Cervantes's poem "Refugee Ship" as an illustration of the critical thinking/critical reading connection.

Refugee Ship

like wet cornstarch
I slide past mi abuelita's[1] eyes
bible placed by her side
she removes her glasses
the pudding thickens

mama raised me with no language
I am an orphan to my spanish name
the words are foreign, stumbling on my tongue
I stare at my reflection in the mirror
brown skin, black hair

I feel I am a captive
aboard the refugee ship
a ship that will never dock
a ship that will never dock

Lorna Dee Cervantes

[1] **mi abuelita's eyes:** my grandmother's eyes

First the students reacted to the title and stated that the poem made them feel sad and that it invoked comparisons with the plight of the Vietnamese, with the predicament of other immigrant groups who came earlier to the United States, and with the tragedy of the Haitian and Chinese boat people. As they pondered the significance of the title in relation to the story of a grandmother and a granddaughter, they expressed feelings, discovered personal associations, and asked questions about the text. They also realized that they needed to step back, to cast their personal associations aside, and to develop an interpretation of the work that focused on the relationship of the grandmother and her granddaughter and the speaker's connection to her heritage. They gathered information from the poem and focused first on understanding the grandmother's character through analyzing the objects associated with her: "glasses," "bible," and her gesture of taking off her spectacles. They concluded that she was a traditional Latina grandmother, unable to understand the speaker, her granddaughter. Some descriptive details (the images of "cornstarch" and "pudding [that] thickens") puzzled them. They wondered, "What is 'like wet cornstarch'?"; "What does the image have to do with the portrayal of the granddaughter?"; "What is the speaker like?" "Why is she described as an 'orphan' and as a 'captive'?" They began by making observations, and then they started analyzing the stated and implied meanings of the words and images of the poem.

The students concluded that the grandmother and granddaughter exist in separate worlds. The granddaughter, the speaker, cannot communicate with her grandmother because the latter cannot speak or understand English. The persona (the speaker in the poem) has learned "no language"; she has not learned Spanish and, therefore, she finds herself with "words [that] are foreign, stumbling on [her] tongue," her Spanish heritage lost. The granddaughter yearns to know Spanish, to communicate with her grandmother, and to learn more about her people. As the students began deciphering the meaning of the words and images, they realized that "wet cornstarch" is a necessary ingredient that "thick[ens]" a pudding; and that the "pudding" then suggests the emotional distance between grandmother and granddaughter, a distance that the speaker cannot dissolve or resolve. As the students formed interpretations about the meaning of the work, they also realized that the speaker feels as if she lives like a "captive" on a "refugee ship/a ship that will never dock." One student exclaimed, "The movement of the ship—anxiety—never to be able to dock, to find stability, to understand her roots, to have a home"; and another reflected, "The repetition of the last line adds emphasis and sadness." Finally, a student concluded, "Both people are lost, not at home in America, and lost to each other."

The class discussion dynamically progressed from observation to selection of details, to analysis of language, to interpretation, and to judgment. The students moved beyond their first impressions of the work and discovered multiple layers of implied meanings. They also evaluated the work and determined that each word, phrase, and image evoked vivid and significant ideas. A deceptively simple poem presented a compelling vision of loss of heritage, language, and connection with one's past.

CRITICAL ANALYSIS OF LITERATURE: A CLASSROOM EXPERIENCE

Examine this more expansive model of the critical reading process that emerged during a class discussion of Theodore Roethke's "My Papa's Waltz."

My Papa's Waltz

The whiskey on your breath
Could make a small boy dizzy;
But I hung on like death:
Such waltzing was not easy.

We romped until the pans
Slid from the kitchen shelf;
My mother's countenance
Could not unfrown itself.

The hand that held my wrist
Was battered on one knuckle;
At every step you missed
My right ear scraped a buckle.

You beat time on my head
With a palm caked hard by dirt,
Then waltzed me off to bed
Still clinging to your shirt.

The teacher asked students to record their initial responses to the poem in the form of a cluster that she put on the board:

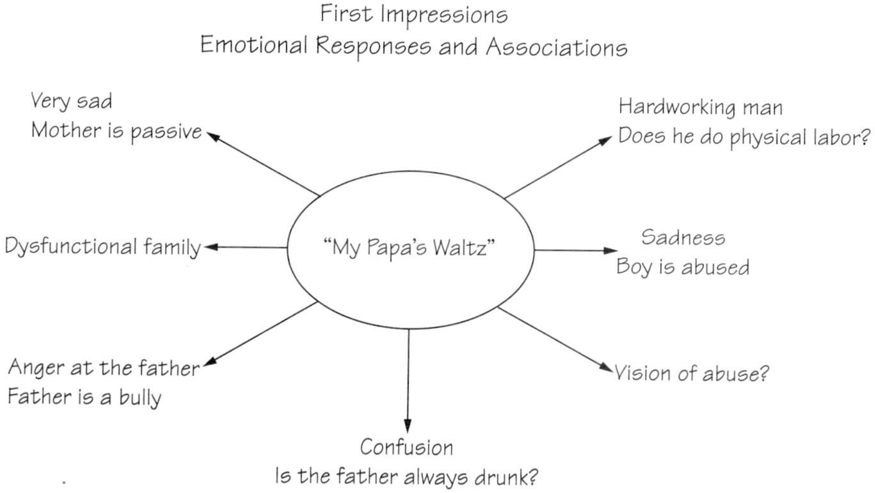

Next she had students focus on key words and questions and group their observations into patterns of meaning. The students asked, for example, whether the waltz suggested a moment of closeness, albeit tainted, between father and son or a relationship between an abusive parent and child. Witness the next cluster that they formed and their list of several patterns of meaning.

<u>The basic facts</u>: Drunken father, a dance between father and child
Scene: The kitchen—The dance creates a mess—pans fall down
Fun or Frenzy?

Patterns of Meaning/Questions and Interpretations

- Is the boy hoping that the dance will never end? (Is it a moment of closeness, or is the boy clinging to an abusive father?)
- Why is the "waltzing . . . not easy"? Is the boy struggling to hold on, afraid to let go, or is he "clinging" affectionately to a staggering father?
- Is the father too drunk to notice that he is wounding his child?
- Is the father deliberately abusing his son or is he drunk and careless, carried away by the moment of dancing? Is he happy dancing with his son?
- Is he actually "waltzing" or does the dance imply both the predictable pattern of the relationship and the father's unpredictable treatment of his child?
- Does the child predictably return to the same parent for punishment or affection?
- What is the source of the mother's anger? Is the mother frowning because her husband is creating a ruckus and keeping her son up too long? Or because he is abusive and she can't stop him? Is there a distance between mother and father?

The class in the process of analyzing the poem for meaning also noted these effective poetic techniques:

- The rhythm, rhyme, and four-line stanzas are unobtrusive and fit the waltzing motif.
- The images of the dance are powerful.
- The perspective of the child works.

Finally, the class formed interpretations of the poem. The class was divided in its analysis of the meaning of the work. Some students believed that the speaker was presenting a moment between an alcoholic father who was negligent and careless but who loved his child. This group of students thought that the poem depicts a moment of bonding between father and son, represented in the boy's "clinging" to the father's shirt as he was danced "off to bed." However, the other group of students determined that the father was abusive. They pointed to the images of cruelty in the poem: The boy's ear "scraped a buckle"; The father was "beat[ing] time on [the boy's] head" while the boy "hung on like death." Both groups examined the work carefully, dissecting word and image, constructing patterns of meaning and interpretations. "Who was right?" they asked. The teacher assured students that several interpretations of a work were valid as long as they returned to the text to test their evolving interpretation and to find evidence to support their ideas. At this point she also suggested the possibility of doing biographical research or of reading criticism of the work. Although biographical information may be misleading, it also may illuminate a writer's choices: a portrayal of a character's dilemma, a plot element, or a symbolic motif. It is important to realize, the teacher suggested, that his poem is based on Roethke's memory of a "dance" with his father, that the poet's father was a florist and owned a greenhouse (hence, "the palm caked hard by dirt"), and, therefore, that the ambiguities in the poem may reflect the ambivalent response of a son to a father and the fuzziness of memory.

As the students examined their responses to "My Papa's Waltz," they began to understand the various processes involved in critical reading. Many of the analyses and evaluations they agreed upon. Then they uncovered disagreements. Ultimately, they decided that the poem had multiple layers of meaning and that they could entertain several points of view at once as they tested their conclusions against the words on the page, the words of others in the class and critical sources. They learned that class discussion, dialogue, and research enhanced the critical reading process. Finally, in the course of discussion, they also discovered the wholeness of the process. In reading any text, we do not separate modes of feeling and thinking, but simultaneously engage in many critical acts of interpretation. We react, remember, associate, observe, infer from information, form conclusions, analyze, interpret, evaluate, and judge. These processes lead to a deepened appreciation of the phenomena and texts of our world.

CHAPTER 2

The Reading Process

READER RESPONSE

To be frank, not every reading experience becomes a full, rich, interpretation of a text. Many times we read simply to garner information, as when we survey road signs, food labels, or sets of instructions. We may read newspapers, letters, and textbooks in our college classes; and the main aim may be solely to summarize information. At other times, we may wish to read a book on a level approaching pure emotional response and appreciation. Often, while we read, our minds are wandering, not concentrating on the work. However, the process of critical reading that we wish to emphasize is one in which the reader is fully involved, responding on many levels of feeling and thinking. We do not simply scan words on a page; we form emotional reactions, gather information, construct patterns of meaning, analyze, interpret, and evaluate a work to determine its effectiveness and its worth.

THE READING/WRITING CONNECTION

Writing helps develop the reading process and keeps it active and critical. The following are some procedures for reading and reacting to a text, called *reader response strategies,* all of which involve writing. These procedures include *glossing* and *annotating, brainstorming* and *questioning, freewriting, journal writing, notetaking,* and *"think" writings.*

Glossing and Annotating

Examine a series of reader responses written by students about Gloria Anzaldúa's poem, "horse," from her autobiography, *Borderlands: La Frontera—The New Mestiza.* You may react to this poem in many ways. Reading theorists suggest that you first preview the work by looking at the title and by scanning the poem to gain an overview of it. Then read the passage again to learn content and to write notes about your reactions to the text. This process is called *glossing* and *annotating.* When you gloss a work, you read it to understand content; and you take notes, called *annotations,* as you read. You may make comments in the margins, underline the title and key words, and record reactions or questions. You create a map of the reading so that you know its structure and key points. You also discover your own questions, reactions, and initial responses. After you have completed your marginal annotations, you might make *end comments* that include the key ideas and describe the impact of the work on you. Analyze this annotation and end comment for "horse":

Why the title?
Why small letters?

horse

(para la gente de Hargill, Texas[1])

Is this a true story? What does the dedication mean?

Horse is free, powerful.

Look at ing verbs: power-action

Great horse running in the fields
come thundering toward
the outstretched hands
nostrils flaring at the corn
only it was knives in the hidden hands
can a horse smell tempered steel?

*Shift to death and destruction

Key: hobbled crippled horse

Anoche[2] some kids cut up a horse
it was night and the pueblo[3] slept
the Mexicans mutter among themselves:
they hobbled the two front legs
the two hind legs, kids aged sixteen
but they're gringos
and the sheriff won't do a thing
he's just say boys will be boys
just following their instincts.

Contrast Spanish words vs. anglos
Spanish gringo

Mexican World
Narrative form
Build up of story

Horse— ← Soul of people

Horse— symbol of Mexican identity

Mexican people?

But it's the mind that kills
the animal the mexicanos murmur
killing it would have been a mercy
black horse running in the dark
came thundering toward
the outstretched hands
nostrils flaring at the smell
only it was knives in the hidden hands
did it pray all night for morning?

Repetition— Contrast
Power of horse vs. crippling

It was the owner came running
30.30 in his hand
put the caballo[4] out of its pain
the Chicanos shake their heads
turn away some rich father
fished out his wallet

A Mexican must put horse out or pain. Mexican people go home to die.

---

[1] **para la gente de Hargill, Texas:** for the people of Hargill, Texas.

[2] **Anoche:** last night.

[3] **pueblo:** town or village.

[4] **caballo:** horse.

held out the folds of green
as if green could staunch red
pools dripping from the ribbons
on the horse's flanks
could cast up testicles
grow back the ears on the horse's head
no ears of corn but sheaths
hiding blades of steel
earth drinking blood sun rusting it
in that small Texas town
the mexicanos shuffle their feet
shut their faces stare at the ground.

Strong images of blood. Graphic. Is the horse castrated?

What does the corn symbolize?

Boys "get off." Money is power.

Corn—symbol of sustenance, replaced by knives, death. Opposition.

Dead horse neighing in the night
come thundering toward the open faces
hooves iron-shod hurling lightning
only it is red red in the moonlight
in their sleep the gringos cry out
the mexicanos mumble if you're Mexican
you are born old.

Why are hooves hurling lightning? Is it anger at racism?

Repetition of color

Gringos cry out—why?

Cycle of racism?

End Comment: Does this poem use a true story of boys crippling and mutilating a horse to suggest the pain and suffering of Mexicans in Texas facing prejudice and racism?

Brainstorming and Questioning

Another notetaking process is *brainstorming,* a process in which you write down ideas and comments in any order without attention to sequence, logic, or sentence structure. Register as many of your reactions as you can as your mind "storms" through a work. Jot single words or phrases without worrying about creating coherent, grammatical sentences and without worrying about organization and development. This technique allows you to sketch the range of your responses; later you can select certain ideas to compose your essay. One focused form of brainstorming is generating a list of questions concerning the work. You may use the reporter's questions (Who? What? When? Where? Why? How?) to trigger your explorations. Examine Mark Greenberg's brainstorming exercise for "horse":

Who is the "great horse"? Symbol?
Who is the speaker?
Who has the knives?
Why are they hidden?
Why did they do it?
The sheriff is hateful.

How can he use such lame excuses—"boys will be boys?" I'm a man, and I would never participate in such a terrible act.
Why does the father cover for the son? My dad would kill me.
The dead horse can thunder, can hurl lightning?
Is this the poet's retelling of the story? Autobiographical?
The horse, in many images, has many meanings.
Social tensions—inequalities between gringos and Mexicans.
Finally something about race relations.
A true story?

In his exercise, Greenberg's questions focus on the events of the poem, on the cruelty, and on his reactions to the sheriff who excuses and to the father who covers for the barbaric actions of the "boys." His responses direct Greenberg to the beginning of an interpretation: a poem about "inequalities between gringos and Mexicans" and "race relations."

Freewriting

Another method to express your responses, reactions, questions, associations, and analysis of the work is to freewrite immediately after you finish reading. *Freewriting* is a process in which you give yourself a certain amount of time, say, five minutes, to compose sentences without stopping and without censoring your thoughts. Write without stopping, without worrying, and without rereading—just keep going. Do not worry about grammar, spelling, punctuation, or meaning. Freewriting is a way to unleash ideas, to discover your own responses and ideas. It is a way to bypass the part of the writer's self who is the editor and critic, that part of the self that blocks and censors the process of discovery. Often it is helpful not only to freewrite immediately after a first reading, but also to freewrite after several readings. You can compose a first sample, then isolate one idea from that work, and draft another version based on that idea. This second activity is called *focused freewriting*. You may create a series of freewritings that prompt you to discover your full reactions and to develop your thoughts into an essay.

Here are two examples of freewriting about "horse":

horse
Frances Gonzalez

The poem presents a powerful set of contrasts between the soul of the Mexican people and what happens to people when there is racism. The horse is powerful, black, free. The "thundering" gives a feeling of strength and force. Then the horse is "hobbled"; racism cripples. The black horse "running" "thundering" is contrasted with the impotence of the powerlessness of the Mexicans who "mumble" "shake their heads" "shuffle" "stare at the ground" and "mumble." They seem weak, yet there is some hope. For the "dead horse" in the night "comes thundering" "hurling lightning"—that "lightning" is "red red."

Does that mean that the Mexicans will rebel against injustice—that eventually justice will be done? Is the poet "hurling lightning" hoping to cry out—hoping her words will be heard that people will learn and speak "from the mind" in a different way? Not a way that kills?

horse
Julie Miller

I love the feeling of freedom at the beginning of the poem. There are such powerful images of the horse—running, "thundering"—"nostrils flaring." The horse is powerful and alive—then I knew danger was coming in the image of the knives. Why did the boys cut up the horse? Why would anyone do anything that senseless? I thought that it was so brutal and cruel that the horse was mutilated. It was hard to read. What did the horse symbolize? Did it symbolize the Mexicans? The "gringos" just think nothing of cutting up the horse. In the same way the white world in Texas is stopping Mexicans from having opportunities. The poem is asking people to feel the way the Mexicans are treated unfairly. The way they are being oppressed. The white world wins—The "rich father" pays off the owner. The boys aren't punished. The gringos have power. I understand the lines "if you're Mexican/you are born old." You are born with the knowledge of prejudice. This poem makes a powerful plea for understanding injustice.

Journal Writing

You may chart your reading responses by keeping a journal: an informal record of your thoughts and impressions. Your instructor already may have asked you to write a personal journal. A *reader response journal* provides an opportunity for you to write informally about the works that you read and encourages an expansion of the process of personal writing. The methods previously discussed are appropriate for a reader response journal in which you may include glosses and annotations (if you include the works), brainstorming notes and questions, freewrites, and responses to texts. In your reader response journal, you may write significant ideas and quotations. You may focus on any one of the following subjects:

Explication, analyses (explanations of the works)

Personal response (feelings-reactions to the works)

Likes/dislikes

Associations with other characters, other works, other readings, themes, issues, current events, materials in other classes

Associations with events in your life

Responses to characters

Responses to key events

Responses to key passages or to quotations

Responses to issues presented (social, political)

Judgments of characters

Arguments with the writer, with key ideas, with characters' views

Arguments with positions presented in class discussion

Creative writing (stories, poems, plays)

Imitations of style

Monologues in the voices of characters

Again, as in freewriting, you need not worry about grammar, punctuation, spelling, or logical presentation of subject matter. Follow your own responses, ideas, and questions; and let them take over. A journal entry, however, may be more developed and more structured than a freewrite. You may be asked to revise your reactions as developed paragraphs. Your journal may become the source of ideas for essays. In your journal, you may have a record not only of your reading responses, but also of your emotional and intellectual development.

In this entry about "horse," Mark Greenberg summarizes information, reacts to descriptive language, begins to respond to details in the poem, and ends with his feelings about the message of the work.

horse

The black horse "thundered" toward the boys because they beckoned it. How could they summon a "great horse," the Mexican, only to cut it to pieces with knives, knives hidden in their hands? They tortured the animal because they believed that they had a right to do so. The "red red" blood, the flaying, excited them. They expected their fathers to pay for their cruelty and the owner of the horse to kill it—to finish their game. They exercised rights which they believed came with the color of their skin, with their social and economic positions. Little did they know that the dark horse would invade their dreams and make them "cry out," the dead horse—"red red"—"hurling lightning" through their dreams forever.

Notetaking and the Double-Entry Notebook

Another method of becoming an active reader is to keep a *double-entry notebook,* a form of notetaking adapted from theorist Ann Berthoff, who contends that writing and reading processes involve us in continually "interpreting our interpretations." Berthoff suggests that readers sometimes recognize only one level of reaction to a text—summary of main information—and neglect other levels of thinking provoked by the words: reactions, associations, questionings, analysis, synthesis, and theorizing. The double-entry notebook, or *dialectical notebook* as Berthoff calls it, prompts readers to be aware of all acts of interpretation and creates what Berthoff calls "the continuing audit of meaning." The journal entries provide readers with records of what they think about their own thinking.

For a double-entry notebook, we recommend that you write on the left-hand page of a notebook the facts, key points, and main information from a work. On the right-hand page, write all of your other responses, feelings, associations, questions, comparisons with other ideas, and interpretations. The notes need to be recorded as the reading takes place so that you capture your mind in action. Alternate from the left-hand page to the right-hand page. Keep writing back and forth from fact to reaction, analysis, questions, and comments. The double-entry notebook results in a more complete response to a work. You are, therefore, much better prepared to write an essay about the text.

Examine the beginning and the conclusion of Mark Greenberg's double-entry notebook concerning "horse":

horse
Gloria Anzaldúa

Title "horse"	Symbolic. Why no caps?
para la gente de Hargill	I don't know Spanish, but I can guess that the words mean—"For the people of Hargill." Why does she dedicate the poem? Is it a true story?
Great horse running thundering nostrils flaring	The horse is powerful, beautiful, expectant. Progressives add power and action. Good parallel constructions.
Knives in hidden hands	Why offer corn and hide knives? Who?
Question about smelling steel	Rhetorical? Good sounds. Does steel have a smell?
"Anoche"	"Night"? "Last night"? "The night before"? "At night"?
The Mexicans slept, and boys cut up a horse	The straight story. Incredible cruelty. A narrative poem.
The Mexicans "mutter"	They cannot protest aloud.
The "gringos" hobbled the legs	How did they conceive of such cruelty? The horse is like the Mexicans—hobbled.
Sheriff "boys will be boys" following instincts	The law does not apply to gringos. What is wrong with us? This racism is blatant.
It's the mind that kills the animal	This statement is like a thesis sentence. It clearly emphasizes the situation of the Mexicans.

Mexicans "murmur"	Again, they cannot speak loudly.
Killing would have been mercy	These boys feel no sadness, have no mercy. The suffering seems unbearable. The writer must want me to feel this pain.
Repetition of images and event black horse thundering outstretched hands flaring nostrils corn—knives	Now that I know about the knives, the repetition is incredibly effective. The horse represents everything and everyone who was ever destroyed by promises of kindness and who was nurtured only to be conquered, tortured, or killed. This poem is difficult to read, to face, and to accept. The horse symbolizes the Mexicans.

❋ ❋ ❋

Dead horse neighing in night thundering hooves "iron-shod" hurling lightning	Paradox—unravels in dreams Retribution for the knives.
"red red in moonlight"	The horse has turned red, transformation. Blood, anger, revenge?
"gringos" "cry out"	The horse enters their dreams; they are not absolved; they have not triumphed. They have received a life sentence of nightmares.
The Mexicanos "mumble" "If you're Mexican/you are born old."	They do not speak. They are not empowered by the horse which hurls lightning. They are born old in a corrupt and oppressive environment. I want racism to disappear. I want a world which includes everyone. I want it now.

Note the writer's questions, analysis of the portrait and the symbolism of the horse, and inferences about the knife and the central action of the poem. Notice also the judgments about the boys' behavior and about the effectiveness of the verbs and images. The double-entry exercise prompted the writer to engage in all aspects of critical thinking and analysis.

"Think" Writings

Your instructor may assign as homework informal paragraphs or mini-essays with designated topics or questions that relate to the readings. Some instructors prefer not to incorporate freewriting or journals in a course because they think that these forms of writing are too subjective and unstructured and will not necessarily provoke in-depth analysis of works. They concentrate, instead, on more objective and formal modes of response to the assigned works. These "think" writings, however, like the more personal forms of reaction, prompt you to explore your responses to a literary work, direct your thinking, prepare you for participating in class discussion and for writing the essay about literature, and stimulate analysis and reflection. The questions may focus on a particular issue or theme of the work or a specific literary technique (for example, the symbolism in "horse"). Your instructor may collect these writings on a weekly or monthly basis or may ask you to select several of them as part of a writing portfolio. In addition, your instructor may ask you to frame these "think" questions yourself, to become a class discussion leader, and to present these topics as the opening to class discussion or as the basis of collaborative work. Finally, your instructor may ask you to participate in an online discussion group and to respond to "think" questions as part of your work in the course. (See chapter 8 for an example of an online dialogue in response to a question about *The Tempest.*)

Possibilities for "think" writing topics include the following:

First and final impressions of a work

In-depth analysis of a key passage

Treatment of a literary technique

Selection and response to a quotation

Focus on a particular theme

Debate with a position suggested by a reading

Letter to an author or to a character

Note Esther Martinez's short paragraph written in response to this "think" question: "What does the poem suggest about the American dream?" Note how she connects the horse with the identity of Mexican Americans and then compares the mutilation of the horse with the destruction of the American dream for Mexican Americans.

This is a poem about racism. Whites against Mexicans. There are a lot of ways that the poet shows the "inferiority" of the Mexicans. "horse" is not capitalized. Although the horse is a powerful, passionate animal, "thundering," "nostrils flaring," the horse is treated as inferior. The description of the kids hacking away at the horse symbolizes the Mexicans being beaten down, harassed. The castration symbolizes the Mexicans' shame. Their culture, way of life, traditions are seen as less special, their lifestyle as inferior. Is it *wrong just because gringos say it's wrong? Are they not entitled to opportunity? What happens to their dreams for themselves, for their lives?*

Critical analysis requires your active involvement in the process. These forms of reader response—glossing, annotating, brainstorming and questioning, freewriting, journal writing, keeping a double-entry notebook, and "think" writings—will help you become a more involved reader and lead to richer, fuller, more complex interpretations and judgments of literary works.

SOME FINAL CONSIDERATIONS ABOUT THE READING PROCESS

These methods of reader response enable us to discover ideas and to unpeel the layers of our reactions to a work. They also validate our approaches to literature. They remind us that the reading process is both objective and subjective—objective, because we interpret verifiable texts; subjective, because we are unique in our reactions to those texts. We create meanings as a result of our own perspectives, gender, ethnic and class backgrounds, cultural contexts, personalities, and values. Reading is an interactive process. The writer, who has a particular perspective, personality, and background and who is part of a particular culture at a specific time in history, creates a work and invests it with a set of meanings. The reader, who, likewise, is a product of individual traits and cultural influences at a particular point in history, brings ideas and values to the work and derives meaning from the work. The text acts on the reader; the reader creates a particular version (interpretation) of the text.

Certain aspects of literature, however, may be more widely comprehended. *Hamlet's famous soliloquy* generally may be understood as an exploration of questions concerning suicide. "Do Not Go Gentle into That Good Night" by Dylan Thomas generally will be considered a meditation on mortality. Yet each period's writers, each culture's writers, reinterpret these objective judgments, guided by emotional, personal, and social concerns. Each literary work, then, represents both a moment in history and in culture and a moment in an individual reader's and writer's life.

Would Harriet Beecher Stowe have written her antislavery novel, *Uncle Tom's Cabin,* if she had not been the daughter of an abolitionist minister, if she had not been driven by moral outrage and financial need, if she had not known the patterns of slave narratives, if she had not herself seen a place where runaway slaves had crossed the Ohio River to freedom? In each century, readers interpret Stowe's fiction differently. During her lifetime, readers in New England were moved by her novel to struggle to abolish slavery; her book was a bestseller. However, some present readers criticize her sentimentality and her depiction of the black slave.

Interpretations will vary, but some analyses of a work seem more valid than others. To justify our interpretations, we return continually to the work as the primary source, and we share our views with others in a community of readers in order to discuss and to compare ideas. In dialogue with others, we may critique; and we may change our ideas and impressions. We may agree with an interpretation that differs from our original conclusion. We can enlarge our understanding of a work as we engage in the cyclic activities required by thinking, reading, and writing. Through these processes, which are *recursive,* to which we continuously return, we develop new perspectives on a work. For example, we may reread "Refugee Ship" and suddenly decide to study the poem from the point of view of the grandmother who cannot understand her granddaughter. The "glasses," the "bible," and the "pudding" assume new connotations as we shift attention from the speaker to the situation of another character in the work. In the process, we recognize that critical reading activities lead to a more comprehensive understanding of literature.

CHAPTER 3

The Writing Process: Writing the Essay about Literature

When you approach the task of writing about literature, you may worry that you will not understand the text, that you will miss its hidden messages, and that you will not give the responses the instructor expects. You might believe that you have nothing to say. Such anxieties are natural—and groundless. Keep in mind that writing essays about literature evolves from the processes of critical thinking and reader response described in chapters 1 and 2. These multifaceted activities provide no right or wrong answers.

You will not be asked to write compositions that pose correct answers, although you will be expected to provide thoughtful interpretations supported by careful reading of a work. As you learn to trust your own thinking, you also will learn to trust your own acts of interpretation. Remember that you have valuable insights to contribute and that you will have opportunities to question, to test ideas with your peers and instructor, and to construct more developed interpretations that confirm, deny, or expand your initial views of a work.

INTERRELATED STAGES OF WRITING

Writing essays about literature follows directly from procedures for reader response. You should realize, however, that an essay is not composed in a short burst of reader reaction or in moments of brilliant creative insights. Rather, the best essays result from many, many hours of thinking; and they take shape on paper in interrelated stages that include the following:

1. **Prewriting:** Discovering and planning ideas for writing.
2. **Shaping:** Organizing, outlining, and structuring ideas with an audience in mind.
3. **Drafting:** Composing and concentrating on organization, development, and fluency.
4. **Revising and Editing:** Sharpening wording, sentence structure, and style; rearranging, deleting, and clarifying; checking for sentence variety and correct usage.
5. **Proofreading:** Correcting grammar, spelling, and punctuation.

These stages do not always occur in this sequential order; they vary from person to person and from writing task to writing task. Some people draft, edit, and proofread as they work. Others quickly write a first draft and check spelling, grammar, and punctuation later. Different writing situations dictate different processes: a laboratory report, a meditative essay, a journal, and a research paper all require distinct approaches to writing. Whatever your task, you will probably engage in many of these activities before you submit the final version of your essay. Consider each of these stages in detail.

Prewriting

Prewriting, the first stage of the process, takes place even before beginning a first draft and involves finding ideas for composing. As you prewrite, you discover subject matter, approach, and **point of view** (attitude to the subject matter). Various prewriting strategies include these techniques—annotating, brainstorming, taking notes, listing, freewriting, clustering, mapping, and journal writing—and talking with others. You also will select the form of your essay: think about the requirements of your assignment (page length and designated rhetorical mode—exposition, argument, research—for example). Then consider the purpose of your assignment, your main goal in writing. Some central purposes for writing are the following: to express yourself, to inform, to argue, or to create a literary work. You will begin to define your audience. In writing about literary subjects, you may assume that your audience is your instructor and your classmates—people who are familiar with the works that you discuss. Your instructor may designate such different audiences for your material as the campus newspaper or some group interested in the subject. Considerations of point of view, purpose, and audience constitute the **rhetorical situation** of a writing.

Shaping

The second stage of the writing process involves clear definition of focus, point of view, tone, tentative **thesis** (main idea), and topics for discussion. In terms of point of view and tone, you need to decide how you want your essay to sound to the reader. Will you write formally or informally? Will you sound sympathetic, involved, or angry? Will you be lyrical, meditative, or persuasive? These decisions fall into place as you determine your thesis, topics, method of organization, and relationship to audience. At this point, you assess your audience, determine the direction of thesis and topics, and develop and shape supporting evidence with your audience in mind. Then you map ideas, plan your writing, and create informal or formal outlines.

Drafting

The third stage of the writing process is drafting. In creating versions of essays, you still consider not only purpose, requirements of the assignment, and audience, but also development and organization. You may recast your thesis, alter points, delete and add supporting information (quotations, facts, and specific paraphrased examples from the text), and sharpen language.

Revising and Editing

The fourth stage of the writing process involves revising and editing your essay. Consider your relationship with your audience, and ask yourself if you have organized and developed points with a particular audience in mind. Ask yourself if your tone and point of view are appropriate, if they are likely to interest your readers, and if they are convincing and strong. Examine your introduction to determine if it will capture your readers' attention and establish your purpose and thesis. Determine whether you have sufficiently developed your thesis and supporting points. Evaluate your conclusion and decide if it conveys the proper emphasis. Rewriting sometimes requires reviewing ideas and clarifying points—perhaps, even rethinking the entire piece—but it also involves fine tuning through editing, through changes in word choice, and through small alterations of order and structure.

Proofreading

Proofreading is the final stage of the writing process. Check your final draft for grammatical, punctuation, spelling, and typographical errors. For example, if you have trouble with sentence fragments, review sentence structure. If you tend to confuse "it's" and "its," reread your paper with this problem in mind. Examine the manuscript to ensure that it still follows the original requirements of the assignment.

Composing on a Computer

Many students compose directly on a computer. After jotting down some preliminary notes, they may draft immediately on the computer and embed the processes of prewriting, shaping, drafting, revising, and editing. If you work in this manner, here are some useful strategies to consider:

- Create a file folder; then enter and save prewriting (e.g., brainstorming, notes, and outlines). You may want to refer to this work later on in the process.
- Archive versions of your essay. Again, you don't want to lose important information that may not be contained in your final draft. You may want to refer to it later.
- If you work from a single paragraph, exploratory draft and then use your cut-and-paste function to block out separate introductory, body, and concluding paragraphs, make sure these paragraphs and sentences within a paragraph proceed logically from point to point. Check the progression of ideas. As you rearrange and delete text, you should make

sure your ideas still cohere. Check your transitional expressions; add transition words as necessary to create a fluid essay.

- As you expand and develop ideas, take the time to return to the text for further evidence. Note significant facts, quotes, and specifics in the margins of a draft. Then revise. It is difficult to draft and to find supporting evidence at the same time. (See Esther Martinez's work in chapter 3.)
- Leave time to evaluate a version of your essay. Print out a penultimate copy for review. It is crucial to see your work as a whole in order to assess it.
- And, of course, use your spell check and proofread thoroughly.
- Always save your work on disk.

Summary

There are as many composing processes as there are students and writing situations. You need to work through the process in *your* own way; the omission of the stages of composing can lead to weaknesses in your final draft. For example, if you do not spend enough time planning your writing, your essay may be disorganized and unconvincing. If you do not spend enough time prewriting and exploring ideas, you may submit a final draft that is lifeless and undeveloped. If you do not spend enough time editing and proofreading, you may create a work so riddled with distracting grammatical errors and spelling mistakes that your essay will fail to convince your readers of the merit of your ideas. Each stage of the writing process is necessary to the development of a strong essay.

THE WRITING PROCESS: AN EXAMPLE

As an exercise in reading, responding, and writing, assume that your instructor has asked you to create a short essay, a literary analysis of a poem, building on one of your "think" writings. Esther Martinez chose to expand her treatment of "horse," concentrating on such specific literary techniques as symbolism, diction, and imagery.

Esther began her paper by doing the assigned "think" writing. She next jotted down some notes and observations and created a thesis and a mini-outline.

Notes on "horse"

What are the words for literary essays? Diction, word choice, irony, imagery.

Diction: Repetition

"Great horse"
"Thundering"
"Mexicans mutter"

Thesis: Through diction, repetition, imagery, the author clearly portrays the injustice experienced by Mexican Americans.

Diction
Repetition
Imagery
Symbolism

Additional Notes:

Tone changes from awe to disgust and frenzy

There is tension, craziness

Money is power

White man rules

Instead of killing the horse—they watch it suffer in a pool of blood

Description of kids works. Testicles—shame

Title—'horse'—lowercase

After jotting down these notes and developing a thesis, she wrote a short exploratory draft and noted details that she wanted to include. In her second draft, she more systematically focused on symbolism, diction, and imagery. Following her instructor's suggestions, she treated each technique in a separate paragraph and she developed the symbolism of the horse and compared it with the state of the Mexican Americans. In her third draft she more clearly organized and developed the essay, devoting a paragraph to each literary technique, and she included an historical reference that places the boys' actions within a particular historical context. This context explains and deepens the symbolic motif in the poem. The boys' actions not only represent the aberrant, violent, and racist behavior of adolescents, but they also mirror the prejudice directed at Mexican Americans and experienced by those who have been on the margins in this country from its inception. Perhaps what is most significant is that Esther's involvement with the work began with her own connection to her Mexican American heritage. Notice how her passion fuels her analysis, yet she retains the capacity to "stand back" and objectively analyze the work. What emerges is a complex and thoughtful treatment of a powerful poem.

Esther Martinez's First Exploratory Draft and Notes (Written at Home)

In the poem entitled, "horse" by Gloria Anzaldúa, the poet describes a symbolic situation of teenage boys killing a horse and the consequences of their action. Through the title, syntax, diction, and immagry [imagery] and foreshadowing [symbolism] the peot [poet] makes a statement about the power of money and the white man by showing the injustice shown to Mexicans.

Action

Through diction, the Mexican people are characterized along with their suffering. The "great horse" gallops and "some kids" follow as "Mexicans mutter among themselves" in anticipation [(knowing)] and knowing. This powerful horse racing through the field symbolizes the Mexican people and their culture. Great care is taken in describing the power of the horse as it races through the field symbolizing the Mexican people and their culture. On the other hand, the white teens are simply "some kids" showing the Mexican people are threatened and attacked mentally and physically by the—it [because] doesn't matter who killed the horse and their identity won't matter because whites don't get in trouble for lashing out at Mexicans. The Mexicans are aware of what is going on, but are unable to stop what is happening. The tension of the poem mounts . . . "Hidden hands" await the horse that "cast up testicles."

The poem can be related to all races

The hidden hands ~~conotate~~ connote the . . . ?
~~Immagery~~ Imagery creates a powerful picture of the helplessness of the oppressed Mexican people and their reaction to the situation. The "mexicanos murmur" and "shuffle their feet" as their "faces stare at the ground." The image created shows the inferiority felt by the Mexicans who shuffle their feet in nervous anticipation and a desire to lash out at their oppressor. However, they aren't ~~alowed~~ allowed to speak out or act, so in shame and helplessness they listen, wait, watch, ~~wisper.~~ whisper. The "folds of green" cover the stain of the "earth drinking blood."

tempered steel—unbreakable, unbendable, powerful, strong

Symbolism is used throughout the poem to help show the brutality of racism.

- boys pretending to feed horse
- weapon hidden in corn
- money
- can money replace/make all injury to Mexicans in the U.S. go away?

Second draft
(Turned in to Instructor)

In the poem "horse" by Gloria Anzaldúa, the poet describes a symbolic situation of teenage boys killing a horse and the consequences of their action. Through symbolism, diction and imagery the poet makes a statement about the power of money and the white man by demonstrating the injustice shown to Mexicans.

Commas

Excellent opening

Excellent thesis

Solid topics

Symbolism is used throughout the poem to help show the brutality of racism. In the poem a "horse [runs]" toward open palms holding tempting "ears of corn," not knowing there is "tempered steel" hidden within. The situation symbolizes the characteristic injustice of whites that in past history have been known to befriend a foe and gain trust in order to defeat "the enemy." This tactic was used when the whites coaxed the Indians out of hiding by declaring peace and giving them land to live on. When the Native Americans settled, the Europeans slaughtered the people, burnt the village, and destroyed the corn. The tempered steel symbolizes, not only the weapons used to mutilate the horse, but also the Americans who are powerful, cold, and unjust.

Could you give more pointed historical information?

Vague—too general

You could expand with historical references and explanations.

Divide into two paragraphs—separate topics

Diction and imagery create a powerful picture of the oppressed Mexican people and their reaction to the situation in the poem. "Folds of green" sneak out of a father's wallet, money that is to correct the injustice performed on the "great horse" that "some kids" mutilated. Much care is taken in describing the "great horse" as it races through the field. There is a passion and power behind it's "thundering" gallop, "flaring" "nostrils" and "iron-shod" hooves. The white teens, however, are simply described as "some kids"—showing that the identity of the whites doesn't and won't matter, because whites don't get in trouble for racism. Money is used to resolve the situation, however, money isn't capable of wiping away the pain, suffering, shame felt by the victims. The "*mexicanos* murmur" and "shuffle their feet" and "their faces stare at the ground." The images created show the inferiority felt by the Mexicans who desire to defend their lifestyle and culture. However, they aren't allowed to speak out or act, so in shame and helplessness they listen, wait, watch, whisper.

Excellent discussion of imagery of the horse

its → it's = it is

Good use of particular details from text

Excellent analysis of wording

Careful, no comma!

comma splice

Solid focus on verbs to describe Mexicanos

Excellent interpretation and portrayal of the Mexicanos

Solid parallelism in wording

"If you're Mexican you are born old," the poem concludes. From birth, Mexicans must struggle for their lives—not only against the injustice of racism, but also against poverty. Their childhood is snatched away as quickly as it's given. The poem "horse" can be related to any race or people ~~or~~ with a particular lifestyle suffering from persecution. The title itself—in all lowercase letters—signifies a people looked at as inferior.

Careful, format for including lines of poetry: use slash between lines

Excellent point

Focus on closing image. How can the image of the "dead horse" contrast with the image of Mexicanos who are born old? Expand analysis of closing. Is this an emphatic closing sentence?

Instructor's Comments

I am impressed with your process of revision. You revise beautifully—what a difference between your initial "think" writing and drafts. This essay has a solid thesis, is well-organized, well-developed, persuasive. Work on the concluding images in the poem and your conclusion.

Question

How does the image of the "dead horse" contrast with the image of Mexicanos who are "born old"? Develop your conclusion further.

Final Draft

Add comma

In the poem "horse" by Gloria Anzaldúa, the poet describes a symbolic situation of teenage boys' killing a horse and the consequences of their action. Through symbolism, diction and imagery the poet makes a statement about the power of money and the white man by demonstrating the injustice shown to Mexicans.

Careful, add commas!

Solid thesis

Symbolism is used throughout the poem to help show the brutality of racism. In the poem, a "horse [runs]" toward open palms holding tempting ears of "corn," not knowing there is "tempered steel" hidden within. The situation symbolizes the characteristic injustice of whites that in past history have been known to befriend a foe and gain trust in order to defeat "the enemy." This tactic was used when the whites coaxed the Indians out of hiding by declaring peace and giving them land to live on. When the Native Americans settled, the Europeans slaughtered the people, burnt the village, and destroyed the corn. In *American Slavery, American Freedom* Edmund Morgan wrote:

Excellent use of historical reference

Again, add comma

> Since the Indians were better woodsmen than the English and virtually impossible to track down, the method was to feign peaceful intentions, let them settle down and plant their corn wherever

Excellent inclusion of a quote

> they chose, and then just before harvest, fall upon them, killing as many as possible and burning the corn.
>
> (Zinn 13)

The tempered steel symbolizes not only the weapons used to mutilate the horse, but also the Americans who are powerful, cold, and unjust.

Diction is used to reveal the arrogance of the whites, [*the spirit of the Mexicans,*] and the cruelty shown to the Mexicans. The father "[fishes] out his wallet" [*Again, add comma*] intending to correct the injustice performed on the "great horse" that "some kids" mutilated. Much care is taken in describing the "great horse" as it races through the field. There is a passion and power behind it's [*its again!*] "thundering" gallop, "flaring" nostrils, and "iron-shod" hooves. [*Transition needed. However, that power doesn't protect the Mexicans. The teens have the power to destroy.*] The white ~~teens, however,~~ adolescents are simply described as "some kids"—showing that the identity of the whites doesn't and won't matter, [*No comma*] because whites don't get punished for racism. The father lightly and carelessly pulls out his wallet—confident that money will resolve the situation. Money, however, isn't capable of wiping away the pain, suffering, and shame felt by the victims.

Through imagery, a powerful picture is painted of the reactions of both the perpetrators and the oppressed Mexican people. The neighing horse hurtles toward the "open faces" of the sleeping gringos who "cry out" in desperation. [*Excellent expanded treatment*] The reader can clearly see the white boys waking up night after night—faces pale and clammy with perspiration, mouths open in shock and terror after having yet another nightmare. The whites are forever haunted by the images and brutality of their actions—an inadequate penance. With the *mexicanos* in lowercase and italicized, the reader feels compelled to whisper the phrase, and, in turn, to experience the same anxiety, tension, and anticipation felt by the tormented people. The image created also shows the inferiority felt by the Mexicans who desire to defend their lifestyle and culture. However, they aren't allowed to speak out or act, so in shame and helplessness they listen, wait, watch, whisper.

Because "mexicanos" is written in

[Margin: wording needs to be clearer]

[Margin: comma again]

"If you're Mexican/you are born old," the poem concludes. From birth, Mexicans must struggle for their lives—not only against the injustice of racism, but also against poverty. Their childhood is snatched away as quickly as it's given. The phrase "dead horse neighing in the night"—shows that although the Mexicans' voices are stifled, they will not give up in their struggle for equality and justice. The poem "horse" can be related to any race, people, or lifestyle suffering from persecution. [The title itself—in all lowercase letters—signifies a people viewed as inferior.]

,however,

[Margin: Change the order of sentences for greater emphasis in conclusion]

[Margin: Again—re-order closing sentences]

Work Cited

Zinn, Howard. *A People's History of the United States: 1492–Present.* New York: Harper Perennial, 1995.

INSTRUCTOR'S COMMENTS

A wonderful essay, Esther. You analyze the themes of the poem beautifully. Excellent added treatment of the imagery.
Work on:

- *Transitions*
- *Progression of thought from sentence to sentence*
- *Commas*

STUDENT'S COMMENTS

I chose to analyze the poem "horse" because I was able to relate to the message. I felt anger and frustration as I read the poem and wanted to expose the truth of the poem. My family is Hispanic and has suffered because of racism and oppression, and because of the personal experience, I thought, with my emotions raging, I would be able to write an effective paper. I was also able to relate to the past suffering the Native Americans experienced. It was remarkable and horrifying to see the hatred and cruelty that hasn't died in America, but, instead, is thriving.

Peer Evaluation

Be aware that you may exchange early drafts of your essays with a peer for feedback if your instructor so desires, or your instructor may read and comment on drafts of your writing. Three levels of peer critique are helpful:

1. *Provide Initial Reaction.* A peer may give you an initial emotional response and react to specific sections of the work in terms of his or her feelings and thoughts about the work.
2. *Indicate Organizational Strengths and Weaknesses.* A peer reader can outline the work—pinpointing thesis, key points, and details—to check the progression and development of the writer's arguments. A peer editor also may single out examples that are most convincing and vivid and note areas that are confusing and/or need further development.
3. *Provide an Evaluative Response.* Your instructor or your peer reviewers can provide a detailed evaluation of your essay's focus, thesis, organization, paragraph development, logic, transitions, style, and sentence structure.

It is helpful to evaluate a draft with a set of questions in mind so that the critical responses might provide pointed, productive feedback. Here is a checklist for evaluating a draft of writing:

The Reading/Writing Connection

1. Have I used some form of reader response first to gain ideas?
2. What is the focus of my response? What is my purpose?

Content

3. What is my perspective? my point of view? tone?
4. What is my main idea? My thesis? Who is my audience? Have I structured my thesis and topics with my audience in mind?
5. Do my major points follow from the thesis? Are they appropriate for the audience?

Organization

6. Are my major points arranged in a logical order? Do they build? Do I emphasize my most convincing point?
7. Does my essay have an introduction, middle paragraphs, and a conclusion?
8. Will my introduction interest a reader and give the reader a sense of the direction of my essay?
9. Does my conclusion end emphatically and reinforce my main idea and points? Do I leave the reader with something to consider?

Development

10. Have I included enough evidence (reasons, details, quotations, and examples) from the work to explain my points? Have I explained the examples sufficiently?
11. Have I included this evidence properly? Have I used proper quoting techniques and proper techniques for paraphrasing?

Grammar, Style, Sentence Sense

12. Have I written about the work in the present tense?
13. Have I maintained a consistent tone? (e.g., objective? personal? persuasive? meditative?)
14. Am I satisfied with wording, sentence structure, patterns of sentences (emphasis, variety)? Have I avoided repetitive wording and phrasing?
15. Have I created coherence by repeating key words, by creating transitions from point to point, and by using parallelism?
16. Have I shifted levels of diction?
17. Is my word choice specific, pointed, not vague?
18. Have I checked the final draft for grammar, punctuation, and spelling errors?

SPECIAL REQUIREMENTS FOR WRITING ABOUT LITERATURE

Several special requirements for writing about literature are important to note. First, compose primarily in the present tense. Use the past tense to refer only to events in a text that clearly took place in the past. For example, in "horse," you would use the present tense to describe the horse's mythic running in the night, but you would use the past tense to describe the animal's mutilation because that event occurred before the speaker begins her story.

Another important feature of writing about literature is the inclusion of quotations from the work. When you quote, be careful to cite the exact quotation and to insert ellipses (. . .) for any information that you delete within a quotation; use four periods (. . . .) for any part of a sentence that you delete at the end of the quotation. Block and indent quotations of more than four lines of prose or three lines of poetry. You also must make the quotation consistent with the preceding discussion. Use brackets to insert any changes in wording so that the quotation fits content and presentation of ideas and so that it makes sense. For example, consider this sentence from Martinez's essay: "In the poem, a 'horse [runs]' toward open palms." The writer changed "ran" to "runs" to keep the tense consistent.

Select sufficient quotations from the work as evidence. Your writing will be more persuasive if you include specifics from the work. Remember the student's weaving of quotations into her discussion of "horse." Be aware, however, that it is disastrous to overload your analysis with unexplained or extensive quotations. This technique could lead a reader to assume that you have not understood the work fully.

Another important aspect of using evidence from a text is to **paraphrase** correctly. Where you do not use quotations, you still might want to support your points with descriptions, examples, or events in the text by phrasing them in your own words—that is, by paraphrasing the original work. Be careful to choose only your own words in such cases; any of the original language must be placed within quotation marks. Consider this additional example from Martinez's essay: "Much care is taken in describing the 'great horse' as it races through the field." She paraphrases the action of the horse as she also uses a direct quotation from the poem to add emphasis and to name the creature.

FORMS OF THE ESSAY ABOUT LITERATURE

In critical analysis of literature, you experience a complicated process of response. In writing about literature, you focus your energies on one aspect, one strand of your reading experience. Depending on your particular reading and on your goals in writing, you may then compose an essay in response to literature that may assume any of several different forms: response, explication, comparison-contrast, argumentation, critical analysis, review, and research.

Response Essay

A response essay is an analysis of a reader's emotional response to a work. In this kind of paper, you explain both your reading experience and the parts of the work that evoke your reaction. For example, you might respond to Luisa Valenzuela's story "I'm Your Horse in the Night" (chapter 7) by discussing your mounting horror and disgust as the characters suffer torture and death at the hands of the government police in Argentina. You may want to proceed sequentially through the story to discuss the stages and aspects of your response. Or you may focus on one main emotional reaction and explore its components: the elements of the story that provoke your reaction.

Explication Essay

Another form of response, explication, is a careful analysis of the work to examine its meaning. In this type of essay, the writer proceeds through the text methodically and analyzes those aspects of the work and the writer's technique that create the themes. Usually explications of meaning are done on short texts so that the work can be analyzed in depth and treated fully. For example, a student may explore a theme of Emily Dickinson's "My Life Had Stood—" (chapter 4) by carefully examining each line, each image, and each stanza and by finding the strands of connection revealed by this process. Such analysis demonstrates aspects of the poem (wording, imagery, figurative language, point of view, tone, rhythm, and rhyme) that develop Dickinson's message. You may organize the essay by treating each part of the text as a separate paragraph or by organizing in terms of poetic techniques; that is, have each technique serve as a topic for a middle paragraph.

Comparison/Contrast Essay

In this form of essay, you may compare and/or contrast two works to find similarities and differences. Then you may have to decide to concentrate on treatment of theme, character, style, or technique. Instructors often specify the subject of the comparison and ask students to compare two characters in two different stories, to evaluate two poems with similar themes, or to assess two plays to determine which treatment of character or theme seems more effective.

There are two major organizational patterns for a comparison/contrast essay. You may treat first one text and then the other in successive paragraphs: this format is labeled *block* or *side-by-side* organization. For example, you might devote several paragraphs to a given theme, such as coming of age in "A White Heron," followed immediately by several paragraphs on the same theme in "Barn Burning" (chapter 4). This type of pattern is sometimes not effective because it separates the discussion of the two works and confuses or loses the reader. The other pattern relies on *point-by-point* or *alternating* organization. In this form of the essay, each of the middle (body) paragraphs presents the treatment of a key topic (point) in both of the works.

For example, in a discussion of coming of age in "A White Heron" and in "Barn Burning," one middle paragraph might focus on the innocence of the main protagonist. The next paragraph might explain each protagonist's capability for moral decision making as a prerequisite for growing beyond childhood. In every paragraph, the writer would consider first "A White Heron" and then "Barn Burning." This method keeps the topics for comparison foremost in the reader's mind and allows the reader to weigh and compare the evidence from each story.

Block or Side-by-Side			Point-by-Point		
Introduction—Thesis			Introduction—Thesis		
Middle Paragraphs			Middle Paragraphs		
Work A		"A White Heron"	**Topic 1**		Innocence of protagonist
	Topic 1	Innocence of protagonist		**Work A**	"A White Heron"
	Topic 2	Capacity for moral decisions		**Work B**	"Barn Burning"
Work B		"Barn Burning"	**Topic 2**		Capacity for moral decisions
	Topic 1	Innocence of protagonist		**Work A**	"A White Heron"
	Topic 2	Capacity for moral decisions		**Work B**	"Barn Burning"
Conclusion			Conclusion		

Argumentation Essay

An argument presents your point of view, your opinion (position), reasons, and supporting evidence. For an argumentative paper on literature, you take a particular position regarding the text; and then you defend your position by providing reasons and supporting evidence from the text. As in other forms of argument, you will need to create a sound thesis, defend your thesis with logical reasoning, and provide sufficient evidence to prove your points and to convince the reader. In addition, you need to consider the opposing point of view: to evaluate and to analyze arguments in opposition to yours. An example of an argumentative question follows:

Do you agree that Oedipus creates his destiny? (See chapter 7.) To write about this query, you would take a position and compose an argumentative essay in response to the assignment.

You can structure your response in any of several ways. You might consider one classical pattern of argument:

Opening paragraph:	Presentation of argumentative thesis
Second paragraph:	Acknowledgment of opposition—rebuttal
Subsequent paragraphs:	Reasons and proof
Closing paragraph:	Reinforcement of your position. The rebuttal of the opposition may also be placed in the next to last or closing paragraph.

Critical Analysis Essay

In a *critical analysis,* you are asked to analyze a literary work according to a single principle: theme, character, style, or a particular technique of fiction, poetry, drama, or nonfiction. For example, you may be asked to explore one theme of "Hills Like White Elephants" (chapter 6); or you might be asked to analyze the character of the woman in that story; your instructor may ask you to analyze Hemingway's style; or you might be asked to focus on the imagery of the hills or the symbolism of the title. In each case, you isolate one level of a work and explore its function and its impact. Critical analysis often leads to judgments of effectiveness. Is the theme treated compellingly? Is the character portrayal moving? believable? Is the imagery powerful? Is Hemingway's style effective?

Evaluation and Review Essay

Evaluation and *review* are forms of critical analysis that focus on determining the effectiveness of a work. When you are asked to evaluate a text, you compare the text with chosen standards and come to conclusions about its worth and effectiveness. You might evaluate Athol Fugard's *"Master Harold" . . . and the Boys* (chapter 8), for example, and conclude that its characters, dialogue, conflict, and themes create a drama of great power.

A *review* is a particular form of evaluative response that often follows this set pattern:

Paragraph One:	General assessment of a work. Relevant background information.
Paragraph Two:	Summary of key features of the work. (The reviewer assumes that the reader has not yet seen or read the work.)
Paragraph Three:	Strengths
Paragraph Four:	Weaknesses
Conclusion:	A general recommendation

Reviews are a common form of both academic and journalistic prose. Many instructors in college courses require book, magazine, or film reviews. Consequently, this form is a valuable one to learn.

The Research Essay

The *research paper* is a writing assignment that involves searching beyond the text to find information that expands your understanding of the work. Research opens the text to different interpretations and enriches the reading experience. Research may move in different directions. You may explore any one of the following areas:

- *Biographical research:* Research on the writer's life. Exploration of the connections between the writer's life and art.
- *Research on the historical, cultural, political, philosophical, or sociological background of the work.*
- *Reading of criticism that treats the work.* This reading of another's exploration of the text will help you understand it and, perhaps, explain aspects that are puzzling. Critics provide you with alternative interpretations.
- *Reading of specific forms of literary criticism.* Historical, cultural, social, formalist, feminist, deconstructive. (See Appendix B.) These particular schools of literary criticism will provide you with frameworks and theories that will help you read the work in particular ways and place it in new intellectual contexts.

In each instance, once you write about secondary sources, you must cite the sources of the information and give adequate documentation for the works that you quote or paraphrase. One accepted method of documenting information in essays about literature is MLA (Modern Language Association of America) citation form as recommended in the *MLA Handbook for Writers of Research Papers.* The MLA citation form involves two steps: citations of references in the work itself and a "Works Cited" page that contains all of your primary and secondary sources in alphabetical order by author's last name. The MLA citations within the discussion sections of your paper include two parts: author, page. If the author's name is presented in your essay, you only indicate page number. If an author has written two books, you should include an abbreviated title in the citation. Note the following excerpt from a rough draft of a student research essay on Sylvia Plath's theme of transcendence. The writer, Kevin Stoffel, contends that an examination of the drafts of Plath's poems reveals a transformation of suffering into images of power, autonomy, and purity. Note the correct form of MLA citation. You can find a complete discussion of MLA documentation and of this research paper in Appendix B.

Plath's poems were an outlet for her constant pain. From her swings and fits of mania and depression, she drew on the theme of transcendence. The transformation of this theme, from its early stages to its final state, can be seen in the drafts of the poems, "Fever 103°," "Ariel," and "Edge."

In a statement prepared by a BBC reading, Plath wrote of "Fever 103°":

> This poem is about two kinds of fire—the fires of hell, which merely agonize, and the fires of heaven which purify. During the poem, the first sort of fire suffers into the second. (Newman 62)

"Fever 103°" is one of several poems in which fire serves to bring about a sense of purity equivalent to a type of transcendence, a movement to a higher plane.

SUMMARY

The recursive processes of critical thinking, reader response, and composing the essay about literature develop new capacities for understanding texts in different genres—fiction, poetry, drama, and nonfiction. As you read, analyze, and write about selections in the thematic anthology that follows, you not only will find yourself more interested in issues like those presented in Gloria Anzaldúa's poem, "horse," but you also will find your life enriched by the insights and ideas provided by the study of these works.

PART TWO

Thematic Anthology

CHAPTER 4

INITIATION AND IDENTITY

I came to explore the wreck.
The words are purposes.
The words are maps.
I came to see the damage that was done
and the treasures that prevail.

Adrienne Rich, "Diving into the Wreck"

It is not possible to define the self without acts of consciousness, without surveying "the damage that was done/and the treasures that prevail"; similarly, it is not possible to grow without being challenged by experience and by cultural mores. When we are young, we live in a seemingly idyllic world. As we mature, we face the experiences that affect our innocence, that complicate our lives, and that provide the basis for growth and for the development of identity.

For characters in literary works, loss of innocence often comes in facing the transitory nature of life, the facts of birth and death, as in Sarah Orne Jewett's "A White Heron," Walt Whitman's "Out of the Cradle Endlessly Rocking," and Robert Frost's "Birches." Or the protagonist learns the limits of moral responsibility, as in William Faulkner's "Barn Burning." Part of the inevitable process of maturing becomes facing disappointment, learning that adults are not always wise or correct in their views of the world, and gaining an understanding, often painful, of the discrepancy between the ideal and the real, between the dream and the reality. Such struggle and disillusionment are portrayed in Diane Wakoski's "Wind Secrets," Countee Cullen's "Incident," Liliana Heker's "The Stolen Party," and Lorna Dee Cervantes's "Uncle's First Rabbit."

Literary rites of passage include knowledge of discrimination, of sexuality, of violence, and of disillusionment with the adult world. Certainly Barbara Kingsolver's young protagonist in "Rose-Johnny" gains this knowledge of prejudice. In the Thematic Preview, Luisa Valenzuela's "The Verb to Kill," Joyce Carol Oates's "Where Are You Going, Where Have You Been?" and Margaret Atwood's "Game After Supper" depict characters grappling with the emergence of their sexuality and questioning their sexual roles. In these works, sexuality has a violent edge and destructive consequences. William S. Kowinski's "Kids in the Mall" and David Elkind's "Our Hurried Children" warn us about the negative effects that malls and other aspects of mass culture have upon the development of selfhood.

Adolescence is not necessarily a dangerous phase of life; it may be a time of great growth, challenge, and joy. Many works affirmatively portray the physical energy and vitality of adolescence. Witness the exuberance of the teenage boys in Gary Soto's "Oranges" and the equally positive expression of selfhood in Nikki Giovanni's "Ego Tripping." However, other works in this chapter portray the debilitating confusions of adolescence: Audre Lorde's "Hanging Fire," Sandra Cisneros's "The Monkey Garden," and Janice Mirikitani's "Suicide Note."

In some cases, the vitality of adolescence emerges from the drive to rebel. Members of ethnic groups who experience alienation in North American culture often use rebellion to gain an understanding of prejudice and to reject societal mores. Louise Erdrich's runaways from the "Indian Boarding School" experience the effects of racism and run to break free of societal constraints.

Experiencing discrimination can lead to an awareness of difference and to confusion about cultural heritage. Should we aspire to assimilate or to embrace our cultural legacies, or are we caught between worlds? These alternatives plague the speakers in Cathy Song's "Lost Sister" and Sandra Cisneros's "My Name."

The process of coming of age differs for men and for women and from culture to culture. Many times literary characters decide to reject the mores, the cultural norms of their societies; they deem them corrupt, destructive. The African American persona in Rita Dove's "Adolescence I, II, III" experiences phases of her emerging womanhood. "Black Hair," Gary Soto's partially autobiographical poem of growing up in the barrio, presents a struggle to attain manhood, a struggle that reflects the realities of his Chicano background; yet his need "To become a man," to please his father, becomes mythic in its proportions.

One outcome of these challenges is the consolidation of identity—"the treasures that prevail": the movement from confusion to a surer, albeit not necessarily static, sense of the adult self. Confusion and development persist into adulthood (the twenties, thirties, forties). We continue to face experiences, as do Raymond Carver's narrator in "Cathedral" and Flannery O'Connor's grandmother in "A Good Man Is Hard to Find," that challenge us to define and to redefine self. We separate from and align ourselves with others as Lewis Thomas metaphorically suggests in "The Medusa and the Snail." In William Shakespeare's *Hamlet,* the ghost of the father appears to haunt the son; the profound loss of the father serves as a symbol for the continual insistence and intrusion of the past into the present. Hamlet must try to resolve such conflicts in order to live as an adult.

As readers we are cognizant that acts of writing, acts of communication, are revelatory. Like Adrienne Rich, we know that words are the "purposes," the "maps," by which we come to know ourselves and to find our ways into the world.

THEMATIC PREVIEW: COMBINING THE GENRES

The Verb to Kill

Luisa Valenzuela

Translated by Helen Lane

Luisa Valenzuela (1938–), born in Buenos Aires, Argentina, grew up in a literary atmosphere. After graduating from the University of Buenos Aires, Valenzuela worked for a number of magazines and newspapers and traveled widely in Europe, North America, and Latin America. In 1963, she published her first novel, The Lizard's Tale; *in 1966, she published her first collection of short stories,* Clara. *They have been followed by volumes including* Strange Things Happen Here *(1976),* Other Weapons *(1985), and* Open Door *(1989). Valenzuela has been praised by critics for the boldness and experimentation of her fiction.*

1976

1 He kills—he killed—he will kill—he has killed—he had killed—he will have killed—he would have killed—he is killing—he was killing—he has been killing—he would have been killing—he will have been killing—he will be killing—he would be killing—he may kill.

2 We decided that none of these tenses or moods suited him. Did he kill, will he kill, will he have killed? We think he *is* killing, with every step, with every breath, with every . . . We don't like him to get close to us but we come across him when we go clam-digging on the beach. We walk from north to south, and he comes from south to north, closer to the dunes, as if looking for pebbles. He looks at us and we look at him—did he kill, will he kill, would he have killed, is he killing? We put down the sack with the clams and hold each other's hand till he passes. He doesn't throw so much as one little pebble at us, he doesn't even look at us, but afterward we're too weak in the knees to go on digging clams.

3 The other day he walked by us and right afterward we found an injured sea gull on the beach. We took the poor thing home and on the way we told it that we were good, not like him, that it didn't have to be afraid of us, and we even covered it up with my jacket so the cold wind wouldn't hurt its broken wing. Later we ate it in a stew. A little tough, but tasty.

4 The next day we went back to run on the beach. We didn't see him and we didn't find a single injured sea gull. He may be bad, but he's got something that attracts animals. For example, when we were fishing: hours without a bite until he suddenly showed up and then we caught a splendid sea bass. He didn't look at our catch or smile, and it's good he didn't because he looked more like a murderer than ever with his long bushy hair and gleaming eyes. He just went on gathering his pebbles as though nothing were wrong, thinking about the girls that he has killed, will kill, kills.

5 When he passes by we're petrified—will it be our turn someday? In school we conjugate the verb *to kill* and the shiver that goes up our spine isn't the same as when we see him passing on the beach, all puffed up with pride and gathering his pebbles. The shiver on the beach is lower down in our bodies and more stimulating, like sea air. He gathers all those pebbles to cover up the graves of his victims—very small, transparent pebbles that he holds up to the sun and looks through from time to time so as to make certain that the sun exists. Mama says that if he spends all day looking for pebbles, it's because he *eats* them. Mama can't think about anything but food, but I'm sure he eats something else. The last breath of his victims, for example. There's nothing more nourishing than the last sigh, the one that brings with it everything that a person has gathered over the years. He must have some secret for trapping this essence that escapes his victims, and that's why he doesn't need vitamins. My sister and I are afraid he'll catch us some night and kill us to absorb everything that we've been eating over the last few years. We're terribly afraid because we're well nourished, Mama has always seen to it that we eat balanced meals and we've never lacked for fruit or vegetables even though they're very expensive in this part of the country. And clams have lots of iodine, Mama says, and fish are the healthiest food there is even though the taste of it bores us but why should he be bored because while he kills his victims (always girls, of course) he must do those terrible things to them that my sister and I keep imagining, just for fun. We spend hours talking about the things that he does to his victims before killing them just for fun. The papers often talk about degenerates like him but he's one of the worst because that's all he eats. The other day we spied on him while he was talking to the lettuce he has growing in his garden (he's crazy as well as degenerate). He was saying affectionate things to it and we were certain it was poisoned lettuce. For our part we don't say anything to lettuce, we have to eat it with oil and lemon even though it's disgusting, all because Mama says it has lots of vitamins. And now we have to swallow vitamins for him, what a bother, because the better fed we are the happier we'll make him and the more he'll like doing those terrible things the papers talk about and we imagine, just before killing us so as to gulp down our last breath full of vitamins in one big mouthful. He's going to do a whole bunch of things so repulsive we'll be ashamed to tell anybody, and we only say them in a whisper when we're on the beach and there's nobody within miles. He's going to take our last breath and then he'll be as strong as a bull to go kill other little girls like us. I hope he catches Pocha. But I hope he doesn't do any of those repulsive things to her before killing her because she might like it, the dirty thing. I hope he kills her straightaway by plunging a knife in her belly. But he'll have his fun with us for a long time because we're pretty and he'll like our bodies and our voices when we scream. And we will scream and scream but nobody will hear us because he's going to take us to a place very far away and then he will put in our mouths that terrible thing we know he has. Pocha already told us about it—he must have an enormous thing that he uses to kill his victims.

6 An enormous one, even though we've never seen it. To show how brave we are, we tried to watch him while he made peepee, but he saw us and chased us away. I wonder why he didn't want to show it to us. Maybe it's because he wants to surprise us on our last day here and catch us while we're pure so's to get more pleasure. That must be it. He's saving himself for our last day and that's why he doesn't try to get close to us.

7 Not anymore.

8 Papa finally lent us the rifle after we asked and asked for it to hunt rabbits. He told us we were big girls now, that we can go out alone with the rifle if we want to, but to be careful, and he said it was a reward for doing so well in school. It's true we're doing well in school. It isn't hard at all to learn to conjugate verbs:

9 He will be killed—he is killed—he has been killed.

Explorations of the Text

1. Notice the verb tenses and moods at the beginning. The narrator says "We decided that none of these tenses or moods suited him." Why?
2. Characterize the boy. What are his alleged actions?
3. Explain the emphasis on "breath."
4. What is the relationship between sexuality and death?
5. Explore the significance of the images of the beach, of birds and fish, and of vegetables.
6. Trace the verb "to kill" through the story. What do you conclude?
7. What does the ending mean? What has really happened to the boy? Will there be consequences for the girls?

The Reading/Writing Connection

1. "Think" Topic: What is fantastic and what is real in this story?
2. Gloss the text. Examine the sentence structure. How does Valenzuela establish the voice of the speaker? What impact does the voice have? Respond to these questions in a journal entry.

Ideas for Writing

1. Discuss the significance of violence in this work.
2. Compare the experience of adolescent fear and fantasy in this story with the situations in other works such as "Where Are You Going, Where Have You Been?" or "Game After Supper."

Where Are You Going, Where Have You Been?

Joyce Carol Oates

Joyce Carol Oates (1938–), born in Lockport, New York, studied at Syracuse University and the University of Wisconsin. With the publication of The Garden of Earthly Delights *(1967) and* Expensive People *(1968), she became famous. In 1969, her novel,* them, *won the National Book Award. Known for her prolific and varied writing, Oates, professor of humanities at Princeton University, has published almost fifty books: novels, short fiction, poetry, essays, and literary criticism. Recent works include* Because It Is Bitter, and Because It Is My Heart *(1991) and* Haunted: Tales of the Grotesque *(1994). Oates based her most famous story, "Where Are You Going, Where Have You Been?" on an article in* Life *magazine about a murderer, Charles Schmid of Tucson, Arizona.*

1970

To Bob Dylan

Her name was Connie. She was fifteen and she had a quick nervous giggling habit of craning her neck to glance into mirrors or checking other people's faces to make sure her own was all right. Her mother, who noticed everything and knew everything and who hadn't much reason any longer to look at her own face, always scolded Connie about it. "Stop gawking at yourself, who are you? You think you're so pretty?" she would say. Connie would raise her eyebrows at these familiar complaints and look right through her mother, into a shadowy vision of herself as she was right at that moment: she knew she was pretty and that was everything. Her mother had been pretty once too, if you could believe those old snapshots in the album, but now her looks were gone and that was why she was always after Connie. "Why don't you keep your room clean like your sister? How've you got your hair fixed—what the hell stinks? Hair spray? You don't see your sister using that junk."

Her sister June was twenty-four and still lived at home. She was a secretary in the high school Connie attended, and if that wasn't bad enough—with her in the same building—she was so plain and chunky and steady that Connie had to hear her praised all the time by her mother and her mother's sisters. June did this, June did that, she saved money and helped clean the house and cooked and Connie couldn't do a thing, her mind was all filled with trashy daydreams. Their father was away at work most of the time and when he came home he wanted supper and he read the newspaper at supper and after supper he went to bed. He didn't bother talking much to them, but around his bent head Connie's mother kept picking at her until Connie wished her mother were dead and she herself were dead and it were all over. "She makes me want to throw up sometimes," she complained to her friends. She had a high, breathless, amused voice which made everything she said sound a little forced, whether it was sincere or not.

There was one good thing: June went places with girlfriends of hers, girls who were just as plain and steady as she, and so when Connie wanted to do that her mother had no objections. The father of Connie's best girlfriend drove the girls the three miles to town and left them off at a shopping plaza, so that they could walk through the stores or go to a movie, and when he came to pick them up again at eleven he never bothered to ask what they had done.

They must have been familiar sights, walking around that shopping plaza in their shorts and flat ballerina slippers that always scuffed the sidewalk, with charm bracelets jingling on their thin wrists; they would lean together to whisper and laugh secretly if someone passed by who amused or interested them. Connie had long dark blond hair that drew anyone's eye to it, and she wore part of it pulled up on her head and puffed out and the rest of it she let fall down her back. She wore a pullover jersey blouse that looked one way when she was at home and another way when she was away from home. Everything about her had two sides to it, one for home and one for anywhere that was not home: her walk that could be childlike and bobbing, or languid enough to make anyone think she was hearing music in her head, her mouth which was pale and smirking most of the time, but bright and pink on these evenings out, her laugh which was cynical and drawling at home—"Ha, ha, very funny"—but high-pitched and nervous anywhere else, like the jingling of the charms on her bracelet.

5 Sometimes they did go shopping or to a movie, but sometimes they went across the highway, ducking fast across the busy road, to a drive-in restaurant where older kids hung out. The restaurant was shaped like a big bottle, though squatter than a real bottle, and on its cap was a revolving figure of a grinning boy who held a hamburger aloft. One night in midsummer they ran across, breathless with daring, and right away someone leaned out a car window and invited them over, but it was just a boy from high school they didn't like. It made them feel good to be able to ignore him. They went up through the maze of parked and cruising cars to the bright-lit, fly-infested restaurant, their faces pleased and expectant as if they were entering a sacred building that loomed out of the night to give them what haven and what blessing they yearned for. They sat at the counter and crossed their legs at the ankles, their thin shoulders rigid with excitement, and listened to the music that made everything so good: the music was always in the background like music at a church service, it was something to depend upon.

A boy named Eddie came in to talk with them. He sat backward on his stool, turning himself jerkily around in semicircles and then stopping and turning again, and after a while he asked Connie if she would like something to eat. She said she did and so she tapped her friend's arm on her way out—her friend pulled her face up into a brave droll look—and Connie said she would meet her at eleven, across the way. "I just hate to leave her like that," Connie said earnestly, but the boy said that she wouldn't be alone for long. So they went out to his car and on the way Connie couldn't help but let her eyes wander over the windshields and faces all around her, her face gleaming with a joy that had nothing to do with Eddie or even this place; it might have been the music. She drew her shoulders up and sucked in her breath with the pure pleasure of being alive, and just at that moment she happened to glance at a face just a few feet from hers. It was a boy with shaggy black hair, in a convertible jalopy painted gold. He stared at her and then his lips widened into a grin. Connie slit her eyes at him and turned away, but she couldn't help glancing back and there he was still watching her. He wagged a finger and laughed and said, "Gonna get you, baby," and Connie turned away again without Eddie noticing anything.

She spent three hours with him, at the restaurant where they ate hamburgers and drank Cokes in wax cups that were always sweating, and then down an alley a mile or so away, and when he left her off at five to eleven only the movie house was still open at the plaza. Her girlfriend was there, talking with a boy. When Connie came up and the two girls smiled at each other and Connie said, "How was the movie?" and the girl said, "*You* should know." They rode off with the girl's father, sleepy and pleased, and Connie couldn't help but look at the darkened shopping plaza with its big empty parking lot and its signs that were faded and ghostly now, and over at the drive-in restaurant where cars were still circling tirelessly. She couldn't hear the music at this distance.

Next morning June asked her how the movie was and Connie said, "So-so."

She and that girl and occasionally another girl went out several times a week that way, and the rest of the time Connie spent around the house—it was summer vacation—getting in her mother's way and thinking, dreaming, about the boys she met. But all the boys fell back and dissolved into a single face that was not even a face, but an idea, a feeling, mixed up with the urgent insistent pounding of the music and the humid night air of July. Connie's mother kept dragging her back to the daylight by finding things for her to do or saying, suddenly, "What's this about the Pettinger girl?"

10 And Connie would say nervously, "Oh, her. That dope." She always drew thick clear lines between herself and such girls, and her mother was simple and kindly enough to believe her. Her mother was so simple, Connie thought, that it was maybe cruel to fool her so much. Her mother went scuffling around the house in old bedroom slippers and complained over the telephone to one sister about the other, then the other called up and the two of them complained about the third one. If June's name was mentioned her mother's tone was approving, and if Connie's name was mentioned it was disapproving. This did not really mean she disliked Connie and actually Connie thought that her mother preferred her to June because she was prettier, but the two of them kept up a pretense of exasperation, a sense that they were tugging and struggling over something of little value to either of them. Sometimes, over coffee, they were almost friends, but something would come up—some vexation that was like a fly buzzing suddenly around their heads—and their faces went hard with contempt.

One Sunday Connie got up at eleven—none of them bothered with church—and washed her hair so that it could dry all day long, in the sun. Her parents and sister were going to a barbecue at an aunt's house and Connie said no, she wasn't interested, rolling her eyes to let her mother know just what she thought of it. "Stay home alone then," her mother said sharply. Connie sat out back in a lawn chair and watched them drive away, her father quiet and bald, hunched around so that he could back the car out, her mother with a look that was still angry and not at all softened through the windshield, and in the back seat poor old June all dressed up as if she didn't know what a barbecue was, with all the running yelling kids and the flies. Connie sat with her eyes closed in the sun, dreaming and dazed with the warmth about her as if this were a kind of love, the caresses of love, and her mind slipped over onto thoughts of the boy she had been with the night before and how nice he had been, how sweet it always was, not the way someone like June would suppose but sweet, gentle, the way it was in movies and promised in songs; and when she opened her eyes she hardly knew where she was, the back yard ran off into weeds and a fence line of trees and behind it the sky was perfectly blue and still. The asbestos "ranch house" that was now three years old startled her—it looked small. She shook her head as if to get awake.

It was too hot. She went inside the house and turned on the radio to drown out the quiet. She sat on the edge of her bed, barefoot, and listened for an hour and a half to a program called XYZ Sunday Jamboree, record after record of hard, fast, shrieking songs she sang along with, interspersed by exclamations from "Bobby King": "An' look here you girls at Napoleon's—Son and Charley want you to pay real close attention to this song coming up!"

And Connie paid close attention herself, bathed in a glow of slow-pulsed joy that seemed to rise mysteriously out of the music itself and lay languidly about the airless little room, breathed in and breathed out with each gentle rise and fall of her chest.

After a while she heard a car coming up the drive. She sat up at once, startled, because it couldn't be her father so soon. The gravel kept crunching all the way in from the road—the driveway was long—and Connie ran to the window. It was a car she didn't know. It was an open jalopy, painted a bright gold that caught the sunlight opaquely. Her heart began to pound and her fingers snatched at her hair, checking it, and she whispered "Christ, Christ," wondering how bad she looked. The car came to a stop at the side door and the horn sounded four short taps as if this were a signal Connie knew.

15 She went into the kitchen and approached the door slowly, then hung out the screen door, her bare toes curling down off the step. There were two boys in the car and now she recognized the driver: he had shaggy, shabby black hair that looked crazy as a wig and he was grinning at her.

"I ain't late, am I?" he said.

"Who the hell do you think you are?" Connie said.

"Toldja I'd be out, didn't I?"

"I don't even know who you are."

20 She spoke sullenly, careful to show no interest or pleasure, and he spoke in a fast bright monotone. Connie looked past him to the other boy, taking her time. He had fair brown hair, with a lock that fell onto his forehead. His

sideburns gave him a fierce, embarrassed look, but so far he hadn't even bothered to glance at her. Both boys wore sunglasses. The driver's glasses were metallic and mirrored everything in miniature.

"You wanta come for a ride?" he said.

Connie smirked and let her hair fall loose over one shoulder.

"Don'tcha like my car? New paint job," he said. "Hey."

"What?"

"You're cute."

She pretended to fidget, chasing flies away from the door.

"Don'tcha believe me, or what?" he said.

"Look, I don't even know who you are," Connie said in disgust.

"Hey, Ellie's got a radio, see. Mine's broke down." He lifted his friend's arm and showed her the little transistor the boy was holding, and now Connie began to hear the music. It was the same program that was playing inside the house.

"Bobby King?" she said.

"I listen to him all the time. I think he's great."

"He's kind of great," Connie said reluctantly.

"Listen, that guy's *great.* He knows where the action is."

Connie blushed a little, because the glasses made it impossible for her to see just what this boy was looking at. She couldn't decide if she liked him or if he was just a jerk, and so she dawdled in the doorway and wouldn't come down or go back inside. She said, "What's all that stuff painted on your car?"

"Can'tcha read it?" He opened the door very carefully, as if he was afraid it might fall off. He slid out just as carefully, planting his feet firmly on the ground, the tiny metallic world in his glasses slowing down like gelatine hardening and in the midst of it Connie's bright green blouse. "This here is my name, to begin with," he said. ARNOLD FRIEND was written in tarlike black letters on the side, with a drawing of a round grinning face that reminded Connie of a pumpkin, except it wore sunglasses. "I wanta introduce myself, I'm Arnold Friend and that's my real name and I'm gonna be your friend, honey, and inside the car's Ellie Oscar, he's kinda shy." Ellie brought his transistor radio up to his shoulder and balanced it there. "Now these numbers are a secret code, honey," Arnold Friend explained. He read off the numbers 33, 19, 17 and raised his eyebrows at her to see what she thought of that, but she didn't think much of it. The left rear fender had been smashed and around it was written, on the gleaming gold background: DONE BY CRAZY WOMAN DRIVER. Connie had to laugh at that. Arnold Friend was pleased at her laughter and looked up at her. "Around the other side's a lot more—you wanta come and see them?"

"No."

"Why not?"

"Why should I?"

"Don'tcha wanta see what's on the car? Don'tcha wanta go for a ride?"

"I don't know."

"Why not?"

"I got things to do."

"Like what?"

"Things."

45 He laughed as if she had said something funny. He slapped his thighs. He was standing in a strange way, leaning back against the car as if he were balancing himself. He wasn't tall, only an inch or so taller than she would be if she came down to him. Connie liked the way he was dressed, which was the way all of them dressed: tight faded jeans stuffed into black, scuffed boots, a belt that pulled his waist in and showed how lean he was, and a white pullover shirt that was a little soiled and showed the hard small muscles of his arms and shoulders. He looked as if he probably did hard work, lifting and carrying things. Even his neck looked muscular. And his face was a familiar face, somehow: the jaw and chin and cheeks slightly darkened, because he hadn't shaved for a day or two, and the nose long and hawklike, sniffing as if she were a treat he was going to gobble up and it was all a joke.

"Connie, you ain't telling the truth. This is your day set aside for a ride with me and you know it," he said, still laughing. The way he straightened and recovered from his fit of laughing showed that it had been all fake.

"How do you know what my name is?" she said suspiciously.

"It's Connie."

"Maybe and maybe not."

50 "I know my Connie," he said, wagging his finger. Now she remembered him even better, back at the restaurant, and her cheeks warmed at the thought of how she sucked in her breath just at the moment she passed him—how she must have looked at him. And he had remembered her. "Ellie and I come out here especially for you," he said. "Ellie can sit in back. How about it?"

"Where?"

"Where what?"

"Where're we going?"

He looked at her. He took off the sunglasses and she saw how pale the skin around his eyes was, like holes that were not in shadow but instead in light. His eyes were like chips of broken glass that catch the light in an amiable way. He smiled. It was as if the idea of going for a ride somewhere, to some place, was a new idea to him.

55 "Just for a ride, Connie sweetheart."

"I never said my name was Connie," she said.

"But I know what it is. I know your name and all about you, lots of things," Arnold Friend said. He had not moved yet but stood still leaning back against the side of his jalopy. "I took a special interest in you, such a pretty girl, and found out all about you like I know your parents and sister are gone somewheres and I know where and how long they're going to be gone, and I know who you were with last night, and your best girlfriend's name is Betty. Right?"

He spoke in a simple lilting voice, exactly as if he were reciting the words to a song. His smile assured her that everything was fine. In the car Ellie turned up the volume on his radio and did not bother to look around at them.

"Ellie can sit in the back seat," Arnold Friend said. He indicated his friend with a casual jerk of his chin, as if Ellie did not count and she should not bother with him.

"How'd you find out all that stuff?" Connie said.

"Listen: Betty Schultz and Tony Fitch and Jimmy Pettinger and Nancy Pettinger," he said, in a chant. "Raymond Stanley and Bob Hutter—"

"Do you know all those kids?"

"I know everybody."

"Look, you're kidding. You're not from around here."

"Sure."

"But—how come we never saw you before?"

"Sure you saw me before," he said. He looked down at his boots, as if he were a little offended. "You just don't remember."

"I guess I'd remember you," Connie said.

"Yeah?" He looked up at this, beaming. He was pleased. He began to mark time with the music from Ellie's radio, tapping his fists lightly together. Connie looked away from his smile to the car, which was painted so bright it almost hurt her eyes to look at it. She looked at that name. ARNOLD FRIEND. And up at the front fender was an expression that was familiar—MAN THE FLYING SAUCERS. It was an expression kids had used the year before, but didn't use this year. She looked at it for a while as if the words meant something to her that she did not yet know.

"What're you thinking about? Huh?" Arnold Friend demanded. "Not worried about your hair blowing around in the car, are you?"

"No."

"Think I maybe can't drive good?"

"How do I know?"

"You're a hard girl to handle. How come?" he said. "Don't you know I'm your friend? Didn't you see me put my sign in the air when you walked by?"

"What sign?"

"My sign." And he drew an X in the air, leaning out toward her. They were maybe ten feet apart. After his hand fell back to his side the X was still in the air, almost visible. Connie let the screen door close and stood perfectly still inside it, listening to the music from her radio and the boy's blend together. She stared at Arnold Friend. He stood there so stiffly relaxed, pretending to be relaxed, with one hand idly on the door handle as if he were keeping himself up that way and had no intention of ever moving again. She recognized most things about him, the tight jeans that showed his thighs and buttocks and the greasy leather boots and the tight shirt, and even that slippery friendly smile of his, that sleepy dreamy smile that all the boys used to get across ideas they didn't want to put into words. She recognized all this and also the singsong way he talked, slightly mocking, kidding, but serious and a little melancholy, and she recognized the way he tapped one fist against the other in homage of the perpetual music behind him. But all these things did not come together.

She said suddenly, "Hey, how old are you?"

His smile faded. She could see then that he wasn't a kid, he was much older—thirty, maybe more. At this knowledge her heart began to pound faster.

"That's a crazy thing to ask. Can'tcha see I'm your own age?"

80 "Like hell you are."

"Or maybe a coupla years older, I'm eighteen."

"Eighteen?" she said doubtfully.

He grinned to reassure her and lines appeared at the corners of his mouth. His teeth were big and white. He grinned so broadly his eyes became slits and she saw how thick the lashes were, thick and black as if painted with a black tarlike material. Then he seemed to become embarrassed, abruptly, and looked over his shoulder at Ellie. "*Him,* he's crazy," he said. "Ain't he a riot, he's a nut, a real character." Ellie was still listening to the music. His sunglasses told nothing about what he was thinking. He wore a bright orange shirt unbuttoned halfway to show his chest, which was a pale, bluish chest and not muscular like Arnold Friend's. His shirt collar was turned up all around and the very tips of the collar pointed out past his chin as if they were protecting him. He was pressing the transistor radio up against his ear and sat there in a kind of daze, right in the sun.

"He's kinda strange," Connie said.

85 "Hey, she says you're kinda strange! Kinda strange!" Arnold Friend cried. He pounded on the car to get Ellie's attention. Ellie turned for the first time and Connie saw with shock that he wasn't a kid either—he had a fair, hairless face, cheeks reddened slightly as if the veins grew too close to the surface of his skin, the face of a forty-year-old baby. Connie felt a wave of dizziness rise in her at this sight and she stared at him as if waiting for something to change the shock of the moment, make it all right again. Ellie's lips kept shaping words, mumbling along with the words blasting in his ear.

"Maybe you two better go away," Connie said faintly.

"What? How come?" Arnold Friend cried. "We come out here to take you for a ride. It's Sunday." He had the voice of the man on the radio now. It was the same voice, Connie thought. "Don'tcha know it's Sunday all day and honey, no matter who you were with last night today you're with Arnold Friend and don't you forget it!—Maybe you better step out here," he said, and this last was in a different voice. It was a little flatter, as if the heat was finally getting to him.

"No. I got things to do."

"Hey."

90 "You two better leave."

"We ain't leaving until you come with us."

"Like hell I am—"

"Connie, don't fool around with me. I mean, I mean, don't fool *around,*" he said, shaking his head. He laughed incredulously. He placed his sunglasses on top of his head, carefully, as if he were indeed wearing a wig, and brought the stems down behind his ears. Connie stared at him, another wave of dizziness and fear rising in her so that for a moment he wasn't even in focus but was just a blur, standing there against his gold car, and she had the idea that he had driven up the driveway all right but had come from nowhere before that and belonged nowhere and that everything about him and even about the music that was so familiar to her was only half real.

"If my father comes and sees you—"

95 "He ain't coming. He's at a barbecue."

"How do you know that?"

"Aunt Tillie's. Right now they're—uh—they're drinking. Sitting around," he said vaguely, squinting as if he were staring all the way to town and over to Aunt Tillie's back yard. Then the vision seemed to get clear and he nodded energetically. "Yeah. Sitting around. There's your sister in a blue dress, huh? And high heels, the poor sad bitch—nothing like you, sweetheart! And your mother's helping some fat woman with the corn, they're cleaning the corn—husking the corn—"

"What fat woman?" Connie cried.

"How do I know what fat woman, I don't know every goddam fat woman in the world!" Arnold laughed.

100 "Oh, that's Mrs. Hornby . . . Who invited her?" Connie said. She felt a little light-headed. Her breath was coming quickly.

"She's too fat. I don't like them fat. I like them the way you are, honey," he said, smiling sleepily at her. They stared at each other for a while, through the screen door. He said softly, "Now what you're going to do is this: you're going to come out that door. You're going to sit up front with me and Ellie's going to sit in the back, the hell with Ellie, right? This isn't Ellie's date. You're my date. I'm your lover, honey."

"What? You're crazy—"

"Yes, I'm your lover. You don't know what that is, but you will," he said. "I know that too. I know all about you. But look: it's real nice and you couldn't ask for nobody better than me, or more polite. I always keep my word. I'll tell you how it is, I'm always nice at first, the first time. I'll hold you so tight you won't think you have to try to get away or pretend anything because you'll know you can't. And I'll come inside you where it's all secret and you'll give in to me and you'll love me—"

"Shut up! You're crazy!" Connie said. She backed away from the door. She put her hands against her ears as if she'd heard something terrible, something not meant for her. "People don't talk like that, you're crazy," she muttered. Her heart was almost too big now for her chest and its pumping made sweat break out all over her. She looked out to see Arnold Friend pause and then take a step toward the porch lurching. He almost fell. But, like a clever drunken man, he managed to catch his balance. He wobbled in his high boots and grabbed hold of one of the porch posts.

105 "Honey?" he said. "You still listening?"

"Get the hell out of here!"

"Be nice, honey. Listen."

"I'm going to call the police—"

He wobbled again and out of the side of his mouth came a fast spat curse, an aside not meant for her to hear. But even this "Christ!" sounded forced. Then he began to smile again. She watched this smile come, awkward as if he were smiling from inside a mask. His whole face was a mask, she thought wildly, tanned down onto his throat but then running out as if he had plastered makeup on his face but had forgotten about his throat.

110 "Honey—? Listen, here's how it is. I always tell the truth and I promise you this: I ain't coming in that house after you."

"You better not! I'm going to call the police if you—if you don't—"

"Honey," he said, talking right through her voice, "honey, I'm not coming in there but you are coming out here. You know why?"

She was panting. The kitchen looked like a place she had never seen before, some rooms she had run inside but which wasn't good enough, wasn't going to help her. The kitchen window had never had a curtain, after three years, and there were dishes in the sink for her to do—probably—and if you ran your hand across the table you'd probably feel something sticky there.

"You listening, honey? Hey?"

115 "—going to call the police—"

"Soon as you touch the phone I don't need to keep my promise and can come inside. You won't want that."

She rushed forward and tried to lock the door. Her fingers were shaking. "But why lock it," Arnold Friend said gently, talking right into her face. "It's just a screen door. It's just nothing." One of his boots was at a strange angle, as if his foot wasn't in it. It pointed out to the left, bent at the ankle. "I mean, anybody can break through a screen door and glass and wood and iron or anything else if he needs to, anybody at all and specially Arnold Friend. If the place got lit up with a fire honey you'd come runnin' out into my arms, right into my arms an' safe at home—like you knew I was your lover and'd stopped fooling around. I don't mind a nice shy girl but I don't like no fooling around." Part of those words were spoken with a slight rhythmic lilt, and Connie somehow recognized them—the echo of a song from last year, about a girl rushing into her boyfriend's arms and coming home again—

Connie stood barefoot on the linoleum floor, staring at him. "What do you want?" she whispered.

"I want you," he said.

120 "What?"

"Seen you that night and thought, that's the one, yes sir. I never needed to look any more."

"But my father's coming back. He's coming to get me. I had to wash my hair first—" She spoke in a dry, rapid voice, hardly raising it for him to hear.

"No, your Daddy is not coming and yes, you had to wash your hair and you washed it for me. It's nice and shining and all for me, I thank you, sweetheart," he said, with a mock bow, but again he almost lost his balance. He had to bend and adjust his boots. Evidently his feet did not go all the way down; the boots must have been stuffed with something so that he would seem taller. Connie stared out at him and behind him Ellie in the car, who seemed to be looking off toward Connie's right into nothing. This Ellie said, pulling the words out of the air one after another as if he were just discovering them, "You want me to pull out the phone?"

"Shut your mouth and keep it shut," Arnold Friend said, his face red from bending over or maybe from embarrassment because Connie had seen his boots. "This ain't none of your business."

125 "What—what are you doing? What do you want?" Connie said. "If I call the police they'll get you, they'll arrest you—"

"Promise was not to come in unless you touch the phone, and I'll keep that promise," he said. He resumed his erect position and tried to force his shoulders back. He sounded like a hero in a movie, declaring something important. He spoke too loudly and it was as if he were speaking to someone behind Connie. "I ain't made plans for coming in that house where I don't belong but just for you to come out to me, the way you should. Don't you know who I am?"

"You're crazy," she whispered. She backed away from the door but did not want to go into another part of the house, as if this would give him permission to come through the door. "What do you . . . You're crazy, you . . ."

"Huh? What're you saying, honey?"

Her eyes darted everywhere in the kitchen. She could not remember what it was, this room.

130 "This is how it is, honey; you come out and we'll drive away, have a nice ride. But if you don't come out we're gonna wait till your people come home and then they're all going to get it."

"You want that telephone pulled out?" Ellie said. He held the radio away from his ear and grimaced, as if without the radio the air was too much for him.

"I toldja shut up, Ellie," Arnold Friend said, "you're deaf, get a hearing aid, right? Fix yourself up. This little girl's no trouble and's gonna be nice to me, so Ellie keep to yourself, this ain't your date—right? Don't hem in on me. Don't hog. Don't crush. Don't bird dog. Don't trail me," he said in a rapid meaningless voice, as if he were running through all the expressions he'd learned but was no longer sure which one of them was in style, then rushing on to new ones, making them up with his eyes closed, "Don't crawl under my fence, don't squeeze in my chipmunk hole, don't sniff my glue, suck my popsicle, keep your own greasy fingers on yourself!" He shaded his eyes and peered in at Connie, who was backed against the kitchen table. "Don't mind him honey he's just a creep. He's a dope. Right? I'm the boy for you and like I said you come out here nice like a lady and give me your hand, and nobody else gets hurt, I mean, your nice old bald-headed daddy and your mummy and your sister in her high heels. Because listen: why bring them in this?"

"Leave me alone," Connie whispered.

"Hey, you know that old woman down the road, the one with the chickens and stuff—you know her?"

135 "She's dead!"

"Dead? What? You know her?" Arnold Friend said.

"She's dead—"

"Don't you like her?"

"She dead—she's—she isn't there any more—"

140 "But don't you like her, I mean, you got something against her? Some grudge or something?" Then his voice dipped as if he were conscious of a rudeness. He touched the sunglasses perched on top of his head as if to make sure they were still there. "Now you be a good girl."

"What are you going to do?"

"Just two things, or maybe three," Arnold Friend said. "But I promise it won't last long and you'll like me the way you get to like people you're close to. You will. It's all over for you here, so come on out. You don't want your people in any trouble, do you?"

She turned and bumped against a chair or something, hurting her leg, but she ran into the back room and picked up the telephone. Something roared in her ear, a tiny roaring, and she was so sick with fear that she could do nothing but listen to it—the telephone was clammy and very heavy and her fingers groped down to the dial but were too weak to touch it. She began to scream into the phone, into the roaring. She cried out, she cried for her mother, she felt her breath start jerking back and forth in her lungs as if it were something Arnold Friend were stabbing her with again and again with no tenderness. A noisy sorrowful wailing rose all about her and she was locked inside it the way she was locked inside this house.

After a while she could hear again. She was sitting on the floor with her wet back against the wall.

145 Arnold Friend was saying from the door, "That's a good girl. Put the phone back."

She kicked the phone away from her.

"No, honey. Pick it up. Put it back right."

She picked it up and put it back. The dial tone stopped.

"That's a good girl. Now you come outside."

150 She was hollow with what had been fear, but what was now just an emptiness. All that screaming had blasted it out of her. She sat, one leg cramped under her, and deep inside her brain was something like a pinpoint of light that kept going and would not let her relax. She thought, I'm not going to see my mother again. She thought, I'm not going to sleep in my bed again. Her bright green blouse was all wet.

Arnold Friend said, in a gentle-loud voice that was like a stage voice. "The place where you came from ain't there any more, and where you had in mind to go is canceled out. This place you are now—inside your daddy's house—is nothing but a cardboard box I can knock down any time. You know that and always did know it. You hear me?"

She thought, I have got to think. I have to know what to do.

"We'll go out to a nice field, out in the country here where it smells so nice and it's sunny," Arnold Friend said. "I'll have my arms tight around you so you won't need to try to get away and I'll show you what love is like, what it does. The hell with this house! It looks solid all right," he said. He ran a fingernail down the screen and the noise did not make Connie shiver, as it would have the day before. "Now put your hand on your heart, honey. Feel that? That feels solid too, but we know better, be nice to me, be sweet like you can because what else is there for a girl like you but to be sweet and pretty and give in?—and get away before her people come back?"

She felt her pounding heart. Her hand seemed to enclose it. She thought for the first time in her life that it was nothing that was hers, that belonged to her, but just a pounding, living thing inside this body that wasn't really hers either.

155 "You don't want them to get hurt," Arnold Friend went on. "Now get up, honey. Get up all by yourself."

She stood.

"Now turn this way. That's right. Come over here to me—Ellie, put that away, didn't I tell you? You dope. You miserable creepy dope," Arnold Friend said. His words were not angry but only part of an incantation. The incantation was kindly. "Now come out through the kitchen to me honey, and let's see a smile, try it, you're a brave sweet little girl and now they're eating corn and hot dogs cooked to bursting over an outdoor fire, and they don't know one thing about you and never did and honey you're better than them because not a one of them would have done this for you."

Connie felt the linoleum under her feet; it was cool. She brushed her hair back out of her eyes. Arnold Friend let go of the post tentatively and opened his arms for her, his elbows pointing in toward each other and his wrists limp, to show that this was an embarrassed embrace and a little mocking, he didn't want to make her self-conscious.

She put out her hand against the screen. She watched herself push the door slowly open as if she were safe back somewhere in the other doorway, watching this body and this head of long hair moving out into the sunlight where Arnold Friend waited.

160 "My sweet little blue-eyed girl," he said, in a half-sung sigh that had nothing to do with her brown eyes but was taken up just the same by the vast sunlit reaches of the land behind him and on all sides of him, so much land that Connie had never seen before and did not recognize except to know that she was going to it.

Explorations of the Text

1. Joyce Carol Oates wrote this story after listening to Bob Dylan's "It's All Over Now, Baby Blue." What are the roles of music, sex, restaurants, malls, and cars in this work?
2. Characterize Connie. Why is her sense of her own identity so vague?
3. Why does the narrator say of Connie that "everything about her had two sides to it"?
4. How do Arnold's car and clothes reflect his character?

5. What is Ellie's role in the story?
6. What does the religious imagery suggest? Explore the references to fairy tales in the story.
7. Interpret the ending. Does Arnold commit rape and murder?
8. Compare this story with Luisa Valenzuela's "The Verb to Kill." What does each writer suggest about adolescent sexuality?

The Reading/Writing Connection

1. "Think" Topic: Gothic literature is characterized by gloomy settings, mysterious and violent events, and an atmosphere of death and decay. Discuss the gothic elements in this story.
2. Does Connie lack inner resources? Respond to this question in a paragraph.

Ideas for Writing

1. Is this story still relevant to contemporary teenage culture? Using Kowinski's "Kids in the Mall" as a resource, construct an argument which addresses this question.
2. Why would this story win a prize? Evaluate the work. Consider such elements of fiction as point of view, conflict, character development, language, and tone (see chapter 9).

Game After Supper

Margaret Atwood

Margaret Atwood (1939–) was born in Ottawa, Ontario, Canada, and grew up in northern Ontario, Quebec, and Toronto. She was educated at the University of Toronto, Radcliffe College, and Harvard University. Atwood has written more than twenty books of fiction, poetry, and nonfiction. Her writing is distinguished by its eloquence and its provocativeness. Atwood's works include Surfacing *(1972),* Bluebeard's Egg *(1983),* The Handmaid's Tale *(1985), and* Alias, Grace *(1996). She works in many genres, including science fiction, historical fiction, satire, black comedy, and realistic fiction.*

1970

This is before electricity,
it is when there were porches.

On the sagging porch an old man
is rocking. The porch is wooden,

the house is wooden and grey;
in the living room which smells of
smoke and mildew, soon
the woman will light the kerosene lamp.

There is a barn but I am not in the barn;
there is an orchard too, gone bad,
its apples like soft cork
but I am not there either.

I am hiding in the long grass
with my two dead cousins,
the membrane grown already
across their throats.

We hear crickets and our own hearts
close to our ears;
though we giggle, we are afraid.

From the shadows around
the corner of the house
a tall man is coming to find us:

He will be an uncle,
if we are lucky.

Explorations of the Text

1. What does the locale (the porch, the house, barn, orchard) signify in relation to the rest of the poem?
2. What is the "game after supper"? Why are they hiding? What do they fear?
3. Who is the "tall man"? What does he symbolize?
4. Discuss the significance of the lines: "He will be an uncle, / if we are lucky."

The Reading/Writing Connection

1. Respond to the settings in the poem.
2. Freewrite about the associations that this poem evokes in you.
3. Gloss the poem and list those words and phrases that create the mood of the poem. Write a short paragraph about Atwood's method of establishing the mood.

Ideas for Writing

1. Compare this initiation experience with incidents in "The Verb to Kill"; in "Where Are You Going . . ."; and in "Adolescence I, II, III."

KIDS IN THE MALL

William S. Kowinski

A poet, fiction writer, and critic, William Severini Kowinski studied at Knox College and has been a writer and editor for the Boston Phoenix *and* Washington Newsworks. *He has published in numerous magazines including* Esquire, New Times, *and* The New York Times Magazine. *His book,* The Malling of America: An Inside Look at the Great Consumer Paradise *(1985), is an investigation of the effects of shopping malls on the lives of adolescents.*

1985

Butch heaved himself up and loomed over the group. "Like it was different for me," he piped. "My folks used to drop me off at the shopping mall every morning and leave me all day. It was like a big free babysitter, you know? One night they never came back for me. Maybe they moved away. Maybe there's some kind of a Bureau of Missing Parents I could check with."

—Richard Peck
Secrets of the Shopping Mall
a novel for teenagers

From his sister at Swarthmore, I'd heard about a kid in Florida whose mother picked him up after school every day, drove him straight to the mall, and left him there until it closed—all at his insistence. I'd heard about a boy in Washington who, when his family moved from one suburb to another, pedaled his bicycle five miles every day to get back to his old mall, where he once belonged.

These stories aren't unusual. The mall is a common experience for the majority of American youth; they have probably been going there all their lives. Some ran within their first large open space, saw their first fountain, bought their first toy, and read their first book in a mall. They may have smoked their first cigarette or first joint or turned them down, had their first kiss or lost their virginity in the mall parking lot. Teenagers in America now spend more time in the mall than anywhere else but home and school. Mostly it is their choice, but some of that mall time is put in as the result of two-paycheck and single-parent households, and the lack of other viable alternatives. But are these kids being harmed by the mall?

I wondered first of all what difference it makes for adolescents to experience so many important moments in the mall. They are, after all, at play in the fields of its little world and they learn its ways; they adapt to it and make it adapt to them. It's here that these kids get their street sense, only it's mall sense. They are learning the ways of a large-scale artificial environment: its subtleties and flexibilities, its particular pleasures and resonances, and the attitudes it fosters.

5 The presence of so many teenagers for so much time was not something mall developers planned on. In fact, it came as a big surprise. But kids became a fact of mall life very early, and the International Council of Shopping Centers found it necessary to commission a study, which they published along with a guide to mall managers on how to handle the teenage incursion.

The study found that "teenagers in suburban centers are bored and come to the shopping centers mainly as a place to go. Teenagers in suburban centers spent more time fighting, drinking, littering and walking than did their urban counterparts, but presented fewer overall problems." The report observed that "adolescents congregated in groups of two to four and predominantly at locations selected by them rather than management." This probably had something to do with the decision to install game arcades, which allow management to channel these restless adolescents into naturally contained areas away from major traffic points of adult shoppers.

The guide concluded that mall management should tolerate and even encourage the teenage presence because, in the words of the report, "The vast majority support the same set of values as does shopping center management." *The same set of values* means simply that mall kids are already preprogrammed to be consumers and that the mall can put the finishing touches to them as hard-core, lifelong shoppers just like everybody else. That, after all, is what the mall is about. So it shouldn't be surprising that in spending a lot of time there, adolescents find little that challenges the assumption that the goal of life is to make money and buy products, or that just about everything else in life is to be used to serve those ends.

Growing up in a high-consumption society already adds inestimable pressure to kids' lives. Clothes consciousness has invaded the grade schools, and popularity is linked with having the best, newest clothes in the currently acceptable styles. Even what they read has been affected. "Miss [Nancy] Drew wasn't obsessed with her wardrobe," noted *The Wall Street Journal,* "but today the mystery in teen fiction for girls is what outfit the heroine will wear next." Shopping has become a survival skill and there is certainly no better place to learn it than the mall, where its importance is powerfully reinforced and certainly never questioned.

The mall as a university of suburban materialism, where Valley Girls and Boys from coast to coast are educated in consumption, has its other lessons in this era of change in family life and sexual mores and their economic and social ramifications. The plethora of products in the mall, plus the pressure on teens to buy them, may contribute to the phenomenon that psychologist David Elkind calls "the hurried child": kids who are exposed to too much of the adult world too quickly, and must respond with a sophistication that belies their still-tender emotional development. Certainly the adult products marketed for children—form-fitting designer jeans, sexy tops for preteen girls—add to the social pressure to look like an adult, along with the home-grown need to understand adult finances (why mothers must work) and adult emotions (when parents divorce).

10 Kids spend so much time at the mall partly because their parents allow it and even encourage it. The mall is safe, it doesn't seem to harbor any unsavory activities, and there is adult supervision; it is, after all, a controlled environment. So the temptation, especially for working parents, is to let the mall be their babysitter. At least the kids aren't watching TV. But the mall's role as a surrogate mother may be more extensive and more profound.

Karen Lansky, a writer living in Los Angeles, has looked into the subject and she told me some of her conclusions about the effects on its teenaged denizens of the mall's controlled and controlling environment. "Structure is the dominant idea, since true 'mall rats' lack just that in their home lives," she said, "and adolescents about to make the big leap into growing up crave more structure than our modern society cares to acknowledge." Karen pointed out some of the elements malls supply that kids used to get from their families, like warmth (Strawberry Shortcake dolls and similar cute and cuddly merchandise), old-fashioned mothering ("We do it all for you," the fast-food slogan), and even home cooking (the "homemade" treats at the food court).

The problem in all this, as Karen Lansky sees it, is that while families nurture children by encouraging growth through the assumption of responsibility and then by letting them rest in the bosom of the family from the rigors of growing up, the mall as a structural mother encourages passivity and consumption, as long as the kid doesn't make trouble. Therefore all they learn about becoming adults is how to act and how to consume.

Kids are in the mall not only in the passive role of shoppers—they also work there, especially as fast-food outlets infiltrate the mall's enclosure. There they learn how to hold a job and take responsibility, but still within the same value context. When *CBS Reports* went to Oak Park Mall in suburban Kansas City, Kansas, to tape part of their hour-long consideration of malls, "After the Dream Comes True," they interviewed a teenaged girl who worked in a fast-food outlet there. In a sequence that didn't make the final program, she described the major goal of her present life, which was to perfect the curl on top of the ice-cream cones that were her store's speciality. If she could do that, she would be moved from the lowly soft-drink dispenser to the more prestigious ice-cream division, the curl on top of the status ladder at her restaurant. These are the achievements that are important at the mall.

Other benefits of such jobs may also be overrated, according to Laurence D. Steinberg of the University of California at Irvine's social ecology department, who did a study on teenage employment. Their jobs, he found, are generally simple, mindlessly repetitive and boring. They don't really learn anything, and the jobs don't head anywhere. Teenagers also work primarily with other teenagers; even their supervisors are often just a little older than they are. "Kids need to spend time with adults," Steinberg told me. "Although they get benefits from peer relationships, without parents and other adults it's a one-sided socialization. They hang out with each other, have age-segregated jobs, and watch TV."

15 Perhaps much of this is not so terrible or even so terribly different. Now that they have so much more to contend with in their lives, adolescents probably need more time to spend with other adolescents without adult impositions, just to sort things out. Though it is more concentrated in the mall (and therefore perhaps a clearer target), the value system there is really the dominant one of the whole society. Attitudes about curiosity, initiative, self-expression, empathy, and disinterested learning aren't necessarily made in the mall; they are mirrored there, perhaps a bit more intensely—as through a glass brightly.

Besides, the mall is not without its educational opportunities. There are bookstores, where there is at least a short shelf of classics at great prices, and other books from which it is possible to learn more than how to do sit-ups. There are tools, from hammers to VCRs, and products, from clothes to records, that can help the young find and express themselves. There are older people with stories, and places to be alone or to talk one-on-one with a kindred spirit. And there is always the passing show.

The mall itself may very well be an education about the future. I was struck with the realization, as early as my first forays into Greengate, that the mall is only one of a number of enclosed and controlled environments that are part of the lives of today's young. The mall is just an extension, say, of those large suburban schools—only there's Karmelkorn instead of chem lab, the ice rink instead of the gym: It's high school without the impertinence of classes.

Growing up, moving from home to school to the mall—from enclosure to enclosure, transported in cars—is a curiously continuous process, without much in the way of contrast or contact with unenclosed reality. Places must tend to blur into one another. But whatever differences and dangers there are in this, the skills these adolescents are learning may turn out to be useful in their later lives. For we seem to be moving inexorably into an age of preplanned and regulated environments, and this is the world they will inherit.

Still, it might be better if they had more of a choice. One teenaged girl confessed to *CBS Reports* that she sometimes felt she was missing something by hanging out at the mall so much. "But I'm here," she said, "and this is what I have."

Explorations of the Text

1. How does the opening quotation from Richard Peck's *Secrets of the Shopping Mall* establish the point of view, tone, and concerns of the essay?
2. Why does Kowinski include several personal anecdotes in the opening paragraph?
3. What negative effects does Kowinski attribute to teenagers' "hanging out"? Is he persuasive?
4. In what ways does Kowinski suggest that teenagers benefit at all from the experience? Do you agree with his conclusions?

5. How is Connie in "Where Are You Going, Where Have You Been?" similar to the adolescents presented in this essay? How is Connie a product of mall culture?

The Reading/Writing Connection

1. Did you "hang out" as a teenager? Describe your "hang out" and your friends. You may want to write a dialogue.
2. "Think" Topic: Agree or disagree with Karen Lansky's statement that the mall is a surrogate mother figure that "encourages passivity and consumption."

Ideas for Writing

1. Go to a mall and observe; write about your impressions. Or interview people in a shopping mall about their reactions to mall culture.
2. Write an argument: refute or agree with Kowinski's position or the position of one of the experts quoted in his essay.
3. Is Connie an example of one of Elkind's "hurried children"?

FICTION

A White Heron

Sarah Orne Jewett

Born in South Berwick, Maine, Theodora Sarah Orne Jewett (1849–1909) graduated from Berwick Academy. She began writing stories under a pseudonym for the Atlantic *magazine. In 1877, she published her first collection,* Deephaven. *It was followed by the story collections,* A White Heron, and Other Stories *(1886) and* The King of Folly Island *(1888), and the novels,* A Country Doctor *(1988) and* The Country of Pointed Firs *(1896). Jewett stated that she wrote about those "country characters and landscapes to which (she herself) belonged, and which (she) had been taught to love with all (her) heart."*

1886

I

The woods were already filled with shadows one June evening, just before eight o'clock, though a bright sunset still glimmered faintly among the trunks of the trees. A little girl was driving home her cow, a plodding, dilatory, provoking creature in her behavior, but a valued companion for all that. They were going away from the western light, and striking deep into the dark woods, but their feet were familiar with the path, and it was no matter whether their eyes could see it or not.

There was hardly a night the summer through when the old cow could be found waiting at the pasture bars; on the contrary, it was her greatest pleasure to hide herself away among the high huckleberry bushes, and though she wore a loud bell she had made the discovery that if one stood perfectly still it would not ring. So Sylvia had to hunt for her until she found her, and call Co'! Co'! with never an answering Moo, until her childish patience was quite spent. If the creature had not given good milk and plenty of it, the case would have seemed very different to her owners. Besides, Sylvia had all the time there was, and very little use to make of it. Sometimes in pleasant weather it was a consolation to look upon the cow's pranks as an intelligent attempt to play hide and seek, and as the child had no playmates she lent herself to this amusement with a good deal of zest. Though this chase had been so long that the wary animal herself had given an unusual signal of her whereabouts, Sylvia had only laughed when she came upon Mistress Moolly at the swamp-side, and urged her affectionately homeward with a twig of birch leaves. The old cow was not inclined to wander farther, she even turned in the right direction for once as they left the pasture, and stepped along the road at a good pace. She was quite ready to be milked now, and seldom stopped to browse. Sylvia wondered what her grandmother would say because they were so late. It was a great while since she had left home at half past five o'clock, but everybody knew the difficulty of making this errand a short one. Mrs. Tilley had chased the horned torment too many summer evenings herself to blame any one else for lingering, and was only thankful as she waited that she had Sylvia, nowadays, to give such valuable assistance. The good woman suspected that Sylvia loitered occasionally on her own account; there never was such a child for straying about out-of-doors since the world was made! Everybody said that it was a good change for a little maid who had tried to grow for eight years in a crowded manufacturing town, but, as for Sylvia herself, it seemed as if she never had been alive at all before she came to live at the farm. She thought often with wistful compassion of a wretched dry geranium that belonged to a town neighbor.

" 'Afraid of folks,' " old Mrs. Tilley said to herself, with a smile, after she had made the unlikely choice of Sylvia from her daughter's houseful of children, and was returning to the farm. " 'Afraid of folks,' they said! I guess she won't be troubled no great with 'em up to the old place!" When they reached the door of the lonely house and stopped to unlock it, and the cat came to purr loudly, and rub against them, a deserted pussy, indeed, but fat with young robins, Sylvia whispered that this was a beautiful place to live in, and she never should wish to go home.

The companions followed the shady wood-road, the cow taking slow steps, and the child very fast ones. The cow stopped long at the brook to drink, as if the pasture were not half a swamp, and Sylvia stood still and waited, letting her bare feet cool themselves in the shoal water, while the great twilight moths struck softly against her. She waded on through the brook as the cow moved away, and listened to the thrushes with a heart that beat fast with pleasure. There was a stirring in the great boughs overhead. They were full of little birds and beasts that seemed to be wide-awake, and going about their world, or else saying good-night to each other in sleepy twitters. Sylvia herself felt sleepy as she walked along. However, it was not much farther to the house, and the air was soft and sweet. She was not often in the woods so late as this, and it made her feel as if she were a part of the gray shadows and the moving leaves. She was just thinking how long it seemed since she first came to the farm a year ago, and wondering if everything went on in the noisy town just the same as when she was there; the thought of the great red-faced boy who used to chase and frighten her made her hurry along the path to escape from the shadow of the trees.

5 Suddenly this little woods-girl was horror-stricken to hear a clear whistle not very far away. Not a bird's whistle, which would have a sort of friendliness, but a boy's whistle, determined, and somewhat aggressive. Sylvia left the cow to whatever sad fate might await her, and stepped discreetly aside into the bushes, but she was just too late. The enemy had discovered her, and called out in a very cheerful and persuasive tone. "Halloa, little girl, how far is it to the road?" and trembling Sylvia answered almost inaudibly, "A good ways."

She did not dare to look boldly at the tall young man, who carried a gun over his shoulder, but she came out of her bush and again followed the cow, while he walked alongside.

"I have been hunting for some birds," the stranger said kindly, "and I have lost my way, and need a friend very much. Don't be afraid," he added gallantly. "Speak up and tell me what your name is, and whether you think I can spend the night at your house, and go out gunning early in the morning."

Sylvia was more alarmed than before. Would not her grandmother consider her much to blame? But who could have foreseen such an accident as this? It did not appear to be her fault, and she hung her head as if the stem of it were broken, but managed to answer, "Sylvy," with much effort when her companion again asked her name.

Mrs. Tilley was standing in the doorway when the trio came into view. The cow gave a loud moo by way of explanation.

10 "Yes, you'd better speak up for yourself, you old trial! Where'd she tucked herself away this time, Sylvy?" Sylvia kept an awed silence; she knew by instinct that her grandmother did not comprehend the gravity of the situation. She must be mistaking the stranger for one of the farmer-lads of the region.

The young man stood his gun beside the door, and dropped a heavy game-bag beside it; then he bade Mrs. Tilley good evening, and repeated his wayfarer's story, and asked if he could have a night's lodging.

"Put me anywhere you like," he said. "I must be off early in the morning, before day; but I am very hungry, indeed. You can give me some milk at any rate, that's plain."

"Dear sakes, yes," responded the hostess, whose long slumbering hospitality seemed to be easily awakened. "You might fare better if you went out on the main road a mile or so, but you're welcome to what we've got. I'll milk right off, and you make yourself at home. You can sleep on husks or feathers," she proffered graciously. "I raised them all myself. There's good pasturing for geese just below here towards the ma'sh. Now step round and set a plate for the gentleman, Sylvy!" And Sylvia promptly stepped. She was glad to have something to do, and she was hungry herself.

It was a surprise to find so clean and comfortable a little dwelling in this New England wilderness. The young man had known the horrors of its most primitive housekeeping, and the dreary squalor of that level of society which does not rebel at the companionship of hens. This was the best thrift of an old-fashioned farmstead, though on such a small scale that it seemed like a hermitage. He listened eagerly to the old woman's quaint talk, he watched Sylvia's pale face and shining gray eyes with ever growing enthusiasm, and insisted that this was the best supper he had eaten for a month; then, afterward, the new-made friends sat down in the doorway together while the moon came up.

15 Soon it would be berry time, and Sylvia was a great help at picking. The cow was a good milker, though a plaguy thing to keep track of, the hostess gossiped frankly, adding presently that she had buried four children, so that Sylvia's mother, and a son (who might be dead) in California were all the children she had left. "Dan, my boy, was a great hand to go gunning," she

explained sadly. "I never wanted for pa'tridges or gray squer'ls while he was to home. He's been a great wand'rer, I expect, and he's no hand to write letters. There, I don't blame him, I'd ha' seen the world myself if it had been so I could."

"Sylvia takes after him," the grandmother continued affectionately, after a minute's pause. "There ain't a foot o' ground she don't know her way over, and the wild creatur's counts her one o' themselves. Squer'ls she'll tame to come an' feed right out o' her hands, and all sorts o' birds. Last winter she got the jay-birds to bangeing here, and I believe she'd 'a' scanted herself of her own meals to have plenty to throw out amongst 'em, if I hadn't kep' watch. Anything but crows, I tell her, I'm willin' to help support,—though Dan he went an' tamed one o' them that did seem to have reason same as folks. It was round here a good spell after he went away. Dan an' his father they didn't hitch,—but he never held up his head ag'in after Dan had dared him an' gone off."

The guest did not notice this hint of family sorrows in his eager interest in something else.

"So Sylvy knows all about birds, does she?" he exclaimed, as he looked round at the little girl who sat, very demure but increasingly sleepy, in the moonlight. "I am making a collection of birds myself. I have been at it ever since I was a boy." (Mrs. Tilley smiled.) "There are two or three very rare ones I have been hunting for these five years. I mean to get them on my own ground if they can be found."

"Do you cage 'em up?" asked Mrs. Tilley doubtfully, in response to this enthusiastic announcement.

"Oh, no, they're stuffed and preserved, dozens and dozens of them," said the ornithologist, "and I have shot or snared every one myself. I caught a glimpse of a white heron three miles from here on Saturday, and I have followed it in this direction. They have never been found in this district at all. The little white heron, it is," and he turned again to look at Sylvia with the hope of discovering that the rare bird was one of her acquaintances.

But Sylvia was watching a hop toad in the narrow footpath.

"You would know the heron if you saw it," the stranger continued eagerly. "A queer tall white bird with soft feathers and long thin legs. And it would have a nest perhaps in the top of a high tree, made of sticks, something like a hawk's nest."

Sylvia's heart gave a wild beat; she knew that strange white bird, and had once stolen softly near where it stood in some bright green swamp grass, away over at the other side of the woods. There was an open place where the sunshine always seemed strangely yellow and hot, where tall, nodding rushes grew, and her grandmother had warned her that she might sink in the soft black mud underneath and never be heard of more. Not far beyond were the salt marshes and beyond those was the sea, the sea which Sylvia wondered and dreamed about, but never had looked upon, though its great voice could often be heard above the noise of the woods on stormy nights.

"I can't think of anything I should like so much as to find that heron's nest," the handsome stranger was saying. "I would give ten dollars to anybody who could show it to me," he added desperately, "and I mean to spend my whole vacation hunting for it if need be. Perhaps it was only migrating, or had been chased out of its region by some bird of prey."

Mrs. Tilley gave amazed attention to all this, but Sylvia still watched the toad, not divining, as she might have done at some calmer time, that the creature wished to get to its hole under the doorstep, and was much hindered by the unusual spectators at that hour of the evening. No amount of thought, that night, could decide how many wished-for treasures the ten dollars, so lightly spoken of, would buy.

The next day the young sportsman hovered about the woods, and Sylvia kept him company, having lost her first fear of the friendly lad, who proved to be most kind and sympathetic. He told her many things about the birds and what they knew and where they lived and what they did with themselves. And he gave her a jackknife, which she thought as great a treasure as if she were a desert-islander. All day long he did not once make her troubled or afraid except when he brought down some unsuspecting singing creature from its bough. Sylvia would have liked him vastly better without his gun; she could not understand why he killed the very birds he seemed to like so much. But as the day waned, Sylvia still watched the young man with loving admiration. She had never seen anybody so charming and delightful: the woman's heart, asleep in the child, was vaguely thrilled by a dream of love. Some premonition of that great power stirred and swayed these young foresters who traversed the solemn woodlands with soft-footed silent care. They stopped to listen to a bird's song; they pressed forward again eagerly, parting the branches—speaking to each other rarely and in whispers; the young man going first and Sylvia following, fascinated, a few steps behind, with her gray eyes dark with excitement.

She grieved because the longed-for white heron was elusive, but she did not lead the guest, she only followed, and there was no such thing as speaking first. The sound of her own unquestioned voice would have terrified her—it was hard enough to answer yes or no when there was need of that. At last evening began to fall, and they drove the cow home together, and Sylvia smiled with pleasure when they came to the place where she heard the whistle and was afraid only the night before.

II

Half a mile from home, at the farther edge of the woods, where the land was highest, a great pine-tree stood, the last of its generation. Whether it was left for a boundary mark, or for what reason, no one could say; the woodchoppers who had felled its mates were dead and gone long ago, and a whole forest of sturdy trees, pines and oaks and maples, had grown again. But the stately head of this old pine towered above them all and made a landmark for sea and shore miles and miles away. Sylvia knew it well. She had always believed that whoever climbed to the top of it could see the ocean; and the little girl had often laid her hand on the great rough trunk and looked up wistfully at those dark boughs that the wind always stirred, no matter how hot and still the air might be below. Now she thought of the tree with a new excitement, for why, if one climbed it at break of day, could not one see all the world, and easily discover whence the white heron flew, and mark the place, and find the hidden nest?

What a spirit of adventure, what wild ambition! What fancied triumph and delight and glory for the later morning when she could make known the secret! It was almost too real and too great for the childish heart to bear.

All night the door of the little house stood open, and the whippoorwills came and sang upon the very step. The young sportsman and his old hostess were sound asleep, but Sylvia's great design kept her broad awake and watching. She forgot to think of sleep. The short summer night seemed as long as the winter darkness, and at last when the whippoorwills ceased, and she was afraid the morning would after all come too soon, she stole out of the house and followed the pasture path through the woods, hastening toward the open ground beyond, listening with a sense of comfort and companionship to the drowsy twitter of a half-awakened bird, whose perch she had jarred in passing. Alas, if the great wave of human interest which flooded for the first time this dull little life should sweep away the satisfactions of an existence heart to heart with nature and the dumb life of the forest!

There was the huge tree asleep yet in the paling moonlight, and small and hopeful Sylvia began with utmost bravery to mount to the top of it, with tingling, eager blood coursing the channels of her whole frame, with her bare feet and fingers, that pinched and held like bird's claws to the monstrous ladder reaching up, up, almost to the sky itself. First she must mount the white oak tree that grew alongside, where she was almost lost among the dark branches and the green leaves heavy and wet with dew; a bird fluttered off its nest, and a red squirrel ran to and fro and scolded pettishly at the harmless housebreaker. Sylvia felt her way easily. She had often climbed there, and knew that higher still one of the oak's upper branches chafed against the pine trunk, just where its lower boughs were set close together. There, when she made the dangerous pass from one tree to the other, the great enterprise would really begin.

She crept out along the swaying oak limb at last, and took the daring step across into the old pine-tree. The way was harder than she thought; she must reach far and hold fast, the sharp dry twigs caught and held her and scratched her like angry talons, the pitch made her thin little fingers clumsy and stiff as she went round and round the tree's great stem, higher and higher upward. The sparrows and robins in the woods below were beginning to wake and twitter to the dawn, yet it seemed much lighter there aloft in the pine-tree, and the child knew that she must hurry if her project were to be of any use.

The tree seemed to lengthen itself out as she went up, and to reach farther and farther upward. It was like a great main-mast to the voyaging earth; it must truly have been amazed that morning through all its ponderous frame as it felt this determined spark of human spirit creeping and climbing from higher branch to branch. Who knows how steadily the least twigs held themselves to advantage this light, weak creature on her way! The old pine must have loved his new dependent. More than all the hawks, and bats, and moths, and even the sweet-voiced thrushes, was the brave, beating heart of the solitary gray-eyed child. And the tree stood still and held away the winds that June morning while the dawn grew bright in the east.

Sylvia's face was like a pale star, if one had seen it from the ground, when the last thorny bough was past, and she stood trembling and tired but wholly triumphant, high in the tree-top. Yes, there was the sea with the dawning sun making a golden dazzle over it, and toward that glorious east flew two hawks with slow-moving pinions.[1] How low they looked in the air from that height when before one had only seen them far up, and dark against the blue sky. Their gray feathers were as soft as moths; they seemed only a little way from the tree, and Sylvia felt as if she too could go flying away among the clouds. Westward, the woodlands and farms reached miles and miles into the distance; here and there were church steeples, and white villages; truly it was a vast and awesome world.

The birds sang louder and louder. At last the sun came up bewilderingly bright. Sylvia could see the white sails of ships out at sea, and the clouds that were purple and rose-colored and yellow at first began to fade away. Where was the white heron's nest in the sea of green branches, and was this wonderful sight and pageant of the world the only reward for having climbed to such a giddy height? Now look down again, Sylvia, where the green marsh is set among the shining birches and dark hemlocks; there where you saw the white heron once you will see him again; look, look! a white spot of him like a single floating feather comes up from the dead hemlock and grows larger, and rises, and comes close at last, and goes by the landmark pine with steady sweep of wing and outstretched slender neck and crested head. And wait! wait! do not move a foot or a finger, little girl, do not send an arrow of light and consciousness from your two eager eyes, for the heron has perched on a pine bough not far beyond yours, and cries back to his mate on the nest, and plumes his feathers for the new day!

The child gives a long sigh a minute later when a company of shouting cat-birds comes also to the tree, and vexed by their fluttering and lawlessness the solemn heron goes away. She knows his secret now, the wild, light, slender bird that floats and wavers, and goes back like an arrow presently to his home in the green world beneath. Then Sylvia, well satisfied, makes her perilous way down again, not daring to look far below the branch she stands on, ready to cry sometimes because her fingers ache and her lamed feet slip. Wondering over and over again what the stranger would say to her, and what he would think when she told him how to find his way straight to the heron's nest.

"Sylvy, Sylvy!" called the busy old grandmother again and again, but nobody answered, and the small husk bed was empty, and Sylvia had disappeared.

The guest waked from a dream, and remembering his day's pleasure hurried to dress himself that it might sooner begin. He was sure from the way the

[1] Parts of a bird's wing; wings or feathers.

shy little girl looked once or twice yesterday that she had at least seen the white heron, and now she must really be persuaded to tell. Here she comes now, paler than ever, and her worn old frock is torn and tattered, and smeared with pine pitch. The grandmother and the sportsman stand in the door together and question her, and the splendid moment has come to speak of the dead hemlock-tree by the green marsh.

But Sylvia does not speak after all, though the old grandmother fretfully rebukes her, and the young man's kind appealing eyes are looking straight in her own. He can make them rich with money; he has promised it, and they are poor now. He is so well worth making happy, and he waits to hear the story she can tell.

No, she must keep silence! What is it that suddenly forbids her and makes her dumb? Has she been nine years growing, and now, when the great world for the first time puts out a hand to her, must she thrust it aside for a bird's sake? The murmur of the pine's green branches is in her ears, she remembers how the white heron came flying through the golden air and how they watched the sea and the morning together, and Sylvia cannot speak; she cannot tell the heron's secret and give its life away.

Dear loyalty, that suffered a sharp pang as the guest went away disappointed later in the day, that could have served and followed him and loved him as a dog loves! Many a night Sylvia heard the echo of his whistle haunting the pasture path as she came home with the loitering cow. She forgot even her sorrow at the sharp report of his gun and the piteous sight of thrushes and sparrows dropping silent to the ground, their songs hushed and their pretty feathers stained and wet with blood. Were the birds better friends than their hunter might have been,—who can tell? Whatever treasures were lost to her, woodlands and summer-time, remember! Bring your gifts and graces and tell your secrets to this lonely country child!

Explorations of the Text

1. What is the relationship of landscapes to character? What is the significance of the girl's name?
2. Characterize the ornithologist. Why does Sylvia want to please the young man? What are the complications?
3. What is the relationship between the grandmother and Sylvia?
4. Why does Sylvia save the bird? How does she decide?
5. How does this story differ in theme and style from Faulkner's "Barn Burning?" What elements are similar?

The Reading/Writing Connection

1. In a journal entry, describe female initiation in Jewett's story. What does Sylvia learn?

2. Freewrite and react to the depiction of nature in this work.
3. Write a monologue in the voice of the ornithologist.
4. "Think" Topic: Does Sylvia do the right thing in not revealing the location of the heron?

Ideas for Writing

1. Write about the conflict between love and principle in "A White Heron."
2. Compare the depiction of hunting and violence in "A White Heron" and in "Uncle's First Rabbit."

Barn Burning

William Faulkner

William Faulkner (1897–1962) lived most of his life in Oxford, Mississippi. His literary career began in New Orleans, where he wrote newspaper stories for the Times-Picayune. *With the assistance of the writer Sherwood Anderson, whom he met in New Orleans, Faulkner published his first novel,* Soldier's Pay *(1926). In his major novels, considered among the greatest of the twentieth century, he created an imaginary region near Oxford called Yoknapatawpha County, chronicling its history in* The Sound and the Fury *(1929),* As I Lay Dying *(1930),* Light in August *(1932),* Absalom, Absalom! *(1936),* The Hamlet *(1940), and* Go Down, Moses *(1942). His short fiction can be found in* The Collected Stories of William Faulkner *(1951). Faulkner received the Nobel Prize for Literature in 1949.*

1938

The store in which the Justice of the Peace's court was sitting smelled of cheese. The boy, crouched on his nail keg at the back of the crowded room, knew he smelled cheese, and more; from where he sat he could see the ranked shelves close-packed with the solid, squat, dynamic shapes of tin cans whose labels his stomach read, not from the lettering which meant nothing to his mind but from the scarlet devils and the silver curve of fish—this, the cheese which he knew he smelled and the hermetic meat[1] which his intestines believed he smelled coming in intermittent gusts momentary and brief between the other constant one, the smell and sense just a little of fear because mostly of despair and grief, the old fierce pull of blood. He could not see the table where the Justice sat and before which his father and his father's enemy (*our enemy* he thought in that despair; *ourn! mine and his both! He's my father!*) stood, but he could hear them, the two of them that is, because his father had said no word yet:

"But what proof have you, Mr. Harris?"

[1] Canned meat.

"I told you. The hog got into my corn. I caught it up and sent it back to him. He had no fence that would hold it. I told him so, warned him. The next time I put the hog in my pen. When he came to get it I gave him enough wire to patch up his pen. The next time I put the hog up and kept it. I rode down to his house and saw the wire I gave him still rolled on to the spool in his yard. I told him he could have the hog when he paid me a dollar pound fee. That evening a nigger came with the dollar and got the hog. He was a strange nigger. He said, 'He say to tell you wood and hay kin burn.' I said, 'What?' 'That what he say to tell you,' the nigger said. 'Wood and hay kin burn.' That night my barn burned. I got the stock out but I lost the barn."

"Where is the nigger? Have you got him?"

5 "He was a strange nigger, I tell you. I don't know what became of him."

"But that's not proof. Don't you see that's not proof?"

"Get that boy up here. He knows." For a moment the boy thought too that the man meant his older brother until Harris said. "Not him. The little one. The boy," and, crouching, small for his age, small and wiry like his father, in patched and faded jeans even too small for him, with straight, uncombed, brown hair and eyes gray and wild as storm scud, he saw the men between himself and the table part and become a lane of grim faces, at the end of which he saw the Justice, a shabby, collarless, graying man in spectacles, beckoning him. He felt no floor under his bare feet; he seemed to walk beneath the palpable weight of the grim turning faces. His father, stiff in his black Sunday coat donned not for the trial but for the moving, did not even look at him. *He aims for me to lie,* he thought, again with that frantic grief and despair. *And I will have to do hit.*

"What's your name, boy?" the Justice said.

"Colonel Sartoris Snopes," the boy whispered.

10 "Hey?" the Justice said. "Talk louder. Colonel Sartoris? I reckon anybody named for Colonel Sartoris in this country can't help but tell the truth, can they?" The boy said nothing. *Enemy! Enemy!* he thought; for a moment he could not even see, could not see that the Justice's face was kindly nor discern that his voice was troubled when he spoke to the man named Harris: "Do you want me to question this boy?" But he could hear, and during those subsequent long seconds there was absolutely no sound in the crowded little room save that of quiet and intent breathing it was as if he had swung outward at the end of a grape vine, over a ravine, and at the top of the swing had been caught in a prolonged instant of mesmerized gravity, weightless in time.

"No!" Harris said violently, explosively. "Damnation! Send him out of here!" Now time, the fluid world, rushed beneath him again, the voices coming to him again through the smell of cheese and sealed meat, the fear and despair and the old grief of blood:

"This case is closed. I can't find against you, Snopes, but I can give you advice. Leave this country and don't come back to it."

His father spoke for the first time, his voice cold and harsh, level, without emphasis: "I aim to. I don't figure to stay in a country among people who . . ." he said something unprintable and vile, addressed to no one.

"That'll do," the Justice said, "Take your wagon and get out of this country before dark. Case dismissed."

His father turned, and he followed the stiff black coat, the wiry figure walking a little stiffly, from where a Confederate provost's man's musket ball had taken him in the heel on a stolen horse thirty years ago, followed the two backs now, since his older brother had appeared from somewhere in the crowd, no taller than the father but thicker, chewing tobacco steadily, between the two lines of grim-faced men and out of the store and across the worn gallery and down the sagging steps and among the dogs and half-grown boys in the mild May dust, where as he passed a voice hissed:

"Barn burner!"

Again he could not see, whirling; there was a face in a red haze, moonlike, bigger than the full moon, the owner of it half again his size, he leaping in the red haze toward the face, feeling no blow, feeling no shock when his head struck the earth, scrabbling up and leaping again, feeling no blow this time either and tasting no blood, scrabbling up to see the other boy in full flight and himself already leaping into pursuit as his father's hand jerked him back, the harsh, cold voice speaking above him: "Go get in the wagon."

It stood in a grove of locusts and mulberries across the road. His two hulking sisters in their Sunday dresses and his mother and her sister in calico and sunbonnets were already in it, sitting on and among the sorry residue of the dozen and more movings which even the boy could remember—the battered stove, the broken beds and chairs, the clock inlaid with mother-of-pearl, which would not run, stopped at some fourteen minutes past two o'clock of a dead and forgotten day and time, which had been his mother's dowry. She was crying, though when she saw him she drew her sleeve across her face and began to descend from the wagon. "Get back," the father said.

"He's hurt, I got to get some water and wash his . . ."

"Get back in the wagon," his father said. He got in too, over the tail-gate. His father mounted to the seat where the older brother already sat and struck the gaunt mules two savage blows with the peeled willow, but without heat. It was not even sadistic; it was exactly that same quality which in later years would cause his descendants to over-run the engine before putting a motor car into motion, striking and reining back in the same movement. The wagon went on, the store with its quiet crowd of grimly watching men dropped behind; a curve in the road hid it. *Forever* he thought. *Maybe he's done satisfied now, now that he has . . .* stopping himself, not to say it aloud even to himself. His mother's hand touched his shoulder.

"Does hit hurt?" she said.

"Naw," he said. "Hit don't hurt. Lemme be."

"Can't you wipe some of the blood off before hit dries?"

"I'll wash tonight," he said. "Lemme be, I tell you."

The wagon went on. He did not know where they were going. None of them ever did or ever asked, because it was always somewhere, always a house of sorts waiting for them a day or two days or even three days away. Likely his father had already arranged to make a crop on another farm before he . . . Again he had to stop himself. He (the father) always did. There was something about his wolflike independence and even courage when the advantage was at least neutral which impressed strangers, as if they got from his latent ravening ferocity not so much a sense of dependability as a feeling that his ferocious conviction in the rightness of his own actions would be of advantage to all whose interest lay with his.

That night they camped, in a grove of oaks and beeches where a spring ran. The nights were still cool and they had a fire against it, of a rail lifted from a nearby fence and cut into lengths—a small fire, neat, niggard almost, a shrewd fire; such fires were his father's habit and custom always, even in freezing weather. Older, the boy might have remarked this and wondered why not a big one; why should not a man who had not only seen the waste and extravagance of war, but who had in his blood an inherent voracious prodigality with mate-rial not his own, have burned everything in sight? Then he might have gone astep farther and thought that that was the reason; that niggard blaze was theliving fruits of nights passed during those four years in the woods hiding fromall men, blue or grey, with his strings of horses (captured horses, he calledthem). And older still, he might have divined the true reason: that the elementof fire spoke to some deep mainspring of his father's being, as the element ofsteel or of powder spoke to other men, as the one weapon for the preservationof integrity, else breath were not worth the breathing, and hence to be re-garded with respect and used with discretion.

But he did not think this now and he had seen those same niggard blazes all his life. He merely ate his supper beside it and was already half asleep over his iron plate when his father called him, and once more he followed the stiff back, the stiff and ruthless limp, up the slope and on to the starlit road where, turning, he could see his father against the stars but without face or depth—a shape black, flat, and bloodless as though cut from tin in the iron folds of the frockcoat which had not been made for him, the voice harsh like tin and without heat like tin:

"You were fixing to tell them. You would have told him." He didn't answer. His father struck him with the flat of his hand on the side of the head, hard but without heat, exactly as he had struck the two mules at the store, exactly as he would strike either of them with any stick in order to kill a horse fly, his voice still without heat or anger: "You're getting to be a man. You got to learn. You got to learn to stick to your own blood or you ain't going to have any blood to stick to you. Do you think either of them, any man there this morning, would? Don't you know all they wanted was a chance to get at me because they knew I had them beat? Eh?" Later, twenty years later, he was to tell himself, "If I had said they wanted only truth, justice, he would have hit me again." But now he said nothing. He was not crying. He just stood there. "Answer me," his father said.

"Yes," he whispered. His father turned.

"Get on to bed. We'll be there tomorrow."

Tomorrow they were there. In the early afternoon the wagon stopped before a paintless two-room house identical almost with the dozen others it had stopped before even in the boy's ten years, and again, as on the other dozen occasions, his mother and aunt got down and began to unload the wagon, although his two sisters and his father and brother had not moved.

"Likely hit ain't fitten for hawgs," one of the sisters said.

"Nevertheless, fit it will and you'll hog it and like it," his father said. "Get out of them chairs and help your Ma unload."

The two sisters got down, big, bovine, in a flutter of cheap ribbons; one of them drew from the jumbled wagon bed a battered lantern, the other a worn broom. His father handed the reins to the older son and began to climb stiffly over the wheel. "When they get unloaded, take the team to the barn and feed them." Then he said, and at first the boy thought he was still speaking to his brother: "Come with me."

"Me?" he said.

"Yes," his father said. "You."

"Abner," his mother said. His father paused and looked back—the harsh level stare beneath the shaggy, graying, irascible brows.

"I reckon I'll have a word with the man that aims to begin tomorrow owning me body and soul for the next eight months."

They went back up the road. A week ago—or before last night, that is—he would have asked where they were going, but not now. His father had struck him before last night but never before had he paused afterward to explain why; it was as if the blow and the following calm, outrageous voice still rang, repercussed, divulging nothing to him save the terrible handicap of being young, the light weight of his few years, just heavy enough to prevent his soaring free of the world as it seemed to be ordered but not heavy enough to keep footed solid in it, to resist it and try to change the course of its events.

Presently he could see the grove of oaks and cedars and the other flowering trees and shrubs where the house would be, though not the house yet. They walked beside a fence massed with honeysuckle and Cherokee roses and came to a gate swinging open between two brick pillars, and now, beyond a sweep of drive, he saw the house for the first time and at that instant he forgot his father and the terror and despair both, and even when he remembered his father again (who had stopped) the terror and despair did not return. Because, for all the twelve movings, they had sojourned until now in a poor country, a land of small farms and fields and houses, and he had never seen a house like this before. *Hit's big as a courthouse* he thought quietly, with a surge of peace and joy whose reason he could not have thought into words, being too young for that: *They are safe from him. People whose lives are a part of this peace and dignity are beyond his touch, he no more to them than a buzzing wasp: capable of stinging for a little moment but that's all; the spell of this peace and dignity rendering even the barns and stable and cribs which belong to it impervious to the puny flames he might contrive . . .* this, the peace and joy, ebbing for an instant as he looked again at the stiff black back, the stiff and implacable limp of the figure which was not dwarfed by the house, for the reason that it had never looked big anywhere and which now, against the serene columned backdrop, had more than ever that impervious quality of something cut ruthlessly from tin, depthless, as though, sidewise to the sun, it would cast no shadow. Watching him, the boy remarked the absolutely undeviating course which his father held and saw the stiff foot come squarely down in a pile of fresh droppings where a horse had stood in the drive and which his father could have avoided by a simple change of stride. But it ebbed only for a moment, though he could not have thought this into words either, walking on in the spell of the house, which he could even want but without envy, without sorrow, certainly never with that ravening and jealous rage which unknown to him walked in the ironlike black coat before him: *Maybe he will feel it too. Maybe it will even change him now from what maybe he couldn't help but be.*

They crossed the portico. Now he could hear his father's stiff foot as it came down on the boards with clocklike finality, a sound out of all proportion to the displacement of the body it bore and which was not dwarfed either by the white door before it, as though it had attained to a sort of vicious and ravening minimum not to be dwarfed by anything—the flat, wide, black hat, the formal coat of broadcloth which had once been black but which had now that friction-glazed greenish cast of the bodies of old house flies, the lifted sleeve which was too large, the lifted hand like a curled claw. The door opened so promptly that the boy knew the Negro must have been watching them all the time, an old man with neat grizzled hair, in a linen jacket, who stood barring the door with his body, saying "Wipe yo foots, white man, fo you come in here. Major ain't home nohow."

"Get out of my way, nigger," his father said, without heat too, flinging the door back and the Negro also and entering, his hat still on his head. And now the boy saw the prints of the stiff foot on the doorsill and saw them appear on the pale rug behind the machinelike deliberation of the foot which seemed to bear (or transmit) twice the weight which the body compassed. The Negro was shouting "Miss Lula! Miss Lula!" somewhere behind them, then the boy, deluged as though by a warm wave by a suave turn of carpeted stair and a pendant glitter of chandeliers and a mute gleam of gold frames, heard the swift feet and saw her too, a lady—perhaps he had never seen her like before either—in a gray, smooth gown with lace at the throat and an apron tied at the waist and the sleeves turned back, wiping cake or biscuit dough from her hands with a towel as she came up the hall, looking not at his father at all but at the tracks on the blond rug with an expression of incredulous amazement.

"I tried," the Negro cried. "I tole him to . . ."

"Will you please go away?" she said in a shaking voice. "Major de Spain is not at home. Will you please go away?"

His father had not spoken again. He did not speak again. He did not even look at her. He just stood stiff in the center of the rug, in his hat, the shaggy iron-gray brows twitching slightly above the pebble-colored eyes as he appeared to examine the house with brief deliberation. Then with the same deliberation he turned; the boy watched him pivot on the good leg and saw the stiff foot drag round the arc of the turning, leaving a final long and fading smear. His father never looked at it, he never once looked down at the rug. The Negro held the door. It closed behind them, upon the hysteric and indistinguishable woman-wail. His father stopped at the top of the steps and scraped his boot clean on the edge of it. At the gate he stopped again. He stood for a moment, planted stiffly on the stiff foot, looking back at the house. "Pretty and white, ain't it?" he said. "That's sweat. Nigger sweat. Maybe it ain't white enough yet to suit him. Maybe he wants to mix some white sweat with it."

Two hours later the boy was chopping wood behind the house within which his mother and aunt and the two sisters (the mother and aunt, not the two girls, he knew that; even at this distance and muffled by walls the flat loud voices of the two girls emanated an incorrigible idle inertia) were setting up the stove to prepare a meal, when he heard the hooves and saw the linen-clad man on a fine sorrel mare, whom he recognized even before he saw the rolled rug in front of the Negro youth following on a fat bay carriage horse—a suffused, angry face vanishing, still at full gallop, beyond the corner of the house where his father and brother were sitting in the two tilted chairs; and a moment later, almost before he could have put the axe down, he heard the hooves again and watched the sorrel mare go back out of the yard, already galloping again. Then his father began to shout one of the sisters' names, who presently emerged backward from the kitchen door dragging the rolled rug along the ground by one end while the other sister walked behind it.

"If you ain't going to tote, go on and set up the wash pot," the first said.

"You, Sarty!" the second shouted. "Set up the wash pot!" His father appeared at the door, framed against that shabbiness, as he had been against that other bland perfection, impervious to either, the mother's anxious face at his shoulder.

"Go on," the father said. "Pick it up." The two sisters stooped, broad, lethargic; stooping, they presented an incredible expanse of pale cloth and a flutter of tawdry ribbons.

"If I thought enough of a rug to have to git hit all the way from France I wouldn't keep hit where folks coming in would have to tromp on hit," the first said. They raised the rug.

"Abner," the mother said. "Let me do it."

"You go back and git dinner," his father said. "I'll tend to this."

From the woodpile through the rest of the afternoon the boy watched them, the rug spread flat in the dust beside the bubbling wash pot, the two sisters stooping over it with that profound and lethargic reluctance, while the father stood over them in turn, implacable and grim, driving them though never raising his voice again. He could smell the harsh homemade lye they were using; he saw his mother come to the door once and look toward them with an expression not anxious now but very like despair; he saw his father turn, and he fell to with the axe and saw from the corner of his eye his father raise from the ground a flattish fragment of field stone and examine it and return to the pot, and this time his mother actually spoke: "Abner. Abner. Please don't. Please, Abner."

Then he was done too. It was dusk; the whippoorwills had already begun. He could smell coffee from the room where they would presently eat the cold food remaining from the mid-afternoon meal, though when he entered the house he realized they were having coffee again because there was a fire on the hearth, before which the rug now lay spread over the backs of the two chairs. The tracks of his father's foot were gone. Where they had been were now long, water-cloudy scoriations resembling the sporadic course of a Lilliputian[2] mowing machine.

55 It still hung there while they ate the cold food and then went to bed, scattered without order or claim up and down the two rooms, his mother in one bed, where his father would later lie, the older brother in the other, himself, the aunt, and the two sisters on pallets on the floor. But his father was not in bed yet. The last thing the boy remembered was the depthless, harsh silhouette of the hat and coat bending over the rug and it seemed to him that he had not even closed his eyes when the silhouette was standing over him, the fire almost dead behind it, the stiff foot prodding him awake. "Catch up the mule," his father said.

When he returned with the mule his father was standing in the black door, the rolled rug over his shoulder. "Ain't you going to ride?" he said.

"No. Give me your foot."

He bent his knee into his father's hand, the wiry, surprising power flowed smoothly, rising, he rising with it, on to the mule's bare back (they had owned a saddle once; the boy could remember it though not when or where) and with the same effortlessness his father swung the rug up in front of him. Now in the starlight they retraced the afternoon's path, up the dusty road rife with honeysuckle, through the gate and up the black tunnel of the drive to the lightless house, where he sat on the mule and felt the rough warp of the rug drag across his thighs and vanish.

"Don't you want me to help?" he whispered. His father did not answer and now he heard again that stiff foot striking the hollow portico with that wooden and clocklike deliberation, that outrageous overstatement of the weight it carried. The rug, hunched, not flung (the boy could tell that even in the darkness) from his father's shoulder, struck the angle of wall and floor with a sound unbelievably loud, thunderous, then the foot again, unhurried and enormous; a light came on in the house and the boy sat, tense, breathing steadily and quietly and just a little fast, though the foot itself did not increase its beat at all, descending the steps now; now the boy could see him.

60 "Don't you want to ride now?" he whispered. "We kin both ride now," the light within the house altering now, flaring up and sinking. *He's coming down the stairs now,* he thought. He had already ridden the mule up beside the horse block; presently his father was up behind him and he doubled the reins over and slashed the mule across the neck, but before the animal could begin to trot the hard, thin arm came round him, the hard, knotted hand jerking the mule back to a walk.

In the first red rays of the sun they were in the lot, putting plow gear on the mules. This time the sorrel mare was in the lot before he heard it at all, the

[2] Referring to Lilliput, an imaginary island in Jonathan Swift's *Gulliver's Travels,* the inhabitants of which were six inches tall; diminutive.

rider collarless and even bareheaded, trembling, speaking in a shaking voice as the woman in the house had done, his father merely looking up once before stooping again to the hame he was buckling, so that the man on the mare spoke to his stooping back:

"You must realize you have ruined that rug. Wasn't there anybody here, any of your women . . ." He ceased, shaking, the boy watching him, the older brother leaning now in the stable door, chewing, blinking slowly and steadily at nothing apparently. "It cost a hundred dollars. But you never had a hundred dollars. You never will. So I'm going to charge you twenty bushels of corn against your crop. I'll add it in your contract and when you come to the commissary you can sign it. That won't keep Mrs. de Spain quiet but maybe it will teach you to wipe your feet off before you enter her house again."

Then he was gone. The boy looked at his father, who still had not spoken or even looked up again, who was now adjusting the logger-head in the hame.

"Pap," he said. His father looked at him—the inscrutable face, the shaggy brows beneath which the gray eyes glinted coldly. Suddenly the boy went toward him, fast, stopping as suddenly. "You done the best you could!" he cried. "If he wanted hit done different why didn't he wait and tell you how? He won't git no twenty bushels! He won't git none! We'll get hit and hide hit! I kin watch . . ."

"Did you put the cutter back in that straight stock like I told you?"

"No, sir," he said.

"Then go do it."

That was Wednesday. During the rest of that week he worked steadily, at what was within his scope and some which was beyond it, with an industry that did not need to be driven nor even commanded twice; he had this from his mother, with the difference that some at least of what he did he liked to do, such as splitting wood with the half-size axe which his mother and aunt had earned, or saved money somehow, to present him with at Christmas. In company with the two older women (and on one afternoon even one of the sisters), he built pens for the shoat and the cow which were a part of his father's contract with the landlord, and one afternoon, his father being absent, gone somewhere on one of the mules, he went to the field.

They were running a middle buster now, his brother holding the plow straight while he handled the reins, and walking beside the straining mule, the rich black soil shearing cool and damp against his bare ankles, he thought *Maybe this is the end of it. Maybe even that twenty bushels that seems hard to have to pay for just a rug will be a cheap price for him to stop forever and always from being what he used to be;* thinking, dreaming now, so that his brother had to speak sharply to him to mind the mule: *Maybe he even won't collect the twenty bushels. Maybe it will all add up and balance and vanish—corn, rug, fire; the terror and grief, the being pulled two ways like between two teams of horses—gone, done with forever and ever.*

Then it was Saturday; he looked up from beneath the mule he was harnessing and saw his father in the black coat and hat. "Not that," his father said. "The wagon gear." And then, two hours later, sitting in the wagon bed behind his father and brother on the seat, the wagon accomplished a final curve, and he saw the weathered paintless store with its tattered tobacco- and patent-medicine posters and the tethered wagons and saddle animals below the gallery. He mounted the gnawed steps behind father and brother, and there again was the lane of quiet, watching faces for the three of them to walk through. He saw the man in spectacles sitting at the plank table and he did not need to be told this was Justice of the Peace; he sent one glare of fierce, exultant, partisan defiance at the man in collar and cravat now, whom he had seen but twice in his life, and that on a galloping horse, who now wore on his face an expression not of rage but of amazed unbelief which the boy could not have known was at the incredible circumstance of being sued by one of his own tenants, and came and stood against his father and cried at the Justice: "He ain't done it! He ain't burnt . . ."

"Go back to the wagon," his father said.

"Burnt?" the Justice said. "Do I understand this rug was burned too?"

"Does anybody here claim it was?" his father said. "Go back to the wagon." But he did not, he merely retreated to the rear of the room, crowded as that other had been, but not to sit down this time, instead, to stand pressing among the motionless bodies, listening to the voices:

"And you claim twenty bushels of corn is too high for the damage you did to the rug?"

"He brought the rug to me and said he wanted the tracks washed out of it. I washed the tracks out and took the rug back to him."

"But you didn't carry the rug back to him in the same condition it was in before you made the tracks on it."

His father did not answer, and now for perhaps half a minute there was no sound at all save that of breathing, the faint, steady suspiration of complete and intent listening.

"You decline to answer that, Mr. Snopes?" Again his father did not answer. "I'm going to find against you, Mr. Snopes. I'm going to find that you were responsible for the injury to Major de Spain's rug and hold you liable for it. But twenty bushels of corn seems a little high for a man in your circumstances to have to pay. Major de Spain claims it cost a hundred dollars. October corn will be worth about fifty cents. I figure that if Major de Spain can stand a ninety-five-dollar loss on something he paid cash for, you can stand a five-dollar loss you haven't earned yet. I hold you in damages to Major de Spain to the amount of ten bushels of corn over and above your contract with him, to be paid to him out of your crop at gathering time. Court adjourned."

It had taken no time hardly, the morning was but half begun. He thought they would return home and perhaps back to the field, since they were late, far behind all other farmers. But instead his father passed on behind the wagon, merely indicating with his hand for the older brother to follow with it, and crossed the road toward the blacksmith shop opposite, pressing on after his father, overtaking him, speaking, whispering up at the harsh, calm face beneath the weathered hat: "He won't git no ten bushels neither. He won't git one. We'll . . ." until his father glanced for an instant down on him, the face absolutely calm, the grizzled eyebrows tangled above the cold eyes, the voice almost pleasant, almost gentle:

"You think so? Well, we'll wait till October anyway."

The matter of the wagon—the setting of a spoke or two and the tightening of the tires—did not take long either, the business of the tires accomplished by driving the wagon into the spring branch behind the shop and letting it stand there, the mules nuzzling into the water from time to time, and the boy on the seat with the idle reins, looking up the slope and through the sooty tunnel of the shed where the slow hammer rang and where his father sat on an upended cypress bolt, easily, either talking or listening, still sitting there when the boy brought the dripping wagon up out of the branch and halted it before the door.

"Take them on to the shade and hitch," his father said. He did so and returned. His father and the smith and a third man squatting on his heels inside the door were talking, about crops and animals; the boy, squatting too in the ammoniac dust and hoof-parings and scales of rust, heard his father tell a long and unhurried story out of the time before the birth of the older brother even when he had been a professional horsetrader. And then his father came up beside him where he stood before a tattered last year's circus poster on the other side of the store, gazing rapt and quiet at the scarlet horses, the incredible poisings and convolutions of tulle and tights and the painted leers of comedians, and said, "It's time to eat."

But not at home. Squatting beside his brother against the front wall, he watched his father emerge from the store and produce from a paper sack a segment of cheese and divided it carefully and deliberately into three with his pocket knife and produce crackers from the same sack. They all three squatted on the gallery and ate slowly, without talking; then in the store again, they drank from a tin dipper tepid water smelling of the cedar bucket and of living beech trees. And still they did not go home. It was a horse lot this time, a tall rail fence upon and along which men stood and sat and out of which one by one horses were led, to be walked and trotted and then cantered back and forth along the road while the slow swapping and buying went on and the sun began to slant westward, they—the three of them—watching and listening, the older brother with his muddy eyes and his steady inevitable tobacco, the father commenting now and then on certain of the animals, to no one in particular.

It was after sundown when they reached home. They ate supper by lamplight, then, sitting on the doorstep, the boy watched the night fully accomplish, listening to the whippoorwills and the frogs, when he heard his mother's voice: "Abner! No! No! Oh, God, Oh, God, Abner!" and he rose, whirled, and saw the altered light through the door where a candle stub now burned in a bottle neck on the table and his father, still in the hat and coat, at once formal and burlesque as though dressed carefully for some shabby and ceremonial violence, emptying the reservoir of the lamp back into the five-gallon kerosene can from which it had been filled, while the mother tugged at his arm until he shifted the lamp to the other hand and flung her back, not savagely or viciously, just hard, into the wall, her hands flung out against the wall for balance, her mouth open and in her face the same quality of hopeless despair as had been in her voice. Then his father saw him standing in the door.

85 "Go to the barn and get that can of oil we were oiling the wagon with," he said. The boy did not move. Then he could speak.

"What . . ." he cried. "What are you . . ."

"Go get that oil," his father said. "Go."

Then he was moving, running, outside the house, toward the stable: this the old habit, the old blood which he had not been permitted to choose for himself, which had been bequeathed him willy nilly and which had run for so long (and who knew where, battening on what of outrage and savagery and lust) before it came to him. *I could keep on,* he thought, *I could run on and on and never look back, never need to see his face again. Only I can't. I can't,* the rusted can in his hand now, the liquid sloshing in it as he ran back to the house and into it, into the sound of his mother's weeping in the next room, and handed the can to his father.

"Ain't you going to even send a nigger?" he cried. "At least you sent a nigger before!"

90 This time his father didn't strike him. The hand came even faster than the blow had, the same hand which had set the can on the table with almost excruciating care flashing from the can toward him too quick for him to follow it, gripping him by the back of his shirt and on to tiptoe before he had seen it quit the can, the face stooping at him in breathless and frozen ferocity, the cold, dead voice speaking over him to the older brother who leaned against the table, chewing with that steady, curious, sidewise motion of cows:

"Empty the can into the big one and go on. I'll catch up with you."

"Better tie him up to the bedpost," the brother said.

"Do like I told you," the father said. Then the boy was moving, his bunched shirt and the hard, bony hand between his shoulder-blades, his toes just touching the floor, across the room and into the other one, past the sisters sitting with spread heavy thighs in the two chairs over the cold hearth, and to where his mother and aunt sat side by side on the bed, the aunt's arms about the mother's shoulders.

"Hold him," the father said. The aunt made a startled movement. "Not you," the father said. "Lennie. Take hold of him. I want to see you do it." His mother took him by the wrist. "You'll hold him better than that. If he gets loose don't you know what he is going to do? He will go up yonder." He jerked his head toward the road. "Maybe I'd better tie him."

95 "I'll hold him," his mother whispered.

"See you do then." Then his father was gone, the stiff foot heavy and measured upon the boards, ceasing at last.

Then he began to struggle. His mother caught him in both arms, he jerking and wrenching at them. He would be stronger in the end, he knew that. But he had not time to wait for it. "Lemme go!" he cried. "I don't want to have to hit you!"

"Let him go!" the aunt said. "If he don't go, before God, I am going up there myself!"

"Don't you see I can't?" his mother cried. "Sarty! Sarty! No! No! Help me, Lizzie!"

100 Then he was free. His aunt grasped at him but it was too late. He whirled, running, his mother stumbled forward on to her knees behind him, crying to the nearer sister: "Catch him, Net! Catch him!" But that was too late too, the sister (the sisters were twins, born at the same time, yet either of them now gave the impression of being, encompassing as much living meat and volume and weight as any other two of the family) not yet having begun to rise from the chair, her head, face, alone merely turned, presenting to him in the flying instant an astonishing expanse of young female features untroubled by any surprise even, wearing only an expression of bovine interest. Then he was out of the room, out of the house, in the mild dust of the starlit road and the heavy rifeness of honeysuckle, the pale ribbon unspooling with terrific slowness under his running feet, reaching the gate at last and turning in, running, his heart and lungs drumming, on up the drive toward the lighted house, the lighted door. He did not knock, he burst in, sobbing for breath, incapable for the moment of speech; he saw the astonished face of the Negro in the line jacket without knowing when the Negro had appeared.

"De Spain!" he cried, panted. "Where's . . ." then he saw the white man too emerging from a white door down the hall. "Barn!" he cried. "Barn!"

"What?" the white man said. "Barn?"

"Yes!" the boy cried. "Barn!"

"Catch him!" the white man shouted.

105 But it was too late this time too. The Negro grasped his shirt, but the entire sleeve, rotten with washing, carried away, and he was out that door too and in the drive again, and had actually never ceased to run even while he was screaming into the white man's face.

Behind him the white man was shouting. "My horse! Fetch my horse!" and he thought for an instant of cutting across the park and climbing the fence into the road, but he did not know the park nor how high the vine-massed fence might be and he dared not risk it. So he ran on down the drive, blood and breath roaring; presently he was in the road again though he could not see it. He could not hear either: the galloping mare was almost upon him before he heard her, and even then he held his course, as if the very urgency of his wild grief and need must in a moment more find him wings, waiting until the ultimate instant to hurl himself aside and into the weed-choked roadside ditch as the horse thundered past and on, for an instant in furious silhouette against the stars, the tranquil early summer night sky which, even before the shape of the horse and rider vanished, strained abruptly and violently upward: a long, swirling roar incredible and soundless, blotting the stars, and he springing up and into the road again, running again, knowing it was too late yet still running even after he heard the shot and, an instant later, two shots, pausing now without knowing he had ceased to run, crying "Pap! Pap!," running again before he knew he had begun to run, stumbling, tripping over something and scrabbling up again without ceasing to run, looking backward over his shoulder at the glare as he got up, running on among the invisible trees, panting, sobbing, "Father! Father!"

At midnight he was sitting on the crest of a hill. He did not know it was midnight and he did not know how far he had come. But there was no glare behind him now and he sat now, his back toward what he had called home for four days anyhow, his face toward the dark woods which he would enter when breath was strong again, small, shaking steadily in the chill darkness, hugging himself into the remainder of his thin, rotten shirt, the grief and despair now no longer terror and fear but just grief and despair. *Father. My father,* he thought. "He was brave!" he cried suddenly, aloud but not loud, no more than a whisper: "He was! He was in the war! He was in Colonel Sartoris' cav'ry!" not knowing that his father had gone to that war a private in the fine old European sense, wearing no uniform, admitting the authority of and giving fidelity to no man or army or flag, going to war as Malbrouck[3] himself did: for booty—it meant nothing and less than nothing to him if it were enemy booty or his own.

The slow constellations wheeled on. It would be dawn and then sun-up after a while and he would be hungry. But that would be tomorrow and now he was only cold, and walking would cure that. His breathing was easier now and he decided to get up and go on, and then he found that he had been asleep because he knew it was almost dawn, the night almost over. He could tell that from the whippoorwills. They were everywhere now among the dark trees below him, constant and inflectioned and ceaseless, so that, as the instant for giving over to the day birds drew nearer and nearer, there was no interval at all between them. He got up. He was a little stiff, but walking would cure that too as it would the cold, and soon there would be the sun. He went on down the hill, toward the dark woods within which the liquid silver voices of the birds called unceasing—the rapid and urgent beating of the urgent and quiring heart of the late spring night. He did not look back.

Explorations of the Text

1. Describe the courtroom scene at the beginning of the story. How does Sarty feel and react?
2. Why does the boy feel "peace and joy" when he sees Major de Spain's house?
3. What are the father's values? Does the boy renounce them? Does the boy really betray the father?
4. What image characterizes the women in the story? What do you conclude?
5. What concepts of justice emerge in "Barn Burning"? What is implied about the evolution of justice from rudimentary to more civilized ideas?

[3] Hero of an old French ballad ("Malbrouck s'en va-t-en guerre"); the original Malbrouck was the English Duke of Marborough (1650–1722), accused of profiteering during wartime (1702–13).

6. Trace the changes in Sarty's character. Be specific.
7. Read the last two paragraphs carefully. Is the ending pessimistic or optimistic? Which words give evidence for a conclusion?
8. Faulkner is noted for his complex style. Is the style appropriate in this story?

The Reading/Writing Connection

1. "Think Topic": In a paragraph, discuss the logic of each participant in the courtroom scene.
2. Evaluate Faulkner's technique in the opening of the story.

Ideas for Writing

1. Describe the father's past and explain his actions in the story. Does the reader have any sympathy for him?
2. How does Faulkner portray women in "Barn Burning"?
3. Write on one of the following themes: betrayal, guilt and redemption, or sins of the father.

The Stolen Party

Liliana Heker

Born in Argentina, Liliana Heker (1943–) published her first volume of short stories, Those Who Beheld the Burning Bush, *when she was still a teenager. Later she served as the editor of the literary journal* The Platypus *during the years of Argentina's dictatorship, when many writers "disappeared" and many who objected to oppression were tortured and killed by death squads.*

1982

As soon as she arrived she went straight to the kitchen to see if the monkey was there. It was: what a relief! She wouldn't have liked to admit that her mother had been right. *Monkeys at a birthday?* her mother had sneered. *Get away with you, believing any nonsense you're told!* She was cross, but not because of the monkey, the girl thought; it's just because of the party.

"I don't like you going," she told her. "It's a rich people's party."

"Rich people go to Heaven too," said the girl, who studied religion at school.

"Get away with Heaven," said the mother. "The problem with you, young lady, is that you like to fart higher than your ass."

5 The girl didn't approve of the way her mother spoke. She was barely nine, and one of the best in her class.

"I'm going because I've been invited," she said. "And I've been invited because Luciana is my friend. So there."

"Ah yes, your friend," her mother grumbled. She paused. "Listen, Rosaura," she said at last. "That one's not your friend. You know what you are to them? The maid's daughter, that's what."

Rosaura blinked hard: she wasn't going to cry. Then she yelled: "Shut up! You know nothing about being friends!"

Every afternoon she used to go to Luciana's house and they would both finish their homework while Rosaura's mother did the cleaning. They had their tea in the kitchen and they told each other secrets. Rosaura loved everything in the big house, and she also loved the people who lived there.

"I'm going because it will be the most lovely party in the whole world, Luciana told me it would. There will be a magician, and he will bring a monkey and everything."

The mother swung around to take a good look at her child, and pompously put her hands on her hips.

"Monkeys at a birthday?" she said. "Get away with you, believing any nonsense you're told!"

Rosaura was deeply offended. She thought it unfair of her mother to accuse other people of being liars simply because they were rich. Rosaura too wanted to be rich, of course. If one day she managed to live in a beautiful palace, would her mother stop loving her? She felt very sad. She wanted to go to that party more than anything else in the world.

"I'll die if I don't go," she whispered, almost without moving her lips.

And she wasn't sure whether she had been heard, but on the morning of the party she discovered that her mother had starched her Christmas dress. And in the afternoon, after washing her hair, her mother rinsed it in apple vinegar so that it would be all nice and shiny. Before going out, Rosaura admired herself in the mirror, with her white dress and glossy hair, and thought she looked terribly pretty.

Señora Ines seemed to notice. As soon as she saw her, she said:

"How lovely you look today, Rosaura."

Rosaura gave her starched skirt a slight toss with her hands and walked into the party with a firm step. She said hello to Luciana and asked about the monkey. Luciana put on a secretive look and whispered into Rosaura's ear: "He's in the kitchen. But don't tell anyone, because it's a surprise."

Rosaura wanted to make sure. Carefully she entered the kitchen and there she saw it: deep in thought, inside its cage. It looked so funny that the girl stood there for while, watching it, and later, every so often, she would slip out of the party unseen and go and admire it. Rosaura was the only one allowed into the kitchen. Señora Ines had said: "You yes, but not the others, they're much too boisterous, they might break something." Rosaura had never broken anything. She even managed the jug of orange juice, carrying it from the kitchen into the dining room. She held it carefully and didn't spill a single drop. And Señora Ines had said: "Are you sure you can manage a jug as big as that?" Of course she could manage. She wasn't a butterfingers, like the others. Like that blonde girl with the bow in her hair. As soon as she saw Rosaura, the girl with the bow had said:

"And you? Who are you?"

"I'm a friend of Luciana," said Rosaura.

"No," said the girl with the bow, "you are not a friend of Luciana because I'm her cousin and I know all her friends. And I don't know you."

"So what," said Rosaura. "I come here every afternoon with my mother and we do our homework together."

"You and your mother do your homework together?" asked the girl, laughing.

"I and Luciana do our homework together," said Rosaura, very seriously.

The girl with the bow shrugged her shoulders.

"That's not being friends," she said. "Do you go to school together?"

"No."

"So where do you know her from?" said the girl, getting impatient.

Rosaura remembered her mothers's words perfectly. She took a deep breath.

"I'm the daughter of the employee," she said.

Her mother had said very clearly: "If someone asks, you say you're the daughter of the employee; that's all." She also told her to add: "And proud of it." But Rosaura thought that never in her life would she dare say something of the sort.

"What employee?" said the girl with the bow. "Employee in a shop?"

"No," said Rosaura angrily. "My mother doesn't sell anything in any shop, so there."

"So how come she's an employee?" said the girl with the bow.

Just then Señora Ines arrived saying *shh shh,* and asked Rosaura if she wouldn't mind helping serve out the hotdogs, as she knew the house so much better than the others.

"See?" said Rosaura to the girl with the bow, and when no one was looking she kicked her in the shin.

Apart from the girl with the bow, all the others were delightful. The one she liked best was Luciana, with her golden birthday crown; and then the boys. Rosaura won the sack race, and nobody managed to catch her when they played tag. When they split into two teams to play charades, all the boys wanted her for their side. Rosaura felt she had never been so happy in all her life.

But the best was still to come. The best came after Luciana blew out the candles. First the cake. Señora Ines had asked her to help pass the cake around, and Rosaura had enjoyed the task immensely, because everyone called out to her, shouting "Me, me!" Rosaura remembered a story in which there was a queen who had the power of life or death over her subjects. She had always loved that, having the power of life or death. To Luciana and the boys she gave the largest pieces, and to the girl with the bow she gave a slice so thin one could see through it.

After the cake came the magician, tall and bony, with a fine red cape. A true magician: he could untie handkerchiefs by blowing on them and make a chain with links that had no openings. He could guess what cards were pulled out from a pack, and the monkey was his assistant. He called the monkey "partner." "Let's see here, partner," he would say, "turn over a card." And, "Don't run away, partner: time to work now."

The final trick was wonderful. One of the children had to hold the monkey in his arms and the magician said he would make him disappear.

"What, the boy?" they all shouted.

"No, the monkey!" shouted back the magician.

Rosaura thought that this was truly the most amusing party in the whole world.

The magician asked a small fat boy to come and help, but the small fat boy got frightened almost at once and dropped the monkey on the floor. The magician picked him up carefully, whispered something in his ear, and the monkey nodded almost as if he understood.

"You mustn't be so unmanly, my friend," the magician said to the fat boy.

"What's unmanly?" said the fat boy.

The magician turned around as if to look for spies.

"A sissy," said the magician. "Go sit down."

Then he stared at all the faces, one by one. Rosaura felt her heart tremble.

"You, with the Spanish eyes," said the magician. And everyone saw that he was pointing at her.

She wasn't afraid. Neither holding the monkey, nor when the magician made him vanish; not even when, at the end, the magician flung his red cape over Rosaura's head and uttered a few magic words . . . and the monkey reappeared, chattering happily, in her arms. The children clapped furiously. And before Rosaura returned to her seat, the magician said:

"Thank you very much, my little countess."

She was so pleased with the compliment that a while later, when her mother came to fetch her, that was the first thing she told her.

"I helped the magician and he said to me, 'Thank you very much, my little countess.' "

It was strange because up to then Rosaura had thought that she was angry with her mother. All along Rosaura had imagined that she would say to her: "See that the monkey wasn't a lie?" But instead she was so thrilled that she told her mother all about the wonderful magician.

Her mother tapped her on the head and said: "So now we're a countess!"

But one could see that she was beaming.

And now they both stood in the entrance, because a moment ago Señora Ines, smiling, had said: "Please wait here a second."

Her mother suddenly seemed worried.

"What is it?" she asked Rosaura.

"What is what?" said Rosaura. "It's nothing; she just wants to get the presents for those who are leaving, see?"

She pointed at the fat boy and at a girl with pigtails who were also waiting there, next to their mothers. And she explained about the presents. She knew, because she had been watching those who left before her. When one of the girls was about to leave, Señora Ines would give her a bracelet. When a boy left, Señora Ines gave him a yo-yo. Rosaura preferred the yo-yo because it sparkled, but she didn't mention that to her mother. Her mother might have said: "So why don't you ask for one, you blockhead?" That's what her mother was like. Rosaura didn't feel like explaining that she'd be horribly ashamed to be the odd one out. Instead she said:

"I was the best-behaved at the party."

And she said no more because Señora Ines came out into the hall with two bags, one pink and one blue.

First she went up to the fat boy, gave him a yo-yo out of the blue bag, and the fat boy left with his mother. Then she went up to the girl and gave her a bracelet out of the pink bag, and the girl with the pigtails left as well.

Finally she came up to Rosaura and her mother. She had a big smile on her face and Rosaura liked that. Señora Ines looked down at her, then looked up at her mother, and then said something that made Rosaura proud:

"What a marvelous daughter you have, Herminia."

For an instant, Rosaura thought that she'd give her two presents: the bracelet and the yo-yo. Señora Ines bent down as if about to look for something. Rosaura also leaned forward, stretching out her arm. But she never completed the movement.

Señora Ines didn't look in the pink bag. Nor did she look in the blue bag. Instead she rummaged in her purse. In her hand appeared two bills.

"You really and truly earned this," she said handing them over. "Thank you for all your help, my pet."

Rosaura felt her arms stiffen, stick close to her body, and then she noticed her mother's hand on her shoulder. Instinctively she pressed herself against her mother's body. That was all. Except her eyes. Rosaura's eyes had a cold, clear look that fixed itself on Señora Ines's face.

Señora Ines, motionless, stood there with her hand outstretched. As if she didn't dare draw it back. As if the slightest change might shatter an infinitely delicate balance.

Explorations of the Text

1. What is the central conflict between the mother and Rosaura?
2. What fantasies does Rosaura invent about herself and about her life?
3. How does Heker weave a subtle pattern of servitude into Rosaura's participation in the party?
4. In the episode with the monkey, what is the role of the fat boy? What does the incident symbolize?
5. Why does Señora Ines offer Rosaura money? What does Rosaura's "cold, clear look" suggest? What is the "infinitely delicate balance" at the end?
6. Two pairs of mothers and daughters appear in this story. What do you learn about the social status and world views of these characters?

7. How would you characterize the tone of this story? Why?
8. How do details contribute to the theme of the story? What can you learn about subtlety, about irony, and about organization from Liliana Heker?

The Reading/Writing Connection

1. How is the party "stolen"? Respond to this question in a journal entry.
2. Write a paragraph, and continue the story.
3. "Think" Topic: What characterizes children's perceptions of prejudice or stereotyping in the works by Heker and by Countee Cullen?

Ideas for Writing

1. How does point of view contribute to the development of the themes in this work?
2. Write about a "stolen party" from your childhood or adolescence. What did you realize? Or compare a party that you attended as a child with Rosaura's experience.

ROSE-JOHNNY

Barbara Kingsolver

Barbara Kingsolver (1955–) was born in Kentucky and educated at DePauw University and the University of Arizona. She published her first novel, The Bean Trees, *in 1989. Subsequent novels include* Animal Dreams *(1990) and* The Poisonwood Bible *(1998). She has also published a collection of short stores,* Homeland and Other Stories *(1989), a collection of essays,* High Tide in Tuscon: Essays for Now and Never *(1995), a collection of poems,* Another America *(1992), and a nonfiction book,* Holding the Line: Women in the Great Arizona Mine Strike of 1983 *(1989). Kingsolver has described the goal of her fiction as first to entertain and second to educate.*

1989

Rose-Johnny wore a man's haircut and terrified little children, although I will never believe that was her intention. For her own part she inspired in us only curiosity. It was our mothers who took this fascination and wrung it, through daily admonitions, into the most irresistible kind of horror. She was like the old wells, covered with ancient rotting boards and overgrown with weeds, that waited behind the barns to swallow us down: our mothers warned us time and again not to go near them, and still were certain that we did.

My own mother was not one of those who had a great deal to say about her, but Walnut Knobs was a small enough town so that a person did not need to be told things directly. When I had my first good look at her, at close range, I was ten years old. I fully understood the importance of the encounter.

What mattered to me at the time, though, was that it was something my sister had not done before me. She was five years older, and as a consequence there was hardly an achievement in my life, nor even an article of clothing, that had not first been Mary Etta's. But, because of the circumstances of my meeting Rose-Johnny, I couldn't tell a living soul about it, and so for nearly a year I carried the secret torment of a great power that can't be used. My agitation was not relieved but made worse when I told the story to myself, over and over again.

She was not, as we always heard, half man and half woman, something akin to the pagan creatures whose naked torsos are inserted in various shocking ways into parts of animal bodies. In fact, I was astonished by her ordinariness. It is true that she wore Red Wing boots like my father. And also there was something not quite womanly in her face, but maybe any woman's face would look the same with that haircut. Her hair was coal black, cut flat across the top of her round head, so that when she looked down I could see a faint pale spot right on top where the scalp almost surfaced.

5 But the rest of her looked exactly like anybody's mother in a big flowered dress without a waistline and with two faded spots in front, where her bosom rubbed over the counter when she reached across to make change or wipe away the dust.

People say there is a reason for every important thing that happens. I was sent to the feed store, where I spoke to Rose-Johnny and passed a quarter from my hand into hers, because it was haying time. And because I was small for my age. I was not too small to help with tobacco setting in the spring, in fact I was better at it than Mary Etta, who complained about the stains on her hands, but I was not yet big enough to throw a bale of hay onto the flatbed. It was the time of year when Daddy complained about not having boys. Mama said that at least he oughtn't to bother going into town for the chicken mash that day because Georgeann could do it on her way home from school.

Mama told me to ask Aunt Minnie to please ma'am give me a ride home. "Ask her nice to stop off at Lester Wall's store so you can run in with this quarter and get five pound of laying mash."[1]

I put the quarter in my pocket, keeping my eye out to make certain Mary Etta understood what I had been asked to do. Mary Etta had once told me that I was no better than the bugs that suck on potato vines, and that the family was going to starve to death because of my laziness. It was one of the summer days when we were on our knees in the garden picking off bugs and dropping them into cans of coal oil. She couldn't go into town with Aunt Minnie to look at dress patterns until we finished with the potato bugs. What she said, exactly, was that if I couldn't work any harder than that, then she might just as well

[1] A type of boiled grain, bran, or meal, fed warm to horses, cattle, and chickens.

throw *me* into a can of coal oil. Later she told me she hadn't meant it, but I intended to remember it nonetheless.

❋ ❋ ❋

Aunt Minnie taught the first grade and had a 1951 Dodge. That is how she referred to her car whenever she spoke of it. It was the newest automobile belonging to anyone related to us, although some of the Wilcox cousins had once come down to visit from Knoxville in a Ford they were said to have bought the same year it was made. But I saw that car and did not find it nearly as impressive as Aunt Minnie's, which was white and immense and shone like glass. She paid a boy to polish it every other Saturday.

10 On the day she took me to Wall's, she waited in the car while I went inside with my fist tight around the quarter. I had never been in the store before, and although I had passed by it many times and knew what could be bought there, I had never imagined what a wonderful combination of warm, sweet smells of mash and animals and seed corn it would contain. The dust lay white and thin on everything like a bridal veil. Rose-Johnny was in the back with a water can, leaning over into one of the chick tubs. The steel rang with the sound of confined baby birds, and a light bulb shining up from inside the tub made her face glow white. Mr. Wall, Rose-Johnny's Pa, was in the front of the store talking to two men about a horse. He didn't notice me as I crept up to the counter. It was Rose-Johnny who came forward to the cash register.

"And what for you, missy?"

She is exactly like anybody's mama, was all I could think, and I wanted to reach and touch her flowered dress. The two men were looking at me.

"My mama needs five pound of laying mash and here's a quarter for it." I clicked the coin quickly onto the counter.

"Yes, ma'am." She smiled at me, but her boots made heavy, tired sounds on the floor. She made her way slowly, like a duck in water, over to the row of wooden bins that stood against the wall. She scooped the mash into a paper bag and weighed it, then shoved the scoop back into the bin. A little cloud of dust rose out of the mash up into the window. I watched her from the counter.

15 "Don't your mama know she's wasting good money on chicken mash? Any fool chicken will eat corn." I jumped when the man spoke. It was one of the two, and they were standing so close behind me I would have had to look right straight up to see their faces. Mr. Wall was gone.

"No sir, they need mash," I said to the man's boots.

"What's that?" It was the taller man doing the talking.

"They need mash," I said louder. "To lay good sturdy eggs for selling. A little mash mixed in with the corn. Mama says it's got oster shells in it."

"Is that a fact," he said. "Did you hear that, Rose-Johnny?" he called out. "This child says you put oster shells in that mash. Is that right?

20 When Rose-Johnny came back to the cash register she was moon-eyed. She made quick motions with her hands and pushed the bag at me as if she didn't know how to talk.

"Do you catch them osters yourself, Rose-Johnny? Up at Jackson Crick?" The man was laughing. The other man was quiet.

Rose-Johnny looked all around and up at the ceiling. She scratched at her short hair, fast and hard, like a dog with ticks.

When the two men were gone I stood on my toes and leaned over the counter as far as I could. "Do you catch the osters yourself?"

She hooked her eyes right into mine, the way the bit goes into the mule's mouth and fits just so, one way and no other. Her eyes were the palest blue of any I had ever seen. Then she threw back her head and laughed so hard I could see the wide, flat bottoms of her back teeth, and I wasn't afraid of her.

When I left the store, the two men were still outside. Their boots scuffed on the front-porch floorboards, and the shorter one spoke.

"Child, how much did you pay that woman for the chicken mash?"

"A quarter," I told him.

He put a quarter in my hand. "You take this here, and go home and tell your daddy something. Tell him not never to send his little girls to Wall's feed store. Tell him to send his boys if he has to, but not his little girls." His hat was off, and his hair lay back in wet orange strips. A clean line separated the white top of his forehead from the red-burned hide of his face. In this way, it was like my father's face.

"No, sir, I can't tell him, because all my daddy's got is girls."

"That's George Bowles's child, Bud," the tall man said. "He's just got the two girls."

"Then tell him to come for hisself," Bud said. His eyes had the sun in them, and looked like a pair of new pennies.

Aunt Minnie didn't see the man give me the quarter because she was looking at herself in the side-view mirror of the Dodge. Aunt Minnie was older than Mama, but everyone mistook her for the younger because of the way she fixed herself up. And, of course, Mama was married. Mama said if Aunt Minnie ever found a man she would act her age.

When I climbed in the car she was pulling gray hairs out of her part. She said it was teaching school that caused them, but early gray ran in my mama's family.

She jumped when I slammed the car door. "All set?"

"Yes, ma'am," I said. She put her little purple hat back on her head and slowly pushed the long pin through it. I shuddered as she started up the car.

Aunt Minnie laughed. "Somebody walked over your grave."

"I don't have a grave," I said. "I'm not dead."

"No, you most certainly are not. That's just what they say when a person shivers like that." She smiled. I liked Aunt Minnie most of the time.

"I don't think they mean your real grave, with you in it," she said after a minute. "I think it means the place where your grave is going to be someday."

I thought about this for a while. I tried to picture the place, but could not. Then I thought about the two men outside Wall's store. I asked Aunt Minnie why it was all right for boys to do some things that girls couldn't.

"Oh, there's all kinds of reasons," she said. "Like what kinds of things, do you mean?"

"Like going into Wall's feed store."

"Who told you that?"

"Somebody."

45 Aunt Minnie didn't say anything.

Then I said, "It's because of Rose-Johnny, isn't it?"

Aunt Minnie raised her chin just a tiny bit. She might have been checking her lipstick in the mirror, or she might have been saying yes.

"Why?" I asked.

"Why what?"

50 "Why because of Rose-Johnny?"

"I can't tell you that, Georgeann."

"Why can't you tell me?" I whined. "Tell me."

The car rumbled over a cattle grate. When we came to the crossing, Aunt Minnie stepped on the brake so hard we both flopped forward. She looked at me. "Georgeann, Rose-Johnny is a Lebanese. That's all I'm going to tell you. You'll understand better when you're older."

When I got home I put the laying mash in the henhouse. The hens were already roosting high above my head, clucking softly into their feathers and shifting back and forth on their feet. I collected the eggs as I did every day, and took them into the house. I hadn't yet decided what to do about the quarter, and so I held on to it until dinnertime.

55 Mary Etta was late coming down, and even though she had washed and changed she looked pale as a haunt from helping with the haying all day. She didn't speak and she hardly ate.

"Here, girls, both of you, eat up these potatoes," Mama said after a while. "There's not but just a little bit left. Something to grow on."

"I don't need none then," Mary Etta said. "I've done growed all I'm going to grow."

"Don't talk back to your mama," Daddy said.

"I'm not talking back. It's the truth." Mary Etta looked at Mama. "Well, it is."

60 "Eat a little bite, Mary Etta. Just because you're in the same dresses for a year don't mean you're not going to grow no more."

"I'm as big as you are, Mama."

"All right then." Mama scraped the mashed potatoes onto my plate. "I expect now you'll be telling me you don't want to grow no more either," she said to me.

"No, ma'am, I won't," I said. But I was distressed, and looked sideways at the pink shirtwaist I had looked forward to inheriting along with the grown-up shape that would have to be worn inside it. Now it appeared that I was condemned to my present clothes and potato-shaped body; keeping these forever seemed to me far more likely than the possibility of having clothes that, like the Wilcox automobile, had never before been owned. I ate my potatoes quietly. Dinner was almost over when Daddy asked if I had remembered to get the laying mash.

"Yes, sir. I put it in the henhouse." I hesitated. "And here's the quarter back. Mr. Wall gave me the mash for nothing."

"Why did he do that?" Mama asked.

Mary Etta was staring like the dead. Even her hair looked tired, slumped over the back of her chair like a long black shadow.

"I helped him out," I said. "Rose-Johnny wasn't there, she was sick, and Mr. Wall said if I would help him clean out the bins and dust the shelves and water the chicks, then it wouldn't cost me for the laying mash."

"And Aunt Minnie waited while you did all that?"

"She didn't mind," I said. "She had some magazines to look at."

It was the first important lie I had told in my life, and I was thrilled with its power. Every member of my family believed I had brought home the laying mash in exchange for honest work.

I was also astonished at how my story, once I had begun it, wouldn't finish. "He wants me to come back and help him again the next time we need something," I said.

"I don't reckon you let on like we couldn't pay for the mash?" Daddy asked sternly.

"No, sir. I put the quarter right up there on the counter. But he said he needed the help. Rose-Johnny's real sick."

He looked at me like he knew. Like he had found the hole in the coop where the black snake was getting in. But he just said, "All right. You can go, if Aunt Minnie don't mind waiting for you."

"You don't have to say a thing to her about it," I said. "I can walk home the same as I do ever day. Five pound of mash isn't nothing to carry."

"We'll see," Mama said.

That night I believed I would burst. For a long time after Mary Etta fell asleep I twisted in my blankets and told the story over to myself, both the true and false versions. I talked to my doll, Miss Regina. She was a big doll, a birthday present from my Grandma and Grandpa Bowles, with a tiny wire crown and lovely long blond curls.

"Rose-Johnny isn't really sick," I told Miss Regina. "She's a Lebanese."

❄ ❄ ❄

I looked up the word in Aunt Minnie's Bible dictionary after school. I pretended to be looking up St. John the Baptist but then turned over in a hurry to the *L*'s while she was washing her chalkboards. My heart thumped when I found it, but I read the passage quickly, several times over, and found it empty. It said the Lebanese were a seafaring people who built great ships from cedar trees. I couldn't believe that even when I was older I would be able, as Aunt Minnie promised, to connect this with what I had seen of Rose-Johnny. Nevertheless, I resolved to understand. The following week I went back to the store, confident that my lie would continue to carry its own weight.

Rose-Johnny recognized me. "Five pounds of laying mash," she said, and this time I followed her to the feed bins. There were flecks of white dust in her hair.

"Is it true you come from over the sea?" I asked her quietly as she bent over with the scoop.

She laughed and rolled her eyes. "A lot of them says I come from the moon," she said, and I was afraid she was going to be struck dumb and animal-eyed as she was the time before. But, when she finished weighing the bag, she just said, "I was born in Slate Holler, and that's as far from here as I ever been or will be."

"Is that where you get the osters from?" I asked, looking into the mash and trying to pick out which of the colored flecks they might be.

Rose-Johnny looked at me for a long time, and then suddenly laughed her big laugh. "Why, honey child, don't you know? Osters comes from the sea."

She rang up twenty-five cents on the register, but I didn't look at her.

"That was all, wasn't it?"

I leaned over the counter and tried to put tears in my eyes, but they wouldn't come. "I can't pay," I said. "My daddy said to ask you if I could do some work for it. Clean up or something."

"Your daddy said to ask me that? Well, bless your heart," she said. "Let me see if we can't find something for you to do. Bless your little heart, child, what's your name?"

"Georgeann," I told her.

"I'm Rose-Johnny," she said, and I did not say that I knew it, that like every other child I had known it since the first time I saw her in town, when I was five or six, and had to ask Mama if it was a man or a lady.

"Pleased to meet you," I said.

We kept it between the two of us: I came in every week to help with the pullets and the feed, and took home my mash. We did not tell Mr. Wall, although it seemed it would not have mattered one whit to him. Mr. Wall was in the store so seldom that he might not have known I was there. He kept to himself in the apartment at the back where he and Rose-Johnny lived.

It was she who ran the store, kept the accounts, and did the orders. She showed me how to feed and water the pullets and ducklings and pull out the sick ones. Later I learned how to weigh out packages of seed and to mix the different kinds of mash. There were lists nailed to the wall telling how much cracked corn and oats and grit to put in. I followed the recipes with enormous care, adding tiny amounts at a time to the bag on the hanging scales until the needle touched the right number. Although she was patient with me, I felt slow next to Rose-Johnny, who never had to look at the lists and used the scales only to check herself. It seemed to me she knew how to do more things than anyone I had ever known, woman or man.

She also knew the names of all the customers, although she rarely spoke to them. Sometimes such a change came over her when the men were there that it wasn't clear to me whether she was pretending or had really lost the capacity to speak. But afterward she would tell me their names and everything about them. Once she told me about Ed Charney, Sr. and Bud Mattox, the two men I had seen the first day I was in the store. According to Rose-Johnny, Ed had an old red mule he was in the habit of mistreating. "But even so," she said, "Ed's mule don't have it as bad as Bud's wife." I never knew how she acquired this knowledge.

When she said "Bud Mattox," I remembered his penny-colored eyes and connected him then with all the Mattox boys at school. It had never occurred to me that eyes could run in families, like early gray.

Occasionally a group of black-skinned children came to the store, always after hours. Rose-Johnny opened up for them. She called each child by name, and asked after their families and the health of their mothers' laying hens.

The oldest one, whose name was Cleota, was shaped like Mary Etta. Her hair was straight and pointed, and smelled to me like citronella candles. The younger girls had plaits that curved out from their heads like so many handles. Several of them wore dresses made from the same bolt of cloth, but they were not sisters. Rose-Johnny filled a separate order for each child.

I watched, but didn't speak. The skin on their heels and palms was creased, and as light as my own. Once, after they had left, I asked Rose-Johnny why they only came into the store when it was closed.

"People's got their ways," she said, stoking up the wood stove for the night. Then she told me all their names again, starting with Cleota and working down. She looked me in the eye. "When you see them in town, you speak. Do you hear? By *name*. I don't care who is watching."

❄ ❄ ❄

I was allowed to spend half an hour or more with Rose-Johnny nearly every day after school, so long as I did not neglect my chores at home. Sometimes on days that were rainy or cold Aunt Minnie would pick me up, but I preferred to walk. By myself, without Mary Etta to hurry me up.

As far as I know, my parents believed I was helping Mr. Wall because of Rose-Johnny's illness. They had no opportunity to learn otherwise, though I worried that someday Aunt Minnie would come inside the store to fetch me, instead of just honking, or that Daddy would have to go to Wall's for something and see for himself that Rose-Johnny was fit and well. Come springtime he would be needing to buy tobacco seed.

It was soon after Christmas when I became consumed with a desire to confess. I felt the lies down inside me like cold, dirty potatoes in a root cellar, beginning to sprout and crowd. At night I told Miss Regina of my dishonesty and the things that were likely to happen to me because of it. In so doing, there were several times I nearly confessed by accident to Mary Etta.

"Who's going to wring your neck?" she wanted to know, coming into the room one night when I thought she was downstairs washing the supper dishes.

"Nobody," I said, clutching Miss Regina to my pillow. I pretended to be asleep. I could hear Mary Etta starting to brush her hair. Every night before she went to bed she sat with her dress hiked up and her head hung over between her knees, brushing her hair all the way down to the floor. This improved the circulation to the hair, she told me, and would prevent it turning. Mary Etta was already beginning to get white hairs.

105 "Is it because Mama let you watch Daddy kill the cockerels? Did it scare you to see them jump around like that with their necks broke?"

"I'm not scared," I murmured, but I wanted so badly to tell the truth that I started to cry. I knew, for certain, that something bad was going to happen. I believe I also knew it would happen to my sister, instead of me.

"Nobody's going to hurt you," Mary Etta said. She smoothed my bangs and laid my pigtails down flat on top of the quilt. "Give me Miss Regina and let me put her up for you now, so you won't get her hair all messed up."

I let her have the doll. "I'm not scared about the cockerels, Mary Etta. I promise." With my finger, under the covers, I traced a cross over my heart.

❄ ❄ ❄

When Rose-Johnny fell ill I was sick with guilt. When I first saw Mr. Wall behind the counter instead of Rose-Johnny, so help me God, I prayed this would be the day Aunt Minnie would come inside to get me. Immediately after, I felt sure God would kill me for my wickedness. I pictured myself falling dead beside the oat bin. I begged Mr. Wall to let me see her.

110 "Go on back, littl'un. She told me you'd be coming in," he said.

I had never been in the apartment before. There was little in it beyond the necessary things and a few old photographs on the walls, all of the same woman. The rooms were cold and felt infused with sickness and an odor I incorrectly believed to be medicine. Because my father didn't drink, I had never before encountered the smell of whiskey.

Rose-Johnny was propped on the pillows in a lifeless flannel gown. Her face changed when she saw me, and I remembered the way her face was lit by the light bulb in the chick tub, the first time I saw her. With fresh guilt I threw myself on her bosom.

"I'm sorry. I could have paid for the mash. I didn't mean to make you sick." Through my sobs I heard accusing needly wheezing sounds in Rose-Johnny's chest. She breathed with a great pulling effort.

"Child, don't talk foolish."

❄ ❄ ❄

115 As weeks passed and Rose-Johnny didn't improve, it became clear that my lie was prophetic. Without Rose-Johnny to run the store, Mr. Wall badly needed my help. He seemed mystified by his inventory and was rendered helpless by any unusual demand from a customer. It was March, the busiest time for the store. I had turned eleven, one week before Mary Etta turned sixteen. These seven days out of each year, during which she was only four years older, I considered to be God's greatest gifts to me.

The afternoon my father would come in to buy the vegetable garden and tobacco seed was an event I had rehearsed endlessly in my mind. When it finally did transpire, Mr. Wall's confusion gave such complete respectability to my long-standing lie that I didn't need to say a word myself in support of it. I waited on him with dignity, precisely weighing out his tobacco seed, and even recommended to him the white runner beans that Mr. Wall had accidentally overstocked, and which my father did not buy.

Later on that same afternoon, after the winter light had come slanting through the dusty windows and I was alone in the store cleaning up, Cleota and the other children came pecking at the glass. I let them in. When I had filled all the orders Cleota unwrapped their coins, knotted all together into a blue handkerchief. I counted, and counted again. It was not the right amount, not even half.

"That's what Miss Rose-Johnny ast us for it," Cleota said. "Same as always." The smaller children—Venise, Anita, Little-Roy, James—shuffled and elbowed each other like fighting cocks, paying no attention. Cleota gazed at me calmly, steadily. Her eyebrows were two perfect arches.

"I thank you very much," I said, and put the coins in their proper places in the cash drawer.

120 During that week I also discovered an epidemic of chick droop in the pullets. I had to pull Mr. Wall over by the hand to make him look. There were more sick ones than well.

"It's because it's so cold in the store," I told him. "They can't keep warm. Can't we make it warmer in here?"

Mr. Wall shrugged at the wood stove, helpless. He could never keep a fire going for long, the way Rose-Johnny could.

"We have to try. The one light bulb isn't enough," I said. The chicks were huddled around the bulb just the way the men would collect around the stove in the mornings to say howdy-do to Mr. Wall and warm up their hands on the way to work. Except the chicks were more ruthless: they climbed and shoved, and the healthy ones pecked at the eyes and feet of the sick ones, making them bleed.

I had not noticed before what a very old man Mr. Wall was. As he stared down at the light, I saw that his eyes were covered with a film. "How do we fix them up?" he asked me.

125 "We can't. We've got to take the sick ones out so they won't all get it. Rose-Johnny puts them in that tub over there. We give them water and keep them warm, but it don't do any good. They've got to die."

He looked so sad I stood and patted his old freckled hand.

I spent much more time than before at the store, but no longer enjoyed it particularly. Working in the shadow of Rose-Johnny's expertise, I had been a secret witness to a wondrous ritual of counting, weighing, and tending. Together we created little packages that sailed out like ships to all parts of the country, giving rise to gardens and barnyard life in places I had never even seen. I felt superior to my schoolmates, knowing that I had had a hand in the creation of their families' poultry flocks and their mothers' kitchen gardens. By contrast, Mr. Wall's bewilderment was pathetic and only increased my guilt. But each day I was able to spend a little time in the back rooms with Rose-Johnny.

There were rumors about her illness, both before and after the fact. It did not occur to me that I might have been the source of some of the earlier rumors. But, if I didn't think of this, it was because Walnut Knobs was overrun with tales of Rose-Johnny, and not because I didn't take notice of the stories. I did.

The tales that troubled me most were those about Rose-Johnny's daddy. I had heard many adults say that he was responsible for her misfortune, which I presumed to mean her short hair. But it was also said that he was a colored man, and this I knew to be untrue. Aunt Minnie, when I pressed her, would offer nothing more than that if it were up to her I wouldn't go near either one of them, advice which I ignored. I was coming to understand that I would not hear the truth about Rose-Johnny from Aunt Minnie or anyone else. I knew, in a manner that went beyond the meanings of words I could not understand, that she was no more masculine than my mother or aunt, and no more lesbian than Lebanese. Rose-Johnny was simply herself, and alone.

130 And yet she was such a capable woman that I couldn't believe she would be sick for very long. But as the warm weather came she grew sluggish and pale. Her slow, difficult breathing frightened me. I brought my schoolbooks and read to her from the foot of the bed. Sometimes the rather ordinary adventures of the boy in my reader would make her laugh aloud until she choked. Other times she fell asleep while I read, but then would make me read those parts over again.

She worried about the store. Frequently she would ask about Mr. Wall and the customers, and how he was managing. "He does all right," I always said. But eventually my eagerness to avoid the burden of further lies, along with the considerable force of my pride, led me to confess that I had to tell him nearly everything. "He forgets something awful," I told her.

Rose-Johnny smiled. "He used to be as smart as anything, and taught me. Now I've done taught you, and you him again." She was lying back on the pillows with her eyes closed and her plump hands folded on her stomach.

"But he's a nice man," I said. I listened to her breathing. "He don't hurt you does he? Your pa?"

Nothing moved except her eyelids. They opened and let the blue eyes out at me. I looked down and traced my finger over the triangles of the flying-geese patch on the quilt. I whispered, "Does he make you cut off your hair?"

135 Rose-Johnny's eyes were so pale they were almost white, like ice with water running underneath. "He cuts it with a butcher knife. Sometimes he chases me all the way down to the river." She laughed a hissing laugh like a boy, and she had the same look the yearling calves get when they are cornered and jump the corral and run to the woods and won't be butchered. I understood then that Rose-Johnny, too, knew the power of a lie.

❄ ❄ ❄

It was the youngest Mattox boy who started the fight at school on the Monday after Easter. He was older than me, and a boy, so nobody believed he would hit me, but when he started the name calling I called them right back, and he threw me down on the ground. The girls screamed and ran to get the teacher, but by the time she arrived I had a bloody nose and had bitten his arm wonderfully hard.

Miss Althea gave me her handkerchief for my nose and dragged Roy Mattox inside to see the principal. All the other children stood in a circle, looking at me.

"It isn't true, what he said," I told them. "And not about Rose-Johnny either. She isn't a pervert. I love her."

"Pervert," one of the boys said.

I marveled at the sight of my own blood soaking through the handkerchief. "I love her," I said.

I did not get to see Rose-Johnny that day. The door of Wall's store was locked. I could see Mr. Wall through the window, though, so I banged on the glass with the flats of my hands until he came. He had the strong medicine smell on his breath.

"Not today, littl'un." The skin under his eyes was dark blue.

"I need to see Rose-Johnny." I was irritated with Mr. Wall, and did not consider him important enough to prevent me from seeing her. But evidently he was.

"Not today," he said. "We're closed." He shut the door and locked it.

I shouted at him through the glass. "Tell her I hit a boy and bit his arm, that was calling her names. Tell her I fought with a boy, Mr. Wall."

The next day the door was open, but I didn't see him in the store. In the back, the apartment was dark except for the lamp by Rose-Johnny's bed. A small brown bottle and a glass stood just touching each other on the night table. Rose-Johnny looked asleep but made a snuffing sound when I climbed onto the bottom of the bed.

"Did your daddy tell you what I told him yesterday?"

She said nothing.

"Is your daddy sick?"

"My daddy's dead," she said suddenly, causing me to swallow a little gulp of air. She opened her eyes, then closed them again. "Pa's all right, honey, just stepped out, I imagine." She stopped to breathe between every few words. "I didn't mean to give you a fright. Pa's not my daddy, he's my mama's daddy."

I was confused. "And your real daddy's dead?"

She nodded. "Long time."

"And your mama, what about her? Is she dead too?"

"Mm-hmm," she said, in the same lazy sort of way Mama would say it when she wasn't really listening.

"That her?" I pointed to the picture over the bed. The woman's shoulders were bare except for a dark lace shawl. She was looking backward toward you, over her shoulder.

Rose-Johnny looked up at the picture, and said yes it was.

"She's pretty," I said.

"People used to say I looked just like her." Rose-Johnny laughed a wheezy laugh, and coughed.

"Why did she die?"

Rose-Johnny shook her head. "I can't tell you that."

"Can you when I'm older?"

She didn't answer.

"Well then, if Mr. Wall isn't your daddy, then the colored man is your daddy," I said mostly to myself.

She looked at me. "Is that what they say?"

I shrugged.

"Does no harm to me. Every man is some color," she said.

"Oh," I said.

"My daddy was white. After he died my mama loved another man and he was brown."

"What happened then?"

"What happened then," she said. "Then they had a sweet little baby Johnny." Her voice was more like singing than talking, and her eyes were so peacefully closed I was afraid they might not open again. Every time she breathed there was the sound of a hundred tiny birds chirping inside her chest.

"Where's he?"

"Mama's Rose and sweet little baby Johnny," she sang it like an old song. "Not nothing bad going to happen to them, not nobody going to take her babies." A silvery moth flew into the lamp and clicked against the inside of the lampshade. Rose-Johnny stretched out her hand toward the night table. "I want you to pour me some of that bottle."

I lifted the bottle carefully and poured the glass half full. "That your medicine?" I asked. No answer. I feared this would be another story without an end, without meaning. "Did somebody take your mama's babies?" I persisted.

"Took her man, is what they did, and hung him up from a tree." She sat up slowly on her elbows, and looked straight at me. "Do you know what lynched is?"

"Yes, ma'am," I said, although until that moment I had not been sure.

"People will tell you there's never been no lynchings north of where the rivers don't freeze over. But they done it. Do you know where Jackson Crick is, up there by Floyd's Mill?" I nodded. "They lynched him up there, and drowned her baby Johnny in Jackson Crick, and it was as froze as you're ever going to see it. They had to break a hole in the ice to do it." She would not stop looking right into me. "In that river. Poor little baby in that cold river. Poor Mama, what they did to Mama. And said they would do to me, when I got old enough."

She didn't drink the medicine I poured for her, but let it sit. I was afraid to hear any more, and afraid to leave. I watched the moth crawl up the outside of the lampshade.

And then, out of the clear blue, she sat up and said, "But they didn't do a thing to me!" The way she said it, she sounded more like she ought to be weighing out bags of mash than sick in bed. "Do you want to know what Mama did?"

I didn't say.

180 "I'll tell you what she did. She took her scissors and cut my hair right off, every bit of it. She said, 'From now on, I want you to be Rose and Johnny both.' And then she went down to the same hole in the crick where they put baby Johnny in."

I sat with Rose-Johnny for a long time. I patted the lump in the covers where her knees were, and wiped my nose on my sleeve. "You'd better drink your medicine, Rose-Johnny," I said. "Drink up and get better now," I told her. "It's all over now."

❄ ❄ ❄

It was the last time I saw Rose-Johnny. The next time I saw the store, more than a month later, it was locked and boarded up. Later on, the Londroski brothers took it over. Some people said she had died. Others thought she and Mr. Wall had gone to live somewhere up in the Blue Ridge, and opened a store there. This is the story I believed. In the years since, when passing through that part of the country, I have never failed to notice the Plymouth Rocks and Rhode Islands scratching in the yards, and the tomato vines tied up around the back doors.

❄ ❄ ❄

I would like to stop here and say no more, but there are enough half-true stories in my past. This one will have to be heard to the end.

Whatever became of Rose-Johnny and her grandfather, I am certain that their going away had something to do with what happened on that same evening to Mary Etta. And I knew this to be my fault.

185 It was late when I got home. As I walked I turned Rose-Johnny's story over and over, like Grandpa Bowles's Indian penny with the head on both sides. You never could stop turning it over.

When I caught sight of Mama standing like somebody's ghost in the front doorway I thought she was going to thrash me, but she didn't. Instead she ran out into the yard and picked me up like she used to when I was a little girl, and carried me into the house.

"Where's Daddy?" I asked. It was suppertime, but there was no supper.

"Daddy's gone looking for you in the truck. He'll be back directly, when he don't find you."

"Why's he looking for me? What did I do?"

190 "Georgeann, some men tried to hurt Mary Etta. We don't know why they done it, but we was afraid they might try to hurt you."

"No, ma'am, nobody hurt me," I said quietly. "Did they kill her?" I asked.

"Oh Lordy no," Mama said, and hugged me. "She's all right. You can go upstairs and see her, but don't bother her if she don't want to be bothered."

Our room was dark, and Mary Etta was in bed crying. "Can I turn on the little light?" I asked. I wanted to see Mary Etta. I was afraid that some part of her might be missing.

"If you want to."

195 She was all there: arms, legs, hair. Her face was swollen, and there were marks on her neck.

"Don't stare at me," she said.

"I'm sorry." I looked around the room. Her dress was hanging over the chair. It was her best dress, the solid green linen with covered buttons and attached petticoat that had taken her all winter to make. It was red with dirt and torn nearly in half at the bodice.

"I'll fix your dress, Mary Etta. I can't sew as good as you, but I can mend," I said.

"Can't be mended," she said, but then tried to smile with her swollen mouth. "You can help me make another one."

"Who was it that done it?" I asked.

"I don't know." She rolled over and faced the wallpaper. "Some men. Three or four of them. Some of them might have been boys, I couldn't tell for sure. They had things over their faces."

"What kind of things?"

"I don't know. Just bandanners and things." She spoke quietly to the wall. "You know how the Mattoxes have those funny-colored eyes? I think some of them might of been Mattoxes. Don't tell, Georgeann. Promise."

I remembered the feeling of Roy Mattox's muscle in my teeth. I did not promise.

"Did you hit them?"

"No. I screamed. Mr. Dorsey come along the road."

"What did they say, before you screamed?"

"Nothing. They just kept saying, 'Are you the Bowles girl, are you the Bowles girl?' And they said nasty things."

"It was me they was looking for," I said. And no matter what anyone said, I would not believe otherwise. I took to my bed and would not eat or speak to anyone. My convalescence was longer than Mary Etta's. It was during that time that I found my sister's sewing scissors and cut off all my hair and all of Miss Regina's. I said that my name was George-Etta, not Georgeann, and I called my doll Rose-Johnny.

For the most part, my family tolerated my distress. My mother retrimmed my hair as neatly as she could, but there was little that could be done. Every time I looked in the mirror I was startled and secretly pleased to see that I looked exactly like a little boy. Mama said that when I went back to school I would have to do the explaining for myself. Aunt Minnie said I was going through a stage and oughtn't to be pampered.

But there was only a month left of school, and my father let Mary Etta and me stay home to help set tobacco. By the end of the summer my hair had grown out sufficiently so that no explanations were needed. Miss Regina's hair, of course, never grew back.

Explorations of the Text

1. How is suspense created at the beginning of the story?
2. Why do you think Georgeann tells the lie about the quarter?

3. Why does she want to work at the feed store? What attracts her to Rose-Johnny?
4. Characterize Rose-Johnny. What do you learn about her from her appearance, gestures, actions, dialogue?
5. What repetitions of plot occur in the story? Why do the men assault Mary Etta?
6. Why does Georgeann say her name is George-Etta?
7. What is the significance of the last line—of the doll's hair staying cut?
8. What is the narrative perspective? What are the aspects of a child's perspective? Of an adult looking back and recalling a child's experiences?
9. Compare Georgeann's coming of age with Rosaura's in "The Stolen Party" or with the narrator's in "The Monkey Garden." What do these characters learn about life and the world?

The Reading/Writing Connection

1. "Think" Topic: In an interview Barbara Kingsolver revealed that she "often [chose] to tell stories in the voices of fairly unsophisticated people. Children are . . . [a] good choice because they haven't lived long enough yet to get sophisticated." What is the impact of her point of view? Is it successful?
2. Journal Entry: Write about a moment when you felt different from others or when you observed or experienced prejudice.

Ideas for Writing

1. In that same interview, Kingsolver suggested that she "invented this story, which got wilder and wilder but had everything to do with prejudices of small towns in the South and how they rein people in or cut them free." Discuss the theme of conformity in this work and in "Barn Burning."
2. Analyze the character of Rose-Johnny or of Georgeann.

A Good Man Is Hard to Find

Flannery O'Connor

Flannery O'Connor (1925–64) was born in Savannah, Georgia. After being educated at Georgia State College for Women and the University of Iowa, O'Connor published her first novel, Wise Blood, *in 1952. Afflicted by lupus, the same disease that killed her father, O'Connor lived most her life with her mother on the family farm in Milledgeville, Georgia. She is best known for short stories, collected in* A Good Man

Is Hard to Find *(1955), the posthumous* Everything That Rises Must Converge *(1965), and* The Complete Stories *(1971), which won the National Book Award. Considered by many critics to be one of the finest American short story writers, O'Connor wrote stories distinguished by their violence, their use of the grotesque, and their deep spiritual concerns.*

1955

The grandmother didn't want to go to Florida. She wanted to visit some of her connections in east Tennessee and she was seizing at every chance to change Bailey's mind. Bailey was the son she lived with, her only boy. He was sitting on the edge of his chair at the table, bent over the orange sports section of the *Journal.* "Now look here, Bailey," she said, "see here, read this," and she stood with one hand on her thin hip and the other rattling the newspaper at his bald head. "Here this fellow that calls himself The Misfit is aloose from the Federal Pen and headed toward Florida and you read here what it says he did to these people. Just you read it. I wouldn't take my children in any direction with a criminal like that aloose in it. I couldn't answer to my conscience if I did."

Bailey didn't look up from his reading so she wheeled around then and faced the children's mother, a young woman in slacks, whose face was as broad and innocent as a cabbage and was tied around with a green head-kerchief that had two points on the top like a rabbit's ears. She was sitting on the sofa, feeding the baby his apricots out of a jar. "The children have been to Florida before," the old lady said. "You all ought to take them somewhere else for a change so they would see different parts of the world and be broad. They never have been to east Tennessee."

The children's mother didn't seem to hear her but the eight-year-old boy, John Wesley, a stocky child with glasses, said, "If you don't want to go to Florida, why dontcha stay at home?" He and the little girl, June Star, were reading the funny papers on the floor.

"She wouldn't stay at home to be queen for a day," June Star said without raising her yellow head.

5 "Yes and what would you do if this fellow, The Misfit, caught you?" the grandmother asked.

"I'd smack his face," John Wesley said.

"She wouldn't stay at home for a million bucks," June Star said. "Afraid she'd miss something. She has to go everywhere we go."

"All right, Miss," the grandmother said. "Just remember that the next time you want me to curl your hair."

June Star said her hair was naturally curly.

10 The next morning the grandmother was the first one in the car, ready to go. She had her big black valise that looked like the head of a hippopotamus in one corner, and underneath it she was hiding a basket with Pitty Sing, the cat, in it. She didn't intend for the cat to be left alone in the house for three days because he would miss her too much and she was afraid he might brush against

one of the gas burners and accidentally asphyxiate himself. Her son, Bailey, didn't like to arrive at a motel with a cat.

She sat in the middle of the back seat with John Wesley and June Star on either side of her. Bailey and the children's mother and the baby sat in front and they left Atlanta at eight forty-five with the mileage on the car at 55890. The grandmother wrote this down because she thought it would be interesting to say how many miles they had been when they got back. It took them twenty minutes to reach the outskirts of the city.

The old lady settled herself comfortably, removing her white cotton gloves and putting them up with her purse on the shelf in front of the back window. The children's mother still had on slacks and still had her head tied up in a green kerchief, but the grandmother had on a navy blue straw sailor hat with a bunch of white violets on the brim and a navy blue dress with a small white dot in the print. Her collars and cuffs were white organdy trimmed with lace and at her neckline she had pinned a purple spray of cloth violets containing a sachet. In case of an accident, anyone seeing her dead on the highway would know at once that she was a lady.

She said she thought it was going to be a good day for driving, neither too hot nor too cold, and she cautioned Bailey that the speed limit was fifty-five miles an hour and that the patrolmen hid themselves behind billboards and small clumps of trees and sped out after you before you had a chance to slow down. She pointed out interesting details of the scenery: Stone Mountain; the blue granite that in some places came up to both sides of the highway; the brilliant red clay banks slightly streaked with purple; and the various crops that made rows of green lace-work on the ground. The trees were full of silver-white sunlight and the meanest of them sparkled. The children were reading comic magazines and their mother had gone back to sleep.

"Let's go through Georgia fast so we won't have to look at it much," John Wesley said.

"If I were a little boy," said the grandmother, "I wouldn't talk about my native state that way. Tennessee has the mountains and Georgia has the hills."

"Tennessee is just a hillbilly dumping ground," John Wesley said, "and Georgia is a lousy state too."

"You said it," June Star said.

"In my time," said the grandmother, folding her thin veined fingers, "children were more respectful of their native states and their parents and everything else. People did right then. Oh look at the cute little pickaninny!" she said and pointed to a Negro child standing in the door of a shack. "Wouldn't that make a picture, now?" she asked and they all turned and looked at the little Negro out of the back window. He waved.

"He didn't have any britches on," June Star said.

"He probably didn't have any," the grandmother explained. "Little niggers in the country don't have things like we do. If I could paint, I'd paint that picture," she said.

The children exchanged comic books.

The grandmother offered to hold the baby and the children's mother passed him over the front seat to her. She set him on her knee and bounced him and told him about the things they were passing. She rolled her eyes and screwed up her mouth and stuck her leathery thin face into his smooth bland one. Occasionally he gave her a faraway smile. They passed a large cotton field with five or six graves fenced in the middle of it, like a small island. "Look at the graveyard!" the grandmother said, pointing it out. "That was the old family burying ground. That belonged to the plantation."

"Where's the plantation?" John Wesley asked.

"Gone With the Wind," said the grandmother. "Ha. Ha."

25 When the children finished all the comic books they had brought, they opened the lunch and ate it. The grandmother ate a peanut butter sandwich and an olive and would not let the children throw the box and the paper napkins out the window. When there was nothing else to do they played a game by choosing a cloud and making the other two guess what shape it suggested. John Wesley took one the shape of a cow and June Starr guessed a cow and John Wesley said, no, an automobile, and June Star said he didn't play fair, and they began to slap each other over the grandmother.

The grandmother said she would tell them a story if they would keep quiet. When she told a story, she rolled her eyes and waved her head and was very dramatic. She said once when she was a maiden lady she had been courted by a Mr. Edgar Atkins Teagarden from Jasper, Georgia. She said he was a very good-looking man and a gentleman and that he brought her a watermelon every Saturday afternoon with initials cut in it, E. A. T. Well, one Saturday, she said, Mr. Teagarden brought the watermelon and there was nobody at home and he left it on the front porch and returned in his buggy to Jasper, but she never got the watermelon, she said, because a nigger boy ate it when he saw the initials, E. A. T.! This story tickled John Wesley's funny bone and he giggled and giggled but June Star didn't think it was any good. She said she wouldn't marry a man that just brought her a watermelon on Saturday. The grandmother said she would have done well to marry Mr. Teagarden because he was a gentleman and had bought Coca-Cola stock when it first came out and that he had died only a few years ago, a very wealthy man.

They stopped at The Tower for barbecued sandwiches. The Tower was a part stucco and part wood filling station and dance hall set in a clearing outside of Timothy. A fat man named Red Sammy Butts ran it and there were signs stuck here and there on the building and for miles up and down the highway saying, TRY RED SAMMY'S FAMOUS BARBECUE. NONE LIKE FAMOUS RED SAMMY'S! RED SAM! THE FAT BOY WITH THE HAPPY LAUGH! A VETERAN! RED SAMMY'S YOUR MAN!

Red Sammy was lying on the bare ground outside The Tower with his head under a truck while a gray monkey about a foot high, chained to a small chinaberry tree, chattered nearby. The monkey sprang back into the tree and got on the highest limb as soon as he saw the children jump out of the car and run toward him.

Inside, The Tower was a long dark room with a counter at one end and tables at the other and dancing space in the middle. They all sat down at a board table next to the nickelodeon and Red Sam's wife, a tall burnt-brown woman with hair and eyes lighter than her skin, came and took their order. The children's mother put a dime in the machine and played "The Tennessee Waltz," and the grandmother said that tune always made her want to dance. She asked Bailey if he would like to dance but he only glared at her. He didn't have a naturally sunny disposition like she did and trips made him nervous. The grandmother's brown eyes were very bright. She swayed her head from side to side and pretended she was dancing in her chair. June Star said play something she could tap to so the children's mother put in another dime and played a fast number and June Star stepped out onto the dance floor and did her tap routine.

30 "Ain't she cute?" Red Sam's wife said, leaning over the counter. "Would you like to come be my little girl?"

"No I certainly wouldn't," June Star said. "I wouldn't live in a broken-down place like this for a million bucks!" and she ran back to the table.

"Ain't she cute?" the woman repeated, stretching her mouth politely.

"Aren't you ashamed?" hissed the grandmother.

Red Sam came in and told his wife to quit lounging on the counter and hurry up with these people's order. His khaki trousers reached just to his hip bones and his stomach hung over them like a sack of meal swaying under his shirt. He came over and sat down at a table nearby and let out a combination sign and yodel. "You can't win," he said. "You can't win," and he wiped his sweating red face off with a gray handkerchief. "These days you don't know who to trust," he said. "Ain't that the truth?"

35 "People are certainly not nice like they used to be," said the grandmother.

"Two fellers come in here last week," Red Sammy said, "driving a Chrysler. It was a old beat-up car but it was a good one and these boys looked all right to me. Said they worked at the mill and you know I let them fellers charge the gas they bought? Now why did I do that?"

"Because you're a good man!" the grandmother said at once.

"Yes'm, I suppose so," Red Sam said as if he were struck with this answer.

His wife brought the orders, carrying the five plates all at once without a tray, two in each hand and one balanced on her arm. "It isn't a soul in this green world of God's that you can trust," she said. "And I don't count nobody out of that, not nobody," she repeated, looking at Red Sammy.

40 "Did you read about the criminal, The Misfit, that's escaped?" asked the grandmother.

"I wouldn't be a bit surprised if he didn't attact this place right here," said the woman. "If he hears about it being here, I wouldn't be none surprised to see him. If he hears it's two cent in the cash register, I wouldn't be a tall surprised if he . . ."

"That'll do," Red Sam said. "Go bring these people their Co'-Colas," and the woman went off to get the rest of the order.

"A good man is hard to find," Red Sammy said. "Everything is getting terrible. I remember the day you could go off and leave your screen door unlatched. Not no more."

He and the grandmother discussed better times. The old lady said that in her opinion Europe was entirely to blame for the way things were now. She said the way Europe acted you would think we were made of money and Red Sam said it was no use talking about it, she was exactly right. The children ran outside into the white sunlight and looked at the monkey in the lacy chinaberry tree. He was busy catching fleas on himself and biting each one carefully between his teeth as if it were a delicacy.

45 They drove off again into the hot afternoon. The grandmother took cat naps and woke up every few minutes with her own snoring. Outside of Toombsboro she woke up and recalled an old plantation that she had visited in this neighborhood once when she was a young lady. She said the house had six white columns across the front and that there was an avenue of oaks leading up to it and two little wooden trellis arbors on either side in front where you sat down with your suitor after a stroll in the garden. She recalled exactly which road to turn off to get to it. She knew that Bailey would not be willing to lose any time looking at an old house, but the more she talked about it, the more she wanted to see it once again and find out if the little twin arbors were still standing. "There was a secret panel in this house," she said craftily, not telling the truth but wishing that she were, "and the story went that all the family silver was hidden in it when Sherman[1] came through but it was never found . . ."

"Hey!" John Wesley said. "Let's go see it! We'll find it! We'll poke all the woodwork and find it! Who lives there? Where do you turn off at? Hey Pop, can't we turn off there?"

"We never have seen a house with a secret panel!" June Star shrieked. "Let's go to the house with the secret panel! Hey Pop, can't we go see the house with the secret panel!"

"It's not far from here, I know," the grandmother said. "It wouldn't take over twenty minutes."

Bailey was looking straight ahead. His jaw was as rigid as a horseshoe. "No," he said.

50 The children began to yell and scream that they wanted to see the house with the secret panel. John Wesley kicked the back of the front seat and June Star hung over her mother's shoulder and whined desperately into her ear that they never had any fun even on their vacation, that they could never do what THEY wanted to do. The baby began to scream and John Wesley kicked the back of the seat so hard that his father could feel the blows in his kidney.

"All right!" he shouted and drew the car to a stop at the side of the road. "Will you all shut up? Will you just shut up for one second? If you don't shut up, we won't go anywhere."

[1] William Tecumseh Sherman (1820–91). Union general during the Civil War.

"It would be very educational for them," the grandmother murmured.

"All right," Bailey said, "but get this: this is the only time we're going to stop for anything like this. This is the one and only time."

"The dirt road that you have to turn down is about a mile back," the grandmother directed. "I marked it when we passed."

"A dirt road," Bailey groaned.

After they had turned around and were headed toward the dirt road, the grandmother recalled other points about the house, the beautiful glass over the front doorway and the candle-lamp in the hall. John Wesley said that the secret panel was probably in the fireplace.

"You can't go inside this house," Bailey said. "You don't know who lives there."

"While you all talk to the people in front, I'll run around behind and get in a window," John Wesley suggested.

"We'll all stay in the car," his mother said.

They turned onto the dirt road and the car raced roughly along in a swirl of pink dust. The grandmother recalled the times when there were no paved roads and thirty miles was a day's journey. The dirt road was hilly and there were sudden washes in it and sharp curves on dangerous embankments. All at once they would be on a hill, looking down over the blue tops of trees for miles around, then the next minute, they would be in a red depression with the dust-coated trees looking down on them.

"This place had better turn up in a minute," Bailey said, "or I'm going to turn around."

The road looked as if no one had traveled on it in months.

"It's not much farther," the grandmother said and just as she said it, a horrible thought came to her. The thought was so embarrassing that she turned red in the face and her eyes dilated and her feet jumped up, upsetting her valise in the corner. The instant the valise moved, the newspaper top she had over the basket under it rose with a snarl and Pitty Sing, the cat, sprang onto Bailey's shoulder.

The children were thrown to the floor and their mother, clutching the baby, was thrown out the door onto the ground; the old lady was thrown into the front seat. The car turned over once and landed right-side-up in a gulch off the side of the road. Bailey remained in the driver's seat with the cat—gray-striped with a broad white face and an orange nose—clinging to his neck like a caterpillar.

As soon as the children saw they could move their arms and legs, they scrambled out of the car, shouting, "We've had an ACCIDENT!" The grandmother was curled up under the dashboard, hoping she was injured so that Bailey's wrath would not come down on her all at once. The horrible thought she had had before the accident was that the house she had remembered so vividly was not in Georgia but in Tennessee.

Bailey removed the cat from his neck with both hands and flung it out the window against the side of a pine tree. Then he got out of the car and started looking for the children's mother. She was sitting against the side of the red gutted ditch, holding the screaming baby, but she only had a cut down her face and a broken shoulder. "We've had an ACCIDENT!" the children screamed in a frenzy of delight.

"But nobody's killed," June Star said with disappointment as the grandmother limped out of the car, her hat still pinned to her head but the broken front brim standing up at a jaunty angle and the violet spray hanging off the side. They all sat down in the ditch, except the children, to recover from the shock. They were all shaking.

"Maybe a car will come along," said the children's mother hoarsely.

"I believe I have injured an organ," said the grandmother, pressing her side, but no one answered her. Bailey's teeth were clattering. He had on a yellow sport shirt with bright blue parrots designed in it and his face was as yellow as the shirt. The grandmother decided that she would not mention that the house was in Tennessee.

70 The road was about ten feet above and they could see only the tops of the trees on the other side of it. Behind the ditch they were sitting in there were more woods, tall and dark and deep. In a few minutes they saw a car some distance away on top of a hill, coming slowly as if the occupants were watching them. The grandmother stood up and waved both arms dramatically to attract their attention. The car continued to come on slowly, disappeared around a bend and appeared again, moving even slower, on top of the hill they had gone over. It was a big black battered hearse-like automobile. There were three men in it.

It came to a stop just over them and for some minutes, the driver looked down with a steady expressionless gaze to where they were sitting, and didn't speak. Then he turned his head and muttered something to the other two and they got out. One was a fat boy in black trousers and a red sweat shirt with a silver stallion embossed on the front of it. He moved around on the right side of them and stood staring, his mouth partly open in a kind of loose grin. The other had on khaki pants and a blue striped coat and a gray hat pulled down very low, hiding most of his face. He came around slowly on the left side. Neither spoke.

The driver got out of the car and stood by the side of it, looking down at them. He was an older man than the other two. His hair was just beginning to gray and he wore silver-rimmed spectacles that gave him a scholarly look. He had a long creased face and didn't have on any shirt or undershirt. He had on blue jeans that were too tight for him and was holding a black hat and a gun. The two boys also had guns.

"We've had an ACCIDENT!" the children screamed.

The grandmother had the peculiar feeling that the bespectacled man was someone she knew. His face was as familiar to her as if she had known him all her life but she could not recall who he was. He moved away from the car and began to come down the embankment, placing his feet carefully so that he wouldn't slip. He had on tan and white shoes and no socks, and his ankles were red and thin. "Good afternoon," he said. "I see you all had you a little spill."

75 "We turned over twice!" said the grandmother.

"Oncet," he corrected. "We seen it happen. Try their car and see will it run, Hiram," he said quietly to the boy with the gray hat.

"What you got that gun for?" John Wesley asked. "Whatcha gonna do with that gun?"

"Lady," the man said to the children's mother, "would you mind calling them children to sit down by you? Children make me nervous. I want all you all to sit down right there together where you're at."

"What are you telling us what to do for?" June Star asked.

Behind them the line of woods gaped like a dark open mouth. "Come here," said their mother.

"Look here now," Bailey began suddenly, "We're in a predicament! We're in . . ."

The grandmother shrieked. She scrambled to her feet and stood staring. "You're The Misfit!" she said. "I recognized you at once!"

"Yes'm," the man said, smiling slightly as if he were pleased in spite of himself to be known, "but it would have been better for all of you, lady, if you hadn't of reckernized me."

Bailey turned his head sharply and said something to his mother that shocked even the children. The old lady began to cry and The Misfit reddened.

"Lady," he said, "don't you get upset. Sometimes a man says things he don't mean. I don't reckon he meant to talk to you thataway."

"You wouldn't shoot a lady, would you?" the grandmother said and removed a clean handkerchief from her cuff and began to slap at her eyes with it.

The Misfit pointed the toe of his shoe into the ground and made a little hole and then covered it up again. "I would hate to have to," he said.

"Listen," the grandmother almost screamed, "I know you're a good man. You don't look a bit like you have common blood. I know you must come from nice people!"

"Yes mam," he said, "finest people in the world." When he smiled he showed a row of strong white teeth. "God never made a finer woman than my mother and my daddy's heart was pure gold," he said. The boy with the red sweat shirt had come around behind them and was standing with his gun at his hip. The Misfit squatted down on the ground. "Watch them children, Bobby Lee," he said. "You know they make me nervous." He looked at the six of them huddled together in front of him and he seemed to be embarrassed as if he couldn't think of anything to say. "Ain't a cloud in the sky," he remarked, looking up at it. "Don't see no sun but don't see no cloud either."

"Yes, it's a beautiful day," said the grandmother. "Listen," she said, "you shouldn't call yourself The Misfit because I know you're a good man at heart. I can just look at you and tell."

"Hush!" Bailey yelled. "Hush! Everybody shut up and let me handle this!" He was squatting in the position of a runner about to sprint forward but he didn't move.

"I pre-chate that, lady," The Misfit said and drew a little circle in the ground with the butt of his gun.

"It'll take a half a hour to fix this here car," Hiram called, looking over the raised hood of it.

"Well, first you and Bobby Lee get him and that little boy to step over yonder with you," The Misfit said, pointing to Bailey and John Wesley. "The boys want to ast you something," he said to Bailey. "Would you mind stepping back in them woods there with them?"

95 "Listen," Bailey began, "we're in a terrible predicament! Nobody realizes what this is," and his voice cracked. His eyes were as blue and intense as the parrots in his shirt and he remained perfectly still.

The grandmother reached up to adjust her hat brim as if she were going to the woods with him but it came off in her hand. She stood staring at it and after a second she let it fall on the ground. Hiram pulled Bailey up by the arm as if he were assisting an old man. John Wesley caught hold of his father's hand and Bobby Lee followed. They went off toward the woods and just as they reached the dark edge, Bailey turned and supporting himself against a gray naked pine trunk, he shouted, "I'll be back in a minute, Mama, wait on me!"

"Come back this instant!" his mother shrilled but they all disappeared into the woods.

"Bailey Boy!" the grandmother called in a tragic voice but she found she was looking at The Misfit squatting on the ground in front of her. "I just know you're a good man," she said desperately. "You're not a bit common!"

"Nome, I ain't a good man," The Misfit said after a second as if he had considered her statement carefully, "but I ain't the worst in the world neither. My daddy said I was a different breed of dog from my brothers and sisters. 'You know,' Daddy said, 'it's some that can live their whole life out without asking about it and it's others has to know why it is, and this boy is one of the latters. He's going to be into everything!' " He put on his black hat and looked up suddenly and then away deep into the woods as if he were embarrassed again. "I'm sorry I don't have on a shirt before you ladies," he said, hunching his shoulders slightly. "We buried our clothes that we had on when we escaped and we're just making do until we can get better. We borrowed these from some folks we met," he explained.

100 "That's perfectly all right," the grandmother said. "Maybe Bailey has an extra shirt in his suitcase."

"I'll look and see terrectly," The Misfit said.

"Where are they taking him?" the children's mother screamed.

"Daddy was a card himself," The Misfit said. "You couldn't put anything over on him. He never got in trouble with the Authorities though. Just had the knack of handling them."

"You could be honest too if you'd only try," said the grandmother. "Think how wonderful it would be to settle down and live a comfortable life and not have to think about somebody chasing you all the time."

105 The Misfit kept scratching in the ground with the butt of his gun as if he were thinking about it. "Yes'm, somebody is always after you," he murmured.

The grandmother noticed how thin his shoulder blades were just behind his hat because she was standing up looking down on him. "Do you ever pray?" she asked.

He shook his head. All she saw was the black hat wiggle between his shoulder blades. "Nome," he said.

There was a pistol shot from the woods, followed closely by another. Then silence. The old lady's head jerked around. She could hear the wind move through the tree tops like a long satisfied insuck of breath. "Bailey Boy!" she called.

"I was a gospel singer for a while," The Misfit said. "I been most everything. Been in the arm service, both land and sea, at home and abroad, been twict married, been an undertaker, been with the railroads, plowed Mother Earth, been in a tornado, seen a man burnt alive oncet," and looked up at the children's mother and the little girl who were sitting close together, their faces white and their eyes glassy; "I even seen a woman flogged," he said.

"Pray, pray," the grandmother began, "pray, pray . . ."

"I never was a bad boy that I remember of," The Misfit said in an almost dreamy voice, "but somewheres along the line I done something wrong and got sent to the penitentiary. I was buried alive," and he looked up and held her attention to him by a steady stare.

"That's when you should have started to pray," she said. "What did you do to get sent to the penitentiary that first time?"

"Turn to the right, it was a wall," The Misfit said, looking up again at the cloudless sky. "Turn to the left, it was a wall. Look up it was a ceiling, look down it was a floor. I forget what I done, lady. I set there and set there, trying to remember what it was I done and I ain't recalled it to this day. Oncet in a while, I would think it was coming to me, but it never come."

"Maybe they put you in by mistake," the old lady said vaguely.

"Nome," he said. "It wasn't no mistake. They had the papers on me."

"You must have stolen something," she said.

The Misfit sneered slightly. "Nobody had nothing I wanted," he said. "It was a head-doctor at the penitentiary said what I had done was kill my daddy but I known that for a lie. My daddy died in nineteen ought nineteen of the epidemic flu and I never had a thing to do with it. He was buried in the Mount Hopewell Baptist churchyard and you can go there and see for yourself."

"If you would pray," the old lady said, "Jesus would help you."

"That's right," The Misfit said.

"Well then, why don't you pray?" she asked trembling with delight suddenly.

"I don't want no hep," he said. "I'm doing all right by myself."

Bobby Lee and Hiram came ambling back from the woods. Bobby Lee was dragging a yellow shirt with bright blue parrots in it.

"Thow me that shirt, Bobby Lee," The Misfit said. The shirt came flying at him and landed on his shoulder and he put it on. The grandmother couldn't name what the shirt reminded her of. "No, lady," The Misfit said while he was buttoning it up, "I found out the crime don't matter. You can do one thing or you can do another, kill a man or take a tire off his car, because sooner or later you're going to forget what it was you done and just be punished for it."

The children's mother had begun to make heaving noises as if she couldn't get her breath. "Lady," he asked, "would you and that little girl like to step off yonder with Bobby Lee and Hiram and join your husband?"

125 "Yes, thank you," the mother said faintly. Her left arm dangled helplessly and she was holding the baby, who had gone to sleep, in the other. "Hep that lady up, Hiram," The Misfit said as she struggled to climb out of the ditch, "and Bobby Lee, you hold onto that little girl's hand."

"I don't want to hold hands with him," June Star said. "He reminds me of a pig."

The fat boy blushed and laughed and caught her by the arm and pulled her off into the woods after Hiram and her mother.

Alone with The Misfit, the grandmother found that she had lost her voice. There was not a cloud in the sky nor any sun. There was nothing around her but woods. She wanted to tell him that he must pray. She opened and closed her mouth several times before anything came out. Finally she found herself saying, "Jesus, Jesus," meaning, Jesus will help you, but the way she was saying it, it sounded as if she might be cursing.

"Yes'm," The Misfit said as if he agreed. "Jesus thown everything off balance. It was the same case with Him as with me except He hadn't committed any crime and they could prove I had committed one because they had the papers on me. Of course," he said, "they never shown me my papers. That's why I sign myself now. I said long ago, you get you a signature and sign everything you do and keep a copy of it. Then you'll know what you done and you can hold up the crime to the punishment and see do they match and in the end you'll have something to prove you ain't been treated right. I call myself The Misfit," he said, "because I can't make what all I done wrong fit what all I gone through in punishment."

130 There was a piercing scream from the woods, followed closely by a pistol report. "Does it seem right to you, lady, that one is punished a heap and another ain't punished at all?"

"Jesus!" the old lady cried. "You've got good blood! I know you wouldn't shoot a lady! I know you come from nice people! Pray! Jesus, you ought not to shoot a lady. I'll give you all the money I've got!"

"Lady," The Misfit said, looking beyond her far into the woods, "there never was a body that give the undertaker a tip."

There were two more pistol reports and the grandmother raised her head like a parched old turkey hen crying for water and called, "Bailey Boy, Bailey Boy!" as if her heart would break.

"Jesus was the only One that ever raised the dead." The Misfit continued, "and He shouldn't have done it. He thrown everything off balance. If He did what He said, then it's nothing for you to do but throw away everything and follow Him, and if He didn't, then it's nothing for you to do but enjoy the few minutes you got left the best way you can—by killing somebody or burning down his house or doing some other meanness to him. No pleasure but meanness," he said and his voice had become almost a snarl.

135 "Maybe He didn't raise the dead," the old lady mumbled, not knowing what she was saying and feeling so dizzy that she sank down in the ditch with her legs twisted under her.

"I wasn't there so I can't say He didn't," The Misfit said. "I wisht I had of been there," he said, hitting the ground with his fist. "It ain't right I wasn't there because if I had of been there I would of known. Listen lady," he said in a high voice, "if I had of been there I would of known and I wouldn't be like I am now." His voice seemed about to crack and the grandmother's head cleared for an instant. She saw the man's face twisted close to her own as if he were going to cry and she murmured, "Why you're one of my babies. You're one of my own children!" She reached out and touched him on the shoulder. The Misfit sprang back as if a snake had bitten him and shot her three times through the chest. Then he put his gun down on the ground and took off his glasses and began to clean them.

Hiram and Bobby Lee returned from the woods and stood over the ditch, looking down at the grandmother who half sat and half lay in a puddle of blood with her legs crossed under her like a child's and her face smiling up at the cloudless sky.

Without his glasses, The Misfit's eyes were red-rimmed and pale and defenseless-looking. "Take her off and throw her where you thrown the others," he said, picking up the cat that was rubbing itself against his leg.

"She was talker, wasn't she?" Bobby Lee said, sliding down the ditch with a yodel.

140 "She would of been a good woman," The Misfit said, "if it had been somebody there to shoot her every minute of her life."

"Some fun!" Bobby Lee said.

"Shut up, Bobby Lee," The Misfit said. "It's no real pleasure in life."

Explorations of the Text

1. Analyze the grandmother's character. Examine her relationship with her grandchildren, her son, and with her daughter-in-law. Discuss her concept of being a lady.
2. Discuss the episode in The Tower restaurant and the symbolism of the monkey.
3. What causes the accident?
4. What is your view of The Misfit? Is he a homicidal serial killer or a demented prophet?
5. Does the grandmother change? Does The Misfit change? Examine the grandmother's final confrontation with The Misfit.
6. Explore the significance of The Misfit statement: " 'She would of been a good woman,' . . . 'if it had been somebody there to shoot her every minute of her life.' "
7. Discuss the significance of the title.

The Reading/Writing Connection

1. List your questions about this story. Then answer one of them in a paragraph.
2. "Think" Topic: Is this a story about salvation or damnation?
3. Journal Entry: React to Red Sam's statement: " 'These days you don't know who to trust.' "
4. Debate Topic: "The grandmother has become a good woman." Argue pro or con.

Ideas for Writing

1. Compare the treatment of violence in this story with "Where Are You Going, Where Have You Been?" or compare the endings of both stories.
2. Compare the grandmother's "coming of age" with the narrator's in "Cathedral."
3. Compare the spiritual vision in "Cathedral" with that of "A Good Man Is Hard to Find." Refer to the student essay anthologized in this chapter.

CATHEDRAL

Raymond Carver

Raymond Carver (1938–89) grew up in Oregon. He studied creative writing with John Gardner at Chico State College, earned his B.A. from Humboldt State College, and studied at the University of Iowa. He taught at a number of colleges, principally Syracuse University. He achieved fame for his short stories, a form of which he was a master. His first collection of stories, Will You Please Be Quiet, Please? *was nominated for the National Book Award in 1976. He subsequently published ten more collections of stories and poetry, including* What We Talk About When We Talk About Love *(1981),* Cathedral *(1984), and* Where I'm Calling From *(1988). With Richard Ford and Tobias Wolff, Carver was considered one of the leading members of the literary school of "dirty realism," fiction that focused on the minute, and frequently unpleasant, details of people's daily lives.*

1984

This blind man, an old friend of my wife's, he was on his way to spend the night. His wife had died. So he was visiting the dead wife's relatives in Connecticut. He called my wife from his in-laws'. Arrangements were made. He would come by train, a five-hour trip, and my wife would meet him at the station. She hadn't seen him since she worked for him one summer in Seattle ten years ago. But she and the blind man had kept in touch. They made tapes and mailed them back and forth. I wasn't enthusiastic about his visit. He was no one I knew. And his being blind bothered me. My idea of blindness came from the movies. In the movies, the blind moved slowly and never laughed. Sometimes they were led by seeing-eye dogs. A blind man in my house was not something I looked forward to.

That summer in Seattle she had needed a job. She didn't have any money. The man she was going to marry at the end of the summer was in officers' training school. He didn't have any money, either. But she was in love with the guy, and he was in love with her, etc. She'd seen something in the paper: HELP WANTED—*Reading to Blind Man,* and a telephone number. She phoned and went over, was hired on the spot. She'd worked with this blind man all summer. She read stuff to him, case studies, reports, that sort of thing. She helped him organize his little office in the county social-service department. They'd become good friends, my wife and the blind man. How do I know these things? She told me. And she told me something else. On her last day in the office, the blind man asked if he could touch her face. She agreed to this. She told me he touched his fingers to every part of her face, her nose—even her neck! She never forgot it. She even tried to write a poem about it. She was always trying to write a poem. She wrote a poem or two every year, usually after something really important had happened to her.

When we first started going out together, she showed me the poem. In the poem, she recalled his fingers and the way they had moved around over her face. In the poem, she talked about what she had felt at the time, about what went through her mind when the blind man touched her nose and lips. I can remember I didn't think much of the poem. Of course, I didn't tell her that. Maybe I just don't understand poetry. I admit it's not the first thing I reach for when I pick up something to read.

Anyway, this man who'd first enjoyed her favors, the officer-to-be, he'd been her childhood sweetheart. So okay. I'm saying that at the end of the summer she let the blind man run his hands over her face, said goodbye to him, married her childhood etc., who was now a commissioned officer, and she moved away from Seattle. But they'd kept in touch, she and the blind man. She made the first contact after a year or so. She called him up one night from an Air Force base in Alabama. She wanted to talk. They talked. He asked her to send him a tape and tell him about her life. She did this. She sent the tape. On the tape, she told the blind man about her husband and about their life together in the military. She told the blind man she loved her husband but she didn't like it where they lived and she didn't like it that he was a part of the military-industrial thing. She told the blind man she'd written a poem and he was in it. She told him that she was writing a poem about what it was like to be an Air Force officer's wife. The poem wasn't finished yet. She was still writing it. The blind man made a tape. He sent her the tape. She made a tape. This went on for years. My wife's officer was posted to one base and then another. She sent tapes from Moody AFB, McGuire, McConnell, and finally Travis, near Sacramento, where one night she got to feeling lonely and cut off from people she kept losing in that moving-around life. She got to feeling she couldn't go it another step. She went in and swallowed all the pills and capsules in the medicine chest and washed them down with a bottle of gin. Then she got into a hot bath and passed out.

But instead of dying, she got sick. She threw up. Her officer—why should he have a name? he was the childhood sweetheart, and what more does he want?—came home from somewhere, found her, and called the ambulance. In time, she put it all on a tape and sent the tape to the blind man. Over the years, she put all kinds of stuff on tapes and sent the tapes off lickety-split. Next to writing a poem every year, I think it was her chief means of recreation. On one tape, she told the blind man she'd decided to live away from her officer for a time. On another tape, she told him about her divorce. She and I began going out, and of course she told her blind man about it. She told him everything, or so it seemed to me. Once she asked me if I'd like to hear the latest tape from the blind man. This was a year ago. I was on the tape, she said. So I said okay, I'd listen to it. I got us drinks and we settled down in the living room. We made ready to listen. First she inserted the tape into the player and adjusted a couple of dials. Then she pushed a lever. The tape squeaked and someone began to talk in this loud voice. She lowered the volume. After a few minutes of harmless chitchat, I heard my own name in the mouth of this stranger, this blind man I didn't even know! And then this: "From all you've said about him, I can only conclude—" But we were interrupted, a knock at the door, something, and we didn't ever get back to the tape. Maybe it was just as well. I'd heard all I wanted to.

Now this same blind man was coming to sleep in my house.

"Maybe I could take him bowling," I said to my wife. She was at the draining board doing scalloped potatoes. She put down the knife she was using and turned around.

"If you love me," she said, "you can do this for me. If you don't love me, okay. But if you had a friend, any friend, and the friend came to visit, I'd make him feel comfortable." She wiped her hands with the dish towel.

"I don't have any blind friends," I said.

"You don't have *any* friends," she said. "Period. Besides," she said, "goddamn it, his wife's just died! Don't you understand that? The man's lost his wife!"

I didn't answer. She'd told me a little about the blind man's wife. Her name was Beulah. Beulah! That's a name for a colored woman.

"Was his wife a Negro?" I asked.

"Are you crazy?" my wife said. "Have you just flipped or something?" She picked up a potato. I saw it hit the floor, then roll under the stove. "What's wrong with you?" she said. "Are you drunk?"

"I'm just asking," I said.

Right then my wife filled me in with more detail than I cared to know. I made a drink and sat at the kitchen table to listen. Pieces of the story began to fall into place.

Beulah had gone to work for the blind man the summer after my wife had stopped working for him. Pretty soon Beulah and the blind man had themselves a church wedding. It was a little wedding—who'd want to go to such a wedding in the first place?—just the two of them, plus the minister and the minister's wife. But it was a church wedding just the same. It was what Beulah had wanted, he's said. But even then Beulah must have been carrying the cancer in her glands. After they had been inseparable for eight years—my wife's word, *inseparable*—Beulah's health went into a rapid decline. She died in a Seattle hospital room, the blind man sitting beside the bed and holding on to her hand. They'd married, lived and worked together, slept together—had sex, sure—and then the blind man had to bury her. All this without his having ever seen what the goddamned woman looked like. It was beyond my understanding. Hearing this, I felt sorry for the blind man for a little bit. And then I found myself thinking what a pitiful life this woman must have led. Imagine a woman who could never see herself as she was seen in the eyes of her loved one. A woman who could go on day after day and never receive the smallest compliment from her beloved. A woman whose husband could never read the expression on her face, be it misery or something better. Someone who could wear makeup or not—what difference to him? She could, if she wanted, wear green eye-shadow around one eye, a straight pin in her nostril, yellow slacks and purple shoes, no matter. And then to slip off into death, the blind man's hand on her hand, his blind eyes streaming tears—I'm imagining now—her last thought maybe this: that he never even knew what she looked like, and she on an express to the grave. Robert was left with a small insurance policy and half of a twenty-peso Mexican coin. The other half of the coin went into the box with her. Pathetic.

So when the time rolled around, my wife went to the depot to pick him up. With nothing to do but wait—sure, I blamed him for that—I was having a drink and watching the TV when I heard the car pull into the drive. I got up from the sofa with my drink and went to the window to have a look.

I saw my wife laughing as she parked the car. I saw her get out of the car and shut the door. She was still wearing a smile. Just amazing. She went around to the other side of the car to where the blind man was already starting to get out. This blind man, feature this, he was wearing a full beard! A beard on a blind man! Too much, I say. The blind man reached into the back seat and dragged out a suitcase. My wife took his arm, shut the car door, and, talking all the way, moved him down the drive and then up the steps to the front porch. I turned off the TV. I finished my drink, rinsed the glass, dried my hands. Then I went to the door.

My wife said, "I want you to meet Robert. Robert, this is my husband. I've told you all about him." She was beaming. She had this blind man by his coat sleeve.

20 The blind man let go of his suitcase and up came his hand.

I took it. He squeezed hard, held my hand, and then he let it go.

"I feel like we've already met," he boomed.

"Likewise," I said. I didn't know what else to say. Then I said, "Welcome. I've heard a lot about you." We began to move then, a little group, from the porch into the living room, my wife guiding him by the arm. The blind man was carrying his suitcase in his other hand. My wife said things like, "To your left here, Robert. That's right. Now watch it, there's a chair.

That's it. Sit down right here. This is the sofa. We just bought this sofa two weeks ago."

I started to say something about the old sofa. I'd liked that old sofa. But I didn't say anything. Then I wanted to say something else, small-talk, about the scenic ride along the Hudson. How going *to* New York, you should sit on the right-hand side of the train, and coming *from* New York, the left-hand side.

25 "Did you have a good train ride?" I said. "Which side of the train did you sit on, by the way?"

"What a question, which side!" my wife said. "What's it matter which side?" she said.

"I just asked," I said.

"Right side," the blind man said. "I hadn't been on a train in nearly forty years. Not since I was a kid. With my folks. That's been a long time. I'd nearly forgotten the sensation. I have winter in my beard now," he said. "So I've been told, anyway. Do I look distinguished, my dear?" the blind man said to my wife.

"You look distinguished, Robert," she said. "Robert," she said. "Robert, it's just so good to see you."

30 My wife finally took her eyes off the blind man and looked at me. I had the feeling she didn't like what she saw. I shrugged.

I've never met, or personally known, anyone who was blind. This blind man was late forties, a heavy-set, balding man with stooped shoulders, as if he carried a great weight there. He wore brown slacks, brown shoes, a light-brown shirt, a tie, a sports coat. Spiffy. He also had this full beard. But he didn't use a cane and he didn't wear dark glasses. I'd always thought dark glasses were a must for the blind. Fact was, I wished he had a pair. At first glance, his eyes looked like anyone else's eyes. But if you looked close, there was something different about them. Too much white in the iris, for one thing, and the pupils seemed to move around in the sockets without his knowing it or being able to stop it. Creepy. As I stared at his face, I saw the left pupil turn in toward his nose while the other made an effort to keep in one place. But it was only an effort, for that eye was on the roam without his knowing it or wanting it to be.

I said, "Let me get you a drink. What's your pleasure? We have a little of everything. It's one of our pastimes."

"Bub, I'm a Scotch man myself," he said fast enough in this big voice.

"Right," I said. Bub! "Sure you are. I knew it."

35 He let his fingers touch his suitcase, which was sitting alongside the sofa. He was taking his bearings. I didn't blame him for that.

"I'll move that up to your room," my wife said.

"No, that's fine," the blind man said loudly. "It can go up when I go up."

"A little water with the Scotch?" I said.

"Very little," he said.

40 "I knew it," I said.

He said, "Just a tad. The Irish actor, Barry Fitzgerald? I'm like that fellow. When I drink water, Fitzgerald said, I drink water. When I drink whiskey, I drink whiskey." My wife laughed. The blind man brought his hand up under his beard. He lifted his beard slowly and let it drop.

I did the drinks, three big glasses of Scotch with a splash of water in each. Then we made ourselves comfortable and talked about Robert's travels. First the long flight from the West Coast to Connecticut, we covered that. Then from Connecticut up here by train. We had another drink concerning that leg of the trip.

I remembered having read somewhere that the blind didn't smoke because, as speculation had it, they couldn't see the smoke they exhaled. I thought I knew that much and that much only about blind people. But this blind man smoked his cigarette down to the nubbin and then lit another one. This blind man filled his ashtray and my wife emptied it.

When we sat down at the table for dinner, we had another drink. My wife heaped Robert's plate with cube steak, scalloped potatoes, green beans. I buttered him up two slices of bread. I said, "Here's bread and butter for you." I swallowed some of my drink. "Now let us pray," I said, and the blind man lowered his head. My wife looked at me, her mouth agape. "Pray the phone won't ring and the food doesn't get cold," I said.

We dug in. We ate everything there was to eat on the table. We ate like there was no tomorrow. We didn't talk. We ate. We scarfed. We grazed that table. We were into serious eating. The blind man had right away located his foods, he knew just where everything was on his plate. I watched with admiration as he used his knife and fork on the meat. He'd cut two pieces of meat, fork the meat into his mouth, and then go all out for the scalloped potatoes, the beans next, and then he'd tear off a hunk of buttered bread and eat that. He'd follow this up with a big drink of milk. It didn't seem to bother him to use his fingers once in a while, either.

We finished everything, including half a strawberry pie. For a few moments, we sat as if stunned. Sweat beaded on our faces. Finally, we got up from the table and left the dirty plates. We didn't look back. We took ourselves into the living room and sank into our places again. Robert and my wife sat on the sofa. I took the big chair. We had us two or three more drinks while they talked about the major things that had come to pass for them in the past ten years. For the most part, I just listened. Now and then I joined in. I didn't want him to think I'd left the room, and I didn't want her to think I was feeling left out. They talked of things that had happened to them—to them!—these past ten years. I waited in vain to hear my name on my wife's sweet lips: "And then my dear husband came into my life"—something like that. But I heard nothing of the sort. More talk of Robert. Robert had done a little of everything, it seemed, a regular blind jack-of-all-trades. But most recently he and his wife had had an Amway distributorship, from which, I gathered, they'd earned their living, such as it was. The blind man was also a ham radio operator. He talked in his loud voice about conversations he'd had with fellow operators in Guam, in the Philippines, in Alaska, and even in Tahiti. He said he'd have a lot of friends there if he ever wanted to go visit those places. From time to time, he'd turn his blind face toward me, put his hand under his beard, ask me something. How long had I been in my present position? (Three years.) Did I like my work? (I didn't.) Was I going to stay with it? (What were the options?) Finally, when I thought he was beginning to run down, I got up and turned on the TV.

My wife looked at me with irritation. She was heading toward a boil. Then she looked at the blind man and said, "Robert, do you have a TV?"

The blind man said, "My dear, I have two TVs. I have a color set and a black-and-white thing, an old relic. It's funny, but if I turn the TV on, and I'm always turning it on, I turn on the color set. It's funny, don't you think?"

I didn't know what to say to that. I had absolutely nothing to say to that. No opinion. So I watched the news program and tried to listen to what the announcer was saying.

"This is a color TV," the blind man said. "Don't ask me how, but I can tell."

"We traded up a while ago," I said.

The blind man had another taste of his drink. He lifted his beard, sniffed it, and let it fall. He leaned forward on the sofa. He positioned his ashtray on the coffee table, then put the lighter to his cigarette. He leaned back on the sofa and crossed his legs at the ankles.

My wife covered her mouth, and then she yawned. She stretched. She said, "I think I'll go upstairs and put on my robe. I think I'll change into something else. Robert, you make yourself comfortable," she said.

"I'm comfortable," the blind man said.

"I want you to feel comfortable in this house," she said.

"I am comfortable," the blind man said.

After she'd left the room, he and I listened to the weather report and then to the sports roundup. By that time, she'd been gone so long I didn't know if she was going to come back. I thought she might have gone to bed. I wished she'd come back downstairs. I didn't want to be left alone with a blind man. I asked him if he wanted another drink, and he said sure. Then I asked if he wanted to smoke some dope with me. I said I'd just rolled a number. I hadn't, but I planned to do so in about two shakes.

"I'll try some with you," he said.

"Damn right," I said. "That's the stuff."

I got our drinks and sat down on the sofa with him. Then I rolled us two fat numbers. I lit one and passed it. I brought it to his fingers. He took it and inhaled.

"Hold it as long as you can," I said. I could tell he didn't know the first thing.

My wife came back downstairs wearing her pink robe and her pink slippers.

"What do I smell?" she said.

"We thought we'd have us some cannabis," I said.

My wife gave me a savage look. Then she looked at the blind man and said, "Robert, I didn't know you smoked."

He said, "I do now, my dear. There's a first time for everything. But I don't feel anything yet."

"This stuff is pretty mellow," I said. "This stuff is mild. It's dope you can reason with," I said. "It doesn't mess you up."

"Not much it doesn't, bub," he said, and laughed.

My wife sat on the sofa between the blind man and me. I passed her the number. She took it and toked and then passed it back to me. "Which way is this going?" she said. Then she said, "I shouldn't be smoking this. I can hardly keep my eyes open as it is. That dinner did me in. I shouldn't have eaten so much."

"It was the strawberry pie," the blind man said. "That's what did it," he said, and he laughed his big laugh. Then he shook his head.

"There's more strawberry pie," I said.

"Do you want some more, Robert?" my wife said.

"Maybe in a little while," he said.

We gave our attention to the TV. My wife yawned again. She said, "Your bed is made up when you feel like going to bed, Robert. I know you must have had a long day. When you're ready to go to bed, say so." She pulled his arm. "Robert?"

He came to and said, "I've had a real nice time. This beats tapes, doesn't it?"

I said, "Coming at you," and I put the number between his fingers. He inhaled, held the smoke, and then let it go. It was like he'd been doing it since he was nine years old.

"Thanks, bub," he said. "But I think this is all for me. I think I'm beginning to feel it," he said. He held the burning roach out for my wife.

"Same here," she said. "Ditto. Me, too." She took the roach and passed it to me. "I may just sit here for a while between you two guys with my eyes closed. But don't let me bother you, okay? Either one of you. If it bothers you, say so. Otherwise, I may just sit here with my eyes closed until you're ready to go to bed," she said. "Your bed's made up, Robert, when you're ready. It's right next to our room at the top of the stairs. We'll show you up when you're ready. You wake me up now, you guys, if I fall asleep." She said that and then she closed her eyes and went to sleep.

The news program ended. I got up and changed the channel. I sat back down on the sofa. I wished my wife hadn't pooped out. Her head lay across the back of the sofa, her mouth open. She'd turned so that her robe had slipped away from her legs, exposing a juicy thigh. I reached to draw her robe back over her, and it was then that I glanced at the blind man. What the hell! I flipped the robe open again.

"You say when you want some strawberry pie," I said.

"I will," he said.

I said, "Are you tired? Do you want me to take you up to your bed? Are you ready to hit the hay?"

"Not yet," he said. "No, I'll stay up with you, bub. If that's all right. I'll stay up until you're ready to turn in. We haven't had a chance to talk. Know what I mean? I feel like me and her monopolized the evening." He lifted his beard and he let it fall. He picked up his cigarettes and his lighter.

"That's all right," I said. Then I said, "I'm glad for the company."

And I guess I was. Every night I smoked dope and stayed up as long as I could before I fell asleep. My wife and I hardly ever went to bed at the same time. When I did go to sleep, I had these dreams. Sometimes I'd wake up from one of them, my heart going crazy.

Something about the church and the Middle Ages was on the TV. Not your run-of-the-mill TV fare. I wanted to watch something else. I turned to the other channels. But there was nothing on them, either. So I turned back to the first channel and apologized.

"Bub, it's all right," the blind man said. "It's fine with me. Whatever you want to watch is okay. I'm always learning something. Learning never ends. It won't hurt me to learn something tonight. I got ears," he said.

We didn't say anything for a time. He was leaning forward with his head turned at me, his right ear aimed in the direction of the set. Very disconcerting. Now and then his eyelids drooped and then they snapped open again. Now and then he put his fingers into his beard and tugged, like he was thinking about something he was hearing on the television.

On the screen, a group of men wearing cowls was being set upon and tormented by men dressed in skeleton costumes and men dressed as devils. The men dressed as devils wore devil masks, horns, and long tails. This pageant was part of a procession. The Englishman who was narrating the thing said it took place in Spain once a year. I tried to explain to the blind man what was happening.

"Skeletons," he said. "I know about skeletons," he said, and he nodded.

The TV showed this one cathedral. Then there was a long, slow look at another one. Finally, the picture switched to the famous one in Paris, with its flying buttresses and its spires reaching up to the clouds. The camera pulled away to show the whole of the cathedral rising above the skyline.

There were times when the Englishman who was telling the thing would shut up, would simply let the camera move around over the cathedrals. Or else the camera would tour the countryside, men in fields walking behind oxen. I waited as long as I could. Then I felt I had to say something. I said, "They're showing the outside of this cathedral now. Gargoyles. Little statues carved to look like monsters. Now I guess they're in Italy. Yeah, they're in Italy. There's paintings on the walls of this one church."

"Are those fresco paintings, bub?" he asked, and he sipped from his drink.

I reached for my glass. But it was empty. I tried to remember what I could remember. "You're asking me are those frescoes?" I said. "That's a good question. I don't know."

The camera moved to a cathedral outside Lisbon. The differences in the Portuguese cathedral compared with the French and Italian were not that great. But they were there. Mostly the interior stuff. Then something occurred to me, and I said, "Something has occurred to me. Do you have any idea what a cathedral is? What they look like, that is? Do you follow me? If somebody says cathedral to you, do you have any notion what they're talking about? Do you know the difference between that and a Baptist church, say?"

He let the smoke dribble from his mouth. "I know they took hundreds of workers fifty or a hundred years to build," he said. "I just heard the man say that, of course. I know generations of the same families worked on a cathedral. I heard him say that, too. The men who began their life's work on them, they never lived to see the completion of their work. In that wise, bub, they're no different from the rest of us, right?" He laughed. Then his eyelids drooped again. His head nodded. He seemed to be snoozing. Maybe he was imagining himself in Portugal. The TV was showing another cathedral now. This one was in Germany. The Englishman's voice droned on. "Cathedrals," the blind man said. He sat up and rolled his head back and forth. "If you want the truth, bub, that's about all I know. What I just said. What I heard him say. But maybe you could describe one to me? I wish you'd do it. I'd like that. If you want to know, I really don't have a good idea."

I stared hard at the shot of the cathedral on the TV. How could I even begin to describe it? But say my life depended on it. Say my life was being threatened by an insane guy who said I had to do it or else.

I stared some more at the cathedral before the picture flipped off into the countryside. There was no use. I turned to the blind man and said, "To begin with, they're very tall." I was looking around the room for clues. "They reach way up. Up and up. Toward the sky. They're so big, some of them, they have to have these supports. To help hold them up, so to speak. These supports are called buttresses. They remind me of viaducts, for some reason. But maybe you don't know viaducts, either? Sometimes the cathedrals have devils and such carved into the front. Sometimes lords and ladies. Don't ask me why this is," I said.

He was nodding. The whole upper part of his body seemed to be moving back and forth.

100 "I'm not doing so good, am I?" I said.

He stopped nodding and leaned forward on the edge of the sofa. As he listened to me, he was running his fingers through his beard. I wasn't getting through to him, I could see that. But he waited for me to go on just the same. He nodded, like he was trying to encourage me. I tried to think what else to say. "They're really big," I said. "They're massive. They're built of stone. Marble, too, sometimes. In those olden days, when they built cathedrals, men wanted to be close to God. In those olden days, God was an important part of everyone's life. You could tell this from their cathedral-building. I'm sorry," I said, "but it looks like that's the best I can do for you. I'm just no good at it."

"That's all right, bub," the blind man said. "Hey, listen. I hope you don't mind my asking you. Can I ask you something? Let me ask you a simple question, yes or no. I'm just curious and there's no offense. You're my host. But let me ask if you are in any way religious? You don't mind my asking?"

I shook my head. He couldn't see that, though. A wink is the same as a nod to a blind man. "I guess I don't believe in it. In anything. Sometimes it's hard. You know what I'm saying?"

"Sure, I do," he said.

105 "Right," I said.

The Englishman was still holding forth. My wife sighed in her sleep. She drew a long breath and went on with her sleeping.

"You'll have to forgive me," I said. "But I can't tell you what a cathedral looks like. It just isn't in me to do it. I can't do any more than I've done."

The blind man sat very still, his head down, as he listened to me.

I said, "The truth is, cathedrals don't mean anything special to me. Nothing. Cathedrals. They're something to look at on late-night TV. That's all they are."

110 It was then that the blind man cleared his throat. He brought something up. He took a handkerchief from his back pocket. Then he said, "I get it, bub. It's okay. It happens. Don't worry about it," he said. "Hey, listen to me. Will you do me a favor? I got an idea. Why don't you find us some heavy paper? And a pen. We'll do something. We'll draw one together. Get us a pen and some heavy paper. Go on, bub, get the stuff," he said.

So I went upstairs. My legs felt like they didn't have any strength in them. They felt like they did after I'd done some running. In my wife's room, I looked around. I found some ballpoints in a little basket on her table. And then I tried to think where to look for the kind of paper he was talking about.

Downstairs, in the kitchen, I found a shopping bag with onion skins in the bottom of the bag. I emptied the bag and shook it. I brought it into the living room and sat down with it near his legs. I moved some things, smoothed the wrinkles from the bag, spread it out on the coffee table.

The blind man got down from the sofa and sat next to me on the carpet.

He ran his fingers over the paper. He went up and down the sides of the paper. The edges, even the edges. He fingered the corners.

115 "All right," he said. "All right, let's do her."

He found my hand, the hand with the pen. He closed his hand over my hand. "Go ahead, bub, draw," he said. "Draw. You'll see. I'll follow along with you. It'll be okay. Just begin now like I'm telling you. You'll see. Draw," the blind man said.

So I began. First I drew a box that looked like a house. It could have been the house I lived in. Then I put a roof on it. At either end of the roof, I drew spires. Crazy.

"Swell," he said. "Terrific. You're doing fine," he said. "Never thought anything like this could happen in your lifetime, did you, bub? Well, it's a strange life, we all know that. Go on now. Keep it up."

I put in windows with arches. I drew flying buttresses.[1] I hung great doors. I couldn't stop. The TV station went off the air. I put down the pen and closed and opened my fingers. The blind man felt around over the paper. He

[1] A crucial part of the architecture of Gothic cathedrals; an external support arch that carries an outward and downward thrust to a solid buttress, thereby creating a vertical thrust against a masonry wall to help hold the structure.

moved the tips of his fingers over the paper, all over what I had drawn, and he nodded.

"Doing fine," the blind man said.

I took up the pen again, and he found my hand. I kept at it. I'm no artist. But I kept drawing just the same.

My wife opened up her eyes and gazed at us. She sat up on the sofa, her robe hanging open. She said, "What are you doing? Tell me, I want to know."

I didn't answer her.

The blind man said, "We're drawing a cathedral. Me and him are working on it. Press hard," he said to me. "That's right. That's good," he said. "Sure. You got it, bub. I can tell. You didn't think you could. But you can, can't you? You're cooking with gas now. You know what I'm saying? We're going to really have us something here in a minute. How's the old arm?" he said. "Put some people in there now. What's a cathedral without people?"

My wife said, "What's going on? Robert, what are you doing? What's going on?"

"It's all right," he said to her. "Close your eyes now," the blind man said to me.

I did it. I closed them just like he said.

"Are they closed?" he said. "Don't fudge."

"They're closed," I said.

"Keep them that way," he said. He said, "Don't stop now. Draw."

So we kept on with it. His fingers rode my fingers as my hand went over the paper. It was like nothing else in my life up to now.

Then he said, "I think that's it. I think you got it," he said. "Take a look. What do you think?"

But I had my eyes closed. I thought I'd keep them that way for a little longer. I thought it was something I ought to do.

"Well?" he said. "Are you looking?"

My eyes were still closed. I was in my house. I knew that. But I didn't feel like I was inside anything.

"It's really something," I said.

Explorations of the Text

1. Examine the character of the speaker: his attitudes, values, actions, speech.
2. Why does only the blind man have a name? Describe his attitudes, his physical characteristics, and his capacity for friendship.
3. What is the nature of the relationship between the wife and Robert? Between the wife and the narrator?
4. Why does the woman leave Robert and the narrator together? Is her action deliberate?

5. Does the incident concerning the cathedral have religious meaning? What is the symbolism of the title? In what way does the narrator change at the end of the story?
6. Compare and contrast the themes concerning blindness in *Oedipus Rex* (chapter 7) and in "Cathedral."

The Reading/Writing Connection

1. "Think" Topic: What does the narrator mean when he says, "I didn't feel like I was inside anything"?
2. Journal Entry: extend the narrative: write about possible changes in the narrator when the blind man leaves.

Ideas for Writing

1. Write a character analysis of the wife that takes into account her first marriage, her suicide attempt, her friendship with Robert, and her present life.
2. Explore the symbolism of the cathedral.
3. Carver mentions television numerous times in the opening paragraphs of the story. Why? Use evidence from the story to support your thesis.

POETRY

Wind Secrets

Diane Wakoski

Diane Wakoski (1937–) was born in Whittier, California. Wakoski, educated at the University of California, Berkeley, has held a number of jobs, including working in a bookstore, teaching high school English, and teaching at universities. Her more than twenty volumes of poetry include Coins and Coffins *(1962),* The Man Who Shook Hands *(1978), and* Medea the Sorceress *(1991). Much of Wakoski's poetry concerns itself with creating a personal mythology for the writer.*

1966

I like the wind
with its puffed cheeks and closed eyes.
Nice wind.
I like its gentle sounds
and fierce bites.
When I was little
I used to sit by the black, potbellied stove and stare
at a spot on the ceiling,
while the wind breathed and blew
outside.

"Nice wind,"
I murmured to myself.

I would ask mother when she kneeled to tie my shoes
what the wind said.

Mother knew.

And the wind whistled and roared outside
while the coals opened their eyes in anger
at me.
I would hear mother crying under the wind.
"Nice wind," I said,
But my heart leapt like a darting fish.
I remember the wind better than any sound.
It was the first thing I heard
with blazing ears,
a sound that didn't murmur and coo,
and the sounds wrapped round my head
and huffed open my eyes.

It was the first thing I heard
besides my father beating my mother.
The sounds slashed at my ears like scissors.
Nice wind.

The wind blows
while the glowing coals from the stove look at me
with angry eyes.
Nice wind.
Nice wind.
Oh, close your eyes.
There was nothing I could do.

Explorations of the Text

1. Discuss the speaker's point of view. Is it a child's or an adult's voice? Explain.
2. What comparisons create the dramatic effects and momentum in the poem? What do they suggest about the child's state of mind?
3. Explore the symbolism of the "eyes." Whose "eyes" are they?

The Reading/Writing Connection

1. Do a freewrite response to this poem.
2. Journal Entry: Create a moment from childhood in which you use nature imagery to suggest your state of mind (You may create a poem or a drawing for this entry).

Ideas for Writing

1. Write a monologue in the voice of the mother.
2. Discuss the use of figurative language in this poem. How does the language develop the theme?
3. Compare this poem with "Incident." Focus on loss of innocence.

Incident

Countee Cullen

Born in New York City, Countee Cullen (1903–46) was a central figure in the Harlem Renaissance. He published his first collection of poems, Color, *in 1925 when he was a student at New York University. He received a Guggenheim Fellowship and published* Black Christ and Other Poems *in France in 1929. Cullen also wrote a novel and children's stories. He collaborated with his friend Arna Bontemps on a play,* St. Louis Woman, *which became a popular Broadway musical in 1946.*

1925

Once riding in old Baltimore,
    Heart-filled, head-filled with glee,
I saw a Baltimorean
    Keep looking straight at me.

Now I was eight and very small,
    And he was no whit bigger,
And so I smiled, but he poked out
    His tongue and called me, "Nigger."

I saw the whole of Baltimore
    From May until December:
Of all the things that happened there
    That's all that I remember.

Explorations of the Text

1. What is the nature of the interaction between the two boys?
2. Why does the speaker remember nothing more than the incident, even though he stayed in Baltimore from "May until December"?
3. See how much Cullen conveys in few and simple words. How can you transfer this power of compression in poetry to forms of nonfiction?
4. What aspects of this poem are similar to the story by Heker?

The Reading/Writing Connection

1. In a paragraph compare your experience of prejudice with the persona in the poem.
2. "Think" Topic: Compare the reactions of the persona with those in the works by Heker and Erdrich.

Ideas for Writing

1. What do its form and rhyme add to this poem?
2. What is the power of language? What are the effects of the use of the term *nigger?*

Uncle's First Rabbit

Lorna Dee Cervantes

Born in San Francisco and educated in California, Lorna Dee Cervantes (1954–) is active in the Chicano community and in literary affairs. In 1976, she founded Mango Publications, a small press that publishes a literary journal and both Mexican American and multicultural books. Her first volume of poetry, Emplumada *(1981), received high praise from critics. Her second volume of poems,* From the Cables of Genocide, *was published in 1991.*

1981

He was a good boy
making his way through
the Santa Barbara[1] pines,
sighting the blast of fluff
as he leveled the rifle,
and the terrible singing began.
He was ten years old,
hunting my grandpa's supper.
He had dreamed of running,
shouldering the rifle to town,
selling it, and taking the next
train out.
    Fifty years
have passed and he still hears
that rabbit "just like a baby."
He remembers how the rabbit
stopped keening under the butt
of his rifle, how he brought
it home with tears streaming
down his blood soaked jacket.
"That bastard. That bastard."
He cried all night and the week
after, remembering that voice
like his dead baby sister's,
remembering his father's drunken
kicking that had pushed her
into birth. She had a voice
like that, growing faint
at its end; his mother rocking,
softly, keening. He dreamed
of running, running
the bastard out of his life.

[1] A city in California.

He would forget them, run down
the hill, leave his mother's
silent waters, and the sounds
of beating night after night,
When war came,
he took the man's vow. He was
finally leaving and taking
the bastard's last bloodline
with him. At war's end, he could
still hear her, her soft
body stiffening under water
like a shark's. The color
of the water, darkening, soaking,
as he clung to what was left
of a ship's gun. Ten long hours
off the coast of Okinawa,[2] he sang
so he wouldn't hear them.
He pounded their voices out
of his head, and awakened
to find himself slugging the bloodied
face of his wife.
Fifty years
have passed and he has not run
the way he dreamed. The Paradise
pines shadow the bleak hills
to his home. His hunting hounds,
dead now. His father, long dead.
His wife, dying, hacking in the bed
she has not let him enter for the last
thirty years. He stands looking,
he mouths the words, "Die you bitch.
I'll live to watch you die." He turns,
entering their moss-soft livingroom.
He watches out the picture window
and remembers running: how he'll
take the new pickup to town, sell it,
and get the next train out.

Explorations of the Text

1. What events relate to the killing of the rabbit? Why is it compared to a baby?

[2] One of the islands of the Ryukyu group, part of Japan, occupied by the United States from 1945 to 1972, when it was returned to Japan.

2. What is the narrator's point of view?
3. How has the uncle changed in fifty years?
4. Why does the uncle not leave? Will he ever leave?
5. What connections can you find between this poem and "Barn Burning"?

The Reading/Writing Connection

1. Paraphrase this poem in a paragraph.
2. Respond to the actions of the uncle. Freewrite.

Ideas for Writing

1. Gloss the poem, focusing on the speaker's attitude toward killing the rabbit. Which words provide clues or evidence for your position?
2. Analyze the uncle's character.
3. Compare this presentation of hunting with the hunting scene in Alberto Moravia's "The Chase" (in chapter 6).

OUT OF THE CRADLE ENDLESSLY ROCKING

Walt Whitman

Walt Whitman (1819–92) was born on Long Island. Until the early 1850s, he moved among printing, writing, and teaching jobs in New York. The first edition of his Leaves of Grass *was published in 1855 and consisted of twelve untitled poems, including the work eventually titled "Song of Myself." Whitman spent the rest of his life revising* Leaves of Grass, *editing the poems in it and adding new ones. The spacious, unconventional verse patterns in* Leaves of Grass *have had a profound and lasting effect on North and South American poetry.*

1859

Out of the cradle endlessly rocking,
Out of the mocking-bird's throat, the musical shuttle,
Out of the Ninth-month[1] midnight,
Over the sterile sands and the fields beyond, where the child leaving his bed wander'd alone, bareheaded, barefoot,
Down from the shower'd halo,
Up from the mystic play of shadows twining and twisting as if they were alive,
Out from the patches of briers and blackberries,
From the memories of the bird that chanted to me,
From your memories sad brother, from the fitful risings and fallings I heard,

[1] Quaker name for September.

From under that yellow half-moon late-risen and swollen as if with tears,
From those beginning notes of yearning and love there in the mist,
From the thousand responses of my heart never to cease,
From the myriad thence-arous'd words,
From the word stronger and more delicious than any,
For such as now they start the scene revisiting,
As a flock, twittering, rising, or overhead passing,
Borne hither, ere all eludes me, hurriedly,
A man, yet by these tears a little boy again,
Throwing myself on the sand, confronting the waves,
I, chanter of pains and joys, uniter of here and hereafter,
Taking all hints to use them, but swiftly leaping beyond them,
A reminiscence sing.

Once Paumanok,
When the lilac-scent was in the air and Fifth-month grass was growing,
Up this seashore in some briers,
Two feather'd guests from Alabama, two together,
And their nest, and four light-green eggs spotted with brown,
And every day the he-bird to and fro near at hand,
And every day the she-bird crouch'd on her nest, silent, with bright eyes,
And every day I, a curious boy, never too close, never disturbing them,
Cautiously peering, absorbing, translating.

Shine! shine! shine!
Pour down your warmth, great sun!
While we bask, we two together.
Two together!
Winds blow south, or winds blow north,
Day come white, or night come black,
Home, or rivers and mountains from home,
Singing all time, minding no time,
While we two keep together.

Till of a sudden,
May-be kill'd, unknown to her mate,
One forenoon the she-bird crouch'd not on the nest,
Nor return'd that afternoon, nor the next,
Nor ever appear'd again.

And thenceforward all summer in the sound of the sea,
And at night under the full of the moon in calmer weather,
Over the hoarse surging of the sea,
Or flitting from brier to brier by day,
I saw, I heard at intervals the remaining one, the he-bird,
The solitary guest from Alabama.

Blow! blow! blow!
Blow up sea-winds along Paumanok's shore;
I wait and I wait till you blow my mate to me.

Yes, when the stars glisten'd,
All night long on the prong of a moss-scallop'd stake,
Down almost amid the slapping waves,
Sat the lone singer wonderful causing tears.
He call'd on his mate,
He pour'd forth the meanings which I of all men know.

Yes my brother I know,
The rest might not, but I have treasur'd every note,
For more than once dimly down to the beach gliding,
Silent, avoiding the moonbeams, blending myself with the shadows,
Recalling now the obscure shapes, the echoes, the sounds and sights after their sorts,
The white arms out in the breakers tirelessly tossing,
I, with bare feet, a child, the wind wafting my hair,
Listen'd long and long.

Listen'd to keep, to sing, now translating the notes,
Following you my brother.

Soothe! soothe! soothe!
Close on its wave soothes the wave behind,
And again another behind embracing and lapping, every one close,
But my love soothes not me, not me.

Low hangs the moon, it rose late,
It is lagging—O I think it is heavy with love, with love.

O madly the sea pushes upon the land,
With love, with love.

O night! do I not see my love fluttering out among the breakers?
What is that little black thing I see there in the white?

Loud! loud! loud!
Loud I call to you, my love!

High and clear I shoot my voice over the waves,
Surely you must know who is here, is here,
You must know who I am, my love.

Low-hanging moon!
What is that dusky spot in your brown yellow?
O it is the shape, the shape of my mate!
O moon do not keep her from me any longer.

Land! land! O land!
Whichever way I turn, O I think you could give me my mate back again if you only would,
For I am almost sure I see her dimly whichever way I look.
O rising stars!
Perhaps the one I want so much will rise, will rise with some of you.

O throat! O trembling throat!
Sound clearer through the atmosphere!
Pierce the woods, the earth,
Somewhere listening to catch you must be the one I want.

Shake out carols!
Solitary here, the night's carols!
Carols of lonesome love! death's carols!
Carols under that lagging, yellow, waning moon!
O under that moon where she droops down into the sea!
O reckless despairing carols.

But soft! sink low!
Soft! let me just murmur,
And do you wait a moment you husky-nois'd sea,
For somewhere I believe I heard my mate responding to me,
So faint, I must be still, be still to listen,
But not altogether still, for then she might not come immediately to me.

Hither my love!
Here I am! here!
With this just-sustain'd note I announce myself to you,
This gentle call is for you my love, for you.

Do not be decoy'd elsewhere,
That is the whistle of the wind, it is not my voice,
That is the fluttering, the fluttering of the spray,
Those are the shadows of leaves.

O darkness! O in vain!
O I am very sick and sorrowful.
O brown halo in the sky near the moon, drooping upon the sea!
O troubled reflection in the sea!

O throat! O throbbing heart!
And I singing uselessly, uselessly all the night.

O past! O happy life! O songs of joy!
In the air, in the woods, over fields,
Loved! loved! loved! loved! loved!
But my mate no more, no more with me!
We two together no more.

The aria[2] sinking,
All else continuing, the stars shining,
The winds blowing, the notes of the bird continuous echoing,
With angry moans the fierce old mother incessantly moaning,
On the sands of Paumanok's shore gray and rustling,
The yellow half-moon enlarged, sagging down, drooping, the face of the sea almost touching
The boy ecstatic, with his bare feet the waves, with his hair the atmosphere dallying,
The love in the heart long pent, now loose, now at last tumultuously bursting,
The aria's meaning, the ears, the soul, swiftly depositing,
The strange tears down the cheeks coursing,
The colloquy there, the trio, each uttering,
The undertone, the savage old mother incessantly crying,
To the boy's soul's questions sullenly timing, some drown'd secret hissing,
To the outsetting bard.[3]

Demon or bird! (said the boy's soul,)
Is it indeed toward your mate you sing? or is it really to me?
For I, that was a child, my tongue's use sleeping, now I have heard you,
Now in a moment I know what I am for, I awake,
And already a thousand singers, a thousand songs, clearer, louder and more sorrowful than yours,
A thousand warbling echoes have started to live within me, never to die.

O you singer solitary, singing by yourself, projecting me,
O solitary me listening, never more shall I cease perpetuating you,
Never more shall I escape, never more the reverberations,
Never more the cries of unsatisfied love be absent from me,
Never again leave me to be the peaceful child I was before what there in the night,
By the sea under the yellow and sagging moon,
The messenger there arous'd, the fire, the sweet hell within,
The unknown want, the destiny of me.

---

[2] A song performed by a single voice in opera.

[3] A poet.

O give me the clew! (it lurks in the night here somewhere,)
O if I am to have so much, let me have more!

A word then, (for I will conquer it,)
The word final, superior to all,
Subtle, sent up—what is it?—I listen;
Are you whispering it, and have been all the time, you sea waves?
Is that it from your liquid rims and wet sands?

Whereto answering, the sea,
Delaying not, hurrying not,
Whisper'd me through the night, and very plainly before daybreak,
Lisp'd to me the low and delicious word death,
And again death, death, death, death,
Hissing melodious, neither like the bird nor like my arous'd child's heart,
But edging near as privately for me rustling at my feet,
Creeping thence steadily up to my ears and laving me softly all over,
Death, death, death, death, death.

Which I do not forget,
But fuse the song of my dusky demon and brother,
That he sang to me in the moonlight on Paumanok's gray beach,
With the thousand responsive songs at random,
My own songs awaked from that hour,
And with them the key, the word up from the waves,
The word of the sweetest song and all songs,
The strong and delicious word which, creeping to my feet,
(Or like some old crone rocking the cradle, swathed in sweet garments,
  bending aside,)
The sea whisper'd me.

Explorations of the Text

1. About what does the speaker reminisce? What is the speaker's motivation for this "reminiscence" song?
2. What is the mood of the prologue?
3. What is the message of the he-bird's lament? Is the personification effective?
4. What does the boy learn of life through the "reminiscence" song? What does the adult speaker learn?
5. Explore the connections of birth, love, and death expressed in this poem.
6. Whitman is known for his organic free verse (poetry that has music, form, and rhythm, but not a standard metric or rhythmic pattern); see

the Glossary and chapter 10. How does Whitman's free verse work in this poem?

7. How does Whitman make use of musical form?

The Reading/Writing Connection

1. Choose one line from the poem, and in a journal entry respond to the line.
2. Freewrite about one of the following symbols: star, bird, or sea.
3. Study the he-bird's song. Create a free verse monologue spoken by a bird or other creature. In a concrete manner, convey an abstract idea, such as loss, betrayal, death, or love.

Ideas for Writing

1. Analyze the persona. (See lines 1–21 and 130–182.)
2. What do the repeated symbols of the star, bird, and sea suggest?

BIRCHES

Robert Frost

Robert Frost (1874–1963) was born in California but moved to New England after his father died when Frost was eleven. He attended Dartmouth College and Harvard University. Frost attempted, among other things, to run his own farm before moving his family to England, where he published his first book of poems, A Boy's Will *(1913), which drew favorable reviews from Ezra Pound. Pound assisted the publication of Frost's second book,* North of Boston *(1914), the success of which encouraged Frost to return to New England. For almost the next half-century, Frost enjoyed tremendous popular success. He also taught and lectured at colleges including Amherst, Dartmouth, and Harvard. His subsequent volumes include* New Hampshire *(1923) and* The Poetry of Robert Frost *(1969). Of poetry, Frost said that it should begin "in delight" and end "in wisdom."*

1916

When I see birches bend to left and right
Across the lines of straighter darker trees,
I like to think some boy's been swinging them.
But swinging doesn't bend them down to stay.
Ice-storms do that. Often you must have seen them
Loaded with ice a sunny winter morning
After a rain. They click upon themselves
As the breeze rises, and turn many-colored

As the stir cracks and crazes their enamel.
Soon the sun's warmth makes them shed crystal shells
Shattering and avalanching on the snow-crust—
Such heaps of broken glass to sweep away
You'd think the inner dome of heaven had fallen.
They are dragged to the withered bracken[1] by the load,
And they seem not to break; though once they are bowed
So low for long, they never right themselves:
You may see their trunks arching in the woods
Years afterwards, trailing their leaves on the ground
Like girls on hands and knees that throw their hair
Before them over their heads to dry in the sun.
But I was going to say when Truth broke in
With all her matter-of-fact about the ice-storm
I should prefer to have some boy bend them
As he went out and in to fetch the cows—
Some boy too far from town to learn baseball,
Whose only play was that he found himself,
Summer or winter, and could play alone.
One by one he subdued his father's trees
By riding them down over and over again
Until he took the stiffness out of them,
And not one but hung limp, not one was left
For him to conquer. He learned all there was
To learn about not launching out too soon
And so not carrying the tree away
Clear to the ground. He always kept his poise
To the top branches, climbing carefully
With the same pains you use to fill a cup
Up to the brim, and even above the brim.
Then he flung outward, feet first, with a swish,
Kicking his way down through the air to the ground.
So was I once myself a swinger of birches.
And so I dream of going back to be.
It's when I'm weary of considerations,
And life is too much like a pathless wood
Where your face burns and tickles with the cobwebs
Broken across it, and one eye is weeping
From a twig's having lashed across it open.
I'd like to get away from earth awhile
And then come back to it and begin over.
May no fate willfully misunderstand me
And half grant what I wish and snatch me away

[1] A large fern; a cluster or thicket of ferns.

Not to return. Earth's the right place for love:
I don't know where it's likely to go better.
I'd like to go by climbing a birch tree,
And climb black branches up a snow-white trunk
Toward heaven, till the tree could bear no more,
But dipped its top and set me down again.
That would be good both going and coming back.
One could do worse than be a swinger of birches.

Explorations of the Text

1. Describe the persona's stance and point of view at the beginning of the poem.
2. Explore the symbolism of the central action of the poem: the "bend[ing]" of the branches caused by "ice-storms" and created by a boy's "riding them down over and over again."
3. Discuss the speaker's realization at the end of the poem (lines 40–58). Why "could [he] do worse than be a swinger of birches"?
4. Compare the poem's view of innocence and experience with that of "Wind Secrets" or of "The Monkey Garden."

The Reading/Writing Connection

1. Journal Entry: Compare events or phases in your own life with the symbolic states of life presented in the poem.
2. Write a double-entry notebook for this poem. What do you learn from this writing exercise? Write your conclusions in a short essay.

Ideas for Writing

1. Create a dialogue among the speakers in several of the anthologized poems in this section on the subject of initiation and realization.
2. Explicate this poem, and focus on point of view, imagery, symbolism, and them.

Black Hair

Gary Soto

Gary Soto (1952–), born in Fresno, California, won the American Book Award for his volume of autobiographical essays, Living Up the Street *(1984). His volumes of poetry include* The Element of San Joaquin *(1977),* The Tale of Sunlight *(1978), and* Black Hair *(1985). He has edited* Pieces of the Heart: New Chicano Fiction *(1993). Soto teaches Chicano Studies and English at the University of California at*

Berkeley. Among other honors, he has received a Guggenheim Fellowship and the Academy of American Poets Award.

1985

At eight I was brilliant with my body.
In July, that ring of heat
We all jumped through, I sat in the bleachers
Of Romain Playground, in the lengthening
Shade that rose from our dirty feet.
The game before us was more than baseball.
It was a figure—Hector Moreno
Quick and hard with turned muscles,
His crouch the one I assumed before an altar
Of worn baseball cards, in my room.

I came here because I was Mexican, a stick
Of brown light in love with those
Who could do it—the triple and hard slide,
The gloves eating balls into double plays.
What could I do with 50 pounds, my shyness,
My black torch of hair, about to go out?
Father was dead, his face no longer
Hanging over the table or our sleep,
And mother was the terror of mouths
Twisting hurt by butter knives.

In the bleachers I was brilliant with my body,
Waving players in and stomping my feet,
I chewed sunflower seeds. I drank water
And bit my arm through the late innings.
When Hector lined balls into deep
Center, in my mind I rounded the bases
With him, my face flared, my hair lifting
Beautifully, because we were coming home
To the arms of brown people.

Explorations of the Text

1. What is the speaker's view of Hector Moreno? What does Hector Moreno represent?
2. How are the speaker's attitudes toward being Mexican and toward baseball intertwined?
3. What is the nature of the narrator's relationship with his father and his mother?
4. What is the significance of the image of "black hair"?

5. Contrast the speaker's position in this poem with the experience of the teenagers in "Indian Boarding School: The Runaways."

The Reading/Writing Connection

1. Why are sports important to teenagers? Respond to this question in a journal entry.
2. "Think" Topic: What ways have ethnic groups found to break cultural barriers in the United States? How has North American culture changed as a result?

Ideas for Writing

1. Write about the possible meanings and connotations of the word *brilliant* in "Black Hair."
2. Hector Moreno is the speaker's hero. Write about a hero in your own life.

Oranges

Gary Soto

1985

The first time I walked
With a girl, I was twelve,
Cold, and weighted down
With two oranges in my jacket.
December. Frost cracking
Beneath my steps, my breath
Before me, then gone,
As I walked toward
Her house, the one whose
Porch light burned yellow
Night and day, in any weather.
A dog barked at me, until
She came out pulling
At her gloves, face bright
With rouge. I smiled,
Touched her shoulder, and led
Her down the street, across
A used car lot and a line
Of newly planted trees,
Until we were breathing
Before a drugstore. We
Entered, the tiny bell

Bringing a saleslady
Down a narrow aisle of goods.
I turned to the candies
Tiered like bleachers,
And asked what she wanted—
Light in her eyes, a smile
Starting at the corners
Of her mouth. I fingered
A nickel in my pocket,
And when she lifted a chocolate
That cost a dime,
I didn't say anything.
I took the nickel from
My pocket, then an orange,
And set them quietly on
The counter. When I looked up,
The lady's eyes met mine,
And held them, knowing
Very well what it was all
About.

Outside,
A few cars hissing past,
Fog hanging like old
Coats between the trees.
I took my girl's hand
In mine for two blocks,
Then released it to let
Her unwrap the chocolate.
I peeled my orange
That was so bright against
The gray of December
That, from some distance,
Someone might have thought
I was making a fire in my hands.

Explorations of the Text

1. Discuss the significance of the purchase at the drugstore.
2. Explore the symbolism of peeling the paper from the chocolate, peeling the orange, and the last line. What do these images suggest?
3. Examine the images associated with weather. How does the time of year enhance the mood of the poem?

The Reading/Writing Connection

1. In a journal entry, write about your first date.
2. Write a monologue in the voice of the young girl.
3. "Think" Topic: How does the outside world, the environment, influence the speaker's experience? Are there clues in the poem?

Ideas for Writing

1. What do the last two lines of the poem mean? Do they present a satisfying conclusion?
2. Compare the state of mind of the speaker with that of Audre Lorde's adolescent girl in "Hanging Fire."

ADOLESCENCE—I
ADOLESCENCE—II
ADOLESCENCE—III

Rita Dove

Rita Dove (1952–) was born in Akron, Ohio. She began teaching at Arizona State University and is currently a professor at the University of Virginia. In 1987, she was awarded the Pulitzer Prize for poetry for Thomas and Beulah, *poems based loosely on the lives of Dove's maternal grandparents. In 1993, her* Selected Poems *was published, and she was appointed Poet Laureate of the United States, not only the first African American, but also the youngest person ever to receive this honor.*

1980

Adolescence—I

In water-heavy nights behind grandmother's porch
We knelt in the tickling grasses and whispered:
Linda's face hung before us, pale as a pecan,
And it grew wise as she said:
    "A boy's lips are soft,
    As soft as baby's skin."
The air closed over her words.
A firefly whirred near my ear, and in the distance
I could hear streetlamps ping
Into miniature suns
Against a feathery sky.

Adolescence—II

Although it is night, I sit in the bathroom, waiting.
Sweat prickles behind my knees, the baby-breasts are alert.
Venetian blinds slice up the moon; the tiles quiver in pale strips.

Then they come, the three seal men with eyes as round
As dinner plates and eyelashes like sharpened tines.
They bring the scent of licorice. One sits in the washbowl,
One on the bathtub edge; one leans against the door.
"Can you feel it yet?" they whisper.
I don't know what to say, again. They chuckle,

Patting their sleek bodies with their hands.
"Well, maybe next time." And they rise,
Glittering like pools of ink under moonlight,

And vanish. I clutch at the ragged holes
They leave behind, here at the edge of darkness.
Night rests like a ball of fur on my tongue.

Adolescence—III

With Dad gone, Mom and I worked
The dusky rows of tomatoes.
As they glowed orange in sunlight
And rotted in shadow, I too
Grew orange and softer, swelling out
Starched cotton slips.

The texture of twilight made me think of
Lengths of Dotted Swiss.[1] In my room
I wrapped scarred knees in dresses
That once went to big-band dances;
I baptized my earlobes with rosewater.
Along the window-sill, the lipstick stubs
Glittered in their steel shells.

Looking out at the rows of clay
And chicken manure, I dreamed how it would happen:
He would meet me by the blue spruce,
A carnation over his heart, saying,
"I have come for you, Madam;
I have loved you in my dreams."

---

[1] A muslin material with raised dots.

At his touch, the scabs would fall away.
Over his shoulder, I see my father coming toward us:
He carries his tears in a bowl,
And blood hangs in the pine-soaked air.

Explorations of the Text

I.

1. What is the focus of the girls' gatherings?
2. What are the mood and tone of the poem? What images create the mood and tone?
3. What is the meaning of the images of "suns," "firefly," and "feathers"?

II.

1. Who are the "seal men"? Explore their symbolic significance.
2. For what does she wait?
3. How does the mood change in this section?
4. Explain the line, "Night rests like a ball of fur on my tongue."

III.

1. What are the roles of the mother and the father?
2. Explore the symbolism of "tomatoes," "sunlight," and "twilight."
3. What is the meaning of the closing lines concerning the father: "He carries his tears in a bowl" and "blood hangs in the pine-soaked air"? What are the consequences of sexual awakening?

The Reading/Writing Connection

1. "Think" Topic: How do the views of female sexuality change in these three poems?

Ideas for Writing

1. Characterize the stages of adolescence in the three poems.
2. Compare Dove's view of coming of age as a female with Soto's view of coming in age in "Oranges" and in "Black Hair."

Hanging Fire

Audre Lorde

Audre Lorde (1934–92) was born in New York City of West Indian parents. She attended National University of Mexico, Hunter College, and Columbia University, where she received her M.L.S. She subsequently worked as a librarian and taught school, and she spent a year at Tougaloo College, Mississippi, as poet-in-residence. Lorde taught writing and English at several colleges before becoming professor of English at Hunter College in 1980. Her volumes of poetry include Cables to Rage *(1970),* Coal *(1976), and* The Black Unicorn *(1978). She also wrote an account of her courageous struggle with breast cancer and mastectomy,* The Cancer Journals *(1980), and a prose autobiography,* Zami: A New Spelling of My Name *(1982).*

1978

I am fourteen
and my skin has betrayed me
the boy I cannot live without
still sucks his thumb
in secret
how come my knees are
always so ashy
what if I die
before morning
and momma's in the bedroom
with the door closed.

I have to learn how to dance
in time for the next party
my room is too small for me
suppose I die before graduation
they will sing sad melodies
but finally
tell the truth about me
There is nothing I want to do
and too much
that has to be done
and momma's in the bedroom
with the door closed.

Nobody even stops to think
about my side of it
I should have been on Math Team
my marks were better than his

why do I have to be
the one
wearing braces
I have nothing to wear tomorrow
will I live long enough
to grow up
and momma's in the bedroom
with the door closed.

Explorations of the Text

1. Characterize the voice and the tone of the speaker.
2. Discuss the speaker's conflict. What is her view of her body?
3. What is "momma's" role in her life?
4. Discuss the impact of the repetition in the poem.
5. What does the poem reveal about being "fourteen"? Explore the meaning of the title.

The Reading/Writing Connection

1. Freewrite about being an adolescent.
2. "Think" Topic: Does the poem present a realistic portrait of early adolescence?

Ideas for Writing

1. Compare the vision of adolescence in this work with those in "Oranges," "Black Hair," and "Adolescence I, II, III."
2. How can parents help adolescents negotiate this difficult stage of life? Write a letter to the mother in this poem.

Ego Tripping

Nikki Giovanni

Nikki Giovanni (1943–), born and educated in Tennessee, has taught creative writing at Rutgers University and other colleges. Currently, she teaches at Virginia Polytechnic University. A prolific poet, her volumes of poetry include Ego Tripping and Other Poems *(1973),* Cotton Candy on a Rainy Day *(1978),* Spin a Soft Black Song *(1985),* Sacred Cows and Other Edibles *(1988), and* Blues: For All the Changes: New Poems *(1999).*

1973

(there may be a reason why)

I was born in the congo
I walked to the fertile crescent and built
the sphinx[1]
I designed a pyramid so tough that a star
that only glows every one hundred years falls
into the center giving divine perfect light
I am bad

I sat on the throne
drinking nectar with allah[2]
I got hot and sent an ice age to europe
to cool my thirst
My oldest daughter is nefertiti[3]
the tears from my birth pains
created the nile[4]
I am a beautiful woman

I gazed on the forest and burned
out the sahara desert
with a packet of goat's meat
and a change of clothes
I crossed it in two hours
I am a gazelle so swift
so swift you can't catch me

For a birthday present when he was three
I gave my son hannibal[5] an elephant
He gave me rome for mother's day
My strength flows ever on

[1] A mythical creature with the head of a human or animal, the body of a lion, and the wings of an eagle. One of the famous monuments in ancient Egypt, near the pyramids. In Greek mythology, the Sphinx proposed a riddle to Oedipus; and when he answered it, she killed herself.

[2] In Islam, the name of God; Supreme Being.

[3] An Egyptian queen (fourteenth century B.C.), known for her beauty.

[4] Longest river in Africa, flowing north from Lake Victoria to the Mediterranean.

[5] A Carthaginian general who crossed the Mediterranean and the Alps and attacked Italy. Carthage—a country in North Africa.

My son noah built new/ark and
I stood proudly at the helm
as we sailed on a soft summer day
I turned myself into myself and was
jesus
men intone my loving name

All praises All praises
I am the one who would save

I sowed diamonds in my back yard
My bowels deliver uranium
the filings from my fingernails are
semi-precious jewels
On a trip north
I caught a cold and blew
My nose giving oil to the arab world
I am so hip even my errors are correct
I sailed west to reach east and had to round off
the earth as I went
The hair from my head thinned and gold was laid
across three continents

I am so perfect so divine so ethereal so surreal
I cannot be comprehended
except by my permission

I mean . . . I . . . can fly
like a bird in the sky . . .

Explorations of the Text

1. What is the speaker's view of herself? What character traits does she attribute to herself?
2. How is the title a clue to the meaning of the poem? In what ways does the poem extend its themes beyond the ego?
3. How does the poet use such devices from oral tradition as exaggeration and **anaphora** (repetition) to create an impact?
4. How does humor contribute to the poem's effect?
5. Identify the historical and anthropological references in the poem. How do these allusions enrich this work?
6. Contrast the speaker's sense of self with the persona's identity in "Suicide Note," "Oranges," or "My Name."

The Reading/Writing Connection

1. Do a double-entry for a section of the poem as preparation for one of the assigned ideas for writing.
2. "Think" Topic: What are the advantages and disadvantages of **hyperbole** (exaggeration)? Use details from this poem to support your position.

Ideas for Writing

1. Analyze the voice and tone of the speaker of this poem.
2. How does the tone contribute to the meaning of the poem?
3. Write a short essay that explicates one of the allusions in the poem.

My Name and The Monkey Garden from *The House on Mango Street*

Sandra Cisneros

Sandra Cisneros (1954–) was born in Chicago to a Mexican American mother and a Mexican father. She has worked as an arts administrator and college recruiter and has taught both high school dropouts and university students. Her publications include The House on Mango Street *(1984),* Woman Hollering Creek and Other Stories *(1991), and* Loose Woman *(1994). In spare, poetic language that resembles prose poetry, Cisneros explores issues of the Chicana/o community.*

My Name

1984

In English my name means hope. In Spanish it means too many letters. It means sadness, it means waiting. It is like the number nine. A muddy color. It is the Mexican records my father plays on Sunday mornings when he is shaving, songs like sobbing.

It was my great-grandmother's name and now it is mine. She was a horse woman too, born like me in the Chinese year of the horse—which is supposed to be bad luck if you're born female—but I think this is a Chinese lie because the Chinese, like the Mexicans, don't like their women strong.

My great-grandmother. I would've liked to have known her, a wild horse of a woman, so wild she wouldn't marry. Until my great-grandfather threw a sack over her head and carried her off. Just like that, as if she were a fancy chandelier. That's the way he did it.

And the story goes she never forgave him. She looked out the window her whole life, the way so many women sit their sadness on an elbow. I wonder if she made the best with what she got or was she sorry because she couldn't be all the things she wanted to be. Esperanza. I have inherited her name, but I don't want to inherit her place by the window.

At school they say my name funny as if the syllables were made out of tin and hurt the roof of your mouth. But in Spanish my name is made out of a softer something, like silver, not quite as thick as sister's name—Magdalena—which is uglier than mine. Magdalena who at least can come home and become Nenny. But I am always Esperanza.

I would like to baptize myself under a new name, a name more like the real me, the one nobody sees. Esperanza as Lisandra or Maritza or Zeze the X. Yes. Something like Zeze the X will do.

Explorations of the Text

1. How does the narrator view her name?
2. Discuss the character of the great-grandmother.
3. Why does the narrator want to rename herself?

The Reading/Writing Connection

1. In a paragraph explore the significance of your name as Cisneros does. Do you think your name fits your personality? Or choose a new name for yourself. Why did you choose the name?

Ideas for Writing

1. What does the story of the great-grandmother symbolize to Esperanza?
2. What does the imagery of language and names signify in this work?

The Monkey Garden

1984

The monkey doesn't live there anymore. The monkey moved—to Kentucky—and took his people with him. And I was glad because I couldn't listen anymore to his wild screaming at night, the twangy yakkety-yak of the people who owned him. The green metal cage, the porcelain table top, the family that spoke like guitars. Monkey, family, table. All gone.

And it was then we took over the garden we had been afraid to go into when the monkey screamed and showed its yellow teeth.

There were sunflowers big as flowers on Mars and thick cockscombs bleeding the deep red fringe of theater curtains. There were dizzy bees and bow-tied fruit flies turning somersaults and humming in the air. Sweet sweet peach trees. Thorn roses and thistle and pears. Weeds like so many squinty-eyed stars and brush that made your ankles itch and itch until you washed with soap and water. There were big green apples hard as knees. And everywhere the sleepy smell of rotting wood, damp earth and dusty hollyhocks thick and perfumy like the blue-blond hair of the dead.

Yellow spiders ran when we turned rocks over and pale worms blind and afraid of light rolled over in their sleep. Poke a stick in the sandy soil and a few blue-skinned beetles would appear, an avenue of ants, so many crusty lady bugs. This was a garden, a wonderful thing to look at in the spring. But bit by bit, after the monkey left, the garden began to take over itself. Flowers stopped obeying the little bricks that kept them from growing beyond their paths. Weeds mixed in. Dead cars appeared overnight like mushrooms. First one and then another and then a pale blue pickup with the front windshield missing. Before you knew it, the monkey garden became filled with sleepy cars.

Things had a way of disappearing in the garden, as if the garden itself ate them, or, as if with its old-man memory, it put them away and forgot them. Nenny found a dollar and a dead mouse between two rocks in the stone wall where the morning glories climbed, and once when we were playing hide and seek, Eddie Vargas laid his head beneath a hibiscus tree and fell asleep there like a Rip Van Winkle until somebody remembered he was in the game and went back to look for him.

This, I suppose, was the reason why we went there. Far away from where our mothers could find us. We and a few old dogs who lived inside the empty cars. We made a club-house once on the back of that old blue pickup. And besides, we liked to jump from the roof of one car to another and pretend they were giant mushrooms.

Somebody started the lie that the monkey garden had been there before anything. We liked to think the garden could hide things for a thousand years. There beneath the roots of soggy flowers were the bones of murdered pirates and dinosaurs, the eye of a unicorn turned to coal.

This is where I wanted to die and where I tried one day but not even the monkey garden would have me. It was the last day I would go there.

Who was it that said I was getting too old to play the games? Who was it I didn't listen to? I only remember that when the others ran, I wanted to run too, up and down and through the monkey garden, fast as the boys, not like Sally who screamed if she got her stockings muddy.

I said, Sally, come on, but she wouldn't. She stayed by the curb talking to Tito and his friends. Play with the kids if you want, she said, I'm staying here. She could be stuck-up like that if she wanted to, so I just left.

It was her own fault too. When I got back Sally was pretending to be mad . . . something about the boys having stolen her keys. Please give them back to me, she said punching the nearest one with a soft fist. They were laughing. She was too. It was a joke I didn't get.

I wanted to go back with the other kids who were still jumping on cars, still chasing each other through the garden, but Sally had her own game.

One of the boys invented the rules. One of Tito's friends said you can't get the keys back unless you kiss us and Sally pretended to be mad at first but she said yes. It was that simple.

I don't know why, but something inside me wanted to throw a stick. Something wanted to say no when I watched Sally going into the garden with Tito's buddies all grinning. It was just a kiss, that's all. A kiss for each one. So what, she said.

Only how come I felt angry inside. Like something wasn't right. Sally went behind that old blue pickup to kiss the boys and get her keys back, and I ran up three flights of stairs to where Tito lived. His mother was ironing shirts. She was sprinkling water on them from an empty pop bottle and smoking a cigarette.

Your son and his friends stole Sally's keys and now they won't give them back unless she kisses them and right now they're making her kiss them, I said all out of breath from the three flights of stairs.

Those kids, she said, not looking up from her ironing.

That's all?

What do you want me to do, she said, call the cops? And kept on ironing.

I looked at her a long time, but couldn't think of anything to say, and ran back down the three flights to the garden where Sally needed to be saved. I took three big sticks and a brick and figured this was enough.

But when I got there Sally said go home. Those boys said, leave us alone. I felt stupid with my brick. They all looked at me as if *I* was the one that was crazy and made me feel ashamed.

And then I don't know why but I had to run away. I had to hide myself at the other end of the garden, in the jungle part, under a tree that wouldn't mind if I lay down and cried a long time. I closed my eyes like tight stars so that I wouldn't, but I did. My face felt hot. Everything inside hiccupped.

I read somewhere in India there are priests who can will their heart to stop beating. I wanted to will my blood to stop, my heart to quit its pumping. I wanted to be dead, to turn into the rain, my eyes melt into the ground like two black snails. I wished and wished. I closed my eyes and willed it, but when I got up my dress was green and I had a headache.

I looked at my feet in their white socks and ugly round shoes. They seemed far away. They didn't seem to be my feet anymore. And the garden that had been such a good place to play didn't seem mine either.

Explorations of the Text

1. Discuss the symbolism of the monkey and the garden. Examine the details and images of the garden.
2. Interpret the following: "Things had a way of disappearing in the garden, as if the garden itself ate them." Discuss the irony of this statement in the light of Esperanza's realization at the end of the chapter.
3. Why does Esperanza "[want] to be dead"? What does she learn about "the monkey garden"? What happens to her there?
4. Contrast the world of the teenagers and that of the adults.

5. Compare Esperanza's awakening to sexuality with that of the persona in "Adolescence I, II, III."

The Reading/Writing Connection

1. As preparation for class discussion, list questions you have about this reading. After class discussion, write a short paragraph focusing on one of your initial questions and then your response after the class explored the work.
2. Gloss and annotate the text, noting color images or images of disappearance and loss.
3. Write an end comment discussing the significance of these images.

Ideas for Writing

1. Using your gloss as prewriting material, create a short essay on Cisneros's use of color or on themes of loss in "The Monkey Garden."
2. Contrast Esperanza's persona in "My Name" with that of "The Monkey Garden."

Lost Sister

Cathy Song

Cathy Song (1955–) won the Yale Younger Poets Award for her first book, Picture Bride *(1983), in which she wrote about her Korean grandmother, who was purchased as a mail-order bride on the basis of her photograph. In her second volume of poetry,* Frameless Windows, Squares of Light *(1988), Song expanded her analysis of family, of heritage, and of the past.*

1983

1

In China,
even the peasants
named their first daughters
Jade—
the stone that in the far fields
could moisten the dry season,
could make men move mountains
for the healing green of the inner hills
glistening like slices of winter melon.

And the daughters were grateful:
They never left home.
To move freely was a luxury
stolen from them at birth.
Instead, they gathered patience,
learning to walk in shoes
the size of teacups,
without breaking—
the arc of their movements
as dormant as the rooted willow,
as redundant as the farmyard hens.
But they traveled far
in surviving,
learning to stretch the family rice,
to quiet the demons,
the noisy stomachs.

2

There is a sister
across the ocean,
who relinquished her name,
diluting jade green
with the blue of the Pacific.
Rising with a tide of locusts,
she swarmed with others
to inundate another shore.
In America,
there are many roads
and women can stride along with men.

But in another wilderness,
the possibilities,
the loneliness,
can strangulate like jungle vines.
The meager provisions and sentiments
of once belonging—
fermented roots, Mah-Jong[1] tiles and firecrackers—set but
a flimsy household
in a forest of nightless cities.
A giant snake rattles above,
spewing black clouds into your kitchen.

[1] Chinese game, similar to dominoes.

Dough-faced landlords
slip in and out of your keyholes,
making claims you don't understand,
tapping into your communication systems
of laundry lines and restaurant chains.

You find you need China:
your one fragile identification,
a jade link
handcuffed to your wrist.
You remember your mother
who walked for centuries,
footless—
and like her,
you have left no footprints,
but only because
there is an ocean in between,
the unremitting space of your rebellion.

Explorations of the Text

1. What view emerges in Part 1 of women's roles in China?
2. Why does the speaker state that "even the peasants/named their first daughters/Jade"?
3. What is the conflict for first-generation Chinese American women presented in the poem?
4. How are the "daughter" and "mother" similar in the end?

The Reading/Writing Connection

1. "Think" Topic: In Part 2, the poet depicts the "lost sister" in America. What are the consequences of rebellion?

Ideas for Writing

1. Why do the Chinese women who have immigrated to the United States still need China?
2. Discuss the symbolism of jade.

INDIAN BOARDING SCHOOL: THE RUNAWAYS

Louise Erdrich

Louise Erdrich (1954–) was born in Minnesota to a French Chippewa mother and a German father. She was educated at Dartmouth College and Johns Hopkins University. Her first volume of poems, Jacklight *(1984), and her first novel,* Love Medicine *(1984), both won major awards and established her as an important literary presence. Her work has explored Native American life in twentieth-century America, with her novels forming parts of a larger whole. Erdrich's novels include* The Beet Queen *(1986),* Tracks *(1988),* The Bingo Palace *(1994),* Tales of Burning Love *(1996), and* The Antelope Wife *(1998).*

1984

Home's the place we head for in our sleep.
Boxcars stumbling north in dreams
don't wait for us. We catch them on the run.
The rails, old lacerations that we love,
shoot parallel across the face and break
just under Turtle Mountains.[1] Riding scars
you can't get lost. Home is the place they cross.

The lame guard strikes a match and makes the dark
less tolerant. We watch through cracks in boards
as the land starts rolling, rolling till it hurts
to be here, cold in regulation clothes.
We know the sheriff's waiting at midrun
to take us back. His car is dumb and warm.
The highway doesn't rock, it only hums
like a wing of long insults. The worn-down welts
of ancient punishments lead back and forth.
All runaways wear dresses, long green ones,
the color you would think shame was. We scrub
the sidewalks down because it's shameful work.
Our brushes cut the stone in watered arcs
and in the soak frail outlines shiver clear
a moment, things us kids pressed on the dark
face before it hardened, place, remembering
delicate old injuries, the spines of names and leaves.

[1] The location of a Chippewa Indian reservation in North Dakota.

Explorations of the Text

1. Who are the runaways?
2. What has the school done to or for the children? What is the root of their fear?
3. What does home mean to them? Discuss locations and landscape in the poem.
4. In what sense is the poem realistic? fantastic? In what sense does it recreate a recurring experience?
5. Who is the enemy? Is it the school? the sheriff? the guard?
6. How are "insults" to the land and the punishments of the children connected? Why are the welts "worn-down"?
7. Follow the order of the narrative in each stanza. How is the poem organized?

The Reading/Writing Connection

1. Choose the most powerful lines in this poem. What makes them strong? Freewrite about them.
2. "Think" Topic: Does running away help or hinder rites of passage into the adult world?

Ideas for Writing

1. Explore the imagery concerning punishment and pain in this poem.
2. Compare the portrayal of running away in this poem and in "Barn Burning."

SUICIDE NOTE

Janice Mirikitani

Janice Mirikitani (1942–) spent her early childhood interned in a concentration camp for Japanese Americans in Rohwer, Arkansas, during World War II. Although her first volume of poems, Awake in the River, *was not published until 1978, Mirikitani's influence has been profound, especially among younger Asian American poets. Her subsequent volumes of poetry include* Shedding Silence *(1987) and* We the Dangerous *(1995). Mirikitani has edited and co-edited numerous anthologies. She is president of the Glide Foundation of San Francisco.*

1987

. . An Asian American college student was reported to have jumped to her death from her dormitory window. Her body was found two days later under a

deep cover of snow. Her suicide note contained an apology to her parents for having received less than a perfect four point grade average . . .

How many notes written . . .
ink smeared like birdprints in snow.

not good enough   not pretty enough   not smart enough
dear mother and father.
I apologize
for disappointing you.
I've worked very hard,
not good enough
harder, perhaps to please you.
If only I were a son, shoulders broad
as the sunset threading through pine,
I would see the light in my mother's
eyes, or the golden pride reflected
in my father's dream
of my wide, male hands worthy of work
and comfort.
I would swagger through life
muscled and bold and assured,
drawing praises to me
like currents in the bed of wind, virile
with confidence.
not good enough   not strong enough   not good enough

I apologize.
Tasks do not come easily.
Each failure, a glacier.
Each disapproval, a bootprint.
Each disappointment,
ice above my river.
So I have worked hard.
not good enough
My sacrifice I will drop
bone by bone, perched
on the ledge of my womanhood,
fragile as wings.
not strong enough
It is snowing steadily
surely not good weather
for flying—this sparrow
sillied and dizzied by the wind
on the edge.
not smart enough

I make this ledge my altar
to offer penance.
This air will not hold me,
The snow burdens my crippled wings,
my tears drop like bitter cloth
softly into the gutter below.
  not good enough   not strong enough   not smart enough
        Choices thin as shaved
        ice. Notes shredded
        drift like snow
on my broken body,
covers me like whispers
of sorries
sorries.
Perhaps when they find me
they will bury
my bird bones beneath
a sturdy pine
and scatter my feathers like
unspoken song
over this white and cold and silent
breast of earth.

Explorations of the Text

1. Discuss the point of view of the speaker. Why does she "apologize"?
2. Analyze the speaker's relationship with her parents.
3. What drives the speaker to suicide? Why does she depict herself as a "sparrow" "on the edge"?
4. How do the images of sun, wind, and snow develop the themes of the poem?
5. Examine the form of the poem. How does the stanzaic form enhance meaning?
6. Discuss the impact of the variations of the repeated line: "not good enough   not strong enough   not smart enough"? Why does she use all lowercase letters for this lament?

The Reading/Writing Connection

1. "Think" Topic: Are the parents' behavior and expectations the cause of their daughter's suicide? Argue pro or con in a mini-essay.
2. Journal Entry: Is the poem's characterization of the young woman believable? What pressures do today's college students face?

Ideas for Writing

1. Does gender figure in the persona's sense of self-worth? Would the poem differ if a man were the central protagonist? In what ways?
2. Compare the portrayal of the young woman in this poem with the women in "Lost Sister."

Poems for Further Reading

When I consider how my light is spent

John Milton (1608–74)

1655

When I consider how my light is spent
Ere half my days, in this dark world and wide,
And that one talent which is death to hide[1]
Lodged with me useless, though my soul more bent
To serve therewith my Maker, and present
My true account, lest he returning chide;
"Doth God exact day-labor, light denied?"
I fondly[2] ask; but Patience to prevent[3]
That murmur, soon replies, "God doth not need
Either man's work or his own gifts; who best
Bear his mild yoke, they serve him best. His state
Is kingly. Thousands at his bidding speed
And post o'er land and ocean without rest:
They also serve who only stand and wait."

There Was a Child Went Forth

Walt Whitman (1819–92)

1855

There was a child went forth every day,
And the first object he look'd upon, that object he became,
And that object became part of him for the day or a certain part of the day,
Or for many years or stretching cycles of years.

[1] Reference to Christ's "Parable of the Talents" (Matthew 25:14ff) in which a servant is chastised for not using his talent (a monetary unit): an intended pun. Note also play on words in "use," meaning using or interest.

[2] Foolishly.

[3] To forestall.

The early lilacs became part of this child,
And grass and white and red morning-glories, and white and red clover, and the song of the phoebe-bird,
And the Third-month lambs and the sow's pink-faint litter, and the mare's foal and the cow's calf,
And the noisy brood of the barnyard or by the mire of the pond-side,
And the fish suspending themselves so curiously below there, and the beautiful curious liquid,
And the water-plants with their graceful flat heads, all became part of him.
The field-sprouts of Fourth-month and Fifth-month became part of him,
Winter-grain sprouts and those of the light-yellow corn, and the esculent roots of the garden,
And the apple-trees cover'd with blossoms and the fruit afterward, and wood-berries, and the commonest weeds by the road,
And the old drunkard staggering home from the outhouse of the tavern whence he had lately risen,
And the schoolmistress that pass'd on her way to the school,
And the friendly boys that pass'd, and the quarrelsome boys,
And the tidy and fresh-cheek'd girls, and the barefoot negro boy and girl,
And all the changes of city and country wherever he went.

His own parents, he that had father'd him and she that had conceiv'd him in her womb and birth'd him,
They gave this child more of themselves than that,
They gave him afterward every day, they became part of him.

The mother at home quietly placing the dishes on the supper-table,
The mother with mild words, clean her cap and gown, a wholesome odor falling off her person and clothes as she walks by,
The father, strong, self-sufficient, manly, mean, anger'd, unjust,
The blow, the quick loud word, the tight bargain, the crafty lure,
The family usages, the language, the company, the furniture, the yearning and swelling heart,
Affection that will not be gainsay'd, the sense of what is real, the thought if after all it should prove unreal,
The doubts of day-time and the doubts of night-time, the curious whether and how,
Whether that which appears so is so, or is it all flashes and specks?
Men and women crowding fast in the streets, if they are not flashes and specks what are they?
The streets themselves and the façades of houses, and goods in the windows,
Vehicles, teams, the heavy-plank'd wharves, the huge crossing at the ferries,
The village on the highland seen from afar at sunset, the river between,
Shadows, aureola and mist, the light falling on roofs and gables of white or brown two miles off,
The schooner near by sleepily dropping down the tide, the little boat slack-tow'd astern,

The hurrying tumbling waves, quick-broken crests, slapping,
The strata of color'd clouds, the long bar of maroon-tint away solitary by itself, the spread of purity it lies motionless in,
The horizon's edge, the flying sea-crow, the fragrance of salt marsh and shore mud,
These became part of that child who went forth every day, and who now goes, and will always go forth every day.

My Life Had Stood—

Emily Dickinson (1830–86)

c. 1863

My Life had stood—a Loaded Gun—
In Corners—till a Day
The Owner passed—identified—
And carried Me away—

And now We roam in Sovereign Woods—
And now We hunt the Doe—
And every time I speak for Him—
The Mountains straight reply—

And do I smile, such cordial light
Upon the Valley glow—
It is as a Vesuvian[1] face
Had let its pleasure through—

And when at Night—Our good Day done—
I guard My Master's Head—
'Tis better than the Eider-Duck's
Deep Pillow[2]—to have shared—

To foe of His—I'm deadly foe—
None stir the second time—
On whom I lay a Yellow Eye—
Or an emphatic Thumb—

Though I than He—may longer live
He longer must—than I—
For I have but the power to kill,
Without—the power to die—

[1] Resembling Mount Vesuvius, a volcano in Italy.
[2] Eider down; referring to soft feathers from the female Eider-Duck.

Fern Hill

Dylan Thomas (1914–53)

1946

Now as I was young and easy under the apple boughs
About the lilting house and happy as the grass was green,
The night above the dingle[1] starry,
Time let me hail and climb
Golden in the heydays of his eyes,
And honoured among wagons I was prince of the apple towns
And once below a time I lordly had the trees and leaves
Trail with daisies and barley
Down the rivers of the windfall light.

And as I was green and carefree, famous among the barns
About the happy yard and singing as the farm was home,
In the sun that is young once only,
Time let me play and be
Golden in the mercy of his means,
And green and golden I was huntsman and herdsman, the calves
Sang to my horn, the foxes on the hills barked clear and cold,
And the sabbath rang slowly
In the pebbles of the holy streams.

All the sun long it was running, it was lovely, the hay
Fields high as the house, the tunes from the chimneys, it was air
And playing, lovely and watery
And fire green as grass.
And nightly under the simple stars
As I rode to sleep the owls were bearing the farm away,
All the moon long I heard, blessed among stables, the night-jars[2]
Flying with the ricks,[3] and the horses
Flashing into the dark.

And then to awake, and the farm, like a wanderer white
With the dew, come back, the cock on his shoulder: it was all
Shining, it was Adam and maiden,
The sky gathered again
And the sun grew round that very day.
So it must have been after the birth of the simple light
In the first, spinning place, the spellbound horses walking warm

[1] A narrow valley or shady dell.
[2] Any old world goat-sucker (a nocturnal European bird).
[3] A pile of straw or hay.

Out of the whinnying green stable
On to the fields of praise.

And honoured among foxes and pheasants by the gay house
Under the new made clouds and happy as the heart was long,
In the sun born over and over,
I ran my heedless ways,
My wishes raced through the house high hay
And nothing I cared, at my sky blue trades, that time allows
In all his tuneful turning so few and such morning songs
Before the children green and golden
Follow him out of grace,

Nothing I cared, in the lamb white days, that time would take me
Up to the swallow thronged loft by the shadow of my hand,
In the moon that is always rising,
Nor that riding to sleep
I should hear him fly with the high fields
And wake to the farm forever fled from the childless land.
Oh as I was young and easy in the mercy of his means,
Time held me green and dying
Though I sang in my chains like the sea.

Leavetaking

Greg Delanty (1958–)

1992

After you board the train, you sit & wait,
to begin your first real journey alone.
You read to avoid the window's awkwardness,
knowing he's anxious to catch your eye,
loitering out in never-ending rain,
to wave, a bit shy, another final goodbye;
you are afraid of having to wave too soon.

And for the moment you think it's the train
next to you has begun, but it is yours,
and your face, pressed to the windowpane,
is distorted & numbed by the icy glass,
pinning your eyes upon your father,
as he cranes to defy your disappearing train.
Both of you waving, eternally, to each other.

DRAMA

Hamlet

William Shakespeare

William Shakespeare (1564–1616), the most widely known writer of English literature, was born in Stratford-on-Avon, England. By 1592, Shakespeare had become an accomplished actor and playwright in London. With several other actors, Shakespeare formed a syndicate to build a new playhouse, The Globe, one of the most famous theaters of its time. Shakespeare wrote thirty-seven plays and is believed to have played such supporting roles as the ghost of Hamlet's father.

The dramas in the accepted canon—works authentically Shakespeare's—are generally arranged into four categories: comedies, histories, tragedies, and romances. Of the tragedies, Hamlet *remains the most frequently staged and analyzed.*

1603

Dramatis Personae

Claudius, King of Denmark
Hamlet, son to the late, and nephew to the present King
Polonius, Lord Chamberlain
Horatio, friend to Hamlet
Laertes, son to Polonius
Voltimand
Cornelius
Rosencrantz
Guildenstern
Osric
A Gentleman
} courtiers
A Priest
Marcellus
Bernardo
} officers
Francisco, a soldier
Reynaldo, servant to Polonius
Players
Two Clowns, gravediggers
Fortinbras, Prince of Norway
A Captain
English Ambassadors
Gertrude, Queen of Denmark, and mother to Hamlet
Ophelia, daughter to Polonius
Lords, Ladies, Officers, Soldiers, Sailors, Messengers, and other Attendants
Ghost of Hamlet's father
Scene—Denmark.

Act I

Scene I. Elsinore. A platform[1] before the castle.

(Francisco at his post. Enter to him Bernardo.)

Bernardo: Who's there?
Francisco: Nay, answer me. Stand, and unfold yourself.[2]
Bernardo: Long live the King![3]
Francisco: Bernardo?
Bernardo: He.
Francisco: You come most carefully upon your hour.
Bernardo: 'Tis now struck twelve. Get thee to bed, Francisco.
Francisco: For this relief much thanks. 'Tis bitter cold,

---

[1] **platform:** the level space on the ramparts where the cannon were mounted.
[2] **unfold yourself:** reveal who you are. [3] **Long . . . King:** probably the password for the night.

And I am sick at heart.
Bernardo: Have you had quiet guard?
Francisco: Not a mouse stirring.
Bernardo: Well, good night.
If you do meet Horatio and Marcellus,
The rivals[4] of my watch, bid them make haste.
Francisco: I think I hear them. Stand, ho! Who is there!

(Enter Horatio and Marcellus.)

Horatio: Friends to this ground.
Marcellus: And liegemen[5] to the Dane.
Francisco: Give you good night.
Marcellus: Oh, farewell, honest soldier.
Who hath relieved you?
Francisco: Bernardo hath my place.
Give you good night. *(Exit.)*
Marcellus: Holloa! Bernardo!
Bernardo: Say,
What, is Horatio there?
Horatio: A piece of him.
Bernardo: Welcome, Horatio. Welcome, good Marcellus.
Marcellus: What, has this thing appeared again tonight?
Bernardo: I have seen nothing.
Marcellus: Horatio says 'tis but our fantasy,[6]
And will not let belief take hold of him
Touching this dreaded sight twice seen of us.
Therefore I have entreated him along
With us to watch the minutes of this night,
That if again this apparition come,
He may approve our eyes[7] and speak to it.
Horatio: Tush, tush, 'twill not appear.
Bernardo: Sit down awhile,
And let us once again assail your ears,
That are so fortified against our story,
What we have two nights seen.
Horatio: Well, sit we down,
And let us hear Bernardo speak of this.
Bernardo: Last night of all,
When yond same star that's westward from the pole[8]
Had made his course to illume[9] that part of heaven
Where now it burns, Marcellus and myself,
The bell then beating one—

(Enter Ghost.)

Marcellus: Peace, break thee off. Look where it comes again!
Bernardo: In the same figure, like the King that's dead.
Marcellus: Thou art a scholar.[10] Speak to it, Horatio.
Bernardo: Looks it not like the King? Mark it, Horatio.
Horatio: Most like. It harrows[11] me with fear and wonder.
Bernardo: It would be spoken to.
Marcellus: Question it, Horatio.
Horatio: What art thou that usurp'st this time of night,
Together with[12] that fair and warlike form
In which the majesty of buried Denmark[13]
Did sometimes march? By Heaven I charge thee, speak!
Marcellus: It is offended.
Bernardo: See, it stalks away!
Horatio: Stay! Speak, speak! I charge thee, speak!

(Exit Ghost.)

Marcellus: 'Tis gone, and will not answer.

---

[4] **rivals:** partners. [5] **liegemen:** loyal subjects. [6] **fantasy:** imagination.
[7] **approve our eyes:** verify what we have seen. [8] **pole:** Polestar. [9] **illume:** light.
[10] **scholar:** As Latin was the proper language in which to address and exorcise evil spirits, a scholar was necessary. [11] **harrows:** distresses; lit., plows up. [12] **Together with:** i.e., appearing in. [13] **majesty . . . Denmark:** the dead King.

Bernardo: How now, Horatio! You tremble and look pale.
Is not this something more than fantasy?
What think you on 't?
Horatio: Before my God, I might not this believe
Without the sensible and true avouch
Of mine own eyes.[14]
Marcellus: Is it not like the King?
Horatio: As thou art to thyself.
Such was the very armor he had on
When he the ambitious Norway combated.
So frowned he once when, in an angry parle,[15]
He smote the sledded Polacks[16] on the ice.
'Tis strange.
Marcellus: Thus twice before, and jump at this dead hour,[17]
With martial stalk hath he gone by our watch.
Horatio: In what particular thought to work I know not,
But in the gross and scope[18] of my opinion
This bodes some strange eruption[19] to our state.
Marcellus: Good now, sit down and tell me, he that knows,
Why this same strict and most observant watch
So nightly toils[20] the subject[21] of the land;
And why such daily cast of brazen cannon
And foreign mart[22] for implements of war;
Why[23] such impress[24] of shipwrights, whose sore task
Does not divide the Sunday from the week;
What might be toward,[25] that this sweaty haste
Doth make the night joint laborer with the day.
Who is 't that can inform me?
Horatio: That can I,
At least the whisper goes so. Our last King,
Whose image even but now appeared to us,
Was, as you know, by Fortinbras of Norway,
Thereto pricked[26] on by a most emulate[27] pride,
Dared to the combat, in which our valiant Hamlet—
For so this side of our known world esteemed him—
Did slay this Fortinbras. Who[28] by a sealed compact,[29]
Well ratified by law and heraldry,[30]
Did forfeit, with his life, all those his lands
Which he stood seized of[31] to the conqueror.
Against the which, a moiety competent[32]

---

[14] **Without . . . eyes:** unless my own eyes had vouched for it. **sensible:** perceived by my senses. [15] **parle:** parley. [16] **sledded Polacks:** There has been much controversy about this phrase. Q_1 and Q_2 read "sleaded Pollax." F_1 reads "sledded Pollax." Either the late King smote his heavy (leaded) poleax on the ice, or else he attacked the Poles in their sledges. There is no further reference to this incident. [17] **jump . . . hour:** just at deep midnight. [18] **gross . . . scope:** general conclusion. [19] **eruption:** violent disturbance. [20] **toils:** wearies. [21] **subject:** subjects. [22] **foreign mart:** purchase abroad. [23] **Why . . . day:** i.e., workers in shipyards and munition factories are working night shifts and Sundays. [24] **impress:** conscription. [25] **toward:** in preparation. [26] **pricked:** spurred. [27] **emulate:** jealous. [28] **Who . . . Hamlet:** i.e., before the combat it was agreed that the victor should win the land of the vanquished. [29] **sealed compact:** formal agreement. [30] **heraldry:** The heralds were responsible for arranging formal combats. [31] **seized of:** possessed of, a legal term. [32] **moiety competent:** adequate portion.

Was gagèd[33] by our King, which had returned
To the inheritance of Fortinbras
Had he been vanquisher, as by the same covenant
And carriage of the article designed[34]
His fell to Hamlet. Now, sir, young Fortinbras,
Of unimprovèd mettle[35] hot and full,
Hath in the skirts[36] of Norway here and there
Sharked[37] up a list of lawless resolutes,[38]
For food and diet,[39] to some enterprise
That hath a stomach[40] in 't. Which is no other—
As it doth well appear unto our state—
But to recover of us, by strong hand
And terms compulsatory,[41] those foresaid lands
So by his father lost. And this, I take it,
Is the main motive of our preparations,
The source of this our watch and the chief head[42]
Of this posthaste and romage[43] in the land.

Bernardo: I think it be no other but e'en so.
Well may it sort[44] that this portentous figure
Comes armèd through our watch, so like the King
That was and is the question of these wars.

Horatio: A mote[45] it is to trouble the mind's eye.
In the most high and palmy[46] state of Rome,
A little ere the mightiest Julius fell,
The graves stood tenantless, and the sheeted[47] dead
Did squeak and gibber[48] in the Roman streets.
As stars[49] with trains of fire and dews of blood,
Disasters[50] in the sun, and the moist star[51]
Upon whose influence Neptune's empire stands
Was sick almost to doomsday with eclipse.
And even the like precurse[52] of fierce events,
As harbingers[53] preceding still the fates
And prologue to the omen[54] coming on,
Have Heaven and earth together demonstrated
Unto our climatures[55] and countrymen.
(Re-enter Ghost.) But soft, behold! Lo where it comes again!
I'll cross it,[56] though it blast me. Stay, illusion!
If thou hast any sound, or use of voice,
Speak to me.

[33] **gaged:** pledged. [34] **carriage . . . designed:** fulfillment of the clause in the agreement. [35] **unimproved mettle:** untutored, wild material, nature. [36] **skirts:** outlying parts. [37] **Sharked:** collected indiscriminately, as a shark bolts its prey. [38] **lawless resolutes:** gangsters. [39] **diet:** maintenance. [40] **stomach:** resolution. [41] **terms compulsatory:** force. [42] **chief head:** main purpose. [43] **posthaste . . . romage:** urgency and bustle. [44] **Well . . . sort:** it would be a natural reason. [45] **mote:** speck of dust. [46] **palmy:** flourishing. [47] **sheeted:** in their shrouds. [48] **gibber:** utter strange sounds. [49] **As stars:** The sense of the passage is here broken; possibly a line has been omitted after l. 116. [50] **Disasters:** unlucky signs. [51] **moist star:** the moon, which influences the tides. [52] **precurse:** forewarning. [53] **harbingers:** forerunners. The harbinger was an officer of the Court who was sent ahead to make the arrangements when the Court went on progress. [54] **omen:** disaster. [55] **climatures:** regions. [56] **cross it:** stand in its way.

If[57] there be any good thing to be done
That may to thee do ease and grace to me,[58]
Speak to me.
If thou art privy to[59] thy country's fate,
Which, happily,[60] foreknowing may avoid,
Oh, speak!
Or if thou hast uphoarded in thy life
Extorted[61] treasure in the womb of earth,
For which, they say, you spirits oft walk in death,
Speak of it. Stay, and speak! *(The cock crows.*[62]*)* Stop it, Marcellus.

Marcellus: Shall I strike at it with my partisan?[63]

Horatio: Do, if it will not stand.

Bernardo: 'Tis here!

Horatio: 'Tis here!

Marcellus: 'Tis gone! *(Exit Ghost.)*
We do it wrong, being so majestical,
To offer it the show of violence,
For it is as the air invulnerable,
And our vain blows malicious mockery.

Bernardo: It was about to speak when the cock crew.

Horatio: And then it started like a guilty thing
Upon a fearful[64] summons. I have heard
The cock, that is the trumpet to the morn,
Doth with his lofty and shrill-sounding throat
Awake the god of day, and at his warning,
Whether in sea or fire, in earth or air,
The extravagant and erring[65] spirit hies
To his confíne.[66] And of the truth herein
This present object made probation.[67]

Marcellus: It faded on the crowing of the cock.
Some say that ever 'gainst[68] that season comes
Wherein Our Saviour's birth is celebrated,
The bird of dawning singeth all night long.
And then, they say, no spirit dare stir abroad,
The nights are wholesome, then no planets[69] strike,
No fairy takes[70] nor witch hath power to charm,
So hallowed and so gracious is the time.

Horatio: So have I heard and do in part believe it.
But look, the morn, in russet mantle clad,
Walks o'er the dew of yon high eastward hill.
Break we our watch up, and by my advice
Let us impart what we have seen tonight
Unto young Hamlet, for upon my life,
This spirit, dumb to us, will speak to him.
Do you consent we shall acquaint him with it,
As needful in our loves, fitting our duty?

---

[57] **If . . . speak:** In popular belief there were four reasons why the spirit of a dead man should *walk:* (a) to reveal a secret, (b) to utter a warning, (c) to reveal concealed treasure, (d) to reveal the manner of its death. Horatio thus adjures the ghost by three potent reasons, but before he can utter the fourth the cock crows. [58] **grace to me:** bring me into a state of spiritual grace. [59] **privy to:** have secret knowledge of. [60] **happily:** by good luck. [61] **Extorted:** evilly acquired. [62] s.d., **cock crows:** i.e., a sign that dawn is at hand. See ll. 147–64. [63] **partisan:** spear-like weapon. [64] **fearful:** causing fear. [65] **extravagant . . . erring:** both words mean "wandering." [66] **confine:** place of confinement. [67] **probation:** proof. [68] **'gainst:** in anticipation of. [69] **planets:** Planets were supposed to bring disaster. [70] **takes:** bewitches.

Marcellus: Let's do 't, I pray. And I this morning know
Where we shall find him most conveniently.

(Exeunt.)

Scene II. A room of state in the castle.

(Flourish.[1] *Enter the King, Queen, Hamlet, Polonius, Laertes, Voltimand, Cornelius, Lords, and Attendants.)*

King: Though yet of Hamlet our dear brother's death
The memory be green,[2] and that it us befitted
To bear our hearts in grief and our whole kingdom
To be contracted in one brow of woe,[3]
Yet so far hath discretion[4] fought with nature[5]
That we with wisest sorrow think of him,
Together with remembrance of ourselves.
Therefore our sometime sister,[6] now our Queen,
The imperial jointress[7] to this warlike state,
Have we, as 'twere with a defeated joy—
With an auspicious and a dropping eye,[8]
With mirth in funeral and with dirge in marriage,
In equal scale weighing delight and dole[9]—
Taken to wife. Nor have we herein barred
Your better wisdoms,[10] which have freely gone
With this affair along. For all, our thanks.
Now follows that you know. Young Fortinbras,
Holding a weak supposal[11] of our worth,
Or thinking by our late dear brother's death
Our state to be disjoint and out of frame,
Colleagued with the dream of his advantage,[12]
He hath not failed to pester us with message
Importing the surrender of those lands
Lost by his father, with all bonds of law,[13]
To our most valiant brother. So much for him.
Now for ourself, and for this time of meeting.
Thus much the business is: We have here writ
To Norway, uncle of young Fortinbras—
Who, impotent and bedrid, scarcely hears
Of this his nephew's purpose—to suppress
His further gait[14] herein, in that the levies,
The lists[15] and full proportions,[16] are all made
Out of his subject.[17] And we here dispatch
You, good Cornelius, and you, Voltimand,

---

[1] **Flourish:** fanfare of trumpets. [2] **green:** fresh. [3] **contracted . . . woe:** i.e., every subject's forehead should be puckered with grief. [4] **discretion:** common sense. [5] **nature:** natural sorrow. [6] **sister:** sister-in-law. [7] **jointress:** partner by marriage. [8] **auspicious . . . eye:** an eye at the same time full of joy and tears. [9] **dole:** grief. [10] **barred . . . wisdoms:** i.e., in taking this step we have not shut out your advice. As is obvious throughout the play, the Danes chose their King by election and not by right of birth. [11] **weak supposal:** poor opinion. [12] **Colleagued . . . advantage:** uniting himself with this dream that here was a good opportunity. [13] **with . . . law:** legally binding. [14] **gait:** progress. [15] **lists:** rosters. [16] **proportions:** military establishments. [17] **subject:** subjects.

For bearers of this greeting to old Norway,
Giving to you no further personal power
To business with the King more than the scope[18]
Of these delated articles[19] allow.
Farewell, and let your haste commend[20] your duty.

Cornelius & Voltimand: In that and all things will we show our duty.

King: We doubt it nothing. Heartily farewell.

(Exeunt Voltimand and Cornelius.)

And now, Laertes, what's the news with you?
You told us of some suit[21]—what is 't, Laertes?
You cannot speak of reason to the Dane
And lose your voice. What wouldst thou beg, Laertes,
That shall not be my offer, not thy asking?
The head is not more native[22] to the heart,
The hand more instrumental[23] to the mouth,
Than is the throne of Denmark to thy father.
What wouldst thou have, Laertes?

Laertes: My dread[24] lord,
Your leave and favor to return to France,
From whence though willingly I came to Denmark
To show my duty in your coronation,
Yet now, I must confess, that duty done,
My thoughts and wishes bend again toward France
And bow them to your gracious leave and pardon.

King: Have you your father's leave? What says Polonius?

Polonius: He hath, my lord, wrung from me my slow leave
By laborsome petition, and at last
Upon his will[25] I sealed my hard consent.[26]
I do beseech you give him leave to go.

King: Take thy fair hour, Laertes, time be thine,
And thy best graces spend[27] it at thy will!
But now, my cousin[28] Hamlet, and my son—

Hamlet: *(Aside.)* A little more than kin and less than kind.[29]

King: How is it that the clouds still hang on you?

Hamlet: Not so, my lord. I am too much i' the sun.

Queen: Good Hamlet, cast thy nighted color[30] off.
And let thine eye look like a friend on Denmark.
Do not forever with thy vailèd lids[31]
Seek for thy noble father in the dust.
Thou know'st 'tis common—all that lives must die,
Passing through nature to eternity.

Hamlet: Aye, madam, it is common.

---

[18] **scope:** limit. [19] **delated articles:** detailed instructions. Claudius is following usual diplomatic procedure. Ambassadors sent on a special mission carried with them a letter of introduction and greeting to the King of the foreign Court and detailed instructions to guide them in the negotiations. [20] **commend:** display; lit., recommend. [21] **suit:** petition. [22] **native:** closely related. [23] **instrumental:** serviceable. [24] **dread:** dreaded, much respected. [25] **will:** desire. [26] **sealed . . . consent:** agreed to, but with great reluctance. [27] **best . . . spend:** i.e., use your time well. [28] **cousin:** kinsman. The word was used for any near relation. [29] **A . . . kind:** too near a relation (uncle-father) and too little natural affection. **kind:** affectionate. [30] **nighted color:** black. Hamlet alone is in deep mourning; the rest of the Court wear gay clothes. [31] **vailed lids:** lowered eyelids.

Queen: If it be,
Why seems it so particular with thee?

Hamlet: Seems, madam! Nay, it is. I know not "seems."
'Tis not alone my inky cloak, good Mother,
Nor customary suits of solemn black,
Nor windy suspiration of forced breath—
No, nor the fruitful river[32] in the eye,
Nor the dejected havior of the visage,[33]
Together with all forms, moods, shapes of grief—
That can denote me truly. These indeed seem,
For they are actions that a man might play.[34]
But I have that within which passeth show,
These but the trappings[35] and the suits of woe.

King: 'Tis sweet and commendable in your nature, Hamlet,
To give these mourning duties to your father.
But you must know your father lost a father,
That father lost, lost his, and the survivor bound
In filial obligation for some term
To do obsequious sorrow.[36] But to perséver
In obstinate condolement[37] is a course
Of impious stubbornness, 'tis unmanly grief.
It shows a will most incorrect to Heaven,
A heart unfortified,[38] a mind impatient,
An understanding simple and unschooled.
For what we know must be and is as common
As any the most vulgar[39] thing to sense,
Why should we in our peevish opposition
Take it to heart? Fie! 'Tis a fault to Heaven,
A fault against the dead, a fault to nature,
To reason most absurd, whose common theme
Is death of fathers, and who still hath cried,
From the first corse[40] till he that died today,
"This must be so." We pray you throw to earth
This unprevailing[41] woe, and think of us
As of a father. For let the world take note,
You are the most immediate[42] to our throne,
And with no less nobility of love
Than that which dearest father bears his son
Do I impart toward you. For your intent
In going back to school[43] in Wittenberg,
It is most retrograde[44] to our desire.
And we beseech you bend you[45] to remain
Here in the cheer and comfort of our eye,
Our chiefest courtier, cousin, and our son.

Queen: Let not thy mother lose her prayers, Hamlet.

---

[32] **fruitful river:** stream of tears. [33] **dejected . . . visage:** downcast countenance. [34] **play:** act, as in a play. [35] **trappings:** ornaments. [36] **obsequious sorrow:** the sorrow usual at funerals. [37] **obstinate condolement:** lamentation disregarding the will of God. [38] **unfortified:** not strengthened with the consolation of religion. [39] **vulgar:** common. [40] **corse:** corpse. There is unconscious irony in this remark, for the first corpse was that of Abel, also slain by his brother. [41] **unprevailing:** futile. [42] **most immediate:** next heir. [43] **school:** university. [44] **retrograde:** contrary. [45] **bend you:** incline.

I pray thee, stay with us, go not to Wittenberg.
Hamlet: I shall in all my best obey you, Madam.
King: Why, 'tis a loving and a fair reply.
Be as ourself in Denmark. Madam, come,
This gentle and unforced accord of Hamlet
Sits smiling to my heart. In grace whereof,
No jocund health that Denmark drinks today
But the great cannon[46] to the clouds shall tell,
And the King's rouse[47] the Heaven shall bruit[48] again,
Respeaking earthly thunder. Come away.

(Flourish. Exeunt all but Hamlet.)

Hamlet: Oh, that this too too solid flesh would melt,
Thaw, and resolve itself into a dew!
Or that the Everlasting had not fixed
His canon[49] 'gainst self-slaughter! Oh, God! God!
How weary, stale, flat, and unprofitable
Seem to me all the uses[50] of this world!
Fie on 't, ah, fie! 'Tis an unweeded garden,
That grows to seed, things rank[51] and gross in nature
Possess it merely.[52] That it should come to this!
But two months dead! Nay, not so much, not two.
So excellent a King, that was, to this,
Hyperion[53] to a satyr.[54] So loving to my mother
That he might not beteem[55] the winds of heaven
Visit her face too roughly. Heaven and earth!
Must I remember? Why, she would hang on him
As if increase of appetite had grown
By what it fed on. And yet within a month—
Let me not think on 't.—Frailty, thy name is woman!—
A little month, or ere those shoes were old
With which she followed my poor father's body,
Like Niobe[56] all tears.—Why she, even she—
Oh, God! A beast that wants discourse of reason[57]
Would have mourned longer—married with my uncle,
My father's brother, but no more like my father
Than I to Hercules. Within a month,
Ere yet the salt of most unrighteous tears
Had left the flushing in her gallèd[58] eyes,
She married. Oh, most wicked speed, to post[59]
With such dexterity[60] to incestuous sheets!
It is not, nor it cannot, come to good.
But break, my heart, for I must hold my tongue!

(Enter Horatio, Marcellus, and Bernardo.)

Horatio: Hail to your lordship!

---

[46] **great cannon:** This Danish custom of discharging cannon when the King proposed a toast was much noted by Englishmen. [47] **rouse:** deep drink. [48] **bruit:** sound loudly, echo. [49] **canon:** rule, law. [50] **uses:** ways. [51] **rank:** coarse. [52] **merely:** entirely. [53] **Hyperion:** the sun god. [54] **satyr:** a creature half man, half goat—ugly and lecherous. [55] **beteem:** allow. [56] **Niobe:** She boasted of her children, to the annoyance of the goddess Artemis, who slew them all. Thereafter Niobe became so sorrowful that she changed into a rock everlastingly dripping water. [57] **wants . . . reason:** is without ability to reason. [58] **galled:** sore. [59] **post:** hasten. [60] **dexterity:** nimbleness.

Hamlet: I am glad to see you well.
Horatio—or I do forget myself.
Horatio: The same, my lord, and your poor servant ever.
Hamlet: Sir, my good friend—I'll change that name[61] with you.
And what make you from Wittenberg, Horatio?
Marcellus?
Marcellus: My good lord?
Hamlet: I am very glad to see you. *(To Bernardo.)* Good even, sir.
But what, in faith, make you from Wittenberg?
Horatio: A truant disposition, good my lord.
Hamlet: I would not hear your enemy say so,
Nor shall you do my ear that violence
To make it truster of your own report
Against yourself. I know you are no truant.
But what is your affair in Elsinore?
We'll teach you to drink deep[62] ere you depart.
Horatio: My lord, I came to see your father's funeral.
Hamlet: I pray thee do not mock me, fellow student.
I think it was to see my mother's wedding.
Horatio: Indeed, my lord, it followed hard upon.
Hamlet: Thrift, thrift, Horatio! The funeral baked meats
Did coldly furnish forth the marriage tables.[63]
Would I had met my dearest[64] foe in Heaven
Or ever I had seen that day, Horatio!
My father!—Methinks I see my father.
Horatio: Oh, where, my lord?
Hamlet: In my mind's eye, Horatio.
Horatio: I saw him once. He was a goodly King.
Hamlet: He was a man, take him for all in all.
I shall not look upon his like again.
Horatio: My lord, I think I saw him yesternight.
Hamlet: Saw? Who?
Horatio: My lord, the King your father.
Hamlet: The King my father!
Horatio: Season your admiration[65] for a while
With an attent[66] ear till I may deliver,
Upon the witness of these gentlemen,
This marvel to you.
Hamlet: For God's love, let me hear.
Horatio: Two nights together had these gentlemen,
Marcellus and Bernardo, on their watch
In the dead vast and middle of the night,[67]
Been thus encountered. A figure like your father,
Armed at point exactly, cap-a-pie,[68]
Appears before them and with solemn march
Goes slow and stately by them. Thrice he walked
By their oppressed and fear-surprisèd eyes
Within his truncheon's[69] length, whilst they, distilled[70]
Almost to jelly with the act of fear,
Stand dumb, and speak not to him. This to me
In dreadful secrecy impart they did,
And I with them the third night kept the watch.
Where, as they had delivered, both in time,

[61] **that name:** i.e., friend. [62] **drink deep:** For more on the drunken habits of the Danes, see I.iv. 8–38. [63] **Thrift . . . tables:** they hurried on the wedding for economy's sake, so that the remains of food served at the funeral might be used cold for the wedding. **baked meats:** feast. [64] **dearest:** best-hated. [65] **Season . . . admiration:** moderate your wonder. [66] **attent:** attentive. [67] **dead . . . night:** deep, silent midnight. [68] **at . . . cap-a-pie:** complete in every detail, head to foot. [69] **truncheon:** a general's staff. [70] **distilled:** melted.

Form of the thing, each word made true and good,
The apparition comes. I knew your father.
These hands are not more like.
Hamlet: But where was this?
Marcellus: My lord, upon the platform where we watched.
Hamlet: Did you not speak to it?
Horatio: My lord, I did,
But answer made it none. Yet once methought
It lifted up it[71] head and did address
Itself to motion, like as it would speak.
But even then the morning cock crew loud,
And at the sound it shrunk in haste away
And vanished from our sight.
Hamlet: 'Tis very strange.
Horatio: As I do live, my honored lord, 'tis true,
And we did think it writ down in our duty
To let you know of it.
Hamlet: Indeed, indeed, sirs, but this troubles me.
Hold you the watch tonight?
Marcellus & Bernardo: We do, my lord.
Hamlet: Armed, say you?
Marcellus & Bernardo: Armed, my lord.
Hamlet: From top to toe?
Marcellus & Bernardo: My lord, from head to foot.
Hamlet: Then saw you not his face?
Horatio: Oh yes, my lord, he wore his beaver[72] up.
Hamlet: What, looked he frowningly?
Horatio: A countenance more in sorrow than in anger.
Hamlet: Pale, or red?
Horatio: Nay, very pale.
Hamlet: And fixed his eyes upon you?
Horatio: Most constantly.
Hamlet: I would I had been there.
Horatio: It would have much amazed you.
Hamlet: Very like, very like. Stayed it long?
Horatio: While one with moderate haste might tell[73] a hundred.
Marcellus & Bernardo: Longer, longer.
Horatio: Not when I saw 't.
Hamlet: His beard was grizzled?[74] No?
Horatio: It was as I have seen it in his life,
A sable silvered.[75]
Hamlet: I will watch tonight.
Perchance 'twill walk again.
Horatio: I warrant it will.
Hamlet: If it assume my noble father's person,
I'll speak to it though Hell itself should gape
And bid me hold my peace. I pray you all,
If you have hitherto concealed this sight,
Let it be tenable[76] in your silence still,
And whatsoever else shall hap tonight,
Give it an understanding, but no tongue.
I will requite[77] your loves. So fare you well.
Upon the platform, 'twixt eleven and twelve,
I'll visit you.
All: Our duty to your Honor.
Hamlet: Your loves, as mine to you. Farewell.

(Exeunt all but Hamlet.)

My father's spirit in arms! All is not well.
I doubt[78] some foul play. Would the night were come!
Till then sit still, my soul. Foul deeds will rise.

---

[71] **it:** its. [72] **beaver:** front part of the helmet, which could be raised. [73] **tell:** count. [74] **grizzled:** gray. [75] **sable silvered:** black mingled with white. [76] **tenable:** held fast. [77] **requite:** repay. [78] **doubt:** suspect.

Though all the earth o'erwhelm them, to men's eyes. *(Exit.)*

Scene III. A room in Polonius's house.

(Enter Laertes and Ophelia.)

Laertes: My necessaries[1] are embarked. Farewell.
And, Sister, as the winds give benefit
And convoy is assistant,[2] do not sleep,
But let me hear from you.

Ophelia: Do you doubt that?

Laertes: For Hamlet, and the trifling of his favor,[3]
Hold it a fashion and a toy in blood,[4]
A violet in the youth of primy[5] nature,
Forward, not permanent, sweet, not lasting,
The perfume and suppliance of a minute[6]—
No more.

Ophelia: No more but so?

Laertes: Think it no more.
For Nature crescent does not grow alone
In thews and bulk,[7] but as this temple[8] waxes
The inward service of the mind and soul
Grows wide withal. Perhaps he loves you now,
And now no soil nor cautel[9] doth besmirch
The virtue of his will.[10] But you must fear,
His greatness weighed,[11] his will is not his own.
For he himself is subject to his birth.
He may not, as unvalued persons do,
Carve[12] for himself, for on his choice depends
The safety and health of this whole state,
And therefore must his choice be circumscribed[13]
Unto the voice and yielding of that body
Whereof he is the head. Then if he says he loves you,
It fits your wisdom so far to believe it
As he in his particular act and place
May give his saying deed, which is no further
Than the main voice of Denmark goes withal.
Then weigh what loss your honor may sustain
If with too credent[14] ear you list his songs,
Or lose your heart, or your chaste treasure[15] open
To his unmastered importunity.
Fear it, Ophelia, fear it, my dear sister,
And keep you in the rear[16] of your affection,
Out of the shot and danger of desire.
The chariest maid is prodigal enough
If she unmask her beauty to the moon.
Virtue itself 'scapes not calumnious strokes.
The canker galls the infants[17] of the spring
Too oft before their buttons[18] be disclosed,
And in the morn and liquid dew of youth
Contagious blastments[19] are most imminent.

---

[1] **necessaries:** baggage. [2] **convoy . . . assistant:** means of conveyance is available. [3] **favor:** i.e., toward you. [4] **toy in blood:** trifling impulse. [5] **primy:** springtime; i.e., youthful. [6] **perfume . . . minute:** perfume which lasts only for a minute. [7] **For . . . bulk:** for natural growth is not only in bodily bulk. [8] **temple:** i.e., the body. [9] **cautel:** deceit. [10] **will:** desire. [11] **His . . . weighed:** when you consider his high position. [12] **Carve:** choose. [13] **circumscribed:** restricted. [14] **credent:** credulous. [15] **chaste treasure:** the treasure of your chastity. [16] **in . . . rear:** i.e., farthest from danger. [17] **canker . . . infants:** maggot harms the unopened buds. [18] **buttons:** buds. [19] **Contagious blastments:** infectious blasts.

Be wary, then, best safety lies in fear.
Youth to itself rebels, though none else near.[20]

Ophelia: I shall the effect of this good lesson keep
As watchman to my heart. But, good my brother,
Do not, as some ungracious pastors do,
Show me the steep and thorny way to Heaven
Whilst, like a puffed[21] and reckless libertine,
Himself the primrose path of dalliance[22] treads
And recks not his own rede.[23]

Laertes: Oh, fear me not.
I stay too long. But here my father comes.
(Enter Polonius.) A double blessing is a double grace,
Occasion smiles[24] upon a second leave.

Polonius: Yet here, Laertes! Aboard, aboard, for shame!
The wind sits in the shoulder of your sail
And you are stayed[25] for. There, my blessing with thee!
And these few precepts in thy memory
Look thou charácter.[26] Give thy thoughts no tongue,
Nor any unproportioned[27] thought his act.
Be thou familiar, but by no means vulgar.
Those friends thou hast, and their adoption tried,[28]
Grapple them to thy soul with hoops of steel,
But do not dull thy palm with entertainment[29]
Of each new-hatched unfledged[30] comrade. Beware
Of entrance to a quarrel, but being in,
Bear 't that the opposèd may beware of thee.
Give every man thy ear, but few thy voice.[31]
Take each man's censure,[32] but reserve thy judgment.
Costly thy habit[33] as thy purse can buy,
But not expressed in fancy[34]—rich, not gaudy.
For the apparel oft proclaims the man,
And they in France of the best rank and station
Are of a most select and generous chief in that.[35]
Neither a borrower nor a lender be,
For loan oft loses both itself and friend
And borrowing dulls the edge of husbandry.[36]
This above all: To thine own self be true,
And it must follow, as the night the day,
Thou canst not then be false to any man.
Farewell. My blessing season[37] this in thee!

Laertes: Most humbly do I take my leave, my lord.

Polonius: The time invites you. Go, your servants tend.[38]

---

[20] **though . . . near:** without anyone else to encourage it. [21] **puffed:** panting. [22] **primrose . . . dalliance:** i.e., the pleasant way of love-making. [23] **recks . . . rede:** takes no heed of his own advice. [24] **Occasion smiles:** i.e., here is a happy chance. [25] **stayed:** waited. [26] **charácter:** inscribe. [27] **unproportioned:** unsuitable. [28] **adoption tried:** friendship tested by experience. [29] **dull . . . entertainment:** let your hand grow callous with welcome. [30] **unfledged:** lit., newly out of the egg, immature. [31] **Give . . . voice:** listen to everyone but commit yourself to few. [32] **censure:** opinion. [33] **habit:** dress. [34] **expressed in fancy:** fantastic. [35] **Are . . . that:** A disputed line; this is the F reading. Q_2 reads "Or of the most select and generous, chief in that"; i.e., the best noble and gentle families are very particular in their dress. **generous:** of gentle birth. [36] **husbandry:** economy. [37] **season:** bring to fruit. [38] **tend:** attend.

Laertes: Farewell, Ophelia, and remember well
What I have said to you.
Ophelia: 'Tis in my memory locked,
And you yourself shall keep the key of it.
Laertes: Farewell. *(Exit.)*
Polonius: What is 't, Ophelia, he hath said to you?
Ophelia: So please you, something touching the Lord Hamlet.
Polonius: Marry,[39] well bethought.[40]
'Tis told me he hath very oft of late
Given private time to you, and you yourself
Have of your audience been most free and bounteous.
If it be so—as so 'tis put on me,
And that in way of caution—I must tell you
You do not understand yourself so clearly
As it behooves[41] my daughter and your honor.
What is between you? Give me up the truth.
Ophelia: He hath, my lord, of late made many tenders[42]
Of his affection to me.
Polonius: Affection! Pooh! You speak like a green girl,
Unsifted[43] in such perilous circumstance.
Do you believe his tenders, as you call them?
Ophelia: I do not know, my lord, what I should think.
Polonius: Marry, I'll teach you. Think yourself a baby
That you have ta'en these tenders[44] for true pay,
Which are not sterling.[45] Tender yourself more dearly,
Or—not to crack the wind of[46] the poor phrase,
Running it thus—you'll tender me a fool.
Ophelia: My lord, he hath importuned me with love
In honorable fashion.
Polonius: Aye, fashion[47] you may call it. Go to, go to.
Ophelia: And hath given countenance to his speech,[48] my lord,
With almost all the holy vows of Heaven.
Polonius: Aye, springes[49] to catch woodcocks.[50] I do know,
When the blood burns, how prodigal[51] the soul
Lends the tongue vows. These blazes,[52] daughter,
Giving more light than heat, extinct in both,
Even in their promise as it is a-making,
You must not take for fire. From this time
Be something scanter of your maiden presence,
Set your entreatments at a higher rate
Than a command to parley.[53] For Lord Hamlet,
Believe so much in him, that he is young,
And with a larger tether[54] may he walk
Than may be given you. In few,[55] Ophelia,

---

[39] **Marry:** Mary, by the Virgin Mary. [40] **well bethought:** well remembered.
[41] **behooves:** is the duty of. [42] **tenders:** offers. [43] **Unsifted:** untried.
[44] **tenders . . . tender:** Polonius puns on "tenders," counters (used for money in games); "tender," value; "tender," show. [45] **sterling:** true currency. [46] **crack . . . of:** i.e., ride to death. [47] **fashion:** mere show. [48] **given . . . speech:** confirmed his words.
[49] **springes:** snares. [50] **woodcocks:** foolish birds. [51] **prodigal:** extravagantly.
[52] **blazes:** flashes, quickly extinguished *(extinct)*. [53] **Set . . . parley:** when you are asked to see him do not regard it as a command to negotiate. **parley:** meeting to discuss terms. [54] **tether:** rope by which a grazing animal is fastened to its peg. [55] **In few:** in short.

Do not believe his vows, for they are brokers,[56]
Not of that dye which their investments[57] show,
But mere implorators[58] of unholy suits,
Breathing like sanctified and pious bawds[59]
The better to beguile. This is for all.
I would not, in plain terms, from this time forth
Have you so slander any moment leisure[60]
As to give words or talk with the Lord Hamlet.
Look to 't, I charge you. Come your ways.

Ophelia: I shall obey, my lord. *(Exeunt.)*

Scene IV. The platform

(Enter Hamlet, Horatio, and Marcellus.)

Hamlet: The air bites shrewdly.[1] It is very cold.
Horatio: It is a nipping and an eager[2] air.
Hamlet: What hour now?
Horatio: I think it lacks of twelve.
Marcellus: No, it is struck.
Horatio: Indeed? I heard it not. It then draws near the season
Wherein the spirit held his wont to walk.

(A flourish of trumpets, and ordnance shot off within.[3])

What doth this mean, my lord?

Hamlet: The King doth wake[4] tonight and takes his rouse,[5]
Keeps wassail,[6] and the swaggering upspring reels.[7]
And as he drains his draughts of Rhenish[8] down,
The kettledrum and trumpet thus bray out
The triumph of his pledge.
Horatio: Is it a custom?
Hamlet: Aye, marry, is 't.
But to my mind, though I am native here
And to the manner born, it is a custom
More honored in the breach than the observance.
This heavy-headed revel[9] east and west
Makes us traduced and taxed of[10] other nations.
They clepe[11] us drunkards, and with swinish phrase
Soil our addition,[12] and indeed it takes
From our achievements, though performed at height,[13]
The pith and marrow of our attribute.[14]
So oft it chances in particular men,
That for some vicious mole[15] of nature in them,
As in their birth—wherein they are not guilty,
Since nature cannot choose his origin—
By the o'ergrowth of some complexion,[16]

---

[56] **brokers:** traveling salesmen. [57] **investments:** garments. [58] **implorators:** men who solicit. [59] **bawds:** keepers of brothels. F_1 and Q_2 read "bond," an easy misprint for "baud"—the Elizabethan spelling of "bawd." [60] **slander . . . leisure:** misuse any moment of leisure.

[1] **shrewdly:** bitterly. [2] **eager:** sharp. [3] **within:** off stage. [4] **wake:** "makes a night of it." [5] **rouse:** See I.ii. 127, n. [6] **wassail:** revelry. [7] **swaggering . . . reels:** reel in a riotous dance. [8] **Rhenish:** Rhine wine. [9] **heavy-headed revel:** drinking that produces a thick head. [10] **traduced . . . of:** disgraced and censured by. [11] **clepe:** call. [12] **soil . . . addition:** smirch our honor. **addition:** lit., title of honor added to a man's name. [13] **though . . . height:** though of the highest merit. [14] **pith . . . attribute:** essential part of our honor; i.e., we lose the honor due to our achievements because of our reputation for drunkenness. [15] **mole:** blemish. [16] **o'ergrowth . . . complexion:** some quality allowed to overbalance the rest.

Oft breaking down the pales[17] and forts of reason,
Or by some habit that too much o'erleavens[18]
The form of plausive[19] manners, that these men—
Carrying, I say, the stamp of one defect,
Being Nature's livery,[20] or Fortune's star[21]—
Their virtues else—be they as pure as grace,
As infinite as man may undergo—
Shall in the general censure take corruption
From that particular fault. The dram of eale
Doth all the noble substance of a doubt
To his own scandal.[22]

(Enter Ghost.)

Horatio: Look, my lord, it comes!

Hamlet: Angels and ministers of grace defend us!
Be thou a spirit of health or goblin damned,[23]
Bring with thee airs from Heaven or blasts from Hell,
Be thy intents wicked or charitable,
Thou comest in such a questionable[24] shape
That I will speak to thee. I'll call thee Hamlet,
King, Father, royal Dane. Oh, answer me!
Let me not burst in ignorance, but tell
Why thy canónized[25] bones, hearsèd[26] in death,
Have burst their cerements,[27] why the sepulcher
Wherein we saw thee quietly inurned[28]
Hath oped his ponderous and marble jaws
To cast thee up again. What may this mean,
That thou, dead corse, again, in complete steel,[29]
Revisit'st thus the glimpses of the moon,
Making night hideous, and we fools[30] of nature
So horridly to shake our disposition[31]
With thoughts beyond the reaches of our souls?
Say, why is this? Wherefore? What should we do?

(Ghost beckons Hamlet.)

Horatio: It beckons you to go away with it,
As if it some impartment[32] did desire

[17] **pales:** defenses. [18] **o'erleavens:** mixes with. [19] **plausive:** agreeable. [20] **Nature's livery:** i.e., inborn. [21] **Fortune's star:** the result of ill luck. [22] **The . . . scandal:** This is the most famous of all disputed passages in Shakespeare's plays. The general meaning is clear: "a small portion of evil brings scandal on the whole substance, however noble." "Eale" is an Elizabethan spelling and pronunciation of "evil," as later in Q_2; "deale" is the spelling and pronunciation of "Devil." The difficulty lies in "of a doubt," which is obviously a misprint for some such word as "corrupt"; but to be satisfactory it must fit the meter and be a plausible misprint. So far, although many guesses have been made, none is wholly convincing. The best is perhaps "often dout"—often put out. [23] **spirit . . . damned:** a holy spirit or damned fiend. Hamlet, until convinced at the end of the play scene (III.ii.), is perpetually in doubt whether the ghost which he sees is a good spirit sent to warn him, a devil sent to tempt him into some damnable action, or a hallucination created by his own diseased imagination. [24] **questionable:** inviting question. [25] **canonized:** buried with full rites according to the canon of the Church. [26] **hearsed:** buried. [27] **cerements:** waxen shroud, used to wrap the bodies of the illustrious dead. [28] **inurned:** buried. [29] **complete steel:** full armor. [30] **fools:** dupes. [31] **disposition:** nature. [32] **impartment:** communication.

To you alone.
Marcellus: Look with what courteous action
It waves you to a more removèd ground.
But do not go with it.
Horatio: No, by no means.
Hamlet: It will not speak. Then I will follow it.
Horatio: Do not, my lord.
Hamlet: Why, what should be the fear?
I do not set my life as a pin's fee,[33]
And for my soul, what can it do to that,
Being a thing immortal as itself?
It waves me forth again. I'll follow it.
Horatio: What if it tempt you toward the flood, my lord,
Or to the dreadful summit of the cliff
That beetles o'er[34] his base into the sea,
And there assume some other horrible form
Which might deprive your sovereignty of reason[35]
And draw you into madness? Think of it.
The very place puts toys of desperation,[36]
Without more motive, into every brain
That looks so many fathoms to the sea
And hears it roar beneath.
Hamlet: It waves me still.
Go on. I'll follow thee.
Marcellus: You shall not go, my lord.
Hamlet: Hold off your hands.
Horatio: Be ruled. You shall not go.
Hamlet: My fate cries out,
And makes each petty artery in this body
As hardy as the Nemean lion's nerve.[37]
Still am I called. Unhand me, gentlemen.
By Heaven, I'll make a ghost of him that lets[38] me!
I say, away! Go on. I'll follow thee.

(Exeunt Ghost and Hamlet.)

Horatio: He waxes desperate with imagination.
Marcellus: Let's follow. 'Tis not fit thus to obey him.
Horatio: Have after. To what issue will this come?
Marcellus: Something is rotten in the state of Denmark.
Horatio: Heaven will direct it.
Marcellus: Nay, let's follow him.
(Exeunt.)

Scene V. Another part of the platform.

(Enter Ghost and Hamlet.)

Hamlet: Whither wilt thou lead me? Speak. I'll go no further.
Ghost: Mark me.
Hamlet: I will.
Ghost: My hour is almost come
When I to sulphurous and tormenting flames
Must render up myself.
Hamlet: Alas, poor ghost!
Ghost: Pity me not, but lend thy serious hearing
To what I shall unfold.
Hamlet: Speak. I am bound to hear.
Ghost: So art thou to revenge, when thou shalt hear.
Hamlet: What?
Ghost: I am thy father's spirit,
Doomed for a certain term to walk the night
And for the day confined to fast in fires
Till the foul crimes done in my days of nature

---

[33] **fee:** value. [34] **beetles o'er:** juts out over. [35] **sovereignty of reason:** control of your reason over your actions. [36] **toys of desperation:** desperate fancies. [37] **Nemean . . . nerve:** sinew of a fierce beast slain by Hercules. [38] **lets:** hinders.

Are burnt and purged away. But that I am forbid
To tell the secrets of my prison house,
I could a tale unfold whose lightest word
Would harrow up thy soul, freeze thy young blood,
Make thy two eyes, like stars, start from their spheres,[1]
Thy knotted and combinèd[2] locks to part
And each particular[3] hair to stand an[4] end
Like quills upon the fretful porpentine.[5]
But this eternal blazon[6] must not be
To ears of flesh and blood. List, list, oh, list!
If thou didst ever thy dear father love—

Hamlet: Oh, God!

Ghost: Revenge his foul and most unnatural murder.

Hamlet: Murder!

Ghost: Murder most foul, as in the best[7] it is,
But this most foul, strange, and unnatural.

Hamlet: Haste me to know 't, that I, with wings as swift
As meditation or the thoughts of love,
May sweep to my revenge.

Ghost: I find thee apt,
And duller shouldst thou be than the fat[8] weed
That roots itself in ease[9] of Lethe wharf[10]
Wouldst thou not stir in this. Now, Hamlet, hear.
'Tis given out that, sleeping in my orchard,
A serpent stung me—so the whole ear of Denmark
Is by a forgèd process[11] of my death
Rankly abused. But know, thou noble youth,
The serpent that did sting thy father's life
Now wears his crown.

Hamlet: Oh, my prophetic soul!
My uncle!

Ghost: Aye, that incestuous, that adulterate beast,
With witchcraft of his wit, with traitorous gifts—
O wicked wit and gifts, that have the power
So to seduce!—won to his shameful lust
The will of my most seeming-virtuous Queen.
O Hamlet, what a falling-off was there!
From me, whose love was of that dignity
That it went hand in hand even with the vow
I made to her in marriage, and to decline
Upon a wretch whose natural gifts were poor
To those of mine!
But virtue, as it never will be moved
Though lewdness court it in a shape of Heaven,[12]
So Lust, though to a radiant angel linked,
Will sate itself[13] in a celestial bed
And prey on garbage.
But soft! Methinks I scent the morning air.

---

[1] **spheres:** the circles in which the planets and stars were supposed to move. [2] **knotted . . . combined:** the hair that lies together in a mass. [3] **particular:** individual. [4] **an:** on. [5] **porpentine:** porcupine. [6] **eternal blazon:** description of eternity. [7] **in . . . best:** i.e., murder is foul even when there is a good excuse. [8] **fat:** thick, slimy, motionless. [9] **in ease:** undisturbed. [10] **Lethe wharf:** the bank of Lethe, the river of forgetfulness in the underworld. [11] **forged process:** false account. [12] **lewdness . . . Heaven:** though wooed by Lust disguised as an angel. [13] **state itself:** gorge.

Brief let me be. Sleeping within my orchard,
My custom always of the afternoon,
Upon my secure hour[14] thy uncle stole
With juice of cursèd hebenon[15] in a vial,
And in the porches[16] of my ears did pour
The leperous distillment,[17] whose effect
Holds such an enmity with blood of man
That swift as quicksilver it courses through
The natural gates and alleys of the body,
And with a sudden vigor it doth posset[18]
And curd, like eager[19] droppings into milk,
The thin and wholesome blood. So did it mine,
And a most instant tetter barked[20] about,
Most lazarlike,[21] with vile and loathsome crust,
All my smooth body.
Thus was I, sleeping, by a brother's hand
Of life, of crown, of Queen, at once dispatched—
Cut off even in the blossoms of my sin,[22]
Unhouseled, disappointed, unaneled,[23]
No reckoning made, but sent to my account
With all my imperfections on my head.
Oh, horrible! Oh, horrible, most horrible!
If thou hast nature[24] in thee, bear it not.
Let not the royal bed of Denmark be
A couch for luxury[25] and damned incest.
But, howsoever thou pursuest this act,
Taint not thy mind, nor let thy soul contrive
Against thy mother aught. Leave her to Heaven
And to those thorns that in her bosom lodge
To prick and sting her. Fare thee well at once!
Thy glowworm shows the matin[26] to be near,
And 'gins to pale his uneffectual[27] fire.
Adieu, adieu, adieu! Remember me.
(Exit.)

Hamlet: O all you host of Heaven! O earth! What else?
And shall I couple Hell? Oh, fie! Hold, hold, my heart,
And you, my sinews, grow not instant old
But bear me stiffly up. Remember thee!
Aye, thou poor ghost, while memory holds a seat
In this distracted globe.[28] Remember thee!
Yea, from the table[29] of my memory
I'll wipe away all trivial fond[30] recórds,
All saws[31] of books, all forms,[32] all pressures[33] past,

---

[14] **secure hour:** time of relaxation. [15] **hebenon:** probably henbane, a poisonous plant. [16] **porches:** entrances. [17] **leperous distillment:** distillation causing leprosy. [18] **posset:** curdle. [19] **eager:** acid. [20] **tetter barked:** eruption formed a bark. [21] **lazarlike:** like leprosy. [22] **Cut . . . sin:** cut off in a state of sin and so in danger of damnation. [23] **Unhouseled . . . unaneled:** without receiving the sacrament, not properly prepared, unanointed—without extreme unction. [24] **nature:** natural feelings. [25] **luxury:** lust. [26] **matin:** morning. [27] **uneffectual:** made ineffectual by daylight. [28] **globe:** i.e., head. [29] **table:** notebook. Intellectual young men carried notebooks in which they recorded good sayings and notable observations. [30] **fond:** trifling. [31] **saws:** wise sayings. [32] **forms:** images in the mind. [33] **pressures:** impressions.

That youth and observation copied there,
And thy commandment all alone shall live
Within the book and volume of my brain,
Unmixed with baser matter. Yes, by Heaven!
O most pernicious woman!
O villain, villain, smiling, damnèd villain!
My tables—meet it is I set it down
(Writing.) That one may smile, and smile, and be a villain.
At least I'm sure it may be so in Denmark.
So, Uncle, there you are. Now to my word.[34]
It is "Adieu, adieu! Remember me."
I have sworn 't.

Horatio & Marcellus: *(Within.)* My lord, my lord!

(Enter Horatio and Marcellus.)

Marcellus: Lord Hamlet!
Horatio: Heaven secure him!
Hamlet: So be it!
Marcellus: Illo, ho, ho,[35] my lord!
Hamlet: Hillo, ho, ho, boy! Come, bird, come.
Marcellus: How is 't, my noble lord?
Horatio: What news, my lord?
Hamlet: Oh, wonderful!
Horatio: Good my lord, tell it.
Hamlet: No, you will reveal it.
Horatio: Not I, my lord, by Heaven.
Marcellus: Nor I, my lord.
Hamlet: How say you, then, would heart of man once think it?
But you'll be secret?
Horatio & Marcellus: Aye, by Heaven, my lord.
Hamlet: There's ne'er a villain dwelling in all Denmark
But he's an arrant[36] knave.
Horatio: There needs no ghost, my lord, come from the grave
To tell us this.
Hamlet: Why, right, you are i' the right.
And so, without more circumstance[37] at all,
I hold it fit that we shake hands and part—
You as your business and desire shall point you,
For every man hath business and desire,
Such as it is. And for my own poor part,
Look you, I'll go pray.
Horatio: These are but wild and whirling[38] words, my lord.
Hamlet: I'm sorry they offend you, heartily,
Yes, faith, heartily.
Horatio: There's no offense, my lord.
Hamlet: Yes, by Saint Patrick, but there is, Horatio,
And much offense too. Touching this vision here,
It is an honest[39] ghost, that let me tell you.
For your desire to know what is between us,
O'ermaster 't as you may. And now, good friends,
As you are friends, scholars, and soldiers,
Give me one poor request.
Horatio: What is 't, my lord? We will.
Hamlet: Never make known what you have seen tonight.
Horatio & Marcellus: My lord, we will not.
Hamlet: Nay, but swear 't.
Horatio: In faith,
My lord, not I.
Marcellus: Nor I, my lord, in faith.
Hamlet: Upon my sword.

[34] **word:** cue. [35] **Illo . . . ho:** the falconer's cry to recall the hawk. [36] **arrant:** out-and-out. [37] **circumstance:** ceremony. [38] **whirling:** violent. [39] **honest:** true.

Marcellus: We have sworn, my lord, already.
Hamlet: Indeed, upon my sword,[40] indeed.
Ghost: *(Beneath.)* Swear.
Hamlet: Ah, ha, boy! Say'st thou so? Art thou there, truepenny?[41]
Come on. You hear this fellow in the cellarage.
Consent to swear.
Horatio: Propose the oath, my lord.
Hamlet: Never to speak of this that you have seen,
Swear by my sword.
Ghost: *(Beneath.)* Swear.
Hamlet: *Hic et ubique?*[42] Then we'll shift our ground.
Come hither, gentlemen,
And lay your hands again upon my sword.
Never to speak of this that you have heard,
Swear by my sword.
Ghost: *(Beneath.)* Swear.
Hamlet: Well said, old mole! Canst work i' the earth so fast?
A worthy pioner![43] Once more remove,[44] good friends.
Horatio: Oh, day and night, but this is wondrous strange!
Hamlet: And therefore as a stranger give it welcome.
There are more things in Heaven and earth, Horatio,
Than are dreamt of in your philosophy.
But come,
Here, as before, never, so help you mercy,
How strange or odd soe'er I bear myself,
As I perchance hereafter shall think meet
To put an antic disposition[45] on,
That you, at such times seeing me, never shall,
With arms encumbered[46] thus, or this headshake,
Or by pronouncing of some doubtful phrase,
As "Well, well, we know," or "We could an if we would,"
Or "If we list to speak," or "There be, an if they might,"
Or such ambiguous giving out, to note
That you know aught of me. This not to do,
So grace and mercy at your most need help you,
Swear.
Ghost: *(Beneath.)* Swear.
Hamlet: Rest, rest, perturbèd spirit!
(They swear.) So, gentlemen,
With all my love I do commend me to you.
And what so poor a man as Hamlet is
May do to express his love and friending[47] to you,
God willing, shall not lack. Let us go in together.
And still your fingers on your lips, I pray.
The time is out of joint. Oh, cursèd spite
That ever I was born to set it right!
Nay, come, let's go together. *(Exeunt.)*

Act II

Scene I. A room in Polonius's house.

(Enter Polonius and Reynaldo.)

Polonius: Give him this money and these notes, Reynaldo.
Reynaldo: I will, my lord.
Polonius: You shall do marvelous wisely, good Reynaldo.
Before you visit him, to make inquire
Of his behavior.
Reynaldo: My lord, I did intend it.

---

[40] **upon . . . sword:** on the cross made by the hilt of the sword; but for soldiers the sword itself was a sacred object. [41] **truepenny:** old boy. [42] **Hic et ubique:** here and everywhere. [43] **pioner:** miner. [44] **remove:** move. [45] **antic disposition:** mad behavior. [46] **encumbered:** folded. [47] **friending:** friendship.

Polonius: Marry, well said, very well said. Look you, sir,
Inquire me first what Danskers[1] are in Paris,
And how, and who, what means,[2] and where they keep,[3]
What company, at what expense, and finding
By this encompassment and drift of question[4]
That they do know my son, come you more nearer
Than your particular demands will touch it.[5]
Take you, as 'twere, some distant knowledge of him,
As thus, "I know his father and his friends,
And in part him." Do you mark this, Reynaldo?

Reynaldo: Aye, very well, my lord.

Polonius: "And in part him, but," you may say, "not well.
But if 't be he I mean, he's very wild,
Addicted so and so"—and there put on him
What forgeries[6] you please. Marry, none so rank[7]
As may dishonor him, take heed of that,
But, sir, such wanton, wild, and usual slips
As are companions noted and most known
To youth and liberty.

Reynaldo: As gaming, my lord.

Polonius: Aye, or drinking, fencing,[8] swearing, quarreling,
Drabbing.[9] You may go so far.

Reynaldo: My lord, that would dishonor him.

Polonius: Faith, no, as you may season[10] it in the charge.
You must not put another scandal on him,
That he is open to incontinency.[11]
That's not my meaning. But breathe his faults so quaintly[12]
That they may seem the taints of liberty,
The flash and outbreak of a fiery mind,
A savageness in unreclaimèd[13] blood,
Of general assault.[14]

Reynaldo: But, my good lord—

Polonius: Wherefore should you do this?

Reynaldo: Aye, my lord,
I would know that.

Polonius: Marry, sir, here's my drift,[15]
And I believe it is a fetch of warrant.[16]
You laying these slight sullies[17] on my son,
As 'twere a thing a little soiled i' the working,
Mark you,
Your party in converse, him you would sound,
Having ever seen[18] in the prenominate[19] crimes
The youth you breathe of guilty, be assured
He closes with you in this consequence[20]—
"Good sir," or so, or "friend," or "gentleman,"

[1] **Danskers:** Danes. [2] **what means:** what their income is. [3] **keep:** live. [4] **encompassment . . . question:** roundabout method of questioning. [5] **your . . . it:** i.e., you won't get at the truth by straight questions. [6] **forgeries:** inventions. [7] **rank:** gross. [8] **fencing:** A young man who haunted fencing schools would be regarded as quarrelsome and likely to belong to the sporting set. [9] **Drabbing:** whoring. [10] **season:** qualify. [11] **open . . . incontinency:** So long as Laertes does his drabbing inconspicuously Polonius would not be disturbed. [12] **quaintly:** skillfully. [13] **unreclaimed:** naturally wild. [14] **Of . . . assault:** common to all men. [15] **drift:** intention. [16] **fetch . . . warrant:** trick warranted to work. [17] **sullies:** blemishes. [18] **Having . . . seen:** if ever he has seen. [19] **prenominate:** aforementioned. [20] **closes . . . consequence:** follows up with this reply.

According to the phrase or the addition[21]
Of man and country.

Reynaldo: Very good, my lord.

Polonius: And then, sir, does he this—he does—What was I about to say? By the mass, I was about to say something. Where did I leave?

Reynaldo: At "closes in the consequence," or "friend or so," and "gentleman."

Polonius: At "closes in the consequence," aye, marry,
He closes with you thus: "I know the gentleman.
I saw him yesterday, or t'other day,
Or then, or then, with such, or such, and, as you say,
There was a' gaming, there o'ertook in 's rouse,
There falling out at tennis."[22] Or perchance,
"I saw him enter such a house of sale,"
Videlicet,[23] a brothel, or so forth.
See you now,
Your bait of falsehood takes this carp of truth.
And thus do we of wisdom and of reach,[24]
With windlasses[25] and with assays of bias,[26]
By indirections find directions out.[27]
So, by my former lecture and advice,
Shall you my son. You have me, have you not?

Reynaldo: My lord, I have.

Polonius: God be wi' ye, fare ye well.

Reynaldo: Good my lord!

Polonius: Observe his inclination in[28] yourself.

Reynaldo: I shall, my lord.

Polonius: And let him ply his music.

Reynaldo: Well, my lord.

Polonius: Farewell! *(Exit Reynaldo.)*
(Enter Ophelia.) How now, Ophelia! What's the matter?

Ophelia: Oh, my lord, my lord, I have been so affrighted!

Polonius: With what, i' the name of God?

Ophelia: My lord, as I was sewing in my closet,[29]
Lord Hamlet, with his doublet[30] all unbraced,
No hat upon his head, his stockings fouled,
Ungartered and down-gyved[31] to his ankle,
Pale as his shirt, his knees knocking each other,
And with a look so piteous in purport
As if he had been loosèd out of Hell
To speak of horrors, he comes before me.

Polonius: Mad for thy love?

Ophelia: My lord, I do not know,
But truly I do fear it.

Polonius: What said he?

Ophelia: He took me by the wrist and held me hard.
Then goes he to the length of all his arm,
And with his other hand thus o'er his brow,
He falls to such perusal of my face
As he would draw it. Long stayed he so.
At last, a little shaking of mine arm,
And thrice his head thus waving up and down,
He raised a sigh so piteous and profound

[21] **addition:** title. [22] **tennis:** Visitors to France were much impressed by the enthusiasm of all classes of Frenchmen for tennis, which in England was mainly a courtier's game. [23] **Videlicet:** namely, "viz." [24] **wisdom . . . reach:** of far-reaching wisdom. [25] **windlasses:** roundabout methods. [26] **assays of bias:** making our bowl take a curved course. [27] **indirections . . . out:** by indirect means come at the direct truth. [28] **in:** for. [29] **closet:** private room. [30] **doublet:** the short close-fitting coat which was braced to the hose by laces. When a man was relaxing or careless of appearance, he *unbraced,* as a modern man takes off his coat or unbuttons his waistcoat. [31] **down-gyved:** hanging around his ankles like fetters.

As it did seem to shatter all his bulk
And end his being. That done, he lets me go.
And with his head over his shoulder turned,
He seemed to find his way without his eyes;
For out o' doors he went without their helps,
And to the last bended their light on me.

Polonius: Come, go with me. I will go seek the King.
This is the very ecstasy[32] of love,
Whose violent property fordoes[33] itself
And leads the will to desperate undertakings
As oft as any passion under heaven
That does afflict our natures. I am sorry.
What, have you given him any hard words of late?

Ophelia: No, my good lord, but, as you did command,
I did repel his letters and denied
His access to me.

Polonius: That hath made him mad.
I am sorry that with better heed and judgment
I had not quoted[34] him. I feared he did but trifle
And meant to wreck thee, but beshrew[35] my jealousy!
By Heaven, it is as proper[36] to our age
To cast beyond ourselves[37] in our opinions
As it is common for the younger sort
To lack discretion. Come, go we to the King.
This must be known, which, being kept close, might move
More grief to hide than hate to utter love.[38]
Come. *(Exeunt.)*

Scene II. A room in the castle.

(Flourish. Enter King, Queen, Rosencrantz, Guildenstern, and Attendants.)

King: Welcome, dear Rosencrantz and Guildenstern!
Moreover[1] that we much did long to see you,
The need we have to use you did provoke
Our hasty sending. Something have you heard
Of Hamlet's transformation—so call it,
Sith[2] nor the exterior nor the inward man
Resembles that it was. What it should be,
More than his father's death, that thus hath put him
So much from the understanding of himself
I cannot dream of. I entreat you both
That, being of so young days brought up with him
And sith so neighbored to his youth and havior[3]
That you vouchsafe your rest[4] here in our Court
Some little time, so by your companies
To draw him on to pleasures, and to gather
So much as from occasion you may glean,
Whether aught to us unknown afflicts him thus
That opened lies within our remedy.[5]

[32] **ecstasy:** frenzy. [33] **property fordoes:** natural quality destroys. [34] **quoted:** observed carefully. [35] **beshrew:** a plague on. [36] **proper:** natural. [37] **cast . . . ourselves:** be too clever. [38] **which . . . love:** by being kept secret it may cause more sorrow than it will cause anger by being revealed; i.e., the King and Queen may be angry at the thought of the Prince's marrying beneath his proper rank.
[1] **Moreover:** in addition to the fact that. [2] **Sith:** since. [3] **neighbored . . . havior:** so near to his youthful manner of living. [4] **vouchsafe . . . rest:** consent to stay. [5] **opened . . . remedy:** if revealed, might be put right by us.

Queen: Good gentlemen, he hath much talked of you,
And sure I am two men there art not living
To whom he more adheres.[6] If it will please you
To show us so much gentry[7] and goodwill
As to expend your time with us a while
For the supply and profit of our hope,[8]
Your visitation shall receive such thanks
As fits a king's remembrance.

Rosencrantz: Both your Majesties
Might, by the sovereign power you have of us,
Put your dread pleasures more into command
Than to entreaty.

Guildenstern: But we both obey,
And here give up ourselves, in the full bent[9]
To lay our service freely at your feet,
To be commanded.

King: Thanks, Rosencrantz and gentle Guildenstern.

Queen: Thanks, Guildenstern and gentle Rosencrantz.
And I beseech you instantly to visit
My too-much-changèd son. Go, some of you,
And bring these gentlemen where Hamlet is.

Guildenstern: Heavens make our presence and our practices
Pleasant and helpful to him!

Queen: Aye, amen!
(Exeunt Rosencrantz, Guildenstern, and some Attendants.)

(Enter Polonius.)

Polonius: The ambassadors from Norway, my good lord,
Are joyfully returned.

King: Thou still[10] hast been the father of good news.

Polonius: Have I, my lord? I assure my good liege
I hold my duty as I hold my soul,
Both to my God and to my gracious King.
And I do think, or else this brain of mine
Hunts not the trail of policy so sure
As it hath used to do,[11] that I have found
The very cause of Hamlet's lunacy.

King: Oh, speak of that. That do I long to hear.

Polonius: Give first admittance to the ambassadors.
My news shall be the fruit[12] to that great feast.

King: Thyself do grace[13] to them and bring them in. *(Exit Polonius.)*
He tells me, my dear Gertrude, he hath found
The head and source of all your son's distemper.[14]

Queen: I doubt it is no other but the main,[15]
His father's death and our o'erhasty marriage.

King: Well, we shall sift him.

(Re-enter Polonius, with Voltimand and Cornelius.)

Welcome, my good friends!
Say, Voltimand, what from our brother Norway?

Voltimand: Most fair return of greetings and desires.
Upon our first,[16] he sent out to suppress
His nephew's levies, which to him appeared
To be a preparation 'gainst the Polack,

---

[6] **To . . . adheres:** whom he regards more highly. [7] **gentry:** courtesy. [8] **supply . . . hope:** to bring a profitable conclusion to our hope. [9] **in . . . bent:** stretched to our uttermost. [10] **still:** always. [11] **Hunts . . . do:** is not so good at following the scent of political events as it used to be. [12] **fruit:** the dessert, which comes at the end of the feast. [13] **do grace:** honor; i.e., by escorting them into the royal presence. [14] **distemper:** mental disturbance. [15] **main:** principal cause. [16] **first:** i.e., audience.

But better looked into, he truly found
It was against your Highness, whereat, grieved
That so his sickness, age, and impotence
Was falsely borne in hand,[17] sends out arrests
On Fortinbras; which he, in brief, obeys,
Receives rebuke from Norway, and in fine[18]
Makes vow before his uncle never more
To give the assay of arms[19] against your Majesty.
Whereon old Norway, overcome with joy,
Gives him three thousand crowns in annual fee
And his commission to employ those soldiers,
So levied as before, against the Polack.
With an entreaty, herein further shown,

(Giving a paper.)

That it might please you to give quiet pass[20]
Through your dominions for this enterprise,
On such regards of safety and allowance[21]
As therein are set down.

King: It likes[22] us well,
And at our more considered time we'll read,
Answer, and think upon this business.
Meantime we thank you for your well-took labor.
Go to your rest. At night we'll feast together.
Most welcome home!

(Exeunt Voltimand and Cornelius.)

Polonius: This business is well ended.
My liege, and madam, to expostulate[23]
What majesty should be, what duty is,
Why day is day, night night, and time is time,
Were nothing but to waste night, day, and time.
Therefore, since brevity is the soul of wit
And tediousness the limbs and outward flourishes,[24]
I will be brief. Your noble son is mad.
Mad call I it, for to define true madness,
What is 't but to be nothing else but mad?
But let that go.

Queen: More matter, with less art.[25]

Polonius: Madam, I swear I use no art at all.
That he is mad, 'tis true. 'Tis true 'tis pity,
And pity 'tis 'tis true—a foolish figure,[26]
But farewell it, for I will use no art.
Mad let us grant him, then. And now remains
That we find out the cause of this effect,
Or rather say the cause of this defect,
For this effect defective comes by cause.
Thus it remains and the remainder thus.
Perpend.[27]
I have a daughter—have while she is mine—
Who in her duty and obedience, mark,
Hath given me this. Now gather and surmise.[28]

---

[17] **borne in hand:** imposed upon. [18] **in fine:** in the end. [19] **give . . . arms:** make an attack. [20] **quiet pass:** unmolested passage. [21] **regards . . . allowance:** safeguard and conditions. [22] **likes:** pleases. [23] **expostulate:** indulge in an academic discussion. [24] **flourishes:** ornaments. [25] **art:** ornament. [26] **figure:** i.e., a figure of speech. [27] **Perpend:** note carefully. [28] **surmise:** guess the meaning.

(Reads.)

"To the celestial, and my soul's idol, the most beautified[29] Ophelia—"
That's an ill phrase, a vile phrase, "beautified" is a vile phrase. But you shall hear. Thus: *(Reads.)*
"In her excellent white bosom, these," and so forth.

Queen: Came this from Hamlet to her?

Polonius: Good madam, stay awhile, I will be faithful.
(Reads.) "Doubt thou the stars are fire,
Doubt that the sun doth move,
Doubt truth to be a liar,
But never doubt I love.
"O dear Ophelia, I am ill at these numbers,[30] I
have not art to reckon my groans, but that I love thee
best, O most best, believe it. Adieu.
"Thine evermore, most dear lady, whilst this
machine[31] is to him, Hamlet."
This in obedience hath my daughter shown me,
And more above, hath his solicitings,
As they fell out by time, by means and place,
All given to mine ear.

King: But how hath she
Received his love?

Polonius: What do you think of me?

King: As of a man faithful and honorable.

Polonius: I would fain prove so. But what might you think,
When I had seen this hot love on the wing—
As I perceived it, I must tell you that,
Before my daughter told me—what might you
Or my dear Majesty your Queen here think
If I had played the desk or table book,[32]
Or given my heart awinking, mute and dumb,
Or looked upon this love with idle sight—
What might you think? No, I went round[33] to work,
And my young mistress thus I did bespeak:[34]
"Lord Hamlet is a Prince, out of thy star.[35]
This must not be." And then I prescripts[36] gave her
That she should lock herself from his resort,
Admit no messengers, receive no tokens.
Which done, she took the fruits of my advice.
And he, repulsèd, a short tale to make,
Fell into a sadness, then into a fast,
Thence to a watch, thence into a weakness,
Thence to a lightness,[37] and by this declension[38]
Into the madness wherein now he raves
And all we mourn for.

King: Do you think this?

Queen: It may be, very like.

Polonius: Hath there been such a time, I'd fain know that,
That I have positively said "'Tis so"
When it proved otherwise?

King: Not that I know.

Polonius: *(Pointing to his head and shoulder.)* Take this from this, if this be otherwise.

---

[29] **beautified:** beautiful. [30] **numbers:** verses. [31] **machine:** i.e., body, an affected phrase. [32] **desk . . . book:** i.e., acted as silent go-between (desks and books being natural post offices for a love letter), or been a recipient of secrets but took no action (as desks and notebooks are the natural but inanimate place for keeping secrets). [33] **round:** straight. [34] **bespeak:** address. [35] **out . . . star:** above your destiny. [36] **prescripts:** instructions. [37] **Fell . . . lightness:** Hamlet's case history, according to Polonius, develops by stages—melancholy, loss of appetite, sleeplessness, physical weakness, mental instability, and finally madness. [38] **declension:** decline.

If circumstances lead me, I will find
Where truth is hid, though it were hid indeed
Within the center.[39]

King: How may we try it further?

Polonius: You know sometimes he walks four hours together.
Here in the lobby.

Queen: So he does indeed.

Polonius: At such a time I'll loose[40] my daughter to him.
Be you and I behind an arras[41] then.
Mark the encounter. If he love her not,
And be not from his reason fall'n thereon,
Let me be no assistant for a state,
But keep a farm and carters.[42]

King: We will try it.

Queen: But look where sadly the poor wretch comes reading.

Polonius: Away, I do beseech you, both away.
I'll board[43] him presently. *(Exeunt King, Queen, and Attendants.)*

(Enter Hamlet, reading.) Oh, give me leave, How does my good Lord Hamlet?

Hamlet: Well, God-a-mercy.

Polonius: Do you know me, my lord?

Hamlet: Excellent well. You are a fishmonger.[44]

Polonius: Not I, my lord.

Hamlet: Then I would you were so honest a man.

Polonius: Honest, my lord!

Hamlet: Aye, sir, to be honest, as this world goes, is to be one man picked out of ten thousand.

Polonius: That's very true, my lord.

Hamlet: For if the sun breed maggots[45] in a dead dog, being a god[46] kissing carrion[47]—Have you a daughter?

Polonius: I have, my lord.

Hamlet: Let her not walk i' the sun. Conception is a blessing, but not as your daughter may conceive—friend, look to 't.

Polonius: *(Aside.)* How say you by that? Still harping on my daughter. Yet he knew me not at first, he said I was a fishmonger. He is far gone, far gone. And truly in my youth I suffered much extremity for love, very near this. I'll speak to him again.—What do you read, my lord?

Hamlet: Words, words, words.

Polonius: What is the matter, my lord?

Hamlet: Between who?

Polonius: I mean the matter that you read, my lord.

Hamlet: Slanders, sir. For the satirical rogue says here that old men have gray beards, that their faces are wrinkled, their eyes purging thick amber and plum-tree gum, and that they have a plentiful lack of wit, together with most weak hams.[48] All which, sir, though I most powerfully and potently believe, yet I hold it not honesty to have it thus set down; for yourself, sir, should be old as I am if like a crab you could go backward.

Polonius: *(Aside.)* Though this be madness, yet there is method[49] in 't.—Will you walk out of the air, my lord?

Hamlet: Into my grave.

Polonius: Indeed, that's out of the air. *(Aside.)* How pregnant[50] sometimes his replies are! A happiness[51] that often

---

[39] **center:** the very center of the earth. [40] **loose:** turn loose. [41] **arras:** tapestry hanging. [42] **keep . . . carters:** i.e., turn country squire—like Justice Shallow. [43] **board:** accost. [44] **fishmonger:** Hamlet is now in his "antic disposition," enjoying himself by fooling Polonius. [45] **sun . . . maggots:** a general belief. [46] **god:** Q_2 and F_1 read "good." [47] **carrion:** flesh. [48] **hams:** knee joints. [49] **method:** order, sense. [50] **pregnant:** apt, meaningful. [51] **happiness:** good turn of phrase.

madness hits on, which reason and sanity could not so prosperously be delivered of. I will leave him, and suddenly contrive the means of meeting between him and my daughter.—My honorable lord, I will most humbly take my leave of you.

Hamlet: You cannot, sir, take from me anything that I will more willingly part withal—except my life, except my life, except my life.

Polonius: Fare you well, my lord.

Hamlet: These tedious old fools!

(Enter Rosencrantz and Guildenstern.)

Polonius: You go to seek the Lord Hamlet. There he is.

Rosencrantz: *(To Polonius.)* God save you, sir!

(Exit Polonius.)

Guildenstern: My honored lord!

Rosencrantz: My most dear lord!

Hamlet: My excellent good friends![52] How dost thou, Guildenstern? Ah, Rosencrantz! Good lads, how do you both?

Rosencrantz: As the indifferent[53] children of the earth.

Guildenstern: Happy in that we are not overhappy. On Fortune's cap we are not the very button.[54]

Hamlet: Nor the soles of her shoe?

Rosencrantz: Neither, my lord.

Hamlet: Then you live about her waist, or in the middle of her favors?

Guildenstern: Faith, her privates[55] we.

Hamlet: In the secret parts of Fortune? Oh, most true, she is a strumpet. What's the news?

Rosencrantz: None, my lord, but that the world's grown honest.

Hamlet: Then is Doomsday near. But your news is not true. Let me question more in particular. What have you, my good friends, deserved at the hands of Fortune, that she sends you to prison hither?

Guildenstern: Prison, my lord!

Hamlet: Denmark's a prison.

Rosencrantz: Then is the world one.

Hamlet: A goodly one, in which there are many confines,[56] wards,[57] and dungeons, Denmark being one o' the worst.

Rosencrantz: We think not so, my lord.

Hamlet: Why, then 'tis none to you, for there is nothing either good or bad but thinking makes it so. To me it is a prison.

Rosencrantz: Why, then your ambition[58] makes it one. 'Tis too narrow for your mind.

Hamlet: Oh, God, I could be bounded in a nutshell and count myself a king of infinite space were it not that I have bad dreams.

Guildenstern: Which dreams indeed are ambition, for the very substance of the ambitious[59] is merely the shadow of a dream.

Hamlet: A dream itself is but a shadow.

Rosencrantz: Truly, and I hold ambition of so airy and light a quality that it is but a shadow's shadow.

Hamlet: Then are our beggars bodies, and our monarchs and outstretched heroes the beggars' shadows.[60] Shall we to the Court? For, by my fay,[61] I cannot reason.[62]

---

[52] **My . . . friends:** As soon as Polonius has gone, Hamlet drops his assumed madness and greets Rosencrantz and Guildenstern naturally. [53] **indifferent:** neither too great nor too little. [54] **button:** i.e., at the top. [55] **privates:** with a pun on "private parts" and "private," not concerned with politics. [56] **confines:** places of confinement. [57] **wards:** cells. [58] **your ambition:** Rosencrantz is feeling after one possible cause of Hamlet's melancholy—thwarted ambition. [59] **substance . . . ambitious:** that on which an ambitious man feeds his fancies. [60] **Then . . . shadows:** i.e., by your reasoning beggars are the only men of substance, for kings and heroes are by nature ambitious and therefore "the shadows of a dream." **outstretched:** of exaggerated reputation. [61] **fay:** faith. [62] **reason:** argue.

Rosencrantz & Guildenstern: We'll wait upon you.[63]

Hamlet: No such matter. I will not sort[64] you with the rest of my servants, for, to speak to you like an honest man, I am most dreadfully attended.[65] But in the beaten way of friendship, what make you at Elsinore?

Rosencrantz: To visit you, my lord, no other occasion.

Hamlet: Beggar that I am, I am even poor in thanks, but I thank you. And sure, dear friends, my thanks are too dear a halfpenny.[66] Were you not sent for? Is it your own inclining? Is it a free visitation?[67] Come, deal justly with me. Come, come. Nay, speak.

Guildenstern: What should we say, my lord?

Hamlet: Why, anything, but to the purpose.[68] You were sent for, and there is a kind of confession in your looks which your modesties have not craft enough to color.[69] I know the good King and Queen have sent for you.

Rosencrantz: To what end, my lord?

Hamlet: That you must teach me. But let me conjure[70] you, by the rights of our fellowship,[71] by the consonancy[72] of our youth, by the obligation of our ever preserved love, and by what more dear a better proposer could charge you withal, be even[73] and direct with me, whether you were sent for, or no.

Rosencrantz: *(Aside to Guildenstern.)* What say you?

Hamlet: *(Aside.)* Nay, then, I have an eye of you.—If you love me, hold not off.

Guildenstern: My lord, we were sent for.

Hamlet: I will tell you why. So shall my anticipation prevent your discovery, and your secrecy to the King and Queen molt no feather.[74] I have of late—but wherefore I know not—lost all my mirth, forgone all custom of exercises, and indeed it goes so heavily with my disposition that this goodly frame the earth seems to me a sterile promontory. This most excellent canopy,[75] the air, look you, this brave o'erhanging firmament,[76] this majestical roof fretted[77] with golden fire—why, it appears no other thing to me than a foul and pestilent congregation of vapors. What a piece of work is a man! How noble in reason! How infinite in faculty![78] In form and moving[79] how express[80] and admirable! In action how like an angel! In apprehension how like a god! The beauty of the world! The paragon of animals! And yet, to me, what is this quintessence[81] of dust? Man delights not me—no, nor woman neither, though by your smiling you seem to say so.

Rosencrantz: My lord, there was no such stuff in my thoughts.

Hamlet: Why did you laugh, then, when I said "Man delights not me"?

Rosencrantz: To think, my lord, if you delight not in man, what lenten entertainment[82] the players shall receive from you. We coted[83] them on the way, and hither are they coming to offer you service.

Hamlet: He that plays the King shall be welcome, His Majesty shall have tribute

---

[63] **wait . . . you:** be your servants. [64] **sort:** class. [65] **dreadfully attended:** my attendants are a poor crowd. [66] **too . . . halfpenny:** not worth a halfpenny. [67] **free visitation:** voluntary visit. [68] **anything . . . purpose:** anything so long as it is not true. [69] **color:** conceal. [70] **conjure:** make solemn appeal to. [71] **fellowship:** comradeship. [72] **consonancy:** concord. [73] **even:** straight. [74] **So . . . feather:** i.e., so by my telling you first you will not be obliged to betray the secrets of the King. **prevent:** forestall. **molt no feather:** be undisturbed. [75] **canopy:** covering. [76] **firmament:** sky. [77] **fretted:** ornamented. [78] **faculty:** power of the mind. [79] **moving:** movement. [80] **express:** exact. [81] **quintessence:** perfection; the fifth essence, which would be left if the four elements were taken away. [82] **lenten entertainment:** meager welcome. [83] **coted:** overtook.

of me. The adventurous knight shall use his foil and target,[84] the lover shall not sigh gratis, the humorous man[85] shall end his part in peace, the clown shall make those laugh whose lungs are tickle o' the sere,[86] and the lady shall say her mind freely or the blank verse shall halt[87] for 't. What players are they?

Rosencrantz: Even those you were wont to take such delight in, the tragedians of the city.

Hamlet: How chances it they travel? Their residence, both in reputation and profit, was better both ways.[88]

Rosencrantz: I[89] think their inhibition[90] comes by the means of the late innovation.[91]

Hamlet: Do they hold the same estimation they did when I was in the city? Are they so followed?

Rosencrantz: No, indeed are they not.

Hamlet: How comes it? Do they grow rusty?

Rosencrantz: Nay, their endeavor keeps in the wonted pace.[92] But there is, sir, an eyrie[93] of children, little eyases,[94] that cry out on the top of question[95] and are most tyrannically[96] clapped for 't. These are now the fashion, and so berattle[97] the common stages[98]—so they call them—that many wearing rapiers are afraid of goose quills[99] and dare scare come thither.

Hamlet: What, are they children? Who maintains 'em? How are they escoted?[100] Will they pursue the quality[101] no longer than they can sing? Will they not say afterward, if they should grow themselves to common players—as it is most like if their means are no better—their writers do them wrong to make them exclaim against their own succession?[102]

Rosencrantz: Faith, there has been much to-do on both sides, and the nation holds it no sin to tarre[103] them to controversy. There was for a while no money bid for argument[104] unless the poet and the player went to cuffs[105] in the question.

Hamlet: Is 't possible?

Guildenstern: Oh, there has been much throwing-about of brains.

Hamlet: Do the boys carry it away?

Rosencrantz: Aye, that they do, my lord, Hercules and his load[106] too.

Hamlet: It is not very strange, for my uncle is King of Denmark, and those that would make mows[107] at him while my father lived give twenty, forty, fifty, a hundred ducats apiece for his picture in little. 'Sblood,[108] there is something in this more than natural, if philosophy could find it out.

(Flourish of trumpets within.)

---

[84] **foil . . . target:** rapier and small shield. [85] **humorous man:** the man who specializes in character parts. [86] **are . . . sere:** explode at a touch. The *sere* is part of the trigger mechanism of a gun which if "ticklish" will go off at a touch. [87] **halt:** limp. [88] **Their . . . ways:** i.e., if they stayed in the city, it would bring them more profit and fame. [89] **I . . . too** (ll. 386–426: This reference to the stage war between the Children's Companies is one of the several topical references in *Hamlet.* [90] **inhibition:** formal prohibition. [91] **innovation:** riot. [92] **endeavor . . . pace:** they try as hard as ever. [93] **eyrie:** nest. [94] **eyases:** young hawks. [95] **cry . . . question:** either "cry in a shrill voice" or perhaps "cry out the latest detail of the dispute." [96] **tyrannically:** outrageously. [97] **berattle:** abuse. [98] **common stages:** the professional players. The boys acted in "private" playhouses. [99] **goose quills:** pens; i.e., of such as Ben Jonson. [100] **escoted:** paid. [101] **quality:** acting profession. [102] **exclaim . . . succession:** abuse the profession to which they will afterward belong. [103] **tarre:** urge on to fight; generally used of encouraging a dog. [104] **argument:** plot of a play. [105] **went to cuffs:** boxed each others' ears. [106] **Hercules . . . load:** Hercules carrying the globe on his shoulders was the sign of the Globe Playhouse. [107] **mows:** grimaces. [108] **'Sblood:** by God's blood.

Guildenstern: There are the players.

Hamlet: Gentlemen, you are welcome to Elsinore. Your hands. Come then. The appurtenance of welcome is fashion and ceremony.[109] Let me comply[110] with you in this garb,[111] lest my extent[112] to the players—which, I tell you, must show fairly outward—should more appear like entertainment[113] than yours. You are welcome. But my uncle-father and aunt-mother are deceived.

Guildenstern: In what, my dear lord?

Hamlet: I am but mad north-northwest.[114] When the wind is southerly,[115] I know a hawk from a handsaw.[116]

(Re-enter Polonius.)

Polonius: Well be with you, gentlemen!

Hamlet: Hark you, Guildenstern, and you too—at each ear a hearer. That great baby you see there is not yet out of his swaddling clouts.[117]

Rosencrantz: Happily he's the second time come to them, for they say an old man is twice a child.

Hamlet: I will prophesy he comes to tell me of the players, mark it. You say right, sir. O' Monday morning, 'twas so indeed.

Polonius: My lord, I have news to tell you.

Hamlet: My lord, I have news to tell you. When Roscius[118] was an actor in Rome—

Polonius: The actors are come hither, my lord.

Hamlet: Buzz, buzz![119]

Polonius: Upon my honor—

Hamlet: Then came each actor on his ass—

Polonius: The[120] best actors in the world, either for tragedy, comedy, history, pastoral, pastoral-comical, historical-pastoral, tragical-historical, tragical-comical-historical-pastoral, scene individable[121] or poem unlimited.[122] Seneca cannot be too heavy, nor Plautus[123] too light. For the law of writ[124] and the liberty,[125] these are the only men.

Hamlet: O Jephthah,[126] judge of Israel, what a treasure hadst thou!

Polonius: What a treasure had he, my lord?

Hamlet: Why,

"One[127] fair daughter, and no more,
The which he lovèd passing well."

Polonius: *(Aside.)* Still[128] on my daughter.

Hamlet: Am I not i' the right, old Jephthah?

Polonius: If you call me Jephthah, my lord, I have a daughter that I love passing well.

Hamlet: Nay, that follows not.

Polonius: What follows, then, my lord?

Hamlet: Why,

"As by lot, God wot,"[129]
and then you know,
"It came to pass, as most like it was—"

---

[109] **appurtenance . . . ceremony:** that which pertains to welcome is formal ceremony. [110] **comply:** use the formality of welcome; i.e., shake hands with you. [111] **garb:** fashion. [112] extent: outward behavior. [113] **entertainment:** welcome. [114] **north-northwest:** i.e., 327° (out of 360°) of the compass. [115] **wind is southerly:** The south wind was considered unhealthy. [116] **hawk . . . handsaw:** Either "handsaw" is a corruption of "heronshaw," heron, or a hawk is a tool like a pickax. The phrase means "I'm not so mad as you think." [117] **clouts:** clothes. [118] **Roscius:** the most famous of Roman actors. [119] **Buzz, buzz:** slang for "stale news." [120] **The . . . men:** Polonius reads out the accomplishments of the actors from the license which they have presented him. [121] **scene individable:** i.e., a play preserving the unities. [122] **poem unlimited:** i.e., a play that disregards the rules. [123] **Seneca . . . Plautus:** the Roman writers of tragedy and comedy with whose plays every educated man was familiar. [124] **law of writ:** the critical rules; i.e., classical plays. [125] **liberty:** plays freely written; i.e., "modern" drama. [126] **Jephthah:** The story of Jephthah is told in Judges, Chapter II. He vowed that if successful against the Ammonites he would sacrifice the first creature to meet him on his return, which was his daughter. [127] **One . . . was:** Quotations from a ballad of Jephthah. [128] **Still:** always. [129] **wot:** knows.

the first row[130] of the pious chanson[131] will show you more, for look where my abridgement[132] comes. *(Enter four or five Players.)* You are welcome, masters, welcome all. I am glad to see thee well. Welcome, good friends. Oh, my old friend![133] Why, thy face is valanced[134] since I saw thee last. Comest thou to beard[135] me in Denmark? What, my young lady[136] and mistress! By 'r Lady, your ladyship is nearer to Heaven than when I saw you last, by the altitude of a chopine.[137] Pray God your voice, like a piece of uncurrent gold, be not cracked within the ring.[138] Masters, you are all welcome. We'll e'en to 't like French falconers,[139] fly at anything we see. We'll have a speech straight. Come, give us a taste of your quality[140]—come, a passionate speech.

1. Player: What speech, my good lord?

Hamlet: I heard thee speak me a speech once, but it was never acted, or if it was, not above once; for the play, I remember, pleased not the million, 'twas caviar[141] to the general.[142] But it was—as I received it, and others, whose judgments in such matters cried in the top of mine[143]—an excellent play, well digested[144] in the scenes, set down with as much modesty[145] as cunning. I remember one said there were no sallets[146] in the lines to make the matter savory, nor no matter in the phrase that might indict the author of affection,[147] but called it an honest method, as wholesome as sweet, and by very much more handsome than fine.[148] One speech in it I chiefly loved. 'Twas Aeneas' tale to Dido,[149] and thereabout of it especially where he speaks of Priam's[150] slaughter. If it lives in your memory, begin at this line—let me see, let me see—

"The rugged Pyrrhus,[151] like th' Hyrcanian beast,[152]—"
It is not so. It begins with "Pyrrhus."
"The[153] rugged Pyrrhus, he whose sable[154] arms,
Black as his purpose, did the night resemble
When he lay couchèd in the ominous[155] horse,[156]
Hath now this dread and black complexion smeared

---

[130] **row:** line. [131] **pious chanson:** godly poem. [132] **abridgement:** entertainment. [133] **old friend:** i.e., the leading player. [134] **valanced:** bearded. A valance is a fringe hung round the sides and bottom of a bed. [135] **beard:** dare, with a pun on "valanced." [136] **young lady:** i.e., the boy who takes the woman's parts. [137] **chopine:** lady's shoe with thick cork sole. [138] **cracked . . . ring:** Before coins were milled on the rim they were liable to crack. When the crack reached the ring surrounding the device, the coin was no longer valid. [139] **French falconers:** They were famous for their skill in hawking. [140] **quality:** skill as an actor. [141] **caviar:** sturgeon's roe, a Russian delicacy not then appreciated (or known) by any but gourmets. [142] **general:** common herd. [143] **cried . . . mine:** surpassed mine. [144] **digested:** composed. [145] **modesty:** moderation. [146] **sallets:** tasty bits. [147] **phrase . . . affection:** nothing in the language which could charge the author with affectation. [148] **fine:** subtle. [149] **Aeneas' . . . Dido:** the story of the sack of Troy as told by Aeneas to Dido, Queen of Carthage. The original is in Virgil's *Aeneid.* A similar speech occurs in Marlowe's play *Dido, Queen of Carthage.* [150] Priam: the old King of Troy. [151] **Pyrrhus:** the son of Achilles, one of the Greeks concealed in the Wooden Horse. [152] Hyrcanian beast: the tiger. [153] **The . . . gods:** The speech may be from some lost play of *Dido* and *Aeneas,* but more likely it is Shakespeare's own invention. It is written in the heavy elaborate style still popular in the dramas of the Admiral's Men. The first player delivers it with excessive gesture and emotion. [154] **sable: black.** [155] ominous: fateful. [156] **horse:** the Wooden Horse by which a small Greek force was enabled to make a secret entry into Troy.

With heraldry[157] more dismal. Head to foot
Now is he total gules, horridly tricked
With blood of fathers, mothers, daughters, sons,
Baked and impasted[158] with the parching streets
That lend a tyrannous and a damnèd light
To their lord's murder. Roasted in wrath and fire,
And thus o'ersized with coagulate gore,[159]
With eyes like carbuncles, the hellish Pyrrhus
Old grandsire Priam seeks."
So proceed you.

Polonius: 'Fore God, my lord, well spoken, with good accent and good discretion.

1. Player: "Anon he finds him
Striking too short at Greeks. His antique sword,
Rebellious to his arm, lies where it falls,
Repugnant to command.[160] Unequal matched,
Pyrrhus at Priam drives, in rage strikes wide,
But with the whiff and wind of his fell sword
The unnerved father falls. Then senseless Ilium,[161]
Seeming to feel this blow, with flaming top
Stoops to his base,[162] and with a hideous crash
Takes prisoner Pyrrhus' ear. For lo! his sword,
Which was declining[163] on the milky[164] head
Of reverend Priam, seemed i' the air to stick.
So as a painted tyrant[165] Pyrrhus stood,
And like a neutral to his will and matter,[166]
Did nothing.
But as we often see, against[167] some storm
A silence in the heavens, the rack[168] stand still,
The bold winds speechless and the orb[169] below
As hush as death, anon the dreadful thunder
Doth rend the region[170]—so after Pyrrhus' pause
Arousèd vengeance sets him new awork.
And never did the Cyclops'[171] hammers fall
On Mars's armor, forged for proof eterne,[172]
With less remorse[173] than Pyrrhus' bleeding sword
Now falls on Priam.
Out, out, thou strumpet, Fortune! All you gods,
In general synod[174] take away her power,
Break all the spokes and fellies[175] from her wheel,

[157] **heraldry:** painting. The image of heraldic painting is kept up in *gules* (the heraldic term for red) and *tricked* (painted). [158] **impasted:** turned into a crust by the heat of the burning city. [159] **o'ersized . . . gore:** covered over with congealed blood. [160] **Repugnant to command:** refusing to be used. [161] **Ilium:** the citadel of Troy. [162] **stoops . . . base:** collapses. [163] **declining:** bending toward. [164] **milky:** milk-white. [165] **painted tyrant:** as in the painting of a tyrant. [166] **neutral . . . matter:** one midway (*neutral*) between his desire (*will*) and action (*matter*). [167] **against:** just before. [168] **rack:** the clouds in the upper air. [169] **orb:** world. [170] **region:** the country round. [171] **Cyclops':** of Titans, giants who aided Vulcan, the blacksmith god, to make armor for Mars, the war god. [172] **proof eterne:** everlasting protection. [173] **remorse:** pity. [174] **synod:** council. [175] **fellies:** the pieces forming the circumference of a wooden wheel.

And bowl the round nave[176] down the hill of Heaven
As low as to the fiends!"

Polonius: This is too long.

Hamlet: It shall to the barber's, with your beard. Prithee, say on. He's for a jig[177] or a tale of bawdry, or he sleeps. Say on. Come to Hecuba.

1. Player: "But who, oh, who had seen the mobled[178] Queen—"

Hamlet: "The mobled Queen"?

Polonius: That's good, "mobled Queen" is good.

1. Player: "Run barefoot up and down, threatening the flames
With bisson rheum,[179] a clout[180] upon that head
Where late the diadem stood, and for a robe,
About her lank and all o'erteemed[181] loins
A blanket, in the alarm of fear caught up.
Who this had seen, with tongue in venom steeped
'Gainst Fortune's state would treason have pronounced.[182]
But if the gods themselves did see her then,
When she saw Pyrrhus make malicious sport
In mincing with his sword her husband's limbs,
The instant burst of clamor that she made,
Unless things mortal move them not at all,
Would have made milch[183] the burning eyes of Heaven
And passion in the gods."

Polonius: Look whether he has not turned his color and has tears in 's eyes. Prithee, no more.

Hamlet: 'Tis well; I'll have thee speak out the rest of this soon. Good my lord, will you see the players well bestowed?[184] Do you hear, let them be well used, for they are the abstract and brief chronicles of the time.[185] After your death you were better have a bad epitaph than their ill report while you live.

Polonius: My lord, I will use them according to their desert.[186]

Hamlet: God's bodykins,[187] man, much better. Use every man after his desert and who shall 'scape whipping? Use them after your own honor and dignity. The less they deserve, the more merit is in your bounty. Take them in.

Polonius: Come, sirs.

Hamlet: Follow him, friends. We'll hear a play tomorrow. *(Exit Polonius with all the Players but the First.)* Dost thou hear me, old friend? Can you play *The Murder of Gonzago?*

1. Player: Aye, my lord.

Hamlet: We'll ha 't tomorrow night. You could, for a need, study a speech of some dozen or sixteen lines which I would set down and insert in 't, could you not?

1. Player: Aye, my lord.

Hamlet: Very well. Follow that lord, and look you mock him not. *(Exit First Player.)* My good friends, I'll leave you till night. You are welcome to Elsinore.

Rosencrantz: Good my lord!

Hamlet: Aye, so, God be wi' ye! *(Exeunt Rosencrantz and Guildenstern.)* Now I am alone.

---

[176] **nave:** center of the wheel. [177] **jig:** bawdy dance. [178] **mobled:** muffled. [179] **bisson rheum:** blinding moisture. [180] **clout:** rag. [181] **o'erteemed:** exhausted by bearing children; she had borne fifty-two. [182] **Who . . . pronounced:** anyone who had seen this sight would with bitter words have uttered treason against the tyranny of Fortune. [183] **milch:** milky, i.e., dripping moisture. [184] **bestowed:** housed. [185] **abstract . . . time:** they summarize and record the events of our time. Elizabethan players were often in trouble for too saucily commenting on their betters in plays dealing with history or contemporary events and persons. [186] **desert:** rank. [187] **God's bodykins:** by God's little body.

Oh, what a rogue and peasant slave am I!
Is it not monstrous that this player here,
But in a fiction, in a dream of passion,[188]
Could force his soul so to his own conceit[189]
That from her working[190] all his visage wanned,[191]
Tears in his eyes, distraction[192] in 's aspect,[193]
A broken voice, and his whole function[194] suiting
With forms to his conceit? And all for nothing!
For Hecuba!
What's Hecuba to him or he to Hecuba,
That he should weep for her? What would he do
Had he the motive and the cue for passion
That I have? He would drown the stage with tears
And cleave the general ear[195] with horrid speech,
Make mad the guilty and appal the free,[196]
Confound the ignorant, and amaze indeed
The very faculties of eyes and ears.
Yet I,
A dull and muddy-mettled[197] rascal, peak,[198]
Like John-a-dreams,[199] unpregnant of my cause,[200]
And can say nothing—no, not for a King
Upon whose property[201] and most dear life
A damned defeat[202] was made. Am I a coward?
Who[203] calls me villain? Breaks my pate across?
Plucks off my beard and blows it in my face?
Tweaks me by the nose? Gives me the lie i' the throat
As deep as to the lungs? Who does me this?
Ha!
'Swounds,[204] I should take it. For it cannot be
But I am pigeon-livered[205] and lack gall[206]
To make oppression bitter, or ere this
I should have fatted all the region kites
With this slave's offal.[207] Bloody, bawdy villain!
Remorseless, treacherous, lecherous, kindless[208] villain!
Oh, vengeance!
Why, what an ass am I! This is most brave,
That I, the son of a dear father murdered,
Prompted to my revenge by Heaven and Hell,
Must, like a whore, unpack my heart with words
And fall a-cursing like a very drab,[209]
A scullion![210]
Fie upon 't! Foh! About, my brain! Hum, I have heard

---

[188] **dream of passion:** imaginary emotion. [189] **conceit:** imagination. [190] **her working:** i.e., the effect of imagination. [191] **wanned:** went pale. [192] **distraction:** frenzy. [193] **aspect:** countenance. [194] **function:** behavior. [195] **general ear:** ears of the audience. [196] **free:** innocent. [197] **muddy-mettled:** made of mud, not iron. [198] **peak:** mope. [199] **John-a-dreams:** "Sleepy Sam." [200] **unpregnant . . . cause:** barren of plans for vengeance. [201] **property:** personality, life. [202] **defeat:** ruin. [203] **Who . . . this:** Hamlet runs through all the insults which provoked a resolute man to mortal combat. **pate:** head. **lie . . . throat:** the bitterest of insults. [204] **'Swounds:** by God's wounds. [205] **pigeon-livered:** "as gentle as a dove." [206] **gall:** spirit. [207] **I . . . offal:** before this I would have fed this slave's (i.e., the King's) guts to the kites. **fatted:** made fat. [208] **kindless:** unnatural. [209] **drab:** "moll." [210] **scullion:** the lowest of the kitchen servants.

That guilty creatures sitting at a play
Have by the very cunning of the scene
Been struck so to the soul that presently[211]
They have proclaimed their malefactions;[212]
For murder, though it have no tongue, will speak
With most miraculous organ. I'll have these players
Play something like the murder of my father
Before mine uncle. I'll observe his looks,
I'll tent[213] him to the quick. If he but blench,[214]
I know my course. The spirit that I have seen
May be the Devil, and the Devil hath power
To assume a pleasing shape. Yea, and perhaps
Out of my weakness and my melancholy,
As he is very potent with such spirits,
Abuses me to damn me.[215] I'll have grounds[216]
More relative than this.[217] The play's the thing
Wherein I'll catch the conscience of the King.

(Exit.)

Act III

Scene I. A room in the castle.

(Enter King, Queen, Polonius, Ophelia, Rosencrantz, and Guildenstern.)

King: And can you, by no drift of circumstance,[1]
Get from him why he puts on this confusion,
Grating[2] so harshly all his days of quiet
With turbulent and dangerous lunacy?

Rosencrantz: He does confess he feels himself distracted,
But from what cause he will by no means speak.

Guildenstern: Nor do we find him forward to be sounded,[3]
But, with a crafty madness, keeps aloof
When we would bring him on to some confession
Of his true state.

Queen: Did he receive you well?

Rosencrantz: Most like a gentleman.

Guildenstern: But with much forcing of his disposition.[4]

Rosencrantz: Niggard of question,[5] but of our demands
Most free in his reply.

Queen: Did you assay him
To any pastime?[6]

Rosencrantz: Madam, it so fell out that certain players
We o'erraught[7] on the way. Of these we told him,
And there did seem in him a kind of joy
To hear of it. They are about the Court,
And, as I think, they have already order
This night to play before him.

Polonius: 'Tis most true.
And he beseeched me to entreat your Majesties
To hear and see the matter.

---

[211] **presently:** immediately. [212] **proclaimed . . . malefactions:** shouted out their crimes. [213] **tent:** probe. [214] **blench:** flinch. [215] **Abuses . . . me:** i.e., deceives me so that I may commit the sin of murder that will bring me to damnation. [216] **grounds:** reasons for actions. [217] **relative . . . this:** i.e., more convincing than the appearance of a ghost.

[1] **drift of circumstance:** circumstantial evidence, hint. [2] **grating:** disturbing. [3] **forward . . . sounded:** eager to be questioned. [4] **much . . . disposition:** making a great effort to be civil to us. [5] **Niggard of question:** not asking many questions. [6] **Did . . . pastime:** did you try to interest him in any amusement. [7] **o'erraught:** overtook.

King: With all my heart, and it doth much content me
To hear him so inclined.
Good gentlemen, give him a further edge,[8]
And drive his purpose on to these delights.

Rosencrantz: We shall, my lord.

(Exeunt Rosencrantz and Guildenstern.)

King: Sweet Gertrude, leave us too,
For we have closely[9] sent for Hamlet hither,
That he, as 'twere by accident, may here
Affront[10] Ophelia.
Her father and myself, lawful espials,[11]
Will so bestow ourselves that, seeing unseen,
We may of their encounter frankly judge
And gather by him, as he is behaved,[12]
If 't be the affliction of his love or no
That thus he suffers for.

Queen: I shall obey you.
And for your part, Ophelia, I do wish
That your good beauties be the happy cause
Of Hamlet's wildness. So shall I hope your virtues
Will bring him to his wonted way[13] again,
To both your honors.

Ophelia: Madam, I wish it may.
(Exit Queen.)

Polonius: Ophelia, walk you here.
Gracious,[14] so please you,
We will bestow outselves. *(To Ophelia.)* Read on this book,[15]
That show of such an exercise may color
Your loneliness. We are oft to blame in this—
'Tis too much proved—that with devotion's visage[16]
And pious action we do sugar o'er
The Devil himself.

King: *(Aside.)* Oh, 'tis too true!
How smart a lash that speech doth give my conscience!
The harlot's cheek, beautied with plastering art,
Is not more ugly to the thing that helps it[17]
Than is my deed to my most painted[18] word.
Oh, heavy burden!

Polonius: I hear him coming. Let's withdraw, my lord.

(Exeunt King and Polonius.)
(Enter Hamlet.[19])

Hamlet: To be, or not to be—that is the question.
Whether 'tis nobler in the mind to suffer
The slings and arrows of outrageous[20] fortune,
Or to take arms against a sea[21] of troubles
And by opposing end them. To die, to sleep—
No more, and by a sleep to say we end
The heartache and the thousand natural shocks
That flesh is heir to. 'Tis a consummation[22]
Devoutly to be wished. To die, to sleep,

---

[8] **edge:** encouragement. [9] **closely:** secretly. [10] **Affront:** encounter. [11] **lawful espials:** who are justified in spying on him. [12] **by . . . behaved:** from him, from his behavior. [13] **wonted way:** normal state. [14] **Gracious:** your Majesty—addressed to the King. [15] **book:** i.e., of devotions. [16] **devotion's visage:** an outward appearance of religion. [17] **ugly . . . it:** i.e., lust, which is the cause of its artificial beauty. [18] **painted:** i.e., false. [19] **Enter Hamlet:** In Q_1 the King draws attention to Hamlet's approach with the words "See where he comes poring upon a book." Hamlet is again reading, and is too much absorbed to notice Ophelia. [20] **outrageous:** cruel. [21] **sea:** i.e., an endless turmoil. [22] **consummation:** completion.

To sleep—perchance to dream. Aye, there's the rub,[23]
For in that sleep of death what dreams may come
When we have shuffled off this mortal coil[24]
Must give us pause. There's the respect[25]
That makes calamity of so long life.[26]
For who would bear the whips and scorns of time,
The oppressor's wrong, the proud man's contumely[27]
The pangs of déspised love, the law's delay,
The insolence of office[28] and the spurns
That patient merit of the unworthy takes,[29]
When he himself might his quietus[30] make
With a bare bodkin?[31] Who would fardels[32] bear,
To grunt and sweat under a weary life,
But that the dread of something after death,
The undiscovered country from whose bourn[33]
No traveler returns, puzzles the will,[34]
And makes us rather bear those ills we have
Than fly to others that we know not of?
Thus[35] conscience does make cowards of us all,
And thus the native hue[36] of resolution
Is sicklied o'er with the pale cast[37] of thought,
And enterprises of great pitch[38] and moment
With this regard their currents turn awry
And lose the name of action.[39]—Soft you now!
The fair Ophelia! Nymph, in thy orisons[40]
Be all my sins remembered.

Ophelia: Good my lord,
How does your Honor for this many a day?
Hamlet: I humbly thank you—well, well, well.
Ophelia: My lord, I have remembrances of yours
That I have longed long to redeliver.
I pray you now receive them.
Hamlet: No, not I.
I never gave you aught.
Ophelia: My honored lord, you know right well you did,
And with them words of so sweet breath composed
As made the things more rich. Their perfume lost,
Take these again, for to the noble mind
Rich gifts wax poor when givers prove unkind.
There, my lord.
Hamlet: Ha, ha! Are you honest?[41]
Ophelia: My lord?
Hamlet: Are you fair?

---

[23] **rub:** impediment. See App. 13. [24] **shuffled . . . coil:** cast off this fuss of life. [25] **respect:** reason. [26] **makes . . . life:** makes it a calamity to have to live so long. [27] **contumely:** insulting behavior. [28] **insolence of office:** insolent behavior of government officials. [29] **spurns . . . takes:** insults which men of merit have patiently to endure from the unworthy. [30] **quietus:** discharge. [31] **bodkin:** dagger. [32] **fardels:** burdens, the coolie pack. [33] **bourn:** boundary. [34] **will:** resolution, ability to act. [35] **Thus . . . action:** the religious fear that death may not be the end makes men shrink from heroic actions. [36] **native hue:** natural color. [37] **cast:** color. [38] **pitch:** height; used of the soaring flight of a hawk. [39] **With . . . action:** by brooding on this thought great enterprises are diverted from their course and fade away. [40] **orisons:** prayers. [41] **honest:** chaste.

Ophelia: What means your lordship?

Hamlet: That if you be honest and fair, your honesty should admit no discourse to your beauty.[42]

Ophelia: Could beauty, my lord, have better commerce than with honesty?

Hamlet: Aye, truly, for the power of beauty will sooner transform honesty from what it is to a bawd[43] than the force of honesty can translate beauty into his likeness. This was sometime a paradox,[44] but now the time gives it proof. I did love you once.

Ophelia: Indeed, my lord, you made me believe so.

Hamlet: You should not have believed me, for virtue cannot so inoculate our old stock but we shall relish[45] of it. I loved you not.

Ophelia: I was the more deceived.

Hamlet: Get thee to a nunnery. Why wouldst thou be a breeder of sinners? I am myself indifferent honest,[46] but yet I could accuse me of such things that it were better my mother had not borne me. I am very proud, revengeful, ambitious, with more offenses at my beck[47] than I have thoughts to put them in, imagination to give them shape, or time to act them in. What should such fellows as I do crawling between heaven and earth? We are arrant knaves all. Believe none of us. Go thy ways to a nunnery.[48] Where's your father?

Ophelia: At home, my lord.

Hamlet: Let the doors be shut upon him, that he may play the fool nowhere but in 's own house. Farewell.

Ophelia: Oh, help him, you sweet Heavens!

Hamlet: I thou dost marry, I'll give thee this plague for thy dowry: Be thou as chaste as ice, as pure as snow—thou shalt not escape calumny.[49] Get thee to a nunnery, go. Farewell. Or if thou wilt needs marry, marry a fool, for wise men know well enough what monsters[50] you make of them. To a nunnery, go, and quickly too. Farewell.

Ophelia: O heavenly powers, restore him!

Hamlet: I have heard of your paintings[51] too, well enough. God hath given you one face and you make yourselves another. You jig,[52] you amble,[53] and you lisp,[54] and nickname God's creatures, and make your wantonness your ignorance.[55] Go to, I'll no more on 't—it hath made me mad. I say we will have no more marriages. Those that are married already, all but one, shall live; the rest shall keep as they are. To a nunnery, go. *(Exit.)*

Ophelia: Oh, what a noble mind is here o'erthrown!
The courtier's, soldier's, scholar's, eye, tongue, sword—
The expectancy and rose[56] of the fair state,
The glass[57] of fashion and the mold of form,[58]
The observed of all observers—quite, quite down!
And I, of ladies most deject and wretched,
That sucked the honey of his music vows,

---

[42] **That . . . beauty:** if you are chaste and beautiful your chastity should have nothing to do with your beauty—because (so Hamlet thinks in his bitterness) beautiful women are seldom chaste. [43] **bawd:** brothel-keeper. [44] **paradox:** statement contrary to accepted opinion. [45] **relish:** have some trace. [46] **indifferent honest:** moderately honorable. [47] **at . . . beck:** waiting to come when I beckon. [48] **nunnery:** i.e., a place where she will be removed from temptation. [49] **calumny:** slander.
[50] **monsters:** horned beasts, cuckolds. [51] **paintings:** using make-up. [52] **jig:** dance lecherously. [53] **amble:** walk artificially. [54] **lisp:** talk affectedly.
[55] **nickname . . . ignorance:** give things indecent names and pretend to be too simple to understand their meanings. [56] **expectancy . . . rose:** bright hope. The rose is used as a symbol for beauty and perfection. [57] **glass:** mirror. [58] **mold of form:** perfect pattern of manly beauty.

Now see that noble and most sovereign reason,
Like sweet bells jangled, out of tune and harsh,
That unmatched[59] form and feature of blown[60] youth
Blasted with ecstasy.[61] Oh, woe is me,
To have seen what I have seen, see what I see!

(Re-enter King and Polonius.)

King: Love! His affections[62] do not that way tend,
Nor what he spake, though it lacked form a little,
Was not like madness. There's something in his soul
O'er which his melancholy sits on brood,[63]
And I do doubt the hatch and the disclose[64]
Will be some danger. Which for to prevent,
I have in quick determination
Thus set it down: He shall with speed to England,
For the demand of our neglected tribute.
Haply[65] the seas and countries different
With variable objects[66] shall expel
This something-settled[67] matter in his heart
Whereon his brains still beating puts him thus
From fashion of himself.[68] What think you on 't?

Polonius: It shall do well. But yet do I believe
The origin and commencement of his grief
Sprung from neglected love. How now, Ophelia!
You need not tell us what Lord Hamlet said,
We heard it all. My lord, do as you please,
But, if you hold it fit, after the play
Let his Queen mother all alone entreat him
To show his grief. Let her be round[69] with him,
And I'll be placed, so please you, in the ear
Of all their conference. If she find him not,
To England send him, or confine him where
Your wisdom best shall think.

King: It shall be so.
Madness in great ones must not unwatched go.

(Exeunt.)

Scene II. A hall in the castle.

(Enter Hamlet and Players.)

Hamlet: Speak the speech,[1] I pray you, as I pronounced it to you, trippingly[2] on the tongue. But if you mouth[3] it, as many of your players do, I had as lief[4] the town crier spoke my lines. Nor do not saw the air too much with your hand, thus, but use all gently. For in the very torrent, tempest, and, as I may say, whirlwind of passion, you must acquire and beget a temperance that may give it smoothness. Oh, it offends me

---

[59] **unmatched:** unmatchable. [60] **blown:** perfect, like an open flower at its best. [61] **Blasted . . . ecstasy:** ruined by madness. [62] **affections:** state of mind. [63] **sits . . . brood:** sits hatching. [64] **doubt . . . disclose:** suspect the brood which will result. [65] **Haply:** perhaps. [66] **variable objects:** novel sights. [67] **something-settled:** somewhat settled; i.e., not yet incurable. [68] **puts . . . himself:** i.e., separates him from his normal self. [69] **round:** direct.

[1] **the speech:** which he has written. The whole passage which follows is Shakespeare's own comment on the actor's art and states the creed and practice of his company as contrasted with the more violent methods of Edward Alleyn and his fellows.

[2] **trippingly:** smoothly, easily. [3] **mouth:** "ham" it. [4] **lief:** soon.

to the soul to hear a robustious[5] periwig-pated[6] fellow tear a passion to tatters, to very rags, to split the ears of the groundlings,[7] who for the most part are capable of nothing but inexplicable dumb shows[8] and noise. I would have such a fellow whipped for o'erdoing Termagant[9]—it out-Herods Herod. Pray you, avoid it.

1. Player: I warrant your Honor.

Hamlet: Be not too tame neither, but let your own discretion be your tutor. Suit the action to the word, the word to the action, with this special observance, that you o'erstep not the modesty of nature. For anything so overdone is from[10] the purpose of playing, whose end, both at the first and now, was and is to hold as 'twere the mirror up to Nature—to show Virtue her own feature, scorn her own image, and the very age and body of the time his form and pressure.[11] Now this overdone or come tardy off, though it make the unskillful laugh, cannot but make the judicious grieve, the censure of the which one[12] must in your allowance o'erweigh a whole theater of others. Oh, there be players[13] that I have seen play, and heard others praise—and that highly, not to speak it profanely—that neither having the accent of Christians nor the gait of Christian, pagan, nor man, have so strutted and bellowed that I have thought some of Nature's journeymen[14] had made men, and not made them well, they imitated humanity so abominably.

1. Player: I hope we have reformed that indifferently[15] with us, sir.

Hamlet: Oh, reform it altogether. And let those that play your clowns[16] speak no more than is set down for them. For there be of them that will themselves laugh, to set on some quantity of barren spectators to laugh too, though in the meantime some necessary question of the play be then to be considered. That's villainous, and shows a most pitiful[17] ambition in the fool that uses it. Go, make you ready. *(Exeunt Players. Enter Polonius, Rosencrantz, and Guildenstern.)* How now, my lord! Will the King hear this piece of work?

Polonius: And the Queen too, and that presently.

Hamlet: Bid the players make haste. *(Exit Polonius.)* Will you two help to hasten them?

Rosencrantz & Guildenstern: We will, my lord.

(Exeunt Rosencrantz and Guildenstern.)

Hamlet: What ho! Horatio!

[5] **robustious:** ranting. [6] **periwig-pated:** wearing a wig. [7] **groundlings:** the poorer spectators, who stood in the yard of the playhouse. [8] **dumb shows:** an old-fashioned dramatic device, still being used by the Admiral's Men: before a tragedy, and sometimes before each act, the characters mimed the action which was to follow.
[9] **Termagant:** God of the Saracens, who, like Herod, was presented in early stage plays as a roaring tyrant. [10] **from:** contrary to. [11] **very . . . pressure:** an exact reproduction of the age. **form:** shape. **pressure:** imprint (of a seal). [12] **the . . . one:** i.e., the judicious spectator. [13] **there . . . players:** An obvious attack on Alleyn.
[14] **journeymen:** hired workmen, not masters of the trade. [15] **indifferently:** moderately. [16] **those . . . clowns:** A hit at Will Kempe, the former clown of Shakespeare's company. Q_1 adds the passage "And then you have some again that keep one suit of jests, as a man is known by one suit of apparel, and gentlemen quote his jests down in their tables before they come to the play, as thus: 'Cannot you stay till I eat my porridge?' and 'You owe me a quarter's wages,' and 'My coat wants a cullison,' and 'Your beer is sour,' and blabbering with his lips, and thus keeping in his cinquepace of jests, when God knows the warm clown cannot make a jest unless by chance, as the blind man catcheth a hare. Masters tell him of it." [17] **pitiful:** contemptible.

(Enter Horatio.)

Horatio: Here, sweet lord, at your service.
Hamlet: Horatio, thou art e'en as just a man
As e'er my conversation coped[18] withal.
Horatio: Oh, my dear lord—
Hamlet: Nay, do not think I flatter,
For what advancement[19] may I hope from thee,
That no revénue hast but thy good spirits
To feed and clothe thee? Why should the poor be flattered?
No, let the candied[20] tongue lick absurd pomp
And crook the pregnant hinges of the knee
Where thrift may follow fawning.[21] Dost thou hear?
Since my dear soul was mistress of her choice
And could of men distinguish, her election
Hath sealed[22] thee for herself. For thou hast been
As one in suffering all that suffers nothing,
A man that fortune's buffets and rewards
Hast ta'en with equal thanks. And blest are those
Whose blood and judgment are so well commingled
That they are not a pipe[23] for fortune's finger
To sound what stop she please. Give me that man
That is not passion's slave, and I will wear him
In my heart's core—aye, in my heart of heart,
As I do thee. Something too much of this.
There is a play tonight before the King.
One scene of it comes near the circumstance
Which I have told thee of my father's death.
I prithee when thou seest that act afoot,
Even with the very comment[24] of thy soul
Observe my uncle. If his occulted[25] guilt
Do not itself unkennel[26] in one speech
It is a damnèd ghost[27] that we have seen
And my imaginations are as foul
As Vulcan's[28] stithy.[29] Give him heedful note,[30]
For I mine eyes will rivet to his face,
And after we will both our judgments join
In censure of his seeming.[31]
Horatio: Well, my lord.
If he steal aught the whilst this play is playing,
And 'scape detecting, I will pay the theft.
Hamlet: They are coming to the play. I must be idle.[32]
Get you a place.

(Danish march. A flourish. Enter King, Queen, Polonius, Ophelia, Rosencrantz, Guildenstern, and other Lords attendant, with the Guard carrying torches.)

[18] **coped:** met. [19] **advancement:** promotion. [20] **candied:** sugared over with hypocrisy. [21] **crook . . . fawning:** bend the ready knees whenever gain will follow flattery. [22] **sealed:** set a mark on. [23] **pipe:** an instrument that varies its notes. [24] **comment:** close observation. [25] **occulted:** concealed. [26] **unkennel:** come to light; lit., force a fox from his hole. [27] **damned ghost:** evil spirit. [28] **Vulcan:** the blacksmith god. [29] **stithy:** smithy. [30] **heedful note:** careful observation. [31] **censure . . . seeming:** judgment on his looks. [32] **be idle:** seem crazy.

King: How fares our cousin Hamlet?

Hamlet: Excellent, i' faith, of the chameleon's dish. I eat the air, promise-crammed. You cannot feed capons so.[33]

King: I have nothing with this answer,[34] Hamlet. These words are not mine.

Hamlet: No, nor mine now.[35] *(To Polonius.)* My lord, you played once i' the university, you say?

Polonius: That did I, my lord, and was accounted a good actor.

Hamlet: What did you enact?

Polonius: I did enact Julius Caesar. I was killed i' the Capitol. Brutus killed me.

Hamlet: It was a brute part of him to kill so capital a calf there. Be the players ready?

Rosencrantz: Aye, my lord, they stay upon your patience.[36]

Queen: Come hither, my dear Hamlet, sit by me.

Hamlet: No, good Mother, here's metal more attractive.

Polonius: *(To the King.)* Oh ho! Do you mark that?

Hamlet: Lady, shall I lie in your lap?

(Lying down at Ophelia's feet.)

Ophelia: No, my lord.

Hamlet: I mean, my head upon your lap?

Ophelia: Aye, my lord.

Hamlet: Do you think I meant country matters?[37]

Ophelia: I think nothing, my lord.

Hamlet: That's a fair thought to lie between maids' legs.

Ophelia: What is, my lord?

Hamlet: Nothing.

Ophelia: You are merry, my lord.

Hamlet: Who, I?

Ophelia: Aye, my lord.

Hamlet: Oh God, your only jig-maker.[38] What should a man do but be merry? For look you how cheerfully my mother looks, and my father died within 's two hours.

Ophelia: Nay, 'tis twice two months, my lord.

Hamlet: So long? Nay, then, let the Devil wear black, for I'll have a suit of sables.[39] Oh heavens! Die two months ago, and not forgotten yet? Then there's hope a great man's memory may outlive his life half a year. But, by 'r Lady, he must build churches then, or else shall he suffer not thinking on, with the hobbyhorse,[40] whose epitaph is "For, oh, for oh, the hobbyhorse is forgot."

(Hautboys[41] play. The dumb show enters.[42] Enter a King and a Queen very lovingly, the Queen embracing him and he her. She kneels, and makes show of protestation unto him. He takes her up, and declines his head upon her neck, lays him down upon a bank of flowers. She, seeing him asleep, leaves him. Anon comes in a fellow, takes off his crown, kisses it, and pours poison in the King's

---

[33] **Excellent . . . so:** Hamlet takes "fare" literally as "what food are you eating." The chameleon was supposed to feed on air. **promise-crammed:** stuffed, like a fattened chicken (*capon*)—but with empty promises. [34] **I . . . answer:** I cannot make any sense of your answer. [35] **nor . . . now:** i.e., once words have left the lips they cease to belong to the speaker. [36] **stay . . . patience:** wait for you to be ready. [37] **country matters:** something indecent. [38] **jig-maker:** composer of jigs. [39] **suit of sables:** a quibble on "sable," black, and "sable," gown trimmed with sable fur, worn by wealthy old gentlemen. [40] **hobbyhorse:** imitation horse worn by performers in a morris dance, an amusement much disapproved of by the godly. [41] **Hautboys:** oboes. [42] **The dumb show enters:** Critics have been disturbed because this dumb show cannot be exactly paralleled in any other Elizabethan play, and because the King is apparently not disturbed by it. Shakespeare's intention, however, in presenting a play within a play is to produce something stagy and artificial compared with the play proper. Moreover, as Hamlet has already complained, dumb shows were often inexplicable.

ears, and exit. The Queen returns, finds the King dead, and makes passionate action. The Poisoner, with some two or three Mutes, comes in again, seeming to lament with her. The dead body is carried away. The Poisoner woos the Queen with gifts. She seems loath and unwilling awhile, but in the end accepts his love. Exeunt.)

Ophelia: What means this, my lord?

Hamlet: Marry, this is miching mallecho.[43] It means mischief.

Ophelia: Belike this show imports the argument[44] of the play.

(Enter Prologue.)

Hamlet: We shall know by this fellow. The players cannot keep counsel, they'll tell all.

Ophelia: Will he tell us what this show meant?

Hamlet: Aye, or any show that you'll show him. Be not you ashamed to show, he'll not shame to tell you what it means.

Ophelia: You are naught,[45] you are naught. I'll mark the play.

Prologue: For us, and for our tragedy,
Here stooping to your clemency,
We beg your hearing patiently.

Hamlet: Is this a prologue, or the posy of a ring?[46]

Ophelia: 'Tis brief, my lord.

Hamlet: As woman's love.

(Enter two Players, King and Queen.)

Player King: Full[47] thirty times hath Phoebus' cart[48] gone round
Neptune's[49] salt wash and Tellus'[50] orbèd ground,
And thirty dozen moons with borrowed sheen[51]
About the world have times twelve thirties been,
Since love our hearts and Hymen[52] did our hands
Unite commutual[53] in most sacred bands.

Player Queen: So many journeys may the sun and moon
Make us again count o'er ere love be done!
But, woe is me, you are so sick of late,
So far from cheer and from your former state,
That I distrust[54] you. Yet, though I distrust,
Discomfort you, my lord, it nothing must.
For women's fear and love holds quantity[55]
In neither aught or in extremity.[56]
Now what my love is, proof hath made you know,
And as my love is sized, my fear is so.
Where love is great, the littlest doubts are fear,
Where little fears grow great, great love grows there.

Player King: Faith, I must leave thee,[57] love, and shortly too,
My operant powers[58] their functions leave to do.
And thou shalt live in this fair world behind,
Honored, beloved, and haply one as kind
For husband shalt thou—

---

[43] **miching mallecho:** slinking mischief. [44] **argument:** plot. She too is puzzled by the dumb show. [45] **naught:** i.e., disgusting. [46] **posy . . . ring:** It was a pretty custom to inscribe rings with little mottoes or messages, which were necessarily brief. [47] **Full . . . twain:** The play is deliberately written in crude rhyming verse, full of ridiculous and bombastic phrases. [48] **Phoebus' cart:** the chariot of the sun. [49] **Neptune:** the sea god. [50] **Tellus:** the earth goddess. [51] **borrowed sheen:** light borrowed from the sun. [52] **Hymen:** god of marriage. [53] **commutual:** mutually. [54] **distrust:** am anxious about. [55] **quantity:** proportion. [56] **In . . . extremity:** either nothing or too much. [57] **leave thee:** i.e., die. [58] **operant powers:** bodily strength.

Player Queen: Oh, confound the rest!
Such love must needs be treason in my breast.
In second husband let me be accurst!
None wed the second but who killed the first.

Hamlet: *(Aside.)* Wormwood,[59] wormwood.

Player Queen: The instances[60] that second marriage move
Are base respects of thrift,[61] but none of love.
A second time I kill my husband dead
When second husband kisses me in bed.

Player King: I do believe you think what now you speak,
But what we do determine oft we break.
Purpose is but the slave to memory,
Of violent birth but poor validity,
Which now, like fruit unripe, sticks on the tree
But fall unshaken when they mellow be.
Most necessary 'tis that we forget
To pay ourselves what to ourselves is debt.
What to ourselves in passion we propose,
That passion ending, doth the purpose lose.
The violence of either grief or joy
Their own enactures[62] with themselves destroy.
Where joy most revels, grief doth most lament,
Grief joys, joy grieves, on slender accident.
This world is not for aye,[63] nor 'tis not strange
That even our loves should with our fortunes change,
For 'tis a question left us yet to prove
Whether love lead fortune or else fortune love.
The great man down, you mark his favorite flies,
The poor advanced makes friends of enemies.
And hitherto doth love on fortune tend,
For who not needs shall never lack a friend,
And who in want a hollow friend doth try
Directly seasons[64] him his enemy.
But, orderly to end where I begun,
Our wills and fates do so contráry run
That our devices still are overthrown,
Our thoughts are ours, their ends none of our own.
So think thou wilt no second husband wed,
But die thy thoughts when thy first lord is dead.

Player Queen: Nor earth to me give food nor Heaven light!
Sport and repose lock from me day and night!
To desperation turn my trust and hope!
An anchor's[65] cheer in prison be my scope!
Each opposite that blanks[66] the face of joy
Meet what I would have well and it destroy!
Both here and hence pursue me lasting strife
If, once a widow, ever I be wife!

Hamlet: If she should break it now!

Player King: 'Tis deeply sworn. Sweet, leave me here a while.
My spirits grow dull, and fain I would beguile
The tedious day with sleep. *(Sleeps.)*

Player Queen: Sleep rock thy brain,
And never come mischance betwéen us twain!

(Exit.)

[59] **Wormwood:** bitterness. [60] **instances:** arguments. [61] **respects of thrift:** considerations of gain. [62] **enactures:** performance. [63] **aye:** ever. [64] **seasons:** ripens into. [65] **anchor:** anchorite, hermit. [66] **blanks:** makes pale.

Hamlet: Madam, how like you this play?

Queen: The lady doth protest too much, methinks.

Hamlet: Oh, but she'll keep her word.

King: Have you heard the argument?[67] Is there no offense in 't?

Hamlet: No, no, they do but jest, poison in jest—no offense i' the world.

King: What do you call the play?

Hamlet: *The Mousetrap.*[68] Marry, how? Tropically.[69] This play is the image of a murder done in Vienna. Gonzago is the Duke's name, his wife, Baptista. You shall see anon. 'Tis a knavish piece of work, but what o' that? Your Majesty, and we that have free[70] souls, it touches us not. Let the galled jade wince, our withers are unwrung.[71]

(Enter Lucianus.) This is one Lucianus, nephew to the King.

Ophelia: You are as good as a chorus,[72] my lord.

Hamlet: I could interpret between you and your love, if I could see the puppets dallying.[73]

Ophelia: You are keen, my lord, you are keen.

Hamlet: I would cost you a groaning to take off my edge.

Ophelia: Still better, and worse.

Hamlet: So you must take your husbands.[74] Begin, murderer. Pox, leave thy damnable faces and begin. Come, the croaking raven doth bellow for revenge.

Lucianus: Thoughts black, hands apt, drugs fit, and time agreeing,
Confederate season, else no creature[75] seeing,
Thou mixture rank of midnight weeds collected,
With Hecate's ban[76] thrice blasted, thrice infected,
Thy natural magic and dire property[77]
On wholesome life usurp immediately.

(Pours the poison into the sleeper's ear.)

Hamlet: He poisons him i' the garden for his estate.[78] His name's Gonzago. The story is extant, and written in very choice Italian. You shall see anon how the murderer gets the love of Gonzago's wife.

Ophelia: The King rises.

Hamlet: What, frighted with false fire![79]

Queen: How fares my lord?

Polonius: Give o'er the play.

King: Give me some light. Away!

Polonius: Lights, lights, lights!

(Exeunt all but Hamlet and Horatio.)

Hamlet: "Why, let the stricken deer go weep,
The hart ungallèd play,
For some must watch while some must sleep.
Thus runs the world away."
Would not this, sir, and a forest of feathers[80]—if the rest of my

---

[67] **argument:** plot. When performances were given at Court it was sometimes customary to provide a written or printed synopsis of the story for the distinguished spectators. [68] **Mousetrap:** The phrase was used of a device to entice a person to his own destruction (OED). [69] **Tropically:** figuratively, with a pun on "trap." [70] **free:** innocent. [71] **galled . . . unwrung:** let a nag with a sore back flinch when the saddle is put on; our shoulders (being ungalled) feel no pain. [72] **chorus:** the chorus sometimes introduced the characters and commented on what was to follow. [73] **puppets dallying:** Elizabethan puppets were crude marionettes, popular at fairs. While the figures were put through their motions, the puppet master explained what was happening. [74] **So . . . husbands:** i.e., as the marriage service expresses it, "for better, for worse." [75] **confederate . . . creature:** the opportunity conspiring with me, no other creature. [76] **Hecate's ban:** the curse of Hecate, goddess of witchcraft. [77] **property:** nature. [78] **estate:** kingdom. [79] **false fire:** a mere show. [80] **forest of feathers:** set of plumes, much worn by players.

fortunes turn Turk[81] with me—with two Provincial roses[82] on my razed[83] shoes, get me a fellowship[84] in a cry[85] of players, sir?

Horatio: Half a share.

Hamlet: A whole one, I.
"For thou dost know, O Damon[86] dear,
This realm dismantled[87] was
Of Jove himself, and now reigns here
A very, very—pajock."[88]

Horatio: You might have rhymed.

Hamlet: O good Horatio, I'll take the ghost's word for a thousand pound. Didst perceive?

Horatio: Very well, my lord.

Hamlet: Upon the talk of the poisoning?

Horatio: I did very well note him.

Hamlet: Ah, ha! Come, some music! Come, the recorders![89]
"For if the King like not the comedy,
Why then, belike, he likes it not,
perdy."[90]
Come, some music!

(Re-enter Rosencrantz and Guildenstern.)

Guildenstern: Good my lord, vouchsafe me a word with you.

Hamlet: Sir, a whole history.

Guildenstern: The King, sir—

Hamlet: Aye, sir, what of him?

Guildenstern: Is in his retirement marvelous distempered.[91]

Hamlet: With drink, sir?

Guildenstern: No, my lord, rather with choler.[92]

Hamlet: Your wisdom should show itself more richer to signify this to the doctor, for me to put him to his purgation[93] would perhaps plunge him into far more choler.

Guildenstern: Good my lord, put your discourse into some frame,[94] and start not so wildly from my affair.

Hamlet: I am tame, sir. Pronounce.

Guildenstern: The Queen your mother, in most great affliction of spirit, hath sent me to you.

Hamlet: You are welcome.

Guildenstern: Nay, good my lord, this courtesy is not of the right breed. If it shall please you to make me a wholesome answer, I will do your mother's commandment. If not, your pardon and my return shall be the end of my business.

Hamlet: Sir, I cannot.

Guildenstern: What, my lord?

Hamlet: Make you a wholesome answer, my wit's diseased. But, sir, such answer as I can make you shall command, or rather, as you say, my mother. Therefore no more, but to the matter. My mother, you say—

Rosencrantz: Then thus she says. Your behavior hath struck her into amazement and admiration.[95]

Hamlet: Oh, wonderful son that can so astonish a mother! But is there no sequel at the heels of this mother's admiration? Impart.

Rosencrantz: She desires to speak with you in her closet ere you go to bed.

Hamlet: We shall obey, were she ten times our mother. Have you any further trade with us?

Rosencrantz: My lord, you once did love me.

---

[81] **turn Turk:** turn heathen, and treat me cruelly. [82] **Provincial roses:** rosettes, worn on the shoes. [83] **razed:** slashed, ornamented with cuts. [84] **fellowship:** partnership. [85] **cry:** pack. [86] **Damon:** Damon and Pythias were types of perfect friends. [87] **dismantled:** robbed. [88] **pajock:** peacock, a strutting, lecherous bird. These verses, and the lines above, may have come from some ballad, otherwise lost. [89] **recorders:** wooden pipes. [90] **perdy:** by God. [91] **distempered:** disturbed: but Hamlet takes the word in its other sense of "drunk." [92] **choler:** anger, which Hamlet again pretends to understand as meaning "biliousness." [93] **put . . . purgation:** "give him a dose of salts." [94] **frame:** shape; i.e., "please talk sense." [95] **admiration:** wonder.

Hamlet: So I do still, by these pickers and stealers.[96]

Rosencrantz: Good my lord, what is your cause of distemper? You do surely bar the door upon your own liberty if you deny your griefs[97] to your friend.

Hamlet: Sir, I lack advancement.[98]

Rosencrantz: How can that be when you have the voice of the King himself for your succession in Denmark?

Hamlet: Aye, sir, but "While the grass grows"[99]—the proverb is something musty. *(Re-enter Players with recorders.)* Oh, the recorders![100] Let me see one. To withdraw[101] with you—why do you go about to recover the wind[102] of me, as if you would drive me into a toil?[103]

Guildenstern: O my lord, if my duty be too bold, my love is too unmannerly.[104]

Hamlet: I do not well understand that. Will you play upon this pipe?

Guildenstern: My lord, I cannot.

Hamlet: I pray you.

Guildenstern: Believe me, I cannot.

Hamlet: I do beseech you.

Guildenstern: I know no touch of it, my lord.

Hamlet: It is as easy as lying. Govern these ventages[105] with your fingers and thumb, give it breath with your mouth, and it will discourse most eloquent music. Look you, these are the stops.

Guildenstern: But these cannot I command to any utterance of harmony, I have not the skill.

Hamlet: Why, look you now, how unworthy a thing you make of me! You would play upon me, you would seem to know my stops, you would pluck out the heart of my mystery, you would sound me from my lowest note to the top of my compass—and there is much music, excellent voice, in this little organ—yet cannot you make it speak. 'Sblood, do you think I am easier to be played on than a pipe? Call me what instrument you will, though you can fret[106] me, you cannot play upon me. *(Re-enter Polonius.)* God bless you, sir!

Polonius: My lord, the Queen would speak with you, and presently.

Hamlet: Do you see yonder cloud that's almost in shape of a camel?

Polonius: By the mass, and 'tis like a camel indeed.

Hamlet: Methinks it is like a weasel.

Polonius: It is backed like a weasel.

Hamlet: Or like a whale?

Polonius: Very like a whale.

Hamlet: Then I will come to my mother by and by. They fool me to the top of my bent.[107] I will come by and by.

Polonius: I will say so. *(Exit Polonius.)*

Hamlet: "By and by" is easily said. Leave me, friends. *(Exeunt all but Hamlet.)*
'Tis now the very witching time[108] of night,
When churchyards yawn and Hell itself breathes out
Contagion[109] to this world. Now could I drink hot blood,
And do such bitter business as the day
Would quake to look on. Soft! Now to my mother.
O heart, lose not thy nature, let not ever

---

[96] **pickers . . . stealers:** i.e., hands—an echo from the Christian's duty in the catechism to keep his hands "from picking and stealing." [97] **deny . . . griefs:** refuse to tell your troubles. [98] **advancement:** promotion. Hamlet harks back to his previous interview with Rosencrantz and Guildenstern. [99] **While . . . grows:** the proverb ends "the steed starves." [100] **recorders:** wooden pipes. [101] **withdraw:** go aside. Hamlet leads Guildenstern to one side of the stage. [102] **recover . . . wind:** a hunting metaphor; approach me with the wind against you. [103] **toil:** net. [104] **if . . . unmannerly:** if I exceed my duty by asking these questions, then my affection for you shows lack of manners; i.e., forgive me if I have been impertinent. [105] **ventages:** holes, stops. [106] **fret:** annoy, with a pun on the frets or bars on stringed instruments by which the fingering is regulated. [107] **top . . . bent:** to the utmost. [108] **witching time:** when witches perform their foul rites. [109] **Contagion:** infection.

The soul of Nero[110] enter this firm bosom.
Let me be cruel, not unnatural.
I will speak daggers to her, but use none.
My tongue and soul in this be hypocrites,
How in my words soever she be shent,[111]
To give them seals[112] never, my soul, consent!

(Exit.)

Scene III. A room in the castle.

(Enter King, Rosencrantz, and Guildenstern.)

King: I like him not, nor stands it safe with us
To let his madness range.[1] Therefore prepare you.
I your commission will forthwith dispatch,
And he to England shall along with you.
The terms of our estate[2] may not endure
Hazard so near us as doth hourly grow
Out of his lunacies.

Guildenstern: We will ourselves provide.[3]
Most holy and religious fear[4] it is
To keep those many many bodies safe
That live and feed upon your Majesty.

Rosencrantz: The single and peculiar[5] life is bound
With all the strength and armor of the mind
To keep itself from noyance,[6] but much more
That spirit upon whose weal[7] depends and rests
The lives of many. The cease of majesty[8]
Dies not alone, but like a gulf[9] doth draw
What's near it with it. It is a massy[10] wheel
Fixed on the summit of the highest mount,
To whose huge spokes ten thousand lesser things
Are mortised[11] and adjoined; which, when it falls,
Each small annexment, petty consequence,[12]
Attends[13] the boisterous ruin. Never alone
Did the King sigh but with a general groan.

King: Arm you, I pray you, to this speedy voyage,
For we will fetters put upon this fear,
Which now goes too free-footed.

Rosencrantz & Guildenstern: We will haste us.

(Exeunt Rosencrantz and Guildenstern.)
(Enter Polonius.)

Polonius: My lord, he's going to his mother's closet.
Behind the arras I'll convey myself
To hear the process.[14] I'll warrant she'll tax[15] him home.
And, as you said,[16] and wisely was it said,
'Tis meet that some more audience than a mother,
Since nature makes them partial, should o'erhear

---

[110] **Nero:** Nero killed his own mother. Hamlet is afraid that in the interview to come he will lose all self-control. [111] **shent:** rebuked. [112] **give . . . seals:** ratify words by actions.
[1] **range:** roam freely. [2] **terms . . . estate:** i.e., one in my position. [3] **ourselves provide:** make our preparations. [4] **fear:** anxiety. [5] **peculiar:** individual. [6] **noyance:** injury. [7] **weal:** welfare. [8] **cease of majesty:** death of a king. [9] **gulf:** whirlpool. [10] **massy:** massive. [11] **mortised:** firm. [12] **annexment . . . consequence:** attachment, smallest thing connected with it. [13] **Attends:** waits on, is involved in. [14] **process:** proceeding. [15] **tax:** censure. [16] **as . . . said:** Actually Polonius himself had said it.

The speech, of vantage.[17] Fare you well, my liege.
I'll call upon you ere you go to bed
And tell you what I know.

King: Thanks, dear my lord. *(Exit Polonius.)*
Oh, my offense is rank,[18] it smells to Heaven.
It hath the primal eldest curse[19] upon 't,
A brother's murder. Pray can I not,
Though inclination be as sharp as will.[20]
My stronger guilt defeats my strong intent,
And like a man to double business bound,
I stand in pause where I shall first begin,
And both neglect. What if this cursèd hand
Were thicker than itself with brother's blood,
Is there not rain enough in the sweet heavens
To wash it white as snow? Whereto serves mercy
But to confront the visage of offense?[21]
And what's in prayer but this twofold force,
To be forestalled[22] ere we come to fall
Or pardoned being down? Then I'll look up,
My fault is past. But oh, what form of prayer
Can serve my turn? "Forgive me my foul murder"?
That cannot be, since I am still possessed
Of those effects[23] for which I did the murder—
My crown, mine own ambition, and my Queen.
May one be pardoned and retain the offense?[24]
In the corrupted currents[25] of this world
Offense's gilded hand may shove by justice,
And oft 'tis seen the wicked prize[26] itself
Buys out the law. But 'tis not so above.
There is no shuffling, there the action lies
In his true nature,[27] and we ourselves compelled
Even to the teeth and forehead[28] of our faults
To give in evidence. What then? What rests?
Try what repentance can. What can it not?
Yet what can it when one cannot repent?
Oh, wretched state! Oh, bosom black as death!
Oh, limèd[29] soul, that struggling to be free
Art more engaged![30] Help, angels! Make assay![31]
Bow, stubborn knees, and heart with strings of steel,
Be soft as sinews of the newborn babe!
All may be well. *(Retires and kneels.)*

(Enter Hamlet.)

Hamlet: Now might I do it pat, now he is praying,
And now I'll do 't. And so he goes to Heaven,[32]

---

[17] **of vantage:** from a place of vantage; i.e., concealment. [18] **rank:** foul. [19] **primal . . . curse:** the curse laid upon Cain, the first murderer, who also slew his brother. [20] **will:** desire. [21] **confront . . . offense:** look crime in the face. [22] **forestalled:** prevented. [23] **effects:** advantages. [24] **offense:** i.e., that for which he has offended. [25] **currents:** courses, ways. [26] **wicked prize:** the proceeds of the crime. [27] **there . . . nature:** in Heaven the case is tried on its own merits. [28] **teeth . . . forehead:** i.e., face to face. [29] **limed:** caught as in birdlime. [30] **engaged:** stuck fast. [31] **assay:** attempt. [32] **And . . . Heaven:** Praying, Claudius is in a state of grace.

And so am I revenged. That would be scanned:
A villain kills my father, and for that
I, his sole son, do this same villain send
To Heaven.
Oh, this is hire and salary,[33] not revenge.
He took my father grossly,[34] full of bread,
With all his crimes broad blown, as flush[35] as May,
And how his audit[36] stands who knows save Heaven?
But in our circumstance and course of thought,[37]
'Tis heavy with him. And am I then revenged,
To take him in the purging of his soul,
When he is fit and seasoned,[38] for his passage?
No.
Up, sword, and know thou a more horrid hent.[39]
When he is drunk asleep, or in his rage,
Or in the incestuous pleasure of his bed—
At gaming, swearing, or about some act
That has no relish of salvation in 't—
Then trip him, that his heels may kick at Heaven
And that his soul may be as damned and black
As Hell, whereto it goes. My mother stays.
This physic but prolongs thy sickly days. *(Exit.)*

King: *(Rising.)* My words fly up, my thoughts remain below.
Words without thoughts never to Heaven go.

(Exit.)

Scene IV. The Queen's closet.

(Enter Queen and Polonius.)

Polonius: He will come straight. Look you lay home to[1] him.
Tell him his pranks have been too broad[2] to bear with,
And that your grace hath screened and stood between
Much heat and him. I'll sconce me[3] even here.
Pray you, be round with him.

Hamlet: *(Within.)* Mother, Mother, Mother!

Queen: I'll warrant you,
Fear me not. Withdraw, I hear him coming.

(Polonius hides behind the arras.)
(Enter Hamlet.)

Hamlet: Now, Mother, what's the matter?

Queen: Hamlet, thou hast thy father much offended.

Hamlet: Mother, you have my father much offended.

Queen: Come, come, you answer with an idle[4] tongue.

Hamlet: Go, go, you question with a wicked tongue.

Queen: Why, how now, Hamlet!

Hamlet: What's the matter now?

Queen: Have you forgot me?

Hamlet: No, by the rood,[5] not so.
You are the Queen, your husband's brother's wife,

[33] **hire . . . salary:** i.e., a kind of action deserving pay. [34] **grossly:** i.e., when he was in a state of sin. [35] **broad . . . flush:** in full blossom, as luxuriant. [36] **audit:** account. [37] **circumstance . . . thought:** as it appears to my mind. [38] **seasoned:** ripe. [39] **hent:** opportunity.

[1] **lay . . . to:** be strict with. [2] **broad:** unrestrained. Polonius is thinking of the obvious insolence of the remarks about second marriage in the play scene. [3] **sconce me:** hide myself. [4] **idle:** foolish. [5] **rood:** crucifix.

And—would it were not so!—you are my mother.

Queen: Nay, then, I'll set those to you that can speak.

Hamlet: Come, come, and sit you down. You shall not budge,
You go not till I set you up a glass[6]
Where you may see the inmost part of you.

Queen: What wilt thou do? Thou wilt not murder me?
Help, help, ho!

Polonius: *(Behind.)* What ho! Help, help, help!

Hamlet: *(Drawing.)* How now! A rat?
Dead, for a ducat, dead! *(Makes a pass through the arras.)*

Polonius: *(Behind.)* Oh, I am slain! *(Falls and dies.)*

Queen: Oh me, what hast thou done?

Hamlet: Nay, I know not. Is it the King?

Queen: Oh, what a rash and bloody deed is this!

Hamlet: A bloody deed! Almost as bad, good Mother,
As kill a king and marry with his brother.

Queen: As kill a king!

Hamlet: Aye, lady, 'twas my word.

(Lifts up the arras and discovers Polonius.)

Thou wretched, rash, intruding fool, farewell!
I took thee for thy better. Take thy fortune.
Thou find'st to be too busy is some danger.
Leave wringing of your hands. Peace! Sit you down,
And let me wring your heart. For so I shall
If it be made of penetrable stuff,
If damnèd custom have not brassed[7] it so
That it be proof and bulwark against sense.

Queen: What have I done that thou darest wag thy tongue
In noise so rude against me?

Hamlet: Such an act
That blurs the grace and blush of modesty,
Calls virtue hypocrite, takes off the rose
From the fair forehead of an innocent love,
And sets a blister[8] there—makes marriage vows
As false as dicers' oaths. Oh, such a deed
As from the body of contraction[9] plucks
The very soul, and sweet religion makes
A rhapsody of words.[10] Heaven's face doth glow,
Yea, this solidity and compound mass,[11]
With tristful visage, as against the doom,[12]
Is thought-sick at the act.

Queen: Aye me, what act
That roars so loud and thunders in the index?[13]

Hamlet: Look here upon this picture,[14] and on this,
The counterfeit presentment[15] of two brothers.
See what a grace was seated on this brow—

---

[6] **glass:** looking-glass. [7] **brassed:** made brazen; i.e., impenetrable. [8] **sets a blister:** brands as a harlot. [9] **contraction:** the marriage contract. [10] **rhapsody of words:** string of meaningless words. [11] **solidity . . . mass:** i.e., solid earth. [12] **tristful . . . doom:** sorrowful face, as in anticipation of Doomsday. [13] **in . . . index:** i.e., if the beginning (*index,* i.e., table of contents) is so noisy, what will follow? [14] **picture:** Modern producers usually interpret the pictures as miniatures, Hamlet wearing one of his father, Gertrude one of Claudius. In the eighteenth century, wall portraits were used. [15] **counterfeit presentment:** portrait.

Hyperion's curls, the front[16] of Jove himself,
An eye like Mars, to threaten and command,
A station[17] like the herald Mercury[18]
New-lighted[19] on a heaven-kissing hill,
A combination[20] and a form indeed
Where every god did seem to set his seal[21]
To give the world assurance of a man.
This was your husband. Look you now what follows.
Here is your husband, like a mildewed ear,
Blasting his wholesome brother. Have you eyes?
Could you on this fair mountain leave to feed
And batten[22] on this moor? Ha! Have you eyes?
You cannot call it love, for at your age
The heyday[23] in the blood is tame, it's humble,
And waits upon the judgment. And what judgment
Would step from this to this? Sense[24] sure you have,
Else could you not have motion.[25] But sure that sense
Is apoplexed;[26] for madness would not err,
Nor sense to ecstasy[27] was ne'er so thralled[28]
But it reserved some quantity of choice
To serve in such a difference.[29] What devil was 't
That thus hath cozened[30] you at hoodman-blind?[31]
Eyes without feeling, feeling without sight,
Ears without hands or eyes, smelling sans[32] all,
Or but a sickly part of one true sense
Could not so mope.[33]
Oh, shame! Where is thy blush? Rebellious[34] Hell,
If thou canst mutine[35] in a matron's bones,
To flaming youth let virtue be as wax
And melt in her own fire. Proclaim no shame
When the compulsive ardor[36] gives the charge,
Since frost itself as actively doth burn,
And reason panders[37] will.

Queen: O Hamlet, speak no more.
Thou turn'st mine eyes into my very soul,
And there I see such black and grainèd[38] spots
As will not leave their tinct.[39]

Hamlet: Nay, but to live
In the rank sweat of an enseamèd[40] bed,
Stewed in corruption, honeying and making love
Over the nasty sty—

Queen: Oh, speak to me no more,
These words like daggers enter in my ears.
No more, sweet Hamlet!

---

[16] **front:** forehead. [17] **station:** figure; lit., standing. [18] **Mercury:** messenger of the gods, and one of the most beautiful. [19] **New-lighted:** newly alighted. [20] **combination:** i.e., of physical qualities. [21] **set . . . seal:** guarantee as a perfect man. [22] **batten:** glut yourself. [23] **heyday:** excitement. [24] **Sense:** feeling. [25] **Motion:** desire. [26] **apoplexed:** paralyzed. [27] **ecstasy:** excitement, passion. [28] **thralled:** enslaved. [29] **serve . . . difference:** to enable you to see the difference between your former and your present husband. [30] **cozened:** cheated. [31] **hoodman-blind:** blind-man's-buff. [32] **sans:** without. [33] **mope:** be dull. [34] **Rebellious . . . will:** i.e., if the passion *(Hell)* of a woman of your age is uncontrollable *(rebellious),* youth can have no restraints; there is no shame in a young man's lust when the elderly are just as eager and their reason (which should control desire) encourages them. [35] **mutine:** mutiny. [36] **compulsive ardor:** compelling lust. [37] **panders:** acts as go-between. [38] **grained:** dyed in the grain. [39] **tinct:** color. [40] **enseamed:** greasy.

Hamlet: A murderer and a villain,
A slave that is not twentieth part the tithe[41]
Of your precedent[42] lord, a vice of kings,[43]
A cutpurse[44] of the empire and the rule,
That from a shelf the precious diadem stole
And put it in his pocket!

Queen: No more!

Hamlet: A king of shreds and patches—
(Enter Ghost.) Save me, and hover o'er me with your wings,
You heavenly guards! What would your gracious figure?

Queen: Alas, he's mad!

Hamlet: Do you not come your tardy son to chide
That, lapsed in time and passion, lets go by
The important acting of your dread command?[45]
Oh, say!

Ghost: Do not forget. This visitation
Is but to whet thy almost blunted purpose.
But look, amazement on thy mother sits.
Oh, step between her and her fighting soul.
Conceit[46] in weakest bodies strongest works.
Speak to her, Hamlet.

Hamlet: How is it with you, lady?

Queen: Alas, how is 't with you
That you do bend your eye on vacancy[47]
And with the incorporal[48] air do hold discourse?
Forth at your eyes your spirits wildly peep,
And as the sleeping soldiers in the alarm,
Your bedded[49] hairs, like life in excrements,[50]
Start up and stand an[51] end. O gentle son,
Upon the heat and flame of thy distemper[52]
Sprinkle cool patience. Whereon do you look?

Hamlet: On him, on him! Look you how pale he glares!
His form and cause conjoined,[53] preaching to stones,
Would make them capable.[54] Do not look upon me,
Lest with this piteous action you convert
My stern effects.[55] Then what I have to do
Will want true color—tears perchance for blood.

Queen: To whom to you speak this?

Hamlet: Do you see nothing there?

Queen: Nothing at all, yet all that is I see.

Hamlet: Nor did you nothing hear?

Queen: No, nothing but ourselves.

Hamlet: Why, look you there! Look how it steals away!
My father, in his habit as he lived!
Look where he goes, even now, out at the portal!

(Exit Ghost.)

Queen: This is the very coinage of your brain.

---

[41] **tithe:** tenth part. [42] **precedent:** former. [43] **vice of kings:** caricature of a king. [44] **cutpurse:** thief. [45] **That . . . command:** who has allowed time to pass and passion to cool and neglects the urgent duty of obeying your dread command. [46] **Conceit:** imagination. [47] **vacancy:** empty space. [48] **incorporal:** bodiless. [49] **bedded:** evenly laid. [50] **excrements:** anything that grows out of the body, such as hair or fingernails: here hair. [51] **an:** on. [52] **distemper:** mental disturbance. [53] **form . . . conjoined:** his appearance and the reason for his appearance joined. [54] **capable:** i.e., of feeling. [55] **convert . . . effects:** change the stern action which should follow.

This bodiless creation ecstasy[56]
Is very cunning in.

Hamlet: Ecstasy!
My pulse, as yours, doth temperately keep time,
And makes as healthful music. It is not madness
That I have uttered. Bring me to the test
And I the matter will reword, which madness
Would gambol[57] from. Mother, for love of grace,
Lay not that flattering unction[58] to your soul,
That not your trespass but my madness speaks.
It will but skin and film the ulcerous place,
Whiles rank corruption, mining[59] all within,
Infects unseen. Confess yourself to Heaven,
Repent what's past, avoid what is to come,
And do not spread the compost[60] on the weeds
To make them ranker. Forgive me this my virtue,
For in the fatness[61] of these pursy[62] times
Virtue itself of vice must pardon beg—
Yea, curb[63] and woo for leave to do him good.

Queen: O Hamlet, thou hast cleft my heart in twain.

Hamlet: Oh, throw away the worser part of it,
And live the purer with the other half.
Good night. But go not to my uncle's bed.
Assume a virtue if you have it not.
That[64] monster, custom, who all sense doth eat,
Of habits devil,[65] is angel yet in this,
That to the use[66] of actions fair and good
He likewise gives a frock or livery
That aptly[67] is put on. Refrain tonight,
And that shall lend a kind of easiness
To the next abstinence, the next more easy.
For use almost can change the stamp[68] of nature,
And either the Devil,[69] or throw him out
With wondrous potency. Once more, good night.
And when you are desirous to be blest,
I'll blessing beg of you. For this same lord,

(Pointing to Polonius.)

I do repent; but Heaven hath pleased it so,
To punish me with this, and this with me,
That I must be their scourge and minister.
I will bestow[70] him, and will answer well
The death I gave him. So again good night.
I must be cruel only to be kind.
Thus bad begins, and worse remains behind.
One word more, good lady.

Queen: What shall I do?

---

[56] **ecstasy:** madness. [57] **gambol:** start away. [58] **unction:** healing ointment. [59] **mining:** undermining. [60] **compost:** manure. [61] **fatness:** grossness. [62] **pursy:** bloated. [63] **curb:** bow low. [64] **That . . . on:** i.e., custom (bad habits) like an evil monster destroys all sense of good and evil, but yet can become an angel (good habits) when it makes us perform good actions as mechanically as we put on our clothes. [65] **devil:** This is the Q_2 reading; the passage is omitted in F_1. Probably the word should be "evil." [66] **use:** practice. [67] **aptly:** readily. [68] **stamp:** impression. [69] **either the Devil:** some verb such as shame" or "curb" has been omitted. [70] **bestow:** get rid of.

Hamlet: Not this, by no means, that I bid you do.
Let the bloat[71] king tempt you again to bed,
Pinch wanton[72] on your cheek, call you his mouse,
And let him, for a pair of reechy[73] kisses
Or paddling in your neck with his damned fingers,
Make you to ravel[74] all this matter out,
That I essentially am not in madness,
But mad in craft. 'Twere good you let him know.
For who that's but a Queen, fair, sober, wise,
Would from a paddock,[75] from a bat, a gib,[76]
Such dear concernings[77] hide? Who would do so?
No, in despite[78] of sense and secrecy,
Unpeg the basket on the house's top,
Let the birds fly, and like the famous ape,[79]
To try conclusions,[80] in the basket creep
And break your own neck down.

Queen: Be thou assured if words be made of breath
And breath of life, I have no life to breathe
What thou hast said to me.

Hamlet: I must to England. You know that?

Queen: Alack,
I had forgot. 'Tis so concluded on.

Hamlet: There's letters sealed, and my two school fellows,
Whom I will trust as I will adders fanged,
They bear the mandate.[81] They must sweep my way,
And marshal me to knavery. Let it work,
For 'tis the sport to have the enginer[82]
Hoist with his own petar.[83] And 't shall go hard
But I will delve one yard below their mines
And blow them at the moon: Oh, 'tis most sweet
When in one line two crafts[84] directly meet.
This man shall set me packing.
I'll lug the guts into the neighbor room.
Mother, good night. Indeed this counselor
Is now most still, most secret, and most grave
Who was in life a foolish prating knave.
Come, sir, to draw toward an end with you.
Good night, Mother. *(Exeunt severally,[85] Hamlet dragging in Polonius.)*

Act IV

Scene I. A room in the castle.

(Enter King, Queen, Rosencrantz, and Guildenstern.)

King: There's matter[1] in these sighs, these profound heaves,

---

[71] **bloat:** bloated. [72] **wanton:** lewdly. [73] **reechy:** foul. [74] **ravel:** unravel, reveal. [75] **paddock:** toad. [76] **gib:** tomcat. [77] **dear concernings:** important matters. [78] **despite:** spite. [79] **famous ape:** The story is not known, but evidently told of an ape that let the birds out of their cage and, seeing them fly, crept into the cage himself and jumped out, breaking his own neck. [80] **try conclusions:** repeat the experiment. [81] **mandate:** command. [82] **enginer:** engineer. [83] **petar:** petard, land mine. [84] **crafts:** devices. [85] **Exeunt severally:** i.e., by separate exits. In F_1 there is no break here. The King enters as soon as Hamlet has dragged the body away. Q_2 marks the break. The act division was first inserted in a quarto of 1676.

[1] **matter:** something serious.

You must translate. 'Tis fit we understand them.
Where is your son?

Queen: Bestow this place[2] on us a little while.

(Exeunt Rosencrantz and Guildenstern.)

Ah, mine own lord, what have I seen tonight!

King: What, Gertrude? How does Hamlet?

Queen: Mad as the sea and wind when both contend
Which is the mightier. In his lawless fit,
Behind the arras hearing something stir,
Whips out his rapier, cries "A rat, a rat!"
And in this brainish apprehension[3] kills
The unseen good old man.

King: Oh, heavy deed!
It had been so with us had we been there.
His liberty is full of threats to all,
To you yourself, to us, to everyone.
Alas, how shall this bloody deed be answered?
It will be laid to us, whose providence[4]
Should have kept short,[5] restrained and out of haunt,[6]
This mad young man. But so much was our love
We would not understand what was most fit,
But, like the owner of a foul disease,
To keep it from divulging[7] let it feed
Even on the pith[8] of life. Where is he gone?

Queen: To draw apart the body he hath killed,
O'er whom his very madness, like some ore
Among a mineral of metals base,
Shows itself pure. He weeps for what is done.

King: O Gertrude, come away!
The sun no sooner shall the mountains touch
But we will ship him hence. And this vile deed
We must, with all our majesty and skill,
Both countenance[9] and excuse. Ho, Guildenstern!

(Re-enter Rosencrantz and Guildenstern.)

Friends both, go join you with some further aid.
Hamlet in madness hath Polonius slain,
And from his mother's closet hath he dragged him.
Go seek him out, speak fair, and bring the body
Into the chapel. I pray you, haste in this.

(Exeunt Rosencrantz and Guildenstern.)

Come, Gertrude, we'll call up our wisest friends,
And let them know both what we mean to do
And what's untimely done,[10]
Whose whisper o'er the world's diameter
As level as the cannon to his blank[11]
Transports his poisoned shot, may miss our name
And hit the woundless air. Oh, come away!
My soul is full of discord and dismay.
(Exeunt.)

---

[2] **Bestow . . . place:** give place, leave us. [3] **brainish apprehension:** mad imagination. [4] **providence:** foresight. [5] **short:** confined. [6] **out of haunt:** away from others. [7] **divulging:** becoming known. [8] **pith:** marrow. [9] **countenance:** take responsibility for. [10] **done:** A half-line has been omitted. Some editors fill the gap with "So, haply slander." [11] **blank:** target.

Scene II. Another room in the castle.

(Enter Hamlet.)

Hamlet: Safely stowed.
Rosencrantz & Guildenstern: (Within) Hamlet! Lord Hamlet!
Hamlet: But soft, what noise? Who calls on Hamlet?
Oh, here they come.

(Enter Rosencrantz and Guildenstern.)

Rosencrantz: What have you done, my lord, with the dead body?
Hamlet: Compounded it with dust, whereto 'tis kin.
Rosencrantz: Tell us where 'tis, that we may take it thence
And bear it to the chapel.
Hamlet: Do not believe it.
Rosencrantz: Believe what?
Hamlet: That I can keep your counsel and not mine own. Besides, to be demanded of a sponge! What replication[1] should be made by the son of a king?
Rosencrantz: Take you me for a sponge, my lord?
Hamlet: Aye, sir, that soaks up the King's countenance,[2] his rewards, his authorities. But such officers do the King best service in the end. He keeps them, like an ape, in the corner of his jaw, first mouthed, to be last swallowed. When he needs what you have gleaned, it is but squeezing you and, sponge, you shall be dry again.
Rosencrantz: I understand you not, my lord.
Hamlet: I am glad of it. A knavish speech sleeps in a foolish ear.[3]
Rosencrantz: My lord, you must tell us where the body is; and go with us to the King.
Hamlet: The body is with the King, but the King is not with the body.[4] The King is a thing—
Guildenstern: A thing, my lord?
Hamlet: Of nothing. Bring me to him. Hide fox, and all after.[5]

(Exeunt.)

Scene III. Another room in the castle.

(Enter King, attended.)

King: I have sent to seek him, and to find the body.
How dangerous is it that this man goes loose!
Yet must not we put the strong law on him.
He's loved of the distracted[1] multitude,
Who like not in their judgment but their eyes;[2]
And where 'tis so, the offender's scourge[3] is weighed,
But never the offense. To bear[4] all smooth and even,
This sudden sending him away must seem
Deliberate pause.[5] Diseases desperate grown
By desperate appliance are relieved,
Or not at all.
(Enter Rosencrantz.) How now! What hath befall'n?
Rosencrantz: Where the dead body is bestowed, my lord,
We cannot get from him.
King: But where is he?
Rosencrantz: Without, my lord, guarded, to know your pleasure.
King: Bring him before us.

---

[1] **replication:** answer. [2] **countenance:** favor. [3] **A . . . ear:** a fool never understands the point of a sinister speech. [4] **The . . . body:** Hamlet deliberately bewilders his companions. [5] **Hide . . . after:** a form of the game of hide-and-seek. With these words Hamlet runs away from them.

[1] **distracted:** bewildered. [2] **like . . . eyes:** whose likings are swayed not by judgment but by looks. [3] **scourge:** punishment. [4] **bear:** make. [5] **Deliberate pause:** the result of careful planning.

Rosencrantz: Ho, Guildenstern! Bring in my lord.

(Enter Hamlet and Guildenstern.)

King: Now, Hamlet, where's Polonius?

Hamlet: At supper.

King: At supper! Where?

Hamlet: Not where he eats, but where he is eaten. A certain convocation of politic worms[6] are e'en at him. Your worm is your only emperor for diet. We fat all creatures else to fat us, and we fat ourselves for maggots. Your fat king and your lean beggar is but variable service,[7] two dishes, but to one table. That's the end.

King: Alas, alas!

Hamlet: A man may fish with the worm that hath eat of a king, and eat of the fish that hath fed of that worm.

King: What dost thou mean by this?

Hamlet: Nothing but to show you how a king may go a progress[8] through the guts of a beggar.

King: Where is Polonius?

Hamlet: In Heaven—send thither to see. If your messenger find him not there, seek him i' the other place yourself. But indeed if you find him not within this month, you shall nose him as you go up the stairs into the lobby.

King: *(To some Attendants)* Go seek him there.

Hamlet: He will stay till you come.

(Exeunt Attendants.)

King: Hamlet, this deed, for thine especial safety,
Which we do tender,[9] as we dearly grieve
For that which thou hast done, must send thee hence
With fiery quickness. Therefore prepare thyself.
The bark is ready and the wind at help,[10]
The associates tend,[11] and every thing is bent[12]
For England.

Hamlet: For England?

King: Aye, Hamlet.

Hamlet: Good.

King: So is it if thou knew'st our purposes.

Hamlet: I see a cherub that sees them.
But, come, for England! Farewell, dear Mother.

King: Thy loving father, Hamlet.

Hamlet: My mother. Father and mother is man and wife, man and wife is one flesh, and so, my mother. Come, for England! *(Exit.)*

King: Follow him at foot,[13] tempt[14] him with speed aboard.
Delay it not, I'll have him hence tonight.
Away! For everything is sealed and done
That else leans on the affair. Pray you make haste.

(Exeunt Rosencrantz and Guildenstern.)

And, England, if my love thou hold'st at aught—
As my great power thereof may give thee sense,
Since yet thy cicatrice[15] looks raw and red
After the Danish sword, and thy free awe[16]
Pays homage to us—thou mayst not coldly set
Our sovereign process,[17] which imports at full,

---

[6] **convocation . . . worms:** an assembly of political-minded worms. [7] **variable service:** choice of alternatives. [8] **go a progress:** make a state journey. [9] **tender:** regard highly. [10] **at help:** favorable. [11] **associates tend:** your companions are waiting. [12] **bent:** ready. [13] **at foot:** at his heels. [14] **tempt:** entice. [15] **cicatrice:** scar. There is nothing in the play to explain this incident. [16] **free awe:** voluntary submission. [17] **coldly . . . process:** hesitate to carry out our royal command.

By letters congruing[18] to that effect,
The present[19] death of Hamlet. Do it, England,
For like the hectic[20] in my blood he rages,
And thou must cure me. Till I know 'tis done,
Howe'er my haps,[21] my joys were ne'er begun.

(Exit.)

Scene IV. A plain in Denmark.

(Enter Fortinbras, a Captain and Soldiers, marching.)

Fortinbras: Go, Captain, from me greet the Danish King.
Tell him that by his license Fortinbras
Craves the conveyance of a promised march[1]
Over his kingdom. You know the rendezvous.
If that His Majesty would aught with us,
We shall express our duty in his eye,[2]
And let him know so.
Captain: I will do 't, my lord.
Fortinbras: Go softly on.

(Exeunt Fortinbras and Soldiers.)
(Enter Hamlet, Rosencrantz, Guildenstern, and others.)

Hamlet: Good sir, whose powers[3] are these?
Captain: They are of Norway, sir.
Hamlet: How purposed, sir, I pray you?
Captain: Against some part of Poland.
Hamlet: Who commands them, sir?
Captain: The nephew to old Norway, Fortinbras.
Hamlet: Goes it against the main[4] of Poland, sir,
Or for some frontier?
Captain: Truly to speak, and with no addition,[5]
We go to gain a little patch of ground
That hath in it no profit but the name.
To pay five ducats, five, I would not farm it,
Nor will it yield to Norway or the Pole
A ranker[6] rate should it be sold in fee.[7]
Hamlet: Why, then the Polack never will defend it.
Captain: Yes, it is already garrisoned.
Hamlet: Two thousand souls and twenty thousand ducats
Will not debate the question of this straw.
This is the imposthume of[8] much wealth and peace,
That inward breaks, and shows no cause without
Why the man dies. I humbly thank you, sir.
Captain: God be wi' you, sir. *(Exit.)*
Rosencrantz: Will 't please you go, my lord?
Hamlet: I'll be with you straight. Go a little before.

(Exeunt all but Hamlet.)

How[9] all occasions do inform against[10] me
And spur my dull revenge! What is a man
If his chief good and market[11] of his time
Be but to sleep and feed? A beast, no more.

---

[18] **congruing:** agreeing. [19] **present:** immediate. [20] **hectic:** fever. [21] **Howe'er my haps:** whatever may happen to me.
[1] **Craves . . . march:** asks for permission to transport his army, as had already been promised. [2] **in . . . eye:** before his eyes; i.e., in person. [3] **powers:** forces.
[4] **main:** mainland. [5] **addition:** exaggeration. [6] **ranker:** richer. [7] **in fee:** with possession as freehold. [8] **imposthume of:** inward swelling caused by.
[9] **How . . . worth:** The soliloquy and all the dialogue after the exit of Fortinbras are omitted in F_1. [10] **inform against:** accuse. [11] **market:** profit.

Sure. He that made us with such large discourse,
Looking before and after,[12] gave us not
That capability and godlike reason
To fust[13] in us unused. Now whether it be
Bestial oblivion, or some craven scruple
Of thinking too precisely on the event—
A thought which, quartered, hath but one part wisdom
And ever three parts coward—I do not know
Why yet I live to say "This thing's to do,"
Sith I have cause, and will, and strength, and means
To do 't. Examples gross[14] as earth exhort me.
Witness this army, of such mass and charge,[15]
Led by a delicate and tender Prince
Whose spirit with divine ambition puffed
Makes mouths at the invisible event,[16]
Exposing what is mortal and unsure
To all that fortune, death, and danger dare,
Even for an eggshell.[17] Rightly to be great
Is not to stir without great argument,
But greatly to find quarrel in a straw
When honor's at the stake.[18] How stand I then,
That have a father killed, a mother stained,
Excitements of my reason and my blood,
And let all sleep while to my shame I see
The imminent death of twenty thousand men
That for a fantasy and trick[19] of fame
Go to their graves like beds, fight for a plot
Whereon the numbers cannot try the cause,[20]
Which is not tomb enough and continent[21]
To hide the slain? Oh, from this time forth,
My thoughts be bloody or be nothing worth!

(Exit.)

Scene V. Elsinore. A room in the castle.

(Enter Queen, Horatio, and a Gentleman.)

Queen: I will not speak with her.
Gentleman: She is importunate, indeed distract.[1]
Her mood will needs be pitied.
Queen: What would she have?
Gentleman: She speaks much of her father, says she hears
There's tricks[2] i' the world, and hems[3] and beats her heart,
Spurns enviously[4] at straws, speaks things in doubt
That carry but half-sense. Her speech is nothing,
Yet the unshaped use[5] of it doth move
The hearers to collection.[6] They aim[7] at it,

[12] **such . . . after:** intelligence that enables us to consider the future and the past. [13] **fust:** grow musty. [14] **gross:** large. [15] **charge:** expense. [16] **Makes . . . event:** mocks at the unseen risk. [17] **eggshell:** i.e., worthless trifle. [18] **Rightly . . . stake:** true greatness is a matter of fighting not for a mighty cause but for the merest trifle when honor is concerned. [19] **fantasy . . . trick:** illusion and whim. [20] **Whereon . . . cause:** a piece of ground so small that it would not hold the combatants. [21] **continent:** large enough to contain.

[1] **distract:** out of her mind. [2] **tricks:** trickery. [3] **hems:** makes significant noises. [4] **Spurns enviously:** kicks spitefully. [5] **unshaped use:** disorder. [6] **collection:** i.e., attempts to find a sinister meaning. [7] **aim:** guess.

And botch[8] the words up fit to their own thoughts,
Which, as her winks and nods and gestures yield them,
Indeed would make one think there might be thought,
Though nothing sure, yet much unhappily.

Horatio: 'Twere good she were spoken with, for she may strew
Dangerous conjectures in ill-breeding minds.

Queen: Let her come in.

(Exit Gentleman.)

(Aside) To my sick soul, as sin's true nature is,
Each toy[9] seems prologue to some great amiss.[10]
So full of artless jealousy[11] is guilt,
It spills itself in fearing to be spilt.[12]

(Re-enter Gentleman, with Ophelia.[13])

Ophelia: Where is the beauteous Majesty of Denmark?

Queen: How now, Ophelia!

Ophelia: *(Sings.)*

"How should I your truelove know
From another one?
By his cockle hat[14] and staff
And his sandal shoon."[15]

Queen: Alas, sweet lady, what imports this song?

Ophelia: Say you? nay, pray you, mark. *(Sings.)*

"He is dead and gone, lady,
He is dead and gone,
At his head a grass-green turf,
At his heels a stone."
Oh, oh!

Queen: Nay, but, Ophelia—

Ophelia: Pray you, mark. *(Sings.)*
"White his shroud as the mountain snow—"

(Enter King.)

Queen: Alas, look here, my lord.

Ophelia: *(Sings.)*
"Larded[16] with sweet flowers,
Which bewept to the grave did go
With truelove showers."[17]

King: How do you, pretty lady?

Ophelia: Well, God 'ild[18] you! They say the owl was a baker's daughter.[19] Lord, we know what we are but know not what we may be. God be at your table!

King: Conceit upon her father.

Ophelia: Pray you let's have no words of this, but when they ask you what it means, say you this

(Sings.):

"Tomorrow is Saint Valentine's day,[20]
All in the morning betime,
And I a maid at your window,
To be your Valentine.
"Then up he rose, and donned his clothes,
And dupped[21] the chamber door,
Let in the maid, that out a maid
Never departed more."

King: Pretty Ophelia!

Ophelia: Indeed, la, without an oath, I'll make an end on 't. *(Sings.)*

[8] **botch:** patch. [9] **toy:** trifle. [10] **amiss:** calamity. [11] **artless jealousy:** clumsy suspicion. [12] **It . . . spilt:** guilt reveals itself by its efforts at concealment. [13] **Re-enter . . . Ophelia:** Q_1 notes "Enter Ophelia playing on a lute, and her hair down, singing." [14] **cockle hat:** a hat adorned with a cockleshell worn by pilgrims. [15] **sandal shoon:** sandals, the proper footwear of pilgrims. [16] **Larded:** garnished. [17] **truelove showers:** the tears of his faithful love. [18] **'ild (yield):** reward. [19] **owl . . . daughter:** An allusion to a legend that Christ once went into a baker's shop and asked for bread. The baker's wife gave him a piece but was rebuked by her daughter for giving him too much. Thereupon the daughter was turned into an owl. [20] **Saint . . . day:** February 14, the day when birds are supposed to mate. According to the old belief the first single man then seen by a maid is destined to be her husband. [21] **dupped:** opened.

"By Gis[22] and by Saint Charity,
Alack, and fie for shame!
Young men will do 't, if they come to 't,
By cock, they are to blame.
Quoth she, before you tumbled me,
You promised me to wed."
He answers:
"So would I ha' done, by yonder sun,
An thou hadst not come to my bed."

King: How long hath she been thus?

Ophelia: I hope all will be well. We must be patient. But I cannot choose but weep to think they should lay him i' the cold ground. My brother shall know of it. And so I thank you for your good counsel. Come, my coach! Good night, ladies, good night, sweet ladies, good night, good night. *(Exit.)*

King: Follow her close,[23] give her good watch, I pray you. *(Exit Horatio.)*
Oh, this is the poison of deep grief. It springs
All from her father's death. O Gertrude, Gertrude.
When sorrows come, they come not single spies,[24]
But in battalions! First, her father slain.
Next, your son gone, and he most violent author[25]
Of his own just remove. The people muddied,
Thick and unwholesome in their thoughts and whispers,
For good Polonius' death. And we have done but greenly[26]
In huggermugger[27] to inter him. Poor Ophelia
Divided from herself and her fair judgment,[28]
Without the which we are pictures,[29] or mere beasts.
Last, and as much containing as all these,
Her brother is in secret come from France,
Feeds on his wonder, keeps himself in clouds,
And wants not buzzers[30] to infect his ear
With pestilent speeches of his father's death,
Wherein necessity, of matter beggared,
Will nothing stick our person to arraign[31]
In ear and ear. O my dear Gertrude, this,
Like to a murdering piece,[32] in many places
Gives me superfluous death. *(A noise within.)*

Queen: Alack, what noise is this?

King: Where are my Switzers?[33] Let them guard the door.
(Enter another Gentleman.) What is the matter?

Gentleman: Save yourself, my lord!
The ocean, overpeering of his list,[34]
Eats not the flats[35] with more impetuous haste
Than young Laertes, in a riotous head,[36]
O'erbears your officers. The rabble call him lord.
And as the world were now but to begin,

[22] **Gis . . . cock:** for "Jesus" and "God," both words being used instead of the sacred names, like the modern "Jeez" and "Gee." [23] **close:** closely. [24] **spies:** scouts. [25] **author:** cause. [26] **done . . . greenly:** shown immature judgment. [27] **hugger-mugger:** secret haste, "any which way." [28] **Divided . . . judgment:** no longer able to use her judgment. [29] **pictures:** lifeless imitations. [30] **buzzers:** scandalmongers. [31] **herein . . . arraign:** in which, knowing nothing of the true facts, he may necessarily accuse us. [32] **murdering piece:** cannon loaded with grapeshot. [33] **Switzers:** Swiss bodyguard. [34] **overpeering . . . list:** looking over its boundary; i.e., flooding the mainland. [35] **Eats . . . flats:** floods not the flat country. [36] **in . . . head:** with a force of rioters.

Antiquity forgot, custom not known,
The ratifiers and props of every word,[37]
They cry "Choose we—Laertes shall be King!"
Caps, hands, and tongues applaud it to the clouds—
"Laertes shall be King, Laertes King!"

Queen: How cheerfully on the false trail they cry!
Oh, this is counter,[38] you false Danish dogs!

(Noise within.)

King: The doors are broke.

(Enter Laertes, armed, Danes following.)

Laertes: Where is this King? Sirs, stand you all without.

Danes: No, let's come in.

Laertes: I pray you, give me leave.

Danes: We will, we will.

(They retire without the door.)

Laertes: I thank you. Keep the door. O thou vile King,
Give me my father!

Queen: Calmly, good Laertes.

Laertes: That drop of blood that's calm proclaims me bastard,
Cries cuckold[39] to my father, brands the harlot[40]
Even here, between the chaste unsmirchèd brows
Of my true mother.

King: What is the cause, Laertes,
That thy rebellion looks so giantlike?
Let him go, Gertrude. Do not fear[41] our person.
There's such divinity doth hedge a king[42]
That treason can but peep[43] to what it would,
Acts little of his will. Tell me, Laertes,
Why thou art thus incensed. Let him go, Gertrude.
Speak, man.

Laertes: Where is my father?

King: Dead.

Queen: But not by him.

King: Let him demand his fill.

Laertes: How came he dead? I'll not be juggled with.
To Hell, allegiance! Vows, to the blackest devil!
Conscience and grace, to the profoundest pit!
I dare damnation. To this point I stand,
That both the worlds I give to negligence.[44]
Let come what comes, only I'll be revenged
Most throughly[45] for my father.

King: Who shall stay you?

Laertes: My will, not all the world.
And for my means, I'll husband[46] them so well
They shall go far with little.

King: Good Laertes,
If you desire to know the certainty
Of your dear father's death, is 't writ in your revenge
That, swoopstake,[47] you will draw both friend and foe,
Winner and loser?

Laertes: None but his enemies.

King: Will you know them, then?

---

[37] **Antiquity . . . word:** forgetting ancient rule and ignoring old custom, by which all promises must be maintained. [38] **counter:** in the wrong direction of the scent. [39] **cuckold:** a husband deceived by his wife. [40] **brands . . . harlot:** Convicted harlots were branded with a hot iron. [41] **fear:** fear for. [42] **divinity . . . king:** divine protection surrounds a king as with a hedge. [43] **peep:** look over, not break through. [44] **That . . . negligence:** I do not care what happens to me in this world or the next. [45] **throughly:** thoroughly. [46] **husband:** use economically. [47] **swoopstake:** "sweeping the board."

Laertes: To his good friends thus wide
I'll ope my arms,
And like the kind life-rendering pelican,[48]
Repast[49] them with my blood.
King: Why, now you speak
Like a good child and a true gentleman.
That I am guiltless of your father's death,
And am most sensibly[50] in grief for it,
It shall as level[51] to your judgment pierce
As day does to your eye.
Danes: *(Within.)* Let her come in.
Laertes: How now! What noise is that?
(Re-enter Ophelia.) O heat, dry up my brains! Tears seven times salt
Burn out the sense and virtue of mine eye!
By Heaven, thy madness shall be paid with weight
Till our scale turn the beam.[52] O rose of May![53]
Dear maid, kind sister, sweet Ophelia!
Oh heavens! Is 't possible a young maid's wits
Should be as mortal as an old man's life?
Nature is fine in love, and where 'tis fine
It sends some precious instance of itself
After the thing it loves.[54]
Ophelia: *(Sings.)*
"They bore him barefaced on the bier,
Hey non nonny, nonny, hey nonny,
And in his grave rained many a tear—"
Fare you well, my dove!
Laertes: Hadst thou thy wits and didst persuade revenge,
It could not move thus.
Ophelia: *(Sings.)*
"You must sing down a-down
An you call him a-down-a."
Oh, how the wheel[55] becomes it! It is the false steward, that stole his master's daughter.
Laertes: This nothing's more than matter.[56]
Ophelia: There's[57] rosemary, that's for remembrance—pray you, love, remember. And there is pansies, that is for thoughts.
Laertes: A document[58] in madness, thoughts and remembrance fitted.
Ophelia: There's fennel for you, and columbines. There's rue for you, and here's some for me—we may call it herb of grace o' Sundays. Oh, you must wear your rue with a difference. There's a daisy. I would give you some violets, but they withered all when my father died. They say a' made a good end. *(Sings.)*
"For bonny sweet Robin is all my joy."
Laertes: Thought and affliction, passion, Hell itself,
She turns to favor[59] and to prettiness.

[48] **life-rendering pelican:** The mother pelican was supposed to feed her young with blood from her own breast. [49] **Repast:** feed. [50] **sensibly:** feelingly. [51] **level:** clearly. [52] **turn . . . beam:** weigh down the beam of the scale. [53] **rose of May:** perfection of young beauty. [54] **Nature . . . loves:** i.e., her love for her father was so exquisite that she has sent her sanity after him. Laertes, especially in moments of emotion, is prone to use highly exaggerated speech. [55] **wheel:** explained variously as the spinning wheel, Fortune's wheel, or the refrain. The likeliest explanation is that she breaks into a little dance at the words "You must sing," and that the **wheel** is the turn as she circles round. [56] **This . . . matter:** this nonsense means more than sense. [57] **There's . . . died:** In the language of flowers, each has its peculiar meaning, and Ophelia distributes them appropriately: for her brother rosemary (remembrance) and pansies (thoughts); for the King fennel (flattery) and columbine (thanklessness); for the Queen rue, called also herb o' grace (sorrow), and daisy (light of love). Neither is worthy of violets (faithfulness). [58] **document:** instruction. [59] **favor:** charm.

Ophelia: *(Sings.)*
"And will a' not come again?
And will a' not come again?
No, no, he is dead,
Go to thy deathbed,
He never will come again.

"His beard was as white as snow,
All flaxen was his poll.[60]
He is gone, he is gone,
And we cast away moan.
God ha' mercy on his soul!"
And of all Christian souls, I pray God.
God be wi' you. *(Exit.)*

Laertes: Do you see this, O God?

King: Laertes, I must commune with your grief,
Or you deny me right. Go but apart,
Make choice of whom your wisest friends you will,
And they shall hear and judge 'twixt you and me.
If by direct or by collateral[61] hand
They find us touched,[62] we will our kingdom give,
Our crown, our life, and all that we call ours,
To you in satisfaction. But if not,
Be you content to lend your patience to us
And we shall jointly labor with your soul
To give it due content.

Laertes: Let this be so.
His means of death, his obscure funeral,[63]
No trophy, sword, nor hatchment[64] o'er his bones,
No noble rite nor formal ostentation,[65]
Cry to be heard, as 'twere from Heaven to earth,
That I must call 't in question.

King: So you shall,
And where the offense is let the great ax fall.
I pray you, go with me. *(Exeunt.)*

Scene VI. Another room in the castle.

(Enter Horatio and a Servant.)

Horatio: What are they that would speak with me?

Servant: Seafaring men, sir. They say they have letters for you.

Horatio: Let them come in.
(Exit Servant.)
I do not know from what part of the world
I should be greeted, if not from Lord Hamlet.

(Enter Sailors.)

1. Sailor: God bless you, sir.

Horatio: Let Him bless thee too.

1. Sailor: He shall, sir, an 't please Him. There's a letter for you, sir. It comes from the ambassador that was bound for England—if your name be Horatio, as I am let to know it is.

Horatio: *(Reads.)* "Horatio, when thou shalt have overlooked[1] this, give these fellows some means[2] to the King. They have letters for him. Ere we were two days old at sea, a pirate of very warlike appointment[3] gave us chase. Finding ourselves too slow of sail, we put on a compelled valor, and in the grapple I boarded them. On the instant they got clear of our ship, so I alone became their prisoner. They have dealt with me like thieves of mercy; but they knew

---

[60] **flaxen . . . poll:** white as flax was his head. [61] **collateral:** i.e., as an accessory. [62] **touched:** implicated. [63] **obscure funeral:** Men of rank were buried with much ostentation. To bury Polonius "huggermugger" was thus an insult to his memory and to his family. [64] **hatchment:** device of the coat of arms carried in a funeral and hung up over the tomb. [65] **formal ostentation:** ceremony properly ordered.
[1] **overlooked:** read. [2] **means:** access. [3] **appointment:** equipment.

what they did—I am to do a good turn for them. Let the King have the letters I have sent, and repair thou to me with as much speed as thou wouldest fly death. I have words to speak in thine ear will make thee dumb, yet are they much too light for the bore of the matter.[4] These good fellows will bring thee where I am. Rosencrantz and Guildenstern hold their course for England. Of them I have much to tell thee. Farewell.

"He that thou knowest thine.

"Hamlet"

Come, I will make you way for these your letters,
And do 't the speedier that you may direct me
To him from whom you brought them.

(Exeunt.)

Scene VII. Another room in the castle.

(Enter King and Laertes.)

King: Now must your conscience my acquittance seal,[1]
And you must put me in your heart for friend,
Sith you have heard, and with a knowing ear,
That he which hath your noble father slain
Pursued my life.

Laertes: It well appears. But tell me
Why you proceeded not against these feats,[2]
So crimeful and so capital[3] in nature,
As by your safety, wisdom, all things else,
You mainly were stirred up.

King: Oh, for two special reasons,
Which may to you perhaps seem much unsinewed,[4]
But yet to me they're strong. The Queen his mother
Lives almost by his looks, and for myself—
My virtue or my plague, be it either which—
She's so conjunctive[5] to my life and soul
That as the star moves not but[6] in his sphere,
I could not but by her. The other motive
Why to a public count[7] I might not go
Is the great love the general gender[8] bear him,
Who, dipping all his faults in their affection,[9]
Would, like the spring that turneth wood to stone,[10]
Convert his gyves to graces.[11] So that my arrows,
Too slightly timbered[12] for so loud a wind,
Would have reverted to my bow again
And not where I had aimed them.

Laertes: And so have I a noble father lost,
A sister driven into desperate terms,[13]
Whose worth, if praises may go back again,[14]
Stood challenger on mount of all the age

---

[4] **too . . . matter:** i.e., words fall short, like a small shot fired from a cannon with too wide a bore.

[1] **my . . . seal:** acquit me. [2] **feats:** acts. [3] **capital:** deserving death. [4] **unsinewed:** weak, flabby. [5] **conjunctive:** joined inseparably. [6] **moves . . . but:** moves only in. [7] **count:** trial. [8] **general gender:** common people. [9] **dipping . . . affection:** gilding his faults with their love. [10] **like . . . stone:** In several places in England there are springs of water so strongly impregnated with lime that they will quickly cover with stone anything placed under them. [11] **Convert . . . graces:** regard his fetters as honorable ornaments. [12] **timbered:** shafted. A light arrow is caught by the wind and blown back. [13] **terms:** condition. [14] **if . . . again:** if one may praise her for what she used to be.

For her perfections.[15] But my revenge will come.

King: Break not your sleeps for that. You must not think
That we are made of stuff so flat and dull
That we can let our beard be shook with danger
And think it pastime. You shortly shall hear more.[16]
I loved your father, and we love ourself,
And that, I hope, will teach you to imagine—
(Enter a Messenger, with letters.) How now! What news!

Messenger: Letters, my lord, from Hamlet.
This to your Majesty, this to the Queen.

King: From Hamlet! Who brought them?

Messenger: Sailors, my lord, they say—I saw them not.
They were given me by Claudio, he received them
Of him that brought them.

King: Laertes, you shall hear them.
Leave us. *(Exit Messenger.)*
(Reads.) "High and Mighty, you shall know I am set naked[17] on your kingdom. Tomorrow shall I beg leave to see your kingly eyes, when I shall, first asking your pardon thereunto, recount the occasion of my sudden and more strange return.

"Hamlet"

What should this mean? Are all the rest come back?
Or is it some abuse,[18] and no such thing?

Laertes: Know you the hand?

King: 'Tis Hamlet's character.[19] "Naked!"
And in a postscript here, he says "alone."
Can you advise me?

Laertes: I'm lost in it, my lord. But let him come.
It warms the very sickness in my heart
That I shall live and tell him to his teeth
"Thus didest thou."

King: If it be so, Laertes—
As how should it be so, how otherwise?—
Will you be ruled by me?

Laertes: Aye, my lord,
So you will not o'errule[20] me to a peace.

King: To thine own peace. If he be now returned,
As checking at[21] his voyage, and that he means
No more to undertake it, I will work him
To an exploit now ripe in my device,
Under the which he shall not choose but fall.
And for his death no wind of blame shall breathe,
But even his mother shall uncharge the practice[22]
And call it accident.

Laertes: My lord, I will be ruled,
The rather if you could devise it so
That I might be the organ.[23]

King: It falls right.
You have been talked of since your travel much,
And that in Hamlet's hearing, for a quality
Wherein they say you shine. Your sum of parts[24]
Did not together pluck such envy from him

[15] **Stood . . . perfections:** i.e., her worth challenged the whole world to find one as perfect. [16] **hear more:** i.e., when news comes from England that Hamlet is dead. [17] **naked:** destitute. [18] **abuse:** attempt to deceive. [19] **character:** handwriting. [20] **o'errule:** command. [21] **checking at:** swerving aside from, like a hawk that leaves the pursuit of its prey. [22] **uncharge . . . practice:** not suspect that his death was the result of the plot. [23] **organ:** instrument. [24] **sum of parts:** accomplishments as a whole.

As did that one, and that in my regard
Of the unworthiest siege.[25]
Laertes: What part is that, my lord?
King: A very ribbon in the cap of youth,
Yet needful too; for youth no less becomes
The light and careless livery that it wears
Than settled age his sables and his weeds,[26]
Importing health and graveness. Two months since,
Here was a gentleman of Normandy.
I've seen myself, and served against, the French,
And they can well[27] on horseback; but this gallant
Had witchcraft in 't, he grew unto his seat,
And to such wondrous doing brought his horse
As had he been incorpsed and deminatured[28]
With the brave beast. So far he topped my thought[29]
That I, in forgery of shapes and tricks,[30]
Come short of what he did.
Laertes: A Norman was 't?
King: A Norman.
Laertes: Upon my life, Lamond.
King: The very same.
Laertes: I know him well. He is the brooch[31] indeed
And gem of all the nation.
King: He made confession[32] of you,
And gave you such a masterly report
For art and exercise in your defense,
And for your rapier most especial,
That he cried out 'twould be a sight indeed
If one could match you. The scrimers[33] of their nation,
He swore, had neither motion, guard, nor eye
If you opposed them. Sir, this report of his
Did Hamlet so envenom[34] with his envy
That he could nothing do but wish and beg
Your sudden coming o'er, to play with him.
Now, out of this—
Laertes: What out of this, my lord?
King: Laertes, was your father dear to you?
Or are you like the painting[35] of a sorrow,
A face without a heart?
Laertes: Why ask you this?
King: Not that I think you did not love your father,
But that I know love is begun by time,
And that I see, in passages of proof,[36]
Time qualifies[37] the spark and fire of it.
There lives within the very flame of love
A kind of wick or snuff[38] that will abate it.
And nothing is at a like goodness still,[39]
For goodness, growing to a pleurisy,[40]
Dies in his own too much. That we would do
We should do when we would; for this "would" changes

[25] **siege:** seat, place. [26] **sables . . . weeds:** dignified roles. [27] **can well:** can do well. [28] **incorpsed . . . deminatured:** of one body. [29] **topped my thoughts:** surpassed what I could imagine. [30] **forgery . . . tricks:** imagination of all kinds of fancy tricks. **shapes:** fancies. [31] **brooch:** ornament. [32] **confession:** report. [33] **scrimers:** fencers. [34] **envenom:** poison. [35] **painting:** i.e., imitation. [36] **passages of proof:** experiences which prove. [37] **qualifies:** diminishes. [38] **snuff:** Before the invention of self-consuming wicks for candles, the wick smoldered and formed a ball of soot which dimmed the light and gave out a foul smoke. [39] **still:** always. [40] **pleurisy:** fullness.

And hath abatements and delays as many
As there are tongues, are hands, are accidents,
And then this "should" is like a spendthrift[41] sigh
That hurts by easing. But to the quick o' the ulcer.[42]
Hamlet comes back. What would you undertake
To show yourself your father's son in deed
More than in words?

Laertes: To cut his throat i' the church.[43]

King: No place indeed should murder sanctuarize,[44]
Revenge should have no bounds. But, good Laertes,
Will you do this, keep close within your chamber.
Hamlet returned shall know you are come home.
We'll put on those[45] shall praise your excellence
And set a double varnish on the fame
The Frenchman gave you, bring you in fine[46] together
And wager on your heads. He, being remiss,[47]
Most generous[48] and free from all contriving,[49]
Will not peruse the foils, so that with ease,
Or with a little shuffling, you may choose
A sword unbated,[50] and in a pass of practice[51]
Requite him for your father.

Laertes: I will do 't,
And for that purpose I'll anoint my sword.
I bought an unction[52] of a mountebank[53]
So mortal that but dip a knife in it,
Where it draws blood no cataplasm[54] so rare,
Collected from all simples[55] that have virtue
Under the moon,[56] can save the thing from death
That is but scratched withal. I'll touch my point
With this contagion, that if I gall[57] him slightly,
It may be death.

King: Let's further think of this,
Weigh what convenience both of time and means
May fit us to our shape.[58] If this should fail,
And that our drift look through our bad performance,[59]
'Twere better not assayed. Therefore this project
Should have a back or second, that might hold
If this did blast in proof.[60] Soft! Let me see—
We'll make a solemn wager on your cunnings.
I ha 't.

---

[41] **spendthrift:** wasteful, because sighing was supposed to be bad for the blood.
[42] **quick . . . ulcer:** i.e., to come to the real issue. **quick:** flesh, sensitive part.
[43] **cut . . . church:** i.e., to commit murder in a holy place, which would bring Laertes in danger of everlasting damnation; no crime could be worse. [44] **sanctuarize:** give sanctuary to. [45] **put . . . those:** set on some. [46] **fine:** short. [47] **remiss:** careless. [48] **generous:** noble. [49] **contriving:** plotting. [50] **unbated:** not blunted, with a sharp point. [51] **pass of practice:** treacherous thrust. [52] **unction:** poison. [53] **mountebank:** quack doctor. [54] **cataplasm:** poultice. [55] **simples:** herbs.
[56] **Under . . . moon:** herbs collected by moonlight were regarded as particularly potent.
[57] **gall:** break the skin. [58] **Weigh . . . shape:** consider the best time and method of carrying out a plan. [59] **drift . . . performance:** intention be revealed through bungling.
[60] **blast in proof:** break in trial, like a cannon which bursts when being tested.

When in your motion you are hot and dry—
As make your bouts[61] more violent to that end—
And that he calls for drink, I'll have prepared him
A chalice[62] for the nonce,[63] whereon but sipping,
If he by chance escape your venomed stuck,[64]
Our purpose may hold there. But stay, what noise?
(Enter Queen.) How now, Sweet Queen!

Queen: One woe doth tread upon another's heel.
So fast they follow. Your sister's drowned, Laertes.

Laertes: Drowned! Oh, where?

Queen: There is a willow grows aslant a brook
That shows his hoar[65] leaves in the glassy stream.
There with fantastic garlands did she come
Of crowflowers, nettles, daises, and long purples
That liberal[66] shepherds give a grosser name,
But our cold maids do dead-men's-fingers call them.
There on the pendent[67] boughs her coronet weeds[68]
Clambering to hang, an envious sliver[69] broke,
When down her weedy trophies and herself
Fell in the weeping brook. Her clothes spread wide,
And mermaidlike awhile they bore her up—
Which time she chanted snatches of old tunes,
As one incapable[70] of her own distress,
Or like a creature native and indued[71]
Unto that element. But long it could not be
Till that her garments, heavy with their drink,
Pulled the poor wretch from her melodious lay[72]
To muddy death.

Laertes: Alas, then, she is drowned!

Queen: Drowned, drowned.

Laertes: Too much of water hast thou, poor Ophelia,
And therefore I forbid my tears. But yet
It is our trick[73]—Nature her custom holds,
Let shame say what it will. When these[74] are gone,
The woman will be out.[75] Adieu, my lord.
I have a speech of fire that fain[76] would blaze
But that this folly douts[77] it. *(Exit.)*

King: Let's follow, Gertrude.
How much I had to do to calm his rage!
Now fear I this will give it start again,
Therefore let's follow. *(Exeunt.)*

---

[61] **bouts:** attacks, in the fencing match. [62] **chalice:** cup. [63] **nonce:** occasion. [64] **stuck:** thrust. [65] **hoar:** gray. The underside of the leaves of the willow are silver-gray. [66] **liberal:** coarse-mouthed. [67] **pendent:** hanging over the water. [68] **coronet weeds:** wild flowers woven into a crown. [69] **envious sliver:** malicious branch. [70] **incapable:** not realizing. [71] **indued:** endowed; i.e., a creature whose natural home is the water (*element*). [72] **lay:** song. [73] **But . . . trick:** it is our habit; i.e., to break into tears of great sorrow. [74] **these:** i.e., my tears. [75] **woman . . . out:** I shall be a man again. [76] **fain:** willingly. [77] **douts:** puts out.

Act V

Scene I. A churchyard.

(Enter two Clowns,[1] with spades, etc.)

1. Clown: Is she to be buried in Christian burial[2] that willfully seeks her own salvation?

2. Clown: I tell thee she is, and therefore make her grave straight.[3] The crowner[4] hath sat on her, and finds it Christian burial.

1. Clown: How can that be, unless she drowned herself in her own defense?

2. Clown: Why, 'tis found so.

1. Clown: It must be "se offendendo,"[5] it cannot be else. For here lies the point. If I drown myself wittingly,[6] it argues an act, and an act hath three branches—it is to act, to do, and to perform. Argal,[7] she drowned herself wittingly.

2. Clown: Nay, but hear you, goodman delver.[8]

1. Clown: Give me leave. Here lies the water, good. Here stands the man, good. If the man go to this water and drown himself, it is will he, nill he[9] he goes, mark you that; but if the water come to him and drown him, he drowns not himself. Argal, he that is not guilty of his own death shortens not his own life.

2. Clown: But is this law?

1. Clown: Aye, marry, is 't, crowner's quest[10] law.

2. Clown: Will you ha' the truth on 't? If this had not been a gentlewoman, she should have been buried out o' Christian burial.

1. Clown: Why, there thou say'st. And the more pity that great folks should have countenance[11] in this world to drown or hang themselves more than their even[12] Christian. Come, my spade. There is no ancient gentlemen but gardeners, ditchers, and gravemakers. They hold up[13] Adam's profession.

2. Clown: Was he a gentleman?

1. Clown: A' was the first that ever bore arms.[14]

2. Clown: Why, he had none.

1. Clown: What, art a heathen? How dost thou understand the Scripture? The Scripture says Adam digged. Could he dig without arms? I'll put another question to thee. If thou answerest me not to the purpose, confess thyself—

2. Clown: Go to.

1. Clown: What is he that builds stronger than either the mason, the shipwright, or the carpenter?

2. Clown: The gallows-maker, for that frame outlives a thousand tenants.

1. Clown: I like thy wit well, in good faith. The gallows does well, but how does it well? It does well to those that do ill. Now thou dost ill to say the gallows is built stronger than the church; argal, the gallows may do well to thee. To 't again, come.

2. Clown: Who builds stronger than a mason, a shipwright, or a carpenter?

1. Clown: Aye, tell me that, and unyoke.[15]

2. Clown: Marry, now I can tell.

1. Clown: To 't.

2. Clown: Mass,[16] I cannot tell.

(Enter Hamlet and Horatio, afar off.)

---

[1] **Clowns:** countrymen. [2] **Christian burial:** Suicides were not allowed burial in consecrated ground, but were buried at crossroads. The gravediggers and the priest are professionally scandalized that Ophelia should be allowed Christian burial solely because she is a lady of the Court. [3] **straight:** straightway. [4] **crowner:** coroner. [5] **se offendendo:** for **defendendo,** in self-defense. [6] **wittingly:** with full knowledge. [7] **Argal:** for the Latin **ergo,** therefore. [8] **delver:** digger. [9] **will he, nill he:** willy-nilly, whether he wishes or not. [10] **quest:** inquest. [11] **countenance:** favor. [12] **even:** fellow. [13] **hold up:** support. [14] **bore arms:** had a coat of arms—the outward sign of a gentleman. [15] **unyoke:** finish the job, unyoking the plow oxen being the end of the day's work. [16] **Mass:** by the mass.

1. Clown: Cudgel thy brains no more about it, for your dull ass will not mend his pace with beating, and when you are asked this question next, say "A gravemaker." The houses that he makes last till Doomsday. Go, get thee to Yaughan,[17] fetch me a stoup[18] of liquor.

(Exit Second Clown.)

(First Clown digs, and sings.)

"In youth,[19] when I did love, did love,
Methought it was very sweet,
To contract; oh, the time, for-a my behoove,[20]
Oh, methought, there-a was nothing-a meet."

Hamlet: Has this fellow no feeling for his business, that he sings at grave-making?

Horatio: Custom hath made it in him a property of easiness.[21]

Hamlet: 'Tis e'en so. The hand of little employment hath the daintier sense.[22]

1. Clown: *(Sings.)*

"But age, with his stealing steps,
Hath clawed me in his clutch,
And hath shipped me intil the land[23]
As if I had never been such."

(Throws up a skull.)

Hamlet: That skull had a tongue in it, and could sing once. How the knave jowls[24] it to the ground, as if it were Cain's jawbone, that did the first murder! It might be the pate of a politician which this ass now o'erreaches[25]—one that would circumvent[26] God, might it not?

Horatio: It might, my lord.

Hamlet: Or of a courtier, which could say "Good morrow, sweet lord! How dost thou, good lord?" This might be my lord Such-a-one that praised my lord Such-a-one's horse when he meant to beg it, might it not?

Horatio: Aye, my lord.

Hamlet: Why, e'en so. And now my Lady Worm's chapless,[27] and knocked about the mazzard[28] with a sexton's spade. Here's fine revolution, an we had the trick to see 't. Did these bones cost no more the breeding but to play at loggats[29] with 'em? Mine ache to think on 't.

1. Clown: *(Sings.)*

"A pickax and a spade, a spade,
For and a shrouding sheet—
Oh, a pit of clay for to be made
For such a guest is meet."

(Throws up another skull.)

Hamlet: There's another. Why may not that be the skull of a lawyer?[30] Where be his quiddities now, his quillets, his cases, his tenures, and his tricks? Why does he suffer this rude knave now to knock him about the sconce[31] with a dirty shovel, and will not tell him of his action of battery? Hum! This fellow might be in 's time a great buyer of land, with his statutes, his recognizances, his fines, his double vouchers, his recoveries. Is this the fine[32] of his fines and the recovery of his recoveries,

---

[17] **Yaughan:** apparently an innkeeper near the Globe Theatre. [18] **stoup:** large pot.
[19] **In youth . . . meet:** The song which the gravedigger sings without much care for accuracy or sense was first printed in **Tottel's Miscellany,** I558. [20] **behoove:** benefit.
[21] **property of easiness:** careless habits. [22] **hand . . . sense:** those who have little to do are the most sensitive. [23] **shipped . . . land:** shoved me into the ground.
[24] **jowls:** dashes. [25] **o'erreaches:** gets the better of. [26] **circumvent:** get around.
[27] **chapless:** without jaws. [28] **mazzard:** head, a slang word; lit., drinking-bowl.
[29] **loggats:** a game in which billets of wood or bones were stuck in the ground and knocked over by throwing at them. [30] **lawyer . . . indentures:** Hamlet strings out a number of the legal phrases loved by lawyers: *quiddities:* subtle arguments; *quillets:* quibbles; *tenures:* titles to property; *tricks:* knavery; *statutes:* bonds; *recognizances:* obligation; *fines:* conveyances; *vouchers:* guarantors; *recoveries:* transfers; *indentures:* agreements.
[31] **sconce:** head; lit., blockhouse. [32] **fine:** ending.

to have his fine pate full of fine dirt? Will his vouchers vouch him no more of his purchase, and double ones too, than the length and breadth of a pair of indentures? The very conveyances of his lands will hardly lie in this box,[33] and must the interior himself have no more, ha?

Horatio: Not a jot more, my lord.

Hamlet: Is not parchment made of sheepskins?

Horatio: Aye, my lord, and of calfskins too.

Hamlet: They are sheep and calves which seek out assurance in that. I will speak to this fellow. Whose grave's this, sirrah?

1. Clown: Mine, sir. *(Sings.)*
"Oh, a pit of clay for to be made
For such a guest is meet."

Hamlet: I think it be thine indeed, for thou liest in 't.

1. Clown: You lie out on 't, sir, and therefore 'tis not yours. For my part, I do not lie in 't, and yet it is mine.

Hamlet: Thou does lie in 't, be in 't and say it is thine. 'Tis for the dead, not for the quick, therefore thou liest.

1. Clown: 'Tis a quick lie, sir, 'twill away again, from me to you.

Hamlet: What man dost thou dig it for?

1. Clown: For no man, sir.

Hamlet: What woman, then?

1. Clown: For none, neither.

Hamlet: Who is to be buried in 't?

1. Clown: One that was a woman, sir, but, rest her soul, she's dead.

Hamlet: How absolute[34] the knave is! We must speak by the card,[35] or equivocation[36] will undo us. By the Lord, Horatio, this three years I have taken note of it—the age is grown so picked[37] that the toe of the peasant comes so near the heel of the courtier, he galls his kibe.[38] How long hast thou been a gravemaker?

1. Clown: Of all the days i' the year, I came to 't that day that our last King Hamlet o'ercame Fortinbras.

Hamlet: How long is that since?

1. Clown: Cannot you tell that? Every fool can tell that. It was that very day that young Hamlet was born, he that is mad, and sent into England.

Hamlet: Aye, marry, why was he sent into England?

1. Clown: Why, because a' was mad. A' shall recover his wits there, or, if a' do not, 'tis no great matter there.

Hamlet: Why?

1. Clown: 'Twill not be seen in him there—there the men are as mad as he.

Hamlet: How came he mad?

1. Clown: Very strangely, they say.

Hamlet: How "strangely"?

1. Clown: Faith, e'en with losing his wits.

Hamlet: Upon what ground?

1. Clown: Why, here in Denmark. I have been sexton here, man and boy, thirty years.[39]

Hamlet: How long will a man lie i' the earth ere he rot?

1. Clown: I' faith, if a' be not rotten before a' die—as we have many pocky[40]

---

[33] **box:** coffin. [34] **absolute:** exact. [35] **by . . . card:** exactly. The card is the mariner's compass. [36] **equivocation:** speaking with a double sense. The word was much discussed when *Hamlet* was written. [37] **picked:** refined. [38] **toe . . . kibe:** i.e., the peasant follows the courtier so closely that he rubs the courtier's heel into a blister. From about 1598 onward, writers, especially dramatists, often satirized the practice of yeoman farmers grown rich from war profits in sending their awkward sons to London to learn gentlemanly manners. Ben Jonson portrays two specimens in Stephen in *Every Man in His Humour* and Sogliardo in *Every Man out of His Humour.* [39] **thirty years:** The Clown's chronology has puzzled critics, for the general impression is that Hamlet was much younger. [40] **pocky:** suffering from the pox (venereal disease).

corses nowadays that will scarce hold the laying in—a' will last you some eight year or nine year. A tanner will last you nine year.

Hamlet: Why he more than another?

1. Clown: Why, sir, his hide is so tanned with his trade that a' will keep out water a great while, and your water is a sore decayer of your whoreson[41] dead body. Here's a skull now. This skull has lain in the earth three and twenty years.

Hamlet: Whose was it?

1. Clown: A whoreson mad fellow's it was. Whose do you think it was?

Hamlet: Nay, I know not.

1. Clown: A pestilence on him for a mad rogue! A' poured a flagon of Rhenish on my head once. This same skull, sir, was Yorick's skull, the King's jester.

Hamlet: This?

1. Clown: E'en that.

Hamlet: Let me see. *(Takes the skull.)* Alas, poor Yorick! I knew him, Horatio—a fellow of infinite jest, of most excellent fancy. He hath borne me on his back a thousand times, and now how abhorred in my imagination it is! My gorge rises[42] at it. Here hung those lips that I have kissed I know not how oft. Where be your gibes now? Your gambols? Your songs? Your flashes of merriment that were wont to set the table on a roar? Not one now, to mock your own grinning? Quite chop-fallen?[43] Now get you to my lady's chamber and tell her, let her paint an inch thick, to this favor[44] she must come—make her laugh at that. Prithee, Horatio, tell me one thing.

Horatio: What's that, my lord?

Hamlet: Dost thou think Alexander looked o' this fashion i' the earth?

Horatio: E'en so.

Hamlet: And smelt so? Pah!

(Puts down the skull.)

Horatio: E'en so, my lord.

Hamlet: To what base uses we may return, Horatio! Why may not imagination trace the noble dust of Alexander till he find it stopping a bunghole?[45]

Horatio: 'Twere to consider too curiously[46] to consider so.

Hamlet: No, faith, not a jot, but to follow him thither with modesty[47] enough and likelihood to lead it. As thus: Alexander died, Alexander was buried, Alexander returneth into dust; the dust is earth; of earth we make loam;[48] and why of that loam, whereto he was converted, might they not stop a beer barrel?

"Imperious Caesar, dead and turned to clay,
Might stop a hole to keep the wind away.
Oh, that that earth which kept the world in awe
Should patch a wall to expel the winter's flaw!"[49]
But soft! But soft! Aside—here comes the King.

(Enter Priests,[50] etc., in procession; the corpse of Ophelia, Laertes and Mourners following; King, Queen, their trains, etc.)

---

[41] **whoreson:** bastard, "son of a bitch." [42] **My . . . rises:** I feel sick. **gorge:** throat. [43] **chop-fallen:** downcast, with a pun on "chapless." [44] **favor:** appearance, especially in the face. [45] **bunghole:** the hole in a beer barrel. [46] **curiously:** precisely. [47] **with modesty:** without exaggeration. [48] **loam:** mixture of clay and sand, used in plastering walls. [49] **flaw:** blast. [50] **Enter Priests:** The stage directions in early texts are less elaborate. Q_2 notes, curtly, **Enter K.Q. Laertes and the corse.** F_1 has *Enter King, Queen, Laertes, and a coffin, with Lords attendant.* Q_1 prints *Enter King and Queen, Laertes and other lords, with a Priest after the coffin.* This probably was how the scene was originally staged. The modern directions ignore the whole significance of the "maimed rites"—Ophelia's funeral is insultingly simple.

The Queen, the courtiers—who is this they follow?
And with such maimèd[51] rites? This doth betoken[52]
The corse they follow did with desperate hand
Fordo[53] its own life. 'Twas of some estate.[54]
Couch[55] we awhile, and mark.

(Retiring with Horatio.)

Laertes: What ceremony else?
Hamlet: That is Laertes, a very noble youth. Mark.
Laertes: What ceremony else?
1. Priest: Her obsequies have been as far enlarged
As we have warranty.[56] Her death was doubtful,
And but that great command o'ersways the order,[57]
She should in ground unsanctified have lodged
Till the last trumpet; for[58] charitable prayers,
Shards,[59] flints, and pebbles should be thrown on her.
Yet here she is 'lowed her virgin crants,[60]
Her maiden strewments[61] and the bringing home
Of bell and burial.
Laertes: Must there no more be done?
1. Priest: No more be done.
We should profane the service of the dead
To sing a requiem and such rest to her
As to peace-parted souls.[62]
Laertes: Lay her i' the earth.
And from her fair and unpolluted flesh
May violets spring! I tell thee, churlish priest,
A ministering angel shall my sister be
When thou liest howling.
Hamlet: What, the fair Ophelia!
Queen: (Scattering flowers.) Sweets to the sweet. Farewell!
I hoped thou shouldst have been my Hamlet's wife,
I thought thy bride bed to have decked, sweet maid,
And not have strewed thy grave.
Laertes: Oh, treble woe
Fall ten times treble on that cursèd head
Whose wicked deed thy most ingenious sense[63]
Deprived thee of! Hold off the earth a while
Till I have caught her once more in mine arms.

(Leaps into the grave.)

Now pile your dust upon the quick[64] and dead
Till of this flat a mountain you have made
To o'ertop old Pelion[65] on the skyish[66] head
Of blue Olympus.
Hamlet: *(Advancing.)* What is he whose grief
Bears such an emphasis? Whose phrase of sorrow
Conjures the wandering stars and makes them stand[67]

---

[51] **maimed:** curtailed. [52] **betoken:** indicate. [53] **Fordo:** destroy. [54] **estate:** high rank. [55] **Couch:** lie down. [56] **Her . . . warranty:** the funeral rites have been as complete as may be allowed. [57] **but . . . order:** if the King's command had not overruled the proper procedure. [58] **for:** instead of. [59] **Shards:** pieces of broken crockery. [60] **crants:** wreaths of flowers—a sign that she had died unwed. [61] **maiden strewments:** the flowers strewn on the corpse of a maiden. [62] **peace-parted souls:** souls which departed in peace, fortified with the rites of the Church. [63] **most . . . sense:** lively intelligence. [64] **quick:** living. [65] **Pelion:** When the giants fought against the gods in order to reach Heaven, they tried to pile Mount Pelion and Mount Ossa on Mount Olympus, the highest mountain in Greece. [66] **skyish:** reaching the sky. [67] **stand:** stand still.

Like wonder-wounded hearers? This is I,
Hamlet the Dane. *(Leaps into the grave.)*
Laertes: The Devil take thy soul!

(Grappling with him.)

Hamlet: Thou pray'st not well.
I prithee, take thy fingers from my throat,
For though I am not splenitive[68] and rash,
Yet have I in me something dangerous,
Which let thy wisdom fear. Hold off thy hand.
King: Pluck them asunder.
Queen: Hamlet, Hamlet!
All: Gentlemen—
Horatio: Good my lord, be quiet.

(The Attendants part them, and they come out of the grave.)

Hamlet: Why, I will fight with him upon this theme
Until my eyelids will no longer wag.
Queen: O my son, what theme?
Hamlet: I loved Ophelia. Forty thousand brothers
Could not, with all their quantity of love,
Make up my sum. What wilt thou do for her?
King: Oh, he is mad, Laertes.
Queen: For love of God, forbear him.[69]
Hamlet: 'Swounds,[70] show me that thou'lt do.
Woo 't weep? Woo 't fight? Woo 't fast? Woo 't tear thyself?
Woo 't drink up eisel?[71] Eat a crocodile?
I'll do 't. Dost thou come here to whine?
To outface[72] me with leaping in her grave?
Be buried quick with her, and so will I.
And if thou prate of mountains, let them throw
Millions of acres on us, till our ground,
Singeing his pate against the burning zone,
Make Ossa[73] like a wart! Nay, an thou 'lt mouth,
I'll rant as well as thou.
Queen: This is mere madness.
And thus awhile the fit will work on him.
Anon, as patient as the female dove
When that her golden couplets[74] are disclosed,[75]
His silence will sit drooping.
Hamlet: Hear you, sir.
What is the reason that you use me thus?
I loved you ever. But it is no matter,
Let Hercules himself do what he may,
The cat will mew and dog will have his day.[76] *(Exit.)*
King: I pray thee, good Horatio, wait upon him.

(Exit Horatio.)

(To Laertes) Strengthen your patience in our last night's speech.
We'll put the matter to the present push.[77]
Good Gertrude, set some watch over your son.
This grave shall have a living monument.[78]
An hour of quiet shortly shall we see,
Till then, in patience our proceeding be. *(Exeunt.)*

---

[68] **splenitive:** hot-tempered. [69] **forbear him:** leave him alone. [70] **'Swounds . . . thou:** Hamlet in his excitement cries out that if Laertes wishes to make extravagant boasts of what he will do to show his sorrow, he will be even more extravagant. [71] **eisel:** vinegar. [72] **outface:** brow beat. [73] **Ossa:** See l. 307, n. [74] **couplets:** eggs, of which the dove lays two only. [75] **disclosed:** hatched. [76] **Let . . . day:** i.e., let this ranting hero have his turn; mine will come sometime. [77] **push:** test; lit., thrust of a pike. [78] **living monument:** with the double meaning of "lifelike memorial" and "the death of Hamlet."

Scene II. A hall in the castle.

(Enter Hamlet and Horatio.)

Hamlet: So much for this, sir. Now shall you see the other.
You do remember all the circumstance?
Horatio: Remember it, my lord!
Hamlet: Sir, in my heart there was a kind of fighting
That would not let me sleep. Methought I lay
Worse than the mutines in the bilboes.[1] Rashly,
And praised be rashness for it, let us know,
Our indiscretion sometime serves us well
When our deep plots do pall.[2] And that should learn[3] us
There's a divinity that shapes our ends,
Roughhew them how we will.[4]
Horatio: That is most certain.
Hamlet: Up from my cabin,
My sea gown[5] scarfed[6] about me, in the dark
Groped I to find out them,[7] had my desire,
Fingered their packet, and in fine withdrew
To mine own room again, making so bold,
My fears forgetting manners, to unseal
Their grand commission where I found, Horatio—
Oh royal knavery!—an exact command,
Larded[8] with many several sorts of reasons,
Importing Denmark's health and England's too,
With, ho! such bugs[9] and goblins in my life[10]
That, on the supervise,[11] no leisure bated,[12]
No, not to stay the grinding of the ax,
My head should be struck off.
Horatio: Is 't possible?
Hamlet: Here's the commission. Read it at more leisure
But wilt thou hear me how I did proceed?
Horatio: I beseech you.
Hamlet: Being thus benetted round with villainies—
Ere I could make a prologue to my brains,
They had begun the play—I sat me down,
Devised a new commission, wrote it fair.
I once did hold it, as our statists[13] do,
A baseness to write fair, and labored much
How to forget that learning, but, sir, now
It did me yeoman's service.[14] Wilt thou know
The effect of what I wrote?
Horatio: Aye, good my lord.
Hamlet: An earnest conjuration from the King,
As England was his faithful tributary,

---

[1] **mutines . . . bilboes:** mutineers in the shackles used on board ship. [2] **pall:** fail. [3] **learn:** teach. [4] **There's . . . will:** though we may make the rough beginning, God finishes our designs. [5] **sea gown:** a thick coat with a high collar worn by seamen. [6] **scarfed:** wrapped. [7] **them:** i.e., Rosencrantz and Guildenstern. [8] **Larded:** garnished. [9] **bugs:** bugbears. [10] **in my life:** so long as I was alive. [11] **supervise:** reading. [12] **bated:** allowed. [13] **statists:** statesmen. As scholars who have had to read Elizabethan documents know, the more exalted the writer, the worse his handwriting. As a girl Queen Elizabeth wrote a beautiful script; as Queen her letters are as illegible as any. All but the most confidential documents were copied out in a fair hand by a secretary. [14] **yeoman's service:** faithful service. The most reliable English soldiers were yeomen—farmers and their men.

As love between them like the palm might flourish,
As peace should still her wheaten garland wear
And stand a comma 'tween their amities,[15]
And many suchlike "Ases"[16] of great charge,[17]
That, on the view and knowing of these contents,
Without debatement[18] further, more or less,
He should the bearers put to sudden death,
Not shriving time allowed.[19]

Horatio: How was this sealed?

Hamlet: Why, even in that was Heaven ordinant.[20]
I had my father's signet in my purse,
Which was the model[21] of that Danish seal—
Folded the writ[22] up in the form of the other,
Subscribed[23] it, gave 't the impression,[24] placed it safely,
The changeling[25] never known. Now the next day
Was our sea fight, and what to this was sequent[26]
Thou know'st already.

Horatio: So Guildenstern and Rosencrantz go to 't.

Hamlet: Why, man, they did make love to this employment.
They are not near my conscience, their defeat[27]
Does by their own insinuation[28] grow.
'Tis dangerous when the baser nature comes
Between the pass and fell incensèd points
Of mighty opposites.[29]

Horatio: Why, what a King is this!

Hamlet: Does it not, think'st thee, stand me now upon—
He that hath killed my King and whored my mother,
Popped in between the election and my hopes,[30]
Thrown out his angle[31] for my proper[32] life,
And with such cozenage[33]—is 't not perfect conscience,
To quit[34] him with this arm? And is 't not to be damned,
To let this canker[35] of our nature come
In further evil?

Horatio: It must be shortly known to him from England
What is the issue of the business there.

Hamlet: It will be short. The interim[36] is mine,
And a man's life's no more than to say "One."
But I am very sorry, good Horatio,
That to Laertes I forgot myself,
For by the image of my cause I see

---

[15] **stand . . . amities:** be a connecting link of their friendship. [16] **"Ases":** Official documents were written in flowery language full of metaphorical clauses beginning with "As." Hamlet puns on "asses." [17] **great charge:** "great weight" and "heavy burden." [18] **debatement:** argument. [19] **Not . . . allowed:** without giving them time even to confess their sins. [20] **ordinant:** directing, in control. [21] **model:** copy. [22] **writ:** writing. [23] **Subscribed:** signed. [24] **impression:** of the seal. [25] **changeling:** lit., an ugly child exchanged by the fairies for a fair one. [26] **sequent:** following. [27] **defeat:** destruction. [28] **by . . . insinuation:** because they insinuated themselves into this business. [29] **'Tis . . . opposites:** it is dangerous for inferior men to interfere in a duel between mighty enemies. **pass:** thrust. **fell:** fierce. [30] **Popped . . . hopes:** As is from time to time shown in the play, the Danes chose their King by election. [31] **angle:** fishing rod and line. [32] **proper:** own. [33] **cozenage:** cheating. [34] **quit:** pay back. [35] **canker:** maggot. [36] **interim:** interval; between now and the news from England.

The portraiture of his. I'll court his favors.
But, sure, the bravery[37] of his grief did put me
Into a towering passion.

Horatio: Peace! Who comes here?

(Enter Osric.[38])

Osric: Your lordship is right welcome back to Denmark.

Hamlet: I humbly thank you, sir. Dost know this water fly?[39]

Horatio: No, my good lord.

Hamlet: Thy state is the more gracious,[40] for 'tis a vice to know him. He hath much land, and fertile. Let a beast be lord of beasts and his crib shall stand at the King's mess.[41] 'Tis a chough,[42] but, as I say, spacious[43] in the possession of dirt.

Osric: Sweet lord, if your lordship were at leisure, I should impart a thing to you from His Majesty.

Hamlet: I will receive it, sir, with all diligence of spirit. Put your bonnet to his right use,[44] 'tis for the head.

Osric: I thank your lordship, it is very hot.

Hamlet: No, believe me, 'tis very cold. The wind is northerly.

Osric: It is indifferent[45] cold, my lord, indeed.

Hamlet: But yet methinks it is very sultry and hot, for my complexion—

Osric: Exceedingly, my lord. It is very sultry, as 'twere—I cannot tell how. But, my lord, His Majesty bade me signify to you that he has laid a great wager on your head. Sir, this is the matter—

Hamlet: I beseech you, remember—

(Hamlet moves him to put on his hat.)

Osric: Nay, good my lord, for mine ease, in good faith. Sir, here is newly come to Court Laertes—believe me, an absolute[46] gentleman, full of most excellent differences,[47] of very soft society[48] and great showing.[49] Indeed, to speak feelingly[50] of him, he is the card or calendar of gentry,[51] for you shall find in him the continent of what part a gentleman would see.[52]

Hamlet: Sir,[53] his definement suffers no perdition in you, though I know to divide him inventorially would dizzy

---

[37] **bravery:** excessive show. [38] **Osric:** Osric is a specimen of the fashionable, effeminate courtier. He dresses prettily and talks the jargon of his class, which at this time affected elaborate and allusive metaphors and at all costs avoided saying plain things plainly. [39] **water fly:** a useless little creature that flits about. [40] **Thy . . . gracious:** you are in the better state. [41] **Let . . . mess:** i.e., any man, however low, who has wealth enough will find a good place at Court. **crib:** manger. **mess:** table. [42] **chough:** jackdaw. [43] **spacious:** wealthy. [44] **Put . . . use:** i.e., put your hat on your head. Osric is so nice-mannered that he cannot bring himself to wear his hat in the presence of the Prince. [45] **indifferent:** moderately. [46] **absolute:** perfect. [47] **differences:** qualities peculiar to himself. [48] **soft society:** gentle breeding. [49] **great showing:** distinguished appearance. [50] **feelingly:** with proper appreciation. [51] **card . . . gentry:** the very fashion plate of what a gentleman should be. [52] **continent . . . see:** all the parts that should be in a perfect gentleman. [53] **Sir . . . more:** Hamlet retorts in similar but even more extravagant language. This is too much for Osric (and for most modern readers). Hamlet's words may be paraphrased: "Sir, the description of this perfect gentleman loses nothing in your account of him; though I realize that if one were to try to enumerate his excellences, it would exhaust our arithmetic, and yet"—here he changes the image to one of sailing—"we should still lag behind him as he outsails us. But in the true vocabulary of praise, I take him to be a soul of the greatest worth, and his perfume"—i.e., his personal essence—"so scarce and rare that to speak truly of him, the only thing like him is his own reflection in his mirror, and everyone else who tries to follow him merely his shadow." **yaw:** fall off from the course laid. **verity . . . extolment:** in true praise. **infusion:** essence. **semblable:** resemblance. **trace:** follow. **umbrage:** shadow.

the arithmetic of memory, and yet but yaw neither, in respect of his quick sail. But in the verity of extolment, I take him to be a soul of great article, and his infusion of such dearth and rareness as, to make true diction of him, his semblable is his mirror, and who else would trace him, his umbrage—nothing more.

Osric: Your lordship speaks most infallibly of him.

Hamlet: The concernancy,[54] sir? Why do we wrap the gentleman in our more rawer breath?[55]

Osric: Sir?[56]

Horatio: Is 't not possible to understand in another tongue? You will do 't, sir, really.

Hamlet: What imports the nomination[57] of this gentleman?

Osric: Of Laertes?

Horatio: His purse is empty already, all's golden words are spent.

Hamlet: Of him, sir.

Osric: I know you are not ignorant—

Hamlet: I would you did, sir. Yet, in faith, if you did, it would not much approve[58] me. Well, sir?

Osric: You are not ignorant of what excellence Laertes is—

Hamlet: I dare not confess that, lest I should compare with him in excellence, but to know a man well were to know himself.

Osric: I mean, sir, for his weapon,[59] but in the imputation[60] laid on him by them, in his meed[61] he's unfellowed.[62]

Hamlet: What's his weapon?

Osric: Rapier and dagger.

Hamlet: That's two of his weapons, but, well.

Osric: The King, sir, hath wagered with him six Barbary horses, against the which he has imponed,[63] as I take it, six French rapiers and poniards, with their assigns,[64] as girdle, hanger,[65] and so—three of the carriages, in faith, are very dear to fancy,[66] very responsive to[67] the hilts, most delicate carriages, and of very liberal conceit.[68]

Hamlet: What call you the carriages?

Horatio: I knew you must be edified by the margent[69] ere you had done.

Osric: The carriages, sir, are the hangers.

Hamlet: The phrase would be more germane[70] to the matter if we could carry a cannon by our sides. I would it might be hangers till then. But, on—six Barbary horses against six French swords, their assigns, and three liberal-conceited carriages. That's the French bet against the Danish. Why is this "imponed," as you call it?

Osric: The King, sir, hath laid, sir, that in a dozen passes between yourself and him, he shall not exceed you three hits. He hath laid on twelve for nine,[71] and it would come to immediate trial if your lordship would vouchsafe the answer.

Hamlet: How if I answer no?

Osric: I mean, my lord, the opposition of your person in trial.

Hamlet: Sir, I will walk here in the hall. If it please His Majesty, it is the breathing-time of day with me.[72] Let the foils be

[54] **concernancy:** i.e., what is all this talk about? [55] **Why . . . breath:** why do we discuss the gentleman with our inadequate voices? [56] **Sir:** Osric is completely baffled. [57] **nomination:** naming. [58] **approve:** commend. [59] **his weapon:** i.e., skill with his weapon. [60] **imputation:** reputation. [61] **meed:** merit. [62] **unfellowed:** without an equal. [63] **imponed:** laid down as a stake. [64] **assigns:** that which goes with them. [65] **hanger:** straps by which the scabbard was hung from the belt, for specimens. [66] **dear to fancy:** of beautiful design. [67] **responsive to:** matching. [68] **liberal conceit:** elaborately artistic. [69] **edified . . . margent:** informed by the notes. In Shakespeare's time the notes were often printed in the margin. [70] **germane:** related. [71] **twelve . . . nine:** Laertes has bet the King he will hit Hamlet twelve times before Hamlet hits him nine. [72] **breathing-time . . . me:** time when I take exercise.

brought, the gentleman willing, and the King hold his purpose, I will win for him an I can. If not, I will gain nothing but my shame and the odd hits.

Osric: Shall I redeliver you e'en so?

Hamlet: To this effect, sir, after what flourish[73] your nature will.

Osric: I commend my duty to your lordship.

Hamlet: Yours, yours. *(Exit Osric.)* He does well to commend it himself, there are no tongues else for 's turn.

Horatio: This lapwing[74] runs away with the shell on his head.

Hamlet: He did comply with his dug[75] before he sucked it. Thus has he—and many more of the same breed that I know the drossy[76] age dotes on—only got the tune of the time and outward habit of encounter,[77] a kind of yesty collection[78] which carries them through and through the most fond[79] and winnowed[80] opinions—and do but blow them to their trial, the bubbles are out.[81]

(Enter a Lord.)

Lord: My lord, His Majesty commended him to you by young Osric, who brings back to him that you attend him in the hall. He sends to know if your pleasure hold to play with Laertes, or that you will take longer time.

Hamlet: I am constant to my purpose, they follow the King's pleasure. If his fitness speaks, mine is ready, now or whensoever, provided I be so able as now.

Lord: The King and Queen and all are coming down.

Hamlet: In happy time.[82]

Lord: The Queen desires you to use some gentle entertainment[83] to Laertes before you fall to play.

Hamlet: She well instructs me. *(Exit Lord.)*

Horatio: You will lose this wager, my lord.

Hamlet: I do not think so. Since he went into France I have been in continual practice, I shall win at the odds. But thou wouldst not think how ill all's here about my heart—but it is no matter.

Horatio: Nay, good my lord—

Hamlet: It is but foolery, but it is such a kind of gaingiving[84] as would perhaps trouble a woman.

Horatio: If your mind dislike anything, obey it. I will forestall their repair hither and say you are not fit.

Hamlet: Not a whit, we defy augury.[85] There's special providence in the fall of a sparrow.[86] If it be now, 'tis not to come; if it be not to come, it will be now; if it be not now, yet it will come. The readiness is all. Since no man has aught of what he leaves, what is 't to leave betimes? Let be.

(Enter King, Queen, Laertes, and Lords, Osric and other Attendants with foils; a table and flagons of wine on it.)

King: Come, Hamlet, come, and take this hand from me.

---

[73] **flourish:** fanfare, elaborate phrasing. [74] **lapwing:** a pretty, lively little bird. It is so lively that it can run about the moment it is hatched. [75] **did . . . dug:** was ceremonious with the nipple; i.e., behaved in this fantastic way from his infancy. [76] **drossy:** scummy, frivolous. [77] **tune . . . encounter:** i.e., they sing the same tune as everyone else and have the same society manners. [78] **yesty collection:** frothy catchwords. [79] **fond:** foolish. [80] **winnowed:** light as chaff. Winnowing is the process of fanning the chaff from the grain. [81] **do . . . out:** force them to make sense of their words and they are deflated, as Hamlet has just deflated Osric. [82] **In . . . time:** at a good moment. [83] **gentle entertainment:** kindly treatment; i.e., be reconciled after the brawl in the churchyard. [84] **gaingiving:** misgiving. [85] **augury:** omens. [86] **special . . . sparrow.** The idea comes from Matthew 10:29, "Are not two sparrows sold for a farthing? and one of them shall not fall to the ground without your Father."

(The King puts Laertes' hand into Hamlet's.)

Hamlet: Give me your pardon, sir. I've done you wrong,
But pardon 't, as you are a gentleman.
This presence[87] knows,
And you must needs have heard, how I am punished
With sore distraction. What I have done
That might your nature, honor, and exception[88]
Roughly awake, I here proclaim was madness.
Was 't Hamlet wronged Laertes? Never Hamlet.
If Hamlet from himself be ta'en away,[89]
And when he's not himself does wrong Laertes,
Then Hamlet does it not, Hamlet denies it.
Who does it, then? His madness. If 't be so,
Hamlet is of the faction that is wronged,
His madness is poor Hamlet's enemy.
Sir, in this audience
Let my disclaiming from a purposed evil[90]
Free me so far in your most generous thoughts
That I have shot mine arrow o'er the house,
And hurt my brother.

Laertes: I am satisfied in nature,
Whose motive, in this case, should stir me most
To my revenge. But in my terms of honor
I stand aloof, and will no reconcilement
Till by some elder masters of known honor
I have a voice and precedent of peace
To keep my name ungored.[91] But till that time
I do receive your offered love like love
And will not wrong it.

Hamlet: I embrace it freely,
And will this brother's wager frankly play.
Give us the foils. Come on.

Laertes: Come, one for me.

Hamlet: I'll be your foil,[92] Laertes. In mine ignorance
Your skill shall, like a star i' the darkest night,
Stick[93] fiery off indeed.

Laertes: You mock me, sir.

Hamlet: No, by this hand.

King: Give them the foils, young Osric. Cousin Hamlet,
You know the wager?

Hamlet: Very well, my lord.
Your Grace has laid the odds o' the weaker side.

King: I do not fear it, I have seen you both.
But since he is bettered,[94]
We have therefore odds.

Laertes: This is too heavy, let me see another.

Hamlet: This likes[95] me well. These foils have all a length?[96] *(They prepare to play.)*

Osric: Aye, my good lord.

King: Set me the stoups[97] of wine upon that table.
If Hamlet give the first or second hit,

---

[87] **presence:** the whole Court. [88] **exception:** resentment. [89] **If . . . away:** i.e., Hamlet mad is not Hamlet. [90] **Let . . . evil:** let my declaration that I did not intend any harm. [91] **I . . . ungored:** I bear you no grudge so far as concerns my personal feelings, which would most readily move me to vengeance; but as this matter touches my honor, I cannot accept your apology until I have been assured by those expert in matters of honor that I may so do without loss of reputation. [92] **foil:** Hamlet puns on the other meaning of foil—tin foil set behind a gem to give it luster. [93] **Stick . . . off:** Shine out. [94] **bettered:** considered your superior. [95] **likes:** pleases. [96] **have . . . length:** are all of equal length. [97] **stoups:** drinking vessels.

Or quit[98] in answer of the third exchange,
Let all the battlements their ordnance fire.
The King shall drink to Hamlet's better breath,
And in the cup a union[99] shall he throw
Richer than that which four successive kings
In Denmark's crown have worn. Give me the cups,
And let the kettle[100] to the trumpet speak,
The trumpet to the cannoneer without,
The cannon to the Heavens, the Heaven to earth,
"Now the King drinks to Hamlet."
Come, begin,
And you, the judge, bear a wary eye.

Hamlet: Come on, sir.
Laertes: Come, my lord. *(They play.)*
Hamlet: One.
Laertes: No.
Hamlet: Judgment.
Osric: A hit, a very palpable[101] hit.
Laertes: Well, again.
King: Stay, give me drink. Hamlet, this pearl is thine[102]—
Here's to thy health.

(Trumpets sound, and cannon shot off within.)

Give him the cup.

Hamlet: I'll play this bout first. Set it by a while.
Come. *(They play.)*
Another hit, what say you?
Laertes: A touch, a touch, I do confess.
King: Our son shall win.
Queen: He's fat[103] and scant of breath.
Here, Hamlet, take my napkin, rub thy brows.
The Queen carouses to thy fortune, Hamlet.
Hamlet: Good madam!
King: Gertrude, do not drink.
Queen: I will, my lord, I pray you pardon me.

(She drinks.)

King: *(Aside.)* It is the poisoned cup, it is too late.
Hamlet: I dare not drink yet, madam—by and by.
Queen: Come, let me wipe thy face.
Laertes: My lord, I'll hit him now.
King: I do not think 't.
Laertes: *(Aside.)* And yet 'tis almost against my conscience.
Hamlet: Come, for the third, Laertes. You but dally.[104]
I pray you pass with your best violence,
I am afeard you make a wanton of me.[105]
Laertes: Say you so? Come on. *(They play.)*
Osric: Nothing, neither way.
Laertes: Have at you now!

(Laertes wounds Hamlet; then, in scuffling, they change rapiers,[106] and Hamlet wounds Laertes.)

King: Part them, they are incensed.
Hamlet: Nay, come, again. *(The Queen falls.)*
Osric: Look to the Queen there, ho!
Horatio: They bleed on both sides. How is it, my lord?
Osric: How is 't, Laertes?
Laertes: Why, as a woodcock to mine own springe,[107] Osric,

---

[98] **quit:** strike back. [99] **union:** a large pearl. [100] **kettle:** kettledrum. [101] **palpable:** clear. [102] **this . . . thine:** With these words the King drops the poisoned pearl into the cup intended for Hamlet. [103] **fat:** out of condition. [104] **dally:** play. [105] **make . . . me:** treat me like a child by letting me win. [106] **they . . . rapiers:** With the exchange of rapiers, Hamlet wounds Laertes with the pointed and poisoned weapon. [107] **springe:** snare.

I am justly killed with mine own treachery.

Hamlet: How does the Queen?

King: She swounds to see them bleed.

Queen: No, no, the drink, the drink!—O my dear Hamlet—
The drink, the drink! I am poisoned. *(Dies.)*

Hamlet: Oh, villainy! Ho! Let the door be locked.
Treachery! Seek it out. *(Laertes falls.)*

Laertes: It is here, Hamlet. Hamlet, thou art slain.
No medicine in the world can do thee good,
In thee there is not half an hour of life.
The treacherous instrument is in thy hand,
Unbated and envenomed. The foul practice
Hath turned itself on me. Lo, here I lie
Never to rise again. Thy mother's poisoned.
I can no more. The King, the King's to blame.

Hamlet: The point envenomed too!
Then, venom, to thy work. *(Stabs the King.)*

All: Treason! Treason!

King: Oh, yet defend me, friends, I am but hurt.

Hamlet: Here, thou incestuous, murderous, damnèd Dane,
Drink off this potion. Is thy union[108] here?
Follow my mother. *(King dies.)*

Laertes: He is justly served.
It is a poison tempered[109] by himself.
Exchange forgiveness with me, noble Hamlet.
Mine and my father's death come not upon thee,[110]
Nor thine on me! *(Dies.)*

Hamlet: Heaven make thee free of it![111] I follow thee,
I am dead, Horatio. Wretched Queen, adieu!
You that look pale and tremble at this chance,
That are but mutes or audience to this act,
Had I but time—as this fell[112] sergeant,[113] Death,
Is strict in his arrest—oh, I could tell you—
But let it be. Horatio, I am dead,
Thou livest. Report me and my cause aright
To the unsatisfied.[114]

Horatio: Never believe it.
I am more an antique Roman[115] than a Dane.
Here's yet some liquor left.

Hamlet: As thou 'rt a man,
Give me the cup. Let go—by Heaven, I'll have 't.
O good Horatio, what a wounded name,
Things standing thus unknown, shall live behind me!
If thou didst ever hold me in thy heart,
Absent thee from felicity a while,
And in this harsh world draw thy breath in pain
To tell my story. *(March afar off, and shot within.)*
What warlike noise is this?

Osric: Young Fortinbras, with conquest come from Poland,
To the ambassadors of England gives
This warlike volley.

Hamlet: Oh, I die, Horatio,
The potent poison quite o'ercrows[116] my spirit.

---

[108] **union:** pearl. [109] **tempered:** mixed. [110] **come . . . thee:** are not on your head. [111] **Heaven . . . it:** God forgives you. [112] **fell:** dread. [113] **sergeant:** the officer of the Court who made arrests. [114] **unsatisfied:** who do not know the truth. [115] **antique Roman:** like Cato and Brutus, who killed themselves rather than survive in a world which was unpleasing to them. [116] **o'ercrows:** overpowers.

I cannot live to hear the news from England,
But I do prophesy the election[117] lights
On Fortinbras. He has my dying voice.[118]
So tell him, with the occurrents, more and less,
Which have solicited.[119] The rest is silence. *(Dies.)*

Horatio: Now cracks a noble heart. Good night, sweet Prince,
And flights of angels sing thee to thy rest!

(March within.)

Why does the drum come hither?

(Enter Fortinbras, and the English Ambassadors, with drum, colors, and Attendants.)

Fortinbras: Where is this sight?

Horatio: What is it you would see?
If aught of woe or wonder, cease your search.

Fortinbras: This quarry cries on havoc.[120] O proud Death,
What feast is toward[121] in thine eternal cell
That thou so many princes at a shot
So bloodily hast struck?

1. Ambassador: The sight is dismal,
And our affairs from England come too late.
The ears are senseless that should give us hearing,
To tell him his commandment is fulfilled,
That Rosencrantz and Guildenstern are dead.
Where should we have our thanks?

Horatio: Not from his mouth
Had it the ability of life to thank you.
He never gave commandment for their death.
But since, so jump[122] upon this bloody question,[123]
You from the Polack wars, and you from England,
Are here arrived, give order that these bodies
High on a stage be placèd to the view,
And let me speak to the yet unknowing world
How these things came about. So shall you hear
Of carnal, bloody, and unnatural acts,
Of accidental judgments, casual slaughters,
Of deaths put on by cunning and forced cause,
And, in this upshot, purposes mistook
Fall'n on the investors' heads.[124] All this can I
Truly deliver.

Fortinbras: Let us haste to hear it,
And call the noblest to the audience.
For me, with sorrow I embrace my fortune.
I have some rights of memory[125] in this kingdom,
Which now to claim my vantage[126] doth invite me.

Horatio: Of that I shall have also cause to speak,
And from his mouth whose voice will draw on more.[127]
But let this same be presently performed,
Even while men's minds are wild, lest more mischance

---

[117] **election:** as King of Denmark. [118] **voice:** support. [119] **occurrents . . . solicited:** events great and small which have caused me to act. [120] **quarry . . . havoc:** heap of slain denotes a pitiless slaughter. [121] **toward:** being prepared. [122] **jump:** exactly. [123] **question:** matter. [124] **carnal . . . heads:** These lines sum up the whole tragedy. [125] **rights of memory:** rights that will be remembered; i.e., with the disappearance of all the family of the original King Hamlet the situation reverts to what it was before the death of Fortinbras' father. [126] **vantage:** i.e., my advantage, there being none to dispute my claim. [127] **voice . . . more:** i.e., Hamlet's dying voice will strengthen your claim.

On plots and errors happen.

Fortinbras: Let four captains
Bear Hamlet, like a soldier, to the stage.
For he was likely, had he been put on,[128]
To have proved most royally. And for his passage
The soldiers' music and the rites of war
Speak loudly for him.
Take up the bodies. Such a sight as this
Becomes the field, but here shows much amiss.
Go, bid the soldiers shoot.

(A dead march. Exeunt, bearing off the bodies; after which a peal of ordnance is shot off.)

Explorations of the Text

Act I

1. Discuss the first scene in *Hamlet.* What is wrong in the State of Denmark?
2. Why does Claudius ask Hamlet to abandon his "impious stubbornness"?
3. In Act I, Scene ii, what does Hamlet reveal about himself in his first **soliloquy** (a speech directed to the audience recreating thoughts not known to other characters)?
4. What do Laertes and Polonius believe about Ophelia's love for Hamlet? What do they want her to do?
5. What does Polonius's advice (Act I, Scene iii) reveal of life at court?
6. What does the ghost tell Hamlet? What is his request?

Act II

1. How is Hamlet changed by his father's death and by his mother's remarriage? Is he mad, or is he pretending to be mad (II, i)?
2. What do you learn about Polonius through his diagnosis of and reaction to Hamlet's madness (II, ii)?

Act III

1. Why does Hamlet find it difficult to avenge his father? Explain his famous soliloquy, which begins "To be or not to be."
2. Consider Hamlet's treatment of Ophelia in Act III, Scene i. Find evidence that Hamlet knows that Claudius and Polonius listen to this conversation.
3. Why does Ophelia become insane?
4. How does "The Murder of Gonzago," the play-within-the-play, relate to *Hamlet?* What does Hamlet learn from Claudius' reaction?

[128] **had . . . on:** had he become King.

5. Is Claudius a good ruler, a loving husband and father, and a reasonable man?
6. Why does Hamlet not kill Claudius at prayer?
7. Interpret Hamlet's treatment of Gertrude in Act III. What crimes does Hamlet believe that Gertrude has committed?
8. Is Polonius a wise counselor, sycophant, hypocrite, and/or fool?
9. Is Laertes' desire to avenge the death of Polonius less or more justified than Hamlet's mandate for revenge?

Act IV

1. How does Claudius manipulate Laertes? To what extent does Laertes comply?
2. Identify the conflicts in *Hamlet.* Which is the central conflict?

Act V

1. In the scene with the gravediggers, how does the comedy function in relation to the themes of the play?
2. What does Hamlet tell Horatio about life? How has Hamlet changed (V, i)?
3. Polonius, Rosencrantz, Guildenstern, Ophelia, Laertes, Gertrude, Claudius, and Hamlet all die in *Hamlet.* Who is responsible for these deaths—Claudius and/or Hamlet?
4. Explain the appearance of Fortinbras (V, i). Is this a tragedy of state as well as a personal tragedy?

The Reading/Writing Connection

1. Select a famous or intriguing line or passage from this play, and write about it. Consider language, tone, character, conflict, or theme. Add personal reflections.
2. Choose a character from the play, and write a description of appearance, voice, personality, habits, motives, conflicts, virtues, and/or flaws.

Ideas for Writing

1. Write an analysis of Hamlet's character. Refer to literary criticism if you wish.
2. Discuss a relationship in *Hamlet.* (Suggestions: Hamlet and Ophelia, Hamlet and Gertrude, Claudius and Gertrude, Hamlet and Laertes, or Hamlet and Horatio)

3. Consider a famous quotation from *Hamlet* in relation to two other works in this chapter.
4. Compose an essay on the theme of betrayal, revenge, or love in this play.
5. Read about the Globe Theater and about the staging and production of *Hamlet.* Write a paper on a topic that emerges from this research.

NONFICTION

Our Hurried Children from *The Hurried Child: Growing Up Too Fast Too Soon*

David Elkind

David Elkind (1931–) was born in Detroit, Michigan. Elkind, educated at the University of California, Los Angeles, where he received his undergraduate degree and his doctorate in psychology, is a practicing child psychologist. He has written several books concerned with child development and the factors influencing it. Currently, Elkind is chair of the Department of Child Study at Tufts University.

1981

The concept of childhood, so vital to the traditional American way of life, is threatened with extinction in the society we have created. Today's child has become the unwilling, unintended victim of overwhelming stress—the stress borne of rapid, bewildering social change and constantly rising expectations. The contemporary parent dwells in a pressure-cooker of competing demands, transitions, role changes, personal and professional uncertainties, over which he or she exerts slight direction. We seek release from stress whenever we can, and usually the one sure ambit of our control is the home. Here, if nowhere else, we enjoy the fact (or illusion) of playing a determining role. If child-rearing necessarily entails stress, then by hurrying children to grow up, or by treating them as adults, we hope to remove a portion of our burden of worry and anxiety and to enlist our children's aid in carrying life's load. We do not mean our children harm in acting thus—on the contrary, as a society we have come to imagine that it is good for young people to mature rapidly. Yet we do our children harm when we hurry them through childhood.

The principal architect of our modern notion of childhood was the French philosopher Jean-Jacques Rousseau. It was he who first criticized the educational methods for presenting materials from a uniquely adult perspective, reflecting adult values and interests. Classical *paideia*—that is, the value of transmitting a cultural-social heritage—was a good thing, said Rousseau, but the learning process must take the child's perceptions and stage of development into account. In his classic work *Emile,* Rousseau wrote, "Childhood has its own way of seeing, thinking, and feeling, and nothing is more foolish than to try to substitute ours for theirs." More specifically, he observed that children matured in four stages, and just as each stage had its own characteristics, it should also have a corresponding set of appropriate educational objectives.

This idea of childhood as a distinct phase preceding adult life became inextricably interwoven with the modern concepts of universal education and the small, nuclear family (mother, father, children—not the extended family of earlier eras) in the late eighteenth and early nineteenth centuries, the heyday of the original Industrial Revolution. The transition is well explained by futurologist Alvin Toffler: "As work shifted out of the fields and the home, children had to be prepared for factory life. . . . If young people could be prefitted in the industrial system, it would vastly ease the problems of industrial discipline later on. The result was another central structure of all [modern] societies: mass education."

In addition to free, universal, public education, the emergent society tended to create smaller family units. Toffler writes, "To free workers for factory labor, key functions of the family were parcelled out to new specialized institutions. Education of the child was turned over to schools. Care of the aged was turned over to the poor houses or old-age homes or nursing homes. Above all, the new society required mobility. It needed workers who would follow jobs from place to place. . . . Torn apart by migration to the cities, battered by economic storms, families stripped themselves of unwanted relatives, grew smaller, more mobile, more suited to the needs of the [work place]."

5 While industrialization proceeded apace, the cultural recognition of childhood as a discrete life phase was given strong social reinforcement in the late nineteenth century with the establishment of child psychology as a scientific discipline. Work in this field began with the so-called baby biographies—minutely detailed accounts by observant parents of their infants' behavior. Bronson Alcott, father of Louisa May, contributed one such study, as did Milicent Shinn. Jean Piaget, the celebrated Swiss psychologist, carried on the tradition when he took time off from his collective studies of children to observe at close range (and write about) his own three offspring.

Around the turn of the century, G. Stanley Hall, generally regarded as the founder of the laboratory study of children, initiated the ill-fated "Child Study Movement." The extensive questionnaires he designed that parents and teachers administered to children by the thousands proved to be terribly error-prone and inexact. However, Hall had more success in founding Clark University, and the school's department of child psychology, carefully cultivated by Hall, led the nation in research and training in the new field, producing scientists of the eminence of Arnold Gessell and Lewis Terman.

After the Second World War, child psychology entered its boom period. Whereas before the war there were only two scientific journals reporting research in child development, today there are more than a dozen. All university departments of psychology include psychologists who are studying topics as varied as adolescence, learning in infants, socialization, peer interaction, sexual development, attachment and loss, the measurement of intelligence, learning disabilities, language acquisition, and so on. In short, we have accumulated a large library of data and knowledge about the period of life we call childhood. It is indeed no small irony that at the very time the stress of social life and change is threatening the existence of childhood, we know far more about childhood than we have ever known in the past.

What is even more curious is the degree to which this scientific knowledge is available to and consumed by the general public, for the research explosion in child study has been matched by a corresponding blaze of popular books about children. Often, well-known child psychologists undertake to "translate" scientific finds into useful applications. As early as 1894, the renowned psychologist T. Emmet Holt informed readers of his book *Care and Feeding of Children* how to prevent chafing: "First, not too much or too strong soap should be used; secondly, careful rinsing of the body, thirdly, not too vigorous rubbing, either during or after the bath; fourthly, the very free use of dusting powder in all the folds of the skin. . . . This is of the utmost importance in very fat infants." Holt was merely the first in a seemingly endless line of distinguished (and not so distinguished) "translators" of scientific child psychology into a popular idiom. Perhaps the two best-known are Arnold Gesell's *The Child from Birth to Five* and the incomparably influential *Infant and Child Care* by Benjamin Spock. Yet each year an awesome number of books, some very well written and others less so, appear with titles like (to consider just 1977) *Raising Happy Healthy Children, For Love of Children, Parenting, The Parent Book, Living with Your Hyperactive Children,* and *Helping Your Child Learn Right from Wrong.* Workshops and courses are available in every community in the country to guide and assist adults involved with the rearing of young people. If we hurry children to grow up too fast today, then, it is surely not done out of ignorance.

Miniature Adults

Today's pressures on middle-class children to grow up fast begin in early childhood. Chief among them is the pressure for early intellectual attainment, deriving from a changed perception of precocity. Several decades ago precocity was looked upon with great suspicion. The child prodigy, it was thought, turned out to be a neurotic adult; thus the phrase "early ripe, early rot!" Trying to accelerate children's acquisition of academic skills was seen as evidence of bad parenting.

10 A good example of this type of attitude is provided by the case of William James Sidis, the son of a psychiatrist. Sidis was born at the turn of the century and became a celebrated child prodigy who entered Harvard College at the age of eleven. His papers on higher mathematics gave the impression that he would make major contributions in this area. Sidis soon attracted the attention of the media, who celebrated his feats as a child. But Sidis never went further and seemed to move aimlessly from one job to another. In 1930 James Thurber wrote a profile of Sidis in the *New Yorker* magazine entitled "Where Are They Now?"; he described Sidis's lonely and pitiful existence in which his major preoccupation was collecting streetcar transfers from all over the world.

Such attitudes, however, changed markedly during the 1960s when parents were bombarded with professional and semiprofessional dicta on the importance of learning in the early years. If you did not start teaching children when they were young, parents were told, a golden opportunity for learning would be lost. Today, tax-supported kindergartens are operating in almost every state, and children are admitted at increasingly earlier ages. (In many cities a child born before January 1 can enter kindergarten the preceding

September, making his or her effective entrance age four.) Once enrolled in kindergarten, children are now often presented with formal instruction in reading and math once reserved for the later grades.

How did this radical turnabout in attitudes happen? There are probably many reasons, but a major one was the attack on "progressive" education that occurred in the fifties and that found much education material dated. The Russian launching of the Sputnik in 1957 drove Americans into a frenzy of self-criticism about education and promoted the massive curriculum movement of the 1960s that brought academics from major universities into curriculum writing. Unfortunately, many academics knew their discipline but didn't know children and were unduly optimistic about how fast and how much children could learn. This optimism was epitomized in Jerome Bruner's famous phrase, "That any subject can be taught effectively in some intellectually honest form to any child at any stage of development." What a shift from "early ripe, early rot"!

The trend toward early academic pressure was further supported by the civil rights movement, which highlighted the poor performance of disadvantaged children in our schools. Teachers were under attack by avant-garde educators such as John Holt, Jonathan Kozol, and Herbert Kohl, and they were forced to defend their lack of success by shifting the blame. Their children did not do well because they came inadequately prepared. It was not what was going on in the classroom but what had not gone on at home that was the root of academic failure among the disadvantaged; hence Head Start, hence busing, which by integrating students would equalize background differences.

One consequence of all this concern for the early years was the demise of the "readiness" concept. The concept of readiness had been extolled by developmental psychologists such as Arnold Gesell who argues for the biological limitations on learning. Gesell believed that children were not biologically ready for learning to read until they had attained a Mental Age (a test score in which children are credited with a certain number of months for each correct answer) of six and one-half years. But the emphasis on early intervention and early intellectual stimulation (even of infants) made the concept of readiness appear dated and old-fashioned. In professional educational circles readiness, once an honored educational concept, is now in disrepute.

15 The pressure for early academic achievement is but one of many contemporary pressures on children to grow up fast. Children's dress is another. Three or four decades ago, prepubescent boys wore short pants and knickers until they began to shave; getting a pair of long pants was a true rite of passage. Girls were not permitted to wear makeup or sheer stockings until they were in their teens. For both sexes, clothing set children apart. It signaled adults that these people were to be treated differently, perhaps indulgently; it made it easier for children to act as children. Today even preschool children wear miniature versions of adult clothing. From overalls to LaCoste shirts to scaled-down designer fashions, a whole range of adult costumes is available to children. (Along with them is a wide choice of corresponding postures such as those of young teenagers modeling designer jeans.) Below is an illustration from a recent article by Susan Ferraro entitled "Hotsy Totsy."

It was a party like any other: ice cream and cake, a donkey poster and twelve haphazard tails, and a door prize for everyone including Toby, the birthday girl's little brother who couldn't do anything but smear icing.

"Ooh," sighed seven-year-old Melissa as she opened her first present. It was Calvin Klein jeans. "Aah," she gasped at the second box revealed a bright new top from Gloria Vanderbilt. There were Christian Dior undies from grandma—a satiny little chemise and matching bloomer bottoms—and mother herself had fallen for a marvelous party outfit from Yves St. Laurent. Melissa's best friend gave her an Izod sports shirt, complete with alligator emblem. Added to that a couple of books were, indeed, very nice and predictable—except for the fancy doll one guest's eccentric mother insisted on bringing.

When children dress like adults they are more likely to behave as adults do, to imitate adult actions. It is hard to walk like an adult male wearing corduroy knickers that make an awful noise. But boys in long pants can walk like men, and little girls in tight jeans can walk like women. It is more difficult today to recognize that children are children and not miniature adults, because children dress and move like adults.

Another evidence of the pressure to grow up fast is the change in the programs of summer camps for children. Although there are still many summer camps that offer swimming, sailing, horseback riding, archery, and camp fires—activities we remember from our own childhood—an increasing number of summer camps offer specialized training in many different areas, including foreign languages, tennis, baseball, dance, music, and even computers.

Among such camps the most popular seem to be those that specialize in competitive sports: softball, weight training, tennis, golf, football, basketball, hockey, soccer, lacrosse, gymnastics, wrestling, judo, figure skating, surfing. "Whatever the sport there's a camp (or ten or a hundred of them) dedicated to teaching the finer points. Often these camps are under the direction, actual or nominal, of a big name in a particular sport, and many have professional athletes on their staffs. The daily routine is rigorous, with individual and/or group lessons, practice sessions and tournaments, complete with trophies. And, to cheer the athletes on with more pep and polish, cheerleaders and song girls can also attend."

The change in the programs of summer camps reflects the new attitude that the years of childhood are not to be frittered away by engaging in activities merely for fun. Rather, the years are to be used to perfect skills and abilities that are the same as those of adults. Children are early initiated into the rigors of adult competition. Competitive sports for children are becoming ever more widespread and include everything from Little League to Pee Wee hockey. The pressure to engage in organized, competitive sports at camp and at home is one of the most obvious pressures on contemporary children to grow up fast.

20 There are many other pressures as well. Many children today travel across the country, and indeed across the world, alone. The so-called unaccompanied minor has become so commonplace that airlines have instituted special rules

and regulations for them. The phenomenon is a direct result of the increase in middle-class divorces and the fact that one or the other parent moves to another part of the country or world. Consequently, the child travels to visit one parent or the other. Children also fly alone to see grandparents or to go to special camps or training facilities.

While some children really do not like to travel alone, others enjoy it. This young man's story is illustrative:

> *Louic Villeneuve, nine, who lives in Cambridge, flies to Montreal alone each summer to visit his mother and to stay in the city where he spent the first five years of his life. "He loves it," said his father. "Once there weren't enough seats in the back of the plane so I had to go first class," Louic said, "there was so much food." The only problem Louic finds is adults who ask him which he likes better, Montreal or Boston. No matter which he answers, Louic has found, someone is unhappy. When his father flew with him recently, Louic commented, "I wish you weren't with me." A child alone, he seems to have discovered, gets more attention, more crayons, and more food than one travelling with a parent.*

Although airline personnel take good care of unaccompanied children and some children like Louic enjoy traveling alone, it is very stressful for other children. Young children in particular may feel that they are abandoning their parent, or are being abandoned, or both. Being in an airplane with strange people and going to a different living arrangement, children are required to make adaptations that are more appropriate to older children and adults.

Other facets of society also press children to grow up fast. Lawyers, for example, are encouraging children to sue their parents for a variety of grievances. In California, four-and-one-half-year-old Kimberely Ann Alpin, who was born out of wedlock, is suing her father for the right to visit with him. The father, who provides support payments, does not want to see Kimberely. Whatever the decision, or the merits of the case, it illustrates the tendency of child-advocates to accord adult legal right to children. In West Hartford, Connecticut, David Burn, age 16, legally "divorced" his parents under a new state law in 1980. While such rights may have some benefits, they also put children in a difficult and often stressful position vis-à-vis their parents.

The media too, including music, books, films, and television, increasingly portray young people as precocious and present them in more or less explicit sexual or manipulative situations. Such portrayals force children to think they should act grown up before they are ready. In the movie *Little Darlings* the two principals—teenage girls—are in competition as to who will lose her virginity first. Similarly, teen music extols songs such as "Take Your Time (Do It Right)" and "Do That to Me One More Time," which are high on the charts of teen favorites. Television also promotes teenage erotica with features detailing such themes as teenage prostitution. According to some teenagers, the only show on television where playing hard to get is not regarded as stupid is "Laverne and Shirley."

25 The media promote not only teenage sexuality but also the wearing of adult clothes and the use of adult behaviors, language, and interpersonal strategies. Sexual promotion occurs in the context of other suggestions and models for growing up fast. A Jordache jean commercial, which depicts a young girl piggy-back on a young boy, highlights clothing and implicit sexuality as well as adult expressions, hairstyles, and so on. Likewise, in the film *Foxes,* four teenage girls not only blunder into sexual entanglements but also model provocative adult clothing, makeup, language, and postures. Thus the media reinforce the pressure on children to grow up fast in their language, thinking, and behavior.

But can young people be hurried into growing up fast emotionally as well? Psychologists and psychiatrists recognize that emotions and feelings are the most complex and intricate part of development. Feelings and emotions have their own timing and rhythm and cannot be hurried. Young teenagers may look and behave like adults but they usually don't feel like adults. (Watch a group of teenagers in a children's playground as they swing on the swings and teeter on the teeter-totters.) Children can grow up fast in some ways but not in others. Growing up emotionally is complicated and difficult under any circumstances but may be especially so when children's behavior and appearance speak "adult" while their feelings cry "child."

The Child Inside

Some of the more negative consequences of hurrying usually become evident in adolescence, when the pressures to grow up fast collide with institutional prohibitions. Children pushed to grow up fast suddenly find that many adult prerogatives—which they assumed would be their prerogative—such as smoking, drinking, driving, and so on, are denied them until they reach a certain age. Many adolescents feel betrayed by a society that tells them to grow up fast but also to remain a child. Not surprisingly, the stresses of growing up fast often result in troubled and troublesome behavior during adolescence.

In a recent article, Patricia O'Brien gave some examples of what she called "the shrinking of childhood." Her examples reflect a rush to experiment that is certainly one consequence of growing up fast:

> *Martin L (not his real name) confronted his teenager who had stayed out very late the night before. The son replied, "Look, Dad, I've done it all—drugs, sex, and booze, there is nothing left I don't know about." This young man is twelve years old!*
>
> *In Washington, D.C., area schools administrators estimate that many thousands of teenagers are alcoholics, with an estimated 30,000 such young people in Northern Virginia alone.*

The rush to experiment is perhaps most noticeable in teenage sexual behavior. Although survey data are not always as reliable as one might wish, the available information suggests that there has been a dramatic increase in the number of sexually active teenage girls in the last decade. Melvin Zelnick and John F. Kanther, professors of public health at Johns Hopkins University in Baltimore, conclude that nearly 50 percent of the total population of teenage girls between the ages of fifteen and nineteen (about 10.3 million females) have had premarital sex. The percentage has nearly doubled since the investigators first undertook their study in 1971. "Things that supported remaining a virgin in the past—the fear of getting pregnant, being labelled the 'town pump,' or whatever have disappeared," observes Zelnick.

30 Young people themselves are very much aware of this trend. "I'd say half the girls in my graduating class are virgins," says an eighteen-year-old high school senior from New Iberia, Louisiana. "But you wouldn't believe those freshmen and sophomores. By the time they graduate there aren't going to be any virgins left."

There are a number of disturbing consequences of this sexual liberation. The number of teenage pregnancies is growing at a startling rate. About 10 percent of all teenage girls, one million in all, get pregnant each year and the number keeps increasing. About 600,000 teenagers give birth each year, and the sharpest increase in such births is for girls under fourteen! In addition, venereal disease is a growing problem among teenagers, who account for 25 percent of the one million or so cases of gonorrhea each year.

The causes of this enhanced sexual activity among young people today are many and varied. The age of first menstruation, for example, has dropped from age seventeen about a century ago to age twelve and half today. Fortunately this seems to be the lower limit made possible by good health care and nutrition. However, this age of first menstruation has remained stable over the past decade, so it cannot account for the increased sexual activity of young women during this period. Other contributing factors include rapid changes in social values, women's liberation, the exploding divorce rate, the decline of parental and institutional authority, and the fatalistic sense, not often verbalized, that we are all going to die in a nuclear holocaust anyway, so "what the hell, have a good time."

Although the media are quick to pick up these sexual trends and exploit them for commercial purposes (for example, the cosmetics for girls four to nine years old currently being marketed by toy manufacturers), the immediate adult model is perhaps the most powerful and the most pervasive. Married couples are generally discreet about their sexuality in front of their offspring—in part because of a natural tendency to avoid exposing children to what they might not understand, but also because by the time the children are born, much of the romantic phase of the relationship for many couples is in the past.

But single parents who are dating provide a very different model for children. Quite aside from confrontations such as that in *Kramer vs. Kramer* wherein the son encounters the father's naked girlfriend, single parents are likely to be much more overtly sexual than married couples. With single parents, children may witness the romantic phase of courtship—the hand-holding, the eye-gazing, the constant touching and fondling. This overt sexuality, with all the positive affection it demonstrates, may encourage young people to look for something similar.

It is also true, as Professor Mavis Hetherington of the University of Virginia has found in her research, that daughters of divorced women tend to be more sexually oriented, more flirtatious with men than daughters of widowed mothers or daughters from two-parent homes. Because there are more teenage daughters from single-parent homes today than ever before, this too could contribute to enhanced sexual activity of contemporary teenage girls.

While it is true that some young people in every past generation have engaged in sex at an early age, have become pregnant, contracted venereal disease, and so on, they were always a small proportion of the population. What is new today are the numbers, which indicate that pressures to grow up fast are social and general rather than familial and specific (reflecting parental biases and needs). The proportion of young people who are abusing drugs, are sexually active, and are becoming pregnant is so great that we must look to the society as a whole for a full explanation, not to just the parents who mirror it.

Parallelling the increased sexuality of young people is an increase in children of what in adults are known as stress diseases. Pediatricians report a greater incidence of such ailments as headaches, stomachaches, allergic reactions, and so on in today's youngsters than in previous generations. Type A behavior (high-strung, competitive, demanding) has been identified in children and associated with heightened cholesterol levels. It has also been associated with parental pressure for achievement.

Another negative reflection of the pressure to grow up fast is teenage (and younger) crime. During 1980, for example, New York police arrested 12,762 children aged sixteen and under on felony charges. In Chicago the figure for the same period was 18,754 charges. Having worked for juvenile courts, I am sure that these figures are underestimated. Many children who have committed felonies are released without a formal complaint so that they will not have a police record. The children who are "booked" have usually had several previous encounters with the law.

The following examples, recent cases from the New York Police Department, illustrate the sort of activities for which children get arrested:

- On 27 February 1981, a boy who had to stand on tiptoes to speak to the bank teller made off with $118 that he had secured at gunpoint. He was nine years old, the youngest felon ever sought by the F.B.I.
- A ten-year-old Brooklyn girl was apprehended in December after she snatched a wallet from a woman's purse. Police said it was the girl's nineteenth arrest.
- One of four suspects captured in the murder of a policeman in Queens on 12 January 1981 was a fifteen-year-old youth.
- A thirteen-year-old Bronx boy was arrested in March 1981 on charges that he killed two elderly women during attempted purse snatchings.
- Another thirteen-year-old boy had a record of thirty-two arrests when seized last year on a charge of attempted murder. He later confessed to an incredible 200 plus felonies.

40 Such crimes are not being committed just by poor disadvantaged youth who are acting out against a society prejudiced against them. Much teenage crime is committed by middle-class youngsters. However, it tends to be concealed because police and parents try to protect the children; but sometimes this is not possible. One case involved a thirteen-year-old Long Island boy who was killed by three teenagers who stomped on him and strangled him by stuffing stones down his throat. He was attacked because he accidentally discovered that the other boys had stolen an old dirt bike worth only a couple of dollars. It was one of the most brutal and gruesome murders to be committed on Long Island.

How can pressure to grow up fast contribute to crime among teenagers from affluent backgrounds? Consider the case of John Warnock Hinckley, Jr., the young man who shot President Reagan and others on March 31, 1981. Unlike other assassins such as Lee Harvey Oswald, who shot President Kennedy, John Hinckley came from a respected upper-class family. Young Hinckley's father had built a prosperous business, and he and his wife had brought up three bright children. The family was religious, law-abiding, and socially conscious. Before and after the family moved from Dallas to Denver, Mrs. Hinckley made it a point to stay home to raise the children. Mr. Hinckley, though busy with his business, always made it a point to take his children camping, on family outings, and the like.

> *In line with this model upbringing, the three children—especially Scott, the eldest, now 32—and Diane, now 29—were viewed as popular, intelligent and good looking. Scott, for example, was a scholarly athlete at Highland Park High School, the most prestigious public high school in the Dallas area. He was a member of an academic honorary group, the student council and the chess club and he was a varsity tennis player. At Vanderbilt University in Nashville, Tenn., Scott the fraternity man earned academic honors in mechanical engineering and went on to become the Singapore branch manager of Reading & Bates Inc. a Tulsa based oil company.*
>
> *Diane is just as memorable. The blond beauty was the head cheerleader, a home-coming princess, an honor student, and a member of the choir and of the student council during her years at Highland Park High. At well-heeled Southern Methodist University in Dallas, she joined a sorority, majored in education, and met her future husband, Stephen Sims, who now is a Dallas insurance executive. Friends describe her today as a "model housewife" with two small children, a red brick house, and a two-car garage.*

John Hinckley also did well in his early school career. He was active in sports and in the Cub Scouts. In the eighth grade, he was too small to make the basketball team but he handed out towels and led cheers from the bench. In the seventh and ninth grades he was elected president of his homeroom. But the pressure of Highland Park High School was apparently too much for John. From an outgoing cheerful boy, he became progressively more quiet and withdrawn, eventually preferring to practice his guitar alone at home than to be out with his friends.

Unlike his brother and sister, who went to expensive private schools, John elected to go to Texas Tech, a public institution. But he did not fraternize and often enrolled in courses that he never attended. Tendencies toward political extremism began to emerge. John joined and was eventually expelled from the Naturalist Socialist Party of America (a neo-Nazi party). He was expelled from the group because, according to another member, "We thought he was either deranged or could become an agent provocateur of violence."

John left college, was out of touch with his parents, and began the aimless drifting that was suddenly given direction and motivation by the desire to shoot the President. That this act was to gain the attention of a movie actress may be true in part, but the actress also had the same first name as his mother—Jodi.

John Hinckley's case shows how the pressure to achieve and to achieve early can bring about personality disorder and emotional disturbance. Had John been born into a different family, had his brother and sister not been so successful, he might have found himself. But in Erik Erikson's terms, John's older brother—by being at the same time athlete, scholar, and social leader—preempted all of the personal identities held out as valuable by his parents. Consequently, John adopted a negative identify—one of extremism, aloneness, social disruption—the negative of what his parents valued.

The pressure to grow up fast, to achieve early in the area of sports, academics, and social interaction, is very great in middle-class America. There is no room today for the "late bloomers," the children who come into their own later in life rather than earlier (John might have been one of these). Children have to achieve success early or they are regarded as losers. It has gone so far that many parents refuse to have their children repeat or be retained in kindergarten—despite all the evidence that this is the best possible time to retain a child. "But," the parents say, "how can we tell our friends that our son failed kindergarten?"

John Hinckley's solution to the problem of early achievement and success was attaining notoriety, catching people's attention with negative rather than positive accomplishments. But there are many other solutions to this pressure to achieve early. One such solution is to join a cult, such as the "Moonies." What characterizes such cults is that they accept young people unconditionally, regardless of academic success or failure. The cults, in effect, provide an accepting family that does not demand achievement in return for love, although cults do demand obedience and adherence to a certain moral ethic. Even rebellious young people find it easy to adhere to these rules in the atmosphere of acceptance and lack of pressure and competition offered by the cult group. Cult membership is another form of negative identity in which young people adopt a group identity rather than an individual one.

A case in point is the Christ Commune (a pseudonym), a branch of the best-organized and most rapidly growing sect of what has been called the Jesus movement. The Commune is a summer camp where members come from their homes for a few months each year. The population (about one hundred) consists of young adults between the ages of fifteen and thirty (average age twenty-one) who are white and come from large (four to eight children), middle-class families. Most have completed high school and some have done college work. One gets the impression they are young people who have not distinguished themselves socially, academically, or athletically and who have held boring, low-paying jobs.

The group offers a strict moral code, a rigid behavioral program, and a sense of mission, of being chosen by and working for God through the mediation of Christ. The members work hard—they get up at 4:30 A.M. and go to sleep at 11:00 P.M. They seem happy with simple food (little meat, water to drink, peanut butter sandwiches for lunch) and strenuous work six days a week. Entertainment and recreation are limited to sitting in a common room, talking, singing spirituals, and engaging in spontaneous prayer.

50 Such communes, the Jesus movement, and other religious groups are attractive to young people whose personal styles are at variance with those of the larger society. Such groups offer recognition and status to young people who tend to be noncompetitive, anti-intellectual, and spiritual in orientation. Thus the groups provide a needed haven from the pressure to grow up fast, to achieve early, and to make a distinctive mark in life.

The last phenomenon in relation to hurrying to be discussed here is teenage suicide. Currently, suicide is the third leading cause of death during the teen years—preceded only by death via accidents and homicide. An American Academy of Pediatrics report on teenage suicide indicates a large increase in the number of suicides by adolescents in the last decade—the number is now about 5000 per year. For young people between the ages of fifteen to nineteen, the number of suicides per year doubled during the period from 1968 to 1976. The data for young adolescents of ages ten to fourteen are even more distressing: the number of suicides was 116 in 1968 and rose to 158 by 1976.

For every suicide completed, some 50 to 200 are attempted but not successful. Adolescents from all walks of life, all races, religions, and ethnic groups commit or attempt to commit suicide. Boys are generally more successful than girls because they use more lethal methods—boys tend to shoot or hang themselves whereas girls are more likely to overdose on pills or to cut their wrists. "For most adolescents," the pediatric report concludes, "suicide represents an attempt to resolve a difficult conflict, escape an intolerable living arrangement or punish important individuals in their lives."

To illustrate how hurrying can contribute to teenage suicide, consider the data from the most affluent suburbs of Chicago, a ten-mile stretch of communities along Chicago's northside lakefront that is one of the richest areas in the country. It is the locale chosen by director Robert Redford for the movie *Ordinary People.* The median income per family is about $60,000. Children in these areas attend excellent schools, travel about the world on vacations, are admitted to the best and most prestigious private colleges, and often drive their own cars (which can sometimes be a Mercedes). These are children of affluence who would seem to have it made.

And yet, this cluster of suburbs has the highest number of teenage suicides per year in the state, and almost in the nation. There has been a 250 percent increase in suicides per year over the past decade. These figures are dismaying not only in and of themselves but because the community has made serious efforts at suicide prevention, including the training of teachers in suicide detection and the provision of a twenty-four-hour hot line. One hot line, provided by Chicago psychoanalyst Joseph Pribyl, receives some 150 calls per month. But the suicides continue.

A nineteen-year-old from Glencoe, Illinois, says, "We have an outrageous number of suicides for a community our size." One of this teenager's friends cut her wrist and two others drove their cars into trees. "Growing up here you are handed everything on a platter, but something else is missing. The one thing parents don't give is love, understanding, and acceptance of you as a person." And Isadora Sherman, of Highland Park's Jewish Family and Community Service says, "People give their kids a lot materially, but expect a lot in return. No one sees his kids as average, and those who don't perform are made to feel like failures."

Chicago psychiatrist Harold Visotsky succinctly states how pressure to achieve at an early age, to grow up and be successful fast can contribute to teenage suicide: "People on the lower end of the social scale expect less than these people. Whatever anger the poor experience is acted out in antisocial ways—vandalism, homicide, riots—and the sense of shared misery in the lower income groups prevents people from feeling so isolated. With well-to-do kids, *the rattle goes in the mouth and the foot goes on the social ladder.* The competition ethic takes over, making a child feel even more alone. He's more likely to take it out on himself than society."

Adolescents are very audience conscious. Failure is a public event, and the adolescent senses the audience's disapproval. It is the sense that "everyone knows" that is so painful and that can lead to attempted and successful suicides in adolescents who are otherwise so disposed. Hurrying our children has, I believe, contributed to the extraordinary rise in suicide rates among young people over the past decade.

All Grown Up and No Place to Go

Sigmund Freud was once asked to describe the characteristics of maturity, and he replied: *lieben und arbeiten* ("loving and working"). The mature adult is one who can love and allow himself or herself to be loved and who can work productively, meaningfully, and with satisfaction. Yet most adolescents, and certainly all children, are really not able to work or to love in the mature way that Freud had in mind. Children love their parents in a far different way from how they will love a real or potential mate. And many, probably most, young people will not find their life work until they are well into young adulthood.

When children are expected to dress, act, and think as adults, they are really being asked to playact, because all of the trappings of adulthood do not in any way make them adults in the true sense of *lieben und arbeiten.* It is ironic that the very parents who won't allow their children to believe in Santa Claus or the Easter Bunny (because they are fantasy and therefore dishonest) allow their children to dress and behave as adults without any sense of the tremendous dishonesty involved in allowing children to present themselves in this grown-up way.

60 It is even more ironic that practices once considered the province of lower-class citizens now have the allure of middle-class chic. Divorce, single parenting, dual-career couples, and unmarried couples living together were common among the lower class decades ago. Such arrangements were prompted more often than not by economic need, and the children of low-income families were thus pressured to grow up fast out of necessity. They were pitied and looked down upon by upper- and middle-class parents, who helped provide shelters like the Home for Little Wanderers in Boston.

Today the middle class has made divorce its status symbol. And single parenting and living together without being married are increasingly commonplace. Yet middle-class children have not kept pace with the adjustments these adult changes require. In years past a child in a low-income family could appreciate the need to take on adult responsibilities early; families needed the income a child's farm or factory labor would bring, and chores and child-rearing tasks had to be allocated to even younger members of the family. But for the middle-income child today, it is hard to see the necessity of being relegated to a baby sitter or sent to a nursery school or a day care center when he or she has a perfectly nice playroom and yard at home. It isn't the fact of parents' being divorced that is so distressing to middle-class children, but rather that often it seems so unnecessary, so clearly a reflection of parent and not child need. As we shall see, it is the feeling of being used, of being exploited by parents, of losing the identity and uniqueness of childhood without just cause that constitute the major stress of hurrying and account for so much unhappiness among affluent young people today.

It is certainly true that the trend toward obscuring the divisions between children and adults is part of a broad egalitarian movement in this country that seeks to overcome the barriers separating the sexes, ethnic and racial groups, and the handicapped. We see these trends in unisex clothing and hairstyles, in the call for equal pay for equal work, in the demands for affirmative action, and in the appeals and legislation that provide the handicapped with equal opportunities for education and meaningful jobs.

From this perspective, the contemporary pressure for children to grow up fast is only one symptom of a much larger social phenomenon in this country—a movement toward true equality, toward the ideal expressed in our Declaration of Independence. While one can only applaud this movement with respect to the sexes, ethnic and racial groups, and the handicapped, its unthinking extension to children is unfortunate.

Children need time to grow, to learn, and to develop. To treat them differently from adults is not to discriminate against them but rather to recognize their special estate. Similarly, when we provide bilingual programs for Hispanic children, we are not discriminating against them but are responding to the special needs they have, which, if not attended to, would prevent them from attaining a successful education and true equality. In the same way, building ramps for handicapped students is a means to their attaining equal opportunity. Recognizing special needs is not discriminatory; on the contrary, it is the only way that true equality can be attained.

All children have, vis-à-vis adults, special needs—intellectual, social, and emotional. Children do not learn, think, or feel in the same way as adults. To ignore these differences, to treat children as adults, is really not democratic or egalitarian. If we ignore the special needs of children, we are behaving just as if we denied Hispanic or Indian children bilingual programs, or denied the handicapped their ramps and guideposts. In truth, the recognition of a group's special needs and accommodation to those needs are the only true ways to insure equality and true equal opportunity.

Explorations of the Text

1. Paraphrase Elkind's central thesis in paragraph 1. Do you agree with him?
2. According to Elkind, what are the reasons for this change in the view of "childhood" and child rearing? What "pressures" do children in North American society face?
3. What are the "negative consequences" for today's children of "grow[ing] up fast"?
4. What does Elkind propose as a solution?
5. What forms of evidence does Elkind include to support his points? Is his argument persuasive?
6. Connect Elkind's views of childhood with Connie's situation in "Where Are You Going, Where Have You Been?" with the personas in "Suicide Note," or with Twilight Bey's in "Twilight Bey" (See chapter 7).

The Reading/Writing Connection

1. Outline Elkind's argument as preparation for class discussion.
2. "Think" Topic: Choose one statement from the essay. Write a paragraph response, agreeing or disagreeing with Elkind's views.
3. Debate Topic: "Are children's lives today too hurried?"

Ideas for Writing

1. Do you agree with Elkind's view of childhood? What solutions would you propose?
2. Choose a character from one of the works in this chapter (for example, the speaker in "Suicide Note"). Have that character write a letter to Elkind. Or choose a character from a popular television show and have that character write a letter to Elkind in which he/she responds to Elkind's argument.

The Medusa and the Snail

Lewis Thomas

Lewis Thomas (1931–93), born in New York City, graduated from Princeton University and from Harvard Medical School. He was president of the Memorial Sloan-Kettering Cancer Center in New York and also taught at the University of Minnesota, New York University–Bellevue, and Yale Medical School. The Lives of a Cell *(1974), his first book of essays, won the National Book Award. His other volumes include* Late Night Thoughts on Listening to Mahler's Ninth Symphony *(1985) and* The Fragile Species *(1992).*

1979

We've never been so self-conscious about our selves as we seem to be these days. The popular magazines are filled with advice on things to do with a self: how to find it, identify it, nurture it, protect it, even, for special occasions, weekends, how to lose it transiently. There are instructive books, best sellers on self-realization, self-help, self-development. Groups of self-respecting people pay large fees for three-day sessions together, learning self-awareness. Self-enlightenment can be taught in college electives.

You'd think, to read about it, that we'd only just now discovered selves. Having long suspected that there was *something alive* in there, running the place, separate from everything else, absolutely individual and independent, we've celebrated by giving it a real name. My self.

It is an interesting word, formed long ago in much more social ambiguity than you'd expect. The original root was *se* or *seu,* simply the pronoun of the third person, and most of the descendant words, except "self" itself, were constructed to allude to other, somehow connected people; "sibs" and "gossips," relatives and close acquaintances, came from *seu. Se* was also used to indicate something outside or apart, hence words like "separate," "secret," and "segregate." From an extended root *swedh* it moved into Greek as *ethnos,* meaning people of one's own sort, and *ethos,* meaning the customs of such people. "Ethics" means the behavior of people like one's self, one's own ethnics.

We tend to think of our selves as the only wholly unique creations in nature, but it is not so. Uniqueness is so commonplace a property of living things that there is really nothing at all unique about it. A phenomenon can't be unique and universal at the same time. Even individual, free-swimming bacteria can be viewed as unique entities, distinguishable from each other even when they are the progeny of a single clone. Spudich and Koshland have recently reported that motile microorganisms of the same species are like solitary eccentrics in their swimming behavior. When they are searching for food, some tumble in one direction for precisely so many seconds before quitting, while others tumble differently and for different, but characteristic, periods of time. If you watch them closely, tethered by their flagellae to the surface of an antibody-coated slide, you can tell them from each other by the way they twirl, as accurately as though they had different names.

5 Beans carry self-labels, and are marked by these as distinctly as a mouse by his special smell. The labels are glycoproteins, the lectins, and may have something to do with negotiating the intimate and essential attachment between the bean and the nitrogen-fixing bacteria which live as part of the plant's flesh, embedded in root nodules. The lectin from one line of legume has a special affinity for the surfaces of the particular bacteria which colonize that line, but not for bacteria from other types of bean. The system seems designed for the maintenance of exclusive partnerships. Nature is pieced together by little snobberies like this.

Coral polyps are biologically self-conscious. If you place polyps of the same genetic line together, touching each other, they will fuse and become a single polyp, but if the lines are different, one will reject the other.

Fish can tell each other apart as individuals, by the smell of self. So can mice, and here the olfactory discrimination is governed by the same H_2 locus which contains the genes for immunologic self-marking.

The only living units that seem to have no sense of privacy at all are the nucleated cells that have been detached from the parent organism and isolated in a laboratory dish. Given the opportunity, under the right conditions, two cells from wildly different sources, a yeast cell, say, and a chicken erythrocyte, will touch, fuse, and the two nuclei will then fuse as well, and the new hybrid cell will now divide into monstrous progeny. Naked cells, lacking self-respect, do not seem to have any sense of self.

The markers of self, and the sensing mechanisms responsible for detecting such markers, are conventionally regarded as mechanisms for maintaining individuality for its own sake, enabling one kind of creature to defend and protect itself against all the rest. Selfness, seen thus, is for self-preservation.

10 In real life, though, it doesn't seem to work this way. The self-marking of invertebrate animals in the sea, who must have perfected the business long before evolution got around to us, was set up in order to permit creatures of one kind to locate others, not for predation but to set up symbiotic households. The anemones who live on the shells of crabs are precisely finicky; so are the crabs. Only a single species of anemone will find its way to only a single species of crab. They sense each other exquisitely, and live together as though made for each other.

Sometimes there is such a mix-up about selfness that two creatures, each attracted by the molecular configuration of the other, incorporate the two selves to make a single organism. The best story I've ever heard about this is the tale told of the nudibranch and medusa living in the Bay of Naples. When first observed, the nudibranch, a common sea slug, was found to have a tiny vestigial parasite, in the form of a jellyfish, permanently affixed to the ventral surface near the mouth. In curiosity to learn how the medusa got there, some marine biologists began searching the local waters for earlier developmental forms, and discovered something amazing. The attached parasite, although apparently so specialized as to have given up living for itself, can still produce offspring, for they are found in abundance at certain seasons of the year. They drift through the upper waters, grow up nicely and astonishingly, and finally become full-grown, handsome, normal jellyfish. Meanwhile, the snail produces snail larvae, and these too begin to grow normally, but not for long. While still extremely small, they become entrapped in the tentacles of the medusa and then engulfed within the umbrella-shaped body. At first glance, you'd believe the medusae are now the predators, paying back for earlier humiliations, and the snails the prey. But no. Soon the snails, undigested and insatiable, begin to eat, browsing away first at the radial canals, then the borders of the rim, finally the tentacles, until the jellyfish becomes reduced in substance by being eaten while the snail grows correspondingly in size. At the end, the arrangement is back to the first scene, with the full-grown nudibranch basking, and nothing left of the jellyfish except the round, successfully edited parasite, safely affixed to the skin near the mouth.

It is a confusing tale to sort out, and even more confusing to think about. Both creatures are designed for this encounter, marked as selves as that they can find each other in the waters of the Bay of Naples. The collaboration, if you want to call it that, is entirely specific; it is only this species of medusa and only this kind of nudibranch that can come together and live this way. And, more surprising, they cannot live in any other way; they depend for their survival on each other. They are not really selves, they are specific *others.*

The thought of these creatures gives me an odd feeling. They do not remind me of anything, really. I've never heard of such a cycle before. They are bizarre, that's it, unique. And at the same time, like a vaguely remembered dream, they remind me of the whole earth at once. I cannot get my mind to stay still and think it through.

Explorations of the Text

1. Why does Thomas give the definition and etymology of "self"? How can a writer use definitions without being predictable or trite?
2. What are the examples of "unique entities" in the essay? How do they add to the conception of self?
3. What is symbiosis? How do the medusa and the snail differ from other symbiotic relationships in nature?
4. What is disturbing about the medusa and the snail?
5. Why does Thomas end the essay with uncertainties and state, "I cannot get my mind to stay still and think it through"?
6. What analogy does Thomas imply in "The Medusa and the Snail"? What can a writer learn about the use and rhetorical power of analogy from this work?

The Reading/Writing Connection

1. "Think" Topic: Do you agree with Thomas's first statement: "We've never been so self-conscious about our selves as we seem to be these days"?

2. Consider interdependence as a prerequisite for selfhood. How much privacy does an individual need? Respond to this question in a paragraph.

Ideas for Writing

1. Use Thomas's ideas as the beginning of an inquiry into the nature of identity.
2. Construct your own analogy for identity and relationships, and use Thomas's work as a model.

Student Essay: Personal Response

Response to Greg Delanty's "Leavetaking"

Staci Anna Marie Ferris

Staci Ferris is a student at Berea College, where she is majoring in German and secondary education. She wrote this essay (in the form of a letter to the author) as an assignment in an introduction to poetry class.

Dear Greg,

Your poem "Leavetaking" brought memories flowing back into my mind. Memories of the day that I left my home and family in Switzerland and headed to college on a train. Memories of many tears and yet memories of excitement. Reading your poem was like having someone read my mind and put the memories of that day on paper. I am amazed at how much alike our feelings and experiences were about leaving home.

The first thing about the poem that struck me as a coincidence was the train. I also left home a little more than two months ago on a train. When you talk about "sit[ting] and wait[ing]/to begin your first real journey alone," as I read, memories of the day of leavetaking began to flow back into my mind as vividly as the day I left. I remember stepping on the train and taking my seat next to the window. On the other side of the window was my family. I felt as if I were already over the ocean, and they still were at home in Switzerland. I felt the window's "awkwardness." The window of the train was like a barrier between home and the future, my future. I could not look at them out the window for fear that I would break out into tears.

But yet at the same time I wanted to look at them, to capture the memory of every line of my family's faces, hair, the clothes that they were wearing, and, most importantly, the look in their eyes. Everyone had looks of sadness on their faces and tears in their eyes, except my little cousins who were too young to understand what was happening—that I was going to be away for a long time. My cousins were all standing there with ice cream in their hands, smiling and waving. All I could think was how I wished that I was that little again and wasn't on the train about to leave. I only looked at them at short glances thinking what would happen if I just jumped off the train and decided to stay home. But I continued to sit on the train for what seemed an eternity.

Another line that struck me was "you are afraid of having to wave too soon." I remember that I was too afraid to wave because I thought that once I began to wave the train would move, and I would be slowly moving down the track away from my family and home. I kept thinking—my "face pressed to the windowpane"—that if I didn't wave, then the train wouldn't move; I could just sit there forever taking short glances at my family. However, finally the train began to move, and I got a funny feeling in the pit of my stomach, a sick feeling perhaps. I began to wave out the window at my family, and they waved back. They were crying and waving, and I was doing the same. All of us waving, "eternally, to each other," hoping that I wasn't really leaving and that they could still see me. As the miles passed and the mountains became practically invisible, I realized that I had left home and my family to start this new journey, new beginning, a new chapter of my life: a chapter filled with new people and places, but still containing my family and my home. However, I would be living at a distance from them and not seeing them as much.

Greg, your poem took me back to a very important and vivid day in my life. Thank you for reminding me of that day and the moment that the train started to move on the tracks.

Yours truly,
Staci Ferris

Student Essay: Character Analysis

Spiritual Evolution of Literary Characters

Joella Knapp

This essay corresponds to assignment 22 at the end of this chapter. Joella Knapp is a student at State University of New York–New Paltz, where she is majoring in creative writing and marketing. She wrote this essay during her freshman year in a composition course.

In his short story "Cathedral" Raymond Carver addresses spirituality and the journey to inner peace through physical and spiritual visions. Throughout the story, the narrator, a married man, does not seem to be exceedingly stimulated by his life, yet he makes no effort to remedy this tediousness. His wife, on the other hand, tries to understand and reach that higher level of understanding and happiness by writing poems. Their marriage is not particularly happy, and they each have their own prejudices which complicate their efforts, or lack of efforts, to find peace and tranquility within themselves and their lives. This is clear when Robert, a friend of the wife's comes to visit, and the husband states, "My wife finally took her eyes off the blind man and looked at me. I had the feeling she didn't like what she saw. I shrugged" (116). The narrator's lack of concern shows how much he regards his wife's opinion of him, the one person whose opinion is supposed to mean the most. With his apathetic attitude he manages to push himself farther away from spiritual fulfillment. Robert may be physically blind, but the narrator is spiritually blind.

Robert's spirituality gives him direction in his life; he wants to live within his soul and savor all the little things in life. He relishes his life; he had a marvelous marriage, and warm memories of his wife, his friends, and almost every aspect of his life. This type of spiritual serenity is resting within the narrator's and his wife's reach, if only they would cast off the blinding robes of prejudice in favor of enlightenment. Their prejudices against each other and people who are different blind them to their morose existence. The narrator does not bother himself with the search. His wife is frustrated with her husband's lack of concern and with her own ineptitude that inspires the substance for her fascination with Robert and her resentment toward her husband. "You don't have *any* friends (114)," she angrily mocks him, and perhaps it is comments like this one which drive him to smoke marijuana every night and lose himself within the placating depths of the hallucinogenic television (114). The narrator's prejudices and his discomfort around people who are "different" from him probably contribute largely to his lack of friends. Also, he has heard many myths about people who are "different," like blind people, for example. He says, "This blind man, feature this, he was wearing a full beard! A beard on a blind man! Too much, I say" (115).

The narrator also believes that if you are physically blind you cannot have a fulsome and rewarding relationship. Indeed, he stereotypes what he believes Robert's marriage was like, stating:

> Pretty soon Beulah and the blind man had themselves a church wedding. It was a little wedding—who'd want to

> go to such a wedding in the first place? After they had been inseparable for eight years—my wife's word, inseparable. All this without his having ever seen what the goddamned woman looked like. It was beyond my understanding. Hearing this I felt sorry for the blind man for a little bit. And then I found myself thinking what a pitiful life this woman must have led. Imagine a woman who could never see herself as she was seen in the eyes of her loved one (114-115).

The narrator thinks that a blind man's wedding is below him and sneers upon their love and their devotion. He sneers upon their happiness simply because Robert is blind. He believes that physical blindness impedes spiritual love, but Beulah and Robert loved each other with far more voracity than the narrator and his wife probably ever will love each other. Robert and Beulah are the epitome of the happy couple; the relationship between the narrator and his wife can in no way compare to his stunning example of contentment, as they are the quintessence of the dejected and dysfunctional couple.

The narrator and his wife can see each other, but when they look into the eyes of their "loved" one what do they see? Do they even want to see themselves as their loved one sees them? Throughout the night of Robert's visit, the narrator's wife never smiles at him, and he "wait[s] in vain to hear [his] name on [his] wife's sweet lips: 'And then my dear husband came into my life'—something like that. But [he] hear[s] nothing of the sort" (117). She does not include him at all in her conversation with Robert, and he would not be included at all if Robert did not attempt to involve him. The narrator's relationship with his wife is further demoralized by his thoughts of Robert at his own wife's funeral. "Robert was left with a small insurance policy and half of a twenty-peso Mexican coin. The other half of the coin went into the box with her. Pathetic." (115). The narrator's assessment of these circumstances exhibits his lack of comprehension of the deep love that Robert and Beulah shared and further supports the dysfunctional nature of his own relationship with his wife.

Under these circumstances it is almost safe to say that whatever love might have existed between the narrator and his wife is close to being snuffed out. This is also emphasized by the fact that they never go to bed at the same time and by his wife's obvious condemnation of her husband's attempts to converse with Robert. She does not support him; she doesn't want him to be a part of her relationship with Robert. The narrator's desire for her to think of him in conversation indicates that, although he is not really searching for spirituality, he is probably the more sensitive one of the two in their relationship.

Another aspect of their deteriorating marriage is their lack of spirituality. They are not really spiritual people as the narrator so blatantly exhibits at dinnertime through his dialogues. "'Here's bread and butter for you.' I swallowed some of my drink. 'Now let us pray,' I said, and the blind man lowered his head. [His] wife looked at [him], her mouth agape. 'Pray the phone won't ring and the food doesn't get cold'" (117). This exchange could be interpreted as a missed opportunity; it could have represented a type of communion until the narrator adds his little personal touch to the "prayer." Communion is supposed to be food for the soul; it nourishes the soul and helps it grow, but the way that they eat their food suggests that they gain very little nourishment. As the narrator describes it: "We dug in. We ate everything there was to eat on the table. We ate like there was no tomorrow. We didn't talk. We ate. We scarfed. We grazed the table. We were into serious eating" (117). Unlike the typical family dinner where the family speaks, at this table there is a dysfunctional family who stuffs their faces in order to avoid conversation and awkwardness, almost like they are trying to stuff the void in their lives with food.

A second chance to connect spiritually occurs when Robert and the narrator share a joint. This could represent the sharing of the wine at communion. It is here that they first begin to make their tedious progress towards spiritual connection. Also, the narrator could be using the cannabis in an attempt to fill up the holes in his life, to smooth over and make up for all the spiritual enlightenment he lacks. Although his wife smokes the "number" too, she gives the narrator "a savage look" for asking Robert to smoke with him (118). This could be because she believes Robert is too good to enjoy her husband's—and her own—habits. Her efforts to keep them apart is emphasized by her decision to smoke after Robert does, to stop when he stops, and then, as she says, to "just sit here for a while between you two guys with my eyes closed . . . you wake me up now, you guys, if I fall asleep" (119). While she does fall asleep, she maintains a physical barrier between the two of them by staying on the couch instead of going to bed as she normally does.

As his wife sleeps, the narrator and Robert watch/listen to a television show about cathedrals. Since the narrator is so inept in communicating, he cannot convey the physical image of the cathedral to Robert. When Robert asks the narrator "[A]re you in any way religious?" and when the narrator responds, "I guess I don't believe in it. In anything" (121), then a very important problem is answered: The narrator's lackluster life and his lack of spirituality go hand in hand. Yet the semblance of being close to something so big and so inspiring as a cathedral blesses Robert and the narrator with the ability to enjoy life at a startling new pinnacle of sensory delight. It gives them a new insight and meaning in their lives.

Robert is like a messenger from God in a way because he helps the narrator to discover his spirituality. This transpires when Robert suggests that they attempt to draw a cathedral together. Robert directs the activity, and the narrator contemplates it as follows:

> "Close your eyes now" the blind man said to me. . . . "Don't stop now. Draw." . . . His fingers rode my fingers as my hand went over the paper. It was like nothing else in my life up to now.
>
> Then he said, "I think that's it. I think you got it," he said. "Take a look. What do you think?"
>
> But I had my eyes closed. I thought I'd keep them that way a little longer. I thought it was something I ought to do.
>
> . . . I was in my house. I knew that. But I didn't feel like I was inside anything.
>
> "It's really something," I said. (123)

The emotion he expresses here represents a major milestone in the narrator's life. He has found his own spirituality. He has found new meaning in his life, a new way of looking at things. He can be compared to Oedipus in that neither man had much direction throughout their lives; they did what was required of them and that was it. And with "blindness" both reached soaring levels of peace and enlightenment. They became more in touch with themselves and the world around them. Blindness gave them their appreciation of life and proved to be the inspiration they needed to incite the germination of their mental and spiritual freedom. It set them free.

Writing Assignments

1. a. What makes you proud of your background? Freewrite.

   b. Compare your view of cultural pride and identity with the views in two of the following poems: "Ego Tripping," "Indian Boarding School: The Runaways," "Lost Sister," and "Suicide Note."

2. a. Compare the view of gaining sexual awareness and identity for men and for women in any of the works in this chapter.
   b. Interview several people about their experiences in gaining sexual awareness.
   c. Based on the works in this chapter and/or your interviews, write an essay that classifies ways in which adolescents acquire sexual knowledge.
3. Rites of passage may be characterized as those that involve loss, those that entail facing death, those that include isolation, and those that involve gaining new knowledge. Analyze two or three of the works in the chapter according to one of these categories.
4. Compare Elkind's view of adolescence with that of one of the other works in this chapter.
5. Coming of age and initiation experiences prompt adolescents either to accept or to reject adult responsibilities. Analyze the conflicts of a character in one of the works in this chapter in light of this idea.
6. Use one of these topic areas as the basis for an essay on a rite of passage: driving, flying, running, being caged, facing the self, hunting, lying.
7. a. Freewrite on a coming-of-age ritual you have experienced, for example, a bar mitzvah.
   b. Read about coming-of-age rituals in a particular culture. Take notes. Examine the origins, the evolution, and the current practice of the ritual (for example, bar mitzvah in Jewish culture). Write an outline, draft, revision, and final version of a research paper concerning one such ritual.
8. Contrast views of cultural identity in this chapter.
9. a. List the ways in which you have assimilated and the ways in which you have asserted your identity.
   b. Write about a single event that symbolizes the conflict between assimilation and assertion of identity.
   c. Coming of age involves coming to terms with one's culture. Discuss the struggle between acceptance and rejection of cultural roots as it is presented in several works in the chapter.
10. Discuss how a scene or vignette from a story or play functions in the development of a particular character.
11. Many of the works in this chapter depend on *irony*. Choose two or three selections, and discuss the function and effects of irony. (Suggestions: "The Verb to Kill," "Barn Burning," "The Stolen Party," "Rose-Johnny," and/or *Hamlet*.)
12. a. Write a journal entry on your search for selfhood.
    b. Compare your process of individuation with the struggles of a character in a work in this chapter.

c. Discuss the themes concerning the search for self in two works in this chapter in relation to concepts of individuation and symbiosis in Lewis Thomas' "The Medusa and the Snail."

13. a. Write a journal entry on a coming-of-age experience.

    b. Compare your experience with the conflict concerning the coming of age of a character in one of the works in this chapter.

14. Discuss the connection between "Kids in the Mall" and "Where Are You Going, Where Have You Been?" or "Our Hurried Children" and Oates' story.

15. Initiation stories often involve the spilling of blood. Using examples from the works in this chapter, argue in support or refutation of such an assertion.

16. Choose two or three works that exemplify the theme of initiation at different ages. What similarities and differences are apparent?

17. a. Interview your parents or other adults about conflicts between parents and children in adolescence.

    b. Interview several teenagers about their perspectives concerning conflicts between parents and adolescents.

    c. Write a summary of these responses.

    d. Write an essay that compares these perspectives.

18. Explore the connection between sexuality and violence in the works in the Thematic Preview: Valenzuela's "The Verb to Kill," Oates' "Where Are You Going, Where Have You Been?" Atwood's "Game After Supper," and Kowinski's "Kids in the Mall."

19. Discuss stages of coming of age presented in Robert Frost's "Birches," and then apply these rites of passage to the situations of two characters in two works in this chapter.

20. Choose several stories in this chapter and discuss whether those stories' portrayal of adolescence is still relevant today.

21. Analyze the search for self-experienced by one character in one of the works in this chapter.

22. Explore your personal responses to one of the works in this chapter. You may frame your response as a letter to the writer.

CHAPTER 5

FAMILY

"We live our lives like chips in a kaleidoscope always part of patterns that are larger than ourselves and somehow more than the sum of their parts."

Salvadore Minuchin, *Family Kaleidoscope*

We live as part of a kaleidoscope that is "larger than ourselves." The chips of the patterns are variegated, beautiful, and complex. The first movers of the pattern are family members. They provide the initial forms of bonding; they provide the crucial experiences of security and insecurity, of love and hate. These early relationships of intimacy, connection, and conflict with parents and siblings influence our responses to the world.

Our memories of those relationships and experiences change. As children, we become conscious of our parents' power over us, the ways in which their needs and values have shaped ours; and conversely, as adults, we recognize the ways in which we have emerged as distinct individuals. As we grow, we understand the family—its benefits, its disadvantages, and its enduring importance in our lives.

The Thematic Preview presents visions of complicated relationships between parents and children. In Nathaniel Hawthorne's "Rappaccini's Daughter," a father's obsession shapes his daughter's destiny, while John Millington Synge's "Riders to the Sea" portrays a mother's fierce determination to stop her son from breaking away—to avoid inevitable separation. His desire to wander, to flee, has tragic consequences. In "Those Winter Sundays" by Robert Hayden, the speaker remembers his childhood and finally understands his father's silences that created a gulf between them. In the excerpts from bell hooks' autobiography, *bone black,* the writer grapples with her memories of an authoritarian father and his effect on her mother's and her own life.

Literature is replete with images of the father as the authority figure, as the protector, and as the provider. What happens when fathers fail in these obligations? This failure is also discussed by Junot Diaz in "Fiesta 1980." Authority and absence become swords—damaging a child's individuality and sense of integrity. Sometimes children perceive fathers as unapproachable and silent. The absence of the father becomes as formative as the authoritarian presence. Witness Sylvia Plath's speaker's inability to talk to "Daddy": "the tongue stuck in [her] jaw."

Relationships with fathers are also life-giving and nurturing. Fathers demonstrate their values and teach their children to live in the world. In Simon

Ortiz's "My Father's Song," the father gives his son a philosophy of existing in accord with nature. In "Persimmons" by Li-Young Lee and in "Digging" by Seamus Heaney, the speakers explore the legacies that their fathers left them, particularly gifts of will, mind, and spirit that influenced their development of artistry. In "The Sign in My Father's Hands," Martin Espada portrays a father who is viewed as almost miraculous by his adoring son.

Like fathers' bonds with their children, mothers' relationships with their sons and daughters are life-giving and nurturing and yet fraught with anxiety and danger. Amy Tan's "Scar" presents a daughter who primally bonds with her mother, whereas Jamaica Kincaid's "Girl" humorously portrays a mother who attempts to direct her daughter's life and a "girl" who both conforms and desires to be free. Positive images of mothers and daughters emerge in Anne Sexton's "My Little Girl, My Stringbean, My Lovely Woman" and in Maxine Kumin's "Making the Jam Without You." Other poets create voices of daughters who assert their selfhood in different keys. In Lyn Lifshin's "My Mother and the Bed" and in Audre Lorde's "From the House of Yemanjá," the daughters, threatened by the physical and emotional energy of enormous and powerful mother figures, struggle to break free. In Kumin's "Making the Jam Without You," the speaker recognizes the intense bond between mothers and daughters and the inevitable need for the mother to be only a "sliver" in the daughter's adult life. She recognizes the obligation of parents to release their children.

These works concerning parents and children, then, are stories of love and nurture as well as of loss and recognition of loss—the parents' recognition of overwhelming spiritual, physical, and emotional ties with their children. Ben Jonson in "On My First Son," Amiri Baraka in "Preface to a Twenty Volume Suicide Note," and W. D. Snodgrass in "Heart's Needle" cope with their understanding that these ties are fragile.

The works also emphasize the difficulties of parenting; they acknowledge that fate, circumstance, economic conditions, and culture influence parenting. In Tillie Olsen's "I Stand Here Ironing," the mother's perceived failures are shaped by social and economic circumstances, and she mourns not only her lost connection with her daughter, but also her own powerlessness. Like the mother in "I Stand Here Ironing," Pat Mora's speaker in "Elena" experiences a powerlessness brought about by her isolation in North America—she is unable to help her children because she cannot speak English and, therefore, cannot comprehend them or their world.

Some stories demonstrate the mistakes of parents, and they record the anger of the children who perceive that parents have failed them—failed them because of their own limits, failed them because of desires for their children to be perfect, to be like them, and to compensate for their deficiencies. In "Ruth's Song," Gloria Steinem portrays her mother as a woman defeated by marriage. The mother's weaknesses determined the course of her child's life. As an adult, Steinem comes to terms with her mother's madness and with the limits of love and of understanding.

The same kaleidoscope of relationships exists among siblings and friends. In James Baldwin's "Sonny's Blues," we find two brothers, opposites and unable to communicate, who begin to discover a common ground because of tragedies in their lives. In Lorraine Hansberry's *A Raisin in the Sun,* a sister and a brother seek to define their identities in a threatening urban landscape while their mother struggles to keep the family intact and preserve their culture. In Sherman Alexie's "This Is What It Means to Say Phoenix, Arizona," we discover two friends, almost brothers, who are irretrievably bound together by the circumstances of their lives and fated to nurture each other.

Several stories and poems affirm kinship ties, those bonds with others that become sources of strength. "Krik? Krak!" presents Edwidge Danticat's exploration of her complex female ancestry that both confines her and challenges her to explore her creativity. In "The Idea of Ancestry," Etheridge Knight gains spiritual sustenance in his jail cell from the forty-seven pictures of his relatives. As he says, "I am all of them,/they are all of me, I am me, they are they, and I have no children/to float in the space between." An appreciation of ancestry provides identity, continuity, and a way of facing one's present and of ancestral ties, our senses of self, and our sense of community. These bonds exist as our "lineage," our roots, as Margaret Walker suggests.

THEMATIC PREVIEW: COMBINING THE GENRES

Rappaccini's Daughter

Nathaniel Hawthorne

Nathaniel Hawthorne (1804–64) was born in Salem, Massachusetts, and educated at Bowdoin College. Twenty-two years separate his first novel, Fanshawe *(1828), from his second,* The Scarlet Letter *(1850), time during which he hones his skills as a writer by working on the short stories that were collected in* Twice-Told Tales *(1837) and* Mosses from an Old Manse *(1846). Hawthorne wrote three other novels:* The House of the Seven Gables *(1851),* The Blithedale Romance *(1853), and* The Marble Faun *(1860). Hawthorne's fiction is marked by its use of symbol and allegory and its concern with sin.*

1846

A young man, named Giovanni Guasconti, came, very long ago, from the more southern region of Italy, to pursue his studies at the University of Padua. Giovanni, who had but a scanty supply of gold ducats[1] in his pocket, took lodgings in a high gloomy chamber of an old edifice which looked not unworthy to have been the palace of a Paduan noble, and which, in fact, exhibited over its entrance the armorial bearings of a family long since extinct. The young stranger, who was not unstudied in the great poem of his country, recollected that one of the ancestors of this family, and perhaps an occupant of this very mansion, had been pictured by Dante as a partaker of the immortal agonies of his Inferno.[2] These reminiscences and associations, together with the tendency to heartbreak natural to a young man for the first time out of his native sphere, caused Giovanni to sigh heavily as he looked around the desolate and ill-furnished apartment.

"Holy Virgin, signor!" cried old Dame Lisabetta, who, won by the youth's remarkable beauty of person was kindly endeavoring to give the chamber a habitable air, "what a sigh was that to come out of a young man's heart! Do you find this old mansion gloomy? For the love of Heaven, then, put your head out of the window, and you will see as bright sunshine as you have left in Naples."

Guasconti mechanically did as the old woman advised, but could not quite agree with her that the Paduan sunshine was as cheerful as that of southern Italy. Such as it was, however, it fell upon a garden beneath the window and expended its fostering influences on a variety of plants, which seemed to have been cultivated with exceeding care.

"Does this garden belong to the house?" asked Giovanni.

---

[1] Gold coins.

[2] In *Inferno* 18:71, Dante mentions an unnamed Paduan nobleman among those who have committed crimes against Nature.

5 "Heaven forbid, signor, unless it were fruitful of better pot herbs than any that grow there now," answered old Lisabetta. "No; that garden is cultivated by the own hands of Signor Giacomo Rappaccini, the famous doctor, who, I warrant him, has been heard of as far as Naples. It is said that he distils these plants into medicines that are as potent as a charm. Oftentimes you may see the signor doctor at work, and perchance the signora, his daughter, too, gathering the strange flowers that grow in the garden."

The old woman had now done what she could for the aspect of the chamber; and, commending the young man to the protection of the saints, took her departure.

Giovanni still found no better occupation than to look down into the garden beneath his window. From its appearance, he judged it to be one of those botanic gardens which were of earlier date in Padua than elsewhere in Italy or in the world. Or, not improbably, it might once have been the pleasure-place of an opulent family; for there was the ruin of a marble fountain in the centre, sculptured with rare art, but so wofully shattered that it was impossible to trace the original design from the chaos of remaining fragments. The water, however, continued to gush and sparkle into the sunbeams as cheerfully as ever. A little gurgling sound ascended to the young man's window and made him feel as if the fountain were an immortal spirit that sung its song unceasingly and without heeding the vicissitudes around it, while one century imbodied it in marble and another scattered the perishable garniture on the soil. All about the pool into which the water subsided grew various plants, that seemed to require a plentiful supply of moisture for the nourishment of gigantic leaves, and, in some instances, flowers gorgeously magnificent. There was one shrub in particular, set in a marble vase in the midst of the pool, that bore a profusion of purple blossoms, each of which had the lustre and richness of a gem; and the whole together made a show so resplendent that it seemed enough to illuminate the garden, even had there been no sunshine. Every portion of the soil was peopled with plants and herbs, which, if less beautiful, still bore tokens of assiduous care, as if all had their individual virtues, known to the scientific mind that fostered them. Some were placed in urns, rich with old carving, and others in common garden pots; some crept serpent-like along the ground or climbed on high, using whatever means of ascent was offered them. One plant had wreathed itself round a statue of Vertumnus,[3] which was thus quite veiled and shrouded in a drapery of hanging foliage, so happily arranged that it might have served a sculptor for a study.

While Giovanni stood at the window he heard a rustling behind a screen of leaves, and became aware that a person was at work in the garden. His figure soon emerged into view, and showed itself to be that of no common laborer, but a tall, emaciated, sallow, and sickly-looking man, dressed in a scholar's garb of black. He was beyond the middle term of life, with gray hair, a thin, gray beard, and a face singularly marked with intellect and cultivation,

[3] The Roman god of the seasons.

but which could never, even in his more youthful days, have expressed much warmth of heart.

Nothing could exceed the intentness with which this scientific gardener examined every shrub which grew in his path: it seemed as if he was looking into their inmost nature, making observations in regard to their creative essence, and discovering why one leaf grew in this shape and another in that, and wherefore such and such flowers differed among themselves in hue and perfume. Nevertheless, in spite of this deep intelligence on his part, there was no approach to intimacy between himself and these vegetable existences. On the contrary, he avoided their actual touch or the direct inhaling of their odors with a caution that impressed Giovanni most disagreeably; for the man's demeanor was that of one walking among malignant influences, such as savage beasts, or deadly snakes, or evil spirit, which, should he allow them one moment of license, would wreak upon him some terrible fatality. It was strangely frightful to the young man's imagination to see this air of insecurity in a person cultivating a garden, that most simple and innocent of human toils, and which has been alike the joy and labor of the unfallen parents of the race. Was this garden, then, the Eden of the present world? And this man, with such a perception of harm in what his own hands caused to grow,—was he the Adam?

10 The distrustful gardener, while plucking away the dead leaves or pruning the too luxuriant growth of the shrubs, defended his hands with a pair of thick gloves. Nor were these his only armor. When, in his walk through the garden, he came to the magnificent plant that hung its purple gems beside the marble fountain, he placed a kind of mask over his mouth and nostrils, as if all this beauty did but conceal a deadlier malice; but, finding his task still too dangerous, he drew back, removed the mask, and called loudly, but in the infirm voice of a person affected with inward disease,—

"Beatrice! Beatrice!"

"Here am I, my father. What would you?" cried a rich and youthful voice from the window of the opposite house—a voice as rich as a tropical sunset, and which made Giovanni, though he knew not why, think of deep hues of purple or crimson and of perfumes heavily delectable. "Are you in the garden?"

"Yes, Beatrice," answered the gardener; "and I need your help."

Soon there emerged from under a sculptured portal the figure of a young girl, arrayed with as much richness of taste as the most splendid of the flowers, beautiful as the day, and with a bloom so deep and vivid that one shade more would have been too much. She looked redundant with life, health, and energy; all of which attributes were bound down and compressed, as it were, and girdled tensely, in their luxuriance, by her virgin zone.[4] Yet Giovanni's fancy must have grown morbid while he looked down into the garden; for the impression which the fair stranger made upon him was as if here were another flower, the human sister of those vegetable ones, as beautiful as they, more

[4] Her belt, "virgin" because Beatrice appears to be an unmarried girl.

beautiful than the richest of them, but still to be touched only with a glove, nor to be approached without a mask. As Beatrice came down the garden path, it was observable that she handled and inhaled the odor of several of the plants which her father had most sedulously avoided.

"Here, Beatrice," said the latter, "see how many needful offices require to be done to our chief treasure. Yet, shattered as I am, my life might pay the penalty of approaching it so closely as circumstances demand. Henceforth, I fear, this plant must be consigned to your sole charge."

"And gladly will I undertake it," cried again the rich tones of the young lady, as she bent towards the magnificent plant and opened her arms as if to embrace it. "Yes, my sister, my splendor, it shall be Beatrice's task to nurse and serve thee; and thou shalt reward her with thy kisses and perfumed breath, which to her is as the breath of life."

Then, with all the tenderness in her manner that was so strikingly expressed in her words, she busied herself with such attentions as the plant seemed to require; and Giovanni, at his lofty window, rubbed his eyes, and almost doubted whether it were a girl tending her favorite flower, or one sister performing the duties of affection to another. The scene soon terminated. Whether Dr. Rappaccini had finished his labors in the garden, or that his watchful eye had caught the stranger's face, he now took his daughter's arm and retired. Night was already closing in; oppressive exhalations seemed to proceed from the plants and steal upward past the open window; and Giovanni, closing the lattice, went to this couch and dreamed of a rich flower and beautiful girl. Flower and maiden were different, and yet the same, and fraught with some strange peril in either shape.

But there is an influence in the light of morning that tends to rectify whatever errors of fancy, or even of judgment, we may have incurred during the sun's decline, or among the shadows of the night, or in the less wholesome glow of moonshine. Giovanni's first movement, on starting from sleep, was to throw open the window and gaze down into the garden which his dreams had made so fertile of mysteries. He was surprised, and a little ashamed, to find how real and matter-of-fact an affair it proved to be, in the first rays of the sun which gilded the dewdrops that hung upon leaf and blossom, and while giving a brighter beauty to each rare flower, brought every thing within the limits of ordinary experience. The young man rejoiced that, in the heart of the barren city, he had the privilege of overlooking this spot of lovely and luxuriant vegetation. It would serve, he said to himself, as a symbolic language to keep him in communion with Nature. Neither the sickly and thoughtworn Dr. Giacomo Rappaccini, it is true, nor his brilliant daughter, were now visible; so that Giovanni could not determine how much of the singularity which he attributed to both was due to their own qualities and how much to his wonder-working fancy; but he was inclined to take a most rational view of the whole matter.

In the course of the day he paid his respects to Signor Pietro Baglioni, professor of medicine in the university, a physician of eminent repute, to whom Giovanni had brought a letter of introduction. The professor was an elderly personage, apparently of genial nature and habits that might almost be called jovial. He kept the young man to dinner, and made himself very agreeable by the freedom and liveliness of his conversation, especially when warmed by a flask or two of Tuscan wine. Giovanni, conceiving that men of science, inhabitants of the same city, must needs be on familiar terms with one another, took an opportunity to mention the name of Dr. Rappaccini. But the professor did not respond with so much cordiality as he had anticipated.

"Ill would it become a teacher of the divine art of medicine," said Professor Pietro Baglioni, in answer to a question of Giovanni, "to withhold due and well-considered praise of a physician so eminently skilled as Rappaccini; but, on the other hand, I should answer it but scantily to my conscience were I to permit a worthy like yourself, Signor Giovanni, the son of an ancient friend, to imbibe erroneous ideas respecting a man who might hereafter chance to hold your life and death in his hands. The truth is, our worshipful Dr. Rappaccini has as much science as any member of the faculty—with perhaps one single exception—in Padua, or all Italy; but there are certain grave objections to his professional character."

"And what are they?" asked the young man.

"Has my friend Giovanni any disease of body or heart, that he is so inquisitive about physicians?" said the professor, with a smile. "But as for Rappaccini, it is said of him—and I, who know the man well, can answer for its truth—that he cares infinitely more for science than for mankind. His patients are interesting to him only as subjects for some new experiment. He would sacrifice human life, his own among the rest, or whatever else was dearest to him, for the sake of adding so much as a grain of mustard seed to the great heap of his accumulated knowledge."

"Methinks he is an awful[5] man indeed," remarked Guasconti, mentally recalling the cold and purely intellectual aspect of Rappaccini. "And yet, worshipful professor, is it not a noble spirit? Are there many men capable of so spiritual a love or science?"

"God forbid," answered the professor, somewhat testily; "at least, unless they take sounder views of the healing art than those adopted by Rappaccini. It is his theory that all medicinal virtues are comprised within those substances which we term vegetable poisons. These he cultivates with his own hands, and is said even to have produced new varieties of poison, more horribly deleterious than Nature, without the assistance of this learned person, would ever have plagued the world withal. That the signor doctor does less mischief than might be expected with such dangerous substances, is undeniable. Now and then, it must be owned, he has effected, or seemed to effect, a marvellous cure; but, to tell you my private mind, Signor Giovanni, he should receive little credit for such instances of success,—they being probably the work of chance,—but should be held strictly accountable for his failures, which may justly be considered his own work."

[5] Frightful, inspiring fear; dreadful.

25 The youth might have taken Baglioni's opinions with many grains of allowance had he known that there was a professional warfare of long continuance between him and Dr. Rappaccini, in which the latter was generally thought to have gained the advantage. If the reader be inclined to judge for himself, we refer him to certain black-letter tracts on both sides, preserved in the medical department of the University of Padua.

"I know not, most learned professor," returned Giovanni, after musing on what had been said of Rappaccini's exclusive zeal for science,—"I know not how dearly this physician may love his art; but surely there is one object more dear to him. He has a daughter."

"Aha!" cried the professor, with a laugh. "So now our friend Giovanni's secret is out. You have heard of this daughter, whom all the young men in Padua are wild about, though not half a dozen have ever had the good hap to see her face. I know little of the Signora Beatrice save that Rappaccini is said to have instructed her deeply in his science, and that, young and beautiful as fame reports her, she is already qualified to fill a professor's chair. Perchance her father destines her for mine! Other absurd rumors there be, not worth talking about or listening to. So now, Signor Giovanni, drink off your glass of lachryma."[6]

Guasconti returned to his lodgings somewhat heated with the wine he had quaffed, and which caused his brain to swim with strange fantasies in reference to Dr. Rappaccini and the beautiful Beatrice. On his way, happening to pass by a florist's, he bought a fresh bouquet of flowers.

Ascending to his chamber, he seated himself near the window, but within the shadow thrown by the depth of the wall, so that he could look down into the garden with little risk of being discovered. All beneath his eye was a solitude. The strange plants were basking in the sunshine, and now and then nodding gently to one another, as if in acknowledgment of sympathy and kindred. In the midst, by the shattered fountain, grew the magnificent shrub, with its purple gems clustering all over it; they glowed in the air, and gleamed back again out of the depths of the pool, which thus seemed to overflow with colored radiance from the rich reflection that was steeped in it. At first, as we have said, the garden was a solitude. Soon, however,—as Giovanni had half hoped, half feared, would be the case,—a figure appeared beneath the antique sculptured portal, and came down between the rows of plants, inhaling their various perfumes as if she were one of those beings of old classic fable that lived upon sweet odors. On again beholding Beatrice, the young man was even startled to perceive how much her beauty exceeded his recollection of it; so brilliant, so vivid, was its character, that she glowed amid the sunlight, and, as Giovanni whispered to himself, positively illuminated the more shadowy intervals of the garden path. Her face being now more revealed than on the former occasion, he was struck by its expression of simplicity and sweetness—qualities that had not entered into his idea of her character, and which made him ask anew what manner of mortal she might be. Nor did he fail again

[6] Italian wine, grown near Mount Vesuvius; lachrymal also pertains to tears.

to observe, or imagine, an analogy between the beautiful girl and the gorgeous shrub that hung its gemlike flowers over the fountain—a resemblance which Beatrice seemed to have indulged a fantastic humor in heightening, both by the arrangement of her dress and the selection of its hues.

30 Approaching the shrub, she threw open her arms, as with a passionate ardor, and drew its branches into an intimate embrace—so intimate that her features were hidden in its leafy bosom and her glistening ringlets all intermingled with the flowers.

"Give me thy breath, my sister," exclaimed Beatrice; "for I am faint with common air. And give me this flower of thine, which I separate with gentlest fingers from the stem and place it close beside my heart."

With these words the beautiful daughter of Rappaccini plucked one of the richest blossoms of the shrub, and was about to fasten it in her bosom. But now, unless Giovanni's draughts of wine had bewildered his senses, a singular incident occurred. A small orange-colored reptile, of the lizard or chameleon species, chanced to be creeping along the path, just at the feet of Beatrice. It appeared to Giovanni,—but, at the distance from which he gazed, he could scarcely have seen any thing so minute,—it appeared to him, however, that a drop or two of moisture from the broken stem of the flower descended upon the lizard's head. For an instant the reptile contorted itself violently, and then lay motionless in the sunshine. Beatrice observed this remarkable phenomenon, and crossed herself, sadly, but without surprise; nor did she therefore hesitate to arrange the fatal flower in her bosom. There it blushed, and almost glimmered with the dazzling effect of a precious stone, adding to her dress and aspect the one appropriate charm which nothing else in the world could have supplied. But Giovanni, out of the shadow of his window, bent forward and shrank bank, and murmured and trembled.

"Am I awake? Have I my senses?" said he to himself. "What is this being? Beautiful shall I call her, or inexpressibly terrible?"

Beatrice now strayed carelessly through the garden, approaching closer beneath Giovanni's window, so that he was compelled to thrust his head quite out of its concealment in order to gratify the intense and painful curiosity which she excited. At this moment there came a beautiful insect over the garden wall: it had, perhaps, wandered through the city, and found no flowers or verdure among those antique haunts of men until the heavy perfumes of Dr. Rappaccini's shrubs had lured it from afar. Without alighting on the flowers, this winged brightness seemed to be attracted by Beatrice, and lingered in the air and fluttered about her head. Now, here it could not be but that Giovanni Guasconti's eyes deceived him. Be that as it might, he fancied that, while Beatrice was gazing at the insect with childish delight, it grew faint and fell at her feet; its bright wings shivered; it was dead—from no cause that he could discern, unless it were the atmosphere of her breath. Again Beatrice crossed herself and sighed heavily as she bent over the dead insect.

35 An impulsive movement of Giovanni drew her eyes to the window. There she beheld the beautiful head of the young man—rather a Grecian than an Italian head, with fair, regular features, and a glistening of gold among his ringlets—gazing down upon her like a being that hovered in mid air. Scarcely

knowing what he did, Giovanni threw down the bouquet which he had hitherto held in his hand.

"Signora," said he, "there are pure and healthful flowers. Wear them for the sake of Giovanni Guasconti."

"Thanks, signor," replied Beatrice, with her rich voice, that came forth as it were like a gush of music, and with a mirthful expression half childish and half womanlike. "I accept your gift, and would fain recompense it with this precious purple flower; but, if I toss it into the air, it will not reach you. So Signor Guasconti must even content himself with my thanks."

She lifted the bouquet from the ground, and then, as if inwardly ashamed at having stepped aside from her maidenly reserve to respond to a stranger's greeting, passed swiftly homeward through the garden. But, few as the moments were, it seemed to Giovanni, when she was on the point of vanishing beneath the sculptured portal, that his beautiful bouquet was already beginning to wither in her grasp. It was an idle thought; there could be no possibility of distinguishing a faded flower from a fresh one at so great a distance.

For many days after this incident the young man avoided the window that looked into Dr. Rappaccini's garden, as if something ugly and monstrous would have blasted his eyesight had he been betrayed into a glance. He felt conscious of having put himself, to a certain extent, within the influence of an unintelligible power by the communication which he had opened with Beatrice. The wisest course would have been, if his heart were in any real danger, to quit his lodging and Padua itself at once; the next wiser, to have accustomed himself, as far as possible, to the familiar and daylight view of Beatrice—thus bringing her rigidly and systematically within the limits of ordinary experience. Least of all, while avoiding her sight, ought Giovanni to have remained so near this extraordinary being that the proximity and possibility even of intercourse should give a kind of substance and reality to the wild vagaries which his imagination ran riot continually in producing. Guasconti had not a deep heart—or, at all events, its depths were not sounded now; but he had a quick fancy, and an ardent southern temperament, which rose every instant to a higher fever pitch. Whether or not Beatrice possessed those terrible attributes, that fatal breath, the affinity with those so beautiful and deadly flowers which were indicated by what Giovanni had witnessed, she had at least instilled a fierce and subtle poison in his system. It was not love, although her rich beauty was a madness to him; nor horror, even while he fancied her spirit to be imbued with the same baneful essence that seemed to pervade her physical frame; but a wild offspring of both love and horror that had each parent in it, and burned like one and shivered like the other. Giovanni knew not what to dread; still less did he know what to hope; yet hope and dread kept a continual warfare in his breast, alternately vanquishing one another and starting up afresh to renew the contest. Blessed are all simple emotions, be they dark or bright! It is the lurid intermixture of the two that produces the illuminating blaze of the infernal regions.

Sometimes he endeavored to assuage the fever of his spirit by a rapid walk through the streets of Padua or beyond its gates: his footsteps kept time with the throbbings of his brain, so that the walk was apt to accelerate itself to a race. One day he found himself arrested; his arm was seized by a portly personage, who had turned back on recognizing the young man and expended much breath in overtaking him.

"Signor Giovanni! Stay, my young friend!" cried he. "Have you forgotten me? That might well be the case if I were as much altered as yourself."

It was Baglioni, whom Giovanni had avoided ever since their first meeting, from a doubt that the professor's sagacity would look too deeply into his secrets. Endeavoring to recover himself, he stared forth wildly from his inner world into the outer one and spoke like a man in a dream.

"Yes; I am Giovanni Guasconti. You are Professor Pietro Baglioni. Now let me pass!"

"Not yet, not yet, Signor Giovanni Guasconti," said the professor, smiling, but at the same time scrutinizing the youth with an earnest glance. "What! did I grow up side by side with your father? and shall his son pass me like a stranger in these old streets of Padua? Stand still, Signor Giovanni; for we must have a word or two before we part."

45 "Speedily, then, most worshipful professor, speedily," said Giovanni, with feverish impatience. "Does not your worship see that I am in haste?"

Now, while he was speaking there came a man in black along the street, stooping and moving feebly like a person in inferior health. His face was all overspread with a most sickly and sallow hue, but yet so pervaded with an expression of piercing and active intellect that an observer might easily have overlooked the merely physical attributes and have seen only this wonderful energy. As he passed, this person exchanged a cold and distant salutation with Baglioni, but fixed his eyes upon Giovanni with an intentness that seemed to bring out whatever was within him worthy of notice. Nevertheless, there was a peculiar quietness in the look, as if taking merely a speculative, not a human, interest in the young man.

"It is Dr. Rappaccini!" whispered the professor when the stranger had passed. "Has he ever seen your face before?

"Not that I know," answered Giovanni, starting at the name.

He *has* seen you! he must have seen you!" said Baglioni, hastily. "For some purpose or other, this man of science is making a study of you. I know that look of his! It is the same that coldly illuminates his face as he bends over a bird, a mouse, or a butterfly; which, in pursuance of some experiment, he has killed by the perfume of a flower; a look as deep as Nature itself, but without Nature's warmth of love. Signor Giovanni, I will stake my life upon it, you are the subject of one of Rappaccini's experiments!"

50 "Will you make a fool of me?" cried Giovanni, passionately. "*That,* signor professor, were an untoward experiment."

"Patience! patience! replied the imperturbable professor. "I tell thee, my poor Giovanni, that Rappaccini has a scientific interest in thee. Thou hast fallen into fearful hands! And the Signora Beatrice,—what part does she act in this mystery?"

But Guasconti, finding Baglioni's pertinacity intolerable, here broke away, and was gone before the professor could again seize his arm. He looked after the young man intently and shook his head.

"This must not be," said Baglioni to himself. "The youth is the son of my old friend, and shall not come to any harm from which the arcana[7] of medical science can preserve him. Besides, it is too insufferable an impertinence in Rappaccini thus to snatch the lad out of my own hands, as I may say, and make use of him for his infernal experiments. This daughter of his! It shall be looked to. Perchance, most learned Rappaccini, I may foil you where you little dream of it!"

Meanwhile Giovanni had pursued a circuitous route, and at length found himself at the door of his lodgings. As he crossed the threshold he was met by old Lisabetta, who smirked and smiled, and was evidently desirous to attract his attention; vainly, however, as the ebullition of his feelings had momentarily subsided into a cold and dull vacuity. He turned his eyes full upon the withered face that was puckering itself into a smile, but seemed to behold it not. The old dame, therefore, laid her grasp upon his cloak.

"Signor! signor!" whispered she, still with a smile over the whole breadth of her visage, so that it looked not unlike a grotesque carving in wood, darkened by centuries. "Listen, signor! There is a private entrance into the garden!"

"What do you say?" exclaimed Giovanni, turning quickly about, as if an inanimate thing should start into feverish life. "A private entrance into Dr. Rappaccini's garden?"

"Hush, hush! not so loud!" whispered Lisabetta, putting her hand over his mouth. "Yes; into the worshipful doctor's garden, where you may see all his fine shrubbery. Many a young man in Padua would give gold to be admitted among those flowers."

Giovanni put a piece of gold into her hand.

"Show me the way," said he.

A surmise, probably excited by his conversation with Baglioni, crossed his mind, that this interposition of old Lisabetta might perchance be connected with the intrigue, whatever were its nature, in which the professor seemed to suppose that Dr. Rappaccini was involving him. But such a suspicion, though it disturbed Giovanni, was inadequate to restrain him. The instant that he was aware of the possibility of approaching Beatrice, it seemed an absolute necessity of his existence to do so. It mattered not whether she were angel or demon; he was irrevocably within her sphere, and must obey the law that whirled him onward, in ever-lessening circles, towards a result which he did not attempt to foreshadow; and yet, strange to say, there came across him a sudden doubt whether this intense interest on his part were not delusory; whether it were really of so deep and positive a nature as to justify him in now thrusting himself into an incalculable position; whether it were not merely the fantasy of a young man's brain, only slightly or not at all connected with his heart.

He paused, hesitated, turned half about, but again went on. His withered guide led him along several obscure passages, and finally undid a door,

---

[7] Secrets.

through which, as it was opened, there came the sight and sound of rustling leaves, with the broken sunshine glimmering among them. Giovanni stepped forth, and, forcing himself through the entanglement of a shrub that wreathed its tendrils over the hidden entrance, stood beneath his own window in the open area of Dr. Rappaccini's garden.

How often is it the case that, when impossibilities have come to pass and dreams have condensed their misty substance into tangible realities, we find ourselves calm, and even coldly self-possessed, amid circumstances which it would have been a delirium of joy or agony to anticipate! Fate delights to thwart us thus. Passion will choose his own time to rush upon the scene, and lingers sluggishly behind when an appropriate adjustment of events would seem to summon his appearance. So was it now with Giovanni. Day after day his pulses had throbbed with feverish blood at the improbably idea of an interview with Beatrice, and of standing with her, face to face, in this very garden, basking in the Oriental sunshine of her beauty, and snatching from her full gaze the mystery which he deemed the riddle of his own existence. But now there was a singular and untimely equanimity within this breast. He threw a glance around the garden to discover if Beatrice or her father were present, and, perceiving that he was alone, began a critical observation of the plants.

The aspect of one and all of them dissatisfied him; their gorgeousness seemed fierce, passionate, and even unnatural. There was hardly an individual shrub which a wanderer, straying by himself through a forest, would not have been startled to find growing wild, as if an unearthly face had glared at him out of the thicket. Several also would have shocked a delicate instinct by an appearance of artificialness indicating that there had been such commixture, and, as it were, adultery of various vegetable species, that the production was not longer of God's making, but the monstrous offspring of man's depraved fancy, glowing with only an evil mockery of beauty. They were probably the result of experiment, which in one or two cases had succeeded in mingling plants individually lovely into a compound possessing the questionable and ominous character that distinguished the whole growth of the garden. In fine, Giovanni recognized but two or three plants in the collection, and those of a kind that he well knew to be poisonous. While busy with these contemplations he heard the rustling of a silken garment, and, turning, beheld Beatrice emerging from beneath the sculptured portal.

Giovanni had not considered with himself what should be his deportment; whether he should apologize for his intrusion into the garden, or assume that he was there with the privity at least, if not by the desire, of Dr. Rappaccini or his daughter; but Beatrice's manner placed him at his ease, though leaving him still in doubt by what agency he had gained admittance. She came lightly along the path and met him near the broken fountain. There was surprise in her face, but brightened by a simple and kind expression of pleasure.

65 "You are a connoisseur in flowers, signor," said Beatrice, with a smile, alluding to the bouquet which he had flung her from the window. "It is no marvel, therefore, if the sight of my father's rare collection has tempted you to take a nearer view. If he were here, he could tell you many strange and interesting

facts as to the nature and habits of these shrubs; for he has spent a lifetime in such studies, and this garden is his world."

"And yourself, lady," observed Giovanni, "if fame says true,—you likewise are deeply skilled in the virtues indicated by these rich blossoms and these spicy perfumes. Would you deign to be my instructress, I should prove an apter scholar than if taught by Signor Rappaccini himself."

"Are there such idle rumors?" asked Beatrice, with the music of a pleasant laugh. "Do people say that I am skilled in my father's science of plants? What a jest is there! No; though I have grown up among these flowers, I know no more of them than their hues and perfume; and sometimes methinks I would fain rid myself of even that small knowledge. There are many flowers here, and those not the least brilliant, that shock and offend me when they meet my eye. But pray, signor, do not believe these stories about my science. Believe nothing of me save what you see with your own eyes."

"And must I believe all that I have seen with my own eyes?" asked Giovanni, pointedly, while the recollection of former scenes made him shrink. "No, signora; you demand too little of me. Bid me believe nothing save what comes from your own lips."

It would appear that Beatrice understood him. There came a deep flush to her cheek; but she looked full into Giovanni's eyes, and responded to his gaze of uneasy suspicion with a queenlike haughtiness.

"I do so bid you, signor," she replied. "Forget whatever you may have fancied in regard to me. If true to the outward senses, still it may be false in its essence; but the words of Beatrice Rappaccini's lips are true from the depths of the heart outward. Those you may believe."

A fervor glowed in her whole aspect and beamed upon Giovanni's consciousness like the light of truth itself; but while she spoke there was a fragrance in the atmosphere around her, rich and delightful, though evanescent, yet which the young man, from an indefinable reluctance, scarcely dared to draw into his lungs. It might be the odor of the flowers. Could it be Beatrice's breath which thus embalmed her words with a strange richness, as if by steeping them in her heart? A faintness passed like a shadow over Giovanni and flitted away; he seemed to gaze through the beautiful girl's eyes into her transparent soul, and felt no more doubt or fear.

The tinge of passion that had colored Beatrice's manner vanished; she became gay, and appeared to derive a pure delight from her communion with the youth not unlike what the maiden of a lonely island might have felt conversing with a voyager from the civilized world. Evidently her experience of life had been confined within the limits of that garden. She talked now about matters as simple as the daylight or summer clouds, and now asked questions in reference to the city, or Giovanni's distant home, his friends, his mother, and his sisters—questions indicating such seclusion, and such lack of familiarity with modes and forms, that Giovanni responded as if to an infant. Her spirit gushed out before him like a fresh rill that was just catching its first glimpse of the sunlight and wondering at the reflections of earth and sky which were flung into its bosom. There came thoughts, too, from a deep source, and fantasies of a gemlike brilliancy, as if diamonds and rubies sparkled upward among the bubbles of the fountain. Ever and anon there gleamed across the young man's mind a sense of wonder that he should be walking side by side with the being who had so wrought upon his imagination, whom he had idealized in such hues of terror, in whom he had positively witnessed such manifestations of dreadful attributes—that he should be conversing with Beatrice like a brother, and should find her so human and so maidenlike. But such reflections were only momentary; the effect of her character was too real not to make itself familiar at once.

In this free intercourse they had strayed through the garden, and now, after many turns among its avenues, were come to the shattered fountain, beside which grew the magnificent shrub, with its treasury of flowing blossoms. A fragrance was diffused from it which Giovanni recognized as identical with that which he had attributed to Beatrice's breath, but incomparably more powerful. As her eyes fell upon it, Giovanni beheld her press her hand to her bosom as if her heart were throbbing suddenly and painfully.

"For the first time in my life," murmured she, addressing the shrub, "I had forgotten thee."

"I remember, signora," said Giovanni, "that you once promised to reward me with one of these living gems for the bouquet which I had the happy boldness to fling to your feet. Permit me now to pluck it as a memorial of this interview."

He made a step towards the shrub with extended hand; but Beatrice darted forward, uttering a shriek that went through his heart like a dagger. She caught his hand and drew it back with the whole force of her slender figure. Giovanni felt her touch thrilling through his fibres.

"Touch it not!" exclaimed she, in a voice of agony. "Not for thy life! It is fatal!"

Then, hiding her face, she fled from him and vanished beneath the sculptured portal. As Giovanni followed her with his eyes, he beheld the emaciated figure and pale intelligence of Dr. Rappaccini, who had been watching the scene, he knew not how long, within the shadow of the entrance.

No sooner was Guasconti alone in his chamber than the image of Beatrice came back to his passionate musings, invested with all the witchery that had been gathering around it ever since his first glimpse of her, and now likewise imbued with a tender warmth of girlish womanhood. She was human; her nature was endowed with all gentle and feminine qualities; she was worthiest to be worshipped; she was capable, surely, on her part, of the height and heroism of love. Those tokens which he had hitherto considered as proofs of a frightful peculiarity in her physical and moral system were now either forgotten or by the subtle sophistry of passion transmitted into a golden crown of enchantment, rendering Beatrice the more admirable by so much as she was the more unique. Whatever had looked ugly was not beautiful; or, if incapable of such a change, it stole away and hid itself among those shapeless half ideas which throng the dim region beyond the daylight of our perfect consciousness. Thus did he spend the night, nor fell asleep until the dawn had begun to awake the slumbering flowers in Dr. Rappaccini's garden, whither Giovanni's dreams doubtless led him. Up rose the sun in his due season, and, flinging his beams upon the young man's eyelids, awoke him to a sense of pain. When thoroughly aroused, he became sensible of a burning and tingling agony in his hand—in his right hand—the very hand which Beatrice had grasped in her own when he was on the point of plucking one of the gemlike flowers. On the back of that hand there was now a purple print like that of four small fingers, and the likeness of a slender thumb upon his wrist.

O, how stubbornly does love,—or even that cunning semblance of love which flourishes in the imagination, but strikes no depth of root into the heart,—how stubbornly does it hold its faith until the moment comes when it is doomed to vanish into thin mist! Giovanni wrapped a handkerchief about his hand and wondered what evil thing had stung him, and soon forgot his pain in a revery of Beatrice.

After the first interview, a second was in the inevitable course of what we call fate. A third; a fourth; and a meeting with Beatrice in the garden was no longer an incident in Giovanni's daily life, but the whole space in which he might be said to live; for the anticipation and memory of that ecstatic hour made up the remainder. Nor was it otherwise with the daughter of Rappaccini. She watched for the youth's appearance and flew to his side with confidence as unreserved as if they had been playmates from early infancy—as if they were such playmates still. If, by any unwonted chance, he failed to come at the appointed moment, she stood beneath the window and sent up the rich sweetness of her tones to float around him in his chamber and echo and reverberate throughout his heart—"Giovanni! Giovanni! Why tarriest thou? Come down!" And down he hastened into that Eden of poisonous flowers.

But, with all this intimate familiarity, there was still a reserve in Beatrice's demeanor, so rigidly and invariably sustained that the idea of infringing it scarcely occurred to his imagination. By all appreciable signs, they loved; they had looked love with eyes that conveyed the holy secret from the depths of one soul into the depths of the other, as if it were too sacred to be whispered by the way; they had even spoken love in those gushes of passion when their spirits darted forth in articulated breath like tongues of long hidden flame; and yet there had been no seal of lips, no clasp of hands, nor any slightest caress such as love claims and hallows. He had never touched one of the gleaming ringlets of her hair; her garment—so marked was the physical barrier between them—had never been waved against him by a breeze. On the few occasions when Giovanni had seemed tempted to overstep the limit, Beatrice grew so sad, so stern, and withal wore such a look of desolate separation, shuddering at itself, that not a spoken word was requisite to repel him. At such times he was startled at the horrible suspicions that rose, monster-like, out of the caverns of his heart and stared him in the face; his love grew thin and faint as the morning mist; his doubts alone had substance. But, when Beatrice's face brightened again after the momentary shadow, she was transformed at once from the mysterious, questionable being whom he had watched with so much awe and horror; she was now the beautiful and unsophisticated girl whom he felt that his spirit knew with a certainty beyond all other knowledge.

A considerable time had now passed since Giovanni's last meeting with Baglioni. One morning, however, he was disagreeably surprised by a visit from the professor, whom he had scarcely thought of for whole weeks, and would willingly have forgotten still longer. Given up as he had long been to a pervading excitement, he could tolerate no companions except upon condition of their perfect sympathy with his present state of feeling. Such sympathy was not to be expected from Professor Baglioni.

The visitor chatted carelessly for a few moments about the gossip of the city and the university, and then took up another topic.

85 "I have been reading an old classic author lately," said he, "and met with a story that strangely interested me. Possibly you may remember it. It is of an Indian prince, who sent a beautiful woman as a present to Alexander the Great. She was as lovely as the dawn and gorgeous as the sunset; but what especially distinguished her was a certain rich perfume in her breath—richer than a garden of Persian roses. Alexander, as was natural to a youthful conqueror, fell in love at first sight with this magnificent stranger; but a certain sage physician, happening to be present, discovered a terrible secret in regard to her."

"And what was that?" asked Giovanni, turning his eyes downward to avoid those of the professor.

"That this lovely woman," continued Baglioni, with emphasis, "had been nourished with poisons from her birth upward, until her whole nature was so imbued with them that she herself had become the deadliest poison in existence. Poison was her element of life. With that rich perfume of her breath she blasted the very air. Her love would have been poison—her embrace death. Is not this a marvellous tale?"

"A childish fable," answered Giovanni, nervously starting from his chair. "I marvel how your worship finds time to read such nonsense among your graver studies."

"By the by," said the professor, looking uneasily about him, "what singular fragrance is this in your apartment? Is it the perfume of your gloves? It is faint, but delicious; and yet, after all, by no means agreeable. Were I to breathe it long, methinks it would make me ill. It is like the breath of a flower; but I see no flowers in the chamber."

90 "Nor are there any," replied Giovanni, who had turned pale as the professor spoke; "nor, I think, is there any fragrance except in your worship's imagination. Odors, being a sort of element combined of the sensual and the spiritual, are apt to deceive us in this matter. The recollection of a perfume, the bare idea of it, may easily be mistaken for a present reality."

"Ay; but my sober imagination does not often play such tricks," said Baglioni; "and, were I to fancy any kind of odor, it would be that of some vile apothecary drug, wherewith my fingers are likely enough to be imbued. Our worshipful friend Rappaccini, as I have heard, tinctures his medicaments with odors richer than those of Araby.[8] Doubtless, likewise, the fair and learned Signora Beatrice would minister to her patients with draughts as sweet as a maiden's breath; but woe to him that sips them!"

Giovanni's face evinced many contending emotions. The tone in which the professor alluded to the pure and lovely daughter of Rappaccini was a torture to his soul; and yet the intimation of a view of her character, opposite to his own, gave instantaneous distinctness to a thousand dim suspicions, which now grinned at him like so many demons. But he strove hard to quell them and to respond to Baglioni with a true lover's perfect faith.

"Signor professor," said he, "you were my father's friend; perchance, too, it is your purpose to act a friendly part towards his son. I would fain feel nothing towards you save respect and deference; but I pray you to observe, signor, that there is one subject on which we must not speak. You know not the Signora Beatrice. You cannot, therefore, estimate the wrong—the blasphemy, I may even say—that is offered to her character by a light or injurious word."

"Giovanni! my poor Giovanni!" answered the professor, with a calm expression of pity. "I know this wretched girl far better than yourself. You shall hear the truth in respect to the poisoner Rappaccini and his poisonous daughter; yes, poisonous as she is beautiful. Listen; for, even should you do violence to my gray hairs, it shall not silence me. That old fable of the Indian woman has become a truth by the deep and deadly science of Rappaccini and in the person of the lovely Beatrice."

Giovanni groaned and hid his face.

"Her father," continued Baglioni, "was not restrained by natural affection from offering up his child in this horrible manner as the victim of his insane zeal for science; for, let us do him justice, he is as true a man of science as ever distilled his own heart in an alembic. What, then, will be your fate? Beyond a doubt you are selected as the material of some new experiment. Perhaps the result is to be death; perhaps a fate more awful still. Rappaccini, with what he calls the interest of science before his eyes, will hesitate at nothing."

"It is a dream," muttered Giovanni to himself; "surely it is a dream."

"But," resumed the professor, "be of good cheer, son of my friend. It is not yet too late for the rescue. Possibly we may even succeed in bringing back this miserable child within the limits of ordinary nature, from which her father's madness has estranged her. Behold this little silver vase! It was wrought by the hands of the renowned Benvenuto Cellini,[9] and is well worthy to be a love gift to the fairest dame in Italy. But its contents are invaluable. One little sip of this antidote would have rendered the most virulent poisons of the Borgias[10] innocuous. Doubt not that it will be as efficacious against those

[8] Arabia.

[9] Benvenuto Cellini (1500–71), an Italian sculptor.

[10] Notorious, powerful Italian Renaissance family, noted for cruelty and political intrigues.

of Rappaccini. Bestow the vase, and the precious liquid within it, on your Beatrice, and hopefully await the result."

Baglioni laid a small, exquisitely wrought silver vial on the table and withdrew, leaving what he had said to produce its effect upon the young man's mind.

"We will thwart Rappaccini yet," thought he, chuckling to himself, as he descended the stairs; "but, let us confess the truth of him, he is a wonderful man—a wonderful man indeed; a vile empiric,[11] however, in his practice, and therefore not to be tolerated by those who respect the good old rules of the medical profession."

Throughout Giovanni's whole acquaintance with Beatrice, he had occasionally, as we have said, been haunted by dark surmises as to her character; yet so thoroughly had she made herself felt by him as a simple, natural, most affectionate, and guileless creature, that the image now held up by Professor Baglioni looked as strange and incredible as if it were not in accordance with his own original conception. True, there were ugly recollections connected with his first glimpses of the beautiful girl; he could not quite forget the bouquet that withered in her grasp, and the insect that perished amid the sunny air, by no ostensible agency save the fragrance of her breath. These incidents, however, dissolving in the pure light of her character, had no longer the efficacy of facts, but were acknowledged as mistaken fantasies, by whatever testimony of the senses they might appear to be substantiated. There is something truer and more real than what we can see with the eyes and touch with the finger. On such better evidence had Giovanni founded his confidence in Beatrice, though rather by the necessary force of her high attributes than by any deep and generous faith on his part. But now his spirit was incapable of sustaining itself at the height to which the early enthusiasm of passion had exalted it; he fell down, grovelling among earthly doubts, and defiled therewith the pure whiteness of Beatrice's image. Not that he gave her up; he did but distrust. He resolved to institute some decisive test that should satisfy him, once for all, whether there were those dreadful peculiarities in her physical nature which could not be supposed to exist without some corresponding monstrosity of soul. His eyes, gazing down afar, might have deceived him as to the lizard, the insect, and the flowers; but if he could witness, at the distance of a few paces, the sudden blight of one fresh and healthful flower in Beatrice's hand, there would be room for no further question. With this idea he hastened to the florist's and purchased a bouquet that was still gemmed with the morning dewdrops.

It was now the customary hour of his daily interview with Beatrice. Before descending into the garden, Giovanni failed not to look at his figure in the mirror—a vanity to be expected in a beautiful young man, yet, as displaying itself at that troubled and feverish moment, the token of a certain shallowness of feeling and insincerity of character. He did gaze, however, and said to himself

[11] Charlatan.

that his features had never before possessed so rich a grace, nor his eyes such vivacity, nor his cheeks so warm a hue of superabundant life.

"At least," thought he, "her poison has not yet insinuated itself into my system. I am no flower to perish in her grasp."

With that thought he turned his eyes on the bouquet, which he had never once laid aside from his hand. A thrill of indefinable horror shot through his frame on perceiving that those dewy flowers were already beginning to droop; they wore the aspect of things that had been fresh and lovely yesterday. Giovanni grew white as marble, and stood motionless before the mirror, staring at his own reflection there as at the likeness of something frightful. He remembered Baglioni's remark about the fragrance that seemed to pervade the chamber. It must have been the poison in his breath! Then he shuddered—shuddered at himself. Recovering from his stupor, he began to watch with curious eye a spider that was busily at work hanging its web from the antique cornice of the apartment, crossing and recrossing the artful system of interwoven lines—as vigorous and active a spider as ever dangled from an old ceiling. Giovanni bent towards the insect, and emitted a deep, long breath. The spider suddenly ceased its toil; the web vibrated with a tremor originating in the body of the small artisan. Again Giovanni sent forth a breath, deeper, longer, and imbued with a venomous feeling out of his heart: he knew not whether he were wicked, or only desperate. The spider made a convulsive gripe with his limbs and hung dead across the window.

"Accursed! accursed!" muttered Giovanni, addressing himself. "Hast thou grown so poisonous that this deadly insect perishes by thy breath?"

At that moment a rich, sweet voice came floating up from the garden.

"Giovanni! Giovanni! It is past the hour! Why tarriest thou? Come down!"

"Yes," muttered Giovanni again. "she is the only being whom my breath may not slay! Would that it might!"

He rushed down, and in an instant was standing before the bright and loving eyes of Beatrice. A moment ago his wrath and despair had been so fierce that he could have desired nothing so much as to wither her by a glance; but with her actual presence there came influences which had too real an existence to be at once shaken off; recollections of the delicate and benign power of her feminine nature, which had so often enveloped him in a religious calm; recollections of many a holy and passionate outgush of her heart, when the pure fountain had been unsealed from its depths and made visible in its transparency to his mental eye; recollections which, had Giovanni known how to estimate them, would have assured him that all this ugly mystery was but an earthly illusion, and that, whatever mist of evil might seem to have gathered over her, the real Beatrice was a heavenly angel. Incapable as he was of such high faith, still her presence had not utterly lost its magic. Giovanni's rage was quelled into an aspect of sullen insensibility. Beatrice, with a quick spiritual sense, immediately felt that there was a gulf of blackness between them which neither he nor she could pass. They walked on together, sad and silent, and came thus to the marble fountain and to its pool of water on the ground, in the midst of which grew the shrub that bore gemlike blossoms. Giovanni was affrighted at the eager enjoyment—the appetite, as it were—with which he found himself inhaling the fragrance of the flowers.

110 "Beatrice," asked he, abruptly, "whence came this shrub?"

"My father created it," answered she, with simplicity.

"Created it! created it!" repeated Giovanni. "What mean you, Beatrice?"

"He is a man fearfully acquainted with the secrets of Nature," replied Beatrice; "and, at the hour when I first drew breath, this plant sprang from the soil, the offspring of his science, of his intellect, while I was but his earthly child. Approach it not!" continued she, observing with terror that Giovanni was drawing nearer to the shrub. "It has qualities that you little dream of. But I, dearest Giovanni,—I grew up and blossomed with the plant and was nourished with its breath. It was my sister, and I loved it with a human affection; for, alas!—hast thou not suspected it?—there was an awful doom."

Here Giovanni frowned so darkly upon her that Beatrice paused and trembled. But her faith in his tenderness reassured her, and made her blush that she had doubted for an instant.

115 "There was an awful doom," she continued, "The effect of my father's fatal love of science, which estranged me from all society of my kind. Until Heaven sent thee, dearest Giovanni, O, how lonely was thy poor Beatrice!"

"Was it a hard doom?" asked Giovanni, fixing his eyes upon her.

"Only of late have I known how hard it was," answered she, tenderly. "O, yes; but my heart was torpid, and therefore quiet."

Giovanni's rage broke forth from his sullen gloom like a lightning flash out of a dark cloud.

"Accursed one!" cried he, with venomous scorn and anger. "And, finding thy solitude wearisome, thou hast severed me likewise from all the warmth of life and enticed me into thy region of unspeakable horror!"

120 "Giovanni!" exclaimed Beatrice, turning her large bright eyes upon his face. The force of his words had not found it way into her mind; she was merely thunderstruck.

"Yes, poisonous thing!" repeated Giovanni, beside himself with passion. "Thou hast done it! Thou hast blasted me! Thou hast filled my veins with poison! Thou hast made me as hateful, as ugly, as loathsome and deadly a creature as thyself—a world's wonder of hideous monstrosity! Now, if our breath be happily as fatal to ourselves as to all other, let us join our lips in one kiss of unutterable hatred, and so die!"

"What has befallen me?" murmured Beatrice, with a low moan out of her heart. "Holy Virgin, pity me, a poor heart-broken child!"

"Thou, —dost thou pray?" cried Giovanni, still with the same fiendish scorn. "Thy very prayers, as they come from thy lips, taint the atmosphere with death. Yes, yes; let us pray! Let us to church and dip our fingers in the holy water at the portal! They that come after us will perish as by a pestilence! Let us sign crosses in the air! It will be scattering curses abroad in the likeness of holy symbols!"

"Giovanni," said Beatrice, calmly, for her grief was beyond passion, "why dost thou join thyself with me thus in those terrible words? I, it is true, am the horrible thing thou namest me. But thou,—what hast thou to do, save with one other shudder at my hideous misery to go forth out of the garden and mingle with thy race, and forget that there ever crawled on earth such a monster as poor Beatrice?"

125 Dost thou pretend ignorance?" asked Giovanni, scowling upon her. "Behold! this power have I gained from the pure daughter of Rappaccini."

There was a swarm of summer insects flitting through the air in search of the food promised by the flower odors of the fatal garden. They circled round Giovanni's head, and were evidently attracted towards him by the same influence which had drawn them for an instant within the sphere of several of the shrubs. He sent forth a breath among them, and smiled bitterly at Beatrice as at least a score of the insects fell dead upon the ground.

"I see it! I see it!" shrieked Beatrice. "It is my father's fatal science! No, no, Giovanni; it was not I! Never! never! I dreamed only to love thee and be with thee a little time, and so to let thee pass away, leaving but thine image in mine heart; for, Giovanni, believe it, though my body be nourished with poison, my spirit is God's creature, and craves love as its daily food. But my father,—he has united us in this fearful sympathy. Yes; spurn me, tread upon me, kill me! O, what is death after such words as thine? But it was not I. Not for a world of bliss would I have done it."

Giovanni's passion had exhausted itself in its outburst from his lips. There now came across him a sense, mournful, and not without tenderness, of the intimate and peculiar relationship between Beatrice and himself. They stood, as it were, in an utter solitude, which would be made none the less solitary by the densest throng of human life. Ought not, then, the desert of humanity around them to press this insulated pair closer together? If they should be cruel to one another, who was there to be kind to them? Besides, thought Giovanni, might there not still be a hope of his returning within the limits of ordinary nature, and leading Beatrice, the redeemed Beatrice, by the hand? O, weak, and selfish, and unworthy spirit, that could dream of an earthly union and earthly happiness as possible, after such deep love had been so bitterly wronged as was Beatrice's love by Giovanni's blighting words! No, no; there could be no such hope. She must pass heavily, with that broken heart, across the borders of Time—she must bathe her hurts in some fount of paradise, and forget her grief in the light of immortality, and *there* be well.

But Giovanni did not know it.

130 "Dear Beatrice," said he, approaching her, while she shrank away as always at his approach, but now with a different impulse, "dearest Beatrice, our fate is not yet so desperate. Behold! there is a medicine, potent, as a wise physician has assured me, and almost divine in its efficacy. It is composed of ingredients the most opposite to those by which thy awful father has brought this calamity upon thee and me. It is distilled of blessed herbs. Shall we not quaff it together, and thus be purified from evil?"

"Give it me!" said Beatrice, extending her hand to receive the little silver vial which Giovanni took from his bosom. She added, with a peculiar emphasis, "I will drink; but do thou await the result."

She put Baglioni's antidote to her lips; and, at the same moment, the figure of Rappaccini emerged from the portal and came slowly towards the marble fountain. As he drew near, the pale man of science seemed to gaze with a triumphant expression at the beautiful youth and maiden, as might an artist who should spend his life in achieving a picture or a group of statuary and finally be satisfied with his success. He paused; his bent form grew erect with conscious power; he spread out his hands over them in the attitude of a father imploring a blessing upon his children; but those were the same hands that had thrown poison into the stream of their lives. Giovanni trembled. Beatrice shuddered nervously, and pressed her hand upon her heart.

"My daughter," said Rappaccini, "thou art no longer lonely in the world. Pluck one of those precious gems from thy sister shrub and bid thy bridegroom wear it in his bosom. It will not harm him now. My science and the sympathy between thee and him have so wrought within his system that he now stands apart from common men, as thou dost, daughter of my pride and triumph, from ordinary women. Pass on, then, through the world, most dear to one another and dreadful to all besides!"

"My father," said Beatrice, feebly—and still as she spoke she kept her hand upon her heart,—"wherefore didst thou inflict this miserable doom upon thy child?"

135 "Miserable!" exclaimed Rappaccini. "What mean you, foolish girl." Dost thou deem it misery to be endowed with marvellous gifts against which no power nor strength could avail an enemy—misery, to be able to quell the mightiest with a breath—misery, to be as terrible as thou art beautiful? Wouldst thou, then, have preferred the condition of a weak woman, exposed to all evil and capable of none?"

"I would fain have been loved, not feared," murmured Beatrice, sinking down upon the ground. "But now it matters not. I am going, father, where the evil which thou hast striven to mingle with my being will pass away like a dream—like the fragrance of these poisonous flowers, which will no longer taint my breath among the flowers of Eden. Farewell, Giovanni! Thy words of hatred are like lead within my heart; but they, too, will fall away as I ascend. O, was there not, from the first, more poison in thy nature than in mine?"

To Beatrice,—so radically had her earthly part been wrought upon by Rappaccini's skill,—as poison had been life, so the powerful antidote was death; and thus the poor victim of man's ingenuity and of thwarted nature, and of the fatality that attends all such efforts of perverted wisdom, perished there, at the feet of her father and Giovanni. Just at that moment Professor Pietro Baglioni looked forth from the window, and called loudly, in a tone of triumph mixed with horror, to the thunderstricken man of science,—

"Rappaccini! Rappaccini! and is *this* the upshot of your experiment?"

Explorations of the Text

1. The garden is a central setting and symbol in the story. How do different characters view the garden? Consider Beatrice, Giovanni, Rappaccini, and Baglioni.
2. Trace the development of Beatrice's and Giovanni's relationship. Identify at least three important stages. What qualities of each are attractive to the other?
3. Analyze the family relationships in the story. How do Rappaccini and Baglioni function as Giovanni's fathers? In what ways is the garden's "magnificent shrub" the sister of Beatrice? In what ways are Beatrice and Giovanni brother and sister? How does Rappaccini function as Beatrice's sole parent?
4. What role does Dame Lisabetta play in the family?
5. Why does Giovanni give Beatrice Baglioni's medicine? Do you believe that he is justified in doing so? Why does Beatrice drink the potion? Should she have done so? Give your reasons.
6. How are evil and virtue defined in the story?
7. What views emerge of science, faith, and fate?

The Reading/Writing Connection

1. "Think" Topic: How might the story be different if Dr. Rappaccini or Beatrice were the narrator? Choose one of these characters and write a monologue in his/her voice.
2. Journal Entry: Does Beatrice have any free will or agency? Respond.
3. Debate Topic: Is Giovanni responsible for Beatrice's death? Or is her father responsible for her fate?

Ideas for Writing

1. Compare the visions of fate and free will presented in "Riders to the Sea" and in this work.
2. Compare the family relationships in this work with those in "Riders to the Sea."
3. Create a feminist analysis of the story.

THOSE WINTER SUNDAYS

Robert Hayden

Robert Hayden (1913–80) was born in Detroit, Michigan. He attended Detroit City College (now Wayne State University) and the University of Michigan. He garnered many honors and fellowships and in 1976 became the first African American poet to be chosen Consultant in Poetry to the Library of Congress. His works include Heart-Shape in the Dust *(1940),* Words in Mourning Time *(1970), and* Robert Hayden: Collected Poems *(1982).*

1962

Sundays too my father got up early
and put his clothes on in the blueblack cold,
then with cracked hands that ached
from labor in the weekday weather made
banked fires blaze. No one ever thanked him.

I'd wake and hear the cold splintering, breaking.
When the rooms were warm, he'd call,
and slowly I would rise and dress,
fearing the chronic angers of that house,

Speaking indifferently to him,
who had driven out the cold
and polished my good shoes as well.
What did I know, what did I know
of love's austere and lonely offices?

Explorations of the Text

1. What hints about the father's work does Hayden provide?
2. Which details define the family's economic condition?
3. What do the images of cold and warmth suggest about the life of the family?
4. Discuss the "chronic angers" of the house.
5. What meanings are suggested by the speaker's question: "What did I know/of love's austere and lonely offices?"
6. In what ways has the speaker's attitude toward his father changed now that he is an adult?

The Reading/Writing Connection

1. Journal Entry: Write about an incident from childhood, a Saturday or Sunday morning at home with a parent. You might begin with: "Sunday mornings, I . . . ."
2. "Think" Topic: Interpret the quotation from Paul Simon's song, "The Sound of Silence": "Silence like a cancer grows." Connect it with the conflict of the speaker in this poem.

Ideas for Writing

1. Compare the barriers between fathers and sons in Hayden's poem and in other works in this chapter. Cite your personal experience and observation, too.
2. *Explicate* (examine line by line) this poem. Concentrate on point of view, imagery, theme.

Riders to the Sea

John Millington Synge

John Millington Synge (1871–1909), the youngest of five children, was born to Protestant English parents near Dublin, Ireland. He graduated from Trinity College, Dublin, and spent ten years traveling the Continent. In Paris, he met William Butler Yeats, who suggested Synge visit the Aran Islands off the west coast of Ireland, which Synge did in 1899. The trip had a profound and lasting effect on him. Synge's first play, In the Shadow of the Glen, *was produced at Dublin's Abbey Theater in 1905. It was followed by* Riders to the Sea *(1904), and Synge's masterpiece,* The Playboy of the Western World *(1907). With Yeats and other playwrights and artists, Synge created a legendary Irish theater at the Abbey and was responsible for the renaissance of Irish literature at the beginning of the twentieth century.*

1904

Characters

Maurya, an old woman
Bartley, her son
Cathleen, her daughter
Nora, a younger daughter
Men and Women

An island off the west of Ireland.

Cottage kitchen, with nets, oil-skins, spinning-wheel, some new boards standing by the wall, etc. Cathleen, a girl of about twenty finishes kneading cake, and puts it down on the pot-oven by the fire; then wipes her hands, and begins to spin at the wheel. Nora, a young girl, puts her head in at the door.

Nora *(In a low voice.):* Where is she?
Cathleen: She's lying down, God help her, and may be sleeping, if she's able.

(Nora comes in softly, and takes a bundle from under her shawl.)

Cathleen *(Spinning the wheel rapidly.)*: What is it you have?

Nora: The young priest is after bringing them. It's a shirt and a plain stocking were got off a drowned man in Donegal.[1]

(Cathleen stops her wheel with a sudden movement, and leans out to listen.)

Nora: We're to find out if it's Michael's they are, some time herself will be down looking by the sea.

Cathleen: How would they be Michael's, Nora? How would he go the length of that way to the Far North?

Nora: The young priest says he's known the like of it. "If it's Michael's they are," says he, "you can tell herself he's got a clean burial by the grace of God, and if they're not his, let no one say a word about them, for she'll be getting her death," says he, "with crying and lamenting."

(The door which Nora half closed is blown open by a gust of wind.)

Cathleen *(Looking out anxiously.):* Did you ask him would he stop Bartley going this day with the horses to the Galway[2] fair?

Nora: "I won't stop him," says he, "but let you not be afraid. Herself does be saying prayers half through the night, and the Almighty God won't leave her destitute," says he, "with no son living."

Cathleen: Is the sea bad by the white rocks, Nora?

Nora: Middling bad, God help us. There's a great roaring in the west, and it's worse it'll be getting when the tide's turned to the wind. *(She goes over to the table with the bundle.)* Shall I open it now?

Cathleen: Maybe she'd wake up on us, and come in before we'd done. *(Coming to the table.)* It's a long time we'll be, and the two of us crying.

Nora *(Goes to the inner door and listens.):* She's moving about on the bed. She'll be coming in a minute.

Cathleen: Give me the ladder, and I'll put them up in the turf-loft, the way she won't know of them at all, and maybe when the tide turns she'll be going down to see would he be floating from the east.

(They put the ladder against the gable of the chimney; Cathleen goes up a few steps and hides the bundle in the turf-loft. Maurya comes from the inner room.)

Maurya *(Looking up at Cathleen and speaking querulously.):* Isn't it turf enough you have for this day and evening?

Cathleen: There's a cake baking at the fire for a short space *(Throwing down the turf.)* and Bartley will want it when the tide turns if he goes to Connemara.[3]

(Nora picks up the turf and puts it round the pot-oven.)

---

[1] County in Northwestern Ireland; in Ulster.
[2] City in West Central Ireland.
[3] Region of West Ireland.

Maurya *(Sitting down on a stool at the fire.)*: He won't go this day with the wind rising from the south and west. He won't go this day, for the young priest will stop him surely.

Nora: He'll not stop him, Mother, and I heard Eamon Simon and Stephen Pheety and Colum Shawn saying he would go.

Maurya: Where is he itself?

Nora: He went down to see would there be another boat sailing in the week, and I'm thinking it won't be long till he's here now, for the tide's turning at the green head, and the hooker's[4] tacking from the east.

Cathleen: I hear some one passing the big stones.

Nora *(Looking out.)*: He's coming now, and he in a hurry.

Bartley *(Comes in and looks round the room; speaking sadly and quietly.)*: Where is the bit of new rope, Cathleen, was bought in Connemara?

Cathleen *(Coming down.)*: Give it to him, Nora; it's on a nail by the white boards. I hung it up this morning, for the pig with the black feet was eating it.

Nora *(Giving him a rope.)*: Is that it, Bartley?

Maurya: You'd do right to leave that rope, Bartley, hanging by the boards. *(Bartley takes the rope.)* It will be wanting in this place, I'm telling you, if Michael is washed up tomorrow morning, or the next morning, or any morning in the week, for it's a deep grave we'll make him by the grace of God.

Bartley *(Beginning to work with the rope.)*: I've no halter the way I can ride down on the mare, and I must go now quickly. This is the one boat going for two weeks or beyond it, and the fair will be a good fair for horses I heard them saying below.

Maurya: It's a hard thing they'll be saying below if the body is washed up and there's no man in it to make the coffin, and I after giving a big price for the finest white boards you'd find in Connemara. *(She looks round at the boards.)*

Bartley: How would it be washed up, and we after looking each day for nine days, and a strong wind blowing a while back from the west and south?

Maurya: If it wasn't found itself, that wind is raising the sea, and there was a star up against the moon, and it rising in the night. If it was a hundred horses, or a thousand horses you had itself, what is the price of a thousand horses against a son where there is one son only?

Bartley *(Working at the halter, to Cathleen.)*: Let you go down each day, and see the sheep aren't jumping in on the rye, and if the jobber[5] comes you can sell the pig with the black feet if there is a good price going.

Maurya: How would the like of her get a good price for a pig?

---

[4] One-masted fishing boat used on the English and Irish coast. [5] Wholesaler.

Bartley *(To Cathleen.):* If the west wind holds with the last bit of the moon let you and Nora get up weed enough for another cock[6] for the kelp. It's hard set we'll be from this day with no one in it but one man to work.

Maurya: It's hard set we'll be surely the day you're drowned'd with the rest. What way will I live and the girls with me, and I an old woman looking for the grave?

(Bartley lays down the halter, takes off his old coat, and puts on a newer one of the same flannel.)

Bartley *(To Nora.):* Is she coming to the pier?

Nora *(Looking out.):* She's passing the green head and letting fall her sails.

Bartley *(Getting his purse and tobacco.):* I'll have half an hour to go down, and you'll see my coming again in two days, or in three days, or maybe in four days if the wind is bad.

Maurya *(Turning round to the fire, and putting her shawl over her head.):* Isn't it a hard and cruel man won't hear a word from an old woman, and she holding him from the sea?

Cathleen: It's the life of a young man to be going on the sea, and who would listen to an old woman with one thing and she saying it over?

Bartley *(Taking the halter.):* I must go now quickly. I'll ride down on the red mare, and the gray pony'll run behind me. . . . The blessing of God on you. *(He goes out.)*

Maurya *(Crying out as he is in the door.):* He's gone now, God spare us, and we'll not see him again. He's gone now, and when the black night is falling I'll have no son left me in the world.

Cathleen: Why wouldn't you give him your blessing and he looking round in the door? Isn't it sorrow enough is on every one in this house without your sending him out with an unlucky word behind him and a hard word in his ear?

(Maurya takes up the tongs and begins raking the fire aimlessly without looking round.)

Nora *(Turning toward her.):* You're taking away the turf from the cake.

Cathleen *(Crying out.):* The Son of God forgive us, Nora, we're after forgetting his bit of bread. *(She comes over to the fire.)*

Nora: And it's destroyed he'll be going till dark night, and he after eating nothing since the sun went up.

Cathleen *(Turning the cake out of the oven.):* It's destroyed he'll be, surely. There's no sense left on any person in a house where an old woman will be talking forever.

(Maurya sways herself on her stool.)

[6] A small pile for burning seaweed into kelp (used as fertilizer).

Cathleen *(Cutting off some of the bread and rolling it in a cloth; to Maurya.):* Let you go down now to the spring well and give him this and he passing. You'll see him then and the dark word will be broken, and you can say "God speed you," the way he'll be easy in his mind.

Maurya *(Taking the bread.):* Will I be in it as soon as himself?

Cathleen: If you go now quickly.

Maurya *(Standing up unsteadily.):* It's hard set I am to walk.

Cathleen *(Looking at her anxiously.):* Give her the stick, Nora, or maybe she'll slip on the big stones.

Nora: What stick?

Cathleen: The stick Michael brought from Connemara.

Maurya *(Taking a stick Nora gives her.):* In the big world the old people do be leaving things after them for their sons and children, but in this place it is the young men do be leaving things behind for them that do be old.

(She goes out slowly. Nora goes over to the ladder.)

Cathleen: Wait, Nora, maybe she'd turn back quickly. She's that sorry, God help her, you wouldn't know the thing she'd do.

Nora: Is she gone round by the bush?

Cathleen *(Looking out.):* She's gone now. Throw it down quickly, for the Lord knows when she'll be out of it again.

Nora *(Getting the bundle from the loft.):* The young priest said he'd be passing tomorrow, and we might go down and speak to him below if it's Michael's they are surely.

Cathleen *(Taking the bundle.):* Did he say what way they were found?

Nora *(Coming down.):* "There were two men," says he, "and they rowing round with poteen[7] before the cocks crowed, and the oar of one of them caught the body, and they passing the black cliffs of the north."

Cathleen *(Trying to open the bundle.):* Give me a knife, Nora, the string's perished with the salt water, and there's a black knot on it you wouldn't loosen in a week.

Nora *(Giving her a knife.):* I've heard tell it was a long way to Donegal.

Cathleen *(Cutting the string.):* It is surely. There was a man in here a while ago—the man sold us that knife—and he said if you set off walking from the rocks beyond, it would be seven days you'd be in Donegal.

Nora: And what time would a man take, and he floating?

(Cathleen opens the bundle and takes out a bit of a stocking. They look at them eagerly.)

Cathleen *(In a low voice.):* The Lord spare us, Nora! isn't it a queer hard thing to say if it's his they are surely?

---

[7] Illegally distilled whiskey.

Nora: I'll get his shirt off the hook the way we can put the one flannel on the other. *(She looks through some clothes hanging in the corner.)* It's not with them, Cathleen, and where will it be?

Cathleen: I'm thinking Bartley put it on him in the morning, for his own shirt was heavy with the salt in it. *(Pointing to the corner.)* There's a bit of a sleeve was of the same stuff. Give me that and it will do.

(Nora brings it to her and they compare the flannel.)

Cathleen: It's the same stuff, Nora; but if it is itself aren't there great rolls of it in the shops of Galway, and isn't it many another man may have a shirt of it as well as Michael himself?

Nora *(Who has taken up the stocking and counted the stitches, crying out.):* It's Michael, Cathleen, it's Michael; God spare his soul, and what will herself say when she hears this story, and Bartley on the sea?

Cathleen *(Taking the stocking.):* It's a plain stocking.

Nora: It's the second one of the third pair I knitted, and I put up threescore stitches, and I dropped four of them.

Cathleen *(Counts the stitches.):* It's that number is in it. *(Crying out.)* Ah, Nora, isn't it a bitter thing to think of him floating that way to the Far North, and no one to keen[8] him but the black hags that do be flying on the sea?

Nora *(Swinging herself round, and throwing out her arms on the clothes.):* And isn't it a pitiful thing when there is nothing left of a man who was a great rower and fisher, but a bit of an old shirt and a plain stocking?

Cathleen *(After an instant.):* Tell me is herself coming, Nora? I hear a little sound on the path.

Nora *(Looking out.):* She is, Cathleen. She's coming up to the door.

Cathleen: Put these things away before she'll come in. Maybe it's easier she'll be after giving her blessing to Bartley, and we won't let on we've heard anything the time he's on the sea.

Nora *(Helping Cathleen to close the bundle.):* We'll put them here in the corner.

(They put them into a hole in the chimney corner. Cathleen goes back to the spinning-wheel.)

Nora: Will she see it was crying I was?

Cathleen: Keep your back to the door the way the light'll not be on you.

(Nora sits down at the chimney corner, with her back to the door. Maurya comes in very slowly, without looking at the girls, and goes over to her stool at the other side of the fire. The cloth with the bread is still in her hand. The girls look at each other, and Nora points to the bundle of bread.)

[8] Ritualized lamentation for the dead; wailing with deep sorrow about the dead.

Cathleen *(After spinning for a moment.):* You didn't give him his bit of bread? *(Maurya begins to keen softly, without turning round.)*

Cathleen: Did you see him riding down?

(Maurya goes on keening.)

Cathleen *(A little impatiently.):* God forgive you; isn't it a better thing to raise your voice and tell what you seen, than to be making lamentation for a thing that's done? Did you see Bartley, I'm saying to you.

Maurya *(With a weak voice.):* My heart's broken from this day.

Cathleen *(As before.):* Did you see Bartley?

Maurya: I seen the fearfulest thing.

Cathleen *(Leaves her wheel and looks out.):* God forgive you; he's riding the mare now over the green head, and the gray pony behind him.

Maurya *(Starts, so that her shawl falls back from her head and shows her white tossed hair. With a frightened voice.):* The gray pony behind him.

Cathleen *(Coming to the fire.):* What is it ails you, at all?

Maurya *(Speaking very slowly.):* I've seen the fearfulest thing any person has seen, since the day Bride Dara seen the dead man with a child in his arms.

Cathleen and Nora: Uah.

(They crouch down in front of the old woman at the fire.)

Nora: Tell us what it is you seen.

Maurya: I went down to the spring well, and I stood there saying a prayer to myself. Then Bartley came along, and he riding on the red mare with the gray pony behind him. *(She puts up her hands, as if to hide something from her eyes.)* The Son of God spare us, Nora!

Cathleen: What is it you seen?

Maurya: I seen Michael himself.

Cathleen *(Speaking softly.):* You did not, Mother; it wasn't Michael you seen for his body is after being found in the Far North, and he's got a clean burial by the grace of God.

Maurya *(A little defiantly.):* I'm after seeing him this day, and he riding and galloping. Bartley came first on the red mare; and I tried to say, "God speed you," but something choked the words in my throat. He went by quickly; and "the blessing of God on you," says he, and I could say nothing. I looked up then, and I crying, at the gray pony, and there was Michael upon it—with fine clothes on him, and new shoes on his feet.

Cathleen *(Begins to keen.):* It's destroyed we are from this day. It's destroyed, surely.

Nora: Didn't the young priest say the Almighty God wouldn't leave her destitute with no son living?

Maurya *(In a low voice, but clearly.):* It's little the like of him knows of the sea. . . . Bartley will be lost now, and let you call in Eamon and make me a good coffin out of the white boards, for I won't live after them. I've had a husband, and a husband's father, and six sons in this house—six fine men, though it was a hard birth I had with every one of them and they coming to the world—and some of them were found and some of them were not found, but they're gone now the lot of them. . . . There was Stephen, and Shawn, were lost in the great wind, and found after in the Bay of Gregory of the Golden Mouth, and carried up the two of them on the one plank, and in by that door.

(She pauses for a moment, the girls start as if they heard something through the door that is half open behind them.)

Nora *(In a whisper.):* Did you hear that, Cathleen? Did you hear a noise in the northeast?

Cathleen *(In a whisper.):* There's some one after crying out by the seashore.

Maurya *(Continues without hearing anything.):* There was Sheamus and his father, and his own father again, were lost in a dark night, and not a stick or sign was seen of them when the sun went up. There was Patch after was drowned out of a curagh that turned over. I was sitting here with Bartley, and he a baby, lying on my two knees, and I seen two women, and three women, and four women coming in, and they crossing themselves, and not saying a word. I looked out then, and there were men coming after them, and they holding a thing in the half of a red sail, and water dripping out of it—it was a dry day, Nora—and leaving a track to the door.

(She pauses again with her hand stretched out toward the door. It opens softly and old women begin to come in, crossing themselves on the threshold, and kneeling down in front of the stage with red petticoats over their heads.)

Maurya *(Half in a dream, to Cathleen.):* Is it Patch, or Michael, or what is it at all?

Cathleen: Michael is after being found in the Far North, and when he is found there how could he be here in this place?

Maurya: There does be a power of young men floating round in the sea, and what way would they know if it was Michael they had, or another man like him, for when a man is nine days in the sea, and the wind blowing, it's hard set his own mother would be to say what man was it.

Cathleen: It's Michael, God spare him, for they're after sending us a bit of his clothes from the Far North.

(She reaches out and hands Maurya the clothes that belonged to Michael. Maurya stands up slowly, and takes them in her hands. Nora looks out.)

Nora: They're carrying a thing among them and there's water dripping out of it and leaving a track by the big stones.

Cathleen *(In a whisper to the women who have come in.):* Is it Bartley it is?

One of the Women: It is surely, God rest his soul.

(Two younger women come in and pull out the table. Then men carry in the body of Bartley, laid on a plank, with a bit of a sail over it, and lay it on the table.)

Cathleen *(To the women, as they are doing so.):* What way was he drowned?

One of the Women: The gray pony knocked him into the sea, and he was washed out where there is a great surf on the white rocks.

(Maurya has gone over and knelt down at the head of the table. The women are keening softly and swaying themselves with a slow movement. Cathleen and Nora kneel at the other end of the table. The men kneel near the door.)

Maurya *(Raising her head and speaking as if she did not see the people around her.):* They're all gone now, and there isn't anything more the sea can do to me. . . . I'll have no call now to be up crying and praying when the wind breaks from the south, and you can hear the surf is in the east, and the surf is in the west, making a great stir with the two noises, and they hitting one on the other. I'll have no call now to be going down and getting Holy Water in the dark nights after Samhain,[9] and I won't care what way the sea is when the other women will be keening. *(To Nora.)* Give me the Holy Water, Nora, there's a small sup still on the dresser.

(Nora gives it to her.)

Maurya *(Drops Michael's clothes across Bartley's feet, and sprinkles the Holy Water over him.):* It isn't that I haven't prayed for you, Bartley, to the Almighty God. It isn't that I haven't said prayers in the dark night till you wouldn't know what I'd be saying; but it's a great rest I'll have now, and it's time surely. It's a great rest I'll have now, and great sleeping in the long nights after Samhain, if it's only a bit of wet flour we do have to eat, and maybe a fish that would be stinking.

(She kneels down again, crossing herself, and saying prayers under her breath.)

Cathleen *(To an old man.):* Maybe yourself and Eamon would make a coffin when the sun rises. We have fine white boards herself bought. God help her, thinking Michael would be found, and I have a new cake you can eat while you'll be working.

The Old Man *(Looking at the boards.):* Are there nails with them?

Cathleen: There are not, Colum; we didn't think of the nails.

Another Man: It's a great wonder she wouldn't think of the nails, and all the coffins she's seen made already.

Cathleen: It's getting old she is, and broken.

(Maurya stands up again very slowly and spreads out the pieces of Michael's clothes beside the body, sprinkling them with the last of the Holy Water.)

Nora *(In a whisper to Cathleen.):* She's quiet now and easy; but the day Michael was drowned you could hear her crying out from this to the spring well. It's fonder she was of Michael, and would any one have thought that?

---

[9] Similar to all hallows, a holiday which falls on November 1 and marks the beginning of winter; it is celebrated with harvest rites and a Feast of the Dead.

Cathleen *(Slowly and clearly.):* An old woman will be soon tired with anything she will do, and isn't it nine days herself is after crying and keening, and making great sorrow in the house?

Maurya *(Puts the empty cup mouth downwards on the table, and lays her hands together on Bartley's feet.):* They're all together this time, and the end is come. May the Almighty God have mercy on Bartley's soul, and on Michael's soul, and on the souls of Sheamus and Patch, and Stephen and Shawn; *(Bending her head.)* and may He have mercy on my soul, Nora, and on the soul of every one is left living in the world.

(She pauses, and the keen rises a little more loudly from the women, then sinks away.)

Maurya *(Continuing.):* Michael has a clean burial in the Far North, by the grace of the Almighty God. Bartley will have a fine coffin out of the white boards, and a deep grave surely. What more can we want than that? No man at all can be living forever, and we must be satisfied.

(She kneels down again and the curtain falls slowly.)

Explorations of the Text

1. What does the initial dialogue between Nora and Cathleen reveal about the protagonists' world? What do they fear?
2. Discuss the characters of Nora, Cathleen, and Bartley as individuals and as family members. How are they different from each other?
3. How do the sisters realize their brother is dead? Interpret the symbolism of Michael's clothes.
4. What is the meaning of Maurya's vision of Michael "on the red mare with the gray pony behind him"? Why is Maurya so concerned with a proper burial and coffin?
5. Consider Maurya's character. What has been her role as a mother? How does she handle the deaths of her sons?
6. Why does Maurya claim: "They're all gone now, and there isn't anything more the sea can do to me"? Do you believe her when she claims, "No man at all can be living forever, and we must be satisfied"?
7. Do the images of sea, surf, and wind change in the play? Are they negative or positive?
8. Compare the view of fate in this work with themes of "Rappaccini's Daughter."

The Reading/Writing Connection

1. "Think" Topic: Synge's play is about people living on a small island off the coast of Ireland in the early 1900s. Does the fate of these people have relevance for us today? Why?

2. Discuss rituals of mourning and experiences of grief in a journal entry. (You may wish to refer to your own experience.)

Ideas for Writing

1. Choose a detail of the play—a stage direction, a gesture, an aspect of scene, a prop, an image—and analyze its relationship to theme.
2. Distinguish between the roles and concerns of men and of women in the play.
3. What does Synge believe about the power of the sea?
4. Synge has been quoted as saying, "The drama, like the symphony, does not teach or prove anything." After reading *Riders to the Sea,* do you agree with him?

BONE BLACK
Chapters 49, 50, and 51

bell hooks

bell hooks (1955–), born Gloria Watkins in Kentucky and educated at Stanford University, published her first book, Ain't I a Woman: Black Women and Feminism, *in 1981. A prolific writer, hooks has pursued the role of public intellectual, seeking to bring her concerns with matters of race and gender to a broad audience. Her books include* Talking Back: Thinking Feminist, Thinking Black *(1989), and* Teaching to Transgress: Education as the Price of Freedom *(1994). hooks teaches at the City College of New York and the City University of New York Graduate Center.*

1996

49

1 They have never heard their mama and daddy fussing or fighting. They have heard him be harsh, complain that the house should be cleaner, that he should not have to come home from work to a house that is not cleaned just right. They know he gets mad. When he gets mad about the house he begins to clean it himself to show that he can do better. Although he never cooks he knows how. He would not be able to judge her cooking if he did not cook himself. They are afraid of him when he is mad. They go upstairs to get out of his way. He does not come upstairs. Taking care of children is not a man's work. It does not concern him. He is not even interested—that is, unless something goes wrong. Then he can show her that she is not very good at parenting. They know they have a good mama, the best. Even though they fear him they are not moved by his opinions. She tries to remember a time when she felt loved by him. She remembers it as being the time when she was a baby girl, a small girl. She remembers him taking her places, taking her to the world inhabited by black men, the barbershop, the pool hall. He took his affections away from her

abruptly. She never understood why, only that they went and did not come back. She remembered trying to do whatever she could to bring them back, only they never came. Growing up she stopped trying. He mainly ignored her. She mainly tried to stay out of his way. In her own way she grew to hate wanting his love and not being able to get it. She hated that part of herself that kept wanting his love or even just his approval long after she could see that he was never, never going to give it.

2 Out of nowhere he comes home from work angry. He reaches the porch yelling and screaming at the woman inside—yelling that she is his wife, he can do with her what he wants. They do not understand what is happening. He is pushing, hitting, telling her to shut up. She is pleading—crying. He does not want to hear, to listen. They catch his angry words in their hands like lightning bugs—store them in a jar to sort them out later. Words about other men, about phone calls, about how he had told her. They do not know what he has told her. They have never heard them talk in an angry way.

3 She thinks of all the nights she lies awake in her bed hearing the woman's voice, her mother's voice, hearing his voice. She wonders if it is then that he is telling her everything—warning her. Yelling, screaming, hitting: they stare at the red blood that trickles through the crying mouth. They cannot believe this pleading, crying woman, this woman who does not fight back, is the same person they know. The person they know is strong, gets things done, is a woman of ways and means, a woman of action. They do not know her still, paralyzed, waiting for the next blow, pleading. They do not know their mama afraid. Even if she does not hit back they want her to run, to run and to not stop running. She wants her to hit him with the table light, the ashtray, the one near her hand. She does not want to see her like this, not fighting back. He notices them, long enough to tell them to get out, go upstairs. She refuses to move. She cannot move. She cannot leave her mama alone. When he says What are you staring at, do you want some, too? she is afraid enough to move. She will not take her orders from him. She asks the woman if it is right to leave her alone. The woman—her mother—nods her head yes. She still stands still. It is his movement in her direction that sends her up the stairs. She cannot believe all her sisters and her brother are not taking a stand, that they go to sleep. She cannot bear their betrayal. When the father is not looking she creeps down the steps. She wants the woman to know that she is not alone. She wants to bear witness.

4 They say she is near death, that we must go and see her because it may be the last time. I will not go. I have my own ideas about death. I see her all the time. I see her as she moves about the house doing things, cooking, cleaning, fussing. I refuse to go. I cannot tell them why, that I do not want to have the last sight of her be there in the white hospital bed, surrounded by strangers and the smell of death. She does not die. She comes home angry, not wanting to see the uncaring daughter, the one who would not even come to say good-bye. She is in control. She is not yet ready to love. She does not understand. Upstairs in my hiding place I cry. They tell her she is upstairs crying and will not stop. She sends me orders to stop crying right this minute, that I have nothing to cry about, that she should be crying to have such a terrible daughter. When I go to her, sitting on the bed, with my longing and my tears she knows that

she breaks my heart a little. She thinks I break her heart a little. She cannot know the joy we feel that she is home, alive.

50

5 All that she does not understand about marriage, about men and women, is explained to her one night. In her dark place on the stairs she is seeing over and over again the still body of the woman pleading, crying, the moving body of the man angry, yelling. She sees that the man has a gun. She hears him tell the woman that he will kill her. She sits in her place on the stair and demands to know of herself is she able to come to the rescue, is she willing to fight, is she ready to die. Her body shakes with the answers. She is fighting back the tears. When he leaves the room she comes to ask the woman if she is all right, if there is anything she can do. The woman's voice is full of tenderness and hurt. She is in her role as mother. She tells her daughter to go upstairs and go to sleep, that everything will be all right. The daughter does not believe her. Her eyes are pleading. She does not want to be told to go. She hovers in the shadows. When he returns he tells her that he has told her to get her ass upstairs. She does not look at him. He turns to the woman, tells her to leave, tells her to take the daughter with her.

6 The woman does not protest. She moves like a robot, hurriedly throwing things into suitcases, boxes. She says nothing to the man. He is still screaming, muttering. When she tries to say to him he is wrong, so wrong, he is more angry, threatening. All the neat drawers are emptied out on the bed, all the precious belongings that can be carried, stuffed, are to be taken. There is sorrow in every gesture, sorrow and pain—like a dust collecting on everything, so thick she can gather it in her hands. She is seeing that the man owns everything, that the woman has only her clothes, her shoes, and other personal belongings. She is seeing that the woman can be told to go, can be sent away in the silent, long hours of the night. She is hearing in her head the man's threats to kill. She can feel the cool metal as if it is resting against her cheek. She can hear the click, the blast. She can see the woman's body falling. No, it is not her body, it is the body of love. She witnesses the death of love. If love were alive she believes it would stop everything. It would steady the man's voice, calm his rage. Love would take the woman's hand, caress her cheek and with a clean handkerchief wipe her eyes. The gun is pointed at love. He lays it on the table. He wants his wife to finish her packing, to go.

7 She is again in her role as mother. She tells the daughter that she does not have to flee in the middle of the night, that it is not her fight. The daughter is silent, staring into the woman's eyes. She is looking for the bright lights, the care and adoration she has shown the man. The eyes are dark with grief, swollen. She feels that a fire inside the woman is dying out, that she is cold. She is sure the woman will freeze to death if she goes out into the night alone. She takes her hand, ready to go with her. Yet she hopes there will be no going. She hopes when the mother's brother comes he will be strong enough to take love's body and give it, mouth-to-mouth, the life it has lost. She hopes he will talk to the man, guide him. When he finally comes, her

mother's favorite brother, she cannot believe the calm way he lifts suitcase, box, sack, carries them to the car without question. She cannot bear his silent agreement that the man is right, that he has done what men are able to do. She cannot take the bits and pieces of her mother's heart and put them together again.

51

8 I am always fighting with mama. Everything has come between us. She no longer stands between me and all that would hurt me. She is hurting me. This is my dream of her—that she will stand between me and all that hurts me, that she will protect me at all cost. It is only a dream. In some way I understand that it has to do with marriage, that to be the wife to the husband she must be willing to sacrifice even her daughters for his good. For the mother it is not simple. She is always torn. She works hard to fulfill his needs, our needs. When they are not the same she must maneuver, manipulate, choose. She has chosen. She has decided in his favor. She is a religious woman. She has been told that a man should obey god, that a woman should obey man, that children should obey their fathers and mothers, particularly their mothers. I will not obey.

9 She says that she punishes me for my own good. I do not know what it is I have done this time. I know that she is ready with her switches, that I am to stand still while she lashes out again and again. In my mind there is the memory of a woman sitting still while she is being hit, punished. In my mind I am remembering how much I want that woman to fight back. Before I can think clearly my hands reach out, grab the switches, are raised as if to hit her back. For a moment she is stunned, unbelieving. She is shocked. She tells me that I must never *ever* as long as I live raise my hand against my mother. I tell her I do not have a mother. She is even more shocked. Enraged, she lashes out again. This time I am still. This time I cry. I see the hurt in her eyes when I say I do not have a mother. I am ready to be punished. My desire was to stop the pain, not to hurt. I am ashamed and torn. I do not want to stand still and be punished but I never want to hurt mama. It is better to hurt than to cause her pain. She warns me that she will tell daddy when he comes home, that I will be punished again. I cannot understand her acts of betrayal. I cannot understand that she must be against me to be for him. He and I are strangers. Deep in the night we parted from one another, knowing that nothing would ever be the same. He did not say good-bye. I did not look him in the face. Now we avoid one another. He speaks to me through her.

10 Although they act as if everything between them is the same, that life is as it was. It is only a game. They pretend. There is no pain in the pretense. Everything is hidden. Secrets find a way out in sleep. My sisters say to mama She cries in her sleep, calls out. In her sleep is the place of remembering. It is the place where there is no pretense. She is dreaming always the same dream. A movie is showing. It is a tragic story of jealousy and lost love. It is called *Crime of Passion.* In the movie a man has killed his wife and daughter. He has killed his wife because he believes she has lovers. He has killed the daughter

because she witnesses the death of the wife. When they go to trial all the remaining family come to speak on behalf of the man. At his job he is calm and quiet, a hardworking man, a family man. Neighbors come to testify that the dead woman was young and restless, that the daughter was wild and rebellious. Everyone sympathizes with the man. His story is so sad that they begin to weep. All their handkerchiefs are clean and white. Like flags waving, they are a signal of peace, of surrender. They are a gesture to the man that he can go on with life.

Explorations of the Text

1. Why do you think that bell hooks writes about herself and her family in third person? What impact does this narrative point of view have? Characterize hooks's autobiographical persona and voice.
2. Discuss the narrator's views of her mother, of her father, and of their marriage. How are the dynamics of their relationship governed by social conditioning?
3. Analyze the narrator's relationship with her father. How does their bond change as she ages?
4. Why is her father enraged? What is her mother's response? To what does the narrator want to "bear witness"?
5. Does the narrator have any power to help her mother?
6. Why is a "fire inside [her mother] dying out"?
7. Compare the speaker's realizations about family dynamics with the persona's awareness expressed in "Winter Sundays."

The Reading/Writing Connection

1. Journal Entry: Write a letter to one of your parents expressing your feelings concerning an issue or experience about which you have kept silent. Or say something that you have always wanted to express to them (positive or negative).
2. Respond in a freewrite to this quotation: "A fire inside the woman is dying out. . . ."
3. "Think" Topic: The "silent agreement that the man is right" is still operative today. In a paragraph agree or disagree with this statement.

Ideas for Writing

1. Compare the father-daughter bond in this work with Rappaccini's relationship with his daughter.
2. How do parental power and control shape the destinies of the children in the works in this thematic cluster?

FICTION

I Stand Here Ironing

Tillie Olsen

Tillie Olsen (1913–), born in Omaha, Nebraska, is the daughter of blue-collar workers who fled czarist Russia after the 1905 revolution. She grew up in poverty and at age fifteen quit high school to help support her family during the Depression. Celebrated as a crusader for the feminist movement and other causes, Olsen was presented the O. Henry Award in 1961 for Tell Me a Riddle. *Her first novel,* Yonnondio, *started in 1934, finally was published in 1974;* Silences, *a study exploring circumstances that interfere with women's creativity, appeared in 1978.*

1953

I stand here ironing, and what you asked me moves tormented back and forth with the iron.

"I wish you would manage the time to come and talk with me about your daughter. I'm sure you can help me understand her. She's a youngster who needs help and whom I'm deeply interested in helping."

"Who needs help." . . . Even if I came, what good would it do? You think because I am her mother I have a key, or that in some way you could use me as a key? She has lived for nineteen years. There is all that life that has happened outside of me, beyond me.

And when is there time to remember, to sift, to weigh, to estimate, to total? I will start and there will be an interruption and I will have to gather it all together again. Or I will become engulfed with all I did or did not do, with what should have been and what cannot be helped.

5 She was a beautiful baby. The first and only one of our five that was beautiful at birth. You do not guess how new and uneasy her tenancy in her now-loveliness. You did not know her all those years she was thought homely, or see her poring over her baby pictures, making me tell her over and over how beautiful she had been—and would be, I would tell her—and was now, to the seeing eye. But the seeing eyes were few or nonexistent. Including mine.

I nursed her. They feel that's important nowadays. I nursed all the children, but with her, with all the fierce rigidity of first motherhood, I did like the books then said. Though her cries battered me to trembling and my breasts ached with swollenness, I waited till the clock decreed.

Why do I put that first? I do not even know if it matters, or if it explains anything.

She was a beautiful baby. She blew shining bubbles of sound. She loved motion, loved light, loved color and music and textures. She would lie on the floor in her blue overalls patting the surface so hard in ecstasy her hands and feet would blur. She was a miracle to me, but when she was eight months old I had to leave her daytimes with the woman downstairs to whom she was no miracle at all, for I worked or looked for work and for Emily's father, who "could no longer endure" (he wrote in his good-bye note) "sharing want with us."

I was nineteen. It was the pre-relief, pre-WPA[1] world of the Depression. I would start running as soon as I got off the streetcar, running up the stairs, the place smelling sour, and awake or asleep to startle awake, when she saw me she would break into a clogged weeping that could not be comforted, a weeping I can hear yet.

After a while I found a job hashing at night so I could be with her days, and it was better. But it came to where I had to bring her to his family and leave her.

It took a long time to raise the money for her fare back. Then she got chicken pox and I had to wait longer. When she finally came, I hardly knew her, walking quick and nervous like her father, looking like her father, thin, and dressed in a shoddy red that yellowed her skin and glared at the pockmarks. All the baby loveliness gone.

She was two. Old enough for nursery school they said, and I did not know then what I know now—the fatigue of the long day, and the lacerations of group life in the kinds of nurseries that are only parking places for children.

Except that it would have made no difference if I had known. It was the only place there was. It was the only way we could be together, the only way I could hold a job.

And even without knowing, I knew. I knew the teacher that was evil because all these years it has curdled into my memory, the little boy hunched in the corner, her rasp, "why aren't you outside, because Alvin hits you? that's no reason, go out, scaredy." I knew Emily hated it even if she did not clutch and implore "don't go Mommy" like the other children, mornings.

She always had a reason why we should stay home. Momma, you look sick. Momma, I feel sick. Momma, the teachers aren't there today, they're sick. Momma, we can't go, there was a fire there last night. Momma, it's a holiday today, no school, they told me.

But never a direct protest, never rebellion. I think of our others in their three-, four-year-oldness—the explosions, the tempers, the denunciations, the demands—and I feel suddenly ill. I put the iron down. What in me demanded that goodness in her? And what was the cost, the cost to her of such goodness?

The old man living in the back once said in his gentle way: "You should smile at Emily more when you look at her." What *was* in my face when I looked at her? I loved her. There were all the acts of love.

It was only with the others I remembered what he said, and it was the face of joy, and not of care or tightness or worry I turned to them—too late for Emily. She does not smile easily, let alone almost always as her brothers and

[1] Works Progress Administration: a federal agency that administered public works to relieve unemployment from 1935 to 1943.

sisters do. Her face is closed and sombre, but when she wants, how fluid. You must have seen it in her pantomimes, you spoke of her rare gift for comedy on the stage that rouses a laughter out of the audience so dear they applaud and applaud and do not want to let her go.

Where does it come from, that comedy? There was none of it in her when she came back to me that second time, after I had had to send her away again. She had a new daddy now to learn to love, and I think perhaps it was a better time.

20 Except when we left her alone nights, telling ourselves she was old enough.

"Can't you go some other time, Mommy, like tomorrow?" she would ask. "Will it be just a little while you'll be gone? Do you promise?"

The time we came back, the front door open, the clock on the floor in the hall. She rigid awake. "It wasn't just a little while. I didn't cry. Three times I called you, just three times, and then I ran downstairs to open the door so you could come faster. The clock talked loud. I threw it away, it scared me what it talked."

She said the clock talked loud again that night I went to the hospital to have Susan. She was delirious with the fever that comes before red measles, but she was fully conscious all the week I was gone and the week after we were home when she could not come near the new baby or me.

She did not get well. She stayed skeleton thin, not wanting to eat, and night after night she had nightmares. She would call for me, and I would rouse from exhaustion to sleepily call back: "You're all right, darling, go to sleep, it's just a dream," and if she still called, in a sterner voice, "now go to sleep, Emily, there's nothing to hurt you." Twice, only twice, when I had to get up for Susan anyhow, I went in to sit with her.

25 Now when it is too late (as if she would let me hold and comfort her like I do the others) I get up and go to her at once at her moan or restless stirring. "Are you awake, Emily? Can I get you something?" And the answer is always the same: "No, I'm all right, go back to sleep, Mother."

They persuaded me at the clinic to send her away to a convalescent home in the country where "she can have the kind of food and care you can't manage for her, and you'll be free to concentrate on the new baby." They still send children to that place. I see pictures on the society page of sleek young women planning affairs to raise money for it, or dancing at the affairs, or decorating Easter eggs or filling Christmas stockings for the children.

They never have a picture of the children so I do not know if the girls still wear those gigantic red bows and the ravaged looks on the every other Sunday when parents can come to visit "unless otherwise notified"—as we were notified the first six weeks.

Oh it is a handsome place, green lawns and tall trees and fluted flower beds. High up on the balconies of each cottage the children stand, the girls in their red bows and white dresses, the boys in white suits and giant red ties. The parents stand below shrieking up to be heard and the children shriek down to be heard, and between them the invisible wall "Not to Be Contaminated by Parental Germs or Physical Affection."

There was a tiny girl who always stood hand in hand with Emily. Her parents never came. One visit she was gone. "They moved her to Rose Cottage," Emily shouted in explanation. "They don't like you to love anybody here."

She wrote once a week, the labored writing of a seven-year-old. "I am fine. How is the baby. If I write my leter nicly I will have a star. Love" There never was a star. We wrote every other day, letters she could never hold or keep but only hear read—once. "We simply do not have room for children to keep any personal possessions," they patiently explained when we pieced one Sunday's shrieking together to plead how much it would mean to Emily, who loved so to keep things, to be allowed to keep her letters and cards.

Each visit she looked frailer. "She isn't eating," they told us.

(They had runny eggs for breakfast or mush with lumps, Emily said later, I'd hold it in my mouth and not swallow. Nothing ever tasted good, just when they had chicken.)

It took us eight months to get her released home, and only the fact that she gained back so little of her seven lost pounds convinced the social worker.

I used to try to hold and love her after she came back, but her body would stay stiff, and after a while she'd push away. She ate little. Food sickened her, and I think much of life too. Oh she had physical lightness and brightness, twinkling by on skates, bouncing like a ball up and down up and down over the jump rope, skimming over the hill; but these were momentary.

She fretted about her appearance, thin and dark and foreign-looking at a time when every little girl was supposed to look or thought she should look a chubby blonde replica of Shirley Temple. The doorbell sometimes rang for her, but no one seemed to come and play in the house or be a best friend. Maybe because we moved so much.

There was a boy she loved painfully through two school semesters. Months later she told me how she had taken pennies from my purse to buy him candy. "Licorice was his favorite and I brought him some every day, but he still liked Jennifer better'n me. Why, Mommy?" The kind of question for which there is no answer.

School was a worry to her. She was not glib or quick in a world where glibness and quickness were easily confused with ability to learn. To her overworked and exasperated teachers she was an overconscientious "slow learner" who kept trying to catch up and was absent entirely too often.

I let her be absent, though sometimes the illness was imaginary. How different from my now-strictness about attendance with the others. I wasn't working. We had a new baby, I was home anyhow. Sometimes, after Susan grew old enough, I would keep her home from school, too, to have them all together.

Mostly Emily had asthma, and her breathing, harsh and labored, would fill the house with a curiously tranquil sound. I would bring the two old dresser mirrors and her boxes of collections to her bed. She would select beads and single earrings, bottle tops and shells, dried flowers and pebbles, old postcards and scraps, all sorts of oddments; then she and Susan would play Kingdom, setting up landscapes and furniture, peopling them with action.

40 Those were the only times of peaceful companionship between her and Susan. I have edged away from it, that poisonous feeling between them, that terrible balancing of hurts and needs I had to do between the two, and did so badly, those earlier years.

Oh there are conflicts between the others too, each one human, needing, demanding, hurting, taking—but only between Emily and Susan, no, Emily toward Susan that corroding resentment. It seems so obvious on the surface, yet it is not obvious. Susan, the second child, Susan, golden- and curly-haired and chubby, quick and articulate and assured, everything in appearance and manner Emily was not; Susan, not able to resist Emily's precious things, losing or sometimes clumsily breaking them; Susan telling jokes and riddles to company for applause while Emily sat silent (to say to me later: that was *my* riddle, Mother, I told it to Susan); Susan, who for all the five years' difference in age was just a year behind Emily in developing physically.

I am glad for that slow physical development that widened the difference between her and her contemporaries, though she suffered over it. She was too vulnerable for that terrible world of youthful competition, of preening and parading, of constant measuring of yourself against every other, of envy, "If I had that copper hair," "If I had that skin. . . ." She tormented herself enough about not looking like the others, there was enough of the unsureness, the having to be conscious of words before you speak, the constant caring—what are they thinking of me? without having it all magnified by the merciless physical drives.

Ronnie is calling. He is wet and I change him. It is rare there is such a cry now. That time of motherhood is almost behind me when the ear is not one's own but must always be racked and listening for the child cry, the child call. We sit for a while and I hold him, looking out over the city spread in charcoal with its soft aisles of light. *"Shoogily,"* he breathes and curls closer. I carry him back to bed, asleep. *Shoogily.* A funny word, a family word, inherited from Emily, invented by her to say: *comfort.*

In this and other ways she leaves her seal, I say aloud. And startle at my saying it. What do I mean? What did I start to gather together, to try and make coherent? I was at the terrible, growing years. War years. I do not remember them well. I was working, there were four smaller ones now, there was not time for her. She had to help be a mother, and housekeeper, and shopper. She had to set her seal. Mornings of crisis and near hysteria trying to get lunches packed, hair combed, coats and shoes found, everyone to school or Child Care on time, the baby ready for transportation. And always the paper scribbled on by a smaller one, the book looked at by Susan then mislaid, the homework not done. Running out to that huge school where she was one, she was lost, she was a drop; suffering over the unpreparedness, stammering and unsure in her classes.

45 There was so little time left at night after the kids were bedded down. She would struggle over books, always eating (it was in those years she developed her enormous appetite that is legendary in our family) and I would be ironing, or preparing food for the next day, or writing V-mail to Bill, or tending the

baby. Sometimes, to make me laugh, or out of her despair, she would imitate happenings or types at school.

I think I said once: "Why don't you do something like this in the school amateur show?" One morning she phoned me at work, hardly understandable through the weeping: "Mother, I did it. I won, I won; they gave me first prize; they clapped and clapped and wouldn't let me go."

Now suddenly she was Somebody, and as imprisoned in her difference as she had been in anonymity.

She began to be asked to perform at other high schools, even in colleges, then at city and statewide affairs. The first one we went to, I only recognized her that first moment when thin, shy, she almost drowned herself into the curtains. Then: Was this Emily? The control, the command, the convulsing and deadly clowning, the spell, then the roaring, stamping audience, unwilling to let this rare and precious laughter out of their lives.

Afterwards: You ought to do something about her with a gift like that—but without money or knowing how, what does one do? We have left it all to her, and the gift has as often eddied inside, clogged and clotted, as been used and growing.

She is coming. She runs up the stairs two at a time with her light graceful step, and I know she is happy tonight. Whatever it was that occasioned your call did not happen today.

"Aren't you ever going to finish the ironing, Mother? Whistler[2] painted his mother in a rocker. I'd have to paint mine standing over an ironing board." This is one of her communicative nights and she tells me everything and nothing as she fixes herself a plate of food out of the icebox.

She is so lovely. Why did you want me to come in at all? Why were you concerned? She will find her way.

She starts up the stairs to bed. "Don't get me up with the rest in the morning." "But I thought you were having midterms." "Oh, those," she comes back in, kisses me, and says quite lightly, "in a couple of years when we'll all be atom-dead they won't matter a bit."

She has said it before. She *believes* it. But because I have been dredging the past, and all that compounds a human being is so heavy and meaningful in me, I cannot endure it tonight.

I will never total it all. I will never come in to say: She was a child seldom smiled at. Her father left me before she was a year old. I had to work her first six years when there was work, or I sent her home and to his relatives. There were years she had care she hated. She was dark and thin and foreign-looking in a world where the prestige went to blondeness and curly hair and dimples, she was slow where glibness was prized. She was a child of anxious, not proud, love. We were poor and could not afford for her the soil of easy growth. I was a young mother, I was a distracted mother. There were other children pushing up, demanding. Her younger sister seemed all that she was not. There were

[2] James (Abbott) McNeill Whistler (1834–1903), United States painter and etcher.

years she did not want me to touch her. She kept too much in herself, her life was such she had to keep too much in herself. My wisdom came too late. She has much to her and probably little will come of it. She is a child of her age, of depression, of war, of fear.

Let her be. So all that is in her will not bloom—but in how many does it? There is still enough left to live by. Only help her to know—help make it so there is cause for her to know—that she is more than this dress on the ironing board, helpless before the iron.

Explorations of the Text

1. How does the mother view her daughter Emily as a baby?
2. How do economic and social circumstances affect the mother's ability to take care of Emily?
3. Characterize Emily as a baby and at different stages in her life. According to the narrator, what needs, yearnings, and conflicts shape the daughter's view of herself?
4. Analyze the images describing Emily's body. How do societal conceptions of beauty figure in Emily's development?
5. What are reasons for the conflict between Emily and Susan?
6. How does the mother feel about herself as a parent? Is she a "good mother"? Is she to blame for what has happened to Emily?
7. Explore the significance of the title and the symbol of ironing. Discuss Tillie Olsen's critique of woman's position in society?
8. How does the opening, the interchange between the unnamed social worker and the mother, develop the story?
9. What vision of parenting is presented in the story? How much control do parents possess? How much depends on fate or circumstance?

The Reading/Writing Connection

1. "Think" Topic: What effect does the first-person point of view have on the story? Rewrite several passages in third person. How does the perspective change?
2. Write a monologue in the voice of Emily, and present her version of her upbringing. Or write a letter from Emily to her mother.

Ideas for Writing

1. Compare this story with "Scar."
2. Some psychologists suggest that "wounds" in childhood may later become sources of creativity. Is there support for this theory in the story?
3. Continue the story. What is going to happen to Emily?

Fiesta 1980

Junot Diaz

Junot Diaz (1968–) was born in Santo Domingo, Dominican Republic, and educated at Rutgers and Cornell universities. He has published his fiction in many magazines, including The New Yorker, Story, *and* Paris Review. *His first collection of stories,* Drown, *was published in 1996. He teaches in the creative writing program at Syracuse University. Diaz won the 1998 Eugene McDermott Award.*

Mami's youngest sister—my tía[1] Yrma—finally made it to the United States that year. She and tío[2] Miguel got themselves an apartment in the Bronx, off the Grand Concourse and everybody decided that we should have a party. Actually, my pops decided, but everybody—meaning Mami, tía Yrma, tío Miguel and their neighbors—thought it a dope idea. On the afternoon of the party Papi came back from work around six. Right on time. We were all dressed by then, which was a smart move on our part. If Papi had walked in and caught us lounging around in our underwear, he would have kicked our asses something serious.

He didn't say nothing to nobody, not even my moms. He just pushed past her, held up his hand when she tried to talk to him and headed right into the shower. Rafa gave me the look and I gave it back to him; we both knew Papi had been with that Puerto Rican woman he was seeing and wanted to wash off the evidence quick.

Mami looked really nice that day. The United States had finally put some meat on her; she was no longer the same flaca[3] who had arrived here three years before. She had cut her hair short and was wearing tons of cheap-ass jewelry which on her didn't look too lousy. She smelled like herself, like the wind through a tree. She always waited until the last possible minute to put on her perfume because she said it was a waste to spray it on early and then have to spray it on again once you got to the party.

We—meaning me, my brother, my little sister and Mami—waited for Papi to finish his shower. Mami seemed anxious, in her usual dispassionate way. Her hands adjusted the buckle of her belt over and over again. That morning, when she had gotten us up for school, Mami told us that she wanted to have a good time at the party. I want to dance, she said, but now, with the sun sliding out of the sky like spit off a wall, she seemed ready just to get this over with.

5 Rafa didn't much want to go to no party either, and me, I never wanted to go anywhere with my family. There was a baseball game in the parking lot outside and we could hear our friends, yelling, Hey, and, Cabrón, to one

---

[1] Aunt.

[2] Uncle.

[3] Thin woman.

another. We heard the pop of a ball as it sailed over the cars, the clatter of an aluminum bat dropping to the concrete. Not that me or Rafa loved baseball; we just liked playing with the local kids, thrashing them at anything they were doing. By the sounds of the shouting, we both knew the game was close, either of us could have made a difference. Rafa frowned and when I frowned back, he put up his fist. Don't you mirror me, he said.

Don't you mirror me, I said.

He punched me—I would have hit him back but Papi marched into the living room with his towel around his waist, looking a lot smaller than he did when he was dressed. He had a few strands of hair around his nipples and a surly closed-mouth expression, like maybe he'd scalded his tongue or something.

Have you eaten? he asked Mami.

She nodded. I made you something.

10 You didn't let him eat, did you?

Ay, Dios mío,[4] she said, letting her arms fall to her side.

Ay, Dios mîo is right, Papi said.

I was never supposed to eat before our car trips, but earlier, when she had put out our dinner of rice, beans and sweet platanos, guess who had been the first one to clean his plate? You couldn't blame Mami really, she had been busy—cooking, getting ready, dressing my sister Madai. I should have reminded her not to feed me but I wasn't that sort of son.

Papi turned to me. Coño, muchacho,[5] why did you eat?

15 Rafa had already started inching away from me. I'd once told him I considered him a low-down chickenshit for moving out of the way every time Papi was going to smack me.

Collateral damage, Rafa had said. Ever heard of it?

No.

Look it up.

Chickenshit or not, I didn't dare glance at him. Papi was old-fashioned; he expected your undivided attention when you were getting your ass whupped. You couldn't look him in the eye either—that wasn't allowed. Better to stare at his belly button, which was perfectly round and immaculate. Papi pulled me to my feet by my ear.

20 If you throw up—

I won't, I cried, tears in my eyes, more out of reflex than pain.

Ya, Ramón, ya. It's not his fault, Mami said.

They've know about this party forever. How did they think we were going to get there? Fly?

He finally let go of my ear and I sat back down. Madai was too scared to open her eyes. Being around Papi all her life had turned her into a major-league wuss. Anytime Papi raised his voice her lip would start trembling, like some specialized tuning fork. Rafa pretended that he had knuckles to crack

[4] My God.

[5] Boy.

and when I shoved him, he gave me a *Don't start* look. But even that little bit of recognition made me feel better.

I was the one who was always in trouble with my dad. It was like my God-given duty to piss him off, to do everything the way he hated. Our fights didn't bother me too much. I will wanted him to love me, something that never seemed strange or contradictory until years later, when he was out of our lives.

By the time my ear stopped stinging Papi was dressed and Mami was crossing each one of us, solemnly, like we were heading off to war. We said, in turn, Bendición,[6] Mami, and she poked us in our five cardinal spots while saying, Que Dios te bendiga.[7]

This was how all our trips began, the words that followed me every time I left the house.

None of us spoke until we were inside Papi's Volkswagen van. Brand-new, lime-green and bought to impress. Oh, we were impressed, but me, every time I was in that VW and Papi went above twenty miles an hour, I vomited. I'd never had trouble with cars before—that van was like my curse. Mami suspected it was the upholstery. In her mind, American things—appliances, mouthwash, funny-looking upholstery—all seemed to have an intrinsic badness about them. Papi was careful about taking me anywhere in the VW, but when he had to, I rode up front in Mami's usual seat so I could throw up out a window.

¿Cómo te sientas?[8] Mami asked over my shoulder when Papi pulled onto the turnpike. She had her hand on the base of my neck. One thing about Mami, her palms never sweated.

I'm OK, I said, keeping my eyes straight ahead. I definitely didn't want to trade glances with Papi. He had this one look, furious and sharp, that always left me feeling bruised.

Toma. Mami handed me four mentas.[9] She had thrown three out of her window at the beginning of our trip, an offering to Eshú; the rest were for me.

I took one and sucked it slowly, my tongue knocking it up against my teeth. We passed Newark Airport without any incident. If Madai had been awake she would have cried because the planes flew so close to the cars.

How's he feeling? Papi asked.

Fine, I said. I glanced back at Rafa and he pretended like he didn't see me. That was the way he was, at school and at home. When I was in trouble, he didn't know me. Madai was solidly asleep, but even with her face all wrinkled up and drooling she looked cute, her hair all separated into twists.

I turned around and concentrated on the candy. Papi even started to joke that we might not have to scrub the van out tonight. He was beginning to loosen up, not checking his watch too much. Maybe he was thinking about that

[6] Benediction.

[7] May God bless you.

[8] How do you feel?

[9] Candies.

Puerto Rican woman or maybe he was just happy that we were all together. I could never tell. At the toll, he was feeling positive enough to actually get out of the van and search around under the basket for dropped coins. It was something he had once done to amuse Madai, but now it was habit. Cars behind us honked their horns and I slid down in my seat. Rafa didn't care; he grinned back at the other cars and waved. His actual job was to make sure no cops were coming. Mami shook Madai awake and as soon as she saw Papi stooping for a couple of quarters she let out this screech of delight that almost took off the top of my head.

That was the end of the good times. Just outside the Washington Bridge, I started feeling woozy. The smell of the upholstery got all up inside my head and I found myself with a mouthful of saliva. Mami's hand tensed on my shoulder and when I caught Papi's eye, he was like, No way. Don't do it.

The first time I got sick in the van Papi was taking me to the library. Rafa was with us and he couldn't believe I threw up. I was famous for my steel-lined stomach. A third-world childhood could give you that. Papi was worried enough that just as quick as Rafa could drop off the books we were on our way home. Mami fixed me one of her honey-and-onion concoctions and that made my stomach feel better. A week later we tried the library again and on this go-around I couldn't get the window open in time. When Papi got me home, he went and cleaned out the van himself, an expression of askho on his face. This was a big deal, since Papi almost never cleaned anything himself. He came back inside and found me sitting on the couch feeling like hell.

It's the car, he said to Mami. It's making him sick.

This time the damage was pretty minimal, nothing Papi couldn't wash off the door with a blast of the hose. He was pissed, though; he jammed his finger into my cheek, a nice solid thrust. That was the way he was with his punishments: imaginative. Earlier that year I'd written an essay in school called "My Father the Torturer," but the teacher made me write a new one. She thought I was kidding.

We drove the rest of the way to the Bronx in silence. We only stopped once, so I could brush my teeth. Mami had brought along my toothbrush and a tube of toothpaste and while every car known to man sped by us she stood outside with me so I wouldn't feel alone.

Tío Miguel was about seven feet tall and had his hair combed up and out, into a demi-fro. He gave me and Rafa big spleen-crushing hugs and then kissed Mami and finally ended up with Madai on his shoulder. The last time I'd seen Tío was at the airport, his first day in the United States. I remembered how he hadn't seemed all that troubled to be in another country.

He looked down at me. Carajo,[10] Yunior, you look horrible!

He threw up, my brother explained.

---

[10] Darn.

I pushed Rafa. Thanks a lot, ass-face.

Hey, he said. Tío asked.

Tío clapped a bricklayer's hand on my shoulder. Everybody gets sick sometimes, he said. You should have seen me on the plane over here. Dios mío! He rolled his Asian-looking eyes for emphasis. I thought we were all going to die.

Everybody could tell he was lying. I smiled like he was making me feel better.

Do you want me to get you a drink? Tío asked. We got beer and rum.

Miguel, Mami said. He's young.

Young? Back in Santo Domingo, he'd be getting laid by now.

Mami thinned her lips, which took some doing.

Well, it's true, Tío said.

So, Mami, I said. When do I get to go visit the D.R.?

That's enough, Yunior.

It's the only pussy you'll ever get, Rafa said to me in English.

Not counting your girlfriend, of course.

Rafa smiled. He had to give me that one.

Papi came in from parking the van. He and Miguel gave each other the sort of handshakes that would have turned my fingers into Wonder bread.

Coño, compa'i,[11] ¿cómo va todo? they said to each other.

Tía came out then, with an apron on and maybe the longest Lee Press-On Nails I've ever seen in my life. There was this one guru motherfucker in the *Guinness Book of World Records* who had longer nails, but I tell you, it was close. She gave everybody kisses, told me and Rafa how guapo we were—Rafa, of course, believed her—told Madai how bella[12] she was, but when she got to Papi, she froze a little, like maybe she'd seen a wasp on the tip of his nose, but then kissed him all the same.

Mami told us to join the other kids in the living room. Tío said, Wait a minute, I want to show you the apartment. I was glad Tía said, Hold on, because from what I'd seen so far, the place had been furnished in Contemporary Dominican Tacky. The less I saw, the better. I mean, I liked plastic sofa covers but damn, Tío and Tía had taken it to another level. They had a disco ball hanging in the living room and the type of stucco ceilings that looked like stalactite heaven. The sofas all had golden tassels dangling from their edges. Tía came out of the kitchen with some people I didn't know and by the time she got done introducing everybody, only Papi and Mami were given the guided tour of the four-room third-floor apartment. Me and Rafa joined the kids in the living room. They'd already started eating. We were hungry, one of the girls explained, a pastelito in hand. The boy was about three years younger than me but the girl who'd spoken, Leti, was my age. She and another girl were on the sofa together and they were cute as hell.

---

[11] Darn, compadre. How are you all? How's everything?

[12] *Guapo*—handsome; *bella*—beautiful.

Leti introduced them: the boy was her brother Wilquins and the other girl was her neighbor Mari. Leti had some serious tetas and I could tell that my brother was going to gun for her. His taste in girls was predictable. He sat down right between Leti and Mari and by the way they were smiling at him I knew he'd do fine. Neither of the girls gave me more than a cursory one-two, which didn't bother me. Sure, I liked girls but I was always too terrified to speak to them unless we were arguing or I was calling them stupidos, which was one of my favorite words that year. I turned to Wilquins and asked him what there was to do around here. Mari, who had the lowest voice I'd ever heard, said, He can't speak.

What does that mean?

He's mute.

65 I looked at Wilquins incredulously. He smiled and nodded, as if he'd won a prize or something.

Does he understand? I asked.

Of course he understands, Rafa said. He's not dumb.

I could tell Rafa had said that just to score point with the girls. Both of them nodded. Low-voice Mari said, He's the best student in his grade.

I thought, Not bad for a mute. I sat next to Wilquins. After about two seconds of TV Wilquins whipped out a bag of dominos and motioned to me. Did I want to play? Sure. Me and him played Rafa and Leti and we whupped their collective asses twice, which put Rafa in a real bad mood. He looked at me like maybe he wanted to take a swing, just one to make him feel better. Leti kept whispering into Rafa's ear, telling him it was OK.

70 In the kitchen I could hear my parents slipping into their usual modes. Papi's voice was loud and argumentative; you didn't have to be anywhere near him to catch his drift. And Mami, you had to put cups to your ears to hear hers. I went into the kitchen a few times—once so the tíos could show off how much bullshit I'd been able to cram in my head the last few years; another time for a bucket-sized cup of soda. Mami and Tía were frying tostones and the last of the pastelitos. She appeared happier now and the way her hands worked on our dinner you would think she had a life somewhere else making rare and precious things. She nudged Tía every now and then, shit they must have been doing all their lives. As soon as Mami saw me though, she gave me the eye. Don't stay long, that eye said. Don't piss your old man off.

Papi was too busy arguing about Elvis to notice me. Then somebody mentioned María Montez and Papi barked, María Montez? Let me tell *you* about María Montez, compa'i.[13]

Maybe I was used to him. His voice—louder than most adults'—didn't bother me none, though the other kids shifted uneasily in their seats. Wilquins was about to raise the volume on the TV, but Rafa said, I wouldn't do that. Muteboy had balls, though. He did it anyway and then sat down. Wilquins's pop came into the living room a second later, a bottle of Presidente in hand.

[13] A Hispanic actress.

That dude must have had Spider-senses or something. Did you raise that? he asked Wilquins and Wilquins nodded.

Is this your house? his pops asked. He looked ready to beat Wilquins silly but he lowered the volume instead.

See, Rafa said. You nearly got your ass *kicked.*

75 I met the Puerto Rican woman right after Papi had gotten the van. He was taking me on short trips, trying to cure me of my vomiting. It wasn't really working but I looked foward to our trips, even though at the end of each one I'd be sick. These were the only times me and Papi did anything together. When we were alone he treated me much better, like maybe I was his son or something.

Before each drive Mami would cross me.

Bendición, Mami, I'd say.

She'd kiss my forehead. Que Dios te bendiga. And then she would give me a handful of mentas because she wanted me to be OK. Mami didn't think these excursions would cure anything, but the one time she had brought it up to Papi he had told her to shut up, what did she know about anything anyway?

Me and Papi didn't talk much. We just drove around our neighborhood. Occasionally he'd ask, How is it?

80 And I'd nod, no matter how I felt.

One day I was sick outside of Perth Amboy. Instead of taking me home he went the other way on Industrial Avenue, stopping a few minutes later in front of a light blue house I didn't recognize. It reminded me of the Easter eggs we colored at school, the ones we threw out the bus windows at other cars.

The Puerto Rican woman was there and she helped me clean up. She had dry papery hands and when she rubbed the towel on my chest, she did it hard, like I was a bumper she was waxing. She was very thin and had a cloud of brown hair rising above her narrow face and the sharpest blackest eyes you've ever seen.

He's cute, she said to Papi.

Not when he's throwing up, Papi said.

85 What's your name? she asked me. Are you Rafa?

I shook my head.

Then it's Yunior, right?

I nodded.

You're the smart one, she said, suddenly happy with herself. Maybe you want to see my books?

90 They weren't hers. I recognized them as ones my father must have left in her house. Papi was a voracious reader, couldn't even go cheating without a paperback in his pocket.

Why don't you go watch TV? Papi suggested. He was looking at her like she was the last piece of chicken on earth.

We got plenty of channels, she said. Use the remote if you want.

The two of them went upstairs and I was too scared of what was happening to poke around. I just sat there, ashamed, expecting something big and fiery to crash down on our heads. I watched a whole hour of the news before Papi came downstairs and said, Let's go.

About two hours later the women laid out the food and like always nobody but the kids thanked them. It must be some Dominican tradition or something. There was everything I liked—chicharrones,[14] fried chicken, tostones,[15] sancocho,[16] rice, fried cheese, yuca, avocado, potato salad, a meteor-sized hunk of pernil,[17] even a tossed salad which I could do without—but when I joined the other kids around the serving table, Papi said, Oh no you don't, and took the paper plate out of my hand. His fingers weren't gentle.

What's wrong now? Tía asked, handing me another plate.

He ain't eating, Papi said. Mami pretended to help Rafa with the pernil.

Why can't he eat?

Because I said so.

I nodded.

And if your brother gives you any food, I'll beat him too. Right here in front of everybody. ¿Entiendes?[18]

I nodded again. I wanted to kill him and he must have sensed it because he gave my head a little shove.

All the kids watched me come in and sit down in front of the TV.

What's wrong with your dad? Leti asked.

He's a dick, I said.

Rafa shook his head. Don't say that shit in front of people.

Easy for you to be nice when you're eating, I said.

Hey, if I was a pukey little baby, I wouldn't get no food either.

I almost said something back but I concentrated on the TV. I wasn't going to start it. No fucking way. So I watched Bruce Lee beat Chuck Norris into the floor of the Colosseum and tried to pretend that there was no food anywhere in the house. It was Tía who finally saved me. She came into the living room and said, Since you ain't eating, Yunior, you can at least help me get some ice.

I didn't want to, but she mistook my reluctance for something else.

I already asked your father.

She held my hand while we walked; Tía didn't have any kids but I could tell she wanted them. She was the sort of relative who always remembered your birthday but who you only went to visit because you had to. We didn't get past the first-floor landing before she opened her pocketbook and handed me the first of three pastelitos[19] she had smuggled out of the apartment.

Go ahead, she said. And as soon as you get inside make sure you brush your teeth.

Thanks a lot, Tía, I said.

Those pastelitos didn't stand a chance.

[14] Pork fritters.

[15] Thick, fried plantains.

[16] Soup, beef broth with potato, corn, yuca.

[17] Pork leg.

[18] Understand?

[19] Round, small empanadas or meatpies.

115 She sat next to me on the stair and smoked her cigarette. All the way down on the first floor and we could still hear the music and the adults and the television. Tía looked a ton like Mami; the two of them were both short and light-skinned. Tía smiled a lot and that was what set them apart the most.

How is it at home, Yunior?

What do you mean?

How's it going in the apartment? Are you kids OK?

I knew an interrogation when I heard one, no matter how sugar-coated it was. I didn't say anything. Don't get me wrong, I loved my tía, but something told me to keep my mouth shut. Maybe it was family loyalty, maybe I just wanted to protect Mami or I was afraid that Papi would find out—it could have been anything really.

120 Is your mom all right?

I shrugged.

Have there been lots of fights?

None, I said. Too many shrugs would have been just as bad as an answer. Papi's at work too much.

Work, Tía said, like it was somebody's name she didn't like.

125 Me and Rafa we didn't talk much about the Puerto Rican woman. When we ate dinner at her house, the few times Papi had taken us over there, we still acted like nothing was out of the ordinary. Pass the ketchup, man. No sweat, bro. The affair was like a hole in our living room floor, one we'd gotten so used to circumnavigating that we sometimes forgot it was there.

By midnight all the adults were crazy dancing. I was sitting outside Tía's bedroom—where Madai was sleeping—trying not to attract attention. Rafa had me guarding the door; he and Leti were in there too, with some of the other kids, getting busy no doubt. Wilquins had gone across the hall to bed so I had me and the roaches to mess around with.

When I peered into the main room I saw about twenty moms and dads dancing and drinking beers. Every now and then somebody yelled, Quisqueya! And then everybody else would yell and stomp their feet. From what I could see my parents seemed to be enjoying themselves.

Mami and Tía spent a lot of time side by side, whispering, and I kept expecting something to come of this, a brawl maybe. I'd never once been out with my family when it hadn't turned to shit. We weren't even theatrical or straight crazy like other families. We fought like sixth-graders, without any real dignity. I guess the whole night I'd been waiting for a blowup, something between Papi and Mami. This was how I always figured Papi would be exposed, out in public, where everybody would know.

You're a cheater!

130 But everything was calmer than usual. And Mami didn't look like she was about to say anything to Papi. The two of them danced every now and then but they never lasted more than a song before Mami joined Tía again in whatever conversation they were having.

I tried to imagine Mami before Papi. Maybe I was tired, or just sad, thinking about the way my family was. Maybe I already knew how it would all end up in a few years, Mami without Papi, and that was why I did it. Picturing her alone wasn't easy. It seemed like Papi had always been with her, even when we were waiting in Santo Domingo for him to send for us.

The only photograph our family had of Mami as a young woman, before she married Papi, was the one that somebody took of her at an election party that I found one day while rummaging for money to go to the arcade. Mami had it tucked into her immigration papers. In the photo, she's surrounded by laughing cousins I will never meet, who are all shiny from dancing, whose clothes are rumpled and loose. You can tell it's night and hot and that the mosquitos have been biting. She sits straight and even in a crowd she stands out, smiling quietly like maybe she's the one everybody's celebrating. You can't see her hands but I imagined they're knotting a straw or a bit of thread. This was the woman my father met a year later on the Malecón,[20] the woman Mami thought she'd always be.

Mami must have caught me studying her because she stopped what she was doing and gave me a smile, maybe her first one of the night. Suddenly I wanted to go over and hug her, for no other reason than I loved her, but there were about eleven fat jiggling bodies between us. So I sat down on the tiled floor and waited.

I must have fallen asleep because the next thing I knew Rafa was kicking me and saying, Let's go. He looked like he'd been hitting those girls off; he was all smiles. I got to my feet in time to kiss Tía and Tío good-bye. Mami was holding the serving dish she had brought with her.

135 Where's Papi? I asked.

He's downstairs, bringing the van around. Mami leaned down to kiss me.

You were good today, she said.

And then Papi burst in and told us to get the hell downstairs before some pendejo[21] cop gave him a ticket. More kisses, more handshakes and then we were gone.

I don't remember being out of sorts after I met the Puerto Rican woman, but I must have been because Mami only asked me questions when she thought something was wrong in my life. It took her about ten passes but finally she cornered me one afternoon when we were alone in the apartment. Our upstairs neighbors were beating the crap out of their kids, and me and her had been listening to it all afternoon. She put her hand on mine and said, Is everything OK, Yunior? Have you been fighting with your brother?

140 Me and Rafa had already talked. We'd been in the basement, where our parents couldn't hear us. He told me that yeah, he knew about her.

Papi's taken me there twice now, he said.

---

[20] Embankment (literally): Walk by the ocean.

[21] Idiot.

Why didn't you tell me? I asked.

What the hell was I going to say? *Hey, Yunior, guess what happened yesterday? I met Papi's sucia!*[22]

I didn't say anything to Mami either. She watched me, very very closely. Later I would think, maybe if I had told her, she would have confronted him, would have done something, but who can know these things? I said I'd been having trouble in school and like that everything was back to normal between us. She put her hand on my shoulder and squeezed and that was that.

* * *

145 We were on the turnpike, just past Exit 11, when I started feeling it again. I sat up from leaning against Rafa. His fingers smelled and he'd gone to sleep almost as soon as he got into the van. Madai was out too but at least she wasn't snoring.

In the darkness, I saw that Papi had a hand on Mami's knee and that the two of them were quiet and still. They weren't slumped back or anything; they were both wide awake, bolted into their seats. I couldn't see either of their faces and no matter how hard I tried I could not imagine their expressions. Neither of them moved. Every now and then the van was filled with the bright rush of somebody else's headlights. Finally I said, Mami, and they both looked back, already knowing what was happening.

Explorations of the Text

1. Analyze the point of view and tone of the narrator. Discuss the narrator's role in his family. Discuss his relationship with his siblings. Why does his father single him out for punishment?
2. What main impression do you gain of Papi's and Mami's characters. What distinguishes their relationship? What are the reasons for the breakdown of their marriage?
3. Why does the story center on the fiesta? What is the significance of the last encounter between Mami and Papi?
4. Why does the narrator vomit in the car? Explore the symbolism of this action.
5. What is the impact of the inclusion of Spanish words and colloquial language?
6. Compare the father-son relationship in this story with the one in "This Is What It Means to Say Phoenix, Arizona."

[22] Lover.

The Reading/Writing Connection

1. Journal Entry: "What is unspoken in family life wields great power." Relate this quotation to your own life experiences.
2. Gloss and annotate the text; note images of words versus silence. Then freewrite about the work and concentrate on this theme.

Ideas for Writing

1. Write a character analysis of the narrator or of Papi.
2. Compare Mami to Elena, the speaker in Pat Mora's poem.
3. Write an essay on themes of estrangement and loss in this story.

Sonny's Blues

James Baldwin

James Baldwin (1924–87) was born and raised in Harlem, a district on New York's Manhattan Island. He grew up in a large family, and his stepfather was an evangelical preacher. An excellent student, Baldwin wrote from an early age. Although several well-known publications accepted his essays and short stories and although Richard Wright helped him win a fellowship, it was not until he moved to Europe in 1948 that Baldwin's creative powers came to fruition. His first novel, Go Tell It on the Mountain *(1953), is about a Harlem teenager's conflicts with a repressive father; his first play,* The Amen Corner *(1955), which deals with the pentecostal faith, represents Baldwin's search for his racial heritage. These were followed by* Notes of a Native Son *(1955), the 1956 novel* Giovanni's Room, Nobody Knows My Name: More Notes of a Native Son *(1961), and* The Fire Next Time *(1963).*

1957

I read about it in the paper, in the subway, on my way to work. I read it, and I couldn't believe it, and I read it again. Then perhaps I just stared at it, at the newsprint spelling out his name, spelling out the story. I stared at it in the swinging lights of the subway car, and in the faces and bodies of the people, and in my own face, trapped in the darkness which roared outside.

It was not to be believed and I kept telling myself that, as I walked from the subway station to the high school. And at the same time I couldn't doubt it. I was scared, scared for Sonny. He became real to me again. A great block of ice got settled in my belly and kept melting there slowly all day long, while I taught my classes algebra. It was a special kind of ice. It kept melting, sending trickles of ice water all up and down my veins, but it never got less. Sometimes it hardened and seemed to expand until I felt my guts were going to come spilling out or that I was going to choke or scream. This would always be at a moment when I was remembering some specific thing Sonny had once said or done.

When he was about as old as the boys in my classes his face had been bright and open, there was a lot of copper in it; and he'd had wonderfully direct brown eyes, and great gentleness and privacy. I wondered what he looked like now. He had been picked up, the evening before, in a raid on an apartment downtown, for peddling and using heroin.

I couldn't believe it: but what I mean by that is that I couldn't find any room for it anywhere inside me. I had kept it outside me for a long time. I hadn't wanted to know. I had had suspicions, but I didn't name them, I kept putting them away. I told myself that Sonny was wild, but he wasn't crazy. And he'd always been a good boy, he hadn't ever turned hard or evil or disrespectful, the way kids can, so quick, so quick, especially in Harlem. I didn't want to believe that I'd ever see my brother going down, coming to nothing, all that light in his face gone out, in the condition I'd already seen so many others. Yet it had happened and here I was, talking about algebra to a lot of boys who might, every one of them for all I knew, be popping off needles every time they went to the head. Maybe it did more for them than algebra could.

5 I was sure that the first time Sonny had ever had horse, he couldn't have been much older than these boys were now. These boys, now, were living as we'd been living then, they were growing up with a rush and their heads bumped abruptly against the low ceiling of their actual possibilities. They were filled with rage. All they really knew were two darknesses, the darkness of their lives, which was now closing in on them, and the darkness of the movies, which had blinded them to that other darkness, and in which they now, vindictively, dreamed, at once more together than they were at any other time, and more alone.

When the last bell rang, the last class ended, I let out my breath. It seemed I'd been holding it for all that time. My clothes were wet—I may have looked as though I'd been sitting in a steam bath, all dressed up, all afternoon. I sat alone in the classroom a long time. I listened to the boys outside, downstairs, shouting and cursing and laughing. Their laughter struck me for perhaps the first time. It was not the joyous laughter which—God knows why—one associates with children. It was mocking and insular, its intent was to denigrate. It was disenchanted, and in this, also, lay the authority of their curses. Perhaps I was listening to them because I was thinking about my brother and in them I heard my brother. And myself.

One boy was whistling a tune, at once very complicated and very simple, it seemed to be pouring out of him as though he were a bird, and it sounded very cool and moving through all that harsh, bright air, only just holding its own through all those other sounds.

I stood up and walked over to the window and looked down into the courtyard. It was the beginning of the spring and the sap was rising in the boys. A teacher passed through them every now and again, quickly, as though he or she couldn't wait to get out of that courtyard, to get those boys out of their sight and off their minds. I started collecting my stuff. I thought I'd better get home and talk to Isabel.

The courtyard was almost deserted by the time I got downstairs. I saw this boy standing in the shadow of a doorway, looking just like Sonny. I almost called his name. Then I saw that it wasn't Sonny, but somebody we used to know, a boy from around our block. He'd been Sonny's friend. He'd never been mine, having been too young for me, and, anyway, I'd never liked him. And now, even though he was a grown-up man, he still hung around that block, still spent hours on the street corners, was always high and raggy. I used to run into him from time to time and he'd often work around to asking me for a quarter or fifty cents. He always had some real good excuse, too, and I always gave it to him, I don't know why.

10 But now, abruptly, I hated him. I couldn't stand the way he looked at me, partly like a dog, partly like a cunning child. I wanted to ask him what the hell he was doing in the school courtyard.

He sort of shuffled over to me, and he said, "I see you got the papers. So you already know about it."

"You mean about Sonny? Yes, I already know about it. How come they didn't get you?"

He grinned. It made him repulsive and it also brought to mind what he'd looked like as a kid. "I wasn't there. I stay away from them people."

"Good for you." I offered him a cigarette and I watched him through the smoke. "You come all the way down here just to tell me about Sonny?"

15 "That's right." He was sort of shaking his head and his eyes looked strange, as though they were about to cross. The bright sun deadened his damp dark brown skin and it made his eyes look yellow and showed up the dirt in his kinked hair. He smelled funky. I moved a little away from him and I said, "Well, thanks. But I already know about it and I got to get home."

"I'll walk you a little ways," he said. We started walking. There were a couple of kids still loitering in the courtyard and one of them said goodnight to me and looked strangely at the boy beside me.

"What're you going to do?" he asked me. "I mean, about Sonny?"

"Look. I haven't seen Sonny for over a year, I'm not sure I'm going to do anything. Anyway, what the hell *can* I do?"

"That's right," he said quickly, "ain't nothing you can do. Can't much help old Sonny no more, I guess."

20 It was what I was thinking and so it seemed to me he had no right to say it.

"I'm surprised at Sonny, though," he went on—he had a funny way of talking, he looked straight ahead as though he were talking to himself—"I thought Sonny was a smart boy, I thought he was too smart to get hung."

"I guess he thought so too," I said sharply, "and that's how he got hung. And now about you? You're pretty goddamn smart, I bet."

Then he looked directly at me, just for a minute. "I ain't smart," he said. "If I was smart, I'd have reached for a pistol a long time ago."

"Look. Don't tell *me* your sad story, if it was up to me, I'd give you one." Then I felt guilty—guilty, probably, for never having supposed that the poor bastard *had* a story of his own, much less a sad one, and I asked, quickly, "What's going to happen to him now?"

25 He didn't answer this. He was off by himself some place. "Funny thing," he said, and from his tone we might have been discussing the quickest way to get to Brooklyn, "when I saw the papers this morning, the first thing I asked myself was if I had anything to do with it. I felt sort of responsible."

I began to listen more carefully. The subway station was on the corner, just before us, and I stopped. He stopped, too. We were in front of a bar and he ducked slightly, peering in, but whoever he was looking for didn't seem to be there. The juke box was blasting away with something black and bouncy and I half watched the barmaid as she danced her way from the juke box to her place behind the bar. And I watched her face as she laughingly responded to something someone said to her, still keeping time to the music. When she smiled one saw the little girl, one sensed the doomed, still-struggling woman beneath the battered face of the semi-whore.

"I never give Sonny nothing," the boy said finally, "but a long time ago I come to school high and Sonny asked me how it felt." He paused, I couldn't bear to watch him, I watched the barmaid, and I listened to the music which seemed to be causing the pavement to shake. "I told him it felt great." The music stopped, the barmaid paused and watched the juke box until the music began again. "It did."

All this way carrying me some place I didn't want to go. I certainly didn't want to know how it felt. It filled everything, the people, the houses, the music, the dark, quick-silver barmaid, with menace: and this menace was their reality.

"What's going to happen to him now?" I asked again.

30 "They'll send him away some place and they'll try to cure him." He shook his head. "Maybe he'll even think he's kicked the habit. Then they'll let him loose"—he gestured, throwing his cigarette into the gutter. "That's all."

"What do you mean, that's *all?*"

But I knew what he meant.

"I mean, that's *all.*" He turned his head and looked at me, pulling down the corners of his mouth. "Don't you know what I mean?" he asked, softly.

"How the hell would I know what you mean?" I almost whispered it. I don't know why.

35 "That's right," he said to the air, "how would he know what I mean?" He turned toward me again, patient and calm, and yet I somehow felt him shaking, shaking as though he were going to fall apart. I felt that ice in my guts again, the dread I'd felt all afternoon; and again I watched the barmaid, moving about the bar, washing glasses, and singing. "Listen. They'll let him out and then it'll just start all over again. That's what I mean."

"You mean—they'll let him out. And then he'll just start working his way back in again. You mean he'll never kick the habit. Is that what you mean?"

"That's right," he said, cheerfully. "You see what I mean."

"Tell me," I said at last, "why does he want to die? He must want to die, he's killing himself, why does he want to die?"

He looked at me in surprise. He licked his lips. "He don't want to die. He wants to live. Don't nobody want to die, ever."

40 Then I wanted to ask him—too many things. He could not have answered, or if he had, I could not have borne the answers. I started walking. "Well, I guess it's none of my business."

"It's going to be rough on old Sonny," he said. We reached the subway station. "This is your station?" he asked. I nodded. I took one step down. "Damn!" he said, suddenly. I looked up at him. He grinned again. "Damn it if I didn't leave all my money home. You ain't got a dollar on you, have you? Just for a couple of days, is all."

All at once something inside gave and threatened to come pouring out of me. I didn't hate him any more, I felt that in another moment I'd start crying like a child.

"Sure," I said. "Don't swear." I looked in my wallet and didn't have a dollar, I only had a five. "Here," I said. "That hold you?"

He didn't look at it—he didn't want to look at it. A terrible, closed look came over his face, as though he were keeping the number on the bill a secret from him and me. "Thanks," he said, and now he was dying to see me go. "Don't worry about Sonny. Maybe I'll write him or something."

45 "Sure," I said. "You do that. So long."

"Be seeing you," he said. I went down the steps.

And I didn't write Sonny or send him anything for a long time. When I finally did, it was just after my little girl died, he wrote me back a letter which made me feel like a bastard.

Here's what he said:

Dear Brother,

You don't know how much I needed to hear from you. I wanted to write you many a time but I dug how much I must have hurt you and so I didn't write. But now I feel like a man who's been trying to climb up out of some deep, real deep and funky hole and just saw the sun up there, outside. I got to get outside.

I can't tell you much about how I got here. I mean I don't know how to tell you. I guess I was afraid of something or I was trying to escape from something and you know I have never been very strong in the head (smile). I'm glad Mama and Daddy are dead and can't see what's happened to their son and I swear if I'd known what I was doing I would never have hurt you so, you and a lot of other fine people who were nice to me and who believed in me.

I don't want you to think it had anything to do with me being a musician. It's more than that. Or maybe less than that. I can't get anything straight in my head down here and I try not to think about what's going to happen to me when I get outside again. Sometime I think I'm going to flip and never get outside and sometime I think I'll come straight back, I tell you one thing, though. I'd rather blow my brains out than go through this again. But that's what they all say, so they tell me. If I tell you when I'm coming to New York and if you could meet me, I sure would appreciate it. Give my love to Isabel and the kids and I was sure sorry to hear about little Gracie. I wish I could be like Mama and say the Lord's will be done, but I don't know it seems to me that trouble is the one thing that never does get stopped and I don't know what good it does to blame it on the Lord. But maybe it does some good if you believe it.

Your brother,
Sonny

Then I kept in constant touch with him and I sent him whatever I could and I went to meet him when he came back to New York. When I saw him many things I thought I had forgotten came flooding back to me. This was because I had begun, finally, to wonder about Sonny, about the life that Sonny lived inside. This life, whatever it was, had made him older and thinner and it had deepened the distant stillness in which he had always moved. He looked very unlike my baby brother. Yet, when he smiled, when we shook hands, the baby brother I'd never known looked out from the depths of his private life, like an animal waiting to be coaxed into the light.

"How you been keeping?" he asked me.

"All right. And you?"

"Just fine." He was smiling all over his face. "It's good to see you again."

"It's good to see you."

The seven years' difference in our ages lay between us like a chasm: I wondered if these years would ever operate between us as a bridge. I was remembering, and it made it hard to catch my breath, that I had been there when he was born; and I had heard the first words he had ever spoken. When he started to walk, he walked from our mother straight to me. I caught him just before he fell when he took the first steps he ever took in this world.

"How's Isabel?"

"Just fine. She's dying to see you."

"And the boys?"

"They're fine, too. They're anxious to see their uncle."

"Oh, come on. You know they don't remember me."

"Are you kidding? Of course they remember you."

He grinned again. We got into a taxi. We had a lot to say to each other, far too much to know how to begin.

As the taxi began to move, I asked, "You still want to go to India?"

He laughed. "You still remember that. Hell, no. This place is Indian enough for me."

"It used to belong to them," I said.

And he laughed again. "They damn sure knew what they were doing when they got rid of it."

Years ago, when he was around fourteen, he'd been all hipped on the idea of going to India. He read books about people sitting on rocks, naked, in all kinds of weather, but mostly bad, naturally, and walking barefoot through hot coals and arriving at wisdom. I used to say that it sounded to me as though they were getting away from wisdom as fast as they could. I think he sort of looked down on me for that.

"Do you mind," he asked, "if we have the driver drive alongside the park? On the west side—I haven't seen the city in so long."

"Of course not," I said. I was afraid that I might sound as though I were humoring him, but I hoped he wouldn't take it that way.

So we drove along, between the green of the park and the stony, lifeless elegance of hotels and apartment buildings, toward the vivid, killing streets of our childhood. These streets hadn't changed, though housing projects jutted up out of them now like rocks in the middle of a boiling sea. Most of the houses in which we had grown up had vanished, as had the stores from which we had stolen, the basements in which we had first tried sex, the rooftops from which we had hurled tin cans and bricks. But houses exactly like the houses of our past yet dominated the landscape, boys exactly like the boys we once had been found themselves smothering in these houses, came down into the streets for light and air and found themselves encircled by disaster. Some escaped the trap, most didn't. Those who got out always left something of themselves behind, as some animals amputate a leg and leave it in the trap. It might be said, perhaps, that I had escaped, after all, I was a school teacher; or that Sonny had, he hadn't lived in Harlem for years. Yet, as the cab moved uptown through streets which seemed, with a rush, to darken with dark people, and as I covertly studied Sonny's face, it came to me that what we both were seeking through our separate cab windows was that part of ourselves which had been left behind. It's always at the hour of trouble and confrontation that the missing member aches.

70 We hit 110th Street and started rolling up Lenox Avenue. And I'd known this avenue all my life, but it seemed to me again, as it had seemed on the day I'd first heard about Sonny's trouble, filled with a hidden menace which was its very breath of life.

"We almost there," said Sonny.

"Almost." We were both too nervous to say anything more.

We live in a housing project. It hasn't been up long. A few days after it was up it seemed uninhabitably new, now, of course, it's already rundown. It looks like a parody of the good, clean, faceless life—God knows the people who live in it do their best to make it a parody. The beat-looking grass lying around isn't enough to make their lives green, the hedges will never hold out the streets, and they know it. The big windows fool no one, they aren't big enough to make space out of no space. They don't bother with the windows, they watch the TV screen instead. The playground is most popular with the children who don't play at jacks, or skip rope, or roller skate, or swing, and they can be found in it after dark. We moved in partly because it's not too far from where I teach, and partly for the kids; but it's really just like the houses in which Sonny and I grew up. The same things happen, they'll have the same things to remember. The moment Sonny and I started into the house I had the feeling that I was simply bringing him back into the danger he had almost died trying to escape.

Sonny has never been talkative. So I don't know why I was sure he'd be dying to talk to me when supper was over the first night. Everything went fine, the oldest boy remembered him, and the youngest boy liked him, and Sonny had remembered to bring something for each of them; and Isabel, who is really much nicer than I am, more open and giving, had gone to a lot of trouble about dinner and was genuinely glad to see him. And she's always been able to tease Sonny in a way that I haven't. It was nice to see her face so vivid again and to hear her laugh and watch her make Sonny laugh. She wasn't, or, anyway, she didn't seem to be, at all uneasy or embarrassed. She chatted as though there were no subject which had to be avoided and she got Sonny past his first, faint stiffness. And thank God she was there, for I was filled with that icy dread again. Everything I did seemed awkward to me, and everything I said sounded freighted with hidden meaning. I was trying to remember everything I'd heard about dope addiction and I couldn't help watching Sonny for signs. I wasn't doing it out of malice. I was trying to find out something about my brother. I was dying to hear him tell he was safe.

75 "Safe!" my father grunted, whenever Mama suggested trying to move to a neighborhood which might be safer for children. "Safe, hell! Ain't no place safe for kids, nor nobody."

He always went on like this, but he wasn't, ever, really as bad as he sounded, not even on weekends, when he got drunk. As a matter of fact, he was always on the lookout for "something a little better," but he died before he found it. He died suddenly, during a drunken weekend in the middle of the war, when Sonny was fifteen. He and Sonny hadn't ever got on too well. And this was partly because Sonny was the apple of his father's eye. It was because he loved Sonny so much and was frightened for him, that he was always fighting with him. It doesn't do any good to fight with Sonny. Sonny just moves back, inside himself, where he can't be reached. But the principal reason that they never hit it off is that they were so much alike. Daddy was big and rough and loud-talking, just the opposite of Sonny, but they both had—that same privacy.

Mama tried to tell me something about this, just after Daddy died. I was home on leave from the army.

This was the last time I ever saw my mother alive. Just the same, this picture gets all mixed up in my mind with pictures I had of her when she was younger. The way I always see her is the way she used to be on a Sunday afternoon, say, when the old folks were talking after the big Sunday dinner. I always see her wearing pale blue. She'd be sitting on the sofa. And my father would be sitting in the easy chair, not far from her. And the living room would be full of church folks and relatives. There they sit, in chairs all around the living room, and the night is creeping up outside, but nobody knows it yet. You can see the darkness growing against the windowpanes and you hear the street noises every now and again, or maybe the jangling beat of a tambourine from one of the churches close by, but it's real quiet in the room. For a moment nobody's talking, but every face looks darkening, like the sky outside. And my mother rocks a little from the waist, and my father's eyes are closed. Everyone is looking at something a child can't see. For a minute they've forgotten the children. Maybe a kid is lying on the rug, half asleep. Maybe somebody's got a kid in his lap and is absent-mindedly stroking the kid's head. Maybe there's a kid, quiet and big-eyed, curled up on a big chair in the corner. The silence, the darkness coming, and the darkness in the faces frightens the child obscurely. He hopes that the hand which strokes his forehead will never stop—will never die. He hopes that there will never come a time when the old folks won't be sitting around the living room, talking about where they've come from, and what they've seen, and what's happened to them and their kinfolk.

But something deep and watchful in the child knows that this is bound to end, is already ending. In a moment someone will get up and turn on the light. Then the old folks will remember the children and they won't talk any more that day. And when light fills the room, the child is filled with darkness. He knows that every time this happens he's moved just a little closer to that darkness outside. The darkness outside is what the old folks have been talking about. It's what they've come from. It's what they endure. The child knows that they won't talk any more because if he knows too much about what's happened to *them,* he'll know too much too soon, about what's going to happen to *him.*

80 The last time I talked to my mother, I remember I was restless. I wanted to get out and see Isabel. We weren't married then and we had a lot to straighten out between us.

There Mama sat, in black, by the window. She was humming an old church song, *Lord, you brought me from a long ways off.* Sonny was out somewhere. Mama kept watching the streets.

"I don't know," she said, "if I'll ever see you again, after you go off from here. But I hope you'll remember the things I tried to teach you."

"Don't talk like that," I said, and smiled. "You'll be here a long time yet."

She smiled, too, but she said nothing. She was quiet for a long time. And I said, "Mama, don't you worry about nothing. I'll be writing all the time, and you be getting the checks. . . ."

85 "I want to talk to you about your brother," she said, suddenly. "If anything happens to me he ain't going to have nobody to look out for him."

"Mama," I said, "ain't nothing going to happen to you *or* Sonny. Sonny's all right. He's a good boy and he's got good sense."

"It ain't a question of his being a good boy," Mama said, "nor of his having good sense. It ain't only the bad ones, nor yet the dumb ones that gets sucked under." She stopped, looking at me. "Your Daddy once had a brother," she said, and she smiled in a way that made me feel she was in pain. "You didn't never know that, did you?"

"No," I said, "I never knew that," and I watched her face.

"Oh, yes," she said, "your Daddy had a brother." She looked out of the window again. "I know you never saw your Daddy cry. But *I* did—many a time, through all these years."

90 I asked her, "What happened to his brother? How come nobody's ever talked about him?"

This was the first time I ever saw my mother look old.

"His brother got killed," she said, "when he was just a little younger than you are now. I knew him. He was a fine boy. He was maybe a little full of the devil, but he didn't mean nobody no harm."

Then she stopped and the room was silent, exactly as it had sometimes been on those Sunday afternoons. Mama kept looking out into the streets.

"He used to have a job in the mill," she said, "and, like all young folks, he just liked to perform on Saturday nights. Saturday nights, him and your father would drift around to different places, go to dances and things like that, or just sit around with people they knew, and your father's brother would sing, he had a fine voice, and play along with himself on his guitar. Well, this particular Saturday night, him and your father was coming home from some place, and they were both a little drunk and there was a moon that night, it was bright like day. Your father's brother was feeling kind of good, and he was whistling to himself, and he had his guitar slung over this shoulder. They was coming down a hill and beneath them was a road that turned off from the highway. Well, your father's brother, being always kind of frisky, decided to run down this hill, and he did, with that guitar banging and clanging behind him, and he ran across the road, and he was making water behind a tree. And your father was sort of amused at him and he was still coming down the hill, kind of slow. Then he heard a car motor and that same minute his brother stepped from behind the tree, into the road, in the moonlight. And he started to cross the road. And your father started to run down the hill, he says he don't know why. This car was full of white men. They was all drunk, and when they seen your father's brother they let out a great whoop and holler and they aimed the car straight at him. They was having fun, they just wanted to scare him, the way they do sometimes, you know. But they was drunk. And I guess the boy, being drunk, too, and scared, kind of lost his head. By the time he jumped it was too late. Your father says he heard his brother scream when the car rolled over him, and he heard the wood of that guitar when it give, and he heard them strings go flying, and he heard them white men shouting, and the car kept on a-going and it ain't stopped till this day. And, time your father got down the hill, his brother weren't nothing but blood and pulp."

95 Tears were gleaming on my mother's face. There wasn't anything I could say.

"He never mentioned it," she said, "because I never let him mention it before you children. Your Daddy was like a crazy man that night and for many a night thereafter. He says he never in his life seen anything as dark as that road after the lights of that car had gone away. Weren't nothing, weren't nobody on that road, just your Daddy and his brother and that busted guitar. Oh, yes. Your Daddy never did really get right again. Till the day he died he weren't sure but that every white man he saw was the man that killed his brother."

She stopped and took out her handkerchief and dried her eyes and looked at me.

"I ain't telling you all this," she said, "to make you scared or bitter or to make you hate nobody. I'm telling you this because you got a brother. And the world ain't changed."

I guess I didn't want to believe this. I guess she saw this in my face. She turned away from me, toward the window again, searching those streets.

100 "But I praise my Redeemer," she said at last, "that He called your Daddy home before me. I ain't saying it to throw no flowers at myself, but, I declare, it keeps me from feeling too cast down to know I helped your father get safely through this world. Your father always acted like he was the roughest, strongest man on earth. And everybody took him to be like that. But if he hadn't had *me* there—to see his tears!"

She was crying again. Still, I couldn't move. I said, "Lord, Lord, Mama, I didn't know it was like that."

"Oh, honey," she said, "there's a lot that you don't know. But you are going to find it out." She stood up from the window and came over to me. "You got to hold on to your brother," she said, "and don't let him fall, no matter what it looks like is happening to him and no matter how evil you gets with him. You going to be evil with him many a time. But don't you forget what I told you, you hear?"

"I won't forget," I said. "Don't you worry, I won't forget. I won't let nothing happen to Sonny."

My mother smiled as though she were amused at something she saw in my face. Then, "You may not be able to stop nothing from happening. But you got to let him know you's *there*."

105 Two days later I was married, and then I was gone. And I had a lot of things on my mind and I pretty well forgot my promise to Mama until I got shipped home on a special furlough for her funeral.

And after the funeral, with just Sonny and me alone in the empty kitchen, I tried to find out something about him.

"What do you want to do?" I asked him.

"I'm going to be a musician," he said.

For he had graduated, in the time I had been away, from dancing to the juke box to finding out who was playing what, and what they were doing with it, and he had bought himself a set of drums.

110 "You mean, you want to be a drummer?" I somehow had the feeling that being a drummer might be all right for other people but not for my brother Sonny.

"I don't think," he said, looking at me very gravely, "that I'll ever be a good drummer. But I think I can play a piano."

I frowned. I'd never played the role of the older brother quite so seriously before, had scarcely ever, in fact, *asked* Sonny a damn thing. I sensed myself in the presence of something I didn't really know how to handle, didn't understand. So I made my frown a little deeper as I asked: "What kind of musician do you want to be?"

He grinned, "How many kinds do you think there are?"

"Be *serious,*" I said.

115 He laughed, throwing his head back, and then looked at me. "I *am* serious."

"Well, then, for Christ's sake, stop kidding around and answer a serious question. I mean, do you want to be a concert pianist, you want to play classical music and all that, or—or what?" Long before I finished he was laughing again. "For Christ's *sake,* Sonny!"

He sobered, but with difficulty. "I'm sorry, But you sound so—*scared!*" and he was off again.

"Well, you may think it's funny now, baby, but it's not going to be so funny when you have to make your living at it, let me tell you *that.*" I was furious because I knew he was laughing at me and I didn't know why.

"No," he said, very sober now, and afraid, perhaps, that he'd hurt me. "I don't want to be a classical pianist. That isn't what interests me. I mean"—he paused, looking hard at me, as though his eyes would help me to understand, and then gestured helplessly, as though perhaps his hand would help—"I mean, I'll have a lot of studying to do, and I'll have to study *everything,* but, I mean, I want to play *with*—jazz musicians." He stopped, "I want to play jazz," he said.

120 Well, the word had never before sounded as heavy, as real, as it sounded that afternoon in Sonny's mouth. I just looked at him and I was probably frowning a real frown by this time. I simply couldn't see why on earth he'd want to spend his time hanging around nightclubs, clowning around on bandstands, while people pushed each other around a dance floor. It seemed—beneath him, somehow. I had never thought about it before, had never been forced to, but I suppose I had always put jazz musicians in a class with what Daddy called "good-time people."

"Are you *serious?*"

"Hell, *yes,* I'm serious."

He looked more helpless than ever, and annoyed, and deeply hurt.

I suggested, helpfully: "You mean—like Louis Armstrong?"[1]

125 His face closed as though I'd struck him. "No. I'm not talking about none of that old-time, down home crap."

"Well, look, Sonny, I'm sorry, don't get mad. I just don't altogether get it, that's all. Name somebody—you know, a jazz musician you admire."

"Bird."

"Who?"

"Bird! Charlie Parker![2] Don't they teach you nothing in the goddamn army?"

130 I lit a cigarette. I was surprised and then a little amused to discover that I was trembling. "I've been out of touch," I said. "You'll have to be patient with me. Now. Who's this Parker character?"

[1] Famous jazz trumpet player.

[2] Famous jazz musician, nicknamed Bird.

"He's just one of the greatest jazz musicians alive," said Sonny, sullenly, his hands in his pockets, his back to me. "Maybe *the* greatest," he added, bitterly, "that's probably why *you* never heard of him."

"All right," I said, "I'm ignorant. I'm sorry. I'll go out and buy all the cat's records right away, all right?"

"It don't," said Sonny, with dignity, "make any difference to me. I don't care what you listen to. Don't do me no favors."

I was beginning to realize that I'd never seen him so upset before. With another part of my mind I was thinking that this would probably turn out to be one of those things kids go through and that I shouldn't make it seem important by pushing it too hard. Still, I didn't think it would do any harm to ask: "Doesn't all this take a lot of time? Can you make a living at it?"

135 He turned back to me and half leaned, half sat, on the kitchen table. "Everything takes time," he said, "and—well, yes, sure, I can make a living at it. But what I don't seem to be able to make you understand is that it's the only thing I want to do."

"Well, Sonny," I said, gently, "you know people can't always do exactly what they *want* to do—"

"*No,* I don't know that," said Sonny, surprising me. "I think people *ought* to do what they want to do, what else are they alive for?"

"You getting to be a big boy," I said desperately, "it's time you started thinking about your future."

"I'm thinking about my future," said Sonny, grimly. "I think about it all the time."

140 I gave up. I decided, if he didn't change his mind, that we could always talk about it later. "In the meantime," I said, "you got to finish school." We had already decided that he'd have to move in with Isabel and her folks. I knew this wasn't the ideal arrangement because Isabel's folks are inclined to be dicty[3] and they hadn't especially wanted Isabel to marry me. But I didn't know what else to do. "And we have to get you fixed up at Isabel's."

There was a long silence. He moved from the kitchen table to the window. "That's a terrible idea. You know it yourself."

"Do you have a *better* idea?"

He just walked up and down the kitchen for a minute. He was as tall as I was. He had started to shave. I suddenly had the feeling that I didn't know him at all.

He stopped at the kitchen table and picked up my cigarettes. Looking at me with a kind of mocking, amused defiance, he put one between his lips. "You mind?"

145 "You smoking already?"

He lit the cigarette and nodded, watching me through the smoke. "I just wanted to see if I'd have the courage to smoke in front of you." He grinned and

[3] Putting on fine airs.

blew a great cloud of smoke to the ceiling. "It was easy." He looked at my face. "Come on, now. I bet you was smoking at my age, tell the truth."

I didn't say anything but the truth was on my face, and he laughed. But now there was something very strained in his laugh. "Sure. And I bet that ain't all you was doing."

He was frightening me a little. "Cut the crap," I said. "We already decided that you was going to go and live at Isabel's. Now what's got into you all of a sudden?"

"*You* decided it," he pointed out. "*I* didn't decide nothing." He stopped in front of me, leaning against the stove, arms loosely folded. "Look, brother. I don't want to stay in Harlem no more, I really don't." He was very earnest. He looked at me, then over toward the kitchen window. There was something in his eyes I'd never seen before, some thoughtfulness, some worry all his own. He rubbed the muscle of one arm. "It's time I was getting out of here."

"Where do you want to *go,* Sonny?"

"I want to join the army. Or the navy, I don't care. If I say I'm old enough, they'll believe me."

Then I got mad. It was because I was so scared. "You must be crazy. You goddamn fool, what the hell do you want to go and join the *army* for?"

"I just told you. To get out of Harlem."

"Sonny, you haven't even finished *school.* And if you really want to be a musician, how do you expect to study if you're in the *army?*"

He looked at me, trapped, and in anguish. "There's ways. I might be able to work out some kind of deal. Anyway, I'll have the G.I. Bill when I come out."

"*If* you come out." We stared at each other. "Sonny, please. Be reasonable. I know the setup is far from perfect. But we got to do the best we can."

"I ain't learning nothing in school," he said. "Even when I go." He turned away from me and opened the window and threw his cigarette out into the narrow alley. I watched his back. "At least, I ain't learning nothing you'd want me to learn." He slammed the window so hard I thought the glass would fly out, and turned back to me. "And I'm sick of the stink of these garbage cans!"

"Sonny," I said, "I know how you feel. But if you don't finish school now, you're going to be sorry later that you didn't." I grabbed him by the shoulders. "And you only got another year. It ain't so bad. And I'll come back and I swear I'll help you do *whatever* you want to do. Just try to put up with it till I come back. Will you please do that? For me?"

He didn't answer and he wouldn't look at me.

"Sonny. You hear me?"

He pulled away. "I hear you. But you never hear anything *I* say."

I didn't know what to say to that. He looked out of the window and then back at me. "OK," he said, and sighed. "I'll try."

Then I said, trying to cheer him up a little, "They got a piano at Isabel's. You can practice on it."

And as a matter of fact, it did cheer him up for a minute. "That's right," he said to himself. "I forgot that." His face relaxed a little. But the worry, the thoughtfulness, played on it still, the way shadows play on a face which is staring into the fire.

165 But I thought I'd never hear the end of that piano. At first, Isabel, would write me, saying how nice it was that Sonny was so serious about his music and how, as soon as he came in from school, or wherever he had been when he was supposed to be at school, he went straight to that piano and stayed there until suppertime. And, after supper, he went back to that piano and stayed there until everybody went to bed. He was at the piano all day Saturday and all day Sunday. Then he bought a record player and started playing records. He'd play one record over and over again, all day long sometimes, and he'd improvise along with it on the piano. Or he'd play one section of the record, one chord, one change, one progression, then he'd do it on the piano. Then back to the record. Then back to the piano.

Well, I really don't know how they stood it. Isabel finally confessed that it wasn't like living with a person at all, it was like living with sound. And the sound didn't make any sense to her, didn't make any sense to any of them—naturally. They began, in a way, to be afflicted by this presence that was living in their home. It was as though Sonny were some sort of god, or monster. He moved in an atmosphere which wasn't like theirs at all. They fed him and he ate, he washed himself, he walked in and out of their door; he certainly wasn't nasty or unpleasant or rude, Sonny isn't any of those things; but it was as though he were all wrapped up in some cloud, some fire, some vision all his own; and there wasn't any way to reach him.

At the same time, he wasn't really a man yet, he was still a child, and they had to watch out for him in all kinds of ways. They certainly couldn't throw him out. Neither did they dare to make a great scene about that piano because even they dimly sensed, as I sensed, from so many thousands of miles away, that Sonny was at that piano playing for his life.

But he hadn't been going to school. One day a letter came from the school board and Isabel's mother got it—there had, apparently, been other letters but Sonny had torn them up. This day, when Sonny came in, Isabel's mother showed him the letter and asked where he'd been spending his time. And she finally got it out of him that he'd been down in Greenwich Village, with musicians and other characters, in a white girl's apartment. And this scared her and she started to scream at him and what came up, once she began—though she denies it to this day—was what sacrifices they were making to give Sonny a decent home and how little he appreciated it.

Sonny didn't play the piano that day. By evening, Isabel's mother had calmed down but then there was the old man to deal with, and Isabel herself. Isabel says she did her best to be calm but she broke down and started crying. She says she just watched Sonny's face. She could tell, by watching him, what was happening with him. And what was happening was that they penetrated his cloud, they had reached him. Even if their fingers had been a thousand times more gentle than human fingers ever are, he could hardly help feeling that they had stripped him naked and were spitting on that nakedness. For he also had to see that his presence, that music, which was life or death to him, had been torture for them and that they had endured it, not at all for his sake, but only for mine. And Sonny couldn't take that. He can take it a little better today than he could then but he's still not very good at it and, frankly, I don't know anybody who is.

170 The silence of the next few days must have been louder than the sound of all the music ever played since time began. One morning, before she went to work, Isabel was in his room for something and she suddenly realized that all of his records were gone. And she knew for certain that he was gone. And he was. He went as far as the navy would carry him. He finally sent me a postcard from some place in Greece and that was the first I knew that Sonny was still alive. I didn't see him any more until we were both back in New York and the war had long been over.

He was a man by then, of course, but I wasn't willing to see it. He came by the house from time to time, but we fought almost every time we met. I didn't like the way he carried himself, loose and dreamlike all the time, and I didn't like his friends, and his music seemed to be merely an excuse for the life he led. It sounded just that weird and disordered.

Then we had a fight, a pretty awful fight, and I didn't see him for months. By and by I looked him up, where he was living, in a furnished room in the Village, and I tried to make it up. But there were lots of other people in the room and Sonny just lay on his bed, and he wouldn't come downstairs with me, and he treated these other people as though they were his family and I weren't. So I got mad and then he got mad, and then I told him that he might just as well be dead as live the way he was living. Then he stood up and he told me not to worry about him any more in life, that he *was* dead as far as I was concerned. Then he pushed me to the door and the other people looked on as though nothing were happening, and he slammed the door behind me. I stood in the hallway, staring at the door. I heard somebody laugh in the room and then the tears came to my eyes. I started down the steps, whistling to keep from crying. I kept whistling to myself, *You going to need me, baby, one of these cold, rainy days.*

I read about Sonny's trouble in the spring. Little Grace died in the fall. She was a beautiful little girl. But she only lived a little over two years. She died of polio and she suffered. She had a slight fever for a couple of days, but it didn't seem like anything and we just kept her in bed. And we would certainly have called the doctor, but the fever dropped, and she seemed to be all right. So we thought it had just been a cold. Then, one day, she was up, playing, Isabel was in the kitchen fixing lunch for the two boys when they'd come in from school, and she heard Grace fall down in the living room. When you have a lot of children you don't always start running when one of them falls, unless they start screaming or something. And, this time, Grace was quiet. Yet, Isabel says that when she heard that *thump* and then that silence, something happened in her to make her afraid. And she ran to the living room and there was little Grace on the floor, all twisted up, and the reason she hadn't screamed was that she couldn't get her breath. And when she did scream, it was the worst sound, Isabel says, that she'd ever heard in all her life, and she still hears it sometimes in her dreams. Isabel will sometimes wake me up with a low, moaning, strangled sound and I have to be quick to awaken her and hold her to me and where Isabel is weeping against me seems a mortal wound.

I think I may have written Sonny the very day that little Grace was buried. I was sitting in the living room in the dark, by myself, and I suddenly thought of Sonny. My trouble made his real.

175 One Saturday afternoon, when Sonny had been living with us, or, anyway, been in our house, for nearly two weeks, I found myself wandering aimlessly about the living room, drinking from a can of beer, and trying to work up the courage to search Sonny's room. He was out, he was usually out whenever I was home, and Isabel had taken the children to see their grandparents. Suddenly I was standing still in front of the living room window, watching Seventh Avenue. The idea of searching Sonny's room made me still. I scarcely dared to admit to myself what I'd be searching for. I didn't know what I'd do if I found it. Or if I didn't.

On the sidewalk across from me, near the entrance to a barbecue joint, some people were holding an old-fashioned revival meeting. The barbecue cook, wearing a dirty white apron, his conked hair reddish and metallic in the pale sun, and a cigarette between his lips, stood in the doorway, watching them. Kids and older people paused in their errands and stood there, along with some older men and a couple of very tough-looking women who watched everything that happened on the avenue, as though they owned it, or were maybe owned by it. Well, they were watching this, too. The revival was being carried on by three sisters in black, and a brother. All they had were their voices and their Bibles and a tambourine. The brother was testifying and while he testified two of the sisters stood together, seeming to say, amen, and the third sister walked around with the tambourine outstretched and a couple of people dropped coins into it. Then the brother's testimony ended and the sister who had been taking up the collection dumped the coins into her palm and transferred them to the pocket of her long black robe. Then she raised both hands, striking the tambourine against the air, and then against one hand, and she started to sing. And the two other sisters and the brother joined in.

It was strange, suddenly, to watch, though I had been seeing these street meetings all my life. So, of course, had everybody else down there. Yet, they paused and watched and listened and I stood still at the window. *"Tis the old ship of Zion,"* they sang, and the sister with the tambourine kept a steady, jangling beat, *"it has rescued many a thousand!"* Not a soul under the sound of their voices was hearing this song for the first time, not one of them had been rescued. Nor had they seen much in the way of rescue work being done around them. Neither did they especially believe in the holiness of the three sisters and the brother, they knew too much about them, knew where they lived, and how. The woman with the tambourine, whose voice dominated the air, whose face was bright with joy, was divided by very little from the woman who stood watching her, a cigarette between her heavy, chapped lips, her hair a cuckoo's nest, her face scarred and swollen from many beatings, and her black eyes glittering like coal. Perhaps they both knew this, which was why, when, as rarely, they addressed each other, they addressed each other as Sister. As the singing filled the air the watching, listening faces underwent a change, and eyes focusing on something within; the music seemed to soothe a poison out of them; and time seemed, nearly, to fall away from the sullen, belligerent, battered faces, as though they were fleeing back to their first condition, while dreaming of their last. The barbecue cook half shook his head and smiled, and dropped his cigarette and disappeared into his joint. A man fumbled in his pockets for change and stood holding it in his hand impatiently, as though he had just remembered a pressing appointment further up the avenue. He looked furious. Then I saw Sonny, standing on the edge of the crowd. He was carrying a wide, flat notebook with a green cover, and it made him look, from where I was standing, almost like a schoolboy. The coppery sun brought out the copper in his skin, he was very faintly smiling, standing very still. Then the singing stopped, the tambourine turned into a collection plate again. The furious man dropped in his coins and vanished, so did a couple of the women, and Sonny dropped some change in the plate, looking directly at the woman with a little smile. He started across the avenue, toward the house. He has a slow, loping walk, something like the way Harlem hipsters walk, only he's imposed on this his own half-beat. I had never really noticed it before.

I stayed at the window, both relieved and apprehensive. As Sonny disappeared from my sight, they began singing again. And they were still singing when his key turned in the lock.

"Hey," he said.

180 "Hey, yourself. You want some beer?"

"No. Well, maybe." But he came up to the window and stood beside me, looking out. "What a warm voice," he said.

They were singing *If I could only hear my mother pray again!*

"Yes," I said, "and she can sure beat that tambourine."

"But what a terrible song," he said, and laughed. He dropped his notebook on the sofa and disappeared into the kitchen. "Where's Isabel and the kids?"

185 "I think they went to see their grandparents. You hungry?"

"No." He came back into the living room with his can of beer. "You want to come some place with me tonight?"

I sensed, I don't know how, that I couldn't possibly say no. "Sure. Where?"

He sat down on the sofa and picked up his notebook and started leafing through it. "I'm going to sit in with some fellows in a joint in the Village."

"You mean, you're going to play, tonight?"

190 "That's right." He took a swallow of his beer and moved back to the window. He gave me a sidelong look. "If you can stand it."

"I'll try," I said.

He smiled to himself and we both watched as the meeting across the way broke up. The three sisters and the brother, heads bowed, were singing *God be with you till we meet again.* The faces around them were very quiet. Then the song ended. The small crowd dispersed. We watched the three women and the lone man walk slowly up the avenue.

"When she was singing before," said Sonny, abruptly, "her voice reminded me for a minute of what heroin feels like sometimes—when it's in your veins. It makes you feel sort of warm and cool at the same time. And distant. And—and sure." He sipped his beer, very deliberately not looking at me. I watched his face. "It makes you feel—in control. Sometimes you've got to have that feeling."

"Do you?" I sat down slowly in the easy chair.

195 "Sometimes." He went to the sofa and picked up his notebook again. "Some people do."

"In order," I asked, "to play?" And my voice was very ugly, full of contempt and anger.

"Well"—he looked at me with great, troubled eyes, as though, in fact, he hoped his eyes would tell me things he could never otherwise say—"they *think* so. And *if* they think so—!"

"And what do *you* think?" I asked.

He sat on the sofa and put his can of beer on the floor. "I don't know," he said, and I couldn't be sure if he were answering my question or pursuing his thoughts. He face didn't tell me. "It's not so much to *play.* It's to *stand* it, to be able to make it at all. On any level." He frowned and smiled: "In order to keep from shaking to pieces."

200 "But these friends of yours," I said, "they seem to shake themselves to pieces pretty goddamn fast."

"Maybe." He played with the notebook. And something told me that I should curb my tongue, that Sonny was doing his best to talk, that I should listen. "But of course you only know the ones that've gone to pieces. Some don't—or at least they haven't *yet* and that's just about all *any* of us can say." He paused. "And then there are some who just live, really, in hell, and they know it and they see what's happening and they go right on. I don't know." He sighed, dropped the notebook, folded his arms. "Some guys, you can tell from the way they play, they on something *all* the time. And you can see that, well, it makes something real for them. But of course," he picked up his beer from the floor and sipped it and put the can down again, "they *want* to, too, you've got to see that. Even some of them that say they don't—*some,* not all."

"And what about you?" I asked—I couldn't help it. "What about you? Do *you* want to?"

He stood up and walked to the window and remained silent for a long time. Then he sighed. "Me," he said. Then: "While I was downstairs before, on my way here, listening to that woman sing, it struck me all of a sudden how much suffering she must have had to go through—to sing like that. It's *repulsive* to think you have to suffer that much."

I said: "But there's no way not to suffer—is there, Sonny?"

205 "I believe not," he said and smiled, "but that's never stopped anyone from trying." He looked at me. "Has it?" I realized, with this mocking look, that

there stood between us, forever, beyond the power of time or forgiveness, the fact that I had held silence—so long!—when he had needed human speech to help him. He turned back to the window. "No, there's no way not to suffer. But you try all kinds of ways to keep from drowning in it, to keep on top of it, and to make it seem—well, like *you.* Like you did something, all right, and now you're suffering for it. You know?" I said nothing. "Well you know," he said, impatiently, "why *do* people suffer? Maybe it's better to do something to give it a reason, *any* reason."

"But we just agreed," I said, "that there's no way not to suffer. Isn't it better, then, just to—take it?"

"But nobody just takes it," Sonny cried, "that's what I'm telling you! *Everybody* tries not to. You're just hung up on the *way* some people try—it's not *your* way!"

The hair on my face began to itch, my face felt wet. "That's not true," I said, "that's not true. I don't give a damn what other people do, I don't even care how they suffer. I just care how *you* suffer." And he looked at me. "Please believe me," I said, "I don't want to see you—die—trying not to suffer."

"I won't," he said, flatly, "die trying not to suffer. At least, not any faster than anybody else."

210 "But there's no need," I said, trying to laugh, "is there? in killing yourself."

I wanted to say more, but I couldn't. I wanted to talk about will power and how life could be—well, beautiful. I wanted to say that it was all within; but was it? or, rather, wasn't that exactly the trouble? And I wanted to promise that I would never fail him again. But it would all have sounded—empty words and lies.

So I made the promise to myself and prayed that I would keep it.

"It's terrible sometimes, inside," he said, "that's what's the trouble. You walk these streets, black and funky and cold, and there's not really a living ass to talk to, and there's nothing shaking, and there's no way of getting it out—that storm inside. You can't talk it and you can't make love with it, and when you finally try to get with it and play it, you realize *nobody's* listening. So *you've* got to listen. You got to find a way to listen."

And then he walked away from the window and sat on the sofa again, as though all the wind had suddenly been knocked out of him. "Sometimes you'll do *anything* to play, even cut your mother's throat." He laughed and looked at me. "Or your brother's." Then he sobered. "Or your own." Then: "Don't worry. I'm all right now and I think I'll *be* all right. But I can't forget—where I've been. I don't mean just the physical place I've been, I mean where I've *been.* And *what* I've been."

215 "What have you been, Sonny?" I asked.

He smiled—but sat sideways on the sofa, his elbow resting on the back, his fingers playing with his mouth and chin, not looking at me. "I've been something I didn't recognize, didn't know I could be. Didn't know anybody could be." He stopped, looking inward, looking helplessly young, looking old.

"I'm not talking about it now because I feel *guilty* or anything like that—maybe it would be better if I did, I don't know. Anyway, I can't really talk about it. Not to you, not to anybody," and now he turned and faced me. "Sometimes, you know, and it was actually when I was most *out* of the world, I felt that I was in it, that I was *with* it, really, and I could play or I didn't really have to *play,* it just came out of me, it was there. And I don't know how I played, thinking about it now, but I know I did awful things, those times, sometimes, to people. Or it wasn't that I *did* anything to them—it was that they weren't real." He picked up the beer can; it was empty; he rolled it between his palms: "And other times—well, I needed a fix, I needed to find a place to lean, I needed to clear a space to *listen*—and I couldn't find it, and I—went crazy, I did terrible things to *me,* I was terrible *for* me." He began pressing the beer can between his hands, I watched the metal begin to give. It glittered, as he played with it, like a knife, and I was afraid he would cut himself, but I said nothing. "Oh well, I can never tell you. I was all by myself at the bottom of something, stinking and sweating and crying and shaking, and I smelled it, you know? *my* stink, and I thought I'd die if I couldn't get away from it and yet, all the same, I knew that everything I was doing was just locking me in with it. And I didn't know," he paused, still flattening the beer can, "I didn't know, I still *don't* know, something kept telling me that maybe it was good to smell your own stink, but I didn't think that *that* was what I'd been trying to do—and—who can stand it?" and he abruptly dropped the ruined beer can, looking at me with a small, still smile, and then rose, walking to the window as though it were the lodestone rock. I watched his face, he watched the avenue. "I couldn't tell you when Mama died—but the reason I wanted to leave Harlem so bad was to get away from drugs. And then, when I ran away, that's what I was running from—really. When I came back, nothing had changed, *I* hadn't changed, I was just—older." And he stopped, drumming with his fingers on the windowpane. The sun had vanished, soon darkness would fall. I watched his face. "It can come again," he said, almost as though speaking to himself. Then he turned to me. "It can come again," he repeated. "I just want you to know that."

"All right," I said, at last. "So it can come again, All right."

He smiled, but the smile was sorrowful. "I had to try to tell you," he said.

"Yes," I said. "I understand that."

220 "You're my brother," he said, looking straight at me, and not smiling at all.

"Yes," I repeated, "yes. I understand that."

He turned back to the window, looking out. "All that hatred down there," he said, "all that hatred and misery and love. It's a wonder it doesn't blow the avenue apart."

We went to the only nightclub on a short, dark street, downtown. We squeezed through the narrow, chattering, jampacked bar to the entrance of the big room, where the bandstand was. And we stood there for a moment, for the lights were very dim in this room and we couldn't see. Then, "Hello, boy," said a voice and an enormous black man, much older than Sonny or myself, erupted out of all that atmospheric lighting and put an arm around Sonny's shoulder. "I been sitting right here," he said, "waiting for you."

He had a big voice, too, and heads in the darkness turned toward us.

Sonny grinned and pulled a little away, and said, "Creole, this is my brother. I told you about him."

Creole shook my hand. "I'm glad to meet you, son," he said, and it was clear that he was glad to meet me *there,* for Sonny's sake. And he smiled, "You got a real musician in *your* family," and he took his arm from Sonny's shoulder and slapped him, lightly, affectionately, with the back of his hand.

"Well. Now I've heard it all," said a voice behind us. This was another musician, and a friend of Sonny's, a coal-black, cheerful-looking man, built close to the ground. He immediately began confiding to me, at the top of his lungs, the most terrible things about Sonny, his teeth gleaming like a lighthouse and his laugh coming up out of him like the beginning of an earthquake. And it turned out that everyone at the bar knew Sonny, or almost everyone; some were musicians, working there, or nearby, or not working, some were simply hangers-on, and some were there to hear Sonny play. I was introduced to all of them and they were all very polite to me. Yet it was clear that, for them, I was only Sonny's brother. Here, I was in Sonny's world. Or, rather: his kingdom. Here, it was not even a question that his veins bore royal blood.

They were going to play soon and Creole installed me, by myself, at a table in a dark corner. Then I watched them, Creole, and the little black man, and Sonny, and the others, while they horsed around, standing just below the bandstand. The light from the bandstand spilled just a little short of them and, watching them laughing and gesturing and moving about, I had the feeling that they, nevertheless, were being most careful not to step into that circle of light too suddenly: that if they moved into the light too suddenly, without thinking, they would perish in flame. Then, while I watched, one of them, the small, black man, moved into the light and crossed the bandstand and started fooling around with his drums. Then—being funny and being, also, extremely ceremonious—Creole took Sonny by the arm and led him to the piano. A woman's voice called Sonny's name and a few hands started clapping. And Sonny, also being funny and being ceremonious, and so touched, I think, that he could have cried, but neither hiding it nor showing it, riding it like a man, grinned, and put both hands to his heart and bowed from the waist.

Creole then went to the bass fiddle and a lean, very bright-skinned brown man jumped up on the bandstand and picked up his horn. So there they were, and the atmosphere on the bandstand and in the room began to change and tighten. Someone stepped up to the microphone and announced them. Then there were all kinds of murmurs. Some people at the bar shushed others. The waitress ran around, frantically getting in the last orders, guys and chicks got closer to each other, and the lights on the bandstand, on the quartet, turned to a kind of indigo. Then they all looked different there. Creole looked about him for the last time, as though he were making certain that all his chickens were in the coop, and then he—jumped and struck the fiddle. And there they were.

230 All I know about music is that not many people ever really hear it. And even then, on the rare occasions when something opens within, and the music enters, what we mainly hear, or hear corroborated, are personal, private, vanishing evocations. But the man who creates the music is hearing something else, is dealing with the roar rising from the void and imposing order on it as it hits the air. What is evoked in him, then, is of another order, more terrible because it has no words, and triumphant, too, for that same reason. And his triumph, when he triumphs, is ours. I just watched Sonny's face. His face was troubled, he was working hard, but he wasn't with it. And I had the feeling that, in a way, everyone on the bandstand was waiting for him, both waiting for him and pushing him along. But as I began to watch Creole, I realized that it was Creole who held them all back. He had them on a short rein. Up there, keeping the beat with his whole body, wailing on the fiddle, with his eyes half closed, he was listening to everything, but he was listening to Sonny. He was having a dialogue with Sonny. He wanted Sonny to leave the shoreline and strike out for the deep water. He was Sonny's witness that deep water and drowning were not the same thing—he had been there, and he knew. And he wanted Sonny to know. He was waiting for Sonny to do the things on the keys which would let Creole know that Sonny was in the water.

And, while Creole listened, Sonny moved, deep within, exactly like someone in torment. I had never before thought of how awful the relationship must be between the musician and his instrument. He has to fill it, this instrument, with the breath of life, his own. He has to make it do what he wants it to do. And a piano is just a piano. It's made out of so much wood and wires and little hammers and big ones, and ivory. While there's only so much you can do with it, the only way to find this out is to try; to try and make it do everything.

And Sonny hadn't been near a piano for over a year. And he wasn't on much better terms with his life, not the life that stretched before him now. He and the piano stammered, started one way, got scared, stopped; started another way, panicked, marked time, started again; then seemed to have found a direction, panicked again, got stuck. And the face I saw on Sonny I'd never seen before. Everything had been burned out of it, and, at the same time, things usually hidden were being burned in, by the fire and fury of the battle which was occurring in him up there.

Yet, watching Creole's face as they neared the end of the first set, I had the feeling that something had happened, something I hadn't heard. Then they finished, there was scattered applause, and then, without an instant's warning, Creole started into something else, it was almost sardonic, it was *Am I Blue*. And, as though he commanded, Sonny began to play. Something began to happen. And Creole let out the reins. The dry, low, black man said something awful on the drums, Creole answered, and the drums talked back. Then the horn insisted, sweet and high, slightly detached perhaps, and Creole listened, commenting now and then, dry, and driving, beautiful and calm and old. Then they all came together again, and Sonny was part of the family again. I could tell this from his face. He seemed to have found, right there beneath his fingers, a damn brand-new piano. It seemed that he couldn't get over it. Then, for awhile, just being happy with Sonny, they seemed to be agreeing with him that brand-new pianos certainly were a gas.

Then Creole stepped forward to remind them that what they were playing was the blues. He hit something in all of them, he hit something in me, myself, and the music tightened and deepened, apprehension began to beat the air. Creole began to tell us what the blues were all about. They were not about anything very new. He and his boys up there were keeping it new, at the risk of ruin, destruction, madness, and death, in order to find new ways to make us listen. For, while the tale of how we suffer, and how we are delighted, and how we may triumph is never new, it always must be heard. There isn't any other tale to tell, it's the only light we've got in all this darkness.

235 And this tale, according to that face, that body, those strong hands on those strings, has another aspect in every country, and a new depth in every generation. Listen, Creole seemed to be saying, listen. Now these are Sonny's blues. He made the little black man on the drums know it, and the bright, brown man on the horn. Creole wasn't trying any longer to get Sonny in the water. He was wishing him Godspeed. Then he stepped back, very slowly, filling the air with the immense suggestion that Sonny speak for himself.

Then they all gathered around Sonny and Sonny played. Every now and again one of them seemed to say, amen. Sonny's fingers filled the air with life, his life. But that life contained so many others. And Sonny went all the way back, he really began with the spare, flat statement of the opening phrase of the song. Then he began to make it his. It was very beautiful because it wasn't hurried and it was no longer a lament. I seemed to hear with what burning he had made it his, with what burning we had yet to make it ours, how we could cease lamenting. Freedom lurked around us and I understood, at last, that he could help us to be free if we would listen, that he would never be free until we did. Yet, there was no battle in his face now. I heard what he had gone through, and would continue to go through until he came to rest in earth. He had made it his: that long line, of which we knew only Mama and Daddy. And he was giving it back, as everything must be given back, so that, passing through death, it can live forever. I saw my mother's face again, and felt, for the first time, how the stones of the road she had walked on must have bruised her feet. I saw the moonlit road where my father's brother died. And it brought something else back to me, and carried me past it, I saw my little girl again and felt Isabel's tears again, and I felt my own tears begin to rise. And I was yet aware that this was only a moment, that the world waited outside, as hungry as a tiger, and that trouble stretched above us, longer than the sky.

Then it was over. Creole and Sonny let out their breath, both soaking wet, and grinning. There was a lot of applause and some of it was real. In the dark, the girl came by and I asked her to take drinks to the bandstand. There was a long pause, while they talked up there in the indigo light and after awhile I saw a girl put a Scotch and milk on top of the piano for Sonny. He didn't seem to notice it, but just before they started playing again, he sipped from it and looked toward me, and nodded. Then he put it back on top of the piano. For me, then, as they began to play again, it glowed and shook above my brother's head like the very cup of trembling.[4]

Explorations of the Text

1. After reading the first paragraph, what do you predict about the **narrator** and about the **plot** of the story? Why is the narrator's face "trapped in the darkness which roared outside"? What does the "darkness . . . outside" signify to the children? To the adult narrator? To us as readers?
2. Explore the metaphor of "the block of ice." What does the metaphor reveal about the narrator's feelings for Sonny?
3. What characterizes the narrator's relationship with his brother at the beginning of the story?
4. Characterize the narrator. What is revealed about his personality in his constant position as an onlooker (at the window in the schoolroom, at the window in his apartment, at the jazz club)?
5. Compare and contrast the narrator and Sonny. Why have they grown up differently?
6. Why does Sonny turn to the life of the streets? drugs? What importance does music play in his life?
7. Why does the relationship between the narrator and Sonny change? What are the narrator's feelings for his brother at the end of the story?
8. What is the meaning of the scene in the club at the end? What does the narrator realize? What does the scotch and milk cocktail that the narrator sends up to Sonny symbolize?
9. The story is told through a series of **flashbacks.** What would the story lose if it were structured chronologically?

The Reading/Writing Connection

1. Baldwin published this story in 1957 about life in Harlem. Does this vision of life still seem real? What might Baldwin write about today?
2. Freewrite and respond to a nonverbal art form (a photograph, a painting, a piece of music) so that someone unfamiliar with the work can share your feelings.
3. "Think" Topic: Will Sonny be saved by music?

[4] An allusion to the Bible, Isaiah 51:22; "I have taken out of thine hand the cup of trembling . . . thou shalt no more drink it again. . . ."

Ideas for Writing

1. Is violence part of the life of the nuclear family? Explore this **theme** in the works of Hayden, Diaz, and/or Baldwin.
2. How do the images of light and darkness function in this story? What do they suggest about growing up in Harlem?
3. Imagine Sonny's future.
4. What are the causes of Sonny's problems? Propose possible solutions. (Use Journal Entry 1 as a beginning.)

This Is What It Means to Say Phoenix, Arizona

Sherman Alexie

Sherman Alexie (1966–), a Spokane/Coeur d'Alene Indian, was born on the Spokane Indian Reservation in Wellpinit, Washington. He graduated from Washington State University. By the time his first novel, Reservation Blues *(1995), was published, Alexie had published over three hundred poems, stories, essays, and reviews. His other works include a novel,* Indian Killer *(1996), and the short story collections,* The Lone Ranger and Tonto Fistfight in Heaven *(1993), which served as the basis for the 1998 film* Smoke Signals, *and* The Toughest Indian in the World *(2000).*

1993

Just after Victor lost his job at the Bureau of Indian Affairs, he also found out that his father had died of a heart attack in Phoenix, Arizona. Victor hadn't seen his father in a few years, had only talked to him on the telephone once or twice, but there still was a genetic pain, which was as real and immediate as a broken bone. Victor didn't have any money. Who does have money on a reservation, except the cigarette and fireworks salespeople? His father had a savings account waiting to be claimed, but Victor needed to find a way to get from Spokane to Phoenix. Victor's mother was just as poor as he was, and the rest of the family didn't have any use at all for him. So Victor called the tribal council.

"Listen," Victor said. "My father just died. I need some money to get to Phoenix to make arrangements."

"Now, Victor," the council said, "you know we're having a difficult time financially."

"But I thought the council had special funds set aside for stuff like this."

5 "Now, Victor, we do have some money available for the proper return of tribal members' bodies. But I don't think we have enough to bring your father all the way back from Phoenix."

"Well," Victor said. "It ain't going to cost all that much. He had to be cremated. Things were kind of ugly. He died of a heart attack in his trailer and nobody found him for a week. It was really hot, too. You get the picture."

"Now, Victor, we're sorry for your loss and the circumstances. But we can really only afford to give you one hundred dollars."

"That's not even enough for a plane ticket."

"Well, you might consider driving down to Phoenix."

10 "I don't have a car. Besides, I was going to drive my father's pickup back up here."

"Now, Victor," the council said, "we're sure there is somebody who could drive you to Phoenix. Or could anybody lend you the rest of the money?"

"You know there ain't nobody around with that kind of money."

"Well, we're sorry, Victor, but that's the best we can do."

Victor accepted the tribal council's offer. What else could he do? So he signed the proper papers, picked up his check, and walked over to the Trading Post to cash it.

15 While Victor stood in line, he watched Thomas Builds-the-Fire standing near the magazine rack talking to himself. Like he always did. Thomas was a storyteller whom nobody wanted to listen to. That's like being a dentist in a town where everybody has false teeth.

Victor and Thomas Builds-the-Fire were the same age, had grown up and played in the dirt together. Ever since Victor could remember, it was Thomas who had always had something to say.

Once, when they were seven years old, when Victor's father still lived with the family, Thomas closed his eyes and told Victor this story: "Your father's heart is weak. He is afraid of his own family. He is afraid of you. Late at night, he sits in the dark. Watches the television until there's nothing but that white noise. Sometimes he feels like he wants to buy a motorcycle and ride away. He wants to run and hide. He doesn't want to be found."

Thomas Builds-the-Fire had known that Victor's father was going to leave, known it before anyone. Now Victor stood in the Trading Post with a one-hundred-dollar check in his hand, wondering if Thomas knew that Victor's father was dead, if he knew what was going to happen next.

Just then, Thomas looked at Victor, smiled, and walked over to him.

20 "Victor, I'm sorry about your father," Thomas said.

"How did you know about it?" Victor asked.

"I heard it on the wind. I heard it from the birds. I felt it in the sunlight. Also, your mother was just in here crying."

"Oh," Victor said and looked around the Trading Post. All the other Indians stared, surprised that Victor was even talking to Thomas. Nobody talked to Thomas anymore because he told the same damn stories over and over again. Victor was embarrassed, but he thought that Thomas might be able to help him. Victor felt a sudden need for tradition.

"I can lend you the money you need," Thomas said suddenly. "But you have to take me with you."

25 "I can't take your money," Victor said. "I mean, I haven't hardly talked to you in years. We're not really friends anymore."

"I didn't say we were friends. I said you had to take me with you."

"Let me think about it."

Victor went home with his one hundred dollars and sat at the kitchen table. He held his head in his hands and thought about Thomas Builds-the-Fire, remembered little details, tears and scars, the bicycle they shared for a summer, so many stories.

Thomas Builds-the-Fire sat on the bicycle, waiting in Victor's yard. He was ten years old and skinny. His hair was dirty because it was the Fourth of July.

"Victor," Thomas yelled. "Hurry up. We're going to miss the fireworks."

After a few minutes, Victor ran out of his family's house, vaulted over the porch railing, and landed gracefully on the sidewalk.

Thomas gave him the bike and they headed for the fireworks. It was nearly dark and the fireworks were about to start.

"You know," Thomas said, "it's strange how us Indians celebrate the Fourth of July. It ain't like it was our independence everybody was fighting for."

"You think about things too much," Victor said. "It's just supposed to be fun. Maybe Junior will be there."

"Which Junior? Everybody on this reservation is named Junior."

The fireworks were small, hardly more than a few bottle rockets and a fountain. But it was enough for two Indian boys. Years later, they would need much more.

Afterward, sitting in the dark, fighting off mosquitoes, Victor turned to Thomas Builds-the-Fire.

"Hey," Victor said. "Tell me a story."

Thomas closed his eyes and told this story: "There were these two Indian boys who wanted to be warriors. But it was too late to be warriors in the old way. All the horses were gone. So the two Indian boys stole a car and drove to the city. They parked the stolen car in the front of the police station and then hitchhiked back home to the reservation. When they got back, all their friends cheered and their parents' eyes shone with pride. 'You were very brave,' everybody said to the two Indian boys. 'Very brave.' "

"Ya-hey," Victor said. "That's a good one. I wish I could be a warrior."

"Me too." Thomas said.

Victor sat at his kitchen table. He counted his one hundred dollars again and again. He knew he needed more to make it to Phoenix and back. He knew he needed Thomas Builds-the-Fire. So he put his money in his wallet and opened the front door to find Thomas on the porch.

"Ya-hey, Victor," Thomas said. "I knew you'd call me."

Thomas walked into the living room and sat down in Victor's favorite chair.

"I've got some money saved up," Thomas said. "It's enough to get us down there, but you have to get us back."

"I've got this hundred dollars," Victor said. "And my dad had a savings account I'm going to claim."

"How much in your dad's account?"

"Enough. A few hundred."

"Sounds good. When we leaving?"

50 When they were fifteen and had long since stopped being friends, Victor and Thomas got into a fistfight. That is, Victor was really drunk and beat Thomas up for no reason at all. All the other Indian boys stood around and watched it happen. Junior was there and so were Lester, Seymour, and a lot of others.

The beating might have gone on until Thomas was dead if Norma Many Horses hadn't come along and stopped it.

"Hey, you boys," Norma yelled and jumped out of her car. "Leave him alone."

If it had been someone else, even another man, the Indian boys would've just ignored the warnings. But Norma was a warrior. She was powerful. She could have picked up any two of the boys and smashed their skulls together. But worse than that, she would have dragged them all over to some tepee and made them listen to some elder tell a dusty old story.

The Indian boys scattered, and Norma walked over to Thomas and picked him up.

55 "Hey, little man, are you O.K.?" she asked.

Thomas gave her a thumbs-up.

"Why they always picking on you?"

Thomas shook his head, closed his eyes, but no stories came to him, no words or music. He just wanted to go home, to lie in his bed and let his dreams tell the stories for him.

* * *

Thomas Builds-the-Fire and Victor sat next to each other in the airplane, coach section. A tiny white woman had the window seat. She was busy twisting her body into pretzels. She was flexible.

60 "I have to ask," Thomas said, and Victor closed his eyes in embarrassment.

"Don't," Victor said.

"Excuse me, miss," Thomas asked. "Are you a gymnast or something?"

"There's no something about it," she said. "I was first alternate on the 1980 Olympic team."

"Really?" Thomas asked.

65 "Really."

"I mean, you used to be a world-class athlete?" Thomas asked.

"My husband thinks I still am."

Thomas Builds-the-Fire smiled. She was a mental gymnast too. She pulled her leg straight up against her body so that she could've kissed her kneecap.

"I wish I could do that," Thomas said.

70 Victor was ready to jump out of the plane. Thomas, that crazy Indian storyteller with ratty old braids and broken teeth, was flirting with a beautiful Olympic gymnast. Nobody back home on the reservation would ever believe it.

"Well," the gymnast said. "It's easy. Try it."

Thomas grabbed at his leg and tried to pull it up into the same position as the gymnast's. He couldn't even come close, which made Victor and the gymnast laugh.

"Hey," she asked. "You two are Indian, right?"

"Full-blood," Victor said.

75 "Not me," Thomas said. "I'm half magician on my mother's side and half clown on my father's."

They all laughed.

"What are your names?" she asked.

"Victor and Thomas."

"Mine is Cathy. Pleased to meet you all."

80 The three of them talked for the duration of the flight. Cathy the gymnast complained about the government, how they screwed the 1980 Olympic team by boycotting the games.[1]

"Sounds like you all got a lot in common with Indians," Thomas said.

Nobody laughed.

After the plane landed in Phoenix and they had all found their way to the terminal, Cathy the gymnast smiled and waved goodbye.

"She was really nice," Thomas said.

85 "Yeah, but everybody talks to everybody on airplanes," Victor said.

"You always used to tell me I think too much," Thomas said. "Now it sounds like you do."

"Maybe I caught it from you."

"Yeah."

Thomas and Victor rode in a taxi to the trailer where Victor's father had died.

90 "Listen," Victor said as they stopped in front of the trailer. "I never told you I was sorry for beating you up that time."

"Oh, it was nothing. We were just kids and you were drunk."

"Yeah, but I'm still sorry."

"That's all right."

Victor paid for the taxi, and the two of them stood in the hot Phoenix summer. They could smell the trailer.

95 "This ain't going to be nice," Victor said. "You don't have to go in."

"You're going to need help."

Victor walked to the front door and opened it. The stink rolled out and made them both gag. Victor's father had lain in that trailer for a week in hundred-degree temperatures before anyone had found him. And the only reason anyone found him was the smell. They needed dental records to identify him. That's exactly what the coroner said. They needed dental records.

"Oh, man," Victor said. "I don't know if I can do this."

"Well, then don't."

---

[1] To protest the Soviet military action in Afghanistan, sixty-two nations including the United States boycotted the 1980 Olympics held in Moscow.

100 "But there might be something valuable in there."

"I thought his money was in the bank."

"It is. I was talking about pictures and letters and stuff like that."

"Oh," Thomas said as he held his breath and followed Victor into the trailer.

When Victor was twelve, he stepped into an underground wasps' nest. His foot was caught in the hole and no matter how hard he struggled, Victor couldn't pull free. He might have died there, stung a thousand times, if Thomas Builds-the-Fire had not come by.

105 "Run," Thomas yelled and pulled Victor's foot from the hole. They ran then, hard as they ever had, faster than Billy Mills, faster than Jim Thorpe,[2] faster than the wasps could fly.

Victor and Thomas ran until they couldn't breathe, ran until it was cold and dark outside, ran until they were lost and it took hours to find their way home. All the way back, Victor counted his stings.

"Seven," Victor said. "My lucky number."

* * *

Victor didn't find much to keep in the trailer. Only a photo album and a stereo. Everything else had that smell stuck in it or was useless anyway. "I guess this is all," Victor said. "It ain't much."

"Better than nothing," Thomas said.

110 "Yeah, and I do have the pickup."

"Yeah," Thomas said. "It's in good shape."

"Dad was good about that stuff."

"Yeah, I remember your dad."

"Really?" Victor asked. "What do you remember?"

115 Thomas Builds-the-Fire closed his eyes and told this story: "I remember when I had this dream that told me to go to Spokane, to stand by the falls in the middle of the city and wait for a sign. I knew I had to go there but I didn't have a car. Didn't have a license. I was only thirteen. So I walked all the way, took me all day, and I finally made it to the falls. I stood there for an hour waiting. Then your dad came walking up. 'What the hell are you doing here?' he asked me. I said, 'Waiting for a vision.' Then your father said, 'All you're going to get here is mugged.' So he drove me over to Denny's bought me dinner, and then drove me home to the reservation. For a long time, I was mad because I thought my dreams had lied to me. But they hadn't. Your dad was my vision. *Take care of each other* is what my dreams were saying. *Take care of each other.*"

Victor was quiet for a long time. He searched his mind for memories of his father, found the good ones, found a few bad ones, added it all up, and smiled.

[2] U.S. athletes who were Native American.

"My father never told me about finding you in Spokane," Victor said.

"He said he wouldn't tell anybody. Didn't want me to get in trouble. But he said I had to watch out for you as part of the deal."

"Really?"

"Really. Your father said you would need the help. He was right."

"That's why you came down here with me, isn't it?" Victor asked.

"I came because of your father."

Victor and Thomas climbed into the pickup, drove over to the bank, and claimed the three hundred dollars in the savings account.

Thomas Builds-the-Fire could fly.

Once, he jumped off the roof of the tribal school and flapped his arms like a crazy eagle. And he flew. For a second he hovered, suspended above all the other Indian boys, who were too smart or too scared to jump too.

"He's flying," Junior yelled, and Seymour was busy looking for the trick wires or mirrors. But it was real. As real as the dirt when Thomas lost altitude and crashed to the ground.

He broke his arm in two places.

"He broke his wing, he broke his wing, he broke his wing," all the Indian boys chanted as they ran off, flapping their wings, wishing they could fly too. They hated Thomas for his courage, his brief moment as a bird. Everybody has dreams about flying. Thomas flew.

One of his dreams came true for just a second, just enough to make it real.

Victor's father, his ashes, fit in one wooden box with enough left over to fill a cardboard box.

"He always was a big man," Thomas said.

Victor carried part of his father out to the pickup, and Thomas carried the rest. They set him down carefully behind the seats, put a cowboy hat on the wooden box and a Dodgers cap on the cardboard box. That was the way it was supposed to be.

"Ready to head back home?" Victor asked.

"It's going to be a long drive."

"Yeah, take a couple days, maybe."

"We can take turns," Thomas said.

"O.K.," Victor said, but they didn't take turns. Victor drove for sixteen hours straight north, made it halfway up Nevada toward home before he finally pulled over.

"Hey, Thomas," Victor said. "You got to drive for a while."

"O.K."

Thomas Builds-the-Fire slid behind the wheel and started off down the road. All through Nevada, Thomas and Victor had been amazed at the lack of animal life, at the absence of water, of movement.

"Where is everything?" Victor had asked more than once.

Now, when Thomas was finally driving, they saw the first animal, maybe the only animal in Nevada. It was a long-eared jackrabbit.

"Look," Victor yelled. "It's alive."

Thomas and Victor were busy congratulating themselves on their discovery when the jackrabbit darted out into the road and under the wheels of the pickup.

"Stop the goddamn car," Victor yelled, and Thomas did stop and backed the pickup to the dead jackrabbit.

"Oh, man, he's dead," Victor said as he looked at the squashed animal.

"Really dead."

"The only thing alive in this whole state and we just killed it."

"I don't know," Thomas said. "I think it was suicide."

Victor looked around the desert, sniffed the air, felt the emptiness and loneliness, and nodded his head.

"Yeah," Victor said. "It had to be suicide."

"I can't believe this," Thomas said. "You drive for a thousand miles and there ain't even any bugs smashed on the windshield. I drive for ten seconds and kill the only living thing in Nevada."

"Yeah," Victor said. "Maybe I should drive."

"Maybe you should."

Thomas Builds-the-Fire walked through the corridors of the tribal school by himself. Nobody wanted to be anywhere near him because of all those stories. Story after story.

Thomas closed his eyes and this story came to him: "We are all given one thing by which our lives are measured, one determination. Mine are the stories that can change or not change the world. It doesn't matter which, as long as I continue to tell the stories. My father, he died on Okinawa in World War II,[3] died fighting for this country, which had tried to kill him for years. My mother, she died giving birth to me, died while I was still inside her: She pushed me out into the world with her last breath. I have no brothers or sisters. I have only my stories, which came to me before I even had the words to speak. I learned a thousand stories before I took my first thousand steps. They are all I have. It's all I can do."

Thomas Builds-the-Fire told his stories to all those who would stop and listen. He kept telling them long after people had stopped listening.

Victor and Thomas made it back to the reservation just as the sun was rising. It was the beginning of a new day on earth, but the same old shit on the reservation.

"Good morning," Thomas said.

---

[3] Okinawa, one of the largest of the Ryukyu Islands, occupied by U.S. forces 1945–72 and returned to Japan in 1972.

160 "Good morning."

The tribe was waking up, ready for work, eating breakfast, reading the newspaper, just like everybody else does. Willene LeBret was out in her garden, wearing a bathrobe. She waved when Thomas and Victor drove by.

"Crazy Indians made it," she said to herself and went back to her roses.

Victor stopped the pickup in front of Thomas Build-the-Fire's HUD house. They both yawned, stretched a little, shook dust from their bodies.

"I'm tired," Victor said.

165 "Of everything," Thomas added.

They both searched for words to end the journey. Victor needed to thank Thomas for his help and for the money, and to make the promise to pay it all back.

"Don't worry about the money," Thomas said. "It don't make any difference anyhow."

"Probably not, enit?"

"Nope."

170 Victor knew that Thomas would remain the crazy storyteller who talked to dogs and cars, who listened to the wind and pine trees. Victor knew that he couldn't really be friends with Thomas, even after all that had happened. It was cruel but it was real. As real as the ash, as Victor's father, sitting behind the seats.

"I know how it is," Thomas said. "I know you ain't going to treat me any better than you did before. I know your friends would give you too much shit about it."

Victor was ashamed of himself. Whatever happened to the tribal ties, the sense of community? The only real thing he shared with anybody was a bottle and broken dreams. He owed Thomas something, anything.

"Listen," Victor said and handed Thomas the cardboard box that contained half of his father. "I want you to have this."

Thomas took the ashes and smiled, closed his eyes, and told this story: "I'm going to travel to Spokane Falls one last time and toss these ashes into the water. And your father will rise like a salmon, leap over the bridge, over me, and find his way home. It will be beautiful. His teeth will shine like silver, like a rainbow. He will rise, Victor, he will rise."

175 Victor smiled.

"I was planning on doing the same thing with my half," Victor said. "But I didn't imaging my father looking anything like a salmon. I thought it'd be like cleaning the attic or something. Like letting things go after they've stopped having any use."

"Nothing stops, cousin," Thomas said. "Nothing stops."

Thomas Builds-the-Fire got out of the pickup and walked up his driveway. Victor started the pickup and began the drive home.

"Wait," Thomas yelled suddenly from his porch. "I just got to ask one favor."

180 Victor stopped the pickup, leaned out the window, and shouted back.

"What do you want?" he asked.

"Just one time when I'm telling a story somewhere, why don't you stop and listen?" Thomas asked.

"Just once?"

"Just once."

Victor waved his arms to let Thomas know that the deal was good. It was a fair trade. That's all Thomas had ever wanted from his whole life. So Victor drove his father's pickup toward home while Thomas went into his house, closed the door behind him, and heard a new story come to him in the silence afterward.

Explorations of the Text

1. How do the settings—real and imagined—create the context, atmosphere, and mood of the story (i.e., the Indian reservation; the plane; the trailer in Phoenix, Arizona; the desert in Nevada; and the falls in Spokane)?
2. Analyze Thomas's and Victor's characters. Why weren't they friends in childhood? How do they differ?
3. Discuss the stages of the journey. What do the two protagonists learn by the end of the trip? How does the gymnast function as a character foil?
4. Interpret the symbolism of the falls in Spokane and of Thomas's dream.
5. Explore the significance of storytelling as a motif in the story.
6. Are the flashbacks and dream sequences an effective means of exposition? Does the structure of the story work?
7. Compare the views of heritage presented in this work with those ideas expressed in "Heritage" (chapter 8) and "The Idea of Ancestry."
8. Compare the father-son relationships in "My Father's Song," "Persimmons," "Digging," and this work.

The Reading/Writing Connection

1. List questions that you have about this story. After class discussion of the work, return to your questions and answer one of them.
2. Freewrite about your initial impression of the work. After class discussion, write a second freewrite. Compare your first and final impressions. How have your views of the work changed?
3. "Think" Topic: Who is the true "warrior"—Victor or Thomas?
4. Journal Entry: Read this poetic excerpt from the film script for *Smoke Signals*—Sherman Alexie's film adaptation of this story—then answer this question: "Do we forgive our fathers?" You may substitute "mothers" for "fathers." Respond.

Do we forgive our fathers for leaving us too often or
forever when we were little? Maybe for scaring us with
unexpected rage or making us nervous because there never
seemed to be any rage there at all?

Do we forgive our fathers for marrying or not marrying
our mother? For divorcing or not divorcing our mothers?
And shall we forgive them for their excesses of warmth or
coldness?

Shall we forgive them for pushing or leaning? For shutting
doors? For speaking only through layers of cloth, or never
speaking, or never being silent?

Do we forgive our fathers in our age or in theirs? Or in
their deaths? Saying it to them or not saying it? If we
forgive our fathers what is left?

Ideas for Writing

1. Connect themes of the poem with those of the story.
2. Watch *Smoke Signals.* Compare the story and the film. Or compare the poetic excerpt (which is the conclusion of the script) with the story's ending. Which has more power—the written or visual form?

SCAR FROM *THE JOY LUCK CLUB*

Amy Tan

Amy Tan (1952–) was born in Oakland, California, shortly after her parents immigrated to the United States from China. She was educated at San Francisco State University and San Jose University. In 1989, she published her first book of fiction, The Joy Luck Club. *Her novels include* The Kitchen God's Wife *(1991),* The Hundred Secret Senses *(1996), and* The Bonesetter's Daughter *(2001). In her work, Tan explores her Chinese heritage and the relationships between generations, especially those between Chinese immigrants to America and their children.*

1989

When I was a young girl in China, my grandmother told me my mother was a ghost. This did not mean my mother was dead. In those days, a ghost was anything we were forbidden to talk about. So I knew Popo wanted me to forget my mother on purpose, and this is how I came to remember nothing of her. The life that I knew began in the large house in Ningpo with the cold hallways and tall stairs. This was my uncle and auntie's family house, where I lived with Popo and my little brother.

But I often heard stories of a ghost who tried to take children away, especially strong-willed little girls who were disobedient. Many times Popo said aloud to all who could hear that my brother and I had fallen out of the bowels of a stupid goose, two eggs that nobody wanted, not even good enough to crack over rice porridge. She said this so that the ghosts would not steal us away. So you see, to Popo we were also very precious.

All my life, Popo scared me. I became even more scared when she grew sick. This was in 1923, when I was nine years old. Popo had swollen up like an overripe squash, so full her flesh had gone soft and rotten with a bad smell. She would call me into her room with the terrible stink and tell me stories. "An-mei," she said, calling me by my school name. "Listen carefully." She told me stories I could not understand.

One was about a greedy girl whose belly grew fatter and fatter. This girl poisoned herself after refusing to say whose child she carried. When the monks cut open her body, they found inside a large white winter melon.

5 "If you are greedy, what is inside you is what makes you always hungry," said Popo.

Another time, Popo told me about a girl who refused to listen to her elders. One day this bad girl shook her head so vigorously to refuse her auntie's simple request that a little white ball fell from her ear and out poured all her brains, as clear as chicken broth.

"Your own thoughts are so busy swimming inside that everything else gets pushed out," Popo told me.

Right before Popo became so sick she could no longer speak, she pulled me close and talked to me about my mother. "Never say her name," she warned. "To say her name is to spit on your father's grave."

The only father I knew was a big painting that hung in the main hall. He was a large, unsmiling man, unhappy to be so still on the wall. His restless eyes followed me around the house. Even from my room at the end of the hall, I could see my father's watching eyes. Popo said he watched me for any signs of disrespect. So sometimes, when I had thrown pebbles at other children at school, or had lost a book through carelessness, I would quickly walk by my father with a know-nothing look and hide in a corner of my room where he could not see my face.

10 I felt our house was so unhappy, but my little brother did not seem to think so. He rode his bicycle through the courtyard, chasing chickens and other children, laughing over which ones shrieked the loudest. Inside the quiet house, he jumped up and down on Uncle and Auntie's best feather sofas when they were away visiting village friends.

But even my brother's happiness went away. One hot summer day when Popo was already very sick, we stood outside watching a village funeral procession marching by our courtyard. Just as it passed our gate, the heavy framed picture of the dead man toppled from its stand and fell to the dusty ground. An old lady screamed and fainted. My brother laughed and Auntie slapped him.

My auntie, who had a very bad temper with children, told him he had no *shou,* no respect for ancestors or family, just like our mother. Auntie had a tongue like hungry scissors eating silk cloth. So when my brother gave her a sour look, Auntie said our mother was so thoughtless she had fled north in a big hurry, without taking the dowry furniture from her marriage to my father, without bringing her ten pairs of silver chopsticks, without paying respect to my father's grave and those of our ancestors. When my brother accused Auntie of frightening our mother away, Auntie shouted that our mother had married a man named Wu Tsing who already had a wife, two concubines, and other bad children.

And when my brother shouted that Auntie was a talking chicken without a head, she pushed my brother against the gate and spat on his face.

"You throw strong words at me, but you are nothing," Auntie said. "You are the son of a mother who has so little respect she has become *ni,* a traitor to our ancestors. She is so beneath others that even the devil must look down to see her."

15 That is when I began to understand the stories Popo taught me, the lessons I had to learn for my mother. "When you lose your face, An-mei," Popo often said, "it is like dropping your necklace down a well. The only way you can get it back is to fall in after it."

Now I could imagine my mother, a thoughtless woman who laughed and shook her head, who dipped her chopsticks many times to eat another piece of sweet fruit, happy to be free of Popo, her unhappy husband on the wall, and her two disobedient children. I felt unlucky that she was my mother and unlucky that she had left us. These were the thoughts I had while hiding in the corner of my room where my father could not watch me.

I was sitting at the top of the stairs when she arrived. I knew it was my mother even though I had not seen her in all my memory. She stood just inside the doorway so that her face became a dark shadow. She was much taller than my auntie, almost as tall as my uncle. She looked strange, too, like the missionary ladies at our school who were insolent and bossy in their too-tall shoes, foreign clothes, and short hair.

My auntie quickly looked away and did not call her by name or offer her tea. An old servant hurried away with a displeased look. I tried to keep very still, but my heart felt like crickets scratching to get out of a cage. My mother must have heard, because she looked up. And when she did, I saw my own face looking back at me. Eyes that stayed wide open and saw too much.

In Popo's room my auntie protested, "Too late, too late," as my mother approached the bed. But this did not stop my mother.

20 "Come back, stay here," murmured my mother to Popo. "*Nuyer* is here. You daughter is back." Popo's eyes were open, but now her mind ran in many different directions, not staying long enough to see anything. If Popo's mind had been clear she would have raised her two arms and flung my mother out of the room.

I watched my mother, seeing her for the first time, this pretty woman with her white skin and oval face, not too round like Auntie's or sharp like Popo's. I saw that she had a long white neck, just like the goose that had laid me. That she seemed to float back and forth like a ghost, dipping cool cloths to lay on Popo's bloated face. As she peered into Popo's eyes, she clucked soft worried sounds. I watched her carefully, yet it was her voice that confused me, a familiar sound from a forgotten dream.

When I returned to my room later that afternoon, she was there, standing tall. And because I remember Popo told me not to speak her name, I stood there, mute. She took my hand and led me to the settee. And then she also sat down as though we had done this every day.

My mother began to loosen my braids and brush my hair with long sweeping strokes.

"An-mei, you have been a good daughter?" she asked, smiling a secret look.

I looked at her with my know-nothing face, but inside I was trembling. I was the girl whose belly held a colorless winter melon.

"An-mei, you know who I am," she said with a small scold in her voice. This time I did not look for fear my head would burst and my brains would dribble out of my ears.

She stopped brushing. And then I could feel her long smooth fingers rubbing and searching under my chin, finding the spot that was my smooth-neck scar. As she rubbed this spot, I became very still. It was as though she were rubbing the memory back into my skin. And then her hand dropped and she began to cry, wrapping her hands around her own neck. She cried with a wailing voice that was so sad. And then I remembered the dream with my mother's voice.

I was four years old. My chin was just above the dinner table, and I could see my baby brother sitting on Popo's lap, crying with an angry face. I could hear voices praising a steaming dark soup brought to the table, voices murmuring politely, *"Ching! Ching!"*—Please, eat!

And then the talking stopped. My uncle rose from his chair. Everyone turned to look at the door, where a tall woman stood. I was the only one who spoke.

"Ma," I had cried, rushing off my chair, but my auntie slapped my face and pushed me back down. Now everyone was standing up and shouting, and I heard my mother's voice crying, "An-mei! An-mei!" Above this noise, Popo's shrill voice spoke.

"Who is this ghost? Not an honored widow. Just a number-three concubine. If you take your daughter, she will become like you. No face. Never able to lift up her head."

Still my mother shouted for me to come. I remember her voice so clearly now. An-mei! An-mei! I could see my mother's face across the table. Between us stood the soup pot on its heavy chimney-pot stand—rocking slowly, back and forth. And then with one shout this dark boiling soup spilled forward and fell all over my neck. It was as though everyone's anger were pouring all over me.

This was the kind of pain so terrible that a little child should never remember it. But it is still in my skin's memory. I cried out loud only a little, because soon my flesh began to burst inside and out and cut off my breathing air.

I could not speak because of this terrible choking feeling. I could not see because of all the tears that poured out to wash away the pain. But I could hear my mother's crying voice. Popo and Auntie were shouting. And then my mother's voice went away.

35 Later that night Popo's voice came to me.

"An-mei, listen carefully." Her voice had the same scolding tone she used when I ran up and down the hallway. "An-mei, we have made your dying clothes and shoes for you. They are all white cotton."

I listened, scared.

"An-mei," she murmured, now more gently. "Your dying clothes are very plain. They are not fancy, because you are still a child. If you die, you will have a short life and you will still owe your family a debt. Your funeral will be very small. Our mourning time for you will be very short."

And then Popo said something that was worse than the burning on my neck.

40 "Even your mother has used up her tears and left. If you do not get well soon, she will forget you."

Popo was very smart. I came hurrying back from the other world to find my mother.

Every night I cried so that both my eyes and my neck burned. Next to my bed sat Popo. She would pour cool water over my neck from the hollowed cup of a large grapefruit. She would pour and pour until my breathing became soft and I could fall asleep. In the morning, Popo would use her sharp fingernails like tweezers and peel off the dead membranes.

In two years' time, my scar became pale and shiny and I had no memory of my mother. That is the way it is with a wound. The wound begins to close in on itself, to protect what is hurting so much. And once it is closed, you no longer see what is underneath, what started the pain.

I worshipped this mother from my dream. But the woman standing by Popo's bed was not the mother of my memory. Yet I came to love this mother as well. Not because she came to me and begged me to forgive her. She did not. She did not need to explain that Popo chased her out of the house when I was dying. This I knew. She did not need to tell me she married Wu Tsing to exchange one unhappiness for another. I knew this as well.

45 Here is how I came to love my mother. How I saw in her my own true nature. What was beneath my skin. Inside my bones.

It was late at night when I went to Popo's room. My auntie said it was Popo's dying time and I must show respect. I put on a clean dress and stood between my auntie and uncle at the foot of Popo's bed. I cried a little, not too loud.

I saw my mother on the other side of the room. Quiet and sad. She was cooking a soup, pouring herbs and medicines into the steaming pot. And then I saw her pull up her sleeve and pull out a sharp knife. She put this knife on the softest part of her arm. I tried to close my eyes, but could not.

And then my mother cut a piece of meat from her arm. Tears poured from her face and blood spilled to the floor.

My mother took her flesh and put it in the soup. She cooked magic in the ancient tradition to try to cure her mother this one last time. She opened Popo's mouth, already too tight from trying to keep her spirit in. She fed her this soup, but that night Popo flew away with her illness.

Even though I was young, I could see the pain of the flesh and the worth of the pain.

This is how a daughter honors her mother. It is *shou* so deep it is in your bones. The pain of the flesh is nothing. The pain you must forget. Because sometimes that is the only way to remember what is in your bones. You must peel off your skin, and that of your mother, and her mother before her. Until there is nothing. No scar, no skin, no flesh.

Explorations of the Text

1. Why is An-Mei Hsu's mother considered a "ghost" by the family? Why is she a "ghost" to the little girl?
2. Why does Popo tell the child scary stories?
3. What are An-Mei's feelings about her father? Explain the symbolism of the portrait.
4. What motivates Auntie's behavior? What effect do her actions have on An-Mei and on her brother?
5. What are the connotations of "luck" in this story?
6. Does An-Mei feel that her mother loves her when her mother returns?
7. What are the symbolic implications of the scenes in which An-Mei becomes sick because the soup spilled and in which An-Mei's mother cuts her own flesh and puts it into the soup for her mother, Popo?

The Reading/Writing Connection

1. "Think" Topic: What is the importance of the scar? Discuss the meaning of this passage: "In two years' time, my scar became pale and shiny and I had no memory of my mother. That is the way it is with a wound. The wound begins to close in on itself, to protect what is hurting so much. And once it is closed, you no longer see what is underneath, what started the pain."

2. What does the closing paragraph reveal? What is meant by "You must peel off your skin, and that of your mother, and her mother before her. Until there is nothing. No scar, no skin, no flesh"? Create a double-entry for the ending of the work.

Ideas for Writing

1. What does "Scar" imply about the relationships between parents and children in Chinese society? How are children supposed to behave? What values are important?
2. Explore the theme of intense connectedness between mothers and their daughters and sons in "Girl," "From the House of Yemanjá," and/or "Scar."
3. Explore the theme of loss between parents and children in "Scar," "Elena," "Persimmons," "Daddy," and/or "Ruth's Song."
4. What do images or dreams suggest about the hold of the past in "Scar," "This Is What It Means to say Phoenix, Arizona," "Making the Jam Without You," and/or "Ruth's Song"?

POETRY

On My First Son[1]

Ben Jonson

Ben Jonson (1572(?)–1637) was born in London, attended Westminster School, then became apprenticed as a bricklayer. For a short time, he served as a soldier in the Netherlands, before returning to England, marrying, and working as an actor and playwright. Jonson's first original play, Every Man in His Humor, *was performed in 1598. Jonson wrote satirical plays that assailed Elizabethan and Jacobean morals and his fellow playwrights, including* Volpone, or The Fox *(1605) and* The Alchemist *(1610). Among Jonson's* Epigrams *(1616) is a poem mourning the death of his seven-year-old son Benjamin, who died of the plague in 1603 while Jonson was away.*

1616

Farewell, thou child of my right hand,[2] and joy;
My sin was too much hope of thee, loved boy;
Seven years thou wert lent to me, and I thee pay,
Exacted by thy fate, on the just day.
Oh, could I lose all father, now! For why
Will man lament the state he should envy?
To have so soon scaped world's, and flesh's rage,
And, if no other misery, yet age?
Rest in soft peace, and, asked, say here doth lie
Ben Jonson his best piece of poetry,
For whose sake, henceforth, all his vows be such,
As what he loves may never like too much.

Explorations of the Text

1. How does the **allusion** to the Hebrew source of the child's name create an effect in the opening?
2. What **metaphoric reference** does Jonson make in lines 3 and 4? How does the metaphor strengthen the lament?
3. Explain the lines: "Oh, could I lose all father, now! For why/Will man lament the state he should envy?/To have so soon scaped world's and flesh's rage."

[1] Jonson's oldest son, Benjamin, died in 1603 on his seventh birthday.

[2] Translated literally from the Hebrew, the name means Ben—"son of"—and Jamin—"my right hand."

4. What poetic device is evident in "soft peace"? What is its effect upon a reader?
5. Why does the speaker call his son "his best piece of poetry"?
6. What is revealed in the closing couplet?
7. What is the rhyme scheme? How does rhyme reinforce meaning?

The Reading/Writing Connection

1. Discuss the responses of a parent who has lost a child as they are revealed in the poem.

Ideas for Writing

1. **Explicate** this poem.
2. Discuss the grief of the loss of children in "Heart's Needle," "On My First Son," and "Elena."

PREFACE TO A TWENTY VOLUME SUICIDE NOTE

Amiri Baraka

Born Everett LeRoi Jones in Newark, New Jersey, Amiri Baraka (1934–) changed his name in 1967. He attended Rutgers and Howard Universities before serving two and a half years in the U.S. Air Force. During the early 1960s, Baraka lived in Greenwich Village, obtained master's degrees in philosophy and German, and socialized with writers of the Beat movement. His first book of poetry, Preface to a Twenty Volume Suicide Note, *was published in 1961. Famous for his poetry and his plays, Baraka has received the Obie Award; fellowships from the Guggenheim, Rockefeller, and John Whitney Foundations; an American Book Award; and prizes from the International Art Festival, the National Endowment of the Arts, and the New Jersey Council for the Arts.*

1961

For Kellie Jones, born 16 May 1959

Lately, I've become accustomed to the way
The ground opens up and envelops me
Each time I go out to walk the dog.
Or the broad-edged silly music the wind
Makes when I run for a bus . . .

Things have come to that.

And now, each night I count the stars,
And each night I get the same number.
And when they will not come to be counted,
I count the holes they leave.

Nobody sings anymore.

And then last night, I tiptoed up
To my daughter's room and heard her
Talking to someone, and when I opened
The door, there was no one there . . .
Only she on her knees, peeking into

Her own clasped hands.

Explorations of the Text

1. What is the mood of the speaker in the opening lines? What images suggest his feelings?
2. What is the significance of music—the absence of song—in this poem?
3. What is the significance of the daughter's gesture of peeking into her own clasped hands?
4. What does the title mean? How does it explain the closing line?
5. Why does Baraka have three short lines, separated as stanzas? How do they convey the message of the poem?
6. Why does Baraka begin stanzas with "Lately," "And now," and "And then"? What do these transition words accomplish?
7. How does the speaker feel about his daughter? What does she represent to him?

The Reading/Writing Connection

1. "Think" Topic: Do you think that the experience of parenting differs for mothers and for fathers? Refer to two works that you have read.

Ideas for Writing

1. How does Baraka use figurative language in this poem? Is the figurative language effective?
2. What do children represent and give to their parents in two of the following poems: "Preface to a Twenty Volume Suicide Note," "Heart's Needle," "Making the Jam Without You," "My Little Girl, My Stringbean, My Lovely Woman"?

Heart's Needle

W. D. Snodgrass

William Dewitt Snodgrass (1926–) was born in Wilkinsburg, Pennsylvania. He attended Geneva College, interrupting his undergraduate work with military service at the end of World War II. Snodgrass received his B.A., M.A., and M.F.A. degrees from the University of Iowa. Although credited as a co-founder of the Confessional school of poetry, Snodgrass eschews the term and association with it. Even so, the self-analytic style that distinguishes his Pulitzer Prize–winning first collection, Heart's Needle *(1959), was widely imitated by students of the Confessional mode. Snodgrass's subsequent volumes of poetry, among them* After Experience *(1967) and* The Führer Bunker: A Cycle of Poems in Progress *(1977), attempt in their concern with social, philosophical, and historical subjects to move into more public spheres.*

1959

1.

Child of my winter, born
When the new fallen soldiers froze
In Asia's steep ravines and fouled the snows,[1]
When I was torn

By love I could not still,
By fear that silenced my cramped mind
To that cold war[2] where, lost, I could not find
My peace in my will,

All those days we could keep
Your mind a landscape of new snow
Where the chilled tenant-farmer finds, below,
His fields asleep

In their smooth covering, white
As quilts to warm the resting bed
Of birth or pain, spotless as paper spread
For me to write,

---

[1] Reference to the Korean War.

[2] Another reference to the Korean War.

And thinks: Here lies my land
Unmarked by agony, the lean foot
Of the weasel tracking, the thick trapper's boot;
And I have planned

My chances to restrain
The torments of demented summer or
Increase the deepening harvest here before
It snows again.

Explorations of the Text

1. Why does Snodgrass address his daughter as "child of my winter"?
2. What is the speaker's crisis? Why is he "torn" by love and fear?
3. How do the images of "landscape of new snow" and "fields asleep" characterize a father's relationship with a daughter?
4. Why does the poet use images of war? How do these images relate to the love the speaker "could not still"?
5. What is the significance of the seasonal imagery in the poem? How do the images of snow change?
6. What is his final wish for his daughter in the closing stanzas?
7. Where does Snodgrass use **personification**? What does the technique accomplish?

The Reading/Writing Connection

1. Compare Baraka's and Snodgrass's states of mind, their relationships with their daughters, and their wishes for their children.
2. Compare your mood, state of mind, or the state of a relationship to a landscape. Try this approach: "When I am . . . (Fill in with a mood), my mind becomes like . . . (fill in with descriptive detail). Expand the simile, and extend it.

Ideas for Writing

1. What common pain of divorce does this poem portray? Which images support your analysis?
2. Is this poem or Baraka's "Preface to a Twenty Volume Suicide Note" more powerful? Why?

The Sign in My Father's Hands

Martin Espada

Martin Espada (1957–), born in Brooklyn, New York, has worked at jobs ranging from bouncer to tenant lawyer. Espada, a professor at the University of Massachusetts, Amherst, has won two National Endowment of the Arts Fellowships, a Massachusetts Artists' Fellowship, a PEN/Revson Fellowship, and the Patterson Poetry Price. His volumes of poetry include Immigrant Iceboy's Bolero *(1982),* Rebellion Is the Circle of a Lover's Hand *(1990), and* Imagine the Angels of Bread *(1996).*

1996

for Frank Espada

The beer company
did not hire Blacks or Puerto Ricans,
so my father joined the picket line
at the Schaefer Beer Pavilion, New York World's Fair,
amid the crowds glaring with canine hostility.
But the cops brandished nightsticks
and handcuffs to protect the beer,
and my father disappeared.

In 1964, I had never tasted beer,
and no one told me about the picket signs
torn in two by the cops of brewery.
I knew what dead was: dead was a cat
overrun with parasites and dumped
in the hallway incinerator.
I knew my father was dead.
I went mute and filmy-eyed, the slow boy
who did not hear the question in school.
I sat studying his framed photograph
like a mirror, my darker face.

Days later, he appeared in the doorway
grinning with his gilded tooth.
Not dead, though I would come to learn
that sometimes Puerto Ricans die
in jail, with bruises no one can explain
swelling their eyes shut.
I would learn too that "boycott"
is not a boy's haircut,
that I could sketch a picket line
on the blank side of a leaflet.

That day my father returned
from the netherworld
easily as riding the elevator to apartment 14-F,
and the brewery cops could only watch
in drunken disappointment.
I searched my father's hands
for a sign of the miracle.

Explorations of the Text

1. Discuss the point of view and perspective of the speaker. How does the speaker view his father?
2. Paraphrase the action of the poem. What has happened to the speaker's father?
3. Explore the connotations of the word "gilded." How does this particular word choice suggest a theme of the work?
4. What is "the miracle"?
5. Discuss the symbolism of the title.
6. Compare the persona's father with the speaker's father in "My Father's Song."

The Reading/Writing Connection

1. "Think" Topic: What is the father's mythic journey?

Ideas for Writing

1. Compare the use of mythic allusions in this work and in "Persimmons."

DADDY

Sylvia Plath

Sylvia Plath (1932–63) was born in Boston, Massachusetts, the daughter of German immigrants who both taught at Boston University. Plath attended Smith College in Massachusetts, where she won a contest that sent her to work for a national magazine in New York, much like the protagonist of her novel, The Bell Jar *(1963). Plath won a Fullbright Scholarship to Cambridge University in England, where she met the poet Ted Hughes. They were married in 1956 and moved to Smith College, where Plath taught for a short time. The couple returned to England, where they had two children before separating. Plath's first volume of poems,* The Colossus, *appeared in 1960. She committed suicide in 1963 at the age of thirty, leaving the manuscript containing the highly acclaimed posthumous collection of poems,* Ariel *(1965). Like*

Anne Sexton and Robert Lowell, she is considered a Confessional poet. When Plath was eight years old, her father died, an event from which she never seemed to recover. Biographical accounts show some connection between the man in "Daddy" and her father; however, Plath herself stated that the two should not be confused. When she read the poem for the BBC, she suggested that the poem's speaker suffers from an Electra complex.

1962

You do not do, you do not do
Any more, black shoe
In which I have lived like a foot
For thirty years, poor and white,
Barely daring to breathe or Achoo.

Daddy, I have had to kill you.
You died before I had time—
Marble-heavy, a bag full of God,
Ghastly statue[1] with one grey toe
Big as a Frisco seal

And a head in the freakish Atlantic
Where it pours bean green over blue
In the waters off beautiful Nauset.[2]
I used to pray to recover you.
Ach, du.[3]

In the German tongue, in the Polish town
Scraped flat by the roller
Of wars, wars, wars.
But the name of the town is common.
My Polack friend

Says there are a dozen or two.
So I never could tell where you
Put your foot, your root,
I never could talk to you.
The tongue stuck in my jaw.

---

[1] The Colossus at Rhodes, a gigantic statue of Apollo protecting the harbor at Rhodes; the Colossus was known as one of the seven wonders of the world.

[2] A place on the shore on Cape Cod in Massachusetts.

[3] "Oh, you" (translation from German).

It stuck in a barb wire snare.
Ich, ich, ich, ich,[4]
I could hardly speak.
I thought every German was you.
And the language obscene

An engine, an engine
Chuffing me off like a Jew.
A Jew to Dachau, Auschwitz, Belsen.[5]
I began to talk like a Jew.
I think I may well be a Jew.

The snows of the Tyrol,[6] the clear beer of Vienna
Are not very pure or true.
With my gypsy ancestress and my weird luck
And my Taroc pack and my Taroc pack
I may be a bit of a Jew.

I have always been scared of *you*,
With your Luftwaffe,[7] your gobbledygoo.
And your neat moustache
And your Aryan[8] eye, bright blue.
Panzer-man,[9] panzer-man, O You—

Not God but a swastika
So black no sky could squeak through.
Every woman adores a Fascist,
The boot in the face, the brute
Brute heart of a brute like you.

You stand at the blackboard, daddy,
In the picture I have of you,
A cleft in your chin instead of your foot
But no less a devil for that, no not
Any less the black man who

---

[4] "I, I, I, I" (translation from German).

[5] Locations of concentration camps.

[6] Region of the Alps in West Austria and Northern Italy.

[7] The German air force.

[8] Of or pertaining to a presumed ethnic type descended from early speakers of Indo-European languages; a term used by the Nazi party in World War II to denote racial purity.

[9] A *panzer* is a "tank" (translation from German).

Bit my pretty red heart in two.
I was ten when they buried you.
At twenty I tried to die
And get back, back, back to you.
I thought even the bones would do.

But they pulled me out of the sack,
And they stuck me together with glue.
And then I knew what to do.
I made a model of you,
A man in black with a Meinkampf[10] look

And a love of the rack and the screw.[11]
And I said I do, I do.
So daddy, I'm finally through.
The black telephone's off at the root,
The voices just can't worm through.

If I've killed one man, I've killed two—
The vampire who said he was you
And drank my blood for a year,
Seven years, if you want to know.
Daddy, you can lie back now.

There's a stake in your fat black heart
And the villagers never liked you.
They are dancing and stamping on you.
They always *knew* it was you.
Daddy, daddy, you bastard, I'm through.

Explorations of the Text

1. What is the significance of the "black shoe"?
2. To what nursery rhyme does the poet allude? How does the allusion dictate the rhyme scheme? What is the emotional effect of the dominant sounds of the rhyme scheme?
3. How does the speaker first present her father? Why does she envision him as "Marble-heavy, a bag full of God"?
4. Why does she compare her father to a German? a Nazi? Why does she compare herself to a Jew?
5. Why does she compare her father to a "devil"?
6. Why does the speaker try to kill herself at twenty?

[10] Book written by Hitler; *My Struggle* (translation from German).

[11] Instruments of torture.

7. Why does the speaker state: "If I've killed one man, I've killed two"?
8. To what does the movie imagery in the last stanza refer? What is the effect of Plath's use of black humor?
9. Compare Plath's vision with the characterization of the father in "Rappaccini's Daughter."

The Reading/Writing Connection

1. "Think" Topic: Plath described the persona as a girl with an Electra complex. What is an Electra complex? Is this an adequate explanation for the behavior of the persona in the poem?

Ideas for Writing

1. How does Plath use sound and rhyme in "Daddy"? How do these techniques develop themes of the poem?
2. Why is the persona so angry at "Daddy"? Is the conflict resolved? Is she "through"?
3. Compare the point of view and tone of the speaker in this poem with that of one speaker in another poem in this chapter.

My Father's Song

Simon Ortiz

Simon Ortiz (1941–), an Acoma Pueblo Indian, was born in Albuquerque, New Mexico. Between 1961 and 1969 Ortiz attended college, interrupting his education to serve in the U.S. Army in Vietnam from 1963 to 1966. In 1969, he won a Discovery Award from the National Endowment for the Arts. In 1976, Going for the Rain, *his first major collection of poems, was published. Subsequent volumes include* A Good Journey *(1977),* Fight Back: For the Sake of the People, For the Sake of the Land *(1980), and* From Sand Creek: Rising in This House Which Is Our America *(1981). Ortiz's work focuses on the entwined destinies of the Native Americans and other cultures, alienation of human beings from their roots; and his dream for producing harmony between humans and nature.*

1976

Wanting to say things,
I miss my father tonight.
His voice, the slight catch,
the depth from his thin chest,
the tremble of emotion
in something he has just said
to his son, his song:

We planted corn one Spring at Acu—
we planted several times
but this one particular time
I remember the soft damp sand
in my hand.

My father had stopped at one point
to show me an overturned furrow;
the plowshare had unearthed
the burrow nest of a mouse
in the soft moist sand.

Very gently, he scooped tiny pink animals
into the palm of his hand
and told me to touch them.
We took them to the edge
of the field and put them in the shade
of a sand moist clod.

I remember the very softness
of cool and warm sand and tiny alive mice
and my father saying things.

Explorations of the Text

1. Who is the speaker in the first stanza of the poem? Who is the speaker in the last four stanzas?
2. What picture emerges of the father in the first stanza? What images give you clues?
3. What does "his song" suggest about the speaker, his father, and his grandfather?
4. Why does the poet repeat the image of "damp sand"? How do the associations of "sand" change or build?
5. What is the significance of the central images of "cool and warm sand" and "tiny alive mice"? What do the furrows and the ploughing suggest?
6. What inheritance does the grandfather want to give to his son? What does the father want to leave to the speaker?

The Reading/Writing Connection

1. Freewrite. Respond to the philosophy of life presented in the poem.
2. Contrast the inability to communicate in "Daddy" with the memory of voice in "My Father's Song."

Ideas for Writing

1. Explicate and evaluate this poem. (See chapter 10.)
2. What is the relation of human beings to the earth in "My Father's Song"?
3. Compare the vision of inheritance enunciated in this work with the sense of tradition presented in "Krik? Krak!"

Persimmons

Li-Young Lee

Li-Young Lee (1957–) was born in Indonesia to Chinese parents. In 1957, his father was jailed by then-dictator Sukarno for nineteen months, sixteen of which were spent in a leper colony. After his father escaped, the family fled the country, settling in western Pennsylvania. Lee's culturally diverse background is evident in his love of both the Chinese poetry and Bible verses recited to him by his classically educated parents. His first volume of poetry, Rose, *was published in 1986; his second volume,* The City in Which I Love You, *won the Lamont Prize for Poetry in 1990.*

1986

In sixth grade Mrs. Walker
slapped the back of my head
and made me stand in the corner
for not knowing the difference
between *persimmon* and *precision.*
How to choose
persimmons. This is precision.
Ripe ones are soft and brown-spotted.
Sniff the bottoms. The sweet one
will be fragrant. How to eat:
put the knife away, lay down newspaper.
Peel the skin tenderly, not to tear the meat.
Chew the skin, suck it,
and swallow. Now, eat
the meat of the fruit,
so sweet,
all of it, to the heart.

Donna undresses, her stomach is white.
In the yard, dewy and shivering
with crickets, we lie naked,
face-up, face-down.
I teach her Chinese.

Crickets: *chiu chiu.* Dew: I've forgotten.
Naked: I've forgotten.
Ni, wo: you and me.
I part her legs,
remember to tell her
she is beautiful as the moon.

Other words
that got me into trouble were
fight and *fright, wren* and *yarn.*
Fight was what I did when I was frightened,
fright was what I felt when I was fighting.
Wrens are small, plain birds,
yarn is what one knits with.
Wrens are soft as yarn.
My mother made birds out of yarn.
I loved to watch her tie the stuff;
a bird, a rabbit, a wee man.

Mrs. Walker brought a persimmon to class
and cut it up
so everyone could taste
a *Chinese apple.* Knowing
it wasn't ripe or sweet, I didn't eat
but watched the other faces.

My mother said every persimmon has a sun
inside, something golden, glowing,
warm as my face.

Once, in the cellar, I found two wrapped in newspaper,
forgotten and not yet ripe.
I took them and set both on my bedroom windowsill,
where each morning a cardinal
sang, *The sun, the sun.*

Finally understanding
he was going blind,
my father sat up all one night
waiting for a song, a ghost.
I gave him the persimmons,
swelled, heavy as sadness,
and sweet as love.

This year, in the muddy lighting
of my parent's cellar, I rummage, looking

for something I lost.
My father sits on the tired, wooden stairs,
black cane between his knees,
hand over hand, gripping the handle.

He's so happy that I've come home.
I ask how his eyes are, a stupid question.
All gone, he answers.

Under some blankets, I find a box.
Inside the box I find three scrolls.
I sit beside him and untie
three paintings by my father:
Hibiscus leaf and a white flower.
Two cats preening.
Two persimmons, so full they want to drop from the cloth.

He raises both hands to touch the cloth,
asks, *Which is this?*

This is persimmons, Father.

Oh, the feel of the wolftail on the silk,
the strength, the tense
precision in the wrist.
I painted them hundreds of times
eyes closed. These I painted blind.
Some things never leave a person:
scent of the hair of one you love,
the texture of persimmons,
in your palm, the ripe weight.

Explorations of the Text

1. Characterize the voice and the tone of the speaker.
2. What do the images of persimmons suggest about the speaker's background? Attitude toward his heritage? Relationship with his father?
3. Why does the poet insert the love scene in stanza 2?
4. List the words that the speaker confuses and then discuss their significance.
5. Explore the meaning of the dialogue between father and son in the last six stanzas. What does the son learn about their relationship? Analyze the play on words of "sun" and "son."
6. What gifts of mind and spirit does the father give to his son? What value does the father want to pass on to his child?

The Reading/Writing Connection

1. Write a monologue in the voice of the father.
2. Journal Entry: Imagine other incidents between father and son. Create a series of scenes and narrative moments.
3. Gloss and annotate the poem; focus on images of China. What do you learn?

Ideas for Writing

1. "Think" Topic: Are the fathers in "Persimmons" and in "Those Winter Sundays" good fathers? Do they nurture their sons? Are the speakers good sons? Do they relate to and know their fathers?
2. In a journal entry discuss how cultural expectations have shaped the father's and son's lives in "Persimmons."

DIGGING

Seamus Heaney

Seamus Heaney (1939–   ) was born into a Roman Catholic family in predominantly Protestant Northern Ireland. Educated at Queen's University, Belfast, Heaney became part of a group of young Northern Irish poets. His first book of poems, Digging, *was published in 1966. Subsequent volumes include* North *(1975),* Station Island *(1984), and* Seeing Things *(1991). Despite Heaney's commitment to the Catholic cause in Northern Island, he moved to the Republic of Ireland in 1972 and divides his time with the United States, where he teaches at Harvard University. He was awarded the Nobel Price for Literature in 1995. His poetry is marked by its concern with the natural world, with Irish history, and with the language of everyday speech.*

1966

Between my finger and my thumb
The squat pen rests; snug as a gun.

Under my window, a clean rasping sound
When the spade sinks into gravelly ground:
My father, digging. I look down

Till his straining rump among the flowerbeds
Bends low, comes up twenty years away
Stooping in rhythm through potato drills
Where he was digging.

The coarse boot nestled on the lug, the shaft
Against the inside knee was levered firmly.
He rooted out tall tops, buried the bright edge deep
To scatter new potatoes that we picked
Loving their cool hardness in our hands.
By God, the old man could handle a spade.
Just like his old man.

My grandfather cut more turf in a day
Than any other man on Toner's bog.
Once I carried him milk in a bottle
Corked sloppily with paper. He straightened up
To drink it, then fell to right away

Nicking and slicing neatly, heaving sods
Over his shoulder, going down and down
For the good turf. Digging.

The cold smell of potato mould, the squelch and slap
Of soggy peat, the curt cuts of an edge
Through living roots awaken in my head.
But I've no spade to follow men like them.

Between my finger and my thumb
The squat pen rests.
I'll dig with it.

Explorations of the Text

1. Contrast the speaker's sense of vocation with his representation of his father's and grandfather's work. Explicate the line: "The squat pen rests." Why does he use the word "squat"?
2. How does the poet describe the father's and grandfather's "digging"? What metaphors are used to describe their labors?
3. What does the speaker realize about his ancestry?
4. Explore the multiple meanings of the title, "Digging."

The Reading/Writing Connection

1. Journal Entry: Contrast a physical act or gesture that you associate with a grandparent or with a parent and one of your own. What do you learn about your connection with your past?
2. "Think" Topic: What views of labor and of artistry are expressed in this work?

Ideas for Writing

1. Create a dialogue among three fathers presented in three poems in this chapter.
2. Explicate this poem: Focus on point of view, tone, imagery, structure, and word choice.

The House of Yemanjá[1]

Audre Lorde

Audre Lorde (1934–92) was born in New York City of West Indian parents. She attended National University of Mexico, Hunter College, and Columbia University, where she received her M.L.S. She subsequently worked as a librarian and taught school, and she spent a year at Tougaloo College, Mississippi, as poet-in-residence. Lorde taught writing and English at several colleges before becoming professor of English at Hunter College in 1980. Her volumes of poetry include Cables to Rage *(1970),* Coal *(1976), and* The Black Unicorn *(1978). She also wrote an account of her courageous struggle with breast cancer and mastectomy,* The Cancer Journals *(1980), and a prose autobiography,* Zami: A New Spelling of My Name *(1982).*

1978

My mother had two faces and a frying pot
where she cooked up her daughters
into girls
before she fixed our dinner.
My mother had two faces
and a broken pot
where she hid out a perfect daughter
who was not me
I am the sun and moon and forever hungry
for her eyes.
I bear two women upon my back
one dark and rich and hidden
in the ivory hungers of the other
mother

[1] "Mother of the other *Orisha* [Yoruban deities], Yemanjá is also the goddess of oceans. Rivers are said to flow from her breasts. One legend has it that a son tried to rape her. She fled until she collapsed, and from her breasts, the rivers flowed. Another legend says that a husband insulted Yemanjá's long breasts, and when she fled with her pots he knocked her down. From her breasts flowed the rivers, and from her body then sprang forth all the other *Orisha.* River-smooth stones are Yemanjá's symbol, and the sea is sacred to her followers. Those who please her are blessed with many children" [Lorde's note].

pale as a witch
yet steady and familiar

brings me bread and terror
in my sleep
her breasts are huge exciting anchors
in the midnight storm.

All this has been
before
in my mother's bed
time has no sense
I have no brothers
and my sisters are cruel.

Mother I need
mother I need
mother I need your blackness now
as the august earth needs rain.
I am
the sun and moon and forever hungry
the sharpened edge
where day and night shall meet
and not be
one.

Explorations of the Text

1. Why does the speaker insist that her mother "had two faces"? What do the "two faces" represent for the speaker?
2. What was the speaker's relationship as a child with her mother? as an adult? What does the adult "need" from her mother?
3. What is the significance of the broken pot (line 6)? Why is the pot "broken"?
4. What is the effect of the repetition of the line in the last stanza?
5. What is the symbolism of "the sharpened edge/where day and night shall meet/and not be/one"? Why shall "day and night" "not be/one"?
6. Explain the title: "From the House of Yemanjá." What is the role of the mythological **allusion** to Yemanjá in the poem?

The Reading/Writing Connection

1. Create a **monologue** in the voice of the mother or a **dialogue** between the mother and daughter.

2. The poem presents primarily metaphors, with few specific examples of the mother's behavior. Create a catalogue of specific actions for the mother that would exemplify her "two faces."
3. Create a metaphor for your upbringing. You may begin with "My mother or father was. . . ."

Ideas for Writing

1. Write a dialogue between the persona in this poem and her mother.
2. Do the allusions to mythology and to fairy tale strengthen the poem? Explain.

My Mother and the Bed

Lyn Lifshin

Lyn Lifshin (1944–), born in Burlington, Vermont, published her first collection of poems, Why Is the House Dissolving? *in 1968, although she had been writing poetry since age three. Many critics consider her finest work to be about historical subjects. In the* Shaker House Poems *(1976), Lifshin captures the essence of early American Shaker religious communities; her poetic reflections on early Eskimo culture of the Arctic are contained in* Leaning South *(1977). During her career, Lifshin has taught writing and poetry at universities and colleges throughout the United States and has received numerous awards for her poetry. She also has edited an important collection of women's autobiographical writing,* Ariadne's Thread: A Collection of Contemporary Women's Journals *(1982).*

1968

No, not that way she'd
say when I was 7, pulling
the bottom sheet smooth,
you've got to saying
hospital corners

I wet the bed much later
than I should, until
just writing this I
hadn't thought of
the connection

My mother would never
sleep on sheets someone
else had I never
saw any stains on hers
tho her bedroom was

a maze of powder   hair
pins   black dresses
Sometimes she brings her
own sheets to my house,
carries toilet seat covers

Did anybody sleep
in my   she always asks
Her sheets   her hair
she says the rooms here
smell funny

We drive at 3 am
slowly into Boston and
strip what looks like
two clean beds as the
sky gets light   I

smooth on the form
fitted flower bottom,
she redoes it

She thinks of my life
as a bed only she
can make right

Explorations of the Text

1. What does the symbol of the bed reveal about each stage of the speaker's life? What does it suggest about the relationship of the speaker and her mother?
2. What conclusions do you draw about the character of the mother?
3. What is the significance of the closing stanza of the poem?
4. Does the humor in the poem add to or detract from the message?
5. Do you think the lack of punctuation enhances the poem? Why? In what ways?

The Reading/Writing Connection

1. "Think" Topic: Based on your own experience and observations, what truths about the mother-daughter relationship does the poem suggest? Is the poem realistic? Why? Why not?
2. Gloss the poem; note examples of humor. What role does humor play in this poem?

Ideas for Writing

1. Write a humorous portrayal of your relationship with a family member. You may write a poem. Use a thematic motif (e.g., the bed).
2. Analyze your essay. Is the humor effective?

GIRL

Jamaica Kincaid

Jamaica Kincaid (1949–) was born in Antigua in the West Indies. Kincaid emigrated to the United States to attend college, which she found "a dismal failure." She is now a naturalized citizen, living in New York City and in Burlington, Vermont. Her first collection of short stories, At the Bottom of the River *(1983), won the Morton Dauwen Zabel Award of the American Academy and Institute of Arts and Letters. Her subsequent volumes have included* Annie John *(1985),* The Autobiography of My Mother *(1996), and* My Brother *(1997).*

"Girl" was Kincaid's first published piece of fiction (in The New Yorker,*) written in 1977 after reading Elizabeth Bishop's "In the Waiting Room." She drafted it in one rush of energy, and it is one long sentence.*

1977

Wash the white clothes on Monday and put them on the stone heap; wash the color clothes on Tuesday and put them on the clothesline to dry; don't walk barehead in the hot sun; cook pumpkin fritters in very hot sweet oil; soak your little cloths right after you take them off; when buying cotton to make yourself a nice blouse, be sure that it doesn't have gum on it, because that way it won't hold up well after a wash; soak salt fish overnight before you cook it; is it true that you sing benna[1] in Sunday school?; always eat your food in such a way that it won't turn someone else's stomach; on Sundays try to walk like a lady and not like the slut you are so bent on becoming; don't sing benna in Sunday school; you mustn't speak to wharf-rat boys, not even to give directions; don't eat fruits on the street—flies will follow you; *but I don't sing benna on Sundays at all and never in Sunday school;* this is how to sew on a button; this is how to make a button-hole for the button you have just sewed on; this is how to hem a dress when you see the hem coming down and so to prevent yourself from looking like the slut I know you are so bent on becoming; this is how you iron your father's khaki shirt so that it doesn't have a crease; this is how you iron your father's khaki pants so that they don't have a crease, this is how you grow okra—far from the house, because okra tree

[1] Calypso music.

harbors red ants: when you are growing dasheen,[2] make sure it gets plenty of water or else it makes your throat itch when you are eating it; this is how you sweep a corner; this is how you sweep a whole house; this is how you sweep a yard; this is how you smile to someone you don't like too much; this is how you smile to someone you don't like at all; this is how you smile to someone you like completely; this is how you set a table for tea; this is how you set a table for dinner; this is how you set a table for dinner with an important guest; this is how you set a table for lunch; this is how you set a table for breakfast; this is how to behave in the presence of men who don't know you very well, and this way they won't recognize immediately the slut I have warned you against becoming; be sure to wash every day, even if it is with your own spit; don't squat down to play marbles—you are not a boy, you know; don't pick people's flowers—you might catch something; don't throw stones at blackbirds, because it might not be a blackbird at all; this is how to make a bread pudding; this is how to make doukona,[3] this is how to make pepper pot;[4] this is how to make a good medicine for a cold; this is how to make a good medicine to throw away a child before it even becomes a child; this is how to catch a fish; this is how to throw back a fish you don't like, and that way something bad won't fall on you; this is how to bully a man; this is how a man bullies you; this is how to love a man, and if this doesn't work there are other ways, and if they don't work don't feel too bad about giving up; this is how to spit up in the air if you feel like it, and this is how to move quick so that it doesn't fall on you; this is how to make ends meet; always squeeze bread to make sure it's fresh; *but what if the baker won't let me feel the bread?;* you mean to say that after all you are really going to be the kind of woman who the baker won't let near the bread?

Explorations of the Text

1. Who speaks which lines in the poem?
2. The speech is a single sentence filled with commands. What do they suggest about the main speaker's intentions? Characterize the speaker.
3. What is the main speaker's tone? What is the significance of the variations of the phrase, "not like the slut you are so bent on becoming"?
4. What do the girl's lines reveal about her character? about her relationship with the speaker?
5. Why does the speaker say, "You mean to say that after all you are really going to be the kind of woman who the baker won't let near the bread?"
6. What vision of female roles emerges in this piece?

[2] A kind of potato.

[3] A spicy pudding made of plantains.

[4] A kind of stew.

7. What is the impact of the repeated phrasing, of the parallel structure, and of its form as a single sentence?

The Reading/Writing Connection

1. Create an imitation of this speech as a mother/father giving advice to a child in North America. You may create the voice of your parent talking to you.
2. Become a representative figure and give advice (e.g., a teenager giving advice about how to be a "teen" in North America to a foreign student; a senior giving advice to a college freshman).
3. Create a comparable version of "Girl" for a "Boy."

Ideas for Writing

1. What motivates the mother's speech? Is her approach effective? Why? Why not?
2. Compare the character of the speaker with that of the mother in "Krik? Krak!"

My Little Girl, My Stringbean, My Lovely Woman

Anne Sexton

Anne Sexton (1928–74) was born in Newton, Massachusetts. She attended Garland Junior College in Massachusetts and taught high school and college. After suffering one of many nervous breakdowns, Sexton was urged by a psychiatrist to try writing poetry. She did so with immediate success; the poet Robert Lowell was one of her mentors. She published her first book of poems, To Bedlam and Part Way Back, *in 1960. In 1967, she won the Pulitzer Prize for Poetry for* Live or Die. *With Lowell, Sexton is associated with the Confessional school of poetry, drawing on intensely personal subject matter for her poems. She committed suicide in 1974. Sexton's* Complete Poems *were published in 1981.*

1964

My daughter, at eleven
(almost twelve), is like a garden.

Oh, darling! Born in that sweet birthday suit
and having owned it and known it for so long,
now you must watch high noon enter—

noon, that ghost hour.
Oh, funny little girl—this one under a blueberry sky,
this one! How can I say that I've known
just what you know and just where you are?

It's not a strange place, this odd home
where your face sits in my hand
so full of distance,
so full of its immediate fever.
The summer has seized you,
as when, last month in Amalfi,[1] I saw
lemons as large as your desk-side globe—
that miniature map of the world—
and I could mention, too,
the market stalls of mushrooms
and garlic buds all engorged.
Or I think even of the orchard next door,
where the berries are done
and the apples are beginning to swell.
And once, with our first backyard,
I remember I planted an acre of yellow beans
we couldn't eat.

Oh, little girl,
my stringbean,
how do you grow?
You grow this way.
You are too many to eat.

I hear
as in a dream
the conversation of the old wives
speaking of *womanhood.*
I remember that I heard nothing myself.
I was alone.
I waited like a target.

Let high noon enter—
the hour of the ghosts.
Once the Romans believed
that noon was the ghost hour,
and I can believe it, too,
under that startling sun,

[1] Town in Italy.

and someday they will come to you,
someday, men bare to the waist, young Romans
at noon where they belong,
with ladders and hammers
while no one sleeps.

But before they enter
I will have said,
Your bones are lovely,
and before their strange hands
there was always this hand that formed.

Oh, darling, let your body in,
let it tie you in,
in comfort.
What I want to say, Linda,
is that women are born twice.
If I could have watched you grow
as a magical mother might,
if I could have seen through my magical transparent belly,
there would have been such ripening within:
your embryo,
the seed taking on its own,
life clapping the bedpost,
bones from the pond,
thumbs and two mysterious eyes,
the awfully human head,
the heart jumping like a puppy,
the important lungs,
the becoming—
while it becomes!
as it does now,
a world of its own,
a delicate place.

I say hello
to such shakes and knockings and high jinks,
such music, such sprouts,
such dancing-mad-bears of music,
such necessary sugar,
such goings-on!

Oh, little girl,
my stringbean,
how do you grow?
You grow this way.
You are too many to eat.

What I want to say, Linda,
is that there is nothing in your body that lies.
All that is new is telling the truth.
I'm here, that somebody else,
an old tree in the background.

Darling,
stand still at your door,
sure of yourself, a white stone, a good stone—
as exceptional as laughter
you will strike fire,
that new thing!

Explorations of the Text

1. What is the significance of the garden imagery? What is the meaning of the refrain?
2. The poem shifts from garden imagery to birth imagery. What do "birth" and "womb" images suggest about the speaker's view of her daughter's imminent adolescence?
3. What does "high noon" signify?
4. What does the speaker envision as her role in her daughter's life?
5. Explore the significance of the statement that "women are born twice."
6. What are the speaker's final wishes for her daughter expressed in the last two stanzas? How will she help her daughter in adolescence?
7. Contrast the image of the mother who "waited like a target" with the image of the daughter who "will strike fire."
8. Compare the speaker's relationship with her daughter with relationships in poems by Baraka, Snodgrass, and Kumin.

The Reading/Writing Connection

1. "Think" Topic: How does Sexton use nursery and children's rhymes? How do the rhymes develop the poem's themes?
2. Journal Entry: Based on your experience, develop advice about growing up and about sexuality, and write it in the form of a letter to an adolescent.

Ideas for Writing

1. What are the speaker's feelings toward her daughter? How does the tone of the poem reveal her attitude? Which specific words and phrases create the tone?

2. Sexton's, Lifshin's, Lorde's, and Kincaid's works portray intense bonds between mothers and daughters. What differences appear in these writers' treatments of mother-daughter relationships?

ELENA

Pat Mora

Pat Mora (1942–) was born in El Paso, Texas. She has written poetry, Chants *(1984),* Borders *(1986), and* Communion *(1991); essays,* Napantla: Essays from the Land in the Middle *(1993); and children's books,* A Birthday Basket for Tia *(1992),* Pablo's Tree *(1994), and* Tomas and the Library Lady *(1997). Mora, awarded a Kellogg Fellowship in 1986, has worked as a teacher and as a museum creator.*

1984

My Spanish isn't enough
I remember how I'd smile
listening to my little ones,
understanding every word they'd say,
their jokes, their songs, their plots.
Vamos a pedirle dulces a mamá. Vamos.[1]
But that was in Mexico.
Now my children go to American high schools.
They speak English. At night they sit around
the kitchen table, laugh with one another.
I stand by the stove and feel dumb, alone.
I bought a book to learn English.
My husband frowned, drank more beer.
My oldest said, "Mamá, he doesn't want you
to be smarter than he is." I'm forty,
embarrassed at mispronouncing words,
embarrassed at the laughter of my children,
the grocer, the mailman. Sometimes I take
my English book and lock myself in the bathroom,
say the thick words softly,
for if I stop trying, I will be deaf
when my children need my help.

Explorations of the Text

1. What is the speaker's conflict in "Elena"?
2. Discuss images of power and powerlessness in the poem. Explore the connotation of the words "deaf" and "dumb" in the poem.
3. Explore the theme of silencing in the work.

[1] "Let's go ask mama for sweets. Let's go."

The Reading/Writing Connection

1. Journal Entry: Write a letter, monologue, or diary entry in Elena's voice.
2. "Think" Topic: Create a dialogue between Elena and the father in "Persimmons" on the subject of living in North America.

Ideas for Writing

1. Compare the character of Elena with that of the speaker in "Refugee Ship."
2. Explore themes of exile in this poem with that of "Lost Sister."

Making the Jam Without You

Maxine Kumin

Maxine Kumin (1925–) was born in Philadelphia and educated at Radcliffe College. Kumin married, had three children, then enrolled in writing workshops at the Boston Center for Adult Education. There she met Anne Sexton, with whom she had a celebrated friendship, collaborating on four children's books with her. In 1973, Kumin received the Pulitzer Price for Poetry for her fourth volume, Up Country: Poems of New England. *Along with five other poetry collections, including her* Selected Poems: 1960–1990 *(1997), Kumin has published several novels, twenty-two children's books, a collection of short stories, and two volumes of essays. She has lectured at universities across the country.*

1970

for Judy

Old daughter, small traveler
asleep in a German featherbed
under the eaves in a postcard town
of turrets and towers,
I am putting a dream in your head.
Listen! Here it is afternoon.
The rain comes down like bullets.
I stand in the kitchen,
that harem of good smells
where we have bumped hips and
cracked the cupboards with our talk
while the stove top danced with pots
and it was not clear who did
the mothering. Now I am

crushing blackberries
to make the annual jam
in a white cocoon of steam.

Take it, my sleeper. Redo it
in any of your three
languages and nineteen years.
Change the geography.
Let there be a mountain,
the fat cows on it belled
like a cathedral. Let

there be someone beside you
as you come upon the ruins
of a schloss,[1] all overgrown
with a glorious thicket,
its brambles soft as wool.
Let him bring the buckets
crooked on his angel arms
and may the berries, vaster
than any forage in
the mild hills of New Hampshire,
drop in your pail, plum size,
heavy as the eyes
of any honest dog
and may you bear them
home together to a square
white unreconstructed kitchen
not unlike this one.
Now may your two heads
touch over the kettle,
over the blood of the berries
that drink up sugar and sun,
over that tar-thick boil
love cannot stir down.
More plainly than
the bric-a-brac of shelves
filling with jelly glasses,
more surely than
the light driving through them
trite as rubies, I see him
as pale as paraffin beside you.
I see you cutting
fresh baked bread to spread it
with the bright royal fur.

[1] Castle.

At this time
I lift the flap of your dream
and slip out thinner than a sliver
as your two mouths open
for the sweet stain of purple.

Explorations of the Text

1. What mood and tone are established by the speaker's imagined scene of the girl asleep "under the eaves in a postcard town"?
2. What is the mother's dream? What is the effect of the dream images (fanciful, mysterious)?
3. What is the significance of the **simile,** "the rain comes down like bullets"?
4. How does the poet develop the symbol of the berries? In what ways do the meanings of the berries change and build?
5. What is the speaker's position in the last stanza? Why does she "slip out thinner than a sliver"?
6. What is the speaker's final wish for her daughter?

The Reading/Writing Connection

1. Write a monologue in the speaker's voice, and make explicit her dreams for her daughter. As a parent, would you have similar hopes?
2. "Think" Topic: How does Kumin use the imagery of the berries?

Ideas for Writing

1. What images indicate a symbiotic relationship between mother and daughter? Which images evoke the mother's letting go of the daughter?
2. Compare this poem with Lifshin's, Synge's, and Lorde's visions.

LINEAGE

Margaret Walker

Margaret Walker (1915–), born in Birmingham, Alabama, was educated at Northwestern University and the University of Iowa and worked as a magazine editor, social worker, and college lecturer in English. She was the first African American woman to win the Yale Younger Poets Award, being honored for her volume, For My People *(1942). Her second book,* Jubilee *(1965), a historical novel, took Walker thirty years to complete, during which she married a disabled veteran, raised four children, taught full-time, and earned a Ph.D. Her second volume of poems was the highly acclaimed* Prophets for a New Day *(1970).*

1942

My grandmothers were strong.
They followed plows and bent to toil.
They moved through fields sowing seed.
They touched earth and grain grew.
They were full of sturdiness and singing.
My grandmothers were strong.

My grandmothers are full of memories
Smelling of soap and onions and wet clay
With veins rolling roughly over quick hands
They have many clean words to say.
My grandmothers were strong.
Why am I not as they?

Explorations of the Text

1. What portrait of the grandmothers emerges from the specific details and concrete, physical images Walker uses to describe them?
2. What is the significance of "They touched earth and grain grew" and "They have many clean words to say"?
3. What is the meaning of the closing question? How does the speaker view herself in relation to her grandmothers?
4. How do repetition and parallel structure work in the poem? What is their impact?
5. What does the title mean?
6. Why are kin and the memories of kin important?

The Reading/Writing Connection

1. Create a one-paragraph character portrait or poem about someone whom you admire through using specific details and physical, concrete images.

Ideas for Writing

1. Compare or contrast Edwidge Danticat's, Margaret Walker's, and Etheridge Knight's views of the role of the artist in the preservation of cultural legacies.

The Idea of Ancestry

Etheridge Knight

Etheridge Knight (1931–) grew up in Indianapolis. He was sentenced to prison for twenty years in 1960 and began writing poetry and short stories during this period explaining: "I died in Korea from a shrapnel wound and narcotics resurrected me. I died in 1960 from a prison sentence and poetry brought me back to life." In 1968, when he was released on parole, he published a remarkable volume, Poems from Prison *(1968). It was followed the same year by* Black Voices from Prison.

1968

1

Taped to the wall of my cell are 47 pictures: 47 black
faces: my father, mother, grandmothers (1 dead), grand-
fathers (both dead), brothers, sisters, uncles, aunts,
cousins (1st & 2nd), nieces, and nephews. They stare
across the space at me sprawling on my bunk. I know
their dark eyes, they know mine. I know their style,
they know mine. I am all of them, they are all of me;
they are farmers, I am a thief, I am me, they are thee.

I have at one time or another been in love with my mother,
1 grandmother, 2 sisters, 2 aunts (1 went to the asylum),
and 5 cousins. I am now in love with a 7 yr old niece
(she sends me letters written in large block print, and
her picture is the only one that smiles at me).

I have the same name as 1 grandfather, 3 cousins, 3 nephews,
and 1 uncle. The uncle disappeared when he was 15, just took
off and caught a freight (they say). He's discussed each year
when the family has a reunion, he causes uneasiness in
the clan, he is an empty space. My father's mother, who is 93
and who keeps the Family Bible with everybody's birth dates
(and death dates) in it, always mentions him. There is no
place in her Bible for "whereabouts unknown."

Each fall the graves of my grandfathers call me, the brown
hills and red gullies of mississippi send out their electric
messages, galvanizing my genes. Last yr / like a salmon quitting
the cold ocean-leaping and bucking up his birthstream / I
hitchhiked my way from L.A. with 16 caps[1] in my pocket and a

[1] Capsules or vials of drugs.

monkey on my back.[2] And I almost kicked it with the kinfolks.
I walked barefooted in my grandmother's backyard / I smelled the old
land and the woods / I sipped cornwhiskey from fruit jars with the men /
I flirted with the women / I had a ball till the caps ran out
and my habit came down. That night I looked at my grandmother
and split / my guts were screaming for junk[3] / but I was almost
contented / I had almost caught up with me.
(The next day in Memphis I cracked a croaker's crib for a fix.)

This yr there is a gray stone wall damming my stream, and when
the falling leaves stir my genes, I pace my cell or flop on my bunk
and stare at 47 black faces across the space. I am all of them,
they are all of me, I am me, they are thee, and I have no children
to float in the space between.

Explorations of the Text

1. What is the importance of the setting?
2. What does the refrain "I am all of them, they are all of me" suggest?
3. Discuss the concept of the extended family in each stanza. What is the progression?
4. What is the meaning of the line, "I cracked a croaker's crib for a fix"?
5. How do the speaker's ancestors help him to survive? Do the closing lines of the poem offer clues?
6. How do the levels of style (e.g., slang, Biblical language) add to the effect of the poem?
7. Find lines that state a thesis of the poem.

The Reading/Writing Connection

1. "Think" Topic: What is one "Idea of Ancestry" in this poem and in "Lineage"?
2. Assume that you are confined in a room or in a space for a prolonged period. How would you choose to decorate the walls? Or select one character from this chapter and create a room for him or her. Respond in a journal entry.

[2] Being high; having a drug habit.

[3] Heroin.

Ideas for Writing

1. What consequences of incarceration are expressed in this poem?
2. Write about the African American concept of extended family and of community. Use this poem and other works in this chapter to support your analysis.

Poems for Further Reading

Lord Randal

Anonymous

(Collected 1882)

"O where hae[1] ye been, Lord Randal, my son?
O where hae ye been, my handsome young man?"
"I hae been to the wild wood; mother, make my bed soon,
For I'm weary wi' hunting, and fain wald[2] lie down."

"Where gat[3] ye your dinner, Lord Randal, my son?
Where gat ye your dinner, my handsome young man?"
"I din'd wi' my true-love; mother, make my bed soon,
For I'm weary wi' hunting, and fain wald lie down."

"What gat ye to your dinner, Lord Randal, my son?
What gat ye to your dinner, my handsome young man?"
"I gat eels boil'd in broo;[4] mother, make my bed soon,
For I'm weary wi' hunting, and fain wald lie down."

"What became of your bloodhounds, Lord Randal, my son?
What became of your bloodhounds, my handsome young man?"
"O they swell'd and they died; mother, make my bed soon,
For I'm weary wi' hunting, and fain wald lie down."

"O I fear ye are poison'd, Lord Randal, my son!
I fear ye are poison'd, my handsome young man!"
"O yes! I am poison'd; mother, make my bed soon,
For I'm sick at the heart, and I fain wald lie down."

---

[1] Have.

[2] Would like to.

[3] Got.

[4] Broth.

To My Dear and Loving Husband

Anne Bradstreet (1612?–72)

1678

If ever two were one, then surely we.
If ever man were loved by wife, then thee;
If ever wife was happy in a man,
Compare with me, ye women, if you can.
I prize thy love more than whole mines of gold
Or all the riches that the East doth hold.
My love is such that rivers cannot quench,
Nor ought but love from thee, give recompense.
Thy love is such I can no way repay,
The heavens reward thee manifold, I pray.
Then while we live, in love let's so persevere
That when we live no more, we may live ever.

The Sailor's Mother

William Wordsworth (1770–1850)

1807

One morning (raw it was and wet—
A foggy day in winter time)
A Woman on the road I met,
Not old, though something past her prime:
Majestic in her person, tall and straight;
And like a Roman matron's was her mien and gait.

The ancient spirit is not dead;
Old times, thought I, are breathing there;
Proud was I that my country bred
Such strength, a dignity so fair:
She begged an alms, like one in poor estate;
I looked at her again, nor did my pride abate.

When from these lofty thoughts I woke,
"What is it," said I, "that you bear,
Beneath the covert of your Cloak,
Protected from this cold damp air?"
She answered, soon as she the question heard,
"A simple burthen, Sir, a little Singing-bird."

And, thus continuing, she said,
"I had a Son, who many a day

Sailed on the seas, but he is dead;
In Denmark he was cast away:
And I have travelled weary miles to see
If aught which he had owned might still remain for me.

"The bird and cage they both were his:
'Twas my Son's bird; and neat and trim
He kept it: many voyages
The singing-bird had gone with him;
When last he sailed, he left the bird behind;
From bodings, as might be, that hung upon his mind.

"He to a fellow-lodger's care
Had left it, to be watched and fed,
And pipe its song in safety;—there
I found it when my Son was dead;
And now, God help me for my little wit!
I bear it with me, Sir;—he took so much delight in it."

The Slave Mother

Frances Ellen Watkins Harper (1825–1911)

1854

Heard you that shriek? It rose
So wildly on the air.
It seemed as if a burden'd heart
Was breaking in despair.

Saw you those hands so sadly clasped—
The bowed the feeble head—
The shuddering of that fragile form—
That look of grief and dread?

Saw you the sad, imploring eye?
Its every glance was pain,
As if a storm of agony
Were sweeping through the brain.

She is a mother, pale with fear,
Her boy clings to her side,
And in her kirtle[1] vainly tries
His trembling form to hide.

[1] Loose-fitting gown.

He is not hers, although she bore
    For him a mother's pains;
He is not hers, although her blood
    Is coursing through his veins!

He is not hers, for cruel hands
    May rudely tear apart
The only wreath of household love
    That binds her breaking heart.

His love has been a joyous light
    That o'er her pathway smiled,
A fountain gushing ever new,
    Amid life's desert wild.

His lightest word has been a tone
    Of music round her heart,
Their lives a streamlet blent in one—
    Oh, Father! must they part?

They tear him from her circling arms,
    Her last and fond embrace.
Oh! never more may her sad eyes
    Gaze on his mournful face.

No marvel, then, these bitter shrieks
    Disturb the listening air:
She is a mother, and her heart
    Is breaking in despair.

Piano

D. H. Lawrence (1885–1930)

1918

Softly, in the dusk, a woman is singing to me;
Taking me back down the vista of years, till I see
A child sitting under the piano, in the boom of the tingling strings
And pressing the small, poised feet of a mother who smiles as she sings.

In spite of myself, the insidious mastery of song
Betrays me back, till the heart of me weeps to belong
To the old Sunday evenings at home, with winter outside
And hymns in the cozy parlour, the tinkling piano our guide.

So now it is vain for the singer to burst into clamour
With the great black piano appassionato. The glamour
Of childish days is upon me, my manhood is cast
Down in the flood of remembrance, I weep like a child for the past.

Odyssey

Harold A. Zlotnik (1914–)

1948

(For My Daughter)

Take this, my child, O World, and
give her strength
As durable as grass that hugs the
earth
In its vicissitudes; insure the length
Of summer days, uncradling from
birth
A sky of living with that pine ter-
rain
Of solitude; and let forgiveness
grow
Pervasive as the democratic rain
In hostile moments. Just as others
know
Compassion past their grief, let her
receive
That night-wind as the balm for
desert heat
Her cool, diurnal hope, and soon
perceive
The beacon stars in crisis or retreat,
And mix her blood divinely with the
sun
For faith to burn in glory and be
won.

DRAMA

A Raisin in the Sun

Lorraine Hansberry

Lorraine Hansberry (1930–65) was born in Chicago. After attending the University of Wisconsin, she moved to New York City, where she married and wrote A Raisin in the Sun *(1959), which was an instant success. Actively involved in the civil rights movement, Hansberry was much in demand as a speaker. Her subsequent plays failed to equal the fame of her first, until the posthumously produced* To Be Young, Gifted, and Black *(1968), which was adapted from her earlier writing and which enjoyed a successful run off-Broadway.*

1959

A Raisin in the Sun *was first presented by Philip Rose and David J. Cogan at the Ethel Barrymore Theatre, New York City, March 11, 1959, with the following cast:*

(In order of appearance)

Ruth Younger	Ruby Dee
Travis Younger	Glynn Turman
Walter Lee Younger (Brother)	Sidney Poitier
Beneatha Younger	Diana Sands
Lena Younger (Mama)	Claudia McNeil
Joseph Asagai	Ivan Dixon
George Murchison	Louis Gossett
Karl Lindner	John Fiedler
Bobo	Lonne Elder III
Moving Men	Ed Hall, Douglas Turner

The action of the play is set in Chicago's Southside, sometime between World War II and the present.

Act One

Scene 1. Friday morning.

Scene 2. The following morning.

Act Two

Scene 1. Later, the same day.

Scene 2. Friday night, a few weeks later.

Scene 3. Moving day, one week later.

Act Three

An hour later.

Directed by Lloyd Richards
Designed and lighted by Ralph Alswang
Costumes by Virginia Volland

Act One

Scene I

The Younger living room would be a comfortable and well-ordered room if it were not for a number of indestructible contradictions to this state of being. Its furnishings are typical and undistinguished and their primary feature now is that they have clearly had to accommodate the living of too many people for too many years—and they are tired. Still, we can see that at some time, a time probably no longer remembered by the family (except perhaps for Mama), the furnishings of this room were actually selected with care and love and even hope—and brought to this apartment and arranged with taste and pride.

That was a long time ago. Now the once loved pattern of the couch upholstery has to fight to show itself from under acres of crocheted doilies and couch covers which have themselves finally come to be more important than the upholstery. And here a table or a chair has been moved to disguise the worn places in the carpet; but the carpet has fought back by showing its weariness, with depressing uniformity, elsewhere on its surface.

Weariness has, in fact, won in this room. Everything has been polished, washed, sat on, used, scrubbed too often. All pretenses but living itself have long since vanished from the very atmosphere of this room.

Moreover, a section of this room, for it is not really a room unto itself, though the landlord's lease would make it seem so, slopes backward to provide a small kitchen area, where the family prepares the meals that are eaten in the living room proper, which must also serve as dining room. The single window that has been provided for these "two" rooms is located in this kitchen area. The sole natural light the family may enjoy in the course of a day is only that which fights its way through this little window.

At left, a door leads to a bedroom which is shared by Mama and her daughter, Beneatha. At right, opposite, is a second room (which in the beginning of the life of this apartment was probably a breakfast room) which serves as a bedroom for Walter and his wife, Ruth.

Time: Sometime between World War II and the present.

Place: Chicago's Southside.

At Rise: It is morning dark in the living room. Travis is asleep on the make-down bed at center. An alarm clock sounds from within the bedroom at right, and presently Ruth enters from that room and closes the door behind her. She crosses sleepily toward the window. As she passes her sleeping son she reaches down and shakes him a little. At the window she raises the shade and a dusky Southside morning light comes in feebly. She fills a pot with water and puts it on to boil. She calls to the boy, between yawns, in a slightly muffled voice.

Ruth is about thirty. We can see that she was a pretty girl, even exceptionally so, but now it is apparent that life has been little that she expected, and disappointment has already begun to hang in her face. In a few years, before thirty-five even, she will be known among her people as a "settled woman."

She crosses to her son and gives him a good, final, rousing shake.

Ruth: Come on now, boy, it's seven-thirty! *(Her son sits up at last, in a stupor of sleepiness.)* I say hurry up, Travis! You ain't the only person in the world got to use a bathroom! *(The child, a sturdy, handsome little boy of ten or eleven, drags himself out of the bed and almost blindly takes his towels and "today's clothes" from drawers and a closet and goes out to the bathroom, which is in an outside hall and which is shared by another family or families on the same floor. Ruth crosses to the bedroom door at right and opens it and calls in to her husband.)* Walter Lee! . . . It's after seven-thirty! Lemme see you do some waking up in there now! *(She waits.)* You better get up from there, man! It's after seven-thirty I tell you. *(She waits again.)* All right, you just go ahead and lay there and next thing you know Travis be finished and Mr. Johnson'll be in there and you'll be fussing and cussing round here like a mad man! And be late too! *(She waits, at the end of patience.) Walter Lee*—it's time for you to get up!

(She waits another second and then starts to go into the bedroom but is apparently satisfied that her husband has begun to get up. She stops, pulls the door to, and returns to the kitchen area. She wipes her face with a moist cloth and runs her fingers through her sleep-disheveled hair in a vain effort and ties an apron around her housecoat. The bedroom door at right opens and her husband stands in the doorway in his pajamas, which are rumpled and mismated. He is a lean, intense young man in his middle thirties, inclined to quick nervous movements and erratic speech habits—and always in his voice there is a quality of indictment.)

Walter: Is he out yet?

Ruth: What you mean *out?* He ain't hardly got in there good yet.

Walter *(Wandering in, still more oriented to sleep than to a new day.):* Well, what was you doing all that yelling for if I can't even get in there yet? *(Stopping and thinking.)* Check coming today?

Ruth: They *said* Saturday and this is just Friday and I hopes to God you ain't going to get up here first thing this morning and start talking to me 'bout no money 'cause I 'bout don't want to hear it.

Walter: Something the matter with you this morning?

Ruth: No—I'm just sleepy as the devil. What kind of eggs you want?

Walter: Not scrambled. *(Ruth starts to scramble eggs.)* Paper come? *(Ruth points impatiently to the rolled up* Tribune *on the table, and he gets it and spreads it out and vaguely reads the front page.)* Set off another bomb yesterday.

Ruth *(Maximum indifference.):* Did they?

Walter *(Looking up.):* What's the matter with you?

Ruth: Ain't nothing the matter with me. And don't keep asking me that this morning.

Walter: Ain't nobody bothering you. *(Reading the news of the day absently again.)* Say Colonel McCormick is sick.

Ruth *(Affecting tea-party interest.):* Is he now? Poor thing.

Walter *(Sighing and looking at his watch.):* Oh, me. *(He waits.)* Now what is that boy doing in that bathroom all this time? He just going to have to start getting up earlier. I can't be being late to work on account of him fooling around in there.

Ruth *(Turning on him.):* Oh, no he ain't going to be getting up no earlier no such thing! It ain't his fault that he can't get to bed no earlier nights 'cause he got a bunch of crazy good-for-nothing clowns sitting up running their mouths in what is supposed to be his bedroom after ten o'clock at night . . .

Walter: That's what you mad about, ain't it? The things I want to talk about with my friends just couldn't be important in your mind, could they?

(He rises and finds a cigarette in her handbag on the table and crosses to the little window and looks out, smoking and deeply enjoying this first one.)

Ruth *(Almost matter of factly, a complaint too automatic to deserve emphasis.):* Why you always got to smoke before you eat in the morning?

Walter *(At the window.):* Just look at 'em down there . . . Running and racing to work . . . *(He turns and faces his wife and watches her a moment at the stove, and then, suddenly.)* You look young this morning, baby.

Ruth *(Indifferently.):* Yeah?

Walter: Just for a second—stirring them eggs. It's gone now—just for a second it was—you looked real young again. *(Then, drily.)* It's gone now—you look like yourself again.

Ruth: Man, if you don't shut up and leave me alone.

Walter *(Looking out to the street again.):* First thing a man ought to learn in life is not to make love to no colored woman first thing in the morning. You all some evil people at eight o'clock in the morning.

(Travis appears in the hall doorway, almost fully dressed and quite wide awake now, his towels and pajamas across his shoulders. He opens the door and signals for his father to make the bathroom in a hurry.)

Travis *(Watching the bathroom.):* Daddy, come on!

(Walter gets his bathroom utensils and flies out to the bathroom.)

Ruth: Sit down and have your breakfast, Travis.

Travis: Mama, this is Friday. *(Gleefully.)* Check coming tomorrow, huh?

Ruth: You get your mind off money and eat your breakfast.

Travis *(Eating.):* This is the morning we supposed to bring the fifty cents to school.

Ruth: Well, I ain't got no fifty cents this morning.

Travis: Teacher say we have to.

Ruth: I don't care what teacher say. I ain't got it. Eat your breakfast, Travis.

Travis: I *am* eating.

Ruth: Hush up now and just eat!

(The boy gives her an exasperated look for her lack of understanding and eats grudgingly.)

Travis: You think Grandmama would have it?

Ruth: No! And I want you to stop asking your grandmother for money, you hear me?

Travis *(Outraged.):* Gaaaleee! I don't ask her, she just gimme it sometimes!

Ruth: Travis Willard Younger—I got too much on me this morning to be—

Travis: Maybe Daddy—

Ruth: *Travis!*

(The boy hushes abruptly. They are both quiet and tense for several seconds.)

Travis *(Presently.):* Could I maybe go carry some groceries in front of the supermarket for a little while after school then?

Ruth: Just hush, I said. *(Travis jabs his spoon into his cereal bowl viciously, and rests his head in anger upon his fists.)* If you through eating, you can get over there and make up your bed.

(The boy obeys stiffly and crosses the room, almost mechanically, to the bed and more or less carefully folds the covering. He carries the bedding into his mother's room and returns with his books and cap.)

Travis *(Sulking and standing apart from her unnaturally.):* I'm gone.

Ruth *(Looking up from the stove to inspect him automatically.):* Come here. *(He crosses to her and she studies his head.)* If you don't take this comb and fix this here head, you better! *(Travis puts down his books with a great sign of oppression, and crosses to the mirror. His mother mutters under her breath about his "slubbornness.")* 'Bout to march out of here with that head looking just like chickens slept in it! I just don't know where you get your slubborn ways . . . And get your jacket, too. Looks chilly out this morning.

Travis *(With conspicuously brushed hair and jacket.):* I'm gone.

Ruth: Get carfare and milk money— *(Waving one finger.)* and not a single penny for no caps, you hear me?

Travis: *(With sullen politeness.):* Yes'm.

(He turns in outrage to leave. His mother watches after him as in his frustration he approaches the door almost comically. When she speaks to him, her voice has become a very gentle tease.)

Ruth *(Mocking; as she thinks he would say it.):* Oh, Mama makes me so mad sometimes, I don't know what to do! *(She waits and continues to his back as he stands stock-still in front of the door.)* I wouldn't kiss that woman good-bye for nothing in this world this morning! *(The boy finally turns around and rolls his eyes at her, knowing the mood has changed and he is vindicated; he does not, however, move toward her yet.)* Not for nothing in this world! *(She finally laughs aloud at him and holds out her arms to him and we see that it is a way between them, very old and practiced. He crosses to her and allows her to embrace him warmly but keeps his face fixed with masculine rigidity. She holds him back from her presently and looks at him and runs her fingers over the features of his face. With utter gentleness—.)* Now—whose little old angry man are you?

Travis *(The masculinity and gruffness start to fade at last.):* Aw gaalee—Mama . . .

Ruth *(Mimicking.):* Aw—gaaaaalleeeee, Mama! *(She pushes him, with rough playfulness and finality, toward the door.)* Get on out of here or you going to be late.

Travis *(In the face of love, new aggressiveness.):* Mama, could I *please* go carry groceries?

Ruth: Honey, it's starting to get so cold evenings.

Walter *(Coming in from the bathroom and drawing a make-believe gun from a make-believe holster and shooting at his son.):* What is it he wants to do?

Ruth: Go carry groceries after school at the supermarket.

Walter: Well, let him go . . .

Travis *(Quickly, to the ally.):* I *have* to—she won't gimme the fifty cents . . .

Walter *(To his wife only.):* Why not?

Ruth *(Simply, and with flavor.):* 'Cause we don't have it.

Walter *(To Ruth only.):* What you tell the boy things like that for? *(Reaching down into his pants with a rather important gesture.)* Here, son—

(He hands the boy the coin, but his eyes are directed to his wife's. Travis takes the money happily.)

Travis: Thanks, Daddy.

(He start out. Ruth watches both of them with murder in her eyes. Walter stands and stares back at her with defiance, and suddenly reaches into his pocket again on an afterthought.)

Walter *(Without even looking at his son, still staring hard at his wife.):* In fact, here's another fifty cents . . . Buy yourself some fruit today—or take a taxi cab to school or something!

Travis: Whoopee—

(He leaps up and clasps his father around the middle with his legs, and they face each other in mutual appreciation; slowly Walter Lee peeks around the boy to catch the violent rays from his wife's eyes and draws his head back as if shot.)

Walter: You better get down now—and get to school, man.

Travis *(At the door.):* O.K. Good-bye.

(He exits.)

Walter *(After him, pointing with pride.):* That's *my* boy. *(She looks at him in disgust and turns back to her work.)* You know what I was thinking 'bout in the bathroom this morning?

Ruth: No.

Walter: How come you always try to be so pleasant!

Ruth: What is there to be pleasant 'bout!

Walter: You want to know what I was thinking 'bout in the bathroom or not!

Ruth: I know what you was thinking 'bout.

Walter *(Ignoring her.):* 'Bout what me and Willy Harris was talking about last night.

Ruth *(Immediately—a refrain.):* Willy Harris is a good-for-nothing loud mouth.

Walter: Anybody who talks to me has got to be a good-for-nothing loud mouth, ain't he? And what you know about who is just a good-for-nothing loud mouth? Charlie Atkins was just a "good-for-nothing loud mouth" too, wasn't he! When he wanted me to go in the dry-cleaning business with him. And now—he's grossing a hundred thousand a year. A hundred thousand dollars a year! You still call *him* a loud mouth!

Ruth *(Bitterly.):* Oh, Walter Lee . . .

(She folds her head on her arms over on the table.)

Walter *(Rising and coming to her and standing over her.):* You tired, ain't you? Tired of everything. Me, the boy, the way we live—this beat-up hole—everything. Ain't you? *(She doesn't look up, doesn't answer.)* So tired—moaning and groaning all the time, but you wouldn't do nothing to help, would you? You couldn't be on my side that long for nothing, could you?

Ruth: Walter, please leave me alone.

Walter: A man needs for a woman to back him up . . .

Ruth: Walter—

Walter: Mama would listen to you. You know she listen to you more than she do me and Bennie. She think more of you. All you have to do is just sit down with her when you drinking your coffee one morning and talking 'bout things like you do and— *(He sits down beside her and demonstrates graphically what he thinks her methods and tone should be.)*—you just sip your coffee, see, and say easy like that you been thinking 'bout that deal Walter Lee is so interested in, 'bout the store and all, and sip some more coffee, like what you saying ain't really that important to you— And the next thing you know, she be listening good and asking you questions and when I come home—I can tell her the details. This ain't no fly-by-night proposition, baby. I mean we figured it out, me and Willy and Bobo.

Ruth *(With a frown.):* Bobo?

Walter: Yeah. You see, this little liquor store we got in mind cost seventy-five thousand and we figured the initial investment on the place be 'bout thirty thousand, see. That be ten thousand each. Course, there's a couple of hundred you got to pay so's you don't spend your life just waiting for them clowns to let your license get approved—

Ruth: You mean graft?

Walter *(Frowning impatiently.)*: Don't call it that. See there, that just goes to show you what women understand about the world. Baby, don't *nothing* happen for you in this world 'less you pay *somebody* off!

Ruth: Walter, leave me alone! *(She raises her head and stares at him vigorously—then says, more quietly.)* Eat your eggs, they gonna be cold.

Walter *(Straightening up from her and looking off.)*: That's it. There you are. Man say to his woman: I got me a dream. His woman say: Eat your eggs. *(Sadly, but gaining power.)* Man say: I got to take hold of this here world, baby! And a woman will say: Eat your eggs and go to work. *(Passionately now.)* Man say: I got to change my life, I'm choking to death, baby! And his woman say—*(In utter anguish as he brings his fists down on his thighs.)*—Your eggs is getting cold!

Ruth *(Softly.)*: Walter, that ain't none of our money.

Walter *(Not listening at all or even looking at her.)*: This morning, I was lookin' in the mirror and thinking about it . . . I'm thirty-five years old; I been married eleven years and I got a boy who sleeps in the living room—*(Very, very quietly.)*—and all I got to give him is stories about how rich white people live . . .

Ruth: Eat your eggs, Walter.

Walter: *Damn my eggs . . . damn all the eggs that ever was!*

Ruth: Then go to work.

Walter *(Looking up at her.)*: See—I'm trying to talk to you 'bout myself—*(Shaking his head with the repetition.)*—and all you can say is eat them eggs and go to work.

Ruth *(Wearily.)*: Honey, you never say nothing new. I listen to you every day, every night and every morning, and you never say nothing new. *(Shrugging.)* So you would rather *be* Mr. Arnold than be his chauffeur. So—I would *rather* be living in Buckingham Palace.

Walter: That is just what is wrong with the colored woman in this world . . . Don't understand about building their men up and making 'em feel like they somebody. Like they can do something.

Ruth *(Drily, but to hurt.)*: There *are* colored men who do things.

Walter: No thanks to the colored woman.

Ruth: Well, being a colored woman, I guess I can't help myself none.

(She rises and gets the ironing board and sets it up and attacks a huge pile of rough-dried clothes, sprinkling them in preparation for the ironing and then rolling them into tight fat balls.)

Walter *(Mumbling.)*: We one group of men tied to a race of women with small minds.

(His sister Beneatha enters. She is about twenty, as slim and intense as her brother. She is not as pretty as her sister-in-law, but her lean, almost intellectual face has a handsomeness of its own. She wears a bright-red flannel nightie, and her thick hair stands wildly about her head. Her speech is a mixture of many things; it is different from the rest of the family's insofar as education has permeated her sense of English—and perhaps the Midwest rather than the South has finally—at last—won out in her inflection; but not altogether, because over all of it is a soft slurring and transformed use of vowels which is the decided influence of the Southside. She passes through the room without looking at either Ruth or Walter and goes to the outside door and looks, a little blindly, out to the bathroom. She sees that it has been lost to the Johnsons. She closes the door with a sleepy vengeance and crosses to the table and sits down a little defeated.)

Beneatha: I am going to start timing those people.

Walter: You should get up earlier.

Beneatha *(Her face in her hands. She is still fighting the urge to go back to bed.):* Really—would you suggest dawn? Where's the paper?

Walter *(Pushing the paper across the table to her as he studies her almost clinically, as though he has never seen her before.):* You a horrible-looking chick at this hour.

Beneatha *(Drily.):* Good morning, everybody.

Walter *(Senselessly.):* How is school coming?

Beneatha *(In the same spirit.):* Lovely. Lovely. And you know, biology is the greatest. *(Looking up at him.)* I dissected something that looked just like you yesterday.

Walter: I just wondered if you've made up your mind and everything.

Beneatha *(Gaining in sharpness and impatience.):* And what did I answer yesterday morning—and the day before that?

Ruth *(From the ironing board, like someone disinterested and old.):* Don't be so nasty, Bennie.

Beneatha *(Still to her brother.):* And the day before that and the day before that!

Walter *(Defensively.):* I'm interested in you. Something wrong with that? Ain't many girls who decide—

Walter *and* **Beneatha** *(In unison.):* —"to be a doctor."

(Silence.)

Walter: Have we figured out yet just exactly how much medical school is going to cost?

Ruth: Walter Lee, why don't you leave that girl alone and get out of here to work?

Beneatha *(Exits to the bathroom and bangs on the door.):* Come on out of there, please!

Walter *(Looking at his sister intently.):* You know the check is coming tomorrow.

Beneatha *(Turning on him with a sharpness all her own.):* That money belongs to Mama, Walter, and it's for her to decide how she wants to use it. I don't care if she wants to buy a house or a rocket ship or just nail it up somewhere and look at it. It's hers. Not ours—*hers.*

Walter *(Bitterly.):* Now ain't that fine! You just got your mother's interest at heart, ain't you, girl? You such a nice girl—but if Mama got that money she can always take a few thousand and help you through school too—can't she?

Beneatha: I have never asked anyone around here to do anything for me!

Walter: No! And the line between asking and just accepting when the time comes is big and wide—ain't it!

Beneatha *(With fury.):* What do you want from me, Brother—that I quit school or just drop dead, which!

Walter: I don't want nothing but for you to stop acting holy 'round here. Me and Ruth done made some sacrifices for you—why can't you do something for the family?

Ruth: Walter, don't be dragging me in it.

Walter: You are in it—Don't you get up and go work in somebody's kitchen for the last three years to help put clothes on her back?

Ruth: Oh, Walter—that's not fair . . .

Walter: It ain't that nobody expects you to get on your knees and say thank you, Brother; thank you, Ruth; thank you, Mama—and thank you, Travis, for wearing the same pair of shoes for two semesters—

Beneatha *(Dropping to her knees.):* Well—I *do*—all right?—thank everybody . . . and forgive me for ever wanting to be anything at all . . . forgive me, forgive me!

Ruth: Please stop it! Your mama'll hear you.

Walter: Who the hell told you you had to be a doctor? If you so crazy 'bout messing 'round with sick people—then go be a nurse like other women—or just get married and be quiet . . .

Beneatha: Well—you finally got it said . . . It took you three years but you finally got it said. Walter, give up; leave me alone—it's Mama's money.

Walter: *He was my father, too!*

Beneatha: So what? He was mine, too—and Travis' grandfather—but the insurance money belongs to Mama. Picking on me is not going to make her give it to you to invest in any liquor stores—*(Underbreath, dropping into a chair.)*—and I for one say, God bless Mama for that!

Walter *(To Ruth.):* See—did you hear? Did you hear!

Ruth: Honey, please go to work.

Walter: Nobody in this house is ever going to understand me.

Beneatha: Because you're a nut.

Walter: Who's a nut?

Beneatha: You—you are a nut. Thee is mad, boy.

Walter *(Looking at his wife and his sister from the door, very sadly.):* The world's most backward race of people, and that's a fact.

Beneatha *(Turning slowly in her chair.):* And then there are all those prophets who would lead us out of the wilderness—*(Walter slams out of the house.)*—into the swamps!

Ruth: Bennie, why you always gotta be pickin' on your brother? Can't you be a little sweeter sometimes? *(Door opens. Walter walks in.)*

Walter *(To Ruth.):* I need some money for carfare.

Ruth *(Looks at him, then warms; teasing, but tenderly.):* Fifty cents? *(She goes to her bag and gets money.)* Here, take a taxi.

(Walter exits. Mama enters. She is a woman in her early sixties, full-bodied and strong. She is one of those women of a certain grace and beauty who wear it so unobtrusively that it takes a while to notice. Her dark-brown face is surrounded by the total whiteness of her hair, and, being a woman who has adjusted to many things in life and overcome many more, her face is full of strength. She has, we can see, wit and faith of a kind that keep her eyes lit and full of interest and expectancy. She is, in a word, a beautiful woman. Her bearing is perhaps most like the noble bearing of the women of the Hereros of Southwest Africa—rather as if she imagines that as she walks she still bears a basket or a vessel upon her head. Her speech, on the other hand, is as careless as her carriage is precise—she is inclined to slur everything—but her voice is perhaps not so much quiet as simply soft.)

Mama: Who that 'round here slamming doors at this hour?

(She crosses through the room, goes to the window, opens it, and brings in a feeble little plant growing doggedly in a small pot on the window sill. She feels the dirt and puts it back out.)

Ruth: That was Walter Lee. He and Bennie was at it again.

Mama: My children and they tempers. Lord, if this little old plant don't get more sun than it's been getting it ain't never going to see spring again. *(She turns from the window.)* What's the matter with you this morning, Ruth? You looks right peaked. You aiming to iron all them things? Leave some for me. I'll get to 'em this afternoon. Bennie honey, it's too drafty for you to be sitting 'round half dressed. Where's your robe?

Beneatha: In the cleaners.

Mama: Well, go get mine and put it on.

Beneatha: I'm not cold, Mama, honest.

Mama: I know—but you so thin . . .

Beneatha *(Irritably.):* Mama, I'm not cold.

Mama *(Seeing the make-down bed as Travis has left it.):* Lord have mercy, look at that poor bed. Bless his heart—he tries, don't he?

(She moves to the bed Travis has sloppily made up.)

Ruth: No—he don't half try at all 'cause he knows you going to come along behind him and fix everything. That's just how come he don't know how to do nothing right now—you done spoiled that boy so.

Mama: Well—he's a little boy. Ain't supposed to know 'bout housekeeping. My baby, that's what he is. What you fix for his breakfast this morning?

Ruth *(Angrily.):* I feed my son, Lena!

Mama: I ain't meddling—*(Underbreath; busy-bodyish.)* I just noticed all last week he had cold cereal, and when it starts getting this chilly in the fall a child ought to have some hot grits or something when he goes out in the cold—

Ruth *(Furious.):* I gave him hot oats—is that all right!

Mama: I ain't meddling. *(Pause.)* Put a lot of nice butter on it? *(Ruth shoots her an angry look and does not reply.)* He likes lots of butter.

Ruth *(Exasperated.):* Lena—

Mama *(To Beneatha. Mama is inclined to wander conversationally sometimes.):* What was you and your brother fussing 'bout this morning?

Beneatha: It's not important, Mama.

(She gets up and goes to look out at the bathroom, which is apparently free, and she picks up her towels and rushes out.)

Mama: What was they fighting about?

Ruth: Now you know as well as I do.

Mama *(Shaking her head.):* Brother still worrying hisself sick about that money?

Ruth: You know he is.

Mama: You had breakfast?

Ruth: Some coffee.

Mama: Girl, you better start eating and looking after yourself better. You almost thin as Travis.

Ruth: Lena—

Mama: Un-hunh?

Ruth: What are you going to do with it?

Mama: Now don't you start, child. It's too early in the morning to be talking about money. It ain't Christian.

Ruth: It's just that he got his heart set on that store—

Mama: You mean that liquor store that Willy Harris want him to invest in?

Ruth: Yes—

Mama: We ain't no business people, Ruth. We just plain working folks.

Ruth: Ain't nobody business people till they go into business. Walter Lee say colored people ain't never going to start getting ahead till they start gambling on some different kinds of things in the world—investments and things.

Mama: What done got into you, girl? Walter Lee done finally sold you on investing.

Ruth: No. Mama, something is happening between Walter and me. I don't know what it is—but he needs something—something I can't give him any more. He needs this chance, Lena.

Mama *(Frowning deeply.):* But liquor, honey—

Ruth: Well—like Walter say—I spec people going to always be drinking themselves some liquor.

Mama: Well—whether they drinks it or not ain't none of my business. But whether I go into business selling it to 'em *is,* and I don't want that on my ledger this late in life. *(Stopping suddenly and studying her daughter-in-law.)* Ruth Younger, what's the matter with you today? You look like you could fall over right there.

Ruth: I'm tired.

Mama: Then you better stay home from work today.

Ruth: I can't stay home. She'd be calling up the agency and screaming at them, "My girl didn't come in today—send me somebody! My girl didn't come in!" Oh, she just have a fit . . .

Mama: Well, let her have it. I'll just call her up and say you got the flu—

Ruth *(Laughing.):* Why the flu?

Mama: 'Cause it sounds respectable to 'em. Something white people get, too. they know 'bout the flu. Otherwise they think you been cut up or something when you tell 'em you sick.

Ruth: I got to go in. We need the money.

Mama: Somebody would of thought my children done all but starved to death the way they talk about money here late. Child, we got a great big old check coming tomorrow.

Ruth *(Sincerely, but also self-righteously.):* Now that's your money. It ain't got nothing to do with me. We all feel like that—Walter and Bennie and me—even Travis.

Mama *(Thoughtfully, and suddenly very far away.):* Ten thousand dollars—

Ruth: Sure is wonderful.

Mama: Ten thousand dollars.

Ruth: You know what you should do, Miss Lena? You should take yourself a trip somewhere. To Europe or South America or someplace—

Mama *(Throwing up her hands at the thought.):* Oh, child!

Ruth: I'm serious. Just pack up and leave! Go on away and enjoy yourself some. Forget about the family and have yourself a ball for once in your life—

Mama *(Drily.):* You sound like I'm just about ready to die. Who'd go with me? What I look like wandering 'round Europe by myself?

Ruth: Shoot—these here rich white women do it all the time. They don't think nothing of packing up they suitcases and piling on one of them big steamships and—swoosh!—they gone, child.

Mama: Something always told me I wasn't no rich white woman.

Ruth: Well—what are you going to do with it then?

Mama: I ain't rightly decided. *(Thinking. She speaks now with emphasis.)* Some of it got to be put away for Beneatha and her schoolin'—and ain't nothing going to touch that part of it. Nothing. *(She waits several seconds, trying to make up her mind about something, and looks at Ruth a little tentatively before going on.)* Been thinking that we maybe could meet the notes on a little old two-story somewhere, with a yard where Travis could play in the summertime, if we use part of the insurance for a down payment and everybody kind of pitch in. I could maybe take on a little day work again, few days a week—

Ruth *(Studying her mother-in-law furtively and concentrating on her ironing, anxious to encourage without seeming to.):* Well, Lord knows, we've put enough rent into this here rat trap to pay for four houses by now . . .

Mama *(Looking up at the words "rat trap" and then looking around and leaning back and sighing—in a suddenly reflective mood—.):* "Rat trap"—yes, that's all it is. *(Smiling.)* I remember just as well the day me and Big Walter moved in here. Hadn't been married but two weeks and wasn't planning on living here no more than a year. *(She shakes her head at the dissolved dream.)* We was going to set away, little by little, don't you know, and buy a little place out in Morgan Park. We had even picked out the house. *(Chuckling a little.)* Looks right dumpy today. But Lord, child, you should know all the dreams I had 'bout buying that house and fixing it up and making me a little garden in the back— *(She waits and stops smiling.)* And didn't none of it happen.

(Dropping her hands in a futile gesture.)

Ruth *(Keeps her head down, ironing.):* Yes, life can be a barrel of disappointments, sometimes.

Mama: Honey, Big Walter would come in here some nights back then and slump down on that couch there and just look at the rug, and look at me and look at the rug and then back at me—and I'd know he was down then . . . really down. *(After a second very long and thoughtful pause; she is seeing back to times that only she can see.)* And then, Lord, when I lost that baby—little Claude—I almost thought I was going to lose Big Walter too. Oh, that man grieved hisself! He was one man to love his children.

Ruth: Ain't nothin' can tear at you like losin' your baby.

Mama: I guess that's how come that man finally worked hisself to death like he done. Like he was fighting his own war with this here world that took his baby from him.

Ruth: He sure was a fine man, all right. I always liked Mr. Younger.

Mama: Crazy 'bout his children! God knows there was plenty wrong with Walter Younger—hard-headed, mean, kind of wild with women—plenty wrong with him. But he sure loved his children. Always wanted them to have something—be something. That's where Brother gets all these notions, I reckon. Big Walter used to say, he's get right wet in the eyes sometimes, lean his head back with the water standing in his eyes and say, "Seem like God didn't see fit to give the black man nothing but dreams—but He did give us children to make them dreams seem worth while." *(She smiles.)* He could talk like that, don't you know.

Ruth: Yes, he sure could. He was a good man, Mr. Younger.

Mama: Yes, a fine man—just couldn't never catch up with his dreams, that's all.

(Beneatha comes in, brushing her hair and looking up to the ceiling, where the sound of a vacuum cleaner has started up.)

Beneatha: What could be so dirty on that woman's rugs that she has to vacuum them every single day?

Ruth: I wish certain young women 'round here who I could name would take inspiration about certain rugs in a certain apartment I could also mention.

Beneatha *(Shrugging.):* How much cleaning can a house need, for Christ's sakes.

Mama *(Not liking the Lord's name used thus.):* Bennie!

Ruth: Just listen to her—just listen!

Beneatha: Oh, God!

Mama: If you use the Lord's name just one more time—

Beneatha *(A bit of a whine.):* Oh, Mama—

Ruth: Fresh—just fresh as salt, this girl!

Beneatha *(Drily.):* Well—if the salt loses its savor—

Mama: Now that will do. I just ain't going to have you 'round here reciting the scriptures in vain—you hear me?

Beneatha: How did I manage to get on everybody's wrong side by just walking into a room?

Ruth: If you weren't so fresh—

Beneatha: Ruth, I'm twenty years old.

Mama: What time you be home from school today?

Beneatha: Kind of late. *(With enthusiasm.)* Madeline is going to start my guitar lessons today.

(Mama and Ruth look up with the same expression.)

Mama: Your *what* kind of lessons?

Beneatha: Guitar.

Ruth: Oh, Father!

Mama: How come you done taken it in your mind to learn to play the guitar?

Beneatha: I just want to, that's all.

Mama *(Smiling.):* Lord, child, don't you know what to do with yourself? How long it going to be before you get tired of this now—like you got tired of that little play-acting group you joined last year? *(Looking at Ruth.)* And what was it the year before that?

Ruth: The horseback-riding club for which she bought that fifty-five-dollar riding habit that's been hanging in the closet ever since!

Mama *(To Beneatha.):* Why you got to flit so from one thing to another, baby?

Beneatha *(Sharply.):* I just want to learn to play the guitar. Is there anything wrong with that?

Mama: Ain't nobody trying to stop you. I just wonders sometimes why you has to flit so from one thing to another all the time. You ain't never done nothing with all that camera equipment you brought home—

Beneatha: I don't flit! I—I experiment with different forms of expression—

Ruth: Like riding a horse?

Beneatha: —People have to express themselves one way or another.

Mama: What is it you want to express?

Beneatha *(Angrily.):* Me! *(Mama and Ruth look at each other and burst into raucous laughter.)* Don't worry—I don't expect you to understand.

Mama *(To change the subject.):* Who you going out with tomorrow night?

Beneatha *(With displeasure.):* George Murchison again.

Mama *(Pleased.):* Oh—you getting a little sweet on him?

Ruth: You ask me, this child ain't sweet on nobody but herself—*(Underbreath.)* Express herself!

(They laugh.)

Beneatha: Oh—I like George all right, Mama. I mean I like him enough to go out with him and stuff, but—

Ruth *(For devilment.):* What does *and stuff* mean?

Beneatha: Mind your own business.

Mama: Stop picking at her now, Ruth. *(A thoughtful pause, and then a suspicious sudden look at her daughter as she turns in her chair for emphasis.)* What *does* it mean?

Beneatha *(Wearily.):* Oh, I just mean I couldn't ever really be serious about George. He's—he's so shallow.

Ruth: Shallow—what do you mean he's shallow? He's *Rich!*

Mama: Hush, Ruth.

Beneatha: I know he's rich. He knows he's rich, too.

Ruth: Well—what other qualities a man got to have to satisfy you, little girl?

Beneatha: You wouldn't even begin to understand. Anybody who married Walter could not possibly understand.

Mama *(Outraged.):* What kind of way is that to talk about your brother?

Beneatha: Brother is a flip—let's face it.

Mama *(To Ruth, helplessly.):* What's a flip?

Ruth *(Glad to add kindling.):* She's saying he's crazy.

Beneatha: Not crazy. Brother isn't really crazy yet—he—he's an elaborate neurotic.

Mama: Hush your mouth!

Beneatha: As for George. Well. George looks good—he's got a beautiful car and he takes me to nice places and, as my sister-in-law says, he is probably the richest boy I will ever get to know and I even like him sometimes—but if the Youngers are sitting around waiting to see if their little Bennie is going to tie up the family with the Murchisons, they are wasting their time.

Ruth: You mean you wouldn't marry George Murchison if he asked you someday? That pretty, rich thing? Honey, I knew you was odd—

Beneatha: No I would not marry him if all I felt for him was what I feel now. Besides, George's family wouldn't really like it.

Mama: Why not?

Beneatha: Oh, Mama—the Murchisons are honest-to-God-real-*live*-rich colored people, and the only people in the world who are more snobbish than rich white people are rich colored people. I thought somebody knew that. I've met Mrs. Murchison. She's a scene!

Mama: You must not dislike people 'cause they well off, honey.

Beneatha: Why not? It makes just as much sense as disliking people 'cause they are poor, and lots of people do that.

Ruth *(A wisdom-of-the-ages manner. To Mama.):* Well, she'll get over some of this—

Beneatha: Get over it? What are you talking about, Ruth? Listen, I'm going to be a doctor. I'm not worried about who I'm going to marry yet—if I ever get married.

Mama *and* **Ruth:** *If!*

Mama: Now, Bennie—

Beneatha: Oh, I probably will . . . but first I'm going to be a doctor, and George, for one, still thinks that's pretty funny. I couldn't be bothered with that. I am going to be a doctor and everybody around here better understand that!

Mama *(Kindly.):* 'Course you going to be a doctor, honey, God willing.

Beneatha *(Drily.):* God hasn't got a thing to do with it.

Mama: Beneatha—that just wasn't necessary.

Beneatha: Well—neither is God. I get sick of hearing about God.

Mama: Beneatha!

Beneatha: I mean it! I'm just tired of hearing about God all the time. What has He got to do with anything? Does he pay tuition?

Mama: You 'bout to get your fresh little jaw slapped!

Ruth: That's just what she needs, all right!

Beneatha: Why? Why can't I say what I want to around here, like everybody else?

Mama: It don't sound nice for a young girl to say things like that—you wasn't brought up that way. Me and your father went to trouble to get you and Brother to church every Sunday.

Beneatha: Mama, you don't understand. It's all a matter of ideas, and God is just one idea I don't accept. It's not important. I am not going out and be immoral or commit crimes because I don't believe in God. I don't even think about it. It's just that I get tired of Him getting credit for all the things the human race achieves through its own stubborn effort. There simply is no blasted God—there is only man and it is he who makes miracles!

(Mama absorbs this speech, studies her daughter and rises slowly and crosses to Beneatha and slaps her powerfully across the face. After, there is only silence and the daughter drops her eyes from her mother's face, and Mama is very tall before her.)

Mama: Now—you say after me, in my mother's house there is still God. *(There is a long pause and Beneatha stares at the floor wordlessly. Mama repeats the phrase with precision and cool emotion.)* In my mother's house there is still God.

Beneatha: In my mother's house there is still God.

(A long pause.)

Mama *(Walking away from Beneatha, too disturbed for triumphant posture. Stopping and turning back to her daughter.):* There are some ideas we ain't going to have in this house. Not long as I am at the head of this family.

Beneatha: Yes, ma'am.

(Mama walks out of the room.)

Ruth *(Almost gently, with profound understanding.):* You think you a woman, Bennie—but you still a little girl. What you did was childish—so you got treated like a child.

Beneatha: I see. *(Quietly.)* I also see that everybody thinks it's all right for Mama to be a tyrant. But all the tyranny in the world will never put a God in the heavens!

(She picks up her books and goes out.)

Ruth *(Goes to Mama's door.):* She said she was sorry.

Mama *(Coming out, going to her plant.):* They frightens me, Ruth. My children.

Ruth: You got good children, Lena. They just a little off sometimes—but they're good.

Mama: No—there's something come down between me and them that don't let us understand each other and I don't know what it is. One done almost lost his mind thinking 'bout money all the time and the other done commence to talk about things I can't seem to understand in no form or fashion. What is it that's changing, Ruth?

Ruth *(Soothingly, older than her years.):* Now . . . you taking it all too seriously. You just got strong-willed children and it takes a strong woman like you to keep 'em in hand.

Mama *(Looking at her plant and sprinkling a little water on it.):* They spirited all right, my children. Got to admit they got spirit—Bennie and Walter. Like this little old plant that ain't never had enough sunshine or nothing—and look at it . . .

(She has her back to Ruth, who has had to stop ironing and lean against something and put the back of her hand to her forehead.)

Ruth *(Trying to keep Mama from noticing.):* You . . . sure . . . loves that little old thing, don't you? . . .

Mama: Well, I always wanted me a garden like I used to see sometimes at the back of the houses down home. This plant is close as I ever got to having one. *(She looks out of the window as she replaces the plant.)* Lord, ain't nothing as dreary as the view from this window on a dreary day, is there? Why ain't you singing this morning, Ruth? Sing that "No Ways Tired." That song always lifts me up so—*(She turns at last to see that Ruth has slipped quietly into a chair, in a state of semiconsciousness.)* Ruth! Ruth honey—what's the matter with you . . . Ruth!

(Curtain.)

Act One

Scene 2

It is the following morning; a Saturday morning, and house cleaning is in progress at the Youngers. Furniture has been shoved hither and yon and Mama is giving the kitchen-area walls a washing down. Beneatha, in dungarees, with a handkerchief tired around her face, is spraying insecticide into the cracks in the walls. As they work, the radio is on and a Southside disk-jockey program is inappropriately filling the house with a rather exotic saxophone blues. Travis, the sole idle one, is leaning on his arms, looking out of the window.

1 **Travis:** Grandmama, that stuff Bennie is using smells awful. Can I go downstairs, please?

Mama: Did you get all them chores done already? I ain't seen you doing much.

Travis: Yes'm—finished early. Where did Mama go this morning?

Mama *(Looking at Beneatha.)*: She had to go on a little errand.

5 **Travis:** Where?

Mama: To tend to her business.

Travis: Can I go outside then?

Mama: Oh, I guess so. You better stay right in front of the house, though . . . and keep a good lookout for the postman.

Travis: Yes'm. *(He starts out and decides to give his Aunt Beneatha a good swat on the legs as he passes her.)* Leave them poor little old cockroaches alone, they ain't bothering you none.

(He runs as she swings the spray gun at him both viciously and playfully. Walter enters from the bedroom and goes to the phone.)

10 **Mama:** Look out there, girl, before you be spilling some of that stuff on that child!

Travis *(Teasing.)*: That's right—look out now!

(He exits.)

Beneatha *(Drily.)*: I can't imagine that it would hurt him—it has never hurt the roaches.

Mama: Well, little boys' hides ain't as tough as Southside roaches.

Walter *(Into phone.)*: Hello—Let me talk to Willy Harris.

15 **Mama:** You better get over there behind the bureau. I seen one marching out of there like Napoleon yesterday.

Walter: Hello, Willy? It ain't come yet. It'll be here in a few minutes. Did the lawyer give you the papers?

Beneatha: There's really only one way to get rid of them, Mama—

Mama: How?

Beneatha: Set fire to this building.

20 **Walter:** Good. Good. I'll be right over.

Beneatha: Where did Ruth go, Walter?

Walter: I don't know.

(He exits abruptly.)

Beneatha: Mama, where did Ruth go?

Mama *(Looking at her with meaning.):* To the doctor, I think.

Beneatha: The doctor? What's the matter? *(They exchange glances.)* You don't think—

Mama *(With her sense of drama.):* Now I ain't saying what I think. But I ain't never been wrong 'bout a woman neither.

(The phone rings.)

Beneatha *(At the phone.):* Hay-lo . . . *(Pause, and a moment of recognition.)* Well—when did you get back! . . . And how was it? . . . Of course I've missed you—in my way . . . This morning? No . . . house cleaning and all that and Mama hates it if I let people come over when the house is like this . . . You *have?* Well, that's different . . . What is it— Oh, what the hell, come on over . . . Right, see you then.

(She hangs up.)

Mama *(Who has listened vigorously, as is her habit.):* Who is that you inviting over here with this house looking like this? You ain't got the pride you was born with!

Beneatha: Asagai doesn't care how houses look, Mama—he's an intellectual.

Mama: *Who?*

Beneatha: Asagai—Joseph Asagai. He's an African boy I met on campus. He's been studying in Canada all summer.

Mama: What's his name?

Beneatha: Asagai, Joseph. Ah-sah-guy . . . He's from Nigeria.

Mama: Oh, that's the little country that was founded by slaves way back . . .

Beneatha: No, Mama—that's Liberia.

Mama: I don't think I never met no African before.

Beneatha: Well, do me a favor and don't ask him a whole lot of ignorant questions about Africans. I mean, do they wear clothes and all that—

Mama: Well, now, I guess if you think we so ignorant 'round here maybe you shouldn't bring your friends here—

Beneatha: It's just that people ask such crazy things. All anyone seems to know about when it comes to Africa is Tarzan—

Mama *(Indignantly.):* Why should I know anything about Africa?

Beneatha: Why do you give money at church for the missionary work?

Mama: Well, that's to help save people.

Beneatha: You mean save them from *heathenism*—

Mama *(Innocently.):* Yes.

Beneatha: I'm afraid they need more salvation from the British and the French.

(Ruth comes in forlornly and pulls off her coat with dejection. They both turn to look at her.)

Ruth *(Dispiritedly.):* Well, I guess from all the happy faces—everybody knows.

Beneatha: You pregnant?

Mama: Lord have mercy, I sure hope it's a little old girl. Travis ought to have a sister.

(Beneatha and Ruth give her a hopeless look for this grandmotherly enthusiasm.)

Beneatha: How far along are you?

Ruth: Two months.

Beneatha: Did you mean to? I mean did you plan it or was it an accident?

Mama: What do you know about planning or not planning?

Beneatha: Oh, Mama.

Ruth *(Wearily.):* She's twenty years old, Lena.

Beneatha: Did you plan it, Ruth?

Ruth: Mind your own business.

Beneatha: It's my business—where is he going to live, on the *roof? (There is silence following the remark as the three women react to the sense of it.)* Gee—I didn't mean that, Ruth, honest. Gee, I don't feel like that at all. I—I think it is wonderful.

Ruth *(Dully.):* Wonderful.

Beneatha: Yes—really.

Mama *(Looking at Ruth, worried.):* Doctor say everything going to be all right?

Ruth *(Far away.):* Yes—she says everything is going to be fine . . .

Mama *(Immediately suspicious.):* "She"— What doctor you went to?

(Ruth folds over, near hysteria.)

Mama *(Worriedly hovering over Ruth.):* Ruth honey—what's the matter with you—you sick?

(Ruth has her fists clenched on her thighs and is fighting hard to suppress a scream that seems to be rising in her.)

Beneatha: What's the matter with her, Mama?

Mama *(Working her fingers in Ruth's shoulder to relax her.):* She be all right. Women gets right depressed sometimes when they get her way. *(Speaking softly, expertly, rapidly.)* Now you just relax. That's right . . . just lean back, don't think 'bout nothing at all . . . nothing at all—

Ruth: I'm all right . . .

(The glass-eyed look melts and then she collapses into a fit of heavy sobbing. The bells rings.)

Beneatha: Oh, my God—that must be Asagai.

Mama *(To Ruth.)*: Come on now, honey. You need to lie down and rest awhile . . . then have some nice hot food.

(They exit, Ruth's weight on her mother-in-law. Beneatha, herself profoundly disturbed, opens the door to admit a rather dramatic-looking young man with a large package.)

Asagai: Hello, Alaiyo—

Beneatha *(Holding the door open and regarding him with pleasure.)*: Hello . . . *(Long pause.)* Well—come in. And please excuse everything. My mother was very upset about my letting anyone come here with the place like this.

Assagai *(Coming into the room.)*: You look disturbed too . . . Is something wrong?

Beneatha *(Still at the door, absently.)*: Yes . . . we've all got acute ghetto-itus. *(She smiles and comes toward him, finding a cigarette and sitting.)* So—sit down! How was Canada?

Asagai *(A sophisticate.)*: Canadian.

Beneatha *(Looking at him.)*: I'm very glad you are back.

Asagai *(Looking back at her in turn.)*: Are you really?

Beneatha: Yes—very.

Asagai: Why—you were quite glad when I went away. What happened?

Beneatha: You went away.

Asagai: Ahhhhhhhh.

Beneatha: Before—you wanted to be so serious before there was time.

Asagai: How much time must there be before one knows what one feels?

Beneatha: *(Stalling this particular conversation. Her hands pressed together, in a deliberately childish gesture.)*: What did you bring me?

Asagai *(Handing her the package.)*: Open it and see.

Beneatha: *(Eagerly opening the package and drawing out some records and the colorful robes of a Nigerian woman.)*: Oh, Asagai! . . . You got them for me! . . . How beautiful . . . and the records too! *(She lifts out the robes and runs to the mirror with them and holds the drapery up in front of herself.)*

Asagai *(Coming to her at the mirror.)*: I shall have to teach you how to drape it properly. *(He flings the material about her for the moment and stands back to look at her.)* Ah—*Oh-pay-gay-day, oh-gbah-mu-shay. (A Yoruba exclamation for admiration.)* You wear it well . . . very well . . . mutilated hair and all.

Beneatha *(Turning suddenly.)*: My hair—what's wrong with my hair?

Asagai *(Shrugging.)*: Were you born with it like that?

Beneatha *(Reaching up to touch it.)*: No . . . of course not.

(She looks back to the mirror, disturbed.)

Asagai *(Smiling.)*: How then?

Beneatha: You know perfectly well how . . . as crinkly as yours . . . that's how.

Asagai: And it is ugly to you that way?

Beneatha: *(Quickly.):* Oh, no—not ugly . . . *(More slowly, apologetically.)* But it's so hard to manage when it's, well—raw.

Asagai: And so to accommodate that—you mutilate it every week?

Beneatha: It's not mutilation!

Asagai *(Laughing aloud at her seriousness.):* Oh . . . please! I am only teasing you because you are so very serious about these things. *(He stands back from her and folds his arms across his chest as he watches her pulling at her hair and frowning in the mirror.)* Do you remember the first time you met me at school? . . . *(He laughs.)* You came up to me and you said—and I thought you were the most serious little thing I had ever seen—you said: *(He imitates her.)* "Mr. Asagai—I want very much to talk with you. About Africa. You see, Mr. Asagai, I am looking for my *identity!*"

(He laughs.)

Beneatha *(Turning to him, not laughing.):* Yes—

(Her face is quizzical, profoundly disturbed.)

Asagai *(Still teasing and reaching out and taking her face in his hands and turning her profile to him.):* Well . . . it is true that this is not so much a profile of a Hollywood queen as perhaps as a queen of the Nile— *(A mock dismissal of the important of the question.)* But what does it matter? Assimilationism is so popular in your country.

Beneatha *(Wheeling, passionately, sharply.):* I am not an assimilationist!

Asagai *(The protest hangs in the room for a moment and Asagai studies her, his laughter fading.):* Such a serious one. *(There is a pause.)* So—you like the robes? You must take excellent care of them—they are from my sister's personal wardrobe.

Beneatha *(With incredulity.):* You—you sent all the way home—for me?

Asagai *(With charm.):* For you—I would do much more . . . Well, that is what I came for. I must go.

Beneatha: Will you call me Monday?

Asagai: Yes . . . We have a great deal to talk about. I mean about identity and time and all that.

Beneatha: Time?

Asagai: Yes. About how much time one needs to know what one feels.

Beneatha: You never understood that there is more than one kind of feeling which can exist between a man and a woman—or, at least, there should be.

Asagai: *(Shaking his head negatively but gently.):* No. Between a man and a woman there need be only one kind of feeling. I have that for you . . . Now even . . . right this moment . . .

Beneatha: I know—and by itself—it won't do. I can find that anywhere.

Asagai: For a woman it should be enough.

Beneatha: I know—because that's what it says in all the novels that men write. But it isn't. Go ahead and laugh—but I'm not interested in being someone's little episode in America or—*(With feminine vengeance.)*—one of them! *(Asagai has burst into laughter again.)* That's funny as hell, huh!

Asagai: It's just that every American girl I have known has said that to me. White—black—in this you are all the same. And the same speech, too!

Beneatha *(Angrily.):* Yuk, yuk, yuk!

Asagai: It's how you can be sure that the world's most liberated women are not liberated at all. You all talk about it too much!

(Mama enters and is immediately all social charm because of the presence of a guest.)

Beneatha: Oh—Mama—this is Mr. Asagai.

Mama: How do you do?

Asagai *(Total politeness to an elder.):* How do you do, Mrs. Younger. Please forgive me for coming at such an outrageous hour on a Saturday.

Mama: Well, you are quite welcome. I just hope you understand that our house don't always look like this. *(Chatterish.)* You must come again. I would love to hear all about—*(Not sure of the name)*—your country. I think it's so sad the way our American Negroes don't know nothing about Africa 'cept Tarzan and all that. And all that money they pour into these churches when they ought to be helping you people over there drive out them French and Englishmen done taken away your land.

(The mother flashes a slightly superior look at her daughter upon completion of the recitation.)

Asagai *(Taken aback by this sudden and acutely unrelated expression of sympathy.):* Yes . . . yes . . .

Mama *(Smiling at him suddenly and relaxing and looking him over.):* How many miles is it from here to where you come from?

Asagai: Many thousands.

Mama *(Looking at him as she would Walter.):* I bet you don't half look after yourself, being away from your mama either. I spec you better come 'round here from time to time and get yourself some decent home-cooked meals . . .

Asagai *(Moved.):* Thank you. Thank you very much. *(They are all quiet, then—)* Well . . . I must go. I will call you Monday, Alaiyo.

Mama: What's that he call you?

Asagai: Oh—"Alaiyo." I hope you don't mind. It is what you would call a nickname, I think. It is a Yoruba word. I am a Yoruba.

Mama *(Looking at Beneatha.):* I—I thought he was from—

Asagai *(Understanding.):* Nigeria is my country. Yoruba is my tribal origin—

Beneatha: You didn't tell us what Alaiyo means . . . for all I know, you might be calling me Little Idiot or something . . .

Asagai: Well . . . let me see . . . I do not know how just to explain it . . . The sense of a thing can be so different when it changes languages.

Beneatha: You're evading.

Asagai: No—really it is difficult . . . *(Thinking.)* It means . . . it means One for Whom Bread—Food—Is Not Enough. *(He looks at her.)* Is that all right?

Beneatha *(Understanding, softly.):* Thank you.

Mama *(Looking from one to the other and not understanding any of it.):* Well . . . that's nice . . . You must come see us again—Mr.—

Asagai: Ah-sah-guy . . .

Mama: Yes . . . Do come again.

Asagai: Good-bye.

(He exits.)

Mama *(After him.):* Lord, that's a pretty thing just went out here! *(Insinuatingly, to her daughter.)* Yes, I guess I see why we done commence to get so interested in Africa 'round here. Missionaries my aunt Jenny!

(She exits.)

Beneatha: Oh, Mama! . . .

(She picks up the Nigerian dress and holds it up to her in front of the mirror again. She sets the headdress on haphazardly and then notices her hair again and clutches at it and then replaces the headdress and frowns at herself. Then she starts to wriggle in front of the mirror as she thinks a Nigerian woman might. Travis enters and regards her.)

Travis: You cracking up?

Beneatha: Shut up.

(She pulls the headdress off and looks at herself in the mirror and clutches at her hair again and squinches her eyes as if trying to imagine something. Then, suddenly, she gets her raincoat and kerchief and hurriedly prepares for going out.)

Mama *(Coming back into the room.):* She's resting now. Travis, baby, run next door and ask Miss Johnson to please let me have a little kitchen cleanser. This here can is empty as Jacob's kettle.

Travis: I just came in.

Mama: Do as you told. *(He exits and she looks at her daughter.)* Where you going?

Beneatha *(Halting at the door.):* To become a queen of the Nile!

(She exits in a breathless blaze of glory. Ruth appears in the bedroom doorway.)

Mama: Who told you to get up?

Ruth: Ain't nothing wrong with me to be lying in no bed for. Where did Bennie go?

Mama *(Drumming her fingers.):* Far as I could make out—to Egypt. *(Ruth just looks at her.)* What time is it getting to?

Ruth: Ten twenty. And the mailman going to ring that bell this morning just like he done every morning for the last umpteen years.

(Travis comes in with the cleanser can.)

Travis: She say to tell you that she don't have much.

Mama *(Angrily.):* Lord, some people I could name sure is tight-fisted! *(Directing her grandson.)* Mark two cans of cleanser down on the list there. If she that hard up for kitchen cleanser, I sure don't want to forget to get her none!

Ruth: Lena—maybe the woman is just short on cleanser—

Mama *(Not listening.):* —Much baking powder as she done borrowed from me all these years, she could of done gone into the baking business!

(The bell sounds suddenly and sharply and all three are stunned—serious and silent—mid-speech. In spite of all the other conversations and distractions of the morning, this is what they have been waiting for, even Travis, who looks helplessly from his mother to his grandmother. Ruth is the first to come to life again.)

Ruth *(To Travis.):* Get down them steps, boy!

(Travis snaps to life and flies out to get the mail.)

Mama *(Her eyes wide, her hand to her breast.):* You mean it done really come?

Ruth *(Excited.)* Oh, Miss Lena!

Mama *(Collecting herself.):* Well . . . I don't know what we all so excited about 'round here for. We known it was coming for months.

Ruth: That's a whole lot different from having it come and being able to hold it in your hands . . . a piece of paper worth ten thousand dollars . . . *(Travis bursts back into the room. He holds the envelope high above his head, like a little dancer, his face is radiant and he is breathless. He moves to his grandmother with sudden slow ceremony and puts the envelope into her hands. She accepts it, and then merely holds it and looks at it.)* Come on! Open it . . . Lord have mercy, I wish Walter Lee was here!

Travis: Open it, Grandmama!

Mama *(Staring at it.):* Now you all be quiet. It's just a check.

Ruth: Open it . . .

Mama *(Still staring at it.):* Now don't act silly . . . We ain't never been no people to act silly 'bout no money—

Ruth *(Swiftly.):* We ain't never had none before—*open it!*

(Mama finally makes a good strong tear and pulls out the thin blue slice of paper and inspects it closely. The boy and his mother study it raptly over Mama's shoulders.)

Mama: *Travis! (She is counting off with doubt.)* Is that the right number of zeros.

Travis: Yes'm . . . ten thousand dollars. Gaalee, Grandmama, you rich.

Mama *(She holds the check away from her, still looking at it. Slowly her face sobers into a mask of unhappiness.):* Ten thousand dollars. *(She hands it to Ruth.)* Put it away somewhere, Ruth. *(She does not look at Ruth; her eyes seem to be seeing something somewhere very far off.)* Ten thousand dollars they give you. Ten thousand dollars.

Travis *(To his mother, sincerely.):* What's the matter with Grandmama—don't she want to be rich?

Ruth *(Distractedly.):* You go on out and play now, baby. *(Travis exits. Mama start wiping dishes absently, humming intently to herself. Ruth turns to her, with kind exasperation.)* You've gone and got yourself upset.

Mama *(Not looking at her.):* I spec if it wasn't for you all . . . I would just put that money away or give it to the church or something.

Ruth: Now what kind of talk is that. Mr. Younger would just be plain mad if he could hear you talking foolish like that.

Mama *(Stopping and staring off.):* Yes . . . he sure would. *(Sighing.)* We got enough to do with that money, all right. *(She halts then, and turns and looks at her daughter-in-law hard; Ruth avoids her eyes and Mama wipes her hands with finality and starts to speak firmly to Ruth.)* Where did you go today, girl?

Ruth: To the doctor.

Mama *(Impatiently.):* Now, Ruth . . . you know better than that. Old Doctor Jones is strange enough in his way but there ain't nothing 'bout him make somebody slip and call him "she"—like you done this morning.

Ruth: Well, that's what happened—my tongue slipped.

Mama: You went to see that woman, didn't you?

Ruth *(Defensively, giving herself away.):* What woman you talking about?

Mama *(Angrily.):* That woman who—

(Walter enters in great excitement.)

Walter: Did it come?

Mama *(Quietly.):* Can't you give people a Christian greeting before you start asking about money?

Walter *(To Ruth.):* Did it come? *(Ruth unfolds the check and lays it quietly before him, watching him intently with thoughts of her own. Walter sits down and grasps it close and counts off the zeros.)* Ten thousand dollars— *(He turns suddenly, frantically to his mother and draws some papers out of his breast pocket.)* Mama—look. Old Willy Harris put everything on paper—

Mama: Son—I think you ought to talk to your wife . . . I'll go on out and leave you alone if you want—

Walter: I can talk to her later—Mama, look—

Mama: Son—

Walter: WILL SOMEBODY PLEASE LISTEN TO ME TODAY!

Mama *(Quietly.):* I don't 'low no yellin' in this house, Walter Lee, and you know it—*(Walter stares at them in frustration and starts to speak several times.)* And there ain't going to be no investing in no liquor stores. I don't aim to have to speak on that again.

(A long pause.)

Walter: Oh—so you don't aim to have to speak on that again? So *you* have decided . . . *(Crumpling his papers.)* Well, *you* tell that to my boy tonight when you put him to sleep on the living-room couch . . . *(Turning to Mama and speaking directly to her.)* Yeah—and tell it to my wife, Mama, tomorrow when she has to go out of here to look after somebody else's kids. And tell it to *me,* Mama, every time we need a new pair of curtains and I have to watch *you* go out and work in somebody's kitchen. Yeah, you tell me then!

(Walter starts out.)

Ruth: Where you going?

Walter: I'm going out!

Ruth: Where?

Walter: Just out of this house somewhere—

Ruth *(Getting her coat.):* I'll come too.

Walter: I don't want you to come!

Ruth: I got something to talk to you about, Walter.

Walter: That's too bad.

Mama *(Still quietly.):* Walter Lee—*(She waits and he finally turns and looks at her.)* Sit down.

Walter: I'm a grown man, Mama.

Mama: Ain't nobody said you wasn't grown. But you still in my house and my presence. And as long as you are—you'll talk to your wife civil. Now sit down.

Ruth *(Suddenly.):* Oh, let him go on out and drink himself to death! He makes me sick to my stomach! *(She flings her coat against him and exits to bedroom.)*

Walter *(Violently, flinging the coat after her.):* And you turn mine too, baby! *(Ruth goes into their bedroom and slam the door behind her.)* That was my greatest mistake—

Mama *(Still quietly.):* Walter, what is the matter with you?

Walter: Matter with me? Ain't nothing the matter with *me!*

Mama: Yes there is. Something eating you up like a crazy man. Something more than me not giving you this money. The past few years I been watching it happen to you. You get all nervous acting and kind of wild in the eyes—*(Walter jumps up impatiently at her words.)* I said sit there now, I'm talking to you!

Walter: Mama—I don't need no nagging at me today.

Mama: Seem like you getting to a place where you always tied up in some kind of knot about something. But if anybody ask you 'bout it you just yell at 'em and bust out the house and go out and drink somewheres. Walter Lee, people can't live with that. Ruth's a good, patient girl in her way—but you getting to be too much. Boy, don't make the mistake of driving that girl away from you.

Walter: Why—what she do for me?

Mama: She loves you.

Walter: Mama—I'm going out. I want to go off somewhere and be by myself for a while.

Mama: I'm sorry 'bout your liquor store, son. It just wasn't the thing for us to do. That's what I want to tell you about—

Walter: I got to go out, Mama—

(He rises.)

Mama: It's dangerous, son.

Walter: What's dangerous?

Mama: When a man goes outside his home to look for peace.

Walter *(Beseechingly.):* Then why can't there never be no peace in this house then?

Mama: You done found it in some other house?

Walter: No—there ain't no woman! Why do women always think there's a woman somewhere when a man gets restless. *(Coming to her.)* Mama—Mama—I want so many things . . .

Mama: Yes, son—

Walter: I want so many things that they are driving me kind of crazy . . . Mama—look at me.

Mama: I'm looking at you. You a good-looking boy. You got a job, a nice wife, a fine boy and—

Walter: A job. *(Looks at her.)* Mama, a job? I open and close car doors all day long. I drive a man around in his limousine and I say, "Yes, sir: no, sir; very good, sir; shall I take the Drive, sir?" Mama, that ain't no kind of job . . . that ain't nothing at all. *(Very quietly.)* Mama, I don't know if I can make you understand.

Mama: Understand what, baby?

Walter *(Quietly.):* Sometimes it's like I can see the future stretched out in front of me—just plain as day. The future, Mama. Hanging over there at the edge of my days. Just waiting for me—a big, looming blank space—full of *nothing*. Just waiting for *me*. *(Pause.)* Mama—sometimes when I'm downtown and pass them cool, quiet-looking restaurants where them white boys are sitting back and talking 'bout things . . . sitting there turning deals worth millions of dollars . . . sometimes I see guys don't look much older than me—

Mama: Son—how come you talk so much 'bout money?

Walter *(With immense passion.):* Because it is life, Mama!

Mama *(Quietly.):* Oh—*(Very quietly.)* So now it's life. Money is life. Once upon a time freedom used to be life—now it's money. I guess the world really do change . . .

Walter: No—it was always money, Mama. We just didn't know about it.

Mama: No . . . something has changed. *(She looks at him.)* You something new, boy. In my time we was worried about not being lynched and getting to the North if we could and how to stay alive and still have a pinch of dignity too . . . Now here come you and Beneatha—talking 'bout things we ain't never even thought about hardly, me and your daddy. You ain't satisfied or proud of nothing we done. I mean that you had a home; that we kept you out of trouble till you was grown; that you don't have to ride to work on the back of nobody's streetcar— You my children—but how different we done become.

Walter: You just don't understand, Mama, you just don't understand.

Mama: Son—do you know your wife is expecting another baby? *(Walter stands, stunned, and absorbs what his mother has said.)* That's what she wanted to talk to you about. *(Walter sinks down into a chair.)* This ain't for me to be telling—but you ought to know. *(She waits.)* I think Ruth is thinking 'bout getting rid of that child.

Walter *(Slowly understanding.)*: No—no—Ruth wouldn't do that.

Mama: When the world gets ugly enough—a woman will do anything for her family. *The part that's already living.*

Walter: You don't know Ruth, Mama, if you think she would do that.

(Ruth opens the bedroom door and stands there a little limp.)

Ruth *(Beaten.)*: Yes I would too, Walter. *(Pause.)* I gave her a five-dollar down payment.

(There is total silence as the man stares at his wife and the mother stares at her son.)

Mama *(Presently.)*: Well—*(Tightly.)* Well—son, I'm waiting to hear you say something . . . I'm waiting to hear how you be your father's son. Be the man he was . . . *(Pause.)* Your wife say she going to destroy your child. And I'm waiting to hear you talk like him and say we a people who give children life, not who destroys them—*(She rises.)* I'm waiting to see you stand up and look like your daddy and say we done give up one baby to poverty and that we ain't going to give up nary another one . . . I'm waiting.

Walter: Ruth—

Mama: If you a son of mine, tell her! *(Walter turns, looks at her and can say nothing. She continues, bitterly.)* You . . . you are a disgrace to your father's memory. Somebody get me my hat.

(Curtain.)

Act Two

Scene I

Time: Later the same day.

At rise: Ruth is ironing again. She has the radio going. Presently Beneatha's bedroom door opens and Ruth's mouth falls and she puts down the iron in fascination.

Ruth: What have we got on tonight!

Beneatha *(Emerging grandly from the doorway so that we can see her thoroughly robed in the costume Asagai brought.)*: You are looking at what a well-dressed Nigerian woman wears—*(She parades for Ruth, her hair completely hidden by the headdress; she is coquettishly fanning herself with an ornate oriental fan, mistakenly more like Butterfly than any Nigerian that ever was.)* Isn't it beautiful? *(She promenades to the radio and, with an arrogant flourish, turns off the good loud blues that is playing.)* Enough of this assimilationist junk! *(Ruth follows her with her eyes as she* *goes to the phonograph and puts on a record and turns and waits ceremoniously for the music to come up. Then, with a shout—)* OCOMOGOSIAY!

(Ruth jumps. The music comes up, a lovely Nigerian melody. Beneatha listens, enraptured, her eyes far away—"back to the past." She begins to dance. Ruth is dumbfounded.)

Ruth: What kind of dance is that?

Beneatha: A folk dance.

Ruth *(Pearl Bailey.):* What kind of folks do that, honey?

Beneatha: It's from Nigeria. It's a dance of welcome.

Ruth: Who you welcoming?

Beneatha: The men back to the village.

Ruth: Where they been?

Beneatha: How should I know—out hunting or something. Anyway, they are coming back now . . .

Ruth: Well, that's good.

Beneatha *(With the record.):*

Alundi, alundi
Alundi alunya
Jop pu a jeepua
Ang gu soooooooooo

Ai yai yae . . .
Ayehaye—alundi . . .

(Walter comes in during this performance; he has obviously been drinking. He leans against the door heavily and watches his sister, at first with distaste. Then his eyes look off—"back to the past"—as he lifts both his fists to the roof, screaming.)

Walter: YEAH . . . AND ETHIOPIA STRETCH FORTH HER HANDS AGAIN! . . .

Ruth *(Drily, looking at him.):* Yes—and Africa sure is claiming her own tonight. *(She gives them both up and starts ironing again.)*

Walter *(All in a drunken, dramatic shout.):* Shut up! . . . I'm digging them drums . . . them drums move me! . . . *(He makes his weaving way to his wife's face and leans in close to her.)* In my *heart of hearts—(He thumps his chest.)*—I am much warrior!

Ruth *(Without even looking up.):* In your heart of hearts you are much drunkard.

Walter *(Coming away from her and starting to wander around the room, shouting.):* Me and Jomo . . . *(Intently, in his sister's face. She has stopped dancing to watch him in this unknown mood.)* That's my man, Kenyatta. *(Shouting and thumping his chest.)* FLAMING SPEAR! HOT DAMN! *(He is suddenly in possession of an imaginary spear and actively spearing enemies all over the room.) OCOMOGOSIAY* . . . THE LION IS WAKING . . .

OWIMOWEH! *(He pulls his shirt open and leaps up on a table and gestures with his spear. The bell rings. Ruth goes to answer.)*

Beneatha *(To encourage Walter, thoroughly caught up with this side of him.): OCOMOGOSIAY,* FLAMING SPEAR!

Walter *(On the table, very far gone, his eyes pure glass sheets. He sees what we cannot, that he is a leader of his people, a great chief, a descendant of Chaka, and that the hour to march has come.):* Listen, my black brothers—

Beneatha: OCOMOGOSIAY!

Walter: —Do you hear the waters rushing against the shores of the coastlands—

Beneatha: OCOMOGOSIAY!

Walter: —Do you hear the screeching of the cocks in yonder hills beyond where the chiefs meet in council for the coming of the mighty war—

Beneatha: OCOMOGOSIAY!

Walter: —Do you hear the beating of the wings of the birds flying over the mountains and the low places of our land—

(Ruth opens the door. George Murchison enters.)

Beneatha: OCOMOGOSIAY!

Walter: —Do you hear the singing of the women, singing the war songs of our fathers to the babies in the great houses . . . singing the sweet war songs? OH, DO YOU HEAR, MY BLACK BROTHERS!

Beneatha *(Completely gone.):* We hear you, Flaming Spear—

Walter: Telling us to prepare for the greatness of the time— *(To George.)* Black Brother!

(He extends his hand for the fraternal clasp.)

George: Black Brother, hell!

Ruth *(Having had enough, and embarrassed for the family.):* Beneatha, you got company—what's the matter with you? Walter Lee Younger, get down off that table and stop acting like a fool . . .

(Walter comes down off the table suddenly and makes a quick exit to the bathroom.)

Ruth: He's had a little to drink . . . I don't know what her excuse is.

George *(To Beneatha.):* Look honey, we're going *to* the theatre—we're not going to be *in* it . . . so go change, huh?

Ruth: You expect this boy to go out with you looking like that?

Beneatha *(Looking at George.):* That's up to George. If he's ashamed of his heritage—

George: Oh, don't be so proud of yourself, Bennie—just because you look eccentric.

Beneatha: How can something that's natural be eccentric?

George: That's what being eccentric means—being natural. Get dressed.

Beneatha: I don't like that, George.

Ruth: Why must you and your brother make an argument out of everything people say?

Beneatha: Because I hate assimilationist Negroes!

Ruth: Will somebody please tell me what assimila-whoever means!

George: Oh, it's just a college girl's way of calling people Uncle Toms—but that isn't what it means at all.

Ruth: Well, what does it mean?

Beneatha *(Cutting George off and staring at him as she replies to Ruth.):* It means someone who is willing to give up his own culture and submerge himself completely in the dominant, and in this case, *oppressive* culture!

George: Oh, dear, dear, dear! Here we go! A lecture on the African past! On our Great West African Heritage! In one second we will hear all about the great Ashanti empires; the great Songhay civilizations; and the great sculpture of Bénin—and then some poetry in the Bantu—and the whole monologue will end with the world *heritage! (Nastily.)* Let's face it, baby, your heritage is nothing but a bunch of raggedy-assed spirituals and some grass huts!

Beneatha: Grass huts! *(Ruth crosses to her and forcibly pushes her toward the bedroom.)* See there . . . you are standing there in your splendid ignorance talking about people who were the first to smelt iron on the face of the earth! *(Ruth is pushing her through the door.)* The Ashanti were performing surgical operations when the English—*Ruth pulls the door to, with Beneatha on the other side, and smiles graciously at George. Beneatha opens the door and shouts the end of the sentence defiantly at George.)*—were still tattooing themselves with blue dragons . . . *(She goes back inside.)*

Ruth: Have a seat, George. *(They both sit. Ruth folds her hands rather primly on her lap, determined to demonstrate the civilization of the family.)* Warm, ain't it? I mean for September. *(Pause.)* Just like they always say about Chicago weather: If it's too hot or cold for you, just wait a minute and it'll change. *(She smiles happily at this cliché of clichés.)* Everybody say it's got to do with them bombs and things they keep setting off. *(Pause.)* Would you like a nice cold beer?

George: No, thank you. I don't care for beer. *(He looks at his watch.)* I hope she hurries up.

Ruth: What time is the show?

George: It's an eight-thirty curtain. That's just Chicago, though. In New York standard curtain time is eight forty.

(He is rather proud of this knowledge.)

Ruth *(Properly appreciating it.):* You get to New York a lot?

George *(Offhand.):* Few times a year.

Ruth: Oh—that's nice. I've never been to New York.

(Walter enters. We feel he has relieved himself, but the edge of unreality is still with him.)

Walter: New York ain't got nothing Chicago ain't. Just a bunch of hustling people all squeezed up together—being "Eastern."

(He turns his face into a screw of displeasure.)

George: Oh—you've been?

Walter: *Plenty* of times.

Ruth *(Shocked at the lie.):* Walter Lee Younger!

Walter *(Staring her down.):* Plenty! *(Pause.)* What we got to drink in this house? Why don't you offer this man some refreshment. *(To George.)* They don't know how to entertain people in this house, man.

George: Thank you—I don't really care for anything.

Walter *(Feeling his head; sobriety coming.):* Where's Mama?

Ruth: She ain't come back yet.

Walter *(Looking Murchison over from head to toe, scrutinizing his carefully casual tweed sports jacket over cashmere V-neck sweater over soft eyelet shirt and tie, and soft slacks, finished off with white buckskin shoes.):* Why all you college boys wear them fairyish-looking white shoes?

Ruth: Walter Lee!

(George Murchison ignores the remark.)

Walter *(To Ruth.):* Well, they look crazy as hell—white shoes, cold as it is.

Ruth *(Crushed.):* You have to excuse him—

Walter: No he don't! Excuse me for what? What you always excusing me for! I'll excuse myself when I needs to be excused! *(A pause.)* They look as funny as them black knee socks Beneatha wears out of here all the time.

Ruth: It's the college *style,* Walter.

Walter: Style, hell. She looks like she got burnt legs or something!

Ruth: Oh, Walter—

Walter *(An irritable mimic.):* Oh, Walter! Oh, Walter! *(To Murchison.)* How's your old man making out? I understand you all going to buy that big hotel on the Drive? *(He finds a beer in the refrigerator, wanders over to Murchison, sipping and wiping his lips with the back of his hand, and straddling a chair backwards to talk to the other man.)* Shrewd move. Your old man is all right, man. *(Tapping his head and half winking for emphasis.)* I mean he knows how to operate. I mean he thinks *big,* you know what I mean, I mean for a *home,* you know? But I think he's kind of running out of ideas now. I'd like to talk to him. Listen, man, I got some plans that could turn this city upside down. I mean I think like he does. *Big.* Invest big, gamble big, hell, lose *big* if you have to, you know what I mean. It's hard to find a man on this whole Southside who understands my kind of thinking—you dig? *(He scrutinizes Murchison again, drinks his beer, squints his eyes, and leans in close, confidential, man to man.)* Me and you ought to sit down and talk sometimes, man. Man, I got me some ideas . . .

Murchison *(With boredom.):* Yeah—sometimes we'll have to do that, Walter.

Walter *(Understanding the indifference, and offended.):* Yeah—well, when you get the time, man. I know you a busy little boy.

Ruth: Walter, please—

Walter *(Bitterly, hurt.):* I know ain't nothing in this world as busy as you colored college boys with your fraternity pins and white shoes . . .

Ruth *(Covering her face with humiliation.):* Oh, Walter Lee—

Walter: I see you all all the time—with the books tucked under your arms—going to your *(British A—a mimic.)* "clahsses." And for what! What the hell you learning over there? Filling up your heads—*(Counting off on his fingers.)*—with the sociology and the psychology—but they teaching you how to be a man? How to take over and run the world? They teaching you how to run a rubber plantation or a steel mill? Naw—just to talk proper and read books and wear white shoes . . .

George *(Looking at him with distaste, a little above it all.):* You're all wacked up with bitterness, man.

Walter *(Intently, almost quietly, between the teeth, glaring at the boy.):* And you—ain't you bitter, man? Ain't you just about had it yet? Don't you see no stars gleaming that you can't reach out and grab? You happy—you contented son-of-a-bitch—you happy? You got it made? Bitter? Man, I'm a volcano. Bitter? Here I am a giant—surrounded by ants! Ants who can't even understand what it is the giant is talking about.

Ruth *(Passionately and suddenly.)* Oh, Walter—ain't you with nobody!

Walter *(Violently.):* No! 'Cause ain't nobody with me! Not even my own mother!

Ruth: Walter, that's a terrible thing to say!

(Beneatha enters, dressed for the evening in a cocktail dress and earrings.)

George: Well—hey, you look great.

Beneatha: Let's go, George. See you all later.

Ruth: Have a nice time.

George: Thanks. Good night. *(To Walter, sarcastically.)* Good night, *Prometheus.*

(Beneatha and George exit.)

Walter *(To Ruth.):* Who is Prometheus?

Ruth: I don't know. Don't worry about it.

Walter *(In fury, pointing after George.):* See there—they get to a point where they can't insult you man to man—they got to go talk about something ain't nobody never heard of!

Ruth: How you know it was an insult? *(To humor him.)* Maybe Prometheus is a nice fellow.

Walter: Prometheus! I bet there ain't even no such thing! I bet that simple-minded clown—

Ruth: Walter—

(She stops what she is doing and looks at him.)

Walter *(Yelling.):* Don't start!

Ruth: Start what?

Walter: Your nagging! Where was I? Who was I with? How much money did I spend?

Ruth *(Plaintively.):* Walter Lee—why don't we just try to talk about it . . .

Walter *(Not listening.):* I been out talking with people who understand me. People who care about the things I got on my mind.

Ruth *(Wearily.):* I guess that means people like Willy Harris.

Walter: Yes, people like Willy Harris.

Ruth *(With a sudden flash of impatience.):* Why don't you all just hurry up and go into the banking business and stop talking about it!

Walter: Why? You want to know why? 'Cause we all tied up in a race of people that don't know how to do nothing but moan, pray, and have babies!

(The line is too bitter even for him and he looks at her and sits down.)

Ruth: Oh, Walter . . . *(Softly.)* Honey, why can't you stop fighting me?

Walter *(Without thinking.):* Who's fighting you? Who even cares about you?

(This line begins the retardation of his mood).

Ruth: Well—*(She waits a long time, and then with resignation starts to put away her things.)* I guess I might as well go on to bed . . . *(More or less to herself.)* I don't know where we lost it . . . but we have . . . *(Then, to him.)* I—I'm sorry about this new baby, Walter. I guess maybe I better go on and do what I started . . . I guess I just didn't realize how bad things was with us . . . I guess I just didn't really realize—*(She starts out to the bedroom and stops.)* You want some hot milk?

Walter: Hot milk?

Ruth: Yes—hot milk.

Walter: Why hot milk?

Ruth: 'Cause after all that liquor you come home with you ought to have something hot in your stomach.

Walter: I don't want no milk.

Ruth: You want some coffee then?

Walter: No, I don't want no coffee. I don't want nothing hot to drink. *(Almost plaintively.)* Why you always trying to give me something to eat?

Ruth *(Standing and looking at him helplessly.):* What else can I give you, Walter Lee Younger?

(She stands and looks at him and presently turns to go out again. He lifts his head and watches her going away from him in a new mood which began to emerge when he asked her "Who cares about you?")

Walter: It's been rough, ain't it, baby? *(She hears and stops but does not turn around and he continues to her back.)* I guess between two people there ain't never as much understood as folks generally thinks there is. I mean like between me and you—*(She turns to face him.)* How we gets to the place where we scared to talk softness to each other. *(He waits, thinking hard himself.)* Why you think it got to be like that? *(He is thoughtful, almost as a child would be.)* Ruth, what is it gets into people ought to be close?

Ruth: I don't know, honey. I think about it a lot.

Walter: On account of you and me, you mean? The way things are with us. The way something done come down between us.

Ruth: There ain't so much between us, Walter . . . Not when you come to me and try to talk to me. Try to be with me . . . a little even.

Walter *(Total honesty.)*: Sometimes . . . sometimes . . . I don't even know how to try.

Ruth: Walter—

Walter: Yes?

Ruth *(Coming to him, gently and with misgiving, but coming to him.)*: Honey . . . life don't have to be like this. I mean sometimes people can do things so that things are better . . . You remember how we used to talk when Travis was born . . . about the way we were going to live . . . the kind of house . . . *(She is stroking his head.)* Well, it's all starting to slip away from us . . .

(Mama enters, and Walter jumps up and shouts at her.)

Walter: Mama, where have you been?

Mama: My—them steps is longer than they used to be. Whew! *(She sits down and ignores him.)* How you feeling this evening, Ruth?

(Ruth shrugs, disturbed some at having been prematurely interrupted and watching her husband knowingly.)

Walter: Mama, where have you been all day?

Mama *(Still ignoring him and leaning on the table and changing to more comfortable shoes.)*: Where's Travis?

Ruth: I let him go out earlier and he ain't come back yet. Boy, is he going to get it!

Walter: Mama!

Mama *(As if she heard him for the first time.)*: Yes, son?

Walter: Where did you go this afternoon?

Mama: I went downtown to tend to some business that I had to tend to.

Walter: What kind of business?

Mama: You know better than to question me like a child, Brother.

Walter *(Rising and bending over the table.)*: Where were you, Mama? *(Bringing his fists down and shouting.)* Mama, you didn't go do something with that insurance money, something crazy?

(The front door opens slowly, interrupting him, and Travis peeks his head in, less than hopefully.)

Travis *(To his mother.)*: Mama, I—

Ruth: "Mama I" nothing! You're going to get it, boy! Get on in that bedroom and get yourself ready!

Travis: But I—

Mama: Why don't you all never let the child explain hisself.

Ruth: Keep out of it now, Lena.

(Mama clamps her lips together, and Ruth advances toward her son menacingly.)

Ruth: A thousand times I have told you not to go off like that—

Mama *(Holding out her arms to her grandson.)*: Well—at least let me tell him something. I want him to be the first one to hear . . . Come here, Travis.

(The boy obeys, gladly.) Travis—*(She takes him by the shoulders and looks into his face.)*—you know that money we got in the mail this morning?

Travis: Yes'm—

Mama: Well—what you think your grandmama gone and done with that money?

Travis: I don't know, Grandmama.

Mama *(Putting her finger on his nose for emphasis.):* She went out and she bought you a house! *(The explosion comes from Walter at the end of the revelation and he jumps up and turns away from all of them in a fury. Mama continues, to Travis.)* You glad about the house? It's going to be yours when you get to be a man.

Travis: Yeah—I always wanted to live in a house.

Mama: All right, gimme some sugar then—(Travis puts his arms around her neck as she watches her son over the boy's shoulder. Then, to Travis, after the embrace.) Now when you say your prayers tonight, you thank God and your grandfather—'cause it was him who give you the house—in his way.

Ruth *(Taking the boy from Mama and pushing him toward the bedroom.):* Now you get out of here and get ready for your beating.

Travis: Aw, Mama—

Ruth: Get on in there—*(Closing the door behind him and turning radiantly to her mother-in-law.)* So you went and did it!

Mama *(Quietly, looking at her son with pain.):* Yes, I did.

Ruth *(Raising both arms classically.): Praise God! (Looks at Walter a moment, who says nothing. She crosses rapidly to her husband.)* Please, honey—let me be glad . . . you be glad too. *(She has laid her hands on his shoulders, but he shakes himself free of her roughly, without turning to face her.)* Oh, Walter . . . a home . . . *a home. (She comes back to Mama.)* Well—where is it? How big is it? How much it going to cost?

Mama: Well—

Ruth: When we moving?

Mama *(Smiling at her.):* First of the month.

Ruth *(Throwing back her head with jubilance.): Praise God!*

Mama *(Tentatively, still looking at her son's back turned against her and Ruth.):* It's—it's a nice house too . . . *(She cannot help speaking directly to him. An imploring quality in her voice, her manner, makes her almost like a girl now.)* Three bedrooms—nice big one for you and Ruth . . . Me and Beneatha still have to share our room, but Travis have one of his own—and—*(With difficulty.)* I figures if the—new baby—is a boy, we could get one of the double-decker outfits . . . And there's a yard with a little patch of dirt where I could maybe get to grow me a few flowers . . . And a nice big basement . . .

Ruth: Walter honey, be glad—

Mama *(Still to his back, fingering things on the table.):* 'Course I don't want to make it sound fancier than it is . . . It's just a plain little old house—but it's made good and solid—and it will be *ours*. Walter Lee—it makes a difference in a man when he can walk on floors that belong to *him* . . .

Ruth: Where is it?

Mama *(Frightened at this telling.):* Well—well—it's out there in Clybourne Park—

(Ruth's radiance fades abruptly, and Walter finally turns slowly to face his mother with incredulity and hostility.)

Ruth: Where?

Mama *(Matter of factly.):* Four o six Clybourne Street, Clybourne Park.

Ruth: Clybourne Park? Mama, there ain't no colored people living in Clybourne Park.

Mama *(Almost idiotically.):* Well, I guess there's going to be some now.

Walter *(Bitterly.)* So that's the peace and comfort you went out and bought for us today!

Mama *(Raising her eyes to meet his finally.):* Son—I just tried to find the nicest place for the least amount of money for my family.

Ruth *(Trying to recover from the shock.):* Well—well—'course I ain't one never been 'fraid of no crackers, mind you—but—well, wasn't there no other houses nowhere?

Mama: Them houses they put up for colored in them areas way out all seem to cost twice as much as other houses. I did the best I could.

Ruth *(Struck senseless with the news, in its various degrees of goodness and trouble, she sits a moment, her fists propping her chin in thought, and then she starts to rise, bringing her fists down with vigor, the radiance spreading from cheek to cheek again.):* Well—well!—All I can say is—if this is my time in life—*my time*—to say good-bye—*(And she builds with momentum as she starts to circle the room with an exuberant, almost tearfully happy release.)*—to these God-damned cracking walls!—*(She pounds the walls.)*—and these marching roaches!—*(She wipes at an imaginary army of marching roaches.)*—and this cramped little closet which ain't now or never was no kitchen! . . . then I say it loud and good, *Hallelujah! and good-bye misery . . . I don't never want to see your ugly face again! (She laughs joyously, having practically destroyed the apartment, and flings her arms up and lets them come down happily, slowly, reflectively, over her abdomen, aware for the first time perhaps that the life therein pulses with happiness and not despair.)* Lena?

Mama *(moved, watching her happiness.):* Yes, honey?

Ruth *(Looking off.):* Is there—is there a whole lot of sunlight?

Mama *(Understanding.):* Yes, child, there's a whole lot of sunlight.

(Long pause.)

Ruth *(Collecting herself and going to the door of the room Travis is in.):* Well—I guess I better see 'bout Travis. *(To Mama.)* Lord, I sure don't feel like whipping nobody today!

(She exits.)

Mama *(The mother and son are left alone now and the mother waits a long time, considering deeply, before she speaks.):* Son—you—you understand what I done, don't you? *(Walter is silent and sullen.)* I—I just seen my family falling apart today . . . just falling to pieces in front of my eyes . . . We couldn't of gone on like we was today. We was going backwards 'stead of forwards—talking 'bout killing babies and wishing each other was dead . . . When it gets like that in life—you just got to do something different, push on out and do something bigger . . . *(She waits.)* I wish you say something, son . . . I wish you'd say how deep inside you, you think I done the right thing.

Walter *(Crossing slowly to his bedroom door and finally turning there and speaking measuredly.):* What you need me to say you done right for? *You* the head of this family. You run our lives like you want to. It was your money and you did what you wanted with it. So what you need for me to say it was all right for? *(Bitterly, to hurt her as deeply as he knows is possible.)* So you butchered up a dream of mine—you—who always talking 'bout your children's dreams . . .

175 **Mama:** Walter Lee—

(He just closes the door behind him. Mama sits alone, thinking heavily.)

(Curtain.)

Act Two

Scene 2

Time: Friday night. A few weeks later.

At rise: Packing crates mark the intention of the family to move. Beneatha and George come in, presumably from an evening out again.

1 **George:** O.K. . . . O.K., whatever you say . . . *(They both sit on the couch. He tries to kiss her. She moves away.)* Look, we've had a nice evening; let's not spoil it, huh? . . .

(He again turns her head and tries to nuzzle in and she turns away from him, not with distaste but with momentary lack of interest; in a mood to pursue what they were talking about.)

Beneatha: I'm *trying* to talk to you.

George: We always talk.

Beneatha: Yes—and I love to talk.

5 **George** *(Exasperated; rising.):* I know it and I don't mind it sometimes . . . I want you to cut it out, see— The moody stuff, I mean. I don't like it. You're a nice-looking girl . . . all over. That's all you need, honey, forget the atmosphere. Guys aren't going to go for the atmosphere—they're going to go for what they see. Be glad for that. Drop the Garbo routine. It doesn't go with you. As for myself, I want a nice—*(Groping.)*—simple—*(Thoughtfully.)* sophisticated girl . . . not a poet—O.K.?

(She rebuffs him again and he starts to leave.)

Beneatha: Why are you angry?

George: Because this is stupid! I don't go out with you to discuss the nature of "quiet desperation" or to hear all about your thoughts—because the world will go on thinking what it thinks regardless—

Beneatha: Then why read books? Why go to school?

George *(With artificial patience, counting on his fingers.):* It's simple. You read books—to learn facts—to get grades—to pass the course—to get a degree. That's all—it has nothing to do with thoughts.

(A long pause.)

Beneatha: I see. *(A longer pause as she looks at him.)* Good night, George.

(George looks at her a little oddly, and starts to exit. He meets Mama coming in.)

George: Oh—hello, Mrs. Younger.

Mama: Hello, George, how you feeling?

George: Fine—fine, how are you?

Mama: Oh, a little tired. You know them steps can get you after a day's work. You all have a nice time tonight?

George: Yes—a fine time. Well, good night.

Mama: Good night. *(He exits. Mama closes the door behind her.)* Hello, honey. What you sitting like that for?

Beneatha: I'm just sitting.

Mama: Didn't you have a nice time?

Beneatha: No.

Mama: No? What's the matter?

Beneatha: Mama, George is a fool—honest. *(She rises.)*

Mama *(Hustling around unloading the packages she has entered with. She stops.):* Is he, baby?

Beneatha: Yes.

(Beneatha makes up Travis' bed as she talks.)

Mama: You sure?

Beneatha: Yes.

Mama: Well—I guess you better not waste your time with no fools.

(Beneatha looks up at her mother, watching her put groceries in the refrigerator. Finally, she gathers up her things and starts into the bedroom. At the door she stops and looks back at her mother.)

Beneatha: Mama—

Mama: Yes, baby—

Beneatha: Thank you.

Mama: For what?

Beneatha: For understanding me this time.

(She exits quickly and the mother stands, smiling a little, looking at the place where Beneatha just stood. Ruth enters.)

Ruth: Now don't you fool with any of this stuff, Lena—

Mama: Oh, I just thought I'd sort a few things out.

(The phone rings. Ruth answers.)

Ruth *(At the phone.)*: Hello—Just a minute. *(Goes to door.)* Walter, it's Mrs. Arnold. *(Waits. Goes back to the phone. Tense.)* Hello. Yes, this is his wife speaking . . . He's lying down now. Yes . . . well, he'll be in tomorrow. He's been very sick. Yes—I know we should have called, but we were so sure he'd be able to come in today. Yes—yes, I'm very sorry. Yes . . . Thank you very much. *(She hands up. Walter is standing in the doorway of the bedroom behind her.)* That was Mrs. Arnold.

Walter *(Indifferently.)*: Was it?

Ruth: She said if you don't come in tomorrow that they are getting a new man . . .

Walter: Ain't that sad—ain't that crying sad.

Ruth: She said Mr. Arnold has had to take a cab for three days . . . Walter, you ain't been to work for three days! *(This is a revelation to her.)* Where you been, Walter Lee Younger? *(Walter looks at her and starts to laugh.)* You're going to lose your job.

Walter: That's right . . .

Ruth: Oh, Walter, and with your mother working like a dog every day—

Walter: That's sad too— Everything is sad.

Mama: What you been doing for these three days, son?

Walter: Mama—you don't know all the things a man what got leisure can find to do in this city . . . What's this—Friday night? Well—Wednesday I borrowed Willy Harris' car and I went for a drive . . . just me and myself and I drove and drove . . . Way out . . . way past South Chicago, and I parked the car and I sat and looked at the steel mills all day long. I just sat in the car and looked at them big black chimneys for hours. Then I drove back and I went to the Green Hat. *(Pause.)* And Thursday—Thursday I borrowed the car again and I got in it and I pointed it the other way and I drove the other way—for hours—way, way up to Wisconsin, and I looked at the farms. I just drove and looked at the farms. Then I drove back and I went to the Green Hat. *(Pause.)* And today—today I didn't get the car. Today I just walked. All over the Southside. And I looked at the Negroes and they looked at me and finally I just sat down on the curb at Thirty-ninth and South Parkway and I just sat there and watched the Negroes go by. And then I went to the Green Hat. You all sad? You all depressed? And you know where I am going right now—

(Ruth goes out quietly.)

Mama: Oh, Big Walter, is this the harvest of our days?

Walter: You know what I like about the Green Hat? *(He turns the radio on and a steamy, deep blues pours into the room.)* I like this little cat they got there who blows a sax . . . He blows. He talks to me. He ain't but 'bout five feet tall and he's got a conked head and his eyes is always closed and he's all music—

Mama *(Rising and getting some papers out of her handbag.)*: Walter—

Walter: And there's this other guy who plays the piano . . . and they got a sound. I mean they can work on some music . . . They got the best little combo in the world in the Green Hat . . . You can just sit there and drink and listen to them three men play and you realize that don't nothing matter worth a damn, but just being there—

Mama: I've helped do it to you, haven't I, son? Walter, I been wrong.

Walter: Naw—you ain't never been wrong about nothing, Mama.

Mama: Listen to me, now. I say I been wrong, son. That I been doing to you what the rest of the world been doing to you. *(She stops and he looks up slowly at her and she meets his eyes pleadingly.)* Walter—what you ain't never understood is that I ain't got nothing, don't own nothing, ain't never really wanted nothing that wasn't for you. There ain't nothing as precious to me . . . There ain't nothing worth holding on to, money, dreams, nothing else—if it means—if it means it's going to destroy my boy. *(She puts her papers in front of him and he watches her without speaking or moving.)* I paid the man thirty-five hundred dollars down on the house. That leaves sixty-five hundred dollars. Monday morning I want you to take this money and take three thousand dollars and put it in a savings account for Beneatha's medical schooling. The rest you put in a checking account—with your name on it. And from now on any penny that come out of it or that go in it is for you to look after. For you to decide. *(She drops her hands a little helplessly.)* It ain't much, but it's all I got in the world and I'm putting it in your hands. I'm telling you to be the head of this family from now on like you supposed to be.

Walter *(Stares at the money.)*: You trust me like that, Mama?

Mama: I ain't never stop trusting you. Like I ain't never stop loving you.

(She goes out, and Walter sits looking at the money on the table as the music continues in its idiom, pulsing in the room. Finally, in a decisive gesture, he gets up and, in a furious action, flings the bedclothes wildly from his son's makeshift bed to all over the floor—with a cry of desperation. Then he picks up the money and goes out in a hurry.)

(Curtain.)

Act Two

Scene 3

Time: Saturday, moving day, one week later.

Before the curtain rises, Ruth's voice, a strident, dramatic church alto, cuts through the silence.

It is, in the darkness, a triumphant surge, a penetrating statement of expectation: "Oh, Lord, I don't feel no ways tired! Children, oh, glory hallelujah!"

As the curtain rises we see that Ruth is alone in the living room, finishing up the family's packing. It is moving day. She is nailing crates and tying cartons. Beneatha enters, carrying a guitar case, and watches her exuberant sister-in-law.

1 **Ruth:** Hey!

Beneatha *(Putting away the case.):* Hi.

Ruth *(Pointing at a package.):* Honey—look in that package there and see what I found on sale this morning at the South Center. *(Ruth gets up and moves to the package and draws out some curtains.)* Lookahere—hand-turned hems!

Beneatha: How do you know the window size out there?

5 **Ruth** *(Who hadn't thought of that.):* Oh— Well, they bound to fit something in the whole house. Anyhow, they was too good a bargain to pass up. *(Ruth slaps her head, suddenly remembering something.)* Oh, Bennie—I meant to put a special note on that carton over there. That's your mama's good china and she wants 'em to be very careful with it.

Beneatha: I'll do it.

(Beneatha finds a piece of paper and starts to draw large letters on it.)

Ruth: You know what I'm going to do soon as I get in that new house?

Beneatha: What?

Ruth: Honey—I'm going to run me a tub of water up to here . . . *(With her fingers practically up to her nostrils.)* And I'm going to get in it—and I am going to sit . . . and sit . . . and sit in that hot water and the first person who knocks to tell *me* to hurry up and come out—

10 **Beneatha:** Gets shot at sunrise.

Ruth *(Laughing happily.):* You said it, sister! *(Noticing how large Beneatha is absent-mindedly making the note.)* Honey, they ain't going to read that from no airplane.

Beneatha *(Laughing herself.):* I guess I always think things have more emphasis if they are big, somehow.

Ruth *(Looking up at her and smiling.):* You and your brother seem to have that as a philosophy of life. Lord, that man—done changed so 'round here. You know—you know what we did last night? Me and Walter Lee?

Beneatha: What?

15 **Ruth** *(Smiling to herself.):* We went to the movies. *(Looking at Beneatha to see if she understands.)* We went to the movies. You know the last time me and Walter went to the movies together?

Beneatha: No.

Ruth: Me neither. That's how long it been. *(Smiling again.)* But we went last night. The picture wasn't much good, but that didn't seem to matter. We went—and we held hands.

Beneatha: Oh, Lord!

Ruth: We held hands—and you know what?

20 **Beneatha:** What?

Ruth: When we come out of the show it was late and dark and all the stores and things was closed up . . . and it was kind of chilly and there wasn't many people on the streets . . . and we was still holding hands, me and Walter.

Beneatha: You're killing me.

(Walter enters with a large package. His happiness is deep in him; he cannot keep still with his new-found exuberance. He is singing and wiggling and snapping his fingers. He puts his package in a corner and puts a phonograph record, which he has brought in with him, on the record player. As the music comes up he dances over to Ruth and tries to get her to dance with him. She gives in at last to his raunchiness and in a fit of giggling allows herself to be drawn into his mood and together they deliberately burlesque an old social dance of their youth.)

Beneatha *(Regarding them a long time as they dance, then drawing in her breath for a deeply exaggerated comment which she does not particularly mean.):* Talk about—olddddddddd-fashionedddddd—Negroes!

Walter *(Stopping momentarily.):* What kind of Negroes?

(He says this in fun. He is not angry with her today, nor with anyone. He starts to dance with his wife again.)

Beneatha: Old-fashioned.

Walter *(As he dances with Ruth.):* You know, when these *New Negroes* have their convention—*(Pointing at his sister.)*—that is going to be the chairman of the Committee on Unending Agitation. *(He goes on dancing, then stops.)* Race, race, race! . . . Girl, I do believe you are the first person in the history of the entire human race to successfully brainwash yourself. *(Beneatha breaks up and he goes on dancing. He stops again, enjoying his tease.)* Damn, even the N double A C P takes a holiday sometimes! *(Beneatha and Ruth laugh. He dances with Ruth some more and starts to laugh and stops and pantomimes someone over an operating table.)* I can just see that chick someday looking down at some poor cat on an operating table before she starts to slice him, saying . . . *(Pulling his sleeves back maliciously.)* "By the way, what are your views on civil rights down there? . . ."

(He laughs at her again and starts to dance happily. The bell sounds.)

Beneatha: Sticks and stones may break my bones but . . . words will never hurt me!

(Beneatha goes to the door and opens it as Walter and Ruth go on with the clowning. Beneatha is somewhat surprised to see a quiet-looking middle-aged white man in a business suit holding his hat and a briefcase in his hand and consulting a small piece of paper.)

Man: Uh—how do you do, miss. I am looking for a Mrs.—*(He looks at the slip of paper.)* Mrs. Lena Younger?

Beneatha *(Smoothing her hair with slight embarrassment.):* Oh—yes, that's my mother. Excuse me. *(She closes the door and turns to quiet the other two.)* Ruth! Brother! Somebody's here. *(Then she opens the door. The man casts a curious quick glance at all of them.)* Uh—come in please.

Man *(Coming in.):* Thank you.

Beneatha: My mother isn't here just now. Is it business?

Man: Yes . . . well, of a sort.

Walter *(Freely, the Man of the House.):* Have a seat. I'm Mrs. Younger's son. I look after most of her business matters.

(Ruth and Beneatha exchange amused glances.)

Man *(Regarding Walter, and sitting.):* Well— My name is Karl Lindner . . .

Walter *(Stretching out his hand.):* Walter Younger. This is my wife—*(Ruth nods politely.)*—and my sister.

Lindner: How do you do.

Walter *(Amiably, as he sits himself easily on a chair, leaning with interest forward on his knees and looking expectantly into the newcomer's face.):* What can we do for you, Mr. Lindner!

Lindner *(Some minor shuffling of the hat and briefcase on his knees.):* Well— I am a representative of the Clybourne Park Improvement Association—

Walter *(Pointing.):* Why don't you sit your things on the floor?

Lindner: Oh—yes. Thank you. *(He slides the briefcase and hat under the chair.)* And as I was saying—I am from the Clybourne Park Improvement Association and we have had it brought to our attention at the last meeting that you people—or at least your mother—has bought a piece of residential property at—*(He digs for the slip of paper again.)*—four o six Clybourne Street . . .

Walter: That's right. Care for something to drink? Ruth, get Mr. Lindner a beer.

Lindner *(Upset for some reason.):* Oh—no, really. I mean thank you very much, but no thank you.

Ruth *(Innocently.):* Some coffee?

Lindner: Thank you, nothing at all.

(Beneatha is watching the man carefully.)

Lindner: Well, I don't know how much you folks know about our organization. *(He is a gentle man; thoughtful and somewhat labored in his manner.)* It is one of these community organizations set up to look after—oh, you know, things like block upkeep and special projects and we also have what we call our New Neighbors Orientation Committee . . .

Beneatha *(Drily.):* Yes—and what do they do?

Lindner *(Turning a little to her and then returning the main force to Walter.):* Well—it's what you might call a sort of welcoming committee, I guess. I mean they, we, I'm the chairman of the committee—go around and see the new people who move into the neighborhood and sort of give them the lowdown on the way we do things out in Clybourne Park.

Beneatha *(With appreciation of the two meanings, which escape Ruth and Walter.):* Un-huh.

Lindner: And we also have the category of what the association calls—*(He looks elsewhere.)*—uh—special community problems . . .

Beneatha: Yes—and what are some of those?

Walter: Girl, let the man talk.

Lindner *(With understated relief.):* Thank you. I would sort of like to explain this thing in my own way. I mean I want to explain to you in a certain way.

Walter: Go ahead.

Lindner: Yes. Well. I'm going to try to get right to the point. I'm sure we'll all appreciate that in the long run.

Beneatha: Yes.

Walter: Be still now!

Lindner: Well—

Ruth *(Still innocently.):* Would you like another chair—you don't look comfortable.

Lindner *(More frustrated than annoyed.):* No, thank you very much. Please. Well—to get right to the point I—*(A great breath, and he is off at last.)* I am sure you people must be aware of some of the incidents which have happened in various part of the city when colored people have moved into certain areas—*(Beneatha exhales heavily and starts tossing a piece of fruit up and down in the air.)* Well—because we have what I think is going to be a unique type of organization in American community life—not only do we deplore that kind of thing—but we are trying to do something about it. *(Beneatha stops tossing and turns with a new and quizzical interest to the man.)* We feel—*(gaining confidence in his mission because of the interest in the faces of the people he is talking to.)*—we feel that most of the trouble in this world, when you come right down to it—*(He hits his knee for emphasis.)*—most of the trouble exists because people just don't sit down and talk to each other.

Ruth *(Nodding as she might in church, pleased with the remark.):* You can say that again, mister.

Lindner *(More encouraged by such affirmation.):* That we don't try hard enough in this world to understand the other fellow's problem. The other guy's point of view.

Ruth: Now that's right.

(Beneatha and Walter merely watch and listen with genuine interest.)

Lindner: Yes—that's the way we feel out in Clybourne Park. And that's why I was elected to come here this afternoon and talk to you people. Friendly like, you know, the way people should talk to each other and see if we couldn't find some way to work this thing out. As I say, the whole business is a matter of *caring* about the other fellow. Anybody can see that you are a nice family of folks, hard working and honest I'm sure. *(Beneatha frowns slightly, quizzically, her head tilted regarding him.)* Today everybody knows what it means to be on the outside of *something*. And of course, there is always somebody who is out to take the advantage of people who don't always understand.

Walter: What do you mean?

Lindner: Well—you see our community is made up of people who've worked hard as the dickens for years to build up that little community. They're not rich and fancy people; just hard-working, honest people who don't really have much but those little homes and a dream of the kind of community they want to raise their children in. Now, I don't say we are perfect and there is a lot wrong in some of the things they want. But you've got to admit that a man, right or wrong, has the right to want to have the neighborhood he lives in a certain kind of way. And at the moment the overwhelming majority of our people out there feel that people get along better, take more of a common interest in the life of the community, when they share a common background. I want you to believe me when I tell you that race prejudice simply doesn't enter into it. It is a matter of the people of Clybourne Park believing, rightly or wrongly, as I say, that for the happiness of all concerned that our Negro families are happier when they live in their *own* communities.

Beneatha *(With a grand and bitter gesture.):* This, friends, is the Welcoming Committee!

Walter *(Dumbfounded, looking at Lindner.):* Is this what you came marching all the way over here to tell us?

Lindner: Well, now we've been having a fine conversation. I hope you'll hear me all the way through.

Walter *(Tightly.):* Go ahead, man.

Lindner: You see—in the face of all things I have said, we are prepared to make your family a very generous offer . . .

Beneatha: Thirty pieces and not a coin less!

Walter: Yeah?

Lindner *(Putting on his glasses and drawing a form out of the briefcase.):* Our association is prepared, through the collective effort of our people, to buy the house from you at a financial gain to your family.

Ruth: Lord have mercy, ain't this the living gall!

Walter: All right, you through?

Lindner: Well, I want to give you the exact terms of the financial arrangement—

Walter: We don't want to hear no exact terms of no arrangement. I want to know if you got any more to tell us 'bout getting together?

Lindner *(Taking off his glasses.):* Well—I don't suppose that you feel . . .

Walter: Never mind how I feel—you got any more to say 'bout how people ought to sit down and talk to each other? . . . Get out of my house, man.

(He turns his back and walks to the door.)

Lindner *(Looking around at the hostile faces and reaching and assembling his hat and briefcase.):* Well—I don't understand why you people are reacting this way. What do you think you are going to gain by moving into a neighborhood where you just aren't wanted and where some elements—well—people can get awful worked up when they feel that their whole way of life and everything they've ever worked for is threatened.

Walter: Get out.

Lindner *(At the door, holding a small card.):* Well—I'm sorry it went like this.

Walter: Get out.

Lindner *(Almost sadly regarding Walter.):* You just can't force people to change their hearts, son.

(He turns and puts his card on a table and exits. Walter pushes the door to with stinging hatred, and stands looking at it. Ruth just sits and Beneatha just stands. They say nothing. Mama and Travis enter.)

Mama: Well—this all the packing got done since I left out of here this morning. I testify before God that my children got all the energy of the dead. What time the moving men due?

Beneatha: Four o'clock. You had a caller, Mama.

(She is smiling, teasingly.)

Mama: Sure enough—who?

Beneatha *(Her arms folded saucily.):* The Welcoming Committee.

(Walter and Ruth giggle.)

Mama *(Innocently.):* Who?

Beneatha: The Welcoming Committee. They said they're sure going to be glad to see you when you get there.

Walter *(Devilishly.):* Yeah, they said they can't hardly wait to see your face.

(Laughter.)

Mama *(Sensing their facetiousness.):* What's the matter with you all?

Walter: Ain't nothing the matter with us. We just telling you 'bout the gentleman who came to see you this afternoon. From the Clybourne Park Improvement Association.

Mama: What he want?

Ruth *(In the same mood as Beneatha and Walter.):* To welcome you, honey.

Walter: He said they can't hardly wait. He said the one thing they don't have, that they just *dying* to have out there is a fine family of colored people! *(To Ruth and Beneatha.)* Ain't that right!

Ruth *and* **Beneatha** *(Mockingly.):* Yeah! He left his card in case—

(They indicate the card, and Mama picks it up and throws it on the floor—understanding and looking off as she draws her chair up to the table on which she has put her plant and some sticks and some cord.)

Mama: Father, give us strength. *(Knowingly—and without fun.)* Did he threaten us?

Beneatha: Oh—Mama—they don't do it like that any more. He talked Brotherhood. He said everybody ought learn how to sit down and hate each other with good Christian fellowship.

(She and Walter shake hands to ridicule the remark.)

Mama *(Sadly.):* Lord, protect us . . .

Ruth: You should hear the money those folks raised to buy the house from us. All we paid and then some.

Beneatha: What they think we going to do—eat 'em?

Ruth: No, honey, marry 'em.

Mama *(Shaking her head.):* Lord, Lord, Lord . . .

Ruth: Well—that's the way the crackers crumble. Joke.

Beneatha *(Laughingly noticing what her mother is doing.):* Mama, what are you doing?

Mama: Fixing my plant so it won't get hurt none on the way . . .

Beneatha: Mama, you going to take *that* to the new house?

Mama: Un-huh—

Beneatha: That raggedy-looking old thing?

Mama *(Stopping and looking at her.):* It expresses *me.*

Ruth *(With delight, to Beneatha.):* So there, Miss Thing!

(Walter comes to Mama suddenly and bends down behind her and squeezes her in his arms with all his strength. She is overwhelmed by the suddenness of it and, though delighted, her manner is like that of Ruth with Travis.)

Mama: Look out now, Boy! You make me mess up my thing here!

Walter *(His face lit, he slips down on his knees beside her, his arms still about her.):* Mama . . . you know what it means to climb up in the chariot?

Mama *(Gruffly, very happy.):* Get on away from me now . . .

Ruth *(Near the gift-wrapped package, trying to catch Walter's eye.):* Psst—

Walter: What the old song say, Mama . . .

Ruth: Walter— Now?

(She is pointing at the package.)

Walter *(Speaking the lines, sweetly, playfully, in his mother's face.):*
I got wings . . . you got wings . . .
All God's children got wings . . .

Mama: Boy—get out of my face and do some work . . .

Walter:
When I get to heaven gonna put on my wings,
Gonna fly all over God's heaven . . .

Beneatha *(Teasingly, from across the room.):* Everybody talking 'bout heaven ain't going there!

Walter *(To Ruth, who is carrying the box across to them.):* I don't know, you think we ought to give her that . . . Seems to me she ain't been very appreciative around here.

Mama *(Eying the box, which is obviously a gift.):* What is that?

Walter *(Taking it from Ruth and putting it on the table in front of Mama.):* Well—what you all think. Should we give it to her?

Ruth: Oh—she was pretty good today.

Mama: I'll good you—

(She turns her eyes to the box again.)

Beneatha: Open it, Mama.

(She stand up, looks at it, turns and looks at all of them, and then presses her hands together and does not open the package.)

Walter *(Sweetly.):* Open it, Mama. It's for you. *(Mama looks in his eyes. It is the first present in her life without its being Christmas. Slowly she opens her package and lifts out, one by one, a brand-new sparkling set of gardening tools. Walter continues, prodding.)* Ruth made up the note—read it . . .

Mama *(Picking up the card and adjusting her glasses.):* "To our own Mrs. Miniver—Love from Brother, Ruth and Beneatha." Ain't that lovely . . .

Travis *(Tugging at his father's sleeve.):* Daddy, can I give her mine now?

Walter: All right, son. *(Travis flies to get his gift.)* Travis didn't want to go in with the rest of us, Mama. He got his own. *(Somewhat amused.)* We don't know what it is . . .

Travis *(Racing back in the room with a large hatbox and putting it in front of his grandmother.):* Here!

Mama: Lord have mercy, baby. You done gone and bought your grandmother a hat?

Travis *(Very proud.):* Open it!

(She does and lifts out an elaborate, but very elaborate, wide gardening hat, and all the adults break up at the sight of it.)

Ruth: Travis, honey, what is that?

Travis *(Who thinks it is beautiful and appropriate.):* It's a gardening hat! Like the ladies always have on in the magazines when they work in their gardens.

Beneatha *(Giggling, fiercely.):* Travis—we were trying to make Mama Mrs. Miniver—not Scarlett O'Hara!

Mama *(Indignantly.):* What's the matter with you all! This here is a beautiful hat! *(Absurdly.)* I always wanted me one just like it!

(She pops it on her head to prove it to her grandson, and the hat is ludicrous and considerably oversized.)

Ruth: Hot dog! Go, Mama!

Walter *(Doubled over with laughter.):* I'm sorry, Mama—but you look like you ready to go out and chop you some cotton sure enough!

(They all laugh except Mama, out of deference to Travis' feelings.)

Mama *(Gathering the boy up to her.):* Bless your heart—this is the prettiest hat I ever owned— *(Walter, Ruth and Beneatha chime in—noisily, festively* *and insincerely congratulating Travis on his gift.)* What are we all standing around here for? We ain't finished packin' yet. Bennie, you ain't packed one book.

(The bell rings.)

Beneatha: That couldn't be the movers . . . it's not hardly two good yet—

(Beneatha goes into her room. Mama starts for door.)

Walter *(Turning, stiffening.):* Wait—wait—I'll get it.

(He stands and looks at the door.)

Mama: You expecting company, son?
Walter *(Just looking at the door.):* Yeah—yeah . . .

(Mama looks at Ruth, and they exchange innocent and unfrightened glances.)

Mama *(Not understanding.):* Well, let them in, son.
Beneatha *(From her room.):* We need some more string.
Mama: Travis—you run to the hardware and get me some string cord.

(Mama goes out and Walter turns and looks at Ruth. Travis goes to a dish for money.)

Ruth: Why don't you answer the door, man?
Walter *(Suddenly bounding across the floor to her.):* 'Cause sometimes it hard to let the future begin! *(Stooping down in her face.)*

I got wings! You got wings!
All God's children got wings!

(He crosses to the door and throws it open. Standing there is a very slight little man in a not too prosperous business suit and with haunted frightened eyes and a hat pulled down tightly, brim up, around his forehead. Travis passes between the men and exits. Walter leans deep in the man's face, still in his jubilance.)

When I get to heaven gonna put on my wings,
Gonna fly all over God's heaven . . .

(The little man just stares at him.)

Heaven—

(Suddenly he stops and looks past the little man into the empty hallway.) *Where's Willy, man?*

Bobo: He ain't with me.
Walter *(Not disturbed.):* Oh—come on in. You know my wife.
Bobo *(Dumbly, taking off his hat.):* Yes—h'you, Miss Ruth.
Ruth *(Quietly, a mood apart from her husband already, seeing Bobo.):* Hello, Bobo.

Walter: You right on time today . . . Right on time. That's the way! *(He slaps Bob on his back.)* Sit down . . . lemme hear.

(Ruth stands stiffly and quietly in back of them, as though somehow she senses death, her eyes fixed on her husband.)

Bobo *(His frightened eyes on the floor, his hat in his hands.):* Could I please get a drink a water, before I tell you about it, Walter Lee?

(Walter does not take his eyes off the man. Ruth goes blindly to the tap and gets a glass of water and brings it to Bobo.)

Walter: There ain't nothing wrong, is there?

Bobo: Lemme tell you—

Walter: Man—didn't nothing go wrong?

Bobo: Lemme tell you—Walter Lee. *(Looking at Ruth and talking to her more than to Walter.)* You know how it was. I got to tell you how it was. I mean first I got to tell you how it was all the way . . . I mean about the money I put in, Walter Lee . . .

Walter *(With taut agitation now.):* What about the money you put in?

Bobo: Well—it wasn't much as we told you—me and Willy— *(He stops.)* I'm sorry, Walter. I got a bad feeling about it. I got a real bad feeling about it . . .

Walter: Man, what you telling me about all this for? . . . Tell me what happened in Springfield . . .

Bobo: Springfield.

Ruth *(Like a dead woman.):* What was supposed to happen in Springfield?

Bobo *(To her.):* This deal that me and Walter went into with Willy— Me and Willy was going to go down to Springfield and spread some money 'round so's we wouldn't have to wait so long for the liquor license . . . That's what we were going to do. Everybody said that was the way you had to do, you understand, Miss Ruth?

Walter: Man—what happened down there?

Bobo *(A pitiful man, near tears.):* I'm trying to tell you, Walter.

Walter *(Screaming at him suddenly.):* THEN TELL ME, GODDAMNIT . . . WHAT'S THE MATTER WITH YOU?

Bobo: Man . . . I didn't go to no Springfield, yesterday.

Walter *(Halted, life hanging in the moment.):* Why not?

Bobo *(The long way, the hard way to tell.):* 'Cause I didn't have no reasons to . . .

Walter: Man, what are you talking about!

Bobo: I'm talking about the fact that when I got to the train station yesterday morning—eight o'clock like we planned . . . Man—*Willy didn't never show up.*

Walter: Why . . . where was he . . . where is he?

Bobo: That's what I'm trying to tell you . . . I don't know . . . I waited six hours . . . I called his house . . . and I waited . . . six hours . . . I waited in that train station six hours . . . *(Breaking into tears.)* That was all the extra money I had in the world . . . *(Looking up at Walter with the tears running down his face.)* Man, Willy is gone.

Walter: Gone, what you mean Willy is gone? Gone where? You mean he went by himself. You mean he went off to Springfield by himself—to take care of getting the license—*(Turns and looks anxiously at Ruth.)* You mean maybe he didn't want too many people in on the business down there? *(Looks to Ruth again, as before.)* You know Willy got his own ways. *(Looks back to Bobo.)* Maybe you was late yesterday and he just went on down there without you. Maybe—maybe—he's been callin' you at home tryin' to tell you what happened or something. Maybe—maybe—he's been callin' you at home tryin' to tell you what happened or something. Maybe—maybe—he just got sick. He's somewhere—he's got to be somewhere. *(Grabs Bobo senselessly by the collar and starts to shake him.)* We just got to find him—me and you got to find him. We got to!

Bobo *(In sudden angry, frightened agony.)*: What's the matter with you, Walter! *When a cat take off with your money he don't leave you no maps!*

Walter *(Turning madly, as though he is looking for Willy in the very room.)*: Willy! . . . Willy . . . don't do it . . . Please don't do it . . . Man, not with that money . . . Man, please, not with that money . . . Oh, God . . . Don't let it be true . . . *(He is wandering around, crying out for Willy and looking for him or perhaps for help from God.)* Man . . . I trusted you . . . Man, I put my life in your hands . . . *(He starts to crumple down on the floor as Ruth just covers her face in horror. Mama opens the door and comes into the room, with Beneatha behind her.)* Man . . . *(He starts to pound the floor with his fists, sobbing wildly.) That money is made out of my father's flesh . . .*

Bobo *(Standing over him helplessly.)*: I'm sorry, Walter . . . *(Only Walter's sobs reply. Bobo puts on his hat.)* I had my life staked on this deal, too . . .

(He exits.)

Mama *(To Walter.)*: Son—*(She goes to him, bends down to him, talks to his bent head.)* Son . . . Is it gone? Son, I gave you sixty-five hundred dollars. Is it gone? All of it? Beneatha's money too?

Walter *(Lifting his head slowly.)*: Mama . . . I never . . . went to the bank at all . . .

Mama *(Not wanting to believe him.)*: You mean . . . your sister's school money . . . you used that too . . . Walter? . . .

Walter: Yessss! . . . All of it . . . It's all gone . . .

(There is total silence. Ruth stands with her face covered with her hands; Beneatha leans forlornly against a wall, fingering a piece of red ribbon from the mother's gift. Mama stops and looks at her son without recognition and then, quite without thinking about it, starts to beat him senselessly in the face. Beneatha goes to them and stops it.)

Beneatha: Mama!

(Mama stops and looks at both of her children and rises slowly and wanders vaguely, aimlessly away from them.)

Mama: I see . . . him . . . night after night . . . come in . . . and look at that rug . . . and then look at me . . . the red showing in his eyes . . . the veins moving in his head . . . I see him grow thin and old before he was forty . . . working and working like somebody's old horse . . . killing himself . . . and you—you give it all away in a day . . .

Beneatha: Mama—

Mama: Oh, God . . . *(She looks up to Him.)* Look down here—and show me the strength.

Beneatha: Mama—

Mama *(Folding over.):* Strength . . .

Beneatha *(Plaintively.):* Mama . . .

Mama: Strength!

(Curtain.)

Act Three

An hour later.

At curtain, there is a sullen light of gloom in the living room, gray light not unlike that which began the first scene of Act One. At left we can see Walter within his room, alone with himself. He is stretched out on the bed, his shirt out and open, his arms under his head. He does not smoke, he does not cry out, he merely lies there, looking up at the ceiling, much as if he were alone in the world.

In the living room Beneatha sits at the table, still surrounded by the now almost ominous packing crates. She sits looking off. We feel that this is a mood struck perhaps an hour before, and it lingers now, full of the empty sound of profound disappointment. We see on a line from her brother's bedroom the sameness of their attitudes. Presently the bell rings and Beneatha rises without ambition or interest in answering. It is Asagai, smiling broadly, striding into the room with energy and happy expectation and conversation.

Asagai: I came over . . . I had some free time. I thought I might help with the packing. Ah, I like the look of packing crates! A household in preparation for a journey! It depresses some people . . . but for me . . . it is another feeling. Something full of the flow of life, do you understand? Movement, progress . . . It makes me think of Africa.

Beneatha: Africa!

Asagai: What kind of a mood is this? Have I told you how deeply you move me?

Beneatha: He gave away the money, Asagai . . .

Asagai: Who gave away what money?

Beneatha: The insurance money. My brother gave it away.

Asagai: Gave it away?

Beneatha: He made an investment! With a man even Travis wouldn't have trusted.

Asagai: And it's gone?

Beneatha: Gone!

Asagai: I've very sorry . . . And you, now?

Beneatha: Me? . . . Me? . . . Me I'm nothing . . . Me. When I was very small . . . we used to take our sleds out in the wintertime and the only hills we had were the ice-covered stone steps of some houses down the street. And we used to fill them in with snow and make them smooth and slide down them all day . . . and it was very dangerous you know . . . far too steep . . . and sure enough one day a kid named Rufus came down too fast and hit the sidewalk . . . and we saw his face just split open right there in front of us . . . And I remember standing there looking at his bloody open face thinking that was the end of Rufus. But the ambulance came and they took him to the hospital and they fixed the broken bones and they sewed it all up . . . and the next time I saw Rufus he just had a little line down the middle of his face . . . I never got over that . . .

Asagai: What?

Beneatha: That that was what one person could do for another, fix him up—sew up the problem, make him all right again. That was the most marvelous thing in the world . . . I wanted to do that. I always thought it was the one concrete thing in the world that a human being could do. Fix up the sick, you know—and make them whole again. This was truly being God . . .

Asagai: You wanted to be God?

Beneatha: No—I wanted to cure. It used to be so important to me. I wanted to cure. It used to matter. I used to care. I mean about people and how their bodies hurt . . .

Asagai: And you've stopped caring?

Beneatha: Yes—I think so.

Asagai: Why?

Beneatha: Because it doesn't seem deep enough, close enough to the truth.

Asagai: Truth? Why is it that you despairing ones always think that only you have the truth? I never thought to see *you* like that. You! Your brother made a stupid, childish mistake—and you are grateful to him. So that now you can give up the ailing human race on account of it. You talk about what good is struggle; what good is anything? Where are we all going? And why are we bothering?

Beneatha: *And you cannot answer it!* All your talk and dreams about Africa and Independence. Independence and then what? What about all the crooks and petty thieves and just plain idiots who will come into power to steal and plunder the same as before—only now they will be black and do it in the name of the new Independence— You cannot answer that.

Asagai *(Shouting over her.): I live the answer! (Pause.)* In my village at home it is the exceptional man who can even read a newspaper . . . or who ever *sees* a book at all. I will go home and much of what I will have to say will seem strange to the people of my village . . . But I will teach and work and things will happen, slowly and swiftly. At times it will seem that nothing changes at all . . . and then again . . . the sudden dramatic events which make history leap into the future. And then quiet again. Retrogression even. Guns, murder, revolution. And I even will have moments when I wonder if the quiet was not better than all that death and hatred. But I will look about my village at the illiteracy and disease and ignorance, and I will not wonder long. And perhaps . . . perhaps I will be a great man . . . I mean perhaps I will hold on to the substance of truth and find my way always with the right course . . . and perhaps for it I will be butchered in my bed some night by the servants of empire . . .

Beneatha: *The martyr!*

Asagai: . . . or perhaps I shall live to be a very old man respected and esteemed in my new nation . . . And perhaps I shall hold office and this is what I'm trying to tell you, Alaiyo; perhaps the things I believe now for my country will be wrong and outmoded, and I will not understand and do terrible things to have things my way or merely to keep my power. Don't you see that there will be young men and women, not British soldiers then, but my own black countrymen . . . to step out of the shadows some evening and slit my then useless throat? Don't you see they have always been there . . . that they always will be. And that such a thing as my own death will be an advance? They who might kill me even . . . actually replenish me!

Beneatha: Oh, Asagai, I know all that.

Asagai: Good! Then stop moaning and groaning and tell me what you plan to do.

Beneatha: Do?

Asagai: I have a bit of a suggestion.

Beneatha: What?

Asagai *(Rather quietly for him.):* That when it is all over—that you come home with me—

Beneatha *(Slapping herself on the forehead with exasperation born of misunderstanding.):* Oh—Asagai—at this moment you decide to be romantic!

Asagai *(Quickly understanding the misunderstanding.):* My dear, young creature of the New World—I do not mean across the city—I mean across the ocean; home—to Africa.

Beneatha *(Slowly understanding and turning to him with murmured amazement.):* To—to Nigeria?

Asagai: Yes! . . . *(Smiling and lifting his arms playfully.)* Three hundred years later the African Prince rose up out of the seas and swept the maiden back across the middle passage over which her ancestors had come—

Beneatha *(Unable to play.):* Nigeria?

Asagai: Nigeria. Home. *(Coming to her with genuine romantic flippancy.)* I will show you our mountains and our stars; and give you cool drinks from gourds and teach you the old songs and the ways of our people—and, in time, we will pretend that—*(Very softly.)*—you have only been away for a day—

(She turns her back to him, thinking. He swings her around and takes her full in his arms in a long embrace which proceeds to passion.)

Beneatha *(Pulling away.):* You're getting me all mixed up—

Asagai: Why?

Beneatha: Too many things—too many things have happened today. I must sit down and think. I don't know what I feel about anything right this minute.

(She promptly sits down and props her chin on her fist.)

Asagai *(Charmed.):* All right, I shall leave you. No—don't get up. *(Touching her, gently, sweetly.)* Just sit awhile and think . . . Never be afraid to sit awhile and think. *(He goes to door and looks at her.)* How often I have looked at you and said, "Ah—so this is what the New World hath finally wrought . . ."

(He exits. Beneatha sits on alone. Presently Walter enters from his room and starts to rummage through things, feverishly looking for something. She looks up and turns in her seat.)

Beneatha *(Hissingly.):* Yes—just look at what the New World hath wrought! . . . Just look! *(She gestures with bitter disgust.)* There he is! Monsieur le petit bourgeois noir—himself! There he is—Symbol of a Rising Class! Entrepreneur! Titan of the system! *(Walter ignores her completely and continues frantically and destructively looking for something and hurling things to floor and tearing things out of their place in his search. Beneatha ignores the eccentricity of his actions and goes on with the monologue of insult.)* Did you dream of yachts on Lake Michigan, Brother? Did you see yourself on that Great Day sitting down at the Conference Table, surrounded by all the mighty bald-headed men in America? All halted, waiting, breathless, waiting for your pronouncements on industry? Waiting for you—Chairman of the Board? *(Walter finds what he is looking for—a small piece of white paper—and pushes it in his pocket and puts on his coat and rushes out without ever having looked at her. She shouts after him.)* I look at you and I see the final triumph of stupidity in the world!

(The door slams and she returns to just sitting again. Ruth comes quickly out of Mama's room.)

Ruth: Who was that?

Beneatha: Your husband.

Ruth: Where did he go?

Beneatha: Who knows—maybe he has an appointment at U.S. Steel.

Ruth *(Anxiously, with frightened eyes.):* You didn't say nothing bad to him, did you?

Beneatha: Bad? Say anything bad to him? No—I told him he was a sweet boy and full of dreams and everything is strictly peachy keen, as the ofay kids say!

(Mama enters from her bedroom. She is lost, vague, trying to catch hold, to make some sense of her former command of the world, but it still eludes her. A sense of waste overwhelms her gait; a measure of apology rides on her shoulders. She goes to her plant, which has remained on the table, looks at it, picks it up and takes it to the window sill and sits it outside, and she stands and looks at it a long moment. Then she closes the window, straightens her body with effort and turns around to her children.)

Mama: Well—ain't it a mess in here, though? *(A false cheerfulness, a beginning of something.)* I guess we all better stop moping around and get some work done. All this unpacking and everything we got to do. *(Ruth raises her head slowly in response to the sense of the line; and Beneatha in similar manner turns very slowly to look at her mother.)* One of you all better call the moving people and tell 'em not to come.

Ruth: Tell 'em not to come?

Mama: Of course, baby. Ain't no need in 'em coming all the way here and having to go back. They charges for that too. *(She sits down, fingers to her brow, thinking.)* Lord, ever since I was a little girl, I always remembers people saying, "Lena—Lena Eggleston, you aims too high all the time. You needs to slow down and see life a little more like it is. Just slow down some." That's what they always used to say down home—"Lord, that Lena Eggleston is a high-minded thing. She'll get her due one day!"

Ruth: No, Lena . . .

Mama: Me and Big Walter just didn't never learn right.

Ruth: Lena, no! We gotta go. Bennie—tell her . . . *(She rises and crosses to Beneatha with her arms outstretched. Beneatha doesn't respond.)* Tell her we can still move . . . the notes ain't but a hundred and twenty-five a month. We got four grown people in this house—we can work . . .

Mama *(To herself.)*: Just aimed too high all the time—

Ruth *(Turning and going to Mama fast—the words pouring out with urgency and desperation.)*: Lena—I'll work . . . I'll work twenty hours a day in all the kitchens in Chicago . . . I'll strap my baby on my back if I have to and scrub all the floors in America and wash all the sheets in America if I have to—but we got move . . . We got to get out of here . . .

(Mama reaches out absently and pats Ruth's hand.)

Mama: No—I sees things differently now. Been thinking 'bout some of the things we could do to fix this place up some. I seen a second-hand bureau over on Maxwell Street just the other day that could fit right there. *(She points to where the new furniture might go. Ruth wanders away from her.)* Would need some new handles on it and then a little varnish and then it look like something brand-new. And—we can put up them new curtains in the kitchen . . . Why this place be looking fine. Cheer us all up so that we forget trouble ever came . . . *(To Ruth.)* And you could get some nice screens to put up in your room round the baby's bassinet . . . *(She looks at* *both of them, pleadingly.)* Sometimes you just got to know when to give up some things . . . and hold on to what you got.

(Walter enters from the outside, looking spent and leaning against the door, his coat hanging from him.)

Mama: Where you been, son?

Walter *(Breathing hard.):* Made a call.

Mama: To who, son?

Walter: To The Man.

Mama: What man, baby?

Walter: The Man, Mama. Don't you know who The Man is?

Ruth: Walter Lee?

Walter: *The Man.* Like the guys in the streets say—The Man. Captain Boss—Mistuh Charley . . . Old Captain Please Mr. Bossman . . .

Beneatha *(Suddenly.):* Lindner!

Walter: That's right! That's good. I told him to come right over.

Beneatha *(Fiercely, understanding.):* For what? What do you want to see him for!

Walter *(Looking at his sister.):* We going to do business with him.

Mama: What you talking 'bout, son?

Walter: Talking 'bout life, Mama. You all always telling me to see life like it is. Well—I laid in there on my back today . . . and I figured it out. Life just like it is. Who gets and who don't get. *(He sits down with his coat on and laughs.)* Mama, you know it's all divided up. Life is. Sure enough. Between the takers and the "tooken." *(He laughs.)* I've figured it out finally. *(He looks around at them.)* Yeah. Some of us always getting "tooken." *(He laughs.)* People like Willy Harris, they don't never get "tooken." And you know why the rest of us do? 'Cause we all mixed up. Mixed up bad. We get to looking 'round for the right and the wrong; and we worry about it and cry about it and stay up nights trying to figure out 'bout the wrong and the right of things all the time . . . And all the time, man, them takers is out there operating, just taking and taking. Willy Harris? Shoot—Willy Harris don't even count. He don't even count in the big scheme of things. But I'll say one thing for old Willy Harris . . . he's taught me something. He's taught me to keep my eye on what counts in this world. Yeah—*(Shouting out a little.)* Thanks, Willy!

Ruth: What did you call that man for, Walter Lee?

Walter: Called him to tell him to come on over to the show. Gonna put on a show for the man. Just what he wants to see. You see, Mama, the man came here today and he told us that them people out there where you want us to move—well they so upset they willing to pay us not to move out there. *(He laughs again.)* And—and oh, Mama—you would of been proud of the way me and Ruth and Bennie acted. We told him to get out . . . Lord have mercy! We told the man to get out. Oh, we was some proud folks this afternoon, yeah. *(He lights a cigarette.)* We were still full of that old-time stuff . . .

Ruth *(Coming toward him slowly.):* You talking 'bout taking them people's money to keep us from moving in that house?

Walter: I ain't just talking 'bout it, baby—I'm telling you that's what's going to happen.

Beneatha: Oh, God! Where is the bottom! Where is the real honest-to-God bottom so he can't go any farther!

Walter: See—that's the old stuff. You and that boy that was here today. You all want everybody to carry a flag and a spear and sing some marching songs, huh? You wanna spend your life looking into things and trying to find the right and the wrong part, huh? Yeah. You know what's going to happen to that boy someday—he'll find himself sitting in a dungeon, locked in forever—and the takers will have the key! Forget it, baby! There ain't no causes—there ain't nothing but taking in this world, and he who takes most is smartest—and it don't make a damn bit of difference *how.*

Mama: You making something inside me cry, son. Some awful pain inside me.

Walter: Don't cry, Mama. Understand. That white man is going to walk in that door able to write checks for more money than we ever had. It's important to him and I'm going to help him . . . I'm going to put on the show, Mama.

Mama: Son—I come from five generations of people who was slaves and sharecroppers—but ain't nobody in my family never let nobody pay 'em no money that was a way of telling us we wasn't fit to walk the earth. We ain't never been that poor. *(Raising her eyes and looking at him.)* We ain't never been that dead inside.

Beneatha: Well—we are dead now. All the talk about dreams and sunlight that goes on in this house. All dead.

Walter: What's the matter with you all! I didn't make this world! It was give to me this way! Hell, yes, I want me some yachts someday! Yes, I want to hang some real pearls 'round my wife's neck. Ain't she supposed to wear no pearls? Somebody tell me—tell me, who decides which women is supposed to wear pearls in this world. I tell you I am a *man*—and I think my wife should wear some pearls in this world!

(This last line hangs a good while and Walter begins to move about the room. The word "Man" has penetrated his consciousness; he mumbles it to himself repeatedly between strange agitated pauses as he moves about.)

Mama: Baby, how you going to feel on the inside?

Walter: Fine! . . . Going to feel fine . . . a man . . .

Mama: You won't have nothing left then, Walter Lee.

Walter *(Coming to her.):* I'm going to feel fine, Mama. I'm going to look that son-of-a-bitch in the eyes and say—*(He falters.)*—and say, "All right, Mr. Lindner—*(He falters even more.)*—that's your neighborhood out there. You got the right to keep it like you want. You got the right to have it like you want. Just write the check and—the house is yours." And, and I am going to say—*(His voice almost breaks.)* And you—you people just put the money in my hand and you won't have to live next to this bunch of stinking niggers! . . . *(He straightens up and moves away from his mother, walking around the room.)* Maybe—maybe I'll get down on my black knees . . . *(He does so; Ruth and Bennie and Mama watch him in frozen horror.)* Captain, Mistuh, Bossman. *(He starts crying.)* A-hee-hee-hee! *(Wringing his hands in profoundly anguished imitation.)* Yassssuh! Great White Father, just gi' ussen de money, fo' God's sake, and we's ain't gwine come out deh and dirty up yo' white folks neighborhood . . .

(He breaks down completely, then gets up and goes into the bedroom.)

Beneatha: That is not a man. That is nothing but a toothless rat.

Mama: Yes—death done come in this here house. *(She is nodding, slowly, reflectively.)* Done come walking in my house. On the lips of my children. You what supposed to be my beginning again. You—what supposed to be my harvest. *(To Beneatha.)* You—you mourning your brother?

Beneatha: He's no brother of mine.

Mama: What you say?

Beneatha: I said that that individual in that room is no brother of mine.

Mama: That's what I thought you said. You feeling like you better than he is today? *(Beneatha does not answer.)* Yes? What you tell him a minute ago? That he wasn't a man? Yes? You give him up for me? You done wrote his epitaph too—like the rest of the world? Well, who give you the privilege?

Beneatha Be on my side for once! You saw what he just did, Mama! You saw him—down on his knees. Wasn't it you who taught me—to despise any man who would do that. Do what he's going to do.

Mama: Yes—I taught you that. Me and your daddy. But I thought I taught you something else too . . . I thought I taught you to love him.

Beneatha: Love him? There is nothing left to love.

Mama: There is always something left to love. And if you ain't learned that, you ain't learned nothing. *(Looking at her.)* Have you cried for that boy today? I don't mean for yourself and for the family 'cause we lost the money. I mean for him; what he been through and what it done to him. Child, when do you think is the time to love somebody the most; when they done good and made things easy for everybody? Well then, you ain't through learning—because that ain't the time at all. It's when he's at his lowest and can't believe in hisself 'cause the world done whipped him so. When you starts measuring somebody, measure him right, child, measure him right. Make sure you done taken into account what hills and valleys he come through before he got to wherever he is.

(Travis bursts into the room at the end of the speech, leaving the door open.)

Travis: Grandmama—the moving men are downstairs! The truck just pulled up.

Mama *(Turning and looking at him.)*: Are they, baby? They downstairs?

(She sighs and sits. Lindner appears in the doorway. He peers in and knocks lightly, to gain attention, and comes in. All turn to look at him.)

Lindner *(Hat and briefcase in hand):* Uh—hello . . .

(Ruth crosses mechanically to the bedroom door and opens it and lets it swing open freely and slowly as the lights come up on Walter within, still in his coat, sitting at the far corner of the room. He looks up and out through the room to Lindner.)

Ruth: He's here.

(A long minute passes and Walter slowly gets up.)

Lindner *(Coming to the table with efficiency, putting his briefcase on the table and starting to unfold papers and unscrew fountain pens.):* Well, I certainly was glad to hear from you people. *(Walter has begun the trek out of the room, slowly and awkwardly, rather like a small boy, passing the back of his sleeve across his mouth from time to time.)* Life can really be so much simpler than people let it be most of the time. Well—with whom do I negotiate? You, Mrs. Younger, or your son here? *(Mama sits with her hands folded on her lap and her eyes closed as Walter advances. Travis goes close to Lindner and looks at the papers curiously.)* Just some official papers, sonny.

Ruth: Travis, you go downstairs.

Mama *(Opening her eyes and looking into Walter's.):* No. Travis, you stay right here. And you make him understand what you doing, Walter Lee. You teach him good. Like Willy Harris taught you. You show where our five generations done come to. Go ahead, son—

Walter *(Looks down into his boy's eyes. Travis grins at him merrily and Walter draws him beside him with his arm lightly around his shoulders.):* Well, Mr. Lindner. *(Beneatha turns away.)* We called you—*(There is a profound, simple groping quality in his speech.)*—because, well, me and my family *(He looks around and shifts from one foot to the other.)* Well—we are very plain people . . .

Lindner: Yes—

Walter: I mean—I have worked as a chauffeur most of my life—and my wife here, she does domestic work in people's kitchens. So does my mother. I mean—we are plain people . . .

Lindner: Yes, Mr. Younger—

Walter *(Really like a small boy, looking down at his shoes and then up at the man.):* And—uh—well, my father, well, he was a laborer most of his life.

Lindner *(Absolutely confused.):* Uh, yes—

Walter *(Looking down at his toes once again.):* My father almost beat a man to death once because this man called him a bad name or something, you know what I mean?

Lindner: No, I'm afraid I don't.

Walter *(Finally straightening up.):* Well, what I mean is that we come from people who had a lot of pride. I mean—we are very proud people. And that's my sister over there and she's going to be a doctor—and we are very proud—

Lindner: Well—I am sure that is very nice, but—

Walter *(Starting to cry and facing the man eye to eye.):* What I am telling you is that we called you over here to tell you that we are very proud and that this is—this is my son, who makes the sixth generation of our family in this country, and that we have all thought about your offer and we have decided to move into our house because my father—my father—he earned it. *(Mama has her eyes closed and is rocking back and forth as though she were in church, with her head nodding the amen yes.)* We don't want to make no trouble for nobody or fight no causes—but we will try to be good neighbors. That's all we got to say. *(He looks the man absolutely in the eyes.)* We don't want your money.

(He turns and walks away from the man.)

115 **Lindner** *(Looking around at all of them.):* I take it then that you have decided to occupy.

Beneatha: That's what the man said.

Lindner *(To Mama in her reverie.):* Then I would like to appeal to you, Mrs. Younger. You are older and wiser and understand things better I am sure . . .

Mama *(Rising.):* I am afraid you don't understand. My son said we was going to move and there ain't nothing left for me to say. *(Shaking her head with double meaning.)* You know how these young folks is nowadays, mister. Can't do a thing with 'em. Good-bye.

Lindner *(Folding up his materials.):* Well—if you are that final about it . . . There is nothing left for me to say. *(He finishes. He is almost ignored by the family, who are concentrating on Walter Lee. At the door Lindner halts and looks around.)* I sure hope you people know what you're doing.

(He shakes his head and exits.)

120 **Ruth** *(Looking around and coming to life.):* Well, for God's sake—if the moving men are here—LET'S GET THE HELL OUT OF HERE!

Mama *(Into action.):* Ain't it the truth! Look at all this here mess. Ruth, put Travis' good jacket on him . . . Walter Lee, fix your tie and tuck your shirt in, you look just like somebody's hoodlum. Lord have mercy, where is my plant? *(She flies to get it amid the general bustling of the family, who are deliberately trying to ignore the nobility of the past moment.)* You all start on down . . . Travis child, don't go empty-handed . . . Ruth, where did I put that box with my skillets in it? I want to be in charge of it myself . . . I'm going to make us the biggest dinner we ever ate tonight . . . Beneatha, what's the matter with them stockings? Pull them things up, girl . . .

(The family starts to file out as two moving men appear and begin to carry out the heavier pieces of furniture, bumping into the family as they move about.)

Beneatha: Mama, Asagai—asked me to marry him today and go to Africa—

Mama *(In the middle of her getting-ready activity.):* He did? You ain't old enough to marry nobody—*(Seeing the moving men lifting one of her chairs* *precariously.)* Darling, that ain't no bale of cotton, please handle it so we can sit in it again. I had that chair twenty-five years . . .

(The movers sigh with exasperation and go on with their work.)

Beneatha *(Girlishly and unreasonably trying to pursue the conversation.):* To go to Africa, Mama—be a doctor in Africa . . .

Mama *(Distracted.):* Yes, baby—

Walter: Africa! What he want you to go to Africa for?

Beneatha: To practice there . . .

Walter: Girl, if you don't get all them silly ideas out your head! You better marry yourself a man with some loot . . .

Beneatha *(Angrily, precisely as in the first scent of the play.):* What have you got to do with who I marry!

Walter: Plenty. Now I think George Murchison—

(He and Beneatha go out yelling at each other vigorously; Beneatha is heard saying that she would not marry George Murchison if he were Adam and she were Eve, etc. The anger is loud and real till their voices diminish. Ruth stands at the door and turns to Mama and smiles knowingly.)

Mama *(Fixing her hat at last.):* Yeah—they something all right, my children . . .

Ruth: Yeah—they're something. Let's go, Lena.

Mama *(Stalling, starting to look around at the house.):* Yes—I'm coming. Ruth—

Ruth: Yes?

Mama *(Quietly, woman to woman.):* He finally come into his manhood today, didn't he? Kind of like a rainbow after the rain . . .

Ruth *(Biting her lip lest her own pride explode in front of Mama.):* Yes, Lena.

(Walter's voice calls for them raucously.)

Mama *(Waving Ruth out vaguely.):* All right, honey—go on down. I be down directly.

(Ruth hesitates, then exits. Mama stands, at last alone in the living room, her plant on the table before her as the lights start to come down. She looks around at all the walls and ceilings and suddenly, despite herself, while the children call below, a great heaving thing rises in her and she puts her fist to her mouth, takes a final desperate look, pulls her coat about her, pats her hat and goes out. The lights dim down. The door opens and she comes back in, grabs her plant, and goes out for the last time.)

(Curtain.)

Explorations of the Text

1. How does the urban setting establish the atmosphere and mood of the play?

2. Characterize Mama. Discuss her relationships with her children. What expectations does she have for their futures?
3. Explore the primary conflicts of the play. What escalates the tension among the characters?
4. What do the two men with whom Beneatha is involved symbolize as directions for her life? What is their thematic significance?
5. How does Walter change in Act Three? What other conflicts within characters are resolved in this act?
6. Concentrate on an aspect of setting or on a stage prop. Is it symbolic? Explain.
7. Is the ending of the play effective?
8. Relate the poem, "Harlem" by Langston Hughes (see p. 886), which serves as the epigraph to the play, to the characters' situations and states of mind.
9. Does *A Raisin in the Sun* present timeless issues?

The Reading/Writing Connection

1. "Think" Topic: Lorraine Hansberry's play was written in the 1950s about problems for a family in urban Chicago. Do you relate to the characters, to the issues presented in the play? Are the events portrayed still relevant today? Argue pro or con.
2. Journal Entry: Write about Beneatha's choices. Have you faced a similar decision?

Ideas for Writing

1. Discuss a central theme of the play. Use evidence from the text to support your interpretation.
2. Compare the poem with the main characters. Or connect the poem with themes of the play.
3. View the film version of this drama. Compare the two works.

NONFICTION

Ruth's Song

Gloria Steinem

Gloria Steinem (1934–) was born in Toledo, Ohio. She attended Smith College and the universities of Delhi and Calcutta in India. After her return to the United States, she worked for the civil rights and peace movements throughout the 1960s. Steinem's best-known article from her early career, "I Was a Playboy Bunny," resulted from an undercover assignment for the 1963 opening of New York City's Playboy Club. In 1968, she co-founded New York *magazine; in 1972 she co-founded* Ms. *magazine. She has been a leading spokesperson for the women's movement. Gloria Steinem has won many awards and fellowships, among them the Ceres Medal from the United Nations and a Woodrow Wilson International Center for Scholars award. Her writings include* The Beach Book *(1963),* Outrageous Acts and Everyday Rebellions *(1983), and* Revolution from Within *(1991). She continues to work for social change.*

1983

Happy or unhappy, families are all mysterious. We have only to imagine how differently we would be described—and will be, after our deaths—by each of the family members who believe they know us. The only question is, Why are some mysteries more important than others?

The fate of my Uncle Ed was a mystery of importance in our family. We lavished years of speculation on his transformation from a brilliant young electrical engineer to the town handyman. What could have changed this elegant, Lincolnesque student voted "Best Dressed" by his classmates to the gaunt, unshaven man I remember? Why did he leave a young son and a first wife of the "proper" class and religion, marry a much less educated woman of the "wrong" religion, and raise a second family in a house near an abandoned airstrip; a house whose walls were patched with metal signs to stop the wind? Why did he never talk about his transformation?

For years, I assumed that some secret and dramatic events of a year he spent in Alaska had made the difference. Then I discovered that the trip had come after his change and probably been made because of it. Strangers he worked for as a much-loved handyman talked about him as one more tragedy of the Depression, and it was true that Uncle Ed's father, my paternal grandfather, had lost his money in the stockmarket Crash and died of (depending on who was telling the story) pneumonia or a broken heart. But the Crash of 1929 also had come long after Uncle Ed's transformation. Another theory was that he was afflicted with a mental problem that lasted most of his life, yet he was supremely competent at his work, led an independent life, and asked for help from no one.

Perhaps he had fallen under the spell of a radical professor in the early days of the century, the height of this country's romance with socialism and anarchism. That was the theory of another uncle on my mother's side. I do remember that no matter how much Uncle Ed needed money, he would charge no more for his work than materials plus 10 percent, and I never saw him in anything other than ancient boots and overalls held up with strategic safety pins. Was he really trying to replace socialism-in-one-country with socialism-in-one-man? If so, why did my grandmother, a woman who herself had run for the school board in coalition with anarchists and socialists, mistrust his judgment so much that she left his share of her estate in trust, even though he was over fifty when she died? And why did Uncle Ed seem uninterested in all other political words and acts? Was it true instead that, as another relative insisted, Uncle Ed had chosen poverty to disprove the myths of Jews and money?

5 Years after my uncle's death, I asked a son in his second family if he had the key to his family mystery. No, he said. He had never known his father any other way. For that cousin, there had been no question. For the rest of us, there was to be no answer.

For many years I also never imagined my mother any way other than the person she had become before I was born. She was just a fact of life when I was growing up; someone to be worried about and cared for; an invalid who lay in bed with eyes closed and lips moving in occasional response to voices only she could hear; a woman to whom I brought an endless stream of toast and coffee, bologna sandwiches and dime pies, in a child's version of what meals should be. She was a loving, intelligent, terrorized woman who tried hard to clean our littered house whenever she emerged from her private world, but who could rarely be counted on to finish one task. In many ways, our roles were reversed: I was the mother and she was the child. Yet that didn't help her, for she still worried about me with all the intensity of a frightened mother, plus the special fears of her own world full of threats and hostile voices.

Even then I suppose I must have known that, years before she was thirty-five and I was born, she had been a spirited adventurous young woman who struggled out of a working-class family and into college, who found work she loved and continued to do, even after she was married and my older sister was there to be cared for. Certainly, our immediate family and nearby relatives, of whom I was by far the youngest, must have remembered her life as a whole and functioning person. She was thirty before she gave up her own career to help my father run the Michigan summer resort that was the most practical of his many dreams, and she worked hard there as everything from bookkeeper to bar manager. The family must have watched this energetic, fun-loving, book-loving woman turn into someone who was afraid to be alone, who could not hang on to reality long enough to hold a job, and who could rarely concentrate enough to read a book.

Yet I don't remember any family speculation about the mystery of my mother's transformation. To the kind ones and those who liked her, this new Ruth was simply a sad event, perhaps a mental case, a family problem to be accepted and cared for until some natural process made her better. To the less kind or those who had resented her earlier independence, she was a willful failure, someone who lived in a filthy house, a woman who simply would not pull herself together.

Unlike the case of my Uncle Ed, exterior events were never suggested as reason enough for her problems. Giving up her own career was never cited as her personal parallel of the Depression. (Nor was there discussion of the Depression itself, though my mother, like millions of others, had made potato soup and cut up blankets to make my sister's winter clothes.) Her fears of dependence and poverty were no match for my uncle's possible political beliefs. The real influence of newspaper editors who had praised her reporting was not taken as seriously as the possible influence of one radical professor.

10 Even the explanation of mental illness seemed to contain more personal fault when applied to my mother. She had suffered her first "nervous breakdown," as she and everyone else called it, before I was born and when my sister was about five. It followed years of trying to take care of a baby, be the wife of a kind but financially irresponsible man with show business dreams, and still keep her much-loved job as reporter and newspaper editor. After many months in a sanatorium, she was pronounced recovered. That is, she was able to take care of my sister again, to move away from the city and the job she loved, and to work with my father at the isolated rural lake in Michigan he was trying to transform into a resort worthy of the big dance bands of the 1930s.

But she was never again completely without the spells of depression, anxiety, and visions into some other world that eventually were to turn her into the nonperson I remember. And she was never again without a bottle of dark, acrid-smelling liquid she called "Doc Howard's medicine": a solution of chloral hydrate that I later learned was the main ingredient of "Mickey Finns" or "knockout drops," and that probably made my mother and her doctor the pioneers of modern tranquilizers. Though friends and relatives saw this medicine as one more evidence of weakness and indulgence, to me it always seemed an embarrassing but necessary evil. It slurred her speech and slowed her coordination, making our neighbors and my school friends believe she was a drunk. But without it, she would not sleep for days, even a week at a time, and her feverish eyes began to see only that private world in which wars and hostile voices threatened the people she loved.

Because my parents had divorced and my sister was working in a far-away city, my mother and I were alone together then, living off the meager fixed income that my mother got from leasing her share of the remaining land in Michigan. I remember a long thanksgiving weekend spent hanging on to her with one hand and holding my eighth-grade assignment of *Tale of Two Cities*[1] in the other, because the war outside our house was so real to my mother that she had plunged her hand through a window, badly cutting her arm in an effort to help us escape. Only when she finally agreed to swallow the medicine could

[1] Novel by Charles Dickens, a nineteenth-century English writer.

she sleep, and only then could I end the terrible calm that comes with crisis and admit to myself how afraid I had been.

No wonder that no relative in my memory challenged the doctor who prescribed this medicine, asked if some of her suffering and hallucinating might be due to overdose or withdrawal, or even consulted another doctor about its use. It was our relief as well as hers.

But why was she never returned even to that first sanatorium? Or to help that might come from other doctors? It's hard to say. Partly, it was her own fear of returning. Partly, it was too little money, and a family's not-unusual assumption that mental illness is an inevitable part of someone's personality. Or perhaps other family members had feared something like my experience when, one hot and desperate summer between the sixth and seventh grade, I finally persuaded her to let me take her to the only doctor from those sanatorium days whom she remembered without fear.

Yes, this brusque old man told me after talking to my abstracted, timid mother for twenty minutes: She definitely belongs in a state hospital. I should put her there right away. But even at that age, *Life* magazine and newspaper exposés had told me what horrors went on inside those hospitals. Assuming there to be no other alternative, I took her home and never tried again.

In retrospect, perhaps the biggest reason my mother was cared for but not helped for twenty years was the simplest: her functioning was not that necessary to the world. Like women alcoholics who drink in their kitchens while costly programs are constructed for executives who drink, or like the homemakers subdued with tranquilizers while male patients get therapy and personal attention instead, my mother was not an important worker. She was not even the caretaker of a very young child, as she had been when she was hospitalized the first time. My father had patiently brought home the groceries and kept our odd household going until I was eight or so and my sister went away to college. Two years later when wartime gas rationing closed his summer resort and he had to travel to buy and sell in summer as well as winter, he said: How can I travel and take care of your mother? How can I make a living? He was right. It was impossible to do both. I did not blame him for leaving once I was old enough to be the bringer of meals and answerer of my mother's questions. ("Has your sister been killed in a car crash?" "Are there German soldiers outside?") I replaced my father, my mother was left with one more way of maintaining a sad status quo, and the world went on undisturbed.

That's why our lives, my mother's from forty-six to fifty-three, and my own from ten to seventeen, were spent alone together. There was one sane winter in a house we rented to be near my sister's college in Massachusetts, then one bad summer spent house-sitting in suburbia while my mother hallucinated and my sister struggled to hold down a summer job in New York. But the rest of those years were lived in Toledo where both my mother and father had been born, and on whose city newspapers an earlier Ruth had worked.

First we moved into a basement apartment in a good neighborhood. In those rooms behind a furnace, I made one last stab at being a child. By pretending to be much sicker with a cold than I really was, I hoped my mother would suddenly turn into a sane and cheerful woman bringing me chicken soup à la Hollywood. Of course, she could not. It only made her feel worse that she could not. I stopped pretending.

But for most of those years, we lived in the upstairs of the house my mother had grown up in and her parents left her—a deteriorating farm house engulfed by the city, with poor but newer houses stacked against it and a major highway a few feet from its sagging front porch. For a while, we could rent the two downstairs apartments to a newlywed factory worker and a local butcher's family. Then the health department condemned our ancient furnace for the final time, sealing it so tight that even my resourceful Uncle Ed couldn't produce illegal heat.

20 In that house, I remember:

. . . lying in the bed my mother and I shared for warmth, listening on the early morning radio to the royal wedding of Princess Elizabeth and Prince Philip being broadcast live, while we tried to ignore and thus protect each other from the unmistakable sounds of the factory worker downstairs beating up and locking up his pregnant wife.

. . . hanging paper drapes I had bought in the dime store; stacking books and papers in the shape of two armchairs and covering them with blankets; evolving my own dishwashing system (I waited until all the dishes were dirty, then put them in the bathtub); and listening to my mother's high praise for these housekeeping efforts to bring order from chaos, though in retrospect I think they probably depressed her further.

. . . coming back from one of the Eagles' Club shows where I and other veterans of a local tap-dancing school made ten dollars a night for two shows, and finding my mother waiting with a flashlight and no coat in the dark cold of the bus stop, worried about my safety walking home.

. . . in a good period, when my mother's native adventurousness came through, answering a classified ad together for an amateur acting troupe that performed Biblical dramas in churches, and doing several very corny performances of *Noah's Ark* while my proud mother shook metal sheets backstage to make thunder.

25 . . . on a hot summer night, being bitten by one of the rats that shared our house and its back alley. It was a terrifying night that turned into a touching one when my mother, summoning courage from some unknown reservoir of love, became a calm, comforting parent who took me to a hospital emergency room despite her terror at leaving home.

. . . coming home from a local library with the three books a week into which I regularly escaped, and discovering that for once there was no need to escape. My mother was calmly planting hollyhocks in the vacant lot next door.

But there were also times when she woke in the early winter dark, too frightened and disoriented to remember that I was at my usual after-school job, and so called the police to find me. Humiliated in front of my friends by sirens and policemen, I would yell at her—and she would bow her head in fear and say "I'm sorry, I'm sorry, I'm sorry," just as she had done so often when my otherwise-kindhearted father had yelled at her in frustration. Perhaps the worst thing about suffering is that it finally hardens the hearts of those around it.

And there were many, many times when I badgered her until her shaking hands had written a small check to cash at the corner grocery and I could leave her alone while I escaped to the comfort of well-heated dime stores that smelled of fresh doughnuts, or to air-conditioned Saturday-afternoon movies that were windows on a very different world.

But my ultimate protection was this: I was just passing through, a guest in the house; perhaps this wasn't my mother at all. Though I knew very well that I was her daughter, I sometimes imagined that I had been adopted and that my real parents would find me, a fantasy I've since discovered is common. (If children wrote more and grownups less, being adopted might be seen not only as a fear but also as a hope.) Certainly, I didn't mourn the wasted life of this woman who was scarcely older than I am now. I worried only about the times when she got worse.

30 Pity takes distance and a certainty of surviving. It was only after our house was bought for demolition by the church next door, and after my sister had performed the miracle of persuading my father to give me a carefree time before college by taking my mother with him to California for a year, that I could afford to think about the sadness of her life. Suddenly, I was far away in Washington, living with my sister and sharing a house with several of her friends. While I finished high school and discovered to my surprise that my classmates felt sorry for me because my mother *wasn't* there, I also realized that my sister, at least in her early childhood, had known a very different person who lived inside our mother, an earlier Ruth.

She was a woman I met for the first time in a mental hospital near Baltimore, a humane place with gardens and trees where I visited her each weekend of the summer after my first year away in college. Fortunately, my sister hadn't been able to work and be our mother's caretaker, too. After my father's year was up, my sister had carefully researched hospitals and found the courage to break the family chain.

At first, this Ruth was the same abstracted, frightened woman I had lived with all those years, though now all the sadder for being approached through long hospital corridors and many locked doors. But gradually she began to talk about her past life, memories that doctors there must have been awakening. I began to meet a Ruth I had never known.

. . . A tall, spirited, auburn-haired high-school girl who loved basketball and reading; who tried to drive her uncle's Stanley Steamer when it was the first car in the neighborhood; who had a gift for gardening and who sometimes, in defiance of convention, wore her father's overalls; a girl with the courage to go to dances even though her church told her that music itself was sinful, and whose sense of adventure almost made up for feeling gawky and unpretty next to her daintier, dark-haired sister.

. . . A very little girl, just learning to walk, discovering the body places where touching was pleasurable, and being punished by her mother who slapped her hard across the kitchen floor.

35 . . . A daughter of a handsome railroad-engineer and a schoolteacher who felt she had married "beneath her"; the mother who took her two daughters on

Christmas trips to faraway New York on an engineer's free railroad pass and showed them the restaurants and theaters they should aspire to—even though they could only stand outside them in the snow.

. . . A good student at Oberlin College, whose freethinking traditions she loved, where friends nicknamed her "Billy"; a student with a talent for both mathematics and poetry, who was not above putting an invisible film of Karo syrup on all the john seats in her dormitory the night of a big prom; a daughter who had to return to Toledo, live with her family, and go to a local university when her ambitious mother—who had scrimped and saved, ghostwritten a minister's sermons, and made her daughters' clothes in order to get them to college at all—ran out of money. At home, this Ruth became a part-time bookkeeper in a lingerie shop for the very rich, commuting to classes and listening to her mother's harsh lectures on the security of becoming a teacher; but also a young woman who was still rebellious enough to fall in love with my father, the editor of her university newspaper, a funny and charming young man who was a terrible student, had no intention of graduating, put on all the campus dances, and was unacceptably Jewish.

I knew from family lore that my mother had married my father twice: once secretly, after he invited her to become the literary editor of his campus newspaper, and once a year later in a public ceremony, which some members of both families refused to attend as the "mixed marriage" of its day.

And I knew that my mother had gone on to earn a teaching certificate. She had used it to scare away truant officers during the winters when, after my father closed the summer resort for the season, we lived in a house trailer and worked our way to Florida or California and back by buying and selling antiques.

But only during those increasingly adventurous weekend outings from the hospital—going shopping, to lunch, to the movies—did I realize that she had taught college calculus for a year in deference to her mother's insistence that she have teaching "to fall back on." And only then did I realize she had fallen in love with newspapers along with my father. After graduating from the university paper, she wrote a gossip column for a local tabloid, under the name "Duncan MacKenzie," since women weren't supposed to do such things, and soon had earned a job as society reporter on one of Toledo's two big dailies. By the time my sister was four or so, she had worked her way up to the coveted position of Sunday editor.

40 It was a strange experience to look into those brown eyes I had seen so often and realize suddenly how much they were like my own. For the first time, I realized that she might really be my mother.

I began to think about the many pressures that might have led up to that first nervous breakdown: leaving my sister who she loved very much with a grandmother whose values my mother didn't share; trying to hold on to a job she loved but was being asked to leave by her husband; wanting very much to go with a woman friend to pursue their own dreams in New York; falling in love with a co-worker at the newspaper who frightened her by being more sexually attractive, more supportive of her work than my father, and perhaps the man she should have married; and finally, nearly bleeding to death with a miscarriage because her own mother had little faith in doctors and refused to get help.

Did those months in the sanatorium brainwash her in some Freudian or very traditional way into making what were, for her, probably the wrong choices? I don't know. It almost doesn't matter. Without extraordinary support to the contrary, she was already convinced that divorce was unthinkable. A husband could not be left for another man, and certainly not for a reason as selfish as a career. A daughter could not be deprived of her father and certainly not be uprooted and taken off to an uncertain future in New York. A bride was supposed to be virginal (not "shop-worn," as my euphemistic mother would have said), and if your husband turned out to be kind, but innocent of the possibility of a woman's pleasure, then just be thankful for kindness.

Of course, other women have torn themselves away from work and love and still survived. But a story my mother told me years later has always symbolized for me the formidable forces arrayed against her.

> *It was early spring, nothing was open yet. There was nobody for miles around. We had stayed at the lake that winter, so I was alone a lot while your father took the car and traveled around on business. You were a baby. Your sister was in school, and there was no phone. The last straw was that the radio broke. Suddenly it seemed like forever since I'd been able to talk with anyone—or even hear the sound of another voice.*
>
> *I bundled you up, took the dog, and walked out to the Brooklyn road. I thought I'd walk the four or five miles to the grocery store, talk to some people, and find somebody to drive me back. I was walking along with Fritzie running up ahead in the empty road—when suddenly a car came out of nowhere and down the hill. It hit Fritzie head on and threw him over to the side of the road. I yelled and screamed at the driver, but he never slowed down. He never looked at us. He never even turned his head.*
>
> *Poor Fritzie was all broken and bleeding, but he was still alive. I carried him and sat down in the middle of the road, with his head cradled in my arms. I was going to make the next car stop and help.*
>
> *But no car ever came. I sat there for hours, I don't know how long, with you in my lap and holding Fritzie, who was whimpering and looking up at me for help. It was dark by the time he finally died. I pulled him over to the side of the road and walked back home with you and washed the blood out of my clothes.*
>
> *I don't know what it was about that one day—it was like a breaking point. When your father came home, I said: "From now on, I'm going with you. I won't bother you. I'll just sit in the car. But I can't bear to be alone again."*

I think she told me that story to show she had tried to save herself, or perhaps she wanted to exorcise a painful memory by saying it out loud. But hearing it made me understand what could have turned her into the woman I remember: a solitary figure sitting in the car, perspiring through the summer, bundled up in winter, waiting for my father to come out of this or that antique shop, grateful just not to be alone. I was there, too, because I was too young to be left at home, and I loved helping my father wrap and unwrap the newspaper around the china and small objects he had bought at auctions and was selling to dealers. It made me feel necessary and grown-up. But sometimes it was hours before we came back to the car again and to my mother who was always patiently, silently waiting.

50 At the hospital and later when Ruth told me stories of her past, I used to say, "But why didn't you leave? Why didn't you take the job? Why didn't you marry the other man?" She would always insist it didn't matter, she was lucky to have my sister and me. If I pressed hard enough, she would add, "If I'd left you never would have been born."

I always thought but never had the courage to say: *But you might have been born instead.*

I'd like to tell you that this story has a happy ending. The best I can do is one that is happier than its beginning.

After many months in that Baltimore hospital, my mother lived on her own in a small apartment for two years while I was in college and my sister married and lived nearby. When she felt the old terrors coming back, she returned to the hospital at her own request. She was approaching sixty by the time she emerged from there and from a Quaker farm that served as a halfway house, but she confounded her psychiatrists' predictions that she would be able to live outside for shorter and shorter periods. In fact, she never returned. She lived more than another twenty years, and for six of them, she was well enough to stay in a rooming house that provided both privacy and company. Even after my sister and her husband moved to a larger house and generously made two rooms into an apartment for her, she continued to have some independent life and many friends. She worked part-time as a "salesgirl" in a china shop; went away with me on yearly vacations and took one trip to Europe with relatives; went to women's club meetings; found a multiracial church that she loved; took meditation courses; and enjoyed many books. She still could not bear to see a sad movie, to stay alone with any of her six grandchildren while they were babies, to live without many tranquilizers, or to talk about those bad years in Toledo. The old terrors were still in the back of her mind, and each day was a fight to keep them down.

It was the length of her illness that had made doctors pessimistic. In fact, they could not identify any serious mental problem and diagnosed her only as having "an anxiety neurosis": low self-esteem, a fear of being dependent, a terror of being alone, a constant worry about money. She also had spells of what now would be called agoraphobia, a problem almost entirely confined to dependent women: fear of going outside the house, and incapacitating anxiety attacks in unfamiliar or public places.

55 Would you say, I asked one of her doctors, that her spirit had been broken? "I guess that's as good a diagnosis as any," he said. "And it's hard to mend anything that's been broken for twenty years."

But once out of the hospital for good, she continued to show flashes of the different woman inside; one with a wry kind of humor, a sense of adventure, and a love of learning. Books on math, physics, and mysticism occupied a lot of her time. ("Religion," she used to say firmly, "begins in the laboratory.") When she visited me in New York during her sixties and seventies, she always told taxi drivers that she was eighty years old ("so they will tell me how young I look"), and convinced theater ticket sellers that she was deaf long before she really was ("so they'll give us seats in the front row"). She made friends easily, with the vulnerability and charm of a person who feels entirely dependent on the approval of others. After one of her visits, every shopkeeper within blocks of my apartment would say, "Oh yes, I know your mother!" At home, she complained that people her own age were too old and stodgy for her. Many of her friends were far younger than she. It was as if she were making up for her own lost years.

She was also overly appreciative of any presents given to her—and that made giving them irresistible. I loved to send her clothes, jewelry, exotic soaps, and additions to her collection of tarot cards. She loved receiving them, though we both knew they would end up stored in boxes and drawers. She carried on a correspondence in German with our European relatives, and exchanges with many other friends, all written in her painfully slow, shaky handwriting. She also loved giving gifts. Even as she worried about money and figured out how to save pennies, she would buy or make carefully chosen presents for grandchildren and friends.

Part of the price she paid for this much health was forgetting. A single reminder of those bad years in Toledo was enough to plunge her into days of depression. There were times when this fact created loneliness for me, too. Only two of us had lived most of my childhood. Now, only one of us remembered. But there were also times in later years when, no matter how much I pled with reporters *not* to interview our friends and neighbors in Toledo, *not* to say that my mother had been hospitalized, they published things that hurt her very much and sent her into a downhill slide.

One the other hand, she was also her mother's daughter, a person with a certain amount of social pride and pretension, and some of her objections had less to do with depression than false pride. She complained bitterly about one report that we had lived in a house trailer. She finally asked angrily: "Couldn't they at least say 'vacation mobile home'?" Divorce was still a shame to her. She might cheerfully tell friends, "I don't know *why* Gloria says her father and I were divorced—we never were." I think she justified this to herself with the idea that they had gone through two marriage ceremonies, one in secret and one in public, but been divorced only once. In fact, they were definitely divorced, and my father had briefly married someone else.

60 She was very proud of my being a published writer, and we generally shared the same values. After her death, I found a mother-daughter morals quiz I once had written for a women's magazine. In her unmistakably shaky

writing, she had recorded her own answers, her entirely accurate imagination of what my answers would be, and a score that concluded our differences were less than those "normal for women separated by twenty-odd years." Nonetheless, she was quite capable of putting a made-up name on her name tag when going to a conservative women's club where she feared our shared identity would bring controversy or even just questions. When I finally got up the nerve to tell her I was signing a 1972 petition of women who publicly said we had had abortions and were demanding the repeal of laws that made them illegal and dangerous, her only reply was sharp and aimed to hurt back. "Every starlet says she's had an abortion," she said. "It's just a way of getting publicity." I knew she agreed that abortion should be a legal choice, but I also knew she would never forgive me for embarrassing her in public.

In fact, her anger and a fairly imaginative ability to wound with words increased in her last years when she was most dependent, most focused on herself, and most likely to need the total attention of others. When my sister made a courageous decision to go to law school at the age of fifty, leaving my mother in a house that not only had many loving teenage grandchildren in it but a kindly older woman as a paid companion besides, my mother reduced her to frequent tears by insisting that this was a family with no love in it, no home-cooked food in the refrigerator; not a real family at all. Since arguments about home cooking wouldn't work on me, my punishment was creative and different. She was going to call up *The New York Times,* she said, and tell them that this was what feminism did: it left old sick women all alone.

Some of this bitterness brought on by failing faculties was eventually solved by a nursing home near my sister's house where my mother not only got the twenty-four-hour help her weakening body demanded, but the attention of affectionate nurses besides. She charmed them, they loved her, and she could still get out for an occasional family wedding. If I ever had any doubts about the debt we owe to nurses, those last months laid them to rest.

When my mother died just before her eighty-second birthday in a hospital room where my sister and I were alternating the hours in which her heart wound slowly down to its last sounds, we were alone together for a few hours while my sister slept. My mother seemed bewildered by her surroundings and the tubes that invaded her body, but her consciousness cleared long enough for her to say: "I want to go home. Please take me home." Lying to her one last time, I said I would. "Okay, honey," she said. "I trust you." Those were her last understandable words.

The nurses let my sister and me stay in the room long after there was no more breath. She had asked us to do that. One of her many fears came from a story she had been told as a child about a man whose coma was mistaken for death. She also had made out a living will requesting that no extraordinary measures be used to keep her alive, and that her ashes be sprinkled in the same stream as my father's.

Her memorial service was in the Episcopalian church that she loved because it fed the poor, let the homeless sleep in its pews, had members of almost every race, and had been sued by the Episcopalian hierarchy for having a woman priest. Most of all, she loved the affection with which its members had welcomed her, visited her at home, and driven her to services. I think she would have liked the Quaker-style informality with which people rose to tell their memories of her. I know she would have loved the presence of many friends. It was to this church that she had donated some of her remaining Michigan property in the hope that it could be used as a multiracial camp, thus getting even with those people in the tiny nearby town who had snubbed my father for being Jewish.

I think she also would have been pleased with her obituary. It emphasized her brief career as one of the early women journalists and asked for donations to Oberlin's scholarship fund so others could go to this college she loved so much but had to leave.

I know I will spend the next years figuring out what her life has left in me.

I realize that I've always been more touched by old people than by children. It's the talent and hopes locked up in a failing body that gets to me; a poignant contrast that reminds me of my mother, even when she was strong.

I've always been drawn to any story of a mother and a daughter on their own in the world. I saw *A Taste of Honey* several times as both a play and a film, and never stopped feeling it. Even *Gypsy* I saw over and over again, sneaking in backstage for the musical and going to the movies as well. I told myself that I was learning the tap-dance routines, but actually my eyes were full of tears.

I once fell in love with a man only because we both belonged to that large and secret club of children who had "crazy mothers." We traded stories of the shameful houses to which we could never invite our friends. Before he was born, his mother had gone to jail for her pacifist convictions. Then she married the politically ambitious young lawyer who had defended her, stayed home and raised many sons. I fell out of love when he confessed that he wished I wouldn't smoke or swear, and he hoped I wouldn't go on working. His mother's plight had taught him self-pity—nothing else.

I'm no longer obsessed, as I was for many years, with the fear that I would end up in a house like that one in Toledo. Now, I'm obsessed instead with the things I could have done for my mother while she was alive, or the things I should have said.

I still don't understand why so many, many years passed before I saw my mother as a person and before I understood that many of the forces in her life are patterns women share. Like a lot of daughters, I suppose I couldn't afford to admit that what had happened to my mother was not all personal or accidental, and therefore could happen to me.

One mystery has finally cleared. I could never understand why my mother hadn't been helped by Pauline, her mother-in-law; a woman she seemed to love more than her own mother. This paternal grandmother had died when I was five, before my mother's real problems began but long after that "nervous breakdown," and I knew Pauline was once a suffragist who addressed Congress, marched for the vote, and was the first woman member of a school board in Ohio. She must have been a courageous and independent woman, yet I could find no evidence in my mother's reminiscences that Pauline had encouraged or helped my mother toward a life of her own.

I finally realized that my grandmother never changed the politics of her own life, either. She was a feminist who kept a neat house for a husband and four antifeminist sons, a vegetarian among five male meat eaters, and a woman who felt so strongly about the dangers of alcohol that she used only paste vanilla; yet she served both meat and wine to the men of the house and made sure their lives and comforts were continued undisturbed. After the vote was won, Pauline seems to have stopped all feminist activity. My mother greatly admired the fact that her mother-in-law kept a spotless house and prepared a week's meals at a time. Whatever her own internal torments, Pauline was to my mother a woman who seemed able to "do it all." "Whither thou goest, I shall go," my mother used to say to her much-loved mother-in-law, quoting the Ruth of the Bible. In the end, her mother-in-law may have added to my mother's burdens of guilt.

75 Perhaps like many later suffragists, my grandmother was a public feminist and a private isolationist. That may have been heroic in itself, the most she could be expected to do, but the vote and a legal right to work were not the only kind of help my mother needed.

The world still missed a unique person named Ruth. Though she longed to live in New York and in Europe, she became a woman who was afraid to take a bus across town. Though she drove the first Stanley Steamer, she married a man who never let her drive.

I can only guess what she might have become. The clues are in moments of spirit or humor.

After all the years of fear, she still came to Oberlin with me when I was giving a speech there. She remembered everything about its history as the first college to admit blacks and the first to admit women, and responded to students with the dignity of a professor, the accuracy of a journalist, and a charm that was all her own.

When she could still make trips to Washington's wealth of libraries, she became an expert genealogist, delighting especially in finding the rogues and rebels in our family tree.

80 Just before I was born, when she had cooked one more enormous meal for all the members of some famous dance band at my father's resort and they failed to clean their plates, she had taken a shotgun down from the kitchen wall and held it over their frightened heads until they had finished the last crumb of strawberry shortcake. Only then did she tell them the gun wasn't loaded. It was a story she told with great satisfaction.

Though sex was a subject she couldn't discuss directly, she had a great appreciation of sensuous men. When a friend I brought home tried to talk to her about cooking, she was furious. ("He came out in the kitchen and talked to me about *stew!*") But she forgave him when we went swimming. She whispered, "He has wonderful legs!"

On her seventy-fifth birthday, she played softball with her grandsons on the beach, and took pride in hitting home runs into the ocean.

Even in the last year of her life, when my sister took her to visit a neighbor's new and luxurious house, she looked at the vertical stripes of a very abstract painting in the hallway and said, tartly, "Is that the price code?"

She worried terribly about being socially accepted herself, but she never withheld her own approval for the wrong reasons. Poverty or style or lack of education couldn't stand between her and a new friend. Though she lived in a mostly white society and worried if I went out with a man of the "wrong" race, just as she had once married a man of the "wrong" religion, she always accepted each person as an individual.

85 "Is he *very* dark?" she once asked worriedly about a friend. But when she met this very dark person, she only said afterward, "What a kind and nice man!"

My father was the Jewish half of the family, yet it was my mother who taught me to have pride in that tradition. It was she who encouraged me to listen to a radio play about a concentration camp when I was little. "You should know that this can happen," she said. Yet she did it just enough to teach, never enough to frighten.

It was she who introduced me to books and a respect for them, to poetry that she knew by heart, and to the idea that you could never criticize someone unless you "walked miles in their shoes."

It was she who sold that Toledo house, the only home she had, with the determination that the money be used to start me in college. She gave both her daughters the encouragement to leave home for four years of independence that she herself had never had.

After her death, my sister and I found a journal she had kept of her one cherished and belated trip to Europe. It was a trip she had described very little when she came home: she always deplored people who talked boringly about their personal travels and showed slides. Nonetheless, she had written a descriptive essay called "Grandma Goes to Europe." She still must have thought of herself as a writer. Yet she showed this long journal to no one.

90 I miss her, but perhaps no more in death than I did in life. Dying seems less sad then having lived too little. But at least we're now asking questions about all the Ruths and all our family mysteries.

If her song inspires that, I think she would be the first to say: It was worth the singing.

Explorations of the Text

1. "Happy or unhappy, families are all mysterious." Does this opening statement provide clues about Steinem's possible purposes in writing?
2. How does Steinem's discussion of her Uncle Ed provide the framework for the portrait of her mother?
3. What are some of the "mysteries" in the life of Steinem's mother?
4. What role must Steinem assume? How does she react to it? What do her short anecdotes reveal about her childhood with her mother?
5. To what possible causes does Steinem trace her mother's breakdown?

6. How has Steinem's life as a child and as an adult been shaped by her mother's life? by her relationship with her mother?
7. Steinem states: "But at least we're now asking questions about all the Ruths and all our family mysteries." How does her mother become a representative figure? What does she represent?
8. Steinem gains control of her material through explicit and implicit comparisons. Examine this structural device. What comparisons guide this essay?
9. The essay begins in "mystery." Does it end in "mystery"?

The Reading/Writing Connection

1. In a mini-essay, explore how the story of Steinem's mother on the road represents (as Steinem suggests) "the formidable forces arrayed against" her mother.
2. "Think" Topic: Does Steinem's process of remembering and writing lead to discovery? Does it lead to a happier ending?

Ideas for Writing

1. Compare the mothers in "The House of Yemanjá," "Riders to the Sea," and this essay.
2. How does Steinem characterize her mother?
3. What revelations about family do you gain from Steinem's essay?
4. Using this work as a model, write about a mysterious relationship in your life.

KRIK? KRAK!

Edwidge Danticat

Edwidge Danticat (1969–) was born in Haiti but lived from the age of twelve in New York. Educated at Barnard College and Brown University, Danticat published her first collection of short stories, Krik? Krak!, *in 1996. Her first novel,* Breath, Eyes, Memory, *appeared in 1994 and was followed by* The Farming of Bones *in 1998. Danticat's awards include a Granta Regional Award for Best Young American Novelist and a Pushcart Prize.*

1996

You remember thinking while braiding your hair that you look a lot like your mother. Your mother who looked like your grandmother and her grandmother before her. Your mother had two rules for living. *Always use your ten fingers,* which in her parlance meant that you should be the best little cook and housekeeper who ever lived.

Your mother's second rule went along with the first. Never have sex before marriage, and even after you marry, you shouldn't say you enjoy it, or your husband won't respect you.

And writing? Writing was as forbidden as dark rouge on the cheeks or a first date before eighteen. It was an act of indolence, something to be done in a corner when you could have been learning to cook.

Are there women who both cook and write? Kitchen poets, they call them. They slip phrases into their stew and wrap meaning around their pork before frying it. They make narrative dumplings and stuff their daughter's mouths so they say nothing more.

5 "What will she do? What will be her passion?" your aunts would ask when they came over to cook on great holidays, which called for cannon salutes back home but meant nothing at all here.

"Her passion is being quiet," your mother would say. "But then she's not being quiet. You hear this scraping from her. Krik? Krak! Pencil, paper. It sounds like someone crying."

Someone was crying. You and the writing demons in your head. You have nobody, nothing but this piece of paper, they told you. Only a notebook made out of discarded fish wrappers, panty-hose cardboard. They were the best confidantes for a lonely little girl.

When you write, it's like braiding your hair. Taking a handful of coarse unruly strands and attempting to bring them unity. Your fingers have still not perfected the task. Some of the braids are long, others are short. Some are thick, others are thin. Some are heavy. Others are light. Like the diverse women in your family. Those whose fables and metaphors, whose similes, and soliloquies, whose diction and *je ne sais quoi* daily slip into your survival soup, by way of their fingers.

You have always had your ten fingers. They curse you each time you force them around the contours of a pen. No, women like you don't write. They carve onion sculptures and potato statues. They sit in a dark corners and braid their hair in new shapes and twists in order to control the stiffness, the unruliness, the rebelliousness.

* * *

10 You remember thinking while braiding your hair that you look a lot like your mother. You remember her silence when you laid your first notebook in front of her. Her disappointment when you told her that words would be your life's work, like the kitchen had always been hers. She was angry at you for not understanding. *And with what do you repay me? With scribbles on paper that are not worth the scratch of a pig's snout.* The sacrifices had been too great.

Writers don't leave any mark in the world. Not the world where we are from. In our world, writers are tortured and killed if they are men. Called lying whores, then raped and killed, if they are women. In our world, if you write, you are a politician, and we know what happens to politicians. They end up in a prison dungeon where their bodies are covered in scalding tar before they're forced to eat their own waste.

The family needs a nurse, not a prisoner. We need to forge ahead with our heads raised, not buried in scraps of throw-away paper. We do not want to bend over a dusty grave, wearing black hats, grieving for you. There are nine hundred and ninety-nine women who went before you and worked their fingers to coconut rind so you can stand here before me holding that torn old notebook that you cradle against your breast like your prettiest Sunday braids. I would rather you had spit in my face.

You remember thinking while braiding your hair that you look like your mother and her mother before her. It was their whispers that pushed you, their murmurs over pots sizzling in your head. A thousand women urging you to speak through the blunt tip of your pencil. Kitchen poets, you call them. Ghosts like burnished branches on a flame tree. These women, they asked for your voice so that they could tell your mother in your place that yes, women like you do speak, even if they speak in a tongue that is hard to understand. Even if it's patois, dialect, Creole.

❋ ❋ ❋

The women in your family have never lost touch with one another. Death is a path we take to meet on the other side. What goddesses have joined, let no one cast asunder. With every step you take, there is an army of women watching over you. We are never any farther than the sweat on your brows or the dust on your toes. Though you walk through the valley of the shadow of death, fear no evil for we are always with you.

❋ ❋ ❋

15 When you were a little girl, you used to dream that you were lying among the dead and all the spirits were begging you to scream. And even now, you are still afraid to dream because you know that you will never be able to do what they say, as they say it, the old spirits that live in your blood.

Most of the women in your life had their heads down. They would wake up one morning to find their panties gone. It is not shame, however, that kept their heads down. They were singing, searching for meaning in the dust. And sometimes, they were talking to faces across the ages, faces like yours and mine.

You thought that if you didn't tell the stories, the sky would fall on your head. You often thought that without the trees, the sky would fall on your head. You learned in school that you have pencils and paper only because the trees gave themselves in unconditional sacrifice. There have been days when the sky was as close as your hair to falling on your head.

This fragile sky has terrified you your whole life. Silence terrifies you more than the pounding of a million pieces of steel chopping away at your flesh. Sometimes, you dream of hearing only the beating of your own heart, but this has never been the case. You have never been able to escape the pounding of a thousand other hearts that have outlived yours by thousands of years. And over the years when you have needed us, you have always cried "Krik?" and we have answered "Krak!" and it has shown us that you have not forgotten us.

❄ ❄ ❄

You remember thinking while braiding your hair that you look a lot like your mother. Your mother, who looked like your grandmother and her grandmother before her. Your mother, she introduced you to the first echoes of the tongue that you now speak when at the end of the day she would braid your hair while you sat between her legs, scrubbing the kitchen pots. While your fingers worked away at the last shadows of her day's work, she would make your braids Sunday-pretty, even during the week.

When she was done she would ask you to name each braid after those nine hundred and ninety-nine women who were boiling in your blood, and since you had written them down and memorized them, the names would come rolling off your tongue. And this was your testament to the way that these women lived and died and lived again.

Explorations of the Text

1. Why does the speaker use the pronoun "you"? Who is her audience?
2. What are the mother's rules for the daughter?
3. What does the phrase "Always use your ten fingers" suggest about the mother's expectations for her daughter's life? Who are the "Kitchen poets"?
4. Consider the images of braiding hair. What do they symbolize about the mother-daughter relationship? About the speaker's relationship with her female ancestry?
5. What is the role of the writer in Haitian society?
6. How does the speaker envision her relationship with her ancestors, with her past?
7. This essay is written in experimental form. Danticat uses descriptive details, narrative fragments, and an interior monologue to convey her thesis and points. Are these techniques effective? Summarize the essay and paraphrase her points in expository prose. Does the essay lose its impact? Why?

The Reading/Writing Connection

1. "Think" Topic: Consider this quotation from T. S. Eliot's "Burnt Norton": "Time present and time past/Are both perhaps present in time future,/And time future contained in time past." How does this quotation relate to the speaker's relationship with the women who "went before [her]"?
2. Journal Entry: What does your hair reveal about you? Or have a dialogue with your hair.

3. In a paragraph, compare the mother in this work with the mother in "Girl."

Ideas for Writing

1. Discuss the portrayal of the writer and writing presented in this work.
2. Is writing a dangerous activity? Argue pro or con.
3. Use your paragraph writing as the basis of a longer essay that compares the mothers in "Girl" and "Krik? Krak!"

Student Essay: Comparison/Contrast
A Collaborative Writing

FATHERS AND SONS

Melissa Del Castillo
Michelle Ing

Melissa Del Castillo and Michelle Ing were both students at the State University of New York at New Paltz. They wrote this assignment, a comparison of the father-son relationships in two poems, as an extra-credit collaboration in a freshman composition course.

In every society, fathers treat their children differently. In some societies, fathers respect their children and care about them and for them while in other societies, fathers don't believe that the children deserve respect. In the poem, "My Father's Song," a father explains to his son how he looks up to his own father and how he learned to respect the things of this world from his father. In the poem, "My Papa's Waltz," a boy explains that he loves his father despite all of his father's abuse. These poems present different kinds of relationships between fathers and sons.

In "My Father's Song," the father, the main speaker in the poem, relates to his son an experience that he had had with his own father. The father and son were walking in a field "one Spring at Acu" when the father noticed "tiny pink animals" in the furrows of a plough. The speaker states: "The plowshare had unearthed/the burrow nest of a mouse/in the soft moist sand." He began talking to his son, relating his "song" to his son, and teaching him to respect nature. The speaker states: "Very gently, he scooped tiny pink animals/into the palm of his hand/and told me to touch them." His father had enough respect for these animals that he carried them to safety. "We took them to the edge/of the field and put them in the shade/of a sand moist clod." His father, a very gentle man, taught his son love and respect for all creatures, and the speaker hopes that he can do the same for his son. He teaches his son to cherish life, and the son feels his father's love, and learns his grandfather's and father's values. He "miss[es]" a father whom he loves and who loves him. The son hopes that he can do the same thing for his children.

In the poem, "My Papa's Waltz," the father-son relationship appears to be a shaky and uncertain one. Although the father is an abusive alcoholic, the son does indeed love him and clings to him seeking affection. There is evidence of the father's abuse in the speaker's statement: "The whiskey on your breath/could make a small boy dizzy." But because the boy loves his father, he is not deterred by the alcohol. The father's behavior is revealed in the images of the boy's dance with the father. The dance is wild and then becomes violent: "We romped until the pans/slid from the kitchen shelf." The pans' sliding from the shelves indicates the father's becoming angry and throwing things. "The hand that held [the son's] wrist" which "was battered on one knuckle" became "battered" perhaps because the father was hitting the mother and son. Even after he beat the boy, the son was still attached to the father because he needed his love. The father "beat time on [his] head" and then "waltzed [him] off to bed/still clinging to [the father's] shirt." The boy will take the abuse as long as he can to be close to his father. The boy will hold on and dance with his papa to gain love. The waltz that the son talks about is like the dance of life—the son "clinging" to the father.

In "My Father's Song," the son respected his father, learned about love and caring from the latter, and hoped he could be a good father; meanwhile, in "My Papa's Waltz," the son, the speaker in the poem, remembers a dance with his father, a moment which represented the whole relationship, his father's lack of respect for him. The father didn't care about him, but his son loved him despite the abuse. In both poems, the sons love their fathers, but the difference is that one father cares, and the other doesn't.

Student Essay: Critical Analysis and Research

Sylvia Plath's "Daddy" and an Analysis of Poetic Language

Anne Cilia

Anne Cilia is a student at State University of New York at New Paltz, where she is majoring in elementary education with a concentration in mathematics. She wrote this essay as a required research project in Composition II.

I used to hate poetry. I could never imagine how poets could write lines and lines of complexities and expect anyone to figure out the meaning. I had not come to a complete appreciation of poetry until recently when I read the poem "Daddy" by Sylvia Plath. This poem intrigued me so much that after reading it I had a strong desire to learn more about it. Sylvia Plath's words are bold and sharp; each line cuts like a razor into "Daddy's" "fat black heart" (line 76) and illustrates how much the narrator was wounded and scarred by this "Daddy." Plath gives the reader much to analyze. Throughout the poem, she uses many poetic devices, such as repetitions, choice of adjectives and colors, creation of tone, and use of sounds to build the themes of the work.

Sylvia Plath uses numerous repetitions in "Daddy." These emphasize certain words and phrases—and especially colors—so that the reader picks up a certain rhythm. For example, she uses the word "black" in abundance, and this rhymes with others she uses throughout, such as "back," "rack," "sack," "pack," and "Polack." These words have an angry, violent effect on the tone though they create a resilient sound. Also, Plath's frequent, pounding use of the word "you" helps to conjure up the anxiety that the narrator is feeling and adds more confusion for the reader, who does not know who "you" is (Boyers 386).

Another device that Plath uses quite well in "Daddy" is her choice of adjectives and colors. Plath could have simply used an everyday, boring vocabulary to write this poem, but she chose to use sharp, echoing words and phrases that resound brilliantly. For example, Plath uses an excellent description in line 47, where she says "a swastika . . . so black no sky could squeak through." Here, the reader can really imagine the extent of darkness of this "black" she is describing. Almost every line of "Daddy" is intense; one good example is line 3 of the 10th stanza: "every women adores a

Fascist." (148). Here, Plath is implying that "all women"—namely, herself—are under some type of brutal authority within their personal relationships. Lawrence R. Ries discusses this particular line along with other lines from "Daddy"; he says that "violence has not replaced love in this poem but has become an integral pat of it" (11). This is a fine example of how word usage develops theme.

Plath also develops theme by creating a particular tone in "Daddy." Her connotations of words create a ridiculing and scornful sound. For example, the words "Ghastly statue," in line 9, give the reader an image of something that is not pleasant to look at, and this adds to the jeering "voice" of the narrator who is offending the "Daddy." Another example of this is the first line of the sixth stanza, which reads "It stuck in a barb wire snare," referring to the narrator's tongue. This bold description lets the reader feel the narrator's pain of not being able to talk; having your tongue "in a barb wire snare" would be extremely painful and appalling, and is only a symbolic method of punishment that the narrator creates for herself in this poem. Some of Plath's words and lines in "Daddy" are a bit off key in comparison to the overall tone of the poem. However, because of her ability to intertwine words together beautifully, they will sound melodic to the common reader. For example, in lines 61-62 the narrator says "they pulled me out of the sack, and they stuck me together with glue." Here, Plath uses very blunt, crude words that do not sound very "pretty" to the human ear, but the overall sound is rhythmic.

Throughout the entire poem, Plath shifts between insolent, contemptuous language and simple, elementary language. She begins the poem simply to sound like a popular nursery rhyme. "you do not do, you do not do, any more, black shoe" and then goes to more advanced language, only to return to juvenile language, and so on. As Steven G. Axelrod puts it "she oscillates between calm reflection ('You stand at the blackboard, daddy,/ In the picture I have of you' [st. 4] and mad incoherence ('Ich, ich, ich, ich' [st. 6]" (57).

Plath makes the conflict of her poem become audible by using particular words and sounds—mainly "oo." As mentioned before, the most prominent word in "Daddy" is "you" and consequently, the most prominent *sound* in the poem is "oo." Moreover, at least one line in every stanza—except for the fourth—ends in an "oo" sound, whether the word be "do," "achoo," "you," "blue," "Jew," "gobbledygoo," "through," "who," "two," "glue," "screw," or "true." Despite the fact that the poem has no distinct pattern or rhyme or rhythm, all of these words—simple as they may sound—are used intentionally to create a sense of rhythm which helps to define the conflict. Caroline K. B. Hall points out that "in these sounds and rhythms, 'Daddy' has clear affinities with the nursery rhyme" (101). A good example of the rhythm created in "Daddy" by the pounding "oo" sound is the very last stanza of the poem:

> There's a stake in your fat black heart
> And the villagers never liked you.
> They are dancing and stamping on you.
> They always knew it was you.
> Daddy, daddy, you bastard, I'm through. (l. 76-80)

These lines help to create the allusion that the narrator is cursing "Daddy" with this repetitive "you," and then with stating "I'm through." Here the narrator—again, Plath herself—is basically announcing that she is "rid of her dead father once and for all" (Simpson 106); therefore, the conflict becomes resolved. Sylvia Plath clearly wanted the poem to have a "nursery rhyme" effect, as it may emphasize the fact that her father died when she was a child, and left her still feeling somewhat childlike[—alone and abandoned—]even with her adult capabilities (Hall 101-103).

"Daddy" is quite hostile-sounding and has very bold descriptive statements. From the beginning, with the (6th) line "Daddy, I have had to kill you" (Plath 396), the reader already anticipates that something dreadful is happening within the context of the poem. Sylvia Plath draws the intrigued reader in with the complexities of each and every line, and the reader then desires to decipher the thematic meaning. Plath herself has commented on the actual meaning of the poem:

> The poem is spoken by a girl with an Electra complex. Her father died while she thought he was God. Her case is complicated by the fact that her father was also a Nazi and her mother very possibly part Jewish. In the daughter the two strains marry and paralyze each other—she has to act out the awful little allegory before she is free of it (Alvarez 382).

Here, one can start to understand that the poem is indeed complex because the narrator is having an identity crisis. Is the narrator identical to Plath? As C. Hoffmann of Kutztown University of Pennsylvania puts it, "examining Plath's life allows her readers to better understand her works." (Hoffmann). In "Daddy," as in any poem, the narrator is not supposed to be thought of as the poet, however, the details in this poem have a direct correlation to some aspects of Plath's short life, such as her father's premature death, her divorce, and her suicide (Axelrod 56-57).

In "Daddy," the meaning of the poem cannot be interpreted with just a glance. To fully understand and appreciate the poem, one must carefully analyze Plath's words as I have learned to do myself. By becoming more open-minded about the art of poetry, I have begun to understand that what lies beneath the "complex" words is what poetry is all about. Poets—especially Sylvia Plath—have an impressive talent that should not be underestimated. Her poem "Daddy" is nothing less than a true masterpiece—this one poem changed my view of poetry completely—and Plath was nothing less than a poetic genius. I wish I could say the same for myself, but right now all I can say is: "I'm through"!

Works Consulted

Alvarez, A. "Sylvia Plath." Young. 381-83.

Axelrod, Steven Gould. *Sylvia Plath: The Wound and the Cure of Words.* Baltimore: Johns Hopkins UP, 1990.

Boyers, Robert. "Sylvia Plath." Young. 383-87.

Geiger, Don. *The Dramatic Impulse in Modern Poetics.* Baton Rouge: Louisiana State UP, 1967.

Hall, Caroline King Barnard. *Sylvia Plath, Revised.* New York: Twayne, 1998.

Hoffmann, C. *A Comprehensive Biography of Sylvia Plath.* Kutztown University of Pennsylvania. <http://www.fortunecity.com/victorian/plath/500/biography1.htm> 21 August 2000.

Nowottny, Winifred. *The Language Poets Use.* London: The Athlone Press, 1962.

Plath, Sylvia. "Daddy." *Legacies.* Eds. Carley Rees Bogarad and Jan Zlotnik Schmidt. New York: Harcourt, 1995. 396-99.

Poetry Exhibits—Sylvia Plath. 5 April 1999. The Academy of American Poets. <http://www.poets.org/LIT/poet/splath.hem> 27 October 1999.

Ries, Lawrence R. *Wolf Masks: Violence in Contemporary Poetry.* Port Washington: Kennikat Press, 1977.

Rylands, George H. W. *Words and Poetry.* New York: AMS, 1972.

Simpson, Louis. *A Revolution in Taste.* New York: Macmillan, 1978.

Young, Robyn V., ed. *Poetry Criticism.* Vol. 1. Detroit: Gale Research, 1991.

Writing Assignments

1. a. Based on the selections in this chapter, freewrite about what you learned regarding the experience of parenting or of childhood that was revelatory to you.

   b. Write a journal entry comparing one example of the parent/child relationship presented in the works in this chapter with your own experience.

   c. Make a list of questions that emerge from these explorations of parent/child relationships. Write an answer to one of these questions. Refer to three works in this chapter.

2. a. Diagram a family tree for the central relationships in your life. Include extended family and friends. Draw straight lines for the relationships that represent solidity and broken lines (– – – –) for those that seem fragile or negative.

   b. Write your conclusions in your journal.

   c. Compare the positive and negative aspects of family dynamics in your life with one work in this chapter.

3. a. Think of a moment from your past—a moment of conflict or of closeness. Write a point-of-view piece, a monologue, for each family member.

   b. After you write these pieces, try several freewrites about characters' conflicts within family settings presented in three works in this chapter. Then create monologues for these characters.

   c. Write an essay about sources of closeness or of conflict between parents and their children. Choose three works from this chapter. Include specific evidence from the texts.

4. Analyze the impact of mothers on their children. What are major issues in mother/daughter relationships evident in works in this chapter? Choose several works for discussion.

5. One important aspect of mothering is the issue of separation from the mother. Is this issue a pattern in the works in this chapter? Are other patterns evident?

6. a. Our views of family change at different stages in our lives. Do a freewrite about several changes in your views of a particular family member. You may begin: "When I was (ten), I thought. . . ."

b. Find two works by the same writer about the same family member. Compare them.

7. Based on selections in this chapter, compare the relationships of fathers and sons to those of fathers and daughters. What conclusions can you draw about the nature of these relationships?

8. a. Define a good parent. (You may do this as either a freewrite or a journal entry.)

   b. Watch several situation comedies about families. What images of parents appear?

   c. Do any television programs present a realistic view of family life? Your analysis may become an argumentative essay.

   d. Compare a comedy from the fifties or sixties with one that is contemporary.

9. a. Interview several people from different ethnic backgrounds. Concentrate on family life, particularly on the roles and responsibilities of parents and of children. What do you conclude?

   b. Based on your interviews and the selections in this chapter, compare the roles of parents or children in two different cultures. Do parents' roles differ? Are there different cultural expectations for children?

   c. Write an analysis of cultural roles for parents and/or children in Tan's "Scar," Baldwin's "Sonny's Blues," or Ortiz's "My Father's Song." (Choose two.)

10. a. Using "Ruth's Song" as a model, write a character sketch about someone who has encouraged the best in you. Make that person come alive.

    b. If you wish, try this inventory for your character: Name, Sex, Age, Height, Weight, Color of Hair and Eyes, Occupation, Mannerisms, Birthplace and Family, Hobbies, Eating Habits, Major Personality Traits, Clothing, Dialogue, Relationships, Key Events That Reveal Character.

    c. To write this sketch, you may want to organize in one of the following ways: by personality traits, by physical description and key events, by monologue or dialogue.

11. a. Freewrite about which work in this chapter has affected you most intensely.

    b. Which work is the most powerful representation of family life? Why?

    c. Which piece is the least successful? Why?

    d. Write an essay about one of your entries. Direct the essay to the writers of the text.

12. Discuss water imagery in three works.

13. Explore the use of allusions to myth, fable, and fairy tale as literary technique in "My Little Girl, My Stringbean, My Lovely Woman," "The House of Yemanjá," and/or "Sonny's Blues."
14. a. Catalogue the qualities of "the good mother" and "the bad mother." What do you conclude?
    b. Compare several works which present visions of good and bad mothers.
    c. Write an essay about a work or works in which the mother's character is stereotypical. Evaluate each portrayal.
    d. You may write about fathers and follow the assignments in a, b, and c above.
15. Explore the idea of kinship, of extended family, and of community as these ideas are depicted in several works in this chapter.
16. Is the idea of the nuclear family in North America being redefined? Defend your position. You may use evidence from the works you have read or do research on this topic to support your argument.
17. Conceive of a definition of the family in the year 2010. What are its attributes? You may use evidence from the works you have read in this chapter, or you may research information to develop your definition.
18. Choose three characters from works in this chapter and create a conversation about family life.
19. Explicate one of the poems in this chapter. Concentrate on point of view, tone, imagery, figurative language, and form. How do these aspects of the work develop theme?
20. Several of the essays in this chapter are autobiographical. Reread these works and determine what creates effective autobiographical writing. (Refer to chapter 13 for directions for analysis.)
21. Examine a common theme in the readings in the Thematic Preview: "Rappaccini's Daughter," "Those Winter Sundays," *Riders to the Sea,* and *Bone Black.* Some suggestions for your consideration are parental control, lack of communication, inevitable loss, or the failures of parenting.

CHAPTER 6

LOVE

It is other people who have separated
You and me.
Come, my lord!
Do not dream of listening
To the between-words of people.
My heart, thinking
"How beautiful he is"
Is like a swift river
[Which] though one dams it and dams it,
Will still break through.

"The Lady of Sakanoye," from the Manyō Shū
(compiled A.D. 760)

From the words of the Manyō Shū, from the love songs of Sappho, from Kalidosa's *Shakuntala,* from "The Song of Solomon," from William Shakespeare's sonnets to Anna Akhmatova's poetry, works have expressed the longing for love. This yearning represents a need deeper than sexual attraction or survival of the species; it represents the desire for connection that emerges as strongly as the urge for food or drink.

The Thematic Preview asks questions about forms of love: What is romantic love? What constitutes romantic fantasy? passion? These questions also are implied in Leslie Silko's "Yellow Woman." The search for love and for fulfillment dominate Shakespeare's "Shall I Compare Thee to a Summer's Day?" and Wakako Yamauchi's *And the Soul Shall Dance.* In "Professions for Women," Virginia Woolf meditates on what it would mean for "a woman . . . [to] [speak] the truth about her passions" and determines that she, Woolf, still doesn't know how to "[tell] the truth about [her] own experiences as a body. . . . " The readings in the rest of the chapter present many aspects of love, and they challenge us to understand these dimensions more fully: young love, marriage, illicit relationships, sexuality, gender differences, social conditioning, cultural patterns—the diverse habits of loving.

Love, romance, and passion fascinate writers and readers. In Ernest Hemingway's "Hills Like White Elephants," the lovers, similar to many young people, begin with unrealistic expectations, with a dream of lasting happiness. The dream fades as they journey together. In contrast, in James

Joyce's "Eveline," the protagonist must decide if the dream is worth pursuing, if falling in love is worth the risk.

Disappointment, loss, and sorrow also are aspects of relationships portrayed in literary works. In marriage, the partners discover the complexities of intimacy—the fulfillment and destruction of William Blake's "The Garden of Love," the garden and the graveyard, the blossoms and the weeds. Njabulo Ndebele's "Death of a Son" portrays a couple, unable to relate to each other, torn apart by the random, pointless shooting of their son. Violence, inherent in apartheid, almost destroys their love. Bobbie Ann Mason's "Shiloh" presents a classic example of a mature marriage in which wife and husband live in separate worlds and fail to recognize the hollow centers of their relationship and of their lives. Matthew Arnold's "Dover Beach" portrays relationship as the solemn answer to the sorrow and loss at the very heart of the human condition: "Ah, love, let us be true to one another."

Some people are true to one another; both Shakespeare's sonnet "Let Me Not to the Marriage of True Minds" and John Donne's "A Valediction Forbidding Mourning" attest to the beauty and the full closeness of love. Liz Rosenberg writes of elderly couples, still in love, transformed by the lasting bond of marriage in "In the End, We Are All Light."

Illicit love always has tantalized men and women with its promise of the forbidden, of the unknown, of the mysteries, of the unconventional—the promise of fulfillment in contrast to the predictability of daily life. Anton Chekhov's characters escape from their dreary marriages in their moment of passion. Pablo Neruda's "Tonight I Can Write" records the deserted lover's sadness. The speaker intones: "Life is so short, forgetting is so long." Indeed, Katherine Anne Porter's Granny Weatherall never recovers from disappointment created by being jilted on her wedding day.

Desire—of the young and old, of the married and unmarried—remains central to the experience of loving. In "To His Coy Mistress," Andrew Marvell's speaker argues with his beloved and urges her to succumb to his plea. Sexual yearning and communion underlie the actions of lovers. Plato theorizes in "The Sexes" from *The Symposium* that this longing for union emerges from a human sense of incompleteness. Each person seeks his or her other half to become "whole" through love. Is each of us half a person? Cherrie Moraga clearly does not believe Plato, but her speaker in "Loving in the War Years" still expresses the same yearning that exists despite the dangers of loving. A similar drive for intimacy is exhibited by the two main characters in Beth Henley's "Am I Blue." Sexual fulfillment reaches a spiritual level in Gary Snyder's "The Bath," in Léopold-Sédar Senghor's "Nuit de Sine," and in Pablo Neruda's "Sweetness, Always." These poems suggest fulfillments that are emotional, sexual, and spiritual. T. S. Eliot's Prufrock both seeks and fears such powerful emotions: he will not "dare."

The pressures of intimacy also cause characters to seek autonomy and reject relationships that obliterate selfhood. For example, Marge Piercy's speaker asks her lover to learn "to love differently": "to have without holding," while Ntozake Shange's lady in blue yells, "Sorry," asserting her independence and rejecting her lover's hold on her.

Conditioned by social mores, men and women have different expectations of roles and behaviors in relationships. D. H. Lawrence's "Tickets, Please" portrays a frightening consequence of the battle of the sexes, while David Ives's "Sure Thing" explores its comic potential. Are men and women doomed to reach out and yet misunderstand each other? Alberto Moravia's "The Chase" and Octavio Paz's "My Life with the Wave" portray male fantasies of love and the disjunction between male dreams and female realities. The men and women in Susan Glaspell's *Trifles* search from clues about motives for murder and create different versions of the crime. Their interpretations reveal the ways in which gender roles shape their views of the world.

Roles for men and for women have been socially constructed. In *The Second Sex,* Simone de Beauvoir contends that women have been objectified and defined as "other." According to de Beauvoir, men have been seen as the dominant presence, women as appendages to men—never subjects, always objects. How does this position shape women's identities and experiences in love relationships? How has the lack of equality affected women's existences? In "The Yellow Wallpaper," Charlotte Perkins Gilman creates a woman driven insane by her role as other. Anna Akhmatova rewrites the story of Lot's wife and gives the nameless woman a life separate from the Biblical representation of her. Anne Sexton's "The Moss of His Skin" presents a powerful critique of a society that stereotypes women. Even language causes and perpetuates women's positions as "other." Huda Naamani understands the power of language to imprison women as she mocks the male "word" in "I Take You an Orange." Seizing the lover's word is the ultimate act of defiance.

Finally, culture also shapes the forms of love. The tradition of arranged marriage in China, in "No Name Woman," comes from a contemporary writer, Maxine Hong Kingston, who has witnessed cultural change and the inevitable conflicts that arise among generations when societal mores are challenged. The narrator confronts her mother's conception of woman's place in society by telling her aunt's tragic story and by breaking the imposed silence, a cultural taboo. Through this act, she redefines her identity as a Chinese woman.

THEMATIC PREVIEW: COMBINING THE GENRES

YELLOW WOMAN

Leslie Marmon Silko

Leslie Marmon Silko (1948–), born in Albuquerque, New Mexico, grew up on the Laguna Pueblo Reservation. Her heritage—Laguna, Mexican, European—provides the material and the inspiration for her writing. A graduate of the University of New Mexico, she now teaches at the University of Arizona in Tucson. Silko published her first novel, Ceremony, *in 1977. Subsequent works include* Storyteller *(1981) and* Almanac of the Dead *(1991). Her fiction and poetry have earned her a grant from the National Endowment for the Arts, a poetry award from the* Chicago Review, *the Pushcart Prize for poetry, and the John D. and Catherine T. MacArthur Foundation Grant.*

1992

I

My thigh clung to his with dampness, and I watched the sun rising up through the tamaracks and willows. The small brown water birds came to the river and hopped across the mud, leaving brown scratches in the alkali-white crust. They bathed in the river silently. I could hear the water, almost at our feet where the narrow fast channel bubbled and washed green ragged moss and fern leaves. I looked at him beside me, rolled in the red blanket on the white river sand. I cleaned the sand out of the cracks between my toes, squinting because the sun was above the willow trees. I looked at him for the last time, sleeping on the white river sand.

I felt hungry and followed the river south the way we had come the afternoon before, following our footprints that were already blurred by lizard tracks and bug trails. The horses were still lying down, and the black one whinnied when he saw me but he did not get up—maybe it was because the corral was made out of thick cedar branches and the horses had not yet felt the sun like I had. I tried to look beyond the pale red mesas to the pueblo. I knew it was there, even if I could not see it, on the sandrock hill above the river, the same river that moved past me now and had reflected the moon last night.

The horse felt warm underneath me. He shook his head and pawed the sand. The bay whinnied and leaned against the gate trying to follow, and I remembered him asleep in the red blanket beside the river. I slid off the horse and tied him close to the other horse. I walked north with the river again, and the white sand broke loose in footprints over footprints.

"Wake up."

5 He moved in the blanket and turned his face to me with his eyes still closed. I knelt down to touch him.

"I'm leaving."

He smiled now, eyes still closed. "You are coming with me, remember?" He sat up now with his bare dark chest and belly in the sun.

"Where?"

"To my place."

10 "And will I come back?"

He pulled his pants on. I walked away from him, feeling him behind me and smelling the willows.

"Yellow Woman," he said.

I turned to face him. "Who are you?" I asked.

He laughed and knelt on the low, sandy bank, washing his face in the river. "Last night you guessed my name, and you knew why I had come."

15 I stared past him at the shallow moving water and tried to remember the night, but I could only see the moon in the water and remember his warmth around me.

"But I only said that you were him and that I was Yellow Woman—I'm not really her—I have my own name and I come from the pueblo on the other side of the mesa. Your name is Silva and you are a stranger I met by the river yesterday afternoon."

He laughed softly. "What happened yesterday has nothing to do with what you will do today, Yellow Woman."

"I know—that's what I'm saying—the old stories about the ka'tsina spirit and Yellow Woman can't mean us."

My old grandpa liked to tell those stories best. There is one about Badger and Coyote who went hunting and were gone all day, and when the sun was going down they found a house. There was a girl living there alone, and she had light hair and eyes and she told them that they could sleep with her. Coyote wanted to be with her all night so he sent Badger into a prairie-dog hole, telling him he thought he saw something in it. As soon as Badger crawled in, Coyote blocked up the entrance with rocks and hurried back to Yellow Woman.

20 "Come here," he said gently.

He touched my neck and I moved close to him to feel his breathing and to hear his heart. I was wondering if Yellow Woman had known who she was—if she knew that she would become part of the stories. Maybe she'd had another name that her husband and relatives called her so that only the ka'tsina from the north and the storytellers would know her as Yellow Woman. But I didn't go on; I felt him all around me, pushing me down into the white river sand.

"Yellow Woman went away with the spirit from the north and lived with him and his relatives. She was gone for a long time, but then one day she came back and she brought twin boys.

"Do you know the story?"

"What story?" He smiled and pulled me close to him as he said this. I was afraid lying there on the red blanket. All I could know was the way he felt, warm, damp, his body beside me. This is the way it happens in the stories. I was thinking, with no thought beyond the moment she meets the ka'tsina spirit and they go.

25 "I don't have to go. What they tell in stories was real only then, back in time immemorial, like they say."

He stood up and pointed at my clothes tangled in the blanket. "Let's go," he said.

I walked beside him, breathing hard because he walked fast, his hand around my wrist. I had stopped trying to pull away from him, because his hand felt cool and the sun was high, drying the river bed into alkali. I will see someone, eventually I will see someone, and then I will be certain that he is only a man—some man from nearby—and I will be sure that I am not Yellow Woman. Because she is from out of time past and I live now and I've been to school and there are highways and pickup trucks that Yellow Woman never saw.

It was an easy ride north on horseback. I watched the change from the cottonwood trees along the river to the junipers that brushed past us in the foothills, and finally there were only piñons, and when I looked up at the rim of the mountain plateau I could see pine trees growing on the edge. Once I stopped to look down, but the pale sandstone had disappeared and the river was gone and the dark lava hills were all around. He touched my hand, not speaking, but always singing softly a mountain song and looking into my eyes.

I felt hungry and wondered what they were doing at home now—my mother, my grandmother, my husband, and the baby. Cooking breakfast, saying, "Where did she go?—maybe kidnapped," and Al going to the tribal police with the details: "She went walking along the river."

30 The house was made with black lava rock and red mud. It was high above the spreading miles of arroyos and long mesas. I smelled a mountain smell of pitch and buck brush. I stood there beside the black horse, looking down on the small, dim country we had passed, and I shivered.

"Yellow Woman, come inside where it's warm."

II

He lit a fire in the stove. It was an old stove with a round belly and an enamel coffeepot on top. There was only the stove, some faded Navajo blankets, and a bedroll and cardboard box. The floor was made of smooth adobe plaster, and there was one small window facing east. He pointed at the box.

"There's some potatoes and the frying pan." He sat on the floor with his arms around his knees pulling them close to his chest and he watched me fry the potatoes. I didn't mind him watching me because he was always watching me—he had been watching me since I came upon him sitting on the river bank trimming leaves from a willow twig with his knife. We ate from the pan and he wiped the grease from his fingers on his Levis.

"Have you brought women here before?" He smiled and kept chewing, so I said, "Do you always use the same tricks?"

35 "What tricks?" He looked at me like he didn't understand.

"The story about being a ka'tsina from the mountains. The story about Yellow Woman."

Silva was silent, his face was calm.

"I don't believe it. Those stories couldn't happen now," I said.

He shook his head and said softly, "But someday they will talk about us, and they will say, 'Those two lived long ago when things like that happened.' "

He stood up and went out. I ate the rest of the potatoes and thought about things—about the noise the stove was making and the sound of the mountain wind outside. I remembered yesterday and the day before, and then I went outside.

I walked past the corral to the edge where the narrow trail cut through the black rim rock. I was standing in the sky with nothing around me but the wind that came down from the mountain peak behind me. I could see faint mountain images in the distance miles across the vast spread of mesa and valleys and plains. I wondered who was over there to feel the mountain wind on those sheer blue edges—who walks on the pine needles in those blue mountains.

"Can you see the pueblo?" Silva was standing behind me.

I shook my head. "We're too far away."

"From here I can see the world." He stepped out on the edge. "The Navajo reservation begins over there." He pointed to the east. "The Pueblo boundaries are over here." He looked below us to the south, where the narrow trail seemed to come from. "The Texans have their ranches over there, starting with that valley, the Concho Valley. The Mexicans run some cattle over there too."

"Do you ever work for them?"

"I steal from them," Silva answered. The sun was dropping behind us and shadows were filling the land below. I turned away from the edge that dropped forever into the valleys below.

"I'm cold," I said; "I'm going inside." I started wondering about this man who could speak the Pueblo language so well but who lived on a mountain and rustled cattle. I decided that this man Silva must be Navajo, because Pueblo men didn't do things like that.

"You must be a Navajo."

Silva shook his head gently. "Little Yellow Woman," he said, "you never give up, do you? I have told you who I am. The Navajo people know me, too." He knelt down and unrolled the bedroll and spread the extra blankets out on a piece of canvas. The sun was down, and the only light in the house came from outside—the dim orange light from sundown.

I stood there and waited for him to crawl under the blankets.

"What are you waiting for?" he said, and I lay down beside him. He undressed me slowly like the night before beside the river—kissing my face gently and running his hands up and down my belly and legs. He took off my pants and then he laughed.

"Why are you laughing?"

"You are breathing so hard."

I pulled away from him and turned my back to him.

He pulled me around and pinned me down with his arms and chest. "You don't understand, do you, little Yellow Woman? You will do what I want."

And again he was all around me with his skin slippery against mine, and I was afraid because I understood that his strength could hurt me. I lay beneath him and I knew that he could destroy me. But later, while he slept beside me, I touched his face and had a feeling—the kind of feeling for him that overcame me that morning along the river. I kissed him on the forehead and he reached out for me.

When I woke up in the morning he was gone. It gave me a strange feeling because for a long time I sat there on the blankets and looked around the little house for some object of his—some proof that he had been there or maybe that he was coming back. Only the blanket and the cardboard box remained. The .30-30 that had been leaning in the corner was gone, and so was the knife I had used the night before. He was gone, and I had my chance to go now. But first I had to eat, because I knew it would be a long walk home.

I found some dried apricots in the cardboard box, and I sat down on a rock at the edge of the plateau rim. There was no wind and the sun warmed me. I was surrounded by silence. I drowsed with apricots in my mouth, and I didn't believe that there were highways or railroads or cattle to steal.

When I woke up, I stared down at my feet in the black mountain dirt. Little black ants were swarming over the pine needles around my foot. They must have smelled the apricots. I thought about my family far below me. They would be wondering about me, because this had never happened to me before. The tribal police would file a report. But if old Grandpa weren't dead he would tell them what happened—he would laugh and say, "Stolen by a ka'tsina, a mountain spirit. She'll come home—they usually do." There are enough of them to handle things. My mother and grandmother will raise the baby like they raised me. Al will find someone else, and they will go on like before, except that there will be a story about the day I disappeared while I was walking along the river. Silva had come for me; he said he had. I did not decide to go. I just went. Moonflowers blossom in the sand hills before dawn just as I followed him. That's what I was thinking as I wandered along the trail through the pine trees.

It was noon when I got back. When I saw the stone house I remembered that I had meant to go home. But that didn't seem important any more, maybe because there were little blue flowers growing in the meadow behind the stone house and the gray squirrels were playing in the pines next to the house. The horses were standing in the corral, and there was a beef carcass hanging on the shady side of a big pine in front of the house. Flies buzzed around the clotted blood that hung from the carcass. Silva was washing his hands in a bucket full of water. He must have heard me coming because he spoke to me without turning to face me.

"I've been waiting for you."

"I went walking in the big pine trees."

I looked into the bucket full of bloody water with brown-and-white animal hairs floating in it. Silva stood there letting his hand drip, examining me intently.

"Are you coming with me?"

"Where?" I asked him.

"To sell the meat in Marquez."

"If you're sure it's O.K."

"I wouldn't ask you if it wasn't," he answered.

He sloshed the water around in the bucket before he dumped it out and set the bucket upside down near the door. I followed him to the corral and watched him saddle the horses. Even beside the horses he looked tall, and I asked him again if he wasn't Navajo. He didn't say anything; he just shook his head and kept cinching up the saddle.

"But Navajos are tall."

"Get on the horse," he said, "and let's go."

The last thing he did before we started down the steep trail was to grab the .30-30 from the corner. He slid the rifle into the scabbard that hung from his saddle.

"Do they ever try to catch you?" I asked.

"They don't know who I am."

"Then why did you bring the rifle?"

"Because we are going to Marquez where the Mexicans live."

III

The trail leveled out on a narrow ridge that was steep on both sides like an animal spine. On one side I could see where the trail went around the rocky gray hills and disappeared into the southeast where the pale sandrock mesas stood in the distance near my home. On the other side was a trail that went west, and as I looked far into the distance I thought I saw the little town. But Silva said no, that I was looking in the wrong place, that I just thought I saw houses. After that I quit looking off into the distance; it was hot and the wildflowers were closing up their deep-yellow petals. Only the waxy cactus flowers bloomed in the bright sun, and I saw every color that a cactus blossom can be: the white ones and the red ones were still buds, but the purple and the yellow were blossoms, open full and the most beautiful of all.

Silva saw him before I did. The white man was riding a big gray horse, coming up the trail toward us. He was traveling fast and the gray horse's feet sent rocks rolling off the trail into the dry tumbleweeds. Silva motioned for me to stop and we watched the white man. He didn't see us right away, but finally his horse whinnied at our horses and he stopped. He looked at us briefly before he loped the gray horse across the three hundred yards that separated us. He stopped his horse in front of Silva, and his young fat face was shadowed by the brim of his hat. He didn't look mad, but his small, pale eyes moved from the blood-soaked gunny sacks hanging from my saddle to Silva's face and then back to my face.

"Where did you get the fresh meat?" the white man asked.

"I've been hunting," Silva said, and when he shifted his weight in the saddle the leather creaked.

"The hell you have, Indian. You've been rustling cattle. We've been looking for the thief for a long time."

The rancher was fat, and sweat began to soak through his white cowboy shirt and the wet cloth stuck to the thick rolls of belly fat. He almost seemed to be panting from the exertion of talking, and he smelled rancid, maybe because Silva scared him.

Silva turned to me and smiled. "Go back up the mountain, Yellow Woman."

The white man got angry when he heard Silva speak in a language he couldn't understand. "Don't try anything, Indian. Just keep riding to Marquez. We'll call the state police from there."

The rancher must have been unarmed because he was very frightened and if he had a gun he would have pulled it out then. I turned my horse around and the rancher yelled, "Stop!" I looked at Silva for an instant and there was something ancient and dark—something I could feel in my stomach—in his eyes, and when I glanced at his hand I saw his finger on the trigger of the .30-30 that was still in the saddle scabbard. I slapped my horse across the flank and the sacks of raw meat swung against my knees as the horse leaped up the trail. It was hard to keep my balance, and once I thought I felt the saddle slipping backward; it was because of this that I could not look back.

I didn't stop until I reached the ridge where the trail forked. The horse was breathing deep gasps and there was a dark film of sweat on its neck. I looked down in the direction I had come from, but I couldn't see the place. I waited. The wind came up and pushed warm air past me. I looked up at the sky, pale blue and full of thin clouds and fading vapor trails left by jets.

I think four shots were fired—I remember hearing four hollow explosions that reminded me of deer hunting. There could have been more shots after that, but I couldn't have heard them because my horse was running again and the loose rocks were making too much noise as they scattered around his feet.

Horses have a hard time running downhill, but I went that way instead of uphill to the mountain because I thought it was safer. I felt better with the horse running southeast past the round gray hills that were covered with cedar trees and black lava rock. When I got to the plain in the distance I could see the dark green patches of tamaracks that grew along the river; and beyond the river I could see the beginning of the pale sandrock mesas. I stopped the horse and looked back to see if anyone was coming; then I got off the horse and turned the horse around, wondering if it would go back to its corral under the pines on the mountain. It looked back at me for a moment and then plucked a mouthful of green tumbleweeds before it trotted back up the trail with its ears pointed forward, carrying its head daintily to one side to avoid stepping on the dragging reins. When the horse disappeared over the last hill, the gunny sacks full of meat were still swinging and bouncing.

IV

I walked toward the river on a wood-hauler's road that I knew would eventually lead to the paved road. I was thinking about waiting beside the road for someone to drive by, but by the time I got to the pavement I had decided it wasn't very far to walk if I followed the river back the way Silva and I had come.

The river water tasted good, and I sat in the shade under a cluster of silvery willows. I thought about Silva, and I felt sad at leaving him; still, there was something strange about him, and I tried to figure it out all the way back home.

I came back to the place on the river bank where he had been sitting the first time I saw him. The green willow leaves that he had trimmed from the branch were still lying there, wilted in the sand. I saw the leaves and I wanted to go back to him—to kiss him and to touch him—but the mountains were too far away now. And I told myself, because I believe it, he will come back sometime and be waiting again by the river.

❋ ❋ ❋

I followed the path up from the river into the village. The sun was getting low, and I could smell supper cooking when I got to the screen door of my house. I could hear their voices inside—my mother was telling my grandmother how to fix the Jell-o and my husband, Al, was playing with the baby. I decided to tell them that some Navajo had kidnapped me, but I was sorry that old Grandpa wasn't alive to hear my story because it was the Yellow Woman stories he liked to tell best.

Explorations of the Text

1. How does the story of Yellow Woman and the ka'tsina function in this work?
2. Describe the relationship between the speaker and Silva. How does it change in each section?
3. How do details about the setting and about the horses emphasize the mythic elements of the story? How do the same details emphasize the sexual fascination between the two characters?
4. Discuss Silva's character. Why does he live a solitary life? Why does he steal cattle? Why does he have a gun?
5. Why does Yellow Woman agree to help Silva sell the meat? What does the symbolism of the dead animal and of the blood signify?
6. Analyze the encounter between Silva and the rancher. Why does the narrator ride down the mountain? Does she make conscious choices?
7. Is the ending optimistic or pessimistic? What roles do imagination and fantasy play in the narrator's actions? What does the story suggest about the power of sexual fantasy?
8. Discuss the depiction of sexual roles in the story. Compare with Maxine Hong Kingston's "No Name Woman."

The Reading/Writing Connection

1. Extend the story to part five. Imitate Silko's style.
2. Freewrite about Silva.
3. "Think" Topic: Does the narrator return to her husband?

Ideas for Writing

1. Analyze the love relationship in this story. Are the male and female roles stereotypical?
2. Compare this vision of love with Senghor's "Nuit de Sine," Yamauchi's *And the Soul Shall Dance,* or Paz's "My Life with the Wave."

Shall I Compare Thee to a Summer's Day?

William Shakespeare

The sonnets of William Shakespeare (1564–1616) are the most prolific, most-loved form of his nondramatic poetry. Numbering 154, the sonnets incorporate images from everyday life, nature, the fine arts, business, law, and, of course, love. The characters and situations of Shakespeare's sonnets signaled a departure from the conventional, more restrictive Petrarchan sonnet tradition and enabled Shakespeare to explore themes of time and death, truth and deceit, beauty and decay and permanence, and love in all of its forms.

1609

Shall I compare thee to a summer's day?
Thou art more lovely and more temperate.
Rough winds do shake the darling buds of May,
And summer's lease hath all too short a date.
Sometimes too hot the eye of heaven shines,
And often is his gold complexion dimmed;
And every fair from fair sometime declines,
By chance, or nature's changing course, untrimmed.
But thy eternal summer shall not fade,
Nor lose possession of that fair thou ow'st;[1]
Nor shall death brag thou wand'rest in his shade,
When in eternal lines to time thou grow'st.
So long as men can breathe or eyes can see,
So long lives this, and this gives life to thee.

Explorations of the Text

1. Why does the speaker consider his loved one more lovely than "a summer's day"? What are the positive qualities of the loved one?
2. List ways in which nature and time change beauty. Interpret lines 3–8.
3. Explain the shift in tone and in subject in line 9. Why does the speaker assure the lover that "eternal summer shall not fade"?

[1] Ownest.

4. What is the relation of art and love? Look carefully at the **couplet** at the end. To what does "this" refer?
5. Which syllables are stressed in the last line? How does this rhythm emphasize the meaning?
6. Identify **metaphors** and **similes** in the sonnet. How do they relate to theme?

The Reading/Writing Connection

1. Write about the timelessness of art and the fragility of beauty in this sonnet. What do you conclude?
2. Freewrite and create a portrait of a loved one through the use of figurative language (e.g., similes and metaphors).

Ideas for Writing

1. Explicate this sonnet. (Focus on imagery, figurative language, formal elements.)

And the Soul Shall Dance

Wakako Yamauchi

Wakako Yamauchi (1924–), born in Westmoreland, California, is the daughter of Japanese immigrants who worked as farmers. She was interned with her family in a camp for Japanese Americans during the Second World War. She later became a freelance writer, and her short stories have appeared in numerous anthologies. Her works include "Songs My Mother Taught Me" (1977), "Surviving the Wasteland Years," and "Maybe" (1990). Her play, And the Soul Shall Dance, *was adapted from the short story of the same name and first performed in Los Angeles in 1977.*

1977

Characters

Murata, 40, Issei[1] farmer.
Hana, Issei wife of Murata.
Masako, 11, Nisei[2] daughter of the Muratas.
Oka, 45, Issei farmer.
Emiko, 30, wife of Oka.
Kiyoko, 14, Oka's daughter.

[1] First-generation Japanese American.
[2] Second-generation Japanese American.

Place and Time

The action of the play takes place on and between two small farms in Southern California's Imperial Valley in the early 1930s.

Act I

Scene 1

Summer 1935, afternoon. Interior of the Murata house. The set is spare. There is a kitchen table, four chairs, a bed, and on the wall, a calendar indicating the year and month: June, 1935. There is a doorway leading to the other room. Props are: a bottle of sake, *two cups, a dish of chiles, a phonograph, and two towels hanging on pegs on the wall. A wide wooden bench sits outside.*

The bathhouse has just burned to the ground due to the carelessness of Masako, Nisei daughter, 11. Off stage there are sounds of Murata, 40, Issei farmer, putting out the fire.

Inside the house Hana Murata, Issei wife, in a drab housedress, confronts Masako (wearing summer dress of the era). Masako is sullen and somewhat defiant. Hana breaks the silence.

Hana: How could you be so careless, Masako? You know you should be extra careful with fire. How often have I told you? Now the whole bathhouse is gone. I told you time and again, when you stoke a fire, you should see that everything is swept into the fireplace.

(Murata enters. He's dressed in old work clothes. He suffers from heat and exhaustion.)

Murata *(Coughing.)*: Shack went up like a match box . . . This kind of weather dries everything . . . just takes a spark to make a bonfire out of dry timber.

Hana: Did you save any of it?

Murata: No. Couldn't . . .

Hana *(To Masako.)*: How many times have I told you . . .

(Masako moves nervously.)

Murata: No use crying about it now. *Shikata ga nai.* It's gone now. No more bathhouse. That's all there is to it.

Hana: But you've got to tell her. Otherwise she'll make the same mistake. You'll be building a bathhouse every year.

(Murata removes his shirt and wipes off his face. He throws his shirt on a chair and sits at the table.)

Murata: *Baka!* Ridiculous!

Masako: I didn't do it on purpose.

(She goes to the bed, opens a book. Hana follows her.)

Hana: I know that but you know what this means? It means we bathe in a bucket . . . inside the house. Carry water in from the pond, heat it on the stove . . . We'll use more kerosene.

Murata: Tub's still there. And the fireplace. We can still build a fire under the tub.

Hana *(Shocked.):* But no walls! Everyone in the country can see us!

Murata: Wait 'til dark then. Wait 'til dark.

Hana: We'll be using a lantern. They'll still see us.

Murata: Angh! Who? Who'll see us? You think everyone in the country waits to watch us take a bath? Hunh? You know how stupid you sound? Ridiculous!

Hana *(Defensively.):* It'll be inconvenient.

(Hana is saved by a rap on the door. Oka, Issei neighbor, 45, enters. He is short and stout, dressed in faded work clothes.)

Oka: Hello! Hello! Oi! What's going on here? Hey! Was there some kind of fire?

(Hana rushes to the door to let Oka in. He stamps the dust from his shoes and enters.)

Hana: Oka-san![3] You just wouldn't believe . . . We had a terrible thing happen.

Oka: Yeah. Saw the smoke from down the road. Thought it was your house. Came rushing over. Is the fire out?

(Murata half rises and sits back again. He's exhausted.)

Murata *(Gesturing.):* Oi, oi. Come in . . . sit down. No big problem. It was just our bathhouse.

Oka: Just the *furoba,* eh?

Murata: Just the bath.

Hana: Our Masako was careless and the *furoba* caught fire. There's nothing left of it but the tub.

(Masako looks up from her book, pained. She makes a very small sound.)

Oka: Long as the tub's there, no problem. I'll help you with it. *(He starts to roll up his sleeves. Murata looks at him.)*

Murata: What . . . now? Now?

Oka: Long as I'm here.

Hana: Oh, Papa. Aren't we lucky to have such friends?

Murata *(To Hana.):* Hell, we can't work on it now. The ashes are still hot. I just now put the damned fire out. Let me rest a while. *(To Oka.)* Oi, how

---

[3] -san: a suffix indicating polite address, similar to Mr., Mrs., or Ms. The suffixes -chan and -kun, found elsewhere in the text, connote affection and familiarity.

about a little *sake?*[4] *(Gesturing to Hana.)* Make *sake* for Oka-san. *(Oka sits at the table. Hana goes to prepare the* sake. *She heats it, gets out the cups and pours it for the men.)* I'm tired . . . I am *tired.*

Hana: Oka-san has so generously offered his help . . .

(Oka is uncomfortable. He looks around and sees Masako sitting on the bed.)

Oka: Hello, there, Masako-chan. You studying?

Masako: No, it's summer vacation.

Murata *(Sucking in his breath.):* Kids nowadays . . . no manners . . .

Hana: She's sulking because I had to scold her.

(Masako makes a small moan.)

Murata: Drink, Oka-san.

Oka *(Swallowing.):* Ahhh, that's good.

Murata: Eh, you not working today?

Oka: No . . . no . . . I took the afternoon off today. I was driving over to Nagatas' when I saw this big black cloud of smoke coming from your yard.

Hana: It went up so fast . . .

Murata: What's up at Nagatas'? *(To Hana.)* Get the chiles out. Oka-san loves chiles.

(Hana opens a jar of chiles and puts them on a plate. She serves the men and gets her mending basket and walks to Masako. Masako makes room for her on the bed.)

Oka *(Helping himself.):* Ah, chiles. *(Murata looks at Oka, the question unanswered.)* Well, I want to see him about my horse. I'm thinking of selling my horse.

Murata: Sell your horse!

Oka *(He scratches his head.):* The fact is, I need some money. Nagata-san's the only one around made money this year, and I'm thinking he might want another horse.

Murata: Yeah, he made a little this year. And he's talking big . . . big! Says he's leasing twenty more acres this fall.

Oka: Twenty acres?

Murata: Yeah. He might want another horse.

Oka: Twenty acres, eh?

Murata: That's what he says. But you know his old woman makes all the decisions. *(Oka scratches his head.)*

Hana: They're doing all right.

Murata: Henh. Nagata-kun's so hen-pecked, it's pathetic. Peko-peko. *(He makes motions of a hen pecking.)*

Oka *(Feeling the strain.):* I better get over there.

Murata: Why the hell you selling your horse?

Oka: I need cash.

---

[4] Alcoholic drink, served heated.

Murata: Oh, yeah. I could use some too. Seems like everyone's getting out of the depression but the poor farmers. Nothing changes for us. We go on and on planting our tomatoes and summer squash and eating them . . . Well, at least it's healthy.

Hana: Papa, do you have lumber?

Murata: Lumber? For what?

Hana: The bath.

Murata *(Impatiently.):* Don't worry about that. We need more *sake* now.

(Hana rises to serve him.)

Oka: You sure Nagata-kun's working twenty more acres?

Murata: Last I heard. What the hell; if you need a few bucks, I can loan you . . .

Oka: A few hundred. I need a few hundred dollars.

Murata: Oh, a few hundred. But what the hell you going to do without a horse? Out here a man's horse is as important as his wife.

Oka *(Seriously.):* I don't think Nagata will buy my wife. *(The men laugh, but Hana doesn't find it so funny. Murata glances at her. She fills the cups again. Oka makes a half-hearted gesture to stop her. Masako watches the pantomine carefully. Oka swallows his drink in one gulp.)* I better get moving.

Murata: What's the big hurry?

Oka: Like to get the horse business done.

Murata: Ehhhh . . . relax. Do it tomorrow. He's not going to die, is he?

Oka *(Laughing.):* Hey he's a good horse. I want to get it settled today. If Nagata-kun won't buy, I got to find someone else. You think maybe Kawaguchi . . . ?

Murata: Not Kawaguchi . . . Maybe Yamamoto.

Hana: What is all the money for, Oka-san? Does Emiko-san need an operation?

Oka: Nothing like that . . .

Hana: Sounds very mysterious.

Oka: No mystery, Mrs. No mystery. No sale, no money, no story.

Murata *(Laughing.):* That's a good one. "No sale, no money, no . . ." Eh, Mama. *(He points to the empty cups. Hana fills the cups and goes back to Masako.)*

Hana *(Muttering.):* I see we won't be getting any work done today. *(To Masako.)* Are you reading again? Maybe we'd still have a bath if you . . .

Masako: I didn't do it on purpose.

Murata *(Loudly.):* I sure hope you know what you're doing. Oka-kun. What'd you do without a horse?

Oka: I was hoping you'd lend me yours now and then . . . *(He looks at Hana.)* I'll pay for some of the feed.

Murata *(Emphatically waving his hand.):* Sure! Sure!

Oka: The fact is, I need that money. I got a daughter in Japan and I just got to send for her this year.

(Hana comes to life. She puts down her mending and sits at the table.)

Hana: A daughter? You have a daughter in Japan? Why, I didn't know you had children. Emiko-san and you . . . I thought you were childless.

Oka *(Scratching his head.):* We are. I was married before.

Murata: You son-of-a-gun!

Hana: Is that so? How old is your daughter?

Oka: Kiyoko must be . . . fifteen now. Yeah, fifteen.

Hana: Fifteen! Oh, that *would* be too old for Emiko-san's child. Is Kiyoko-san living with relatives in Japan?

Oka *(Reluctantly.):* Yeah, with grandparents. With Shizue's parents. Well, the fact is, Shizue, that's my first wife, and Emiko were sisters. They come from a family with no sons. I was a boy when I went to work for the family . . . as an apprentice . . . they're blacksmiths. Later I married Shizue and took on the family name—you know, *yoshi*[5]—because they had no sons. My real name is Sakakihara.

Murata: Sakakihara! That's a great name!

Hana: A magnificent name!

Oka: No one knows me by that here.

Murata: Should have kept that . . . Sakakihara.

Oka *(Muttering.):* I don't even know myself by that name.

Hana: And Shizue-san passed away and you married Emiko-san?

Oka: Oh, yeah. Shizue and I lived with the family for a while and we had the baby . . . that's, you know, Kiyoko . . . *(The liquor has affected him and he's become less inhibited.)* Well, while I was serving apprentice with the family, they always looked down their noses at me. After I married, it got worse . . . That old man . . . Angh! He was terrible! Always pushing me around, making me look bad in front of my wife and kid. That old man was mean . . . ugly!

Murata: Yeah, I heard about that apprentice work—*detchi-boko* . . . Heard it was damned humiliating.

Oka: That's the God's truth!

Murata: Never had to do it myself. I came to America instead. They say *detchi-boko* is bloody hard work.

Oka: The work's all right. I'm not afraid of work. It's the humiliation! I hated them! Pushing me around like I was still a boy . . . Me, a grown man! And married to their daughter! *(Murata groans in sympathy.)* Well, Shizue and I talked it over and we decided the best thing was to get away. We thought if I came to America and made some money . . . you know, send her money until we had enough, I'd go back and we'd leave the family . . . you know, move to another province . . . start a small business, maybe in the city, a noodle shop or something.

Murata: That's everyone's dream. Make money, go home and live like a king.

---

[5] Yoshi is a procedure wherein a man married into a family that has no sons is obliged to carry the wife's family name and continue the lineage [Author's note].

Oka: I worked like a dog. Sent every penny to Shizue. And then she died. She died on me!

(Hana and Murata observe a moment of silence in respect for Oka's anguish.)

Hana: And you married Emiko-san.

Oka: I didn't marry her. They married her to me! Right after Shizue died.

Hana: But Oka-san, you were lucky . . .

Oka: Before the body was cold! No respect! By proxy. The old man wrote me they were arranging a marriage by proxy for me and Emiko. They said she'd grown to be a beautiful woman and would serve me well.

Hana: Emiko-san *is* a beautiful woman.

Oka: And they sent her to me. Took care of everything! Immigration, fare, everything.

Hana: But she's your sister-in-law—Kiyoko's aunt. It's good to keep the family together.

Oka: That's what I thought. But hear this: Emiko was the favored one. Shizue was not so pretty, not so smart. They were grooming Emiko for a rich man—his name was Yamoto—lived in a grand house in the village. They sent her to schools; you know, the culture thing: tea ceremony, you know, all that. They didn't even like me, and suddenly they married her to me.

Murata: Yeah. You don't need all that formal training to make it over here. Just a strong back.

Hana: And a strong will.

Oka: It was all arranged. I couldn't do anything about it.

Hana: It'll be all right. With Kiyoko coming . . .

Oka *(Dubiously.):* I hope so . . . I never knew human beings could be so cruel. You know how they mistreated my daughter? You know after Emiko came over, things got from bad to worse and I *never* had enough money to send to Kiyoko.

Murata: They don't know what it's like here. They think money's picked off the ground here.

Oka: And they treated Kiyoko so bad. They told her I forgot about her. They told her I didn't care—they said I abandoned her. Well, she knew better. She wrote to me all the time and I always told her I'd send for her . . . soon as I got the money. *(He shakes his head.)* I just got to do something this year.

Hana: She'll be happier here. She'll know her father cares.

Oka: Kids tormented her for not having parents.

Murata: Kids are cruel.

Hana: Masako will help her. She'll help her get started at school. She'll make friends . . . she'll be all right.

Oka: I hope so. She'll need friends. *(He considers he might be making a mistake after all.)* What could I say to her? Stay there? It's not what you think over here? I can't help her? I just have to do this thing. I just have to do this one thing for her.

Murata: Sure . . .

Hana: Don't worry. It'll work out fine.

(Murata gestures to Hana. She fills the cup.)

Murata: You talk about selling your horse, I thought you were pulling out.

Oka: I wish I could. But there's nothing else I can do.

Murata: Without money, yeah . . .

Oka: You can go into some kind of business with money, but a man like me . . . no education . . . there's no kind of job I can do. I'd starve in the city.

Murata: Dishwashing, maybe. Janitor . . .

Oka: At least here we can eat. Carrots, maybe, but we can eat.

Murata: All the carrots we been eating 'bout to turn me into a rabbit.

(They laugh. Hana starts to pour more wine for Oka but he stops her.)

Oka: I better not drink any more. Got to drive to Nagata-san's yet. *(He rises and walks over to Masako.)* You study hard, don't you? You'll teach Kiyoko English, eh? When she gets here . . .

Hana: Oh, yes. She will.

Murata: Kiyoko-san could probably teach her a thing or two.

Oka: She won't know about American ways . . .

Masako: I'll help her.

Hana: Don't worry, Oka-san. She'll have a good friend in our Masako. *(They move toward the door.)*

Oka: Well, thanks for the *sake.* I guess I talk too much when I drink. *(He scratches his head and laughs.)* Oh. I'm sorry about the fire. By the way, come to my house for your bath . . . until you build yours again.

Hana *(Hesitantly.):* Oh, uh . . . thank you. I don't know if . . .

Murata: Good! Good! Thanks a lot. I need a good hot bath tonight.

Oka: Tonight, then.

Murata: We'll be there.

Hana *(Bowing.):* Thank you very much. *Sayonara.*[6]

Oka *(Nodding.):* See you tonight.

(Oka leaves. Hana faces her husband as soon as the door closes.)

Hana: Papa, I don't know about going over there.

Murata *(Surprised.):* Why?

Hana: Well, Emiko-san . . .

Murata *(Irritated.):* What's the matter with you? We need a bath and Oka's invited us over.

Hana *(To Masako.):* Help me clear the table. *(Masako reluctantly leaves her book and begins to clear the table.)* Papa, you know we've been neighbors already three, four years and Emiko-san's never been very hospitable.

Murata: She's shy, that's all.

Hana: Not just shy . . . she's strange. I feel like she's pushing me off . . . she makes me feel like—I don't know—like I'm prying or something.

---

[6] Farewell; good-bye; until we see each other again.

Murata: Maybe you are.

Hana: And never put out a cup of tea . . . If she had all that training in the graces . . . why, a cup of tea . . .

Murata: So if you want tea, ask for it.

Hana: I can't do that, Papa. She's strange . . . I don't know . . . *(To Masako.)* When we go there, be very careful not to say anything wrong.

Masako: I never say anything anyway.

Hana *(Thoughtfully.):* Would you believe the story Oka-san just told? Why, I never knew . . .

Murata: There're lot of things you don't know. Just because a man don't . . . talk about them, don't mean he don't feel . . . don't think about . . .

Hana *(Looking around.):* We'll have to take something . . . There's nothing to take . . . Papa, maybe we can dig up some carrots.

Murata: God, Mama, be sensible. They got carrots. Everybody's got carrots.

Hana: Something . . . maybe I should make something.

Murata: Hell, they're not expecting anything.

Hana: It's not good manners to go empty-handed.

Murata: We'll take the *sake.*

(Hana grimaces. Masako sees the record player.)

Masako: I know, Mama. We can take the Victrola! We can play records for Mrs. Oka. Then nobody has to talk.

(Murata laughs.)

(Fade out.)

Scene 2

That evening. We see the exterior wall of the Okas' weathered house. There is a workable screen door and a large screened window. Outside there is a wide wooden bench that can accommodate three or four people. There is one separate chair and a lantern stands against the house.

The last rays of the sun light the area in a soft golden glow. This light grows gray as the scene progresses and it is quite dark at the end of the scene.

Through the screened window, Emiko Oka, Issei woman, 30, can be seen walking erratically back and forth. She wears a drab cotton dress but her grace and femininity come through. Her hair is bunned back in the style of Issei women of the era.

Oka sits cross-legged on the bench. He wears a Japanese summer robe (yukata) and fans himself with a round Japanese fan.

The Muratas enter. Murata carries towels and a bottle of sake. *Hana carries the Victrola, and Masako a package containing their yukatas.*

Oka *(Standing to receive the Muratas.):* Oh, you've come. Welcome!

Murata: Yah . . . Good of you to ask us.

Hana *(Bowing.):* Yes, thank you very much. *(To Masako.)* Say "hello," Masako.

Masako: Hello.
Hana: And "thank you."
Masako: Thank you.

(Oka makes motion of protest. Emiko stops her pacing and watches from the window.)

Hana *(Glancing briefly at the window.):* And how is Emiko-san this evening?
Oka *(Turning toward the house.):* Emi! Emiko!
Hana: That's all right. Don't call her out. She must be busy.
Oka *(Half rising.):* Emiko!

(Emiko comes to the door. Hana starts a deep bow toward the door.)

Murata: *Konbanwa! ("Good evening!")*
Hana: *Konbanwa,* Emiko-san. I feel so bad about this intrusion. Your husband has told you, our bathhouse was destroyed by fire and he graciously invited us to come use yours.

(Emiko shakes her head.)

Oka: I didn't have a chance to . . .

(Hana recovers and nudges Masako.)

Hana: Say hello to Mrs. Oka.
Masako: Hello, Mrs. Oka.

(Hana lowers the Victrola on the bench.)

Oka: What's this? You brought a phonograph?
Masako: It's a Victrola.
Hana *(Laughing indulgently.):* Yes. Masako wanted to bring this over and play some records.
Murata *(Extending the wine.):* Brought a little *sake* too.
Oka *(Taking the bottle.):* Ah, now that I like. Emiko, bring out the cups.

(He waves at his wife, but she doesn't move. He starts to ask again, but decides to get them himself. He enters the house and returns with two cups. Emiko seats herself on the single chair. The Muratas unload their paraphernalia; Oka pours the wine, the men drink, Hana chatters and sorts the records. Masako stands by, helping her.)

Hana: Yes, our Masako loves to play records. I like records too . . . and Papa, he . . .
Murata *(Watching Emiko.):* They take me back home. The only way I can get there . . . in my mind.
Hana: Do you like music, Emiko-san? *(Emiko looks vague but smiles faintly.)* Oka-san, you like them, don't you?
Oka: Yeah. But I don't have a player. No chance to hear them.
Murata: I had to get this for them. They wouldn't leave me alone until I got it. Well . . . a phonograph . . . what the hell, they got to have *some* fun.

Hana: We don't have to play them, if you'd rather not . . .

Oka: Play. Play them.

Hana: I thought we could listen to them and relax *(She extends some records to Emiko.)* Would you like to look through these, Emiko-san? *(Emiko doesn't respond. She pulls out a sack of Bull Durham and starts to roll a cigarette. Hana pushes Masako to her.)* Take these to her. *(Masako moves toward Emiko with the records. Masako stands watching her as she lights her cigarette.)* Some of these are very old. You might know them, Emiko-san. *(She sees Masako watching Emiko.)* Masako, bring those over here. *(She laughs uncomfortably.)* You might like this one, Emiko-san . . . *(She starts the player.)* Do you know it?

(The record whines out "Kago No Tori."[7] *Emiko listens with her head cocked. She smokes her cigarette. She becomes wrapped in nostalgia and memories of the past. Masako watches her carefully.)*

Masako *(Whispering.):* Mama, she's crying.

(Startled, Hana and Murata look toward Emiko.)

Hana *(Pinching Masako.):* Shhh. The smoke is in her eyes.

Murata: Did you bring the record I like, Mama?

(Emiko rises abruptly and enters the house.)

Masako: There were tears, Mama.

Hana: From yawning, Masako. *(Regretfully, to Oka.)* I'm afraid we've offended her.

Oka *(Unaware.):* Hunh? Aw . . . no . . . pay no attention . . . no offense . . .

(Masako looks toward the window. Emiko stands forlornly and slowly drifts into a dance.)

Hana: I'm very sorry. Children, you know . . . they'll say anything, anything that's on their minds.

(Murata notices Masako watching Emiko through the window and tries to divert her attention.)

Murata: The needles. Masako, where're the needles?

Masako *(Still watching.):* I forgot them.

(Hana sees what's going on. Oka is unaware.)

Hana: Masako, go take your bath now. Masako . . .

(Masako reluctantly picks up her towel and leaves.)

Oka: Yeah, yeah . . . take your bath.

Murata *(Sees Emiko still dancing.):* Change the record, Mama.

---

[7] See lyrics at the end of the play.

Oka *(Still unaware.):* That's kind of sad.
Murata: No use to get sick over a record. We're supposed to enjoy.

(Hana stops the record. Emiko disappears from the window. Hana selects a lively ondo[8]*—"Tokyo Ondo.")*

Hana: We'll find something more fun. *(The three begin to tap to the music.)* Can't you just see the festival? The dancers, the bright *kimonos,* the paper lanterns bobbing in the wind, the fireflies . . . How nostalgic . . . Oh, how nostalgic . . .

(From the side of the house Emiko appears. Her hair is down, she wears an old straw hat. She dances in front of the Muratas. They're startled. After the first shock, they watch with frozen smiles. They try to join Emiko's mood but something is missing. Oka is grieved. He finally stands as though he's had enough. Emiko, now close to the door, ducks into the house.)

Hana: That was pretty . . . very nice . . .

(Oka settles down and grunts. Murata clears his throat and Masako returns from her bath.)

Murata: You're done already? *(He's glad to see her.)*
Masako: I wasn't very dirty. The water was too hot.
Murata: Good! Just the way I like it.
Hana: Not dirty?
Murata *(Picking up his towel.):* Come on, Mama . . . scrub my back.
Hana *(Laughing embarrassedly.):* Oh, oh . . . well . . . *(She stops the player.)* Masako, now don't forget . . . crank the machine and change the needle now and then.
Masako: I didn't bring them.
Hana: Oh. Oh . . . all right. I'll be back soon . . . don't forget . . . crank.

(She leaves with her husband. Oka and Masako are alone. Oka is awkward and falsely hearty.)

Oka: So! So you don't like hot baths, eh?
Masako: Not too hot.
Oka *(Laughing.):* I thought you like it real hot. Hot enough to burn the house down. That's a little joke. *(Masako busies herself with the records to conceal her annoyance.)* I hear you're real good in school. Always top of the class.
Masako: It's a small class. Only two of us.
Oka: When Kiyoko comes, you'll help her in school, yeah? You'll take care of her . . . a favor for me, eh?
Masako: Okay.
Oka: You'll be her friend, eh?

---

[8] Leading in singing.

Masako: Okay.

Oka: That's good. That's good. You'll like her. She's a nice girl too. *(Oka stands, yawns, and stretches.)* I'll go for a little walk now.

(He touches his crotch to indicate his purpose. Masako turns her attention to the records and selects one, "The Soul Shall Dance,"[9] *and begins to sway to the music. The song draws Emiko from the house. She looks out the window, sees Masako is alone and begins to slip into a dance.)*

Emiko: Do you like that song, Masa-chan? *(Masako is startled and draws back. She remembers her mother's warning. She doesn't know what to do. She nods.)* That's one of my favorite songs. I remember in Japan I used to sing it so often . . . my favorite song . . . *(She sings along with the record.)*

Akai kuchibiru
Kappu ni yosete
Aoi sake nomya
Kokoro ga odoru . . .

Do you know what that means, Masa-chan?

Masako: I think so . . . The soul will dance?

Emiko: Yes, yes, that's right.

The soul shall dance. Red lips against a glass
Drink the green . . .

Masako: Wine?

Emiko *(Nodding.):* Drink the green wine.

Masako: Green? I thought wine is purple.

Emiko *(Nodding.):* Wine is purple . . . but this is a green liqueur. *(Emiko holds up one of the china cups as though it were crystal, and looks at it as though the light were shining through it and she sees the green liquid.)* It's good . . . it warms your heart.

Masako: And the soul dances.

Emiko: Yes.

Masako: What does it taste like? The green wine . . .

Emiko: Oh, it's like . . . it's like . . .

(The second verse starts. "Kurai yoru yume, Setsunasa yo, Aoi sake nomya, Yume mo odoru . . .")

Masako: In the dark night . . .

Emiko: Dreams are unbearable . . . insufferable . . . *(She turns sad.)*

Masako: Drink the . . .

Emiko *(Nodding.):* Drink the green wine . . .

Masako: And the dreams will dance.

Emiko *(Softly.):* I'll be going back one day . . .

---

[9] Full lyrics are given on pages 575 and 576.

Masako: To where?

Emiko: My home . . . Japan . . . my real home. I'm planning to go back.

Masako: By yourself?

Emiko *(Nodding.):* Oh, yes. It's a secret. You can keep a secret?

Masako: Unhn. I have lots of secrets . . . all my own . . . *(The music stops. Emiko sees Oka approaching and disappears into the house. Masako attends to the record and does not know Emiko is gone.)* Secrets I never tell anyone.

Oka: Secrets? What kind of secrets? What did she say?

Masako: Oh. Nothing.

Oka: What did you talk about?

Masako: Nothing . . . Mrs. Oka was talking about the song. She was telling me what it meant . . . about the soul.

Oka *(Scoffing.):* Heh! What does she know about soul? *(Calming down.)* Ehhh . . . some people don't have them . . . souls.

Masako *(Timidly.):* I thought . . . I think everyone has a soul. I read in a book . . .

Oka *(Laughing.):* Maybe . . . maybe you're right. I'm not an educated man, you know . . . I don't know too much about books. When Kiyoko comes you can talk to her about it. Kiyoko is very . . . *(From inside the house, we hear Emiko begin to sing loudly at the name Kiyoko as though trying to drown it out. Oka stops talking. Then resumes.)* Kiyoko is very smart. You'll have a good time with her. She'll learn your language fast. How old did you say you are?

Masako: Almost twelve.

(By this time Oka and Masako are shouting, trying to be heard above Emiko's singing.)

Oka: Kiyoko is fifteen . . . Kiyoko . . . *(Oka is exasperated. He rushes into the house seething. Masako hears Oka's muffled rage. "Behave yourself" and "kitchigai" come through. Masako slinks to the window and looks in. Oka slaps Emiko around. Masako reacts to the violence. Oka comes out. Masako returns to the bench in time. He pulls his fingers through his hair and sits next to Masako. She very slightly draws away.)* Want me to light a lantern?

Masako *(Shaken.):* No . . . ye- . . . okay . . .

Oka: We'll get a little light here . . .

(He lights the lantern as the Muratas return from their bath. They are in good spirits.)

Murata: Ahhhh . . . Nothing like a good hot bath.

Hana: So refreshing . . .

Murata: A bath should be taken hot and slow. Don't know how Masako gets through so fast.

Hana: She probably doesn't get in the tub.

Masako: I do. *(Everyone laughs.)* Well I do.

(Emiko comes out. She has a large purple welt on her face. She sits on the separate chair, hands folded, quietly watching the Muratas. They look at her with alarm. Oka engages himself with his fan.)

Hana: Oh! Emiko-san . . . what . . . ah-ah . . . whaa . . . *(She draws a deep breath.)* What a nice bath we had . . . such a lovely bath. We do appreciate your hos . . . pitality. Thank you so much.

Emiko: Lovely evening, isn't it?

Hana: Very lovely. Very. Ah, a little warm, but nice . . . Did you get a chance to hear the records? *(Turning to Masako.)* Did you play the records for Mrs. Oka?

Masako: Ye- . . . no . . . The needle was . . .

Emiko: Yes, she did. We played the records together.

Murata: Oh, you played the songs together?

Emiko: Yes . . . yes . . .

Murata: That's nice . . . Masako can understand pretty good, eh?

Emiko: She understand everything . . . everything I say.

Murata *(Withdrawing.):* Oh, yeah? Eh, Mama, we ought to be going . . . *(He closes the player.)* Hate to bathe and run but . . .

Hana: Yes, yes. Tomorrow is a busy day. Come, Masako.

Emiko: Please . . . stay a little longer.

Murata: Eh, well, we got to be going.

Hana: Why, thank you, but . . .

Emiko: It's still quite early.

Oka *(Indicating he's ready to say goodbye.):* Enjoyed the music. And the *sake.*

Emiko: The records are very nice. Makes me remember Japan. I sang those songs . . . those very songs . . . Did you know I used to sing?

Hana *(Politely.):* Why, no . . . no. I didn't know that. You must have a very lovely voice.

Emiko: Yes.

Hana: No, I didn't know that. That's very nice.

Emiko: Yes, I sang. My parents were very strict . . . they didn't like it. They said it was frivolous. Imagine?

Hana: Yes, I can imagine. Things were like that . . . in those days singing was not considered proper for nice . . . I mean, only for women in the profess- . . .

Murata: We better get home, Mama.

Hana: Yes, yes. What a shame you couldn't continue with it.

Emiko: In the city I did do some classics: the dance, and the *koto,* and the flower, and, of course, the tea . . . *(She makes the proper gesture for the different disciplines.)* All those. Even some singing . . . classics, of course.

Hana *(Politely.):* Of course.

Emiko: All of it is so disciplined . . . so disciplined. I was almost a *natori.*[10]

---

[10] Certified artist.

Hana: Oh! How nice.

Emiko: But everything changed.

Hana: Oh!

Emiko: I was sent here to America. *(She glares at Oka.)*

Hana: Oh, too bad . . . I mean, too bad about your *natori.*

Murata *(Loudly to Oka.):* So did you see Nagata today?

Oka: Oh, yeah. Yeah.

Murata: What did he say? Is he interested?

Oka: Yeah. Yeah. He's interested.

Murata: He likes the horse, eh?

Oka: Ah . . . yeah.

Murata: I knew he'd like him. I'd buy him myself if I had the money.

Oka: Well, I have to take him over tomorrow. He'll decide then.

Murata: He'll buy . . . he'll buy. You'd better go straight over to the ticket office and get that ticket. Before you—ha-ha—spend the money.

Oka: Ha-ha. Yeah.

Hana: It'll be so nice when Kiyoko-san comes to join you. I know you're looking forward to it.

Emiko *(Confused.):* Oh . . . oh . . .

Hana: Masako is so happy. It'll be good for her too.

Emiko: I had more freedom in the city . . . I lived with an aunt and she let me . . . She wasn't so strict.

(Murata and Masako have their gear together and stand ready to leave.)

Murata: Good luck on the horse tomorrow.

Oka: Yeah, thanks.

Hana *(Bowing.):* Many, many thanks.

Oka *(Nodding toward the* sake.*):* Thanks for the *sake.*

Hana *(Bowing again.):* Goodnight, Emiko-san. We'll see you again soon. We'll bring the records too.

Emiko *(Softly.):* Those songs . . . those very songs . . .

Murata: Let's go, Mama.

(The Muratas pull away. Light follows them and grows dark on the Okas. The Muratas begin walking home.)

Hana: That was uncomfortable.

Masako: What's the matter with . . .

Hana: Shhhh!

Murata: I guess Oka has his problems.

Masako: Is she really *kitchigai?*

Hana: Of course not. She's not crazy. Don't say that word, Masako.

Masako: I heard Mr. Oka call her that.

Hana: He called her that?

Masako: I . . . I think so.

Hana: You heard wrong, Masako. Emiko-san isn't crazy. She just likes her drinks. She had too much to drink tonight.

Masako: Oh.

Hana: She can't adjust to this life. She can't get over the good times she had in Japan. Well, it's not easy . . . but one has to know when to bend . . . like the bamboo. When the winds blow, bamboo bends. You bend or crack. Remember that, Masako.

Murata *(Laughing wryly.):* Bend, eh? Remember that, Mama.

Hana *(Softly.):* You don't know . . . it isn't ever easy.

Masako: Do you want to go back to Japan, Mama?

Hana: Everyone does.

Masako: Do you, Papa?

Murata: I'll have to make some money first.

Masako: I don't. Not me. Not Kiyoko . . .

Hana: After Kiyoko-san comes, Emiko will have company and things will straighten out. She has nothing to live on but her memories. She doesn't have any friends. At least I have my friends at church . . . at least I have that. She must get awful lonely.

Masako: I know that. She tried to make friends with me.

Hana: She did? What did she say?

Masako: Well, sort of . . .

Hana: What did she say?

Masako: She didn't say anything. I just felt it. Maybe you should be her friend, Mama.

Murata: Poor woman. We could have stayed longer.

Hana: But you wanted to leave. I tried to be friendly. You saw that. It's not easy to talk to Emiko. She either closes up, you can't pry a word from her, or else she goes on and on . . . all that . . . that . . . about the *koto* and tea and the flower . . . I mean, what am I supposed to say? She's so unpredictable. And the drinking . . .

Murata: All right, all right, Mama.

Masako: Did you see her black eye?

Hana *(Calming down.):* She probably hurt herself. She wasn't very steady.

Masako: Oh, no. Mr. Oka hit her.

Hana: I don't think so.

Masako: He hit her. I saw him.

Hana: You saw that? Papa, do you hear that? She saw them. That does it. We're not going there again.

Murata: Aww . . . Oka wouldn't do that. Not in front of a kid.

Masako: Well, they didn't do it in front of me. They were in the house.

Murata: You see . . .

Hana: That's all right. You just have to fix the bathhouse. Either that or we're going to bathe at home . . . in a bucket. We're not going . . . we'll bathe at home. *(Murata mutters to himself.)* What?

Murata: I said all right, it's the bucket then. I'll get to it when I can.

(Hana passes Murata and walks ahead.)

(Fade out.)

Scene 3

Same evening. Lights crossfade to the exterior of the Oka house. The Muratas have just left. Emiko sits on the bench. Her back is to Oka. Oka, still standing, looks at her contemptuously as she takes the bottle and one of the cups to pour herself a drink.

Oka: Nothing more disgusting than a drunk woman. *(Emiko ignores him.)* You made a fool of yourself. *Washi baka ni shite!* You made a fool of me! *(Emiko doesn't move.)*

Emiko: One can only make a fool of one's self.

Oka: You learn that in the fancy schools, eh? *(Emiko examines the pattern on her cup.)* Eh? Eh? Answer me! *(Emiko ignores.)* I'm talking to you. Answer me! *(Menacing.)* You don't get away with that. You think you're so fine . . . *(Emiko looks off into the horizon. Oka turns her roughly around.)* When I talk, you listen! *(Emiko turns away again. Oka pulls the cup from her hand.)* Goddamnit! What'd you think my friends think of you? What kind of ass they think I am? *(He grabs her shoulders.)*

Emiko: Don't touch me . . . don't touch me.

Oka: Who the hell you think you are? "Don't touch me, don't touch me." Who the hell! High and mighty, eh? Too good for me, eh? Don't put on the act for me . . . I know who you are.

Emiko: Tell me who I am, Mister Smart Peasant.

Oka: Shut your fool mouth, goddamnit! Sure! I'll tell you. I know all about you . . . Shizue told me. The whole village knows.

Emiko: Shizue!

Oka: Yeah! Shizue. Embarrassed the hell out of her, your own sister.

Emiko: Embarrassed? I have nothing to be ashamed of. I don't know what you're talking about.

Oka *(Derisively.):* You don't know what I'm talking about. I know. The whole village knows. They're all laughing at you. At me! Stupid Oka got stuck with a second-hand woman. I didn't say anything because . . .

Emiko: I'm not second-hand!

Oka: Who you trying to fool? I know. Knew long time ago . . . Shizue wrote me all about your affairs in Tokyo. The men you were mess- . . .

Emiko: Affairs? Men?

Oka: That man you were messing with . . . I knew all along. I didn't say anything because you . . . I . . .

Emiko: I'm not ashamed of it.

Oka: You're not ashamed! What the hell! Your father thought he was pulling a fast one on me . . . thought I didn't know nothing . . . thought I was some kind of dumb ass . . . I didn't say nothing because Shizue's dead . . . Shizue's dead. I was willing to give you a chance.

Emiko *(Laughing.):* A chance?

Oka: Yeah! A chance! Laugh! Give a *joro* another chance. Sure, I'm stupid . . . dumb.

Emiko: I'm not a whore. I'm true . . . he knows I'm true.

Oka: True! Ha!

Emiko: You think I'm untrue just because I let . . . let you . . . There's only one man for me.

Oka: Let me *(Obscene gesture.)* you? I can do what I want with you. Your father palmed you off on me—like a dog or cat—an animal . . . couldn't do nothing with you. Even that rich dumb Yamoto wouldn't have you. Your father—greedy father—so proud . . . making big plans for you . . . for himself. Ha! The whole village laughing at him . . . *(Emiko hangs her head.)* Shizue told me. And she was working like a dog . . . trying to keep your goddamn father happy . . . doing my work and yours.

Emiko: My work?

Oka: Yeah, your work too! She killed herself working! She killed herself . . . *(He has tender memories of his dull, uncomplaining wife.)* Up in the morning getting the fires started, working the bellows, cleaning the furnace, cooking, and late at night working with the sewing . . . tending the baby . . . *(He mutters.)* The goddamn family killed her. And you . . . you out there in Tokyo with the fancy clothes, doing the *(He sneers.)* dance, the tea, the flower, the *koto,* and the . . . *(Obscene gesture.)*

Emiko *(Hurting.):* Achhhh . . .

Oka: Did you have fun? Did you have fun on your sister's blood? *(Emiko doesn't answer.)* Did you? He must have been a son-of-a-bitch . . . What would make that goddamn greedy old man send his prize mare to a plow horse like me? What kind of bum was he that your father . . .

Emiko: He's not a bum . . . he's not a bum.

Oka: Was he Korean? Was he *Etta?*[11] That's the only thing I could figure.

Emiko: I'm true to him. Only him.

Oka: True? You think he's true to you? You think he waits for you? Remembers you? *Aho!* Think he cares?

Emiko *(Nodding quietly.):* He does.

Oka: And waits ten years? *Baka!* Go back to Japan and see. You'll find out. Go back to Japan. *Kaere!*

Emiko: In time.

Oka: In time? How about now?

Emiko: I can't now.

Oka: Ha! Now! Go now! Who needs you? Who needs you? You think a man waits ten years for a woman? You think you're some kind of . . . of . . . diamond . . . treasure . . . he's going to wait his life for you? Go to him. He's probably married with ten kids. Go to him. Get out! Goddamn *joro* . . . Go! Go!

(Oka sweeps Emiko off the bench.)

Emiko *(Hurting.):* Ahhhh! I . . . I don't have the money. Give me money to . . .

Oka: If I had money I would give it to you ten years ago. You think I been eating this *kuso* for ten years because I like it?

---

[11] Outcast; social class considered outside the mainstream.

Emiko: You're selling the horse . . . Give me the . . .

Oka *(Scoffing.):* That's for Kiyoko. I owe you nothing.

Emiko: Ten years, you owe me.

Oka: Ten years of what? Misery? You gave me nothing. I give you nothing. You want to go, pack your bag and start walking. Try cross the desert. When you get dry and hungry, think about me.

Emiko: I'd die out there.

Oka: Die? You think I didn't die here?

Emiko: I didn't do anything to you.

Oka: No, no you didn't. All I wanted was a little comfort and . . . you . . . no, you didn't. No. So you die. We all die. Shizue died. If she was here, she wouldn't treat me like this . . . *(He thinks of his poor dead wife.)* Ah, I should have brought her with me. She'd be alive now. We'd be poor but happy . . . like . . . like Murata and his wife . . . and the kid . . .

Emiko: I wish she were alive too. I'm not to blame for her dying. I didn't know . . . I was away. I loved her. I didn't want her to die . . . I . . .

Oka *(Softening.):* I know that. I'm not blaming you for that . . . And it's not my fault what happened to you either . . . *(Emiko is silent and Oka mistakes that for a change in attitude. He is encouraged.)* You understand that, eh? I didn't ask for you. It's not my fault you're here in this desert . . . with . . . with me . . . *(Emiko weeps. Oka reaches out.)* I know I'm too old for you. It's hard for me too . . . but this is the way it is. I just ask you be kinder . . . understand it wasn't my fault. Try make it easier for me . . . for yourself too.

(Oka touches her and she shrinks from his touch.)

Emiko: Ach!

Oka *(Humiliated again.):* Goddamn it! I didn't ask for you! *Aho!* If you was smart you'd done as your father said . . . cut out that *saru shibai* with the *Etta* . . . married the rich Yamoto. Then you'd still be in Japan. Not here to make my life so miserable. *(Emiko is silent.)* And you can have your *Etta* . . . and anyone else you want. Take them all on . . . *(Oka is worn out. It's hopeless.)* God, why do we do this all the time? Fighting, fighting all the time. There must be a better way to live . . . there must be another way.

(Oka waits for a response, gives up, and enters the house. Emiko watches him leave and pours herself another drink. The storm has passed, the alcohol takes over. She turns to the door Oka disappeared into.)

Emiko: Because I must keep the dream alive . . . the dream is all I live for. I am only in exile now. Because if I give in, all I've lived before . . . will mean nothing . . . will be for nothing . . . Because if I let you make me believe this is all there is to my life, the dream would die . . . I would die . . . *(She pours another drink and feels warm and good.)*

(Fade out.)

Act II

Scene 1

Mid-September, afternoon. Muratas' kitchen. The calendar reads September. Masako is at the kitchen table with several books. She thumbs through a Japanese magazine. Hana is with her sewing.

Masako: Do they always wear kimonos in Japan, Mama?

Hana: Most of the time.

Masako: I wonder if Kiyoko will be wearing a kimono like this?

Hana *(Peering into Masako's magazine.):* They don't dress like that . . . not for every day.

Masako: I wonder what she's like.

Hana: Probably a lot like you. What do you think she's like?

Masako: She's probably taller.

Hana: Mr. Oka isn't tall.

Masako: And pretty . . .

Hana *(Laughing.):* Mr. Oka . . . Well, I don't suppose she'll look like her father.

Masako: Mrs. Oka is pretty.

Hana: She isn't Kiyoko-san's real mother, remember.

Masako: Oh. That's right.

Hana: But they are related. Well, we'll soon see.

Masako: I thought she was coming in September. It's already September.

Hana: Papa said Oka-san went to San Pedro a few days ago. He should be back soon with Kiyoko-san.

Masako: Didn't Mrs. Oka go too?

Hana *(Glancing toward the Oka house.):* I don't think so. I see lights in their house at night.

Masako: Will they bring Kiyoko over to see us?

Hana: Of course. First thing, probably. You'll be very nice to her, won't you?

(Masako leaves the table and finds another book.)

Masako: Sure. I'm glad I'm going to have a friend. I hope she likes me.

Hana: She'll like you. Japanese girls are very polite, you know.

Masako: We have to be or our Mamas get mad at us.

Hana: Then I should be getting mad at you more often.

Masako: It's often enough already, Mama. *(She opens a hardback book.)* Look at this, Mama . . . I'm going to show her this book.

Hana: She won't be able to read at first.

Masako: I love this story. Mama, this is about people like us—settlers—it's about the prairie. We live in a prairie, don't we?

Hana: Prairie? Does that mean desert?

Masako: I think so.

Hana *(Nodding and looking bleak.):* We live in a prairie.

Masako: It's about the hardships and the floods and droughts and how they have nothing but each other.

Hana *(Nodding.)*: We have nothing but each other. But these people—they're white people.

Masako *(Nodding.)*: Sure, Mama. They come from the east. Just like you and Papa came from Japan.

Hana: We come from the far far east. That's different. White people are different from us.

Masako: I know that.

Hana: White people among white people . . . that's different from Japanese among white people. You know what I'm saying?

Masako: I know that. How come they don't write books about us . . . about Japanese people?

Hana: Because we're nobodies here.

Masako: If I didn't read these, there'd be nothing for me . . .

Hana: Some of the things you read, you're never going to know.

Masako: I can dream, though.

Hana *(Sighing.)*: Sometimes the dreaming makes the living harder. Better to keep your head out of the clouds.

Masako: That's not much fun.

Hana: You'll have fun when Kiyoko-san comes. You can study together, you can sew, and sometime you can try some of those fancy American recipes.

Masako: Mama, you have to have chocolate and cream and things like that.

Hana: We'll get them.

(We hear the putt-putt of Oka's old car. Masako and Hana pause and listen. Masako runs to the window.)

Masako: I think it's them!

Hana: The Okas?

Masako: It's them! It's them!

(Hana stands and looks out. She removes her apron and puts away her sewing.)

Hana: Two of them. Emiko-san isn't with them. Let's go outside.

(Oka and Kiyoko, 14, enter. Oka is wearing his going-out clothes: a sweater, white shirt, dark pants, but no tie. Kiyoko walks behind him. She is short, chunky, broadchested and very self-conscious. Her hair is straight and banded into two shucks. She wears a conservative cotton dress, white socks and two-inch heels. Oka is proud. He struts in, his chest puffed out.)

Oka: Hello, hello . . . We're here. We made it! *(He pushes Kiyoko forward.)* This is my daughter, Kiyoko. *(To Kiyoko.)* Murata-san . . . remember I was talking about? My friends . . .

Kiyoko *(Barely audible, bowing deeply.)*: *Hajimemashite yoroshiku onegai shimasu . . .*

Hana *(Also bowing formally.)*: I hope your journey was pleasant.

Oka *(While the women are still bowing, he pushes Kiyoko toward Masako.)*: This is Masako-chan; I told you about her . . .

(Masako is shocked at Kiyoko's appearance. The girl she expected is already a woman. She stands with her mouth agape and withdraws noticeably. Hana rushes in to fill the awkwardness.)

Hana: Say hello, Masako. My goodness, where are your manners? *(She laughs apologetically.)* In this country they don't make much to-do about manners. *(She stands back to examine Kiyoko.)* My, my, I didn't picture you so grown up. My, my . . . Tell me, how was your trip?

Oka *(Proudly.)*: We just drove in from Los Angeles just this morning. We spent the night in San Pedro and the next two days we spent in Los Angeles . . . you know, Japanese town.

Hana: How nice!

Oka: Kiyoko was so excited. Twisting her head this way and that—couldn't see enough with her big eyes. *(He imitates her fondly.)* She's from the country, you know . . . just a big country girl. Got all excited about the Chinese dinner—we had a Chinese dinner. She never ate it before.

(Kiyoko covers her mouth and giggles.)

Hana: Chinese dinner!

Oka: Oh, yeah. Duck, pakkai, chow mein, seaweed soup . . . the works!

Hana: A feast!

Oka: Oh, yeah. Like a holiday. Two holidays. Two holidays in one.

Hana *(Pushes Masako forward.)*: Two holidays in one! Kiyoko-san, our Masako has been looking forward to meeting you.

Kiyoko *(Bowing again.)*: *Hajimemashite . . .*[12]

Hana: She's been thinking of all sorts of things she can do with you: sewing, cooking . . .

Masako: Oh, Mama.

(Kiyoko covers her mouth and giggles.)

Hana: It's true, Kiyoko-san. She's been looking forward to having a best friend.

(Kiyoko giggles again and Masako pulls away.)

Oka: Kiyoko, you shouldn't be so shy. The Muratas are my good friends and you should feel free with them. Ask anything, say anything . . . right?

Hana: Of course, of course. *(She is slightly annoyed with Masako.)* Masako, go in and start the tea. *(Masako enters the house.)* I'll call Papa. He's in the yard. Papa! Oka-san is here! *(To Kiyoko.)* Now tell me, how was your trip? Did you get seasick?

Kiyoko *(Bowing and nodding.)*: *Eh* ("yes"). A little . . .

Oka: Tell her. Tell her how sick you got.

(Kiyoko covers her mouth and giggles.)

---

[12] Polite greeting.

Hana: Oh, I know, I know. I was too. That was a long time ago. I'm sure things are improved now. Tell me about Japan . . . what is it like now? They say it's so changed . . . modern . . .

Oka: Kiyoko comes from the country . . . backwoods. Nothing changes much there from century to century.

Hana: Ah! That's true. That's why I love Japan. And you wanted to leave. It's unbelievable. To come here!

Oka: She always dreamed about it.

Hana: Well, it's not really that bad.

Oka: No, it's not that bad. Depends on what you make of it.

Hana: That's right. What you make of it. I was just telling Masako today . . .

(Murata enters. He rubs his hands to take off the soil and comes in grinning. He shakes Oka's hand.)

Murata: Oi, oi . . .

Oka: Yah . . . I'm back. This is my daughter.

Murata: No! She's beautiful!

Oka: Finally made it. Finally got her here.

Murata *(To Kiyoko.):* Your father hasn't stopped talking about you all summer.

Hana: And Masako too.

Kiyoko *(Bowing.): Hajimemashite . . .*

Murata *(Acknowledging with a short bow.):* Yah. How'd you like the trip?

Oka: I was just telling your wife—had a good time in Los Angeles. Had a couple of great dinners, took in the cinema—Japanese pictures, bought her some American clothes.

Hana: Oh, you bought that in Los Angeles.

Murata: Got a good price for your horse, eh? Lots of money, eh?

Oka: Nagata's a shrewd bargainer. Heh. It don't take much money to make her happy. She's a country girl.

Murata: That's all right. Country's all right. Country girl's the best.

Oka: Had trouble on the way back.

Murata: Yeah?

Oka: Fan belt broke.

Murata: That'll happen.

Oka: Lucky I was near a gasoline station. We were in the mountains. Waited in a restaurant while it was getting fixed.

Hana: Oh, that was good.

Oka: Guess they don't see Japanese much. Stare? Terrible! Took them a long time to wait on us. Dumb waitress practically threw the food at us. Kiyoko felt bad.

Hana: Ah! That's too bad . . . too bad. That's why I always pack a lunch when we take trips.

Murata: They'll spoil the day for you . . . those barbarians!

Oka: Terrible food too. Kiyoko couldn't swallow the dry bread and bologna.

Hana: That's the food they eat!

Murata: Let's go in . . . have a little wine. Mama, we got wine? This is a celebration.

Hana: I think so . . . a little . . . *(They enter the house talking. Masako has made the tea, and Hana begins to serve the wine.)* How is your mother? Was she happy to see you?

Kiyoko: Oh, she . . . yes . . .

Hana: I just know she was surprised to see you so grown up. Of course, you remember her from Japan, don't you?

Kiyoko *(Nodding.): Eh* ("yes"). I can barely remember. I was very young . . .

Hana: Of course. But you do, don't you?

Kiyoko: She was gone most of the time . . . at school in Tokyo. She was very pretty, I remember that.

Hana: She's still very pretty.

Kiyoko: *Eh.* She was always laughing. She was much younger then.

Hana: Oh now, it hasn't been that long ago.

(Masako leaves the room to go outside. The following dialogue continues muted as light goes dim in the house and focuses on Masako. Emiko enters, is drawn to the Murata window and listens.)

Oka: We stayed at an inn on East First Street. *Shizuokaya.* Whole inn filled with Shizuoka people . . . talking the old dialect. Thought I was in Japan again.

Murata: That right?

Oka: Felt good. Like I was in Japan again.

Hana *(To Kiyoko.):* Did you enjoy Los Angeles?

Kiyoko *(Nodding.): Eh.*

Oka: That's as close as I'll get to Japan.

Murata: *Mattaku na!* That's for sure.

(Outside Masako becomes aware of Emiko.)

Masako: Why don't you go in?

Emiko: Oh. Oh. Why don't you?

Masako: They're all grown-ups in there. I'm not grown up.

Emiko *(Softly.):* All grown-ups . . . Maybe I'm not either. *(Her mood changes.)* Masa-chan, do you have a boy friend?

Masako: I don't like boys. They don't like me.

Emiko: Oh, that will change. You will change. I was like that too.

Masako: Besides, there're none around here . . . Japanese boys . . . There are some at school, but they don't like girls.

Hana *(Calling from the kitchen.):* Masako . . .

(Masako doesn't answer.)

Emiko: Your mother is calling you.

Masako *(Answering her mother.): Nani?* ("What?")

Hana *(From the kitchen.):* Come inside now.

Emiko: You'll have a boy friend one day.

Masako: Not me.

Emiko: You'll fall in love one day. Someone will make the inside of you light up, and you'll know you're in love. *(She relives her own experience.)* Your life will change . . . grow beautiful. It's good, Masa-chan. And this feeling you'll remember the rest of your life . . . will come back to you . . . haunt you . . . keep you alive . . . five, ten years . . . no matter what happens . . . keep you alive.

Hana *(From the kitchen.):* Masako . . . come inside now.

(Masako turns aside to answer and Emiko slips away.)

Masako: What, Mama?

(Hana comes out.)

Hana: Come inside. Don't be so unsociable. Kiyoko wants to talk to you.

Masako *(Watching Emiko leave.):* She doesn't want to talk to me. You're only saying that.

Hana: What's the matter with you? Don't you want to make friends with her?

Masako: She's not my friend. She's your friend.

Hana: Don't be so silly. She's only fourteen.

Masako: Fifteen. They said fifteen. She's your friend. She's an old lady.

Hana: Don't say that.

Masako: I don't like her.

Hana: Shhh! Don't say that.

Masako: She doesn't like me either.

Hana: Ma-chan. Remember your promise to Mr. Oka? You're going to take her to school, teach her the language, teach her the ways of Americans.

Masako: She can do it herself. You did.

Hana: That's not nice, Ma-chan.

Masako: I don't like the way she laughs.

(She imitates Kiyoko holding her hand to her mouth and giggling and bowing.)

Hana: Oh, how awful! Stop that. That's the way the girls do in Japan. Maybe she doesn't like your ways either. That's only a difference in manners. What you're doing now is considered very bad manners. *(She changes tone.)* Ma-chan . . . just wait—when she learns to read and speak, you'll have so much to say to each other. Come on, be a good girl and come inside.

Masako: It's just old people in there, Mama. I don't want to go in.

(Hana calls Kiyoko away from the table and speaks confidentially to her.)

Hana: Kiyoko-san, please come here a minute. Maybe it's better for you to talk to Masako alone. *(Kiyoko leaves the table and walks to Hana outside.)* Masako has a lot of things to tell you about . . . what to expect in school and things . . .

Murata *(Calling from the table.):* Mama, put out something . . . chiles . . . for Oka-san.

(Hana leaves the two girls and enters the house. Kiyoko and Masako stand awkwardly, Kiyoko glancing shyly at Masako.)

Masako: Do you like it here?
Kiyoko *(Nodding.): Eh.*

(There's an uncomfortable pause.)

Masako: School will be starting next week . . .
Kiyoko *(Nodding.): Eh.*
Masako: Do you want to walk to school with me?
Kiyoko *(Nodding.):* Ah.

(Masako rolls her eyes and tries again.)

Masako: I leave at 7:30.
Kiyoko: Ah.

(There's a long pause. Masako finally gives up and moves off stage.)

Masako: I have to do something.

(Kiyoko watches her leave and uncertainly moves back to the house. Hana looks up at Kiyoko coming in alone, sighs, and quietly pulls out a chair for her.)

(Fade out.)

Scene 2

November night. Interior of the Murata house. Lamps are lit. The family is at the kitchen table. Hana sews, Masako does her homework, Murata reads the paper. They're dressed in warm robes and having tea. Outside thunder rolls in the distance and lightning flashes.

Hana: It'll be *ohigan* ("an autumn festival") soon.
Murata: Something to look forward to.
Hana: We will need sweet rice for *omochi* ("rice cakes").
Murata: I'll order it next time I go to town.
Hana *(To Masako.):* How is school? Getting a little harder?
Masako: Not that much. Sometimes the arithmetic is hard.
Hana: How is Kiyoko-san doing? Is she getting along all right?
Masako: She's good in arithmetic. She skipped a grade already.
Hana: Already? That's good news. Only November and she skipped a grade! At this rate she'll be through before you.
Masako: Well, she's older.
Murata: Sure, she's older, Mama.
Hana: Has she made any friends?
Masako: No. She follows me around all day. She understands okay, but she doesn't talk. She talks like, you know . . . she says "ranchi" for lunch and

"ranchi" for ranch too, and like that. Kids laugh and copy behind her back. It's hard to understand her.

Hana: You understand her, don't you?

Masako: I'm used to it. *(Murata smiles secretly.)*

Hana: You should tell the kids not to laugh; after all, she's trying. Maybe you should help her practice those words . . . show her what she's doing wrong.

Masako: I already do. Our teacher told me to do that.

Murata *(Looking up from his paper.):* You ought to help her all you can.

Hana: And remember when you started school you couldn't speak English either.

Masako: I help her.

(Murata rises and goes to the window. The night is cold. Lightning flashes and the wind whistles.)

Murata: Looks like a storm coming up. Hope we don't have a freeze.

Hana: If it freezes, we'll have another bad year. Maybe we ought to start the smudge pots.

Murata *(Listening.):* It's starting to rain. Nothing to do now but pray.

Hana: If praying is the answer, we'd be in Japan now . . . rich.

Murata *(Wryly.):* We're not dead yet. We still have a chance. *(Hana glares at this small joke.)* Guess I'll turn in.

Hana: Go to bed . . . go to bed. I'll sit up and worry.

Murata: If worrying was the answer, we'd be around the world twice and in Japan. Come on, Mama. Let's go to bed. It's too cold tonight to be mad. *(There's an urgent knock on the door. The family react to it.) Dare da!* ("Who is it!") *(Murata goes to the door and pauses.)* Who is it!

Kiyoko *(Weakly.):* It's me . . . help me . . .

(Murata opens the door and Kiyoko enters. She's dressed in a kimono with a shawl thrown over. Her legs are bare except for a pair of straw zori. Her hair is stringy from the rain and she trembles from the cold.)

Murata: My God! Kiyoko-san! What's the matter?

Hana: Kiyoko-san! What is it?

Murata: What happened?

Kiyoko *(Gasping.):* They're fighting . . . they're fighting.

Murata: Ah . . . don't worry . . . those things happen. No cause to worry. Mama, make tea for her. Sit down and catch your breath. I'll take you home when you're ready.

Hana: Papa, I'll take care of it.

Murata: Let me know when you're ready to go home.

Hana: It must be freezing out there. Try to get warm. Try to calm yourself.

Murata: Kiyoko-san . . . don't worry.

(Hana waves Masako and Murata off. Murata leaves. Masako goes to her bed in the kitchen.)

Hana: Papa, I'll take care of it.

Kiyoko *(Looking at Murata's retreating form.):* I came to ask your help.

Hana: You ran down here without a lantern? You could have fallen and hurt yourself.

Kiyoko: I don't care . . . I don't care.

Hana: You don't know, Kiyoko-san. It's treacherous out there . . . snakes, spiders . . .

Kiyoko: I must go back . . . I . . . I . . . you . . . please come with me.

Hana: First, first, we must get you warm . . . Drink your tea.

Kiyoko: But they might kill each other. They're fighting like animals. Help me stop them!

(Hana goes to the stove to warm a pot of soup.)

Hana: I cannot interfere in a family quarrel.

Kiyoko: It's not a quarrel . . . it's a . . .

Hana: That's all it is. A family squabble. You'll see. Tomorrow . . .

(Kiyoko rises and puts her hand on Hana's arm.)

Kiyoko: Not just a squabble . . . please! *(She starts toward the door but Hana restrains her.)*

Hana: Now listen. Listen to me, Kiyoko-san. I've known your father and mother a little while now. I suspect it's been like this for years. Every family has some kind of trouble.

Kiyoko: Not like this . . . not like this.

Hana: Some have it better—some worse. When you get married, you'll understand. Don't worry. Nothing will happen. *(She takes a towel from the wall and dries Kiyoko's hair.)* You're chilled to the bone. You'll catch your death . . .

Kiyoko: I don't care . . . I want to die.

Hana: Don't be silly. It's not that bad.

Kiyoko: They started drinking early in the afternoon. They make some kind of brew and hide it somewhere in the desert.

Hana: It's illegal to make it. That's why they hide it. That home brew is poison to the body . . . and the mind too.

Kiyoko: It makes them crazy. They drink it all the time and quarrel constantly. I was in the other room studying. I try so hard to keep up with school.

Hana: We were talking about you just this evening. Masako says you're doing so well . . . you skipped a grade?

Kiyoko: It's hard . . . hard . . . I'm too old for the class and the children . . . *(She remembers all her problems and starts to cry again.)*

Hana: It's always hard in a new country.

Kiyoko: They were bickering and quarreling all afternoon. Then something happened. All of a sudden I saw them on the floor . . . hitting and . . . and . . . He was hitting her in the stomach, the face . . . I tried to stop them, but they were so . . . drunk.

Hana: There, there . . . It's probably all over now.

Kiyoko: Why does it happen like this? Nothing is right. Everywhere I go . . . Masa-chan is so lucky. I wish my life was like hers. I can hardly remember my real mother.

Hana: Emiko-san is almost a real mother to you. She's blood kin.

Kiyoko: She hates me. She never speaks to me. She's so cold. I want to love her but she won't let me. She hates me.

Hana: I don't think that's true, Kiyoko-san.

Kiyoko: I know it's true.

Hana: No. I don't think you have anything to do with it. It's this place. She hates it. This place is so lonely and alien.

Kiyoko: Then why didn't she go back? Why did they stay here?

Hana: You don't know. It's not so simple. Sometimes I think . . .

Kiyoko: Then why don't they make the best of it here? Like you?

Hana: That isn't easy either. Believe me. *(She goes to the stove to stir the soup.)* Sometimes . . . sometimes the longing for homeland fills me with despair. Will I never return again? Will I never see my mother, my father, my sisters again? But what can one do? There are responsibilities here . . . children . . . *(She draws a sharp breath.)* And another day passes . . . another month . . . another year. Eventually everything passes. *(She takes the soup to Kiyoko.)* Did you have supper tonight?

Kiyoko *(Bowing gratefully.):* Ah. When my . . . my aunt gets like this, she doesn't cook. No one eats. I don't get hungry anymore.

Hana: Cook for yourself. It's important to keep your health.

Kiyoko: I left Japan for a better life here . . .

Hana: It isn't easy for you, is it? But you must remember your filial duty.

Kiyoko: It's so hard.

Hana: But you can make the best of it here, Kiyoko-san. And take care of yourself. You owe that to yourself. Eat. Keep well. It'll be better, you'll see. And sometimes it'll seem worse. But you'll survive. We do, you know . . . we do . . . *(She looks around.)* It's getting late.

Kiyoko *(Apprehensively.):* I don't want to go back.

Hana: You can sleep with Masako tonight. Tomorrow you'll go back. And you'll remember what I told you. *(She puts her arms around Kiyoko, who is overcome with self-pity and begins to weep quietly.)* Life is never easy, Kiyoko-san. Endure. Endure. Soon you'll be marrying and going away. Things will not always be this way. And you'll look back on this . . . this night and you'll . . .

(There is a rap on the door. Hana exchanges glances with Kiyoko and goes to answer it. She opens it a crack. Oka has come looking for Kiyoko. He's dressed in an overcoat and holds a wet newspaper over his head.)

Oka: Ah! I'm sorry to bother you so late at night . . . the fact is . . .

Hana: Oka-san . . .

Oka *(Jovially.):* Good evening, good evening . . . *(He sees Kiyoko.)* Ah . . . there you are . . . Did you have a nice visit?

Hana *(Irritated.)*: Yes, she's here.

Oka *(Still cheerful.)*: Thought she might be. Ready to come home now?

Hana: She came in the rain.

Oka *(Ignoring Hana's tone.)*: That's foolish of you, Kiyoko. You might catch cold.

Hana: She was frightened by your quarreling. She came for help.

Oka *(Laughing with embarrassment.)*: Oh! Kiyoko, that's nothing to worry about. It's just we had some disagreement . . .

Hana: That's what I told her, but she was frightened all the same.

Oka: Children are . . .

Hana: Not children, Oka-san. Kiyoko. Kiyoko was terrified. I think that was a terrible thing to do to her.

Oka *(Rubbing his head.)*: Oh, I . . . I . . .

Hana: If you had seen her a few minutes ago . . . hysterical . . . shaking . . . crying . . . wet and cold to the bone . . . out of her mind with worry.

Oka *(Rubbing his head.)*: Oh . . . I . . . don't know what she was so worried about.

Hana: You. You and Emiko fighting like you were going to kill each other.

Oka *(There's nothing more to hide. He lowers his head in penitence.)*: Aaaaaachhhhhhh . . .

Hana: I know I shouldn't tell you this, but there're one or two things I have to say: You sent for Kiyoko-san and now she's here. You said yourself she had a bad time in Japan, and now she's having a worse time. It isn't easy for her in a strange new country; the least you can do is try to keep her from worrying . . . especially about yourselves. I think it's terrible what you're doing to her . . . terrible!

Oka *(Bowing in deep humility.)*: I am ashamed . . .

Hana: I think she deserves better. I think you should think about that.

Oka *(Still in his bow.)*: I thank you for this reminder. It will never happen again. I promise.

Hana: I don't need that promise. Make it to Kiyoko-san.

Oka *(To Kiyoko.)*: Come with Papa now. He did a bad thing. He'll be a good Papa from now. We won't worry his little girl again. All right? All right?

(They move to the door.)

Kiyoko: Thank you so much. *(She takes Murata's robe and tries to return it.)*

Oka: Madam. I thank you again.

Hana *(To Kiyoko.)*: That's all right. You can bring it back tomorrow. *(Aside to Kiyoko.)* Remember . . . remember what we talked about. *(Loudly.)* Goodnight, Oka-san.

(They leave. Hana goes to Masako, who lies on the bed. She covers her. Murata appears from the bedroom. He's heard it all. He and Hana exchange a glance and together they retire to their room.)

Fade out.

Scene 3

The next morning. The Murata house and yard. Hana and Murata have already left the house to examine the rain damage in the fields. Masako prepares to go to school. She puts on a coat and picks up her books and lunch bag. Meanwhile, Kiyoko slips quietly into the yard. She wears a coat and carries Murata's robe and sets it on the outside bench. Masako walks out and is surprised to see Kiyoko.

Masako: Hi. I thought you'd be . . . sick today.
Kiyoko: Oh. I woke up late.
Masako *(Scrutinizing Kiyoko's face.):* Your eyes are red.
Kiyoko *(Averting her eyes.):* Oh. I . . . got . . . sand in it. Yes.
Masako: Do you want to use eye drops? We have eye drops in the house.
Kiyoko: Oh . . . no. That's all right.
Masako: That's what you call bloodshot.
Kiyoko: Oh.
Masako: My father gets it a lot. When he drinks too much.
Kiyoko: Oh . . .

(Masako notices Kiyoko doesn't have her lunch.)

Masako: Where's your lunch bag?
Kiyoko: I . . . forgot it.
Masako: Did you make your lunch today?
Kiyoko: Yes. Yes, I did. But I forgot it.
Masako: Do you want to go back and get it?
Kiyoko: No, that's all right. *(They are silent for a while.)* We'll be late.
Masako: Do you want to practice your words?
Kiyoko *(Thoughtfully.):* Oh . . .
Masako: Say, "My."
Kiyoko: My?
Masako: Eyes . . .
Kiyoko: Eyes.
Masako: Are . . .
Kiyoko: Are.
Masako: Red.
Kiyoko: Red.
Masako: Your eyes are red. *(Kiyoko doesn't repeat it.)* I . . . *(Kiyoko doesn't cooperate.)* Say, "I."
Kiyoko: I.
Masako: Got . . .
Kiyoko: Got.
Masako: Sand . . . *(Kiyoko balks.)* Say, "I."
Kiyoko *(Sighing.):* I.
Masako: Reft . . .
Kiyoko: Reft.
Masako: My . . .

Kiyoko: My.

Masako: Runch . . .

Kiyoko: Run . . . Lunch. *(She stops.)* Masako-san, you are mean. You are hurting me.

Masako: It's a joke! I was just trying to make you laugh!

Kiyoko: I cannot laugh today.

Masako: Sure you can. You can laugh. Laugh! Like this! *(She makes a hearty laugh.)*

Kiyoko: I cannot laugh when you make fun of me.

Masako: Okay, I'm sorry. We'll practice some other words then, okay? *(Kiyoko doesn't answer.)* Say, "Okay."

Kiyoko *(Reluctantly.):* Okay . . .

Masako: Okay, then . . . um . . . um . . . *(She still teases and talks rapidly.)* Say . . . um . . . "She sells sea shells on the sea shore." *(Kiyoko turns away indignantly.)* Aw, come on, Kiyoko! It's just a joke. Laugh!

Kiyoko *(Imitating sarcastically.):* Ha-ha-ha! Now you say, *"Kono kyaku wa yoku kaki ku kyaku da!"*

Masako: Sure! I can say it! Kono kyaku waki ku kyoku kaku . . .

Kiyoko: That's not right.

Masako: Koki kuki kya . . .

Kiyoko: No.

Masako: Okay, then. You say, "Sea sells she shells . . . shu . . . sss . . ."

(They both laugh, Kiyoko with her hands over her mouth.)

Masako *(Taking Kiyoko's hands from her mouth.):* Not like that! Like this! *(She gives a big belly laugh.)*

Kiyoko: Like this? *((She imitates Masako.)*

Masako: Yeah, that's right! You're not mad anymore?

Kiyoko: I'm not mad anymore.

Masako: Okay. You can share my lunch today because we're . . .

Kiyoko: "Flends?"

(Masako looks at Kiyoko, they giggle and move on. Hana and Murata come in from assessing the storm's damage. They are dressed warmly. Hana is depressed. Murata tries hard to be cheerful.)

Murata: It's not so bad, Mama.

Hana: Half the ranch is flooded . . . at least half.

Murata: No-no. A quarter, maybe. It's sunny today . . . it'll dry.

Hana: The seedlings will rot.

Murata: No, no. It'll dry. It's all right—better than I expected.

Hana: If we have another bad year, no one will lend us money for the next crop.

Murata: Don't worry. If it doesn't drain by tomorrow, I'll replant the worst places. We still have some seed left. Yeah, I'll replant . . .

Hana: More work.

Murata: Don't worry, Mama. It'll be all right.

Hana *(Quietly.):* Papa, where will it end? Will we always be like this—always at the mercy of the weather—prices—always at the mercy of the Gods?

Murata *(Patting Hana's back.):* Things will change. Wait and see. We'll be back in Japan by . . . in two years . . . guarantee . . . Maybe sooner.

Hana *(Dubiously.):* Two years . . .

Murata *(Finds the robe on the bench.):* Ah, look, Mama. Kiyoko-san brought back my robe.

Hana *(Sighing.):* Kiyoko-san . . . poor Kiyoko-san . . . and Emiko-san.

Murata: Ah, Mama. We're lucky. We're lucky, Mama.

(Hana smiles sadly at Murata.)

(Fade out.)

Scene 4

*The following spring, afternoon. Exterior of the Oka house. Oka is dressed to go out. He wears a sweater, long-sleeved white shirt, dark pants, no tie. He puts his foot on the bench to wipe off his shoe with the palm of his hand. He straightens his sleeve, removes a bit of lint and runs his fingers through his hair. He hums under his breath. Kiyoko comes from the house. Her hair is frizzled with a permanent wave, she wears a gaudy new dress and a pair of new shoes. She carries a movie magazine—*Photoplay *or* Modern Screen.

Oka *(Appreciatively.):* Pretty. Pretty.

Kiyoko *(Turning for him.):* It's not too *hadeh?*[13] I feel strange in colors.

Oka: Oh no. Young girls should wear bright colors. There's time enough to wear gray when you get old. Old lady colors. *(Kiyoko giggles.)* Sure you want to go to the picture show? It's such a nice day . . . shame to waste in a dark hall.

Kiyoko: Where else can we go?

Oka: We can go to the Muratas.

Kiyoko: All dressed up?

Oka: Or Nagatas. I'll show him what I got for my horse.

Kiyoko *(Laughing.):* Oh, I love the pictures.

Oka: We don't have many nice spring days like this. Here the season is short. Summer comes in like a dragon . . . right behind . . . breathing fire . . . like a dragon. You don't know the summers here. They'll scare you. *(He tousles Kiyoko's hair and pulls a lock of it. It springs back. He shakes his head in wonder.)* Goddamn. Curly hair. Never thought curly hair could make you so happy.

Kiyoko *(Giggling.):* All the American girls have curly hair.

Oka: Your friend. Masako like it?

Kiyoko *(Nodding.):* She says her mother will never let her get a permanent wave.

---

[13] Gaudy.

Oka: She said that, eh? Bet she's wanting one.

Kiyoko: I don't know about that.

Oka: Bet she's wanting some of your pretty dresses too.

Kiyoko: Her mother makes all her clothes.

Oka: Buying is just as good. Buying is better. No trouble that way.

Kiyoko: Masako's not so interested in clothes. She loves the pictures, but her mother won't let her go. Some day, can we take Masako with us?

Oka: If her mother lets her come. Her mother's got a mind of her own . . . a stiff back.

Kiyoko: But she's nice.

Oka *(Dubiously.)*: Oh, yeah. Can't be perfect, I guess. Kiyoko, after the harvest I'll have money and I'll buy you the prettiest dress in town. I'm going to be lucky this year. I feel it.

Kiyoko: You're already too good to me . . . dresses, shoes, permanent wave . . . movies . . .

Oka: That's nothing. After the harvest, just wait . . .

Kiyoko: Magazines . . . You do enough. I'm happy already.

Oka: You make me happy too, Kiyoko. You make me feel good . . . like a man again . . . *(That statement bothers him.)* One day you're going to make a young man happy. *(Kiyoko giggles.)* Someday we going to move from here.

Kiyoko: But we have good friends here, Papa.

Oka: Next year our lease will be up and we got to move.

Kiyoko: The ranch is not ours?

Oka: No. In America, Japanese cannot own land. We lease and move every two, three years. Next year we going to go someplace where there's young fellows. There's none good enough for you here. *(He watches Kiyoko giggle.)* Yeah. You going to make a good wife. Already a good cook. I like your cooking.

Kiyoko *(A little embarrassed.)*: Shall we go now?

Oka: Yeah. Put the magazine away.

Kiyoko: I want to take it with me.

Oka: Take it with you?

Kiyoko: Last time, after we came back, I found all my magazines torn in half.

Oka *(Looking toward the house.)*: Torn?

Kiyoko: This is the only one I have left.

Oka *(Not wanting to deal with it.)*: All right. All right.

(The two prepare to leave when the door opens. Emiko stands there, her hair is unkempt and she looks wild. She holds an empty can in one hand, the lid in the other.)

Emiko: Where is it?

(Oka tries to make a hasty departure.)

Kiyoko: Where is what?

(Oka pushes Kiyoko ahead of him, still trying to make a getaway.)

Emiko: Where is it? Where is it? What did you do with it? *(Emiko moves toward Oka. He can't ignore her and he stops.)*

Oka *(With false unconcern to Kiyoko.):* Why don't you walk on ahead to the Muratas?

Kiyoko: We're not going to the pictures?

Oka: We'll go. First you walk to the Muratas. Show them your new dress. I'll meet you there.

(Kiyoko picks up a small package and exits. Oka sighs and shakes his head.)

Emiko *(Shaking the can.):* Where is it? What did you do with it?

Oka *(Feigning surprise.):* With what?

Emiko: You know what. You stole it. You stole my money.

Oka: *Your* money?

Emiko: I've been saving that money.

Oka: Yeah? Well, where'd you get it? Where'd you get it, eh? You stole it from me! Dollar by dollar . . . You stole it from me! Out of my pocket!

Emiko: I saved it!

Oka: From my pocket!

Emiko: It's mine! I saved for a long time . . . Some of it I brought from Japan.

Oka: *Bakayuna!*[14] What'd you bring from Japan? Nothing but some useless kimonos. *(Oka starts to leave but Emiko hangs on to him.)*

Emiko: Give back my money! Thief!

Oka *(Swings around and balls his fists but doesn't strike.):* Goddamn! Get off me!

Emiko *(Now pleading.):* Please give it back . . . please . . . please . . . *(She starts to stroke him. Oka pulls her hands away and pushes her from him.) Oni!*

Oka *(Seething.): Oni?* What does that make you? *Oni baba?* Yeah, that's what you are . . . a devil!

Emiko: It's mine! Give it back . . .

Oka: The hell! You think you can live off me and steal my money too? How stupid you think I am?

Emiko *(Tearfully.):* But I've paid . . . I've paid . . .

Oka: With what?

Emiko: You know I've paid.

Oka *(Scoffing.):* You call that paying?

Emiko: What did you do with it?

Oka: I don't have it.

Emiko: It's gone? It's gone?

Oka: Yeah! It's gone. I spent it. The hell! Every last cent.

Emiko: The new clothes . . . the curls . . . restaurants . . . pictures . . . shoes . . . My money . . . my going-home money . . .

Oka: You through?

Emiko: What will I do? What will . . .

---

[14] Stupid woman.

Oka: I don't care what you do. Walk. Use your feet. Swim to Japan. I don't care. I give you no more than you gave me. Now I don't want anything. I don't care what you do. *(He walks away.)*

(Emiko still holds the empty can. Off stage we hear Oka's car door slam and the sound of his old car starting off. Accustomed to crying alone, she doesn't utter a sound. Her shoulders begin to shake, her dry soundless sobs turn to a silent laugh. She wipes the dust gently from the can as though comforting a friend. Her movements become sensuous, her hands move on to her own body, around her throat, over her breasts, to her hips, caressing, soothing, reminding her of her lover's hands.)

(Fade out.)

Scene 5

Same day, late afternoon. Exterior of the Murata house. The light is soft. Hana is sweeping the yard; Masako hangs a glass wind chime on the exposed wall.

Hana *(Directing Masako.):* There . . . there. That's a good place.

Masako: Here?

Hana *(Nodding.):* It must catch the slightest breeze. *(Sighing and listening.)* It brings back so much . . . That's the reason I never hung one before. I guess it doesn't matter much any more . . .

Masako: I thought you liked to think about Japan.

Hana *(Laughing sadly.):* I didn't want to hear that sound so often . . . get too used to it. Sometimes you hear something too often, after a while you don't hear it anymore . . . I didn't want that to happen. The same thing happens to feelings too, I guess. After a while you don't feel any more. You're too young to understand that yet.

Masako: I understand, Mama.

Hana: Wasn't it nice of Kiyoko-san to give us the *furin?*

Masako: I love it. I don't know anything about Japan, but it makes me feel something too.

Hana: Maybe someday when you're grown up, gone away, you'll hear it and remember yourself as this little girl . . . remember this old house, the ranch, and . . . your old mama . . .

Masako: That's kind of scary.

(Emiko enters unsteadily. She carries a bundle wrapped in a colorful scarf "furoshiki." In the packages are two beautiful kimonos.)

Hana: Emiko-san! What a pleasant surprise! Please sit down. We were just hanging the *furin.* It was so sweet of Kiyoko-san to give it to Masako. She loves it.

(Emiko looks mildly interested. She acts as normal as she can throughout the scene, but at times drops her facade, revealing her desperation.)

Emiko: Thank you. *(She sets her bundle on the bench but keeps her hand on it.)*

Hana: Your family was here earlier. *(Emiko smiles vaguely.)* On their way to the pictures, I think. *(To Masako.)* Make tea for us, Ma-chan.

Emiko: Please don't . . .

Hana: Kiyoko-san was looking so nice—her hair all curly . . . Of course, in our day, straight black hair was desirable. Of course, times change.

Emiko: Yes.

Hana: But she did look fine. My, my, a colorful new dress, new shoes, a permanent wave—looked like a regular American girl. Did you choose her dress?

Emiko: No . . . I didn't go.

Hana: You know, I didn't think so. Very pretty, though. I liked it very much. Of course, I sew all Masako's clothes. It saves money. It'll be nice for you to make things for Kiyoko-san too. She'd be so pleased. I know she'd be pleased . . . *(While Hana talks, Emiko plucks nervously at her package. She waits for Hana to stop talking.)* Emiko-san, is everything all right?

Emiko *(Smiling nervously.):* Yes.

Hana: Masako, please go make tea for us. See if there aren't any more of those crackers left. Or did you finish them? *(To Emiko.)* We can't keep anything in this house. She eats everything as soon as Papa brings it home. You'd never know it, she's so skinny. We never have anything left for company.

Masako: We hardly ever have company anyway.

(Hana gives her daughter a strong look, and Masako goes into the house. Emiko is lost in her own thoughts. She strokes her package.)

Hana: Is there something you . . . I can help you with? *(Very gently.)* Emiko-san?

Emiko *(Suddenly frightened.):* Oh no. I was thinking . . . Now that . . . now that . . . Masa-chan is growing up . . . older . . .

Hana *(Relieved.):* Oh, yes. She's growing fast.

Emiko: I was thinking . . . *(She stops, puts the package on her lap and is lost again.)*

Hana: Yes, she *is* growing. Time goes so fast. I think she'll be taller than me soon. *(She laughs weakly, stops and looks puzzled.)*

Emiko: Yes.

(Emiko's depression pervades the atmosphere. Hana is affected by it. The two women sit in silence. A small breeze moves the wind chimes. At the moment light grows dim on the two lonely figures. Masako comes from the house with a tray of tea. The light returns to normal again.)

Hana *(Gently.):* You're a good girl.

(Masako looks first to Emiko then to her mother. She sets the tray on the bench and stands near Emiko, who seems to notice her for the first time.)

Emiko: How are you?

(Hana pours the tea and serves her.)

Hana: Emiko-san, is there something I can do for you?

Emiko: There's . . . I was . . . I . . . Masa-chan will be a young lady soon . . .

Hana: Oh, well, now I don't know about "lady."

Emiko: Maybe she would like a nice . . . nice . . . *(She unwraps her package.)* I have kimonos . . . I wore in Japan for dancing . . . maybe she can . . . if you like, I mean. They'll be nice on her . . . she's so slim . . .

(Emiko shakes out a robe. Hana and Masako are impressed.)

Hana: Ohhhh! Beautiful!

Masako: Oh, Mama! Pretty! *(Hana and Masako finger the material.)* Gold threads, Mama.

Hana: Brocade!

Emiko: Maybe Masa-chan would like them. I mean for her school programs . . . Japanese school . . .

Hana: Oh, no! Too good for country. People will be envious of us . . . wonder where we got them.

Emiko: I mean for festivals . . . *Obon, Hana Matsuri* . . .

Hana: Oh, but you have Kiyoko-san now. You should give them to her. Has she seen them?

Emiko: Oh . . . no . . .

Hana: She'll love them. You should give them to her . . . not our Masako.

Emiko: I thought . . . I mean I was thinking of . . . if you could give me a little . . . if you could pay . . . manage to give me something for . . .

Hana: But these gowns, Emiko-san—they're worth hundreds.

Emiko: I know, but I'm not asking for that. Whatever you can give . . . only as much as you can give.

Masako: Mama?

Hana: Masako, Papa doesn't have that kind of money.

Emiko: Anything you can give . . . anything . . .

Masako: Ask Papa.

Hana: There's no use asking. I know he can't afford it.

Emiko *(Looking at Masako.)*: A little at a time.

Masako: Mama?

Hana *(Firmly.)*: No, Masako. This is a luxury. *(Hana folds the gowns and puts them away. Masako is disappointed. Emiko is devastated. Hana sees this and tries to find some way to help.)* Emiko-san, I hope you understand . . . *(Emiko is silent trying to gather her resources.)* I know you can sell them and get the full price somewhere. Let's see . . . a family with a lot of growing daughters . . . someone who did well last year . . . Nagatas have no girls . . . Umedas have girls but no money . . . Well, let's see . . . Maybe not here in this country town. Ah . . . You can take them to the city, Los Angeles, and sell them to a store . . . or Terminal Island . . . lots of wealthy fishermen there. Yes, that would be the place. Why, it's no problem, Emiko-san. Have your husband take them there. I know you'll get your money. He'll find a buyer. I know he will.

Emiko: Yes.

(Emiko finishes folding and ties the scarf. She sits quietly.)

Hana: Please have your tea. I'm sorry . . . I really would like to take them for Masako but it just isn't possible. You understand, don't you? *(Emiko nods.)* Please don't feel so . . . so bad. It's not really a matter of life or death, is it? Emiko-san?

(Emiko nods again. Hana sips her tea.)

Masako: Mama? If you could ask Papa . . .

Hana: Oh, the tea is cold. Masako could you heat the kettle?

Emiko: No more. I must be going. *(She picks up her package and rises slowly.)*

Hana *(Looking helpless.):* So soon? Emiko-san, please stay. *(Emiko starts to go.)* Masako will walk with you. *(She pushes Masako forward.)*

Emiko: It's not far.

Hana: Emiko-san? You'll be all right?

Emiko: Yes . . . yes . . . yes . . .

Hana *(Calling as Emiko exits.):* I'm sorry, Emiko-san.

Emiko: Yes . . .

(Masako and Hana watch as Emiko leaves. The light grows dim as though a cloud passed over. Emiko exits. Hana strokes Masako's hair.)

Hana: Your hair is so black and straight . . . nice . . .

(They stand close. The wind chimes tinkle; light grows dim. Light returns to normal. Murata enters. He sees this tableau of mother and child and is puzzled.)

Murata: What's going on here?

(The two women part.)

Hana: Oh . . . nothing . . . nothing . . .

Masako: Mrs. Oka was here. She had two kimo- . . .

Hana *(Putting her hand on Masako's shoulder.):* It was nothing . . .

Murata: Eh? What'd she want?

Hana: Later, Papa. Right now, I'd better fix supper.

Murata *(Looking at the sky.):* Strange how that sun comes and goes. Maybe I didn't need to irrigate—looks like rain. *(He remembers and is exasperated.)* Ach! I forgot to shut the water.

Masako: I'll do it, Papa.

Hana: Masako, that gate's too heavy for you.

Murata: She can handle it. Take out the pin and let the gate fall all the way down. All the way. And put the pin back. Don't forget to put the pin back.

Hana: And be careful. Don't fall in the canal.

(Masako leaves.)

Murata: What's the matter with that girl?
Hana: Nothing. Why?
Murata: Usually have to beg her to do . . .
Hana: She's growing up.
Murata: Must be that time of the month.
Hana: Oh, Papa, she's too young for that yet.
Murata *(Genially as they enter the house.):* Got to start some time. Looks like I'll be out-numbered soon. I'm out-numbered already.

(Hana glances at him and quietly sets about preparations for supper. Murata removes his shirt and sits at the table with a paper. Light fades slowly.)

(Fade out.)

Scene 6

Same evening. Exterior, desert. There is at least one shrub. Masako appears, walking slowly. From a distance we hear Emiko singing the song "And the Soul Shall Dance." Masako looks around, sees the shrub and crouches under it. Emiko appears. She's dressed in her beautiful kimono tied loosely at her waist. She carries a branch of sage. Her hair is loose.

Emiko: *Akai kuchibiru / Kappu ni yosete / Aoi sake nomya / Kokoro ga odoru . . . Kurai yoru no yume / Setsu nasa yo . . .*

(She breaks into a dance, laughs mysteriously, turns round and round, acting out a fantasy. Masako stirs uncomfortably. Emiko senses a presence. She stops, drops her branch and walks off stage singing as she goes.)

Emiko: *Aoi sake nomya / Yume mo odoru . . .*

(Masako watches as Emiko leaves. She rises slowly and picks up the branch Emiko has left. She looks at the branch, moves forward a step and looks off to the point where Emiko disappeared. Light slowly fades until only the image of Masako's face remains etched in the mind.)

(Fade out.)

Kokoro Ga Odoru

Akai kuchibiru
Kappu ni yosete
Aoi sake nomya
Kokoro ga odoru

Kurai yoru no yume
Setsu nasa yo
Aoi sake nomya
Yume mo odoru

And the Soul Shall Dance

Red lips
Press against a glass
Drink the green wine
And the soul shall dance

Dark night dreams
Are unbearable
Drink the green wine
And the dreams will dance

Asa no munashisa
Yume wo chirasu
Sora to kokoro wa
Sake shidai

Futari wakare no
Samishisa yo
Hitori sake nomya
Kokoro ga odoru

Morning's reality
Scatter the dreams
Sky and soul
Depend on the wine

The loneliness of
The two apart
Drink the wine alone
And the soul shall dance

LYRICS BY WAKAKO YAMAUCHI

Kago No Tori

Aitasa, mita sa ni
Kowa sa wo wasure
Kurai yomichi wo
Tada hitori

Aini kita no ni
Naze dete awan?
Boku no yobu koe
Wasureta ka?

Anata no yobu koe
Wasure ma senu ga
Deru ni derareru
Kago no tori

The Caged Bird

(She)
In the desire to meet her
And the wish to see her
He forgets his fear and
Walks the dark streets alone.

(He)
Though I've come to tryst
Why do you not come out?
My voice calling you—
Have you forgotten it?

(She)
Your voice calling me
I have not forgotten, but
To leave, to be able to leave—
No choice for the caged bird.

POPULAR SONG

Explorations of the Text

1. Explain the burning of the bathhouse. How does this event function in the play? What are its multiple meanings?
2. Contrast the two marriages. What strengths do you identify? What difficulties become apparent? Find specific scenes to support your conclusions.
3. Consider the characters' reactions to Japan. Who wishes to assimilate? Who does not?
4. Describe the two girls. What is Kiyoko's relationship to Oka, to Masako? What is Oka's attitude toward Kiyoko?
5. Why is alcohol so prominent in the play? What are the consequences?
6. Examine the last scene in *And the Soul Shall Dance.* What has happened to Emiko? Trace the course of her sadness; begin with her lost

love and her desire to return to Japan. Why does Oka take her money? Why does Emiko dance at the end? How do you interpret the dance? What is the impact on Masako?

7. Explain the poems at the end and the title. Focus on the themes of the drama.
8. What are the roles of men and of women in the play? Does anyone break free?
9. What do you learn about the lives of Japanese farmers in the United States in the 1930s? Does anyone experience rootedness or sense of place?
10. Compare the marriages in this play with the relationships in works by Joyce, Gilman, Glaspell, and Ndebele.

The Reading/Writing Connection

1. Yamauchi created this play from a short story with the same title. Rewrite some part of this drama in another genre.
2. "Think" Topic: Write a one-paragraph analysis of one of the characters in *And the Soul Shall Dance.*
3. Write a monologue in the voice of one of the characters.

Ideas for Writing

1. Choose a central scene in this drama; explore character, conflict, dialogue, theme, language, and/or dramatic effect. Evaluate the success of the scene.
2. Write about this drama as an initiation for Masako.
3. Create a character analysis of either Emiko or Masako.

Professions for Women

Virginia Woolf

Virginia Woolf (1882–1941) was born in London. Largely self-educated, Woolf published her first novel, The Voyage Out, *in 1915. She achieved fame with her experimental novels, which include* Mrs. Dalloway *(1925),* To the Lighthouse *(1927), and* The Waves *(1931), and with her essays, which include shorter reviews and critical essays collected in* The Common Reader *(1925) and* The Second Common Reader *(1932) and longer essays concerned with the position of women:* A Room of One's Own *(1929) and* Three Guineas *(1938). With her husband, Leonard, Woolf founded the Hogarth Press in 1917, which published many of the leading writers of the time. Her posthumously published* Letters *(1975–80) and* Diary *(1977–84) give further evidence of her genius.*

1942

1 When your secretary invited me to come here, she told me that your Society is concerned with the employment of women and she suggested that I might tell you something about my own professional experiences. It is true I am a woman; it is true I am employed; but what professional experiences have I had? it is difficult to say. My profession is literature; and in that profession there are fewer experiences for women than in any other, with the exception of the stage—fewer, I mean, that are peculiar to women. For the road was cut many years ago—by Fanny Burney, by Aphra Behn, by Harriet Martineau, by Jane Austen, by George Eliot[1]—many famous women, and many more unknown and forgotten, have been before me, making the path smooth, and regulating my steps. Thus, when I came to write, there were very few material obstacles in my way. Writing was a reputable and harmless occupation. The family peace was not broken by the scratching of a pen. No demand was made upon the family purse. For ten and sixpence one can buy paper enough to write all the plays of Shakespeare—if one has a mind that way. Pianos and models, Paris, Vienna and Berlin, masters and mistresses, are not needed by a writer. The cheapness of writing paper is, of course, the reason why women have succeeded as writers before they have succeeded in the other professions.

2 But to tell you my story—it is a simple one. You have only got to figure to yourselves a girl in a bedroom with a pen in her hand. She had only to move that pen from left to right—from ten o'clock to one. Then it occurred to her to do what is simple and cheap enough after all—to slip a few of those pages into an envelope, fix a penny stamp in the corner, and drop the envelope into the red box at the corner. It was thus that I became a journalist; and my effort was rewarded on the first day of the following month—a very glorious day it was for me—by a letter from an editor containing a cheque for one pound ten shillings and sixpence. But to show you how little I deserve to be called a professional woman, how little I know of the struggles and difficulties of such lives, I have to admit that instead of spending that sum upon bread and butter, rent, shoes and stockings, or butcher's bills, I went out and bought a cat—a beautiful cat, a Persian cat, which very soon involved me in bitter disputes with my neighbours.

3 What could be easier than to write articles and to buy Persian cats with the profits? But wait a moment. Articles have to be about something. Mine, I seem to remember, was about a novel by a famous man. And while I was writing this review, I discovered that if I were going to review books I should need

[1] Famous women writers: Fanny Burney (1752–1840), English novelist and diarist; Aphra Behn (1640–89), English dramatist and novelist; Harriet Martineau (1802–76), English novelist; Jane Austen (1775–1817), English novelist; and George Eliot (1819–80), pen name of Mary Ann Evans, English novelist.

to do battle with a certain phantom. And the phantom was a woman, and when I came to know her better I called her after the heroine of a famous poem, The Angel in the House.[2] It was she who used to come between me and my paper when I was writing reviews. It was she who bothered me and wasted my time and so tormented me that as last I killed her. You who come of a younger and happier generation may not have heard of her—you may not know what I mean by the Angel in the House. I will describe her as shortly as I can. She was intensely sympathetic. She was immensely charming. She was utterly unselfish. She excelled in the difficult arts of family life. She sacrificed herself daily. If there was chicken, she took the leg; if there was a draught she sat in it—in short she was so constituted that she never had a mind or a wish of her own, but preferred to sympathize always with the minds and wishes of others. Above all—I need not say it—she was pure. Her purity was supposed to be her chief beauty—her blushes, her great grace. In those days—the last of Queen Victoria—every house had its Angel. And when I came to write I encountered her with the very first words. The shadow of her wings fell on my page; I heard the rustling of her skirts in the room. Directly, that is to say, I took my pen in hand to review that novel by a famous man, she slipped behind me and whispered: "My dear, you are a young woman.You are writing about a book that has been written by a man. Be sympathetic; be tender; flatter; deceive; use all the arts and wiles of our sex. Never let anybody guess that you have a mind of your own. Above all, be pure." And she made as if to guide my pen. I now record the one act for which I take some credit to myself, though the credit rightly belongs to some excellent ancestors of mine who left me a certain sum of money—shall we say five hundred pounds a year?—so that it was not necessary for me to depend solely on charm for my living. I turned upon her and caught her by the throat. I did my best to kill her. My excuse, if I were to be had up in a court of law, would be that I acted in self-defence. Had I not killed her she would have killed me. She would have plucked the heart out of my writing. For, as I found, directly I put pen to paper, you cannot review even a novel without having a mind of your own, without expressing what you think to be the truth about human relations, morality, sex. And all these questions, according to the Angel in the House, cannot be dealt with freely and openly by women; they must charm, they must conciliate, they must—to put it bluntly—tell lies if they are to succeed. Thus, whenever I felt the shadow of her wing or the radiance of her halo upon my page, I took up the inkpot and flung it at her. She died hard. Her fictitious nature was of great assistance to her. It is far harder to kill a phantom than a reality. She was always creeping back when I thought I had despatched her. Though I flatter myself that I killed her in the end, the struggle was severe; it took much time that had better have been spent upon learning Greek grammar; or in roaming the world in search of adventures. But it was a real experience; it was an experience that was bound to

[2] Woolf took the term from a poem by Coventry Patmore, an English poet and essayist (1823–96).

befall all women writers at that time. Killing the Angel in the House was part of the occupation of a woman writer.

4 But to continue my story. The Angel was dead; what then remained? You may say that what remained was a simple and common object—a young woman in a bedroom with an inkpot. In other words, now that she had rid herself of falsehood, that young woman had only to be herself. Ah, but what is "herself"? I mean, what is a woman? I assure you, I do not know. I do not believe that you know. I do not believe that anybody can know until she has expressed herself in all the arts and professions open to human skill. That indeed is one of the reasons why I have come here—out of respect for you, who are in process of showing us by your experiments what a woman is, who are in process of providing us, by your failures and successes, with that extremely important piece of information.

5 But to continue the story of my professional experiences. I made one pound ten and six by my first review; and I bought a Persian cat with the proceeds. Then I grew ambitious. A Persian cat is all very well, I said; but a Persian cat is not enough. I must have a motor car. And it was thus that I became a novelist—for it is a very strange thing that people will give you a motor car if you will tell them a story. It is a still stranger thing that there is nothing so delightful in the world as telling stories. It is far pleasanter than writing reviews of famous novels. And yet, if I am to obey your secretary and tell you my professional experiences as a novelist, I must tell you about a very strange experience that befell me as a novelist. And to understand it you must try first to imagine a novelist's state of mind. I hope I am not giving away professional secrets if I say that a novelist's chief desire is to be as unconscious as possible. He has to induce in himself a state of perpetual lethargy. He wants life to proceed with the utmost quiet and regularity. He wants to see the same faces, to read the same books, to do the same things day after day, month after month, while he is writing, so that nothing may break the illusion in which he is living—so that nothing may disturb or disquiet the mysterious nosings about, feelings round, darts, dashes and sudden discoveries of that very shy and illusive spirit, the imagination. I suspect that this state is the same both for men and women. Be that as it may, I want you to imagine me writing a novel in a state of trance. I want you to figure to yourselves a girl sitting with a pen in her hand, which for minutes, and indeed for hours, she never dips into the inkpot. The image that comes to my mind when I think of this girl is the image of a fisherman lying sunk in dreams on the verge of a deep lake with a rod held out over the water. She was letting her imagination sweep unchecked round every rock and cranny of the world that lies submerged in the depths of our unconscious being. Now came the experience, the experience that I believe to be far commoner with women writers than with men. The line raced through the girl's fingers. Her imagination had rushed away. It had sought the pools, and depths, the dark places where the largest fish slumber. And then there was a smash. There was an explosion. There was foam and confusion. The imagination had dashed itself against something hard. The girl was roused from her

dream. She was indeed in a state of the most acute and difficult distress. To speak without figure she had thought of something, something about the body, about the passions which it was unfitting for her as a woman to say. Men, her reason told her, would be shocked. The consciousness of what men will say of a woman who speaks the truth about her passions had roused her from her artist's state of unconsciousness. She could write no more. The trance was over. Her imagination could work no longer. This I believe to be a very common experience with women writers—they are impeded by the extreme conventionality of the other sex. For though men sensibly allow themselves great freedom in these respects, I doubt that they realize or can control the extreme severity with which they condemn such freedom in women.

6 These then were two very genuine experiences of my own. These were two of the adventures of my professional life. The first—killing the Angel in the House—I think I solved. She died. But the second, telling the truth about my own experiences as a body, I do not think I solved. I doubt that any woman has solved it yet. The obstacles against her are still immensely powerful—and yet they are very difficult to define. Outwardly, what is simpler than to write books? Outwardly, what obstacles are there for a woman rather than for a man? Inwardly, I think, the case is very different; she has still many ghosts to fight, many prejudices to overcome. Indeed it will be a long time still, I think, before a woman can sit down to write a book without finding a phantom to be slain, a rock to be dashed against. And if this is so in literature, the freest of all professions for women, how is it in the new professions which you are now for the first time entering?

7 Those are the questions that I should like, had I time, to ask you. And indeed, if I have laid stress upon these professional experiences of mine, it is because I believe that they are, though in different forms, yours also. Even when the path is nominally open—when there is nothing to prevent a woman from being a doctor, a lawyer, a civil servant—there are many phantoms and obstacles, as I believe, looming in her way. To discuss and define them is I think of great value and importance; for thus only can the labour be shared, the difficulties be solved. But besides this, it is necessary also to discuss the ends and the aims for which we are fighting, for which we are doing battle with these formidable obstacles. Those aims cannot be taken for granted; they must be perpetually questioned and examined. The whole position, as I see it—here in this hall surrounded by women practising for the first time in history I know not how many different professions—is one of extraordinary interest and importance. You have won rooms of your own in the house hitherto exclusively owned by men. You are able, though not without great labour and effort, to pay the rent. You are earning your five hundred pounds a year. But this freedom is only a beginning; the room is your own, but it is still bare. It has to be furnished; it has to be decorated; it has to be shared. How are you going to furnish it, how are you going to decorate it? With whom are you going to share it, and upon what terms? These, I think are questions of the utmost importance and interest. For the first time in history you are able to ask them; for the first

time you are able to decide for yourselves what the answers should be. Willingly would I stay and discuss those questions and answers—but not tonight. My time is up; and I must cease.

Explorations of the Text

1. How does Woolf view the professions of journalist and writer?
2. Explore the image of the "Angel in the House." What is Woolf's attitude toward this "phantom"? How does the "Angel" affect Woolf's writing career?
3. Discuss Woolf's process of creating a novel. Contrast this process with her work as a journalist.
4. Analyze the "image of a fisherman" and "the girl" extending her line. What is the challenge Woolf faces as a woman writer?
5. Compare Woolf's vision of "telling the truth about [her] own experiences as a body" with Emiko's conflicts in *And the Soul Shall Dance.* Has Emiko solved the problem of expressing her "own experiences as a body"? Why or why not?

The Reading/Writing Connection

1. What does Woolf mean by her "own experiences as a body"? Freewrite in response to this quotation.
2. "Think" Topic: Woolf wrote this essay in 1931. Do you think that women artists today face these same "obstacles"?
3. Write a mini-essay in response to one of the statements or questions in the last paragraph of the essay. Probe the statement or question; relate it to your own observations, experiences, and reading; analyze it; and come to conclusions.

Ideas for Writing

1. Consider Woolf's statement in the last paragraph as a challenge.
2. Explicate the image of a "room of [one's] own."
3. How are women today exercising their "freedom"? "furnish[ing]" "room[s]"?
4. Debate Topic: Do men need to create similar places?
5. Choose a character from this chapter and imagine the kind of "room" this character would create. Create diary entries in the voice of this character.
6. Creative Options: Create a drawing of this room; furnish and decorate it. Or create a poem for a character from this chapter who is now living in a "room of [her] own."

FICTION

Lady with Lapdog

Anton Chekhov Translated by David Magarshack

Anton Chekhov (1860–1904) was born in southern Russia. His short stories and plays were formative in the development of modern, realistic literature. His major plays are The Sea Gull *(1898);* Uncle Vanya *(1899);* The Three Sisters *(1901); and* The Cherry Orchard *(1904). One theme dominates these plays: the protagonists' inabilities to change the circumstances of their lives—their imprisonment in the world of their failed dreams. During the last phase of his life, Chekhov also wrote several volumes of short stories:* Motley Stories *(1886),* Innocent Speeches *(1887),* In The Twilight *(1887), and* Stories *(1889).*

1899

I

The appearance on the front of a new arrival—a lady with a lapdog—became the topic of general conversation. Dmitry Dmitrich Gurov, who had been a fortnight in Yalta[1] and got used to its ways, was also interested in new arrivals. One day, sitting on the terrace of Vernet's restaurant, he saw a young woman walking along the promenade; she was fair, not very tall, and wore a toque;[2] behind her trotted a white pomeranian.

Later he came across her in the park and in the square several times a day. She was always alone, always wearing the same toque, followed by the white pomeranian. No one knew who she was, and she became known simply as the lady with the lapdog.

"If she's here without her husband and without any friends," thought Gurov, "it wouldn't be a bad idea to strike up an acquaintance with her."

He was not yet forty, but he had a twelve-year-old daughter and two schoolboy sons. He had been married off when he was still in his second year at the university, and his wife seemed to him now to be almost twice his age. She was a tall, black-browed woman, erect, dignified, austere, and, as she liked to describe herself, a "thinking person." She was a great reader, preferred the new "advanced" spelling, called her husband by the more formal "Dimitry" and not the familiar "Dmitry"; and though he secretly considered her not particularly intelligent, narrow-minded, and inelegant, he was afraid of her and disliked being at home. He had been unfaithful to her for a long time, he was often unfaithful to her, and that was why, perhaps, he almost always spoke ill of women, and when men discussed women in his presence, he described them as *the lower breed.*

---

[1] A seaport in the Ukraine on the Black Sea.

[2] A kind of hat.

5 He could not help feeling that he had had enough bitter experience to have the right to call them as he pleased, but all the same without *the lower breed* he could not have existed a couple of days. He was bored and ill at ease among men, with whom he was reticent and cold, but when he was among women he felt at ease, he knew what to talk about with them and how to behave, even when he was silent in their company he experienced no feeling of constraint. There was something attractive, something elusive in his appearance, in his character and his whole person that women found interesting and irresistible; he was aware of it, and was himself drawn to them by some irresistible force.

Long and indeed bitter experience had taught him that every new affair, which at first relieved the monotony of life so pleasantly and appeared to be such a charming and light adventure, among decent people and especially among Muscovites, who are so irresolute and so hard to rouse, inevitably developed into an extremely complicated problem and finally the whole situation became rather cumbersome. But at every new meeting with an attractive woman he forgot all about this experience, he wanted to enjoy life so badly and it all seemed so simple and amusing.

And so one afternoon, while he was having dinner at a restaurant in the park, the woman in the toque walked in unhurriedly and took a seat at the table next to him. The way she looked, walked and dressed, wore her hair, told him that she was of good social standing, that she was married, that she was in Yalta for the first time, that she was alone and bored. . . . There was a great deal of exaggeration in the stories about the laxity of morals among the Yalta visitors, and he dismissed them with contempt, for he knew that such stories were mostly made up by people who would gladly have sinned themselves if they had had any idea how to go about it; but when the woman sat down at the table three yards away from him he remembered these stories of easy conquests and excursions to the mountains and the tempting thought of a quiet and fleeting affair, an affair with a strange woman whose very name he did not know, suddenly took possession of him.

He tried to attract the attention of the dog by calling softly to it, and when the pomeranian came up to him he shook a finger at it. The pomeranian growled. Gurov again shook a finger at it.

The woman looked up at him and immediately lowered her eyes.

10 "He doesn't bite," she said and blushed.

"May I give him a bone?" he asked, and when she nodded, he said amiably: "Have you been long in Yalta?"

"About five days."

"And I am just finishing my second week here."

They said nothing for the next few minutes.

15 "Time flies," she said without looking at him, "and yet it's so boring here."

"That's what one usually hears people saying here. A man may be living in Belev and Zhizdra or some other God-forsaken hole and he isn't bored, but the moment he comes here all you hear from him is 'Oh, it's so boring! Oh, the dust!' You'd think he'd come from Granada!"

She laughed. Then both went on eating in silence, like complete strangers; but after dinner they strolled off together, and they embarked on the light playful conversation of free and contented people who do not care where they go or what they talk about. They walked, and talked about the strange light that fell on the sea: the water was of such a soft and warm lilac, and the moon threw a shaft of gold across it. They talked about how close it was after a hot day. Gurov told her that he lived in Moscow, that he was a graduate in philology but worked in a bank, that he had at one time thought of singing in a private opera company but had given up the idea, that he owned two houses in Moscow. . . . From her he learnt that she had grown up in Petersburg, but had got married in the town of S———, where she had been living for the past two years, that she would stay another month in Yalta, and that her husband, who also needed a rest, might join her. She was quite unable to tell him what her husband's job was, whether he served in the offices of the provincial governor or the rural council, and she found this rather amusing herself. Gurov also found out that her name and patronymic were Anna Sergeyevna.

Later, in his hotel room, he thought about her and felt sure that he would meet her again the next day. It had to be. As he went to bed he remembered that she had only recently left her boarding school, that she had been a schoolgirl like his own daughter; he recalled how much diffidence and angularity there was in her laughter and her conversation with a stranger—it was probably the first time in her life she had found herself alone, in a situation when men followed her, looked at her, and spoke to her with only one secret intention, an intention she could hardly fail to guess. He remembered her slender, weak neck, her beautiful grey eyes.

"There's something pathetic about her, all the same," he thought as he fell asleep.

II

20 A week had passed since their first meeting. It was a holiday. It was close indoors, while in the streets a strong wind raised clouds of dust and tore off people's hats. All day long one felt thirsty, and Gurov kept going to the terrace of the restaurant, offering Anna Sergeyevna fruit drinks and ices. There was nowhere to go.

In the evening, when the wind had dropped a little, they went to the pier to watch the arrival of the steamer. There were a great many people taking a walk on the landing pier; some were meeting friends, they had bunches of flowers in their hands. It was there that two peculiarities of the Yalta smart set at once arrested attention: the middle-aged women dressed as if they were still young girls and there was a great number of generals.

Because of the rough sea the steamer arrived late, after the sun had set, and she had to swing backwards and forwards several times before getting alongside the pier. Anna Sergeyevna looked at the steamer and the passengers through her lorgnette, as though trying to make out some friends, and when she turned to Gurov her eyes were sparkling. She talked a lot, asked many abrupt questions, and immediately forgot what it was she had wanted to know; then she lost her lorgnette in the crowd of people.

The smartly dressed crowd dispersed; soon they were all gone, the wind had dropped completely, but Gurov and Anna were still standing there as though waiting to see if someone else would come off the boat. Anna Sergeyevna was no longer talking. She was smelling her flowers without looking at Gurov.

"It's a nice evening," he said. "Where shall we go now? Shall we go for a drive?"

She made no answer.

Then he looked keenly at her and suddenly put his arms round her and kissed her on the mouth. He felt the fragrance and dampness of the flowers and immediately looked around him fearfully; had anyone seen them?

"Let's go to your room," he said softly.

And both walked off quickly.

It was very close in her hotel room, which was full of the smell of the scents she had bought in a Japanese shop. Looking at her now, Gurov thought: "Life is full of strange encounters!" From his past he preserved the memory of carefree, good-natured women, whom love had made gay and who were grateful to him for the happiness he gave them, however short-lived; and of women like his wife, who made love without sincerity, with unnecessary talk, affectedly, hysterically, with such an expression, as though it were not love or passion, but something much more significant; and of two or three very beautiful, frigid women, whose faces suddenly lit up with a predatory expression, an obstinate desire to take, to snatch from life more than it could give; these were women no longer in their first youth, capricious, unreasoning, despotic, unintelligent women, and when Gurov lost interest in them, their beauty merely aroused hatred in him and the lace trimmings on their négligés looked to him then like the scales of a snake.

But here there was still the same diffidence and angularity of inexperienced youth—an awkward feeling; and there was also the impression of embarrassment, as if someone had just knocked at the door. Anna Sergeyevna, this lady with the lapdog, apparently regarded what had happened in a peculiar sort of way, very seriously, as though she had become a fallen woman—so it seemed to him, and he found it odd and disconcerting. Her features lengthened and drooped, and her long hair hung mournfully on either side of her face; she sank into thought in a despondent pose, like a woman taken in adultery in an old painting.

"It's wrong," she said. "You'll be the first not to respect me now."

There was a water-melon on the table. Gurov cut himself a slice and began to eat it slowly. At least half an hour passed in silence.

Anna Sergeyevna was very touching; there was an air of pure, decent, naïve woman about her, a woman who had very little experience of life; the solitary candle burning on the table scarcely lighted up her face, but it was obvious that she was unhappy.

"But, darling, why should I stop respecting you?" Gurov asked. "You don't know yourself what you're saying."

35 "May God forgive me," she said, and her eyes filled with tears. "It's terrible."

"You seem to wish to justify yourself."

"How can I justify myself?" I am a bad, despicable creature. I despise myself and have no thought of justifying myself. I haven't deceived my husband, I've deceived myself. And not only now. I've been deceiving myself for a long time. My husband is, I'm sure, a good and honest man, but, you see, he is a flunkey. I don't know what he does at his office, all I know is that he is a flunkey. I was only twenty when I married him, I was eaten up by curiosity, I wanted something better. There surely must be a different kind of life, I said to myself. I wanted to live. To live, to live! I was burning with curiosity. I don't think you know what I am talking about, but I swear I could no longer control myself, something was happening to me. I could not be held back. I told my husband I was ill, and I came here. . . . Here too I was going about as though in a daze, as though I was mad, and now I've become a vulgar worthless woman whom everyone has a right to despise."

Gurov could not help feeling bored as he listened to her; he was irritated by her naïve tone of voice and her repentance, which was so unexpected and so out of place; but for the tears in her eyes, he might have thought that she was joking or play-acting.

"I don't understand," he said gently, "what it is you want."

40 She buried her face on his chest and clung close to him.

"Please, please believe me," she said. "I love a pure, honest life. I hate immorality. I don't know myself what I am doing. The common people say 'the devil led her astray,' I too can now say about myself that the devil has led me astray."

"There, there . . ." he murmured.

He gazed into her staring, frightened eyes, kissed her, spoke gently and affectionately to her, and gradually she calmed down and her cheerfulness returned; both of them were soon laughing.

Later, when they went out, there was not a soul on the promenade, the town with its cypresses looked quite dead, but the sea was still roaring and dashing itself against the shore; a single launch tossed on the waves, its lamp flickering sleepily.

45 They hailed a cab and drove to Oreanda.

"I've just found out your surname, downstairs in the lobby," said Gurov. "Von Diederitz. Is your husband a German?"

"No. I believe his grandfather was German. He is of the Orthodox faith himself."

In Oreanda they sat on a bench not far from the church, looked down on the sea, and were silent. Yalta could scarcely be seen through the morning mist. White clouds lay motionless on the mountain tops. Not a leaf stirred on the trees, the cicadas chirped, and the monotonous, hollow roar of the sea, coming up from below, spoke of rest, of eternal sleep awaiting us all. The sea had roared like that down below when there was no Yalta or Oreanda, it was roaring now, and it would go on roaring as indifferently and hollowly when we were here no more. And in this constancy, in this complete indifference to life and death of each one of us, there is perhaps hidden the guarantee of our eternal salvation, the never-ceasing movement of life on earth, the never-ceasing movement towards perfection. Sitting beside a young woman who looked so beautiful at the break of day, soothed and enchanted by the sight of all that fairy-land scenery—the sea, the mountains, the clouds, the wide sky—Gurov reflected that, when you came to think of it, everything in the world was really really beautiful, everything but our own thoughts and actions when we lose sight of the higher aims of existence and our dignity as human beings.

Someone walked up to them, a watchman probably, looked at them, and went away. And there seemed to be something mysterious and also beautiful in this fact, too. They could see the Theodosia boat coming towards the pier, lit up by the sunrise, and with no lights.

"There's dew on the grass," said Anna Sergeyevna, breaking the silence.

"Yes. Time to go home."

They went back to town.

After that they met on the front every day at twelve o'clock, had lunch and dinner together, went for walks, admired the sea. She complained of sleeping badly and of her heart beating uneasily, asked the same questions, alternately worried by feelings of jealousy and by fear that he did not respect her sufficiently. And again and again in the park or in the square, when there was no one in sight, he would draw her to him and kiss her passionately. The complete idleness, these kisses in broad daylight, always having to look round for fear of someone watching them, the heat, the smell of the sea, and the constant looming into sight of idle, well-dressed, and well-fed people seemed to have made a new man of him; he told Anna Sergeyevna that she was beautiful, that she was desirable, made passionate love to her, never left her side, while she was often lost in thought and kept asking him to admit that he did not really respect her, that he was not in the least in love with her and only saw in her a vulgar woman. Almost every night they drove out of town, to Oreanda or to the waterfall; the excursion was always a success, and every time their impressions were invariably grand and beautiful.

They kept expecting her husband to arrive. But a letter came from him in which he wrote that he was having trouble with his eyes and implored his wife to return home as soon as possible. Anna Sergeyevna lost no time in getting ready for her journey home.

"It's a good thing I'm going," she said to Gurov. "It's fate."

She took a carriage to the railway station, and he saw her off. The drive took a whole day. When she got into the express train, after the second bell, she said:

"Let me have another look at you. . . . One last look. So."

She did not cry, but looked sad, just as if she were ill, and her face quivered.

"I'll be thinking of you, remembering you," she said. "Good-bye. You're staying, aren't you? Don't think badly of me. We are parting for ever. Yes, it must be so, for we should never have met. Well, good-bye. . . ."

60 The train moved rapidly out of the station; its lights soon disappeared, and a minute later it could not even be heard, just as though everything had conspired to put a quick end to this sweet trance, this madness. And standing alone on the platform gazing into the dark distance, Gurov listened to the chirping of the grasshoppers and the humming of the telegraph wires with a feeling as though he had just woken up. He told himself that this had been just one more affair in his life, just one more adventure, and that it too was over, leaving nothing but a memory. He was moved and sad, and felt a little penitent that the young woman, whom he would never see again, had not been happy with him; he had been amiable and affectionate with her, but all the same in his behavior to her, in the tone of his voice and in his caresses, there was a suspicion of light irony, the somewhat coarse arrogance of the successful male, who was, moreover, almost twice her age. All the time she called him good, wonderful, high-minded; evidently she must have taken him to be quite different from what he really was, which meant that he had involuntarily deceived her.

At the railway station there was already a whiff of autumn in the air; the evening was chilly.

"Time I went north, too," thought Gurov, as he walked off the platform. "High time!"

III

At home in Moscow everything was already like winter: the stoves were heated, and it was still dark in the morning when the children were getting ready to go to school and having breakfast, so that the nurse had to light the lamp for a short time. The frosts had set in. When the first snow falls and the first day one goes out for a ride in a sleigh, one is glad to see the white ground, the white roofs, the air is so soft and wonderful to breathe, and one remembers the days of one's youth. The old lime trees and birches, white with rime, have such a benignant look, they are nearer to one's heart than cypresses and palms, and beside them one no longer wants to think of mountains and the sea.

Gurov had been born and bred in Moscow, and he returned to Moscow on a fine frosty day; and when he put on his fur coat and warm gloves and took a walk down Petrovka Street, and when on Saturday evening he heard the church bells ringing, his recent holiday trip and the places he had visited lost their charm for him. Gradually he became immersed in Moscow life, eagerly reading three newspapers a day and declaring that he never read Moscow papers on principle. Once more, he could not resist the attraction of restaurants, clubs, banquets, and anniversary celebrations, and once more he felt flattered that well-known lawyers and actors came to see him and that in the Medical Club he played cards with a professor as his partner. Once again he was capable of eating a whole portion of the Moscow speciality of sour cabbage and meat served in a frying-pan. . . .

65 Another month and, he thought, nothing but a memory would remain of Anna Sergeyevna; he would remember her as through a haze and only occasionally dream of her with a wistful smile, as he did of the others before her. But over a month passed, winter was at its height, and he remembered her as clearly as though he had only parted from her the day before. His memories haunted him more and more persistently. Every time the voices of his children doing their homework reached him in his study in the stillness of the evening, every time he heard a popular song or some music in a restaurant, every time the wind howled in the chimney—it all came back to him: their walks on the pier, early morning with the mist on the mountains, the Theodosia boat, and the kisses. He kept pacing the room for hours remembering it all and smiling, and then his memories turned into daydreams and the past mingled in his imagination with what was going to happen. He did not dream of Anna Sergeyevna, she accompanied him everywhere like his shadow and followed him wherever he went. Closing his eyes, he saw her as clearly as if she were before him, and she seemed to him lovelier, younger, and tenderer than she had been; and he thought that he too was much better than he had been in Yalta. In the evenings she gazed at him from the bookcase, from the fireplace, from the corner—he heard her breathing, the sweet rustle of her dress. In the street he followed women with his eyes, looking for anyone who resembled her. . . .

He was beginning to be overcome by an overwhelming desire to share his memories with someone. But at home it was impossible to talk of his love, and outside his home there was no one he could talk to. Not the tenants who lived in his house, and certainly not his colleagues in the bank. And what was he to tell them? Had he been in love then? Had there been anything beautiful, poetic, edifying, or even anything interesting about his relations with Anna Sergeyevna? So he had to talk in general terms about love and women, and no one guessed what he was driving at, and his wife merely raised her black eyebrows and said:

"Really, Dimitry, the role of a coxcomb doesn't suit you at all!"

One evening, as he left the Medical Club with his partner, a civil servant, he could not restrain himself, and said:

"If you knew what a fascinating woman I met in Yalta!"

70 The civil servant got into his sleigh and was about to be driven off, but suddenly he turned round and called out:

"I say!"

"Yes?"

"You were quite right; the sturgeon *was* a bit off."

These words, so ordinary in themselves, for some reason hurt Gurov's feelings: they seemed to him humiliating and indecent. What savage manners! What faces! What stupid nights! What uninteresting, wasted days! Crazy gambling at cards, gluttony, drunkenness, endless talk about one and the same thing. Business that was of no use to anyone and talk about one and the same thing absorbed the greater part of one's time and energy, and what was left in the end was a sort of dock-tailed, barren life, a sort of nonsensical existence, and it was impossible to escape from it, just as though you were in a lunatic asylum or a convict chaingang!

Gurov lay awake all night, fretting and fuming, and had a splitting headache the whole of the next day. The following nights too he slept badly, sitting up in bed thinking, or walking up and down his room. He was tired of his children, tired of the bank, he did not feel like going out anywhere or talking about anything.

In December, during the Christmas holidays, he packed his things, told his wife that he was going to Petersburg to get a job for a young man he knew, and set off for the town of S______. Why? He had no very clear idea himself. He wanted to see Anna Sergeyevna, to talk to her, to arrange a meeting, if possible.

He arrived in S______ in the morning and took the best room in a hotel, with a fitted carpet of military grey cloth and an inkstand grey with dust on the table, surmounted by a horseman with raised hand and no head. The hall porter supplied him with all the necessary information: Von Diederitz lived in a house of his own in Old Potter's Street, not far from the hotel. He lived well, was rich, kept his own carriage horses, the whole town knew him. The hall-porter pronounced the name: Dridiritz.

Gurov took a leisurely walk down Old Potter's Street and found the house. In front of it was a long grey fence studded with upturned nails.

"A fence like that would make anyone wish to run away," thought Gurov, scanning the windows and the fence.

As it was a holiday, he thought, her husband was probably at home. It did not matter either way, though, for he could not very well embarrass her by calling at the house. If he were to send in a note it might fall into the hands of the husband and ruin everything. The best thing was to rely on chance. And he kept walking up and down the street and along the fence, waiting for his chance. He watched a beggar enter the gate and the dogs attack him; then, an hour later, he heard the faint indistinct sounds of a piano. That must have been Anna Sergeyevna playing. Suddenly the front door opened and an old woman came out, followed by the familiar white pomeranian. Gurov was about to call to the dog, but his heart began to beat violently and in his excitement he could not remember its name.

He went on walking up and down the street, hating the grey fence more and more, and he was already saying to himself that Anna Sergeyevna had forgotten him and had perhaps been having a good time with someone else, which was indeed quite natural for a young woman who had to look at that damned fence from morning till night. He went back to his hotel room and sat on the sofa for a long time, not knowing what to do, then he had dinner and after dinner a long sleep.

"How stupid and disturbing it all is," he thought, waking up and staring at the dark windows: it was already evening. "Well, I've had a good sleep, so what now? What am I going to do tonight?"

He sat on a bed covered by a cheap grey blanket looking exactly like a hospital blanket, and taunted himself in vexation:

"A *lady* with a lapdog! Some adventure, I must say! Serves you right!"

At the railway station that morning he had noticed a poster announcing in huge letters the first performance of *The Geisha Girl* at the local theatre. He recalled it now, and decided to go to the theatre.

"Quite possibly she goes to first nights," he thought.

The theatre was full. As in all provincial theatres, there was a mist over the chandeliers and the people in the gallery kept up a noisy and excited conversation; in the first row of the stalls stood the local dandies with their hands crossed behind their backs; here, too, in the front seat of the Governor's box, sat the Governor's daughter, wearing a feather boa, while the Governor himself hid modestly behind the portière so that only his hands were visible; the curtain stirred, the orchestra took a long time tuning up. Gurov scanned the audience eagerly as they filed in and occupied their seats.

Anna Sergeyevna came in too. She took her seat in the third row, and when Gurov glanced at her his heart missed a beat and he realized clearly that there was no one in the world nearer and dearer or more important to him than that little woman with the stupid lorgnette in her hand, who was in no way remarkable. That woman lost in a provincial crowd now filled his whole life, was his misfortune, his joy, and the only happiness that he wished for himself. Listening to the bad orchestra and the wretched violins played by second-rate musicians, he thought how beautiful she was. He thought and dreamed.

A very tall, round-shouldered young man with small whiskers had come in with Anna Sergeyevna and sat down beside her; he nodded at every step he took and seemed to be continually bowing to someone. This was probably her husband, whom in a fit of bitterness at Yalta she had called a flunkey. And indeed there was something of a lackey's obsequiousness in his lank figure, his whiskers, and the little bald spot on the top of his head. He smiled sweetly, and the gleaming insignia of some scientific society which he wore in his buttonhole looked like the number on a waiter's coat.

In the first interval the husband went out to smoke and she was left in her seat. Gurov, who also had a seat in the stalls, went up to her and said in a trembling voice and with a forced smile:

"Good evening!"

She looked up at him and turned pale, then looked at him again in panic, unable to believe her eyes, clenching her fan and lorgnette in her hand and apparently trying hard not to fall into a dead faint. Both were silent. She sat and he stood, frightened by her embarrassment and not daring to sit down beside her. The violinists and the flautist began tuning their instruments, and they suddenly felt terrified, as though they were being watched from all the boxes. But a moment later she got up and walked rapidly towards one of the exits; he followed her, and both of them walked aimlessly along corridors and up and down stairs. Figures in all sorts of uniforms—lawyers, teachers, civil servants, all wearing badges—flashed by them: ladies, fur coats hanging on pegs, the cold draught bringing with it the odour of cigarette-ends. Gurov, whose heart was beating violently, thought:

"Oh, Lord, what are all these people, that orchestra, doing here?"

At that moment, he suddenly remembered how after seeing Anna Sergeyevna off he had told himself that evening at the station that all was over and that they would never meet again. But how far they still were from the end!

95 She stopped on a dark, narrow staircase with a notice over it: "To the Upper Circle."

"How you frightened me!" she said, breathing heavily, still looking pale and stunned. "Oh, dear, how you frightened me! I'm scarcely alive. Why did you come? Why?"

"But, please, try to understand, Anna," he murmured hurriedly. "I beg you, please, try to understand. . . ."

She looked at him with fear, entreaty, love, looked at him intently, so as to fix his features firmly in her mind.

"I've suffered so much," she went on, without listening to him. "I've been thinking of you all the time. The thought of you kept me alive. And yet I tried so hard to forget you—why, oh, why did you come?"

100 On the landing above two schoolboys were smoking and looking down, but Gurov did not care. He drew Anna Sergeyevna towards him and began kissing her face, her lips, her hands.

"What are you doing? What are you doing?" she said in horror, pushing him away. "We've both gone mad. You must go back tonight, this minute. I implore you, by all that's sacred . . . Somebody's coming!"

Somebody was coming up the stairs.

"You must go back," continued Anna Sergeyevna in a whisper. "Do you hear? I'll come to you in Moscow. I've never been happy, I'm unhappy now, and I shall never be happy, never! So please don't make me suffer still more. I swear I'll come to you in Moscow. But now we must part. Oh, my sweet, my darling, we must part!"

She pressed his hand and went quickly down the stairs, looking back at him all the time, and he could see from the expression in her eyes that she really was unhappy. Gurov stood listening for a short time, and when all was quiet he went to look for his coat and left the theatre.

IV

105 Anna Sergeyevna began going to Moscow to see him. Every two or three months she left the town of S———, telling her husband that she was going to consult a Moscow gynaecologist, and her husband believed and did not believe her. In Moscow she stayed at the Slav Bazaar and immediately sent a porter in a red cap to inform Gurov of her arrival. Gurov went to her hotel, and no one in Moscow knew about it.

One winter morning he went to her hotel as usual (the porter had called with his message at his house the evening before, but he had not been in). He had his daughter with him, and he was glad of the opportunity of taking her to school, which was on the way to the hotel. Snow was falling in thick wet flakes.

"It's three degrees above zero," Gurov was saying to his daughter, "and yet it's snowing. But then, you see, it's only warm on the earth's surface, in the upper layers of the atmosphere the temperature's quite different."

"Why isn't there any thunder in winter, Daddy?"

He explained that, too. As he was speaking, he kept thinking that he was going to meet his mistress and not a living soul knew about it. He led a double life: one for all who were interested to see, full of conventional truth and conventional deception, exactly like the lives of his friends and acquaintances; and another which went on in secret. And by a kind of strange concatenation of circumstances, possibly quite by accident, everything that was important, interesting, essential, everything about which he was sincere and did not deceive himself, everything that made up the quintessence of his life, went on in secret, while everything that was a lie, everything that was merely the husk in which he hid himself to conceal the truth, like his work at the bank, for instance, his discussions at the club, his ideas of the lower breed, his going to anniversary functions with his wife—all that happened in the sight of all. He judged others by himself, did not believe what he saw, and was always of the opinion that every man's real and most interesting life went on in secret, under cover of night. The personal, private life of an individual was kept a secret, and perhaps that was partly the reason why civilized man was so anxious that his personal secrets should be respected.

110 Having seen his daughter off to her school, Gurov went to the Slav Bazaar. He took off his fur coat in the cloakroom, went upstairs, and knocked softly on the door. Anna Sergeyevna, wearing the grey dress he liked most, tired out by her journey and by the suspense of waiting for him, had been expecting him since the evening before; she was pale, looked at him without smiling, but was in his arms the moment he went into the room. Their kiss was long and lingering, as if they had not seen each other for two years.

"Well," he asked, "how are you getting on there? Anything new?"

"Wait, I'll tell you in a moment. . . . I can't . . ."

She could not speak because she was crying. She turned away from him and pressed her handkerchief to her eyes.

"Well, let her have her cry," he thought, sitting down in an armchair. "I'll wait."

115 Then he rang the bell and ordered tea; while he was having his tea, she was still standing there with her face to the window. She wept because she could not control her emotions, because she was bitterly conscious of the fact that their life was so sad: they could only meet in secret, they had to hide from people, like thieves! Was not their life ruined?

"Please stop crying!" he said.

It was quite clear to him that their love would not come to an end for a long time, if ever. Anna Sergeyevna was getting attached to him more and more strongly, she worshipped him, and it would have been absurd to tell her that all this would have to come to an end one day. She would not have believed it, anyway.

He went up to her and took her by the shoulders, wishing to be nice to her, to make her smile; and at that moment he caught sight of himself in the looking glass.

His hair was already beginning to turn grey. It struck him as strange that he should have aged so much, that he should have lost his good looks in the last few years. The shoulders on which his hands lay were warm and quivering. He felt so sorry for this life, still so warm and beautiful, but probably soon to fade and wilt like his own. Why did she love him so? To women he always seemed different from what he was, and they loved in him not himself, but the man their imagination conjured up and whom they had eagerly been looking for all their lives; and when they discovered their mistake they still loved him. And not one of them had ever been happy with him. Time had passed, he had met women, made love to them, parted from them, but not once had he been in love; there had been everything between them, but no love.

It was only now, when his hair was beginning to turn grey, that he had fallen in love properly, in good earnest for the first time in his life.

He and Anna Sergeyevna loved each other as people do who are very dear and near, as man and wife or close friends love each other; they could not help feeling that fate itself had intended them for one another, and they were unable to understand why he should have a wife and she a husband; they were like two migrating birds, male and female, who had been caught and forced to live in separate cages. They had forgiven each other what they had been ashamed of in the past, and forgave each other everything in their present, and felt that this love of theirs had changed them both.

Before, when he felt depressed, he had comforted himself by all sorts of arguments that happened to occur to him on the spur of the moment, but now he had more serious things to think of, he felt profound compassion, he longed to be sincere, tender. . . .

"Don't cry, my sweet," he said. "That'll do, you've had your cry. . . . Let's talk now, let's think of something."

Then they had a long talk. They tried to think how they could get rid of the necessity of hiding, telling lies, living in different towns, not seeing one another for so long. How were they to free themselves from their intolerable chains?

"How? How?" he asked himself, clutching at his head. "How?"

And it seemed to them that in only a few more minutes a solution would be found and a new, beautiful life would begin; but both of them knew very well that the end was still a long, long way away and that the most complicated and difficult part was only just beginning.

Explorations of the Text

1. Analyze Dmitry Gurov's attitude toward women in Part I. Why has he been "unfaithful" to his wife? Why does he describe women as the "lower breed"?

2. Discuss Anna Sergeyevna's character. Why does she have an affair with Gurov?
3. After lovemaking, why does Anna consider herself "a bad, despicable creature"? Is Gurov sympathetic to her?
4. Explain the symbolism of the landscape of Oreanda.
5. After they return to their homes and spouses, do the feelings of Anna and Gurov for each other change?
6. Interpret the ending. Do Anna and Gurov have a deep commitment to each other? Are they deluded?
7. What critique of Russian society and culture is apparent in the story?

The Reading/Writing Connection

1. "Think" Topic: With which character do you most sympathize? Why?
2. In a journal entry, explore a love relationship that changed your life or that changed you.

Ideas for Writing

1. Chekhov said about his fictional method that he was not a judge of human character; he simply presented problems. Does this story support his view of his fictional strategy?
2. Chekhov is considered a master of the short story. What are his strengths as a fiction writer? (See the evaluation checklist in chapter 9.)
3. Explore the theme of delusion in love or of fatal attraction in this story. You also may refer to another work from this chapter.

Death of a Son

Njabulo S. Ndebele

Njabulo S. Ndebele (1948–) was born and grew up in Charterston Location, a township in South Africa. Educated at Cambridge University and the University of Denver, he teaches African, African American, and English literature at the University College of Roma, Lesotho. His volume of short stories, Fools *(1983), is set in a town like Charterston Location and portrays his childhood world.*

1982

At last we got the body. Wednesday. Just enough time for a Saturday funeral. We were exhausted. Empty. The funeral still ahead of us. We had to find the strength to grieve. There had been no time for grief, really. Only much bewilderment and confusion. Now grief. For isn't grief the awareness of loss?

That is why when we finally got the body, Buntu said: "Do you realize our son is dead?" I realized. Our awareness of the death of our first and only child had been displaced completely by the effort to get his body. Even the horrible events that caused the death: we did not think of them, as such. Instead, the numbing drift of things took over our minds: the pleas, letters to be written, telephone calls to be made, telegrams to be dispatched, lawyers to consult, "influential" people to "get in touch with," undertakers to be contacted, so much walking and driving. That is what suddenly mattered: the irksome details that blur the goal (no matter how terrible it is), each detail becoming a door which, once unlocked, revealed yet another door. Without being aware of it, we were distracted by the smell of the skunk and not by what the skunk had done.

We realized something too, Buntu and I, that during the two-week effort to get our son's body, we had drifted apart. For the first time in our marriage, our presence to each other had become a matter of habit. He was there. He'll be there. And I'll be there. But when Buntu said: "Do you realize our son is dead?" he uttered a thought that suddenly brought us together again. It was as if the return of the body of our son was also our coming together. For it was only at that moment that we really began to grieve; as if our lungs had suddenly begun to take in air when just before, we were beginning to suffocate. Something with meaning began to emerge.

We realized. We realized that something else had been happening to us, adding to the terrible events. Yes, we had drifted apart. Yet, our estrangement, just at that moment when we should have been together, seemed disturbingly comforting to me. I was comforted in a manner I did not quite understand.

5 The problem was that I had known all along that we would have to buy the body anyway. I had known all along. Things would end that way. And when things turned out that way, Buntu could not look me in the eye. For he had said: "Over my dead body! Over my dead body!" as soon as we knew we would be required to pay the police or the government for the release of the body of our child.

"Over my dead body! Over my dead body!" Buntu kept on saying.

Finally, we bought the body. We have the receipt. The police insisted we take it. That way, they would be "protected." It's the law, they said.

I suppose we could have got the body earlier. At first I was confused, for one is supposed to take comfort in the heroism of one's man. Yet, inwardly, I could draw no comfort from his outburst. It seemed hasty. What sense was there to it when all I wanted was the body of my child? What would happen if, as events unfolded, it became clear that Buntu would not give up his life? What would happen? What would happen to him? To me?

For the greater part of two weeks, all of Buntu's efforts, together with friends, relatives, lawyers and the newspapers, were to secure the release of the child's body without the humiliation of having to pay for it. A "fundamental principle."

10 Why was it difficult for me to see the wisdom of the principle? The worst thing, I suppose, was worrying about what the police may have been doing to

the body of my child. How they may have been busy prying it open "to determine the cause of death"?

Would I want to look at the body when we finally got it? To see further mutilations in addition to the "cause of death"? What kind of mother would not want to look at the body of her child? people will ask. Some will say: "It's grief." She is too grief-stricken.

"But still . . . ," they will say. And the elderly among them may say: "Young people are strange."

But how can they know? It was not that I would not want to see the body of my child, but that I was too afraid to confront the horrors of my own imagination. I was haunted by the thought of how useless it had been to have created something. What had been the point of it all? This body filling up with a child. The child steadily growing into something that could be seen and felt. Moving, as it always did, at that time of day when I was all alone at home waiting for it. What had been the point of it all?

How can they know that the mutilation to determine "the cause of death" ripped my own body? Can they think of a womb feeling hunted? Disgorged?

And the milk that I still carried. What about it? What had been the point of it all?

Even Buntu did not seem to sense that that principle, the "fundamental principle," was something too intangible for me at that moment, something that I desperately wanted should assume the form of my child's body. He still seemed far from ever knowing.

I remember one Saturday morning early in our courtship, as Buntu and I walked hand-in-hand through town, window-shopping. We cannot even be said to have been window-shopping, for we were aware of very little that was not ourselves. Everything in those windows was merely an excuse for words to pass between us.

We came across three girls sitting on the pavement, sharing a packet of fish and chips after they had just bought it from a nearby Portuguese cafe. Buntu said: "I want fish and chips too." I said: "So seeing is desire." I said: "My man is greedy!" We laughed. I still remember how he tightened his grip on my hand. The strength of it!

Just then, two white boys coming in the opposite direction suddenly rushed at the girls, and, without warning, one of them kicked the packet of fish and chips out of the hands of the girl who was holding it. The second boy kicked away the rest of what remained in the packet. The girl stood up, shaking her hand as if to throw off the pain in it. Then she pressed it under her armpit as if to squeeze the pain out of it. Meanwhile, the two boys went on their way laughing. The fish and chips lay scattered on the pavement and on the street like stranded boats on a river that had gone dry.

"Just let them do that to you!" said Buntu, tightening once more his grip on my hand as we passed on like sheep that had seen many of their own in the flock picked out for slaughter. We would note the event and wait for our turn. I remember I looked at Buntu, and saw his face was somewhat glum. There seemed no connection between that face and the words of reassurance just uttered. For a while, we went on quietly. It was then that I noticed his grip had grown somewhat limp. Somewhat reluctant. Having lost its self-assurance, it seemed to have been holding on because it had to, not because of a confident sense of possession.

It was not to be long before his words were tested. How could fate work this way, giving to words meanings and intentions they did not carry when they were uttered? I saw that day, how the language of love could so easily be trampled underfoot, or scattered like fish and chips on the pavement, and left stranded and abandoned like boats in a river that suddenly went dry. Never again was love to be confirmed with words. The world around us was too hostile for vows of love. At any moment, the vows could be subjected to the stress of proof. And love died. For words of love need not be tested.

On that day, Buntu and I began our silence. We talked and laughed, of course, but we stopped short of words that would demand proof of action. Buntu knew. He knew the vulnerability of words. And so he sought to obliterate words with acts that seemed to promise redemption.

On that day, as we continued with our walk in town, that Saturday morning, coming up towards us from the opposite direction, was a burly Boer[1] walking with his wife and two children. They approached Buntu and me with an ominously determined advance. Buntu attempted to pull me out of the way, but I never had a chance. The Boer shoved me out of the way, as if clearing a path for his family. I remember, I almost crashed into a nearby fashion display window. I remember, I glanced at the family walking away, the mother and the father each dragging a child. It was for one of those children that I had been cleared away. I remember, also, that as my tears came out, blurring the Boer family and everything else, I saw and felt deeply what was inside of me: a desire to be avenged.

But nothing happened. All I heard was Buntu say: "The dog!" At that very moment, I felt my own hurt vanish like a wisp of smoke. And as my hurt vanished, it was replaced, instead, by a tormenting desire to sacrifice myself for Buntu. Was it something about the powerlessness of the curse and the desperation with which it had been made? The filling of stunned silence with an utterance? Surely it ate into him, revealing how incapable he was of meeting the call of his words.

And so it was, that that afternoon, back in the township, left to ourselves at Buntu's home, I gave in to him for the first time. Or should I say I offered myself to him? Perhaps from some vague sense of wanting to heal something in him? Anyway, we were never to talk about that event. Never. We buried it alive deep inside of me that afternoon. Would it ever be exhumed? All I vaguely felt and knew was that I had the keys to the vault. That was three years ago, a year before we married.

The cause of death? One evening I returned home from work, particularly tired after I had been covering more shootings by the police in the East Rand.

[1] A South African of Dutch lineage.

Then I had hurried back to the office in Johannesburg to piece together on my typewriter the violent scenes of the day, and then to file my report to meet the deadline. It was late when I returned home, and when I got there, I found a crowd of people in the yard. They were those who could not get inside. I panicked. What had happened? I did not ask those who were outside, being desperate to get into the house. They gave way easily when they recognized me.

Then I heard my mother's voice. Her cry rose well above the noise. It turned into a scream when she saw me. "What is it, mother?" I asked, embracing her out of a vaguely despairing sense of terror. But she pushed me away with an hysterical violence that astounded me.

"What misery have I brought you, my child?" she cried. At that point, many women in the room began to cry too. Soon, there was much wailing in the room, and then all over the house. The sound of it! The anguish! Understanding, yet eager for knowledge, I became desperate. I had to hold onto something. The desire to embrace my mother no longer had anything to do with comforting her; for whatever she had done, whatever its magnitude, had become inconsequential. I needed to embrace her for all the anguish that tied everyone in the house into a knot. I wanted to be part of that knot, yet I wanted to know what had brought it about.

Eventually, we found each other, my mother and I, and clasped each other tightly. When I finally released her, I looked around at the neighbors and suddenly had a vision of how that anguish had to be turned into a simmering kind of indignation. The kind of indignation that had to be kept at bay only because there was a higher purpose at that moment: the sharing of concern.

Slowly and with a calmness that surprised me, I began to gather the details of what had happened. Instinctively, I seemed to have been gathering notes for a news report.

It happened during the day, when the soldiers and the police that had been patrolling the township in their Casspirs[2] began to shoot in the streets at random. Need I describe what I did not see? How did the child come to die just at that moment when the police and the soldiers began to shoot at random, at any house, at any moving thing? That was how one of our windows was shattered by a bullet. And that was when my mother, who looked after her grandchild when we were away at work, panicked. She picked up the child and ran to the neighbors. It was only when she entered the neighbor's house that she noticed the wetness of the blanket that covered the child she held to her chest as she ran for the sanctuary of neighbors. She had looked at her unaccountably bloody hand, then she noted the still bundle in her arms, and began at that moment to blame herself for the death of her grandchild . . .

Later, the police, on yet another round of shooting, found people gathered at our house. They stormed in, saw what had happened. At first, they dragged my mother out, threatening to take her away unless she agreed not to say what had happened. But then they returned and, instead, took the body of the child

---

[2] Armored trucks.

away. By what freak of logic did they hope that by this act their carnage would never be discovered?

That evening, I looked at Buntu closely. He appeared suddenly to have grown older. We stood alone in an embrace in our bedroom. I noticed, when I kissed his face, how his once lean face had grown suddenly puffy.

At that moment, I felt the familiar impulse come upon me once more, the impulse I always felt when I sensed that Buntu was in some kind of danger, the impulse to yield something of myself to him. He wore the look of someone struggling to gain control of something. Yet, it was clear he was far from controlling anything. I knew that look. Had seen it many times. It came at those times when I sensed that he faced a wave that was infinitely stronger than he, that it would certainly sweep him away, but that he had to seem to be struggling. I pressed myself tightly to him as if to vanish into him; as if only the two of us could stand up to the wave.

35 "Don't worry," he said. "Don't worry. I'll do everything in my power to right this wrong. Everything. Even if it means suing the police!" We went silent.

I knew that silence. But I knew something else at that moment: that I had to find a way of disengaging myself from the embrace.

Suing the police? I listened to Buntu outlining his plans. "Legal counsel. That's what we need," he said. "I know some people in Pretoria,"[3] he said. As he spoke, I felt the warmth of intimacy between us cooling. When he finished, it was cold. I disengaged from his embrace slowly, yet purposefully. Why had Buntu spoken?

Later, he was to speak again, when all his plans had failed to work: "Over my dead body! Over my dead body!"

He sealed my lips. I would wait for him to feel and yield one day to all the realities of misfortune.

40 Ours was a home, it could be said. It seemed a perfect life for a young couple: I, a reporter; Buntu, a personnel officer at an American factory manufacturing farming implements. He had traveled to the United States and returned with a mind fired with dreams. We dreamed together. Much time we spent, Buntu and I, trying to make a perfect home. The occasions are numerous on which we paged through *Femina, Fair Lady, Cosmopolitan, Home Garden, Car,* as if somehow we were going to surround our lives with the glossiness in the magazines. Indeed, much of our time was spent window-shopping through the magazines. This time, it was different from the window-shopping we did that Saturday when we courted. This time our minds were consumed by the things we saw and dreamed of owning: the furniture, the fridge, TV, videocassette recorders, washing machines, even a vacuum cleaner and every other imaginable thing that would ensure a comfortable modern life.

Especially when I was pregnant. What is it that Buntu did not buy, then? And when the boy was born, Buntu changed the car. A family, he would say, must travel comfortably.

[3] The administrative capital of the Republic of South Africa.

The boy became the center of Buntu's life. Even before he was born, Buntu had already started making inquiries at white private schools. That was where he would send his son, the bearer of his name.

Dreams! It is amazing how the horrible findings of my newspaper reports often vanished before the glossy magazines of our dreams, how I easily forgot that the glossy images were concocted out of the keys of typewriters, made by writers whose business was to sell dreams at the very moment that death pervaded the land. So powerful are words and pictures that even their makers often believe in them.

Buntu's ordeal was long. So it seemed. He would get up early every morning to follow up the previous day's leads regarding the body of our son. I wanted to go with him, but each time I prepared to go he would shake his head. "It's my task," he would say. But every evening he returned, empty-handed, while with each day that passed and we did not know where the body of my child was, I grew restive and hostile in a manner that gave me much pain. Yet Buntu always felt compelled to give a report on each day's events. I never asked for it. I suppose it was his way of dealing with my silence.

One day he would say: "The lawyers have issued a court order that the body be produced. The writ of *habeas corpus*."[4]

On another day he would say: "We have petitioned the Minister of Justice."

On yet another he would say: "I was supposed to meet the Chief Security Officer. Waited the whole day. At the end of the day they said I would see him tomorrow if he was not going to be too busy. They are stalling."

Then he would say: "The newspapers, especially yours, are raising the hue and cry. The government is bound to be embarrassed. It's a matter of time."

And so it went on. Every morning he got up and left. Sometimes alone, sometimes with friends. He always left to bear the failure alone.

How much did I care about lawyers, petitions and Chief Security Officers? A lot. The problem was that whenever Buntu spoke about his efforts, I heard only his words. I felt in him the disguised hesitancy of someone who wanted reassurance without asking for it. I saw someone who got up every morning and left not to look for results, but to search for something he could only have found with me.

And each time he returned, I gave my speech to my eyes. And he answered without my having parted my lips. As a result, I sensed, for the first time in my life, a terrible power in me that could make him do anything. And he would never ever be able to deal with that power as long as he did not silence my eyes and call for my voice.

And so, he had to prove himself. And while he left each morning, I learned to be brutally silent. Could he prove himself without me? Could he? Then I got to know, those days, what I'd always wanted from him. I got to know why I have always drawn him into me whenever I sensed his vulnerability.

[4] Literally translated—to produce the body. Legal jurisdiction to prevent false imprisonment.

I wanted him to be free to fear. Wasn't there greater strength that way? Had he ever lived with his own feelings? And the stress of life in this land: didn't it call out for men to be heroes? And should they live up to it even though the details of the war to be fought may often be blurred? They should.

55 Yet it is precisely for that reason that I often found Buntu's thoughts lacking in strength. They lacked the experience of strife that could only come from a humbling acceptance of fear and then, only then, the need to fight it.

Me? In a way, I have always been free to fear. The prerogative of being a girl. It was always expected of me to scream when a spider crawled across the ceiling. It was known I would jump onto a chair whenever a mouse blundered into the room.

Then, once more, the Casspirs came. A few days before we got the body back, I was at home with my mother when we heard the great roar of truck engines. There was much running and shouting in the streets. I saw them, as I've always seen them on my assignments: the Casspirs. On five occasions they ran down our street at great speed, hurling tear-gas canisters at random. On the fourth occasion, they got our house. The canister shattered another window and filled the house with the terrible pungent choking smoke that I had got to know so well. We ran out of the house gasping for fresh air.

So, this was how my child was killed? Could they have been the same soldiers? Now hardened to their tasks? Or were they new ones being hardened to their tasks? Did they drive away laughing? Clearing paths for their families? What paths?

And was this our home? It couldn't be. It had to be a little bird's nest waiting to be plundered by a predator bird. There seemed no sense to the wedding pictures on the walls, the graduation pictures, birthday pictures, pictures of relatives, and paintings of lush landscapes. There seemed no sense anymore to what seemed recognizably human in our house. It took only a random swoop to obliterate personal worth, to blot out any value there may have been to the past. In desperation, we began to live only for the moment. I do feel hunted.

60 It was on the night of the tear gas that Buntu came home, saw what had happened, and broke down in tears. They had long been in the coming . . .

My own tears welled out too. How much did we have to cry to refloat stranded boats? I was sure they would float again.

A few nights later, on the night of the funeral, exhausted, I lay on my bed, listening to the last of the mourners leaving. Slowly, I became conscious of returning to the world. Something came back after it seemed not to have been there for ages. It came as a surprise, as a reminder that we will always live around what will happen. The sun will rise and set, and the ants will do their endless work, until one day the clouds turn gray and rain falls, and even in the township, the ants will fly out into the sky. Come what may.

My moon came, in a heavy surge of blood. And, after such a long time, I remembered the thing Buntu and I had buried in me. I felt it as if it had just entered. I felt it again as it floated away on the surge. I would be ready for another month. Ready as always, each and every month, for new beginnings.

And Buntu? I'll be with him, now. Always. Without our knowing, all the trying events had prepared for us new beginnings. Shall we not prevail?

Explorations of the Text

1. Why does Buntu not want to pay to have the body returned? Why is the "fundamental principle" so important to him?
2. Why does the narrator not care about this principle? What is her reaction to the death of her child and to the return of the body?
3. What is the purpose of the flashback to the "fish and chips" episode and to the confrontation with the Boers? What do the episodes reveal about the narrator's and Buntu's characters?
4. What is the meaning of the symbolism of the "stranded boats on a river that had gone dry"?
5. In the bedroom on the evening that the child has been killed, how does the narrator respond to the death? How does Buntu respond?
6. Why does Buntu have "to prove himself"?
7. What are the reasons for the rift between Buntu and the narrator? What does the "silence" between them suggest about their relationship and their possibly different ways of dealing with emotions?
8. What does the son represent in their lives?
9. What is the narrator's state of mind at the end of the story? Is the ending believable? falsely optimistic?
10. What do you learn about apartheid in South Africa and its impact on love relationships? family life? development of selfhood?

The Reading/Writing Connection

1. "Think" Topic: "No one is safe in this world." "No one can protect his/her child." Respond to one of these quotations in light of experience in the United States or in another country with which you are familiar.
2. It is unusual for writers to create first-person narrators of the opposite sex. How successfully does Ndebele convey the state of mind of a female narrator who has lost her child?
3. Freewrite and react to the vision of apartheid in this work.

Ideas for Writing

1. Contrast the characters of the narrator and Buntu.

HILLS LIKE WHITE ELEPHANTS

Ernest Hemingway

Ernest Hemingway (1899–1961), born in Oak Park, Illinois, served as an ambulance driver during World War I and was severely wounded. After the war, he lived in Paris among many artists and intellectuals who comprised the "Lost Generation." In 1926, Hemingway published The Sun Also Rises, *which made him famous. He was known for his condensed, allusive style, which was tremendously influential. Hemingway famously compared his writing to the movement of an iceberg, which, he noted, floated largely out of sight, hidden beneath the water but very much there. His subsequent works include* A Farewell to Arms *(1929),* For Whom the Bell Tolls *(1940), and* The Old Man and the Sea, *for which he was awarded the Pulitzer Prize. In 1954, he was awarded the Nobel Prize for Literature.*

1927

The hills across the valley of the Ebro[1] were long and white. On this side there was no shade and no trees and the station was between two lines of rails in the sun. Close against the side of the station there was the warm shadow of the building and a curtain, made of strings of bamboo beads, hung across the open door into the bar, to keep out flies. The American and the girl with him sat at a table in the shade, outside the building. It was very hot and the express from Barcelona would come in forty minutes. It stopped at this junction for two minutes and went on to Madrid.

"What should we drink?" the girl asked. She had taken off her hat and put it on the table.

"It's pretty hot," the man said.

"Let's drink beer."

"Dos cervezas,"[2] the man said into the curtain.

"Big ones?" a woman asked from the doorway.

"Yes. Two big ones."

The woman brought two glasses of beer and two felt pads. She put the felt pads and the beer glasses on the table and looked at the man and the girl. The girl was looking off at the line of hills. They were white in the sun and the country was brown and dry.

"They look like white elephants," she said.

"I've never seen one," the man drank his beer.

"No, you wouldn't have."

"I might have," the man said. "Just because you say I wouldn't have doesn't prove anything."

The girl looked at the bead curtain. "They've painted something on it," she said. "What does it say?"

---

[1] River in Spain.

[2] Two beers.

"Anis del Toro. It's a drink."

"Could we try it?"

The man called "Listen" through the curtain. The woman came out from the bar.

"Four reales."

"We want two Anis del Toro."

"With water?"

"Do you want it with water?"

"I don't know," the girl said. "Is it good with water?"

"It's all right."

"You want them with water?" asked the woman.

"Yes, with water."

"It tastes like licorice," the girl said and put the glass down.

"That's the way with everything."

"Yes," said the girl. "Everything tastes of licorice. Especially all the things you've waited so long for, like absinthe."

"Oh, cut it out."

"You started it," the girl said. "I was being amused. I was having a fine time."

"Well, let's try and have a fine time."

"All right. I was trying. I said the mountains looked like white elephants. Wasn't that bright?"

"That was bright."

"I wanted to try this new drink. That's all we do, isn't it—look at things and try new drinks?"

"I guess so."

The girl looked across the hills.

"They're lovely hills," she said. "They don't really look like white elephants. I just meant the coloring of their skin through the trees."

"Should we have another drink?"

"All right."

The warm wind blew the bead curtain against the table.

"The beer's nice and cool," the man said.

"It's lovely," the girl said.

"It's really an awfully simple operation, Jig," the man said. "It's not really an operation at all."

The girl looked at the ground the table legs rested on.

"I know you wouldn't mind it, Jig. It's really not anything. It's just to let the air in."

The girl did not say anything.

"I'll go with you and I'll stay with you all the time. They just let the air in and then it's all perfectly natural."

"Then what will we do afterward?"

"We'll be fine afterward. Just like we were before."

"What makes you think so?"

"That's the only thing that bothers us. It's the only thing that's made us unhappy."

The girl looked at the bead curtain, put her hand out and took hold of two of the strings of beads.

"And you think then we'll be all right and be happy."

"I know we will. You don't have to be afraid. I've known lots of people that have done it."

"So have I," said the girl. "And afterward they were all happy."

"Well," the man said, "if you don't want to you don't have to. I wouldn't have you do it if you didn't want to. But I know it's perfectly simple."

"And you really want to?"

"I think it's the best thing to do. But I don't want you to do it if you don't really want to."

"And if I do it you'll be happy and things will be like they were and you'll love me?"

"I love you now. You know I love you."

"I know. But if I do it, then it will be nice again if I say things are like white elephants, and you'll like it?"

"I'll love it. I love it now but I just can't think about it. You know how I get when I worry."

"If I do it you won't ever worry?"

"I won't worry about that because it's perfectly simple."

"Then I'll do it. Because I don't care about me."

"What do you mean?"

"I don't care about me."

"Well, I care about you."

"Oh, yes. But I don't care about me. And I'll do it and then everything will be fine."

The girl stood up and walked to the end of the station. Across, on the other side, were fields of grain and trees along the banks of the Ebro. Far away, beyond the river, were mountains. The shadow of a cloud moved across the field of grain and she saw the river through the trees.

"And we could have all this," she said. "And we could have everything and every day we make it more impossible."

"What did you say?"

"I said we could have everything."

"We can have everything."

"No, we can't."

"We can have the whole world."

"No, we can't."

"We can go everywhere."

"No, we can't. It isn't ours any more."

"It's ours."

"No, it isn't. And once they take it away, you never get it back."

"But they haven't taken it away."

"We'll wait and see."

"Come on back in the shade," he said. "You mustn't feel that way."

"I don't feel any way," the girl said. "I just know things."

"I don't want you to do anything that you don't want to do—"

"Nor that isn't good for me," she said. "I know. Could we have another beer?"

"All right. But you've got to realize—"

"I realize," the girl said. "Can't we maybe stop talking?"

They sat down at the table and the girl looked across at the hills on the dry side of the valley and the man looked at her and at the table.

"You've got to realize," he said, "that I don't want you to do it if you don't want to. I'm perfectly willing to go through with it if it means anything to you."

"Doesn't it mean anything to you? We could get along."

"Of course it does. But I don't want anybody but you. I don't want any one else. And I know it's perfectly simple."

"Yes, you know it's perfectly simple."

"It's all right for you to say that, but I do know it."

"Would you do something for me now?"

"I'd do anything for you."

"Would you please please please please please please please stop talking?"

He did not say anything but looked at the bags against the wall of the station. There were labels on them from all the hotels where they had spent nights.

"But I don't want you to," he said, "I don't care anything about it."

"I'll scream," the girl said.

The woman came out through the curtains with two glasses of beer and put them down on the damp felt pads. "The train comes in five minutes," she said.

"What did she say?" asked the girl.

"That the train is coming in five minutes."

The girl smiled brightly at the woman, to thank her.

"I'd better take the bags over to the other side of the station," the man said. She smiled at him.

"All right. Then come back and we'll finish the beer."

He picked up the two heavy bags and carried them around the station to the other tracks. He looked up the tracks but could not see the train. Coming back, he walked through the barroom, where people waiting for the train were drinking. He drank an Anis at the bar and looked at the people. They were all waiting reasonably for the train. He went out through the bead curtain. She was sitting at the table and smiled at him.

"Do you feel better?" he asked.

"I feel fine," she said. "There's nothing wrong with me. I feel fine."

Explorations of the Text

1. What mood is created at the beginning of the story?
2. Examine Jig's and the man's dialogue before the discussion of the operation. What can you infer about the woman's and the man's characters?
3. What is "it"? "the operation"? How does the symbol of the "white elephant" relate to the operation?
4. What is the source of the conflict between Jig and the man?
5. Discuss Jig's state of mind. What are her concerns? Isolate statements that reveal her feelings.
6. What are the man's reasons for wanting her to have "the operation"? Discuss his attitudes toward the woman and their relationship.
7. Why does she want him to "please . . . please stop talking"?
8. Explain the irony of Jig's last statement: "I feel fine. . . . There's nothing wrong with me. I feel fine."
9. Analyze the symbolism of the setting. How does setting develop themes of the story?

The Reading/Writing Connection

1. In a journal entry, write about what you would say to them if you were a marriage counselor.
2. Does Hemingway sympathize with either character? How can you tell?
3. Create a **monologue** in the voice of Jig or of the man several months or years later.

Ideas for Writing

1. Compare Hemingway's view of relationships with Ndebele's portrayal in "Death of a Son."
2. Why does Hemingway choose to present the story almost totally in **dialogue**? Evaluate this technique.
3. Compare Jig's possible feelings about love with the feeling of "the wave" in Paz's "My Life with the Wave."

EVELINE

James Joyce

James Joyce (1882–1941) was the eldest child of a poor, Catholic family in Dublin, Ireland. After graduating from University College, Dublin, he moved to Paris. Joyce lived on the Continent for the rest of his life, returning to Ireland only three times. In 1914, he published his famous collection of short stories, Dubliners. *It was followed by* A Portrait of the Artist as a Young Man *(1916);* Ulysses *(1922), his masterpiece; and* Finnegan's Wake *(1939). Joyce is considered one of the great literary innovators: developing the form of the modern short story and novel, experimenting with stream-of-consciousness, with narrative form, with language, with myth, and with symbol.*

1914

She sat at the window watching the evening invade the avenue. Her head was leaned against the window curtains and in her nostrils was the odour of dusty cretonne.[1] She was tired.

Few people passed. The man out of the last house passed on his way home; she heard his footsteps clacking along the concrete pavement and afterwards crunching on the cinder path before the new red houses. One time there used to be a field there in which they used to play every evening with other people's children. Then a man from Belfast[2] bought the field and built houses in it—not like their little brown houses but bright brick houses with shining roofs. The children of the avenue used to play together in that field—the Devines, the Waters, the Dunns, little Keogh the cripple, she and her brothers and sisters. Ernest, however, never played: he was too grown up. Her father used often to hunt them in out of the field with his blackthorn stick; but usually little Keogh used to keep *nix*[3] and call out when he saw her father coming. Still they seemed to have been rather happy then. Her father was not so bad then; and besides, her mother was alive. That was a long time ago; she and her brothers and sisters were all grown up; her mother was dead. Tizzie Dunn was dead, too, and the Waters had gone back to England. Everything changes. Now she was going to go away like the others, to leave her home.

Home! She looked round the room, reviewing all its familiar objects which she had dusted once a week for so many years, wondering where on earth all the dust came from. Perhaps she would never see again those familiar objects from which she had never dreamed of being divided. And yet during all those years she had never found out the name of the priest whose yellowing photograph hung on the wall above the broken harmonium beside the coloured print of the promises made to Blessed Margaret Mary Alacoque. He had been a school friend of her father. Whenever he showed the photograph to a visitor her father used to pass it with a casual word:

"He is Melbourne now."

5 She had consented to go away, to leave her home. Was that wise? She tried to weigh each side of the question. In her home anyway she had shelter and food; she had those whom she had known all her life about her. Of course she

[1] A heavy cotton material used for draperies and slipcovers.

[2] Capital of present-day Northern Ireland; a city in Ireland before the partition.

[3] Keep watch (slang expression).

had to work hard both in the house and at business. What would they say of her in the Stores when they found out that she had run away with a fellow? Say she was a fool, perhaps; and her place would be filled up by advertisement. Miss Gavan would be glad. She had always had an edge on her, especially whenever there were people listening.

"Miss Hill, don't you see these ladies are waiting?"

"Look lively, Miss Hill, please."

She would not cry many tears at leaving the Stores.

But in her new home, in a distant unknown country, it would not be like that. Then she would be married—she, Eveline. People would treat her with respect then. She would not be treated as her mother had been. Even now, though she was over nineteen, she sometimes felt herself in danger of her father's violence. She knew it was that that had given her the palpitations. When they were growing up he had never gone for her, like he used to go for Harry and Ernest, because she was a girl; but latterly he had begun to threaten her and say what he would do to her only for her dead mother's sake. And now she had nobody to protect her. Ernest was dead and Harry, who was in the church decorating business, was nearly always down somewhere in the country. Besides, the invariable squabble for money on Saturday nights had begun to weary her unspeakably. She always gave her entire wages—seven shillings—and Harry always sent up what he could but the trouble was to get any money from her father. He said she used to squander the money, that she had no head, that he wasn't going to give her his hard-earned money to throw about the streets, and much more, for he was usually fairly bad of a Saturday night. In the end he would give her the money and ask her had she any intention of buying Sunday's dinner. Then she had to rush out as quickly as she could and do her marketing, holding her black leather purse tightly in her hand as she elbowed her way through the crowds and returning home late under her load of provisions. She had hard work to keep the house together and to see that the two young children who had been left to her charge went to school regularly and got their meals regularly. It was hard work—a hard life—but now that she was about to leave it she did not find it a wholly undesirable life.

10 She was about to explore another life with Frank. Frank was very kind, manly, open-hearted. She was to go away with him by the night-boat to be his wife and to live with him in Buenos Ayres where he had a home waiting for her. How well she remembered the first time she had seen him; he was lodging in a house on the main road where she used to visit. It seemed a few weeks ago. He was standing at the gate, his peaked cap pushed back on his head and his hair tumbled forward over a face of bronze. Then they had come to know each other. He used to meet her outside the Stores every evening and see her home. He took her to see *The Bohemian Girl* and she felt elated as she sat in an unaccustomed part of the theatre with him. He was awfully fond of music and sang a little. People knew that they were courting and, when he sang about the lass that loves a sailor, she always felt pleasantly confused. He used to call her Poppens out of fun. First of all it had been an excitement for her to have a fellow and then she had begun to like him. He had tales of distant countries. He

had started as a deck boy at a pound a month on a ship of the Allan Line going out to Canada. He told her the names of the ships he had been on and the names of the different services. He had sailed through the Straits of Magellan[4] and he told her stories of the terrible Patagonians.[5] He had fallen on his feet in Buenos Ayres, he said, and had come over to the old country just for a holiday. Of course, her father had found out the affair and had forbidden her to have anything to say to him.

"I know these sailor chaps," he said.

One day he had quarrelled with Frank and after that she had to meet her lover secretly.

The evening deepened in the avenue. The white of two letters in her lap grew indistinct. One was to Harry; the other was to her father. Ernest had been her favourite but she liked Harry too. Her father was becoming old lately, she noticed; he would miss her. Sometimes he could be very nice. Not long before, when she had been laid up for a day, he had read her out a ghost story and made toast for her at the fire. Another day, when their mother was alive, they had all gone for a picnic to the Hill of Howth. She remembered her father putting on her mother's bonnet to make the children laugh.

Her time was running out but she continued to sit by the window, leaning her head against the window curtain, inhaling the odour of dusty cretonne. Down far in the avenue she could hear a street organ playing. She knew the air. Strange that it should come that very night to remind her of the promise to her mother, her promise to keep the home together as long as she could. She remembered the last night of her mother's illness; she was again in the close dark room at the other side of the hall and outside she heard a melancholy air of Italy. The organ-player had been ordered to go away and given sixpence. She remembered her father strutting back into the sickroom saying:

"Damned Italians! coming over here!"

As she mused the pitiful vision of her mother's life laid its spell on the very quick of her being—that life of commonplace sacrifices closing in final craziness. She trembled as she heard again her mother's voice saying constantly with foolish insistence:

"Derevaun Seraun! Derevaun Seraun!"[6]

She stood up in a sudden impulse of terror. Escape! She must escape! Frank would save her. He would give her life, perhaps love, too. But she wanted to live. Why should she be unhappy? She had a right to happiness. Frank would take her in his arms, fold her in his arms. He would save her.

She stood among the swaying crowd in the station at the North Wall. He held her hand and she knew that he was speaking to her, saying something

---

[4] Channel linking the Atlantic and Pacific oceans at the tip of South America.

[5] People inhabiting the region of Patagonia in southern Argentina and Chile.

[6] **Derevaun Seraun!** This exclamation, according to scholars, has never been completely understood; it is assumed to be gibberish spoken by the mother in her delirium.

about the passage over and over again. The station was full of soldiers with brown baggages. Through the wide doors of the sheds she caught a glimpse of the black mass of the boat, lying in beside the quay[7] wall, with illumined portholes. She answered nothing. She felt her cheek pale and cold and, out of a maze of distress, she prayed to God to direct her, to show her what was her duty. The boat blew a long mournful whistle into the mist. If she went, tomorrow she would be on the sea with Frank, steaming toward Buenos Ayres. Their passage had been booked. Could she still draw back after all he had done for her? Her distress awoke a nausea in her body and she kept moving her lips in silent fervent prayer.

A bell clanged upon her heart. She felt him seize her hand:

"Come!"

All the seas of the world tumbled about her heart. He was drawing her into them: he would drown her. She gripped with both hands at the iron railing.

"Come!"

No! no! No! It was impossible. Her hands clutched the iron in frenzy. Amid the seas she sent a cry of anguish!

"Eveline! Evvy!"

He rushed beyond the barrier and called to her to follow. He was shouted at to go on but he still called to her. She set her white face to him, passive, like a helpless animal. Her eyes gave him no sign of love or farewell or recognition.

Explorations of the Text

1. How do the first two paragraphs create the setting and mood of the story? What details are most significant? What do the details suggest about Eveline's situation?
2. Why is Eveline drawn to Frank? Discuss Eveline's inner conflict.
3. Analyze the symbol of the cretonne curtain and the window.
4. Discuss the conclusion of the story. What is Eveline's epiphany? Do you think that she leaves with Frank?
5. Discuss images of entrapment in this story, in *And the Soul Shall Dance,* and/or in "The Wave."

The Reading/Writing Connection

1. "Think" Topic: Does Eveline leave with Frank? Create a debate in class based on this question. As preparation for the debate, list pros and cons.
2. Journal Entry: Write about leaving home. Consult Greg Delanty's poem, "Leavetaking," and Staci Ferris's Response Essay in chapter 4. What are the challenges? Rewards?

[7] A landing place beside a body of water; a wharf.

3. Continue the narrative. Write a monologue in Frank's or Eveline's voice.

Ideas for Writing

1. Write an essay on risk taking. Use your own experiences and that of two other protagonists in works from this chapter. (Consider, for example, Norma Jean in "Shiloh," or the unnamed wife in "The Chase.")
2. Joyce is considered a master of the modern short story. How do the elements of the story (consult the checklist for fiction in chapter 10) develop themes of the work?
3. Using criteria that you create for a successful short story, evaluate this work.
4. Write an argumentative essay that presents your position about Eveline's leaving home. Use the "Think" topic as prewriting material.

SHILOH

Bobbie Ann Mason

Born in Mayfield, Kentucky, Bobbie Ann Mason (1940–   ) was educated at the University of Kentucky, the State University of New York at Binghamton, and the University of Connecticut. Her first collection of stories, Shiloh and Other Stories *(1982), won the Ernest Hemingway Award for First Fiction. Subsequent works include* Love Life: Stories *(1988),* In Country *(1985),* Spence and Lila *(1988), and* Feather Crowns *(1994). Mason is associated with so-called Kmart realism, which is to say, the use in fiction of icons of popular culture, particularly lower-class culture, to make serious points. She has been awarded fellowships by the National Endowment of the Arts and the Guggenheim Foundation.*

1982

Leroy Moffitt's wife, Norma Jean, is working on her pectorals. She lifts three-pound dumbbells to warm up, then progresses to a twenty-pound barbell. Standing with her legs apart, she reminds Leroy of Wonder Woman.

"I'd give anything if I could just get these muscles to where they're real hard," says Norma Jean. "Feel this arm. It's not as hard as the other one."

"That's 'cause you're right-handed," says Leroy, dodging as she swings the barbell in an arc.

"Do you think so?"

5 "Sure."

Leroy is a truckdriver. He injured his leg in a highway accident four months ago, and his physical therapy, which involves weights and a pulley, prompted Norma Jean to try building herself up. Now she is attending a body-building class. Leroy has been collecting temporary disability since his tractor-trailer jackknifed in Missouri, badly twisting his left leg in its socket. He has a steel pin in his hip. He will probably not be able to drive his rig again. It sits in the backyard, like a gigantic bird that has flown home to roost. Leroy has been home in Kentucky for three months, and his leg is almost healed, but the accident frightened him and he does not want to drive any more long hauls. He is not sure what to do next. In the meantime, he makes things from craft kits. He started by building a miniature log cabin from notched Popsicle sticks. He varnished it and placed it on the TV set, where it remains. It reminds him of a rustic Nativity scene. Then he tried string art (sailing ships on black velvet), a macramé owl kit, a snap-together B-17 Flying Fortress,[1] and a lamp made out of a model truck, with a light fixture screwed in the top of the cab. At first the kits were diversions, something to kill time, but now he is thinking about building a full-scale log house from a kit. It would be considerably cheaper than building a regular house, and besides, Leroy has grown to appreciate how things are put together. He has begun to realize that in all the years he was on the road he never took time to examine anything. He was always flying past scenery.

"They won't let you build a long cabin in any of the new subdivisions," Norma Jean tells him.

"They will if I tell them it's for you," he says, teasing her. Ever since they were married, he has promised Norma Jean he would build her a new home one day. They have always rented, and the house they live in is small and nondescript. It does not even feel like a home, Leroy realizes now.

Norma Jean works at the Rexall drugstore, and she has acquired an amazing amount of information about cosmetics. When she explains to Leroy the three stages of complexion care, involving creams, toners, and moisturizers, he thinks happily of other petroleum products—axle grease, diesel fuel. This is a connection between him and Norma Jean. Since he has been home, he has felt unusually tender about his wife and guilty over his long absences. But he can't tell what she feels about him. Norma Jean has never complained about his traveling; she has never made hurtful remarks, like calling his truck a "widow-maker." He is reasonably certain she has been faithful to him, but he wishes she would celebrate his permanent home-coming more happily. Norma Jean is often startled to find Leroy at home, and he thinks she seems a little disappointed about it. Perhaps he reminds her too much of the early days of their marriage, before he went on the road. They had a child who died as an infant, years ago. They never speak about their memories of Randy, which have almost faded, but now that Leroy is home all the time, they sometimes feel awkward around each other, and Leroy wonders if one of them should mention the child. He has the feeling that they are waking up out of a dream together—that they must create a new marriage, start afresh. They are lucky they are still married. Leroy has read that for most people losing a child destroys the

[1] A model of a heavy bomber used by the U.S. Army in World War II.

marriage—or else he heard this on *Donahue*.[2] He can't always remember where he learns things anymore.

10 At Christmas, Leroy bought an electric organ for Norma Jean. She used to play the piano when she was in high school. "It don't leave you," she told him once. "It's like riding a bicycle."

The new instrument had so many keys and buttons that she was bewildered by it at first. She touched the keys tentatively, pushed some buttons, then pecked out "Chopsticks." It came out in an amplified fox-trot rhythm, with marimba sounds.

"It's an orchestra!" she cried.

The organ had a pecan-look finish and eighteen preset chords, with optional flute, violin, trumpet, clarinet, and banjo accompaniments. Norma Jean mastered the organ almost immediately. At first she played Christmas songs. Then she bought *The Sixties Songbook* and learned every tune in it, adding variations to each with the rows of brightly colored buttons.

"I didn't like these old songs back then," she said. "But I have this crazy feeling I missed something."

15 "You didn't miss a thing," said Leroy.

Leroy likes to lie on the couch and smoke a joint and listen to Norma Jean play "Can't Take My Eyes Off You" and "I'll Be Back." He is back again. After fifteen years on the road, he is finally settling down with the woman he loves. She is still pretty. Her skin is flawless. Her frosted curls resemble pencil trimmings.

Now that Leroy has come home to stay, he notices how much the town has changed. Subdivisions are spreading across western Kentucky like an oil slick. The sign at the edge of town says "Pop: 11,500"—only seven hundred more than it said twenty years before. Leroy can't figure out who is living in all the new houses. The farmers who used to gather around the courthouse square on Saturday afternoons to play checkers and spit tobacco juice have gone. It has been years since Leroy has thought about the farmers, and they have disappeared without his noticing.

Leroy meets a kid named Stevie Hamilton in the parking lot at the new shopping center. While they pretend to be strangers meeting over a stalled car, Stevie tosses an ounce of marijuana under the front seat of Leroy's car. Stevie is wearing orange jogging shoes and a T-shirt that says CHATTAHOOCHEE SUPER-RAT. His father is a prominent doctor who lives in one of the expensive subdivisions in a new white-columned brick house that looks like a funeral parlor. In the phone book under his name there is a separate number, with the listing "Teenagers."

"Where do you get this stuff?" asks Leroy. "From your pappy?"

20 "That's for me to know and you to find out," Stevie says. He is slit-eyed and skinny.

[2] Popular television talk show hosted by Phil Donahue.

"What else you got?"

"What you interested in?"

"Nothing special. Just wondered."

Leroy used to take speed on the road. Now he has to go slowly. He needs to be mellow. He leans back against the car and stays, "I'm aiming to build me a log house, soon as I get time. My wife, though, I don't think she likes the idea."

25 "Well, let me know when you want me again," Stevie says. He has a cigarette in his cupped palm, as though sheltering it from the wind. He takes a long drag, then stomps it on the asphalt and slouches away.

Stevie's father was two years ahead of Leroy in high school. Leroy is thirty-four. He married Norma Jean when they were both eighteen, and their child Randy was born a few months later, but he died at the age of four months and three days. He would be about Stevie's age now. Norma Jean and Leroy were at the drive-in, watching a double feature (*Dr. Strangelove* and *Lover Come Back*), and the baby was sleeping in the back seat. When the first movie ended, the baby was dead. It was the sudden infant death syndrome. Leroy remembers handing Randy to a nurse at the emergency room, as though he were offering her a large doll as a present. A dead baby feels like a sack of flour. "It just happens sometimes," said the doctor, in what Leroy always recalls as a nonchalant tone. Leroy can hardly remember the child anymore, but he still sees vividly a scene from *Dr. Strangelove* in which the President of the United States was talking in a folksy voice on the hot line to the Soviet premier about the bomber accidentally headed toward Russia. He was in the War Room, and the world map was lit up. Leroy remembers Norma Jean standing catatonically beside him in the hospital and himself thinking: Who is this strange girl? He had forgotten who she was. Now scientists are saying that crib death is caused by a virus. Nobody knows anything, Leroy thinks. The answers are always changing.

When Leroy gets home from the shopping center, Norma Jean's mother, Mabel Beasley, is there. Until this year, Leroy has not realized how much time she spends with Norma Jean. When she visits, she inspects the closets and then the plants, informing Norma Jean when a plant is droopy or yellow. Mabel calls the plants "flowers," although there are never any blooms. She also notices if Norma Jean's laundry is piling up. Mabel is a short, overweight woman whose tight, brown-dyed curls look more like a wig than the actual wig she sometimes wears. Today she has brought Norma Jean an off-white dust ruffle she made for the bed; Mabel works in a custom-upholstery shop.

"This is the tenth one I made this year," Mabel says. "I got started and couldn't stop."

"It's real pretty," says Norma Jean.

30 "Now we can hide things under the bed," says Leroy, who gets along with his mother-in-law primarily by joking with her. Mabel has never really forgiven him for disgracing her by getting Norma Jean pregnant. When the baby died, she said that fate was mocking her.

"What's that thing?" Mabel says to Leroy in a loud voice, pointing to a tangle of yarn on a piece of canvas.

Leroy holds it up for Mabel to see. "It's my needlepoint," he explains. "This is a *Star Trek* pillow cover."

"That's what a woman would do," says Mabel. "Great day in the morning!"

"All the big football players on TV do it," he says.

"Why, Leroy, you're always trying to fool me. I don't believe you for one minute. You don't know what to do with yourself—that's the whole trouble. Sewing!"

"I'm aiming to build us a log house," says Leroy. "Soon as my plans come."

"Like *heck* you are," says Norma Jean. She takes Leroy's needlepoint and shoves it into a drawer. "You have to find a job first. Nobody can afford to build now anyway."

Mabel straightens her girdle and says, "I still think before you get tied down y'all ought to take a little run to Shiloh."

"One of these days, Mama," Norma Jean says impatiently.

Mabel is talking about Shiloh, Tennessee. For the past few years, she has been urging Leroy and Norma Jean to visit the Civil War battleground there. Mabel went there on her honeymoon—the only real trip she ever took. Her husband died of a perforated ulcer when Norma Jean was ten, but Mabel, who was accepted into the United Daughters of the Confederacy in 1975, is still preoccupied with going back to Shiloh.

"I've been to kingdom come and back in that truck out yonder," Leroy says to Mabel, "but we never yet set foot in that battleground. Ain't' that something? How did I miss it?"

"It's not even that far," Mabel says.

After Mabel leaves, Norma Jean reads to Leroy from a list she has made. "Things you could do," she announces. "You could get a job as a guard at Union Carbide, where they'd let you set on a stool. You could get on at the lumberyard. You could do a little carpenter work, if you want to build so bad. You could—"

"I can't do something where I'd have to stand up all day."

"You ought to try standing up all day behind a cosmetics counter. It's amazing that I have strong feet, coming from two parents that never had strong feet at all." At the moment Norma Jean is holding on to the kitchen counter, raising her knees one at a time as she talks. She is wearing two-pound ankle weights.

"Don't worry," says Leroy. "I'll do something."

"You could truck calves to slaughter for somebody. You wouldn't have to drive any big old truck for that."

"I'm going to build you this house," says Leroy. "I want to make you a real home."

"I don't want to live in any log cabin."

"It's not a cabin. It's a house."

"I don't care. It looks like a cabin."

"You and me together could lift those logs. It's just like lifting weights."

Norma Jean doesn't answer. Under her breath, she is counting. Now she is marching through the kitchen. She is doing goose steps.

Before his accident, when Leroy came home he used to stay in the house with Norma Jean, watching TV in bed and playing cards. She would cook fried chicken, picnic ham, chocolate pie—all his favorites. Now he is home alone much of the time. In the mornings, Norma Jean disappears, leaving a cooling place in the bed. She eats a cereal called Body Buddies, and she leaves the bowl on the table, with the soggy tan balls floating in a milk puddle. He sees things about Norma Jean that he never realized before. When she chops onions, she stares off into a corner, as if she can't bear to look. She puts on her house slippers almost precisely at nine o'clock every evening and nudges her jogging shoes under the couch. She saves bread heels for the birds. Leroy watches the birds at the feeder. He notices the peculiar way goldfinches fly past the window. They close their wings, then fall, then spread their wings to catch and lift themselves. He wonders if they close their eyes when they fall. Norma Jean closes her eyes when they are in bed. She wants the lights turned out. Even then, he is sure she closes her eyes.

55 He goes for long drives around town. He tends to drive a car rather carelessly. Power steering and an automatic shift make a car feel so small and inconsequential that his body is hardly involved in the driving process. His injured leg stretches out comfortably. Once or twice he has almost hit something, but even the prospect of an accident seems minor in a car. He cruises the new subdivisions, feeling like a criminal rehearsing for a robbery. Norma Jean is probably right about a log house being inappropriate here in the new subdivision. All the houses look grand and complicated. They depress him.

One day when Leroy comes home from a drive he finds Norma Jean in tears. She is in the kitchen making a potato and mushroom-soup casserole, with grated cheese topping. She is crying because her mother caught her smoking.

"I didn't hear her coming. I was standing here puffing away pretty as you please," Norma Jean says, wiping her eyes.

"I knew it would happen sooner or later," says Leroy, putting his arm around her.

"She don't know the meaning of the word 'knock,'" says Norma Jean. "It's a wonder she hadn't caught me years ago."

60 "Think of it this way," Leroy says. "What if she caught me with a joint?"

"You better not let her!" Norma Jean shrieks. "I'm warning you, Leroy Moffitt!"

"I'm just kidding. Here, play me a tune. That'll help you relax."

Norma Jean puts the casserole in the oven and sets the timer. Then she plays a ragtime tune, with horns and banjo, as Leroy lights up a joint and lies on the couch, laughing to himself about Mabel's catching him at it. He thinks of Stevie Hamilton—a doctor's son pushing grass. Everything is funny. The whole town seems crazy and small. He is reminded of Virgil Mathis, a boastful policeman Leroy used to shoot pool with. Virgil recently led a drug bust in a back room at a bowling alley, where he seized ten thousand dollars' worth of marijuana. The newspaper had a picture of him holding up the bags of grass and grinning widely. Right now, Leroy can imagine Virgil breaking down the door and arresting him with a lungful of smoke. Virgil would probably have been alerted to the scene because of all the racket Norma Jean is making. Now she sounds like a hard-rock band. Norma Jean is terrific. When she switches to a Latin-rhythm version of "Sunshine Superman," Leroy hums along. Norma Jean's foot goes up and down, up and down.

"Well, what do you think?" Leroy says, when Norma Jean pauses to search through her music.

65 "What do I think about what?"

His mind has gone blank. Then he says, "I'll sell my rig and build us a house." That wasn't what he wanted to say. He wanted to know what she thought—what she *really* thought—about them.

"Don't start in on that again," says Norma Jean. She begins playing "Who'll Be the Next in Line?"

Leroy used to tell hitchhikers his whole life story—about his travels, his hometown, the baby. He would end with a question: "Well, what do you think?" It was just a rhetorical question. In time, he had the feeling that he'd been telling the same story over and over to the same hitchhikers. He quit talking to hitchhikers when he realized how his voice sounded—whining and self-pitying, like some teenage-tragedy song. Now Leroy has the sudden impulse to tell Norma Jean about himself, as if he had just met her. They have known each other so long they have forgotten a lot about each other. They could become reacquainted. But when the oven timer goes off and she runs to the kitchen, he forgets why he wants to do this.

The next day, Mabel drops by. It is Saturday and Norma Jean is cleaning. Leroy is studying the plans of his log house, which have finally come in the mail. He has them spread out on the table—big sheets of stiff blue paper, with diagrams and numbers printed in white. While Norma Jean runs the vacuum, Mabel drinks coffee. She sets her coffee cup on a blueprint.

70 "I'm just waiting for time to pass," she says to Leroy, drumming her fingers on the table.

As soon as Norma Jean switches off the vacuum, Mabel says in a loud voice, "Did you hear about the datsun dog that killed the baby?"

Norma Jeans says, "The word is 'dachshund.' "

"They put the dog on trial. It chewed the baby's legs off. The mother was in the next room all the time." She raises her voice. "They thought it was neglect."

Norma Jean is holding her ears. Leroy manages to open the refrigerator and get some Diet Pepsi to offer Mabel. Mabel still has some coffee and she waves away the Pepsi.

75 "Datsuns are like that," Mabel says. "They're jealous dogs. They'll tear a place to pieces if you don't keep an eye on them."

"You better watch out what you're saying, Mabel," says Leroy.

"Well, facts is facts."

Leroy looks out the window at his rig. It is like a huge piece of furniture gathering dust in the backyard. Pretty soon it will be an antique. He hears the vacuum cleaner. Norma Jean seems to be cleaning the living room rug again.

Later, she says to Leroy, "She just said that about the baby because she caught me smoking. She's trying to pay me back."

80 "What are you talking about?" Leroy says, nervously shuffling blueprints.

"You know good and well," Norma Jean says. She is sitting in a kitchen chair with her feet up and her arms wrapped around her knees. She looks small and helpless. She says, "The very idea, her bringing up a subject like that! Saying it was neglect."

"She didn't mean that," Leroy says.

"She might not have *thought* she meant it. She always says things like that. You don't know how she goes on."

"But she didn't really mean it. She was just talking."

85 Leroy opens a king-sized bottle of beer and pours it into two glasses, dividing it carefully. He hands a glass to Norma Jean and she takes it from him mechanically. For a long time, they sit by the kitchen window watching the birds at the feeder.

Something is happening. Norma Jean is going to night school. She has graduated from her six-week body-building course and now she is taking an adult-education course in composition at Paducah Community College. She spends her evenings outlining paragraphs.

"First, you have a topic sentence," she explains to Leroy. "Then you divide it up. Your secondary topic has to be connected to your primary topic."

To Leroy, this sounds intimidating. "I never was any good in English," he says.

"It makes a lot of sense."

90 "What are you doing this for, anyhow?"

She shrugs. "It's something to do." She stands up and lifts her dumbbells a few times.

"Driving a rig, nobody cared about my English."

"I'm not criticizing your English."

Norma Jean used to say, "If I lose ten minutes' sleep, I just drag all day." Now she stays up late, writing compositions. She got a B on her first paper—a how-to theme on soup-based casseroles. Recently Norma Jean has been cooking unusual foods—tacos, lasagna, Bombay chicken. She doesn't play the organ anymore, though her second paper was called "Why Music Is Important to Me." She sits at the kitchen table, concentrating on her outlines, while Leroy plays with his log house plans, practicing with a set of Lincoln logs. The thought of getting a truckload of notched, numbered logs scares him, and he wants to be prepared. As he and Norma Jean work together at the kitchen table, Leroy has the hopeful thought that they are sharing something, but he knows he is a fool to think this. Norma Jean is miles away. He knows he is going to lose her. Like Mabel, he is just waiting for time to pass.

95 One day, Mabel is there before Norma Jean gets home from work, and Leroy finds himself confiding in her. Mabel, he realizes, must know Norma Jean better than he does.

"I don't know what's got into that girl," Mabel says. "She used to go to bed with the chickens. Now you say she's up all hours. Plus her a-smoking. I like to died."

"I want to make her this beautiful house," Leroy says, indicating the Lincoln Logs. "I don't think she even wants it. Maybe she was happier with me gone."

"She don't know what to make of you, coming home like this."

"Is that it?"

100 Mabel takes the roof off his Lincoln Log cabin. "You couldn't get *me* in a log cabin," she says. "I was raised in one. It's no picnic, let me tell you."

"They're different now," says Leroy.

"I tell you what," Mabel says, smiling oddly at Leroy.

"What?"

"Take her on down to Shiloh. Y'all need to get out together, stir a little. Her brain's all balled up over them books."

105 Leroy can see traces of Norma Jean's features in her mother's face. Mabel's worn face has the texture of crinkled cotton, but suddenly she looks pretty. It occurs to Leroy that Mabel has been hinting all along that she wants them to take her with them to Shiloh.

"Let's all go to Shiloh," he says. "You and me and her. Come Sunday."

Mabel throws up her hand in protest. "Oh, no, not me. Young folks want to be by theirselves."

When Norma Jean comes in with groceries, Leroy says excitedly, "Your mama here's been dying to go to Shiloh for thirty-five years. It's about time we went, don't you think?"

"I'm not going to butt in on anybody's second honeymoon," Mabel says.

110 "Who's going on a honeymoon, for Christ's sake?" Norma Jean says loudly.

"I never raised no daughter of mine to talk that-a-way," Mabel says.

"You ain't seen nothing yet," says Norma Jean. She starts putting away boxes and cans, slamming cabinet doors.

"There's a log cabin at Shiloh," Mabel says. "It was there during the battle. There's bullet holes in it."

"When are you going to *shut up* about Shiloh, Mama?" asks Norma Jean.

115 "I always thought Shiloh was the prettiest place, so full of history," Mabel goes on. "I just hoped y'all could see it once before I die, so you could tell me about it." Later, she whispers to Leroy, "You do what I said. A little change is what she needs."

"Your name means 'the king,'" Norma Jean says to Leroy that evening. He is trying to get her to go to Shiloh, and she is reading a book about another century.

"Well, I reckon I ought to be right proud."

"I guess so."

"Am I still king around here?"

120 Norma Jean flexes her biceps and feels them for hardness. "I'm not fooling around with anybody, if that's what you mean," she says.

"Would you tell me if you were?"

"I don't know."

"What does *your* name mean?"

"It was Marilyn Monroe's real name."

125 "No kidding!"

"Norma comes from the Normans. They were invaders," she says. She closes her book and looks hard at Leroy. "I'll go to Shiloh with you if you'll stop staring at me."

On Sunday, Norma Jean packs a picnic and they go to Shiloh.[3] To Leroy's relief Mabel says she does not want to come with them. Norma Jean drives, and Leroy, sitting beside her, feels like some boring hitchhiker she has picked up. He tries some conversation, but she answers him in monosyllables. At Shiloh, she drives aimlessly through the park, past bluffs and trails and steep ravines. Shiloh is an immense place, and Leroy cannot see it as a battleground. It is not what he expected. He thought it would look like a golf course. Monuments are everywhere, showing through the thick clusters of trees. Norma Jean passes the log cabin Mabel mentioned. It is surrounded by tourists looking for bullet holes.

"That's not the kind of log house I've got in mind," says Leroy apologetically.

"I know *that.*"

130 "This is a pretty place. Your mama was right."

"It's O.K.," says Norma Jean. "Well, we've seen it. I hope she's satisfied."

They burst out laughing together.

At the park museum, a movie on Shiloh is shown every half hour, but they decide that they don't want to see it. They buy a souvenir Confederate flag for Mabel, and then they find a picnic spot near the cemetery. Norma Jean has brought a picnic cooler, with pimento sandwiches, soft drinks, and Yodels. Leroy eats a sandwich and then smokes a joint, hiding it behind the picnic cooler. Norma Jean has quit smoking altogether. She is picking cake crumbs from the cellophane wrapper, like a fussy bird.

Leroy says, "So the boys in gray ended up in Corinth. The Union soldiers zapped 'em finally. April 7, 1862."

135 They both know that he doesn't know any history. He is just talking about some of the historical plaques they have read. He feels awkward, like a boy on a date with an older girl. They are still just making conversation.

[3] Site of a famous Civil War battle fought in southwestern Tennessee, April 6–7, 1862. The battle resulted in a victory for the North, but there were large numbers of casualties on both sides.

"Corinth is where Mama eloped to," says Norma Jean.

They sit in silence and stare at the cemetery for the Union dead and, beyond, at a tall cluster of trees. Campers are parked nearby, bumper to bumper, and small children in bright clothing are cavorting and squealing. Norma Jean wads up the cake wrapper and squeezes it tightly in her hand. Without looking at Leroy, she says, "I want to leave you."

Leroy takes a bottle of Coke out of the cooler and flips off the cap. He holds the bottle poised near his mouth but cannot remember to take a drink. Finally he says, "No, you don't."

"Yes, I do."

140 "I won't let you."

"You can't stop me."

"Don't do me that way."

Leroy knows Norma Jean will have her own way. "Didn't I promise to be home from now on?" he says.

"In some ways, a woman prefers a man who wanders," says Norma Jean. "That sounds crazy, I know."

145 "You're not crazy."

Leroy remembers to drink from his Coke. Then he says, "Yes, you *are* crazy. You and me could start all over again. Right back at the beginning."

"We *have* started all over again," says Norma Jean. "And this is how it turned out."

"What did I do wrong?"

"Nothing."

150 "Is this one of those women's lib things?" Leroy asks.

"Don't be funny."

The cemetery, a green slope dotted with white markers, looks like a subdivision site. Leroy is trying to comprehend that his marriage is breaking up, but for some reason he is wondering about white slabs in a graveyard.

"Everything was fine till Mama caught me smoking," says Norma Jean, standing up. "That set something off."

"What are you talking about?"

155 "She won't leave me alone—*you* won't leave me alone." Norma Jean seems to be crying, but she is looking away from him. "I feel eighteen again. I can't face that all over again." She starts walking away. "No, it *wasn't* fine. I don't know what I'm saying. Forget it."

Leroy takes a lungful of smoke and closes his eyes as Norma Jean's words sink in. He tries to focus on the fact that thirty-five hundred soldiers died on the grounds around him. He can only think of that war as a board game with plastic soldiers. Leroy almost smiles, as he compares the Confederates' daring attack on the Union camps and Virgil Mathis's raid on the bowling alley. General Grant, drunk and furious, shoved the Southerners back to Corinth,[4] where Mabel and Jet Beasley were married years later, when Mabel was still thin

[4] Corinth, Mississippi.

and good-looking. The next day, Mabel and Jet visited the battleground, and then Norma Jean was born, and then she married Leroy and they had a baby, which they lost, and now Leroy and Norma Jean are here at the same battleground. Leroy knows he is leaving out a lot. He is leaving out the insides of history. History was always just names and dates to him. It occurs to him that building a house of logs is similarly empty—too simple. And the real inner workings of a marriage, like most of history, have escaped him. Now he sees that building a log house is the dumbest idea he could have had. It was clumsy of him to think Norma Jean would want a log house. It was a crazy idea. He'll have to think of something else, quickly. He will wad the blueprints into tight balls and fling them into the lake. Then he'll get moving again. He opens his eyes. Norma Jean has moved away and is walking through the cemetery, following a serpentine[5] brick path.

Leroy gets up to follow his wife, but his good leg is asleep and his bad leg still hurts him. Norma Jean is far away, walking rapidly toward the bluff by the river, and he tries to hobble toward her. Some children run past him, screaming noisily. Norma Jean has reached the bluff, and she is looking out over the Tennessee River. Now she turns toward Leroy and waves her arms. Is she beckoning to him? She seems to be doing an exercise for her chest muscles. The sky is unusually pale—the color of the dust ruffle Mabel made for their bed.

Explorations of the Text

1. What does the opening scene with the barbells reveal about Leroy's and Norma Jean's characters?
2. Why is Leroy building the log house? How has Leroy changed since his accident? How has Norma Jean changed since Leroy first married her?
3. What is Mabel's role in the story?
4. Discuss the significance of the trip to Shiloh. Closely examine the last two paragraphs. Relate the following quotation to themes of the story: "History was always just names and dates to him. . . . And the real inner workings of a marriage, like most of history, have escaped him."
5. Explore the conclusion of the story. What is happening? Does Norma Jean leave Leroy? What are possible interpretations of the ending?

The Reading/Writing Connection

1. Journal Entry: Continue the story. What happens to Norma Jean and to Leroy?

[5] A winding path.

2. Create an exchange of letters between Norma Jean and another character in this chapter. Here is one possible scenario: Have Norma Jean ask this character for advice about her relationship with Leroy.
3. "Think" Topic: Does the story present a realistic view of relationships?
4. Imagine that you are a marriage counselor. What advice would you give Leroy and Norma Jean?

Ideas for Writing

1. Who is responsible for the disintegration of the marriage: Leroy or Norma Jean? Write an argumentative essay defending your position.
2. Bobbie Ann Mason's work is noted for its minimalist style. The story seems straightforward and simply written, yet if one probes, one realizes that every detail builds the symbolic subtext of the work and the themes of the story. Choose one symbolic detail and explore it significance in building theme (e.g., the dust ruffle or the battle of Shiloh).

THE YELLOW WALLPAPER

Charlotte Perkins Gilman

Charlotte Perkins Gilman (1860–1935), born in Hartford, Connecticut, was raised by her mother. After divorcing her first husband, Gilman began to write, to lecture, and to teach. "The Yellow Wallpaper," her most famous story, appeared in 1892 in New England Magazine *and was based on her experience with treatment for postpartum depression. Gilman remarried in 1900. She wrote books about alternate social structures, including* The Home *(1903) and the feminist utopia,* Herland *(1915). She spoke at national and international women's conferences. Gilman committed suicide in 1935, stating that she preferred "chloroform to breast cancer" and that she felt it was her right to do so. Although she suffered from depression all her life, she was a remarkably productive writer and lecturer.*

1892

It is very seldom that mere ordinary people like John and myself secure ancestral halls for the summer.

A colonial mansion, a hereditary estate, I would say a haunted house and reach the height of romantic felicity—but that would be asking too much of fate!

Still I will proudly declare that there is something queer about it.

Else, why should it be let so cheaply? And why have stood so long untenanted?

5 John laughs at me, of course, but one expects that.

John is practical in the extreme. He has no patience with faith, an intense horror of superstition, and he scoffs openly at any talk of things not to be felt and seen and put down in figures.

John is a physician, and *perhaps*—(I would not say it to a living soul, of course, but this is dead paper and a great relief to my mind)—*perhaps* that is one reason I do not get well faster.

You see he does not believe I am sick! And what can one do?

If a physician of high standing, and one's own husband, assures friends and relatives that there is really nothing the matter with one but temporary nervous depression—a slight hysterical tendency[1]—what is one to do?

10 My brother is also a physician, and also of high standing, and he says the same thing.

So I take phosphates[2] or phosphites—whichever it is—and tonics, and air and exercise, and journeys, and am absolutely forbidden to "work" until I am well again.

Personally, I disagree with their ideas.

Personally, I believe that congenial work, with excitement and change, would do me good.

But what is one to do?

15 I did write for a while in spite of them; but it *does* exhaust me a good deal—having to be so sly about it, or else meet with heavy opposition.

I sometimes fancy that in my condition, if I had less opposition and more society and stimulus—but John says the very worst thing I can do is to think about my condition, and I confess it always makes me feel bad.

So I will let it alone and talk about the house.

The most beautiful place! It is quite alone, standing well back from the road, quite three miles from the village. It makes me think of English places that you read about, for there are hedges and walls and gates that lock, and lots of separate little houses for the gardeners and people.

There is a *delicious* garden! I never saw such a garden—large and shady, full of box-bordered paths, and lined with long grape-covered arbors with seats under them.

20 There were greenhouses, but they are all broken now.

There was some legal trouble, I believe, something about the heirs and co-heirs; anyhow, the place has been empty for years.

That spoils my ghostliness, I am afraid, but I don't care—there is something strange about the house—I can feel it.

I even said so to John one moonlight evening, but he said what I felt was a draught, and shut the window.

---

[1] Hysteria was a general nervous condition, often diagnosed in women in the late nineteenth century. Symptoms included tension, anxiety, nervousness, and depression.

[2] A carbonated beverage made of water, fruit syrup, and phosphoric acid, used for medicinal purposes.

I get unreasonably angry with John sometimes. I'm sure I never used to be so sensitive. I think it is due to this nervous condition.

But John says if I feel so I shall neglect proper self-control; so I take pains to control myself—before him, at least, and that makes me very tired.

I don't like our room a bit. I wanted one downstairs that opened onto the piazza and had roses all over the window, and such pretty old-fashioned chintz hangings! But John would not hear of it.

He said there was only one window and not room for two beds, and no near room for him if he took another.

He is very careful and loving, and hardly lets me stir without special direction.

I have a schedule prescription for each hour in the day; he takes all care from me, and so I feel basely ungrateful not to value it more.

He said we came here solely on my account, that I was to have perfect rest and all the air I could get. "Your exercise depends on your strength, my dear," said he, "and your food somewhat on your appetite; but air you can absorb all the time." So we took the nursery at the top of the house.

It is a big, airy room, the whole floor nearly, with windows that look all ways, and air and sunshine galore. It was nursery first, and then playroom and gymnasium, I should judge, for the windows are barred for little children, and there are rings and things in the walls.

The paint and paper look as if a boys' school had used it. It is stripped off—the paper—in great patches all around the head of my bed, about as far as I can reach, and in a great place on the other side of the room low down. I never saw a worse paper in my life. One of those sprawling, flamboyant patterns committing every artistic sin.

It is dull enough to confuse the eye in following, pronounced enough to constantly irritate and provoke study, and when you follow the lame uncertain curves for a little distance they suddenly commit suicide—plunge off at outrageous angles, destroy themselves in unheard-of contradictions.

The color is repellent, almost revolting: a smouldering unclean yellow, strangely faded by the slow-turning sunlight. It is a dull yet lurid orange in some places, a sickly sulphur tint in others.

No wonder the children hated it! I should hate it myself if I had to live in this room long.

There comes John, and I must put this away—he hates to have me write a word.

We have been here two weeks, and I haven't felt like writing before, since that first day.

I am sitting by the window now, up in this atrocious nursery, and there is nothing to hinder my writing as much as I please, save lack of strength.

John is away all day, and even some nights when his cases are serious.

I am glad my case is not serious!

But these nervous troubles are dreadfully depressing.

John does not know how much I really suffer. He knows there is no reason to suffer, and that satisfies him.

Of course it is only nervousness. It does weigh on me so not to do my duty in any way!

I meant to be such a help to John, such a real rest and comfort, and here I am a comparative burden already!

Nobody would believe what an effort it is to do what little I am able—to dress and entertain, and order things.

It is fortunate Mary is so good with the baby. Such a dear baby!

And yet I *cannot* be with him, it makes me so nervous.

I suppose John never was nervous in his life. He laughs at me so about this wallpaper!

At first he meant to repaper the room, but afterward he said that I was letting it get the better of me, and that nothing was worse for a nervous patient than to give way to such fancies.

He said that after the wallpaper was changed it would be the heavy bedstead, and then the barred windows, and then that gate at the head of the stairs, and so on.

"You know the place is doing you good," he said, "and really, dear, I don't care to renovate the house just for a three months' rental."

"Then do let us go downstairs," I said. "There are such pretty rooms there."

Then he took me in his arms and called me a blessed little goose, and said he would go down to the cellar, if I wished, and have it whitewashed into the bargain.

But he is right enough about the beds and windows and things.

It is as airy and comfortable room as anyone need wish, and, of course, I would not be so silly as to make him uncomfortable just for a whim.

I'm really getting quite fond of the big room, all but that horrid paper.

Out of one window I can see the garden—those mysterious deep-shaded arbors, the riotous old-fashioned flowers, and bushes and gnarly trees.

Out of another I get a lovely view of the bay and a little private wharf belonging to the estate. There is a beautiful shaded lane that runs down there from the house. I always fancy I see people walking in these numerous paths and arbors, but John has cautioned me not to give way to fancy in the least. He says that with my imaginative power and habit of story-making, a nervous weakness like mine is sure to lead to all manner of excited fancies, and that I ought to use my will and good sense to check the tendency. So I try.

I think sometimes that if I were only well enough to write a little it would relieve the press of ideas and rest me.

But I find I get pretty tired when I try.

It is so discouraging not to have any advice and companionship about my work. When I get really well, John says we will ask Cousin Henry and Julia down for a long visit; but he says he would as soon put fireworks in my pillow-case as to let me have those stimulating people about now.

I wish I could get well faster.

But I must not think about that. This paper looks to me as if it *knew* what a vicious influence it had!

There is a recurrent spot where the pattern lolls like a broken neck and two bulbous eyes stare at you upside down.

I get positively angry with the impertinence of it and the everlastingness. Up and down and sideways they crawl, and those absurd unblinking eyes are everywhere. There is one place where two breadths didn't match, and the eyes go all up and down the line, one a little higher than the other.

I never saw so much expression in an inanimate thing before, and we all know how much expression they have! I used to lie awake as a child and get more entertainment and terror out of blank walls and plain furniture than most children could find in a toy-store.

I remember what a kindly wink the knobs of our big old bureau used to have, and there was one chair that always seemed like a strong friend.

I used to feel that if any of the other things looked too fierce I could always hop into that chair and be safe.

The furniture in this room is no worse than inharmonious, however, for we had to bring it all from downstairs. I suppose when this was used as a playroom they had to take the nursery things out, and no wonder! I never saw such ravages as the children have made here.

The wallpaper, as I said before, is torn off in spots, and it sticketh closer than a brother—they must have had perseverance as well as hatred.

Then the floor is scratched and gouged and splintered, the plaster itself is dug out here and there, and this great heavy bed, which is all we found in the room, looks as if it had been through the wars.

But I don't mind it a bit—only the paper.

There comes John's sister. Such a dear girl as she is, and so careful of me! I must not let her find me writing.

She is a perfect and enthusiastic housekeeper, and hopes for no better profession. I verily believe she thinks it is the writing which made me sick!

But I can write when she is out, and see her a long way off from these windows.

There is one that commands the road, a lovely shaded winding road, and one that just looks off over the country. A lovely country, too, full of great elms and velvet meadows.

This wallpaper has a kind of sub-pattern in a different shade, a particularly irritating one, for you can only see it in certain lights, and not clearly then.

But in the places where it isn't faded and where the sun is just so—I can see a strange, provoking, formless sort of figure that seems to skulk about behind that silly and conspicuous front design.

There's sister on the stairs!

Well, the Fourth of July is over! The people are all gone, and I am tired out. John thought it might do me good to see a little company, so we just had mother and Nellie and the children down for a week.

Of course I didn't do a thing. Jennie sees to everything now.

But it tired me all the same.

John says if I don't pick up faster he shall send me to Weir Mitchell[3] in the fall.

But I don't want to go there at all. I had a friend who was in his hands once, and she says he is just like John and my brother, only more so!

Besides, it is such an undertaking to go so far.

I don't feel as if it was worthwhile to turn my hand over for anything, and I'm getting dreadfully fretful and querulous.

I cry at nothing, and cry most of the time.

Of course I don't when John is here, or anybody else, but when I am alone.

And I am alone a good deal just now. John is kept in town very often by serious cases, and Jennie is good and lets me alone when I want her to.

So I walk a little in the garden or down that lovely lane, sit on the porch under the roses, and lie down up here a good deal.

I'm getting really fond of the room in spite of the wallpaper. Perhaps *because* of the wallpaper.

It dwells in my mind so!

I lie here on this great immovable bed—it is nailed down, I believe—and follow that pattern about by the hour. It is as good as gymnastics, I assure you. I start, we'll say, at the bottom, down in the corner over there where it has not been touched, and I determine for the thousandth time that I *will* follow that pointless pattern to some sort of a conclusion.

I know a little of the principle of design, and I know this thing was not arranged on any laws of radiation, or alternation, or repetition, or symmetry, or anything else that I ever heard of.

It is repeated, of course, by the breadths, but not otherwise.

Looked at in one way, each breadth stands alone; the bloated curves and flourishes—a kind of "debased Romanesque"[4] with *delirium tremens*[5]—go waddling up and down in isolated columns of fatuity.

But, on the other hand, they connect diagonally, and the sprawling outlines run off in great slanting waves of optic horror, like a lot of wallowing sea-weeds in full chase.

The whole thing goes horizontally, too, at least it seems so, and I exhaust myself in trying to distinguish the order of its going in that direction.

They have used a horizontal breadth for a frieze,[6] and that adds wonderfully to the confusion.

---

[3] American neurologist who invented the "rest cure" for hysteria and who treated Gilman herself.

[4] Style of architecture prevalent from the ninth to twelfth centuries in Europe, characterized by rounded arches and heavy masonry and design.

[5] Condition caused by excessive use of alcohol and characterized by physical trembling and hallucinations.

[6] A decorative band with lettering or sculpture.

100 There is one end of the room where it is almost intact, and there, when the crosslights fade and the low sun shines directly upon it, I can almost fancy radiation after all—the interminable grotesque seems to form around a common center and rush off in headlong plunges of equal distraction.

It makes me tired to follow it. I will take a nap, I guess.

I don't know why I should write this.

I don't want to.

I don't feel able.

105 And I know John would think it absurd. But I *must* say what I feel and think in some way—it is such a relief!

But the effort is getting to be greater than the relief.

Half the time now I am awfully lazy, and lie down ever so much. John says I mustn't lose my strength, and has me take cod liver oil and lots of tonics and things, to say nothing of ale and wine and rare meat.

Dear John! He loves me very dearly, and hates to have me sick. I tried to have a real earnest reasonable talk with him the other day, and tell him how I wish he would let me go and make a visit to Cousin Henry and Julia.

But he said I wasn't able to go, nor able to stand it after I got there; and I did not make out a very good case for myself, for I was crying before I had finished.

110 It is getting to be a great effort for me to think straight. Just this nervous weakness, I suppose.

And dear John gathered me up in his arms, and just carried me upstairs and laid me on the bed, and sat by me and read to me till it tired my head.

He said I was his darling and his comfort and all he had, and that I must take care of myself for his sake, and keep well.

He says no one but myself can help me out of it, that I must use my will and self-control and not let any silly fancies run away with me.

There's one comfort—the baby is well and happy, and does not have to occupy this nursery with the horrid wallpaper.

115 If we had not used it, that blessed child would have! What a fortunate escape! Why, I wouldn't have a child of mine, an impressionable little thing, live in such a room for worlds.

I never thought of it before, but it is lucky that John kept me here after all; I can stand it so much easier than a baby, you see.

Of course I never mention it to them any more—I am too wise—but I keep watch for it all the same.

There are things in that wallpaper that nobody knows about but me, or ever will.

Behind that outside pattern the dim shapes get clearer every day.

120 It is always the same shape, only very numerous.

And it is like a woman stooping down and creeping about behind that pattern. I don't like it a bit. I wonder—I begin to think—I wish John would take me away from here!

It is so hard to talk with John about my case, because he is so wise, and because he loves me so.

But I tried it last night.

It was moonlight. The moon shines in all around just as the sun does.

I hate to see it sometimes, it creeps so slowly, and always comes in by one window or another.

John was asleep and I hated to waken him, so I kept still and watched the moonlight on that undulating wallpaper till I felt creepy.

The faint figure behind seemed to shake the pattern, just as if she wanted to get out.

I got up softly and went to feel and see if the paper *did* move, and when I came back John was awake.

"What is it, little girl?" he said. "Don't go walking about like that—you'll get cold."

I thought it was a good time to talk, so I told him that I really was not gaining here, and that I wished he would take me away.

"Why, darling!" said he. "Our lease will be up in three weeks, and I can't see how to leave before.

"The repairs are not done at home, and I cannot possibly leave town just now. Of course, if you were in any danger, I could and would, but you really are better, dear, whether you can see it or not. I am a doctor, dear, and I know. You are gaining flesh and color, your appetite is better, I feel really much easier about you."

"I don't weigh a bit more," said I, "nor as much; and my appetite may be better in the evening when you are here but it is worse in the morning when you are away!"

"Bless her little heart!" said he with a big hug. "She shall be as sick as she pleases! But now let's improve the shining hours by going to sleep, and talk about it in the morning!"

"And you won't go away?" I asked gloomily.

"Why, how can I, dear? It is only three weeks more and then we will take a nice little trip of a few days while Jennie is getting the house ready. Really, dear, you are better!"

"Better in body perhaps—" I began, and stopped short, for he sat up straight and looked at me with such a stern, reproachful look that I could not say another word.

"My darling," said he, "I beg of you, for my sake and for our child's sake, as well as for your own, that you will never for one instant let that idea enter your mind! There is nothing so dangerous, so fascinating, to a temperament like yours. It is a false and foolish fancy. Can you not trust me as a physician when I tell you so?"

So of course I said no more on that score, and we went to sleep before long. He thought I was asleep first, but I wasn't, and lay there for hours trying to decide whether that front pattern and the back pattern really did move together or separately.

140 On a pattern like this, by daylight, there is a lack of sequence, a defiance of law, that is a constant irritant to a normal mind.

The color is hideous enough, and unreliable enough, and infuriating enough, but the pattern is torturing.

You think you have mastered it, but just as you get well under way in following, it turns a back-somersault and there you are. It slaps you in the face, knocks you down, and tramples upon you. It is like a bad dream.

The outside pattern is a florid arabesque, reminding one of a fungus. If you can imagine a toadstool in joints, an interminable string of toadstools, budding and sprouting in endless convolutions—why, that is something like it.

That is, sometimes!

145 There is one marked peculiarity about this paper, a thing nobody seems to notice but myself, and that is that it changes as the light changes.

When the sun shoots in through the east window—I always watch for that first long, straight ray—it changes so quickly that I never can quite believe it.

That is why I watch it always.

By moonlight—the moon shines in all night when there is a moon—I wouldn't know it was the same paper.

At night in any kind of light, in twilight, candlelight, lamplight, and worst of all by moonlight, it becomes bars! The outside pattern, I mean, and the woman behind it is as plain as can be.

150 I didn't realize for a long time what the thing was that showed behind, that dim sub-pattern, but now I am quite sure it is a woman.

By daylight she is subdued, quiet. I fancy it is the pattern that keeps her so still. It is so puzzling. It keeps me quiet by the hour.

I lie down ever so much now. John says it is good for me, and to sleep all I can.

Indeed he started the habit by making me lie down for an hour after each meal.

It is a very bad habit, I am convinced, for you see, I don't sleep.

155 And that cultivates deceit, for I don't tell them I'm awake—oh, no!

The fact is I am getting a little afraid of John.

He seems very queer sometimes, and even Jennie has an inexplicable look.

It strikes me occasionally, just as a scientific hypothesis, that perhaps it is the paper!

I have watched John when he did not know I was looking, and come into the room suddenly on the most innocent excuses, and I've caught him several times *looking at the paper!* And Jennie too. I caught Jennie with her hand on it once.

160 She didn't know I was in the room, and when I asked her in a quiet, a very quiet voice, with the most restrained manner possible, what she was doing with the paper, she turned around as if she had been caught stealing, and looked quite angry—asked me why I should frighten her so!

Then she said that the paper stained everything it touched, that she had found yellow smooches on all my clothes and John's, and she wished we would be more careful!

Did not that sound innocent? But I know she was studying that pattern and I am determined that nobody shall find it out but myself!

Life is very much more exciting now than it used to be. You see, I have something more to expect, to look forward to, to watch. I really do eat better, and am more quiet than I was.

John is so pleased to see me improve! He laughed a little the other day, and said I seemed to be flourishing in spite of my wallpaper.

I turned it off with a laugh. I had no intention of telling him it was *because* of the wallpaper—he would make fun of me. He might even want to take me away.

I don't want to leave now until I have found it out. There is a week more, and I think that will be enough.

I'm feeling so much better!

I don't sleep much at night, for it is so interesting to watch developments; but I sleep a good deal during the daytime.

In the daytime it is tiresome and perplexing.

There are always new shoots on the fungus, and new shades of yellow all over it. I cannot keep count of them, though I have tried conscientiously. It is the strangest yellow, that wallpaper! It makes me think of all the yellow things I ever saw—not beautiful ones like buttercups, but old, foul, bad yellow things.

But there is something else about that paper—the smell! I noticed it the moment we came into the room, but with so much air and sun it was not bad. Now we have had a week of fog and rain, and whether the windows are open or not, the smell is here.

It creeps all over the house.

I find it hovering in the dining-room, skulking in the parlor, hiding in the hall, lying in wait for me on the stairs.

It gets into my hair.

Even when I go to ride, if I turn my head suddenly and surprise it—there is that smell!

Such a peculiar odor, too! I have spent hours in trying to analyze it, to find what it smelled like.

It is not bad—at first—and very gentle, but quite the subtlest, most enduring odor I ever met.

In this damp weather it is awful. I wake up in the night and find it hanging over me.

It used to disturb me at first. I thought seriously of burning the house—to reach the smell.

But now I am used to it. The only thing I can think of that it is like is the *color* of the paper! A yellow smell.

There is a very funny mark on this wall, low down, near the mopboard. A streak that runs round the room. It goes behind every piece of furniture, except the bed, a long, straight, even *smooch,* as if it had been rubbed over and over.

I wonder how it was done and who did it, and what they did it for. Round and round and round—round and round and round—it makes me dizzy!

I really have discovered something at last.

Through watching so much at night, when it changes so, I have finally found out.

The front pattern *does* move—and no wonder! The woman behind shakes it!

Sometimes I think there are a great many women behind, and sometimes only one, and she crawls around fast, and her crawling shakes it all over.

Then in the very bright spots she keeps still, and in the very shady spots she just takes hold of the bars and shakes them hard.

And she is all the time trying to climb through. But nobody could climb through that pattern—it strangles so; I think that is why it has so many heads.

They get through, and then the pattern strangles them off and turns them upside down, and makes their eyes white!

If those heads were covered or taken off it would not be half so bad.

I think that woman gets out in the daytime!

And I'll tell you why—privately—I've seen her!

I can see her out of every one of my windows!

It is the same woman, I know, for she is always creeping, and most women do not creep by daylight.

I see her in that long shaded lane, creeping up and down. I see her in those dark grape arbors, creeping all around the garden.

I see her on that long road under the trees, creeping along, and when a carriage comes she hides under the blackberry vines.

I don't blame her a bit. It must be very humiliating to be caught creeping by daylight!

I always lock the door when I creep by daylight. I can't do it at night, for I know John would suspect something at once.

And John is so queer now that I don't want to irritate him. I wish he would take another room! Besides, I don't want anybody to get that woman out at night but myself.

I often wonder if I could see her out of all the windows at once.

But, turn as fast as I can, I can only see out of one at one time.

And though I always see her, she *may* be able to creep faster than I can turn! I have watched her sometimes away off in the open country, creeping as fast as a cloud shadow in a wind.

If only that top pattern could be gotten off from the under one! I mean to try it, little by little.

I have found out another funny thing, but I shan't tell it this time! It does not do to trust people too much.

There are only two more days to get this paper off, and I believe John is beginning to notice. I don't like the look in his eyes.

And I heard him ask Jennie a lot of professional questions about me. She had a very good report to give.

She said I slept a good deal in the daytime.

John knows I don't sleep very well at night, for all I'm so quiet!

He asked me all sorts of questions, too, and pretended to be very loving and kind.

As if I couldn't see through him!

Still, I don't wonder he acts so, sleeping under this paper for three months.

It only interests me, but I feel sure John and Jennie are secretly affected by it. Hurrah! This is the last day, but it is enough. John to stay in town over night, and won't be out until this evening.

Jennie wanted to sleep with me—the sly thing; but I told her I should undoubtedly rest better for a night all alone.

That was clever, for really I wasn't alone a bit! As soon as it was moonlight and that poor thing began to crawl and shake the pattern, I got up and ran to help her.

I pulled and she shook. I shook and she pulled, and before morning we had peeled off yards of that paper.

A strip about as high as my head and half around the room.

And then when the sun came and that awful pattern began to laugh at me, I declared I would finish it today!

We go away tomorrow, and they are moving all my furniture down again to leave things as they were before.

Jennie looked at the wall in amazement, but I told her merrily that I did it out of pure spite at the vicious thing.

She laughed and said she wouldn't mind doing it herself, but I must not get tired.

How she betrayed herself that time!

But I am here, and no person touches this paper but Me—not *alive!*

She tried to get me out of the room—it was too patent! But I said it was so quiet and empty and clean now that I believed I would lie down again and sleep all I could, and not to wake me even for dinner—I would call when I woke.

So now she is gone, and the servants are gone, and the things are gone, and there is nothing left but that great bedstead nailed down, with the canvas mattress we found on it.

We shall sleep downstairs tonight, and take the boat home tomorrow.

I quite enjoy the room, now it is bare again.

How those children did tear about here!

This bedstead is fairly gnawed!

But I must get to work.

I have locked the door and thrown the key down into the front path.

I don't want to go out, and I don't want to have anybody come in, till John comes.

I want to astonish him.

I've got a rope up here that even Jennie did not find. If that woman does get out, and tries to get away, I can tie her!

But I forgot I could not reach far without anything to stand on!

This bed will *not* move!

I tried to lift and push it until I was lame, and then I got so angry I bit off a little piece at one corner—but it hurt my teeth.

Then I peeled off all the paper I could reach standing on the floor. It sticks horribly and the pattern just enjoys it! All those strangled heads and bulbous eyes and waddling fungus growths just shriek with derision!

I am getting angry enough to do something desperate. To jump out of the window would be admirable exercise, but the bars are too strong even to try.

Besides I wouldn't do it. Of course not. I know well enough that a step like that is improper and might be misconstrued.

I don't like to *look* out of the windows even—there are so many of those creeping women, and they creep so fast.

I wonder if they all come out of that wallpaper as I did?

But I am securely fastened now by my well-hidden rope—you don't get *me* out in the road there!

I suppose I shall have to get back behind the pattern when it comes night, and that is hard!

It is so pleasant to be out in this great room and creep around as I please!

I don't want to go outside. I won't, even if Jennie asks me to.

For outside you have to creep on the ground, and everything is green instead of yellow.

But here I can creep smoothly on the floor, and my shoulder just fits in that long smooch around the wall, so I cannot lose my way.

Why, there's John at the door!

It is no use, young man, you can't open it!

How he does call and pound!

Now he's crying to Jeannie for an axe.

It would be a shame to break down that beautiful door!

"John dear!" said I in the gentlest voice. "The key is down by the front steps, under a plantain leaf!"

That silenced him for a few moments.

Then he said, very quietly indeed. "Open the door, my darling!"

"I can't," said I. "The key is down by the front door under a plantain leaf!" And then I said it again, several times, very gently and slowly, and said it so often that he had to go and see, and he got it of course, and came in. He stopped short by the door.

"What is the matter?" he cried. "For God's sake, what are you doing!"

I kept on creeping just the same, but I looked at him over my shoulder.

"I've got out at last," said I, "in spite of you and Jane. And I've pulled off most of the paper, so you can't put me back!"

Now why should that man have fainted? But he did, and right across my path by the wall, so that I had to creep over him every time!

Explorations of the Text

1. What attitudes characterize John's treatment of his wife? Do his attitudes contribute to the narrator's situation? Look carefully at terms of endearment.
2. Is the narrator correct in her suspicions about her husband? about her brother? How do her attitudes change in the story?
3. What is the significance of the fact that the narrator's room was originally a nursery?
4. Why does John not want her to write? Why does she want to write?
5. What are the stages in the narrator's psychological breakdown? How are these stages reflected in her obsession with the wallpaper?
6. Who is the "woman" in the wallpaper? Discuss the symbolism of the figure. What does the yellow wallpaper finally symbolize?
7. What does the ending mean? What happens to the narrator? What is the husband's reaction?
8. Explore the point of view and the imagery in this story. How do they contribute to the story's emotional impact?
9. Compare character and theme in this story with those in *And the Soul Shall Dance.*

The Reading/Writing Connection

1. Create a character sketch of the narrator or John. Incorporate specifics from the story.

Ideas for Writing

1. Charlotte Perkins Gilman's doctor, treating her for nervous depression, once told her "never to touch pen, brush or pencil again." Why does Gilman imply that the treatment worsens the condition?
2. "The Yellow Wallpaper" was anthologized as a horror or ghost story for many years. Write a defense of "The Yellow Wallpaper" either as a horror story or as more serious fiction.

Tickets, Please

D. H. Lawrence

D. H. (David Herbert) Lawrence (1885–1930) was born in Nottingham, England, the son of a coal miner and a former schoolteacher. He became a major literary figure with the publication of Sons and Lovers *in 1913. Lawrence's best-known works include* The Rainbow

(1915), Women in Love *(1920), and* Lady Chatterley's Lover *(1928). His shorter works and poems are found in* The Complete Stories *(1961),* Four Short Novels *(1965), and* Complete Poems *(1964). Suffering from tuberculosis and disgusted with his country's industrialism and commercialism, Lawrence spent much of his life traveling through Italy, France, Australia, the United States, and Mexico.*

1922

There is in the Midlands[1] a single-line tramway system which boldly leaves the county town and plunges off into the black, industrial countryside, up hill and down dale, through the long ugly villages of workmen's houses, over canals and railways, past churches perched high and nobly over the smoke and shadows, through stark, grimy cold little marketplaces, tilting away in a rush past cinemas and shops down to the hollow where the collieries[2] are, then up again, past a little rural church, under the ash trees, on in a rush to the terminus, the last little ugly place of industry, the cold little town that shivers on the edge of the wild, gloomy country beyond. There the green and creamy coloured tram-cars seem to pause and purr with curious satisfaction. But in a few minutes—the clock on the turret of the Co-operative Wholesale Society's shops gives the time—away it starts once more on the adventure. Again there are the reckless swoops downhill, bouncing the loops: again the chilly wait in the hill-top market-place: again the breathless slithering round the precipitous drop under the church: again the patient halts at the loops, waiting for the outcoming car: so on and on, for two long hours, till at last the city looms beyond the fat gas-works, the narrow factories draw near, we are in the sordid streets of the great town, once more we sidle to a standstill at our terminus, abashed by the great crimson and cream-coloured city cars, but still perky, jaunty, somewhat dare-devil, green as a jaunty sprig of parsley out of a black colliery garden.

To ride on these cars is always an adventure. Since we are in war-time, the drivers are men unfit for active service: cripples and hunchbacks. So they have the spirit of the devil in them. The ride becomes a steeplechase. Hurray! we have leapt in a clear jump over the canal bridge—now for the four-lane corner. With a shriek and a trail of sparks we are clear again. To be sure, a tram[3] often leaps the rails—but what matter! It sits in a ditch till other trams come to haul it out. It is quite common for a car, parked with one solid mass of living people, to come to a dead halt in the midst of unbroken blackness, the heart of nowhere on a dark night, and for the driver and the girl conductor to call: "All get off—car's on fire!" Instead, however, of rushing out in a panic, the passengers stolidly reply: "Get on—get on! We're not coming out. We're stopping where we are. Push on, George." So till flames actually appear.

---

[1] The central region of England.

[2] A colliery is a coal mine, including area surrounding the mine and buildings.

[3] A tram is a streetcar.

The reason for this reluctance to dismount is that the nights are howling cold, black, and windswept, and a car is a haven of refuge. From village to village the miners travel, for a change of cinema, of girl, of pub. The trams are desperately packed. Who is going to risk himself in the black gulf outside, to wait perhaps an hour for another tram, then to see the forlorn notice "Depot Only," because there is something wrong! Or to greet a unit of three bright cars all so tight with people that they sail past with a howl of derision. Trams that pass in the night.

This, the most dangerous tram-service in England, as the authorities themselves declare, with pride, is entirely conducted by girls, and driven by rash young men, a little crippled, or by delicate young men, who creep forward in terror. The girls are fearless young hussies. In their ugly blue uniform, skirts up to their knees, shapeless old peaked caps on their heads, they have all the *sang-froid*[4] of an old non-commissioned officer. With a tram packed with howling colliers, roaring hymns downstairs and a sort of antiphony of obscenities upstairs, the lasses are perfectly at their ease. They pounce on the youths who try to evade their ticket-machine. They push off the men at the end of their distance. They are not going to be done in the eye—not they. They fear nobody—and everybody fears them.

5 "Hello, Annie!"

"Hello, Ted!"

"Oh, mind my corn, Miss Stone. It's my belief you've got a heart of stone, for you've trod on it again."

"You should keep it in your pocket," replies Miss Stone, and she goes sturdily upstairs in her high boots.

"Tickets, please."

10 She is peremptory, suspicious, and ready to hit first. She can hold her own in ten thousand. The step of that tram-car is her Thermopylae.

Therefore, there is a certain wild romance aboard these cars—and in the sturdy bosom of Annie herself. The time for soft romance is in the morning, between ten o'clock and one, when things are rather slack: that is, except market-day and Saturday. Thus Annie has time to look about her. Then she often hops off her car and into a shop where she has spied something, while the driver chats in the main road. There is very good feeling between the girls and the drivers. Are they not companions in peril, shipments aboard this careering vessel of a tram-car, for ever rocking on the waves of a stormy land.

Then, also, during the easy hours, the inspectors are most in evidence. For some reason, everybody employed in this tram-service is young: there are no grey heads. It would not do. Therefore the inspectors are of the right age, and one, the chief, is also good-looking. See him stand on a wet, gloomy morning, in his long oilskin, his peaked cap well down over his eyes, waiting to board a car. His face ruddy, his small brown moustache is weathered, he has a faint

---

[4] Coolness, calmness, self-possession.

impudent smile. Fairly tall and agile, even in his waterproof, he springs aboard a car and greets Annie.

"Hello, Annie! Keeping the wet out?"

"Trying to."

There are only two people in the car. Inspecting is soon over. Then for a long and impudent chat on the foot-board, a good, easy, twelve-mile chat.

The inspector's name is John Thomas Raynor—always called John Thomas, except sometimes, in malice, Coddy. His face sets in fury when he is addressed, from a distance, with this abbreviation. There is considerable scandal about John Thomas in half a dozen villages. He flirts with the girl conductors in the morning, and walks out with them in the dark night, when they leave their tram-car at the depôt. Of course, the girls quit the service frequently. Then he flirts and walks out with the newcomer: always providing she is sufficiently attractive, and that she will consent to walk. It is remarkable, however, that most of the girls are quite comely, they are all young, and this roving life aboard the car gives them a sailor's dash and recklessness. What matter how they behave when the ship is in port? Tomorrow they will be aboard again.

Annie, however, was something of a Tartar,[5] and her sharp tongue had kept John Thomas at arm's length for many months. Perhaps, therefore, she liked him all the more: for he always came up smiling, with impudence. She watched him vanquish one girl, then another. She could tell by the movement of his mouth and eyes, when he flirted with her in the morning, that he had been walking out with this lass, or the other, the night before. A fine cock-of-the-walk he was. She could sum him up pretty well.

In this subtle antagonism they knew each other like old friends, they were as shrewd with one another almost as man and wife. But Annie had always kept him sufficiently at arm's length. Besides, she had a boy of her own.

The Statutes fair, however, came in November, at Bestwood. It happened that Annie had the Monday night off. It was a drizzling ugly night, yet she dressed herself up and went to the fair-ground. She was alone, but she expected soon to find a pal of some sort.

The roundabouts were veering round and grinding out their music, the side-shows were making as much commotion as possible. In the coconut shies there were no coconuts, but artificial war-time substitutes, which the lads declared were fastened into the irons. There was a sad decline in brilliance and luxury. None the less, the ground was muddy as ever, there was the same crush, the press of faces lighted up by the flares and the electric lights, the same smell of naphtha and a few potatoes, and of electricity.

Who should be the first to greet Miss Annie on the show-ground but John Thomas. He had a black overcoat buttoned up to his chin, and a tweed cap pulled down over his brows, his face between was ruddy and smiling and handy as ever. She knew so well the way his mouth moved.

[5] An intractable person.

She was very glad to have a "boy." To be at the Statutes without a fellow was no fun. Instantly, like the gallant he was, he took her on the dragons, grim-toothed roundabout switchbacks. It was not nearly so exciting as a tram-car actually. But, then, to be seated in a shaking, green dragon, uplifted above the sea of bubble faces, careering in a rickety fashion in the lower heavens, whilst John Thomas leaned over her, his cigarette in his mouth, was after all the right style. She was a plump, quick, alive little creature. So she was quite excited and happy.

John Thomas made her stay on for the next round. And therefore she could hardly for shame repulse him when he put his arm round her and drew her a little nearer to him, in a very warm and cuddly manner. Besides, he was fairly discreet, he kept his movement as hidden as possible. She looked down, and saw that his red, clean hand was out of sight of the crowd. And they knew each other so well. So they warmed up to the fair.

After the dragons they went on the horses. John Thomas paid each time, so she could but be complaisant. He, of course, sat astride on the outer horse—named "Black Bess"—and she sat sideways, towards him, on the inner horse—named "Wildfire." But of course John Thomas was not going to sit discreetly on "Black Bess," holding the brass bar. Round they spun and heaved, in the light. And round he swung on his wooden steed, flinging one leg across her mount, and perilously tipping up and down, across the space, half lying back. laughing at her. He was perfectly happy; she was afraid her hat was on one side, but she was excited.

He threw quoits on a table, and won for her two large, pale blue hat-pins. And then, hearing the noise of the cinemas, announcing another performance, they climbed the boards and went in.

Of course, during these performances pitch darkness falls from time to time, when the machine goes wrong. Then there is a wild whooping, and a loud smacking of simulated kisses. In these moments John Thomas drew Annie towards him. After all, he had a wonderfully warm, cosy way of holding a girl with his arm, he seemed to make such a nice fit. And, after all, it was pleasant to be so held: so very comforting and cosy and nice. He leaned over hear and she felt his breath on her hair; she knew he wanted to kiss her on the lips. And, after all, he was so warm and she fitted in to him so softly. After all, she wanted him to touch her lips.

But the light sprang up; she also started electrically, and put her hat straight. He left his arm lying nonchalantly behind her. Well, it was fun, it was exciting to be at the Statutes with John Thomas.

When the cinema was over they went for a walk across the dark, damp fields. He had all the arts of love-making. He was especially good at holding a girl, when he sat with her on a stile in the black, drizzling darkness. He seemed to be holding her in space, against his own warmth and gratification. And his kisses were soft and slow and searching.

So Annie walked out with John Thomas, though she kept her own boy dangling in the distance. Some of the tram-girls chose to be huffy. But there, you must take things as you find them, in this life.

30 There was no mistake about it, Annie liked John Thomas a good deal. She felt so rich and warm in herself whenever he was near. And John Thomas really liked Annie, more than usual. The soft, melting way in which she could flow into a fellow, as if she melted into his very bones, was something rare and good. He fully appreciated this.

But with a developing acquaintance there began a developing intimacy. Annie wanted to consider him a person, a man: she wanted to take an intelligent interest in him, and to have an intelligent response. She did not want a mere nocturnal presence, which was what he was so far. And she prided herself that he could not leave her.

Here she made a mistake. John Thomas intended to remain a nocturnal presence; he had no idea of becoming an all-round individual to her. When she started to take an intelligent interest in him and his life and his character, he sheered off. He hated intelligent interest. And he knew that the only way to stop it was to avoid it. The possessive female was aroused in Annie. So he left her.

It is no use saying she was not surprised. She was at first startled, thrown out of her count. For she had been so *very* sure of holding him. For a while she was staggered, and everything became uncertain to her. Then she wept with fury, indignation, desolation, and misery. Then she had a spasm of despair. And then, when he came, still impudently, on to her car, still familiar, but letting her see by the movement of his head that he had gone away to somebody else for the time being, and was enjoying pastures new, then she determined to have her own back.

She had a very shrewd idea what girls John Thomas had taken out. She went to Nora Purdy. Nora was a tall, rather pale, but well-built girl, with beautiful yellow hair. She was rather secretive.

35 "Hey!" said Annie, accosting her; then softly: "Who's John Thomas on with now?"

"I don't know," said Nora.

"Why, tha does," said Annie, ironically lapsing into dialect. "Tha knows as well as I do."

"Well, I do, then," said Nora. "It isn't me, so don't bother."

"It's Cissy Meakin, isn't it?"

40 "It is, for all I know."

"Hasn't he got a face on him!" said Annie. "I don't half like his cheek. I could knock him off the foot-board when he comes round at me."

"He'll get dropped on one of these days," said Nora.

"Ay, he will, when somebody makes up their mind to drop it on him. I should like to see him taken down a peg or two, shouldn't you?"

"I shouldn't mind," said Nora.

45 "You've got quite as much cause to as I have," said Annie. "But we'll drop on him one of these days, my girl. What? Don't you want to?"

"I don't mind," said Nora.

But as a matter of fact, Nora was much more vindictive than Annie.

One by one Annie went the round of the old flames. It so happened that Cissy Meakin left the tramway service in quite a short time. Her mother made her leave. Then John Thomas was on the *qui vive.* He cast his eyes over his old flock. And his eyes lighted on Annie. He thought she would be safe now. Besides, he like her.

She arranged to walk home with him on Sunday night. It so happened that her car would be in the depôt at half-past nine: the last car would come in at 10:15. So John Thomas was to wait for her there.

At the depôt the girls had a little waiting-room of their own. It was quite rough, but cosy, with a fire and an oven and a mirror, and table and wooden chairs. The half-dozen girls who knew John Thomas only too well had arranged to take service this Sunday afternoon. So, as the cars began to come in, early, the girls dropped into the waiting-room. And instead of hurrying off home, they sat around the fire and had a cup of tea. Outside was the darkness and lawlessness of war-time.

John Thomas came on the car after Annie, at about a quarter to ten. He poked his head easily into the girls' waiting-room.

"Prayer-meeting?" he asked.

"Ay," said Laura Sharp. "Ladies only."

"That's me!" said John Thomas. It was one of his favourite exclamations.

"Shut the door, boy," said Muriel Baggaley.

"Oh, which side of me?" said John Thomas

"Which tha likes," said Polly Birkin.

He had come in and closed the door behind him. The girls moved in their circle, to make a place for him near the fire. He took off his greatcoat and pushed back his hat.

"Who handles the teapot?" he said.

Nora Purdy silently poured him out a cup of tea.

"Want a bit o' my bread and drippin'?" said Muriel Baggaley to him.

"Ay, give us a bit."

And he began to eat his piece of bread.

"There's no place like home, girls," he said.

They all looked at him as he uttered this piece of impudence. He seemed to be sunning himself in the presence of so many damsels.

"Especially if you're not afraid to go home in the dark," said Laura Sharp.

"Me! By myself I am."

They sat till they heard the last tram come in. In a few minutes Emma Houselay entered.

"Come on, my old duck!" cried Polly Birkin.

"It *is* perishing," said Emma, holding her fingers to the fire.

"But—I'm afraid to, go home in, the dark," sang Laura Sharp, the tune having got into her mind.

"Who're you going with tonight, John Thomas?" asked Muriel Baggaley coolly.

Tonight?" said John Thomas. "Oh, I'm going home by myself tonight—all on my lonely-o."

"That's me!" said Nora Purdy, using his own ejaculation.

The girls laughed shrilly.

"Me as well, Nora," said John Thomas.

"Don't know what you mean," said Laura.

"Yes, I'm toddling," said he, rising and reaching for his overcoat.

"Nay," said Polly. "We're all here waiting for you."

"We've got to be up in good time in the morning," he said, in the benevolent official manner.

They all laughed.

"Nay," said Muriel. "Don't leave us all lonely, John Thomas. Take one!"

"I'll take the lot, if you like," he responded gallantly.

"That you won't, either," said Muriel. "Two's company; seven's too much of a good thing."

"Nay—take one," said Laura. "Fair and square, all above board and say which."

"Ay," cried Annie, speaking for the first time. "Pick, John Thomas; let's hear thee."

"Nay," he said. "I'm going home quiet tonight. Feeling good, for once."

"Whereabouts?" said Annie. "Take a good un, then. But tha's got to take one of us!"

"Nay, how can I take one," he said, laughing uneasily. "I don't want to make enemies."

"You'd only make *one,*" said Annie.

"The chosen *one,*" added Laura.

"Oh, my! Who said girls!" exclaimed John Thomas, again turning as if to escape. "Well—good-night."

"Nay, you've got to make your pick," said Muriel. "Turn your face to the wall, and say which one touches you. Go on—we shall only just touch your back—one of us. Go on—turn your face to the wall, and don't look, and say which one touches you."

He was uneasy, mistrusting them. Yet he had not the courage to break away. They pushed him to a wall and stood him there with his face to it. Behind his back they all grimaced, tittering. He looked so comical. He looked around uneasily.

"Go on!" he cried.

"You're looking—you're looking!" they shouted.

He turned his head away. And suddenly, with a movement like a swift cat, Annie went forward and fetched him a box on the side of the head that sent his cap flying and himself staggering. He started round.

But at Annie's signal they all flew at him, slapping him, pinching him, pulling his hair, though more in fun than in spite or anger. He, however, saw red. His blue eyes flamed with strange fear as well as fury, and he butted through the girls to the door. It was locked. He wrenched at it. Roused, alert, the girls stood round and looked at him. He faced them, at bay. At that moment they were rather horrifying to him, as they stood in their short uniforms. He was distinctly afraid.

"Come on, John Thomas! Come on! Choose!" said Annie.

"What are you after? Open the door," he said.

"We shan't—not till you've chosen!" said Muriel.

"Chosen what?" he said.

"Chosen the one you're going to marry," she replied.

He hesitated a moment.

105 "Open the blasted door," he said, "and get back to your senses." He spoke with official authority.

"You've got to choose!" cried the girls.

"Come on!" cried Annie, looking him in the eye. "Come on! Come on!"

He went forward, rather vaguely. She had taken off her belt, and swinging it, she fetched him a sharp blow over the head with the buckle end. He sprang and seized her. But immediately the other girls rushed upon him, pulling and tearing and beating him. Their blood was now thoroughly up. He was their sport now. They were going to have their own back, out of him. Strange, wild creatures, they hung on him and rushed at him to bear him down. His tunic was torn right up the back. Nora had hold at the back of his collar, and was actually strangling him. Luckily the button burst. He struggled in a wild frenzy of fury and terror, almost mad terror. His tunic was simply torn off his back, his shirt-sleeves were torn away, his arms were naked. The girls rushed at him, clenched their hands on him and pulled at him: or they rushed at him and pushed him, butted him with all their might: or they struck him wild blows. He ducked and cringed and struck sideways. They became more intense.

At last he was down. They rushed on him, kneeling on him. He had neither breath nor strength to move. His face was bleeding with a long scratch, his brow was bruised.

110 Annie knelt on him, the other girls knelt and hung on to him. Their faces were flushed, their hair wild, their eyes were all glittering strangely. He lay at last quite still, with face averted, as an animal lies when it is defeated and at the mercy of the captor. Sometimes his eye glanced back at the wild faces of the girls. His breast rose heavily, his wrists were torn.

"Now, then, my fellow!" gasped Annie at length. "Now then—now—"

At the sound of her terrifying, cold triumph, he suddenly started to struggle as an animal might, but the girls threw themselves upon him with unnatural strength and power, forcing him down.

"Yes—now, then!" gasped Annie at length.

And there was a dead silence, in which the thud of heart-beating was to be heard. It was a suspense of pure silence in every soul.

115 "Now you know where you are," said Annie.

The sight of his white, bare arm maddened the girls. He lay in a kind of trance of fear and antagonism. They felt themselves filled with supernatural strength.

Suddenly Polly started to laugh—to giggle wildly—helplessly—and Emma and Muriel joined in. But Annie and Nora and Laura remained the same, tense, watchful, with gleaming eyes. He winced away from these eyes.

"Yes," said Annie, in a curious low tone, secret and deadly. "Yes! You've got it now. You know what you've done, don't you? You know what you've done."

He made no sound nor sign, but lay with bright, averted eyes, and averted, bleeding face.

"You ought to be *killed,* that's what you ought," said Annie, tensely. "You ought to be *killed.*" And there was a terrifying lust in her voice.

Polly was ceasing to laugh, and giving long-drawn Oh-h-hs and sighs as she came to herself.

"He's got to choose," she said vaguely.

"Oh, yes, he has," said Laura, with vindictive decision.

"Do you hear—do you hear?" said Annie. And with a sharp movement, that made him wince, she turned his face to her.

"Do you hear?" she repeated, shaking him.

But he was quite dumb. She fetched him a sharp slap on the face. He started, and his eyes widened. Then his face darkened with defiance, after all.

"Do you hear?" she repeated.

He only looked at her with hostile eyes.

"Speak!" she said, putting her face devilishly near his.

"What?" he said, almost overcome.

"You've got to *choose!*" she cried, as if it were some terrible menace, and as if it hurt her that she could not exact more.

"What?" he said, in fear.

"Choose your girl, Coddy. You've got to choose her now. And you'll get your neck broken if you play any more of your tricks, my boy. You're settled now."

There was a pause. Again he averted his face. He was cunning in his overthrow. He did not give in to them really—no, not if they tore him to bits.

"All right, then," he said, "I choose Annie." His voice was strange and full of malice. Annie let go of him as if he had been a hot coal.

"He's chosen Annie!" said the girls in chorus.

"Me!" cried Annie. She was still kneeling, but away from him. He was still lying prostrate, with averted face. The girls grouped uneasily around.

"Me!" repeated Annie, with a terrible bitter accent.

Then she got up, drawing away from him with strange disgust and bitterness.

"I wouldn't touch him," she said.

But her face quivered with a kind of agony, she seemed as if she would fall. The other girls turned aside. He remained lying on the floor, with his torn clothes and bleeding, averted face.

"Oh, if he's chosen—" said Polly.

"I don't want him—he can choose again," said Annie, with the same rather bitter hopelessness.

"Get up," said Polly, lifting his shoulder. "Get up."

He rose slowly, a strange, ragged, dazed creature. The girls eyed him from a distance, curiously, furtively, dangerously.

"Who wants him?" cried Laura, roughly.

"Nobody," they answered, with contempt. Yet each one of them waited for him to look at her, hoped he would look at her. All except Annie, and something was broken in her.

He, however, kept his face closed and averted from them all. There was a silence of the end. He picked up the torn pieces of his tunic, without knowing what to do with them. The girls stood about uneasily, flushed, panting, tidying their hair and their dress unconsciously, and watching him. He looked at none of them. He espied his cap in a corner, and went and picked it up. He put it on his head, and one of the girls burst into a shrill, hysteric laugh at the sight he presented. He, however, took no heed, but went straight to where his overcoat hung on a peg. The girls moved away from contact with him as if he had been an electric wire. He put on his coat and buttoned it down. Then he rolled his tunic-rags into a bundle, and stood before the locked door, dumbly.

"Open the door, somebody," said Laura.

"Annie's got the key," said one.

Annie silently offered the key to the girls. Nora unlocked the door.

"Tit for tat, old man," she said. "Show yourself a man, and don't bear a grudge."

But without a word or a sign he had opened the door and gone, his face closed, his head dropped.

"That'll learn him," said Laura.

"Coddy!" said Nora.

"Shut up, for God's sake!" cried Annie fiercely, as if in torture.

"Well, I'm about ready to go, Polly. Look sharp!" said Muriel.

The girls were all anxious to be off. They were tidying themselves hurriedly, with mute, stupefied faces.

Explorations of the Text

1. Discuss the third person narrative point of view. Is it effective? To whom does the narrator seem sympathetic? How would the story have been different if it had been written in first person, told from either John Thomas's or Annie's perspective? Rewrite a section of the story in order to come to conclusions. What do you learn?
2. Why is the World War I setting significant? How does the wartime milieu influence the characters' actions?
3. What motivates Annie to organize the girls? Why does she turn down John Thomas in the end?
4. Why does Annie feel "bitter hopelessness"? Why is she in "agony"?
5. What do you think is Lawrence's view of the fight between John Thomas and the women? What do you think is his view of "the battle of the sexes"?

The Reading/Writing Connection

1. "Think" Topic: Does John Thomas deserve the treatment he received? Why or why not?

2. If this were to take place in 2003, what might the social ramifications be? Who would be seen as right?
3. Compare the pattern of dominance in this story with the relationship between the narrator and "the wave" in Octavio Paz's "My Life with the Wave."

Ideas for Writing

1. This story is loosely based on an event in D. H. Lawrence's life. According to Ian Serraillier, the editor of a volume of Lawrence's early fiction, Lawrence was attacked by "a gang of factory girls." Does this biographical information change your view of the story? How does it shape the narrative perspective?
2. This story almost resembles horror fiction. How does Lawrence create this undercurrent of horror?
3. Create a movie script based on this story. Whom would you cast as the main characters? How would you develop the script? What camera angles would you use? What visual elements and props would you include? After you develop the script, analyze your results. Then in an essay compare the story and the script.

My Life with the Wave

Octavio Paz

Born in Mexico City, Octavio Paz (1914–98) was educated in Catholic schools and graduated from the National University of Mexico. At nineteen, he published his first volume of poetry. His volumes of poetry include Sylvan Moon *(1933),* Salamandra *(1958–61), and* Configurations *(1971). A collected edition of his poems 1957 to 1987 appeared in 1987. He also wrote many volumes of prose. Paz was awarded the Nobel Prize for Literature in 1990. He was an outspoken social critic, a philosopher, an essayist, and a leading figure in the renaissance of Latin American literature.*

1949

When I left that sea, a wave moved ahead of the others. She was tall and light. In spite of the shouts of the others who grabbed her by her floating clothes, she clutched my arm and went off with me leaping. I didn't want to say anything to her, because it hurt me to shame her in front of her friends. Besides, the furious stares of the elders paralyzed me. When we got to town, I explained to her that it was impossible, that life in the city was not what she had been able to imagine with the ingenuity of a wave that had never left the sea. She watched me gravely: "No, your decision is made. You can't go back." I tried sweetness, hardness, irony. She cried, screamed, hugged, threatened. I had to apologize.

The next day my troubles began. How could we get on the train without being seen by the conductor, the passengers, the police? Certainly the rules say nothing in respect to the transport of waves on the railroad, but this same reserve was an indication of the severity with which our act would be judged. After much thought I arrived at the station an hour before departure, took my seat, and, when no one was looking, emptied the water tank for the passengers; then, carefully, poured in my friend.

The first incident came about when the children of a nearby couple declared their noisy thirst. I stopped them and promised them refreshments and lemonade. They were at the point of accepting when another thirsty passenger approached. I was about to invite her also, but the stare of her companion stopped me. The lady took a paper cup, approached the tank, and turned the faucet. Her cup was barely half full when I leaped between the woman and my friend. She looked at me astonished. While I apologized, one of the children turned the faucet again. I closed it violently. The lady brought the cup to her lips:

"Agh, this water is salty."

The boy echoed her. Various passengers rose. The husband called the conductor:

"This man put salt in the water."

The conductor called the Inspector:

"So you put substances in the water?"

The Inspector in turn called the police:

"So you poisoned the water?"

The police in turn called the Captain:

"So you're the poisoner?"

The Captain called three agents. The agents took me to an empty car, amid the stares and whispers of the passengers. At the next station they took me off and pushed and dragged me to the jail. For days no one spoke to me, except during the long interrogations. When I explained my story no one believed me, not even the jailer, who shook his head, saying: "The case is grave, truly grave. You didn't want to poison the children?" One day they brought me before the Magistrate.

"Your case is difficult," he repeated. "I will assign you to the Penal Judge."

A year passed. Finally they judged me. As there were no victims, my sentence was light. After a short time, my day of liberty arrived.

The Chief of the Prison called me in:

"Well, now you're free. You were lucky. Lucky there were no victims. But don't do it again, because the next time won't be so short . . ."

And he stared at me with the same grave stare with which everyone watched me.

The same afternoon I took the train and after hours of uncomfortable traveling arrived in Mexico City. I took a cab home. At the door of my apartment I heard laughter and singing. I felt a pain in my chest, like the smack of a wave of surprise when surprise smacks us across the chest: my friend was there, singing and laughing as always.

20 "How did you get back?"

"Simple: in the train. Someone, after making sure that I was only salt water, poured me in the engine. It was a rough trip: soon I was a white plume of vapor, soon I fell in a fine rain on the machine. I thinned out a lot. I lost many drops."

Her presence changed my life. The house of dark corridors and dusty furniture was filled with air, with sun, with sounds and green and blue reflections, a numerous and happy populace of reverberations and echoes. How many waves is one wave, and how it can make a beach or a rock or jetty out of a wall, a chest, a forehead that it crowns with foam! Even the abandoned corners, the abject corners of dust and debris were touched by her light hands. Everything began to laugh and everywhere shined with teeth. The sun entered the old rooms with pleasure and stayed in my house for hours, abandoning the other houses, the district, the city, the country. And some nights, very late, the scandalized stars watched it sneak from my house.

Love was a game, a perpetual creation. All was beach, sand, a bed of sheets that were always fresh. If I embraced her, she swelled with pride, incredibly tall, like the liquid stalk of a poplar; and soon that thinness flowered into a fountain of white feathers, into a plume of smiles that fell over my head and back and covered me with whiteness. Or she stretched out in front of me, infinite as the horizon, until I too became horizon and silence. Full and sinuous, it enveloped me like music or some giant lips. Her presence was a going and coming of caresses, of murmurs, of kisses. Entered in her waters, I was drenched to the socks and in a wink of an eye I found myself up above, at the height of vertigo, mysteriously suspended, to fall like a stone and feel myself gently deposited on the dryness, like a feather. Nothing is comparable to sleeping in those waters, to wake pounded by a thousand happy light lashes, by a thousand assaults that withdrew laughing.

But never did I reach the center of her being. Never did I touch the nakedness of pain and of death. Perhaps it does not exist in waves, that secret site that renders a woman vulnerable and mortal, that electric button where all interlocks, twitches, and straightens out to then swoon. Her sensibility, like that of women, spread in ripples, only they weren't concentric ripples, but rather excentric, spreading each time farther, until they touched other galaxies. To love her was to extend to remote contacts, to vibrate with far-off stars we never suspected. But her center . . . no, she had no center, just an emptiness as in a whirlwind, that sucked me in and smothered me.

25 Stretched out side by side, we exchanged confidences, whispers, smiles. Curled up, she fell on my chest and there unfolded like a vegetation of murmurs. She sang in my ear, a little snail. She became humble and transparent, clutching my feet like a small animal, calm water. She was so clear I could read all of her thoughts. Certain nights her skin was covered with phosphorescence and to embrace her was to embrace a piece of night tattooed with fire. But she also became black and bitter. At unexpected hours she roared, moaned, twisted. Her groans woke the neighbors. Upon hearing her, the sea wind would scratch at the door of the house or rave in a loud voice on the roof.

Cloudy days irritated her; she broke furniture, said bad words, covered me with insults and green and gray foam. She spit, cried, swore, prophesied. Subject to the moon, to the stars, to the influence of the light of other worlds, she changed her moods and appearance in a way that I thought fantastic, but it was as fatal as the tide.

She began to miss solitude. The house was full of snails and conches, of small sailboats that in her fury she had shipwrecked (together with the others, laden with images, that each night left my forehead and sank in her ferocious or pleasant whirlwinds). How many little treasures were lost in that time! But my boats and the silent song of the snails was not enough. I had to install in the house a colony of fish. I confess that it was not without jealousy that I watched them swimming in my friend, caressing her breasts, sleeping between her legs, adorning her hair with light flashes of color.

Among all those fish there were a few particularly repulsive and ferocious ones, little tigers from the aquarium, with large fixed eyes and jagged and bloodthirsty mouths. I don't know by what aberration my friend delighted in playing with them, shamelessly showing them a preference whose significance I preferred to ignore. She passed long hours confined with those horrible creatures. One day I couldn't stand it any more; I threw open the door and launched after them. Agile and ghostly they escaped my hands while she laughed and pounded me until I fell. I thought I was drowning. And when I was at the point of death, and purple, she deposited me on the bank and began to kiss me, saying I don't know what things. I felt very weak, fatigued and humiliated. And at the same time her voluptuousness made me close my eyes, because her voice was sweet and she spoke to me of the delicious death of the drowned. When I recovered, I began to fear and hate her.

I had neglected my affairs. Now I began to visit friends and renew old and dear relations. I met an old girlfriend. Making her swear to keep my secret, I told her of my life with the wave. Nothing moves women so much as the possibility of saving a man. My redeemer employed all of her arts, but what could a woman, master of a limited number of souls and bodies, do in front of my friend who was always changing—and always identical to herself in her incessant metamorphoses.

Winter came. The sky turned gray. Fog fell on the city. Frozen drizzle rained. My friend cried every night. During the day she isolated herself, quiet and sinister, stuttering a single syllable, like an old woman who grumbles in a corner. She became cold; to sleep with her was to shiver all night and to feel freeze, little by little, the blood, the bones, the thoughts. She turned deep, impenetrable, restless. I left frequently and my absences were each time more prolonged. She, in her corner, howled loudly. With teeth like steel and a corrosive tongue she gnawed the walls, crumbled them. She passed the nights in mourning, reproaching me. She had nightmares, deliriums of the sun, of warm beaches. She dreamt of the pole and of changing into a great block of ice, sailing beneath black skies in nights long as months. She insulted me. She cursed and laughed; filled the house with guffaws and phantoms. She called up the monsters of the depths, blind ones, quick ones, blunt. Charged with electricity, she carbonized all she touched; full of acid, she dissolved whatever she brushed against. Her sweet embraces became knotty cords that strangled me. And her body, greenish and elastic, was an implacable whip that lashed, lashed, lashed. I fled. The horrible fish laughed with ferocious smiles.

There in the mountains, among the tall pines and precipices, I breathed the cold thin air like a thought of liberty. At the end of a month I returned. I had decided. It had been so cold that over the marble of the chimney, next to the extinct fire, I found a statue of ice. I was unmoved by her weary beauty. I put her in a big canvas sack and went out to the streets with the sleeper on my shoulders. In a restaurant in the outskirts I sold her to a waiter friend who immediately began to chop her into little pieces, which he carefully deposited in the buckets where bottles are chilled.

Explorations of the Text

1. What merger of the real and the fantastic propels this story? Why does the narrator compare the sea and an elusive lover?
2. How is the wave like a woman? like a man's fantasy of a woman?
3. Explore the incident of the water fountain. Why is the water "salty"? What does the narrator's imprisonment suggest?
4. Once he returns home, how does her presence at first change his life? What stage of love is depicted?
5. What are the implications of these statements: "But never did I reach the center of her being," and "She had no center, just an emptiness as in a whirlwind, that sucked me in and smothered me"?
6. Why does the narrator have to install a colony of fish? Why does she prefer the "little tigers . . . with large fixed eyes and jagged and bloodthirsty mouths"?
7. Explore the sign of the "drowning" episode. Why does he begin "to fear and hate her"?
8. What is the outcome of their relationship? Explore the symbolic dimension of the wave's association with ice.
9. What visions of romantic love, of sexuality, and of relationships does the story present?
10. Why does Paz depict human love through an affair with a wave instead of an affair with a real lover? What is the impact of this metaphor? Is it effective?

The Reading/Writing Connection

1. Write a parable, fable, or story in magical realism for men's and women's relationships. Or write a feminist fable or fairy tale.
2. "Think" Topic: Why is the woman characterized as a "wave" rather than as an ocean?

Ideas for Writing

1. Examine the text to determine how Paz created the metamorphosis of the woman as ocean lover. Does it lie in the choice of details? verbs? adjectives? figurative language? Comment on Paz's style.
2. Categorize the stages of romantic love in this story.

The Chase

Alberto Moravia

Alberto Moravia (1907–90) was born in Rome. He gained early fame for his first novel, The Time of Indifference *(1929). During the 1930s and 1940s, he earned international acclaim for his novels, which include* Wheel of Fortune *(1937) and* Agostino *(1944). His short story volumes include* Roman Tales *(1956) and* Command and I Will Obey You *(1969). Moravia is known for his penetrating portraits of men and women in love and their struggle to escape the isolation and sterility symptomatic of a materialistic age.*

1967

I have never been a sportsman—or, rather, I have been a sportsman only once, and that was the first and last time. I was a child, and one day, for some reason or other, I found myself together with my father, who was holding a gun in his hand, behind a bush, watching a bird that had perched on a branch not very far away. It was a large, gray bird—or perhaps it was brown—with a long—or perhaps a short—beak; I don't remember. I only remember what I felt at that moment as I looked at it. It was like watching an animal whose vitality was rendered more intense by the very fact of my watching it and of the animal's not knowing that I was watching it.

At that moment, I say, the notion of wildness entered my mind, never again to leave it: everything is wild which is autonomous and unpredictable and does not depend upon us. Then all of a sudden there was an explosion; I could no longer see the bird and I thought it had flown away. But my father was leading the way, walking in front of me through the undergrowth. Finally he stooped down, picked up something, and put it in my hand. I was aware of something warm and soft and I lowered my eyes: there was the bird in the palm of my hand, its dangling, shattered head crowned with a plume of already-thickening blood. I burst into tears and dropped the corpse on the ground, and that was the end of my shooting experience.

I thought again of this remote episode in my life this very day after watching my wife, for the first and also the last time, as she was walking through the streets of the city. But let us take things in order.

What had my wife been like; what was she like now? She once had been, to put it briefly, "wild"—that is, entirely autonomous and unpredictable; latterly she had become "tame"—that is, predictable and dependent. For a long time she had been like the bird that, on that far-off morning in my childhood, I had seen perching on the bough; latterly, I am sorry to say, she had become like a hen about which one knows everything in advance—how it moves, how it eats, how it lays eggs, how it sleeps, and so on.

Nevertheless I would not wish anyone to think that my wife's wildness consisted of an uncouth, rough, rebellious character. Apart from being extremely beautiful, she is the gentlest, politest, most discreet person in the world. Rather her wildness consisted of the air of charming unpredictability, of independence in her way of living, with which during the first years of our marriage she acted in my presence, both at home and abroad. Wildness signified intimacy, privacy, secrecy. Yes, my wife as she sat in front of her dressing table, her eyes fixed on the looking glass, passing the hairbrush with a repeated motion over her long, loose hair, was just as wild as the solitary quail hopping forward along a sun-filled furrow or the furtive fox coming out into a clearing and stopping to look around before running on. She was wild because I, as I looked at her, could never manage to foresee when she would give a last stroke with the hairbrush and rise and come toward me; wild to such a degree that sometimes when I went into our bedroom the smell of her, floating in the air, would have something of the acrid quality of a wild beast's lair.

Gradually she became less wild, tamer. I had had a fox, a quail, in the house, as I have said; then one day I realized that I had a hen. What effect does a hen have on someone who watches it? It has the effect of being, so to speak, an automaton in the form of a bird; automatic are the brief, rapid steps with which it moves about; automatic its hard, terse pecking; automatic the glance of the round eyes in its head that nods and turns; automatic its ready crouching down under the cock; automatic the dropping of the egg wherever it may be and the cry with which it announces that the egg has been laid. Good-by to the fox; good-by to the quail. And her smell—this no longer brought to my mind, in any way, the innocent odor of a wild animal; rather I detected in it the chemical suavity of some ordinary French perfume.

Our flat is on the first floor of a big building in a modern quarter of the town; our windows look out on a square in which there is a small public garden, the haunt of nurses and children and dogs. One day I was standing at the window, looking in a melancholy way at the garden. My wife, shortly before, had dressed to go out; and once again, watching her, I had noticed the irrevocable and, so to speak, invisible character of her gestures and personality; something which gave one the feeling of a thing already seen and already done and which therefore evaded even the most determined observation. And now, as I stood looking at the garden and at the same time wondering why the adorable wildness of former times had so completely disappeared, suddenly my wife came into my range of vision as she walked quickly across the garden in the direction of the bus stop. I watched her and then I almost jumped for joy; in a movement she was making to pull down a fold of her narrow skirt and smooth it over her thigh with the tips of her long, sharp nails, in this movement I recognized the wildness that in the past had made me love her. It was only an instant, but in that instant I said to myself: She's become wild again because she's convinced that I am not there and am not watching her. Then I left the window and rushed out.

But I did not join her at the bus stop; I felt that I must not allow myself to be seen. Instead I hurried to my car, which was standing nearby, got in, and waited. A bus came and she got in together with some other people; the bus started off again and I began following it. Then there came back to me the memory of that one shooting expedition in which I had taken part as a child, and I saw that the bus was the undergrowth with its bushes and trees, my wife the bird perching on the bough while I, unseen, watched it living before my eyes. And the whole town, during this pursuit, became, as though by magic, a fact of nature like the countryside: the houses were hills, the streets valleys, the vehicles hedges and woods, and even the passersby on the pavements had something unpredictable and autonomous—that is, wild—about them. And in my mouth, behind my clenched teeth, there was the acrid, metallic taste of gunfire; and my eyes, usually listless and wandering, had become sharp, watchful, attentive.

These eyes were fixed intently upon the exit door when the bus came to the end of its run. A number of people got out, and then I saw my wife getting out. Once again I recognized, in the manner in which she broke free of the crowd and started off toward a neighboring street, the wildness that pleased me so much. I jumped out of the car and started following her.

10 She was walking in front of me, ignorant of my presence, a tall woman with an elegant figure, long-legged, narrow-hipped, broad-backed, her brown hair falling on her shoulders.

Men turned around as she went past; perhaps they were aware of what I myself was now sensing with an intensity that quickened the beating of my heart and took my breath away: the unrestricted, steadily increasing, irresistible character of her mysterious wildness.

She walked hurriedly, having evidently some purpose in view, and even the fact that she had a purpose of which I was ignorant added to her wildness; I did not know where she was going, just as on that far-off morning I had not known what the bird perching on the bough was about to do. Moreover I thought the gradual, steady increase in this quality of wildness came partly from the fact that as she drew nearer to the object of this mysterious walk there was an increase in her—how shall I express it?—of biological tension, of existential excitement, of vital effervescence. Then, unexpectedly, with the suddenness of a film, her purpose was revealed.

A fair-haired young man in a leather jacket and a pair of corduroy trousers was leaning against the wall of a house in that ancient, narrow street. He was idly smoking as he looked in front of him. But as my wife passed close to him, he threw away his cigarette with a decisive gesture, took a step forward, and seized her arm. I was expecting her to rebuff him, to move away from him, but nothing happened: evidently obeying the rules of some kind of erotic ritual, she went on walking beside the young man. Then after a few steps, with a movement that confirmed her own complicity, she put her arm around her companion's waist and he put his around her.

I understood then that this unknown man who took such liberties with my wife was also attracted by wildness. And so, instead of making a conventional appointment with her, instead of meeting in a café with a handshake, a falsely friendly and respectful welcome, he had preferred, by agreement with her, to take her by surprise—or, rather, to pretend to do so—while she was apparently taking a walk on her own account. All this I perceived by intuition, noticing that at the very moment when he stepped forward and took her arm her wildness had, so to speak, given an upward bound. It was years since I had seen my wife so alive, but alas, the source of this life could not be traced to me.

They walked on thus entwined and then, without any preliminaries, just like two wild animals, they did an unexpected thing: they went into one of the dark doorways in order to kiss. I stopped and watched them from a distance, peering into the darkness of the entrance. My wife was turned away from me and was bending back with the pressure of his body, her hair hanging free. I looked at that long, thick mane of brown hair, which as she leaned back fell free of her shoulders, and I felt at that moment her vitality reached its diapason, just as happens with wild animals when the couple and their customary wildness is redoubled by the violence of love. I watched for a long time and then, since the kiss went on and on and in fact seemed to be prolonged beyond the limits of my power of endurance, I saw that I would have to intervene.

I would have to go forward, seize my wife by the arm—or actually by that hair, which hung down and conveyed so well the feeling of feminine passivity—then hurl myself with clenched fists upon the blond young man. After this encounter I would carry off my wife, weeping, mortified, ashamed, while I was raging and brokenhearted, upbraiding her and pouring scorn upon her.

But what else would this intervention amount to but the shot my father fired at that free, unknowing bird as it perched on the bough? The disorder and confusion, the mortification, the shame, that would follow would irreparably destroy the rare and precious moment of wildness that I was witnessing inside the dark doorway. It was true that this wildness was directed against me; but I had to remember that wildness, always and everywhere, is directed against everything and everybody. After the scene of my intervention it might be possible for me to regain control of my wife, but I should find her shattered and lifeless in my arms like the bird that my father placed in my hand so that I might throw it into the shooting bag.

The kiss went on and on: well, it was a kiss of passion—that could not be denied. I waited until they finished, until they came out of the doorway, until they walked on again still linked together. Then I turned back.

Explorations of the Text

1. Why does the story begin with the incident of the bird? What do you learn about the narrator and his view of his maleness?

2. What does the narrator mean by "wildness"?
3. How has the narrator's wife changed? Explore the significance of the wife's transformation into a "hen about which one knows everything in advance."
4. What is the meaning of "the chase"? the narrator's pursuit of his wife?
5. Why does the narrator decide not to intervene?
6. Consider the narrator's statement in the beginning, when he watches his wife "for the first and also the last time." Why is it the "first" and "the last time"? What will happen after the story ends?
7. How does the hunting anecdote advance the narrative? What does it reveal about the narrator?
8. What critique of marriage, of sexual roles, and of male/female relations emerges in the story?
9. Compare the woman in "The Chase" with the narrator in "Yellow Woman." Who will be happier in her relationship? Why?

The Reading/Writing Connection

1. "Think" Topic: Compare the narrators in this story and in "My Life with the Wave." Are they reliable narrators? Why or why not?
2. Create a monologue spoken by the wife in "The Chase."
3. Does romantic love require a sense of intrigue? In a paragraph, argue pro or con.

Ideas for Writing

1. Rewrite the story with the woman as narrator. Why does the woman have an affair?
2. How is the hunting image central tc the development of character, conflict, and theme in "The Chase"?
3. "The one who loves less has the power in a relationship." Use this statement as the basis for a discussion of "The Chase." Cite other stories and/or personal observations and experience if you wish.

THE JILTING OF GRANNY WEATHERALL

Katherine Anne Porter

Katherine Anne Porter (1890–1980) was born in Indian Creek, Texas. She worked for a time as a newspaperwoman in Chicago and Denver and as a freelance writer in New York. Her first book of stories, Flowering Judas *(1930), was followed by other short story collections and short novels, among them* Noon Wine *(1937),* Pale Horse, Pale Rider

(1939), and Collected Short Stories *(1965). Porter's only novel,* Ship of Fools, *based on the growth of Nazism, which she had witnessed in Germany, appeared in 1962. Porter's work brought her many honors, including the Pulitzer Prize and the National Book Award.*

1930

She flicked her wrist neatly out of Doctor Harry's pudgy careful fingers and pulled the sheet up to her chin. The brat ought to be in knee breeches. Doctoring around the country with spectacles on his nose! "Get along now, take your schoolbooks and go. There's nothing wrong with me."

Doctor Harry spread a warm paw like a cushion on her forehead where the forked green vein danced and made her eyelids twitch. "Now, now, be a good girl, and we'll have you up in no time."

"That's no way to speak to a woman nearly eighty years old just because she's down. I'd have you respect your elders, young man."

"Well, Missy, excuse me." Doctor Harry patted her cheek. "But I've got to warn you, haven't I? You're a marvel, but you must be careful or you're going to be good and sorry."

5 "Don't tell me what I'm going to be. I'm on my feet now, morally speaking. It's Cornelia. I had to go to bed to get rid of her."

Her bones felt loose, and floated around in her skin, and Doctor Harry floated like a balloon around the foot of the bed. He floated and pulled down his waistcoat and swung his glasses on a cord. "Well, stay where you are, it certainly can't hurt you."

"Get along and doctor your sick," said Granny Weatherall. "Leave a well woman alone. I'll call for you when I want you. . . . Where were you forty years ago when I pulled through milk-leg[1] and double pneumonia? You weren't even born. Don't let Cornelia lead you on," she shouted, because Doctor Harry appeared to float up to the ceiling and out. "I pay my own bills, and I don't throw my money away on nonsense!"

She meant to wave good-by, but it was too much trouble. Her eyes closed of themselves, it was like a dark curtain drawn around the bed. The pillow rose and floated under her, pleasant as a hammock in a light wind. She listened to the leaves rustling outside the window. No, somebody was swishing newspapers: no, Cornelia and Doctor Harry were whispering together. She leaped broad awake, thinking they whispered in her ear.

"She was never like this, *never* like this!" "Well, what can we expect?" "Yes, eighty years old. . . ."

10 Well, and what if she was? She still had ears. It was like Cornelia to whisper around doors. She always kept things secret in such a public way. She was always being tactful and kind. Cornelia was dutiful; that was the trouble with her. Dutiful and good: "So good and dutiful," said Granny, "that I'd like to spank her." She saw herself spanking Cornelia and making a fine job of it.

"What'd you say, Mother?"

---

[1] Swelling of the legs, sometimes occurring in women after childbirth.

Granny felt her face tying up in hard knots.

"Can't a body think, I'd like to know?"

"I thought you might want something."

15 "I do. I want a lot of things. First off, go away and don't whisper."

She lay and drowsed, hoping in her sleep that the children would keep out and let her rest a minute. It had been a long day. Not that she was tired. It was always pleasant to snatch a minute now and then. There was always so much to be done, let me see: tomorrow.

Tomorrow was far away and there was nothing to trouble about. Things were finished somehow when the time came; thank God there was always a little margin over for peace: then a person could spread out the plan of life and tuck in the edges orderly. It was good to have everything clean and folded away, with the hair brushes and tonic bottles sitting straight on the white embroidered linen: the day started without fuss and the pantry shelves laid out with rows of jelly glasses and brown jugs and white stone-china jars with blue whirligigs and words painted on them: coffee, tea, sugar, ginger, cinnamon, allspice: and the bronze clock with the lion on top nicely dusted off. The dust that lion could collect in twenty-four hours! The box in the attic with all those letters tied up, well she'd have to go through that tomorrow. All those letters—George's letters and John's letters and her letters to them both—lying around for the children to find afterwards made her uneasy. Yes, that would be tomorrow's business. No use to let them know how silly she had been once.

While she was rummaging around she found death in her mind and it felt clammy and unfamiliar. She had spent so much time preparing for death there was no need for bringing it up again. Let it take care of itself now. When she was sixty she had felt very old, finished, and went around making farewell trips to see her children and grandchildren, with a secret in her mind: This is the very last of your mother, children! Then she made her will and came down with a long fever. That was all just a notion like a lot of other things, but it was lucky too, for she had once for all got over the idea of dying for a long time. Now she couldn't be worried. She hoped she had better sense now. Her father had lived to be one hundred and two years old and had drunk a noggin of strong hot toddy on his last birthday. He told the reporters it was his daily habit, and he owed his long life to that. He had made quite a scandal and was very pleased about it. She believed she'd just plague Cornelia a little.

"Cornelia! Cornelia!" No footsteps, but a sudden hand on her cheek. "Bless you, where have you been?"

20 "Here, mother."

"Well, Cornelia, I want a noggin of hot toddy."

"Are you cold, darling?"

"I'm chilly, Cornelia. Lying in bed stops the circulation. I must have told you that a thousand times."

Well, she could just hear Cornelia telling her husband that Mother was getting childish and they'd have to humor her. The thing that most annoyed her was that Cornelia thought she was deaf, dumb, and blind. Little hasty glances and tiny gestures tossed around her and over her head saying, "Don't cross her, let her have her way, she's eighty years old," and she sitting there as if she lived in a thin glass cage. Sometimes Granny almost made up her mind to pack up and move back to her own house where nobody could remind her every minute that she was old. Wait, wait, Cornelia, till your own children whisper behind your back!

In her day she had kept a better house and had got more work done. She wasn't too old yet for Lydia to be driving eighty miles for advice when one of the children jumped the track, and Jimmy still dropped in and talked things over: "Now, Mammy, you've a good business head, I want to know what you think of this? . . ." Old. Cornelia couldn't change the furniture around without asking. Little things, little things! They had been so sweet when they were little. Granny wished the old days were back again with the children young and everything to be done over. It had been a hard pull, but not too much for her. When she thought of all the food she had cooked, and all the clothes she had cut and sewed, and all the gardens she had made—well, the children showed it. There they were, made out of her, and they couldn't get away from that. Sometimes she wanted to see John again and point to them and say, Well, I didn't do so badly, did I? But that would have to wait. That was for tomorrow. She used to think of him as a man, but now all the children were older than their father, and he would be a child beside her if she saw him now. It seemed strange and there was something wrong in the idea. Why, he couldn't possibly recognize her. She had fenced in a hundred acres once, digging the post holes herself and clamping the wires with just a negro boy to help. That changed a woman. John would be looking for a young woman with the peaked Spanish comb in her hair and the painted fan. Digging post holes changed a woman. Riding country roads in the winter when women had their babies was another thing: sitting up nights with sick horses and sick negroes and sick children and hardly ever losing one. John, I hardly ever lost one of them! John would see that in a minute, that would be something he could understand, she wouldn't have to explain anything!

It made her feel like rolling up her sleeves and putting the whole place to rights again. No matter if Cornelia was determined to be everywhere at once, there were a great many things left undone on this place. She would start tomorrow and do them. It was good to be strong enough for everything, even if all you made melted and changed and slipped under your hands, so that by the time you finished you almost forgot what you were working for. What was it I set out to do? she asked herself intently, but she could not remember. A fog rose over the valley, she saw it marching across the creek swallowing the trees and moving up the hill like an army of ghosts. Soon it would be at the near edge of the orchard, and then it was time to go in and light the lamps. Come in children, don't stay out in the night air.

Lighting the lamps had been beautiful. The children huddled up to her and breathed like little calves waiting at the bars in the twilight. Their eyes followed the match and watched the flame rise and settle in a blue curve, then they moved away from her. The lamp was lit, they didn't have to be scared and hang on to mother any more. Never, never, never more. God, for all my life I thank Thee. Without Thee, my God, I could never have done it. Hail, Mary, full of grace.

I want you to pick all the fruit this year and see that nothing is wasted. There's always someone who can use it. Don't let good things rot for want of using. You waste life when you waste good food. Don't let things get lost. It's bitter to lose things. Now, don't let me get to thinking, not when I am tired and taking a little nap before supper. . . .

The pillow rose about her shoulders and pressed against her heart and the memory was being squeezed out of it: oh, push down the pillow, somebody: it would smother her if she tried to hold it. Such a fresh breeze blowing and such a green day with no threats in it. But he had not come, just the same. What does a woman do when she has put on the white veil and set out the white cake for a man and he doesn't come? She tried to remember. No, I swear he never harmed me but in that. He never harmed me but in that . . . and what if he did? There was the day, the day, but a whirl of dark smoke rose and covered it, crept up and over into the bright field where everything was planted so carefully in orderly rows. That was hell, she knew hell when she saw it. For sixty years she had prayed against remembering him and against losing her soul in the deep pit of hell, and now the two things were mingled in one and the thought of him was a smoky cloud from hell that moved and crept in her head when she had just got rid of Doctor Harry and was trying to rest a minute. Wounded vanity, Ellen, said a sharp voice in the top of her mind. Don't let your wounded vanity get the upper hand of you. Plenty of girls get jilted. You were jilted, weren't you? Then stand up to it. Her eyelids wavered and let in streamers of blue-gray light like tissue paper over her eyes. She must get up and pull the shades down or she'd never sleep. She was in bed again and the shades were not down. How could that happen? Better turn over, hide from the light, sleeping in the light gave you nightmares. "Mother, how do you feel now?" and a stinging wetness on her forehead. But I don't like having my face washed in cold water!

30 Hapsy? George? Lydia? Jimmy? No, Cornelia, and her features were swollen and full of little puddles. "They're coming, darling, they'll all be here soon." Go wash your face, child, you look funny.

Instead of obeying, Cornelia knelt down and put her head on the pillow. She seemed to be talking but there was no sound. "Well, are you tongue-tied? Whose birthday is it? Are you going to give a party?"

Cornelia's mouth moved urgently in strange shapes. "Don't do that, you bother me, daughter."

"Oh, no. Mother, oh, no . . ."

Nonsense. It was strange about children. They disputed your every word. "No what, Cornelia?"

35 "Here's Doctor Harry."

"I won't see that boy again. He just left five minutes ago."

"That was this morning, Mother. It's night now. Here's the nurse."

"This is Doctor Harry, Mrs. Weatherall. I never saw you look so young and happy!"

"Ah, I'll never be young again—but I'd be happy if they'd let me lie in peace and get rested."

40 She thought she spoke up loudly, but no one answered. A warm weight on her forehead, a warm bracelet on her wrist, and a breeze went on whispering, trying to tell her something. A shuffle of leaves in the everlasting hand of God. He blew on them and they danced and rattled. "Mother, don't mind, we're going to give you a little hypodermic." "Look here, daughter, how do ants get in this bed? I saw sugar ants yesterday." Did you send for Hapsy too?

It was Hapsy she really wanted. She had to go a long way back through a great many rooms to find Hapsy standing with a baby on her arm. She seemed to herself to be Hapsy also, and the baby on Hapsy's arm was Hapsy and himself and herself, all at once, and there was no surprise in the meeting. Then Hapsy melted from within and turned flimsy as gray gauze and the baby was a gauzy shadow, and Hapsy came up close and said, "I thought you'd never come," and looked at her very searchingly and said, "You haven't changed a bit!" They leaned forward to kiss, when Cornelia began whispering from a long way off, "Oh, is there anything you want to tell me? Is there anything I can do for you?"

Yes, she had changed her mind after sixty years and she would like to see George. I want you to find George. Find him and be sure to tell him I forgot him. I want him to know I had my husband just the same and my children and my house like any other woman. A good house too and a good husband that I loved and fine children out of him. Better than I hoped for even. Tell him I was given back everything he took away and more. Oh, no, oh, God, no, there was something else besides the house and the man and the children. Oh, surely they were not all? What was it? Something not given back. . . . Her breath crowded down under her ribs and grew into a monstrous frightening shape with cutting edges; it bored up into her head, and the agony was unbelievable: Yes, John, get the Doctor now, no more talk, my time has come.

When this one was born it should be the last. The last. It should have been born first, for it was the one she had truly wanted. Everything came in good time. Nothing left out, left over. She was strong, in three days she would be as well as ever. Better. A woman needed milk in her to have her full health.

"Mother, do you hear me?"

45 "I've been telling you—"

"Mother, Father Connolly's here."

"I went to Holy Communion only last week. Tell him I'm not so sinful as all that."

"Father just wants to speak to you."

He could speak as much as he pleased. It was like him to drop in and inquire about her soul as if it were a teething baby, and then stay on for a cup of tea and a round of cards and gossip. He always had a funny story of some sort, usually about an Irishman who made his little mistakes and confessed them, and the point lay in some absurd thing he would blurt out in the confessional showing his struggles between native piety and original sin. Granny felt easy about her soul. Cornelia, where are your manners? Give Father Connolly a chair. She had her secret comfortable understanding with a few favorite saints who cleared a straight road to God for her. All as surely signed and sealed as the papers for the new Forty Acres. Forever . . . heirs and assigns forever. Since the day the wedding cake was not cut, but thrown out and wasted. The whole bottom dropped out of the world, and there she was blind and sweating with nothing under her feet and the walls falling away. His hand had caught her under the breast, she had not fallen, there was the freshly polished floor with the green rug on it, just as before. He had cursed like a sailor's parrot and said, "I'll kill him for you." Don't lay a hand on him, for my sake leave something to God. "Now, Ellen, you must believe what I tell you. . . ."

So there was nothing, nothing to worry about any more, except sometimes in the night one of the children screamed in a nightmare, and they both hustled out shaking and hunting for the matches and calling, "There, wait a minute, here we are!" John, get the doctor now, Hapsy's time has come. But there was Hapsy standing by the bed in a white cap. "Cornelia, tell Hapsy to take off her cap. I can't see her plain."

Her eyes opened very wide and the room stood out like a picture she had seen somewhere. Dark colors with the shadow rising towards the ceiling in long angles. The tall black dresser gleamed with nothing on it but John's picture, enlarged from a little one, with John's eyes very black when they should have been blue. You never saw him, so how do you know how he looked? But the man insisted the copy was perfect, it was very rich and handsome. For a picture, yes, but it's not my husband. The table by the bed had a linen cover and a candle and a crucifix. The light was blue from Cornelia's silk lampshades. No sort of light at all, just frippery. You had to live forty years with kerosene lamps to appreciate honest electricity. She felt very strong and she saw Doctor Harry with a rosy nimbus around him.

"You look like a saint, Doctor Harry, and I vow that's as near as you'll ever come to it."

"She's saying something."

"I heard you, Cornelia. What's all this carrying-on?"

"Father Connolly's saying—"

Cornelia's voice staggered and bumped like a cart in a bad road. It rounded corners and turned back again and arrived nowhere. Granny stepped up in the cart very lightly and reached for the reins, but a man sat beside her and she knew him by his hands, driving the cart. She did not look in his face, for she knew without seeing, but looked instead down the road where the trees leaned over and bowed to each other and a thousand birds were singing a Mass. She felt like singing too, but she put her hand in the bosom of her dress and pulled out a rosary, and Father Connolly murmured Latin in a very solemn voice and tickled her feet. My God, will you stop that nonsense? I'm a married woman. What if he did run away and leave me to face the priest by myself? I found another a whole world better. I wouldn't have exchanged my husband for anybody except St. Michael himself, and you may tell him that for me with a thank you in the bargain.

Light flashed on her closed eyelids, and a deep roaring shook her. Cornelia, is that lightning? I hear thunder. There's going to be a storm. Close all the windows. Call the children in . . . "Mother, here we are, all of us." "Is that you, Hapsy?" "Oh, no, I'm Lydia. We drove as fast as we could." Their faces drifted above her, drifted away. The rosary fell out of her hands and Lydia put it back. Jimmy tried to help, their hands fumbled together, and Granny closed two fingers around Jimmy's thumb. Beads wouldn't do, it must be something alive. She was so amazed her thoughts ran round and round. So, my dear Lord, this is my death and I wasn't even thinking about it. My children have come to see me die. But I can't, it's not time. Oh, I always hated surprises. I wanted to give Cornelia the amethyst set—Cornelia, you're to have the amethyst set, but Hapsy's to wear it when she wants, and, Doctor Harry, do shut up. Nobody sent for you. Oh, my dear Lord, do wait a minute. I meant to do something about the Forty Acres, Jimmy doesn't need it and Lydia will later on with that worthless husband of hers. I meant to finish the altar cloth and send six bottles of wine to Sister Borgia for her dyspepsia.[2] I want to send six bottles of wine to Sister Borgia, Father Connolly, now don't let me forget.

Cornelia's voice made short turns and tilted over and crashed. "Oh, Mother, oh, Mother, oh, Mother. . . ."

"I'm not going, Cornelia. I'm taken by surprise. I can't go."

You'll see Hapsy again. What about her? "I thought you'd never come." Granny made a long journey outward, looking for Hapsy. What if I don't find her? What then? Her heart sank down and down, there was no bottom to death, she couldn't come to the end of it. The blue light from Cornelia's lampshade drew into a tiny point in the center of her brain, it flickered and winked like an eye, quietly it fluttered and dwindled. Granny lay curled down within herself, amazed and watchful, staring at the point of light that was herself; her body was now only a deeper mass of shadow in an endless darkness and this darkness would curl around the light and swallow it up. God, give a sign!

For the second time there was no sign. Again no bridegroom and the priest in the house. She could not remember any other sorrow because this grief wiped them all away. Oh, no, there's nothing more cruel than this—I'll never forgive it. She stretched herself with a deep breath and blew out the light.

Explorations of the Text

1. Describe the point of view and voice of Granny Weatherall.
2. What do the interchanges between Granny Weatherall and both Cornelia and the doctor reveal about Granny's nature?
3. Analyze Granny's character as a young wife.
4. On her deathbed, whom does Granny Weatherall remember? What has happened to Hapsy?

[2] Indigestion.

5. Examine the symbolism of light, lamplight, shadow, and darkness. How does the symbolism develop themes of the story?
6. Explain the conclusion of the story. Discuss the allusion to the bridegroom. What is the final jilting?

The Reading/Writing Connection

1. "Think" Topic: Explore the symbolism of Granny's name as a starting point for character analysis.
2. Freewrite and react to the portrayal of Granny Weatherall.
3. Write a letter in the voice of George (a letter taken from the box in the attic).

Ideas for Writing

1. Contrast the external (real) and internal (remembered) worlds in the story. How does Porter create a vision of these two worlds?
2. How does first love affect the rest of Granny Weatherall's life? Norma Jean's life in "Shiloh"? Compare the two women's lives.

POETRY

LET ME NOT TO THE MARRIAGE OF TRUE MINDS

William Shakespeare

In this poem, Shakespeare (1564–1616) refers to "The Order of Solemnization of Matrimony" in the Anglican Book of Common Prayer: *"I require that if either of you know any impediments why ye may not be lawfully joined together in matrimony, ye do now confess it."*

1609

Let me not to the marriage of true minds
Admit impediments. Love is not love
Which alters when it alteration finds,
Or bends with the remover to remove.
O no, it is an ever-fixèd mark
That look on tempests and is never shaken;
It is the star to every wand'ring bark,[1]
Whose worth's unknown, although his height[2] be taken.
Love's not Time's fool,[3] though rosy lips and cheeks
Within his bending sickle's compass come;
Love alters not with his brief hours and weeks,
But bears it out[4] even to the edge of doom.[5]
If this be error and upon me proved,
I never writ, nor no man every loved.

Explorations of the Text

1. Why does the persona speak of a "marriage of true minds"?
2. Paraphrase the first two lines. What does the first statement mean?
3. Why does love not "[alter]" or "[bend]"? Why is it "an ever-fixèd mark"?
4. What do the navigational images mean?
5. Look at personification in this sonnet. What is personified? Why? What is the relationship of love and time? Why is love not "Time's fool"?

[1] Small ship.

[2] Altitude.

[3] Slave.

[4] Endures.

[5] The Last Judgment.

6. Discuss the final **couplet.** Solve the **paradox.**
7. Consider the view of love in this sonnet. Is the persona convincing in his contention that true love lasts "even to the edge of doom"?

The Reading/Writing Connection

1. Define love or another abstract idea by stating what it is not. Begin with: Love is not. . . .
2. "Think" Topic: Do you agree with the persona's view of true love.

Ideas for Writing

1. Some critics consider this poem to be Shakespeare's greatest sonnet. Evaluate "Let Me Not to the Marriage of True Minds." (See checklist in chapter 10.)
2. Contrast this poem with Blake's "Garden of Love."

A Valediction Forbidding Mourning

John Donne

John Donne (1571–1631), born into a prominent Catholic family in London during a strongly anti-Catholic time, was educated at Oxford and Cambridge universities. After holding various jobs, Donne converted to Anglicanism, took Anglican orders in 1615 at the age of forty-two, and preached sermons that rank among the greatest of the seventeenth century. He was considered the greatest of the metaphysical poets, whose works combined passion and reason through highly innovative conceits or elaborate metaphors.

1633

As virtuous men pass mildly away,
    And whisper to their souls to go,
Whilst some of their sad friends do say
    The breath goes now, and some say no:

So let us melt, and make no noise,
    No tear-floods, nor sigh-tempests move;
'Twere profanation[1] of our joys
    To tell the laity our love.

Moving of th' earth[2] brings harms and fears;
    Men reckon what it did and meant;

[1] The lovers are like priests, and their love is a mystery.

[2] Earthquakes.

But trepidation of the spheres,[3]
Though greater far, is innocent.

Dull sublunary lovers' love
(Whose soul is sense)[4] cannot admit
Absence, because it doth remove
Those things which elemented it.

But we, by a love so much refined
That ourselves know not what it is,
Inter-assured of the mind,
Care less, eyes, lips, and hands to miss.

Our two souls, therefore, which are one,
Though I must go, endure not yet
A breach, but an expansion,[5]
Like gold to airy thinness beat.

If they be two, they are two so
As stiff twin compasses are two:[6]
Thy soul, the fixed foot, makes no show
To move, but doth, if th' other do.

And though it in the center sit,
Yet when the other far doth roam,
It leans and harkens after it,
And grows erect as that comes home.

Such wilt thou be to me, who must,
Like th' other foot, obliquely run;
Thy firmness makes my circle just,[7]
And makes me end where I begun.

Explorations of the Text

1. To what event does the speaker compare his separation from his beloved in the first stanza?

[3] Prior to Newton's explanation of the equinoxes, people assumed that stars and planets had circular positions. The observation of irregularities (the result of the wobbling of the earth's axis) was explained by the theory of trepidation, a trembling that occurred in outer spheres around the earth.

[4] A completely physical attraction.

[5] Gold is quite malleable.

[6] Compasses used for drawing circles.

[7] Round.

2. What does he mean by the "trepidation of the spheres"?
3. Why can "dull" lovers not part easily? Why can they not tolerate "absence"?
4. What does the "refined" love of the speaker require? (See stanza 5.)
5. How does the gold imagery in lines 21–24 expand the vision of the lovers' communion?
6. Examine the metaphysical **conceit** comparing the lovers to "twin compasses." Is this extended figure effective?
7. Is the speaker's argument against "mourning" persuasive?

The Reading/Writing Connection

1. Many popular songs attest to the difficulty of saying goodbye, of separation. Freewrite about one of these themes.
2. "Think" Topic: Write a letter to the speaker of the poem, responding to his view of love.

Ideas for Writing

1. Both Shakespeare and Donne refer to "the marriage of true minds," a love more refined than ordinary relationship. Take a position on ideal love or on grand passion.
2. Characterize the speaker in the poem; write about his voice, beliefs, attitudes, intelligence, and capacity for love. Use Journal Entry 2 as a beginning.
3. Compare Plato's concept of union with Donne's ideas.

To His Coy Mistress

Andrew Marvell

Andrew Marvell (1621–78) was born in Winchester, England, and educated at Cambridge University. In 1659, he became a member of Parliament and wrote pamphlets and satires on politics. His lyric poetry speaks of love, nature, and God. Most of Marvell's poems were published posthumously in 1681, his satires in 1689. "To His Coy Mistress," Marvell's best-known poem, represents a common literary motif called carpe diem, *which means "seize the day." The poet emphasizes that life is fleeting and urges the person addressed by the speaker—usually a virgin—to enjoy the pleasures of life and of love.*

1681

Had we but world enough and time,
This coyness, lady, were no crime.

We would sit down and think which way
To walk, and pass our long love's day.
Thou by the Indian Ganges'[1] side
Should'st rubies find; I by the tide
Of Humber[2] would complain.[3] I would
Love you ten years before the Flood,
And you should, if you please, refuse
Till the conversion of the Jews.
My vegetable love should grow[4]
Vaster than empires, and more slow.
An hundred years should go to praise
Thine eyes, and on thy forehead gaze,
Two hundred to adore each breast,
But thirty thousand to the rest.
An age at least to every part,
And the last age should show your heart.
For, lady, you deserve this state,
Nor would I love at lower rate.
    But at my back I always hear
Time's wingèd chariot hurrying near,
And yonder all before us lie
Deserts of vast eternity.
Thy beauty shall no more be found,
Nor in thy marble vault shall sound
My echoing song; then worms shall try
That long preserved virginity,
And your quaint honor turn to dust,
And into ashes all my lust.
The grave's a fine and private place,
But none, I think, do there embrace.
    Now therefore, while the youthful-hue
Sits on thy skin like morning glew[5]
And while thy willing soul transpires[6]
At every pore with instant fires,
Now let us sport us while we may;
And now, like amorous birds of prey,
Rather at once our time devour

---

[1] River in India, sacred to Hindus.

[2] Small river that flows through Marvell's hometown of Hull.

[3] Compose love songs.

[4] Slow, unconscious development.

[5] Glow.

[6] Breathes.

Than languish in his slow-chapped[7] power.
Let us roll all our strength and all
Our sweetness up into one ball
And tear our pleasures with rough strife
Thorough the iron gates of life.
Thus, though we cannot make our sun
Stand still, yet we will make him run.

Explorations of the Text

1. In what ways does the speaker suggest the lovers might pass their "long love's day" if only they had time?
2. Why is the lady "coy"?
3. Trace the steps in the argument that begin on lines 1, 21, and 33.
4. What concepts of time and of death does the speaker present? What are the consequences to the beloved?
5. What is the speaker's view of "Time's wingèd chariot"?
6. Why does he suggest that "worms" will "try" her "virginity" and her "quaint honor"? Does the image have sexual connotations?
7. In the conclusion, how does his description of proposed acts of love function? How will the lovers make the sun "run"?
8. How does hyperbole add to the humorous and whimsical tone? Contrast the tone of this poem with "Dover Beach," "The Garden of Love," and "The Flea."

The Reading/Writing Connection

1. In a mini-essay, write a feminist critique of this poem.
2. In a monologue, persuade someone to change his or her attitude or behavior about a love relationship. Use **hyperbole** in an effort to be persuasive.

Ideas for Writing

1. Outline and critique the argument in "To His Coy Mistress."
2. Write a paper on virginity. Consider such questions as abstinence, social and cultural values, peer pressure, and marriage.
3. Read Herrick's "To the Virgins, To Make Much of Time." Would Herrick agree with Marvell?

[7] Slow-jawed.

Dover Beach

Matthew Arnold

Matthew Arnold (1822–88), born at Laliham, Middlesex, England, attended Oxford University. He was professor of poetry at Oxford from 1857 to 1867, then an inspector of schools until 1886. His first volume of poetry, The Strayed Reveller and Other Poems, *appeared in 1849, to be followed by* Empedocles and Other Poems *in 1852. In 1853, Arnold withdrew both volumes from circulation and replaced them with* Poems. *Arnold's prose began to circulate after 1860. The most significant of these works were* Essays in Criticism *and* Culture and Anarchy *(1869). He wrote religious criticism as well as social and political analysis and attempted to improve education, in particular secondary education.*

1851

The sea is calm tonight,
The tide is full, the moon lies fair
Upon the straits; on the French coast the light
Gleams and is gone; the cliffs of England stand,
Glimmering and vast, out in the tranquil bay.
Come to the window, sweet is the night-air!
Only, from the long line of spray
Where the sea meets the moon-blanched land,
Listen! you hear the grating roar
Of pebbles which the waves draw back, and fling,
At their return, up the high strand,
Begin, and cease, and then again begin,
With tremulous cadence slow, and bring
The eternal note of sadness in.[1]
Sophocles long ago
Heard it on the Aegean, and it brought
Into his mind the turbid ebb and flow
Of human misery; we
Find also in the sound a thought,
Hearing it by this distant northern sea.

The Sea of Faith
Was once, too, at the full, and round earth's shore
Lay like the folds of a bright girdle[2] furled.
But now I only hear

[1] A reference to *Antigone* where Sophocles alludes to the tragedies that plague the House of Oedipus as a "mourning tide."

[2] Belt or cord.

Its melancholy, long, withdrawing roar,
Retreating, to the breath
Of the night-wind, down the vast edges drear
And naked shingles[3] of the world.

Ah, love, let us be true
To one another! for the world, which seems
To lie before us like a land of dreams,
So various, so beautiful, so new,
Hath really neither joy, nor love, nor light,
Nor certitude, nor peace, nor help for pain;
And we are here as on a darkling plain
Swept with confused alarms of struggle and flight,
Where ignorant armies clash by night.

Explorations of the Text

1. Compare the initial description with the closing lines (33–37). What is the difference? Are both effective?
2. To whom is the poem addressed? Why?
3. What is "the eternal note of sadness"? What creates the motion and sound of the sea?
4. What is the significance of the "withdrawing roar" of the "Sea of Faith"?
5. What can the lovers do to avoid despair? What can anyone do? Is the speaker hopeful?
6. How would you answer the speaker?
7. Discuss the title and the setting. Is the sadness a modern attitude, or has it always been central to the human condition?

The Reading/Writing Connection

1. In a paragraph, describe the setting and its effect on the persona and on the themes.
2. Write about the sea. Imitate the tone of "Dover Beach."
3. "Think: Topic: Choose the best lines in the poem, and discuss the word choice, sound, and imagery that make them effective.

[3] Beaches covered with small stones or pebbles.

Ideas for Writing

1. M. H. Abrams has called a poem that uses landscape as a prelude to meditation "the greater romantic lyric." The first part creates the setting; the second section presents the meditation; the third transforms the landscape according to the persona's insights. Analyze "Dover Beach" as a lyric in this mode.
2. Write a meditation in lyric or prose form.
3. Explore the sea as setting, character, and/or theme in Arnold and in Paz.

The Garden of Love

William Blake

William Blake (1757–1827), born in London, began drawing at an early age; at fourteen, he was apprenticed to an engraver. Many of the poems he wrote during this period were eventually printed in Poetical Sketches *(1783), his first book of poems. In 1789, Blake wrote and engraved his great poetic work,* Songs of Innocence, *which was followed in 1790 by the prose* The Marriage of Heaven and Hell. *In 1804, he undertook the engravings of his final pieces,* Milton *(1808) and* Jerusalem *(1820). He also engraved his work on copper with the poems surrounded by illustrations that he painted, a process he called "illuminated printing."*

1794

I went to the Garden of Love,
And I saw what I never had seen:
A Chapel was built in the midst,
Where I used to play on the green.

And the gates of this Chapel were shut,
And "Thou shalt not" writ over the door:
So I turned to the Garden of Love
That so many sweet flowers bore;

And I saw it was filled with graves,
And tomb-stones where flowers should be;
And Priests in black gowns were walking their rounds,
And binding with briars my joys and desires.

Explorations of the Text

1. What is the speaker's first sense of love when he "used to play on the green"?

2. What are the obstacles to the experience of love?
3. What are the contradictory sides of love suggested in the images of the "green," "the garden," and "graves"?
4. Analyze the rhyme scheme and the form. How do they create meaning?
5. What critique of organized religion appears in this work?

The Reading/Writing Connection

1. "Love is a time of torment." Comment in a journal entry.
2. "Love is a time of bliss." Comment.
3. Choose a character from one of the short stories in this chapter, and create his/her response to the poem.

Ideas for Writing

1. Compare three views of love presented in three poems in this chapter.
2. Demonstrate the relationship of imagery to theme in this poem.

Sweetness, Always

Pablo Neruda Translated from the Spanish by Alastair Reid

Pablo Neruda (1904–73), born in Chile, received an appointment to the consular service in his twenties, and he served in India and in other Asian countries. In 1934, he received a post in Spain, where he became deeply involved in the Spanish Civil War. As a result, his poetry, which had expressed a romantic view of life, came to express concerns both personal and political. Among his works are Selected Poems of Pablo Neruda *(1961),* The Heights of Macchu Picchu *(1966), and* Pablo Neruda: A New Decade *(1969). His* Collected Poems *has been translated into numerous languages, including English. Neruda was awarded the Nobel Prize for Literature in 1971.*

1958

Why such harsh machinery?
Why, to write down the stuff
and people of every day,
must poems be dressed up in gold,
in old and fearful stone?

I want verses of felt or feather
which scarcely weigh, mild verses
with the intimacy of beds
where people have loved and dreamed.

I want poems stained
by hands and everydayness.

Verses of pastry which melt
into milk and sugar in the mouth,
air and water to drink,
the bites and kisses of love.
I long for eatable sonnets,
poems of honey and flour.

Vanity keeps prodding us
to lift ourselves skyward
or to make deep and useless
tunnels underground.
So we forget the joyous
love-needs of our bodies.
We forget about pastries.
We are not feeding the world.

In Madras[1] a long time since,
I saw a sugary pyramid,
a tower of confectionery—
one level after another,
and in the construction, rubies,
and other blushing delights,
medieval and yellow.

Someone dirtied his hands
to cook up so much sweetness.
Brother poets from here
and there, from earth and sky,
from Medellin,[2] from Veracruz,[3]
Abyssinia,[4] Antofagasta,[5]
do you know the recipe for honeycombs?
Let's forget about all that stone.

Let your poetry fill up
the equinoctial pastry shop
our mouths long to devour—

---

[1] Industrial city in India.

[2] City in Colombia.

[3] Mexican seaport.

[4] Ethiopia.

[5] Coastal city in Chile.

all the children's mouths
and the poor adults' also.
Don't go on without seeing,
relishing, understanding
all these hearts of sugar.
Don't be afraid of sweetness.

With us or without us,
sweetness will go on living
and is infinitely alive,
forever being revived,
for it's in a man's mouth,
whether he's eating or singing,
that sweetness has its place.

Explorations of the Text

1. Whom does the speaker address in the first stanza? Why does he believe that "the stuff/and people of every day" need not be written in "gold" or in "stone"?
2. What kind of poetry does the persona want? Why?
3. Discuss the extended metaphor of "sweetness." What is the connection between love and sweetness?
4. What are the barriers to the poetry of sweetness, to the "eatable sonnets"? What does the speaker mean when he declares, "We are not feeding the world"?
5. Why does he tell about the incident in Madras? Why does he emphasize the cook's dirty hands?
6. Why does he address "brother poets"? Why does he ask the poets to "forget about all that stone"?
7. Why does the speaker say: "Don't be afraid of sweetness"?
8. The speaker contends that sweetness "is infinitely alive," that "it's in a man's mouth." What does he mean?
9. Contrast Neruda's "sweetness" and Arnold's "sadness." What views of life are implied?

The Reading/Writing Connection

1. In a mini-essay, agree or disagree with the speaker's position.
2. Write a short piece in which images of confections represent love. Do *not* be sentimental; control your material.

Ideas for Writing

1. Answer Neruda's "Sweetness, Always." Argue that poetry does not avoid "sweetness" and that poets are not afraid of it.
2. Why does the persona speak only to male poets? Analyze the attitude toward gender presented in the work.
3. Contrast Arnold's vision of "sadness" and Neruda's view of "sweetness." What philosophical stances are suggested?

TONIGHT I CAN WRITE . . .

Pablo Neruda Translated by W. S. Merwin

Tonight I can write the saddest lines.

Write, for example, "The night is shattered
and the blue stars shiver in the distance."

The night wind revolves in the sky and sings.

Tonight I can write the saddest lines.
I loved her, and sometimes she loved me too.

Through nights like this one I held her in my arms.
I kissed her again and again under the endless sky.

She loved me, sometimes I loved her too.
How could one not have loved her great still eyes.

Tonight I can write the saddest lines.
To think that I do not have her. To feel that I have lost her.

To hear the immense night, still more immense without her.
And the verse falls to the soul like dew to the pasture.

What does it matter that my love could not keep her.
The night is shattered and she is not with me.

This is all. In the distance someone is singing. In the distance.
My soul is not satisfied that it has lost her.

My sight searches for her as though to go to her.
My heart looks for her, and she is not with me.

The same night whitening the same trees.
We, of that time, are no longer the same.

I no longer love her, that's certain, but how I loved her.
My voice tried to find the wind to touch her hearing.

Another's. She will be another's. Like my kisses before.
Her voice. Her bright body. Her infinite eyes.

I no longer love her, that's certain, but maybe I love her.
Love is so short, forgetting is so long.

Because through nights like this one I held her in my arms
my soul is not satisfied that it has lost her.

Though this be the last pain that she makes me suffer
and these the last verses that I write for her.

Explorations of the Text

1. Describe the voice and point of view of the persona.
2. Discuss images of night, darkness, and loss in the poem.
3. How do the two-line stanzas deepen mood and heighten themes of the work?
4. Discuss the meaning of this line, "Love is so short, forgetting is so long."

The Reading/Writing Connection

1. What makes this work a powerful love poem? Respond in a freewrite.
2. In a mini-essay, compare the view of love expressed in this poem with your own feelings and experiences.

Ideas for Writing

1. Contrast the view of love in "Sweetness, Always" with the vision of love in this poem.

NUIT DE SINE

Léopold-Sédar Senghor Translated by John Reed and Clive Wake

Léopold-Sédar Senghor (1906–) was born in French West Africa, now the republic of Senegal. He fought to gain independence for Senegal and in 1960 was elected president of the new independent republic. He served in that post until 1981. In addition to being a renowned statesman, he has also written many volumes of poetry and collections of essays, including Ethiopiques *(1956),* Prose and Poetry *(1965), and*

Poems of a Black Orpheus *(1981). He has been a leading spokesperson for the literary movement of* negritude, *arguing the need for crafting a new African tongue, diction, and form, free of imperialism. In 1983, he was elected to the Academie Francaise.*

1945

Woman, rest on my brow your balsam hands, your hands gentler than fur.
The tall palmtrees swinging in the nightwind
Hardly rustle. Not even cradlesongs,
The rhythmic silence rocks us.
Listen to its song, listen to the beating of our dark blood, listen
To the beating of the dark pulse of Africa in the mist of lost villages.
Now the tired moon sinks towards its bed of slack water,
Now the peals of laughter even fall asleep, and the bards themselves
Dandle their heads like children on the banks of their mothers.
Now the feet of the dancers grow heavy and heavy grows the tongue of the singers.
This is the hour of the stars and of the night that dreams
And reclines on this hill of clouds, draped in her long gown of milk.
The roofs of the houses gleam gently. What are they telling so confidently to the stars?
Inside the hearth is extinguished in the intimacy of bitter and sweet scents.
Woman, light the lamp of clear oil, and let the children in bed talk about their ancestors, like their parents.
Listen to the voice of the ancients of Elissa.[1] Like we, exiled,
They did not want to die, lest their seminal flood be lost in the sand.
Let me listen in the smoky hut for the shadowy visit of propitious souls,
My head on your breast glowing, like a kuskus[2] ball smoking out of the fire,
Let me breathe the smell of our dead, let me contemplate and repeat their living voice, let me learn
To live before I sink, deeper than the diver, into the lofty depth of sleep.

Explorations of the Text

1. Whom does the speaker address?
2. What mood is created by the setting? How is that mood intrinsic to the development of the vision of love?
3. Why are memories of "the ancestors" invoked? Why does the speaker want to "breathe the smell" of the dead and "repeat their living voices"?
4. Discuss the speaker's final wish, expressed in the last line.
5. Isolate and discuss the effect of the poem's sensory images.

[1] A village in Guinea.

[2] A spicy dumpling, cooked in soups.

6. Discuss the personification in the poem. What is its impact?
7. What vision of Africa emerges from this poem? Is it solely a poem about love?
8. How is Senghor's vision of passion quite different from the views of Neruda and of Snyder? Why?

The Reading/Writing Connection

1. Create a scene in which you include details from all of the senses to evoke the mood of love.
2. Contrast this poem with Snyder's "The Bath." What do you conclude about the poets' uses of point of view, tone, and imagery?

Ideas for Writing

1. Contrast this poem, written as a dramatic monologue, with "The Love Song of J. Alfred Prufrock." Are they solely about love? How do they differ?

THE BATH

Gary Snyder

Gary Snyder (1930–) was born in San Francisco. He attended the University of California at Berkeley and later studied Zen at a monastery in Kyoto, Japan. Snyder has worked as a seaman, logger, trail crew member, and forester. He first received critical attention for his poetry with Riprap *(1959). Other volumes include* Three Worlds, Three Realms, Six Roads *(1966) and* Songs for Gaia *(1979). Snyder was awarded the Pulitzer Prize for Poetry in 1975 for* Turtle Island.

1974

Washing Kai in the sauna,
The kerosene lantern set on a box
    outside the ground-level window,
Lights up the edge of the iron stove and the
    washtub down on the slab
Steaming air and crackle of waterdrops
    brushed by on the pile of rocks on top
He stands in warm water
Soap all over the smooth of his thigh and stomach
    "Gary don't soap my hair!"
    —his eye-sting fear—
    the soapy hand feeling
    through and around the globes and curves of his body
    up in the crotch,

And washing-tickling out the scrotum, little anus,
his penis curving up and getting hard
as I pull back skin and try to wash it
Laughing and jumping, flinging arms around,
I squat all naked too,
is this our body?

Sweating and panting in the stove-steam hot-stone
cedar-planking wooden bucket water-splashing
kerosene lantern-flicker wind-in-the-pines-out
sierra forest ridges night—
Masa comes in, letting fresh cool air
sweep down from the door
a deep sweet breath
And she tips him over gripping neatly, one knee down
her hair falling hiding one whole side of
shoulder, breast, and belly,
Washes deftly Kai's head-hair
as he gets mad and yells—
The body of my lady, the winding valley spine,
the space between the thighs I reach through,
cup her curving vulva arch and hold it from behind,
a soapy tickle   a hand of grail
The gates of Awe
That open back a turning double-mirror world of
wombs in wombs, in rings,
that start in music,
is this our body?

The hidden place of seed
The veins net flow across the ribs, that gathers
milk and peaks up in a nipple—fits
our mouth—
The sucking milk from this our body sends through
jolts of light; the son, the father,
sharing mother's joy
That brings a softness to the flower of the awesome
open curling lotus gate I cup and kiss
As Kai laughs at his mother's breast he now is weaned
from, we
wash each other,
this our body

Kai's little scrotum up close to his groin,
the seed still tucked away, that moved from us to him

In flows that lifted with the same joys forces
as his nursing Masa later,
playing with her breast,
Or me within her,
Or him emerging,
this is our body:

Clean, and rinsed, and sweating more, we stretch
out on the redwood benches hearts all beating
Quiet to the simmer of the stove,
the scent of cedar
And then turn over,
murmuring gossip of the grasses,
talking firewood,
Wondering how Gen's napping, how to bring him in
soon wash him too—
These boys who love their mother
who loves men, who passes on
her sons to other women;

The cloud across the sky. The windy pines.
the trickle gurgle in the swampy meadow

this is our body.

Fire inside and boiling water on the stove
We sigh and slide ourselves down from the benches
wrap the babies, step outside,

black night & all the stars.

Pour cold water on the back and thighs
Go in the house—stand steaming by the center fire
Kai scampers on the sheepskin
Gen standing hanging on and shouting,

"Bao! bao! bao! bao! bao!"

This is our body. Drawn up crosslegged by the flames
drinking icy water
hugging babies, kissing bellies,

Laughing on the Great Earth

Come out from the bath.

Explorations of the Text

1. Who is the speaker? Who is Kai? What is the nature of the bath in the first section? Describe the setting.
2. What is the speaker's attitude toward Masa in the second section? What images characterize her?
3. Why does Snyder employ such explicit language about bodies and about love? Are the speaker's values different from other peoples'? from other cultures'?
4. How do images of birth and of sexuality function in section 4?
5. What does the speaker reveal about himself in the following lines: "These boys who love their mother/who loves men, who passes on/her sons to other women"?
6. Discuss the refrain and its variations.
7. Describe the scene after the bath—the narrative, the setting, and the personae. What do you conclude?
8. What does the speaker mean by the last line: "Come out from the bath"? To whom does he speak?
9. The poem presents a simple action—a family taking a bath in a sauna—but what larger themes does it also evoke?
10. Compare the relationships in this poem with *And the Soul Shall Dance.* What is the role of the bathhouse in each work?

The Reading/Writing Connection

1. Do you like "The Bath"? Write a reader response journal entry about this poem.
2. Gloss and annotate the poem. Analyze the sexual imagery.

Ideas for Writing

1. Write an essay exploring concepts of the body. Refer to Snyder, to Neruda, and to Woolf.
2. Discuss the spiritual meaning of "The Bath."
3. Argue against the speaker's attitudes. Are they sexist?
4. How does the setting function in developing narrative, personae, and theme?

In the End, We Are All Light

Liz Rosenberg

Liz Rosenberg (1955–), educated at Bennington College and Johns Hopkins University, teaches at the State University of New York at Binghamton. She is a frequent reviewer of poetry, prose, and children's books for publications including the Chicago Tribune *and the* Philadelphia Inquirer. *She was a Kellogg Foundation Fellow and in 1976 won the Atlantic First Award for her story "Memory."* The Angel Poems *(1984) was followed by* The Fire Music *(1986), which won the 1985 Agnes Lynch Stewart Award from the University of Pittsburgh Press, and* Children of Paradise *(1993).*

1986

I love how old men carry purses for their wives,
those stiff light beige or navy wedge-shaped bags
that match the women's pumps,
with small gold clasps that click open and shut.
The men drowse off in medical center waiting rooms,
with bags perched in their laps like big tame birds
too worn to flap away. Within, the wives slowly undress,
put on the thin white robes, consult, come out
and wake the husbands dreaming openmouthed.

And when they both rise up
to take their constitutional,
walk up and down the block, her arms are free as air,
his right hand dangles down.

So I, desiring to shed this skin
for some light silken one,
will tell my husband, "Here, hold this,"
and watch him amble off into the mall among the shining
cans of motor oil, my leather bag
slung over his massive shoulder bone,
so prettily slender-waisted, so forgiving of the ways
we hold each other down, that watching him
I see how men love women, and women men,
and how the burden of the other comes to be
light as a feather blown, more quickly vanishing.

Explorations of the Text

1. Discuss the characters of the "old men" and "their wives." Focus on the simile of the "big tame birds" and on the images of hands.

2. What does the husbands' carrying of their wives' "purses" suggest about their relationships?
3. What is unexpected in this portrayal of marriage and love?
4. What does the speaker conclude from her observations?
5. Characterize the tone of the poem. Does it shift? Look carefully at the images of "light." What word play is evident in the use of "light"?
6. Discuss the speaker's revelation at "how" the burden of the other comes to be/light as a feather blown, more quickly vanishing."
7. What do you learn about long-lasting marriages? about the state of older people in love?
8. Contrast this marriage with that of the couples in *And the Soul Shall Dance* and in *Trifles*.

The Reading/Writing Connection

1. Go to a public place. Observe several couples in love. What does their body language reveal about their relationships?
2. Imagine a young couple whom you know. Describe their lives after fifty years of marriage. Write a scene with them in it.

Ideas for Writing

1. Compare and contrast the state of the newly married with that of people who have been married for many years.
2. Use your first journal entry as the basis of portraits of several couples in love. As Rosenberg does, isolate particular details that evoke visions of the people's characters and relationships.
3. Compare the "old men" and Prufrock.

I Take You an Orange

Huda Naamani Translated from the Arabic by Huda Naamani and Miriam Cooke

Born in Damascus, Syria, Huda Naamani (1930–) earned a law degree from Syrian University and became a court attorney for her uncle's firm. She moved to Beirut, Lebanon, in 1968. She writes regularly for Al-Nahar, *the Beirut newspaper and belongs to the Arab Writers Union. She has published two plays concerning the Lebanese civil war. Her poetry includes* To You *(1970) and* I Was a Point I Was a Circle: An Elegiac Ode *(1975), a collection of patriotic poems about peace.*

1970

I take you an orange and I squeeze you holding you to my face
Spring you blossom in my eyes
A peacock's tail you gaze at me in the dark
I wear you gipsy garb I fold you a nomad's cloak
A flute grass and warmth of sheep flow with you
In the arms of mountains you paint the wreaths of heaven
    And the pains of a goddess

A frame for me I carve you I gild you and
    I fill you with roses
A fish I slaughter you, or a sun
    I bake you
    A star
Lightning flashes from your ring
Your eyes hang on my face coffee grounds honeycombs
Nigerian songs brush my neck, flocks of geese
Your word is suspended on the back of a door a duck's nose

Explorations of the Text

1. What images represent the lover and her beloved? Explain the "orange," the "blossom," the "tail," and the "gipsy garb."
2. Why does the beloved "paint the wreaths of heaven/And the pains of a goddess"? What is the meaning of the opposition?
3. What are the changes in the second stanza? Why does the love become increasingly consuming and violent?
4. In the final stanza, the word of the beloved is negated, "a duck's nose." What has happened?
5. Discuss the ironies of the title.
6. Is this poem a declaration of independence or a call to battle? What is the attitude of the speaker?
7. Are the metaphors powerful? effective? Look at word order.

The Reading/Writing Connection

1. List questions that you have about this work.
2. What surprises do you discover in this poem?

Ideas for Writing

1. Why is "the word" of the beloved the most important issue? Explain the power of language in love.
2. Answer one of your questions.

To Have Without Holding

Marge Piercy

Marge Piercy (1936–) was born in Detroit, Michigan, and was educated at the University of Michigan and Northwestern University. She published her first novel, Going Down Fast, *in 1969. She has written fiction, including* Woman on the Edge of Time *(1976),* Braided Lives *(1982), and* He, She, and It *(1992); and poetry, including* The Moon Is Always Female *(1980),* My Mother's Body *(1985), and* Available Light *(1988). In 1987, she edited* Early Ripening: American Women's Poetry Now.

1980

Learning to love differently is hard,
love with the hands wide open, love
with the doors banging on their hinges,
the cupboard unlocked, the wind
roaring and whimpering in the rooms
rustling the sheets and snapping the blinds
that thwack like rubber bands
in an open palm.

It hurts to love wide open
stretching the muscles that feel
as if they are made of wet plaster,
then of blunt knives, then
of sharp knives.

It hurts to thwart the reflexes
of grab, of clutch, to love and let
go again and again. It pesters to remember
the lover who is not in the bed,
to hold back what is owed to the work
that gutters like a candle in a cave
without air, to love consciously,
conscientiously, concretely, constructively.

I can't do it, you say it's killing
me, but you thrive, you glow
on the street like a neon raspberry,
You float and sail, a helium balloon
bright bachelor's button blue and bobbing
on the cold and hot winds of our breath,
as we make and unmake in passionate
diastole and systole the rhythm

of our unbound bonding, to have
and not to hold, to love
with minimized malice, hunger
and anger moment by moment balanced.

Explorations of the Text

1. Describe the voice and state of mind of the speaker. What is the persona's conflict?
2. How do the image patterns suggest the tension in the relationship?
3. Characterize the lover (See stanza 4).
4. Analyze the use of "air" and wind symbolism. How does this symbolism suggest opposing states of the two lovers?
5. Does the speaker reach any resolution of her dilemma?
6. Contrast the voice of the speaker in this work with Naamani's persona in "I Take You an Orange."

The Reading/Writing Connection

1. Create the lover's response to the speaker.
2. "Think" Topic: Is it possible to love "without holding"; "to love/with minimized malice, hunger/and anger moment by moment balanced"? Respond to this question in a paragraph.

Ideas for Writing

1. Analyze the speaker's conflict in this poem.
2. Compare the speaker's conflict in this poem with the speaker's experience of loving in "The Bath."

Loving in the War Years

Cherrie Moraga

Cherrie Moraga (1952–   ) was born in Whittier, California, and educated at San Francisco State University. With Gloria Anzaldúa, she edited This Bridge Called My Back: Writings by Women of Color *(1981). Her first book,* Loving in the War Years, *appeared in 1983. Subsequent works include a play,* Giving Up the Ghost *(1986), and a collection of prose and poetry,* The Lost Generation *(1993). A self-described Chicana lesbian, Moraga focuses on the situations of all minority communities in her work.*

1983

Loving you is like living
in the war years.
I *do* think of Bogart & Bergman
not clear who's who
but still singin a long smoky
mood into the piano bar
drinks straight up
the last bottle in the house
while bombs split
outside, a broken
world.

A world war going on
but you and I still insisting
in each our own heads
still thinkin how
if I could only make some contact
with that woman across the keyboard
we size each other up
          yes . . .

Loving you has this kind of desperation
to it, like do or die, I
having eyed you from the first
time you made the decision to move
from your stool
to live dangerously.

All on the hunch
that in our exchange of photos
of old girlfriends, names
of cities and memories
back in the states
the fronts we've manned
out here on the continent
all this on the hunch
that *this* time there'll be
no need for resistance.

Loving in the war years
calls for this kind of risking
without a home to call our own
I've got to take you as you come
to me, each time like a stranger
all over again. Not knowing

what deaths you saw today
I've got to take you
as you come, battle bruised
refusing our enemy, fear.

We're all we've got. You and I

maintaining
this wartime morality
where being queer
and female is as rude
as we can get.

Explorations of the Text

1. Why is "loving" "like living/in the war years"? What "world war" is taking place for the speaker?
2. Why does the poem include references to Bogart and to Bergman?
3. Describe the enemy—"fear"?
4. What is the view presented of "being queer/and female"?
5. Contrast the persona's state of being in love with that of Neruda's speaker in "Sweetness, Always."

The Reading/Writing Connection

1. "Think" Topic: Do all love relationships engender fear and vulnerability?

Ideas for Writing

1. Compare this love poem with Adrienne Rich's sonnet, "[My mouth hovers across your breasts]" in the Poems for Further Reading. How do the speakers' senses of love differ?

The Moss of His Skin

Anne Sexton

Young girls in old Arabia were often buried alive next to their dead fathers, apparently as sacrifice to the goddesses of the tribes . . .

Harold Feldman, "Children of the Desert"
Psychoanalysis and Psychoanalytic Review, *Fall 1958*

1960

It was only important
to smile and hold still,
to lie down beside him
and to rest awhile,
to be folded up together
as if we were silk,
to sink from the eyes of mother
and not to talk.
The black room took us
like a cave or a mouth
or an indoor belly.
I held my breath
and daddy was there,
his thumbs, his fat skull,
his teeth, his hair growing
like a field or a shawl.
I lay by the moss
of his skin until
it grew strange. My sisters
will never know that I fall
out of myself and pretend
that Allah[1] will not see
how I hold my daddy
like an old stone tree.

Explorations of the Text

1. What is the purpose of the epigraph?
2. Describe the voice and the point of view of the speaker.
3. What contrasting image patterns emerge in the poem?
4. Explicate the symbolism of the chrysalis.
5. Analyze the closing five lines. What does the speaker view as her fate?
6. Why does she "fall/out of [herself]"?
7. Compare the fate of the persona in this poem with that of the persona in Anna Akhmatova's "Lot's Wife."

The Reading/Writing Connection

1. "Think" Topic: Why does Sexton entitle the work "The Moss of His Skin"? Respond to this question in a paragraph.

[1] The Supreme Being (Islam).

2. Gloss and annotate the text. What contrasting image patterns emerge?
3. Begin a freewrite with this sentence: "It was only important . . . as a boy or as a girl to. . . ."

Ideas for Writing

1. Are the circumstances of the speaker meant to be taken literally? What other experiences for women are implied?

Lot's Wife

Anna Akhmatova Translated from the Russian by D. M. Thomas

Anna Akhmatova (1889–1966), was born in Odessa, Russia, and spent her childhood in St. Petersburg. In 1910, she married Nikolai Gumilev, a poet, who was killed by the Bolsheviks in 1921. Although the couple had been divorced since 1918, Akhmatova and her family were persecuted by the Communists for the next thirty years. None of her poetry was published until after Stalin's death, when she began visiting friends in the West and received a D. Lit from Oxford University in 1965. Her volumes include White Flock, Anno Domini, *and* Poem Without a Hero. *Her great political work, "Requiem," published in 1957, protests the injustices of Stalinism by presenting one woman's endless waiting outside a prison for news of her son.*

1922–24

And the just man trailed God's messenger,
His huge, light shape devoured the black hill.
But uneasiness shadowed his wife and spoke to her:
"It's not too late, you can look back still[1]

At the red towers of Sodom,[2] the place that bore you,
The square in which you sang, the spinning-shed,
At the empty windows of that upper storey
Where children blessed your happy marriage-bed."

Her eyes that were still turning when a bolt
Of pain shot through them, were instantly blind;
Her body turned into transparent salt,
And her swift legs were rooted to the ground.

[1] Lot was the nephew of Abraham. His wife was transformed into a pillar of salt for looking back during their flight from Sodom (Genesis 13–19.)

[2] An ancient city destroyed by God because of its wickedness (Genesis 18–19).

Who mourns one woman in a holocaust?
Surely her death has no significance?
Yet in my heart she never will be lost,
She who gave up her life to steal one glance.

Explorations of the Text

1. Review the story of Sodom and Gomorrah in Genesis 19. Who is the "just man"? "God's messenger"?
2. Explore the significance of the line, "His huge, light shape devoured the black hill." Whose "shape" is it?
3. In Akhmatova's poem, why does Lot's wife look back? What does her glance reveal about women's values and concerns?
4. Why is "uneasiness" personified? What does it signify?
5. What is the significance of the speaker's questions in the last stanza? Why will Lot's wife "never . . . be lost" in the speaker's "heart"?
6. In what ways has Akhmatova changed the story? Why?
7. Why have women always been pillars of salt? What does the salt symbolize?
8. Why is Lot's wife never named? What does this detail suggest about the view of woman's position?

The Reading/Writing Connection

1. Defend the choices of Lot and of his wife. You may write in monologue form.
2. Contrast the characterizations of the women in Akhmatova's poem and in Sexton's "The Moss of His Skin."

Ideas for Writing

1. In *Slaughterhouse Five,* Kurt Vonnegut reflects that it is both necessary and terrifying to look back. Examine the poem in the context of this assertion by Vonnegut. Why is it necessary to look back? Why is it so terrifying?

The Love Song of J. Alfred Prufrock

T. S. Eliot

T. S. (Thomas Stearns) Eliot (1888–1965) was born in St. Louis, Missouri. After graduating from Harvard University, he moved in 1915 to England, where he lived for the rest of his life. Eliot published his first poem when he was a student, "The Love Song of J. Alfred Prufrock" when he was twenty-two, and continued to produce masterpieces including The Waste Land *(1922) and* Four Quarters *(1943). He also wrote influential essays on poetry, gathered in* The Sacred Wood *(1920), and plays including* Murder in the Cathedral *(1935) and* The Cocktail Party *(1950). He was awarded the Nobel Prize for Literature in 1948. Eliot's poetry is noted for its evocative imagery, its range of form and style, and its allusions to myth, to legend, and to works from many traditions.*

1910–11

S'io credessi che mia risposta fosse
A persona che mai tornasse al mondo,
Questa fiamma staria senza piu scosse.
Ma perciocche giammai di questo fondo
Non torno vivo alcun, s'i'odo il vero,
Senza tema d'infamia ti rispondo.[1]

Let us go then, you and I,
When the evening is spread out against the sky
Like a patient etherized upon a table;
Let us go, through certain half-deserted streets,
The muttering retreats
Of restless nights in one-night cheap hotels
And sawdust restaurants with oyster-shells:
Streets that follow like a tedious argument
Of insidious intent
To lead you to an overwhelming question . . .
Oh, do not ask, "What is it?"
Let us go and make our visit.

In the room the women come and go
Talking of Michelangelo.

The yellow fog that rubs its back upon the window-panes,
The yellow smoke that rubs its muzzle on the window-panes
Licked its tongue into the corners of the evening,
Lingered upon the pools that stand in drains,
Let fall upon its back the soot that falls from chimneys,
Slipped by the terrace, made a sudden leap,
And seeing that it was a soft October night,
Curled once about the house, and fell asleep.

---

[1] The epigraph from Dante's *Inferno,* spoken by Guido da Montefeltro, "If I thought that my reply were to someone who could ever return to the world, this flame would shake no more. But since no one has ever returned alive from this place, if what I hear is true, without fear of infamy I answer you," suggests Prufrock's "damnation" and psychological torment.

And indeed there will be time
For the yellow smoke that slides along the street,
Rubbing its back upon the window-panes;
There will be time, there will be time
To prepare a face to meet the faces that you meet;
There will be time to murder and create,
And time for all the works and days[2] of hands
That lift and drop a question on your plate;
Time for you and time for me,
And time yet for a hundred indecisions,
And for a hundred visions and revisions,
Before the taking of a toast and tea.

In the room the women come and go
Talking of Michelangelo.

And indeed there will be time
To wonder, "Do I dare?" and, "Do I dare?"
Time to turn back and descend the stair,
With a bald spot in the middle of my hair—
(They will say: "How his hair is growing thin!")
My morning coat, my collar mounting firmly to the chin,
My necktie rich and modest, but asserted by a simple pin—
(They will say: "But how his arms and legs are thin!")
Do I dare
Disturb the universe?

In a minute there is time
For decisions and revisions which a minute will reverse.

For I have known them all already, known them all:
Have known the evenings, mornings, afternoons,
I have measured out my life with coffee spoons;
I know the voices dying with a dying fall[3]
Beneath the music from a farther room.
So how should I presume?

And I have known the eyes already, known them all—
The eyes that fix you in a formulated phrase,
And when I am formulated, sprawling on a pin,
When I am pinned and wriggling on the wall,
Then how should I begin
To spit out all the butt-ends of my days and ways?
And how should I presume?

---

[2] Reference to a poem by Hesiod, an eighth-century Greek writer.

[3] Allusion to Orsino's speech in Shakespeare's *Twelfth Night* (I, i), "That strain again! It had a dying fall."

And I have known the arms already, known them all—
Arms that are braceleted and white and bare
(But in the lamplight, downed with light brown hair!)
Is it perfume from a dress
That makes me so digress?
Arms that lie along a table, or wrap about a shawl.
And should I then presume?
And how should I begin? . . .

Shall I say, I have gone at dusk through narrow streets
And watched the smoke that rises from the pipes
Of lonely men in shirt-sleeves, leaning out of windows? . . .

I should have been a pair of ragged claws
Scuttling across the floors of silent seas.

And the afternoon, the evening, sleeps so peacefully!
Smoothed by long fingers,
Asleep . . . tired . . . or it malingers,
Stretched on the floor, here beside you and me.
Should I, after tea and cakes and ices,
Have the strength to force the moment to its crisis?
But though I have wept and fasted, wept and prayed,
Though I have seen my head (grown slightly bald) brought in upon a platter,[4]
I am no prophet—and here's no great matter;
I have seen the moment of my greatness flicker,
And I have seen the eternal Footman[5] hold my coat, and snicker,
And in short, I was afraid.

And would it have been worth it, after all,
After the cups, the marmalade, the tea,
Among the porcelain, among some talk of you and me,
Would it have been worth while,
To have bitten off the matter with a smile,
To have squeezed the universe into a ball
To roll it toward some overwhelming question,
To say: "I am Lazarus,[6] come from the dead,
Come back to tell you all, I shall tell you all"—
If one, settling a pillow by her head,
Should say: "That is not what I meant at all.

[4] Reference to John the Baptist, who was beheaded by King Herod (Matthew 14:3–11).

[5] Figure of death or fate.

[6] Lazarus was raised from the dead by Jesus (John 11:1–44).

That is not it, at all."

And would it have been worth while, after all
Would it have been worth while,
After the sunsets and the dooryards and the sprinkled streets,
After the novels, after the teacups, after the skirts that trail along the floor—
And this, and so much more?—
It is impossible to say just what I mean!
But as if a magic lantern threw the nerves in patterns on a screen:
Would it have been worth while
If one, settling a pillow or throwing off a shawl,
And turning toward the window, should say:
"That is not it at all,
That is not what I meant, at all."

* * *

No! I am not Prince Hamlet, nor was meant to be;
Am an attendant lord, one that will do
To swell a progress,[7] start a scene or two,
Advise the prince; no doubt, an easy tool,
Deferential, glad to be of use,
Politic, cautious, and meticulous;
Full of high sentence,[8] but a bit obtuse;
At times, indeed, almost ridiculous—
Almost, at times, the Fool.[9]

I grow old . . . I grow old . . .
I shall wear the bottoms of my trousers rolled.

Shall I part my hair behind? Do I dare to eat a peach?
I shall wear white flannel trousers, and walk upon the beach.
I have heard the mermaids singing, each to each.

I do not think that they will sing to me.

I have seen them riding seaward on the waves
Combing the white hair of the waves blown back
When the wind blows the water white and black.

---

[7] A royal journey (Elizabethan English).

[8] Ideals, sentiments.

[9] Reference to the stock figure of a Fool, appearing in many dramas (e.g., Shakespeare's *King Lear*).

We have lingered in the chambers of the sea
By sea-girls wreathed with seaweed red and brown
Till human voices wake us, and we drown.

Explorations of the Text

1. Identify the "you" and "I." What are the possibilities?
2. What atmosphere do the opening simile of the evening and the personification of "the yellow smoke" and "yellow fog" create?
3. What is the state of mind of the persona, the "I" of the poem, in the first six stanzas? Why is he so concerned with "time"?
4. Why does he ask, "Do I dare/Disturb the universe?" Which details about his appearance (stanza 6) reveal his view of himself?
5. What is the significance of the refrain, "In the room the women come and go / Talking of Michelangelo"?
6. How do the concerns change in the next five stanzas? Whom and what has he "known"? Explore his state of mind.
7. Explain the meaning and impact of the following lines: "I should have been a pair of ragged claws / Scuttling across the floors of silent seas."
8. What is his "crisis" in the last nine stanzas? How do the allusions to John the Baptist, Lazarus, and Hamlet enlarge the scope of his conflict?
9. In the last stanza, what is the significance of the sea imagery and of the mermaids?
10. Conceive of Prufrock's crisis as a journey. Does Prufrock's state of mind change as the journey progresses?
11. Explore Eliot's use of figurative language (personification, simile, metaphor) and irony. What is the impact of these techniques?
12. Examine Eliot's use of repetition and parallelism. What impact do these devices have?
13. Compare Prufrock, Emiko (*And the Soul Shall Dance*), and Minnie Wright (*Trifles*).

The Reading/Writing Connection

1. "Think" Topic: Isolate a simile or metaphor and explain its role in developing a portrait of Prufrock.
2. How does the epigraph from Dante's *Inferno* elucidate themes? Explore the allusions to Hamlet, Lazarus, and John the Baptist.
3. Write a monologue for Prufrock five years after this "love song." What is his future?
4. Use one line from this work as a beginning for your own poem.

Ideas for Writing

1. Create a character analysis of Prufrock. Focus on his appearance, his questions, and his actions.
2. Will Prufrock ever find love? Construct an argumentative response to this question.
3. Do the literary allusions add to or detract from this poem? Do they confuse and intimidate a reader, or do they add depth to Eliot's vision?
4. Is this a "love song"? Why? Why not?
5. Prufrock is considered a modern antihero. Analyze his character in this context.

Poems for Further Reading

To the Virgins, to Make Much of Time

Robert Herrick (1591–1674)

1648

Gather ye rosebuds while ye may,
Old Time is still a-flying;
And this same flower that smiles today,
Tomorrow will be dying.

The glorious lamp of heaven, the sun,
The higher he's a-getting
The sooner will his race be run,
And nearer he's to setting.

That age is best which is the first,
When youth and blood are warmer;
But being spent, the worse, and worst
Times still succeed the former.

Then be not coy, but use your time,
And while ye may, go marry;
For having lost but once your prime,
You may forever tarry.

THE FLEA

John Donne (1572–1631)

1633

Mark[1] but this flea, and mark in this,
How little that which thou deniest me is;
It sucked me first, and now sucks thee,
And in this flea our two bloods mingled be;
Thou know'st that this cannot be said[2]
A sin, nor shame, nor loss of maidenhead,
    Yet this enjoys before it woo,[3]
    And pampered swells with one blood made of two,
    And this, alas, is more than we would do.

Oh stay, three lives in one flea spare,
Where we almost, yea more than married, are.
This flea is you and I, and this
Our marriage bed and marriage temple is;
Though parents grudge, and you, we are met,
And cloistered in these living walls of jet.
    Though use[4] make you apt to kill me
    Let not to that, self-murder added be,
    And sacrilege, three sins in killing three.

Cruel and sudden, hast thou since
Purpled thy nail, in blood of innocence?
Wherein could this flea guilty be,
Except in that drop which it sucked from thee?
Yet thou triumph'st and say'st that thou
Find'st not thy self nor me the weaker now;
    'Tis true, then learn how false fears be;
    Just so much honor, when thou yield'st to me,
    Will waste, as this flea's death took life from thee.

---

[1] Note, look at.

[2] Called.

[3] Marry.

[4] Custom.

She Walks in Beauty

George Gordon, Lord Byron (1788–1824)

1814

She walks in beauty, like the night
Of cloudless climes and starry skies;
And all that's best of dark and bright
Meet in her aspect and her eyes:
Thus mellow'd to that tender light
Which heaven to gaudy day denies.

One shade the more, one ray the less,
Had half impaired the nameless grace
Which waves in every raven tress,
Or softly lightens o'er her face;
Where thoughts serenely sweet express
How pure, how dear their dwelling-place.

And on that cheek, and o'er that brow,
So soft, so calm, yet eloquent,
The smiles that win, the tints that glow,
But tell of days in goodness spent,
A mind at peace with all below,
A heart whose love is innocent!

La Belle Dame sans Merci[1]

John Keats (1795–1821)

1819

O what can ail thee, knight-at-arms,
Alone and palely loitering?
The sedge[2] has withered from the lake,
And no birds sing.

O what can ail thee, knight-at-arms,
So haggard and so woe-begone?
The squirrel's granary is full,
And the harvest's done.

[1] The title taken from a medieval poem means "The Beautiful Lady Without Mercy."
[2] Grasslike or marshlike vegetation growing in wet places.

I see a lily on thy brow,
    With anguish moist and fever dew,
And on thy cheeks a fading rose
    Fast withereth too.

I met a lady in the meads,[3]
    Full beautiful—a faery's child,
Her hair was long, her foot was light,
    And her eyes were wild.

I made a garland for her head,
    And bracelets too, and fragrant zone;[4]
She looked at me as she did love,
    And made sweet moan.

I set her on my pacing steed,
    And nothing else saw all day long,
For sidelong would she bend, and sing
    A faery's song.

She found me roots of relish sweet,
    And honey wild, and manna dew,
And sure in language strange she said,
    "I love thee true."

She took me to her elfin grot,
    And there she wept, and sighed full sore,
And there I shut her wild wild eyes
    With kisses four.

And there she lullèd me asleep,
    And there I dreamed—Ah! woe betide!
The latest[5] dream I ever dreamed
    On the cold hill side.

I saw pale kings and princes too,
    Pale warriors, death-pale were they all;
They cried—"La Belle Dame sans Merci
"Hath thee in thrall!"

[3] Meadows.
[4] Belt.
[5] Last.

I saw their starved lips in the gloam,[6]
With horrid warning gapèd wide,
And I awoke and found me here,
On the cold hill's side.

And this is why I soujourn here,
Alone and palely loitering,
Though the sedge has withered from the lake,
And no birds sing.

How Do I Love Thee?

Elizabeth Barrett Browning (1806–61)

1850

How do I love thee? Let me count the ways.
I love thee to the depth and breadth and height
My soul can reach, when feeling out of sight
For the ends of Being and ideal Grace.
I love thee to the level of everyday's
Most quiet need, by sun and candle-light.
I love thee freely, as men strive for Right;
I love thee purely, as they turn from Praise.
I love thee with the passion put to use
In my old griefs, and with my childhood's faith.
I love thee with a love I seemed to lose
With my lost saints,—I love thee with the breath,
Smiles, tears, of all my life!—and, if God choose,
I shall but love thee better after death.

Eros Turannos

Edgar Arlington Robinson (1869–1935)

1913

She fears him, and will always ask
What fated her to choose him;
She meets in his engaging mask
All reasons to refuse him;
But what she meets and what she fears
Are less than are the downward years,
Drawn slowly to the foamless weirs[1]
Of age, were she to lose him.

---

[6] Twilight.

[1] A small dam or fence in a stream.

Between a blurred sagacity
That once had power to sound him,
And Love, that will not let him be
The Judas[2] that she found him,
Her pride assuages her almost,
As if it were alone the cost.
He sees that he will not be lost,
And waits and looks around him.

A sense of ocean and old trees
Envelopes and allures him;
Tradition, touching all he sees,
Beguiles and reassures him;
And all her doubts of what he says
Are dimmed with what she knows of days—
Till even prejudice delays
And fades, and she secures him.

The falling leaf inaugurates
The reign of her confusion;
The pounding wave reverberates
The dirge of her illusion;
And home, where passion lived and died,
Becomes a place where she can hide,
While all the town and harbor side
Vibrate with her seclusion.

We tell you, tapping on our brows,
The story as it should be,
As if the story of a house
Were told, or ever could be;
We'll have no kindly veil between
Her visions and those we have seen,
As if we guessed what hers have been,
Or what they are or would be.

Meanwhile we do no harm; for they
That with a god have striven,
Not hearing much of what we say,
Take what the god has given;
Though like waves breaking it may be,
Or like a changed familiar tree,
Or like a stairway to the sea
Where down the blind are driven.

[2] Judas Iscariot, the disciple who betrayed Christ; a traitor; a person who commits a treacherous act or an act of betrayal.

What lips my lips have kissed, and where, and why

Edna St. Vincent Millay (1892–1950)

1923

What lips my lips have kissed, and where, and why,
I have forgotten, and what arms have lain
Under my head till morning; but the rain
Is full of ghosts tonight, that tap and sigh
Upon the glass and listen for reply,
And in my heart there stirs a quiet pain
For unremembered lads that not again
Will turn to me at midnight with a cry.
Thus in the winter stands the lonely tree,
Nor knows what birds have vanished one by one,
Yet knows its boughs more silent than before:
I cannot say what loves have come and gone;
I only know that summer sang in me
A little while, that in me sings no more.

LVII

E. E. Cummings (1894–1962)

1931

somewhere i have never travelled,gladly beyond
any experience,your eyes have their silence:
in your most frail gesture are things which enclose me,
or which i cannot touch because they are too near

Note: According to Liveright Publishing, a subsidiary of Norton, and the copyright holder for E. E. Cummings, the convention of setting Cumming's name in lowercase has been made in error. Contrary to popular belief, Cummings never had his name legally changed to an all lowercase spelling, nor did he sign his name in lowercase on letters, legal documents, or paintings. The convention arose when contemporary reviewers noted his habit of writing his poems in all lowercase and began referring to him as "the lowercase mr. cummings" or "mr. lowercase." Cummings, who majored in the classics in college, wrote his poems in lowercase to imitate the ancient Greeks, who did not capitalize the first letter of a sentence. The matter seemed final when Harry Moore wrote the introduction to Norman Friedman's *E. E. Cummings: The Growth of a Writer,* saying that Cummings "had his name put legally into lowercase." There is no record that Cummings ever did so.

your slightest look easily will unclose me
though i have closed myself as fingers,
you open always petal by petal myself as Spring opens
(touching skilfully,mysteriously)her first rose

or if you wish be to close me,i and
my life will shut very beautifully,suddenly,
as when the heart of this flower imagines
the snow carefully everywhere descending;

nothing which we are to perceive in this world equals
the power of your intense fragility:whose texture
compels me with the colour of its countries,
rendering death and forever with each breathing

(i do not know what it is about you that closes
and opens;only something in me understands
the voice of your eyes is deeper than all roses)
nobody,not even the rain,has such small hands

3. My mouth hovers across your breasts

Adrienne Rich (1929–)

1986

My mouth hovers across your breasts
in the short grey winter afternoon
in this bed   we are delicate
and tough   so hot with joy we amaze ourselves
tough   and delicate we play rings
around each other   our daytime candle burns
with its peculiar light   and if the snow
begins to fall outside   filling the branches
and if the night falls   without announcement
these are the pleasures of winter
sudden, wild and delicate   your fingers
exact   my tongue exact at the same moment
stopping to laugh at a joke
my love   hot on your scent   on the cusp of winter

Note: This poem is taken from Rich's series, "Contradictions: Tracking Poems."

DRAMA

Trifles

Susan Glaspell

Susan Glaspell (1882–1948), born in Davenport, Iowa, graduated from Drake University. In 1911, she moved to Greenwich Village; in 1913, she married George Cook; and in 1915, with her husband she founded the Provincetown Players on Cape Cod, Massachusetts. She wrote more than twenty plays, numerous short stories, and novels. In 1930, her drama Alison's House *won the Pulitzer Prize. Glaspell's most famous work is* Trifles *(1916), a one-act play she based on a trial that she covered as a reporter in Iowa and later transformed into a short story, "A Jury of Her Peers."*

1916

The Characters

County Attorney	Hale
Mrs. Peters	Mrs. Hale
Sheriff	

(Scene: The kitchen in the now abandoned farmhouse of John Wright, a gloomy kitchen, and left without having been put in order—unwashed pans under the sink, a loaf of bread outside the bread-box, a dish-towel on the table—other signs of incompleted work. At the rear the outer door opens and the Sheriff comes in followed by the County Attorney and Hale. The Sheriff and Hale are men in middle life, the County Attorney is a young man; all are much bundled up and go at once to the stove. They are followed by two women—the Sheriff's wife first; she is a slight wiry woman, a thin nervous face. Mrs. Hale is larger and would ordinarily be called more comfortable looking, but she is disturbed now and looks fearfully about as she enters. The women have come in slowly, and stand close together near the door.)

County Attorney: *(Rubbing his hands.)* This feels good. Come up to the fire, ladies.

Mrs. Peters: *(After taking a step forward.)* I'm not—cold.

Sheriff: *(Unbuttoning his overcoat and stepping away from the stove as if to mark the beginning of official business.)* Now, Mr. Hale, before we move things about, you explain to Mr. Henderson just what you saw when you came here yesterday morning.

County Attorney: By the way, has anything been moved? Are things just as you left them yesterday?

Sheriff: *(Looking about.)* It's just the same. When it dropped below zero last night I thought I'd better send Frank out this morning to make a fire for us—no use getting pneumonia with a big case on, but I told him not to touch anything except the stove—and you know Frank.

County Attorney: Somebody should have been left here yesterday.

Sheriff: Oh—yesterday. When I had to send Frank to Morris Center for that man who went crazy—I want you to know I had my hands full yesterday. I knew you could get back from Omaha by today and as long as I went over everything here myself—

County Attorney: Well, Mr. Hale, tell just what happened when you came here yesterday morning.

Hale: Harry and I had started to town with a load of potatoes. We came along the road from my place and as I got here I said, "I'm going to see if I can't get John Wright to go in with me on a party telephone." I spoke to Wright about it once before and he put me off, saying folks talked too much anyway, and all he asked was peace and quiet—I guess you know about how much he talked himself; but I thought maybe if I went to the house and talked about it before his wife, though I said to Harry that I didn't know as what his wife wanted made much difference to John—

County Attorney: Let's talk about that later, Mr. Hale. I do want to talk about that, but tell now just what happened when you got to the house.

Hale: I didn't hear or see anything; I knocked at the door, and still it was all quiet inside. I knew they must be up, it was past eight o'clock. So I knocked again, and I thought I heard somebody say, "Come in." I wasn't sure, I'm not sure yet, but I opened the door—this door *(Indicating the door by which the two women are still standing.)* and there in that rocker—*(Pointing to it.)* sat Mrs. Wright.

(They all look at the rocker.)

County Attorney: What—was she doing?

Hale: She was rockin' back and forth. She had her apron in her hand and was kind of—pleating it.

County Attorney: And how did she—look?

Hale: Well, she looked queer.

County Attorney: How do you mean—queer?

Hale: Well, as if she didn't know what she was going to do next. And kind of done up.

County Attorney: How did she seem to feel about your coming?

Hale: Why, I don't think she minded—one way or other. She didn't pay much attention. I said, "How do, Mrs. Wright, it's cold, ain't it?" And she said, "Is it?"—and went on kind of pleating at her apron. Well, I was surprised; she didn't ask me to come up to the stove, or to set down, but just sat there, not even looking at me, so I said, "I want to see John." And then she—laughed. I guess you would call it a laugh. I thought of Harry and the team outside, so I said a little sharp: "Can't I see John?" "No," she says, kind o' dull like. "Ain't he home?" says I. "Yes," says she, "he's home."

"Then why can't I see him?" I asked her, out of patience. "'Cause he's dead," says she. "*Dead?*" says I. She just nodded her head, not getting a bit excited, but rockin' back and forth. "Why—where is he?" says I, not knowing what to say. She just pointed upstairs—like that *(Himself pointing to the room above.)*. I got up, with the idea of going up there. I walked from there to here—then I says, "Why, what did he die of?" "He died of a rope round his neck," says she, and just went on pleatin' at her apron. Well, I went out and called Harry. I thought I might—need help. We went upstairs and there he was lying—

20 **County Attorney:** I think I'd rather have you go into that upstairs, where you can point it all out. Just go on now with the rest of the story.

Hale: Well, my first thought was to get that rope off. It looked . . . *(Stops, his face twitches.)* . . . but Harry, he went up to him, and he said, No, he's dead all right, and we'd better not touch anything. So we went back down stairs. She was still sitting that same way. "Has anybody been notified?" I asked. "No," says she, unconcerned. "Who did this, Mrs. Wright?" said Harry. He said it business-like—and she stopped pleatin' of her apron. "I don't know," she says. "You don't *know?*" says Harry. "No," says she. "Weren't you sleepin' in the bed with him?" says Harry. "Yes," says she, "but I was on the inside." "Somebody slipped a rope round his neck and strangled him and you didn't wake up?" says Harry. "I didn't wake up," she said after him. We must 'a looked as if we didn't see how that could be, for after a minute she said, "I sleep sound." Harry was going to ask her more questions but I said maybe we ought to let her tell her story first to the coroner, or the sheriff, so Harry went fast as he could to Rivers' place, where there's a telephone.

County Attorney: And what did Mrs. Wright do when she knew that you had gone for the coroner?

Hale: She moved from that chair to this one over here *(Pointing to a small chair in the corner.)* and just sat there with her hands held together and looking down. I got a feeling that I ought to make some conversation, so I said I had come in to see if John wanted to put in a telephone, and at that she started to laugh, and then she stopped and looked at me—scared. *(The County Attorney, who has had his notebook out, makes a note.)* I dunno, maybe it wasn't scared. I wouldn't like to say it was. Soon Harry got back, and then Dr. Lloyd came, and you, Mr. Peters, and so I guess that's all I know that you don't.

County Attorney: *(Looking around.)* I guess we'll go upstairs first—and then out to the barn and around there. *(To the Sheriff.)* You're convinced that there was nothing important here—nothing that would point to any motive.

25 **Sheriff:** Nothing here but kitchen things.

(The County Attorney, after again looking around the kitchen, opens the door of a cupboard closet. He gets up on a chair and looks on a shelf. Pulls his hand away, sticky.)

County Attorney: Here's a nice mess.

(The women draw nearer.)

Mrs. Peters: *(To the other woman.)* Oh, her fruit; it did freeze. *(To the County Attorney.)* She worried about that when it turned so cold. She said the fire'd go out and her jars would break.

Sheriff: Well, can you beat the women! Held for murder and worryin' about her preserves.

County Attorney: I guess before we're through she may have something more serious than preserves to worry about.

Hale: Well, women are used to worrying over trifles.

(The two women move a little closer together.)

County Attorney: *(With the gallantry of a young politician.)* And yet, for all their worries, what would we do without the ladies? *(The women do not unbend. He goes to the sink, takes a dipperful of water from the pail and pouring it into a basin, washes his hands. Starts to wipe them on the roller-towel, turns it for a cleaner place.)* Dirty towels! *(Kicks his foot against the pans under the sink.)* Not much of a housekeeper, would you say, ladies?

Mrs. Hale: *(Stiffly.)* There's a great deal of work to be done on a farm.

County Attorney: To be sure. And yet *(With a little bow to her.)* I know there are some Dickson county farmhouses which do not have such roller towels.

(He gives it a pull to expose its full length again.)

Mrs. Hale: Those towels get dirty awful quick. Men's hands aren't always as clean as they might be.

County Attorney: Ah, loyal to your sex, I see. But you and Mrs. Wright were neighbors. I suppose you were friends, too.

Mrs. Hale: *(Shaking her head.)* I've not seen much of her of late years. I've not been in this house—it's more than a year.

County Attorney: And why was that? You didn't like her?

Mrs. Hale: I liked her all well enough. Farmers' wives have their hands full, Mr. Henderson. And then—

County Attorney: Yes—?

Mrs. Hale: *(Looking about.)* It never seemed a very cheerful place.

County Attorney: No—it's not cheerful. I shouldn't say she had the home-making instinct.

Mrs. Hale: Well, I don't know as Wright had, either.

County Attorney: You mean that they didn't get on very well?

Mrs. Hale: No, I don't mean anything. But I don't think a place'd be any cheerfuller for John Wright's being in it.

County Attorney: I'd like to talk more of that a little later. I want to get the lay of things upstairs now.

(He goes to the left, where three steps lead to a stair door.)

Sheriff: I suppose anything Mrs. Peters does'll be all right. She was to take in some clothes for her, you know, and a few little things. We left in such a hurry yesterday.

County Attorney: Yes, but I would like to see what you take, Mrs. Peters, and keep an eye out for anything that might be of use to us.

Mrs. Peters: Yes, Mr. Henderson.

(The women listen to the men's steps on the stairs, then look about the kitchen.)

Mrs. Hale: I'd hate to have men coming into my kitchen, snooping around and criticising.

(She arranges the pans under sink which the County Attorney had shoved out of place.)

Mrs. Peters: Of course it's no more than their duty.

Mrs. Hale: Duty's all right, but I guess that deputy sheriff that came out to make the fire might have got a little of this on. *(Gives the roller towel a pull.)* Wish I'd thought of that sooner. Seems mean to talk about her for not having things slicked up when she had to come away in such a hurry.

Mrs. Peters: *(Who has gone to a small table in the left rear corner of the room, and lifted one end of a towel that covers a pan.)* She had bread set.

(Stands still.)

Mrs. Hale: *(Eyes fixed on a loaf of bread beside the breadbox, which is on a low shelf at the other side of the room. Moves slowly toward it.)* She was going to put this in there. *(Picks up loaf, then abruptly drops it. In a manner of returning to familiar things.)* It's a shame about her fruit. I wonder if it's all gone. *(Gets up on the chair and looks.)* I think there's some here that's all right, Mrs. Peters. Yes—here; *(Holding it toward the window.)* this is cherries, too. *(Looking again.)* I declare I believe that's the only one. *(Gets down, bottle in her hand. Goes to the sink and wipes it off on the outside.)* She'll feel awful bad after all her hard work in the hot weather. I remember the afternoon I put up my cherries last summer.

(She puts the bottle on the big kitchen table, center of the room. With a sigh, is about to sit down in the rocking-chair. Before she is seated realizes what chair it is; with a slow look at it, steps back. The chair, which she has touched, rocks back and forth.)

Mrs. Peters: Well, I must get those things from the front room closet. *(She goes to the door at the right, but after looking into the other room, steps back.)* You coming with me, Mrs. Hale? You could help me carry them.

(They go in the other room; reappear, Mrs. Peters carrying a dress and skirt, Mrs. Hale following with a pair of shoes.)

Mrs. Peters: My, it's cold in there.

(She puts the clothes on the big table, and hurries to the stove.)

Mrs. Hale: *(Examining her skirt.)* Wright was close. I think maybe that's why she kept so much to herself. She didn't even belong to the Ladies Aid. I suppose she felt she couldn't do her part, and then you don't enjoy things when you feel shabby. She used to wear pretty clothes and be lively, when she was Minnie Foster, one of the town girls singing in the choir. But that—oh, that was thirty years ago. This all you was to take in?

Mrs. Peters: She said she wanted an apron. Funny thing to want, for there isn't much to get you dirty in jail, goodness knows. But I suppose just to make her feel more natural. She said they was in the top drawer in this cupboard. Yes, here. And then her little shawl that always hung behind the door. *(Opens stair door and looks.)* Yes, here it is.

(Quickly shuts door leading upstairs.)

Mrs. Hale: *(Abruptly moving toward her.)* Mrs. Peters?

Mrs. Peters: Yes, Mrs. Hale?

Mrs. Hale: Do you think she did it?

Mrs. Peters: *(In a frightened voice.)* Oh, I don't know.

Mrs. Hale: Well, I don't think she did. Asking for an apron and her little shawl. Worrying about her fruit.

Mrs. Peters: *(Starts to speak, glances up, where footsteps are heard in the room above. In a low voice.)* Mr. Peters says it looks bad for her. Mr. Henderson is awful sarcastic in a speech and he'll make fun of her sayin' she didn't wake up.

Mrs. Hale: Well, I guess John Wright didn't wake when they was slipping that rope under his neck.

Mrs. Peters: No, it's strange. It must have been done awful crafty and still. They say it was such a—funny way to kill a man, rigging it all up like that.

Mrs. Hale: That's just what Mr. Hale said. There was a gun in the house. He says that's what he can't understand.

Mrs. Peters: Mr. Henderson said coming out that what was needed for the case was a motive; something to show anger, or—sudden feeling.

Mrs. Hale: *(Who is standing by the table.)* Well, I don't see any signs of anger around here. *(She puts her hand on the dish towel which lies on the table, stands looking down at table, one half of which is clean, the other half messy.)* It's wiped to here. *(Makes a move as if to finish work, then turns and looks at loaf of bread outside the breadbox. Drops towel. In that voice of coming back to familiar things.)* Wonder how they are finding things upstairs. I hope she had it a little more red-up up there. You know, it seems kind of *sneaking*. Locking her up in town and then coming out here and trying to get her own house to turn against her!

Mrs. Peters: But Mrs. Hale, the law is the law.

Mrs. Hale: I s'pose 'tis. *(Unbuttoning her coat.)* Better loosen up your things, Mrs. Peters. You won't feel them when you go out.

(Mrs. Peters takes off her fur tippet, goes to hang it on hook at back of room, stands looking at the under part of the small corner table.)

Mrs. Peters: She was piecing a quilt.

(She brings the large sewing basket and they look at the bright pieces.)

Mrs. Hale: It's log cabin pattern. Pretty, isn't it? I wonder if she was goin' to quilt it or just knot it?

(Footsteps have been heard coming down the stairs. The Sheriff enters followed by Hale and the County Attorney.)

Sheriff: They wonder if she was going to quilt it or just knot it!

(The men laugh; the women look abashed.)

County Attorney: *(Rubbing his hands over the stove.)* Frank's fire didn't do much up there, did it? Well, let's go out to the barn and get that cleared up.

(The men go outside.)

Mrs. Hale: *(Resentfully.)* I don't know as there's anything so strange, our takin' up our time with little things while we're waiting for them to get the evidence. *(She sits down at the big table smoothing out a block with decision.)* I don't see as it's anything to laugh about.

Mrs. Peters: *(Apologetically.)* Of course they've got awful important things on their minds.

(Pulls up a chair and joins Mrs. Hale at the table.)

Mrs. Hale: *(Examining another block.)* Mrs. Peters, look at this one. Here, this is the one she was working on, and look at the sewing! All the rest of it has been so nice and even. And look at this! It's all over the place! Why, it looks as if she didn't know what she was about!

(After she has said this they look at each other, then start to glance back at the door. After an instant Mrs. Hale has pulled at a knot and ripped the sewing.)

Mrs. Peters: Oh, what are you doing, Mrs. Hale?

Mrs. Hale: *(Mildly.)* Just pulling out a stitch or two that's not sewed very good. *(Threading a needle.)* Bad sewing always made me fidgety.

Mrs. Peters: *(Nervously.)* I don't think we ought to touch things.

Mrs. Hale: I'll just finish up this end. *(Suddenly stopping and leaning forward.)* Mrs. Peters?

Mrs. Peters: Yes, Mrs. Hale?

Mrs. Hale: What do you suppose she was so nervous about?

Mrs. Peters: Oh—I don't know. I don't know as she was nervous. I sometimes sew awful queer when I'm just tired. *(Mrs. Hale starts to say something, looks at Mrs. Peters, then goes on sewing.)* Well, I must get these things wrapped up. They may be through sooner than we think. *(Putting apron and other things together.)* I wonder where I can find a piece of paper, and string.

Mrs. Hale: In that cupboard, maybe.

Mrs. Peters: *(Looking in cupboard.)* Why, here's a bird-cage. *(Holds it up.)* Did she have a bird, Mrs. Hale?

Mrs. Hale: Why, I don't know whether she did or not—I've not been here for so long. There was a man around last year selling canaries cheap, but I don't know as she took one; maybe she did. She used to sing real pretty herself.

Mrs. Peters: *(Glancing around.)* Seems funny to think of a bird here. But she must have had one, or why would she have a cage? I wonder what happened to it.

Mrs. Hale: I s'pose maybe the cat got it.

Mrs. Peters: No, she didn't have a cat. She's got that feeling some people have about cats—being afraid of them. My cat got in her room and she was real upset and asked me to take it out.

Mrs. Hale: My sister Bessie was like that. Queer, ain't it?

Mrs. Peters: *(Examining the cage.)* Why, look at this door. It's broke. One hinge is pulled apart.

Mrs. Hale: *(Looking too.)* Looks as if someone must have been rough with it.

Mrs. Peters: Why, yes.

(She brings the cage forward and puts it on the table.)

Mrs. Hale: I wish if they're going to find any evidence they'd be about it. I don't like this place.

Mrs. Peters: But I'm awful glad you came with me, Mrs. Hale. It would be lonesome for me sitting here alone.

Mrs. Hale: It would, wouldn't it? *(Dropping her sewing.)* But I tell you what I do wish, Mrs. Peters. I wish I had come over sometimes when *she* was here. I—*(Looking around the room.)*—wish I had.

Mrs. Peters: But of course you were awful busy, Mrs. Hale—your house and your children.

Mrs. Hale: I could've come. I stayed away because it weren't cheerful—and that's why I ought to have come. I—I've never liked this place. Maybe because it's down in a hollow and you don't see the road. I dunno what it is but it's a lonesome place and always was. I wish I had come over to see Minnie Foster sometimes. I can see now—

(Shakes her head.)

Mrs. Peters: Well, you mustn't reproach yourself, Mrs. Hale. Somehow we just don't see how it is with other folks until—something comes up.

Mrs. Hale: Not having children makes less work—but it makes a quiet house, and Wright out to work all day, and no company when he did come in. Did you know John Wright, Mrs. Peters?

Mrs. Peters: Not to know him; I've seen him in town. They say he was a good man.

Mrs. Hale: Yes—good; he didn't drink, and kept his word as well as most, I guess, and paid his debts. But he was a hard man, Mrs. Peters. Just to pass the time of day with him—*(Shivers.)* Like a raw wind that gets to the bone. *(Pauses, her eye falling on the cage.)* I should think she would 'a wanted a bird. But what do you suppose went with it?

Mrs. Peters: I don't know, unless it got sick and died.

(She reaches over and swings the broken door, swings it again. Both women watch it.)

Mrs. Hale: You weren't raised round here, were you? *(Mrs. Peters shakes her head.)* You didn't know—her?

Mrs. Peters: Not till they brought her yesterday.

Mrs. Hale: She—come to think of it, she was kind of like a bird herself—real sweet and pretty, but kind of timid and—fluttery. How—she—did—change. *(Silence; then as if struck by a happy thought and relieved to get back to everyday things.)* Tell you what, Mrs. Peters, why don't you take the quilt in with you? It might take up her mind.

Mrs. Peters: Why, I think that's a real nice idea, Mrs. Hale. There couldn't possibly be any objection to it, could there? Now, just what would I take? I wonder if her patches are in here—and her things.

(They look in the sewing basket.)

Mrs. Hale: Here's some red. I expect this has got sewing things in it. *(Brings out a fancy box.)* What a pretty box. Looks like something somebody would give you. Maybe her scissors are in here. *(Opens box. Suddenly puts her hand to her nose.)* Why—*(Mrs. Peters bends nearer, then turns her face away.)* There's something wrapped up in this piece of silk.

Mrs. Peters: Why, this isn't her scissors.

Mrs. Hale: *(Lifting the silk.)* Oh, Mrs. Peters—it's—

(Mrs. Peters bends closer.)

Mrs. Peters: It's the bird.

Mrs. Hale: *(Jumping up.)* But, Mrs. Peters—look at it! Its neck! Look at its neck! It's all—other side *to.*

Mrs. Peters: Somebody—wrung—its—neck.

(Their eyes meet. A look of growing comprehension, of horror. Steps are heard outside. Mrs. Hale slips box under quilt pieces, and sinks into her chair. Enter Sheriff and County Attorney. Mrs. Peters rises.)

County Attorney: *(As one turning from serious things to little pleasantries.)* Well, ladies, have you decided whether she was going to quilt it or knot it?

Mrs. Peters: We think she was going to—knot it.

County Attorney: Well, that's interesting, I'm sure. *(Seeing the bird-cage.)* Has the bird flown?

Mrs. Hale: *(Putting more quilt pieces over the box.)* We think the—cat got it.

County Attorney: *(Preoccupied.)* Is there a cat?

(Mrs. Hale glances in a quick covert way at Mrs. Peters.)

Mrs. Peters: Well, not *now.* They're superstitious, you know. They leave.

County Attorney: *(To Sheriff Peters, continuing an interrupted conversation.)* No sign at all of anyone having come from the outside. Their own rope. Now let's go up again and go over it piece by piece. *(They start upstairs.)* It would have to have been someone who knew just the—

(Mrs. Peters sits down. The two women sit there not looking at one another, but as if peering into something and at the same time holding back. When they talk now it is in the manner of feeling their way over strange ground, as if afraid of what they are saying, but as if they can not help saying it.)

Mrs. Hale: She liked the bird. She was going to bury it in that pretty box.

Mrs. Peters: *(In a whisper.)* When I was a girl—my kitten—there was a boy took a hatchet, and before my eyes—and before I could get there—*(Covers her face an instant.)* If they hadn't held me back I would have—*(Catches herself, looks upstairs where steps are heard, falters weakly.)*—hurt him.

Mrs. Hale: *(With a slow look around her.)* I wonder how it would seem never to have had any children around. *(Pause.)* No, Wright wouldn't like the bird—a thing that sang. She used to sing. He killed that, too.

Mrs. Peters: *(Moving uneasily.)* We don't know who killed the bird.

Mrs. Hale: I knew John Wright.

Mrs. Peters: It was an awful thing was done in this house that night, Mrs. Hale. Killing a man while he slept, slipping a rope around his neck that choked the life out of him.

Mrs. Hale: His neck. Choked the life out of him.

(Her hand goes out and rests on the bird-cage.)

Mrs. Peters: *(With rising voice.)* We don't know who killed him. We don't know.

Mrs. Hale: *(Her own feeling not interrupted.)* If there'd been years and years of nothing, then a bird to sing to you, it would be awful—still, after the bird was still.

Mrs. Peters: *(Something within her speaking.)* I know what stillness is. When we homesteaded in Dakota, and my first baby died—after he was two years old, and me with no other then—

Mrs. Hale: *(Moving.)* How soon do you suppose they'll be through, looking for the evidence?

Mrs. Peters: I know what stillness is. *(Pulling herself back.)* The law has got to punish crime, Mrs. Hale.

Mrs. Hale: *(Not as if answering that.)* I wish you'd seen Minnie Foster when she wore a white dress with blue ribbons and stood up there in the choir and sang. *(A look around the room.)* Oh, I *wish* I'd come over here once in a while! That was a crime! That was a crime! Who's going to punish that?

Mrs. Peters: *(Looking upstairs.)* We mustn't—take on.

Mrs. Hale: I might have known she needed help! I know how things can be—for women. I tell you, it's queer, Mrs. Peters. We live close together and we live far apart. We all go through the same things—it's all just a different kind of the same thing. *(Brushes her eyes, noticing the bottle of fruit, reaches out for it.)* If I was you I wouldn't tell her her fruit was gone. Tell her it *ain't.* Tell her it's all right. Take this in to prove it to her. She—she may never know whether it was broke or not.

Mrs. Peters: *(Takes the bottle, looks about for something to wrap it in; takes petticoat from the clothes brought from the other room, very nervously* *begins winding this around the bottle. In a false voice.)* My, it's a good thing the men couldn't hear us. Wouldn't they just laugh! Getting all stirred up over a little thing like a—dead canary. As if that could have anything to do with—with—wouldn't they *laugh!*

(The men are heard coming down stairs.)

Mrs. Hale: *(Under her breath.)* Maybe they would—maybe they wouldn't.

County Attorney: No, Peters, it's all perfectly clear except a reason for doing it. But you know juries when it comes to women. If there was some definite thing. Something to show—something to make a story about—a thing that would connect up with this strange way of doing it—

(The women's eyes meet for an instant. Enter Hale from outer door.)

Hale: Well, I've got the team around. Pretty cold out there.

County Attorney: I'm going to stay here a while by myself. *(To the Sheriff.)* You can send Frank out for me, can't you? I want to go over everything. I'm not satisfied that we can't do better.

Sheriff: Do you want to see what Mrs. Peters is going to take in?

(The County Attorney goes to the table, picks up the apron, laughs.)

County Attorney: Oh, I guess they're not very dangerous things the ladies have picked out. *(Moves a few things about, disturbing the quilt pieces which cover the box. Steps back.)* No, Mrs. Peters doesn't need supervising. For that matter, a sheriff's wife is married to the law. Ever think of it that way, Mrs. Peters?

Mrs. Peters: Not—just that way.

Sheriff: *(Chuckling.)* Married to the law. *(Moves toward the other room.)* I just want you to come in here a minute, George. We ought to take a look at these windows.

County Attorney: *(Scoffingly.)* Oh, windows!

Sheriff: We'll be right out, Mr. Hale.

(Hale goes outside. The Sheriff follows the County Attorney into the other room. Then Mrs. Hale rises, hands tight together, looking intensely at Mrs. Peters, whose eyes make a slow turn, finally meeting Mrs. Hale's. A moment Mrs. Hale holds her, then her own eyes point the way to where the box is concealed. Suddenly Mrs. Peters throws back quilt pieces and tries to put the box in the bag she is wearing. It is too big. She opens box, starts to take bird out, cannot touch it, goes to pieces, stands there helpless. Sound of a knob turning in the other room. Mrs. Hale snatches the box and puts it in the pocket of her big coat. Enter County Attorney and Sheriff.)

County Attorney: *(Facetiously.)* Well, Henry, at least we found out that she was not going to quilt it. She was going to—what is it you call it, ladies?

Mrs. Hale: *(Her hand against her pocket.)* We call it—knot it, Mr. Henderson.

(Curtain.)

Explorations of the Text

1. Characterize Mrs. Hale and Mrs. Peters at the beginning of the play. How do they differ?
2. What clues lead the women to conclude that Minnie Wright killed her husband?
3. How do the men differ from the women? from each other?
4. What do the men discover? Why do they conclude "Nothing here but kitchen things"? What do the women discover?
5. Why do the men and women find different clues about the murder? What does Glaspell imply about the ways in which men and women were conditioned to view the world?
6. Do Mrs. Hale and Mrs. Peters change? Why? How? What makes them sympathize with Minnie Wright? Discuss the symbolism of the broken cage and the dead canary.
7. Characterize Minnie Wright and her husband. Describe their relationship. Why is Minnie Wright absent from the play?
8. Interpret the ending and the title. With what "crime" should Minnie Wright be charged?
9. Compare the marriage of the Wrights with those in other works in this chapter.
10. Compare Glaspell's critique of gender roles and of women's place in society with treatments of these issues by Gilman and Chopin.

The Reading/Writing Connection

1. Write a journal entry in Minnie Wright's voice.
2. Are Mrs. Hale and Mrs. Peters justified in withholding evidence concerning John Wright's murder?
3. "Think" Topic: Discuss the symbolism of the cage.

Ideas for Writing

1. Susan Glaspell claimed that the idea for the play came from a story that she covered as a reporter. Construct your version of her article.
2. What are the strengths and weaknesses of *Trifles?* Consider conflict, characters, setting, theme, symbol, irony, emotion, and/or general effect.
3. After the play was produced, Glaspell wrote a short story, "A Jury of Her Peers," about this subject. Read the story, and decide which version is better. Defend your choice.
4. Should Minnie Wright be found guilty for her actions?

Sure Thing

David Ives

David Ives (1950–), born in Chicago, was educated at Northwestern University and the Yale School of Drama. His collection of one-act plays, All in the Timing, *which includes "Sure Thing," won an Outer Circle Award for playwriting and was nominated for a Drama Desk Award. He has written longer plays, among them* Don Juan in Chicago, *and an opera,* The Secret Garden, *which had its premier at the Pennsylvania Opera Theater. Ives's plays are marked by their wit and invention. In their play with language and their multiple interpretations of and variations on a single moment, Ives's plays exemplify postmodern literature.*

1995

Characters

Bill, in his late twenties
Betty, in her late twenties

Setting

A café table, with a couple of chairs.

Scene

Betty, *reading at the table. An empty chair opposite her.* Bill *enters.*

Bill: Excuse me. Is this chair taken?
Betty: Excuse me?
Bill: Is this taken?
Betty: Yes, it is.
Bill: Oh. Sorry.
Betty: Sure thing.

(A bell rings softly.)

Bill: Excuse me. Is this chair taken?
Betty: Excuse me?
Bill: Is this taken?
Betty: No, but I'm expecting somebody in a minute.
Bill: Oh. Thanks anyway.
Betty: Sure thing.

(A bell rings softly.)

Bill: Excuse me. Is this chair taken?
Betty: No, but I'm expecting somebody very shortly.
Bill: Would you mind if I sit here till he or she or it comes?
Betty: *(Glances at her watch.)* They seem to be pretty late . . .
Bill: You never know who you might be turning down.

Betty: Sorry. Nice try, though.
Bill: Sure thing.

(Bell)

Bill: Is this seat taken?
Betty: No, it's not.
Bill: Would you mind if I sit here?
Betty: Yes, I would.
Bill: Oh.

(Bell)

Bill: Is this chair taken?
Betty: No, it's not.
Bill: Would you mind if I sit here?
Betty: No. Go ahead.
Bill: Thanks. *(He sits. She continues reading.)* Everyplace else seems to be taken.
Betty: Mm-hm.
Bill: Great place.
Betty: Mm-hm.
Bill: What's the book?
Betty: I just wanted to read in quiet, if you don't mind.
Bill: No. Sure thing.

(Bell.)

Bill: Everyplace else seems to be taken.
Betty: Mm-hm.
Bill: Great place for reading.
Betty: Yes, I like it.
Bill: What's the book?
Betty: "The Sound and the Fury."
Bill: Oh. Hemingway.[1]

(Bell)

Bill: What's the book?
Betty: "The Sound and the Fury."
Bill: Oh. Faulkner.[2]
Betty: Have you read it?
Bill: Not . . . actually. I've read *about* it, though. It's supposed to be great.
Betty: It is great.
Bill: I hear it's great. *(Small pause.)* Waiter?

(Bell)

---

[1] Ernest Hemingway (1899–1961). U.S. novelist, short story writer.
[2] William Faulkner (1897–1962). U.S. novelist, short story writer.

Bill: What's the book?
Betty: "The Sound and the Fury."
Bill: Oh. Faulkner.
Betty: Have you read it?
Bill: I'm a Mets fan, myself.

(Bell.)

Betty: Have you read it?
Bill: Yeah, I read it in college.
Betty: Where was college?
Bill: I went to Oral Roberts University.

(Bell.)

Betty: Where was college?
Bill: I was lying. I never really went to college. I just like to party.

(Bell.)

Betty: Where was college?
Bill: Harvard.
Betty: Did you like Faulkner?
Bill: I love Faulkner. I spent a whole winter reading him once.
Betty: I've just started.
Bill: I was so excited after ten pages that I went out and bought everything else he wrote. One of the greatest reading experiences of my life. I mean, all that incredible psychological understanding. Page after page of gorgeous prose. His profound grasp of the mystery of time and human existence. The smells of the earth . . . What do you think?
Betty: I think it's pretty boring.

(Bell.)

Bill: What's the book?
Betty: "The Sound and the Fury."
Bill: Oh! Faulkner!
Betty: Do you like Faulkner?
Bill: I love Faulkner.
Betty: He's incredible.
Bill: I spent a whole winter reading him once.
Betty: I was so excited after ten pages that I went out and bought everything else he wrote.
Bill: All that incredible psychological understanding.
Betty: And the prose is so gorgeous.
Bill: And the way he's grasped the mystery of time—
Betty: —and human existence. I can't believe I've waited this long to read him.
Bill: You never know. You might not have liked him before.
Betty: That's true.

Bill: You might not have been ready for him. You have to hit these things at the right moment or it's no good.
Betty: That's happened to me.
Bill: It's all in the timing. *(Small pause.)* My name's Bill, by the way.
Betty: I'm Betty.
Bill: Hi.
Betty: Hi.

(Small pause.)

Bill: Yes, I thought reading Faulkner was . . . a great experience.
Betty: Yes.

(Small pause.)

Bill: "The Sound and the Fury" . . .

(Another small pause.)

Betty: Well. Onwards and upwards. *(She goes back to her book.)*
Bill: Waiter—?

(Bell.)

Bill: You have to hit these things at the right moment or it's no good.
Betty: That's happened to me.
Bill: It's all in the timing. My name's Bill, by the way.
Betty: I'm Betty.
Bill: Hi.
Betty: Hi.
Bill: Do you come in here a lot?
Betty: Actually I'm just in town for two days from Pakistan.
Bill: Oh. Pakistan.

(Bell.)

Bill: My name's Bill, by the way.
Betty: I'm Betty.
Bill: Hi.
Betty: Hi.
Bill: Do you come in here a lot?
Betty: Every once in a while. Do you?
Bill: No much anymore. Not as much as I used to. Before my nervous breakdown.

(Bell.)

Bill: Do you come in here a lot?
Betty: Why are you asking?
Bill: Just interested.
Betty: Are you really interested, or do you just want to pick me up?
Bill: No, I'm really interested.

Betty: Why would you be interested in whether I come in here a lot?

Bill: Just . . . getting acquainted.

Betty: Maybe you're only interested for the sake of making small talk long enough to ask me back to your place to listen to some music, or because you've just rented some great tape for your VCR, or because you've got some terrific unknown Django Reinhardt[3] record, only all you'll really want to do is fuck—which you won't do very well—after which you'll go into the bathroom and pee very loudly, then pad into the kitchen and get yourself a beer from the refrigerator without asking me whether I'd like anything, and then you'll proceed to lie back down beside me and confess that you've got a girlfriend named Stephanie who's away at medical school in Belgium for a year, and that you've been involved with her—*off and on*—in what you'll call a very intricate relationship, for about *seven YEARS*. None of which *interests* me, mister!

Bill: Okay.

(Bell.)

Bill: Do you come in here a lot?

Betty: Every other day, I think.

Bill: I come in here quite a lot and I don't remember seeing you.

Betty: I guess we must be on different schedules.

Bill: Missed connections.

Betty: Yes. Different time zones.

Bill: Amazing how you can live right next door to somebody in this town and never even know it.

Betty: I know.

Bill: City life.

Betty: It's crazy.

Bill: We probably pass each other in the street every day. Right in front of this place, probably.

Betty: Yep.

Bill: *(Looks around.)* Well, the waiters here sure seem to be in some different time zone. I don't see one anywhere . . . Waiter! *(He looks back.)* So what do you . . . *(He sees that she's gone back to her book.)*

Betty: I beg pardon?

Bill: Nothing. Sorry.

(Bell.)

Betty: I guess we must be on different schedules.

Bill: Missed connections.

Betty: Yes. Different time zones.

---

[3] Famous jazz guitarist, originally named Jean-Baptiste Reinhardt, (1910–43), of Gypsy origin. One of the originals of European jazz, he performed with the Duke Ellington orchestra in 1946.

Bill: Amazing how you can live right next door to somebody in this town and never even know it.

Betty: I know.

Bill: City life.

Betty: It's crazy.

Bill: You weren't waiting for somebody when I came in, were you?

Betty: Actually I was.

Bill: Oh. Boyfriend?

Betty: Sort of.

Bill: What's a sort-of boyfriend?

Betty: My husband.

Bill: Ah-ha.

(Bell.)

Bill: You weren't waiting for somebody when I came in, were you?

Betty: Actually I was.

Bill: Oh. Boyfriend?

Betty: Sort of.

Bill: What's a sort-of boyfriend?

Betty: We were meeting here to break up.

Bill: Mm-hm . . .

(Bell.)

Bill: What's a sort-of boyfriend?

Betty: My lover. Here she comes right now!

(Bell.)

Bill: You weren't waiting for somebody when I came in, were you?

Betty: No, just reading.

Bill: Sort of a sad occupation for a Friday night, isn't it? Reading here, all by yourself?

Betty: Do you think so?

Bill: Well sure. I mean, what's a good-looking woman like you doing out alone on a Friday night?

Betty: Trying to keep away from lines like that.

Bill: No, listen—

(Bell.)

Bill: You weren't waiting for somebody when I came in, were you?

Betty: No, just reading.

Bill: Sort of a sad occupation for a Friday night, isn't it? Reading here all by yourself?

Betty: I guess it is, in a way.

Bill: What's a good-looking woman like you doing out alone on a Friday night? No offense, but . . .

Betty: I'm out alone on a Friday night for the first time in a very long time.

Bill: Oh.

Betty: You see, I just recently ended a relationship.

Bill: Oh.

Betty: Of rather long standing.

Bill: I'm sorry—Well listen, since reading by yourself *is* such a sad occupation for a Friday night, would you like to go elsewhere?

Betty: No . . .

Bill: Do something else?

Betty: No thanks.

Bill: I was headed out to the movies in a while anyway.

Betty: I don't think so.

Bill: Big chance to let Faulkner catch his breath. All those long sentences get him pretty tired.

Betty: Thanks anyway.

Bill: Okay.

Betty: I appreciate the invitation.

Bill: Sure thing.

(Bell.)

Bill: You weren't waiting for somebody when I came in, were you?

Betty: No, just reading.

Bill: Sort of a sad occupation for a Friday night, isn't it? Reading here all by yourself?

Betty: I guess I was trying to think of it as existentially romantic. You know—capuccino, great literature, rainy night . . .

Bill: That only works in Paris. We *could* hop the late plane to Paris. Get on a Concorde. Find a café . . .

Betty: I'm a little short on plane fare tonight.

Bill: Darn it, so am I.

Betty: To tell you the truth, I was headed to the movies after I finished this section. Would you like to come along? Since you can't locate a waiter?

Bill: That's a very nice offer, but—I can't.

Betty: Uh-huh. Girlfriend?

Bill: Two of them, actually. One of them's pregnant, and Stephanie—

(Bell.)

Betty: Girlfriend?

Bill: No, I don't have a girlfriend. Not if you mean the castrating bitch I dumped last night.

(Bell.)

Betty: Girlfriend?

Bill: Sort of. Sort of . . .

Betty: What's a sort-of girlfriend?

Bill: My mother.

(Bell.)

Bill: I just ended a relationship, actually.

Betty: Oh.

Bill: Of rather long standing.

Betty: I'm sorry to hear it.

Bill: This is my first night out alone in a long time. I feel a little bit at sea, to tell you the truth.

Betty: So you didn't stop to talk because you're a Moonie,[4] or you have some weird political affiliation—?

Bill: Nope. Straight-down-the-ticket Republican.

(Bell.)

Straight-down-the-ticket Democrat.

(Bell.)

Can I tell you something about politics?

(Bell.)

I consider myself a citizen of the universe.

(Bell.)

I'm unaffiliated.

Betty: That's a relief. So am I.

Bill: I vote my beliefs.

Betty: Labels are not important.

Bill: Labels are not important, exactly. Like me, for example. I mean, what does it matter if I had a two-point—

(Bell.)

—three-point—

(Bell)

—four-point at college, or if I did come from Pittsburgh—

(Bell)

—Cleveland—

(Bell)

—Westchester County?

Betty: Sure.

Bill: I believe that a man is what he is.

(Bell.)

A person is what he is.

(Bell.)

[4] Member of a religious cult.

A person is what they are.

Betty: I think so, too.

Bill: So what if I admire Trotsky?[5]

(Bell.)

So what if I once had a total body liposuction?

(Bell.)

So what if I don't have a penis?

(Bell.)

So what if I spent a year in the Peace Corps? I was acting on my convictions.

Betty: Convictions are important.

Bill: You just can't hang a sign on a person.

Betty: Absolutely. I'll bet you're a Scorpio.

(Many bells ring.)

Betty: Listen, I was headed to the movies after I finished this section. Would you like to come along?

Bill: That sounds like fun. What's playing?

Betty: A couple of the really early Woody Allen movies.

Bill: Oh.

Betty: Don't you like Woody Allen?

Bill: Sure. I like Woody Allen.

Betty: But you're not crazy about Woody Allen.

Bill: Those early ones kind of get on my nerves.

Betty: Uh-huh.

(Bell.)

Bill: *(Simultaneously.)* **Betty:**

Y'know, I was headed to the . . . I was thinking about . . .

Bill: I'm sorry.

Betty: No, go ahead.

Bill: I was just going to say that I was headed to the movies in a little while, and . . .

Betty: So was I.

Bill: The Woody Allen festival?

Betty: Just up the street.

Bill: Do you like the early ones?

Betty: I think anybody who doesn't ought to be run off the planet.

[5] Leon Trotsky (1879–1940), Russian revolutionary and writer.

Bill: How many times have you seen "Bananas"?[6]
Betty: Eight times.
Bill: Twelve. So are you still interested?
Betty: Do you like Entenmann's crumb cake?
Bill: I went out at two o'clock this morning to buy one. Did you have an Etch-a-Sketch as a child?
Betty: Yes! Do you like brussel sprouts?
Bill: I think they're gross.
Betty: They *are* gross!
Bill: Do you still believe in marriage in spite of current sentiments against it?
Betty: Yes.
Bill: And children?
Betty: Three of them.
Bill: Two girls and a boy.
Betty: Harvard, Vassar, and Brown.
Bill: And will you love me?
Betty: Yes.
Bill: And cherish me forever?
Betty: Yes.
Bill: Do you still want to go to the movies?
Betty: Sure thing.
Bill and Betty *(Together.)*: Waiter!

(Blackout.)

Explorations of the Text

1. Why does Ives choose the names Betty and Bill for his protagonists?
2. What is the significance of the setting—the café? What does the bell signify?
3. Discuss the irony of the repeated line, "Sure thing."
4. How do the interactions between the two characters in each scene differ from one another? How do the scenes build upon one another? Discuss the climactic last interchange.
5. What views of dating and relationships does the play suggest? Are they believable?
6. Discuss the impact of the humor in the play.

[6] A movie produced and directed by Woody Allen.

The Reading/Writing Connection

1. "Think" Topic: Do you relate to the play's vision of the dating game? Create an argumentative mini-essay presenting your response to this question.
2. Using this work as a model, create a dramatic scene or dialogue that conveys a satiric view of relationships. Then in a short paragraph analyze the themes of your work.

Ideas for Writing

1. Analyze this work as an example of the theater of the absurd (refer to chapter 11).

AM I BLUE

Beth Henley

Beth Henley (1952–) was born in Jackson, Mississippi. Henley, educated at Southern Methodist University and the University of Illinois, became a playwright and an actress. Her most famous work is Crimes of the Heart *(1981), for which she received the Pulitzer Prize. She also has been awarded the New York Drama Critics Circle Award and the Oppenheimer Award. Henley wrote this one-act play while she was a student at Southern Methodist University.*

1972

Characters

John Polk	*Seventeen.*
Ashbe	*Sixteen.*
Hilda	*Thirty-five, a waitress.*
Street characters:	Barker, Whore, Bum, Clareece

Settings

A bar, the street, the living room of a run-down apartment

Time

Fall 1968

The scene opens on a street in the New Orleans French Quarter on a rainy blue bourbon night. Various people: a whore, bum, street barker, Clareece appear and disappear along the street. The scene then focuses on a bar where a piano is heard from the back room playing softly and indistinctly "Am I Blue?" The light go up on John Polk, who sits alone at a table. He is seventeen, a bit overweight and awkward. He wears nice clothes, perhaps a navy sweater with large white monograms. His navy raincoat is slung over an empty chair. While drinking, John Polk concentrates on the red-and-black card that he holds in his hand. As soon as the scene is established, Ashbe enters from the street. She is sixteen, wears a flowered plastic rain cap, red galoshes, a butterfly barrette, and jeweled cat eyeglasses. She is carrying a bag full of stolen goods. Her hair is very curly. Ashbe makes her way cautiously to John Polk's table. As he sees her coming, he puts the card into his pocket. She sits in the empty chair and pulls his raincoat over her head.

Ashbe: Excuse me . . . do you mind if I sit here, please?

John Polk *(Looks up at her—then down into his glass.):* What are you doing hiding under my raincoat? You're getting it all wet.

Ashbe: Well, I'm very sorry, but after all, it is a raincoat. *(He tries to pull off coat.)* It was rude of me, I know, but look, I just don't want them to recognize me.

John Polk *(Looking about.):* Who to recognize you?

5 **Ashbe:** Well, I stole these two ashtrays from the Screw Inn, ya know, right down the street. *(She pulls out two glass commercial ashtrays from her white plastic bag.)* Anyway, I'm scared the manager saw me. They'll be after me, I'm afraid.

John Polk: Well, they should be. Look, do you mind giving me back my raincoat? I don't want to be found protecting any thief.

Ashbe *(Coming out from under coat.):* Thief—would you call Robin Hood a thief?

John Polk: Christ.

Ashbe *(Back under coat.):* No, you wouldn't. He was valiant—all the time stealing from the rich and giving to the poor.

10 **John Polk:** But your case isn't exactly the same, is it? You're stealing from some crummy little bar and keeping the ashtrays for yourself. Now give me back my coat.

Ashbe: *(Throws coat at him.):* Sure, take your old coat. I suppose I should have explained—about Miss Marcey. *(Silence.)* Miss Marcey, this cute old lady with a little hump in her back. I always see her in her sun hat and blue print dress. Miss Marcey lives in the apartment building next to ours. I leave all the stolen goods as gifts on her front steps.

John Polk: Are you one of those kleptomaniacs? *(He starts checking his wallet.)*

Ashbe: You mean when people all the time steal and they can't help it?

John Polk: Yeah.

15 **Ashbe:** Oh, no. I'm not a bit careless. Take my job tonight, my very first night job, if you want to know. Anyway, I've been planning it for two months, trying to decipher which bar most deserved to be stolen from. I finally decided on the Screw Inn. Mainly because of the way they're so mean to Mr. Groves. He works at the magazine rack at Diver's Drugstore and is really very sweet, but he has a drinking problem. I don't think that's fair to be mean to people simply because they have a drinking problem—and, well, anyway, you see I'm not just stealing for personal gain. I mean, I don't even smoke.

John Polk: Yeah, well, most infants don't, but then again, most infants don't hang around bars.

Ashbe: I don't see why not, Toulouse Lautrec[1] did.

John Polk: They'd throw me out.

Ashbe: Oh, they throw me out, too, but I don't accept defeat. *(Slowly moves into him.)* Why it's the very same with my pick-pocketing.

(John Polk sneers, turns away.)

It's a very hard art to master. Why, every time I've done it I've been caught.

John Polk: That's all I need is to have some slum kid tell me how good it is to steal. Everyone knows it's not.

Ashbe *(About his drink.):* That looks good. What is it?

John Polk: Hey, would you mind leaving me alone—I just wanted to be alone.

Ashbe: Okay. I'm sorry. How about if I'm quiet?

(John Polk shrugs. He sips drink, looks around, catches her eye; she smiles and sighs.)

I was just looking at your pin. What fraternity are you in?

John Polk: SAE.

Ashbe: Is it a good fraternity?

John Polk: Sure, it's the greatest.

Ashbe: I bet you have lots of friends.

John Polk: Tons.

Ashbe: Are you being serious?

John Polk: Yes.

Ashbe: Hmm. Do they have parties and all that?

John Polk: Yeah, lots of parties, booze, honking horns; it's exactly what you would expect.

Ashbe: I wouldn't expect anything. Why did you join?

John Polk: I don't know. Well, my brother—I guess it was my brother—he told me how great it was, how the fraternity was supposed to get you dates, make you study, solve all your problems.

Ashbe: Gee, does it?

John Polk: Doesn't help you study.

Ashbe: How about dates? Do they get you a lot of dates?

John Polk: Some.

Ashbe: What were the girls like?

John Polk: I don't know—they were like girls.

Ashbe: Did you have a good time?

John Polk: I had a pretty good time.

---

[1] Henn Marie Raymond de Toulouse-Lautrec (1864–1901), French Impressionist painter.

Ashbe: Did you make love to any of them?

John Polk *(To self.):* Oh, Christ—

Ashbe: I'm sorry—I just figured that's why you had the appointment with the whore—'cause you didn't have anyone else—to make love to.

John Polk: How did you know I had the, ah, the appointment?

Ashbe: I saw you put the red card in your pocket when I came up. Those red cards are pretty familiar around here. The house is only about a block or so away. It's one of the best, though, really very plush. Only two murders and a knifing in its whole history. Do you go there often?

John Polk: Yeah, I like to give myself a treat.

Ashbe: Who do you have?

John Polk: What do you mean?

Ashbe: I mean which girl.

(John Polk gazes into his drink.)

Look, I just thought I might know her is all.

John Polk: Know her, ah, how would you know her?

Ashbe: Well, some of the girls from my high school go there to work when they get out.

John Polk: G.G., her name is G.G.

Ashbe: G.G.—Hmm, well, how does she look?

John Polk: I don't know.

Ashbe: Oh, you've never been with her before?

John Polk: No.

Ashbe *(Confidentially.):* Are you one of those kinds that likes a lot of variety?

John Polk: Variety? Sure, I guess I like variety.

Ashbe: Oh, yes, now I remember.

John Polk: What?

Ashbe: G.G., that's just her working name. Her real name is Myrtle Reims; she's Kay Reims's older sister. Kay is in my grade at school.

John Polk: Myrtle? Her name is Myrtle?

Ashbe: I never like the name, either.

John Polk: Myrtle, oh, Christ. Is she pretty?

Ashbe *(Matter-of-fact.):* Pretty, no she's not real pretty.

John Polk: What does she look like?

Ashbe: Let's see . . . she's ahh, well, Myrtle had acne, and there are a few scars left. It's not bad. I think they sort of give her character. Her hair's red, only I don't think it's really red. It sort of fizzles out all over her head. She's got a pretty good figure—big top—but the rest of her is kind of skinny.

John Polk: I wonder if she has a good personality.

Ashbe: Well, she was a senior when I was a freshman; so I never really knew her. I remember she used to paint her fingernails lots of different colors—pink, orange, purple. I don't know, but she kind of scares me. About the only time I ever saw her true personality was around a year ago. I was over at Kay's making a health poster for school. Anyway, Myrtle comes busting in screaming about how she can't find her spangled bra anywhere. Kay and I just sat on the floor cutting pictures of food out of magazines while she was storming about slamming drawers and swearing. Finally, she found it. It was pretty garish—red with black and gold-sequined G's on each cup. That's how I remember the name—G.G.

As Ashbe illustrates the placement of the G's she spots Hilda, the waitress, approaching. Ashbe pulls the raincoat over her head and hides on the floor. Hilda enters through the beaded curtains spilling her tray. Hilda is a woman of few words.)

Hilda: Shit, damn curtain. 'Nuther drink?

John Polk: Ma'am?

Hilda *(Points to drink.):* Vodka Coke?

John Polk: No, thank you. I'm not quite finished yet.

Hilda: Napkins clean.

(Ashbe pulls her bag off the table. Hilda looks at Ashbe, then to John Polk. She walks around the table, as Ashbe is crawling along the floor to escape. Ashbe runs into Hilda 's toes.)

Ashbe: Are those real gold?

Hilda: You again. Out.

Ashbe: She wants me to leave. Why should a paying customer leave? *(Back to Hilda.)* Now I'll have a mint julep and easy on the mint.

Hilda: This preteen with you?

John Polk: Well—I—No—I—

Hilda: IDs.

Ashbe: Certainly, I always try to cooperate with the management.

Hilda *(Looking at John Polk's ID.):* ID, 11-12-50. Date 11-11-68.

John Polk: Yes, but—well, 11-12 is less than two hours away.

Hilda: Back in two hours.

Ashbe: I seem to have left my identification in my gold lamé bag.

Hilda: Well, boo hoo. *(Motions for Ashbe to leave with a minimum of effort. She goes back to table.)* No tip.

Ashbe: You didn't tip her?

John Polk: If figured the drinks were so expensive—I just didn't—

Hilda: No tip!

John Polk: Look, miss, I'm sorry. *(Going through his pockets.)* Here, would you like a—a nickel—wait, wait here's a quarter.

Hilda: Just move ass, sonny. You, too, Barbie.

Ashbe: Ugh, I hate public rudeness. I'm sure I'll refrain from every coming here again.

Hilda: Think I'll go in the back room and cry. *(Ashbe and John Polk exit. Hilda picks up tray and exits through the curtain, tripping again.)* Shit. Damn curtain.

(Ashbe and John Polk are now standing outside under the awning of the bar.)

Ashbe: Gee, I didn't know it was your birthday tomorrow. Happy birthday. Don't be mad. I thought you were at least twenty or twenty-one, really.

John Polk: It's okay. Forget it.

Ashbe *(As they begin walking, various blues are heard coming from the nearby bars.):* It's raining.

John Polk: I know.

Ashbe: Are you going over to the house now?

John Polk: No, not till twelve.

Ashbe: Yeah, the pink-and-blue cards—they mean all night. Midnight till morning. *(At this point a street barker beckons the couple into his establishment. Perhaps he is accompanied by a whore.)*

Barker: Hey, mister, bring your baby on in, buy her a few drinks, maybe tonight ya get lucky.

Ashbe: Keep walking.

John Polk: What's wrong with the place?

Ashbe: The drinks are watery rotgut, and the showgirls are boys.

Barker: Up yours, punk!

John Polk *(Who has now sat down on a street bench.):* Look, just tell me where a cheap bar is. I've got to stay drunk, but I don't have much money left.

Ashbe: Yikes, there aren't too many cheap bars around here, and a lot of them check IDs.

John Polk: Well, do you know of any that don't?

Ashbe: No, not for sure.

John Polk: Oh, God, I need to get drunk.

Ashbe: Aren't you?

John Polk: Some, but I'm losing ground fast. *(By this time a bum who has been traveling drunkenly down the street falls near the couple and begins throwing up.)*

Ashbe: Oh, I know! You can come to my apartment. It's just down the block. We keep one bottle of rum around. I'll serve you a grand drink, three or four if you like.

John Polk *(Fretfully.):* No, thanks.

Ashbe: But, look, we're getting all wet.

John Polk: Sober, too, wet and sober.

Ashbe: Oh, come on! Rain's blurring my glasses.

John Polk: Well, how about your parents? What would they say?

Ashbe: Daddy's out of town and Mama lives in Atlanta; so I'm sure they won't mind. I think we have some cute little marshmallows. *(Pulling on him.)* Won't you really come?

John Polk: You've probably got some gang of muggers waiting to kill me. Oh, all right—what the hell, let's go.

Ashbe: Hurrah! Come on. It's this way. *(She starts across the stage, stops, and picks up an old hat.)* Hey look at this hat. Isn't it something! Here, wear it to keep off the rain.

John Polk *(Throwing hat back onto street.):* No, thanks, you don't know who's worn it before.

Ashbe *(Picking hat back up.)*: That makes it all the more exciting. Maybe it was a butcher's who slaughtered his wife or a silver pirate with a black bird on his throat. Who do you guess?

John Polk: I don't know. Anyway, what's the good of guessing? I mean, you'll never really know.

Ashbe *(Trying the hat on.)*: Yeah, probably not. *(At this point, Ashbe and John Polk reach the front door.)* Here we are. *(Ashbe begins fumbling for her key. Clareece, a teeny-bopper, walks up to John Polk.)*

Clareece: Hey, man, got any spare change?

John Polk *(Looking through his pockets.)*: Let me see—I—

Ashbe *(Coming up between them, giving Clareece a shove.)*: Beat it, Clareece. He's my company.

Clareece *(Walks away and sneers.)*: Oh, shove it, Frizzels.

Ashbe: A lot of jerks live around here. Come on in. *(She opens the door. Lights go up on the living room of a run-down apartment in a run-down apartment house. Besides being merely run-down, the room is a malicious pigsty with colors, paper hats, paper dolls, masks, torn-up stuffed animals, dead flowers and leaves, dress-up clothes, etc., thrown all about.)* My bones are cold. Do you want a towel to dry off?

John Polk: Yes, thank you.

Ashbe *(She picks a towel up off of the floor and tosses it to him.)*: Here. *(He begins drying off as she takes off her rain things; then she begins raking things off the sofa.)* Please do sit down. *(He sits.)* I'm sorry the place is disheveled, but my father's been out of town. I always try to pick up and all before he gets in. Of course he's pretty used to messes. My mother never was too good at keeping things clean.

John Polk: When's he coming back?

Ashbe: Sunday, I believe. Oh, I've been meaning to say—

John Polk: What?

Ashbe: My name's Ashbe Williams.

John Polk: Ashbe?

Ashbe: Yeah, Ashbe.

John Polk: My name's John Polk Richards.

Ashbe: John Polk? They call you John Polk?

John Polk: It's family.

Ashbe *(Putting on socks.)*: These are my favorite socks, the red furry ones.Well, here's some books and magazines to look at while I fix you something to drink. What do you want in your rum?

John Polk: Coke's fine.

Ashbe: I'll see do we have any. I think I'll take some hot Kool-Aid myself. *(She exits to the kitchen.)*

John Polk: Hot Kool-Aid?

Ashbe: It's just Kool-Aid that's been heated, like hot chocolate or hot tea.

John Polk: Sounds great.

Ashbe: Well, I'm used to it. You get so much for your dime it makes it worth your while. I don't buy presweetened, of course, it's better to sugar your own.

John Polk: I remember once I threw up a lot of grape Kool-Aid when I was a kid. I've hated it ever since. Hey, would you check on the time?

Ashbe *(She enters carrying a tray with several bottles of food coloring, a bottle of rum, and a huge glass.):* I'm sorry we don't have Cokes. I wonder if rum and Kool-Aid is good? Oh, we don't have a clock, either. *(She pours a large amount of rum into the large glass.)*

John Polk: I'll just have it with water, then.

Ashbe *(She finds an almost empty glass of water somewhere in the room and dumps it in with the rum.):* Would you like food coloring in the water? It makes a drink all the more aesthetic. Of course, some people don't care for aesthetics.

John Polk: No, thank you, just plain water.

Ashbe: Are you sure? The taste is entirely the same. I put it in all my water.

John Polk: Well—

Ashbe: What color do you want?

John Polk: I don't know.

Ashbe: What's your favorite color?

John Polk: Blue, I guess. *(She puts a few blue drops into the glass—as she has nothing to stir with, she blows into the glass, turning the water blue.)* Thanks.

Ashbe *(Exits. She screams from the kitchen.):* Come on, say come on, cat, eat your fresh good milk.

John Polk: You have a cat?

Ashbe *(Off.):* No.

John Polk: Oh.

Ashbe *(She enters carrying a tray with a cup of hot Kool-Aid and Cheerios and colored marshmallows.):* Here are some Cheerios and some cute little colored marshmallows to eat with your drink.

John Polk: Thanks.

Ashbe: I one time smashed all the big white marshmallows in the plastic bag at the grocery store.

John Polk: Why did you do that?

Ashbe: I was angry. Do you like ceramics?

John Polk: Yes.

Ashbe: My mother makes them. It's sort of her hobby. She is very talented.

John Polk: My mother never does anything. Well, I guess she can shuffle the bridge deck okay.

Ashbe: Actually, my mother is a dancer. She teaches at a school in Atlanta. She's really very talented.

John Polk *(Indicates ceramics.):* She must be to do all these.

Ashbe: Well, Madeline, my older sister, did the blue one. Madeline gets to live with Mama.

John Polk: And you live with your father.

Ashbe: Yeah, but I get to go visit them sometimes.

John Polk: You do ceramics, too?

Ashbe: No, I never learned . . . but I have this great pot holder set. *(Gets up to show him.)* See I make lots of multicolored pot holders and send them to

Mama and Madeline. I also make paper hats. *(Gets material to show him.)* I guess they're more creative, but making pot holders is more relaxing. Here, would you like to make a hat?

John Polk: I don't know, I'm a little drunk.

Ashbe: It's not hard a bit. *(Hands him material.)* Just draw a real pretty design on the paper. It really doesn't have to be pretty, just whatever you want.

John Polk: It's kind of you to give my creative drives such freedom.

Ashbe: Ha, ha, ha, I'll work on my pot holder set a bit.

John Polk: What time is it? I've really got to check on the time.

Ashbe: I know. I'll call the time operator. *(She goes to the phone.)*

John Polk: How do you get along without a clock?

Ashbe: Well, I've been late for school a lot. Daddy has a watch. It's 11:03.

John Polk: I've got a while yet.

Ashbe: *(Twirls back to her chair, drops, and sighs.)*

John Polk: Are you a dancer, too?

Ashbe *(Delighted.):* I can't dance a bit, really. I practice a lot is all, at home in the afternoon. I imagine you go to a lot of dances.

John Polk: Not really, I'm a terrible dancer. I usually get bored or drunk.

Ashbe: You probably drink too much.

John Polk: No, it's just since I've come to college. All you do there is drink more beer and write more papers.

Ashbe: What are you studying for to be?

John Polk: I don't know.

Ashbe: Why don't you become a rancher?

John Polk: Dad wants me to help run his soybean farm.

Ashbe: Soybean farm. Yikes, that's really something. Where is it?

John Polk: Well, I live in the Delta, Hollybluff, Mississippi. Anyway, Dad feels I should go to business school first; you know, so I'll become, well, management minded. Pass the blue.

Ashbe: Is that what you really want to do?

John Polk: I don't know. It would probably be as good as anything else I could do. Dad makes good money. He can take vacations whenever he wants. Sure it'll be a ball.

Ashbe: I'd hate to have to be management minded. *(John Polk shrugs.)* I don't mean to hurt your feelings, but I would really hate to be a management mind. *(She starts walking on her knees, twisting her fists in front of her eyes, and making clicking sounds as a management mind would make.)*

John Polk: Cut it out. Just forget it. The farm could burn down and I wouldn't even have to think about it.

Ashbe *(After a pause.):* Well, what do you want to talk about?

John Polk: I don't know.

Ashbe: When was the last dance you went to?

John Polk: Dances. That's a great subject. Let's see, oh, I don't really remember. It was probably some blind date. God, I hate dates.

Ashbe: Why?

John Polk: Well, they always say that they don't want popcorn and they wind up eating all of yours.

Ashbe: You mean, you hate dates just because they eat your popcorn? Don't you think that's kind of stingy?

John Polk: It's the principle of the thing. Why can't they just say, yes, I'd like some popcorn when you ask them. But, no, they're always so damn coy.

Ashbe: I'd tell my date if I wanted popcorn. I'm not that immature.

John Polk: Anyway, it's not only the popcorn. It's a lot of little things. I've finished coloring. What do I do now?

Ashbe: Now you have to fold it. Here . . . like this. *(She explains the process with relish.)* Say, that's really something.

John Polk: It's kind of funny looking. *(Putting the hat on.)* Yeah, I like it but you could never wear it anywhere.

Ashbe: Well, like what, anyway?

John Polk: Huh?

Ashbe: The things dates do to you that you don't like, the little things.

John Polk: Oh, well just the way they wear those false eyelashes and put their hand on your knee when you're trying to parallel park and keep on giggling and going off to the bathroom with their girlfriends. It's obvious they don't want to go out with me. They just want to go out so that they can wear their new clothes and won't have to sit on their ass in the dormitory. They never want to go out with me. I can never even talk to them.

Ashbe: Well, you can talk to me and I'm a girl.

John Polk: Well, I'm really kind of drunk and you're a stranger . . . Well, I probably wouldn't be able to talk to you tomorrow. That makes a difference.

Ashbe: Maybe it does. *(A bit of a pause, and then, extremely pleased by the idea, she says.)* You know we're alike because I don't like dances, either.

John Polk: I thought you said you practiced . . . in the afternoons.

Ashbe: Well, I like dancing. I just don't like dances. At least not like—well, not like the one our school was having tonight. . . . They're so corny.

John Polk: Yeah, most dances are.

Ashbe: All they serve is potato chips and fruit punch, and then this stupid baby band plays and everybody dances around thinking they're so hot. I frankly wouldn't dance there. I would prefer to wait till I am invited to an exclusive ball. It doesn't really matter which ball, just one where they have huge golden chandeliers and silver fountains and serve delicacies of all sorts and bubble blue champagne. I'll arrive in a pink silk cape. *(Laughing.)* I want to dance in pink!

John Polk: You're mixed up. You're probably one of those people that live in a fantasy world.

Ashbe: I do not. I accept reality as well as anyone. Anyway, you can talk to me, remember. I know what you mean by the kind of girls it's hard to talk to. There are girls a lot that way in the small clique at my school. Really tacky and mean. They expect everyone to be as stylish as they are, and they won't even speak to you in the hall. I don't mind if they don't speak to me, but I really love the orphans, and it hurts my feelings when they are so mean to them.

John Polk: What do you mean—they're mean to the orpheens? *(Notices pun and giggles to self.)*

Ashbe: Oh, well, they sometimes snicker at the orphans' dresses. The orphans usually have hand-me-down, drab, ugly dresses. Once Shelly Maxwell wouldn't let Glinda borrow her pencil, even though she had two. It hurt her feelings.

John Polk: Are you best friends with these orphans?

Ashbe: I hardly know them at all. They're really shy. I just like them a lot. They're the reason I put spells on the girls in the clique.

John Polk: Spells, what do you mean, witch spells?

Ashbe: Witch spells? Not really, mostly just voodoo.

John Polk: Are you kidding? Do you really do voodoo?

Ashbe: Sure, here I'll show you my doll. *(Goes to get doll, comes back with straw voodoo doll. Her air as she returns is one of frightening mystery.)* I know a lot about the subject. Cora she used to wash dishes in the Moonlight Café, told me all about voodoo. She's a real expert on the subject, went to all the meetings and everything. Once she caused a man's throat to rot away and turn almost totally black. She's moved to Chicago now.

John Polk: It doesn't really work. Does it?

Ashbe: Well, not always. The thing about voodoo is that both parties have to believe in it for it to work.

John Polk: Do the girls in school believe in it?

Ashbe: Not really; I don't think. That's where my main problem comes in. I have to make the clique believe in it, yet I have to be very subtle. Mainly, I give reports in English class or Speech.

John Polk: Reports?

Ashbe: On voodoo.

John Polk: That's really kind of sick, you know.

Ashbe: Not really. I don't cast spells that'll do any real harm. Mainly, just the kind of thing to make them think—to keep them on their toes. *(Blue drink intoxication begins to take over and John Polk begins laughing.)* What's so funny?

John Polk: Nothing. I was just thinking what a mean little person you are.

Ashbe: Mean! I'm not mean a bit.

John Polk: Yes, you are mean—*(Picking up color.)* and green, too.

Ashbe: Green?

John Polk: Yes, green with envy of those other girls; so you play all those mean little tricks.

Ashbe: Envious of those other girls, that stupid, close-minded little clique!

John Polk: Green as this marshmallow. *(Eats marshmallow.)*

Ashbe: You think I want to be in some group . . . a sheep like you? A little sheep like you that does everything when he's supposed to do it!

John Polk: Me a sheep—I do what I want!

Ashbe: Ha! I've known you for an hour and already I see you for the sheep you are!

John Polk: Don't take your green meanness out on me.

Ashbe: Not only are you a sheep, you are a *normal* sheep. Give me back my colors! *(Begins snatching colors away.)*

John Polk *(Pushing colors at her.)*: Green and mean! Green and mean! Green and mean! Et cetera.

Ashbe *(Throwing marshmallows at him.)*: That's the reason you're in a fraternity and the reason you're going to manage your mind, and dates—you go out on dates merely because it's expected of you even though you have a terrible time. That's the reason you go to the whorehouse to prove you're a normal man. Well, you're much too normal for me.

John Polk: Infant bitch. You think you're really cute.

Ashbe: That really wasn't food coloring in your drink, it was poison! *(She laughs, he picks up his coat to go, and she stops throwing marshmallows at him.)* Are you going? I was only kidding. For Christ sake, it wasn't really poison. Come on, don't go. Can't you take a little friendly criticism?

John Polk: Look, did you have to bother me tonight? I had enough problems without—*(Phone rings. Both look at phone; it rings for the third time. He stands undecided.)*

Ashbe: Look, wait, we'll make it up. *(She goes to answer phone.)* Hello—Daddy. How are you? . . . I'm fine . . . Dad, you sound funny . . . what? . . . Come on, Daddy, you know she's not here. *(Pause.)* Look, I told you I wouldn't call anymore. You've got her number in Atlanta. *(Pause, as she sinks to the floor.)* Why have you started again? . . . Don't say that. I can tell it. I can. Hey, I have to go to bed now, I don't want to talk anymore, okay? *(Hangs up phone, softly to self.)* Goddamnit.

John Polk *(He has heard the conversation and is taking off his coat.)*: Hey, Ashbe—*(She looks at him blankly, her mind far away.)* You want to talk?

Ashbe: No. *(Slight pause.)* Why don't you look at my shell collection? I have this special shell collection. *(She shows him collection.)*

John Polk: They're beautiful, I've never seen colors like this. *(Ashbe is silent, he continues to himself.)* I used to go to Biloxi[2] a lot when I was a kid . . . one time my brother and I, we camped out on the beach. The sky was purple. I remember it was really purple. We ate pork and beans out of a can. I'd always kinda wanted to do that. Every night for about a week after I got home, I dreamt about these waves foaming over my head and face. It was funny. Did you find these shells or buy them?

Ashbe: Some I found, some I bought. I've been trying to decipher their meaning. Here, listen, do you hear that?

John Polk: Yes.

Ashbe: That's the soul of the sea. *(She listens.)* I'm pretty sure it's the soul of the sea. Just imagine when I decipher the language. I'll know all the secrets of the world.

---

[2] A city in Mississippi on the Gulf of Mexico.

John Polk: Yeah, probably you will. *(Looking into the shell.)* You know, you were right.

Ashbe: What do you mean?

John Polk: About me, you were right. I am a sheep, a normal one. I've been trying to get out of it, but now I'm as big a sheep as ever.

Ashbe: Oh, it doesn't matter. You're company. It was rude of me to say.

John Polk: No, because it was true. I really didn't want to go into a fraternity, I didn't even want to go to college, and I sure as hell don't want to go back to Hollybluff and work the soybean farm till I'm eighty.

Ashbe: I still say you could work on a ranch.

John Polk: I don't know. I wanted to be a minister or something good, but I don't even know if I believe in God.

Ashbe: Yeah.

John Polk: I never used to worry about being a failure. Now I think about it all the time. It's just I need to do something that's—fulfilling.

Ashbe: Fulfilling, yes, I see what you mean. Well, how about college? Isn't it fulfilling? I mean, you take all those wonderful classes, and you have all your very good friends.

John Polk: Friends, yeah, I have some friends.

Ashbe: What do you mean?

John Polk: Nothing—well, I do mean something. Well the hell, let me try to explain. You see it was my "friends," the fraternity guys that set me up with G.G., excuse me, Myrtle, as a gift for my eighteenth birthday.

Ashbe: You mean, you didn't want the appointment?

John Polk: No, I didn't want it. Hey, ah, where did my blue drink go?

Ashbe *(As she hands him the drink.)*: They probably thought you really wanted to go.

John Polk: Yeah, I'm sure they gave a damn what I wanted. They never even asked me. Hell, I would have told them a handkerchief, a pair of argyle socks, but, no, they have to get me a whore just because it's a cool-ass thing to do. They make me sick. I couldn't even stay at the party they gave. All the sweaty T-shirts and moron sex stories—I just couldn't take it.

Ashbe: Is that why you were at the Blue Angel so early?

John Polk: Yeah, I needed to get drunk, but not with them. They're such creeps.

Ashbe: Gosh, so you really don't want to go to Myrtle's?

John Polk: No, I guess not.

Ashbe: Then are you going?

John Polk *(Pause.)*: Yes.

Ashbe: That's wrong. You shouldn't go just to please them.

John Polk: Oh, that's not the point anymore; maybe at first it was, but it's not anymore. Now I have to go for myself—to prove to myself that I'm not afraid.

Ashbe: Afraid? *(Slowly, as she begins to grasp his meaning.)* You mean, you've never slept with a girl before?

John Polk: Well, I've never been in love.

Ashbe *(In amazement.):* You're a virgin?

John Polk: Oh, God.

Ashbe: No, don't feel bad, I am, too.

John Polk: I thought I should be in love—

Ashbe: Well, you're certainly not in love with Myrtle. I mean, you haven't even met her.

John Polk: I know, but, God, I thought maybe I'd never fall in love. What then? You should experience everything—shouldn't you? Oh, what's it matter, everything's so screwed.

Ashbe: Screwed? Yeah, I guess it is. I mean, I always thought it would be fun to have a lot of friends who gave parties and go to dances all dressed up. Like the dance tonight—it might have been fun.

John Polk: Well, why didn't you go?

Ashbe: I don't know. I'm not sure it would have been fun. Anyway, you can't go—alone.

John Polk: Oh, you need a date?

Ashbe: Yeah, or something.

John Polk: Say, Ashbe, ya wanna dance here?

Ashbe: No, I think we'd better discuss your dilemma.

John Polk: What dilemma?

Ashbe: Myrtle. It doesn't seem right you should—

John Polk: Let's forget Myrtle for now. I've got a while yet. Here, have some more of this blue-moon drink.

Ashbe: You're only trying to escape through artificial means.

John Polk: Yeah, you got it. Now, come on. Would you like to dance? Hey, you said you liked to dance.

Ashbe: You're being ridiculous.

John Polk *(Winking at her.):* Dance?

Ashbe: John Polk, I just thought—

John Polk: Hmm?

Ashbe: How to solve your problem—

John Polk: Well—

Ashbe: Make love to me!

John Polk: What?!

Ashbe: It all seems logical to me. It would prove you weren't scared, and you wouldn't be doing it just to impress others.

John Polk: Look, I—I mean I hardly know you—

Ashbe: But we've talked. It's better this way, really. I won't be so apt to point out your mistakes.

John Polk: I'd feel great stripping a twelve-year-old of her virginity.

Ashbe: I'm sixteen! Anyway, I'd be stripping you of yours just as well. I'll go put on some Tiger Claw perfume. *(She runs out.)*

John Polk: Hey, come back! Tiger Claw perfume, Christ.

Ashbe *(Entering.):* I think one should have different scents for different moods.

John Polk: Hey, stop spraying that! You know I'm not going to—well, you'd get neurotic or pregnant or some damn thing. Stop spraying, will you!

Ashbe: Pregnant? You really think I could get pregnant?

John Polk: Sure, it'd be a delightful possibility.

Ashbe: It really wouldn't be bad. Maybe I would get to go to Tokyo for an abortion. I've never been to the Orient.

John Polk: Sure, getting cut on is always a real treat.

Ashbe: Anyway, I might just want to have my dear baby. I could move to Atlanta with Mama and Madeline. It'd be wonderful fun. Why, I could take him to the supermarket, put him in one of those little baby seats to stroll him about. I'd buy peach baby food and feed it to him with a tiny golden spoon. Why, I could take colored pictures of him and send them to you through the mail. Come on—*(Starts putting pillows onto the couch.)* Well, I guess you should kiss me for a start. It's only etiquette; everyone begins with it.

John Polk: I don't think I could even kiss you with a clear conscience. I mean, you're so small, with those little cat-eye glasses and curly hair—I couldn't even kiss you.

Ashbe: You couldn't even kiss me? I can't help it if I have to wear glasses. I got the prettiest ones I could find.

John Polk: Your glasses are fine. Let's forget it, okay?

Ashbe: I know, my lips are too purple, but if I eat carrots, the dye'll come off and they'll be orange.

John Polk: I didn't say anything about your lips being too purple.

Ashbe: Well, what is it? You're just plain chicken, I suppose—

John Polk: Sure, right, I'm chicken, totally chicken. Let's forget it. I don't know how, but somehow this is probably all my fault.

Ashbe: You're darn right it's all your fault. I want to have my dear baby or at least get to Japan. I'm so sick of school I could smash every marshmallow in sight! *(She starts smashing.)* Go on to your skinny pimple whore. I hope the skinny whore laughs in your face, which she probably will because you have an easy face to laugh in.

John Polk: You're absolutely right; she'll probably hoot and howl her damn fizzle red head off. Maybe you can wait outside the door and hear her, give you lots of pleasure, you sadistic little thief.

Ashbe: Thief—was Robin Hood—Oh, what's wrong with this world? I just wasn't made for it is all. I've probably been put in the wrong world, I can see that now.

John Polk: You're fine in this world.

Ashbe: Sure, everyone just views me as an undesirable lump.

John Polk: Who?

Ashbe: You for one.

John Polk *(Pause.)*: You mean because I wouldn't make love to you?

Ashbe: It seems clear to me.

John Polk: But you're wrong, you know.

Ashbe *(To self, softly.)*: Don't pity me.

John Polk: The reason I wouldn't wasn't that—it's just that—well, I like you too much to.

Ashbe: You like me?

John Polk: Undesirable lump, Jesus. Your cheeks, they're—they're—

Ashbe: My cheeks? They're what?

John Polk: They're rosy.

Ashbe: My cheeks are rosy?

John Polk: Yeah, your cheeks, they're really rosy.

Ashbe: Well, they're natural, you know. Say, would you like to dance?

John Polk: Yes.

Ashbe: I'll turn on the radio. *(She turns on radio. Ethel Waters is heard singing "Honey in the Honeycomb." Ashbe begins snapping her fingers.)* Yikes, let's jazz it out. *(They dance.)*

John Polk: Hey, I'm not good or anything—

Ashbe: John Polk.

John Polk: Yeah?

Ashbe: Baby, I think you dance fine! *(They dance on, laughing, saying what they want till end of song. Then a radio announcer comes on and says the 12:00 news will be in five minutes. Billie Holiday or Terry Pierce begins singing, "Am I Blue?")*

John Polk: Dance?

Ashbe: News in five minutes.

John Polk: Yeah.

Ashbe: That means five minutes till midnight.

John Polk: Yeah, I know.

Ashbe: Then you're not—

John Polk: Ashbe, I've never danced all night. Wouldn't it be something to—to dance all night and watch the rats come out of the gutter?

Ashbe: Rats?

John Polk: Don't they come out at night? I hear New Orleans has lots of rats.

Ashbe: Yeah, yeah, it's got lots of rats.

John Polk: Then let's dance all night and wait for them to come out.

Ashbe: All right—but, but how about our feet?

John Polk: Feet?

Ashbe: They'll hurt.

John Polk: Yeah.

Ashbe *(Smiling.):* Okay, then let's dance. *(He takes her hand, and they dance as lights black out and the music soars and continues to play.)*

Explorations of the Text

1. Characterize John Polk and Ashbe. Focus on their gestures, actions, appearance, and dialogue.
2. How are they different from each other? What are their inner conflicts? What are their conflicts with each other?

3. How does their encounter change them?
4. Discuss the symbolism of the dance and of the song "Am I Blue?" in the denouement of the play.
5. What views of identity, family, and relationships emerge in the play?
6. Does the time frame (November 1968) provide clues as to themes of the drama?

The Reading/Writing Connection

1. "Think" Topic: Are John Polk and Ashbe "orphans" even though they are members of families? Respond to this question in a paragraph.
2. What happens to John Polk and Ashbe? Create another scene for this one-act play.

Ideas for Writing

1. Discuss music as a motif in this drama.
2. Write a character analysis of either John Polk or Ashbe. Focus on their appearance, gestures, dialogue, interactions with each other.
3. Contrast the relationship of John Polk and Ashbe with that of Betty and Bill in "Sure Thing."

SORRY

FROM *FOR COLORED GIRLS WHO HAVE CONSIDERED SUICIDE / WHEN THE RAINBOW IS ENUF*

Ntozake Shange

Ntozake Shange (1948–) was born in Brooklyn, New York, and educated at Barnard College and the University of California. Shange is best known for her 1977 "chorepoem,"[1] for colored girls who have considered suicide / when the rainbow is enuf, *which won an Obie award. Her subsequent publications include more chorepoems,* three pieces *(1981), and a poem,* I live in music *(1994). Shange has taught at colleges including Sonoma College, Mills College, and the University of California at Berkeley. She has been named Woman of the Year by* Mademoiselle *magazine and has received the Audelco Award for Best Playwright from the Black Theater Alliance.*

1977

[1] A form of drama in which poetry, music, and dance are intertwined.

lady in blue

one thing i dont need
is any more apologies
i got sorry greetin me at my front door
you can keep yrs
i dont know what to do wit em
they dont open doors
or bring the sun back
they dont make me happy
or get a morning paper
didnt nobody stop usin my tears to wash cars
cuz a sorry

i am simply tired
of collectin
　　　　‘i didn’t know
　　　　i was so important to you’
I’m gonna haveta throw some away
i cant get to the clothes in my closet
for alla the sorries
i’m gonna tack a sign to my door
leave a message by the phone
　　　　‘if you called
　　　　to say yr sorry
　　　　call somebody
　　　　else
　　　　i dont use em anymore’
i let sorry/didnt meanta/& how cd i know abt that
take a walk down a dark & musty street in brooklyn
i’m gonna do exactly what i want to
& i wont be sorry for none of it
letta sorry soothe yr soul/i’m gonna soothe mine

you were always inconsistent
doing something & then bein sorry
beatin my heart to death
talkin bout you sorry
well
i will not call
i’m not goin to be nice
i will raise my voice
& scream & holler
& break things & race the engine
& tell all yr secrets bout yrself to yr face
& i will list in detail everyone of my wonderful lovers

& their ways
i will play oliver lake
loud
& i wont be sorry for none of it

i loved you on purpose
i was open on purpose
i still crave vulnerability & close talk
& i'm not even sorry bout you bein sorry

you can carry all the guilt & grime ya wanna
just dont give it to me
i cant use another sorry
next time
you should admit
you're mean/low-down/triflin/& no count straight
out
steada being sorry alla the time
enjoy being yrself

Explorations of the Text

1. Discuss the point of view and the tone of the speaker, the lady in blue.
2. What is the speaker's attitude toward her lover?
3. What is the impact of the informal language, the idiosyncratic spelling, and the verse form?
4. What realization does the speaker experience?

The Reading/Writing Connection

1. In a journal entry, characterize the speaker. Imagine her dress, gestures, and actions.
2. Create a portrait of the speaker's "beloved." Write a monologue in his voice.

Ideas for Writing

1. Compare the speaker's voice and tone with that of the persona in "I Take You an Orange."
2. Contrast Betty in "Sure Thing" and Ashbe in "Am I Blue" with the lady in blue.
3. Compare this performance piece with that of "Twilight Bey" in chapter 7. What do you notice about treatment of persona, voice, action, and gestures?

NONFICTION

The Sexes from *The Symposium*

Plato Translated by Walter Hamilton

Plato (428–347 B.C.) was born in Athens, Greece, and studied with Socrates. After the latter's execution for heresy in 399 B.C., Plato left Athens for a number of years but returned to found the Academy, often considered the first university. Plato taught philosophy and mathematics there until his death. One of the world's great philosophers, Plato wrote many treatises in the form of dialogues among Socrates and other figures in which the philosopher and his circle debate central, metaphysical questions. In the Symposium, *the dialogue concerns the true nature of love.*

c. 387–367 B.C.

Well, Eryximachus," began Aristophanes,[1] "it is quite true that I intend to take a different line from you and Pausanias. Men seem to me to be utterly insensible of the power of Love; otherwise he would have had the largest temples and altars and the largest sacrifices. As it is, he has none of these things, though he deserves them most of all. For of all the gods he is the most friendly to man, and his helper and physician in those diseases whose cure constitutes the greatest happiness of the human race. I shall therefore try to initiate you into the secret of his power, and you in turn shall teach others.

"First of all, you must learn the constitution of man and the modifications which it has undergone, for originally it was different from what it is now. In the first place there were three sexes, not, as with us, two, male and female; the third partook of the nature of both the others and has vanished, though its name survives. The hermaphrodite was a distinct sex in form as well as in name, with the characteristics of both male and female, but now the name alone remains, and that solely as a term of abuse. Secondly, each human being was a rounded whole, with double back and flanks forming a complete circle; it has four hands and an equal number of legs, and two identically similar faces upon a circular neck, with one head common to both the faces, which were turned in opposite directions. It had four ears and two organs of generation and everything else to correspond. These people could walk upright like us in either direction, backwards or forwards, but when they wanted to run quickly they used all their eight limbs, and turned rapidly over and over in a circle, like tumblers who perform a cart-wheel and return to an upright position. The reason

[1] Aristophanes (448?–385? B.C.), Athenian comic playwright. Eryximachus, Pausanias (following), and Agathon and Socrates (later) are other participants at the banquet, where love is the topic of discussion.

for the existence of three sexes and for their being of such a nature is that originally the male sprang from the sun and the female from the earth, while the sex which was both male and female came from the moon, which partakes of the nature of both sun and earth. Their circular shape and their hoop-like method of progression were both due to the fact that they were like their parents. Their strength and vigour made them very formidable, and their pride was overweening; they attacked the gods, and Homer's story of Ephialtes and Otus attempting to climb up to heaven and set upon the gods is related also of these beings.[2]

"So Zeus and the other gods debated what was to be done with them. For a long time they were at a loss, unable to bring themselves either to kill them by lightning, as they had the giants, and extinguish the race—thus depriving themselves for ever of the honours and sacrifice due from humanity—or to let them go on in their insolence. At last, after much painful thought, Zeus had an idea. "I think," he said, "that I have found a way by which we can allow the human race to continue to exist and also put an end to their wickedness by making them weaker. I will cut each of them in two; in this way they will be weaker, and at the same time more profitable to us by being more numerous. They shall walk upright upon two legs. If there is any sign of wantonness in them after that, and they will not keep quiet, I will bisect them again, and they shall hop on one leg." With these words he cut the members of the human race in half, just like fruit which is to be dried and preserved, or like eggs which are cut with a hair. As he bisected each, he bade Apollo turn round the face and the half-neck attached to it towards the cut side, so that the victim, having the evidence of bisection before his eyes, might behave better in the future. He also bade him heal the wounds. So Apollo turned round the faces, and gathering together the skin, like a purse with drawstrings, on to what is now called the belly, he tied it tightly in the middle of the belly round a single aperture which men call the navel. He smoothed out the other wrinkles, which were numerous, and moulded the chest with a tool like those which cobblers use to smooth wrinkles in the leather on their last. But he left a few on the belly itself round the navel, to remind man of the state from which he had fallen.

"Man's original body having been thus cut in two, each half yearned for the half from which it had been severed. When they met they threw their arms round one another and embraced, in their longing to grow together again, and they perished of hunger and general neglect of their concerns, because they would not do anything apart. When one member of a pair died and the other was left, the latter sought after and embraced another partner, which might be the half either of a female whole (what is now called a woman) or a male. So they went on perishing till Zeus took pity on them, and hit upon a second plan. He moved their reproductive organs to the front: hitherto they had been placed on the outer side of their bodies, and the processes of begetting and birth had

---

[2] Giants Ephialtes and Otus tried to climb to heaven by piling mountain upon mountain.

been carried on not by the physical union of the sexes, but by emission on to the ground, as is the case with grasshoppers. By moving their genitals to the front, as they are now, Zeus made it possible for reproduction to take place by the intercourse of the male with the female. His object in making this change was twofold; if male coupled with female, children might be begotten and the race thus continued, but if male coupled with male, at any rate the desire for intercourse would be satisfied, and men set free from it to turn to other activities and to attend to the rest of the business of life. It is from this distant epoch, then, that we may date the innate love which human beings feel for one another, the love which restores us to our ancient state by attempting to weld two beings into one and to heal the wounds which humanity suffered.

5 "Each of us then is the mere broken tally of a man, the result of a bisection which has reduced us to a condition like that of flat fish, and each of us is perpetually in search of his corresponding tally. Those men who are halves of a being of the common sex, which was called, as I told you, hermaphrodite, are lovers of women, and most adulterers come from this class, as also do women who are mad about men and sexually promiscuous. Women who are halves of a female whole direct their affections towards women and pay little attention to men; Lesbians belong to this category. But those who are halves of a male whole pursue males, and being slices, so to speak, of the male, love men throughout their boyhood, and take pleasure in physical contact with men. Such boys and lads are the best of their generation, because they are the most manly. Some people say that they are shameless, but they are wrong. It is not shamelessness which inspires their behaviour, but high spirit and manliness and virility, which lead them to welcome the society of their own kind. A striking proof of this is that such boys alone, when they reach maturity, engage in public life. When they grow to be men, they become lovers of boys, and it requires the compulsion of convention to overcome their natural disinclination to marriage and procreation; they are quite content to live with one another unwed. In a word, such persons are devoted to lovers in boyhood and themselves lovers of boys in manhood, because they always cleave to what is akin to themselves.

"Whenever the lover of boys—or any other person for that matter—has the good fortune to encounter his own actual other half, affection and kinship and love combined inspire in him an emotion which is quite overwhelming, and such a pair practically refuse ever to be separated even for a moment. It is people like these who form lifelong partnerships, although they would find it difficult to say what they hope to gain from one another's society. No one can suppose that it is mere physical enjoyment which causes the one to take such intense delight in the company of the other. It is clear that the soul of each has some other longing which it cannot express, but can only surmise and obscurely hint at. Suppose Hephaestus with his tools were to visit them as they lie together, and stand over them and ask: "What is it, mortals, that you hope to gain from one another?" Suppose too that when they could not answer he repeated his question in these terms: "Is the object of your desire to be always together as much as possible, and never to be separated from one another day or night? If that is what you want, I am ready to melt and weld you together, so that, instead of two, you shall be one flesh; as long as you live you shall live a common life, and when you die, you shall suffer a common death, and be still one, not two, even in the next world. Would such a fate as this content you, and satisfy your longings?" We know what their answer would be; no one would refuse the offer; it would be plain that this is what everybody wants, and everybody would regard it as the precise expression of the desire which he had long felt but had been unable to formulate, that he should melt into his beloved, and that henceforth they should be one being instead of two. The reason is that this was our primitive condition when we were wholes, and love is simply the name of the desire and pursuit of the whole. Originally, as I say, we were whole beings, before our wickedness caused us to be split by Zeus, as the Arcadians have been split apart by the Spartans.[3] We have reason to fear that if we do not behave ourselves in the sight of heaven, we may be split in two again, like dice which are bisected for tallies, and go about like the people represented in profile on tombstones, sawn in two vertically down the line of our noses. That is why we ought to exhort everyone to conduct himself reverently towards the gods; we shall thus escape a worse fate, and even win the blessing which Love has in his power to bestow, if we take him for our guide and captain. Let no man set himself in opposition to Love—which is the same thing as incurring the hatred of the gods—for if we are his friends and make our peace with him, we shall succeed, as few at present succeed, in finding the person to love who in the strictest sense belongs to us. I know that Eryximachus is anxious to make fun of my speech, but he is not to suppose that in saying this I am pointing at Pausanias and Agathon. They may, no doubt, belong to this class, for they are both unquestionably halves of male wholes, but I am speaking of men and women in general when I say that the way to happiness for our race lies in fulfilling the behests of Love, and in each finding for himself the mate who properly belongs to him; in a word, in returning to our original condition. If that condition was the best, it follows that it is best for us to come as near to it as our present circumstances allow; and the way to do that is to find a sympathetic and congenial object for our affections.

"If we are to praise the god who confers this benefit upon us, it is to Love that our praises should be addressed. It is Love who is the author of our well-being in this present life, by leading us towards what is akin to us, and it is Love who gives us a sure hope that, if we conduct ourselves well in the sight of heaven, he will hereafter make us blessed and happy by restoring us to our former state and healing our wounds.

"There is my speech about Love, Eryximachus, and you will see that it is of quite a different type from yours. Remember my request, and don't make fun of it, but let us hear what each of the others has to say. I should have said 'each of the other two,' for only Agathon and Socrates are left."

[3] The conquering Spartans forced the residents of the Arcadian city of Mantinea to live in four separate villages.

Explorations of the Text

1. Explore the descriptions of the "three sexes," particularly of the "third" sex. How do you react to this description?
2. Describe this myth of the "fall." Compare it to the Biblical creation story and to the fall of Adam and Eve.
3. What is the concept of the "bisection"? How does Aristophanes explain homosexuality and heterosexuality?
4. How does the myth account for love?
5. What will happen if human beings set themselves "in opposition to Love"?
6. According to Aristophanes, what is "the way to happiness" for the race? Why?
7. What are Aristophanes's point of view and tone? Find key words and phrases that reveal his perspective.

The Reading/Writing Connection

1. Create a myth or a fable that provides an explanation for one of the following: a) Why people fall in love; b) The nature of love or relationships; c) The nature of gender roles.
2. "Think" Topic: Take issue with one point in this treatise. Construct a counterargument.

Ideas for Writing

1. Agree or disagree with Aristophanes that happiness lies in "fulfilling the behests of love" and in finding the proper mate.
2. Are we only "half" selves, yearning for completion through our mates or through our love relationships?
3. Compare Aristophanes's (Plato's) views of love with the view in one of the love poems in this chapter.
4. Write in the persona of a character in one of the works in this chapter, and respond to Aristophanes's idea of love.

No Name Woman

Maxine Hong Kingston

Maxine Hong Kingston (1940–) was born in Stockton, California, to parents who immigrated from China. After graduating from the University of California, Kingston moved to Hawaii and taught in secondary schools, colleges, and the University of Hawaii. The Woman Warrior: Memoirs of a Girlhood Among Ghosts, *published in 1976, won the National Book Critics Circle Award. Her second autobiographical volume,* China Men, *was published in 1980. Kingston released her first novel,* Tripmaster Monkey, *in 1989. She now writes full time.*

1976

"You must not tell anyone," my mother said, "what I am about to tell you. In China your father had a sister who killed herself. She jumped into the family well. We say that your father has all brothers because it is as if she had never been born.

"In 1924 just a few days after our village celebrated seventeen hurry-up weddings—to make sure that every young man who went 'out on the road' would responsibly come home—your father and his brothers and your grandfather and his brothers and your aunt's new husband sailed for America, the Gold Mountain. It was your grandfather's last trip. Those lucky enough to get contracts waved good-bye from the decks. They fed and guarded the stowaways and helped them off in Cuba, New York, Bali, Hawaii. "We'll meet in California next year," they said. All of them sent money home.

"I remember looking at your aunt one day when she and I were dressing; I had not noticed before that she had such a protruding melon of a stomach. But I did not think, 'She's pregnant,' until she began to look like other pregnant women, her shirt pulling and the white tops of her black pants showing. She could not have been pregnant, you see, because her husband had been gone for years. No one said anything. We did not discuss it. In early summer she was ready to have the child, long after the time when it could have been possible.

"The village had also been counting. On the night the baby was to be born the villagers raided our house. Some were crying. Like a great saw, teeth strung with lights, files of people walked zigzag across our land, tearing the rice. Their lanterns doubled in the disturbed black water, which drained away through the broken bunds. As the villagers closed in, we could see that some of them, probably men and women we knew well, wore white masks. The people with long hair hung it over their faces. Women with short hair made it stand up on end. Some had tied white bands around their foreheads, arms, and legs.

5 "At first they threw mud and rocks at the house. Then they threw eggs and began slaughtering our stock. We could hear the animals scream their deaths—the roosters, the pigs, a last great roar from the ox. Familiar wild heads flared in our night windows; the villagers encircled us. Some of the faces stopped to peer at us, their eyes rushing like searchlights. The hands flattened against the panes, framed heads, and left red prints.

"The villagers broke in the front and the back doors at the same time, even though we had not locked the doors against them. Their knives dripped with the blood of our animals. They smeared blood on the doors and walls. One woman swung a chicken, whose throat she had slit, splattering blood in red arcs about her. We stood together in the middle of our house, in the family hall with the pictures and tables of the ancestors around us, and looked straight ahead.

"At that time the house had only two wings. When the men came back, we would build two more to enclose our courtyard and a third one to begin a second courtyard. The villagers pushed through both wings, even your grandparents' rooms, to find your aunt's, which was also mine until the men returned. From this room a new wing for one of the younger families would grow. They ripped up her clothes and shoes and broke her combs, grinding them underfoot. They tore her work from the loom. They scattered the cooking fire and rolled the new weaving in it. We could hear them in the kitchen breaking our bowls and banging the pots. They overturned the great waist-high earthenware jugs; duck eggs, pickled fruits, vegetables burst out and mixed in acrid torrents. The old woman from the next field swept a broom through the air and loosed the spirits-of-the-broom over our heads. 'Pig.' 'Ghost.' 'Pig,' they sobbed and scolded while they ruined our house.

"When they left, they took sugar and oranges to bless themselves. They cut pieces from the dead animals. Some of them took bowls that were not broken and clothes that were not torn. Afterward we swept up the rice and sewed it back up into sacks. But the smells from the spilled preserves lasted. Your aunt gave birth in the pigsty that night. The next morning when I went for the water, I found her and the baby plugging up the family well.

"Don't let your father know that I told you. He denies her. Now that you have started to menstruate, what happened to her could happen to you. Don't humiliate us. You wouldn't like to be forgotten as if you had never been born. The villagers are watchful."

10 Whenever she had to warn us about life, my mother told stories that ran like this one, a story to grow up on. She tested our strength to establish realities. Those in the emigrant generations who could not reassert brute survival died young and far from home. Those of us in the first American generations have had to figure out how the invisible world the emigrants built around our childhoods fit in solid America.

The emigrants confused the gods by diverting their curses, misleading them with crooked streets and false names. They must try to confuse their offspring as well, who, I suppose, threaten them in similar ways—always trying to get things straight, always trying to name the unspeakable. The Chinese I know hide their names; sojourners take new names when their lives change and guard their real names with silence.

Chinese-Americans, when you try to understand what things in you are Chinese, how do you separate what is peculiar to childhood, to poverty, insanities, one family, your mother who marked your growing with stories, from what is Chinese? What is Chinese tradition and what is the movies?

If I want to learn what clothes my aunt wore, whether flashy or ordinary, I would have to begin, "Remember Father's drowned-in-the-well sister?" I cannot ask that. My mother has told me once and for all the useful parts. She will add nothing unless powered by Necessity, a riverbank that guides her life. She plants vegetable gardens rather than lawns; she carries the odd-shaped tomatoes home from the fields and eats food left for the gods.

Whenever we did frivolous things, we used up energy; we flew high kites. We children came up off the ground over the melting cones our parents brought home from work and the American movie on New Year's Day—*Oh, You Beautiful Doll* with Betty Grable one year, and *She Wore a Yellow Ribbon* with John Wayne another year. After the one carnival ride each, we paid in guilt; our tired father counted his change on the dark walk home.

15 Adultery is extravagance. Could people who hatch their own chicks and eat the embryos and the heads for delicacies and boil the feet in vinegar for party food, leaving only the gravel, eating even the gizzard lining—could such people engender a prodigal aunt? To be a woman, to have a daughter in starvation time was a waste enough. My aunt could not have been the lone romantic who gave up everything for sex. Women in the old China did not choose. Some man had commanded her to lie with him and be his secret evil. I wonder whether he masked himself when he joined the raid on her family.

Perhaps she encountered him in the fields or on the mountain where the daughters-in-law collected fuel. Or perhaps he first noticed her in the marketplace. He was not a stranger because the village housed no strangers. She had to have dealings with him other than sex. Perhaps he worked an adjoining field, or he sold her the cloth for the dress she sewed and wore. His demand must have surprised, then terrified her. She obeyed him; she always did as she was told.

When the family found a young man in the next village to be her husband, she stood tractably beside the best rooster, his proxy, and promised before they met that she would be his forever. She was lucky that he was her age and she would be the first wife, an advantage secure now. The night she first saw him, he had sex with her. Then he left for America. She had almost forgotten what he looked like. When she tried to envision him, she only saw the black and white face in the group photograph the men had had taken before leaving.

The other man was not, after all, much different from her husband. They both gave orders: she followed. "If you tell your family, I'll beat you. I'll kill you. Be here again next week." No one talked sex, ever. And she might have separated the rapes from the rest of living if only she did not have to buy her oil from him or gather wood in the same forest. I want her fear to have lasted just as long as rape lasted so that the fear could have been contained. No drawn-out fear. But women at sex hazarded birth and hence lifetimes. The fear did not stop but permeated everywhere. She told the man, "I think I'm pregnant." He organized the raid against her.

On nights when my mother and father talked about their life back home, sometimes they mentioned an "outcast table" whose business they still seemed to be settling, their voices tight. In a commensal tradition,[1] where food is precious, the powerful older people made wrongdoers eat alone. Instead of letting them start separate new lives like the Japanese, who could become samurais and geishas, the Chinese family, faces averted but eyes glowering sideways, hung on to the offenders and fed them leftovers. My aunt must have lived in the same house as my parents and eaten at an outcast table. My mother spoke

[1] A tradition that values communal meals—people's sharing of meals.

about the raid as if she had seen it, when she and my aunt, a daughter-in-law to a different household, should not have been living together at all. Daughters-in-law lived with their husbands' parents, not their own; a synonym for marriage in Chinese is "taking a daughter-in-law." Her husband's parents could have sold her, mortgaged her, stoned her. But they had sent her back to her own mother and father, a mysterious act hinting at disgraces not told me. Perhaps they had thrown her out to deflect the avengers.

20 She was the only daughter; her four brothers went with her father, husband, and uncles "out on the road" and for some years became western men. When the goods were divided among the family, three of the brothers took land, and the youngest, my father, chose an education. After my grandparents gave their daughter away to her husband's family, they had dispensed all the adventure and all the property. They expected her alone to keep the traditional ways, which her brothers, now among the barbarians, could fumble without detection. The heavy, deep-rooted women were to maintain the past against the flood, safe for returning. But the rare urge west had fixed upon our family, and so my aunt crossed boundaries not delineated in space.

The work of preservation demands that the feelings playing about in one's guts not be turned into action. Just watch their passing like cherry blossoms. But perhaps my aunt, my forerunner, caught in a slow life, let dreams grow and fade and after some months or years went toward what persisted. Fear at the enormities of the forbidden kept her desires delicate, wire and bone. She looked at a man because she liked the way the hair was tucked behind his ears, or she liked the question-mark line of a long torso curving at the shoulder and straight at the hip. For warm eyes or a soft voice or a slow walk—that's all—a few hairs, a line, a brightness, a sound, a pace, she gave up family. She offered us up for a charm that vanished with tiredness, a pigtail that didn't toss when the wind died. Why, the wrong lighting could erase the dearest thing about him.

It could very well have been, however, that my aunt did not take subtle enjoyment of her friend, but, a wild woman, kept rollicking company. Imagining her free with sex doesn't fit, though. I don't know any women like that, or men either. Unless I see her life branching into mine, she gives me no ancestral help.

To sustain her being in love, she often worked at herself in the mirror, guessing at the colors and shapes that would interest him, changing them frequently in order to hit on the right combination. She wanted him to look back.

On a farm near the sea, a woman who tended her appearance reaped a reputation for eccentricity. All the married women blunt-cut their hair in flaps about their ears or pulled it back in tight buns. No nonsense. Neither style blew easily into heart-catching tangles. And at their weddings they displayed themselves in their long hair for the last time. "It brushed the backs of my knees," my mother tells me. "It was braided, and even so, it brushed the backs of my knees."

25 At the mirror my aunt combed individuality into her bob. A bun could have been contrived to escape into black streamers blowing in the wind or in

quiet wisps about her face, but only the older women in our picture album wear buns. She brushed her hair back from her forehead, tucking the flaps behind her ears. She looped a piece of thread, knotted into a circle between her index fingers and thumbs, and ran the double strand across her forehead. When she closed her fingers as if she were making a pair of shadow geese bite, the string twisted together catching the little hairs. Then she pulled the thread away from her skin, ripping the hairs out neatly, her eyes watering from the needles of pain. Opening her fingers, she cleaned the thread, then rolled it along her hairline and the tops of her eyebrows. My mother did the same to me and my sisters and herself. I used to believe that the expression "caught by the short hairs" meant a captive held with a depilatory string. It especially hurt at the temples, but my mother said we were lucky we didn't have to have our feet bound when we were seven. Sisters used to sit on their beds and cry together, she said, as their mothers or their slaves removed the bandages for a few minutes each night and let the blood gush back into their veins. I hope that the man my aunt loved appreciated a smooth brow, that he wasn't just a tits-and-ass man.

Once my aunt found a freckle on her chin, at a spot that the almanac said predestined her for unhappiness. She dug it out with a hot needle and washed the wound with peroxide.

More attention to her looks than these pullings of hairs and pickings at spots would have caused gossip among the villagers. They owned work clothes and good clothes, and they wore good clothes for feasting the new seasons. But since a woman combing her hair hexes beginnings, my aunt rarely found an occasion to look her best. Women looked like great sea snails—the corded wood, babies, and laundry they carried were the whorls on their backs. The Chinese did not admire a bent back: goddesses and warriors stood straight. Still there must have been a marvelous freeing of beauty when a worker laid down her burden and stretched and arched.

Such commonplace loveliness, however, was not enough for my aunt. She dreamed of a lover for the fifteen days of New Year's, the time for families to exchange visits, money, and food. She plied her secret comb. And sure enough she cursed the year, the family, the village, and herself.

Even as her hair lured her imminent lover, many other men looked at her. Uncles, cousins, nephews, brothers would have looked, too, had they been home between journeys. Perhaps they had already been restraining their curiosity, and they left, fearful that their glances, like a field of nesting birds, might be startled and caught. Poverty hurt, and that was their first reason for leaving. But another, final reason for leaving the crowded house was the never-said.

30 She may have been unusually beloved, the precious only daughter, spoiled and mirror gazing because of the affection the family lavished on her. When her husband left, they welcomed the chance to take her back from the in-laws; she could live like the little daughter for just a while longer. There are stories that my grandfather was different from other people, "crazy ever since the little Jap bayoneted him in the head." He used to put his naked penis on the dinner table, laughing. And one day he brought home a baby girl, wrapped up

inside his brown western-style greatcoat. He had traded one of his sons, probably my father, the youngest, for her. My grandmother made him trade back. When he finally got a daughter of his own, he doted on her. They must have all loved her, except perhaps my father, the only brother who never went back to China, having once been traded for a girl.

Brothers and sisters, newly men and women, had to efface their sexual color and present plain miens.[2] Disturbing hair and eyes, a smile like no other threatened the ideal of five generations living under one roof. To focus blurs, people shouted face to face and yelled from room to room. The immigrants I know have loud voices, unmodulated to American tones even after years away from the village where they called their friendships out across the fields. I have not been able to stop my mother's screams in public libraries or over telephones. Walking erect (knees straight, toes pointed forward, not pigeon-toed, which is Chinese-feminine) and speaking in an inaudible voice, I have tried to turn myself American-feminine. Chinese communication was loud, public. Only sick people had to whisper. But at the dinner table, where the family members came nearest one another, no one could talk, not the outcasts nor any eaters. Every word that falls from the mouth is a coin lost. Silently they gave and accepted food with both hands. A preoccupied child who took his bowl with one hand got a sideways glare. A complete moment of total attention is due everyone alike. Children and lovers have no singularity here, but my aunt used a secret voice, a separate attentiveness.

She kept the man's name to herself throughout her labor and dying; she did not accuse him that he be punished with her. To save her inseminator's name she gave silent birth.

He may have been somebody in her own household, but intercourse with a man outside the family would have been no less abhorrent. All the village were kinsmen, and the titles shouted in loud country voices never let kinship be forgotten. Any man within visiting distance would have been neutralized as a lover—"brother," "younger brother," "older brother"—one hundred and fifteen relationship titles. Parents researched birth charts probably not so much to assure good fortune as to circumvent incest in a population that has but one hundred surnames. Everybody has eight million relatives. How useless then sexual mannerisms, how dangerous.

As if it came from an atavism[3] deeper than fear, I used to add "brother" silently to boys' names. It hexed the boys, who would or would not ask me to dance, and made them less scary and as familiar and deserving of benevolence as girls.

35 But, of course, I hexed myself also—no dates. I should have stood up, both arms waving, and shouted out across libraries, "Hey, you! Love me back." I had no idea, though, how to make attraction selective, how to control its direction and magnitude. If I made myself American-pretty so that the five or

---

[2] Looks.

[3] Reversion to a primitive or an earlier type (or ancestral form).

six Chinese boys in the class fell in love with me, everyone else—the Caucasian, Negro, and Japanese boys—would too. Sisterliness, dignified and honorable, made much more sense.

Attraction eludes control so stubbornly that whole societies designed to organize relationships among people cannot keep order, not even when they bind people to one another from childhood and raise them together. Among the very poor and the wealthy, brothers married their adopted sisters, like doves. Our family allowed some romance, paying adult brides' prices and providing dowries so that their sons and daughters could marry strangers. Marriage promises to turn strangers into friendly relatives—a nation of siblings.

In the village structure, spirits shimmered among the live creatures, balanced and held in equilibrium by time and land. But one human being flaring up into violence could open up a black hole, a maelstrom that pulled in the sky. The frightened villagers, who depended on one another to maintain the real, went to my aunt to show her a personal, physical representation of the break she had made in the "roundness." Misallying couples snapped off the future, which was to be embodied in true offspring. The villagers punished her for acting as if she could have a private life, secret and apart from them.

If my aunt had betrayed the family at a time of large grain yields and peace, when many boys were born, and wings were being built on many houses, perhaps she might have escaped such severe punishment. But the men—hungry, greedy, tired of planting in dry soil, cuckolded—had had to leave the village in order to send food-money home. There were ghost plagues, bandit plagues, wars with the Japanese, floods. My Chinese brother and sister had died of an unknown sickness. Adultery, perhaps only a mistake during good times, became a crime when the village needed food.

The round moon cakes and round doorways, the round tables of graduated size that fit one roundness inside another, round windows and rice bowls—these talismen had lost their power to warn this family of the law: a family must be whole, faithfully keeping the descent line by having sons to feed the old and the dead, who in turn look after the family. The villagers came to show my aunt and her lover-in-hiding a broken house. The villagers were speeding up the circling of events because she was too shortsighted to see that her infidelity had already harmed the village, that waves of consequences would return unpredictably, sometimes in disguise, as now, to hurt her. This roundness had to be made coin-sized so that she would see its circumference: punish her at the birth of her baby. Awaken her to the inexorable. People who refused fatalism because they could invent small resources insisted on culpability. Deny accidents and wrest fault from the stars.

40 After the villagers left, their lanterns now scattering in various directions toward home, the family broke their silence and cursed her. "Aiaa, we're going to die. Death is coming. Death is coming. Look what you've done. You've killed us. Ghost! Dead ghost! You've never been born." She ran out into the fields, far enough from the house so that she could no longer hear their voices, and pressed herself against the earth, her own land no more. When she felt the birth coming, she thought that she had been hurt. Her body seized together. "They've hurt me too much," she thought. "This is gall, and it will kill

me." Her forehead and knees against the earth, her body convulsed and then released her onto her back. The black well of sky and stars went out and out and out forever; her body and her complexity seemed to disappear. She was one of the stars, a bright dot in blackness, without home, without a companion, in eternal cold and silence. An agoraphobia rose in her, speeding higher and higher, bigger and bigger; she would not be able to contain it; there would be no end to fear.

Flayed, unprotected against space, she felt pain return, focusing her body. This pain chilled her—a cold, steady kind of surface pain. Inside, spasmodically, the other pain, the pain of the child, heated her. For hours she lay on the ground, alternately body and space. Sometimes a vision of normal comfort obliterated reality: she saw the family in the evening gambling at the dinner table, the young people massaging their elders' backs. She saw them congratulating one another, high joy on the mornings the rice shoots came up. When these pictures burst, the stars drew yet further apart. Black space opened.

She got to her feet to fight better and remembered that old-fashioned women gave birth in their pigsties to fool the jealous, pain-dealing gods, who do not snatch piglets. Before the next spasms could stop her, she ran to the pigsty, each step a rushing out into emptiness. She climbed over the fence and knelt in the dirt. It was good to have a fence enclosing her, a tribal person alone.

Laboring, this woman who had carried her child as a foreign growth that sickened her every day, expelled it at last. She reached down to touch the hot, wet, moving mass, surely smaller than anything human, and could feel that it was human after all—fingers, toes, nails, nose. She pulled it up on to her belly, and it lay curled there, butt in the air, feet precisely tucked one under the other. She opened her loose shirt and buttoned the child inside. After resting, it squirmed and thrashed and she pushed it up to her breast. It turned its head this way and that until it found her nipple. There, it made little snuffling noises. She clenched her teeth at its preciousness, lovely as a young calf, a piglet, a little dog.

She may have gone to the pigsty as a last act of responsibility: she would protect this child as she had protected its father. It would look after her soul, leaving supplies on her grave. But how would this tiny child without family find her grave when there would be no marker for her anywhere, neither in the earth nor the family hall? No one would give her a family hall name. She had taken the child with her into the wastes. At its birth the two of them had felt the same raw pain of separation, a wound that only the family pressing tight could close. A child with no descent line would not soften her life but only trail after her, ghostlike, begging her to give it purpose. At dawn the villagers on their way to the fields would stand around the fence and look.

45 Full of milk, the little ghost slept. When it awoke, she hardened her breasts against the milk that crying loosens. Toward morning she picked up the baby and walked to the well.

Carrying the baby to the well shows loving. Otherwise abandon it. Turn its face into the mud. Mothers who love their children take them along. It was probably a girl; there is some hope of forgiveness for boys.

"Don't tell anyone you had an aunt. Your father does not want to hear her name. She has never been born." I have believed that sex was unspeakable and words so strong and fathers so frail that "aunt" would do my father mysterious harm. I have thought that my family, having settled among immigrants who had also been their neighbors in the ancestral land, needed to clean their name, and a wrong word would incite the kinspeople even here. But there is more to this silence: they want me to participate in her punishment. And I have.

In the twenty years since I heard this story I have not asked for details nor said my aunt's name; I do not know it. People who can comfort the dead can also chase after them to hurt them further—a reverse ancestor worship. The real punishment was not the raid swiftly inflicted by the villagers, but the family's deliberately forgetting her. Her betrayal so maddened them, they saw to it that she would suffer forever, even after death. Always hungry, always needing, she would have to beg food from other ghosts, snatch and steal it from those whose living descendants give them gifts. She would have to fight the ghosts massed at crossroads for the buns a few thoughtful citizens leave to decoy her away from village and home so that the ancestral spirits could feast unharassed. At peace, they could act like gods, not ghosts, their descent lines providing them with paper suits and dresses, spirit money, paper houses, paper automobiles, chicken, meat, and rice into eternity—essences delivered up in smoke and flames, steam and incense rising from each rice bowl. In an attempt to make the Chinese care for people outside the family, Chairman Mao[4] encourages us now to give our paper replicas to the spirits of outstanding soldiers and workers, no matter whose ancestors they may be. My aunt remains forever hungry. Goods are not distributed evenly among the dead.

My aunt haunts me—her ghost drawn to me because now, after fifty years of neglect, I alone devote pages of paper to her, though not origamied[5] into houses and clothes. I do not think she always means me well. I am telling on her, and she was a spite suicide, drowning herself in the drinking water. The Chinese are always very frightened of the drowned one, whose weeping ghost, wet hair hanging and skin bloated, waits silently by the water to pull down a substitute.

Explorations of the Text

1. Why does the mother tell her story about the narrator's aunt? Why is the aunt considered to have "never been born"?
2. What are the conditions—social, cultural, economic, and personal—that drive the aunt to another man?
3. Why do the villagers storm and raid the house? What do the actions in the scene suggest about the villagers and their values?

[4] Chinese Communist leader (1893–1976).

[5] Origami, the Japanese art of decorative paper folding.

4. What is the purpose of storytelling for these first-generation Chinese American women? What additional motives for the mother's narrative emerge?
5. Why do Chinese "guard their real names with silence"? Why do they want to confuse the gods?
6. Explain: "Adultery is extravagance." Relate the statement to Chinese values and philosophy of life.
7. How does the daughter reinterpret the story of her aunt?
8. How does the daughter view her aunt as her precursor? Look at details of hair and appearance.
9. Why is the aunt's pregnancy so threatening to the society?
10. Why does the aunt give birth in a pigsty? Why does she drown herself and her baby in the well?
11. What are the attitudes toward sexuality, love, marriage, and women's roles in China at the time of this story?
12. Compare the aunt with Emiko in *And the Soul Shall Dance.*

The Reading/Writing Connection

1. Gloss and annotate the text and explore the theme of silence in "No Name Woman."
2. Explain the imagery of the ghost and of the "No Name Woman." Why does she have no name?

Ideas for Writing

1. Consider the title. What are views of language and of identity in this work? What do words mean to the daughter?
2. Write a short scene for a play in which the aunt, Minnie Wright, and Emiko talk with each other. Write monologues and/or dialogue for each character.
3. Examine the theme of initiation in "No Name Woman" and in *And the Soul Shall Dance.*

Woman as Other

Simone de Beauvoir

Simone de Beauvoir (1908–86) had a strict middle class, Catholic upbringing and traced the seeds of her feminism to her repugnance at that restricted social world. She studied philosophy at the Sorbonne, where she met Jean-Paul Sartre and began her career as a writer and as an existential philosopher. A prolific writer, a leftist, an intellectual, and an iconoclast, she wrote philosophical essays and memoirs, chronicling her personal, political, and intellectual development, as well as several novels, of which The Mandarins *(1954) won the* Prix Goncourt. *Her most famous work is* The Second Sex *(1949), one of the most important works of twentieth-century feminism.*

1949

What is a woman?

To state the question is, to me, to suggest, at once, a preliminary answer. The fact that I ask it is in itself significant. A man would never get the notion of writing a book on the peculiar situation of the human male. But if I wish to define myself, I must first of all say: "I am a woman"; on this truth must be based all further discussion. A man never begins by presenting himself as an individual of a certain sex; it goes without saying that he is a man. The terms *masculine* and *feminine* are used symmetrically only as a matter of form, as on legal papers. In actuality the relation of the two sexes is not quite like that of two electrical poles, for man represents both the positive and the neutral, as is indicated by the common use of *man* to designate human beings in general; whereas woman represents only the negative, defined by limiting criteria, without reciprocity. In the midst of an abstract discussion it is vexing to hear a man say: "You think thus and so because you are a woman"; but I know that my only defense is to reply: "I think thus and so because it is true," thereby removing my subjective self from the argument. It would be out of the question to reply: "And you think the contrary because you are a man," for it is understood that the fact of being a man is no peculiarity. A man is in the right in being a man; it is the woman who is in the wrong. It amounts to this: just as for the ancients there was an absolute vertical with reference to which the oblique was defined, so there is an absolute human type, the masculine. Woman has ovaries, a uterus; these peculiarities imprison her in her subjectivity, circumscribe her within the limits of her own nature. It is often said that she thinks with her glands. Man superbly ignores the fact that his anatomy also includes glands, such as the testicles, and that they secrete hormones. He thinks of his body as a direct and normal connection with the world, which he believes he apprehends objectively, whereas he regards the body of woman as a hindrance, a prison, weighed down by everything peculiar to it. "The female is a female by virtue of a certain *lack* of qualities," said Aristotle;[1] "we should regard the female nature as afflicted with a natural defectiveness." And St. Thomas[2] for his part pronounced women to be an "imperfect man," an "incidental" being. This is symbolized in Genesis where Eve is depicted as made from what Bossuet[3] called "a supernumerary bone" of Adam.

---

[1] Greek philosopher (384–322 B.C.).

[2] Saint Thomas Aquinas, ecclesiastical writer and philosopher (1224?-1225–1274).

[3] Jacques Bossuet, French bishop, defended the rights of the French church against papal authority. His literary works include *Funeral Panegyrics* and *Four Great Personages* (1627–1704).

Thus humanity is male and man defines woman not in herself but as relative to him; she is not regarded as an autonomous being. Michelet[4] writes: "Woman, the relative being. . . ." And Benda[5] is most positive in his *Rapport d'Uriel:* "The body of man makes sense in itself quite apart from that of woman, whereas the latter seems wanting in significance by itself. . . . Man can think of himself without woman. She cannot think of herself without man." And she is simply what man decrees; thus she is called "the sex," by which is meant that she appears essentially to the male as a sexual being. For him she is sex—absolute sex, no less. She is defined and differentiated with reference to man and not he with reference to her; she is the incidental, the inessential as opposed to the essential. He is the Subject, he is the Absolute—she is the Other.

The category of the *Other* is as primordial as consciousness itself. In the most primitive societies, in the most ancient mythologies, one finds the expression of a duality—that of the Self and the Other. This duality was not originally attached to the division of the sexes; it was not dependent upon any empirical facts. It is revealed in such works as that of Granet[6] on Chinese thought and those of Dumézil[7] on the East Indies and Rome. The feminine element was at first no more involved in such pairs as Varuna-Mitra, Uranus-Zeus, Sun-Moon, and Day-Night[8] than it was in the contrasts between Good and Evil, lucky and unlucky auspices, right and left, God and Lucifer. Otherness is a fundamental category of human thought.

5 Thus it is that no group ever sets itself up as the One without at once setting up the Other over against itself. If three travelers chance to occupy the same compartment, that is enough to make vaguely hostile "others" out of all the rest of the passengers on the train. In small-town eyes all persons not belonging to the village are "strangers" and suspect; to the native of a country all who inhabit other countries are "foreigners"; Jews are "different" for the anti-Semite, Negroes are "inferior" for American racists, aborigines are "natives" for colonists, proletarians are the "lower class" for the privileged.

Lévi-Strauss,[9] at the end of a profound work on the various forms of primitive societies, reaches the following conclusion: "Passage from the state of Nature to the state of Culture is marked by man's ability to view biological relations as a series of contrasts; duality, alternation, opposition, and symmetry, whether under definite or vague forms, constitute not so much phenomena to be explained as fundamental and immediately given data of social reality."

[4] French historian (1798–1874).

[5] Julian Benda, French novelist and philosopher (1867–1956).

[6] Francois Marius Granet, French painter and watercolorist (1775–1849).

[7] Expert on mythology.

[8] Varuna—Vedic god of skies and sea; Mitra—Vedic god of moon; Uranus—god/father of the Titans in Greek mythology; Zeus—king of the gods in Greek mythology; oppositions.

[9] Claude Lévi-Strauss, French anthropologist (1908–).

These phenomena would be incomprehensible if in fact human society were simply a *Mitsein* or fellowship based on solidarity and friendliness. Things become clear, on the contrary, if, following Hegel,[10] we find in consciousness itself a fundamental hostility toward every other consciousness; the subject can be posed only in being opposed—he sets himself up as the essential, as opposed to the other, the inessential, the object.

But the other consciousness, the other ego, sets up a reciprocal claim. The native traveling abroad is shocked to find himself in turn regarded as a "stranger" by the natives of neighboring countries. As a matter of fact, wars, festivals, trading, treaties, and contests among tribes, nations, and classes tend to deprive the concept *Other* of its absolute sense and to make manifest its relativity; willy-nilly, individuals and groups are forced to realize the reciprocity of their relations. How is it, then, that this reciprocity has not been recognized between the sexes, that one of the contrasting terms is set up as the sole essential, denying any relativity in regard to its correlative and defining the latter as pure otherness? Why is it that women do not dispute male sovereignty? No subject will readily volunteer to become the object, the inessential; it is not the Other who, in defining himself as the Other, establishes the One. The Other is posed as such by the One in defining himself as the One. But if the Other is not to regain the status of being the One, he must be submissive enough to accept this alien point of view. Whence comes this submission in the case of woman?

There are, to be sure, other cases in which a certain category has been able to dominate another completely for a time. Very often this privilege depends upon inequality of numbers—the majority imposes its rule upon the minority or persecutes it. But women are not a minority, like the American Negroes or the Jews; there are as many women as men on earth. Again, the two groups concerned have often been originally independent; they may have been formerly unaware of each other's existence, or perhaps they recognized each other's autonomy. But a historical event has resulted in the subjugation of the weaker by the stronger. The scattering of the Jews, the introduction of slavery into America, the conquests of imperialism are examples in point. In these cases the oppressed retained at least the memory of former days; they possessed in common a past, a tradition, sometimes a religion or a culture.

The parallel drawn by Bebel[11] between women and the proletariat is valid in that neither ever formed a minority or a separate collective unit of mankind. And instead of a single historical event it is in both cases a historical development that explains their status as a class and accounts for the membership of *particular individuals* in that class. But proletarians have not always existed, whereas there have always been women. They are women in virtue of their anatomy and physiology. Throughout history they have always

---

[10] Georg Wilhelm Friedrich Hegel, German philosopher who developed the theory of dialectic (1770–1831).

[11] August Bebel, German Social Democrat leader and writer (1840–1913).

been subordinated to men, and hence their dependency is not the result of a historical event or a social change—it was not something that *occurred.* The reason why otherness in this case seems to be an absolute is in part that it lacks the contingent or incidental nature of historical facts. A condition brought about at a certain time can be abolished at some other time, as the Negroes of Haiti[12] and others have proved; but it might seem that a natural condition is beyond the possibility of change. In truth, however, the nature of things is no more immutably given, once for all, than is historical reality. If woman seems to be the inessential which never becomes the essential, it is because she herself fails to bring about this change. Proletarians say "We"; Negroes also. Regarding themselves as subjects, they transform the bourgeois, the whites, into "others." But women do not say "We," except at some congress of feminists or similar formal demonstration; men say "women," and women use the same word in referring to themselves. They do not authentically assume a subjective attitude. The proletarians have accomplished the revolution in Russia, the Negroes in Haiti, the Indochinese are battling for it in Indochina;[13] but the women's effort has never been anything more than a symbolic agitation. They have gained only what men have been willing to grant; they have taken nothing, they have only received.

10 The reason for this is that women lack concrete means for organizing themselves into a unit which can stand face to face with the correlative unit. They have no past, no history, no religion of their own; and they have no such solidarity of work and interest as that of the proletariat. They are not even promiscuously herded together in the way that creates community feeling among the American Negroes, the ghetto Jews, the workers of Saint-Denis,[14] or the factory hands of Renault.[15] They live dispersed among the males, attached through residence, housework, economic condition, and social standing to certain men—fathers or husbands—more firmly than they are to other women. If they belong to the bourgeoisie, they feel solidarity with men of that class, not with proletarian women; if they are white, their allegiance is to white men, not to Negro women. The proletariat can propose to massacre the ruling class, and a sufficiently fanatical Jew or Negro might dream of getting sole possession of the atomic bomb and making humanity wholly Jewish or black; but woman cannot even dream of exterminating the males. The bond that unites her to her oppressors is not comparable to any other. The division of the sexes is a biological fact, not an event in human history. Male and female stand opposed within a primordial *Mitsein,* and woman has not broken it. The couple is a fundamental unity with its two halves riveted together, and the cleavage of society along the line of sex is impossible. Here is to be found the

[12] Country of the West Indies.

[13] Peninsula of Southeast Asia composed of Vietnam, Laos, Cambodia, Thailand, Burma, and the Malay Peninsula; name given to group of former French colonies.

[14] City in north central France, near Paris.

[15] French car manufacturer.

basic trait of woman: she is the Other in a totality of which the two components are necessary to one another.

One could suppose that this reciprocity might have facilitated the liberation of woman. When Hercules sat at the feet of Omphale[16] and helped with her spinning, his desire for her held him captive; but why did she fail to gain a lasting power? To revenge herself on Jason, Medea[17] killed their children: and this grim legend would seem to suggest that she might have obtained a formidable influence over him through his love for his offspring. In *Lysistrata* Aristophanes[18] gaily depicts a band of women who joined forces to gain social ends through the sexual needs of their men; but this is only a play. In the legend of the Sabine women,[19] the latter soon abandoned their plan of remaining sterile to punish their ravishers. In truth woman has not been socially emancipated through man's need—sexual desire and the desire for offspring—which makes the male dependent for satisfaction upon the female.

Master and slave, also, are united by a reciprocal need, in this case economic, which does not liberate the slave. In the relation of master to slave the master does not make a point of the need that he has for the other; he has in his grasp the power of satisfying this need through his own action; whereas the slave, in his dependent condition, his hope and fear, is quite conscious of the need he has for his master. Even if the need is at bottom equally urgent for both, it always works in favor of the oppressor and against the oppressed. That is why the liberation of the working class, for example, has been slow.

Now, woman has always been man's dependent, if not his slave; the two sexes have never shared the world in equality. And even today woman is heavily handicapped, though her situation is beginning to change. Almost nowhere is her legal status the same as man's, and frequently it is much to her disadvantage. Even when her rights are legally recognized in the abstract, long-standing custom prevents their full expression in the mores. In the economic sphere men and women can almost be said to make up two castes; other things being equal, the former hold the better jobs, get higher wages, and have more opportunity for success than their new competitors. In industry and politics men have a great many more positions and they monopolize the most important posts. In addition to all this, they enjoy a traditional prestige that the education of children tends in every way to support, for the present enshrines the past—and in the past all history has been made by men. At the present time,

---

[16] Hercules—hero of Greek mythology, known for his strength; as a punishment, Zeus condemned Hercules to serve as a slave to Queen Omphale, who required him to dress as a woman and to do women's chores.

[17] Jason—Thessalian hero who journeyed with the Argonauts in search of the Golden Fleece. Medea—a magician or sorceress who aided Jason and later murdered their two children when he betrayed her.

[18] Aristophanes—Athenian dramatist (448–380? B.C.). *Lysistrata,* a comedy by Aristophanes, features a rebellion by women who protest war by denying their husbands sexual favors.

[19] Allusion to the abduction of the Sabine women by the Romans (c. 290 B.C.).

when women are beginning to take part in the affairs of the world, it is still a world that belongs to men—they have no doubt of it at all and women have scarcely any. To decline to be the Other, to refuse to be a party to the deal—this would be for women to renounce all the advantages conferred upon them by their alliance with the superior caste. Man-the-sovereign will provide woman-the-liege with material protection and will undertake the moral justification of her existence; thus she can evade at once both economic risk and the metaphysical risk of a liberty in which ends and aims must be contrived without assistance. Indeed, along with the ethical urge of each individual to affirm his subjective existence, there is also the temptation to forgo liberty and become a thing. This is an inauspicious road, for he who takes it—passive, lost, ruined—becomes henceforth the creature of another's will, frustrated in his transcendence and deprived of every value. But it is an easy road; on it one avoids the strain involved in undertaking an authentic existence. When man makes of woman the *Other,* he may, then, expect her to manifest deep-seated tendencies toward complicity. Thus, woman may fail to lay claim to the status of subject because she lacks definite resources, because she feels the necessary bond that ties her to man regardless of reciprocity, and because she is often very well pleased with her role as the *Other.*

Explorations of the Text

1. Why does de Beauvoir begin with a question? with the need for definition?
2. Do you agree with her assessment that "man represents both the positive and the neutral . . . whereas woman represents only the negative"?
3. What does de Beauvoir mean when she states that woman is "imprison[ed] in her subjectivity" and that "she thinks with her glands"?
4. State in your own words her concept of "the Other." Agree or disagree with her position.
5. Why does de Beauvoir include references to the ideas of "reciprocity" and of "duality"? to master-slave relations?
6. How has woman's sexuality led historically to her position as "Other"? Why have women failed to break out of this position?
7. Outline de Beauvoir's argument. Does she argue through definition, causal analysis, or comparison? Does she argue inductively or deductively? Who is her audience?
8. Why does she include references to Haiti and Indochina, to Jews and African Americans? Why does she include references to Hercules, Jason and Medea, *Lysistrata,* and the Sabine Women? Are the allusions effective?
9. De Beauvoir wrote *The Second Sex* in 1949. Do her ideas still apply to contemporary society? What aspects of women's status have changed?

The Reading/Writing Connection

1. In a short paragraph, define the "Other."
2. "Think" Topic: Do you agree with de Beauvoir's characterization of woman as "Other"?
3. What do you see as a current issue for men and women in North American society? Is de Beauvoir's critique still relevant? Evaluate her arguments. Write a journal response to one of these questions.

Ideas for Writing

1. Compare de Beauvoir's view of the woman as "Other" with the roles of several women in works in this chapter.
2. Conceive of an alternative relationship for men and women. What do you see as ideal?
3. Compare de Beauvoir's argument with Plato's assessment in "The Sexes." How would de Beauvoir respond to Plato?

Student Essay: Explication and Character Analysis

The Jilting of Granny Weatherall

Leigh Grimm

Leigh Grimm graduated as a journalism major from the State University of New York at New Paltz. She recently received a national award for her work and plans to pursue a career as a journalist. She wrote this essay in response to an assignment to compose a character analysis of Granny Weatherall in Freshman Composition.

In "The Jilting of Granny Weatherall" by Katherine Anne Porter, Granny Weatherall, almost eighty years old, lies in a bed in her daughter's house dying. Granny is not consumed by thoughts of her imminent death but by thoughts of the people in her past. There is the sense that her relationships and people in her life have somehow failed her.

When she thinks about how neat and orderly she always kept her house, unlike her daughter Cornelia, Granny remembers a box of old letters in her attic from the two men in her life, George and John. She plans to do something with those letters the next day so that her children do not find them after she is gone. She is afraid that they will read the letters and know what she was like before she was their mother. These letters are the key to why she drifts into the past.

Granny Weatherall drifts off into the past where she can remember her children when they needed her. She would love to be able to go back and do things over again. She remembers her children coming home out of the chilly night air to get warm. She loved the children huddling around her until the house was all lit up. But once the lights were on, they would leave her because they were no longer afraid of the dark. They had no need to cling to her then just as they have no need to cling to her now. Granny Weatherall repeats in her head, "Never, never, never more." All that she has ever wanted was to be needed by her children, and it makes her sad to know that they do not need her anymore. She is happier to think about the way things used to be before her children betray her by growing up.

All through her life she was a strong and independent woman. She became strong when her husband John died leaving her with a house to run and children to support and nurture. She fenced in one hundred acres of land, cooked dozens of meals, made clothes for her family and kept the garden flourishing year after year.

5 In one of her trips to the past, she wonders if John would recognize her after all she has endured. Having to be strong and independent changed her. She says everything changed her, from "Riding country roads in the winter when women had their babies" to "sitting up nights with sick horses and sick negroes and sick children and hardly ever losing one." John also betrayed her by leaving her.

But her children and her husband are not the only ones to betray her. Before she met and married John, she was jilted by another lover. In her wedding gown Granny was left standing at the altar by George. She remembers the cake that never got eaten and the sorrow and embarrassment that she felt. In her head, she still tries to hide the scars of that day. She begins to act like a teenage girl as she asks her children to find George and to tell him that she has forgotten all about him. She wants him to know that she married a man she loved and had beautiful children with him. But the pain of that day forms a shadow that follows her to her death bed. The final jilting is that the pain of that day does not desert her; she never reaches an acceptance of her past—a reconciliation of her own past. She does not find peace and contentment—fulfillment even at the end of her life.

As the moment of death approaches "her body [is] now only a deeper mass of shadow in an endless darkness. . . . " She asks for God to give her a sign. "For the second time there [is] no sign. Again no bridegroom and the priest in the house. She [can] not remember any other sorrow because this grief [wipes] them all away."

By continually drifting into the past, Granny Weatherall shows dissatisfaction with her life. Every relationship comes to some kind of stasis that she found to be difficult and imprisoning. On her death bed she feels that she has missed something all of her life. What she has missed is life itself.

Writing Assignments

1. a. What is platonic or ideal love? Write a definition.
   b. Define your ideal lover.
   c. Discuss platonic or ideal love in Donne, in Shakespeare's "Let Me Not to the Marriage of True Minds," in Senghor, in Snyder, and/or in Rosenberg.
2. a. What is romantic love? Why do people fall in love? Respond in a journal entry.
   b. Explore the vision of romantic love in several works in this chapter.
   c. Compare three views of romantic love and marriage in this chapter.
3. Discuss sexuality in Silko, Snyder, Paz, Senghor, and/or Chekhov.
4. a. What are the major problems in love relationships? Write a journal entry.
   b. Analyze the essay by Woolf. What obstacles does she enumerate?
   c. Write an essay on obstacles in love relationships. Use three works in this chapter to support your points. Refer to Woolf and to your journal entry.
5. Explicate "Let Me Not to the Marriage of True Minds." Concentrate on persona, figurative language, and sonnet form.
6. a. In a journal entry, explore your conceptions of young love, married love, and love in old age.
   b. Categorize kinds of love. Refer to works that represent different states of love.
7. Have any of these works changed your attitude about love? Which ones? Why? Why not?
8. Write about the end of love, the acceptance of loss. Refer to Mason, Akhmatova, Hemingway, Porter, Joyce, and/or Sexton.
9. a. Trace the phases of a relationship you have experienced or observed.
   b. Trace the phases of the love relationship in one of the texts in this chapter.
   c. Compare your relationship with the view of love in one of the works in the text.

10. a. Interview three people from the same cultural background. Ask about gender roles, socialization, and responsibilities.
    b. Write an essay on roles of men and women in that culture. Have gender roles changed in that culture in the twentieth century?
    c. Write an analysis of gender roles in three works in this chapter. You may choose works in other chapters if you wish.
11. a. Interview men about women; women about men. Ask about conceptions of the opposite sex, relationships, and social roles. Summarize your interviews.
    b. Analyze the results of the interviews. What misconceptions do men have about women? Women about men?
    c. "Men and women are doomed never to understand one another." Develop an argument in response to this quotation.
12. a. Freewrite about ways in which men and women might perceive conflict differently.
    b. Choose one experience, and write a monologue for each person involved in the incident.
    c. Based on a work in this chapter, write an essay about how a man and a woman develop different views of a conflict. How does the conflict resolve itself?
13. a. Have you ever felt like an "Other"? Write about this experience in your journal.
    b. In your own words, define "Other." Use your journal entry as a basis for your definition.
    c. Analyze the experience of the woman as "Other" in three works in this chapter.
14. Compare two dramatic monologues. How do voice, tone, and theme develop the personae?
15. What is most important in the development of characters in three works in this chapter? (Choose one genre, and refer to the checklists in chapters 9–12.)
16. Analyze images of the sea in Arnold, Eliot, and Paz.
17. Examine the conflicts and characters in *Trifles* and in *And the Soul Shall Dance*. How does symbolism help to create character and theme?
18. In three works in this chapter, discuss how landscape functions in the development of character, conflict, and theme.
19. "Men are conditioned to fear a full expression of intimacy." Do you agree or disagree? Which works in this chapter support your views?
20. a. Interview another person who has read one of the works in this chapter. Ask questions about speaker, conflict, theme, language, and other literary elements. Summarize your interview.
    b. Write an essay about your interview.

21. Analyze views of romantic love in works in the Thematic Preview.
22. Discuss the "battle of the sexes" as it is depicted in three works in this chapter.
23. Compare Woolf's views of woman's experiences and the challenges for a woman writer with the portrayal of three female characters from three works in this chapter.

CHAPTER 7

War and Injustice

There is a cyclone fence between
ourselves and the slaughter and behind it
we hover in a calm, protected world like
netted fish, exactly like netted fish.
It is either the beginning or the end
of the world, and the choice is ourselves
or nothing.

Carolyn Forché, "Ourselves or Nothing"

For people who have "hover[ed] in a calm, protected world," questions of war and injustice now become urgent. No longer may people assume that they will remain untouched by "the slaughter." The Thematic Preview examines ways in which people are touched by the "slaughter"; the works consider forms of oppression and protest. Luisa Valenzuela's "I'm Your Horse in the Night" depicts the conflicts of a woman caught up in the nightmare of a militaristic regime in Argentina. Wendy Rose's "Three Thousand Dollar Death Song" portrays the devaluation and destruction of the Native American way of life. Sophocles' *Oedipus Rex* and Czeslaw Milosz's "American Ignorance of War" explore moral responses to injustice.

How, then, does one begin? In *Oedipus Rex,* Sophocles suggested an answer two thousand years ago. The individual, he contended, has an obligation to uncover the source of injustice. Oedipus, King of Thebes, attempts to find the cause of the plague in his state. His quest ends in tragedy. Soyinka's speaker in "Telephone Conversation" protests with insolence and humor against discrimination by a prospective landlady. Several other works in this chapter represent aesthetic forms of witnessing injustice as a moral response to the "slaughter": W. H. Auden's "Musée des Beaux Arts," Mary Jo Salter's "Welcome to Hiroshima," and Charlotte Delbo's "Prayer for the Living to Forgive Them for Being Alive."

In the United States, "the beginning" requires awareness. In this case, the awareness emerges from the lives of three female slaves who eventually claimed their freedom. Sojourner Truth connects women's rights with slavery in her famous speech, "Ain't I a Woman?" Harriet Jacobs describes the unbearable sexual exploitation that she and other women suffered in *Incidents in the Life of a Slave Girl.* Susan Griffin thinks of Harriet Tubman, who escaped and worked for the Underground Railroad, which led many slaves to freedom.

Griffin's persona likes to think of Tubman as a model when she contemplates the plight of children who are hungry in the United States today. In another time, Anna Deavere's Smith's "Twilight Bey," the speaker, a gang member, gains an awareness that spurs him to change his way of life and to enlighten others.

African Americans still struggle against discrimination. In "Harlem" Langston Hughes warns about the consequences of living with "a dream deferred." Etheridge Knight describes the loss of Hard Rock's spirit after the latter's visit to the hospital for the criminally insane, a spirit unbroken by prison life. School desegregation and the famous case *Brown* v. *The Board of Education of Topeka, Kansas* are the subjects of Gwendolyn Brooks's "The Chicago Defender Sends a Man to Little Rock." Yet the dream of an ideal, of freedom and of a true America persists. Hughes's "Let America Be America Again" presents an eloquent plea for the dream.

In some critiques of life in the United States, desire for change, for hope, and for love of country appear. Allen Ginsberg's speaker in "America" completes his catalogue of political indictments with the promise that he is "putting [his] queer shoulder to the wheel" while in "The Prism of Race" Manning Marable asks his readers to consider the impact of "race" upon both blacks and whites in North America and to envision means of "transform[ing] our world."

In some of these works, characters respond to injustice with action, with violence, and with activism. Wendy Rose suggests in "Death Song" that those who have violated the bones of Native Americans and who value them only at "three thousand dollars" should begin to fear retribution. Gloria Anzaldúa describes the flaying of a horse by a group of adolescents, "gringos" who believe they have the right to violate anything they choose. The "horse" returns to haunt their dreams. In "For Anna Mae Aquash Whose Spirit Is Present Here and in the Dappled Stars," Joy Harjo memorializes a Native American activist who was murdered in South Dakota. The speaker invokes "the righteous anger of the wind." Maya Angelou's speaker in "Still I Rise" also invokes her righteous anger and voices her resistance to oppression. In both poems images of destruction and renewal are intertwined.

War represents the ultimate form of destruction. Henry Ward Beecher once said, "It is not merely cruelty that leads men to love war, it is excitement." The soldiers in this chapter, however, do not seem to love war. Lao-tzu cautions that triumph or victory be treated as a funeral. In Wilfred Owen's "Dulce et Decorum Est," the speaker describes the terrible deaths of men in World War I. Tim O'Brien suggests that men became soldiers during the Vietnam War in order not to embarrass themselves, their families, and their country. They bear physical and emotional burdens in "The Things They Carried." Shusaku Endō's narrator remembers the weeping of the young men who received their red papers summoning them to battle in "The War Generation," a story—an elegy—about Japan in World War II.

Parents who send their sons and daughters to war do not love the cruelty of war either; they do not find vicarious excitement in their children's service.

They shield themselves from the horrors of war through rationalization and denial. In Luigi Pirandello's "War," the husband and wife mourn the prospect of saying farewell to their son, who has been assigned to the front lines. The patriotic "fat man" in this story finally faces his own grief. The fat man's reaction embodies a human and moral response to suffering, as do the actions of the narrator in Frederick Busch's "Ralph the Duck."

Only Cynthia Ozick in "The Shawl" identifies some of those who love war and find cruelty exciting; she portrays the Nazis, who created the Final Solution, who can toss a girl into an electrified fence as if she were a puppet. The suffering of Rosa and the children, Stella and Magda, demonstrates the horror of the Holocaust and the truth in Beecher's claim that cruelty leads men to love war.

In Argentina and El Salvador, governments reigned in which men loved cruelty and encouraged terror, disappearance, and death. Luisa Valenzuela creates a vivid picture of the vicious torture of an Argentinean woman in "I'm Your Horse in the Night," a woman whose courage and spirit sustain her dream of love. In "The Memory of Elena," Carolyn Forché's narrator and her friend commemorate the deaths of "those who remained/in Buenos Aires." Forché's Salvadoran colonel finds excitement by flaunting his disregard of "the rights of anyone," by throwing severed human ears on the floor to shock his North American visitors. Marjorie Agosin's account of the mothers of the Plaza de Mayo provides a model for collective protest against the government in Argentina in the late 1970s.

Perhaps, Forché is right about Americans "hover[ing] in a calm, protected world." If so, let this time be the beginning of the just world and the end of the unjust. Let it be the beginning of a world in which truth is valued, one in which

> All things human take time,
> time which the damned never seem to have, time for life
> to repair at least the worst of its wounds;
> it took time to wake, time for horror
> to incite revolt, time for the recovery
> of lucidity and will.

Carolyn Forché
"Ourselves or Nothing"

Let this time begin the recovery. Indeed, the works in this chapter attest to the power of art to bring about renewal.

THEMATIC PREVIEW: COMBINING THE GENRES

I'M YOUR HORSE IN THE NIGHT

Luisa Valenzuela (1938–)

Luisa Valenzuela portrays the horrors of the political situation in Argentina through a female speaker who loses her freedom because of her love for a guerilla leader whom she knows only as Beto. Valenzuela left Argentina after the death of dictator Juan Perón in 1974 to escape the military dictatorship that ruled until 1983. Before she fled, she wrote, "Buenos Aires belonged then to violence and to state terrorism, and I could only sit in cafes and brood. Till I decided a book of short stories could be written in a month at those same cafe tables, overhearing scraps of scared conversations, seeping in the general paranoia. Strange Things Happen Here *(1979) was born, and with it a new political awareness. And action."*

1975

The doorbell rang: three short rings and one long one. That was the signal, and I got up, annoyed and a little frightened; it could be them, and then again, maybe not; at these ungodly hours of the night it could be a trap. I opened the door expecting anything except him, face to face, at last.

He came in quickly and locked the door behind him before embracing me. So much in character, so cautious, first and foremost checking his—our—rear guard. Then he took me in his arms without saying a word, not even holding me too tight but letting all the emotions of our new encounter overflow, telling me so much by merely holding me in his arms and kissing me slowly. I think he never had much faith in words, and there he was, as silent as ever, sending me messages in the form of caresses.

We finally stepped back to look at one another from head to foot, not eye to eye, out of focus. And I was able to say Hello showing scarcely any surprise despite all those months when I had no idea where he could have been, and I was able to say

I thought you were fighting up north
I thought you'd been caught
I thought you were in hiding
I thought you'd been tortured and killed
I thought you were theorizing about the revolution in another country

Just one of many ways to tell him I'd been thinking of him, I hadn't stopped thinking of him or felt as if I'd been betrayed. And there he was, always so goddamn cautious, so much the master of his actions.

"Quiet, Chiquita.[1] You're much better off not knowing what I've been up to."

Then he pulled out his treasures, potential clues that at the time eluded me: a bottle of cachaça[2] and a Gal Costa[3] record. What had he been up to in Brazil? What was he planning to do next? What had brought him back, risking his life, knowing they were after him? Then I stopped asking myself questions (quiet, Chiquita, he'd say). Come here, Chiquita, he was saying, and I chose to let myself sink into the joy of having him back again, trying not to worry. What would happen to us tomorrow, and the days that followed?

Cachaça's a good drink. It goes down and up and down all the right tracks, and then stops to warm up the corners that need it most. Gal Costa's voice is hot, she envelops us in its sound and half-dancing, half-floating, we reach the bed. We lie down and keep on staring deep into each other's eyes, continue caressing each other without allowing ourselves to give in to the pure senses just yet. We continue recognizing, rediscovering each other.

Beto, I say, looking at him. I know that isn't his real name, but it's the only one I can call him out loud. He replies:

"We'll make it someday, Chiquita. But let's not talk now."

It's better that way. Better if he doesn't start talking about how we'll make it someday and ruin the wonder of what we're about to attain right now, the two of us, all alone.

"A noite eu so teu cavalo," Gal Costa suddenly sings from the record player.

"I'm your horse in the night," I translate slowly. And so as to bind him in a spell and stop him from thinking about other things:

"It's a saint's song, like in the *macumba.*[4] Someone who's in a trance says she's the horse of the spirit who's riding her, she's his mount."

"Chiquita, you're always getting carried away with esoteric meanings and witchcraft. You know perfectly well that she isn't talking about spirits. If you're my horse in the night it's because I ride you, like this, see? . . . Like this . . . That's all."

It was so long, so deep and so insistent, so charged with affection that we ended up exhausted. I fell asleep with him still on top of me.

I'm your horse in the night.

The goddamn phone pulled me out in waves from a deep well. Making an enormous effort to wake up, I walked over to the receiver, thinking it could be Beto, sure, who was no longer by my side, sure, following his inveterate habit of running away while I'm asleep without a word about where he's gone. To protect me, he says.

[1] Small one, little one (female).

[2] An alcoholic beverage.

[3] Chanteuse.

[4] A polytheistic religion of African origin, practiced mainly by Brazilian blacks in urban areas. A religion involving spirits.

From the other end of the line, a voice I thought belonged to Andrés—the one we call Andrés—began to tell me:

"They found Beto dead, floating down the river near the other bank. It looks as if they threw him alive out of a chopper. He's all bloated and decomposed after six days in the water, but I'm almost sure it's him."

20 "No, it can't be Beto," I shouted carelessly. Suddenly the voice no longer sounded like Andrés: it felt foreign, impersonal.

"You think so?"

"Who is this?" Only then did I think to ask. But that very moment they hung up.

Ten, fifteen minutes? How long must I have stayed there staring at the phone like an idiot until the police arrived? I didn't expect them. But, then again, how could I not? Their hands feeling me, their voices insulting and threatening, the house searched, turned inside out. But I already knew. So what did I care if they broke every breakable object and tore apart my dresser?

They wouldn't find a thing. My only real possession was a dream and they can't deprive me of my dreams just like that. My dream the night before, when Beto was there with me and we loved each other. I'd dreamed it, dreamed every bit of it, I was deeply convinced that I'd dreamed it all in the richest detail, even in full color. And dreams are none of the cops' business.

25 They want reality, tangible facts, the kind I couldn't even begin to give them.

Where is he, you saw him, he was here with you, where did he go? Speak up, or you'll be sorry. Let's hear you sing, bitch, we know he came to see you, where is he, where is he holed up? He's in the city, come on, spill it, we know he came to get you.

I haven't heard a word from him in months. He abandoned me, I haven't heard from him in months. He ran away, went underground. What do I know, he ran off with someone else, he's in another country. What do I know, he abandoned me, I hate him, I know nothing.

(Go ahead, burn me with your cigarettes, kick me all you wish, threaten, go ahead, stick a mouse in me so it'll eat my insides out, pull my nails out, do as you please. Would I make something up for that? Would I tell you he was here when a thousand years ago he left me forever?)

I'm not about to tell them my dreams. Why should they care? I haven't seen that so-called Beto in more than six months, and I loved him. The man simply vanished. I only run into him in my dreams, and they're bad dreams that often become nightmares.

30 Beto, you know now, if it's true that they killed you, or wherever you may be, Beto, I'm your horse in the night and you can inhabit me whenever you wish, even if I'm behind bars. Beto, now that I'm in jail I know that I dreamed you that night; it was just a dream. And if by some wild chance there's a Gal Costa record and a half-empty bottle of cachaça in my house, I hope they'll forgive me: I will them out of existence.

Explorations of the Text

1. Describe the situation and the occasion presented in the opening four paragraphs. Why does Beto prefer not to talk?
2. Form a portrait of Beto from the narrator's statements about him. Consider also the objects he brings with him, his dialogue, and his actions.
3. Describe the relationship between the narrator and Beto. What is the nature of their sexual relationship?
4. Discuss the meanings of the title, "I'm Your Horse in the Night."
5. Why do the police arrest the narrator? How is she able to resist their methods?
6. Explain the narrator's "dream." Why does she decide that the encounter was a dream?
7. Why does she say "And if by some wild chance there's a Gal Costa record and a half-empty bottle of cachaça in my house. I hope they'll forgive me: I will them out of existence"?
8. Examine Valenzuela's narrative technique. Why does she write so many short paragraphs?
9. Compare the political vision in this story to the views in Forché's poems and Agosin's essay.

The Reading/Writing Connection

1. Write about the narrator's dream. Gloss and annotate the text. As an alternative, write a double-entry notebook concerning this story.
2. Ask several people to read this story. Interview them about their responses. How many believe that the narrator fantasized the encounter with Beto?

Ideas for Writing

1. Is this a story about dream or reality? Both? Does it matter? Incorporate question 2 above into your essay.
2. Evaluate this story. Consider character, theme, conflict, form, symbol, and/or other elements of fiction. (See chapter 9.)
3. Compare this story with Forché's "The Colonel." What do you conclude?

Three Thousand Dollar Death Song

Wendy Rose

Born in Oakland, California, Wendy Rose (1948–   ) was educated at the University of California, Berkeley. A Hopi/Miwok, she has taught Native American studies at Berkeley and is a member of many anthropological organizations. Her poetry volumes include Hopi Roadrunner Dancing *(1973),* Builder Kachina: A Home-Going Cycle *(1979),* The Half-breed Chronicles and Other Poems *(1985), and* Bone Dance: New and Selected Poems *(1965–93). She also has written historical works including* Long Division: A Tribal History *(1976). Rose has contributed to anthologies and periodicals, sometimes using the pseudonym Chiron Khanshendel.*

1980

"Nineteen American Indian skeletons from Nevada . . .
valued at $3000 . . ."—Museum invoice, 1975

Is it in cold hard cash? the kind
that dusts the insides of men's pockets
lying silver-polished surface along the cloth.
Or in bills? papering the wallets of they
who thread the night with dark words. Or
checks? paper promises weighing the same
as words spoken once on the other side
of the grown grass and dammed rivers
of history. However it goes, it goes.
Through my body it goes
assessing each nerve, running its edges
along my arteries, planning ahead
for whose hands will rip me
into pieces of dusty red paper,
whose hands will smooth or smatter me
into traces of rubble. Invoiced now,
it's official how our bones are valued
that stretch out pointing to sunrise
or are flexed into one last foetal bend,
that are removed and tossed about,
catalogued, numbered with black ink
on newly-white foreheads.
As we were formed to the white soldier's voice,
so we explode under white students' hands.
Death is a long trail of days
in our fleshless prison.

From this distant point we watch our bones
auctioned with our careful beadwork,

our quilled medicine bundles, even the bridles
of our shot-down horses. You: who have
priced us, you who have removed us: at what cost?
What price the pits where our bones share
a single bit of memory, how one century
turns our dead into specimens, our history
into dust, our survivors into clowns.
Our memory might be catching, you know;
picture the mortars, the arrowheads, the labrets[1]
shaking off their labels like bears
suddenly awake to find the seasons have ended
while they slept. Watch them touch each other,
measure reality, march out the museum door!
Watch as they lift their faces
and smell about for us; watch our bones rise
to meet them and mount the horses once again!
The cost, then, will be paid
for our sweetgrass-smelling having-been
in clam shell beads and steatite,[2]
dentalia and woodpecker scalp, turquoise
and copper, blood and oil, coal
and uranium, children, a universe
of stolen things.

Explorations of the Text

1. Explain the title and the invoice.
2. Why does the speaker ask questions about "cash," "bills," and "checks"? Is her method of questioning effective?
3. Identify the antecedent of "it" in lines 8 to 15.
4. What happens to the bones (lines 15–25)? Interpret the symbolism of colors. Look at the verbs.
5. What is the meaning of the following lines: "Death is a long trail of days/in our fleshless prison"?
6. What is the impact of the idea that the dead might awaken and might "march out the museum door!"? What is the threat that others will "meet them and mount the horses once again"?
7. This poem is divided into two **stanzas.** What does this structure achieve?

[1] Ornaments worn in perforations of the lips.

[2] Talc of grayish green or brown color; soapstone.

The Reading/Writing Connection

1. Freewrite. Respond to the museum invoice.
2. Discuss the title. Does it have a double meaning?
3. "Think" Topic: Discuss the images of money in this poem.

Ideas for Writing

1. Examine all of the imagery concerning money. Use the above "Think" Topic as a beginning.
2. Compare and contrast this poem with Griffin's "I Like to Think of Harriet Tubman."
3. Write an essay on genocide. Refer to this poem, to Ozick's "The Shawl" or to other works in this chapter.

OEDIPUS REX

Sophocles

Although he wrote more than one hundred and twenty dramas, only seven complete plays of Sophocles (496–406 B.C.) survive. Nonetheless, he is considered, with Aeschylus and Euripides, one of the three great Greek tragic dramatists. His first play won the prize over Aeschylus in 468 B.C. By 450 B.C., Sophocles had written at least twenty-four plays and had initiated significant changes in the form of tragedy, most notably that of introducing a third actor to the stage. He won more victories in the play competition than any other writer. In his Poetics, *Aristotle praised Sophocles above other dramatists and used* Oedipus Rex *as a model for his definition of tragedy.*

430 B.C.

Characters

Oedipus, King of Thebes, supposed son of Polybos and Meropê, King and Queen of Corinth
Iokastê, wife of Oedipus and widow of the late King Laïos
Kreon, brother of Iokastê, a prince of Thebes
Teiresias, a blind seer who serves Apollo
Priest
Messenger, from Corinth
Shepherd, former servant of Laïos
Second Messenger, from the palace
Chorus of Theban Elders
Choragos, leader of the Chorus

Antigone and Ismene, young daughters of Oedipus and Iokastê. They appear in the Éxodos but do not speak.
Suppliants, Guards, Servants

The Scene. Before the palace of Oedipus, King of Thebes. A central door and two lateral doors open onto a platform which runs the length of the façade. On the platform, right and left, are altars; and three steps lead down into the orchêstra, or chorus-ground. At the beginning of the action these steps are crowded by suppliants who have brought branches and chaplets of olive leaves and who sit in various attitudes of despair. Oedipus enters.

Prologue

Oedipus: My children, generations of the living
In the line of Kadmos,[1] nursed at his ancient hearth:
Why have you strewn yourselves before these altars
In supplication, with your boughs and garlands?
The breath of incense rises from the city
With a sound of prayer and lamentation.
Children,
I would not have you speak through messengers,
And therefore I have come myself to hear you—
I, Oedipus, who bear the famous name.
(To a Priest.) You, there, since you are eldest in the company,
Speak for them all, tell me what preys upon you,
Whether you come in dread, or crave some blessing:
Tell me, and never doubt that I will help you
In every way I can; I should be heartless
Were I not moved to find you suppliant here.
Priest: Great Oedipus, O powerful king of Thebes!
You see how all the ages of our people
Cling to your altar steps: here are boys
Who can barely stand alone, and here are priests
By weight of age, as I am a priest of God,
And young men chosen from those yet unmarried;
As for the others, all that multitude,
They wait with olive chaplets in the squares,
At the two shrines of Pallas, and where Apollo
Speaks in the glowing embers.
Your own eyes
Must tell you: Thebes is tossed on a murdering sea

[1] **Kadmos:** founder of Thebes.

And can not lift her head from the death surge.
A rust consumes the buds and fruits of the earth;
The herds are sick; children die unborn,
And labor is vain. The god of plague and pyre
Raids like detestable lightning through the city,
And all the house of Kadmos is laid waste,
All emptied, and all darkened: Death alone
Battens upon the misery of Thebes.

You are not one of the immortal gods, we know;
Yet we have come to you to make our prayer
As to the man surest in mortal ways
And wisest in the ways of God. You saved us
From the Sphinx, that flinty singer, and the tribute
We paid to her so long; yet you were never
Better informed than we, nor could we teach you:
A god's touch, it seems, enabled you to help us.

Therefore, O mighty power, we turn to you:
Find us our safety, find us a remedy,
Whether by counsel of the gods or of men.
A king of wisdom tested in the past
Can act in a time of troubles, and act well.
Noblest of men, restore
Life to your city! Think how all men call you
Liberator for your boldness long ago;
Ah, when your years of kingship are remembered,
Let them not say *We rose, but later fell—*
Keep the State from going down in the storm!
Once, years ago, with happy augury,
You brought us fortune; be the same again!
No man questions your power to rule the land:
But rule over men, not over a dead city!
Ships are only hulls, high walls are nothing,
When no life moves in the empty passageways.

Oedipus: Poor children! You may be sure I know
All that you longed for in your coming here.
I know that you are deathly sick; and yet,
Sick as you are, not one is as sick as I.
Each of you suffers in himself alone
His anguish, not another's; but my spirit
Groans for the city, for myself, for you.

I was not sleeping, you are not waking me.
No, I have been in tears for a long while
And in my restless thought walked many ways.

In all my search I found one remedy,
And I have adopted it: I have sent Kreon,
Son of Menoikeus, brother of the queen,
To Delphi, Apollo's place of revelation,
To learn there, if he can,
What act or pledge of mine may save the city.
I have counted the days, and now, this very day,
I am troubled, for he has overstayed his time.
What is he doing? He has been gone too long.
Yet whenever he comes back, I should do ill
Not to take any action the god orders.

Priest: It is a timely promise. At this instant
They tell me Kreon is here.

Oedipus: O Lord Apollo!
May his news be fair as his face is radiant!

Priest: Good news, I gather! he is crowned with bay,
The chaplet is thick with berries.

Oedipus: We shall soon know;
He is near enough to hear us now. *(Enter Kreon.)* O prince:
Brother: son of Menoikeus:
What answer do you bring us from the god?

Kreon: A strong one. I can tell you, great afflictions
Will turn out well, if they are taken well.

Oedipus: What was the oracle? These vague words
Leave me still hanging between hope and fear.

Kreon: Is it your pleasure to hear me with all these
Gathered around us? I am prepared to speak,
But should we not go in?

Oedipus: Speak to them all,
It is for them I suffer, more than for myself.

Kreon: Then I will tell you what I heard at Delphi.
In plain words
The god commands us to expel from the land of Thebes
An old defilement we are sheltering.
It is a deathly thing, beyond cure;
We must not let it feed upon us longer.

Oedipus: What defilement? How shall we rid ourselves of it?

Kreon: By exile or death, blood for blood. It was
Murder that brought the plague-wind on the city.

Oedipus: Murder of whom? Surely the god has named him?

Kreon: My lord: Laïos once ruled this land,
Before you came to govern us.

Oedipus: I know;
I learned of him from others; I never saw him.

Kreon: He was murdered; and Apollo commands us now
To take revenge upon whoever killed him.

Oedipus: Upon whom? Where are they? Where shall we find a clue
To solve that crime, after so many years?
Kreon: Here in this land, he said. Search reveals
Things that escape an inattentive man.
Oedipus: Tell me: Was Laïos murdered in his house,
Or in the fields, or in some foreign country?
Kreon: He said he planned to make a pilgrimage.
He did not come home again.
Oedipus: And was there no one,
No witness, no companion, to tell what happened?
Kreon: They were all killed but one, and he got away
So frightened that he could remember one thing only.
Oedipus: What was that one thing? One may be the key
To everything, if we resolve to use it.
Kreon: He said that a band of highwaymen attacked them,
Outnumbered them, and overwhelmed the king.
Oedipus: Strange, that a highwayman should be so daring—
Unless some faction here bribed him to do it.
Kreon: We thought of that. But after Laïos' death
New troubles arose and we had no avenger.
Oedipus: What troubles could prevent your hunting down the killers?
Kreon: The riddling Sphinx's song
Made us deaf to all mysteries but her own.
Oedipus: Then once more I must bring what is dark to light.
It is most fitting that Apollo shows,
As you do, this compunction for the dead.
You shall see how I stand by you, as I should,
Avenging this country and the god as well,
And not as though it were for some distant friend,
But for my own sake, to be rid of evil.
Whoever killed King Laïos might—who knows?—
Lay violent hands even on me—and soon.
I act for the murdered king in my own interest.

Come, then, my children: leave the altar steps,
Lift up your olive boughs!
One of you go
And summon the people of Kadmos to gather here.
I will do all that I can; you may tell them that. *(Exit a Page.)*
So, with the help of God,
We shall be saved—or else indeed we are lost.
Priest: Let us rise, children. It was for this we came,
And now the king has promised it.
Phoibos[2] has sent us an oracle; may he descend

[2] **Phoibos:** Apollo, god of light and truth.

Himself to save us and drive out the plague. *(Exeunt Oedipus and Kreon into the palace by the central door. The Priest and the Suppliants disperse right and left. After a short pause the Chorus enters the orchêstra.)*

Párados[3]

Strophe 1

Chorus: What is God singing in his profound
Delphi of gold and shadow?
What oracle for Thebes, the sunwhipped city?
Fear unjoints me, the roots of my heart tremble.
Now I remember, O Healer, your power, and wonder:
Will you send doom like a sudden cloud, or weave it
Like nightfall of the past?
Speak to me, tell me, O
Child of golden Hope, immortal Voice.

Antistrophe 1

Let me pray to Athenê, the immortal daughter of Zeus,
And to Artemis her sister
Who keeps her famous throne in the market ring,
And to Apollo, archer from distant heaven—
O gods, descend! Like three streams leap against
The fires of our grief, the fires of darkness;
Be swift to bring us rest!
As in the old time from the brilliant house
Of air you stepped to save us, come again!

Strophe 2

Now our afflictions have no end,
Now all our stricken host lies down
And no man fights off death with his mind;
The noble plowland bears no grain,
And groaning mothers can not bear—
See, how our lives like birds take wing,

---

[3] **Párodos:** The song or ode chanted by the chorus on their entry. It is accompanied by dancing and music played on a flute. The chorus, in this play, represents elders of the city of Thebes. They remain on stage (on a level lower than the principal actors) for the remainder of the play. The choral odes and dances serve to separate one scene from another (there was no curtain in Greek theater) as well as to comment on the action, reinforce the emotion, and interpret the situation. The chorus also performs dance movements during certain portions of the scenes themselves. *Strophe* and *antistrophe* are terms denoting the movement and countermovement of the chorus from one side of their playing area to the other. When the chorus participates in dialogue with the other characters, their lines are spoken by the Choragos, their leader.

Like sparks that fly when a fire soars,
To the shore of the god of evening.

Antistrophe 2

The plague burns on, it is pitiless,
Though pallid children laden with death
Lie unwept in the stony ways,
And old gray women by every path
Flock to the strand about the altars
There to strike their breasts and cry
Worship of Phoibos in wailing prayers:
Be kind, God's golden child!

Strophe 3

There are no swords in this attack by fire,
No shields, but we are ringed with cries.
Send the besieger plunging from our homes
Into the vast sea-room of the Atlantic
Or into the waves that foam eastward of Thrace—
For the day ravages what the night spares—
Destroy our enemy, lord of the thunder!
Let him be riven by lightning from heaven!

Antistrophe 3

Phoibos Apollo, stretch the sun's bowstring,
That golden cord, until it sing for us,
Flashing arrows in heaven!
Artemis, Huntress,
Race with flaring lights upon our mountains!
O scarlet god,[4] O golden-banded brow,
O Theban Bacchos in a storm of Maenads, *(Enter Oedipus, center.)*
Whirl upon Death, that all the Undying hate!
Come with blinding torches, come in joy!

Scene 1

Oedipus: Is this your prayer? It may be answered. Come,
Listen to me, act as the crisis demands,
And you shall have relief from all these evils.

Until now I was a stranger to this tale,
As I had been a stranger to the crime.
Could I track down the murderer without a clue?

[4] **scarlet god:** Bacchos, god of wine and revelry. The Maenads were his female attendants.

But now, friends,
As one who became a citizen after the murder,
I make this proclamation to all Thebans:
If any man knows by whose hand Laïos, son of Labdakos,
Met his death, I direct that man to tell me everything,
No matter what he fears for having so long withheld it.
Let it stand as promised that no further trouble
Will come to him, but he may leave the land in safety.
Moreover: If anyone knows the murderer to be foreign,
Let him not keep silent: he shall have his reward from me.
However, if he does conceal it; if any man
Fearing for his friend or for himself disobeys this edict,
Hear what I propose to do:

I solemnly forbid the people of this country,
Where power and throne are mine, ever to receive that man
Or speak to him, no matter who he is, or let him
Join in sacrifice, lustration, or in prayer.
I decree that he be driven from every house,
Being, as he is, corruption itself to us: the Delphic
Voice of Apollo has pronounced this revelation.
Thus I associate myself with the oracle
And take the side of the murdered king.
As for the criminal, I pray to God—
Whether it be a lurking thief, or one of a number—
I pray that that man's life be consumed in evil and wretchedness.
And as for me, this curse applies no less
If it should turn out that the culprit is my guest here,
Sharing my hearth.
                    You have heard the penalty.
I lay it on you now to attend to this
For my sake, for Apollo's, for the sick
Sterile city that heaven has abandoned.
Suppose the oracle had given you no command:
Should this defilement go uncleansed for ever?
You should have found the murderer: your king,
A noble king, had been destroyed!
                                        Now I,
Having the power that he held before me,
Having his bed, begetting children there
Upon his wife, as he would have, had he lived—
Their son would have been my children's brother,
If Laïos had had luck in fatherhood!
(And now his bad fortune has struck him down)—
I say I take the son's part, just as though
I were his son, to press the fight for him

And see it won! I'll find the hand that brought
Death to Labdakos' and Polydoros' child,
Heir of Kadmos' and Agenor's line.[5]
And as for those who fail me,
May the gods deny them the fruit of the earth,
Fruit of the womb, and may they rot utterly!
Let them be wretched as we are wretched, and worse!

For you, for loyal Thebans, and for all
Who find my actions right, I pray the favor
Of justice, and of all the immortal gods.

Choragos: Since I am under oath, my lord, I swear
I did not do the murder, I can not name
The murderer. Phoibos ordained the search;
Why did he not say who the culprit was?

Oedipus: An honest question. But no man in the world
Can make the gods do more than the gods will.

Choragos: There is an alternative, I think—

Oedipus: Tell me.
Any or all, you must not fail to tell me.

Choragos: A lord clairvoyant to the lord Apollo,
As we all know, is the skilled Teiresias.
One might learn much about this from him, Oedipus.

Oedipus: I am not wasting time:
Kreon spoke of this, and I have sent for him—
Twice, in fact; it is strange that he is not here.

Choragos: The other matter—that old report—seems useless.

Oedipus: What was that? I am interested in all reports.

Choragos: The king was said to have been killed by highwaymen.

Oedipus: I know. But we have no witnesses to that.

Choragos: If the killer can feel a particle of dread,
Your curse will bring him out of hiding!

Oedipus: No.
The man who dared that act will fear no curse. *(Enter the blind seer Teiresias, led by a Page.)*

Choragos: But there is one man who may detect the criminal.
This is Teiresias, this is the holy prophet
In whom, alone of all men, truth was born.

Oedipus: Teiresias: seer: student of mysteries,
Of all that's taught and all that no man tells,
Secrets of Heaven and secrets of the earth:

[5] **Labdakos, Polydoros, Kadmos, and Agenor:** father, grandfather, great-grandfather, and great-great-grandfather of Laïos.

Blind though you are, you know the city lies
Sick with plague; and from this plague, my lord,
We find that you alone can guard or save us.

Possibly you did not hear the messengers?
Apollo, when we sent to him,
Sent us back word that this great pestilence
Would lift, but only if we established clearly
The identity of those who murdered Laïos.
They must be killed or exiled.
Can you use
Birdflight[6] or any art of divination
To purify yourself, and Thebes, and me
From this contagion? We are in your hands.
There is no fairer duty
Than that of helping others in distress.
Teiresias: How dreadful knowledge of the truth can be
When there's no help in truth! I knew this well,
But did not act on it: else I should not have come.
Oedipus: What is troubling you? Why are your eyes so cold?
Teiresias: Let me go home. Bear your own fate, and I'll
Bear mine. It is better so: trust what I say.
Oedipus: What you say is ungracious and unhelpful
To your native country. Do not refuse to speak.
Teiresias: When it comes to speech, your own is neither temperate
Nor opportune. I wish to be more prudent.
Oedipus: In God's name, we all beg you—
Teiresias: You are all ignorant.
No; I will never tell you what I know.
Now it is my misery; then, it would be yours.
Oedipus: What! You do know something, and will not tell us?
You would betray us all and wreck the State?
Teiresias: I do not intend to torture myself, or you.
Why persist in asking? You will not persuade me.
Oedipus: What a wicked old man you are! You'd try a stone's
Patience! Out with it! Have you no feeling at all?
Teiresias: You call me unfeeling. If you could only see
The nature of your own feelings . . .
Oedipus: Why,
Who would not feel as I do? Who could endure
Your arrogance toward the city?

[6] **Birdflight:** Prophets predicted the future or divined the unknown by observing the flight of birds.

Teiresias: What does it matter?
Whether I speak or not, it is bound to come.
Oedipus: Then, if "it" is bound to come, you are bound to tell me.
Teiresias: No, I will not go on. Rage as you please.
Oedipus: Rage? Why not!
And I'll tell you what I think:
You planned it, you had it done, you all but
Killed him with your own hands: if you had eyes,
I'd say the crime was yours, and yours alone.
Teiresias: So? I charge you, then,
Abide by the proclamation you have made:
From this day forth
Never speak again to these men or to me;
You yourself are the pollution of this country.
Oedipus: You dare say that! Can you possibly think you have
Some way of going free, after such insolence?
Teiresias: I have gone free. It is the truth sustains me.
Oedipus: Who taught you shamelessness? It was not your craft.
Teiresias: You did. You made me speak. I did not want to.
Oedipus: Speak what? Let me hear it again more clearly.
Teiresias: Was it not clear before? Are you tempting me?
Oedipus: I did not understand it. Say it again.
Teiresias: I say that you are the murderer whom you seek.
Oedipus: Now twice you have spat out infamy. You'll pay for it!
Teiresias: Would you care for more? Do you wish to be really angry?
Oedipus: Say what you will. Whatever you say is worthless.
Teiresias: I say you live in hideous shame with those
Most dear to you. You can not see the evil.
Oedipus: Can you go on babbling like this for ever?
Teiresias: I can, if there is power in truth.
Oedipus: There is:
But not for you, not for you,
You sightless, witless, senseless, mad old man!
Teiresias: You are the madman. There is no one here
Who will not curse you soon, as you curse me.
Oedipus: You child of total night! I would not touch you;
Neither would any man who sees the sun.
Teiresias: True: it is not from you my fate will come.
That lies within Apollo's competence,
As it is his concern.
Oedipus: Tell me, who made
These fine discoveries? Kreon? or someone else?
Teiresias: Kreon is no threat. You weave your own doom.
Oedipus: Wealth, power, craft of statemanship!
Kingly position, everywhere admired!
What savage envy is stored up against these,

If Kreon, whom I trusted, Kreon my friend,
For this great office which the city once
Put in my hands unsought—if for this power
Kreon desires in secret to destroy me!

He has bought this decrepit fortune-teller, this
Collecter of dirty pennies, this prophet fraud—
Why, he is no more clairvoyant than I am!
Tell us:
Has your mystic mummery ever approached the truth?
When that hellcat the Sphinx was performing here,
What help were you to these people?
Her magic was not for the first man who came along:
It demanded a real exorcist. Your birds—
What good were they? or the gods, for the matter of that?
But I came by,
Oedipus, the simple man, who knows nothing—
I thought it out for myself, no birds helped me!
And this is the man you think you can destroy,
That you may be close to Kreon when he's king!
Well, you and your friend Kreon, it seems to me,
Will suffer most. If you were not an old man,
You would have paid already for your plot.

Choragos: We can not see that his words or yours
Have been spoken except in anger, Oedipus,
And of anger we have no need. How to accomplish
The god's will best: that is what most concerns us.

Teiresias: You are a king. But where argument's concerned
I am your man, as much a king as you.
I am not your servant, but Apollo's.
I have no need of Kreon or Kreon's name.

Listen to me. You mock my blindness, do you?
But I say that you, with both your eyes, are blind:
You can not see the wretchedness of your life,
Nor in whose house you live, no, nor with whom.
Who are your father and mother? Can you tell me?
You do not even know the blind wrongs
That you have done them, on earth and in the world below.
But the double lash of your parents' curse will whip you
Out of this land some day, with only night
Upon your precious eyes.
Your cries then—where will they not be heard?
What fastness of Kithairon[7] will not echo them?

[7] **Kithairon:** the mountain where Oedipus was taken to be exposed as an infant.

And that bridal-descant of yours—you'll know it then,
The song they sang when you came here to Thebes
And found your misguided berthing.
All this, and more, that you can not guess at now,
Will bring you to yourself among your children.

Be angry, then. Curse Kreon. Curse my words.
I tell you, no man that walks upon the earth
Shall be rooted out more horribly than you.
Oedipus: Am I to bear this from him?—Damnation
Take you! Out of this place! Out of my sight!
Teiresias: I would not have come at all if you had not asked me.
Oedipus: Could I have told that you'd talk nonsense, that
You'd come here to make a fool of yourself, and of me?
Teiresias: A fool? Your parents thought me sane enough.
Oedipus: My parents again!—Wait: who were my parents?
Teiresias: This day will give you a father, and break your heart.
Oedipus: Your infantile riddles! Your damned abracadabra!
Teiresias: You were a great man once at solving riddles.
Oedipus: Mock me with that if you like; you will find it true.
Teiresias: It was true enough. It brought about your ruin.
Oedipus: But if it saved this town?
Teiresias *(To the Page.):* Boy, give me your hand.
Oedipus: Yes, boy; lead him away.
—While you are here
We can do nothing. Go; leave us in peace.
Teiresias: I will go when I have said what I have to say.
How can you hurt me? And I tell you again:
The man you have been looking for all this time,
The damned man, the murderer of Laïos,
That man is in Thebes. To your mind he is foreign-born,
But it will soon be shown that he is a Theban,
A revelation that will fail to please.
A blind man,
Who has his eyes now; a penniless man, who is rich now;
And he will go tapping the strange earth with his staff.
To the children with whom he lives now he will be
Brother and father—the very same; to her
Who bore him, son and husband—the very same
Who came to his father's bed, wet with his father's blood.
Enough. Go think that over.
If later you find error in what I have said,
You may say that I have no skill in prophecy.

(Exit Teiresias, led by his Page. Oedipus goes into the palace.)

Ode 1

Strophe 1

Chorus: The Delphic stone of prophecies
Remembers ancient regicide
And a still bloody hand.
That killer's hour of flight has come.
He must be stronger than riderless
Coursers of untiring wind,
For the son[8] of Zeus armed with his father's thunder
Leaps in lightning after him;
And the Furies hold his track, the sad Furies.

Antistrophe 1

Holy Parnassos[9] peak of snow
Flashes and blinds that secret man,
That all shall hunt him down:
Though he may roam the forest shade
Like a bull gone wild from pasture
To rage through glooms of stone.
Doom comes down on him; flight will not avail him;
For the world's heart calls him desolate,
And the immortal voices follow, for ever follow.

Strophe 2

But now a wilder thing is heard
From the old man skilled at hearing Fate in the wing-beat of a bird.
Bewildered as a blown bird, my soul hovers and can not find
Foothold in this debate, or any reason or rest of mind.
But no man ever brought—none can bring
Proof of strife between Thebes' royal house,
Labdakos' line, and the son of Polybos;
And never until now has any man brought word
Of Laïos' dark death staining Oedipus the King.

Antistrophe 2

Divine Zeus and Apollo hold
Perfect intelligence alone of all tales ever told;
And well though this diviner works, he works in his own night;
No man can judge that rough unknown or trust in second sight,
For wisdom changes hands among the wise.
Shall I believe my great lord criminal
At a raging word that a blind old man let fall?

---

[8] **son:** Apollo. [9] **Parnassos:** mountain sacred to Apollo.

I saw him, when the carrion woman[10] faced him of old,
Prove his heroic mind. These evil words are lies.

Scene 2

Kreon: Men of Thebes:
I am told that heavy accusations
Have been brought against me by King Oedipus.

I am not the kind of man to bear this tamely.

If in these present difficulties
He holds me accountable for any harm to him
Through anything I have said or done—why, then,
I do not value life in this dishonor.
It is not as though this rumor touched upon
Some private indiscretion. The matter is grave.
The fact is that I am being called disloyal
To the State, to my fellow citizens, to my friends.
Choragos: He may have spoken in anger, not from his mind.
Kreon: But did you not hear him say I was the one
Who seduced the old prophet into lying?
Choragos: The thing was said; I do not know how seriously.
Kreon: But you were watching him! Were his eyes steady?
Did he look like a man in his right mind?
Choragos: I do not know.
I can not judge the behavior of great men.
But here is the king himself. *(Enter Oedipus.)*
Oedipus: So you dared come back.
Why? How brazen of you to come to my house,
You murderer!
Do you think I do not know
That you plotted to kill me, plotted to steal my throne?
Tell me, in God's name: am I coward, a fool,
That you should dream you could accomplish this?
A fool who could not see your slippery game?
A coward, not to fight back when I saw it?
You are the fool, Kreon, are you not? hoping
Without support or friends to get a throne?
Thrones may be won or bought: you could do neither.
Kreon: Now listen to me. You have talked; let me talk, too.
You can not judge unless you know the facts.
Oedipus: You speak well: there is one fact; but I find it hard
To learn from the deadliest enemy I have.

---

[10] **woman:** the Sphinx.

Kreon: That above all I must dispute with you.
Oedipus: That above all I will not hear you deny.
Kreon: If you think there is anything good in being stubborn
Against all reason, then I say you are wrong.
Oedipus: If you think a man can sin against his own kind
And not be punished for it, I say you are mad.
Kreon: I agree. But tell me: what have I done to you?
Oedipus: You advised me to send for that wizard, did you not?
Kreon: I did. I should do it again.
Oedipus: Very well. Now tell me:
How long has it been since Laïos—
Kreon: What of Laïos?
Oedipus: Since he vanished in that onset by the road?
Kreon: It was long ago, a long time.
Oedipus: And this prophet,
Was he practicing here then?
Kreon: He was; and with honor, as now.
Oedipus: Did he speak of me at that time?
Kreon: He never did,
At least, not when I was present.
Oedipus: But . . . the enquiry?
I suppose you held one?
Kreon: We did, but we learned nothing.
Oedipus: Why did the prophet not speak against me then?
Kreon: I do not know; and I am the kind of man
Who holds his tongue when he has no facts to go on.
Oedipus: There's one fact that you know, and you could tell it.
Kreon: What fact is that? If I know it, you shall have it.
Oedipus: If he were not involved with you, he could not say
That it was I who murdered Laïos.
Kreon: If he says that, you are the one that knows it!—
But now it is my turn to question you.
Oedipus: Put your questions. I am no murderer.
Kreon: First, then: You married my sister?
Oedipus: I married your sister.
Kreon: And you rule the kingdom equally with her?
Oedipus: Everything that she wants she has from me.
Kreon: And I am the third, equal to both of you?
Oedipus: That is why I call you a bad friend.
Kreon: No. Reason it out, as I have done.
Think of this first: Would any sane man prefer
Power, with all a king's anxieties,
To that same power and the grace of sleep?
Certainly not I.
I have never longed for the king's power--only his rights.
Would any wise man differ from me in this?

As matters stand, I have my way in everything
With your consent, and no responsibilities.
If I were king, I should be a slave to policy.
How could I desire a scepter more
Than what is now mine—untroubled influence?
No, I have not gone mad; I need no honors,
Except those with the perquisites I have now.
I am welcome everywhere; every man salutes me,
And those who want your favor seek my ear,
Since I know how to manage what they ask.
Should I exchange this ease for that anxiety?
Besides, no sober mind is treasonable.
I hate anarchy
And never would deal with any man who likes it.
Test what I have said. Go to the priestess
At Delphi, ask if I quoted her correctly.
And as for this other thing: if I am found
Guilty of treason with Teiresias,
Then sentence me to death. You have my word
It is a sentence I should cast my vote for—
But not without evidence!
You do wrong
When you take good men for bad, bad men for good.
A true friend thrown aside—why, life itself
Is not more precious!
In time you will know this well:
For time, and time alone, will show the just man,
Though scoundrels are discovered in a day.

Choragos: This is well said, and a prudent man would ponder it.
Judgments too quickly formed are dangerous.

Oedipus: But is he not quick in his duplicity?
And shall I not be quick to parry him?
Would you have me stand still, hold my peace, and let
This man win everything, through my inaction?

Kreon: And you want—what is it, then? To banish me?

Oedipus: No, not exile. It is your death I want,
So that all the world may see what treason means.

Kreon: You will persist, then? You will not believe me?

Oedipus: How can I believe you?

Kreon: Then you are a fool.

Oedipus: To save myself?

Kreon: In justice, think of me.

Oedipus: You are evil incarnate.

Kreon: But suppose that you are wrong?

Oedipus: Still I must rule.

Kreon: But not if you rule badly.

Oedipus: O city, city!
Kreon: It is my city, too!
Choragos: Now, my lords, be still. I see the queen,
Iokastê, coming from her palace chambers;
And it is time she came, for the sake of you both.
This dreadful quarrel can be resolved through her. *(Enter Iokastê.)*
Iokastê: Poor foolish men, what wicked din is this?
With Thebes sick to death, is it not shameful
That you should rake some private quarrel up?
(To Oedipus.) Come into the house.
—And you, Kreon, go now:
Let us have no more of this tumult over nothing.
Kreon: Nothing? No, sister: what your husband plans for me
Is one of two great evils: exile or death.
Oedipus: He is right.
Why, woman I have caught him squarely
Plotting against my life.
Kreon: No! Let me die
Accurst if ever I have wished you harm!
Iokastê: Ah, believe it, Oedipus!
In the name of the gods, respect this oath of his
For my sake, for the sake of these people here!

Strophe 1

Choragos: Open your mind to her, my lord. Be ruled by her, I beg you!
Oedipus: What would you have me do?
Choragos: Respect Kreon's word. He has never spoken like a fool,
And now he has sworn an oath.
Oedipus: You know what you ask?
Choragos: I do.
Oedipus: Speak on, then.
Choragos: A friend so sworn should not be baited so,
In blind malice, and without final proof.
Oedipus: You are aware, I hope, that what you say
Means death for me, or exile at the least.

Strophe 2

Choragos: No, I swear by Helios, first in heaven!
May I die friendless and accurst,
The worst of deaths, if ever I meant that!
It is the withering fields
That hurt my sick heart:
Must we bear all these ills,
And now your bad blood as well?

Oedipus: Then let him go. And let me die, if I must,
Or be driven by him in shame from the land of Thebes.
It is your unhappiness, and not his talk,
That touches me.
As for him—
Wherever he goes, hatred will follow him.
Kreon: Ugly in yielding, as you were ugly in rage!
Natures like yours chiefly torment themselves.
Oedipus: Can you not go? Can you not leave me?
Kreon: I can.
You do not know me; but the city knows me,
And in its eyes I am just, if not in yours. *(Exit Kreon.)*

Antistrophe 1

Choragos: Lady Iokastê, did you not ask the King to go to his chambers?
Iokastê: First tell me what has happened.
Choragos: There was suspicion without evidence; yet it rankled
As even false charges will.
Iokastê: On both sides?
Choragos: On both.
Iokastê: But what was said?
Choragos: Oh let it rest, let it be done with!
Have we not suffered enough?
Oedipus: You see to what your decency has brought you:
You have made difficulties where my heart saw none.

Antistrophe 2

Choragos: Oedipus, it is not once only I have told you—
You must know I should count myself unwise
To the point of madness, should I now forsake you—
You, under whose hand,
In the storm of another time,
Our dear land sailed out free.
But now stand fast at the helm!
Iokastê: In God's name, Oedipus, inform your wife as well:
Why are you so set in this hard anger?
Oedipus: I will tell you, for none of these men deserves
My confidence as you do. It is Kreon's work,
His treachery, his plotting against me.
Iokastê: Go on, if you can make this clear to me.
Oedipus: He charges me with the murder of Laïos.
Iokastê: Has he some knowledge? Or does he speak from hearsay?
Oedipus: He would not commit himself to such a charge,
But he has brought in that damnable soothsayer
To tell his story.

Iokastê: Set your mind at rest.
If it is a question of soothsayers, I tell you
That you will find no man whose craft gives knowledge
Of the unknowable.
Here is my proof:
An oracle was reported to Laïos once
(I will not say from Phoibos himself, but from
His appointed ministers, at any rate)
That his doom would be death at the hands of his own son—
His son, born of his flesh and of mine!

Now, you remember the story: Laïos was killed
By marauding strangers where three highways meet;
But his child had not been three days in this world
Before the king had pierced the baby's ankles
And left him to die on a lonely mountainside.

Thus, Apollo never caused that child
To kill his father, and it was not Laïos' fate
To die at the hands of his son, as he had feared.
This is what prophets and prophecies are worth!
Have no dread of them.
It is God himself
Who can show us what he wills, in his own way.
Oedipus: How strange a shadowy memory crossed my mind,
Just now while you were speaking; it chilled my heart.
Iokastê: What do you mean? What memory do you speak of?
Oedipus: If I understand you, Laïos was killed
At a place where three roads meet.
Iokastê: So it was said;
We have no later story.
Oedipus: Where did it happen?
Iokastê: Phokis, it is called: at a place where the Theban Way
Divides into the roads toward Delphi and Daulia.
Oedipus: When?
Iokastê: We had the news not long before you came
And proved the right to your succession here.
Oedipus: Ah, what net has God been weaving for me?
Iokastê: Oedipus! Why does this trouble you?
Oedipus Do not ask me yet.
First, tell me how Laïos looked, and tell me
How old he was.
Iokastê: He was tall, his hair just touched
With white; his form was not unlike your own.
Oedipus: I think that I myself may be accurst
By my own ignorant edict.

Iokastê: You speak strangely.
It makes me tremble to look at you, my king.
Oedipus: I am not sure that the blind man can not see.
But I should know better if you were to tell me—
Iokastê: Anything—though I dread to hear you ask it.
Oedipus: Was the king lightly escorted, or did he ride
With a large company, as a ruler should?
Iokastê: There were five men with him in all: one was a herald;
And a single chariot, which he was driving.
Oedipus: Alas, that makes it plain enough!
But who—
Who told you how it happened?
Iokastê: A household servant,
The only one to escape.
Oedipus: And is he still
A servant of ours?
Iokastê: No; for when he came back at last
And found you enthroned in the place of the dead king,
He came to me, touched my hand with his, and begged
That I would send him away to the frontier district
Where only the shepherds go—
As far away from the city as I could send him.
I granted his prayer; for although the man was a slave,
He had earned more than this favor at my hands.
Oedipus: Can he be called back quickly?
Iokastê: Easily.
But why?
Oedipus: I have taken too much upon myself
Without enquiry; therefore I wish to consult him.
Iokastê: Then he shall come.
But am I not one also
To whom you might confide these fears of yours?
Oedipus: That is your right; it will not be denied you,
Now least of all; for I have reached a pitch
Of wild foreboding. Is there anyone
To whom I should sooner speak?

Polybos of Corinth is my father.
My mother is a Dorian: Meropê.
I grew up chief among the men of Corinth
Until a strange thing happened—
Not worth my passion, it may be, but strange.
At a feast, a drunken man maundering in his cups
Cries out that I am not my father's son!

I contained myself that night, though I felt anger
And a sinking heart. The next day I visited

My father and mother, and questioned them. They stormed,
Calling it all the slanderous rant of a fool;
And this relieved me. Yet the suspicion
Remained always aching in my mind;
I knew there was talk; I could not rest;
And finally, saying nothing to my parents,
I went to the shrine at Delphi.

The god dismissed my question without reply;
He spoke of other things.
Some were clear,
Full of wretchedness, dreadful, unbearable:
As, that I should lie with my own mother, breed
Children from whom all men would turn their eyes;
And that I should be my father's murderer.

I heard all this, and fled. And from that day
Corinth to me was only in the stars
Descending in that quarter of the sky,
As I wandered farther and farther on my way
To a land where I should never see the evil
Sung by the oracle. And I came to this country
Where, so you say, King Laïos was killed.

I will tell you all that happened there, my lady.

There were three highways
Coming together at a place I passed;
And there a herald came towards me, and a chariot
Drawn by horses, with a man such as you describe
Seated in it. The groom leading the horses
Forced me off the road at his lord's command;
But as this charioteer lurched over towards me
I struck him in my rage. The old man saw me
And brought his double goad down upon my head
As I came abreast.
He was paid back, and more!
Swinging my club in this right hand I knocked him
Out of his car, and he rolled on the ground.
I killed him.
I killed them all.
Now if that stranger and Laïos were—kin,
Where is a man more miserable than I?
More hated by the gods? Citizen and alien alike
Must never shelter me or speak to me—
I must be shunned by all.
And I myself
Pronounced this malediction upon myself!

Think of it: I have touched you with these hands,
These hands that killed your husband. What defilement!

Am I all evil, then? It must be so,
Since I must flee from Thebes, yet never again
See my own countrymen, my own country,
For fear of joining my mother in marriage
And killing Polybos, my father.
Ah,
If I was created so, born to this fate,
Who could deny the savagery of God?

O holy majesty of heavenly powers!
May I never see that day! Never!
Rather let me vanish from the race of men
Than know the abomination destined me!

Choragos: We too, my lord, have felt dismay at this.
But there is hope: you have yet to hear the shepherd.

Oedipus: Indeed, I fear no other hope is left me.

Iokastê: What do you hope from him when he comes?

Oedipus: This much:
If his account of the murder tallies with yours,
Then I am cleared.

Iokastê: What was it that I said
Of such importance?

Oedipus: Why, "marauders," you said,
Killed the king, according to this man's story.
If he maintains that still, if there were several,
Clearly the guilt is not mine: I was alone.
But if he says one man, singlehanded, did it,
Then the evidence all points to me.

Iokastê: You may be sure that he said there were several;
And can he call back that story now? He can not.
The whole city heard it as plainly as I.
But suppose he alters some detail of it:
He can not ever show that Laïos' death
Fulfilled the oracle: for Apollo said
My child was doomed to kill him; and my child—
Poor baby!—it was my child that died first.

No. From now on, where oracles are concerned,
I would not waste a second thought on any.

Oedipus: You may be right.
But come: let someone go
For the shepherd at once. This matter must be settled.

Iokastê: I will send for him.
I would not wish to cross you in anything,
And surely not in this.—Let us go in. *(Exeunt into the palace.)*

Ode 2

Strophe 1

Chorus: Let me be reverent in the ways of right,
Lowly the paths I journey on;
Let all my words and actions keep
The laws of the pure universe
From highest Heaven handed down.
For Heaven is their bright nurse,
Those generations of the realms of light;
Ah, never of mortal kind were they begot,
Nor are they slaves of memory, lost in sleep:
Their Father is greater than Time, and ages not.

Antistrophe 1

The tyrant is a child of Pride
Who drinks from his great sickening cup
Recklessness and vanity,
Until from his high crest headlong
He plummets to the dust of hope.
That strong man is not strong.
But let no fair ambition be denied;
May God protect the wrestler for the State
In government, in comely policy,
Who will fear God, and on His ordinance wait.

Strophe 2

Haughtiness and the high hand of disdain
Tempt and outrage God's holy law;
And any mortal who dares hold
No immortal Power in awe
Will be caught up in a net of pain:
The price for which his levity is sold.
Let each man take due earnings, then,
And keep his hands from holy things,
And from blasphemy stand apart—
Else the crackling blast of heaven
Blows on his head, and on his desperate heart.
Though fools will honor impious men,
In their cities no tragic poet sings.

Antistrophe 2

Shall we lose faith in Delphi's obscurities,
We who have heard the world's core
Discredited, and the sacred wood
Of Zeus at Elis praised no more?
The deeds and the strange prophecies

Must make a pattern yet to be understood.
Zeus, if indeed you are lord of all,
Throned in light over night and day,
Mirror this in your endless mind:
Our masters call the oracle
Words on the wind, and the Delphic vision blind!
Their hearts no longer know Apollo,
And reverence for the gods has died away.

Scene 3

(Enter Iokastê.)

Iokastê: Princes of Thebes, it has occurred to me
To visit the altars of the gods, bearing
These branches as a suppliant, and this incense.
Our king is not himself: his noble soul
Is overwrought with fantasies of dread,
Else he would consider
The new prophecies in the light of the old.
He will listen to any voice that speaks disaster,
And my advice goes for nothing. *(She approaches the altar, right.)*
To you, then, Apollo,
Lycéan lord, since you are nearest, I turn in prayer.
Receive these offerings, and grant us deliverance
From defilement. Our hearts are heavy with fear
When we see our leader distracted, as helpless sailors
Are terrified by the confusion of their helmsman. *(Enter Messenger.)*
Messenger: Friends, no doubt you can direct me:
Where shall I find the house of Oedipus,
Or, better still, where is the king himself?
Choragos: It is this very place, stranger; he is inside.
This is his wife and mother of his children.
Messenger: I wish her happiness in a happy house,
Blest in all the fulfillment of her marriage.
Iokastê: I wish as much for you: your courtesy
Deserves a like good fortune. But now, tell me:
Why have you come? What have you to say to us?
Messenger: Good news, my lady, for your house and your husband.
Iokastê: What news? Who sent you here?
Messenger: I am from Corinth.
The news I bring ought to mean joy for you,
Though it may be you will find some grief in it.
Iokastê: What is it? How can it touch us in both ways?
Messenger: The word is that the people of the Isthmus
Intend to call Oedipus to be their king.
Iokastê: But old King Polybos—is he not reigning still?

Messenger: No. Death holds him in his sepulchre.
Iokastê: What are you saying? Polybos is dead?
Messenger: If I am not telling the truth, may I die myself.
Iokastê *(To a Maidservant.):* Go in, go quickly; tell this to your master.
O riddlers of God's will, where are you now!
This was the man whom Oedipus, long ago,
Feared so, fled so, in dread of destroying him—
But it was another fate by which he died. *(Enter Oedipus, center.)*
Oedipus: Dearest Iokastê, why have you sent for me?
Iokastê: Listen to what this man says, and then tell me
What has become of the solemn prophecies.
Oedipus: Who is this man? What is his news for me?
Iokastê: He has come from Corinth to announce your father's death!
Oedipus: Is it true, stranger? Tell me in your own words.
Messenger: I can not say it more clearly: the king is dead.
Oedipus: Was it by treason? Or by an attack of illness?
Messenger: A little thing brings old men to their rest.
Oedipus: It was sickness, then?
Messenger: Yes, and his many years.
Oedipus: Ah!
Why should a man respect the Pythian hearth,[11] or
Give heed to the birds that jangle above his head?
They prophesied that I should kill Polybos,
Kill my own father; but he is dead and buried,
And I am here—I never touched him, never,
Unless he died of grief for my departure,
And thus, in a sense, through me. No. Polybos
Has packed the oracles off with him underground.
They are empty words.
Iokastê: Had I not told you so?
Oedipus: You had; it was my faint heart that betrayed me.
Iokastê: From now on never think of those things again.
Oedipus: And yet—must I not fear my mother's bed?
Iokastê: Why should anyone in this world be afraid,
Since Fate rules us and nothing can be foreseen?
A man should live only for the present day.

Have no more fear of sleeping with your mother:
How many men, in dreams, have lain with their mothers!
No reasonable man is troubled by such things.
Oedipus: That is true; only—
If only my mother were not still alive!
But she is alive. I can not help my dread.
Iokastê: Yet this news of your father's death is wonderful.

[11] **Pythian hearth:** Delphi.

Oedipus: Wonderful. But I fear the living woman.
Messenger: Tell me, who is this woman that you fear?
Oedipus: It is Meropê, man; the wife of King Polybos.
Messenger: Meropê? Why should you be afraid of her?
Oedipus: An oracle of the gods, a dreadful saying.
Messenger: Can you tell me about it or are you sworn to silence?
Oedipus: I can tell you, and I will.
Apollo said through his prophet that I was the man
Who should marry his own mother, shed his father's blood
With his own hands. And so, for all these years
I have kept clear of Corinth, and no harm has come—
Though it would have been sweet to see my parents again.
Messenger: And is this the fear that drove you out of Corinth?
Oedipus: Would you have me kill my father?
Messenger: As for that
You must be reassured by the news I gave you.
Oedipus: If you could reassure me, I would reward you.
Messenger: I had that in mind, I will confess: I thought
I could count on you when you returned to Corinth.
Oedipus: No: I will never go near my parents again.
Messenger: Ah, son, you still do not know what you are doing—
Oedipus: What do you mean? In the name of God tell me!
Messenger: —If these are your reasons for not going home.
Oedipus: I tell you, I fear the oracle may come true.
Messenger: And guilt may come upon you through your parents?
Oedipus: That is the dread that is always in my heart.
Messenger: Can you not see that all your fears are groundless?
Oedipus: Groundless? Am I not my parents' son?
Messenger: Polybos was not your father.
Oedipus: Not my father?
Messenger: No more your father than the man speaking to you.
Oedipus: But you are nothing to me!
Messenger: Neither was he.
Oedipus: Then why did he call me son?
Messenger: I will tell you:
Long ago he had you from my hands, as a gift.
Oedipus: Then how could he love me so, if I was not his?
Messenger: He had no children, and his heart turned to you.
Oedipus: What of you? Did you buy me? Did you find me by chance?
Messenger: I came upon you in the woody vales of Kithairon.
Oedipus: And what were you doing there?
Messenger: Tending my flocks.
Oedipus: A wandering shepherd?
Messenger: But your savior, son, that day.
Oedipus: From what did you save me?

Messenger: Your ankles should tell you that.
Oedipus: Ah, stranger, why do you speak of that childhood pain?
Messenger: I pulled the skewer that pinned your feet together.
Oedipus: I have had the mark as long as I can remember.
Messenger: That was why you were given the name you bear.
Oedipus: God! Was it my father or my mother who did it? Tell me!
Messenger: I do not know. The man who gave you to me
Can tell you better than I.
Oedipus: It was not you that found me, but another?
Messenger: It was another shepherd gave you to me.
Oedipus: Who was he? Can you tell me who he was?
Messenger: I think he was said to be one of Laïos' people.
Oedipus: You mean the Laïos who was king here years ago?
Messenger: Yes; King Laïos; and the man was one of his herdsmen.
Oedipus: Is he still alive? Can I see him?
Messenger: These men here
Know best about such things.
Oedipus: Does anyone here
Know this shepherd that he is talking about?
Have you seen him in the fields, or in the town?
If you have, tell me. It is time things were made plain.
Choragos: I think the man he means is that same shepherd
You have already asked to see. Iokastê perhaps
Could tell you something.
Oedipus: Do you know anything
About him, Lady? Is he the man we have summoned?
Is that the man this shepherd means?
Iokastê: Why think of him?
Forget this herdsman. Forget it all.
This talk is a waste of time.
Oedipus: How can you say that,
When the clues to my true birth are in my hands?
Iokastê: For God's love, let us have no more questioning!
Is your life nothing to you?
My own is pain enough for me to bear.
Oedipus: You need not worry. Suppose my mother a slave,
And born of slaves: no baseness can touch you.
Iokastê: Listen to me, I beg you: do not do this thing!
Oedipus: I will not listen; the truth must be made known.
Iokastê: Everything that I say is for your own good!
Oedipus: My own good
Snaps my patience, then; I want none of it.
Iokastê: You are fatally wrong! May you never learn who you are!
Oedipus: Go, one of you, and bring the shepherd here.
Let us leave this woman to brag of her royal name.

Iokastê: Ah, miserable!
That is the only word I have for you now.
That is the only word I can ever have. *(Exit into the palace.)*
Choragos: Why has she left us, Oedipus? Why has she gone
In such a passion of sorrow? I fear this silence:
Something dreadful may come of it.
Oedipus: Let it come!
However base my birth, I must know about it.
The Queen, like a woman, is perhaps ashamed
To think of my low origin. But I
Am a child of Luck; I can not be dishonored.
Luck is my mother; the passing months, my brothers,
Have seen me rich and poor.
If this is so,
How could I wish that I were someone else?
How could I not be glad to know my birth?

Ode 3

Strophe

Chorus: If ever the coming time were known
To my heart's pondering,
Kithairon, now by Heaven I see the torches
At the festival of the next full moon,
And see the dance, and hear the choir sing
A grace to your gentle shade:
Mountain where Oedipus was found,
O mountain guard of a noble race!
May the god[12] who heals us lend his aid,
And let that glory come to pass
For our king's cradling-ground.

Antistrophe

Of the nymphs that flower beyond the years,
Who bore you,[13] royal child,
To Pan of the hills or the timberline Apollo,
Cold in delight where the upland clears,
Or Hermês for whom Kyllenê's heights are piled?
Or flushed as evening cloud,
Great Dionysos, roamer of mountains,
He—was it he who found you there,

[12] **god:** Apollo. [13] **Who bore you:** The chorus is suggesting that perhaps Oedipus is the son of one of the immortal nymphs and of a god—Pan, Apollo, Hermes, or Dionysos. The "sweet god-ravisher" (line 231) is the presumed mother.

And caught you up in his own proud
Arms from the sweet god-ravisher
Who laughed by the Muses' fountains?

Scene 4

Oedipus: Sirs: though I do not know the man,
I think I see him coming, this shepherd we want:
He is old, like our friend here, and the men
Bringing him seem to be servants of my house.
But you can tell, if you have ever seen him.

(Enter Shepherd escorted by Servants.)

Choragos: I know him, he was Laïos' man. You can trust him.
Oedipus: Tell me first, you from Corinth: is this the shepherd
We were discussing?
Messenger: This is the very man.
Oedipus *(To Shepherd.)*: Come here. No, look at me. You must answer
Everything I ask.—You belonged to Laïos?
Shepherd: Yes: born his slave, brought up in his house.
Oedipus: Tell me: what kind of work did you do for him?
Shepherd: I was a shepherd of his, most of my life.
Oedipus: Where mainly did you go for pasturage?
Shepherd: Sometimes Kithairon, sometimes the hills near-by.
Oedipus: Do you remember ever seeing this man out there?
Shepherd: What would he be doing there? This man?
Oedipus: This man standing here. Have you ever seen him before?
Shepherd: No. At least, not to my recollection.
Messenger: And that is not strange, my lord. But I'll refresh
His memory: he must remember when we two
Spent three whole seasons together, March to September,
On Kithairon or thereabouts. He had two flocks;
I had one. Each autumn I'd drive mine home
And he would go back with his to Laïos' sheepfold.—
Is this not true, just as I have described it?
Shepherd: True, yes; but it was all so long ago.
Messenger: Well, then: do you remember, back in those days,
That you gave me a baby boy to bring up as my own?
Shepherd: What if I did? What are you trying to say?
Messenger: King Oedipus was once that little child.
Shepherd: Damn you, hold your tongue!
Oedipus: No more of that!
It is your tongue needs watching, not this man's.
Shepherd: My king, my master, what is it I have done wrong?
Oedipus: You have not answered his question about the boy.
Shepherd: He does not know . . . He is only making trouble . . .
Oedipus: Come, speak plainly, or it will go hard with you.

Shepherd: In God's name, do not torture an old man!
Oedipus: Come here, one of you; bind his arms behind him.
Shepherd: Unhappy king! What more do you wish to learn?
Oedipus: Did you give this man the child he speaks of?
Shepherd: I did.
And I would to God I had died that very day.
Oedipus: You will die now unless you speak the truth.
Shepherd: Yet if I speak the truth, I am worse than dead.
Oedipus *(To Attendant.):* He intends to draw it out, apparently—
Shepherd: No! I have told you already that I gave him the boy.
Oedipus: Where did you get him? From your house? From somewhere else?
Shepherd: Not from mine, no. A man gave him to me.
Oedipus: Is that man here? Whose house did he belong to?
Shepherd: For God's love, my king, do not ask me any more!
Oedipus: You are a dead man if I have to ask you again.
Shepherd: Then . . . Then the child was from the palace of Laïos.
Oedipus: A slave child? or a child of his own line?
Shepherd: Ah, I am on the brink of dreadful speech!
Oedipus: And I of dreadful hearing. Yet I must hear.
Shepherd: If you must be told, then . . .
They said it was Laïos' child;
But it is your wife who can tell you about that.
Oedipus: My wife—Did she give it to you?
Shepherd: My lord, she did.
Oedipus: Do you know why?
Shepherd: I was told to get rid of it.
Oedipus: Oh heartless mother!
Shepherd: But in dread of prophecies . . .
Oedipus: Tell me.
Shepherd: It was said that the boy would kill his own father.
Oedipus: Then why did you give him over to this old man?
Shepherd: I pitied the baby, my king.
And I thought that this man would take him far away
To his own country.
He saved him—but for what a fate!
For if you are what this man says you are,
No man living is more wretched than Oedipus.
Oedipus: Ah God!
It was true!
All the prophecies!
—Now,
O Light, may I look on you for the last time!
I, Oedipus,
Oedipus, damned in his birth, in his marriage damned,
Damned in the blood he shed with his own hand!

(He rushes into the palace.)

Ode 4

Strophe 1

Chorus: Alas for the seed of men.
What measure shall I give these generations
That breathe on the void and are void
And exist and do not exist?
Who bears more weight of joy
Than mass of sunlight shifting in images,
Or who shall make his thought stay on
That down time drifts away?
Your splendor is all fallen.
O naked brow of wrath and tears,
O change of Oedipus!
I who saw your days call no man blest—
Your great days like ghósts góne.

Antistrophe 1

That mind was a strong bow.
Deep, how deep you drew it then, hard archer,
At a dim fearful range,
And brought dear glory down!
You overcame the stranger[14]—
The virgin with her hooking lion claws—
And though death sang, stood like a tower
To make pale Thebes take heart.
Fortress against our sorrow!
True king, giver of laws,
Majestic Oedipus!
No prince in Thebes had ever such renown,
No prince won such grace of power.

Strophe 2

And now of all men ever known
Most pitiful is this man's story:
His fortunes are most changed; his state
Fallen to a low slave's
Ground under bitter fate.
O Oedipus, most royal one!
The great door[15] that expelled you to the light
Gave at night—ah, gave night to your glory:
As to the father, to the fathering son.
All understood too late.
How could that queen whom Laïos won,

[14] **stranger:** the Sphinx. [15] **door:** Iokastê's womb.

The garden that he harrowed at his height,
Be silent when that act was done?

Antistrophe 2

But all eyes fail before time's eye,
All actions come to justice there.
Though never willed, though far down the deep past,
Your bed, your dread sirings,
Are brought to book at last.
Child by Laïos doomed to die,
Then doomed to lose that fortunate little death,
Would God you never took breath in this air
That with my wailing lips I take to cry:
For I weep the world's outcast.
I was blind, and now I can tell why:
Asleep, for you had given ease of breath
To Thebes, while the false years went by.

Exodos[16]

(Enter, from the palace, Second Messenger.)

Second Messenger: Elders of Thebes, most honored in this land,
What horrors are yours to see and hear, what weight
Of sorrow to be endured, if, true to your birth,
You venerate the line of Labdakos!
I think neither Istros nor Phasis, those great rivers,
Could purify this place of all the evil
It shelters now, or soon must bring to light—
Evil not done unconsciously, but willed.

The greatest griefs are those we cause ourselves.
Choragos: Surely, friend, we have grief enough already;
What new sorrow do you mean?
Second Messenger: The queen is dead.
Choragos: O miserable queen! But at whose hand?
Second Messenger: Her own.
The full horror of what happened you can not know,
For you did not see it; but I, who did, will tell you
As clearly as I can how she met her death.

When she had left us,
In passionate silence, passing through the court,
She ran to her apartment in the house,

[16] final scene.

Her hair clutched by the fingers of both hands.
She closed the doors behind her; then, by that bed
Where long ago the fatal son was conceived—
That son who should bring about his father's death—
We heard her call upon Laïos, dead so many years,
And heard her wail for the double fruit of her marriage,
A husband by her husband, children by her child.

Exactly how she died I do not know:
For Oedipus burst in moaning and would not let us
Keep vigil to the end: it was by him
As he stormed about the room that our eyes were caught.
From one to another of us he went, begging a sword,
Hunting the wife who was not his wife, the mother
Whose womb had carried his own children and himself.
I do not know: it was none of us aided him,
But surely one of the gods was in control!
For with a dreadful cry
He hurled his weight, as though wrenched out of himself,
At the twin doors: the bolts gave, and he rushed in.
And there we saw her hanging, her body swaying
From the cruel cord she had noosed about her neck.
A great sob broke from him, heartbreaking to hear,
As he loosed the rope and lowered her to the ground.

I would blot out from my mind what happened next!
For the king ripped from her gown the golden brooches
That were her ornament, and raised them, and plunged them down
Straight into his own eyeballs, crying, "No more,
No more shall you look on the misery about me,
The horrors of my own doing! Too long you have known
The faces of those whom I should never have seen,
Too long been blind to those for whom I was searching!
From this hour, go in darkness!" And as he spoke,
He struck at his eyes—not once, but many times;
And the blood spattered his beard,
Bursting from his ruined sockets like red hail.

So from the unhappiness of two this evil has sprung,
A curse on the man and woman alike. The old
Happiness of the house of Labdakos
Was happiness enough: where is it today?
It is all wailing and ruin, disgrace, death—all
The misery of mankind that has a name—
And it is wholly and for ever theirs.

Choragos: Is he in agony still? Is there no rest for him?

Second Messenger: He is calling for someone to open the doors wide
So that all the children of Kadmos may look upon
His father's murderer, his mother's—no,
I can not say it!
And then he will leave Thebes,
Self-exiled, in order that the curse
Which he himself pronounced may depart from the house.
He is weak, and there is none to lead him,
So terrible is his suffering.
But you will see:
Look, the doors are opening; in a moment
You will see a thing that would crush a heart of stone.

(The central door is opened; Oedipus, blinded, is led in.)

Choragos: Dreadful indeed for men to see.
Never have my own eyes
Looked on a sight so full of fear.

Oedipus!
What madness came upon you, what daemon
Leaped on your life with heavier
Punishment than a mortal man can bear?
No: I can not even
Look at you, poor ruined one.
And I would speak, question, ponder,
If I were able. No.
You make me shudder.
Oedipus: God. God.
Is there a sorrow greater?
Where shall I find harbor in this world?
My voice is hurled far on a dark wind.
What has God done to me?
Choragos: Too terrible to think of, or to see.

Strophe 1

Oedipus: O cloud of night,
Never to be turned away: night coming on,
I can not tell how: night like a shroud!
My fair winds brought me here.
O God. Again
The pain of the spikes where I had sight,
The flooding pain
Of memory, never to be gouged out.
Choragos: This is not strange.
You suffer it all twice over, remorse in pain,
Pain in remorse.

Antistrophe 1

Oedipus: Ah dear friend
Are you faithful even yet, you alone?
Are you still standing near me, will you stay here,
Patient, to care for the blind?
The blind man!
Yet even blind I know who it is attends me,
By the voice's tone—
Though my new darkness hide the comforter.

Choragos: Oh fearful act!
What god was it drove you to rake black
Night across your eyes?

Strophe 2

Oedipus: Apollo. Apollo. Dear
Children, the god was Apollo.
He brought my sick, sick fate upon me.
But the blinding hand was my own!
How could I bear to see
When all my sight was horror everywhere?

Choragos: Everywhere; that is true.

Oedipus: And now what is left?
Images? Love? A greeting even,
Sweet to the senses? Is there anything?
Ah, no, friends: lead me away.
Lead me away from Thebes.
Lead the great wreck
And hell of Oedipus, whom the gods hate.

Choragos: Your misery, you are not blind to that.
Would God you had never found it out!

Antistrophe 2

Oedipus: Death take the man who unbound
My feet on that hillside
And delivered me from death to life! What life?
If only I had died,
This weight of monstrous doom
Could not have dragged me and my darlings down.

Choragos: I would have wished the same.

Oedipus: Oh never to have come here
With my father's blood upon me! Never
To have been the man they call his mother's husband!
Oh accurst! Oh child of evil,
To have entered that wretched bed—
the selfsame one!
More primal than sin itself, this fell to me.

Choragos: I do not know what words to offer you.
You were better dead than alive and blind.

Oedipus: Do not counsel me any more. This punishment
That I have laid upon myself is just.
If I had eyes,
I do not know how I could bear the sight
Of my father, when I came to the house of Death,
Or my mother: for I have sinned against them both
So vilely that I could not make my peace
By strangling my own life.
Or do you think my children,
Born as they were born, would be sweet to my eyes?
Ah never, never! Nor this town with its high walls,
Nor the holy images of the gods.
For I,
Thrice miserable!—Oedipus, noblest of all the line
Of Kadmos, have condemned myself to enjoy
These things no more, by my own malediction
Expelling that man whom the gods declared
To be a defilement in the house of Laïos.
After exposing the rankness of my own guilt,
How could I look men frankly in the eyes?
No, I swear it,
If I could have stifled my hearing at its source,
I would have done it and made all this body
A tight cell of misery, blank to light and sound:
So I should have been safe in my dark mind
Beyond external evil.
Ah Kithairon!
Why did you shelter me? When I was cast upon you,
Why did I not die? Then I should never
Have shown the world my execrable birth.

Ah Polybos! Corinth, city that I believed
The ancient seat of my ancestors: how fair
I seemed, your child! And all the while this evil
Was cancerous within me!
For I am sick
In my own being, sick in my origin.

O three roads, dark ravine, woodland and way
Where three roads met: you, drinking my father's blood,
My own blood, spilled by my own hand: can you remember
The unspeakable things I did there, and the things
I went on from there to do?

O marriage, marriage!
The act that engendered me, and again the act
Performed by the son in the same bed—
Ah, the net
Of incest, mingling fathers, brothers, sons,
With brides, wives, mothers: the last evil
That can be known by men: no tongue can say
How evil!
No. For the love of God, conceal me
Somewhere far from Thebes; or kill me; or hurl me
Into the sea, away from men's eyes for ever.

Come, lead me. You need not fear to touch me.
Of all men, I alone can bear this guilt. *(Enter Kreon.)*

Choragos: Kreon is here now. As to what you ask,
He may decide the course to take. He only
Is left to protect the city in your place.

Oedipus: Alas, how can I speak to him? What right have I
To beg his courtesy whom I have deeply wronged?

Kreon: I have not come to mock you, Oedipus,
Or to reproach you, either.
(To Attendants.)—You, standing there:
If you have lost all respect for man's dignity,
At least respect the flame of Lord Helios:
Do not allow this pollution to show itself
Openly here, an affront to the earth
And Heaven's rain and the light of day. No, take him
Into the house as quickly as you can.
For it is proper
That only the close kindred see his grief.

Oedipus: I pray you in God's name, since your courtesy
Ignores my dark expectation, visiting
With mercy this man of all men most execrable:
Give me what I ask—for your good, not for mine.

Kreon: And what is it that you turn to me begging for?

Oedipus: Drive me out of this country as quickly as may be
To a place where no human voice can ever greet me.

Kreon: I should have done that before now—only,
God's will had not been wholly revealed to me.

Oedipus: But his command is plain: the parricide
Must be destroyed. I am that evil man.

Kreon: That is the sense of it, yes; but as things are,
We had best discover clearly what is to be done.

Oedipus: You would learn more about a man like me?

Kreon: You are ready now to listen to the god.

Oedipus: I will listen. But it is to you
That I must turn for help. I beg you, hear me.

The woman in there—
Give her whatever funeral you think proper:
She is your sister.
—But let me go, Kreon!
Let me purge my father's Thebes of the pollution
Of my living here, and go out to the wild hills,
To Kithairon, that has won such fame with me,
The tomb my mother and father appointed for me,
And let me die there, as they willed I should.
And yet I know
Death will not ever come to me through sickness
Or in any natural way: I have been preserved
For some unthinkable fate. But let that be.
As for my sons, you need not care for them.
They are men, they will find some way to live.
But my poor daughters, who have shared my table,
Who never before have been parted from their father—
Take care of them, Kreon; do this for me.

And will you let me touch them with my hands
A last time, and let us weep together?
Be kind, my lord,
Great prince, be kind!
Could I but touch them,
They would be mine again, as when I had my eyes.

(Enter Antigone and Ismene, attended.)

Ah, God!
Is it my dearest children I hear weeping?
Has Kreon pitied me and sent my daughters?
Kreon: Yes, Oedipus: I knew that they were dear to you
In the old days, and know you must love them still.
Oedipus: May God bless you for this—and be a friendlier
Guardian to you than he has been to me!

Children, where are you?
Come quickly to my hands: they are your brother's—
Hands that have brought your father's once clear eyes
To this way of seeing—
Ah dearest ones,
I had neither sight nor knowledge then, your father
By the woman who was the source of his own life!
And I weep for you—having no strength to see you—,

I weep for you when I think of the bitterness
That men will visit upon you all your lives.
What homes, what festivals can you attend
Without being forced to depart again in tears?
And when you come to marriageable age,
Where is the man, my daughters, who would dare
Risk the bane that lies on all my children?
Is there any evil wanting? Your father killed
His father; sowed the womb of her who bore him;
Engendered you at the fount of his own existence!
That is what they will say of you.
Then, whom
Can you ever marry? There are no bridegrooms for you,
And your lives must wither away in sterile dreaming.

O Kreon, son of Menoikeus!
You are the only father my daughters have,
Since we, their parents, are both of us gone for ever.
They are your own blood: you will not let them
Fall into beggary and loneliness;
You will keep them from the miseries that are mine!
Take pity on them; see, they are only children,
Friendless except for you. Promise me this,
Great prince, and give me your hand in token of it.

(Kreon clasps his right hand.)

Children:
I could say much, if you could understand me,
But as it is, I have only this prayer for you:
Live where you can, be as happy as you can—
Happier, please God, than God has made your father.

Kreon: Enough. You have wept enough. Now go within.
Oedipus: I must; but it is hard.
Kreon: Time eases all things.
Oedipus: You know my mind, then?
Kreon: Say what you desire.
Oedipus: Send me from Thebes!
Kreon: God grant that I may!
Oedipus: But since God hates me . . .
Kreon: No, he will grant your wish.
Oedipus: You promise?
Kreon: I can not speak beyond my knowledge.
Oedipus: Then lead me in.
Kreon: Come now, and leave your children.
Oedipus: No! Do not take them from me!
Kreon: Think no longer

That you are in command here, but rather think
How, when you were, you served your own destruction. *(Exeunt into the house all but the Chorus; the Choragos chants directly to the audience.)*

Choragos: Men of Thebes: look upon Oedipus.

This is the king who solved the famous riddle
And towered up, most powerful of men.
No mortal eyes but looked on him with envy,
Yet in the end ruin swept over him.

Let every man in mankind's frailty
Consider his last day; and let none
Presume on his good fortune until he find
Life, at his death, a memory without pain.

Explorations of the Text

1. Discuss the character of Oedipus. Why is he so impetuous? Why does he not believe Teiresias?
2. Discuss the situation in the play. Why was Oedipus left to die as an infant? Why was he not told about his origins?
3. Discuss the character of Iokastê. Why does she not see the truth?
4. What function does the chorus perform?
5. Discuss Teiresias and Kreon at length.
6. Discuss the nature of prophecy and fate in this tragedy. Does Oedipus have a tragic flaw? (See **hamartia** in the Glossary.) Does fate or character create this tragedy?
7. By the end of the play, what does Oedipus learn about himself, about the gods, about truth?
8. Why is Oedipus' tragedy both personal and political?
9. How does this drama resemble a mystery? Discuss **dramatic irony.** What other devices create suspense?
10. Why does Oedipus blind himself?

The Reading/Writing Connection

1. "Think" Topic: Since seeing and insight are so valuable, why do human beings resist them?
2. Find one example of **dramatic irony** in *Oedipus Rex,* and in a paragraph discuss its function and effectiveness.

Ideas for Writing

1. Explore images of darkness and light in *Oedipus Rex.*
2. Is Oedipus a victim or the agent of his own downfall?
3. How is *Oedipus Rex* a political play?

American Ignorance of War

Czeslaw Milosz

Czeslaw Milosz (1911–) was born in Wilno, Poland. A leader in the Polish literary avant-garde in the 1930s, Milosz immigrated to the United States after the Second World War, settling in California, where he taught at the University of California, Berkeley. He has written essays, including The Captive Mind *(1953), and poetry, including* Facing the River *(1995). His* Collected Poems *appeared in 1990. He received the Nobel Prize for Literature in 1980.*

1953

Are Americans *really* stupid? I was asked in Warsaw. In the voice of the man who posed the question, there was despair, as well as the hope that I would contradict him. This question reveals the attitude of the average person in the people's democracies toward the West: It is despair mixed with a residue of hope.

During the last few years, the West has given these people a number of reasons to despair politically. In the case of the intellectual, other, more complicated reasons come into play. Before the countries of Central and Eastern Europe entered the sphere of the Imperium,[1] they lived through the Second World War. That war was much more devastating there than in the countries of Western Europe. It destroyed not only their economies but also a great many values which had seemed till then unshakable.

Man tends to regard the order he lives in as *natural.* The houses he passes on his way to work seem more like rocks rising out of the earth than like products of human hands. He considers the work he does in his office or factory as essential to the harmonious functioning of the world. The clothes he wears are exactly what they should be, and he laughs at the idea that he might equally well be wearing a Roman toga or medieval armor. He respects and envies a minister of state or a bank director, and regards the possession of a considerable amount of money as the main guarantee of peace and security. He cannot believe that one day a rider may appear on a street he knows well, where cats sleep and children play, and start catching passersby with his lasso. He is accustomed to satisfying those of his physiological needs which are considered

[1] Empire: Sphere of dominance; Soviet Union.

private as discreetly as possible, without realizing that such a pattern of behavior is not common to all human societies. In a word, he behaves a little like Charlie Chaplin in *The Gold Rush,* bustling about in a shack poised precariously on the edge of a cliff.

His first stroll along a street littered with glass from bomb-shattered windows shakes his faith in the "naturalness" of his world. The wind scatters papers from hastily evacuated offices, papers labeled "Confidential" or "Top Secret" that evoke visions of safes, keys, conferences, couriers, and secretaries. Now the wind blows them through the street for anyone to read; yet no one does, for each man is more urgently concerned with finding a loaf of bread. Strangely enough, the world goes on even though the offices and secret files have lost all meaning. Farther down the street, he stops before a house split in half by a bomb, the privacy of people's homes—the family smells, the warmth of the beehive life, the furniture preserving the memory of loves and hatreds—cut open to public view. The house itself, no longer a rock, but a scaffolding of plaster, concrete, and brick; and on the third floor, a solitary white bathtub, rain-rinsed of all recollection of those who once bathed in it. Its formerly influential and respected owners, now destitute, walk the fields in search of stray potatoes. Thus overnight money loses its value and becomes a meaningless mass of printed paper. His walk takes him past a little boy poking a stick into a heap of smoking ruins and whistling a song about the great leader who will preserve the nation against all enemies. The song remains, but the leader of yesterday is already part of an extinct past.

5 He finds he acquires new habits quickly. Once, had he stumbled upon a corpse on the street, he would have called the police. A crowd would have gathered, and much talk and comment would have ensued. Now he knows he must avoid the dark body lying the gutter, and refrain from asking unnecessary questions. The man who fired the gun must have had his reasons; he might well have been executing an Underground sentence.

Nor is the average European accustomed to thinking of his native city as divided into segregated living areas, but a single decree can force him to this new pattern of life and thought. Quarter A may suddenly be designated for one race; B, for a second; C, for a third. As the resettlement deadline approaches, the streets become filled with long lines of wagons, carts, wheelbarrows, and people carrying bundles, beds, chests, caldrons, and bird cages. When all the moves are effected, 2,000 people may find themselves in a building that once housed 200, but each man is at last in the proper area. Then high walls are erected around Quarter C, and daily a given lot of men, women, and children are loaded into wagons that take them off to specially constructed factories where they are scientifically slaughtered and their bodies burned.

And even the rider with the lasso appears, in the form of a military van waiting at the corner of a street. A man passing that corner meets a leveled rifle, raises his hands, is pushed into the van, and from that moment is lost to his family and friends. He may be sent to a concentration camp, or he may face a firing squad, his lips sealed with plaster lest he cry out against the state; but, in any case, he serves as a warning to his fellow men. Perhaps one might escape such a fate by remaining at home. But the father of a family must go out in order to provide bread and soup for his wife and children; and every night they worry about whether or not he will return. Since these conditions last for years, everyone gradually comes to look upon the city as a jungle, and upon the fate of twentieth-century man as identical with that of a caveman living in the midst of powerful monsters.

It was once thought obvious that a man bears the same name and surname throughout his entire life; now it proves wiser for many reasons to change them and to memorize a new and fabricated biography. As a result, the records of the civilian state become completely confused. Everyone ceases to care about formalities, so that marriage, for example, comes to mean little more than living together.

Respectable citizens used to regard banditry as a crime. Today, bank robbers are heroes because the money they steal is destined for the Underground. Usually they are young boys, mothers' boys, but their appearance is deceiving. The killing of a man presents no great moral problem to them.

10 The nearness of death destroys shame. Men and women change as soon as they know that the date of their execution has been fixed by a fat little man with shiny boots and a riding crop. They copulate in public, on the small bit of ground surrounded by barbed wire—their last home on earth. Boys and girls in their teens, about to go off to the barricades to fight against tanks with pistols and bottles of gasoline, want to enjoy their youth and lose their respect for standards of decency.

Which world is "natural"? That which existed before, or the world of war? Both are natural, if both are within the realm of one's experience. All the concepts men live by are a product of the historic formation in which they find themselves. Fluidity and constant change are the characteristics of phenomena. And man is so plastic a being that one can even conceive of the day when a thoroughly self-respecting citizen will crawl on all fours, sporting a tail of brightly colored feathers as a sign of conformity to the order he lives in.

The man of the East cannot take Americans seriously because they have never undergone the experiences that teach men how relative their judgments and thinking habits are. Their resultant lack of imagination is appalling. Because they were born and raised in a given social order and in a given system of values, they believe that any other order must be "unnatural," and that it cannot last because it is incompatible with human nature. But even they may one day know fire, hunger, and the sword. In all probability this is what will occur; for it is hard to believe that when one half of the world is living through terrible disasters, the other half can continue a nineteenth-century mode of life, learning about the distress of its distant fellow men only from movies and newspapers. Recent examples teach us that this cannot be. An inhabitant of Warsaw or Budapest once looked at newsreels of bombed Spain or burning Shanghai, but in the end he learned how these and many other catastrophes appear in actuality. He read gloomy tales of the NKVD[2] until one day he himself had to deal with it. *If something exists in one place, it will exist everywhere.* This is the conclusion he draws from his observations, and so he has no particular faith in the momentary prosperity of America. He suspects that the years 1933–1945 in Europe[3] prefigure what will occur elsewhere. A hard school, where ignorance was punished not by bad marks but by death, has taught him to think sociologically and historically. But it has not freed him from irrational feelings. He is apt to believe in theories that foresee violent changes in the countries of the West, for he finds it unjust that they should escape the hardships he had to undergo.

Explorations of the Text

1. This essay appears in Milosz's first American volume *The Captive Mind* published shortly after World War II and after his defection from Poland in 1951 and thirty-five years before the birth of democracies in Eastern Europe and détente in Soviet Russia. Do you see evidence in the essay of the historical context of this work? To what historical events does the author refer?
2. Why does Milosz begin with the question: "Are Americans really stupid?" What is his perspective in the essay? How does the opening paragraph suggest his point of view, tone, and themes of the essay?
3. Consider Milosz's use of the term "nature." What is "natural" to man? Is he being ironic? Contrast the two views of human nature, modes of living, states of civilization presented in the essay.
4. What does he conclude about the world? Now fifty years after the publication of this essay, do you concur with his views expressed in paragraphs 11 and 12? Have Americans lost their innocence? Their senses of insularity from world events?
5. Compare the view of witnessing expressed in this essay with Oedipus's growth of awareness.

The Reading/Writing Connection

1. "Think" Topic: Do Americans live in a state of willed "ignorance"? Freewrite in response to this question.
2. Choose a statement from this essay that you agree or disagree with. Create a dialogue with the author.
3. Do ordinary citizens bear the responsibility for the living and the dying? Respond in a journal entry.

---

[2] The Soviet secret police, 1935–43.

[3] The years of the rise, dominance, and demise of Nazism.

Ideas for Writing

1. Evaluate Milosz's argument. How does Milosz build his argument? What forms of evidence does he use? Are his techniques effective?
2. Compare Milosz's vision of the response to war with one of the short stories presented in this chapter.
3. Imagine that America has been invaded and occupied by another country. Create a short scene that demonstrates the consequences.
4. Debate Topics: Argue pro or con about one of these contentions.
   - Americans' "lack of imagination is appalling."
   - Americans have never experienced "fire, hunger, and the sword."
   - The state of war is "natural."

FICTION

War

Luigi Pirandello

Luigi Pirandello (1867–1936), born in Sicily, earned his doctorate in philology from Bonn University. A playwright, novelist, short story writer, essayist, and poet, he created "grotesco," the expressionist theater form that deals with the psychological realities underlying social appearances. Pirandello joined the Fascist party in 1924 and was patronized by Mussolini. He won the Nobel Prize for Literature in 1934. Pirandello wrote more than forty plays, including Six Characters in Search of an Author *(1921). He is famous as a playwright and as a writer of short stories.*

1939

The passengers who had left Rome by the night express had had to stop until dawn at the small station of Fabriano in order to continue their journey by the small old-fashioned local joining the main line with Sulmona.

At dawn, in a stuffy and smoky second-class carriage in which five people had already spent the night, a bulky woman in deep mourning was hoisted in—almost like a shapeless bundle. Behind her, puffing and moaning, followed her husband—a tiny man, thin and weakly, his face death-white, his eyes small and bright and looking shy and uneasy.

Having at last taken a seat he politely thanked the passengers who had helped his wife and who had made room for her; then he turned round to the woman trying to pull down the collar of her coat, and politely inquired:

"Are you all right, dear?"

5 The wife, instead of answering, pulled up her collar again to her eyes, so as to hide her face.

"Nasty world," muttered the husband with a sad smile.

And he felt it his duty to explain to his traveling companions that the poor woman was to be pitied, for the war was taking away from her her only son, a boy of twenty to whom both had devoted their entire life, even breaking up their home at Sulmona to follow him to Rome, where he had to go as a student, then allowing him to volunteer for war with an assurance, however, that at least for six months he would not be sent to the front and now, all of a sudden, receiving a wire saying that he was due to leave in three days' time and asking them to go and see him off.

The woman under the big coat was twisting and wriggling, at times growling like a wild animal, feeling certain that all those explanations would not have aroused even a shadow of sympathy from those people who—most likely—were in the same plight as herself. One of them, who had been listening with particular attention, said:

"You should thank God that your son is only leaving now for the front. Mine has been sent there the first day of the war. He has already come back twice wounded and been sent back again to the front."

"What about me? I have two sons and three nephews at the front," said another passenger.

"Maybe, but in our case it is our *only* son," ventured the husband.

"What difference can it make? You may spoil your only son with excessive attentions, but you cannot love him more than you would all your other children if you had any. Paternal love is not like bread that can be broken into pieces and split amongst the children in equal shares. A father gives *all* his love to each one of his children without discrimination, whether it be one or ten, and if I am suffering now for my two sons, I am not suffering half for each of them but double . . ."

"True . . . true . . ." sighed the embarrassed husband, "but suppose (of course we all hope it will never be your case) a father has two sons at the front and he loses one of them, there is still one left to console him . . . while . . ."

"Yes," answered the other, getting cross, "a son left to console him but also a son left for whom he must survive, while in the case of the father of an only son if the son dies the father can die too and put an end to his distress. Which of the two positions is the worse? Don't you see how my case would be worse than yours?"

"Nonsense," interrupted another traveler, a fat, red-faced man with blood-shot eyes of the palest gray.

He was panting. From his bulging eyes seemed to spurt inner violence of an uncontrolled vitality which his weakened body could hardly contain.

"Nonsense," he repeated, trying to cover his mouth with his hand so as to hide the two missing front teeth. "Nonsense. Do we give life to our children for our own benefit?"

The other travelers stared at him in distress. The one who had had his son at the front since the first day of the war sighed: "You are right. Our children do not belong to us, they belong to the Country. . . . "

"Bosh," retorted the fat traveler. "Do we think of the Country when we give life to our children? Our sons are born because . . . well, because they must be born and when they come to life they take our own life with them. This is the truth. We belong to them but they never belong to us. And when they reach twenty they are exactly what we were at their age. We too had a father and mother, but there were so many other things as well . . . girls, cigarettes, illusions, new ties . . . and the Country, of course, whose call we would have answered—when we were twenty—even if father and mother had said no. Now at our age, the love of our Country is still great, of course, but stronger than it is the love for our children. Is there any one of us here who wouldn't gladly take his son's place at the front if he could?"

There was a silence all round, everybody nodding as to approve.

"Why then," continued the fat man, "shouldn't we consider the feelings of our children when they are twenty? Isn't it natural that at their age they should consider the love for their Country (I am speaking of decent boys, of course) even greater than the love for us? Isn't it natural that it should be so, as after all they must look upon us as upon old boys who cannot move any more and must stay at home? If Country exists, if Country is a natural necessity, like bread, of which each of us must eat in order not to die of hunger, somebody must go to defend it. And our sons go, when they are twenty, and they don't want tears, because if they die, they die inflamed and happy (I am speaking, of course, of decent boys). Now, if one dies young and happy, without having the ugly sides of life, the boredom of it, the pettiness, the bitterness of disillusion . . . what more can we ask for him? Everyone should stop crying; everyone should laugh, as I do . . . or at least thank God—as I do—because my son, before dying, sent me a message saying that he was dying satisfied at having ended his life in the best way he could have wished. That is why, as you see, I do not even wear mourning. . . ."

He shook his light fawn coat as to show it; his livid lip over his missing teeth was trembling, his eyes were watery and motionless, and soon after he ended with a shrill laugh which might well have been a sob.

"Quite so . . . quite so . . ." agreed the others.

The woman who, bundled in a corner under her coat, had been sitting and listening had—for the last three months—tried to find in the words of her husband and her friends something to console her in her deep sorrow, something that might show her how a mother should resign herself to send her son not even to death but to a probably dangerous life. Yet not a word had she found amongst the many which had been said . . . and her grief had been greater in seeing that nobody—as she thought—could share her feelings.

But now the words of the traveler amazed and almost stunned her. She suddenly realized that it wasn't the others who were wrong and could not understand her but herself who could not rise up to the same height of those fathers and mothers willing to resign themselves, without crying, not only to the departure of their sons but even to their death.

She lifted her head, she bent over from her corner trying to listen with great attention to the details which the fat man was giving to his companions about the way his son had fallen as a hero, for his King and his Country, happy and without regrets. It seemed to her that she had stumbled into a world she had never dreamt of, a world so far unknown to her and she was so pleased to hear everyone joining in congratulating that brave father who could so stoically speak of his child's death.

Then suddenly, just as if she had heard nothing of what had been said and almost as if waking up from a dream, she turned to the old man, asking him:

"Then . . . is your son really dead?"

Everybody stared at her. The old man, too, turned to look at her, fixing his great, bulging, horribly watery light gray eyes, deep in her face. For some little time he tried to answer, but words failed him. He looked and looked at her, almost as if only then—at that silly, incongruous question—he had suddenly realized at last that his son was really dead—gone for ever—for ever. His face contracted, became horribly distorted, then he snatched in haste a handkerchief from his pocket and, to the amazement of everyone, broke into harrowing, heart-rending, uncontrollable sobs.

Explorations of the Text

1. Discuss the function and effectiveness of the night train as a setting for the story.
2. Describe each of the passengers. What do their physical and emotional traits reveal about their attitudes toward war?
3. Analyze the conversation between the "husband" and the father with two sons. What do you conclude?
4. Why is "the fat man's" speech about love of country so compelling and persuasive? How does his appearance at the end of his speech foreshadow the conclusion of the story?
5. The grieving mother begins to feel "amazed" and "stunned." What is the source of her question: "Then . . . is your son really dead?"
6. What happens to the fat man? What is the meaning of his insight?
7. Consider the economy of Pirandello's style. What do you learn about the value of concise and terse writing?
8. Compare the themes of this story with those in works by O'Brien, Milosz, Ozick, Endō, and/or Delbo.

The Reading/Writing Connection

1. What reasons compel "decent" young people to go to war? Would you go to war?
2. "Think" Topic: Why does "the fat man" rationalize his son's death?
3. Assume that you are about to become a soldier. Write a journal entry about your position on war.

Ideas for Writing

1. Explore the concept of the train journey. What does Pirandello accomplish with this setting?
2. Compare Hemingway's and Pirandello's styles.
3. Analyze the character of "the fat man."
4. Do young people feel more patriotic and bellicose than older people?

The Shawl

Cynthia Ozick

Cynthia Ozick (1928–) was born in New York City. Her writing shows the influence of her extensive reading in Jewish philosophy and the effect of the anti-Semitism that she experienced as a child. Her work includes the novels Trust *(1966) and* The Puttermesser Papers *(1997); a novella,* The Messiah of Stockholm *(1987); and the volumes of short fiction* The Pagan Rabbi and Other Stories *(1971) and* Bloodshed and Three Novellas *(1976). Several of Ozick's short stories have been chosen for* The Best American Short Stories, *notably "The Shawl" and its companion piece, the novella "Rosa." Her work also won first prize in the annual O. Henry Prize Stories collection in 1975, 1981, and 1984.*

1980

Stella, cold, cold, the coldness of hell. How they walked on the roads together, Rosa with Magda curled up between sore breasts, Magda wound up in the shawl. Sometimes Stella carried Magda. But she was jealous of Magda. A thin girl of fourteen, too small, with thin breasts of her own, Stella wanted to be wrapped in a shawl, hidden away, asleep, rocked by the march, a baby, a round infant in arms. Magda took Rosa's nipple, and Rosa never stopped walking, a walking cradle. There was not enough milk; sometimes Magda sucked air; then she screamed. Stella was ravenous. Her knees were tumors on sticks, her elbows chicken bones.

Rosa did not feel hunger; she felt light, not like someone walking but like someone in a faint, in trance, arrested in a fit, someone who is already a floating angel, alert and seeing everything, but in the air, not there, not touching the road. As if teetering on the tips of her fingernails. She looked into Magda's face through a gap in the shawl: a squirrel in a nest, safe, no one could reach her inside the little house of the shawl's windings. The face, very round, a pocket mirror of a face: but it was not Rosa's bleak complexion, dark like cholera, it was another kind of face altogether, eyes blue as air, smooth feathers of hair nearly as yellow as the Star sewn into Rosa's coat. You could think she was one of *their* babies.

Rosa, floating, dreamed of giving Magda away in one of the villages. She could leave the line for a minute and push Magda into the hands of any woman on the side of the road. But if she moved out of line they might shoot. And even if she fled the line for half a second and pushed the shawl-bundle at a stranger, would the woman take it? She might be surprised, or afraid; she might drop the shawl, and Magda would fall out and strike her head and die. The little round head. Such a good child, she gave up screaming, and sucked now only for the taste of the drying nipple itself. The neat grip of the tiny gums. One mite of a tooth tip sticking up in the bottom gum, how shining, an elfin tombstone of white marble, gleaming there. Without complaining, Magda relinquished Rosa's teats, first the left, then the right; both were cracked, not a sniff of milk. The duct crevice extinct, a dead volcano, blind eye, chill hole, so Magda took the corner of the shawl and milked it instead. She sucked and sucked, flooding the threads with wetness. The shawl's good flavor, milk of linen.

It was a magic shawl, it could nourish an infant for three days and three nights. Magda did not die, she stayed alive, although very quiet. A peculiar smell, of cinnamon and almonds, lifted out of her mouth. She held her eyes open every moment, forgetting how to blink or nap, and Rosa and sometimes Stella studied their blueness. On the road they raised one burden of a leg after another and studied Magda's face. "Aryan," Stella said, in a voice grown as thin as a string; and Rosa thought how Stella gazed at Magda like a young cannibal. And the time that Stella said "Aryan," it sounded to Rosa as if Stella had really said, "Let us devour her."

5 But Magda lived to walk. She lived that long, but she did not walk very well, partly because she was only fifteen months old, and partly because the spindles of her legs could not hold up her fat belly. It was fat with air, full and round. Rosa gave almost all her food to Magda, Stella gave nothing; Stella was ravenous, a growing child herself, but not growing much. Stella did not menstruate. Rosa did not menstruate. Rosa was ravenous, but also not; she learned from Magda how to drink the taste of a finger in one's mouth. They were in a place without pity, all pity was annihilated in Rosa, she looked at Stella's bones without pity. She was sure that Stella was waiting for Magda to die so she could put her teeth into the little thighs.

Rosa knew Magda was going to die very soon; she should have been dead already, but she had been buried away deep inside the magic shawl, mistaken there for the shivering mound of Rosa's breasts; Rosa clung to the shawl as if it covered only herself. No one took it away from her. Magda was mute. She never cried. Rosa hid her in the barracks, under the shawl, but she knew that one day someone would inform; or one day someone, not even Stella, would steal Magda to eat her. When Magda began to walk Rosa knew that Magda was going to die very soon, something would happen. She was afraid to fall asleep; she slept with the weight of her thigh on Magda's body; she was afraid she would smother Magda under her thigh. The weight of Rosa was becoming less and less, Rosa and Stella were slowly turning into air.

Magda was quiet, but her eyes were horribly alive, like blue tigers. She watched. Sometimes she laughed—it seemed a laugh, but how could it be? Magda had never seen anyone laugh. Still, Magda laughed at her shawl when the wind blew its corners, the bad wind with pieces of black in it, that made Stella's and Rosa's eyes tear. Magda's eyes were always clear and tearless. She watched like a tiger. She guarded her shawl. No one could touch it; only Rosa could touch it. Stella was not allowed. The shawl was Magda's own baby, her pet, her little sister. She tangled herself up in it and sucked on one of the corners when she wanted to be very still.

Then Stella took the shawl away and made Magda die.

Afterward Stella said: "I was cold."

10 And afterward she was always cold, always. The cold went into her heart: Rosa saw that Stella's heart was cold. Magda flopped onward with her little pencil legs scribbling this way and that, in search of the shawl; the pencils faltered at the barracks opening, where the light began. Rosa saw and pursued. But already Magda was in the square outside the barracks, in the jolly light. It was the roll-call arena. Every morning Rosa had to conceal Magda under the shawl against a wall of the barracks and go out and stand in the arena with Stella and hundreds of others, sometimes for hours, and Magda, deserted, was quiet under the shawl, sucking on her corner. Every day Magda was silent, and so she did not die. Rosa saw that today Magda was going to die, and at the same time a fearful joy ran in Rosa's two palms, her fingers were on fire, she was astonished, febrile: Magda, in the sunlight, swaying on her pencil legs,

was howling. Ever since the drying up of Rosa's nipples, ever since Magda's last scream on the road, Magda had been devoid of any syllable; Magda was a mute. Rosa believed that something had gone wrong with her vocal cords, with her windpipe, with the cave of her larynx; Magda was defective, without a voice; perhaps she was deaf; there might be something amiss with her intelligence; Magda was dumb. Even the laugh that came when the ash-stippled wind made a clown out of Magda's shawl was only the air-blown showing of her teeth. Even when the lice, head lice and body lice, crazed her so that she became as wild as one of the big rats that plundered the barracks at daybreak looking for carrion, she rubbed and scratched and kicked and bit and rolled without a whimper. But now Magda's mouth was spilling a long viscous rope of clamor.

"Maaaa—"

It was the first noise Magda had ever sent out from her throat since the drying up of Rosa's nipples.

"Maaaa . . . aaa!"

Again! Magda was wavering in the perilous sunlight of the arena, scribbling on such pitiful little bent shins. Rosa saw. She saw that Magda was grieving the loss of her shawl, she saw that Magda was going to die. A tide of commands hammered in Rosa's nipples: Fetch, get, bring! But she did not know which to go after first, Magda or the shawl. If she jumped out into the arena to snatch Magda up, the howling would not stop, because Magda would still not have the shawl; but if she ran back into the barracks to find the shawl, and if she found it, and if she came after Magda holding it and shaking it, then she would get Magda back, Magda would put the shawl in her mouth and turn dumb again.

15 Rosa entered the dark. It was easy to discover the shawl. Stella was heaped under it, asleep in her thin bones. Rosa tore the shawl free and flew—she could fly, she was only air—into the arena. The sunheat murmured of another life, of butterflies in summer. The light was placid, mellow. On the other side of the steel fence, far away, there were green meadows speckled with dandelions and deep-colored violets; beyond them, even farther, innocent tiger lilies, tall, lifting their orange bonnets. In the barracks they spoke of "flowers," of "rain": excrement, thick turd-braids, and the slow stinking maroon waterfall that slunk down from the upper bunks, the stink mixed with a bitter fatty floating smoke that greased Rosa's skin. She stood for an instant at the margin of the arena. Sometimes the electricity inside the fence would seem to hum; even Stella said it was only an imagining, but Rosa heard real sounds in the wire: grainy sad voices. The farther she was from the fence, the more clearly the voices crowded at her. The lamenting voices strummed so convincingly, so passionately, it was impossible to suspect them of being phantoms. The voices told her to hold up the shawl, high; the voices told her to shake it, to whip with it, to unfurl it like a flag. Rosa lifted, shook, whipped, unfurled. Far off, very far, Magda leaned across her air-fed belly, reaching out with the rods of her arms. She was high up, elevated, riding someone's shoulder. But the shoulder that carried Magda was not coming toward Rosa and the shawl, it was drifting away, the speck of Magda was moving more and more into the

smoky distance. Above the shoulder a helmet glinted. A light tapped the helmet and sparkled it into a goblet. Below the helmet a black body like a domino and a pair of black boots hurled themselves in the direction of the electrified fence. The electric voices began to chatter wildly. "Maamaa, maaamaaa," they all hummed together. How far Magda was from Rosa now, across the whole square, past a dozen barracks, all the way on the other side! She was no bigger than a moth.

All at once Magda was swimming through the air. The whole of Magda traveled through loftiness. She looked like a butterfly touching a silver vine. And the moment Magda's feathered round head and her pencil legs and balloonish belly and zigzag arms splashed against the fence, the steel voices went mad in their growling, urging Rosa to run and run to the spot where Magda had fallen from her flight against the electrified fence; but of course Rosa did not obey them. She only stood, because if she ran they would shoot, and if she tried to pick up the sticks of Magda's body they would shoot, and if she let the wolf's screech ascending now through the ladder of her skeleton break out, they would shoot; so she took Magda's shawl and filled her own mouth with it, stuffed it in and stuffed it in, until she was swallowing up the wolf's screech and tasting the cinnamon and almond depth of Magda's saliva; and Rosa drank Magda's shawl until it dried.

Explorations of the Text

1. Describe the agony of Rosa, Stella, and Magda as they walk to the camp. What is the attitude of each toward the shawl?
2. Why does Magda's existence remain secret?
3. Explore Stella's relationships with Rosa and with Magda.
4. Examine the agony of Magda's first cry. Consider the language that describes Magda's death. What are the major images?
5. Explain the ending: "Rosa drank Magda's shawl until it dried." Has Ozick chosen the right response for Rosa? Why? Why not?
6. Why does the speaker begin her description of Magda's death only to interrupt it with a fantasy of saving her?
7. How does Stella "make" Magda die? Why is Stella's heart "cold"?
8. Compare the fates of the central characters in works by O'Brien, Endō, Pirandello, and Valenzuela.

The Reading/Writing Connection

1. In a paragraph discuss the symbolism of the shawl.
2. React to Stella's character. Freewrite in your journal.
3. "Think" Topic: Is Stella to be blamed for Magda's death? Argue pro or con.

Ideas for Writing

1. Evaluate the descriptive language in this story. Does it enhance and create meaning?
2. Discuss "The Shawl's" portrayal of the inhumanity and cruelty of the concentration camps during the Holocaust. Is it powerful?
3. Analyze Rosa's or Stella's character.

The War Generation

Shusaku Endō

Shusaku Endō (1923–), born in Tokyo, spent his early childhood in Manchuria, China, then returned to Japan after his parents separated, living with his mother in the home of a Roman Catholic aunt. He received a B.A. from Keio University and studied French literature at Lyon University in France. A playwright, novelist, and short story writer, Endō frequently wrote about the clash between Eastern and Western morals and philosophy. His works include Stained Glass Elegies *(1979) and* The Samurai *(1980).*

1979

Outside it was raining, and the restaurant was crowded. A steaming pot on a white charcoal brazier in front of them, office workers and various other customers blew on their onions and *kiritanpo*[1] before eating them. A young woman dressed in a dark blue kimono with white splashes went from table to table setting down bottles of *sake*.[2]

"Are these seats taken?" a businessman with a young woman in tow asked Konishi.

"No." With this *sake* cup still at his lips, Konishi shook his head sourly. In truth he had wanted this table all to himself.

"Shall we have the fish broth?"

5 "Anything. I'm starving."

She took a cigarette from her brown handbag and began to smoke. Looking at her, Konishi thought of his wife and daughters waiting for him at home. This woman would be about the same age as his oldest girl, but she brought the cigarette to her lips like a habitual smoker. It was a distressing sight.

"Don't you think they're charging a little too much for the year-end party this time?"

"What can we do? We have to go."

Listening without interest to the whispered conversation between these two, Konishi concluded that they must work in the same section at some

[1] A kind of stew, pounded into a mortar and served with chicken.
[2] A kind of alcoholic beverage, made of rice and served warm.

company. Their talk shifted from the cost of the year-end party to backbiting against their co-workers.

10 He consumed a good deal of time slowly drinking down his second bottle of *sake.* At home, his wife and daughters had probably already started dinner. He often stopped off for a few drinks on his way home from work, so his family would wait until seven o'clock and then go ahead and eat without him. Konishi felt more comfortable having them do that than making them wait for him.

As intoxication began to settle in, Konishi thought about the funeral of one of his fellow workers that he had attended the previous day. Mimura had been Personnel Director at the company, and was the same age as Konishi—fifty-two. He had heard that Mimura's blood pressure was a little high, but when the two of them had been tested together a year before in the company examination room, Konishi's blood pressure had been 150, Mimura's around 160. They had talked about how, by taking medicine, the pressure could be held below 200, and so there was nothing to worry about. But Mimura had died suddenly of a heart attack.

A photograph of Mimura, smiling and wearing a golfing hat, had been placed above the Buddhist memorial tablet surrounded by chrysanthemums. To one side sat the drooping figures of Mimura's wife, dressed in mourning kimono, and his son, wearing his high-school uniform. As he pressed his hands together reverently and gazed at Mimura's photograph, Konishi thought that this would be happening to him too before very long. Death, which had until now seemed still some distance away, had suddenly closed in on him with a whirr. In fact, two other funerals he had attended this year were for men in their fifties; he had to be on his guard.

"On my guard . . . ?" he muttered to himself. The woman who was sharing his table was putting fish and onions from the broth into a bowl for her date. The man, puffing on a cigarette, watched her as though he expected such treatment. Doubtless they had already slept together.

I must be on my guard. . . . But what was he supposed to do at this point? He was by no means satisfied with his job, but he had no intention of leaving. Eventually he would become an executive. Thereby he would avoid mandatory retirement. These days he had to feel very grateful for the position he was in. In his youth he had never imagined that his declining years would take their present shape. When he entered the Department of Law, he had planned to become a government official. Those plans had been aborted when he was taken out of school and sent off to war.

15 But Konishi had not been the only one that had happened to. All around him in those days were people who had had to change the direction of their lives because of the war. It was a matter of course for Konishi's generation.

He finished off his second bottle, and while he was debating whether to order a third, the glass door of the restaurant opened with a clatter. In the artificial light the rain looked like needles. A tall, thin woman in a black raincoat, around fifty or so, came into the restaurant.

Her nose was as pronounced as a foreigner's. Flecks of silver streaked her hair, like a foreigner's. Droplets of rain glimmered on her black raincoat. She asked the kimono-clad hostess a brief question and disappeared into a room at the back.

Still holding the empty *sake* bottle in his hand, Konishi let out an unintentional gasp. The man at the next table gave him a peculiar look.

None of the other customers in the restaurant knew who the woman was. But Konishi recognized the middle-aged woman as the violinist Ono Mari.

20 There was not a single clear sky over Tokyo in the days just before Konishi went into the army. Each day was leadenly overcast.

Though he knew it couldn't be the case, he wondered if the ashen skies over Tokyo had something to do with the city being as dark as his own feelings at the time. He had been at the university, and his boarding-house was located at Shinano-machi. Even the main road from there to Shinjuku was always deserted, every store had its glass doors tightly shut and displayed signs reading "Closed." Outside the shops, sandbags, buckets and fire blankets had been stacked in preparation for air raids. But there were no signs of human life.

Every day the sky looked as though it had been stuffed full of tattered cotton swabs. He could remember hearing sounds like faint explosions echoing constantly from the sky.

There was no longer anything resembling classes at the university. Instead, students like Konishi were sent to the F. Heavy Industries factory in Kawasaki, where they assembled airplane parts.

On the wintry mornings, factory workers and students dressed in work clothes and gaiters and carrying knapsacks over their shoulders lined up in single file on the square in front of Kawasaki Station. Buffeted by the cold wind, they waited and waited for their bus to come. Inside Konishi's knapsack he had some soya beans wrapped in paper, the only food that would help in some small way to stave off his hunger throughout the entire day.

25 Towards the end of 1944, the factory suffered a shortage of raw materials, and many machines ground to a halt. Even so, Konishi and the other grease-covered students had to stand in front of their drill presses all day long. Supervisors continued to make their rounds, marking down the names of any students whose work was slack. Those whose names were logged were not given any of the watery porridge that was brought around each day at three o'clock. Diluted as it was, the ravenous students coveted the porridge.

They were starved for more than just food. They likewise craved books. They yearned for heated rooms. They were hungry for human conversation, and for love. And so during the noon break, as they lined up in groups of five or six with their backs to the sunlit concrete wall, they discussed food and books. Then with sighs of longing they talked about certain members of the women's volunteer corps, who worked in a separate building. Dressed in their work pantaloons and wearing headbands, these women sorted the various machine parts. Throughout the factory hung posters that read: "Advance to Attu Island!"[3]

As that year drew to a close, however, one after another of the young men who basked in that noonday sun received their draft notices printed on red paper. Each morning at the factory it was easy to tell from the looks on people's faces just who had received their orders. They would try to force a smile, but the dark, heavy circles under their eyes betrayed them.

"It's come," the latest recipient would announce to everyone in a low voice, as though he were confessing some dark secret.

"When do you leave?"

30 "In two weeks."

Of course, no one mouthed empty phrases like "Congratulations" or "Give it your best!" Sooner or later the same piece of paper would be coming their way. They all stared at the tall factory chimney. Again today the smoke from the chimney swirled straight up into the sombre sky. The scene was unchanged from yesterday or the day before. It seemed as though it would stay that way for eternity.

"When is this war going to end?" No one knew. They felt as though it would linger on and on for ever.

Whenever a new recruit left Tokyo, everyone assembled at Shinjuku or Tokyo Station to see him off. The students formed a circle on the crowded platform and sang their school song in an angry roar. They howled and leaped about, less interested in seeing off their friend than in masking the anxiety and fear that lurked in their own hearts. As the train carrying their comrade vanished from sight, looks of bleak emptiness appeared on the faces of those who had been so boisterous just a few moments before.

1945 came, and still Konishi had not received his induction notice. Around that time the enemy air raids gradually intensified. The previous November the Nakashima Aircraft Plant in Musashino had been bombed, and enemy planes appeared fifteen times the following month. Strangely, F. Factory in Kawasaki was untouched. Often the trains packed with exhausted workers at the end of the day would come to a stop with a groan. Sometimes there appeared to be an attack over the downtown area; from the train windows they could see the sky in that direction glowing a dark red. The train service was often suspended, and Konishi would have to crouch for a long while on a connecting platform at Tokyo Station, staring at the reddened sky, realizing with a start that death was all that lay before them.

35 On 28 February his good friend Inami received his draft notice, and the feeling that his own turn was coming soon struck Konishi with greater force than ever before. The night Inami's orders came, four or five of them gathered in his room for a farewell party. They drank rationed liquor and some watered-down medicinal alcohol they had stolen from the factory. Later that night, the

[3] Island southwest of Alaska, the most western of the Aleutians.

landlord and the owner of an electrical shop who represented the local veterans' association came in and clumsily began to chant some Chinese poetry. "Do your best! Work for your country." They spouted callous words of encouragement. Inami, his face sallow, sat up straight in the student uniform he had not put on for some time.

That night he and Konishi slept in his room under the same blanket. Inami turned over, and Konishi could hear him weeping softly. He listened in silence for a while, then whispered, "I'll be getting drafted too, before long."

"Uh-huh," Inami nodded. He turned so that Konishi could see the profile of his face. "If you want anything of mine, you can have it."

"I don't want any books. My red slip will be coming before I could finish reading any of them."

"Probably. In that case, would you go to a concert in my place? I had to fight to get the ticket. I wanted to go to just one concert before the army got me." He slipped out of bed in his worn-out underwear and rifled through his desk drawer until he found a brown-coloured ticket. Inami was engrossed in music: he had his own record collection, and even had a phonograph in his room.

"Whose concert?"

"Ono Mari on the violin. You've heard of her, haven't you—Ono Mari? They say she's a young genius."

"I've heard the name a lot."

In the dim light from the lamp swathed in a black cloth, Konishi looked at the brown ticket. On the coarse paper had been printed the words: "Ono Mari Solo Violin Concert, March 10." It hardly seemed possible that a concert could be held in Tokyo now that death was everywhere.

"Are you sure I can have this?"

"Please go. In my place."

Inami set out from Shinjuku Station the following morning. The usual clusters of students had gathered in circles on the platform to sing. Inami seemed thinner and shorter than the other students who were boarding the trains. He blinked his eyes behind glasses that kept sliding down his nose, and bowed his head repeatedly to his friends.

On the night of 9 March, a large formation of B-29s attacked Tokyo. The hour was approximately 12 a.m.

There was a strong northerly wind that night. A heavy snow had fallen in Tokyo two or three days earlier, and a thick layer of black ice still remained along the sides of the streets. Around six o'clock, Mari finished rehearsing for the following day's performance at the home of her accompanist, a White Russian named Sapholo, who lived nearby. She returned home, but because of the wind that had stirred up around noon, the long hair that was her trademark kept blowing across her face, and she had to stop many times along the way.

At the age of fourteen, she had left all the older violinists in the dust and taken first place in a music competition sponsored by the Mainichi Newspaper Corporation. Thereafter she attracted many fans. As a young child she had been in poor health, and the rowdy children at elementary school had made fun of her. Unable to endure the atmosphere, she had pleaded with her parents not to make her continue in school; they had agreed to let her pursue her violin and other essential studies at home. Perhaps that was why she was fawned upon there.

50 That evening, as she warmed her legs under the *kotatsu*[4] and ate the potato pie and unsweetened black tea her mother had prepared for her, she discussed with her parents the possibility of going to Manchuria.[5] The Musicians' Patriotic Society had proposed a series of concerts in Manchuria, and if possible she wanted her mother to go with her. Her father, wearing a frayed dressing-gown, agreed that they should go for about half a year, treating it as a kind of evacuation; there would be no air raids in Manchuria, and they would probably not have to contend with food shortages.

"This war should be over within half a year anyway." Her artist father, who had studied in France as a young man, hated the military. He took an active part in air-raid drills and went to pay his respects to departing soldiers, but at the dinner table he often shared his grim outlook on the war situation with his wife and daughter.

Mari eventually grew tired and put her hand to her mouth to yawn. The radio had been playing a song called "Look, a Parachute!," but suddenly it was interrupted by a shrill buzzer, and the announcer began to read a report from the Eastern Military Command.

"Enemy planes have been sighted over the ocean south of the city. They are approaching the mainland." The announcer repeated the words three times.

"It's all right," Mari's mother said. "They're probably just reconnaissance planes."

55 "Why don't we just go to bed instead of putting out the lights," her father replied, extinguishing the coals in the *kotatsu*. "I'm not about to do everything the army wants us to do."

Mari fell asleep in her upstairs room. She had placed her violin case, air-raid hood and knapsack by her pillow, ready for an emergency, and had then dropped off to sleep as swiftly as a shower of falling pebbles. Soon in her dreams the orchestra members began to tune their instruments. The reverberations from the instruments were jumbled and confused, and somehow refused to modulate together as they usually did. Someone was beating on the kettledrum.

"Wake up! Mari, wake up!"

Someone was shouting at her bedside. She opened her eyes and dimly saw her father standing there wearing a metal helmet. Her ears still rang with the discordant strains of the orchestra.

---

[4] Heated charcoal, wrapped in cloth or blankets to preserve warmth and often covered with a box. Used only in winter, the *kotatsu* can be placed in a central location at dinner so that everyone seated for the meal can enjoy the comfort of the heat.

[5] A region in Northeast China, including Heilongjiang, Tilin, and Liaoning provinces and part of Inner Mongolia.

"We've got to get away. It's an air raid! The flames are coming closer to us!"

60 For some reason her father's voice seemed to come from far away. She felt no sense of urgency at the words "air raid." Like a marionette she did as she was instructed and stumbled out of bed. It was then that she realized the noises in her ears were not those of an orchestra tuning up, but the crackling of fires somewhere nearby.

They joined her mother at the foot of the stairs and started for the air-raid shelter in the garden. As they hurried along, they looked up and saw that the sky over Honjo and Fukagawa was a flaming red. There was a popping sound like roasting beans, and they could hear the shouting, clamouring voices of many people. When they reached the shelter, their noses were stung by the smells of straw and damp earth.

"We can't stay here. We've got to run!" her father shouted. To her mother, who was carrying a rucksack and her purse, he called, "Leave that. You don't need it." Carrying just one rucksack on his back, he hurried the two women out through the gate. From the neighbouring Yoshimura house came clattering noises of others preparing to flee; on a road nearby a child cried, "Ma-a-ama!"

The main street was already a maelstrom of people. The sky behind them was a sombre red. In the torrent were a man pulling his belongings along in a bicycle trailer, a young man carrying bedding in a hand-cart and a woman with a blanket wrapped around her body. All of them streamed towards the west, as though drawn by some phantom power. Time and again Mari's father shouted, "Stay together!" Mari realized that the only thing she was carrying was her violin case. Another explosion shook the sky. The white bodies of the B-29s, their arms outstretched, appeared in the searchlights. The anti-aircraft guns opened fire, but the B-29s continued to soar calmly overhead. The wind still blew fiercely. From the distance echoed a succession of thunderous noises, as though a pile-driver were pounding the ground.

At his Shinano-machi boarding-house, Konishi was unable to get to sleep until about 2 a.m., thanks to the searchlights that glanced off his window and the explosion of anti-aircraft guns in the distance. The next morning he learned from the Imperial Headquarters bulletin that part of the city had been indiscriminately bombed by a hundred and thirty B-29s. The information bureau of the Headquarters and the newspapers reported without comment that fifty of the enemy planes had been damaged and fifteen shot down. But that day as he set out for the factory on the sporadically paralysed train line, Konishi saw that nearly all of the downtown sector had been consumed by fire in the previous night's raid. At the plant, workers gathered in small groups here and there, talking in subdued voices. Many of the labourers they were used to seeing had not shown up for work. From the student workforce, Taguchi, Ueno and Fujimoto were absent. A supervisor appeared and roared at the group, "Get back to work!"

65 The ticket he had received from Inami was still carefully tucked into his train pass holder, but as he worked, Konishi began to have doubts that the

concert would be held under the present circumstances. Besides, even if he tried to go to the concert, and there was another air raid like the one the night before, he would not be able to get back to his boarding-house. He decided it would be better not to go. When he reached that conclusion, though, he could hear Inami's plaintive voice echoing in his ears: "I had to fight to get the ticket. Please go in my place." He began to feel that wasting the brown ticket would be akin to betraying his friend. Without even asking, Konishi knew full well what sort of trials Inami was now enduring in the army.

At five o'clock the long, heavy siren announcing the end of the working day blared out. Still uncertain whether or not to go to the concert, Konishi crowded into the bus for Kawasaki Station with the other workers, then transferred to the equally packed train. Those who had found seats and those who dangled from the straps all had their eyes closed, and their faces looked as if they belonged to overworked beasts of burden.

It was pitch black at the deserted Yūraku-chō Station when Konishi got off the train and started walking towards Hibiya Public Hall. Along the way he took some of the paper-wrapped soya beans from his knapsack and chewed them. At the end of the day's labours his legs felt heavy and his stomach empty. When the dark hall at last came into view, he had to sit down on a rock in the park and rest for a while. Then he stood up and walked to the steps of the hall, where about fifty people had gathered by the entrance. Each of them wore gaiters and work pants and carried a knapsack on his shoulders.

As it was nearly six o'clock and the doors still hadn't been opened, someone asked his neighbour in the queue, "Is there going to be a concert or not?" Word of mouth had it that the fires caused by the previous night's air raid had driven both Mari and her accompanist Sapholo from their homes; their whereabouts were unknown, and the hall was presently attempting to contact them. Still no one made a move to leave; they all stood patiently at the entrance.

Two men with stern faces, dressed in patriotic uniforms, appeared and bellowed, "Hmph, what are you doing listening to enemy music in times like these? Go home, all of you!" The group lowered their eyes and said nothing. The men shrugged their shoulders and disappeared.

Before long a timid, middle-aged employee came out of the hall and announced apologetically, "We have not been able to make contact. The concert is cancelled. I'm very sorry."

No one protested. With shadows of resignation flickering on their backs, they silently began to disperse. Feeling somehow relieved, Konishi started to follow them out of the park. Just then a man at the front of the procession called, "She's here!"

Everyone stopped walking. A weary, long-haired girl dressed in men's trousers and carrying a violin case was walking towards the hall with a look of pain on her face. It was Ono Mari.

"There's going to be a concert!" The shout passed from one person to the next like the baton in a relay race. The music enthusiasts turned on their heels like a flock of ducks and went back to the hall.

It was a peculiar concert, the sort not likely to have been seen before or since. The audience filled only half of Hibiya Public Hall, so the patrons dressed in their working clothes picked out seats to their liking and waited eagerly for Ono Mari to make her appearance.

75 Soon Mari came out onto the dusty stage, clutching her violin and bow in one hand. She had not had time to adjust her make-up, and the pained expression lingered as she stood in the centre of the stage. Exhaustion was etched into her face, and the renowned long hair and the wide, almost European eyes seemed agonizingly incongruous with the tattered men's trousers she was wearing. But no one laughed.

"We were burned out of our house," she apologized, the violin and bow dangling from her hands. "The trains couldn't go any further than Yotsuya . . . I walked here from Yotsuya. I had to come . . . knowing this might be my last concert."

She bit her lip, and the audience knew she was choking down her emotions. There was not even a suggestion of applause. Everyone remained silent, pondering what she had just said.

At that moment, Konishi thought, "This just might be the last concert I'll ever hear."

Mari shook her head vigorously to get the hair out of her face, tucked the violin under her chin, leaned forward, bent her slender wrist sharply, and adjusted her bow.

80 From beneath that wrist the strains of Fauré's *Elegy*[6] began to pour out. Not a single cough came from the audience. The tired, begrimed patrons closed their eyes and listened to the music, absorbed in their own private thoughts and individual griefs. The dark, low melody pierced the hearts of each one. As he followed the music, Konishi thought about the dying city of Tokyo. He thought of the scorched, reddish sky he had seen from the station platform. He thought of the drafted workers and students waiting in the chill winter wind for a bus to pick them up at Kawasaki Station. He remembered the thin face of Inami, the tear-stained face he had buried in his bedcovers the night before his induction. Perhaps the air-raid sirens would whine again tonight, and many more people would die. Tomorrow morning Konishi, the other members of the audience and Ono Mari might be reduced to charred grey corpses. Even if he did not die today, before long he would be carted off to the battlefield. When that happened, only the strains of this melody would remain to reach the ears of those who survived.

When she finished the *Elegy,* Mari played Fauré's *Après un réve,* then performed the Saint-Saëns "Rondo Capriccioso"[7] and Beethoven's "Romance." No one even considered the possibility that at any moment the alarms might sound, that the sky might be filled with a deafening roar, and that bombs might start to fall with a screeching howl.

---

[6] François-Félix Fauré, French composer (1843–1924).

[7] Charles Camille Saint-Saëns, French composer (1835–1921).

Something sticky brushed against his head. A spider had woven its web in the *yatsude* plants in front of his house. Konishi clicked his tongue and opened the glass door.

From the parlour he could hear music playing on the television. As a man in his fifties, he could not begin to comprehend the electric guitar music that so delighted his daughters. It sounded to him like nothing more than someone banging noisily on metal buckets.

He was balancing himself with one hand on the shoe cabinet and removing his shoes when his wife came out of the parlour. "Welcome home," she said, and a moment later his second daughter, a high-school girl, appeared and begrudgingly repeated the greeting.

"Clean up the entranceway. How many times do I have to tell you?"

His wife and daughter said nothing. With a sour expression he washed his hands in the bathroom and then gargled, making a sound exactly like a duck. When he had changed his clothes he went into the parlour. The two daughters who had been watching television got abruptly to their feet, looked at him coldly, and muttering, "We've got homework to do," headed for their rooms. Konishi cast a disappointed glance after them.

Konishi's wife chattered as she filled his rice bowl, "Remember I told you that the owner of the Azusa-ya was complaining of stiff shoulders?" The Azusa-ya was a grocery store by the bus stop. "He's gone into hospital. His wife says he's got some kind of growth in his chest. It looks like cancer."

The shop-owner was not much older than Konishi. Once again he felt death closing in on him with a whirring sound. He remembered the funeral of Mimura, his co-worker who had died of a heart attack. No, death was not closing in on them. Since their schooldays, death had always lived alongside the members of his generation. That smouldering red sky he had seen from the platform at Tokyo Station. The buzz of enemy planes that constantly filled the clogged grey skies. Inami had died of an illness on the battlefield in Korea. Other friends had been killed in the South Seas or on islands in the Pacific. Somewhere within, he felt as though the postwar period was just an extension of life that he had been granted.

"Toshiko wants to go on a vacation to Guam with some of her friends." Glumly he continued to eat while his wife went on talking. Her face was fleshy around the eyelids and chin. It occurred to him that when he had seen Ono Mari in the restaurant tonight, her hair was streaked with flecks of silver.

"I saw Ono Mari today," he said, almost to himself.

"Who's she?" His wife smothered a yawn.

Explorations of the Text

1. Describe the occasion and the setting. What do you learn about Konishi in the restaurant?
2. Why does Endō emphasize sky imagery?

3. Discuss Konishi's experience in the factory during the war. Why are the young men so unhappy when the red paper arrives?
4. Analyze the section on Ono Mari and her family. Why is this section in the narrative?
5. Why is Konishi so moved by Ono Mari's appearance in the restaurant many years later? What is the significance of her "hair streaked with flecks of silver"?
6. Examine Konishi's relationships at home. What accounts for his estrangement from his wife and daughters?
7. What are the ironies of the end of the story?
8. Compare the view of the brutality of war in this story with the treatment of the same theme in Pirandello's "War" and in O'Brien's "The Things They Carried."

The Reading/Writing Connection

1. List your preconceptions of the Japanese during World War II. Does this story change your views in any way?
2. React to Konishi's character. What does he fear? Respond to this question in your journal.

Ideas for Writing

1. Characterize Konishi. How does he represent and symbolize the "war generation"?
2. What does the story reveal about life in Japan during World War II? Use exercise 1 in The Reading/Writing Connection as a beginning.
3. What is Ono Mari's role in the story?
4. Compare the attitudes about war and about being a soldier in Endō's story, in Owen's "Dulce et Decorum Est," in O'Brien's "The Things They Carried," and/or in Pirandello's "War."
5. Discuss Endō's use of imagery, tone, and point of view.

The Things They Carried

Tim O'Brien

Tim O'Brien (1946–), born in Austin, Minnesota, was educated at Macalester College and Harvard University. He served in the U.S. Army in Vietnam, ultimately attaining the rank of sergeant, and much of his fiction reflects his experiences of the Vietnam War. His work includes Going After Cacciato *(1978), for which he was awarded the National Book Award;* The Things They Carried *(1990), which was nominated for the Pulitzer Prize;* In the Lake of the Woods *(1994); and* Tomcat in Love *(1998). He is a frequent contributor to magazines and literary journals.*

1990

First Lieutenant Jimmy Cross carried letters from a girl named Martha, a junior at Mount Sebastian College in New Jersey. They were not love letters, but Lieutenant Cross was hoping, so he kept them folded in plastic at the bottom of his rucksack. In the late afternoon, after a day's march, he would dig his foxhole, wash his hands under a canteen, unwrap the letters, hold them with the tips of his fingers, and spend the last hour of light pretending. He would imagine romantic camping trips into the White Mountains in New Hampshire. He would sometimes taste the envelope flaps, knowing her tongue had been there. More than anything, he wanted Martha to love him as he loved her, but the letters were mostly chatty, elusive on the matter of love. She was a virgin, he was almost sure. She was an English major at Mount Sebastian, and she wrote beautifully about her professors and roommates and midterm exams, about her respect for Chaucer[1] and her great affection for Virginia Woolf.[2] She often quoted lines of poetry; she never mentioned the war, except to say, Jimmy, take care of yourself. The letters weighed ten ounces. They were signed "Love, Martha," but Lieutenant Cross understood that "Love" was only a way of signing and did not mean what he sometimes pretended it meant. At dusk, he would carefully return the letters to his rucksack. Slowly, a bit distracted, he would get up and move among his men, checking the perimeter, then at full dark he would return to his hole and watch the night and wonder if Martha was a virgin.

The things they carried were largely determined by necessity. Among the necessities or near necessities were P-38 can openers, pocket knives, heat tabs, wrist watches, dog tags, mosquito repellent, chewing gum, candy, cigarettes, salt tablets, packets of Kool-Aid, lighters, matches, sewing kits, Military Payment Certificates, C rations, and two or three canteens of water. Together, these items weighed between fifteen and twenty pounds, depending upon a man's habits or rate of metabolism. Henry Dobbins, who was a big man, carried extra rations; he was especially fond of canned peaches in heavy syrup over pound cake. Dave Jensen, who practiced field hygiene, carried a toothbrush, dental floss, and several hotel-size bars of soap he'd stolen on R&R in Sydney, Australia. Ted Lavender, who was scared, carried tranquilizers until he was shot in the head outside the village of Than Khe in mid-April. By necessity, and because it was SOP,[3] they all carried steel helmets that weighed five pounds including the liner and camouflage cover. They carried the standard fatigue jackets and trousers. Very few carried underwear. On

[1] Geoffrey Chaucer, English poet, author of *The Canterbury Tales* (1342–1400).

[2] British novelist (1882–1941).

[3] Standard operating procedure.

their feet they carried jungle boots—2.1 pounds—and Dave Jensen carried three pairs of socks and a can of Dr. Scholl's foot powder as a precaution against trench foot. Until he was shot, Ted Lavender carried six or seven ounces of premium dope, which for him was a necessity. Mitchell Sanders, the RTO,[4] carried condoms. Norman Bowker carried a diary. Rat Kiley carried comic books. Kiowa, a devout Baptist, carried an illustrated New Testament that had been presented to him by his father, who taught Sunday school in Oklahoma City, Oklahoma. As a hedge against bad times, however, Kiowa also carried his grandmother's distrust of the white man, his grandfather's old hunting hatchet. Necessity dictated. Because the land was mined and booby-trapped, it was SOP for each man to carry a steel-centered, nylon-covered flak jacket, which weighed 6.7 pounds, but which on hot days seemed much heavier. Because you could die so quickly, each man carried at least one large compress bandage, usually in the helmet band for easy access. Because the nights were cold, and because the monsoons were wet, each carried a green plastic poncho that could be used as a raincoat or ground sheet or makeshift tent. With its quilted liner, the poncho weighed almost two pounds, but it was worth every ounce. In April, for instance, when Ted Lavender was shot, they used his poncho to wrap him up, then to carry him across the paddy, then to lift him into the chopper that took him away.

They were called legs or grunts.

To carry something was to "hump" it, as when Lieutenant Jimmy Cross humped his love for Martha up the hills and through the swamps. In its intransitive form, "to hump" meant "to walk," or "to march," but it implied burdens far beyond the intransitive.

5 Almost everyone humped photographs. In his wallet, Lieutenant Cross carried two photographs of Martha. The first was a Kodachrome snapshot signed "Love," though he knew better. She stood against a brick wall. Her eyes were gray and neutral, her lips slightly open as she stared straight-on at the camera. At night, sometimes, Lieutenant Cross wondered who had taken the picture, because he knew she had boyfriends, because he loved her so much, and because he could see the shadow of the picture taker spreading out against the brick wall. The second photograph had been clipped from the 1968 Mount Sebastian yearbook. It was an action shot—women's volleyball—and Martha was bent horizontal to the floor, reaching, the palms of her hands in sharp focus, the tongue taut, the expression frank and competitive. There was no visible sweat. She wore white gym shorts. Her legs, he thought, were almost certainly the legs of a virgin, dry and without hair, the left knee cocked and carrying her entire weight, which was just over one hundred pounds. Lieutenant Cross remembered touching that left knee. A dark theater, he remembered, and the movie was *Bonnie and Clyde,* and Martha wore a tweed skirt, and during the final scene, when he touched her knee, she turned and looked

[4] Radio telephone operator.

at him in a sad, sober way that made him pull his hand back, but he would always remember the feel of the tweed skirt and the knee beneath it and the sound of the gunfire that killed Bonnie and Clyde, how embarrassing it was, how slow and oppressive. He remembered kissing her good night at the dorm door. Right then, he thought, he should've done something brave. He should've carried her up the stairs to her room and tied her to the bed and touched that left knee all night long. He should've risked it. Whenever he looked at the photographs, he thought of new things he should've done.

What they carried was partly a function of rank, partly of field specialty.

As a first lieutenant and platoon leader, Jimmy Cross carried a compass, maps, code books, binoculars, and a .45-caliber pistol that weighed 2.9 pounds fully loaded. He carried a strobe light and the responsibility for the lives of his men.

As an RTO, Mitchell Sanders carried the PRC-25 radio, a killer, twenty-six pounds with its battery.

As a medic, Rat Kiley carried a canvas satchel filled with morphine and plasma and malaria tablets and surgical tape and comic books and all the things a medic must carry, including M&M's for especially bad wounds, for a total weight of nearly twenty pounds.

10 As a big man, therefore a machine gunner, Henry Dobbins carried the M-60, which weighed twenty-three pounds unloaded, but which was almost always loaded. In addition, Dobbins carried between ten and fifteen pounds of ammunition draped in belts across his chest and shoulders.

As PFCs or Spec 4s, most of them were common grunts and carried the standard M-16 gas-operated assault rifle. The weapon weighed 7.5 pounds unloaded, 8.2 pounds with its full twenty-round magazine. Depending on numerous factors, such as topography and psychology, the riflemen carried anywhere from twelve to twenty magazines, usually in cloth bandoliers, adding on another 8.4 pounds at minimum, fourteen pounds at maximum. When it was available, they also carried M-16 maintenance gear—rods and steel brushes and swabs and tubes of LSA oil—all of which weighed about a pound. Among the grunts, some carried the M-79 grenade launcher, 5.9 pounds unloaded, a reasonably light weapon except for the ammunition, which was heavy. A single round weighed ten ounces. The typical load was twenty-five rounds. But Ted Lavender, who was scared, carried thirty-four rounds when he was shot and killed outside Than Khe, and he went down under an exceptional burden, more than twenty pounds of ammunition, plus the flak jacket and helmet and rations and water and toilet paper and tranquilizers and all the rest, plus the unweighed fear. He was dead weight. There was no twitching or flopping. Kiowa, who saw it happen, said it was like watching a rock fall, or a big sandbag or something—just boom, then down—not like the movies where the dead guy rolls around and does fancy spins and goes ass over teakettle—not like that, Kiowa said, the poor bastard just flat-fuck fell. Boom. Down. Nothing else. It was a bright morning in mid-April. Lieutenant Cross felt the pain. He blamed himself. They stripped off Lavender's canteens and ammo, all the heavy things, and Rat Kiley said the obvious, the guy's dead, and Mitchell Sanders used his radio to report one U.S. KIA[5] and to request a chopper. Then they wrapped Lavender in his poncho. They carried him out to a dry paddy, established security, and sat smoking the dead man's dope until the chopper came. Lieutenant Cross kept to himself. He pictured Martha's smooth young face, thinking he loved her more than anything, more than his men, and now Ted Lavender was dead because he loved her so much and could not stop thinking about her. When the dust-off arrived, they carried Lavender aboard. Afterward they burned Than Khe. They marched until dusk, then dug their holes, and that night Kiowa kept explaining how you had to be there, how fast it was, how the poor guy just dropped like so much concrete. Boom-down, he said. Like cement.

In addition to the three standard weapons—the M-60, M-16, and M-79—they carried whatever presented itself, or whatever seemed appropriate as a means of killing or staying alive. They carried catch-as-catch-can. At various times, in various situations, they carried M-14s and CAR-15s and Swedish Ks and grease guns and captured AK-47s and Chi-Coms and RPGs and Simonov carbines and black-market Uzis and .38-caliber Smith & Wesson handguns and 66 mm LAWs and shotguns and silencers and blackjacks and bayonets and C-4 plastic explosives.[6] Lee Strunk carried a slingshot; a weapon of last resort, he called it. Mitchell Sanders carried brass knuckles. Kiowa carried his grandfather's feathered hatchet. Every third or fourth man carried a Claymore antipersonnel mine—3.5 pounds with its firing device. They all carried fragmentation grenades—fourteen ounces each. They all carried at least one M-18 colored smoke grenade—twenty-four ounces. Some carried CS or tear-gas grenades. Some carried white-phosphorus grenades. They carried all they could bear, and then some, including a silent awe for the terrible power of the things they carried.

In the first week of April, before Lavender died, Lieutenant Jimmy Cross received a good-luck charm from Martha. It was a simple pebble, an ounce at most. Smooth to the touch, it was a milky-white color with flecks of orange and violet, oval-shaped, like a miniature egg. In the accompanying letter, Martha wrote that she had found the pebble on the Jersey shoreline, precisely where the land touched water at high tide, where things came together but also separated. It was this separate-but-together quality, she wrote, that had inspired her to pick up the pebble and to carry it in her breast pocket for several days, where it seemed weightless, and then to send it through the mail, by air, as a token of her truest feelings for him. Lieutenant Cross found this romantic. But he wondered what her truest feelings were, exactly, and what she meant by separate-but-together. He wondered how the tides and waves had come into play on that afternoon along the Jersey shoreline when Martha saw the pebble and bent down to rescue it from geology. He imagined bare feet. Martha was a

[5] Killed in action.

[6] Weaponry.

poet, with the poet's sensibilities, and her feet would be brown and bare, the toenails unpainted, the eyes chilly and somber like the ocean in March, and though it was painful, he wondered who had been with her that afternoon. He imagined a pair of shadows moving along the strip of sand where things came together but also separated. It was phantom jealousy, he knew, but he couldn't help himself. He loved her so much. On the march, through the hot days of early April, he carried the pebble in his mouth, turning it with his tongue, tasting sea salts and moisture. His mind wandered. He had difficulty keeping his attention on the war. On occasion he would yell at his men to spread out the column, to keep their eyes open, but then he would slip away into day-dreams, just pretending, walking barefoot along the Jersey shore, with Martha, carrying nothing. He would feel himself rising. Sun and waves and gentle winds, all love and lightness.

What they carried varied by mission.

15 When a mission took them to the mountains, they carried mosquito netting, machetes, canvas tarps, and extra bug juice.

If a mission seemed especially hazardous, or if it involved a place they knew to be bad, they carried everything they could. In certain heavily mined AOs,[7] where the land was dense with Toe Poppers and Bouncing Betties, they took turns humping a twenty-eight pound mine detector. With its headphones and big sensing plate, the equipment was a stress on the lower back and shoulders, awkward to handle, often useless because of the shrapnel in the earth, but they carried it anyway, partly for safety, partly for the illusion of safety.

On ambush, or other night missions, they carried peculiar little odds and ends. Kiowa always took along his New Testament and a pair of moccasins for silence. Dave Jensen carried night-sight vitamins high in carotin. Lee Strunk carried his slingshot; ammo, he claimed, would never be a problem. Rat Kiley carried brandy and M&M's. Until he was shot, Ted Lavender carried the starlight scope, which weighed 6.3 pounds with its aluminum carrying case. Henry Dobbins carried his girlfriend's pantyhose wrapped around his neck as a comforter. They all carried ghosts. When dark came, they would move out single file across the meadows and paddies to their ambush coordinates, where they would quietly set up the Claymores and lie down and spend the night waiting.

Other missions were more complicated and required special equipment. In mid-April, it was their mission to search out and destroy the elaborate tunnel complexes in the Than Khe area south of Chu Lai. To blow the tunnels, they carried one-pound blocks of pentrite high explosives, four blocks to a man, sixty-eight pounds in all. They carried wiring, detonators, and battery-powered clackers. Dave Jensen carried earplugs. Most often, before blowing the tunnels, they were ordered by higher command to search them, which was considered bad news, but by and large they just shrugged and carried out orders. Because he was a big man, Henry Dobbins was excused from tunnel

[7] Areas of operation.

duty. The others would draw numbers. Before Lavender died there were seventeen men in the platoon, and whoever drew the number seventeen would strip off his gear and crawl in head first with a flashlight and Lieutenant Cross's .45-caliber pistol. The rest of them would fan out as security. They would sit down or kneel, not facing the hole, listening to the ground beneath them, imagining cobwebs and ghosts, whatever was down there—the tunnel walls squeezing in—how the flashlight seemed impossibly heavy in the hand and how it was tunnel vision in the very strictest sense, compression in all ways, even time, and how you had to wiggle in—ass and elbows—a swallowed-up feeling—and how you found yourself worrying about odd things—will your flashlight go dead? Do rats carry rabies? If you screamed, how far would the sound carry? Would your buddies hear it? Would they have the courage to drag you out? In some respects, though not many, the waiting was worse than the tunnel itself. Imagination was a killer.

On April 16, when Lee Strunk drew the number seventeen, he laughed and muttered something and went down quickly. The morning was hot and very still. Not good, Kiowa said. He looked at the tunnel opening, then out across a dry paddy toward the village of Than Khe. Nothing moved. No clouds or birds or people. As they waited, the men smoked and drank Kool-Aid, not talking much, feeling sympathy for Lee Strunk but also feeling the luck of the draw. You win some, you lose some, said Mitchell Sanders, and sometimes you settle for a rain check. It was a tired line and no one laughed.

20 Henry Dobbins ate a tropical chocolate bar. Ted Lavender popped a tranquilizer and went off to pee.

After five minutes, Lieutenant Jimmy Cross moved to the tunnel, leaned down, and examined the darkness. Trouble, he thought—a cave-in maybe. And then suddenly, without willing it, he was thinking about Martha. The stresses and fractures, the quick collapse, the two of them buried alive under all that weight. Dense, crushing love. Kneeling, watching the hole, he tried to concentrate on Lee Strunk and the war, all the dangers, but his love was too much for him, he felt paralyzed, he wanted to sleep inside her lungs and breathe her blood and be smothered. He wanted her to be a virgin and not a virgin, all at once. He wanted to know her. Intimate secrets—why poetry? Why so sad? Why the grayness in her eyes? Why so alone? Not lonely, just alone—riding her bike across campus or sitting off by herself in the cafeteria. Even dancing, she danced alone—and it was the aloneness that filled him with love. He remembered telling her that one evening. How she nodded and looked away. And how, later, when he kissed her, she received the kiss without returning it, her eyes wide open, not afraid, not a virgin's eyes, just flat and uninvolved.

Lieutenant Cross gazed at the tunnel. But he was not there. He was buried with Martha under the white sand at the Jersey shore. They were pressed together, and the pebble in his mouth was her tongue. He was smiling. Vaguely, he was aware of how quiet the day was, the sullen paddies, yet he could not bring himself to worry about matters of security. He was beyond that. He was just a kid at war, in love. He was twenty-two years old. He couldn't help it.

A few moments later Lee Strunk crawled out of the tunnel. He came up grinning, filthy but alive. Lieutenant Cross nodded and closed his eyes while the others clapped Strunk on the back and made jokes about rising from the dead.

Worms, Rat Kiley said. Right out of the grave. Fuckin' zombie.

The men laughed. They all felt great relief.

Spook City, said Mitchell Sanders.

Lee Strunk made a funny ghost sound, a kind of moaning, yet very happy, and right then, when Strunk made that high happy moaning sound, when he went *Ahhooooo,* right then Ted Lavender was shot in the head on his way back from peeing. He lay with his mouth open. The teeth were broken. There was a swollen black bruise under his left eye. The cheekbone was gone. Oh shit, Rat Kiley said, the guy's dead. The guy's dead, he kept saying, which seemed profound—the guy's dead. I mean really.

The things they carried were determined to some extent by superstition. Lieutenant Cross carried his good-luck pebble. Dave Jensen carried a rabbit's foot. Norman Bowker, otherwise a very gentle person, carried a thumb that had been presented to him as a gift by Mitchell Sanders. The thumb was dark brown, rubbery to the touch, and weighed four ounces at most. It had been cut from a VC[8] corpse, a boy of fifteen or sixteen. They'd found him at the bottom of an irrigation ditch, badly burned, flies in his mouth and eyes. The boy wore black shorts and sandals. At the time of his death he had been carrying a pouch of rice, a rifle, and three magazines of ammunition.

You want my opinion, Mitchell Sanders said, there's a definite moral here.

He put his hand on the dead boy's wrist. He was quiet for a time, as if counting a pulse, then he patted the stomach, almost affectionately, and used Kiowa's hunting hatchet to remove the thumb.

Henry Dobbins asked what the moral was.

Moral?

You know. *Moral.*

Sanders wrapped the thumb in toilet paper and handed it across to Norman Bowker. There was no blood. Smiling, he kicked the boy's head, watched the flies scatter, and said, It's like with that old TV show—*Paladin.* Have gun, will travel.

Henry Dobbins thought about it.

Yeah, well, he finally said. I don't see no moral.

There it *is,* man.

Fuck off.

They carried USO[9] stationery and pencils and pens. They carried Sterno, safety pins, trip flares, signal flares, spools of wire, razor blades, chewing tobacco, liberated joss sticks and statuettes of the smiling Buddha, candles, grease pencils, *The Stars and Stripes,* fingernail clippers, Psy Ops[10] leaflets,

[8] Vietcong; North Vietnamese soldier.

[9] United Service Organization.

[10] Psychological operations.

bush hats, bolos, and much more. Twice a week, when the resupply choppers came in, they carried hot chow in green Mermite cans and large canvas bags filled with iced beer and soda pop. They carried plastic water containers, each with a two-gallon capacity. Mitchell Sanders carried a set of starched tiger fatigues for special occasions. Henry Dobbins carried Black Flag insecticide. Dave Jensen carried empty sandbags that could be filled at night for added protection. Lee Strunk carried tanning lotion. Some things they carried in common. Taking turns, they carried the big PRC-77 scrambler radio, which weighed thirty pounds with its battery. They shared the weight of memory. They took up what others could no longer bear. Often, they carried each other, the wounded or weak. They carried infections. They carried chess sets, basketballs, Vietnamese-English dictionaries, insignia of rank, Bronze Stars and Purple Hearts, plastic cards imprinted with the Code of Conduct. They carried diseases, among them malaria and dysentery. They carried lice and ringworm and leeches and paddy algae and various rots and molds. They carried the land itself—Vietnam, the place, the soil—a powdery orange-red dust that covered their boots and fatigues and faces. They carried the sky. The whole atmosphere, they carried it, the humidity, the monsoons, the stink of fungus and decay, all of it, they carried gravity. They moved like mules. By daylight they took sniper fire, at night they were mortared, but it was not battle, it was just the endless march, village to village, without purpose, nothing won or lost. They marched for the sake of the march. They plodded along slowly, dumbly, leaning forward against the heat, unthinking, all blood and bone, simple grunts, soldiering with their legs, toiling up the hills and down into the paddies and across the rivers and up again and down, just humping, one step and then the next and then another, but no volition, no will, because it was automatic, it was anatomy, and the war was entirely a matter of posture and carriage, the hump was everything, a kind of inertia, a kind of emptiness, a dullness of desire and intellect and conscience and hope and human sensibility. Their principles were in their feet. Their calculations were biological. They had no sense of strategy or mission. They searched the villages without knowing what to look for, not caring, kicking over jars of rice, frisking children and old men, blowing tunnels, sometimes setting fires and sometimes not, then forming up and moving on to the next village, then other villages, where it would always be the same. They carried their own lives. The pressures were enormous. In the heat of early afternoon, they would remove their helmets and flak jackets, walking bare, which was dangerous but which helped ease the strain. They would often discard things along the route of march. Purely for comfort, they would throw away rations, blow their Claymores and grenades, no matter, because by nightfall the resupply choppers would arrive with more of the same, then a day or two later still more, fresh watermelons and crates of ammunition and sunglasses and woolen sweaters—the resources were stunning—sparklers for the Fourth of July, colored eggs for Easter. It was the great American war chest—the fruits of science, the smokestacks, the canneries, the arsenals at Hartford, the Minnesota forests, the machine shops, the vast fields of corn and wheat—they carried like freight trains; they carried it on their backs and shoulders—and for all the ambiguities of Vietnam, all the mysteries and unknowns, there was at least the single abiding certainty that they would never be at a loss for things to carry.

40 After the chopper took Lavender away, Lieutenant Jimmy Cross led his men into the village of Than Khe. They burned everything. They shot chickens and dogs, they trashed the village well, they called in artillery and watched the wreckage, then they marched for several hours through the hot afternoon, and then at dusk, while Kiowa explained how Lavender died, Lieutenant Cross found himself trembling.

He tried not to cry. With his entrenching tool, which weighed five pounds, he began digging a hole in the earth.

He felt shame. He hated himself. He had loved Martha more than his men, and as a consequence Lavender was now dead, and this was something he would have to carry like a stone in his stomach for the rest of the war.

All he could do was dig. He used his entrenching tool like an ax, slashing, feeling both love and hate, and then later, when it was full dark, he sat at the bottom of his foxhole and wept. It went on for a long while. In part, he was grieving for Ted Lavender, but mostly it was for Martha, and for himself, because she belonged to another world, which was not quite real, and because she was a junior at Mount Sebastian College in New Jersey, a poet and a virgin and uninvolved, and because he realized she did not love him and never would.

Like cement, Kiowa whispered in the dark. I swear to God—boom-down. Not a word.

45 I've heard this, said Norman Bowker.

A pisser, you know? Still zipping himself up. Zapped while zipping.

All right, fine. That's enough.

Yeah, but you had to see it, the guy just—

I *heard,* man. Cement. So why not shut the fuck *up?*

50 Kiowa shook his head sadly and glanced over at the hole where Lieutenant Jimmy Cross sat watching the night. The air was thick and wet. A warm, dense fog had settled over the paddies and there was the stillness that precedes rain.

After a time Kiowa sighed.

One thing for sure, he said. The Lieutenant's in some deep hurt. I mean that crying jag—the way he was carrying on—it wasn't fake or anything, it was real heavy-duty hurt. The man cares.

Sure, Norman Bowker said.

Say what you want, the man does care.

55 We all got problems.

Not Lavender.

No, I guess not, Bowker said. Do me a favor, though.

Shut up?

That's a smart Indian. Shut up.

60 Shrugging, Kiowa pulled off his boots. He wanted to say more, just to lighten up his sleep, but instead he opened his New Testament and arranged it

beneath his head as a pillow. The fog made things seem hollow and unattached. He tried not to think about Ted Lavender, but then he was thinking how fast it was, no drama, down and dead, and how it was hard to feel anything except surprise. It seemed un-Christian. He wished he could find some great sadness, or even anger, but the emotion wasn't there and he couldn't make it happen. Mostly he felt pleased to be alive. He liked the smell of the New Testament under his cheek, the leather and ink and paper and glue, whatever the chemicals were. He liked hearing the sounds of night. Even his fatigue, it felt fine, the stiff muscles and the prickly awareness of his own body, a floating feeling. He enjoyed not being dead. Lying there, Kiowa admired Lieutenant Jimmy Cross's capacity for grief. He wanted to share the man's pain, he wanted to care as Jimmy Cross cared. And yet when he closed his eyes, all he could think was Boom-down, and all he could feel was the pleasure of having his boots off and the fog curling in around him and the damp soil and the Bible smells and the plush comfort of night.

After a moment Norman Bowker sat up in the dark.

What the hell, he said. You want to talk, *talk*. Tell it to me.

Forget it.

No, man, go on. One thing I hate, it's a silent Indian.

65 For the most part they carried themselves with poise, a kind of dignity. Now and then, however, there were times of panic, when they squealed or wanted to squeal but couldn't, when they twitched and made moaning sounds and covered their heads and said Dear Jesus and flopped around on the earth and fired their weapons blindly and cringed and sobbed and begged for the noise to stop and went wild and made stupid promises to themselves and to God and to their mothers and fathers, hoping not to die. In different ways, it happened to all of them. Afterward, when the firing ended, they would blink and peek up. They would touch their bodies, feeling shame, then quickly hiding it. They would force themselves to stand. As if in slow motion, frame by frame, the world would take on the old logic—absolute silence, then the wind, then sunlight, then voices. It was the burden of being alive. Awkwardly, the men would reassemble themselves, first in private, then in groups, becoming soldiers again. They would repair the leaks in their eyes. They would check for casualties, call in dust-offs, light cigarettes, try to smile, clear their throats and spit and begin cleaning their weapons. After a time someone would shake his head and say, No lie, I almost shit my pants, and someone else would laugh, which meant it was bad, yes, but the guy had obviously not shit his pants, it wasn't that bad, and in any case nobody would ever do such a thing and then go ahead and talk about it. They would squint into the dense, oppressive sunlight. For a few moments, perhaps, they would fall silent, lighting a joint and tracking its passage from man to man, inhaling, holding in the humiliation. Scary stuff, one of them might say. But then someone else would grin or flick his eyebrows and say, Roger-dodger, almost cut me a new asshole, *almost*.

There were numerous such poses. Some carried themselves with a sort of wistful resignation, others with pride or stiff soldierly discipline or good humor or macho zeal. They were afraid of dying but they were even more afraid to show it.

They found jokes to tell.

They used a hard vocabulary to contain the terrible softness. *Greased,* they'd say. *Offed, lit up, zapped while zipping.* It wasn't cruelty, just stage presence. They were actors and the war came at them in 3-D. When someone died, it wasn't quite dying, because in a curious way it seemed scripted, and because they had their lines mostly memorized, irony mixed with tragedy, and because they called it by other names, as if to encyst and destroy the reality of death itself. They kicked corpses. They cut off thumbs. They talked grunt lingo. They told stories about Ted Lavender's supply of tranquilizers, how the poor guy didn't feel a thing, how incredibly tranquil he was.

There's a moral here, said Mitchell Sanders.

70 They were waiting for Lavender's chopper, smoking the dead man's dope.

The moral's pretty obvious, Sanders said, and winked. Stay away from drugs. No joke, they'll ruin your day every time.

Cute, said Henry Dobbins.

Mind-blower, get it? Talk about wiggy—nothing left, just blood and brains.

They made themselves laugh.

75 There it is, they'd say, over and over, as if the repetition itself were an act of poise, a balance between crazy and almost crazy, knowing without going. There it is, which meant be cool, let it ride, because oh yeah, man, you can't change what can't be changed, there it is, there it absolutely and positively and fucking well *is.*

They were tough.

They carried all the emotional baggage of men who might die. Grief, terror, love, longing—these were intangibles, but the intangibles had their own mass and specific gravity, they had tangible weight. They carried shameful memories. They carried the common secret of cowardice barely restrained, the instinct to run or freeze or hide, and in many respects this was the heaviest burden of all, for it could never be put down, it required perfect balance and perfect posture. They carried their reputations. They carried the soldier's greatest fear, which was the fear of blushing. Men killed, and died, because they were embarrassed not to. It was what had brought them to the war in the first place, nothing positive, no dreams of glory or honor, just to avoid the blush of dishonor. They died so as not to die of embarrassment. They crawled into tunnels and walked point and advanced under fire. Each morning, despite the unknowns, they made their legs move. They endured. They kept humping. They did not submit to the obvious alternative, which was simply to close the eyes and fall. So easy, really. Go limp and tumble to the ground and let the muscles unwind and not speak and not budge until your buddies picked you up and lifted you into the chopper that would roar and dip its nose and carry you off to the world. A mere matter of falling, yet no one ever fell. It was not courage, exactly; the object was not valor. Rather, they were too frightened to be cowards.

By and large they carried these things inside, maintaining the masks of composure. They sneered at sick call. They spoke bitterly about guys who had found release by shooting off their own toes or fingers. Pussies, they'd say. Candyasses. It was fierce, mocking talk, with only a trace of envy or awe, but even so, the image played itself out behind their eyes.

They imagined the muzzle against flesh. They imagined the quick, sweet pain, then the evacuation to Japan, then a hospital with warm beds and cute geisha nurses.

80 They dreamed of freedom birds.

At night, on guard, staring into the dark, they were carried away by jumbo jets. They felt the rush of takeoff. *Gone!* they yelled. And then velocity, wings and engines, a smiling stewardess—but it was more than a plane, it was a real bird, a big sleek silver bird with feathers and talons and high screeching. They were flying. The weights fell off, there was nothing to bear. They laughed and held on tight, feeling the cold slap of wind and altitude, soaring, thinking *It's over, I'm gone!*—they were naked, they were light and free—it was all lightness, bright and fast and buoyant, light as light, a helium buzz in the brain, a giddy bubbling in the lungs as they were taken up over the clouds and the war, beyond duty, beyond gravity and mortification and global entanglements—*Sin loi!*[11] they yelled, *I'm sorry, motherfuckers, but I'm out of it, I'm goofed, I'm on a space cruise, I'm gone!*—and it was a restful, disencumbered sensation, just riding the light waves, sailing that big silver freedom bird over the mountains and oceans, over America, over the farms and great sleeping cities and cemeteries and highways and the golden arches of McDonald's. It was flight, a kind of fleeing, a kind of falling, falling higher and higher, spinning off the edge of the earth and beyond the sun and through the vast, silent vacuum where there were no burdens and where everything weighed exactly nothing. *Gone!* they screamed, *I'm sorry but I'm gone!* And so at night, not quite dreaming, they gave themselves over to lightness, they were carried, they were purely borne.

On the morning after Ted Lavender died, First Lieutenant Jimmy Cross crouched at the bottom of his foxhole and burned Martha's letters. Then he burned the two photographs. There was a steady rain falling, which made it difficult, but he used heat tabs and Sterno to build a small fire, screening it with his body, holding the photographs over the tight blue flame with the tips of his fingers.

He realized it was only a gesture. Stupid, he thought. Sentimental, too, but mostly just stupid.

Lavender was dead. You couldn't burn the blame.

[11] Sorry about that.

85 Besides, the letters were in his head. And even now, without photographs, Lieutenant Cross could see Martha playing volleyball in her white gym shorts and yellow T-shirt. He could see her moving in the rain.

When the fire died out, Lieutenant Cross pulled his poncho over his shoulders and ate breakfast from a can.

There was no great mystery, he decided.

In those burned letters Martha had never mentioned the war, except to say, Jimmy, take care of yourself. She wasn't involved. She signed the letters "Love," but it wasn't love, and all the fine lines and technicalities did not matter.

The morning came up wet and blurry. Everything seemed part of everything else, the fog and Martha and the deepening rain.

90 It was a war, after all.

Half smiling, Lieutenant Jimmy Cross took out his maps. He shook his head hard, as if to clear it, then bent forward and began planning the day's march. In ten minutes, or maybe twenty, he would rouse the men and they would pack up and head west, where the maps showed the country to be green and inviting. They would do what they had always done. The rain might add some weight, but otherwise it would be one more day layered upon all the other days.

He was realistic about it. There was that new hardness in his stomach.

No more fantasies, he told himself.

Henceforth, when he thought about Martha, it would be only to think that she belonged elsewhere. He would shut down the daydreams. This was not Mount Sebastian, it was another world, where there were no pretty poems or midterm exams, a place where men died because of carelessness and gross stupidity. Kiowa was right. Boom-down, and you were dead, never partly dead.

95 Briefly, in the rain, Lieutenant Cross saw Martha's gray eyes gazing back at him.

He understood.

It was very sad, he thought. The things men carried inside. The things men did or felt they had to do.

He almost nodded at her, but didn't.

Instead he went back to his maps. He was now determined to perform his duties firmly and without negligence. It wouldn't help Lavender, he knew that, but from this point on he would comport himself as a soldier. He would dispose of his good-luck pebble. Swallow it, maybe, or use Lee Strunk's slingshot, or just drop it along the trail. On the march he would impose strict field discipline. He would be careful to send out flank security, to prevent straggling or bunching up, to keep his troops moving at the proper pace and at the proper interval. He would insist on clean weapons. He would confiscate the remainder of Lavender's dope. Later in the day, perhaps, he would call the men together and speak to them plainly. He would accept the blame for what had happened to Ted Lavender. He would be a man about it. He would look them in the eyes, keeping his chin level, and he would issue the new SOPs in a calm, impersonal tone of voice, an officer's voice, leaving no room for argument or discussion. Commencing immediately, he'd tell them, they would no longer abandon equipment along the route of march. They would police up their acts. They would get their shit together, and keep it together, and maintain it neatly and in good working order.

100 He would not tolerate laxity. He would show strength, distancing himself.

Among the men there would be grumbling, of course, and maybe worse, because their days would seem longer and their loads heavier, but Lieutenant Cross reminded himself that his obligation was not to be loved but to lead. He would dispense with love; it was not now a factor. And if anyone quarreled or complained, he would simply tighten his lips and arrange his shoulders in the correct command posture. He might give a curt little nod. Or he might not. He might just shrug and say Carry on, then they would saddle up and form into a column and move out toward the villages of Than Khe.

Explorations of the Text

1. List the "things" carried by each man. What determines "the things they carried"? Characterize each person.
2. What are the heavy intangible weights carried by these men?
3. Discuss Ted Lavender's death. Why does Lieutenant Cross believe that he is responsible?
4. Evaluate the responses of each character to Lavender's death. What do you conclude?
5. Why does Mitchell Sanders declare "There's a moral here"? Is there a moral? How do you know?
6. The story begins with Lieutenant Cross's fantasies about Martha. How do these fantasies change? Why?
7. What is innovative about this story? Consider characterization, narrative structure, and style.
8. What is the attitude toward war in this story? Compare it to the stances of Ozick and of Endō.

The Reading/Writing Connection

1. Write a reader response journal entry about one of the characters. Discuss the "things" he carried, and theorize about his hopes, demons, and values.
2. Are fantasies destructive, an avoidance of reality, or a method for bearing the unbearable? Respond to this question in a paragraph.

Ideas for Writing

1. "Soldiers are dreamers." Apply this statement to "The Things They Carried." Is dreaming a vital element in the story?

2. Respond to the suggestion that soldiers come to war not out of dreams of glory or honor but out of fear of dishonor.
3. Evaluate this story. What are its major strengths? Use the fiction checklist in chapter 9 for guidance in your evaluation.
4. Create a dialogue in which one of the characters in O'Brien's story responds to "the fat man" in Pirandello's "War."

Ralph the Duck

Frederick Busch

The author of more than twenty books, Frederick Busch (1941–) was educated at Muhlenberg College and Columbia University. He is currently Fairchild Professor of Literature at Colgate University. His novels include The Mutual Friend *(1978),* Girls *(1997), and* The Night Inspector *(1999); his awards include Guggenheim and Ingram-Merrill Fellowships.*

1989

I woke at up 5:25 because the dog was vomiting. I carried seventy-five pounds of heaving golden retriever to the door and poured him onto the silver, moonlit snow. "Good boy," I said because he'd done his only trick. Outside he retched, and I went back up, passing the sofa on which Fanny lay. I tiptoed with enough weight on my toes to let her know how considerate I was while she was deserting me. She blinked her eyes. I swear I heard her blink her eyes. Whenever I tell her that I hear her blink her eyes, she tells me I'm lying; but I can hear the damp slap of lash after I have made her weep.

In bed and warm again, noting the red digital numbers (5:29) and certain that I wouldn't sleep, I didn't. I read a book about men who kill each other for pay or for their honor. I forget which, and so did they. It was 5:45, the alarm would buzz at 6:00, and I would make a pot of coffee and start the wood stove; I would call Fanny and pour her coffee into her mug; I would apologize because I always did, and then she would forgive me if I hadn't been too awful—I didn't think I'd been that bad—and we would stagger through the day, exhausted but pretty sure we were all right, and we'd sleep that night, probably after sex, and then we'd waken in the same bed to the alarm at 6:00, or the dog, if he'd returned to the frozen deer carcass he'd been eating in the forest on our land. He loved what made him sick. The alarm went off, I got into jeans and woolen socks and a sweatshirt, and I went downstairs to let the dog in. He'd be hungry, of course.

I was the oldest college student in America, I thought. But of course I wasn't. There were always ancient women with their parchment for skin who graduated at seventy-nine from places like Barnard and the University of Georgia. I was only forty-two, and I hardly qualified as a student. I patrolled the college at night in a Bronco with a leaky exhaust system, and I went from room to room in the classroom buildings, kicking out students who were studying or humping in chairs—they'd do it *anywhere*—and answering emergency calls with my little blue light winking on top of the truck. I didn't carry a gun or a billy, but I had a flashlight that took six batteries and I'd used it twice on some of my overprivileged northeastern-playboy part-time classmates. On Tuesdays and Thursdays I would awaken at 6:00 with my wife, and I'd do my homework, and work around the house, and go to school at 11:30 to sit there for an hour and a half while thirty-five stomachs growled with hunger and boredom, and this guy gave instruction about books. Because I was on the staff, the college let me take a course for nothing every term. I was getting educated, in a kind of slow-motion way—it would have taken me something like fifteen or sixteen years to graduate, and I would no doubt get an F in gym and have to repeat—and there were time when I respected myself for it. Fanny often did, and that was fair incentive.

I am not unintelligent. *You are not an unintelligent writer,* my professor wrote on my paper about Nathaniel Hawthorne.[1] We had to read short stories, I and the other students, and then we had to write little essays about them. I told how I saw Kafka[2] and Hawthorne in a similar light, and I was not unintelligent, he said. He ran into me at dusk one time, when I answered a call about a dead battery and found out it was him. I jumped his Buick from the Bronco's battery, and he was looking me over, I could tell, while I clamped onto the terminals and cranked it up. He was a tall, handsome guy who never wore a suit. He wore khakis and sweaters, loafers or sneakers, and he was always talking to the female students with the brightest hair and best builds. But he couldn't get a Buick going on an ice-cold night, and he didn't know enough to look for cells going bad. I told him he was going to need a new battery and he looked me over the way men sometimes do with other men who fix their cars for them.

5 "Vietnam?"

I said, "Too old."

"Not at the beginning. Not if you were an adviser. So-called. Or one of the Phoenix Project fellas?"

I was wearing a watch cap made of navy wool and an old Marine fatigue jacket. Slick characters like my professor like it if you're a killer or at least a onetime middleweight fighter. I smiled like I knew something. "Take it easy," I said, and I went back to the truck to swing around the cemetery at the top of the campus. They'd been know to screw in down-filled sleeping bags on horizontal stones up there, and the dean of students didn't want anybody dying of frostbite while joined at the hip to a matriculating fellow resident of our northeastern camp for the overindulged.

He blinked his high beams at me as I went. "You are not an unintelligent driver," I said.

---

[1] Nathaniel Hawthorne (1804–64), U.S. novelist and short story writer.

[2] Franz Kafka (1883–1924), Austrian novelist and short story writer who wrote nightmarish and surreal fiction.

10 Fanny had left me a bowl of something made with sausage and sauerkraut and potatoes, and the dog hadn't eaten too much more than his fair share. He watched me eat his leftovers and then make myself a king-sized drink composed of sourmash whiskey and ice. In our back room, which is on the northern end of the house, and cold for sitting in that close to dawn, I sat and watched the texture of the sky change. It was going to snow, and I wanted to see the storm come up the valley. I woke up that way, sitting in the rocker with its loose right arm, holding a watery drink, and thinking right away of the girl I'd convinced to go back inside. She'd been standing outside her dormitory, looking up at a window that was dark in the midst of all those lighted panes—they never turned a light off, and often left the faucets run half the night—crying onto her bathrobe. She was barefoot in shoe-pacs, the brown ones so many of them wore unlaced, and for all I know she was naked under her robe. She was beautiful, I thought, and she was somebody's red-headed daughter, standing in a quadrangle how many miles from home weeping.

"He doesn't love anyone," the kid told me. "He doesn't love his wife—I mean his ex-wife. And he doesn't love the ex-wife before that, or the one before that. And you know what? He doesn't love me. I don't know anyone who *does!*"

"It isn't your fault if he isn't smart enough to love you," I said, steering her toward the truck.

She stopped. She turned. "You know him?"

I couldn't help it. I hugged her hard, and she let me, and then she stepped back, and of course I let her go. "Don't you *touch* me! Is this sexual harassment? Do you know the rules? Isn't this sexual harassment?"

15 "I'm sorry," I said at the door to the truck. "But I think I have to be able to give you a grade before it counts as harassment."

She got in. I told her we were driving to the dean of students' house. She smelled like marijuana and something very sweet, maybe one of those coffee-with-cream liqueurs you don't buy unless you hate to drink.

As the heat of the truck struck her, she started going kind of clay-gray-green, and I reached across her to open the window.

"You touched my breast!" she said.

"It's the smallest one I've touched all night, I'm afraid."

20 She leaned out the window and gave her rendition of my dog.

But in my rocker, waking up, at whatever time in the morning in my silent house, I thought of her as someone's child. Which made me think of ours, of course. I went for more ice, and I started on a wet breakfast. At the door of the dean of students' house, she'd turned her chalky face to me and asked, "What grade would you give me, then?"

It was a week composed of two teachers locked out of their offices late at night, a Toyota with a flat and no spare, an attempted rape on a senior girl walking home from the library, a major fight outside a fraternity house (broken wrist and significant concussion), and variations on breaking-and-entering. I was scolded by the director of nonacademic services for embracing a student who was drunk; I told him to keep his job, but he called me back because I was right to hug her, he said, and also wrong, but what the hell, and would I please stay. I thought of the fringe benefits—graduation in only sixteen years—so I went back to work.

My professor assigned a story called "A Rose for Emily,"[3] and I wrote him a paper about the mechanics of corpse fucking, and how, since she clearly couldn't screw her dead boyfriend, she was keeping his rotten body in bed because she truly loved him. I called the paper "True Love." He gave me a B and wrote *See me, pls.* In his office after class, his feet up on his deck, he trimmed a cigar with a giant folding knife he kept in his drawer.

"You got to clean the hole out," he said, "or they don't draw."

"I don't smoke," I said.

"Bad habit. Real *habit,* though. I started in smoking 'em in Georgia, in the service. My C.O. smoked 'em. We collaborated on a brothel inspection one time, and we ended up smoking these with a couple of women—" He waggled his eyebrows at me, now that his malehood was established.

"Were the women smoking them too?"

He snorted laughter through his nose while the greasy smoke came curling off his thin, dry lips. "They were pretty smoky, I'll tell ya!" Then he propped his feet—he was wearing cowboy boots that day—and he sat forward. "It's a little hard to explain. But—hell. You just don't say *fuck* when you write an essay for a college prof. Okay?" Like a scoutmaster with a kid he'd caught in the outhouse jerking off: "All right? You don't wanna do that."

"Did it shock you?"

"Fuck, no, it didn't shock me. I just told you. It violates certain proprieties."

"But if I'm writing it to you, like a letter—"

"You're writing it for posterity. For some mythical reader someplace, not just me. You're making a *statement.*"

"Right. My statement said how hard it must be for a woman to fuck with a corpse."

"And a point worth making. I said so. Here."

"But you said I shouldn't say it."

"No. Listen. Just because you're talking about fucking, you don't have to say *fuck.* Does that make it any clearer?"

"No."

"I wish you'd lied to me just now," he said.

I nodded. I did too.

"Where'd you do your service?" he asked.

"Baltimore. Baltimore, Maryland.

"What's in Baltimore?"

"Railroads. I liaised on freight runs of army matériel. I killed a couple of bums on the road with my bare hands, though."

He snorted again, but I could see how disappointed he was. He'd been banking on my having been a murderer. Interesting guy in one of my classes,

[3] A story by William Faulkner.

he must have told some terrific woman at an overpriced meal: I just *know* the guy was a rubout specialist in the Nam, he had to have said. I figured I should come to work wearing my fatigue jacket and a red bandanna tied around my head. Say "Man" to him a couple of times, hang a fist in the air for grief and solidarity, and look terribly worn, exhausted by experiences he was fairly certain that he envied me. His dungarees were ironed, I noticed.

45 On Saturday we went back to the campus because Fanny wanted to see a movie called *The Seven Samurai.* I fell asleep, and I'm afraid I snored. She let me sleep until the auditorium was almost empty. Then she kissed me awake. "Who was screaming in my dream?" I asked her.

"Kurosawa," she said.

"Who?"

"Ask your professor friend."

I looked around, but he wasn't there. "Not an un-weird man," I said.

50 We went home and cleaned up after the dog and put him out. We drank a little Spanish brandy and went upstairs and made love. I was fairly premature, you might say, but one way and another by the time we fell asleep we were glad to be there with each other, and glad that it was Sunday coming up the valley toward us, and nobody with it. The dog was howling at another dog someplace, or at the moon, or maybe just his moon-thrown shadow on the snow. I did not strangle him when I opened the back door and he limped happily past me and stumbled up the stairs. I followed him into our bedroom and groaned for just being satisfied as I got into bed. You'll notice I didn't say fuck.

He stopped me in the hall after class on a Thursday, and asked me How's it going, just one of the kickers drinking sour beer and eating pickled eggs and watching the tube in a country bar. How's it goin. I nodded. I wanted a grade from the man, and I did want to learn about expressing myself. I nodded and made what I thought was a smile. He'd let his mustache grow out and his hair grow longer. He was starting to wear dark shirts with lighter ties. I thought he looked like someone in *The Godfather.* He still wore those light little loafers or his high-heeled cowboy boots. His corduroy pants looked baggy. I guess he wanted them to look that way. He motioned me to the wall of the hallway, and he looked and said, "How about the Baltimore stuff?"

I said, "Yeah?"

"Was that really true?" He was almost blinking, he wanted so much for me to be a damaged Vietnam vet just looking for a bell tower to climb into and start firing from. The college didn't have a bell tower you could get up into, though I'd once spent an ugly hour chasing a drunken ATO down from the roof of the observatory. "You were just clocking through boxcars in Baltimore?"

"I said, "Nah."

55 "I thought so!" He gave a kind of sigh.

"I killed people," I said.

"You know, I could have sworn you did," he said.

I nodded, and he nodded back. I'd made him so happy.

The assignment was to write something to influence somebody. He called it Rhetoric and Persuasion. We read an essay by George Orwell and "A Modest Proposal" by Jonathan Swift. I liked the Orwell better, but I wasn't comfortable with it. He talked about "niggers," and I felt him saying it two ways.

60 I wrote "Ralph the Duck."

Once upon a time, there was a duck named Ralph who didn't have any feathers on either wing. So when the cold wind blew, Ralph said, Brr, and shivered and shook.

What's the matter? Ralph's mommy asked.

I'm *cold,* Ralph said.

Oh, the mommy said. Here. I'll keep you warm.

65 So she spread her big, feathery wings, and hugged Ralph tight, and when the cold wind blew, Ralph was warm and snuggly, and fell fast asleep.

❋ ❋ ❋

The next Thursday, he was wearing canvas pants and hiking boots. He mentioned kind of casually to some of the girls in the class how whenever there was a storm he wore his Lake District walking outfit. He had a big, hairy sweater on. I kept waiting for him to make a noise like a mountain goat. But the girls seemed to like it. His boots made a creaky squeak on the linoleum of the hall when he caught up with me after class.

"As I told you," he said, "it isn't unappealing. It's just—not a college theme."

"Right," I said. "Okay. You want me to do it over?"

"No," he said. "Not at all. The D will remain your grade. But I'll read something else if you want to write it."

70 "This'll be fine," I said.

"Did you understand the assignment?"

"Write something to influence someone—Rhetoric and Persuasion."

We were at his office door and the redheaded kid who had gotten sick in my truck was waiting for him. She looked at me like one of us was in the wrong place, which struck me as accurate enough. He was interested in getting into his office with the redhead, but he remembered to turn around and flash me a grin he seemed to think he was known for.

Instead of going on shift a few hours after class, the way I'm supposed to, I told my supervisor I was sick, and I went home. Fanny was frightened when I came in, because I don't get sick and I don't miss work. She looked at my face and she grew sad. I kissed her hello and went upstairs to change. I always used to change my clothes when I was a kid, as soon as I came from school. I put on jeans and a flannel shirt and thick wool socks, and I made myself a dark drink of sourmash. Fanny poured herself some wine and came into the cold northern room a few minutes later. I was sitting in the rocker, looking over the valley. The wind was lining up a lot of rows of cloud so that the sky looked like a baked trout when you lift the skin off. "It'll snow," I said to her.

75 She sat on the old sofa and waited. After a while, she said, "I wonder why they always call it a mackerel sky?"

"Good eating, mackerel," I said.

Fanny said, "Shit! You're never that laconic unless you feel crazy. What's wrong? Who'd you punch out at the playground?"

"We had to write a composition," I said.

"Did he like it?"

80 "He gave me a D."

"Well, you're familiar enough with D's. I never saw you get this low over a grade."

"I wrote about Ralph the Duck."

She said, "You did?" She said, "Honey." She came over and stood beside the rocker and leaned into me and hugged my head and neck. "Honey," she said. "Honey."

It was the worst of the winter's storms, and one of the worst in years. That afternoon they closed the college, which they almost never do. But the roads were jammed with snow over ice, and now it was freezing rain on top of that, and the only people working at the school that night were the operator who took emergency calls and me. Everyone else had gone home except the students, and most of them were inside. The ones who weren't were drunk, and I kept on sending them in and telling them to act like grown-ups. A number of them said they were, and I really couldn't argue. I had the bright beams on, the defroster set high, the little blue light winking, and a thermos of sourmash and hot coffee that I sipped from every time I had to get out of the truck or every time I realized how cold all that wetness was out there.

85 About eight o'clock, as the rain was turning back to snow and the cold was worse, the roads impossible, just as I was done helping a county sander on the edge of the campus pull a panel truck out of a snowbank, I got the emergency call from the college operator. We had a student missing. The roommate thought the kid was headed for the quarry. This meant I had to get the Bronco up on a narrow road above the campus, above the old cemetery, into all kinds of woods and rough track that I figured would be chocked with ice and snow. Any kid up there would really have to want to be there, and I couldn't go in on foot, because you'd only want to be there on account of drugs, booze, or craziness, and either way I'd be needing blankets and heat, and then a fast ride down to the hospital in town. So I dropped into four-wheel drive to get me up the hill above the campus, bucking snow and sliding on ice, putting all the heater's warmth up onto the windshield because I couldn't see much more than swarming snow. My feet were still cold from the tow job, and it didn't seem to matter that I had on heavy socks and insulated boots I'd coated with waterproofing. I shivered, and I thought of Ralph the Duck.

I had to grind the rest of the way, from the cemetery, in four-wheel low, and in spite of the cold I was smoking my gearbox by the time I was close enough to the quarry—they really did take a lot of rocks for the campus buildings from there—to see I'd have to make my way on foot to where she was. It was a kind of scooped-out shape, maybe four or five stories high, where she stood—well, wobbled is more like it. She was as chalky as she'd been the last time, and her red hair didn't catch the light anymore. It just lay on her like something that had died on top of her head. She was in a white nightgown that was plastered to her body. She had her arms crossed as if she wanted to be warm. She swayed, kind of, in front of the big, dark, scooped-out rock face, where the trees and brush had been cleared for trucks and earthmovers. She looked tiny against all the darkness. From where I stood, I could see the snow driving down in front of the lights I'd left on, but I couldn't see it near her. All it looked like around her was dark. She was shaking with the cold, and she was crying.

I had a blanket with me, and I shoved it down the front of my coat to keep it dry for her, and because I was so cold. I waved. I stood in the lights and I waved. I don't know what she saw—a big shadow, maybe. I surely didn't reassure her, because when she saw me she backed up, until she was near the face of the quarry. She couldn't go any farther.

I called, "Hello! I brought a blanket. Are you cold? I thought you might want a blanket."

Her roommates had told the operator about pills, so I didn't bring her the coffee laced with mash. I figured I didn't have all that much time, anyway, to get her down and pumped out. The booze with whatever pills she'd taken would make her die that much faster.

90 I hated that word. Die. It made me furious with her. I heard myself seething when I breathed. I pulled my scarf and collar up above my mouth. I didn't want her to see how close I might come to wanting to kill her because she wanted to die.

I called, "Remember me?"

I was closer now. I could see the purple mottling of her skin. I didn't know if it was cold or dying. It probably didn't matter much to distinguish between them right now, I thought. That made me smile. I felt the smile, and I pulled the scarf down so she could look at it. She didn't seem awfully reassured.

"You're the sexual harassment guy," she said. She said it very slowly. Her lips were clumsy. It was like looking at a ventriloquist's dummy.

"I gave you an A," I said.

95 "When?"

"It's a joke," I said. "You don't want me making jokes. You want me to give you a nice warm blanket, though. And then you want me to take you home."

She leaned against the rock face when I approached. I pulled the blanket out, then zipped my jacket back up. The snow had stopped. I realized, and that wasn't really a very good sign. It felt like an arctic cold descending in its place. I held the blanket out to her, but she only looked at it.

"You'll just have to turn me in," I said. "I'm gonna hug you again."

She screamed, "No more! I don't want any more hugs!"

100 But she kept her arms on her chest, and I wrapped the blanket around her and stuffed a piece into each of her tight, small fists. I didn't know what to do for her feet. Finally, I got down on my haunches in front of her. She crouched down too, protecting herself.

"No," I said. "No. You're fine."

I took off the woolen mittens I'd been wearing. Mittens keep you warmer than gloves because they trap your hand's heat around the fingers and palms at once. Fanny had knitted them for me. I put a mitten as far onto each of her feet as I could. She let me. She was going to collapse, I thought.

"Now, let's go home," I said. "Let's get you better."

With her funny, stiff lips, she said. "I've been very self-indulgent and weird and I'm sorry. But I'd really like to die." She sounded so reasonable that I found myself nodding in agreement as she spoke.

105 "You can't just die," I said.

"Aren't I dying already?" I took all of them, and then"—she giggled like a child, which of course is what she was—"I borrowed different ones from other people's rooms. See, this isn't some teenage cry for like *help.* Understand? I'm seriously interested in death and I have to like stay out here a little longer and fall asleep. All right?"

"You can't do that," I said. "You ever hear of Vietnam?"

"I saw that move," she said. "With the opera in it? *Apocalypse?* Whatever."

"I was there!" I said. "I killed people! I helped to kill them! And when they die, you see their bones later on. You dream about their bones and blood on the ends of the splintered ones, and this kind of mucous stuff coming out of their eyes. You probably heard of guys having dreams like that, didn't you? Whacked-out Vietnam vets? That's me, see? So I'm telling you, I know about dead people and their eyeballs and everything falling out. And people keep dreaming about the dead people they knew, see? You can't make people dream about you like that! It isn't fair!"

110 "You dream about me?" She was ready to go. She was ready to fall down, and I was going to lift her up and get her to the truck.

"I will," I said. "If you die."

"I want you to," she said. Her lips were hardly moving now. Her eyes were closed. "I want you all to."

I dropped my shoulder and put it into her waist and picked her up and carried her down to the Bronco. She was talking, but not a lot, and her voice leaked down my back. I jammed her into the truck and wrapped the blanket around her better and then put another one down around her feet. I strapped her in with the seat belt. She was shaking, and her eyes were closed and her mouth open. She was breathing. I checked that twice, once when I strapped her in, and then again when I strapped myself in and backed up hard into a sapling and took it down. I got us into first gear, held the clutch in, leaned over to listen for breathing, heard it—heard it—shallow panting, like a kid asleep on your lap for a nap—and then I put the gear in and howled down the hillside on what I thought might be the road.

We passed the cemetery. I told her that was good sign. She didn't respond. I found myself panting too, as if we were breathing for each other. It made me dizzy, but I couldn't stop. We passed the highest dorm, and I dropped the truck into four-wheel high. The cab smelled like burnt oil and hot metal. We were past the chapel now, and the observatory, the president's house, then the bookstore. I had the blue light winking and the V-6 roaring, and I drove on the edge of out-of-control, sensing the skids just before I slid into them, and getting back out of them as I needed to. I took a little fender off once, and a bit of the corner of a classroom building, but I worked us back on course, and all I needed to do now was negotiate the sharp left turn around the Administration Building past the library, then floor it for the straight run to the town's main street and then the hospital.

115 I was panting into the mike, and the operator kept saying, "Say again?"

I made myself slow down some, and I said we'd need stomach pumping, and to get the names of the pills from her friends in the dorm, and I'd be there in less than five or we were crumpled up someplace and dead.

"Roger," the radio said. "Roger all that." My throat tightened and tears came into my eyes. They were helping us, they'd told me: Roger.

I said to the girl, whose head was slumped and whose face looked too blue all through its whiteness, "You know, I had girl once. My wife, Fanny. She and I had small girl one time."

I reached over and touched her cheek. It was cold. The truck swerved, and I got my hands on the wheel. I'd made the turn past the Ad Building using just my left. "I can do it in the dark," I sang to no tune I'd ever learned. "I can do it with one hand." I said to her, "We had a girl child, very small. Now, I do *not* want you dying."

120 I came to the campus gates doing fifty on the ice and snow, smoking the engine, grinding the clutch, and I bounced off a wrought iron fence to give me the curve going left that I needed. On a pool table, it would have been a bank shot worth applause. The town cop picked me up and got out ahead of me and let the street have all the lights and noise it could want. We banged up to the emergency room entrance and I was out and at the other door before the cop on duty, Elmo St. John, could loosen his seat belt. I loosened hers, and they took her away from me. I tried to talk to them, but they made me sit down and do my shaking on a dirty sofa decorated with drawings of little spinning wheels. Somebody brought me hot coffee, I think it was Elmo, but I couldn't hold it.

"They won't," he kept saying to me. "They won't."

"What?"

"You just been sitting there for a minute and a half like St. Vitus dancing, telling me, 'Don't let her die. Don't let her die.' "

"Oh."

125 "You all *right?*"

"How about the kid?"

"They'll tell us soon."

"She better be all right."

"That's right."

130 "She—somebody's gonna have to tell me plenty if she isn't."

"That's right."

"She better not die this time," I guess I said.

Fanny came downstairs to look for me. I was at the northern windows, looking through the mullions down the valley to the faint red line along the mounds and little peaks of the ridge beyond the valley. The sun was going to come up, and I was looking for it.

Fanny stood behind me. I could hear her. I could smell her hair and the sleep on her. The crimson line widened, and I squinted at it. I heard the dog limp in behind her, catching up. He panted and I knew why his panting sounded familiar. She put her hands on my shoulders and arms. I made muscles to impress her with, and then I let them go, and let my head drop down until my chin was on my chest.

135 "I didn't think you'd be able to sleep after that," Fanny said.

"I brought enough adrenaline home to run a football team."

"But you hate being a hero, huh? You're hiding in here because somebody's going to call, or come over, and want to talk to you—her parents for shooting sure, sooner or later. Or is that supposed to be part of the service up at the playground! Saving their suicidal daughters. Almost dying to find them in the woods and driving too fast for *any* weather, much less what we had last night. Getting their babies home. The bastards." She was crying. I knew she would be, sooner or later. I could hear the soft sound of her lashes. She sniffed and I could feel her arm move as she felt for the tissues on the coffee table.

"I have them over here," I said. "On the windowsill."

"Yes." She blew her nose, and the dog thumped his tail. He seemed to think it one of Fanny's finer tricks, and he had wagged for her for thirteen years whenever she'd done it. "Well, you're going to have to talk to them."

140 "I will," I said. "I will." The sun was in our sky now, climbing. We had built the room so we could watch it climb. "I think that jackass with the smile, my prof? She showed up a lot at his office, the last few weeks. He called her 'my advisee,' you know? The way those guys sound about what they're achieving by getting up and shaving and going to work and saying the same thing every day? Every year? Well, she was his advisee, I bet. He was shoving home the old advice."

"She'll be okay," Fanny said. "Her parents will take her home and love her up and get her some help." She began to cry again, then she stopped. She blew her nose, and the dog's tail thumped. She kept a hand between my shoulder and my neck. "So tell me what you'll tell a waiting world. How'd you talk her out?"

"Well, I didn't, really. I got up close and picked her up and carried her is all."

"You didn't say *any*thing?"

"Sure I did. Kid's standing in the snow outside of a lot of pills, you're gonna say something.

145 "So what'd you *say?*"

"I told her stories," I said. "I did Rhetoric and Persuasion."

Fanny said, "Then you go in early on Thursday, you go in half an hour early, and you get that guy to jack up your grade."

Explorations of the Text

1. What is your first impression of the point of view of the narrator? Is he a reliable narrator? Discuss voice and tone.
2. Summarize the main plot and subplots. How do they connect and reinforce each other?
3. Why does Busch include the hints at the relationship between the professor and the redheaded girl? Is this subplot necessary to the development of the story?
4. Discuss the significance of the story of "Ralph the Duck." What does it mean to the narrator and to his wife? To the reader? Discuss the levels of irony in its presentation.
5. Why does the writer include the description of the dog? What is the significance of this detail?
6. Explore the class critique and criticism of the academy presented in the story.
7. Discuss the significance of the repeated line, "Rhetoric and Persuasion."
8. Do you think that the narrator actually went to war? What is the significance of this detail?
9. How does the dialogue develop theme?
10. Compare visions of compassion and community presented in this work with the treatment of this theme in "The Things They Carried."

The Reading/Writing Connection

1. "Think" Topic: Is the narrator a sympathetic character? Why or why not? Explain your impression in a paragraph.
2. Journal Entry: How would this story change if it were narrated in third person from the point of view of the wife? Write a portion of the story from this perspective and analyze the results. What is the impact of the narrative point of view?

Ideas for Writing

1. Discuss war as the central symbol in the story. How does this symbol connect the layers of the plot and suggest themes of the work?
2. How would the narrator of this work respond to "American Ignorance of War"? Construct a letter written by the narrator to Milosz.

POETRY

Musée des Beaux Arts

W. H. Auden

W. H. Auden (1907–73), born in York, England, received a scholarship to Oxford University, where he studied science and engineering before changing his field of study to English. After immigrating to the United States and living there for a number of years, Auden became a citizen in 1946. He taught at colleges including Bryn Mawr and Barnard. Auden's work includes Poems *(1928), and* Some Poems *(1940); and the plays,* The Dance of Death *(1934) and* No More Peace! A Thoughtful Comedy *(1936). He also wrote introductions to many collections of verse and translated a number of works. His many awards include the King's Gold Metal for poetry in 1937 and the Pulitzer Prize for Poetry in 1948.*

1940

About suffering they were never wrong,
The Old Masters: how well they understood
Its human position; how it takes place
While someone else is eating or opening a window or just walking dully
along
How, when the aged are reverently, passionately waiting
For the miraculous birth, there always must be
Children who did not specially want it to happen, skating
On a pond at the edge of the wood:
They never forgot
That even the dreadful martyrdom must run its course
Anyhow in a corner, some untidy spot
Where the dogs go on with their doggy life and the torturer's horse
Scratches its innocent behind on a tree.
In Brueghel's *Icarus,*[1] for instance: how everything turns away
Quite leisurely from the disaster; the ploughman may
Have heard the splash, the forsaken cry,
But for him it was not an important failure; the sun shone
As it had to on the white legs disappearing into the green

[1] Peter Brueghel, Flemish painter (ca. 1525–69), whose painting, "Landscape with the Fall of Icarus," hangs in the Musees Royaux des Beaux-Arts in Brussels, Belgium. Icarus is a classical mythological figure who with his father, Daedalus, designed wings of wax and feathers, which they used to attempt to escape from Crete. Daedalus succeeded, but Icarus flew too close to the sun. The sun melted the boy's wings, and he plunged into the sea and drowned.

Water; and the expensive delicate ship that must have seen
Something amazing, a boy falling out of the sky,
Had somewhere to get to and sailed calmly on.

Explorations of the Text

1. About what were the "Old Masters" correct? What views did the "Old Masters" hold about suffering?
2. Characterize the persona. How does he view suffering? Contrast the speaker's vision with that of the "Old Masters."
3. Discuss the symbolism of Brueghel's painting. How does the symbolism develop themes of the poem?
4. What does the poem suggest about heroism, great deeds, and suffering?
5. How would the father in the story "War" respond to the poem?

The Reading/Writing Connection

1. Respond to the speaker's view of suffering in this poem. Write a letter to the speaker.
2. Compare the views presented in this poem with those in "American Ignorance of War" or in "Three Thousand Dollar Death Song."

Ideas for Writing

1. Compare the view of suffering presented in this work with that of Charlotte Delbo's persona in "Prayer to the Living to Forgive Them for Being Alive."

Weapons at Best

Lao-tzu

Lao-tzu lived during the sixth century B.C. in the ancient state of Ch'u in China. The Tao-te-Ching, *the major document of Taoism, is attributed to his authorship, although it may not be the work of a single person. Some of the* Tao-te-Ching*'s sayings may date from the time of Confucius, but others are certainly later, and the book as a whole may date from 300 B.C. Indeed, the name Lao-tzu may represent a type of sage and not a specific person, though the work attributed to him has continued to be respected in China and throughout the world. The* Tao-te-Ching *is a collection of eighty-one poems or segments that present an eloquent expression of withdrawal from action, the way to virtue.*

c. 500–200 B.C.

Weapons at best are tools of bad omen,
Loathed and avoided by those of the Way.

In the usage of men of good breeding,
Honor is had at the left;
Good omens belong on the left;
Bad omens belong on the right;
And warriors press to the right!
When the general stands at the right
His lieutenant is placed at the left.
So the usage of men of great power
Follows that of the funeral rite.

Weapons are tools of bad omen,
By gentlemen not to be used;
But when it cannot be avoided,
They use them with calm and restraint.
Even in victory's hour
These tools are unlovely to see;
For those who admire them truly
Are men who in murder delight.

As for those who delight to do murder,
It is certain they never can get
From the world what they sought when ambition
Urged them to power and rule.

A multitude slain!—and their death
Is a matter for grief and for tears;
The victory after a conflict
Is a theme for a funeral rite.

Exploration of the Text

1. Why should the person "who has Reason" not rely on arms?
2. What is the difference between "left" and "right" in section 2?
3. Why does Lao-tzu say that one may use arms "when it is unavoidable?" Why does he honor "peace and quietude"?
4. Why should the victor not "rejoice"? Why is taking pleasure in "the slaughter of men" wrong, according to Lao-tzu?
5. Compare this poem with Owen's "Dulce et Decorum Est" and O'Brien's "The Things They Carried."

The Reading/Writing Connection

1. Respond to the following quotation from the *Tao-te-Ching:*

   To quicken but not to own, to make but not to claim.

   To raise but not rule, this is called profound virtue.

2. Explore themes of "Quelling War."

Ideas for Writing

1. Agree or disagree with the following statements: "Arms are unblest among tools and not the superior man's tools. Only when it is unavoidable he uses them."
2. Compare this work with "Arms and the Boy" by Owen (see chapter 10).

Dulce et Decorum Est

Wilfred Owen

Wilfred Owen (1893–1918), born in Shropshire, England, attended the University of London. In 1915, he joined the British army and served in a rifle corps during World War I. After seven months, he was injured and sent to a war hospital in Scotland, where he met another patient, poet Siegfried Sassoon, who encouraged him to write. After recovering from his injury, Owen returned to the battlefield in France and was awarded the Military Cross for gallantry under fire. He was killed while leading troops across the Sombre Canal just a week before the Armistice. His work was collected and published by Sassoon in a volume titled Poems *(1920).*

1920

Bent double, like old beggars under sacks,
Knock-kneed, coughing like hags, we cursed through sludge,
Till on the haunting flares we turned our backs
And towards our distant rest began to trudge.
Men marched asleep. Many had lost their boots
But limped on, blood-shod. All went lame; all blind;
Drunk with fatigue; deaf even to the hoots
Of tired, outstripped Five-Nines[1] that dropped behind.

Gas! Gas! Quick, boys!—An ecstasy of fumbling,
Fitting the clumsy helmets just in time;
But someone still was yelling out and stumbling
And flound'ring like a man in fire or lime . . .

[1] Gas shells.

Dim, through the misty panes and thick green light,
As under a green sea, I saw him drowning.

In all my dreams, before my helpless sight,
He plunges at me, guttering, choking, drowning.

If in some smothering dreams you too could pace
Behind the wagon that we flung him in,
And watch the white eyes writhing in his face,
His hanging face, like a devil's sick of sin;
If you could hear, at every jolt, the blood
Come gargling from the froth-corrupted lungs,
Obscene as cancer, bitter as the cud
Of vile, incurable sores on innocent tongues,—
My friend, you would not tell with such high zest
To children ardent for some desperate glory,
The old Lie: Dulce et decorum est
Pro patria mori.[2]

Explorations of the Text

1. Discuss the **similes** in lines 1 and 2. What images of the young soldiers does Owen present?
2. Find the words with negative **connotations** in stanza 1. Why are the men "lame," "blind," "drunk with fatigue," and "deaf"?
3. Why does Owen shift to the **first person** in the second verse? What effect does this highly personal testimony achieve?
4. Whom does the narrator address as "you" in stanza 4? What is his purpose? Who is the audience?
5. Give a synopsis of the narrative in this poem. What is the attitude of the speaker? Describe the tone.
6. Discuss figures of speech, rhyme scheme, and sound. How do they contribute to the effectiveness of this work?
7. Compare "Dulce et Decorum Est" to "The Things They Carried."

The Reading/Writing Connection

1. "Think" Topic: Gloss and annotate the text; identify and react to the similes in this poem.
2. In a mini-essay, respond to the vision of war in stanza 4 or the attitude toward war in stanza 2.

[2] "It is sweet and fitting to die for one's country."

Ideas for Writing

1. Write an essay that takes a position on Horace's quotation. Refer to works in the chapter to support your points.
2. Explicate this poem. Concentrate on point of view, tone, and imagery. (Look at the analysis of Owen's "Arms and the Boy" in chapter 10 as a model.)
3. Does this poem persuade you that "war is Hell"? Why or why not?

Welcome to Hiroshima

Mary Jo Salter

Mary Jo Salter (1954–), a graduate of Harvard University, teaches at Mount Holyoke College. Her volumes of poetry include Henry Purcell in Japan *(1985) and* Unfinished Painting *(1989). Recent works include* Sunday Skaters *(1994) and* Kiss in Space *(1999).*

1985

is what you first see, stepping off the train:
a billboard brought to you in living English
by Toshiba Electric. While a channel
silent in the TV of the brain

projects those flickering re-runs of a cloud
that brims its risen columnful like beer
and, spilling over, hangs its foamy head,[1]
you feel a thirst for history: what year

it started to be safe to breathe the air,
and when to drink the blood and scum afloat
on the Ohta River.[2] But no, the water's clear,
they pour it for your morning cup of tea

in one of the countless sunny coffee shops
whose plastic dioramas advertise
mutations of cuisine behind the glass:
a pancake sandwich; a pizza someone tops

with a maraschino cherry. Passing by
the Peace Park's floral hypocenter[3] (where
how bravely, or with what mistaken cheer,
humanity erased its own erasure),

---

[1] Reference to the telltale mushroom cloud of the atomic blast.

[2] River in Hiroshima.

[3] Epicenter of the blast.

you enter the memorial museum
and through more glass are served, as on a dish
of blistered grass, three mannequins. Like gloves
a mother clips to coatsleeves, strings of flesh

hang from their fingertips; or as if tied
to recall a duty for us, *Reverence*
the dead whose mourners too shall soon be dead,
but all commemoration's swallowed up

in questions of bad taste, how re-created
horror mocks the grim original,
and thinking at last *They should have left it all*
you stop. This is the wristwatch of a child.

Jammed on the moment's impact, resolute
to communicate some message, although mute,
it gestures with its hands at eight-fifteen
and eight-fifteen and eight-fifteen again

while tables of statistics on the wall
update the news by calling on a roll
of tape, death gummed on death, and in the case
adjacent, an exhibit under glass

is glass itself: a shard the bomb slammed in
a woman's arm at eight-fifteen, but some
three decades on—as if to make it plain
hope's only as renewable as pain,

and as if all the unsung
debasements of the past may one day come
rising to the surface once again—
worked its filthy way out like a tongue.

Explorations of the Text

1. Why does Salter use the "welcome" sign as the title and the first line of the poem? What impact does this wording have?
2. Discuss the persona's response to the exhibits at Hiroshima. How do the exhibits represent the nuclear holocaust? Focus particularly on stanza 5. What messages do these images convey?
3. How does she use visceral, bodily images?
4. Why do the exhibits of the "wristwatch" and "shard of glass" capture the speaker's attention?

5. Explore the conception of witnessing enunciated in the last two stanzas.
6. How do the rhyme, rhythm, and stanzaic form further themes of the poem?

The Reading/Writing Connection

1. Freewrite and respond to the following line: "Humanity erased its own erasure . . ." To what other historical events would this statement apply?
2. Gloss and annotate the poem. Explore the contrasting images of naïve hope versus understanding of pain; or present versus past realities.
3. "Think" Topic: What is the speaker's view of the exhibit? Connect her views with human beings' abilities to witness war.

Ideas for Writing

1. Compare the vision of witnessing war and genocide presented in this work with themes expressed in "American Ignorance of War," "Prayer to the Living to Forgive Them for Being Alive," and "Memory of Elena."
2. Compare the views of war presented in this work with those suggested in "The War Generation."

Let America Be America Again

Langston Hughes

Langston Hughes (1902–67), born in Joplin, Missouri, wrote more than twenty books—poetry, fiction, drama, and nonfiction—becoming the best-known African American writer of his generation. Hughes, educated at Columbia University, published his first book of poems, The Weary Blues, *in 1926. He was a member of the group of writers and artists known as the Harlem Renaissance, who celebrated African American experience an attempted to find literary forms more suited to it. In 1961, Hughes became a member of the National Academy of Arts and Letters. His works include* Shakespeare in Harlem *(1942),* One Way Ticket *(1949), and* Ask Your Mamma *(1961).*

1938

Let America be America again.
Let it be the dream it used to be.
Let it be the pioneer on the plain
Seeking a home where he himself is free.

(America never was America to me.)

Let America be the dream the dreamers dreamed—
Let it be that great strong land of love
Where never kings connive nor tyrants scheme
That any man be crushed by one above.

(It never was America to me.)

O, let my land be a land where Liberty
Is crowned with no false patriotic wreath,
But opportunity is real, and life is free,
Equality is in the air we breathe.

(There's never been equality for me,
Nor freedom in this "homeland of the free.")

Say who are you that mumbles in the dark?
And who are you that draws your veil across the stars?

I am the poor white, fooled and pushed apart,
I am the red man driven from the land.
I am the refugee clutching the hope I seek—
But finding only the same old stupid plan

Of dog eat dog, of mighty crush the weak.
I am the Negro, "problem" to you all.
I am the people, humble, hungry, mean—
Hungry yet today despite the dream.
Beaten yet today—O, Pioneers!
I am the man who never got ahead,
The poorest worker bartered through the years.
Yet I'm the one who dreamt our basic dream
In that Old World while still a serf of kings,
Who dreamt a dream so strong, so brave, so true,
That even yet its mighty daring sings
In every brick and stone, in every furrow turned
That's made America the land it has become.
O, I'm the man who sailed those early seas
In search of what I meant to be my home—
For I'm the one who left dark Ireland's shore,
And Poland's plain, and England's grassy lea,
And torn from Black Africa's strand I came
To build a "homeland of the free."

The free?
Who said the free? Not me?

Surely not me? The millions on relief today?
The millions who have nothing for our pay
For all the dreams we've dreamed
And all the songs we've sung
And all the hopes we've held
And all the flags we've hung,
The millions who have nothing for our pay—
Except the dream we keep alive today.

O, let America be America again—
The land that never has been yet—
And yet must be—the land where *every* man is free.
The land that's mine—the poor man's, Indian's, Negro's, ME—
Who made America,
Whose sweat and blood, whose faith and pain,
Whose hand at the foundry, whose plow in the rain,
Must bring back our mighty dream again.

O, yes,
I say it plain,
America never was America to me,
And yet I swear this oath—
America will be!

Explorations of the Text

1. What does the title mean? Who is the speaker? For whom does he speak?
2. What dreams of America emerge in the first three stanzas? What is the meaning of America in the refrain?
3. Describe the transformation of the speaker which begins in line 19: "I am the poor white, fooled and pushed apart."
4. What criticisms of America does the speaker make? Compare them to Ginsberg's "America." Are the issues similar?
5. Analyze the **paradox:**

   "O let America be America again—
   The land that never has been yet—"
6. How does the speaker's attitude change in the last stanza?
7. Examine Hughes' use of **irony.** (See chapter 11 for a discussion of irony.)
8. Consider the form of this poem—line length, repetition, stanza divisions—and compare this work with Whitman's "Out of the Cradle Endlessly Rocking" in chapter 4.

The Reading/Writing Connection

1. "Think" Topic: Write about one of Hughes' two Americas.
2. Respond to Hughes' poem in a double-entry notebook.
3. Respond to a contemporary event as if you were Hughes. Create a monologue in his voice. Or, how would Twilight Bey respond to Hughes's vision?

Ideas for Writing

1. Write about speaker and voice in "Let America Be America Again."
2. Agree or disagree with Hughes' analysis of America.
3. Explicate and evaluate this poem. Focus on imagery, paradox, tone, irony, and/or form.
4. Compare this poem with Ginsberg's "America."

Harlem

Langston Hughes

1951

What happens to a dream deferred?

Does it dry up
like a raisin in the sun?
Or fester like a sore—
And then run?
Does it stink like rotten meat?
Or crust and sugar over—
like a syrupy sweet?

Maybe it just sags
like a heavy load.

Or does it explode?

Explorations of the Text

1. What is the connection between the title and the opening question?
2. What possible consequences does the speaker suggest?
3. Why does Hughes create so many **similes**? Are they effective? Why does he use so many questions? Are they effective?
4. Why does the persona speak only one declarative sentence?
5. Why is the last question isolated and written in italics? What are the implications? What is the answer?

6. Examine the rhyme scheme and other formal elements in the poem. What makes "Harlem" work?
7. Compare themes in this poem to those in works by Auden, Ginsberg, and Knight.

The Reading/Writing Connection

1. Gloss and annotate the poem, and write an end comment.
2. Journal Entry: Write about "a dream deferred" in your own life. Compare your experience with the lost hopes of the poem.

Ideas for Writing

1. Explicate formal elements—figures of speech, sound, rhyme, and rhythm—in "Harlem."
2. Consider each of the similes and paraphrase them. Write a cause-effect analysis of the "dream deferred."

The Chicago Defender Sends a Man to Little Rock

Gwendolyn Brooks

Gwendolyn Brooks (1917–2000), born in Topeka, Kansas, graduated from Wilson Junior College. A novelist and poet, she taught at a number of colleges and universities, including Columbia University and the University of Wisconsin. Her many works include the novel Maud Martha *(1953) and volumes of poetry, including* Annie Allen *(1949), which won the Pulitzer Prize for Poetry,* The Bean Eaters *(1960), and* To Disembark *(1981). She was the first African American poet to win the Pulitzer Prize, and she received numerous other awards and honors. She was Distinguished Professor of the Arts at the City College of New York in 1971.*

In 1954, the Supreme Court ordered desegregation of schools "with all deliberate speed" in a landmark decision in the case of Brown v. *The Board of Education of Topeka, Kansas.*

1960

In Little Rock[1] the people bear
Babes, and comb and part their hair

[1] Little Rock, Arkansas, scene of one test of the Supreme Court case *(Brown* v. *The Board of Education)* concerning desegregation of schools. Federal troops in 1957 had to be sent to enforce the Supreme Court decision and integrate Little Rock High School.

And watch the want ads, put repair
To roof and latch. While wheat toast burns
A woman waters multiferns.

Time upholds or overturns
The many, tight, and small concerns.

In Little Rock the people sing
Sunday hymns like anything,
Through Sunday pomp and polishing.

And after testament and tunes,
Some soften Sunday afternoons
With lemon tea and Lorna Doones.[2]

I forecast
And I believe
Come Christmas Little Rock will cleave
To Christmas tree and trifle, weave,
From laugh and tinsel, texture fast.

In Little Rock is baseball; Barcarolle.[3]
That hotness in July . . . the uniformed figures raw and implacable
And not intellectual,
Batting the hotness or clawing the suffering dust.
The Open Air Concert, on the special twilight green. . . .
When Beethoven[4] is brutal or whispers to lady-like air.
Blanket-sitters are solemn, as Johann[5] troubles to lean
To tell them what to mean. . . .

There is love, too, in Little Rock. Soft women softly
Opening themselves in kindness,
Or, pitying one's blindness,
Awaiting one's pleasure
In azure
Glory with anguished rose at the root. . . .
To wash away old semi-discomfitures.
They re-teach purple and unsullen blue.
The wispy soils go. And uncertain
Half-havings have they clarified to sures.

---

[2] Cookies.

[3] Venetian boat song with a rowing rhythm or music imitating such songs.

[4] Ludwig van Beethoven, German composer (1770–1827).

[5] Johann Sebastian Bach, German composer (1685–1750).

In Little Rock they know
Not answering the telephone is a way of rejecting life,
That it is our business to be bothered, is our business
To cherish bores or boredom, be polite
To lies and love and many-faceted fuzziness.
I scratch my head, massage the hate-I-had.
I blink across my prim and pencilled pad.
The saga I was sent for is not down.
Because there is a puzzle in this town.
The biggest News I do not dare
Telegraph to the Editor's chair:
"They are like people everywhere."

The angry Editor would reply
In hundred harryings of Why.

And true, they are hurling spittle, rock,
Garbage and fruit in Little Rock.
And I saw coiling storm a-writhe
On bright madonnas. And a scythe
Of men harassing brownish girls.
(The bows and barrettes in the curls
And braids declined away from joy.)

I saw a bleeding brownish boy. . . .

The lariat lynch-wish I deplored.

The loveliest lynchee was our Lord.

Explorations of the Text

1. Examine the first four stanzas, and describe life in Little Rock.
2. Who is the narrator? Why is the narrator in Little Rock?
3. What is the nature of love in Little Rock? Describe the "soft women." Interpret this section carefully.
4. Why is the narrator so puzzled that the citizens of Little Rock "are like people everywhere"? What are the implications of this conclusion?
5. What has the man sent to Little Rock actually seen? What acts of harassment and violence happen there?
6. Why are the last three lines separated into stanzas? What is the effect?
7. What is traditional about the form of this poem?
8. Compare and contrast this poem with works by Hughes, Knight, Deavere Smith, and Ginsberg.

The Reading/Writing Connection

1. Freewrite. Respond to the idea that the people in Little Rock who opposed desegregation "are like people everywhere."
2. "Think" Topic: Is this poem still relevant, or is it an interesting and powerful description of a singular moment in history? Respond to this question in a paragraph.

Ideas for Writing

1. Write a brief research paper on the historical context of this poem.
2. What are the functions of setting in this poem?

Hard Rock Returns to Prison from the Hospital for the Criminal Insane

Etheridge Knight

In this poem, Knight characterizes Hard Rock, "the doer of things" that others only "dreamed of doing," who returns to prison from a mental hospital.

1968

Hard Rock was "known not to take no shit
From nobody," and he had the scars to prove it:
Split purple lips, lumped ears, welts above
His yellow eyes, and one long scar that cut
Across his temple and plowed through a thick
Canopy of kinky hair.

The WORD was that Hard Rock wasn't a mean nigger
Anymore, that the doctors had bored a hole in his head,
Cut out part of his brain, and shot electricity
Through the rest. When they brought Hard Rock back,
Handcuffed and chained, he was turned loose,
Like a freshly gelded stallion, to try his new status.
And we all waited and watched, like indians at a corral,
To see if the WORD was true.

As we waited we wrapped ourselves in the cloak
Of his exploits: "Man, the last time, it took eight
Screws[1] to put him in the Hole." "Yeah, remember when he
Smacked the captain with his dinner tray?" "He set
The record for time in the Hole—67 straight days!"

---

[1] Guards.

"Ol Hard Rock! man, that's one crazy nigger."
And then the jewel of a myth that Hard Rock had once bit
A screw on the thumb and poisoned him with syphilitic spit.

The testing came, to see if Hard Rock was really tame.
A hillbilly called him a black son of a bitch
And didn't lose his teeth, a screw who knew Hard Rock
From before shook him down and barked in his face.
And Hard Rock did *nothing.* Just grinned and looked silly,
His eyes empty like knot holes in a fence.

And even after we discovered that it took Hard Rock
Exactly 3 minutes to tell you his first name,
We told ourselves that he had just wised up,
Was being cool; but we could not fool ourselves for long,

And we turned away, our eyes on the ground. Crushed.
He had been our Destroyer, the doer of things
We dreamed of doing but could not bring ourselves to do,
The fears of years, like a biting whip,
Had cut grooves too deeply across our backs.

Explorations of the Text

1. How does the speaker describe Hard Rock in stanza 1? What does the characterization imply?
2. What is "the WORD" about Hard Rock?
3. Why do the prisoners wrap themselves "in the cloak/Of his exploits"? Are his exploits real? Does it matter?
4. What tests prove that Hard Rock has broken "like a freshly gelded stallion"?
5. Why do the inmates try to fool themselves? Why are they crushed?
6. What does the persona mean when he says, "The fears of years, like a biting whip,/Had cut grooves too deeply across our backs"?
7. What does Hard Rock symbolize? What is the speaker's attitude toward the change in Hard Rock?
8. Compare/contrast Hard Rock and Busch's narrator.

The Reading/Writing Connection

1. "Think" Topic: Characterize Hard Rock. Why is his situation so important to others?
2. Compare Hard Rock and Twilight Bey.

3. In a journal entry, describe a person whose strengths and whose defeat have influenced your life.
4. Which lines are most powerful? Why? Respond to the lines in a freewrite.

Ideas for Writing

1. Compare this poem to Valenzuela's "I'm Your Horse in the Night."
2. What views of prison life emerge in this poem?

AMERICA

Allen Ginsberg

Allen Ginsberg (1926–97) was born in Newark, New Jersey. After graduating from Columbia University, Ginsberg went to San Francisco, where he worked on his long poem, Howl, *which was published in 1956 and which distinguished him as a major Beat writer in the company of Jack Kerouac and William S. Burroughs. The Beat writers were distinguished by their attempt to combine socially marginal behavior with the quest for spiritual enlightenment. During the early 1960s, he traveled extensively; during the late 1960s, he received a Guggenheim fellowship and visited many colleges and universities. Ginsberg taught at City College in New York and Naropa Institute in Colorado. His work,* Collected Poems *(1984), gives a view of American life over several decades, introducing readers to hundreds of personalities of the times.*

1956

America I've given you all and now I'm nothing.
America two dollars and twentyseven cents January 17, 1956.
I can't stand my own mind.
America when will we end the human war?
Go fuck yourself with your atom bomb.
I don't feel good don't bother me.
I won't write my poem till I'm in my right mind.
America when will you be angelic?
When will you take off your clothes?
When will you look at yourself through the grave?
When will you be worthy of your million Trotskyites?[1]
America why are your libraries full of tears?
America when will you send your eggs to India?

[1] Those who believe in principles proposed by Leon Trotsky, especially the adoption of worldwide communism through revolution.

I'm sick of your insane demands.
When can I go into the supermarket and buy what I need with my good looks?
America after all it is you and I who are perfect not the next world.
Your machinery is too much for me.
You made me want to be a saint.
There must be some other way to settle this argument.
Burroughs[2] is in Tangiers[3] I don't think he'll come back it's sinister.
Are you being sinister or is this some form of practical joke?
I'm trying to come to the point.
I refuse to give up my obsession.
America stop pushing I know what I'm doing.
America the plum blossoms are falling.
I haven't read the newspapers for months, everyday somebody goes on trial for murder.
America I feel sentimental about the Wobblies.[4]
America I used to be a communist when I was a kid I'm not sorry.
I smoke marijuana every chance I get.
I sit in my house for days on end and stare at the roses in the closet.
When I go to Chinatown I get drunk and never get laid.
My mind is made up there's going to be trouble.
You should have seen me reading Marx.[5]
My psychoanalyst thinks I'm perfectly right.
I won't say the Lord's Prayer.
I have mystical visions and cosmic vibrations.
America I still haven't told you what you did to Uncle Max after he came over from Russia.

I'm addressing you.
Are you going to let your emotional life be run by Time Magazine?
I'm obsessed by Time Magazine.
I read it every week.
Its cover stares at me every time I slink past the corner candystore.
I read it in the basement of the Berkeley Public Library.
It's always telling me about responsibility. Businessmen are serious.
Movie producers are serious. Everybody's serious but me.
It occurs to me that I am America.
I am talking to myself again.

---

[2] William S. Burroughs, American novelist (1914–97).

[3] Port on the Strait of Gibralter in North Morocco.

[4] Members of the Industrial Workers of the World.

[5] Karl Marx, German philosopher and Socialist (1818–83).

Asia is rising against me.
I haven't got a chinaman's chance.
I'd better consider my national resources.
My national resources consist of two joints of marijuana millions of genitals
an unpublishable private literature that jetplanes 1400 miles
an hour and twentyfive-thousand mental institutions.
I say nothing about my prisons nor the millions of underprivileged who
live in my flowerpots under the light of five hundred suns.
I have abolished the whorehouses of France, Tangiers is the next to go.
My ambition is to be President despite the fact that I'm a Catholic.

America how can I write a holy litany in your silly mood?
I will continue like Henry Ford my strophes are as individual as his
automobiles more so they're all different sexes.
America I will sell you strophes $2500 apiece $500 down on your old strophe
America free Tom Mooney[6]
America save the Spanish Loyalists[7]
America Sacco & Vanzetti must not die[8]
America I am the Scottsboro boys.[9]
America when I was seven momma took me to Communist Cell meetings
they sold us garbanzos a handful per ticket a ticket costs a nickel
and the speeches were free everybody was angelic and sentimental
about the workers it was all so sincere you have no idea what a
good thing the party was in 1835 Scott Nearing was a grand old
man a real mensch Mother Bloor the Silk-strikers' Ewig-Weibliche[10]
made me cry I once saw the Yiddish orator Israel Amter plain.[11]
Everybody must have been a spy.
America you don't really want to go to war.
America it's them bad Russians.
Them Russians them Russians and them Chinamen. And them Russians.
The Russia wants to eat us alive. The Russia's power mad. She wants to take
our cars from out our garages.
Her wants to grab Chicago. Her needs a Red *Reader's Digest.* Her wants our
auto plants in Siberia. Him big bureaucracy running our fillingstations.

---

[6] American Wobbly, convicted for murder in 1916 and pardoned more than twenty years later.

[7] Spaniards, Republicans, who opposed Franco's Nationalists during the Spanish Civil War (1936–39).

[8] Nicola Sacco (1891–1927) and Bartolemeo Vanzetti (1888–1927), American anarchists who were executed.

[9] Nine African American youths convicted of raping two white women; a controversial case because of lack of evidence.

[10] Ewig-Weibliche: "Eternal feminine" in German.

[11] Nearing, Bloor, and Amter; American leftists.

That no good. Ugh. Him make Indians learn read. Him need big black niggers. Hah. Her make us all work sixteen hours a day. Help.
America this is quite serious.
America this is the impression I get from looking in the television set.
America is this correct?
I'd better get right down to the job.
It's true I don't want to join the Army or turn lathes in precision parts factories, I'm nearsighted and psychopathic anyway.
America I'm putting my queer shoulder to the wheel.

Explorations of the Text

1. Describe the speaker. Focus on his character traits, tone, values, and attitudes.
2. In addressing "America" as his audience, to whom does he speak? What are his criticisms of his culture?
3. Why does he state "It occurs to me that I am America./I am talking to myself again"?
4. Analyze the section beginning: "Asia is rising against me." From whose view is the persona speaking? Is this change of point of view effective?
5. Discuss the speaker's vocation as a writer.
6. How are the historical allusions—Spanish Loyalists, Sacco and Vanzetti, Communist cell meetings—important to the poem?
7. Why does he speak in baby talk, in "Indian" dialect? When does the voice shift?
8. What impact does the humor have? Does it develop themes of the work?
9. In the last line, does the speaker change his point of view and attitude? How?
10. Compare this poem to the poems by Brooks and Hughes.

The Reading/Writing Connection

1. Make a catalogue of the criticisms of America. Are they valid?
2. Write a humorous critique about some aspect of life in the United States. Begin with "America, I . . . ."

Ideas for Writing

1. Analyze the speaker in this poem. How does Ginsberg achieve this characterization? Discuss voice, tone, imagery, humor, word choice, and/or theme. Compose a diary entry in the speaker's voice.

2. Compare themes of this poem with another work in this chapter.
3. Compare this poem with Whitman's "Out of the Cradle Endlessly Rocking" in chapter 4.

horse

Gloria Anzaldúa

Gloria Anzaldúa (1942–) was born in Jesus Maria in the Rio Grande Valley of South Texas. She was educated at Pan American University and the University of Texas, Austin. Her first book, This Bridge Called My Back: Writings by Radical Women of Color *(1981), co-edited by Cherrie Moraga, won the 1986 Before Columbus Foundation American Book Award. Anzaldúa has worked in the migrant farmers movement, and she has taught at colleges including the University of Texas, Austin, and Vermont College of Norwich University. Her other works include* Borderlands/La Frontera: The New Mestiza *(1987) and* Making Faces, Making Soul/Haciendo Caras *(1990).*

1987

(para la gente de Hargill, Texas)[1]

Great horse running in the fields
come thundering toward
the outstretched hands
nostrils flaring at the corn
only it was knives in the hidden hands
can a horse smell tempered steel?

Anoche[2] some kids cut up a horse
it was night and the *pueblo*[3] slept
the Mexicans mutter among themselves:
they hobbled the two front legs
the two hind legs, kids aged sixteen
but they're *gringos*[4]
and the sheriff won't do a thing
he'd just say boys will be boys
just following their instincts.

But it's the mind that kills
the animal the *mexicanos* murmur
killing it would have been a mercy

[1] For the people of Hargill, Texas.
[2] Last night.
[3] Village.
[4] Whites.

black horse running in the dark
came thundering toward
the outstretched hands
nostrils flaring at the smell
only it was knives in the hidden hands
did it pray all night for morning?

It was the owner came running
30-30 in his hand
put the *caballo*[5] out of its pain
the Chicanos shake their heads
turn away some rich father
fished out his wallet
held out the folds of green
as if green could staunch red

pools dripping from the ribbons
on the horse's flanks
could cast up testicles
grow back the ears on the horse's head
no ears of corn but sheaths
hiding blades of steel
earth drinking blood sun rusting it
in that small Texas town
the *mexicanos* shuffle their feet
shut their faces stare at the ground.

Dead horse neighing in the night
come thundering toward the open faces
hooves iron-shod hurling lightning

only it is red red in the moonlight
in their sleep the *gringos* cry out
the *mexicanos* mumble if you're Mexican
you are born old.

Explorations of the Text

1. Examine the image of the horse in stanza 1. What is the effect of "the outstretched hands"? of the "knives"? What is the meaning of the corn?
2. Does the story of the boys who cut the horse have symbolic meaning?

[5] Horse.

3. Explain: "It's the mind that kills."
4. Why does the speaker repeat the image of the horse and the hands with the corn and the knives? Is the repetition effective?
5. Why do the Mexicanos "shuffle their feet/shut their faces stare at the ground" and "mumble"?
6. Examine the **paradox** in the next-to-last stanza. How can the dead horse still thunder "toward the open faces"?
7. Why do the gringos "cry"?
8. How do the last two lines convey themes of the work?
9. Discuss symbolism, imagery, and language in this poem. Is the use of Spanish words and phrases effective?
10. Compare the themes of oppression and bigotry in this poem with similar ideas in "Harlem" or "The Chicago Defender Sends a Man to Little Rock."

The Reading/Writing Connection

1. Gloss and annotate the poem, and write an end comment. See the example in chapter 2.
2. React to the situations of the Mexicans and Chicanos. Why are they "born old"? Freewrite.

Ideas for Writing

1. What does the story symbolize about the attitudes of the gringos toward other people, animals, land, things? Do you agree?
2. Compare the ending of this poem and the endings of works by Griffin, Angelou, Rose, and Harjo. Discuss the reversals, the anger, and the desire for change and for retribution.

For Anna Mae Aquash Whose Spirit Is Present Here and in the Dappled Stars

Joy Harjo

Joy Harjo (1951–), a member of the Creek Tribe, was born in Tulsa, Oklahoma. Educated at the University of New Mexico and the University of Iowa, Harjo has taught writing at Arizona State University, Tempe, and at the University of American Indian Arts in Santa Fe, New Mexico. Her volumes of poetry include The Last Song *(1975),* She Has Some Horses *(1985), and* In Mad Love and War *(1990). She has received numerous awards, including one from the American Academy of Poetry and two from the National Endowment of the Arts.*

1990

For we remember the story and must tell it again so we may all live

Beneath a sky blurred with mist and wind,
I am amazed as I watch the violet
heads of crocuses erupt from the stiff earth
after dying for a season,
as I have watched my own dark head
appear each morning after entering
the next world
to come back to this one,
amazed.
It is the way in the natural world to understand the place
the ghost dancers[1] named
after the heart breaking destruction.
Anna Mae,
everything and nothing changes
You are the shimmering young woman
who found her voice
when you were warned to be silent, or have your body cut away
from you like an elegant weed.
You are the one whose spirit is present in the dappled stars.
(They prance and lope like colored horses who stay with us
through the streets of these steely cities. And I have seen them
nuzzling the frozen bodies of tattered drunks
on the corner.)
This morning when the last star is dimming
and the buses grind toward
the middle of the city, I know it is ten years since they buried
you the second time in Lakota, a language that could
free you.
I heard about it in Oklahoma, or New Mexico
how the wind howled and pulled everything down
in a righteous anger.
(It was the women who told me) and we understood wordlessly
the ripe meaning of your murder.
As I understand ten years later after the slow changing
of the seasons
that we have just begun to touch
the dazzling whirlwind of our anger,
we have just begun to perceive the amazed world the ghost
dancers entered
crazily, beautifully.

[1] Dancers who performed the Ghost Dance, a group dance begun by late nineteenth-century Native Americans to promote the return of the dead and the restoration of the spiritual life of the tribe.

Explorations of the Text

1. Describe the setting and season. What is the attitude of the speaker? Explain the following lines: "as I have watched my own dark head/ appear each morning after entering/the next world/to come back to this one,/amazed."
2. What is the place "the ghost dancers named"? How can it be understood?
3. How is Anna Mae invoked and described? Consider the star imagery and the extension of the **metaphor.**
4. What does the speaker mean when she says "I know it is ten years since they buried/you the second time in Lakota, a language that could/free you"?
5. Examine the last five lines. What is "the dazzling whirlwind" of anger? What is "the amazed world the ghost/dancers entered"?
6. Discuss the images of beauty and of destruction in this poem. How do they reveal theme?
7. Compare the political message of this poem to the ideas in Hughes's "Let America Be America Again" and Ginsberg's "America."

The Reading/Writing Connection

1. Imitate this poem, and write to someone who has died for a political cause.
2. Write a double-entry journal on this poem.
3. Freewrite about the line: "everything and nothing changes."

Ideas for Writing

1. Characterize the speaker and Anna Mae.
2. Analyze the imagery in this poem.

I Like to Think of Harriet Tubman

Susan Griffin

Susan Griffin (1943–), born in California, graduated from San Francisco State University. She has worked as a waitress, teacher, house painter, and switchboard operator. Her collection, Made from this Earth: An Anthology of Writings, *(1982) was followed by* Unremembered Country *(1987) and* A Chorus of Stones: The Private Life of War *(1992). Adrienne Rich, one of the foremost feminist critics and poets in the United States, has said that Griffin's work reflects "female anger as power, female presence as transforming force."*

1970

I like to think of Harriet Tubman.[1]
Harriet Tubman who carried a revolver,
who had a scar on her head from a rock thrown
by a slave-master (because she
talked back), and who
had a ransom on her head
of thousands of dollars and who
was never caught, and who
had no use for the law
when the law was wrong,
who defied the law. I like
to think of her.
I like to think of her especially
when I think of the problem of
feeding children.

The legal answer
to the problem of feeding children
is ten free lunches every month,
being equal, in the child's real life,
to eating lunch every other day.
Monday but not Tuesday.
I like to think of the President
eating lunch Monday, but not
Tuesday.
And when I think of the President
and the law, and the problem of
feeding children, I like to
think of Harriet Tubman
and her revolver.

And then sometimes
I think of the President
and other men,
men who practice the law,
who revere the law,
who make the law,
who enforce the law,
who live behind
and operate through
and feed themselves
at the expense of

[1] African American escaped slave and abolitionist; leader of the Underground Railroad, which arranged safe passage for slaves who sought freedom (c. 1820–30).

starving children
because of the law.

Men who sit in paneled offices
and think about vacations
and tell women
whose care it is
to feed children
not to be hysterical
not to be hysterical as in the word
hysterikos, the greek for
womb suffering,
not to suffer in their
wombs,
not to care,
not to bother the men
because they want to think
of other things
and do not want
to take the women seriously.
I want them
to take women seriously.

I want them to think about Harriet Tubman,
and remember,
remember she was beat by a white man
and she lived
and she lived to redress her grievances,
and she lived in swamps
and wore the clothes of a man
bringing hundreds of fugitives from
slavery, and was never caught,
and led an army,
and won a battle,
and defied the laws
because the laws were wrong, I want men
to take us seriously.
I am tired wanting them to think
about right and wrong.
I want them to fear.
I want them to feel fear now
as I have felt suffering in the womb, and
I want them
to know
that there is always a time
there is always a time to make right

what is wrong,
there is always a time
for retribution
and that time
is beginning.

Explorations of the Text

1. Why does the speaker "like to think of Harriet Tubman"? What details of Tubman's life are important to her?
2. What is the speaker's attitude toward the "law"? What is the tone of the second and third stanzas?
3. What is the role of women? Why does the persona want men "to take the women seriously"?
4. Explain: "I want them to think about Harriet Tubman." Why does the speaker want men "to fear"?
5. At the end, what does the speaker mean by "retribution"?
6. Examine the use of repetition as a rhetorical device in the poem. Is it effective?
7. Compare this poem to "horse," "Three Thousand Dollar Death Song," or "For Anna Mae Aquash. . . ."

The Reading/Writing Connection

1. React in a journal entry to the portrait of Harriet Tubman, or react to the speaker's voice.
2. "Think" Topic: Is the "time" for retribution "beginning"? Respond to this quotation in a paragraph.

Ideas for Writing

1. Compare Griffin's poem to Rose's "Three Thousand Dollar Death Song." Focus on persona and themes.
2. Write about a law that you consider to be unjust.
3. What does Griffin believe about the role of women? Is she redefining gender roles? Is she being too dogmatic?

Still I Rise

Maya Angelou

Maya Angelou (1928–), born in St. Louis, Missouri, achieved fame at the age of forty-two with the publication of her first book, the autobiography I Know Why the Caged Bird Sings *(1972). Before that, she had lived a varied life, working as, among other things, a streetcar conductor in San Francisco and an on- and off-Broadway singer and dancer. Since then, Angelou has published four other volumes of autobiography, including* Gather Together in My Name *(1974) and* All God's Children Need Traveling Shoes *(1986), and several volumes of poetry, including* Just Give Me a Cool Drink of Water 'fore I Die *(1971),* And Still I Rise *(1978), and* I Shall Not Be Moved *(1990). She is Reynolds Professor of American Studies at Wake Forest University. Of her work, Angelou has said that she writes for "the Black voice and any ear which can hear it."*

1978

You may write me down in history
With your bitter, twisted lies,
You may trod me in the very dirt
But still, like dust, I'll rise.

Does my sassiness upset you?
Why are you beset with gloom?
'Cause I walk like I've got oil wells
Pumping in my living room.

Just like moons and like suns,
With the certainty of tides,
Just like hopes springing high,
Still I'll rise.

Did you want to see me broken?
Bowed head and lowered eyes?
Shoulders falling down like teardrops,
Weakened by my soulful cries.

Does my haughtiness offend you?
Don't you take it awful hard
'Cause I laugh like I've got gold mines
Diggin' in my own back yard.

You may shoot me with your words,
You may cut me with your eyes,
You may kill me with your hatefulness,
But still, like air, I'll rise.

Does my sexiness upset you?
Does it come as a surprise
That I dance like I've got diamonds
At the meeting of my thighs?

Out of the huts of history's shame
I rise
Up from a past that's rooted in pain
I rise
I'm a black ocean, leaping and wide,
Welling and swelling I bear in the tide.

Leaving behind nights of terror and fear
I rise
Into a daybreak that's wondrously clear
I rise
Bringing the gifts that my ancestors gave,
I am the dream and the hope of the slave.
I rise
I rise
I rise.

Explorations of the Text

1. Characterize the persona and point of view of the poem.
2. Why does Angelou include the images of "oil well," "gold mines," and "diamonds"?
3. How does the persona view her relationship with her past? To what historical events does she refer when she writes about "huts of history's shame," "broken/bowed head," and "nights of terror and fear"?
4. Will she triumph? Why?
5. Discuss the symbolism of "tides" and "ocean."
6. What effect does anaphora create? Does it add to or detract from the poem?
7. Compare the speaker in this poem with the persona in "I Like to Think of Harriet Tubman."

The Reading/Writing Connection

1. Write a poem or a voice piece in which you proclaim triumph or in which you brag about something that you accomplished.
2. Use one line as an opening to your own poem.

Ideas for Writing

1. Compare the speaker in this poem with the one in "Ego Tripping" (See chapter 4). How do both poets use allusions and historical references?
2. Evaluate both poems. Which one do you think is more effective?

Telephone Conversation

Wole Soyinka

Wole Soyinka (1934–) was born in Isara, Nigeria, He attended the University of Ibadan and received a B.A. with honors from the University of Leeds, England. Considered by many critics to be Africa's best writer, Soyinka has published drama, poetry, novels, and nonfiction. Among his works are a novel, The Interpreters *(1965) and a nonfiction volume,* The Man Died: Prison Notes of Wole Soyinka *(1972). Among his many awards is the 1986 Nobel Prize for Literature. Soyinka's writing reflects contemporary Africa's political upheaval and efforts to blend traditional culture with technological advances.*

1967

The price seemed reasonable, location
Indifferent. The landlady swore she lived
Off premises. Nothing remained
But self-confession. "Madam," I warned,
"I hate a wasted journey—I am African."
Silence. Silenced transmission of
Pressurized good-breeding. Voice, when it came,
Lipstick coated, long gold-rolled
Cigarette-holder pipped. Caught I was, foully.
"HOW DARK?" . . . I had not misheard . . . "ARE YOU LIGHT
OR VERY DARK?" Button B. Button A. Stench
Of rancid breath of public hide-and-speak.
Red booth. Red pillar-box. Red double-tiered
Omnibus squelching tar. It *was* real! Shamed
By ill-mannered silence, surrender
Pushed dumbfoundment to beg simplification.
Considerate she was, varying the emphasis—
"ARE YOU DARK? OR VERY LIGHT?" Revelation came.
"You mean—like plain or milk chocolate?"
Her assent was clinical, crushing in its light
Impersonality. Rapidly, wave-length adjusted,
I chose. "West African sepia"—and as afterthought,
"Down in my passport." Silence for spectroscopic
Flight of fancy, till truthfulness clanged her accent
Hard on the mouthpiece. "WHAT'S THAT?" conceding
"DON'T KNOW WHAT THAT IS." "Like brunette."
"THAT'S DARK, ISN'T IT?" "Not altogether.
Facially, I am brunette, but madam, you should see
The rest of me. Palm of my hand, soles of my feet
Are a peroxide blonde. Friction, caused—

Foolishly madam—by sitting down, has turned
My bottom raven black—One moment madam!"—sensing
Her receiver rearing on the thunderclap
About my ears—"Madam," I pleaded, "wouldn't you rather
See for yourself?"

Explorations of the Text

1. In the opening lines, why is the tone reportial? What happens when the persona confesses that he is African?
2. Is the speaker surprised by the question? Where does this situation happen? Examine details in lines 11 to 14.
3. Characterize the persona. What does he intend when he describes his skin as "West African sepia"?
4. Characterize the landlady.
5. Examine the speaker's final description of his skin (beginning in line 28). What is the meaning of the narrator's last question?
6. What does Soyinka accomplish with humor? Compare this poem with the humor in the speech by Sojourner Truth or in Griffin's poem about Harriet Tubman.

The Reading/Writing Connection

1. Create a telephone conversation about renting a room or apartment. Like Soyinka, create a speaker who cannot succeed in his or her quest because of bigotry.
2. Respond in a journal entry to the closing lines of the poem.

Ideas for Writing

1. Analyze the character of the speaker or of the landlady.
2. Discuss humor as a political response. Refer to this poem and to other works that you have read.

The Colonel

Carolyn Forché

Carolyn Forché (1950–) was born in Detroit, Michigan. She attended Michigan State University and Bowling Green State University. Her publications include the volumes of poetry Gathering the Tribes *(1976), which won the Yale University Younger Poets Award;* The Country Between Us *(1981), which was named the Lamont Selection of the Academy of American Poets; and* The Angel of History *(1994).*

Forché lived in El Salvador from 1978 to 1980, working as a journalist and human rights activist, and she has translated the works of Salvadoran poets. She has edited an anthology of poetry of witness: Against Forgetting *(1993).*

1981

What you have heard is true. I was in his house. His wife carried a tray of coffee and sugar. His daughter filed her nails, his son went out for the night. There were daily papers, pet dogs, a pistol on the cushion beside him. The moon swung bare on its black cord over the house. On the television was a cop show. It was in English. Broken bottles were embedded in the walls around the house to scoop the kneecaps from a man's legs or cut his hands to lace. On the windows there were gratings like those in liquor stores. We had dinner, rack of lamb, good wine, a gold bell was on the table for calling the maid. The maid brought green mangoes, salt, a type of bread. I was asked how I enjoyed the country. There was a brief commercial in Spanish. His wife took everything away. There was some talk then of how difficult it had become to govern. The parrot said hello on the terrace. The colonel told it to shut up, and pushed himself from the table. My friend said to me with his eyes: say nothing. The colonel returned with a sack used to bring groceries home. He spilled many human ears on the table. They were like dried peach halves. There is no other way to say this. He took one of them in his hands, shook it in our faces, dropped it into a water glass. It came alive there. I am tired of fooling around he said. As for the rights of anyone, tell your people they can go fuck themselves. He swept the ears to the floor with his arm and held the last of his wine in the air. Something for your poetry, no? he said. Some of the ears on the floor caught this scrap of his voice. Some of the ears on the floor were pressed to the ground.

Explorations of the Text

1. Discuss the details of the colonel's home, family, and dinner. Explain the first statement.
2. Look at the first half of the poem. Do any images **foreshadow** the events of the conclusion?
3. Where does the mood of the poem shift?
4. Why has the colonel collected human ears "like dried peach halves" in a sack? Why does he drop one in a glass of water? Why does he sweep the ears to the floor?
5. What does the colonel mean when he says "I am tired of fooling around. . . . As for the rights of anyone, tell your people they can go fuck themselves"?
6. Does the colonel believe that the ears might serve as images for poetry, or is he being ironic?

7. Explain the ending. How can the disconnected ears be "pressed to the ground"?
8. Discuss the form of this prose poem. Why does the narrator speak in simple, declarative sentences?
9. Compare this poem with Agosin's essay and with Valenzuela's story. Focus on speaker and voice.

The Reading/Writing Connection

1. Freewrite about the colonel's sack of dried human ears.
2. Write a political prose poem that shifts its tone and subject. Use "The Colonel" as a model.
3. In your journal, react to the color imagery in the poem.

Ideas for Writing

1. Discuss the issue of human rights in Forché's poems.
2. Compare this poem to O'Brien's "The Things They Carried." Focus on the images of tokens of war and "the things they carried."
3. Characterize the colonel.

The Memory of Elena

Carolyn Forché

1981

We spend our morning
in the flower stalls counting
the dark tongues of bells
that hang from ropes waiting
for the silence of an hour.
We find a table, ask for *paella,*[1]
cold soup and wine, where a calm
light trembles years behind us.

In Buenos Aires[2] only three
years ago, it was the last time his hand
slipped into her dress, with pearls
cooling her throat and bells like
these, chipping at the night—

[1] A Spanish dish made with rice, saffron, chicken, sausage, and seafood.
[2] A city in Argentina.

As she talks, the hollow
clopping of a horse, the sound
of bones touched together.
The *paella* comes, a bed of rice
and *camarones,*[3] fingers and shells,
the lips of those whose lips
have been removed, mussels
the soft blue of a leg socket.

This is not *paella,* this is what
has become of those who remained
in Buenos Aires. This is the ring
of a rifle report on the stones,
her hand over her mouth,
her husband falling against her.

These are the flowers we bought
this morning, the dahlias tossed
on his grave and bells
waiting with their tongues cut out
for this particular silence.

Explorations of the Text

1. Examine the first stanza. What happens? Which words have negative **connotations** and **foreshadow** the ending?
2. Describe the relationship of Elena and her husband. What does the sensuality of the marriage contribute to the meaning of the poem?
3. Explain the transformation of the images in stanza 3. Examine the "clopping of a horse" and the personification of the food into horrible examples of torture.
4. Why does the speaker become so direct in the fourth verse? What happened to Elena's husband? Why is it presented so simply?
5. Analyze the flowers and the bells in the last verse. Look again at the opening. How has the imagery changed or expanded?
6. Discuss the title, the form of the poem, and the themes. Does the title contain multiple meanings?
7. Compare the themes of political violence in this poem with similar ideas in "The Colonel" and in works by Valenzuela and Agosin.

[3] Shrimp or prawns.

The Reading/Writing Connection

1. Freewrite and react to one of the images in the poem: silence, tongues, bells, flowers, or food.
2. Gloss and annotate the poem, and write an end comment.

Ideas for Writing

1. Explicate this poem. Focus on tone, imagery, and formal elements. Use your annotation as a beginning.
2. Begin a paper on the two poems by Forché with this quotation by Margaret Atwood: "Here is a poetry of courage and passion, which manages to be tender and achingly sensual and what is often called 'political' at the same time."
3. Write about Elena and about those people in Central and South America who mourn the "disappeared." Refer to Agosin's essay.

Prayer to the Living to Forgive Them for Being Alive

Charlotte Delbo

Charlotte Delbo (1913–85) joined the French Resistance with her husband when the Nazis occupied France early in the Second World War. The two were quickly arrested by the French police and handed over to the Gestapo. Delbo's husband was shot almost immediately while she was eventually sent to Auschwitz in 1943. Delbo survived the concentration camp and, after the war, wrote several volumes about her experiences, including None of Us Will Return *(1965),* Useless Knowledge *(1970), and* The Measure of Our Days *(1970).*

1970

You who are passing by
well dressed in all your muscles
clothing which suits you well
or badly
or just about
you who are passing by
full of tumultuous life within your arteries
glued to your skeleton
as you walk with a sprightly step athletic awkward
laughing sullenly, you are all so handsome
so commonplace
so commonplacely like everyone else
so handsome in your commonplaceness
diverse

with this excess of life which keep you
from feeling your bust following your leg
your hand raised to your hat
your hand upon your heart
your kneecap rolling softly in your knee
how can we forgive you for being alive . . .
You who are passing by
well dressed in all your muscles
how can we forgive you
that all are dead
You are walking by and drinking in cafés
you are happy she loves you
or moody worried about money
how how
will you ever be forgiven
by those who died
so that you may walk by
dressed in all your muscles
so that you may drink in cafés
be younger every spring
I beg you
do something
learn a dance step
something to justify your existence
something that gives you the right
to be dressed in your skin in your body hair
learn to walk and to laugh
because it would be too senseless
after all
for so many to have died
while you live
doing nothing with your life.

❄ ❄ ❄

I have returned
from a world beyond knowledge
and now must unlearn
for otherwise I clearly see
I can no longer live.

❄ ❄ ❄

After all
better not to believe
these ghostly tales
for if you do
you'll never sleep again
if you believe

these ghostly phantoms
revenants returning
yet unable to tell
how.

Exploration of the Text

1. Characterize the voice of the speaker. Why does the speaker address the poem to an unknown "you"? How does the persona describe the "you"? Who is the speaker's intended audience?
2. What do you imagine the speaker must "unlearn"?
3. How does the persona characterize her post-Auschwitz self? Why does she use visceral images to describe those who "walk by"?
4. What does she want her audience to learn?
5. Discuss the irony of these lines: "Otherwise I clearly see/I can no longer live." What does she mean by a "world beyond knowledge"?
6. Connect this world with Ozick's concentration camp milieu in "The Shawl."

The Reading/Writing Connection

1. Journal Entry: Does the speaker's turmoil represent a believable response to trauma? To horror?
2. "Think" Topic: Discuss the poet's use of bodily images.

Ideas for Writing

1. Compare the speaker's view of those shielded from horror with Milosz's view of Americans.
2. Relate the speaker's awareness to Oedipus's realizations.

Poems for Further Reading

A Description of the Morning

Jonathan Swift (1667–1745)

1710

Now hardly here and there a hackney-coach
Appearing, showed the ruddy morn's approach.
Now Betty from her master's bed had flown,
And softly stole to discompose her own;
The slip-shod 'prentice from his master's door
Had pared the dirt and sprinkled round the floor.
Now Moll had whirled her mop with dext'rous airs,

Prepared to scrub the entry and the stairs.
The youth with broomy stumps began to trace
The kennel-edge, where wheels had worn the place.[1]
The small-coal man was heard with cadence deep,
Till drowned in shriller notes of chimney-sweep:
Duns at his lordship's gate began to meet;
And brickdust Moll had screamed through half the street.
The turnkey now his flock returning sees,
Duly let out a-nights to steal for fees:[2]
The watchful bailiffs take their silent stands,
And schoolboys lag with satchels in their hands.

London

William Blake (1757–1827)

1794

I wander through each chartered[1] street,
Near where the chartered Thames does flow,
And mark in every face I meet
Marks of weakness, marks of woe.

In every cry of every man,
In every Infant's cry of fear,
In every voice, in every ban,
The mind-forged manacles I hear.

How the Chimney-sweeper's cry
Every black'ning Church appalls;
And the hapless Soldier's sigh
Runs in blood down Palace walls.

But most through midnight streets I hear
How the youthful Harlot's curse
Blasts the new-born Infant's tear,
And blights with plagues the Marriage hearse.

---

[1] The youth is scavenging in the tracks of wheels in the road.

[2] The "turnkey" (the jailer) has let his incarcerated criminals out in the night to steal.

[1] Pre-empted by the State and leased by royal patent.

The Slave Auction

Frances Ellen Watkins Harper (1825–1911)

1854

The sale began—young girls were there,
    Defenceless in their wretchedness,
Whose stifled sobs of deep despair
    Revealed their anguish and distress.

And mothers stood with streaming eyes,
    And saw their dearest children sold;
Unheeded rose their bitter cries,
    While tyrants bartered them for gold.

And woman, with her love and truth—
    For these in sable[1] forms may dwell—
Gaz'd on the husband of her youth,
    With anguish none may paint or tell.

And men, whose sole crime was their hue,
    The impress of their Maker's hand,
And frail and shrinking children, too,
    Were gathered in that mournful band.

Ye who have laid your love to rest,
    And wept above their lifeless clay,
Know not the anguish of that breast,
    Whose lov'd are rudely torn away.

Ye may not know how desolate
    Are bosoms rudely forced to part,
And how a dull and heavy weight
    Will press the life-drops from the heart.

The Man He Killed

Thomas Hardy (1840–1928)

1902

"Had he and I but met
By some old ancient inn,
We should have sat us down to wet
Right many a nipperkin[1]

---

[1] Black.

[1] Half-pint cup.

"But ranged as infantry,
And staring face to face,
I shot at him as he at me,
And killed him in his place.

"I shot him dead because—
Because he was my foe,
Just so: my foe of course he was;
That's clear enough; although

"He thought he'd 'list, perhaps,
Off-hand like—just as I—
Was out of work—had sold his traps[2]—
No other reason why.

"Yes; quaint and curious war is!
You shoot a fellow down
You'd treat if met where any bar is,
Or help to half-a-crown."

SYMPATHY

Paul Laurence Dunbar (1872–1906)

1893

I know what the caged bird feels, alas!
    When the sun is bright on the upland slopes;
When the wind stirs soft through the springing grass,
And the river flows like a stream of glass;
    When the first bird sings and the first bud opens,
And the faint perfume from its chalice steals—
I know what the caged bird feels!

I know why the caged bird beats his wing
    Till its blood is red on the cruel bars;
For he must fly back to his perch and cling
When he fain would be on the bough a-swing;
    And a pain still throbs in the old, old scars
And they pulse again with a keener sting—
I know why he beats his wing!

[2] Personal possessions or property.

I know why the caged bird sings, ah me,
When his wing is bruised and his bosom sore,—
When he beats his bars and he would be free;
It is not a carol of joy or glee,
But a prayer that he sends from his heart's deep core,
But a plea, that upward to Heaven he flings—
I know why the caged bird sings!

Episode of Hands

Hart Crane (1899–1932)

1920

The unexpected interest made him flush.
Suddenly he seemed to forget the pain,—
Consented,—and held out
One finger from the others.

The gash was bleeding, and a shaft of sun
That glittered in and out among the wheels,
Fell lightly, warmly, down into the wound.

And as the fingers of the factory owner's son,
That knew a grip for books and tennis
As well as one for iron and leather,—
As his taut, spare fingers wound the gauze
Around the thick bed of the wound,
His own hands seemed to him
Like wings of butterflies
Flickering in sunlight over summer fields.

The knots and notches,—many in the wide
Deep hand that lay in his,—seemed beautiful.
They were like the marks of wild ponies' play,—
Bunches of new green breaking a hard turf.

And factory sounds and factory thoughts
Were banished from him by that larger, quieter hand
That lay in his with the sun upon it.
And as the bandage knot was tightened
The two men smiled into each other's eyes.

DRAMA

Limbo/Twilight #2
from Twilight Los Angeles 1992

Anna Deavere Smith

Anna Deavere Smith (1950–) is an actress, playwright, and performance artist. A professor at New York University, Smith won an Obie award and was nominated for the 1992 Pulitzer Prize for Drama for Fires in the Mirror: Crown Heights, Brooklyn, and Other Identities. *She also has written* Twilight Los Angeles 1992 *(1994), which addresses the racial situation in Los Angeles after the police trials following the Rodney King beating. Her work is concerned with representing the multiple perspectives of those experiencing contemporary American racial conflicts. According to Smith, "race and class are the big dividing lines in all society."*

1994

(In a Denny's restaurant in a shopping center. Saturday morning, February 1993. He is a gang member. He is short, graceful, very dark skinned. He is soft-spoken and even in his delivery. He is very confident.)

Twilight Bey,
that's my name.
When I was
twelve and thirteen,
I stayed out until, they say,
until the sun come up.
Every night, you know,
and that was my thing.
I was a
watchdog.
You know, I stayed up in the neighborhood,
make sure we wasn't being rolled on and everything,
and when people
came into light
a what I knew,
a lot a people said,
"Well, Twilight, you know,
you a lot smarter and you have a lot more wisdom than those
twice your age."
And what I did, you know,
I was
at home writing one night

and I was writing my name
and I just looked at it and it came ta me:
"twi,"
abbreviation
of the word "twice."
You take a way the "ce."
You have the last word,
"light."
"Light" is a word that symbolizes knowledge, knowing,
wisdom,
within the Koran[1] and the Holy Bible.
Twilight.
I have twice the knowledge of those my age,
twice the understanding of those my age.
So twilight
is
that time
between day and night.
Limbo,
I call it limbo.
So a lot of times when I've brought up ideas to my homeboys,
they say,
"Twilight,
that's before your time,
that's something you can't do now."
When I talked about the truce back in 1988,
that was something they considered before its time,
yet
in 1992
we made it
realistic.
So to me it's like I'm stuck in limbo,
like the sun is stuck between night and day
in the twilight hours.
You know,
I'm in an area not many people exist.
Nighttime to me
is like a lack of sun,
and I don't affiliate
darkness with anything negative.
I affiliate
darkness with what was first,

[1] The sacred text of Islam.

because it was first,
and then relative to my complexion.
I am a dark individual,
and with me stuck in limbo,
I see darkness as myself.
I see the light as knowledge and the wisdom of the world
and understanding others,
and in order for me to be a, to be a true human being,
I can't forever dwell in darkness,
I can't forever dwell in the idea,
of just identifying with people like me and understanding me and mine.
So I'm up twenty-four hours, it feels like,
and, you know,
what I see at nighttime
is,
like,
little kids
between the ages of
eight and eleven
out at three in the morning.
They beatin' up a old man on the bus stop,
a homeless old man.
You know,
I see these things.
I tell 'em, "Hey, man, what ya all doin'?
Whyn't ya go on home?
What ya doin' out this time of night?"
You know,
and then when I'm in my own neighborhood, I'm driving through and I see the living dead, as we call them,
the base heads,
the people who are so addicted on crack,
if they need a hit they be up all night doin' whatever they have to do
to make the money to get the hit.
It's like gettin' a total dose
of what goes on in the daytime creates at night.

Explorations of the Text

1. How does Twilight Bey think that he has changed since he was "twelve and thirteen"?
2. What is the significance of his name?
3. Discuss the images of darkness, light, and "limbo" in the work.

4. How does "limbo" represent Bey's state of mind.
5. What do you think Bey's dreams are for his future? For his people's future?

The Reading/Writing Connection

1. Journal Entry: Compare Twilight's Bey's view of life with your own.
2. "Think" Topic: In a paragraph write about the view of fate and free will presented in this work.

Ideas for Writing

1. Create a talk show that focuses on issues for today's people of color. Include Twilight Bey as one of the speakers.
2. Compare Manning Marable's and Twilight Bey's relationship to their ethnic heritage and environment. How do both men react to their ethnic backgrounds and to their present worlds?
3. Examine the performance pieces by Anna Deavere Smith and Ntozake Shange (See chapter 6). What techniques of performance drama do you notice? How does performance drama differ from a one-act play (see, for example, "Trifles" in chapter 6)?

NONFICTION

"Ain't I a Woman?"

Sojourner Truth

Born into slavery in Ulster County, New York, Sojourner Truth (1797–1883) originally was named Isabella Van Wagener, after Isaac Van Wagener, who bought her and set her free just before New York State abolished slavery in 1827. In 1829, she went to New York City, where she preached in the streets. Taking the name Sojourner Truth in answer to a divine call, she left the city and began preaching and singing at camp meetings across the country. Although she never abandoned her message of God's goodness, she added to her speeches concern for the abolition of slavery and the rights of women. Her brilliant speeches attracted many listeners and made her famous. In his new biography of Sojourner Truth, Carlton Mabee argues that she never spoke these exact words.[1]

1851

Well, children, where there is so much racket there must be something out of kilter. I think that 'twixt the negroes of the South and the women at the North, all talking about rights, the white men will be in a fix pretty soon. But what's all this here talking about?

That man over there says that women need to be helped into carriages, and lifted over ditches, and to have the best place everywhere. Nobody ever helps me into carriages, or over mud-puddles, or gives me any best place! And ain't I a woman? Look at me! Look at my arm! I have ploughed and planted, and gathered into barns, and no man could head me! And ain't I a woman? I could work as much and eat as much as a man—when I could get it—and bear the lash as well! And ain't I a woman? I have borne thirteen children, and seen them most all sold off to slavery, and when I cried out with my mother's grief, none but Jesus heard me! And ain't I a woman?

Then they talk about this thing in the head; what's this they call it? [Intellect, someone whispers.] That's it, honey. What's that got to do with women's rights or negro's rights? If my cup won't hold but a pint, and yours holds a quart, wouldn't you be mean not to let me have my little half-measure full?

---

[1] Sojourner Truth first gave the speech now referred to as the "Ain't I a Woman?" speech at a women's rights convention in Akron, Ohio, in 1851. However, as Nell Painter, Truth's most recent biographer, has pointed out, the version of the speech that we associate with Truth was not written down until twelve years later by the activist Frances Dena Gage, who added to it considerably. For the popular consciousness, Gage's revision of Truth's speech has become the speech itself, inspiring countless people who have read it. It is for this reason that we print this version of Truth's work.

Then that little man in black there, he says women can't have as much rights as men, 'cause Christ wasn't a woman! Where did your Christ come from? Where did your Christ come from? From God and a woman! Man had nothing to do with Him.

5 If the first woman God ever made was strong enough to turn the world upside down all alone, these women together ought to be able to turn it back, and get it right side up again! And now they is asking to do it, the men better let them.

Obliged to you for hearing me, and now old Sojourner ain't got nothing more to say.

Explorations of the Text

1. What is the occasion? Why does Truth connect women's rights with racial issues in the first section of her speech?
2. Examine the vision of woman presented in paragraph 2. What is the effect of the repetition of "ain't I a woman?"
3. What is the argument about intellect?
4. Why does she include religion in her speech? What does she accomplish when she contends that "Man had nothing to do with [Jesus]"? How does she use humor?
5. Consider Truth's version of Eve, "the first woman." Is her argument logical or true?
6. What elements of persuasion does Truth use effectively? (See chapter 12.)
7. Characterize the voice of the speaker.

The Reading/Writing Connection

1. In a journal entry, respond to the vision of "woman" presented in the speech.
2. Why was the speaker doubly vulnerable?

Ideas for Writing

1. Analyze the rhetorical structure of Sojourner Truth's speech. See checklist for nonfiction in chapter 12.
2. Compose a contemporary version of "Ain't I a Woman?"

Incidents in the Life of a Slave Girl

Harriet Jacobs

Harriet Jacobs (1815–97), born a slave in Edenton, North Carolina, was orphaned as a child. Taught to read and write by her owner/ mistress, Jacobs would recount the events of her life in her 1881 Incidents in the Life of a Slave Girl. *Jacob's book was published pseudonymously (under the name Linda Brent) with encouragement from Amy Post, a feminist and abolitionist, and William C. Nell, an African American abolitionist and writer. During the Civil War, Jacobs nursed black solders in Washington, D.C.*

Childhood

I was born a slave; but I never knew it till six years of happy childhood had passed away. My father was a carpenter, and considered so intelligent and skilful in his trade, that, when buildings out of the common line were to be erected, he was sent for from long distances, to be head workman. On condition of paying his mistress two hundred dollars a year, and supporting himself, he was allowed to work at his trade, and manage his own affairs. His strongest wish was to purchase his children; but, though he several times offered his hard earnings for that purpose, he never succeeded. In complexion my parents were a light shade of brownish yellow, and were termed mulattoes. They lived together in a comfortable home; and, though we were all slaves, I was so fondly shielded that I never dreamed I was a piece of merchandise, trusted to them for safe keeping, and liable to be demanded of them at any moment. I had one brother, William, who was two years younger than myself—a bright, affectionate child. I had also a great treasure in my maternal grandmother, who was a remarkable woman in many respects. She was the daughter of a planter in South Carolina, who, at his death, left her mother and his three children free, with money to go to St. Augustine;[1] where they had relatives. It was during the Revolutionary War; and they were captured on their passage, carried back, and sold to different purchasers. Such was the story my grandmother used to tell me; but I do not remember all the particulars. She was a little girl when she was captured and sold to the keeper of a large hotel. I have often heard her tell how hard she fared during childhood. But as she grew older she evinced so much intelligence, and was so faithful, that her master and mistress could not help seeing it was for their interest to take care of such a valuable piece of property. She became an indispensable personage in the household, officiating in all capacities, from cook and wet nurse to seamstress. She was much praised for her cooking; and her nice crackers became so famous in the neighborhood that many people were desirous of obtaining them. In consequence of numerous requests of this kind, she asked permission of her mistress to bake crackers at night, after all the household work was done; and

[1] City in Florida.

she obtained leave to do it, provided she would clothe herself and her children from the profits. Upon these terms, after working hard all day for her mistress, she began her midnight bakings, assisted by her two oldest children. The business proved profitable; and each year she laid by a little, which was saved for a fund to purchase her children. Her master died, and the property was divided among his heirs. The widow had her dower in the hotel, which she continued to keep open. My grandmother remained in her service as a slave; but her children were divided among her master's children. As she had five, Benjamin, the youngest one, was sold, in order that each heir might have an equal portion of dollars and cents. There was so little difference in our ages that he seemed more like my brother than my uncle. He was a bright, handsome lad, nearly white; for he inherited the complexion my grandmother had derived from Anglo-Saxon ancestors. Though only ten years old, seven hundred and twenty dollars were paid for him. His sale was a terrible blow to my grandmother; but she was naturally hopeful, and she went to work with renewed energy, trusting in time to be able to purchase some of her children. She had laid up three hundred dollars, which her mistress one day begged as a loan, promising to pay her soon. The reader probably knows that no promise or writing given to a slave is legally binding; for, according to Southern laws, a slave, *being* property, can *hold* no property. When my grandmother lent her hard earnings to her mistress, she trusted solely to her honor. The honor of a slaveholder to a slave!

To this good grandmother I was indebted for many comforts. My brother Willie and I often received portions of the crackers, cakes, and preserves, she made to sell; and after we ceased to be children we were indebted to her for many more important services.

Such were the unusually fortunate circumstances of my early childhood. When I was six years old, my mother died; and then, for the first time, I learned, by the talk around me, that I was a slave. My mother's mistress was the daughter of my grandmother's mistress. She was the foster sister of my mother; they were both nourished at my grandmother's breast. In fact, my mother had been weaned at three months old, that the babe of the mistress might obtain sufficient food. They played together as children; and, when they became women, my mother was a most faithful servant to her whiter foster sister. On her death-bed her mistress promised that her children should never suffer for any thing; and during her lifetime she kept her word. They all spoke kindly of my dead mother, who had been a slave merely in name, but in nature was noble and womanly. I grieved for her, and my young mind was troubled with the thought who would now take care of me and my little brother. I was told that my home was now to be with her mistress; and I found it a happy one. No toilsome or disagreeable duties were imposed upon me. My mistress was so kind to me that I was always glad to do her bidding, and proud to labor for her as much as my young years would permit. I would sit by her side for hours, sewing diligently, with a heart as free from care as that of any free-born white child. When she thought I was tired, she would send me out to run and jump; and away I bounded, to gather berries or flowers to decorate her room. Those were happy days—too happy to last. The slave child had no thought for the morrow; but there came that blight, which too surely waits on every human being born to be a chattel.

When I was nearly twelve years old, my kind mistress sickened and died. As I saw the cheek grow pale and the eye more glassy, how earnestly I prayed in my heart that she might live! I loved her; for she had been almost like a mother to me. My prayers were not answered. She died, and they buried her in the little churchyard, where, day after day, my tears fell upon her grave.

5 I was sent to spend a week with my grandmother. I was now old enough to begin to think of the future; and again and again I asked myself what they would do with me. I felt sure I should never find another mistress so kind as the one who was gone. She had promised my dying mother that her children should never suffer for any thing; and when I remembered that, and recalled her many proofs of attachment to me, I could not help having some hopes that she had left me free. My friends were almost certain it would be so. They thought she would be sure to do it, on account of my mother's love and faithful service. But, alas! we all know that the memory of a faithful slave does not avail much to save her children from the auction block.

After a brief period of suspense, the will of my mistress was read, and we learned that she had bequeathed me to her sister's daughter, a child of five years old. So vanished our hopes. My mistress had taught me the precepts of God's Word: "Thou shalt love thy neighbor as thyself." "Whatsoever ye would that men should do unto you, do ye even so unto them." But I was her slave, and I suppose she did not recognize me as her neighbor. I would give much to blot out from my memory that one great wrong. As a child, I loved my mistress; and, looking back on the happy days I spent with her, I try to think with less bitterness of this act of injustice. While I was with her, she taught me to read and spell; and for this privilege, which so rarely falls to the lot of a slave, I bless her memory.

She possessed but few slaves; and at her death those were all distributed among her relatives. Five of them were my grandmother's children, and had shared the same milk that nourished her mother's children. Notwithstanding my grandmother's long and faithful service to her owners, not one of her children escaped the auction block. These God-breathing machines are no more, in the sight of their masters, than the cotton they plant, or the horses they tend.

The New Master and Mistress

Dr. Flint, a physician in the neighborhood, had married the sister of my mistress, and I was now the property of their little daughter. It was not without murmuring that I prepared for my new home; and what added to my unhappiness, was the fact that my brother William was purchased by the same family. My father, by his nature, as well as by the habit of transacting business as a skilful mechanic, had more of the feelings of a freeman than is common among slaves. My brother was a spirited boy; and being brought up under such influences, he early detested the name of master and mistress. One day, when his father and his mistress both happened to call him at the same time, he hesitated between the two; being perplexed to know which had the strongest claim upon his obedience. He finally concluded to go to his mistress. When my father reproved him for it, he said, "You both called me, and I didn't know which I ought to go to first."

"You are *my* child," replied our father, "and when I call you, you should come immediately, if you have to pass through fire and water."

Poor Willie! He was now to learn his first lesson of obedience to a master. Grandmother tried to cheer us with hopeful words, and they found an echo in the credulous hearts of youth.

When we entered our new home we encountered cold looks, cold words, and cold treatment. We were glad when the night came. On my narrow bed I moaned and wept, I felt so desolate and alone.

I had been there nearly a year, when a dear little friend of mine was buried. I heard her mother sob, as the clods fell on the coffin of her only child, and I turned away from the grave, feeling thankful that I still had something left to love. I met my grandmother, who said, "Come with me, Linda;" and from her tone I knew that something sad had happened. She led me apart from the people, and then said, "My child, your father is dead." Dead! How could I believe it? He had died so suddenly I had not even heard that he was sick. I went home with my grandmother. My heart rebelled against God, who had taken from me mother, father, mistress, and friend. The good grandmother tried to comfort me. "Who knows the ways of God?" said she. "Perhaps they have been kindly taken from the evil days to come." Years afterwards I often thought of this. She promised to be a mother to her grandchildren, so far as she might be permitted to do so; and strengthened by her love, I returned to my master's. I thought I should be allowed to go to my father's house the next morning; but I was ordered to go for flowers, that my mistress's house might be decorated for an evening party. I spent the day gathering flowers and weaving them into festoons,[2] while the dead body of my father was lying within a mile of me. What cared my owners for that? he was merely a piece of property. Moreover, they thought he had spoiled his children, by teaching them to feel that they were human beings. This was blasphemous doctrine for a slave to teach; presumptuous in him, and dangerous to the masters.

The next day I followed his remains to a humble grave beside that of my dear mother. There were those who knew my father's worth, and respected his memory.

My home now seemed more dreary than ever. The laugh of the little slave children sounded harsh and cruel. It was selfish to feel so about the joy of others. My brother moved about with a very grave face. I tried to comfort him, by saying, "Take courage, Willie; brighter days will come by and by."

"You don't know any thing about it, Linda," he replied. "We shall have to stay here all our days; we shall never be free."

I argued that we were growing older and stronger, and that perhaps we might, before long, be allowed to hire our own time, and then we could earn

[2] A decorative chain or strip hanging between two points.

money to buy our freedom. William declared this was much easier to say than to do; moreover, he did not intend to *buy* his freedom. We held daily controversies upon this subject.

Little attention was paid to the slaves' meals in Dr. Flint's house. If they could catch a bit of food while it was going, well and good. I gave myself no trouble on that score, for on my various errands I passed my grandmother's house, where there was always something to spare for me. I was frequently threatened with punishment if I stopped there; and my grandmother, to avoid detaining me, often stood at the gate with something for my breakfast or dinner. I was indebted to *her* for all my comforts, spiritual or temporal. It was *her* labor that supplied my scanty wardrobe. I have a vivid recollection of the linsey-woolsey[3] dress given me every winter by Mrs. Flint. How I hated it! It was one of the badges of slavery.

While my grandmother was thus helping to support me from her hard earnings, the three hundred dollars she had lent her mistress were never repaid. When her mistress died, her son-in-law, Dr. Flint, was appointed executor. When grandmother applied to him for payment, he said the estate was insolvent, and the law prohibited payment. It did not, however, prohibit him from retaining the silver candelabra, which had been purchased with that money. I presume they will be handed down in the family, from generation to generation.

My grandmother's mistress had always promised her that, at her death, she should be free; and it was said that in her will she made good the promise. But when the estate was settled, Dr. Flint told the faithful old servant that, under existing circumstances, it was necessary she should be sold.

On the appointed day, the customary advertisement was posted up, proclaiming that there would be a "public sale of negroes, horses, &c." Dr. Flint called to tell my grandmother that he was unwilling to wound her feelings by putting her up at auction, and that he would prefer to dispose of her at private sale. My grandmother saw through his hypocrisy; she understood very well that he was ashamed of the job. She was a very spirited woman, and if he was base enough to sell her, when her mistress intended she should be free, she was determined the public should know it. She had for a long time supplied many families with crackers and preserves; consequently, "Aunt Marthy," as she was called, was generally known, and every body who knew her respected her intelligence and good character. Her long and faithful service in the family was also well known, and the intention of her mistress to leave her free. When the day of sale came, she took her place among the chattels, and at the first call she sprang upon the auction-block. Many voices called out, "Shame! Shame! Who is going to sell *you,* aunt Marthy? Don't stand there! That is no place for *you.*" Without saying a word, she quietly awaited her fate. No one bid for her. At last, a feeble voice said, "Fifty dollars." It came from a maiden lady, seventy years old, the sister of my grandmother's deceased mistress. She had lived forty years under the same roof with my grandmother; she knew how faithfully she had served her owners, and how cruelly she had been defrauded of her rights; and she resolved to protect her. The

[3] A coarse sturdy fabric of wool and linen or cotton.

auctioneer waited for a higher bid; but her wishes were respected; no one bid above her. She could neither read nor write; and when the bill of sale was made out, she signed it with a cross. But what consequence was that, when she had a big heart overflowing with human kindness? She gave the old servant her freedom.

At that time, my grandmother was just fifty years old. Laborious years had passed since then; and now my brother and I were slaves to the man who had defrauded her of her money, and tried to defraud her of her freedom. One of my mother's sisters, called Aunt Nancy, was also a slave in his family. She was a kind, good aunt to me; and supplied the place of both housekeeper and waiting maid to her mistress. She was, in fact, at the beginning and end of every thing.

Mrs. Flint, like many southern women, was totally deficient in energy. She had not strength to superintend her household affairs; but her nerves were so strong, that she could sit in her easy chair and see a woman whipped, till the blood trickled from every stroke of the lash. She was a member of the church; but partaking of the Lord's supper did not seem to put her in a Christian frame of mind. If dinner was not served at the exact time on that particular Sunday, she would station herself in the kitchen, and wait till it was dished, and then spit in all the kettles and pans that had been used for cooking. She did this to prevent the cook and her children from eking out their meagre fare with the remains of the gravy and other scrapings. The slaves could get nothing to eat except what she chose to give them. Provisions were weighed out by the pound and ounce, three times a day. I can assure you she gave them no chance to eat wheat bread from her flour barrel. She knew how many biscuits a quart of flour would make, and exactly what size they ought to be.

Dr. Flint was an epicure.[4] The cook never sent a dinner to his table without fear and trembling; for if there happened to be a dish not to his liking, he would either order her to be whipped, or compel her to eat every mouthful of it in his presence. The poor, hungry creature might not have objected to eating it; but she did object to having her master cram it down her throat till she choked.

They had a pet dog, that was a nuisance in the house. The cook was ordered to make some Indian mush[5] for him. He refused to eat, and when his head was held over it, the froth flowed from his mouth into the basin. He died a few minutes after. When Dr. Flint came in, he said the mush had not been well cooked, and that was the reason the animal would not eat it. He sent for the cook, and compelled her to eat it. He thought that the woman's stomach was stronger than the dog's; but her sufferings afterwards proved that he was mistaken. The poor woman endured many cruelties from her master and mistress; sometimes she was locked up, away from her nursing baby, for a whole day and night.

---

[4] A person devoted to sensual pleasure.

[5] Corn meal pudding.

25 When I had been in the family a few weeks, one of the plantation slaves was brought to town, by order of his master. It was near night when he arrived, and Dr. Flint ordered him to be taken to the work house, and tied up to the joist, so that his feet would just escape the ground. In that situation he was to wait till the doctor had taken his tea. I shall never forget that night. Never before, in my life, had I heard hundreds of blows fall, in succession, on a human being. His piteous groans, and his "O, pray don't, massa," rang in my ear for months afterwards. There were many conjectures as to the cause of this terrible punishment. Some said master accused him of stealing corn; others said the slave had quarrelled with his wife, in presence of the overseer, and had accused his master of being the father of her child. They were both black, and the child was very fair.

I went into the work house next morning, and saw the cowhide still wet with blood, and the boards all covered with gore. The poor man lived, and continued to quarrel with his wife. A few months afterwards Dr. Flint handed them both over to a slavetrader. The guilty man put their value into his pocket, and had the satisfaction of knowing that they were out of sight and hearing. When the mother was delivered into the trader's hands, she said, "You *promised* to treat me well." To which he replied, "You have let your tongue run too far; damn you!" She had forgotten that it was a crime for a slave to tell who was the father of her child.

From others than the master persecution also comes in such cases. I once saw a young slave girl dying soon after the birth of a child nearly white. In her agony she cried out, "O Lord, come and take me!" Her mistress stood by, and mocked at her like an incarnate fiend. "You suffer, do you?" she exclaimed. "I am glad of it. You deserve it all, and more too."

The girl's mother said, "The baby is dead, thank God; and I hope my poor child will soon be in heaven, too."

"Heaven!" retorted the mistress. "There is no such place for the like of her and her bastard."

30 The poor mother turned away, sobbing. Her dying daughter called her, feebly, and as she bent over her, I heard her say, "Don't grieve so, mother; God knows all about it; and HE will have mercy upon me."

Her sufferings, afterwards, became so intense, that her mistress felt unable to stay; but when she left the room, the scornful smile was still on her lips. Seven children called her mother. The poor black woman had but the one child, whose eyes she saw closing in death, while she thanked God for taking her away from the greater bitterness of life.

The Loophole of Retreat (Linda Brent Escapes)

A small shed had been added to my grandmother's house years ago. Some boards were laid across the joists at the top, and between these boards and the roof was a very small garret, never occupied by any thing but rats and mice. It was a pent roof, covered with nothing but shingles, according to the southern custom for such buildings. The garret was only nine feet long and seven wide. The highest part was three feet high, and sloped down abruptly to the loose board floor. There was no admission for either light or air. My uncle Phillip, who was a carpenter, had very skilfully made a concealed trap-door, which communicated with the storeroom. He had been doing this while I was waiting in the swamp. The storeroom opened upon a piazza. To this hole I was conveyed as soon as I entered the house. The air was stifling; the darkness total. A bed had been spread on the floor. I could sleep quite comfortably on one side; but the slope was so sudden that I could not turn on the other without hitting the roof. The rats and mice ran over my bed; but I was weary, and I slept such sleep as the wretched may, when a tempest has passed over them. Morning came. I knew it only by the noises I heard; for in my small den day and night were all the same. I suffered for air even more than for light. But I was not comfortless. I heard the voices of my children. There was joy and there was sadness in the sound. It made my tears flow. How I longed to speak to them! I was eager to look on their faces; but there was no hole, no crack, through which I could peep. This continued darkness was oppressive. It seemed horrible to sit or lie in a cramped position day after day, without one gleam of light. Yet I would have chosen this, rather than my lot as a slave, though white people considered it an easy one; and it was so compared with the fate of others. I was never cruelly overworked; I was never lacerated with the whip from head to foot; I was never so beaten and bruised that I could not turn from one side to the other; I never had my heel-strings cut to prevent my running away; I was never chained to a log and forced to drag it about, while I toiled in the fields from morning till night; I was never branded with hot iron, or torn by bloodhounds. On the contrary, I had always been kindly treated, and tenderly cared for, until I came into the hands of Dr. Flint. I had never wished for freedom till then. But though my life in slavery was comparatively devoid of hardships, God pity the woman who is compelled to lead such a life! My food was passed up to me through the trap-door my uncle had contrived; and my grandmother, my uncle Phillip, and aunt Nancy would seize such opportunities as they could, to mount up there and chat with me at the opening. But of course this was not safe in the daytime. It must all be done in darkness. It was impossible for me to move in an erect position, but I crawled about my den for exercise. One day I hit my head against something, and found it was a gimlet. My uncle had left it sticking there when he made the trap-door. I was as rejoiced as Robinson Crusoe could have been at finding such a treasure. It put a lucky thought into my head. I said to myself, "Now I will have some light. Now I will see my children." I did not dare to begin my work during the daytime, for fear of attracting attention. But I groped round; and having found the side next the street, where I could frequently see my children, I stuck the gimlet in and waited for evening. I bored three rows of holes, one above another; then I bored out the interstices between. I thus succeeded in making one hole about an inch long and an inch broad. I sat by it till late into the night, to enjoy the little whiff of air that floated in. In the morning I watched for my children. The first person I saw in the street was Dr. Flint. I had a shuddering, superstitious feeling that it was a bad omen. Several familiar faces passed by. At last I heard the merry laugh of children, and presently two sweet little faces were looking up at me, as though they knew I was there, and were conscious of the joy they imparted. How I longed to *tell* them I was there!

My condition was now a little improved. But for weeks I was tormented by hundreds of little red insects, fine as a needle's point, that pierced through my skin, and produced an intolerable burning. The good grandmother gave me herb teas and cooling medicines, and finally I got rid of them. The heat of my den was intense, for nothing but thin shingles protected me from the scorching summer's sun. But I had my consolations. Through my peeping-hole I could watch the children, and when they were near enough, I could hear their talk. Aunt Nancy brought me all the news she could hear at Dr. Flint's. From her I learned that the doctor had written to New York to a colored woman, who had been born and raised in our neighborhood, and had breathed his contaminating atmosphere. He offered her a reward if she could find out any thing about me. I know not what was the nature of her reply; but he soon after started for New York in haste, saying to his family that he had business of importance to transact. I peeped at him as he passed on his way to the steamboat. It was a satisfaction to have miles of land and water between us, even for a little while; and it was a still greater satisfaction to know that he believed me to be in the Free States. My little den seemed less dreary than it had done. He returned, as he did from his former journey to New York, without obtaining any satisfactory information. When he passed our house next morning, Benny[6] was standing at the gate. He had heard them say that he had gone to find me, and he called out, "Dr. Flint, did you bring my mother home? I want to see her." The doctor stamped his foot at him in a rage, and exclaimed, "Get out of the way, you little damned rascal! If you don't, I'll cut off your head."

Benny ran terrified into the house, saying, "You can't put me in jail again. I don't belong to you now." It was well that the wind carried the words away from the doctor's ear. I told my grandmother of it, when we had our next conference at the trap-door; and begged of her not to allow the children to be impertinent to the irascible old man.

Autumn came, with a pleasant abatement of heat. My eyes had become accustomed to the dim light, and by holding my book or work in a certain position near the aperture I contrived to read and sew. That was a great relief to the tedious monotony of my life. But when winter came, the cold penetrated through the thin shingle roof, and I was dreadfully chilled. The winters there are not so long, or so severe, as in northern latitudes; but the houses are not built to shelter from cold, and my little den was peculiarly comfortless. The kind grandmother brought me bed-clothes and warm drinks. Often I was obliged to lie in bed all day to keep comfortable; but with all my precautions, my shoulders and feet were frostbitten. O, those long, gloomy days, with no object for my eye to rest upon, and no thoughts to occupy my mind, except the dreary past and the uncertain future! I was thankful when there came a day sufficiently mild for me to wrap myself up and sit at the loophole to watch the

[6] Brent's son.

passers by. Southerners have the habit of stopping and talking in the streets, and I heard many conversations not intended to meet my ears. I heard slave-hunters planning how to catch some poor fugitive. Several times I heard allusions to Dr. Flint, myself, and the history of my children, who, perhaps, were playing near the gate. One would say, "I wouldn't move my little finger to catch her, as old Flint's property." Another would say, "I'll catch *any* nigger for the reward. A man ought to have what belongs to him, if he *is* a damned brute." The opinion was often expressed that I was in the Free States. Very rarely did any one suggest that I might be in the vicinity. Had the least suspicion rested on my grandmother's house, it would have been burned to the ground. But it was the last place they thought of. Yet there was no place, where slavery existed, that could have afforded me so good a place of concealment.

Dr. Flint and his family repeatedly tried to coax and bribe my children to tell something they had heard said about me. One day the doctor took them into a shop, and offered them some bright little silver pieces and gay handkerchiefs if they would tell where their mother was. Ellen[7] shrank away from him, and would not speak; but Benny spoke up, and said, "Dr. Flint, I don't know where my mother is. I guess she's in New York; and when you go there again, I wish you'd ask her to come home, for I want to see her; but if you put her in jail, or tell her you'll cut her head off, I'll tell her to go right back."

Preparations for Escape

I hardly expect that the reader will credit me, when I affirm that I lived in that little dismal hole, almost deprived of light and air, and with no space to move my limbs, for nearly seven years. But it is a fact; and to me a sad one, even now; for my body still suffers from the effects of that long imprisonment, to say nothing of my soul. Members of my family, now living in New York and Boston, can testify to the truth of what I say.

Countless were the nights that I sat late at the little loophole scarcely large enough to give me a glimpse of one twinkling star. There, I heard the patrols and slave-hunters conferring together about the capture of runaways, well knowing how rejoiced they would be to catch me.

Season after season, year after year, I peeped at my children's faces, and heard their sweet voices, with a heart yearning all the while to say, "Your mother is here." Sometimes it appeared to me as if ages had rolled away since I entered upon that gloomy, monotonous existence. At times, I was stupefied and listless; at other times I became very impatient to know when these dark years would end, and I should again be allowed to feel the sunshine, and breathe the pure air.

After Ellen left us, this feeling increased. Mr. Sands had agreed that Benny might go to the north whenever his uncle Phillip could go with him; and I was anxious to be there also, to watch over my children, and protect them so far as I was able. Moreover, I was likely to be drowned out of my

[7] Brent's daughter.

den, if I remained much longer; for the slight roof was getting badly out of repair, and uncle Phillip was afraid to remove the shingles, lest some one should get a glimpse of me. When storms occurred in the night, they spread mats and bits of carpet, which in the morning appeared to have been laid out to dry; but to cover the roof in the daytime might have attracted attention. Consequently, my clothes and bedding were often drenched; a process by which the pains and aches in my cramped and stiffened limbs were greatly increased. I revolved various plans of escape in my mind, which I sometimes imparted to my grandmother, when she came to whisper with me at the trap-door. The kind-hearted old woman had an intense sympathy for runaways. She had known too much of the cruelties inflicted on those who were captured. Her memory always flew back at once to the sufferings of her bright and handsome son, Benjamin, the youngest and dearest of her flock. So, whenever I alluded to the subject, she would groan out, "O, don't think of it, child. You'll break my heart." I had no good old aunt Nancy now to encourage me; but my brother William and my children were continually beckoning me to the north.

And now I must go back a few months in my story. I have stated that the first of January was the time for selling slaves, or leasing them out to new masters. If time were counted by heart-throbs, the poor slaves might reckon years of suffering during that festival so joyous to the free. On the New Year's day preceding my aunt's death, one of my friends, named Fanny, was to be sold at auction, to pay her master's debts. My thoughts were with her during all the day, and at night I anxiously inquired what had been her fate. I was told that she had been sold to one master, and her four little girls to another master, far distant; that she had escaped from her purchaser, and was not to be found. Her mother was the old Aggie I have spoken of. She lived in a small tenement belonging to my grandmother, and built on the same lot with her own house. Her dwelling was searched and watched, and that brought the patrols so near me that I was obliged to keep very close in my den. The hunters were somehow eluded; and not long afterwards Benny accidentally caught sight of Fanny in her mother's hut. He told his grandmother, who charged him never to speak of it, explaining to him the frightful consequences; and he never betrayed the trust. Aggie little dreamed that my grandmother knew where her daughter was concealed, and that the stooping form of her old neighbor was bending under a similar burden of anxiety and fear; but these dangerous secrets deepened the sympathy between the two old persecuted mothers.

My friend Fanny and I remained many weeks hidden within call of each other; but she was unconscious of the fact. I longed to have her share my den, which seemed a more secure retreat than her own; but I had brought so much trouble on my grandmother, that it seemed wrong to ask her to incur greater risks. My restlessness increased. I had lived too long in bodily pain and anguish of spirit. Always I was in dread that by some accident, or some contrivance, slavery would succeed in snatching my children from me. This thought drove me nearly frantic, and I determined to steer for the North Star at all hazards. At this crisis, Providence opened an unexpected way for me to escape. My friend Peter came one evening, and asked to speak with me. "Your day has come, Linda," said he. "I have found a chance for you to go to the Free States. You have a fortnight to decide." The news seemed too good to be true; but Peter explained his arrangements, and told me all that was necessary was for me to say I would go. I was going to answer him with a joyful yes, when the thought of Benny came to my mind. I told him the temptation was exceedingly strong, but I was terribly afraid of Dr. Flint's alleged power over my child, and that I could not go and leave him behind. Peter remonstrated earnestly. He said such a good chance might never occur again; that Benny was free, and could be sent to me; and that for the sake of my children's welfare I ought not to hesitate a moment. I told him I would consult with uncle Phillip. My uncle rejoiced in the plan, and bade me go by all means. He promised, if his life was spared, that he would either bring or send my son to me as soon as I reached a place of safety. I resolved to go, but thought nothing had better be said to my grandmother till very near the time of departure. But my uncle thought she would feel it more keenly if I left her so suddenly. "I will reason with her," said he, "and convince her how necessary it is, not only for your sake, but for hers also. You cannot be blind to the fact that she is sinking under her burdens." I was not blind to it. I knew that my concealment was an ever-present source of anxiety, and that the older she grew the more nervously fearful she was of discovery. My uncle talked with her, and finally succeeded in persuading her that it was absolutely necessary for me to seize the chance so unexpectedly offered.

The anticipation of being a free woman proved almost too much for my weak frame. The excitement stimulated me, and at the same time bewildered me. I made busy preparations for my journey, and for my son to follow me. I resolved to have an interview with him before I went, that I might give him cautions and advice, and tell him how anxiously I should be waiting for him at the north. Grandmother stole up to me as often as possible to whisper words of counsel. She insisted upon my writing to Dr. Flint, as soon as I arrived in the Free States, and asking him to sell me to her. She said she would sacrifice her house, and all she had in the world, for the sake of having me safe with my children in any part of the world. If she could only live to know *that* she could die in peace. I promised the dear old faithful friend that I would write to her as soon as I arrived, and put the letter in a safe way to reach her; but in my own mind I resolved that not another cent of her hard earnings should be spent to pay rapacious slaveholders for what they called their property. And even if I had not been unwilling to buy what I had already a right to possess, common humanity would have prevented me from accepting the generous offer, at the expense of turning my aged relative out of house and home, when she was trembling on the brink of the grave.

I was to escape in a vessel; but I forbear to mention any further particulars. I was in readiness, but the vessel was unexpectedly detained several days. Meantime, news came to town of a most horrible murder committed on a fugitive slave, named James. Charity, the mother of this unfortunate young man, had been an old acquaintance of ours. I have told the shocking particulars of his death, in my description of some of the neighboring slaveholders. My grandmother, always nervously sensitive about runaways, was terribly frightened. She felt sure that a similar fate awaited me, if I did not desist from my enterprise. She sobbed, and groaned, and entreated me not to go. Her excessive fear was somewhat contagious, and my heart was not proof against her extreme agony. I was grievously disappointed, but I promised to relinquish my project.

When my friend Peter was apprised of this, he was both disappointed and vexed. He said, that judging from our past experience, it would be a long time before I had such another chance to throw away. I told him it need not be thrown away; that I had a friend concealed near by, who would be glad enough to take the place that had been provided for me. I told him about poor Fanny, and the kind-hearted, noble fellow, who never turned his back upon any body in distress, white or black, expressed his readiness to help her. Aggie was much surprised when she found that we knew her secret. She was rejoiced to hear of such a chance for Fanny, and arrangements were made for her to go on board the vessel the next night. They both supposed that I had long been at the north, therefore my name was not mentioned in the transaction. Fanny was carried on board at the appointed time, and stowed away in a very small cabin. This accommodation had been purchased at a price that would pay for a voyage to England. But when one proposes to go to fine old England, they stop to calculate whether they can afford the cost of the pleasure; while in making a bargain to escape from slavery, the trembling victim is ready to say, "Take all I have, only don't betray me!"

The next morning I peeped through my loophole, and saw that it was dark and cloudy. At night I received news that the wind was ahead, and the vessel had not sailed. I was exceedingly anxious about Fanny, and Peter too, who was running a tremendous risk at my instigation. Next day the wind and weather remained the same. Poor Fanny had been half dead with fright when they carried her on board, and I could readily imagine how she must be suffering now. Grandmother came often to my den, to say how thankful she was I did not go. On the third morning she rapped for me to come down to the storeroom. The poor old sufferer was breaking down under her weight of trouble. She was easily flurried now. I found her in a nervous, excited state, but I was not aware that she had forgotten to lock the door behind her, as usual. She was exceedingly worried about the detention of the vessel. She was afraid all would be discovered, and then Fanny, and Peter, and I, would all be tortured to death, and Phillip would be utterly ruined, and her house would be torn down. Poor Peter! If he should die such a horrible death as the poor slave James had lately done, and all for his kindness in trying to help me, how dreadful it would be for us all! Alas, the thought was familiar to me, and had sent many a sharp pang through my heart. I tried to suppress my own anxiety, and speak soothingly to her. She brought in some allusion to aunt Nancy, the dear daughter she had recently buried, and then she lost all control of herself. As she stood there, trembling and sobbing, a voice from the piazza called out, "Whar is you, aunt Marthy?" Grandmother was startled, and in her agitation opened the door, without thinking of me. In stepped Jenny, the mischievous housemaid, who had tried to enter my room, when I was concealed in the house of my white benefactress. "I's bin huntin ebery whar for you, aunt Marthy," said she. "My missis wants you to send her some crackers." I had slunk down behind a barrel, which entirely screened me, but I imagined that Jenny was looking directly at the spot, and my heart beat violently. My grandmother immediately thought what she had done, and went out quickly with Jenny to count the crackers, locking the door after her. She returned to me, in a few minutes, the perfect picture of despair. "Poor child!" she exclaimed, "my carelessness has ruined you. The boat ain't gone yet. Get ready immediately, and go with Fanny. I ain't got another word to say against it now; for there's no telling what may happen this day."

Uncle Phillip was sent for, and he agreed with his mother in thinking that Jenny would inform Dr. Flint in less than twenty-four hours. He advised getting me on board the boat, if possible; if not, I had better keep very still in my den, where they could not find me without tearing the house down. He said it would not do for him to move in the matter, because suspicion would be immediately excited; but he promised to communicate with Peter. I felt reluctant to apply to him again, having implicated him too much already; but there seemed to be no alternative. Vexed as Peter had been by my indecision, he was true to his generous nature, and said at once that he would do his best to help me, trusting I should show myself a stronger woman this time.

He immediately proceeded to the wharf, and found that the wind had shifted, and the vessel was slowly beating down stream. On some pretext of urgent necessity, he offered two boatmen a dollar apiece to catch up with her. He was of lighter complexion than the boatmen he hired, and when the captain saw them coming so rapidly, he thought officers were pursuing his vessel in search of the runaway slave he had on board. They hoisted sails, but the boat gained upon them, and the indefatigable Peter sprang on board.

The captain at once recognized him. Peter asked him to go below, to speak about a bad bill he had given him. When he told his errand, the captain replied, "Why, the woman's here already; and I've put her where you or the devil would have a tough job to find her."

"But it is another woman I want to bring," said Peter. "*She* is in great distress, too, and you shall be paid any thing within reason, if you'll stop and take her."

"What's her name?" inquired the captain.

"Linda," he replied.

"That's the name of the woman already here," rejoined the captain. "By George! I believe you mean to betray me."

"O!" exclaimed Peter, "God knows I wouldn't harm a hair of your head. I am too grateful to you. But there really *is* another woman in great danger. Do have the humanity to stop and take her!"

After a while they came to an understanding. Fanny, not dreaming I was any where about in that region, had assumed my name, though she called herself Johnson. "Linda is a common name," said Peter, "and the woman I want to bring is Linda Brent."

The captain agreed to wait at a certain place till evening, being handsomely paid for his detention.

Of course, the day was an anxious one for us all. But we concluded that if Jenny had seen me, she would be too wise to let her mistress know of it; and that she probably would not get a chance to see Dr. Flint's family till evening, for I knew very well what were the rules in that household. I afterwards believed that she did not see me; for nothing ever came of it, and she was one of those base characters that would have jumped to betray a suffering fellow being for the sake of thirty pieces of silver.

I made all my arrangements to go on board as soon as it was dusk. The intervening time I resolved to spend with my son. I had not spoken to him for seven years, though I had been under the same roof, and seen him every day, when I was well enough to sit at the loophole. I did not dare to venture beyond the storeroom; so they brought him there, and locked us up together, in a place concealed from the piazza door. It was an agitating interview for both of us. After we had talked and wept together for a little while, he said, "Mother, I'm glad you're going away. I wish I could go with you. I knew you was here; and I have been *so* afraid they would come and catch you!"

I was greatly surprised, and asked him how he had found it out.

He replied, "I was standing under the eaves, one day, before Ellen went away, and I heard somebody cough up over the wood shed. I don't know what made me think it was you, but I did think so. I missed Ellen, the night before she went away; and grandmother brought her back into the room in the night; and I thought maybe she'd been to see *you,* before she went, for I heard grandmother whisper to her, 'Now go to sleep; and remember never to tell.' "

I asked him if he ever mentioned his suspicions to his sister. He said he never did; but after he heard the cough, if he saw her playing with other children on that side of the house, he always tried to coax her round to the other side, for fear they would hear me cough, too. He said he had kept a close lookout for Dr. Flint, and if he saw him speak to a constable, or a patrol, he always told grandmother. I now recollected that I had seen him manifest uneasiness, when people were on that side of the house, and I had at the time been puzzled to conjecture a motive for his actions. Such prudence may seem extraordinary in a boy of twelve years, but slaves, being surrounded by mysteries, deceptions, and dangers, early learn to be suspicious and watchful, and prematurely cautious and cunning. He had never asked a question of grandmother, or uncle Phillip, and I had often heard him chime in with other children, when they spoke of my being at the north.

I told him I was now really going to the Free States, and if he was a good, honest boy, and a loving child to his dear old grandmother, the Lord would bless him, and bring him to me, and we and Ellen would live together. He began to tell me that grandmother had not eaten any thing all day. While he was speaking, the door was unlocked, and she came in with a small bag of money, which she wanted me to take. I begged her to keep a part of it, at least, to pay for Benny's being sent to the north; but she insisted, while her tears were falling fast, that I should take the whole. "You may be sick among strangers," she said, "and they would send you to the poorhouse to die." Ah, that good grandmother!

For the last time I went up to my nook. Its desolate appearance no longer chilled me, for the light of hope had risen in my soul. Yet, even with the blessed prospect of freedom before me, I felt very sad at leaving forever that old homestead, where I had been sheltered so long by the dear old grandmother; where I had dreamed my first young dream of love; and where, after that had faded away, my children came to twine themselves so closely round my desolate heart. As the hour approached for me to leave, I again descended to the storeroom. My grandmother and Benny were there. She took me by the hand, and said, "Linda, let us pray." We knelt down together, with my child pressed to my heart, and my other arm round the faithful, loving old friend I was about to leave forever. On no other occasion has it ever been my lot to listen to so fervent a supplication for mercy and protection. It thrilled through my heart, and inspired me with trust in God.

Peter was waiting for me in the street. I was soon by his side, faint in body, but strong of purpose. I did not look back upon the old place, though I felt that I should never see it again.

Explorations of the Text

1. Describe life in Dr. Flint's home. Explore the treatment of slaves.
2. Characterize the grandmother, Aunt Marthy. What is the importance of the candelabra?
3. Consider the beating of the field slave. What does Jacobs indicate about the cause of the arguments between the man and woman?
4. Characterize Mrs. Flint. What is the position of the jealous mistress? What does Jacobs think of Southern women?
5. Describe the years in the garret. Explain the following quotation: "My body still suffers from the effects of the long imprisonment, to say nothing of my soul."
6. What are the preparations for escape? What aspects of the flight are most memorable?
7. Characterize the narrator. Is she strong? What evidence suggests an answer to the previous question?
8. Determine the point of view, purpose, and audience for this narrative.
9. Compare speakers in this work with those in Sojourner Truth's speech and in Griffin's poem.

The Reading/Writing Connection

1. Write a journal entry in the voice of Dr. Flint, of the grandmother, of Mrs. Flint, or of the narrator.
2. "Think" Topic: Why does sexual exploitation become the central issue of this work?

Ideas for Writing

1. Characterize the narrator.
2. Write about the portraits of slave owners in these excerpts of Jacobs' narrative.

The Prism of Race

Manning Marable

Manning Marable (1950–) was born in Dayton, Ohio. Marable, educated at Earlham College, the University of Wisconsin, and the University of Maryland, is currently professor of History and Political Science and director of the Institute for Research in African American Studies at Columbia University. Marable has pursued the role of public intellectual, and his weekly public affairs commentary, "Along the Color Line," is published in more than 280 journals and newspapers.

1995

Introduction: The Prism of Race

Black and white. As long as I can remember, the fundamentally defining feature of my life, and the lives of my family, was the stark reality of race. Angular and unforgiving, race was so much more than the background for what occurred or the context for our relationships. It was the social gravity which set into motion our expectations and emotions, our language and dreams. Race seemed far more powerful than distinctions between people based on language, nationality, religion or income. Race seemed granite-like, fixed and permanent, as the center of the social universe. The reality of racial discrimination constantly fed the pessimism and doubts that we as black people felt about the apparent natural order of the world, the inherent unfairness of it all, as well as limiting our hopes for a better life somewhere in the distant future.

I am a child of Middle America. I was born in Dayton, Ohio, on 13 May 1950, at the height of McCarthyism[1] and on the eve of the Korean[2] conflict. One of the few rituals I remember about the anti-Communist hysteria sweeping the nation in the fifties were the obligatory exercises we performed in elementary school, "ducking and covering" ourselves beneath small wooden desks in our classroom to shield ourselves from the fallout and blast of a nuclear explosion. Most of what I now recall of growing up in south-central Ohio had little to do with nuclear war or communism, only the omnipresent reality of race.

---

[1] The practice of making accusations of disloyalty, especially of pro-Communist sentiments, that often were unsupported or based on doubtful evidence.

[2] The Korean War (1950–53); between North Korea (supported by Communist China) and South Korea (aided by the United States) and other members of the United Nations.

In the 1950s, Dayton was a predominantly blue-collar, working-class town, situated on the banks of the Great Miami River. Neighborhoods were divided to some extent by class. Oakwood was the well-to-do, WASP-ish community, filled with the corporate executives and professionals who ran the city's enterprises. Dayton View on the northwest side was becoming increasingly Jewish. Kettering and Centerville were unpretentiously middle class, conservative and Republican. But beneath the divisions of income, religion and political affiliation seemed to be the broad polarization rooted in race. There appeared to be two parallel racial universes which cohabited the same city, each with its own set of religious institutions, cultural activities, social centers, clubs, political organizations and schools. African-Americans generally resided west of the Great Miami River. The central core of the ghetto was located along the corridors of West Third and West Fifth Street. With the great migration of southern blacks to Dayton immediately following World War II, the African-American population became much more dense, and began to spread west, out to the city's furthest boundaries.

The black community existed largely in its own world, within the logic of institutions it had created to sustain itself. We were taught to be proud of our history and literature. Every day, on the way to Edison Elementary School, I would feel a surge of pride as we drove past the home of celebrated African-American poet Paul Lawrence Dunbar. My parents, James and June Marable, were school teachers, a solidly middle-class profession by the standards of the status-conscious Negro elite. During the fifties, my father taught at predominantly black Dunbar and Roosevelt high schools during the day; after school was dismissed, he worked as a laborer in the second shift at Dayton tire factory. Although my father had a principal's certificate and a Master's degree, which qualified him to be appointed as a principal, he was constantly passed over by white administrators because of his fiercely independent spirit and self-initiative. Frustrated, my father eventually went into business for himself, borrowing the money to build a private nursery and daycare center for black children on the city's West Side.

5 Because of my parent's education and jobs, we were part of Dayton's Negro middle class. Our family attorney, James McGee, was elected the city's first black mayor after the successes and reforms in the wake of the civil-rights movement. Most of my parents' friends were physicians, dentists, lawyers, school teachers, entrepreneurs and professionals of various types. Despite their pretensions, most middle-class Negroes were barely two or three paychecks from poverty. Many of the businesses that sold consumer goods to blacks, which were located on West Third Street, were white-owned. Our own business sector consisted chiefly of funeral parlors, beauty salons, auto repair shops and small restaurants.

The college-educated Negro middle class had begun purchasing comfortable, spacious homes clustered high on the ridge which overlooked the West Side, not far from the mostly German farm families who lived in Jefferson Township. Poorer black families lived closer to the factories and foundries, near the dirt, smoke and industrial stench I vividly recall even today. Social class and income stratification were not unimportant. There seemed to be striking similarities between the houses and the manner in which working and poor people were dressed on "our" side of town and in "their" working-class neighborhoods. But color was the greatest denominator of all.

On Gettysburg Avenue there were a group of small rental properties and boarding houses which were within walking distance of the Veteran's Administration Hospital on the far West Side. In the front windows of most of these buildings were small cardboard signs, reading simply "No Colored." Blacks legally could not be denied entrance into the hotels or best restaurants downtown, but they were certainly not welcomed. White taxicab drivers often avoided picking up black passengers at the train station. Very few blacks were on the local police force. Black children weren't permitted to use the public swimming pool on Germantown Pike. In most aspects of public and private life, whites acted toward African-Americans as "superiors," and usually expected to be treated deferentially. There were exceptions, certainly. At my elementary school, there were white students who were friendly. There were white teachers who displayed kindness and sincerity towards their black students. But there was always an unbridgeable distance separating us. No white students with whom I attended school ever asked to come to my home. Although my parents taught in the Dayton Public School system, most white teachers and administrators maintained a strictly professional rather than personal relationship towards them. Whites were omnipresent in our lives, frequently as authority figures: politicians, police officers, bank-loan officers, school administrators, tax auditors, grocery-store managers. Race existed as a kind of prism through which we understood and saw the world, distorting and coloring everything before us.

Despite these experiences and numerous examples of discrimination, Dayton, Ohio was never the Deep South. Although the largest department stores downtown rarely employed Negroes, I recall that black customers were usually treated with courtesy. Whites were enrolled in every school I attended. Occasionally, whites attended our black church. Public institutions were largely desegregated. The color line was at its worse where it converged with the boundaries of class inequality. Blacks were treated most differently, for example, when it was also clear that they lacked money or material resources. Conversely, middle-class African-Americans certainly experienced prejudicial behavior by whites, but often encountered a less virulent form of hatred than their sisters and brothers who were poor. The recognition of class mobility and higher education gave a small number of blacks a buffer status from the worst forms of discrimination at a day-to-day level. But despite this relative privilege, we never forgot that we were black.

Every summer, we had the opportunity to encounter a far more racially charged society. At the end of the school year, my family packed our 1957 Chevrolet and traveled south, through Cincinnati and Nashville, along highways and narrow, two-lane country roads. Often at nights we were forced to sleep in the cramped confines of the automobile, because we could find no motel which permitted black people to stay overnight. We would stop along the highway to purchase gasoline, never knowing in advance whether we would be allowed to use the gas station's toilet facilities. If we were stopped for any reason by a highway patrol officer, we had to be prepared for some kind of verbal, racist abuse, and we had absolutely no recourse or appeal against his behavior or actions. Finally, we would arrive at my father's family home, Tuskegee, Alabama, where the sense of racial hostility and discrimination against African-Americans was the central theme of local life. I knew that Tuskegee then was in the midst of a major legal struggle initiated by blacks to outlaw the political gerrymandering of the city that had in effect disfranchised African-Americans.[3] We were taught that any open protest or violation of the norms of Jim Crow segregation was to court retaliation and retribution, personally and collectively. We learned that whites, with few exceptions, saw us as subhuman, without the rights to economic development, political expression and participation, and public accommodation which whites accepted and took for granted for themselves.

10 It was in Tuskegee, during my long visits to Alabama's Black Belt as a child, that many of my basic impressions concerning the relative permanence and inflexibility of race were formed. Part of that consciousness was shaped by the experiences and stories of my father. James Marable was the grandson of slaves, and the second son of thirteen children. His father, Manning Marable, had owned and operated a small sawmill, cutting pulpwood for farm households. Along with other black rural families, they experienced the prism of race in hundreds of different ways, which formed the basic framework of their existence. From being denied the right to vote to being confined to unequal, segregated schools; from being harassed and intimidated by local white police officers to being forced to lower one's eyes when being directly addressed by a white man, "race" was ingrained in the smallest aspects of Southern daily life.

My father rarely talked at length about growing up black in the Deep South. But occasionally, and especially when we were visiting his large, extended family in Tuskegee, he would reflect about his own history, and recall the hostility and rudeness of whites toward himself, his family and his people. He was trying to prepare me for what I would surely experience. One of my father's stories I remember best occurred on a cold, early winter day in 1946. World War II had ended only months before, and millions of young people were going home. My father had served as a master sergeant in a segregated unit in the US Army Air Corps. Arriving in the Anniston, Alabama, bus station, he had to transfer to another local bus to make the final forty-mile trek to his family's home outside Wedowee, Alabama.

My father was wearing his army uniform, proudly displaying his medals. Quietly he purchased his ticket and stood patiently in line to enter the small

[3] Seat of Macon County, east-central Alabama; home of the Tuskegee Institute, founded by Booker T. Washington in 1881. In 1957 the state legislature approved changes in the city's boundaries that resulted in the disenfranchisement of 400 black voters. In 1960 the U.S. Supreme Court declared that act to be unconstitutional.

bus. When my father finally reached the bus driver, the white man was staring intensely at him. With an ugly frown, the driver took a step. "Nigger," he spat at my father, "you look like you're going to give somebody some trouble. You had better wait here for the next bus." My father was immediately confused and angry. "As a soldier, you always felt sort of proud," my dad recalls. This white bus driver's remarks "hit me like a ton of bricks. Here I am, going home, and I'd been away from the South for four years. I wasn't being aggressive."

Dad turned around and saw that he was standing in front of three whites, who had purchased tickets after him. James Marable had forgotten, or had probably repressed, a central rule in the public etiquette of Jim Crow segregation.[4] Black people had to be constantly vigilant not to offend whites in any way. My father was supposed to have stepped out of line immediately, permitting the white patrons to move ahead of him. My father felt a burning sense of rage, which he could barely contain. "You get there some other way, nigger," the driver repeated with a laugh. The bus door shut in my father's face. The bus pulled away into the distance.

There was no other bus going to Wedowee that afternoon. My father wandered from the station into the street, feeling "really disgusted." Nothing he had accomplished in the previous four years, the sacrifices he had made for his country, seemed to matter. The rhetoric of democracy and freedom which had been popularized in the war against fascism rang hollow and empty. Although he eventually obtained a ride home by hitchhiking on the highway, my father never forgot the bitterness and hatred in the bus driver's words. Years later, he still felt his resentment and rage of that winter afternoon in Alabama. "When you go against the grain of racism," he warned me, "you pay for it, one way or another."

15 For both my father and myself, as well as for millions of black people for many generations, the living content of race was simultaneously and continuously created from within and imposed from without. That is, "race" is always an expression of how black people have defined themselves against the system of oppression, as well as a repressive structure of power and privilege which perpetuates an unequal status for African-Americans within a stratified social order. As an identity, race becomes a way of perceiving ourselves within a group. To be black in what seems to be a bipolar racial universe gives one instantly a set of coordinates within space and time, a sense of geographical location along an endless boundary of color. Blackness as a function of the racial superstructure also gives meaning to collective memory; it allows us to place ourselves within a context of racial resistance, within the many struggles for human dignity, for our families and for material resources. This consciousness of racial pride and community awareness gave hope and strength to my grandfather and father; it was also the prime motivation for the Edward Wilmot Blydens, Marcus Garveys and Fannie Lou Hamers throughout black

[4] Laws segregating, discriminating against Negroes.

history.[5] In this way, the prism of race structures the community of the imagination, setting parameters for real activity and collective possibility.

But blackness in a racially stratified society is always simultaneously the "negation of whiteness." To be white is not a sign of culture, or a statement of biology or genetics: it is essentially a power relationship, a statement of authority, a social construct which is perpetuated by systems of privilege, the consolidation of property and status. There is no genius behind the idea of whiteness, only an empty husk filled with a mountain of lies about superiority and a series of crimes against "nonwhite" people. To be black in a white-dominated social order, for instance, means that one's life chances are circumscribed and truncated in a thousand different ways. To be black means that when you go to the bank to borrow money, despite the fact that you have a credit profile identical to your white counterpart, you are nevertheless two or three times more likely to be denied the loan than the white. To be black means that when you are taken to the hospital for emergency health-care treatment, the quality of care you receive will be inadequate and substandard. To be black means that your children will not have the same academic experiences and access to higher learning resources as children in the white suburbs and exclusive urban enclaves. To be black means that your mere physical presence and the reality of your being can trigger surveillance cameras at shops, supermarkets, malls and fine stores everywhere. To be black, male, and to live in central Harlem in the 1990s, for example, means that you will have a life expectancy of forty-nine years of age—less than in Bangladesh. Race constantly represents itself to black people as an apparently unending series of moments of inequality, which constantly challenge us, sapping and draining our physical, mental and moral resources.

Perhaps this is what most white Americans have never fully comprehended about "race": the racism is not just social discrimination, political disfranchisement and acts of extra-legal violence and terror which proliferated under the Jim Crow segregation of my father's South. Nor is racism the so-called "silent discrimination" faced by my generation of African-Americans raised during the civil-rights era, who are still denied access to credit and capital by unfair banking practices, or who encounter the "glass ceiling" inside businesses which limits their job advancement. As its essential core, racism is most keenly felt in its smallest manifestations: the white merchant who drops change on the sales counter, rather than touch the hand of a black person; the white salesperson who follows you into the dressing room when you carry several items of clothing to try on, because he or she suspects that you are trying to steal; the white teacher who deliberately avoids the upraised hand of a Latino student in class, giving white pupils an unspoken yet understood advantage; the white woman who wraps the strap of her purse several times tightly around her arm, just before walking past a black man; the white

[5] Activists for equal rights for blacks. Marcus Garvey (1887–1940), for example, organized the first important American-based black nationalist movement (1919–1926).

taxicab drivers who speed rapidly past African-Americans or Latinos, picking up whites on the next block. Each of these incidents, no matter how small, constructs the logic for the prism of race for the oppressed. We witness clear, unambiguous changes of behavior or language by whites toward us in public and private situations, and we code or interpret such changes as "racial." These minor actions reflect a structure of power, privilege and violence which most blacks can never forget.

The grandchildren of James Marable have never encountered Jim Crow segregation. They have never experienced signs reading "white" and "colored." They have never been refused service at lunch counters, access to hotel accommodation, restaurants or amusement parks, or admission to quality schools. They have never experienced the widespread unemployment, police brutality, substandard housing and the lack of educational opportunity which constitute the everyday lives of millions of African-American youth. For my children—eighteen-year-old Malaika, and sixteen-year old twins, Sojourner and Joshua—Martin Luther King, Jr., Medgar Evers, Fannie Lou Hamer and Ella Baker[6] are distant figures from the pages of black history books. Malcolm X is the charismatic image of Denzel Washington from Spike Lee's film, or perhaps the cinematic impression from several recent hip-hop music videos. "We shall Overcome" is an interesting but somewhat dated melody of the past, not a hopeful and militant anthem projecting an integrated America.

Yet, like my father before them, and like myself, my children are forced to view their world through the racial prism. They complain that their high-school textbooks don't have sufficient information about the activities and events related to African-Americans in the development of American society. In their classrooms, white students who claim to be their friends argue against affirmative action, insisting that the new "victims" of discrimination are overwhelmingly white and male. When Joshua goes to the shopping mall, he is followed and harassed by security guards. If he walks home alone through an affluent white neighborhood, he may be stopped by the police. White children have moved items away from the reach of my son because they have been taught the stereotype that "all blacks steal." Sojourner complains about her white teachers who have been hostile and unsympathetic toward her academic development, or who have given her lower grades for submitting virtually the identical level of work turned in by her white friends. As my daughter Malaika explains: "White people often misjudge you just by the way you look, without getting to know you. This makes me feel angry inside."

20 A new generation of African-Americans who never personally marched for civil rights or Black Power, who never witnessed the crimes of segregation, feel the same rage expressed by my father half a century ago. When they watch the beating of Rodney King on television or the trial of O.J. Simpson, they instantly comprehend the racism of the Los Angeles police officers involved in each case, and the larger racial implications of both incidents. When they

[6] Civil rights activists.

listen to members of Congress complain about "welfare dependency" and "crime," they recognize the racial stereotypes which are lurking just behind the code words. They have come to expect hypocritical behavior from the white "friends" who act cordially towards them at school but refuse to acknowledge or recognize them in another context. Race is a social force which still has real meaning to the generation of my children.

But the problem with the prism of race is that it simultaneously clarifies and distorts social reality. It both illuminates and obscures, creating false dichotomies and distinctions between people where none really exists. The constructive identity of race, the conceptual framework which the oppressed create to interpret their experiences of inequality and discrimination, often clouds the concrete reality of class, and blurs the actual structure of power and privilege. It creates tensions between oppressed groups which share common class interests, but which may have different physical appearances or colors. For example, on the recent debates concerning undocumented immigrants, a narrow racial perspective could convince African-Americans that they should be opposed to the civil rights and employment opportunities of Mexican Americans, Central Americans and other Latino people. We could see Latinos as potential competitors in the labor market rather than as allies in a struggle against corporate capital and conservatives within the political establishment. On affirmative action, a strict racist outlook might view the interest of lower-class and working-class whites as directly conflicting with programs which could increase opportunities for blacks and other people of color. The racial prism creates an illusion that "race" is permanent and finite; but, in reality, "race" is a complex expression of unequal relations which are dynamic and ever-changing. The dialectics of racial thinking pushes black people toward the logic and "us" versus "them," rather than a formulation which cuts across the perceived boundaries of color.

This observation is not a criticism of the world-views of my father, my children, or myself as I grew up in Dayton, Ohio. It is only common sense that most African-Americans perceive and interpret the basic struggle for equality and empowerment in distinctly racial terms. This perspective does speak to our experiences and social reality, but only to a portion of what that reality truly is. The parallel universes of race do not stand still. What was "black" and "white" in Booker T. Washington's Tuskegee of 1895 was not identical to categories of color and race in New Orleans a century ago; both are distinctly different from how we perceive and define race in the USA a generation after legal segregation. There is always a distance between our consciousness and the movement of social forces, between perception and historical reality. "Blackness" must inevitably be redefined in material terms ideologically, as millions of black and Hispanic people from the Caribbean, Africa and Latin America immigrate into the USA, assimilating within hundreds of urban centers and thousands of neighborhoods with other people of color. As languages, religions, cultural traditions and kinship networks among blacks in the USA become increasingly diverse and complex, our consciousness and our ideas of historical struggle against the leviathan of race also shift and move in new directions. This does not mean that "race" has declined in significance; it does mean that what we mean by "race" and how "race" is utilized as a means of dividing the oppressed are once again being transformed in many crucial respects.

At the beginning of the African presence in the Americas, an African-American culture, nationality and consciousness was constructed. Against great odds, inside the oppressive context of slavery and later racial segregation, the racial identity and perspective of resistance, a community empowered by imagination, was developed against the weight of institutional racism. That historic leap of collective self-definition and inner faith must once again occur, now inside the very different environment of mature capitalism. We must begin the process of redefining blackness in a manner which not only interprets but also transforms our world.

Explorations of the Text

1. What is Marable's purpose in his essay? What is his thesis? Paraphrase his thesis statement.
2. What autobiographical examples of the racial divide, of "the color line," are most powerful? Most persuasive? How does the inclusion of these autobiographical examples enhance the essay?
3. Contrast the world of his childhood—Dayton, Ohio—with that of his father's family home—Tuskegee, Alabama.
4. Contrast James Marable's experiences of growing up during Jim Crow segregation with that of his grandchildren.
5. Do you agree with the following statement: "At its essential core, racism is most keenly felt in its smallest manifestations. . . . These minor actions reflect a structure of power, privilege and violence which most blacks can never forget"?
6. What are Marable's conclusions about the "prism of race"? Does he propose solutions to this problem?

The Reading/Writing Connection

1. "Think" Topic: Do racial politics divide us from one another? Create a dialogue on this subject with the author.
2. Choose one statement from this essay. Agree or disagree with it in a paragraph response.

Ideas for Writing

1. Connect one of Marable's conceptions regarding the "color line" or the "prism of race" with one of the poem's about race presented in this chapter.

A Visit to the Mothers of the Plaza de Mayo

Marjorie Agosin Translated by Cola Framzen and Janice Molloy

Marjorie Agosin (1955–), born in Bethesda, Maryland, grew up in Chile, where her Jewish grandparents settled after they fled from Russia. A writer and professor of Spanish at Wellesley College, she has studied in Argentina as a Fulbright scholar. Among her writings are volumes of poetry, Witches and Other Things *(1985) and* Zones of Pain *(1988), and nonfiction,* Pablo Neruda *(1986) and* Mothers of Plaza de Maya *(1992).*

1992

Sunday in the Plaza de Mayo. August. It is almost the end of winter in South America, and the first buds are starting to swell, a sign of the spring we have all been waiting for, one that might bring an answer to one of the most overwhelming and emotional questions of the Argentinean people: the fate of those who disappeared during the evil years of the dirty war, la guerra sucia.[1]

A limpid sun lights up the Plaza de Mayo this Sunday. Young fathers and their children are feeding the pigeons. Everything looks prosperous. The women of the capital are wearing elegant leather suits this season; the children are well-dressed. All these signs of well-being give the eerie sensation that nothing unusual has happened in this plaza. The appearance of normality is deceiving, for this spot where I sit, caressed by the benign sun of early spring, is the same place that has become a major symbol of protest, witness, and denunciation of the crimes committed by the military Juntas of Argentina.

To make a brief recapitulation of recent historical events, the armed forces of Argentina took power on March 16, 1976. They dissolved all political parties; labour unions and all universities were put under government control. Public statements of the Junta declared these measures were taken "to restore order and peace to the country." Similar measures were taken in Chile in 1973 by the Pinochet dictatorship. In both countries, in addition to the official, announced measures, another level of measures was instituted: a subterranean rule began to take shape that used undeclared and unavowed methods of terror, repression, suspicion, torture, disappearance and murder to put down opposition. At first, the victims were known opponents, such as labour union members, university activists, or journalists. Later, the choice of victims was what one can only describe as random. As the crimes increased, so did the need to keep the subterranean war hidden, and the attempts to hide all traces of the horrendous actions became more outrageous. The military embarked on a kind of final solution with their policy of "disappearing" citizens in greater and greater numbers.

As unbelievable as it may seem to us now, what began as a clandestine operation became, with time, routine and bureaucratic. The squads of terror

---

[1] The *dirty war* designates the epoch beginning before the overthrow of the dictator Juan Perón in 1975 until the restoration of democracy and the election of Raúl Alfonsín as President in 1984.

settled down to using teams of men dressed in civilian clothes and driving black Falcons without license plates, who entered homes or places of work at will, in broad daylight or at night, to seize and drag off people who for one reason or another were thought to be suspicious, or who were just unlucky enough to be in that place at that time. Sometimes totally innocent individuals were taken, including children and even babies. Most of those seized went on to endure clandestine prisons, torture, disappearance and, in many cases, death. The open kidnappings sowed an atmosphere of fear and terror throughout the entire population.

5 Now the country is left to relive this painful era, to uncover what was so assiduously covered up. Where are those who disappeared without trace? What happened to the children snatched along with their parents? What happened to the babies that women carried in their arms as they went to prison? What became of the babies born to imprisoned women? We have begun to know answers to some of these questions, but not to all of them, and justice requires an answer to all questions. Mothers, grandmothers, and wives of the disappeared have been forced by tragic necessity to rescue their lost ones from the oblivion intended by the Juntas, to inquire into the destiny of the estimated 9,000 people who disappeared between 1973 and the return to democracy in 1984.

The years from 1973 to 1975 saw many disappearances as well as a series of disruptive activities carried out by urban guerrillas. The actions of both sides created such a climate of mistrust and tension in the country that, for some time, people did not know who was responsible for the kidnappings and killings. Later, it became known that paramilitary groups of the extreme right, operating under the clear protection of the military of the democratically elected Peróns, were responsible for the disappearances. It was not the urban guerrillas as the military tried to pretend.[2]

The political situation in Argentina has always been an anomaly; it is a prosperous country with many natural resources, yet has always been politically unstable. To recapitulate briefly and to shed some light on this situation, in 1930, the Argentinean armed forces overthrew the democratically elected government of Hipólito Irigoyen of the Radical Civic Union Party. Since then, the military has overthrown five other legally elected governments, and has ruled Argentina for a longer period than all of the democratic governments together.

Juan Perón was a colonel who participated in the coupo d'etat that overthrew President Ramon Carillo. He used his position as the head of the National Labour Department to take control of the developing trade unions, which he corrupted and used as a tool for his own personal gains. Perón became president for the first time in 1946 and was overthrown in 1955. In 1973 Perón, who had by then become a cult figure in Argentina, returned to power.

---

[2] It is estimated that half of the total number of disappearances, involving approximately 5,000 persons, occurred in 1976 during the first year of military rule. In 1979, another 35 percent disappeared and in 1978, 15 percent disappeared. Information obtained from the following study: Eduardo Duhalde. *El estado terroísta argentino* ("The Argentinean Terrorist State"). Madrid: Argos Vergara, 1983.

Even though Perón was chosen to be president, there were many fascists in the armed forces, and they were instrumental in the creation of the paramilitary groups even before the coup. After he died in 1974, Isabel, his second wife, became president, but on March 24, 1976 the military took power and the dirty war began. They dismissed the congress and obsessively took on the mission of ridding the country of what they referred to as subversive thought of any kind.[3]

You may be asking yourself, who were these people who disappeared? The answer is anybody at all who might possibly have been perceived as opposing the regime. One did not have to act openly against the dictatorship to be a candidate for a disappearance. One could just think one's own private thoughts and still be found guilty. Statistics show that 30 percent of the disappeared were workers, 21 percent were students, and 10 percent were professionals. The rest included anyone who happened to be caught in the net, including teenagers, housewives, and even babies, as we said earlier.

10 The world, especially a silenced and silent Argentina, has been shaken to learn, from the testimony of survivors and by subsequent excavations of unmarked graves, that the disappeared were tortured and finally killed. Many were thrown into the Rio de la Plata or into the sea from helicopters. Some of the recovered bodies showed death by drowning, that is, that the people were still alive when they were thrown out. Certain groups were subjected to especially sadistic treatment, for instance women and Jews. For the treatment of Jews in captivity, see Jacobo Timmerman's testimony in *Prisoner Without a Name, Cell Without a Number.* Women were not arrested particularly because they were women, but *because* they were women, they were subjected to rape and other violations in addition to torture in the clandestine prisons. It has been determined that a quarter of the disappeared were women, and of those, 10 percent were pregnant at the time of their arrest.

The state of limbo in which the families of the disappeared found themselves caused them to begin a quest to find their loved ones, even if only their bones.[4] In 1975, the mothers and wives of the disappeared started on a tortuous trek of searching which eventually led them to a period of reflection. When they went to police stations or jails to ask about the whereabouts of their children they were often told: "It's your own fault, Señora, for raising a subversive." Or they would say: "Your son is in the underground and is outside the country."

There are many groups of women in Latin America that have developed in authoritarian regimes. For example, in Chile a group of women formed the Asociación de Detenidos-Desaparecidos (Association of the Detained-Disappeared) in order to find their loved ones. This association was founded

[3] For further information, see: Ronald Dworkin. "Report from Hell," *The New York Times Book Review,* Volume XXXIII, Number 12:11–14.

[4] For a detailed account of the treatment of political prisoners, including testimony of survivors, see: Ernesto Sábato, editor. National Commission of the Rights of People (CONADEP). *Nunca Más* ("Never Again"). Buenos Aires: Eudena, 1984.

in 1975, and carries out a variety of protest activities, including night vigils and political marches. A similar group developed in Guatemala in 1979 called Grupo de Ayuda Mutual (Mutual Aid Group). This group consisted of about thirty women who carried out activities similar to those of the association in Chile. The groups vary in size; they usually have between 30 and 50 members. These women's groups are almost always formed by mothers, housewives who have been forced to leave their private spheres and go into the streets to find their loved ones.

Because there still exists in Argentine society the legacy of Spanish culture that treats *mothers* with a certain respect and even veneration, these mothers were treated by police and police officials with superficial politeness, but were never given a straight answer to their questions. With the guidance of leaders such as Perez Esquivel, the Argentinean human rights activist who was awarded the Nobel Peace Prize in 1981, the Mothers began to request concrete actions, such as asking for a writ of habeas corpus to be issued in specific cases. They still received no response to their requests.

The women then asked themselves, What could they do? What power did they actually possess? Who might make an impact in the face of such indifference? Who might have the information they sought? The group now known as the Mothers of the Plaza de Mayo was born in 1977 from this examination of the possibilities available to them. In the beginning, it was not a formal organization but simply a group of women who decided to join together to protest. Their protests took place then as now in this same plaza where children are playing and feeding the pigeons.

15 The Plaza de Mayo was a strategic location for a public demonstration. Here, Argentinean independence was proclaimed in 1810. Here, Juan Perón gave his populist speeches. In fact, the Plaza de Mayo is not only the heart of Buenos Aires, it is the heart of the country. The buildings that surround it include the old Cabildo, the Town Hall; the Presidential Palace called the Casa Rosada ("Pink House") because of its pink stone; and a number of other important government buildings and churches.

In the centre of the plaza, there is an obelisk that celebrates the 400th anniversary of the city's founding. On a cool April day at five o'clock in the afternoon, a few women appear in the plaza and start circling the obelisk. Each one wears a white kerchief on her head with the names of her disappeared ones embroidered around the edge, together with the date of their disappearance. The women march in absolute silence. The demonstrators, the mothers of the Plaza de Mayo, are mainly working- and middle-class women, because these groups were most affected by the repression. There are some upper-class women, but they constitute a minority.

This civic and cooperative action on the part of a handful of women without any political power, for the most part traditional housewives who had never taken part in any public action before, was the *only public protest* made for a long time against the traffickers of death in Argentina. They were the *only* ones to stand up in favor of life. In his book, *The Madwomen of the Plaza de Mayo,* Jean Pierre Bousquet expressed the significance of this first demonstration: "When on a Thursday of April of 1977 at five o'clock in the afternoon, fourteen women, between 40 and 70 years of age, defied the ban on public gatherings promulgated by the all-powerful Military Junta and marched in the Plaza de Mayo to make known their pain and their resolve not to accept having their questions go unanswered, the generals lost their first battle."[5]

The demonstrations every Thursday in the plaza are now an event, a tradition and a symbol that the Argentinean people refuse to submit to fascism, but the example was started and carried on for years by a handful of women. In the beginning, soldiers would appear and simply ask them to disperse. However, as time went on and as the demonstrations grew in size and began to have a public impact, the Junta began to make reprisals. In 1978, they kidnapped the group's first leader, Azuzena Villaflor de Vicenti, together with eleven other members of the group. At about the same time, they also kidnapped two French nuns who they later gave the sadistic name of "The Flying Nuns" because they were thrown into the sea from a helicopter after being tortured. Doña Azuzena suffered terrible tortures and martyrdom. The location of her remains is still unknown. The others kidnapped with her were finally released after an international outcry, organized mostly by the United Nations.

Regardless of this violent action against nuns, the clergy in Argentina has not been involved in protest as it has been in the case of Chile; on the contrary, the clergy has been so quiet that it has been accused of collaborating with the military. Likewise, liberation theology is not an issue for the Mothers.

At the beginning, very few women gathered; the initial number was, to be exact, thirteen. Then, other women followed, and from 1976 to the present there have usually been between 50 and 60 women marching. The same mothers march, but as the years went by and people stopped being so afraid, there were more and more people joining them. Now, people may not necessarily be mothers, but are sympathetic to the cause. The plaza activity is an outward and physical demonstration of the many things that go on in these people's lives. For example, they have weekly meetings and create new strategies of protest. These strategies vary from seeking public support in other nations to organizing national protest involving other human rights organizations. I believe the mothers have become the heroines of Argentinean society, for people realize that they were the only ones who dared to speak in a silent society. Yet they are in a difficult position with regard to President Alfonsín, because the mothers, as the voice of conscience, want all of the people responsible for the murders to be tried. Alfonsín has said that he will only try those who gave the orders.[6]

---

[5] Jean Pierre Bousquet. *Las Locas de la Plaza de Mayo.* Buenos Aires: El Cid, 1982, p. 43.

[6] As of this writing in April of 1986, the nine military officers who governed Argentina through three successive Juntas have been tried in a civilian court and sentenced. The leader of the three-man junta, Videla, received a life sentence, as did Admiral Massera. Ex-president Viola received a 17-year sentence, and ex-president Galtierei was absolved. There is bitterness at this verdict, because, for the most part, the Mothers cannot accept a compromise for the guilty ones. This is a point of contention between the Mothers and the Alfonsín regime.

What is important to remember is that the Mothers of the Plaza de Mayo have a tremendous historical importance. Even if they did not contribute directly to the fall of the military, they serve as an example to other nonviolent groups in Latin America.

It was not until 1979 that the group of women became cohesive enough to organize themselves officially into the Mothers of the Plaza de Mayo. They collected the twenty names necessary to satisfy the legal requirement to form an association at the risk of their lives. They found a location where they could meet and elect their leaders by secret ballot. The leaders have so far been women who are truly fearless, who refuse to be terrorized, and who inspire confidence in others, women such as the present leader, Hebe de Bonafini.

The Mothers began to have an international impact. Some travelled to Europe in 1979 and asked for and were granted an audience with the Pope. However, they really became known world-wide in 1978 when the World Cup Soccer competition was held in Buenos Aires, and the city was filled with journalists from all over the world. The demonstrations in the plaza were photographed and appeared in the newspapers, magazines and on the television screens of the five continents. The Mothers realized then that visibility and publicity were powerful weapons of protest. Though they had no political contacts and no previous experience in political affairs, they showed real shrewdness in planning and continuing their actions. They became more and more effective, in spite of censorship, in spite of silence, in spite of ostracism. Sometimes even members of their own families refused to have anything to do with these women because they were afraid. Many people were afraid to associate with families of the disappeared. It was considered dangerous, and undoubtedly was.

Just as the World Cup brought the cause of the Mothers to the world, a larger public began to be aware of the Argentinean atrocities and the stories of the disappeared through the Argentine movie, *The Official Story,* which tells of a typical middle-class family, unaware of the brutalities. The mother soon begins to suspect that her adopted daughter could be the child of someone who had been kidnapped and murdered. The rest of the movie involves this woman's increasing awareness of the atrocities that took place in her beloved country, and the impact that this knowledge has on her relationship with her husband and child.

25 The Mothers of the Plaza de Mayo are still visible and extremely active, even after the military was pressured to return to the barracks in 1984. The size of the demonstrations has increased with the return to democracy, even though there have been no disappearances since Alfonsín took office. The reason for this increase is that the Mothers have involved other groups in their public protest. When the Mothers are not in the Plaza, they are still attending other gatherings, always fighting, learning, reflecting. They have learned to channel their anxiety and grief into constructive paths, and to invent new political strategies. These women are priestesses—they have come to symbolize the collective conscience of the country.

Nobody can pretend not to see them. Here they are in the bright afternoon light with their white kerchiefs and with the photographs of the disappeared hanging from ribbons around their tired necks. They are willing to use women's true and ineffable recourse in their battle: the body itself as a weapon, exposed, subjected to hunger strikes, to long marches, to all sorts of abuse, at times given over to torture. Students, workers and intellectuals have begun to join them in their demonstrations. On August 2, 1985, more than 80,000 persons joined a march convened by the Mothers, and wound through the centre of Buenos Aires, shouting their slogan: "Justice and punishment for the guilty."

Through the years, the Mothers have learned by necessity to be wary, patient and persistent, and that is the prevailing attitude even now that the much discredited military has been ousted and the popular, democratically elected Alfonsín is president. As one of Alfonsín's first official acts, he appointed a Commission, headed by the writer Ernesto Sábato, to inquire into the fate of the disappeared. The Commission's results are documented in the report called *Nunca Más* (Never Again) (CONADEP, 1984). The first trial has been held, in a civilian court, of the nine major leaders of the three Juntas; the prosecutor has asked for life sentences for some and shorter sentences for others. Some might think the Mothers should be satisfied. But few of them to date have learned the fate of their own children and grandchildren. The original search goes on; their original aims remain the same, that *all* the guilty be brought to justice. They are still asking for "Life for the disappeared and punishment for the guilty." For this reason, the demonstrations of the Mothers of the Plaza de Mayo continue, even though the kidnapping, torture, killing, and imprisonment of innocent Argentineans has stopped under Alfonsín.

In the early years, the Mothers were called the "Madwomen of the Plaza de Mayo," an attempt by the generals and their cohorts to dismiss them and their claims, using the age-old technique of a male-dominated society by calling women regarded as "out of their place" crazy. As mothers, they were treated with certain deference; nevertheless, their attempts to locate their loved ones were seen as being insane actions, which diminished their importance in the eyes of the military. A few centuries ago no doubt they would have been denounced as witches. But these witches, or Madwomen, have survived, have stayed united in spite of all adversities and all divisive methods used against them, including infiltration, kidnapping, torture and murder of some of their members. One cannot detect in them any political discrepancies, nor any desires for power for power's sake. They are determined and courageous; they are witnesses who dared to speak the dreadful truth about the military government. I would like to insist once again that, for years, they acted alone. Not even the Catholic Church, as an institution, supported them, although individual clergy members did. They defied the traditional, patriarchal society as well as the military Junta when they went out into the street and became public figures, and showed themselves ready to accept all the risks implicit in such rebellious activity.

By their public actions, they have become important and influential in Latin American politics. They have learned to use old political techniques in new and dramatic ways. For instance, their silent and passive marches speak louder and more eloquently than any oration could.

30 At the present time, the Argentinean people find themselves staggered by the testimony of survivors being given in the courtrooms. And the Madwomen are now regarded as heroines because they defied the silence. They, themselves, see their work to be the same as ever—to continue to fight until the last criminal is brought to justice.

As I sit sobered by these thoughts, a woman approaches me. She tells me her parents were exterminated in Auschwitz and that her son, 30 years old, disappeared from the University of Buenos Aires. It does not help her that there is now democracy in Argentina. She is still afraid; she will always be afraid. She begs me not to use her name. How can one comprehend such misfortune? How can it be that this woman has now been a victim of two holocausts?

The House of the Mothers is located in Hipólito Irigoyen Street and was donated by the government of Holland. Other governments who might have helped them, such as the United States government, remained silent and offered no aid. When I visited the house, there was tremendous activity. The Mothers bustle about, putting up posters, organizing meetings, receiving visitors. Said one Mother, "Here, there is much pain but much love." The walls are covered with photographs of the disappeared. I notice that most are young, attractive, brimming with good health; there are many young women among them. I cannot help asking myself again, "How can a civilized society descend to such a barbarous level?"

It is Thursday. We are all on our way to the plaza. I find myself walking beside Hebe Bonafini, President of the Mothers; she makes me feel tall and strong. I can think of nothing to say to her but we smile at one another. The women gather around the obelisk, greeting one another, embracing and kissing friends. I think of their sleepless nights. They arrange themselves for another march in favour of life, in defiance of death. They tell me that, while they are marching in the plaza, they feel very close to their children. They feel their children are by their sides. And the truth is, in the plaza where forgetting is not allowed, memory recovers its meaning. Cruelty of human beings to other human beings is judged. The devastation of the young, the workers, the students, the young pregnant women and the grandmothers is remembered, denounced, mourned, judged.

The activities of the Mothers have not changed since democratization in the sense that they continue to go to marches and there still is no answer for the disappearances of their children. The biggest change in the Mothers' group is the attempt to incorporate other human rights organizations in their plight and to pressure for more immediate answers.

35 Another Thursday in August in Buenos Aires. A conspiring sun caresses our skin. The plaza is full of life and movement: couples holding hands, old people enjoying the sun, children and pigeons. The Mothers arrive, immaculate, serene and disturbing in their white kerchiefs with the embroidered

names and dates. Slowly, their healing aura spreads and creates a blue space in this plaza that is now theirs, that now has to belong to them. They form their sacred circle. Earlier, the world watched and supported them, but silent, fearful Argentina averted its eyes. Now the country joins them and weeps with them, because the Mothers fight not only for their own children but for all children. They are marching to win all rights due a free people, to make any violation of those rights unacceptable. The Mothers have a close acquaintance with death but they are completely committed to life.[7]

I wish to express special appreciation to Nora Feminia, to whom I also dedicate this work. She helped me get to know the Mothers and very generously shared her own work with me concerning women and politics in Argentina.

Explorations of the Text

1. Consider the contrasts between the descriptions of the spring and of the past events. Why does Agosin use a narrative frame for this essay?
2. Summarize the historical events presented in paragraphs 3–10. How does this context contribute to an understanding of the actions of the Mothers?
3. Describe the development of resistance to the terror. Why were the Mothers alone? Why did they persist even when some of them were tortured, imprisoned, and murdered?
4. Why did they choose the Plaza de Mayo?
5. Explain the quotation by Jean Pierre Bousquet from *The Madwomen of the Plaza de Mayo.* Does this analysis of the significance of their actions seem accurate?
6. Trace the growth of the organization of the Mothers. Why did they continue to protest after the election of President Alfonsín?
7. What was the importance of the World Cup Soccer competition in Buenos Aires in 1978? Who supported the Mothers? In what manner?
8. Analyze the symbolic language in the following quotation: "Slowly, their healing aura spreads and creates a blue space in this plaza that is now theirs, that now has to belong to them. They form their sacred circle."

---

[7] There are various books concerning the Mothers; for example, see the following books of poetry:

Juan Gelman. *La Junta Luz.* Buenos Aires: Editorial Tierra Firme, 1985.

Vicente Zito Lema. *Mater.* Buenos Aires: Editorial Tierra Firme, 1985.

Also see:

John Simpson and Jana Bennett. *The Disappeared and the Mothers of the Plaza de Mayo.* New York: St. Martin's Press, 1985.

9. Construct an outline of this essay. Does the author simply explain, or does she persuade?
10. Compare and contrast this essay with Valenzuela's story and with Forché's poems. Does Agosin's essay illuminate these other works?

The Reading/Writing Connection

1. In a journal entry, respond to the actions of the "Mothers of the Plaza de Mayo." What is the most powerful part of this story?
2. "Think" Topic: Write a monologue in the voice of one of the mothers.

Ideas for Writing

1. Summarize Agosin's essay.
2. Make connections between Luisa Valenzuela's "I'm Your Horse in the Night" and "A Visit to the Mothers of the Plaza de Mayo."
3. Analyze Agosin's essay as an example of persuasion.

Student Essay: Argument

REALIZATIONS OF THE QUEST FOR VISION: A POLITICAL INTERPRETATION

Carl Ponesse

Carl Ponesse (1967–), born in Newburgh, New York, majored in sociology at the State University of New York New Paltz. His essay presents an argument about the political implications of the quest for vision in three works: N. Scott Momaday's "A Vision Beyond Time and Place," Raymond Carver's "Cathedral," and Sophocles' Oedipus Rex. *Clearly Ponesse favors Momaday's portrait of Old Man Cheney and the spiritual and natural paths that Cheney follows. Ponesse submitted this essay as a midterm examination.*

Socrates believed that "the unexamined life is not worth living." He did not caution that the examination might lead both to vision and to suffering, both to truth and to tragedy, both to transcendence and to despair. In works by Momaday, Carver, and Sophocles the characters realize their quests for vision: each takes a different path; each reaches a different destination; each experiences a different insight; each discovers that personal vision depends upon cultural and political conditions. I would like to argue that each of these writers presents an individual quest that does or could change the body politic.

In "A Vision Beyond Time and Place," N. Scott Momaday describes old man Cheney and his folkways, which can be explained as spirituality tightly integrated with nature. This Native-American view is contrasted with western culture. In his attempt to capture the integration between Native-American society and nature, Momaday speaks of a "testament to the realization of a quest for vision."

This quest is basic to all human beings—the desire to learn, to experience, to come to an understanding of themselves and their origins. This search is determined by society, by the perception of what environment teaches and of what human beings will strive to obtain and to support.

To Momaday, Cheney achieved self-actualization. He was a "man who saw very deeply into the distance . . . one whose vision extended far beyond physical boundaries." The author explains that this vision begins with a reverence for nature, with being overcome at witnessing a sunrise. "Wonder is a principal part of such a vision," explains Momaday. Nature is a universal entity that binds all living things; to experience the wonder of a sunrise is to experience the marvel of human life. The author ties creation to nature, to that which is not seen with the naked eye, to that which has to be seen with the soul. So when the author says, "When old man Cheney looked into the sunrise he saw as far into himself," he realizes that the Native-American values are worthwhile and that the values have been lost in the westernization of our culture.

5 Momaday's differentiation among cultures starts with thoughtful descriptions of Native-American characteristics. "This native vision, this gift of seeing truly, with wonder and delight, into the natural world, is informed by a certain attitude of reference and self-respect." To take Momaday one step further and to critique the westernization of a people, look at what America now believes. In the late 1800s, when the Indians were being pushed to the reaches of the west coast, something enormous was taking hold in existing cities of the United States—The Industrial Revolution. America has since been defined by it and is responsible for its feeding, a feeding that has eaten crucial natural resources. Nature is no longer revered and nurtured. Nature has suffered a damaging, gluttonous transformation because of man's economic diet.

This change has produced a more scientifically advanced society in which wonder and imagination have been replaced by an addiction to electronic media. One work which shows how people's thoughts are dominated by electronic media is

"Cathedral." In this story by Raymond Carver, the main character is identified by secular society. He is tied to his television for entertainment, to marijuana and to alcohol for a heightened state of mind, and to his ignorance for security. He does not even realize his need for a quest for vision, though it is there, as indicated by his use of drugs to gain altered states. These activities do not make him a worthless character. Carver gives him some positive traits—honesty, humor, and a likability that stems from portraying this man, this couch potato, as a universal citizen. For example, when discussing Robert, the narrator assumes a comical, contemporary Archie Bunker attitude: "A blind man in my house was not something I looked forward to."

This character supports the argument concerning electronic media which dominate thought. Here the quest for vision is replaced by television. According to the narrator, "every night I smoked dope and stayed up as long as I could." Television sets, shows, and cinema are mentioned in more than fifteen paragraphs throughout the story. This repetition gives the appearance that this man's nights are totally dominated by the television. In the opening paragraph, he admits, "My idea of blindness came from the movies."

Later this character learns not only that the blind are intuitive, but also that there are totally new ways of experiencing ideas and thought. Robert, the blind man, is able to encourage his host to open his imagination by closing his eyes and seeing with other senses. As the two men draw a cathedral, the narrator is overwhelmed by this sensation. The incident breaks his passivity, his need to be entertained by the television, and frees his imagination. This transcendent moment arouses hope that the main character will embark on a quest for an even greater understanding of himself. "But I didn't feel like I was inside anything." As Momaday describes Cheney's vision, "It is a matter of extrasensory as well as sensory perception." Here the main character and Robert achieve this union. The ending implies that everyone can achieve such union and that our society must change so that individuals can attain their potential.

The quest for vision in *Oedipus Rex* explores another aspect of understanding—truth. In this drama, the spirituality is already formed by society. There is direct interaction among the gods and the characters. What becomes vital in this story is the search for truth that will lead to an understanding of the main character. As king of Thebes, Oedipus is given the duty by the gods to discover the truth about the murder of the previous ruler, Laius. Intertwined with this knowledge is the uncovering of unnatural behavior—incest and patricide. Although it is unknown by Oedipus, his life becomes the vehicle by which the gods enlighten the citizenry.

10 Oedipus' quest for vision is centered wholly on rescuing the city from the throes of deterioration. Through this task, Oedipus turns inward. He is indicted by the seer, Teiresias, who expatiates, "You blame my temper but you do not see your own that lives within you; it is me you chide." This accusation against Oedipus by the seer—one whose vision is not of sight but of knowledge—illuminates one of the major flaws in the character of Oedipus: he is quick to anger; he has a hot temper. For Oedipus, the quest now becomes one of further understanding himself and his place in the world.

Oedipus has the ability to find the truth. He searches for clues and for witnesses until the realization is one which is unmistakable and insufferable. His quest ends with his knowledge that he has murdered his father and married his mother, crimes which lead to his taking of his eyesight. This punishment seems instinctive. He cannot bear to see the truth; he must punish himself as he vowed; his knowledge is too burdensome. For Oedipus, his insight is linked to the god's prophecy, and, therefore, it becomes a lesson to himself and to society.

Others might contend that N. Scott Momaday simply describes and honors the Native-American view of life. Instead, he demonstrates its value for the entire culture, even though he fears that no one in the United States will hear the message. Carver's narrator experiences transcendence through his meeting with the blind man, Robert. One might interpret the story in this individual manner. Why, then, does Carver criticize the media, bigotry, self-absorption and failure to grasp our own lives, if he does not intend a larger critique and change? Sophocles can be and is interpreted as the tragedy of a great man who discovers his own blindness to the truth, a man who runs, not walks, to fulfill his destiny. However, Oedipus also is a king; and his tragedy causes the suffering of his people. His downfall teaches them a painful lesson. It is imperative to view each of these works as eloquent statements about personal and political change. Any exclusion of the political argument diminishes the achievements of these works.

In three genres—essay, fiction, and drama, the writers create characters and themes that seem intensely personal. Old man Cheney, Carver's narrator, and Oedipus all experience revelation. They find truth. However, the themes do not focus simply on one character; they focus on social critique and ultimately on political change. "The personal is the political."

Writing Assignments

1. a. Write a list of positive and negative aspects of life in the United States.
   b. Write an essay on the criticisms of the United States by Ginsberg, Hughes, Brooks, and Knight. Do these writers express hope?
2. What is the relationship between identity and politics?
3. a. Write a list of themes about war.
   b. Write about one of the themes. Refer to three works in this chapter.
4. a. Make double-entry notebooks on Forché's poems.
   b. Summarize Valenzuela's "I'm Your Horse in the Night."
   c. Outline Agosin's essay.
   d. Write a paper on political issues in Central and South America. Refer to Forché, to Valenzuela, and to Agosin. Consider the student essay in this chapter as a model.
5. Compare a work about the Second World War to one about the Vietnam War, e.g., "The War Generation," "The Things They Carried."
6. a. Annotate the works by Endō, Owen, and O'Brien. Concentrate on the soldiers' attitudes concerning war.
   b. Write an essay about the attitudes of soldiers toward war in the works you have annotated.
7. a. Discuss Marable's treatment of racism in the United States.
   b. Connect his view with two of the readings.
8. a. Write about law and justice. When is law just? When is it not?
   b. Is it ever right to disobey the law?
   c. Discuss the disobedience of Sojourner Truth or Harriet Tubman.
9. a. Define cultural history.
   b. Write about your cultural history.
   c. Compare "Three Thousand Dollar Death Song," "horse," and "Prayer to the Living. . . ."
10. a. Gloss and annotate a political protest poem in this chapter. How effectively does the poet convey his/her political message?
    b. Analyze the poem that you have glossed and annotated. How does it achieve its impact? Focus, for example, on tone, imagery, symbolism, word choice, and/or form.
11. Write about parents whose children are endangered by war. Refer to the works by Pirandello and Ozick.
12. a. Write about the horse symbolism in works by Valenzuela, Anzaldúa, Knight, and Harjo.
    b. Write about a specific instance of political terrorism. Create a symbol to represent the terror or the hope.

c. Compare Latino/Latina visions of the United States. Refer to Soto and Cisneros, in chapter 4, Espada in chapter 5, and/or Anzaldúa in this chapter.

13. a. Write about the anger and dreams of retribution in the poems by Angelou, Rose, Anzaldúa, Griffin, and Harjo.

    b. Is anger necessary for social change? Refer to three works in this chapter.

14. Write about the strength of the human spirit and the enduring dream of freedom and equality. Refer to works by Hughes, Griffin, Angelou, Forché, Ginsberg, and/or Agosin.

15. Write an essay on the statement that "Soldiers are dreamers." Refer to the works by O'Brien, Endō, and/or Valenzuela.

16. Create an antiwar argument. Use examples from works in this chapter to prove your points.

17. a. Make a list of political injustices presented in works in this chapter.

    b. Write on one writer's presentation of this issue.

    c. Support a point of view that counters the presentation of one of the works in this chapter.

18. Contrast the characters of three rebels presented in this chapter.

19. Write a research paper on one of the following topics:

    a. The history of Argentina from 1976 to 1983.

    b. Evita or Juan Perón.

    c. Langston Hughes and the Harlem Renaissance.

    d. Tim O'Brien and the Vietnam War.

    e. A conflict between a minority group and the police (e.g., the Los Angeles riots, racial profiling).

    f. The use of chemical weapons in World War I or in another conflict.

    g. Ginsberg and the Beat generation.

    h. Taoism.

    i. Some aspect of women's suffrage.

    j. Some aspect of slavery in the United States, (e.g., the Underground Railroad).

    k. A contemporary site of conflict, civil war, or injustice.

20. Analyze Sophocles's *Oedipus Rex* as a political tragedy. How does personal suffering become or cause public suffering?

21. Write about the forms of and responses to injustice in the works by Valenzuela, Rose, Sophocles, and Milosz in the Thematic Preview.

22. Choose three works from this chapter and focus on their visions of the "natural order of the world." (See Milosz's "American Ignorance of War.")

CHAPTER 8

The Global Village

"What rough beast, its hour come round at last,
Slouches towards Bethlehem to be born?"

W. B. Yeats
"The Second Coming"

We who live in the first decade of the twenty-first century know more about the millennium than William Butler Yeats divined when he imagined a disastrous future—a violent and tumultuous future—symbolized by a monstrous beast. What can we discover in the present world that Yeats could not or did not predict? What will define the next century or the next two thousand years? We can observe with certainty that all people and nations on earth exist in dynamic tensions and in flux. We can admit that Yeats was, to some degree, prophetic. Unlike Yeats, we also can speak of hope and freedom and concede that the projection of visions of the future has become more complex than anyone might have expected.

From a myriad of pressing contemporary issues, we choose to focus on Africa as an example of present tensions in a postcolonial world and of the emergence of new voices and concerns in diverse places. The conflicts between traditional and "western" values are set against a backdrop of civil war in Chinua Achebe's "Girls at War," while the violence of oppression in Africa has created generations of exiles whose views are forged in anger and in remembrance. In his poem, "A Far Cry from Africa," Derek Walcott depicts the results of "colonial policy" and describes his own divided self and divided loyalties between "this Africa" and "the English tongue [he] love[s]."

In the Thematic Preview, several works portray South Africa's system of apartheid, which had tragic consequences for all of the people who lived during that time. Nadine Gordimer's "Amnesty" depicts the effect of apartheid upon a wife who must cope with her husband's imprisonment as a political dissident. Athol Fugard's *"Master Harold" . . . and the Boys* demonstrates the depth of the ideas and practice of racial separation in the best of people. Nikky Finney's "South Africa: When a Woman Is a Rock" demonstrates the power of women to oppose persecution, and Tony Morrison's "Nobel Lecture" suggests the power of language to combat systems of oppression.

Another imperative of living with knowledge of global conflicts becomes insistent exploration and prediction of the future. We know that actions create consequences. What is the nature of the future that we have made? Some visions present dystopias, predictions of disaster, like

W. B. Yeats's warning in "The Second Coming." Wislawa Szymborska's poems, for instance, create visions of worlds in which the "center cannot hold." Kurt Vonnegut's "Harrison Bergeron" describes a world in which enforced conformity leads to the destruction of individuality. Mary Gordon's "Imagination of Disaster" portrays the ultimate catastrophe, a nuclear holocaust and its aftermath. In "Stone Olives," Judith Johnson contends that our past could be our future, that we have caused and witnessed many forms of destruction against children. The poem issues an eloquent plea for remembrance and for change.

Despite all divisiveness and violence, we find hope for the future in the works of many writers. Rainer Maria Rilke demonstrates his belief in the continuous process of transformation as hope for the future, and Rabindranath Tagore engulfs us in the joy and harmony in each life and in the desire to connect with both others and divinity.

Along with the quest for spiritual meaning, humankind has searched for and continues to construct metaphysical systems in order to explain ultimate reality. Two contrasting views were created by Plato in the fifth century B.C. and by Albert Camus in the twentieth century. In "The Allegory of the Cave" from *The Republic,* Plato distinguishes between a world of shadows and his concept of the real world in order to teach people that which is both beautiful and good. Camus, writing from an existential perspective, claims that humans, inhabiting an absurd and meaningless world, remain capable of acts of insight and of will that become redemptive.

Writers also invent myths for human interdependence and community. Adrienne Rich rejects the old "book of myths" in "Diving into the Wreck." As the speaker plunges into the sea to find the sunken ship, "the wreck," she envisions a new world of androgyny in which differences between women and men may be resolved. In Gabriel García Márquez's "The Handsomest Drowned Man in the World," the villagers, through the ceremony of burial, affirm community and the possibility of love through human connection.

We complete this anthology with dreams of renewal. Anna Lee Walters describes a life force, a spirit, that will rejuvenate, as does Mary Oliver in "Ghosts." Moreover, both Terry Tempest Williams in "The Wild Card" and Alice Walker in "Am I Blue?" espouse philosophies of social change and renewal. Still, we balance these versions of rebirth with a cautionary view. Edward Said demands that the reader remember that each of us lives in a state that Gloria Anzaldúa names the "borderlands." Her poem demonstrates that we exist without borders at "crossroads" in a global village that the narrator in Jhumpa Lahiri's "The Third and Final Continent" and the speaker in Agha Shahid Ali's "Postcard from Kashmir" know all too well. We may go back in time to William Shakespeare's *The Tempest* to see this "crossroads" depicted in another way, to witness the collision of old and new worlds and its consequences for creating a harmonious society. Perhaps this place at the "crossroads"—a place envisioned by artists across four centuries—offers us the greatest challenge and the greatest possibilities for visions of community for the twenty-first century.

THEMATIC PREVIEW: COMBINING THE GENRES

AMNESTY

Nadine Gordimer

Nadine Gordimer (1923–) was born in Johannesburg, South Africa. Her first novel, The Lying Days *(1953), is a semi-autobiographical narrative of a young South African woman. Her other novels include* Burgher's Daughter *(1979),* A Sport of Nature *(1987), and* My Son's Story *(1991). Her short stories are collected in* Selected Stories *(1975) and* Jump, and Other Stories *(1991). Gordimer's fiction is acclaimed for its attempt to deal with the complex sociopolitical realities of life in South Africa in a thoughtful, nuanced manner. She was awarded the Nobel Prize for Literature in 1991.*

1991

When we heard he was released I ran all over the farm and through the fence to our people on the next farm to tell everybody. I only saw afterwards I'd torn my dress on the barbed wire, and there was a scratch, with blood, on my shoulder.

He went away from this place nine years ago, signed up to work in town with what they call a construction company—building glass walls up to the sky. For the first two years he came home for the weekend once a month and two weeks at Christmas; that was when he asked my father for me. And he began to pay. He and I thought that in three years he would have paid enough for us to get married. But then he started wearing that T-shirt, he told us he'd joined the union, he told us about the strike, how he was one of the men who went to talk to the bosses because some others had been laid off after the strike. He's always been good at talking, even in English—he was the best at the farm school, he used to read the newspapers the Indian wraps soap and sugar in when you buy at the store.

There was trouble at the hostel where he had a bed, and riots over paying rent in the townships and he told me—just me, not the old ones—that wherever people were fighting against the way we are treated they were doing it for all of us, on the farms as well as the towns, and the unions were with them, he was with them, making speeches, marching. The third year, we heard he was in prison. Instead of getting married. We didn't know where to find him, until he went on trial. The case was heard in a town far away. I couldn't go often to the court because by that time I had passed my Standard 8 and I was working in the farm school. Also my parents were short of money. Two of my brothers who had gone away to work in town didn't send home; I suppose they lived with girl-friends and had to buy things for them. My father and other brother work here for the Boer and the pay is very small, we have two goats, a few cows we're allowed to graze, and a patch of land where my mother can grow vegetables. No cash from that.

When I saw him in the court he looked beautiful in a blue suit with a striped shirt and brown tie. All the accused—his comrades, he said—were well-dressed. The union bought the clothes so that the judge and the prosecutor would know they weren't dealing with stupid *yes-baas* black men who didn't know their rights. These things and everything else about the court and trial he explained to me when I was allowed to visit him in jail. Our little girl was born while the trial went on and when I brought the baby to court the first time to show him, his comrades hugged him and then hugged me across the barrier of the prisoners' dock and they had clubbed together to give me some money as a present for the baby. He chose the name for her Inkululeko.

5 Then the trial was over and he got six years. He was sent to the Island.[1] We all knew about the Island. Our leaders had been there so long. But I have never seen the sea except to colour it in blue at school, and I couldn't imagine a piece of earth surrounded by it. I could only think of a cake of dung, dropped by the cattle, floating in a pool of rain-water they'd crossed, the water showing the sky like a looking-glass, blue. I was ashamed only to think that. He had told me how the glass walls showed the pavement trees and the other buildings in the street and the colours of the cars and the clouds as the crane lifted him on a platform higher and higher through the sky to work at the top of a building.

He was allowed one letter a month. It was my letter because his parents didn't know how to write. I used to go to them where they worked on another farm to ask what message they wanted to send. The mother always cried and put her hands on her head and said nothing, and the old man, who preached to us in the veld every Sunday, said tell my son we are praying, God will make everything all right for him. Once he wrote back, That's the trouble—our people on the farms, they're told God will decide what's good for them so that they won't find the force to do anything to change their lives.

After two years had passed, we—his parents and I—had saved up enough money to go to Cape Town[2] to visit him. We went by train and slept on the floor at the station and asked the way, next day, to the ferry. People were kind; they all knew that if you wanted the ferry it was because you had somebody of yours on the Island.

And there it was—there was the sea. It was green *and* blue, climbing and falling, bursting white, all the way to the sky. A terrible wind was slapping it this way and that; it hid the Island, but people like us, also waiting for the ferry, pointed where the Island must be, far out in the sea that I never thought would be like it really was.

There were other boats, and ships as big as building that go to other places, all over the world, but the ferry is only for the Island, it doesn't go anywhere else in the world, only to the Island. So everybody waiting there was

[1] Robben Island, located off Cape Town, South Africa, the prison where black political prisoners—opponents of apartheid—were incarcerated.

[2] The capital of the Republic of South Africa.

waiting for the Island, there could be no mistake we were not in the right place. We had sweets and biscuits, trousers and a warm coat for him (a woman standing with us said we wouldn't be allowed to give him the clothes) and I wasn't wearing, any more, the old beret pulled down over my head that farm girls wear, I had bought relaxer cream from the man who comes round the farms selling things out of a box on his bicycle, and my hair was combed up thick under a flowered scarf that didn't cover the gold-coloured rings in my ears. His mother had her blanket tied round her waist over her dress, a farm woman, but I looked just as good as any of the other girls there. When the ferry was ready to take us, we stood all pressed together and quiet like the cattle waiting to be let through a gate. One man kept looking round with his chin moving up and down, he was counting, he must have been afraid there were too many to get on and he didn't want to be left behind. We all moved up to the policeman in charge and everyone ahead of us went onto the boat. But when our turn came and he put out his hand for something, I didn't know what.

10 We didn't have a permit. We didn't know that before you come to Cape Town, before you come to the ferry for the Island, you have to have a police permit to visit a prisoner on the Island. I tried to ask him nicely. The wind blew the voice out of my mouth.

We were turned away. We saw the ferry rock, bumping the landing where we stood, moving, lifted and dropped by all that water, getting smaller and smaller until we didn't know if we were really seeing it or one of the birds that looked black, dipping up and down, out there.

The only good thing was one of the other people took the sweets and biscuits for him. He wrote and said he got them. But it wasn't a good letter. Of course not. He was cross with me; I should have found out, I should have known about the permit. He was right—I bought the train tickets, I asked where to go for the ferry, I should have known about the permit. I have passed Standard 8. There was an advice office to go to in town, the churches ran it, he wrote. But the farm is so far from town, we on the farms don't know about these things. It was as he said; our ignorance is the way we are kept down, this ignorance must go.

We took the train back and we never went to the Island—never saw him in the three more years he was there. Not once. We couldn't find the money for the train. His father died and I had to help his mother from my pay. For our people the worry is always money, I wrote. When will we ever have money? Then he sent such a good letter. That's what I'm on the Island for, far away from you, I'm here so that one day our people will have the things they need, land, food, the end of ignorance. There was something else—I could just read the word "power" the prison had blacked out. All his letters were not just for me; the prison officer read them before I could.

He was coming home after only five years!

15 That's what it seemed to me, when I heard—the five years were suddenly disappeared—nothing!—there was no whole year still to wait. I showed my—our—little girl his photo again. That's your daddy, he's coming, you're going

to see him. She told the other children at school, I've got a daddy, just as she showed off about the kid goat she had at home.

We wanted him to come at once, and at the same time we wanted time to prepare. His mother lived with one of his uncles; now that his father was dead there was no house of his father for him to take me to as soon as we married. If there had been time, my father would have cut poles, my mother and I would have baked bricks, cut thatch, and built a house for him and me and the child.

We were not sure what day he would arrive. We only heard on my radio his name and the names of some other who were released. Then at the Indian's store I noticed the newspaper, *The Nation,* written by black people, and on the front a picture of a lot of people dancing and waving—I saw at once it was at that ferry. Some men were being carried on other men's shoulders. I couldn't see which one was him. We were waiting. The ferry had brought him from the Island but we remembered Cape Town is a long way from us. Then he did come. On a Saturday, no school, so I was working with my mother, hoeing and weeding round the pumpkins and mealies, my hair, that I meant to keep nice, tied in an old *doek.* A combi came over the veld and his comrades had brought him. I wanted to run away and wash but he stood there stretching his legs, calling, hey! hey! with his comrades making a noise around him, and my mother started shrieking in the old style aie! aie! and my father was clapping and stamping towards him. He held his arms open to us, this big man in town clothes, polished shoes, and all the time while he hugged me I was holding my dirty hands, full of mud, away from him behind his back. His teeth hit me hard through his lips, he grabbed at my mother and she struggled to hold the child up to him. I thought we would all fall down! Then everyone was quiet. The child hid behind my mother. He picked her up but she turned her head away to her shoulder. He spoke to her gently but she wouldn't speak to him. She's nearly six years old! I told her not to be a baby. She said, That's not him.

The comrades all laughed, we laughed, she ran off and he said, She has to have time to get used to me.

He has put on weight, yes; a lot. You couldn't believe it. He used to be so thin his feet looked too big for him. I used to feel his bones but now—that night—when he lay on me he was so heavy, I didn't remember it was like that. Such a long time. It's strange to get stronger in prison; I though he wouldn't have enough to eat and would come out weak. Everyone said, Look at him—he's a man, now. He laughed and banged his fist on his chest, told them how the comrades exercised in their cells, he would run three miles a day, stepping up and down on one place on the floor of that small cell where he was kept. After we were together at night we used to whisper a long time but now I can feel he's thinking of some things I don't know and I can't worry him with talk. Also I don't know what to say. To ask him what it was like, five years shut away there; or to tell him something about school or about the child. What else has happened, here? Nothing. Just waiting. Sometimes in the daytime I do try to tell him what it was like for me, here at home on the farm, five years. He listens, he's interested, just like he's interested when people from the other farms come to visit and talk to him about little things that happened to them while he was away all that time on the Island. He smiles and nods, asks a couple of questions and then stands up and stretches. I see it's to show them it's enough, his mind is going back to something he was busy with before they came. And we farm people are very slow; we tell things slowly, he used to, too.

He hasn't signed on for another job. But he can't stay at home with us; we thought, after five years over there in the middle of that green and blue sea, so far, he would rest with us a little while. The combi or some car comes to fetch him and he says don't worry, I don't know what day I'll be back. At first I asked, what week, next week? He tried to explain to me: in the Movement it's not like it was in the union, where you do your work every day and after that you are busy with meetings; in the Movement you never know where you will have to go and what is going to come up next. And the same with money. In the Movement, it's not like a job, with regular pay—I know that, he doesn't have to tell me—it's like it was going to the Island, you do it for all our people who suffer because we haven't got money, we haven't got land—look, he said, speaking of my parents', my home, the home that has been waiting for him, with his child: look at this place where the white man owns the ground and lets you squat in mud and tin huts here only as long as you work for him—*Baba* and your brother planting his crops and looking after his cattle, Mama cleaning his house and you in the school without even having the chance to train properly as a teacher. The farmer owns us, he says.

I've been thinking we haven't got a home because there wasn't time to build a house before he came from the Island: but we haven't got a home at all. Now I've understood that.

I'm not stupid. When the comrades come to this place in the combi to talk to him here I don't go away with my mother after we've brought them tea or (if she's made it for the weekend) beer. They like her beer, they talk about our culture and there's one of them who makes a point of putting his arm around my mother, calling her the mama of all of them, the mama of Africa. Sometimes they please her very much by telling her how they used to sing on the Island and getting her to sing an old song we all know from our grandmothers. They join in with their strong voices. My father doesn't like this noise travelling across the veld; he's afraid that if the Boer finds out my man is a political, from the Island, and he's holding meetings on the Boer's land, he'll tell my father to go, and take his family with him. But my brother says if the Boer asks anything just tell him it's a prayer meeting. Then the singing is over; my mother knows she must go away into the house.

I stay, and listen. He forgets I'm there when he's talking and arguing about something I can see is important, more important than anything we could ever have to say to each other when we're alone. But now and then, when one of the other comrades is speaking I see him look at me for a moment the way I will look up at one of my favourite children in school to encourage the child to understand. The men don't speak to me and I don't speak. One of the things they talk about is organizing the people on the farms—the workers, like my father and brother, and like his parents used to be. I learn what all these things are: minimum wage, limitation of working hours, the right to strike, annual leave, accident compensation, pensions, sick and even maternity leave. I am pregnant, at last I have another child inside me, but that's women's business. When they talk about the Big Man, the Old Men, I know who these are: our leaders are also back from prison. I told him about the child coming; he said, And this one belongs to a new country, he'll build the freedom we've fought for! I know he wants to get married but there's no time for that at present. There was hardly time for him to make the child. He comes to me just like he comes here to eat a meal or put on clean clothes. Then he picks up the little girl and swings her round and there!—it's done, he's getting into the combi, he's already turning to his comrade that face of his that knows only what's inside his head, those eyes that move quickly as if he's chasing something you can't see. The little girl hasn't had time to get used to this man. But I know she'll be proud of him, one day!

How can you tell that to a child six years old. But I tell her about the Big Man and the Old Men, our leaders so she'll know that her father was with them on the Island, this man is a great man, too.

25 On Saturday, no school and I plant and weed with my mother, she sings but I don't; I think. On Sunday there's no work, only prayer meetings out of the farmer's way under the trees, and beer drinks at the mud and tin huts where the farmers allow us to squat on their land. I go off on my own as I used to do when I was a child, making up games and talking to myself where no one would hear me or look for me. I sit on a warm stone in the late afternoon, high up, and the whole valley is a path between the hills, leading away from my feet. It's the Boer's farm but that's not true, it belongs to nobody. The cattle don't know that anyone says he owns it, the sheep—they are grey stones, and then they become a thick grey snake moving—don't know. Our huts and the old mulberry tree and the little brown mat of earth that my mother dug over yesterday, way down there, and way over there the clump of trees round the chimneys and the shiny thing that is the TV mast of the farmhouse—they are nothing, on the back of this earth. It could twitch them away like a dog does a fly.

I am up with the clouds. The sun behind me is changing the colours of the sky and the clouds are changing themselves, slowly, slowly. Some are pink, some are white, swelling like bubbles. Underneath is a bar of grey, not enough to make rain. It gets longer and darker, it grows a thin snout and long body and then the end of it is a tail. There's a huge grey rat moving across the sky, eating the sky.

The child remembered the photo; she said *That's not him.* I'm sitting here where I came often when he was on the Island. I came to get away from the others, to wait by myself.

I'm watching the rat, it's losing itself, its shape, eating the sky, and I'm waiting. Waiting for him to come back.

Waiting.

30 I'm waiting to come back home.

Exploration of the Text

1. Describe the narrator's perspective and point of view. How does this narrative perspective suggest the conflict between the husband and wife?
2. Discuss the conflict between the husband and wife. Contrast their philosophies of life.
3. Gordimer describes in detail the facts of the narrator's daily life. Why does she include these specifics?
4. Analyze the images describing "the Island."
5. What is the meaning of the closing image of the story: the "huge grey rat moving across the sky"?
6. What are the ironies of the title?
7. Compare the treatment of gender in this story with that of the poem, "South Africa: When a Woman Is a Rock."

The Reading/Writing Connection

1. "Think" Topic: In a paragraph, contrast the philosophies of life of the husband and of the wife.
2. Journal Entry: What does the work reveal about life in South Africa during apartheid?

Ideas for Writing

1. Summarize the husband's and the wife's positions. Who is right? Is anyone right?
2. Analyze themes in "Amnesty."
3. Compare this story and *"Master Harold" . . . and the Boys.* How do characterization and conflict develop theme?

South Africa: When a Woman Is a Rock

Nikky Finney

Nikky Finney (1957–) was born in Conway, South Carolina. After being educated at Talladega College, she published her first book of poems, On Wings Made of Gauze, *in 1985. Her subsequent work includes* Rice *(1995). A founding member of the Affrilachian Poets, Finney teaches at the University of Kentucky.*

1995

They always put their hands on the women first
They do this for a living

They do it to make a point
cutting away the heart
leaves a hole
big enough for bullets to crawl through

The children are prepared for school
while the ground is prepared for the children
in mourning circles the women gather
they think of a number between one and ten
then guess aloud
then pray they are wrong

Whose names go here
The shoveling dirt asks
whose tiny back fits
This bloody ground
which infant heart is next

They strike the gentle angry women first
and when they do
They do not know
They are touching rock

Lillian Ngoyi
Albertina Sisulu
Florence Matomela[1]

are there
raising the hands   the heads
of the twenty million
who wear coffin lines
like bracelets
on their shoulders

Yea   Swazi
Yea   Xhosa

Yea   Venda
Yea   Zulu[2]

all our rivers are red
and your stomping skips
like a pebble across the Atlantic
it is family here that knows

---

[1] South African freedom fighters.

[2] Native peoples of South Afica.

They have more than touched
The gentle angry women
on the frontlines
where our children are illegal
our men banished
where land offered is no homeland
and boulders born from pebbles
fall instead

Francina Baard
Mary Moodley
Winnie Mandela[3]

ain't no running to the rock
to hide your face
cause rocks will cry out
no hiding place

Yea Swazi   Yea Xhosa
Yea Venda   Yea Zulu

The gentlest
The angriest
The women
live beyond sea level

and

"A nation is never conquered
until the hearts of its women
are on the ground."[4]

Exploration of the Text

1. Who are "they" in the poem?
2. What characterizes the position of the women? The power of women?
3. Discuss the significance of the title.
4. Compare the views of oppression, social protest, and resistance suggested in the work with the other works in the Thematic Preview.

[3] South African freedom fighters.

[4] Native Indian proverb.

The Reading/Writing Connection

1. "Think" Topic: Do you agree with the following quotation: "A nation is never conquered/until the hearts of its women/are on the ground"? Respond to this question in a paragraph.

Ideas for Writing

1. Compare the portrayal of women in this poem with that of the woman in "Amnesty."

"Master Harold" . . . and the Boys

Athol Fugard

Athol Fugard (1932–), born in South Africa, has spent most of his life in Port Elizabeth. His 1961 production of The Blood Knot *was considered shocking because it was the first time black and white actors shared the stage in South Africa. In addition to his many award-winning plays, which include* Boesman and Lena *(1969),* A Lesson from Aloes *(1978), and* The Road to Mecca *(1984), Fugard has written scripts, including those for* Gandhi *(1982) and* The Killing Fields *(1984). In his* Notebooks: 1960–1977, *Fugard describes the relationship between himself and Sam on which he based* "Master Harold" . . . and the Boys, *recalling that Sam was his best friend during his boyhood. Fugard recounts being overwhelmed with shame at his betrayal of his friend.*

1982

The St. George's Park Tea Room on a wet and windy Port Elizabeth[1] afternoon.

Tables and chairs have been cleared and are stacked on one side except for one which stands apart with a single chair. On this table a knife, fork, spoon and side plate in anticipation of a simple meal, together with a pile of comic books.

Other elements: a serving counter with a few stale cakes under glass and a not very impressive display of sweets, cigarettes and cool drinks, etc.; a few cardboard advertising handouts—Cadbury's Chocolate, Coca-Cola—and a blackboard on which an untrained hand has chalked up the prices of Tea, Coffee, Scones, Milkshakes—all flavors—and Cool Drinks; a few sad ferns in pots; a telephone; an old-style jukebox.

There is an entrance on one side and an exit into a kitchen on the other.

[1] Southeastern South African city on the Indian Ocean.

Leaning on the solitary table, his head cupped in one hand as he pages through one of the comic books, is Sam. A black man in his mid-forties. He wears the white coat of a waiter. Behind him on his knees, mopping down the floor with a bucket of water and a rag, is Willie. Also black and about the same age as Sam. He has his sleeves and trousers rolled up.

The year: 1950

Willie *(Singing as he works.):*

"She was scandalizin' my name,
She took my money
She called me honey
But she was scandalizin' my name.
Called it love but was playin' a game . . ."

(He gets up and moves the bucket. Stands thinking for a moment, then, raising his arms to hold an imaginary partner, he launches into an intricate ballroom dance step. Although a mildly comic figure, he reveals a reasonable degree of accomplishment.)

Hey, Sam.

(Sam, absorbed in the comic book, does not respond.)

Hey, Boet Sam!

(Sam looks up.)

I'm getting it. The quickstep. Look now and tell me. *(He repeats the step.)* Well?

Sam *(Encouragingly.):* Show me again.

Willie: Okay, count for me.

Sam: Ready?

Willie: Ready.

Sam: Five, six, seven, eight . . . *(Willie starts to dance.)* A-n-d one two three four . . . and one two three four. . . . *(Ad libbing as Willie dances.)* Your shoulders, Willie . . . your shoulders! Don't look down! Look happy, Willie! Relax, Willie!

Willie *(Desperate but still dancing.):* I am relax.

Sam: No, you're not.

Willie *(He falters.):* Ag no man, Sam! Mustn't talk. You make me make mistakes.

Sam: But you're too stiff.

Willie: Yesterday I'm not straight . . . today I'm too stiff!

Sam: Well, you are. You asked me and I'm telling you.

Willie: Where?

Sam: Everywhere. Try to glide through it.

Willie: Glide?

Sam: Ja, make it smooth. And give it more style. It must look like you're enjoying yourself.

Willie *(Emphatically.)*: I wasn't.

Sam: Exactly.

Willie: How can I enjoy myself? Not straight, too stiff and now it's also glide, give it more style, make it smooth. . . . Haai! Is hard to remember all those things, Boet Sam.

Sam: That's your trouble. You're trying too hard.

Willie: I try hard because it *is* hard.

Sam: But don't let me see it. The secret is to make it look easy. Ballroom must look happy, Willie, not like hard work. It must . . . Ja! . . . it must look like romance.

Willie: Now another one! What's romance?

Sam: Love story with happy ending. A handsome man in tails, and in his arms, smiling at him, a beautiful lady in evening dress!

Willie: Fred Astaire, Ginger Rogers.[2]

Sam: You got it. Tapdance or ballroom, it's the same. Romance. In two weeks' time when the judges look at you and Hilda, they must see a man and a woman who are dancing their way to a happy ending. What I saw was you holding her like you were frightened she was going to run away.

Willie: Ja! Because that is what she wants to do! I got no romance left for Hilda anymore, Boet Sam.

Sam: Then pretend. When you put your arms around Hilda, imagine she is Ginger Rogers.

Willie: With no teeth? You try.

Sam: Well, just remember, there's only two weeks left.

Willie: I know, I know! *(To the jukebox.)* I do it better with music. You got sixpence for Sarah Vaughan?[3]

Sam: That's a slow foxtrot. You're practicing the quickstep.

Willie: I'll practice slow foxtrot.

Sam *(Shaking his head.)*: It's your turn to put money in the jukebox.

Willie: I only got bus fare to go home. *(He returns disconsolately to his work.)* Love story and happy ending! She's doing it all right, Boet Sam, but is not me she's giving happy endings. Fuckin' whore! Three nights now she doesn't come practice. I wind up gramophone, I get record ready and I sit and wait. What happens? Nothing. Ten o'clock I start dancing with my pillow. You try and practice romance by yourself, Boet Sam. Struesgod, she doesn't come tonight I take back my dress and ballroom shoes and I find me new partner. Size twenty-six. Shoes size seven. And now she's also making trouble for me with the baby again. Reports me to Child Wellfed, that I'm not giving her money. She lies! Every week I am giving her money for milk. And how do I know is my baby? Only his hair looks like me. She's fucking around all the time I turn my back. Hilda Samuels is a bitch! *(Pause.)* Hey, Sam!

Sam: Ja.

---

[2] North American dancers and movie stars. [3] Jazz singer.

Willie: You listening?

Sam: Ja.

Willie: So what you say?

Sam: About Hilda?

Willie: Ja.

Sam: When did you last give her a hiding?

Willie *(Reluctantly.):* Sunday night.

Sam: And today is Thursday.

Willie *(He knows what's coming.):* Okay.

Sam: Hiding on Sunday night, then Monday, Tuesday and Wednesday she doesn't come to practice . . . and you are asking me why?

Willie: I said okay, Boet Sam!

Sam: You hit her too much. One day she's going to leave you for good.

Willie: So? She makes me the hell-in too much.

Sam *(Emphasizing his point.): Too* much and *too* hard. You had the same trouble with Eunice.

Willie: Because she also make the hell-in, Boet Sam. She never got the steps right. Even the waltz.

Sam: Beating her up every time she makes a mistake in the waltz? *(Shaking his head.)* No, Willie! That takes the pleasure out of ballroom dancing.

Willie: Hilda is not too bad with the waltz, Boet Sam. Is the quickstep where the trouble starts.

Sam *(Teasing him gently.):* How's your pillow with the quickstep?

Willie *(Ignoring the tease.):* Good! And why? Because it got no legs. That's her trouble. She can't move them quick enough, Boet Sam. I start the record and before halfway Count Basie[4] is already winning. Only time we catch up with him is when gramophone runs down.

(Sam laughs.)

Haaikona, Boet Sam, is not funny.

Sam *(Snapping his fingers.):* I got it! Give her a handicap.

Willie: What's that?

Sam: Give her a ten-second start and then let Count Basie go. Then I put my money on her. Hot favorite in the Ballroom Stakes: Hilda Samuels ridden by Willie Malopo.

Willie *(Turning away.):* I'm not talking to you no more.

Sam *(Relenting.):* Sorry, Willie . . .

Willie: It's finish between us.

Sam: Okay, okay . . . I'll stop.

Willie: You can also fuck off.

Sam: Willie, listen! I want to help you!

Willie: No more jokes?

Sam: I promise.

---

[4] U.S. jazz musician, composer, and bandleader (1904–84).

Willie: Okay. Help me.

Sam *(His turn to hold an imaginary partner.):* Look and learn. Feet together. Back straight. Body relaxed. Right hand placed gently in the small of her back and wait for the music. Don't start worrying about making mistakes or the judges or the other competitors. It's just you, Hilda and the music, and you're going to have a good time. What Count Basie do you play?

Willie: "You the cream in my coffee, you the salt in my stew."

Sam: Right. Give it to me in strict tempo.

Willie: Ready?

Sam: Ready.

Willie: A-n-d . . . *(Singing.)*

"You the cream in my coffee.
You the salt in my stew.
You will always be my
necessity.
I'd be lost without
you. . . ." *(etc.)*

(Sam launches into the quickstep. He is obviously a much more accomplished dancer than Willie. Hally enters. A seventeen-year-old white boy. Wet raincoat and school case. He stops and watches Sam. The demonstration comes to an end with a flourish. Applause from Hally and Willie.)

Hally: Bravo! No question about it. First place goes to Mr. Sam Semela.

Willie *(In total agreement.):* You was gliding with style, Boet Sam.

Hally *(Cheerfully.):* How's it, chaps?

Sam: Okay, Hally.

Willie *(Springing to attention like a soldier and saluting.):* At your service, Master Harold!

Hally: Not long to the big event, hey!

Sam: Two weeks.

Hally: You nervous?

Sam: No.

Hally: Think you stand a chance?

Sam: Let's just say I'm ready to go out there and dance.

Hally: It looked like it. What about you, Willie?

(Willie groans.)

What's the matter?

Sam: He's got leg trouble.

Hally *(Innocently.):* Oh, sorry to hear that, Willie.

Willie: Boet Sam! You promised. *(Willie returns to his work.)*

(Hally deposits his school case and takes off his raincoat. His clothes are a little neglected and untidy: black blazer with school badge, gray flannel trousers in need of an ironing, khaki shirt and tie, black shoes. Sam has fetched a towel for Hally to dry his hair.)

Hally: God, what a lousy bloody day. It's coming down cats and dogs out there. Bad for business, chaps . . . *(Conspiratorial whisper.)* . . . but it also means we're in for a nice quiet afternoon.

Sam: You can speak loud, your Mom's not here.

Hally: Out shopping?

Sam: No. The hospital.

Hally: But it's Thursday. There's no visiting on Thursday afternoons. Is my Dad okay?

Sam: Sounds like it. In fact, I think he's going home.

Hally *(Stopped short by Sam's remark.)*: What do you mean?

Sam: The hospital phoned.

Hally: To say what?

Sam: I don't know. I just heard your Mom talking.

Hally: So what makes you say he's going home?

Sam: It sounded as if they were telling her to come and fetch him.

(Hally thinks about what Sam has said for a few seconds.)

Hally: When did she leave?

Sam: About an hour ago. She said she would phone you. Want to eat?

(Hally doesn't respond.)

Hally, want your lunch?

Hally: I suppose so. *(His mood has changed.)* What's on the menu? . . . as if I don't know.

Sam: Soup, followed by meat pie and gravy.

Hally: Today's?

Sam: No.

Hally: And the soup?

Sam: Nourishing pea soup.

Hally: Just the soup. *(The pile of comic books on the table.)* And these?

Sam: For your Dad. Mr. Kempston brought them.

Hally: You haven't been reading them, have you?

Sam: Just looking.

Hally *(Examining the comics.)*: *Jungle Jim . . . Batman and Robin . . . Tarzan*[5] . . . God, what rubbish! Mental pollution. Take them away.

(Sam exits waltzing into the kitchen. Hally turns to Willie.)

Hally: Did you hear my Mom talking on the telephone, Willie?

Willie: No, Master Hally. I was at the back.

Hally: And she didn't say anything to you before she left?

Willie: She said I must clean the floors.

Hally: I mean about my Dad.

Willie: She didn't say nothing to me about him, Master Hally.

[5] Comic book characters.

Hally *(With conviction.):* No! It can't be. They said he needed at least another three weeks of treatment. Sam's definitely made a mistake. *(Rummages through his school case, finds a book and settles down at the table to read.)* So, Willie!

Willie: Yes, Master Hally! Schooling okay today?

Hally: Yes, okay. . . . *(He thinks about it.)* . . . No, not really. Ag, what's the difference? I don't care. And Sam says you've got problems.

Willie: Big problems.

Hally: Which leg is sore?

(Willie groans.)

Both legs.

Willie: There is nothing wrong with my legs. Sam is just making jokes.

Hally: So then you *will* be in the competition.

Willie: Only if I can find me a partner.

Hally: But what about Hilda?

Sam *(Returning with a bowl of soup.):* She's the one who's got trouble with her legs.

Hally: What sort of trouble, Willie?

Sam: From the way he describes it, I think the lady has gone a bit lame.

Hally: Good God! Have you taken her to see a doctor?

Sam: I think a vet would be better.

Hally: What do you mean?

Sam: What do you call it again when a racehorse goes very fast?

Hally: Gallop?

Sam: That's it!

Willie: Boet Sam!

Hally: "A gallop down the homestretch to the winning post." But what's that got to do with Hilda?

Sam: Count Basie always gets there first.

(Willie lets fly with his slop rag. It misses Sam and hits Hally.)

Hally *(Furious.):* For Christ's sake, Willie! What the hell do you think you're doing!

Willie: Sorry, Master Hally, but it's him. . . .

Hally: Act your bloody age! *(Hurls the rag back at Willie.)* Cut out the nonsense now and get on with your work. And you too, Sam. Stop fooling around.

(Sam moves away.)

No. Hang on. I haven't finished! Tell me exactly what my Mom said.

Sam: I have. "When Hally comes, tell him I've gone to the hospital and I'll phone him."

Hally: She didn't say anything about taking my Dad home?

Sam: No. It's just that when she was talking on the phone . . .

Hally *(Interrupting him.):* No, Sam. They can't be discharging him. She would have said so if they were. In any case, we saw him last night and he wasn't in good shape at all. Staff nurse even said there was talk about taking more X-rays. And now suddenly today he's better? If anything, it sounds more like a bad turn to me . . . which I sincerely hope it isn't. Hang on . . . how long ago did you say she left?

Sam: Just before two . . . *(His wrist watch.)* . . . hour and a half.

Hally: I know how to settle it. *(Behind the counter to the telephone. Talking as he dials.)* Let's give her ten minutes to get to the hospital, ten minutes to load him up, another ten, at the most, to get home and another ten to get him inside. Forty minutes. They should have been home for at least half an hour already. *(Pause—he waits with the receiver to his ear.)* No reply, chaps. And you know why? Because she's at his bedside in hospital helping him pull through a bad turn. You definitely heard wrong.

Sam: Okay.

(As far as Hally is concerned, the matter is settled. He returns to his table, sits down and divides his attention between the book and his soup. Sam is at his school case and picks up a textbook, Modern Graded Mathematics for Standards Nine and Ten. *Opens it at random and laughs at something he sees.)*

Who is this supposed to be?

Hally: Old fart-face Prentice.

Sam: Teacher?

Hally: Thinks he is. And believe me, that is not a bad likeness.

Sam: Has he seen it?

Hally: Yes.

Sam: What did he say?

Hally: Tried to be clever, as usual. Said I was no Leonardo da Vinci[6] and that bad art had to be punished. So, six of the best, and his are bloody good.

Sam: On your bum?

Hally: Where else? The days when I got them on my hands are gone forever, Sam.

Sam: With your trousers down!

Hally: No. He's not quite that barbaric.

Sam: That's the way they do it in jail.

Hally *(Flicker of morbid interest.):* Really?

Sam: Ja. When the magistrate sentences you to "strokes with a light cane."

Hally: Go on.

Sam: They make you lie down on a bench. One policeman pulls down your trousers and holds your ankles, another one pulls your shirt over your head and holds your arms . . .

Hally: Thank you! That's enough.

Sam: . . . and the one that gives you the strokes talks to you gently and for a long time between each one. *(He laughs.)*

Hally: I've heard enough, Sam! Jesus! It's a bloody awful world when you come to think of it. People can be real bastards.

---

[6] Renaissance artist, creator, for example, of the *Mona Lisa* (1452–1519).

Sam: That's the way it is, Hally.

Hally: It doesn't *have* to be that way. There is something called progress, you know. We don't exactly burn people at the stake anymore.

Sam: Like Joan of Arc.[7]

Hally: Correct. If she was captured today, she'd be given a fair trial.

Sam: And then the death sentence.

Hally *(A world-weary sigh.):* I know, I know! I oscillate between hope and despair for this world as well, Sam. But things will change, you wait and see. One day somebody is going to get up and give history a kick up the backside and get it going again.

Sam: Like who?

Hally *(After thought.):* They're called social reformers. Every age, Sam, has got its social reformer. My history book is full of them.

Sam: So where's ours?

Hally: Good question. And I hate to say it, but the answer is: I don't know. Maybe he hasn't even been born yet. Or is still only a babe in arms at his mother's breast. God, what a thought.

Sam: So we just go on waiting.

Hally: Ja, looks like it. *(Back to his soup and the book.)*

Sam *(Reading from the textbook.):* "Introduction: In some mathematical problems only the magnitude . . ." *(He mispronounces the word "magnitude.")*

Hally *(Correcting him without looking up.):* Magnitude.

Sam: What's it mean?

Hally: How big it is. The size of the thing.

Sam *(Reading.):* ". . . a magnitude of the quantities is of importance. In other problems we need to know whether these quantities are negative or positive. For example, whether there is a debit or credit bank balance . . ."

Hally: Whether you're broke or not.

Sam: ". . . whether the temperature is above or below Zero . . ."

Hally: Naught degrees. Cheerful state of affairs! No cash and you're freezing to death. Mathematics won't get you out of that one.

Sam: All these quantities are called . . . *(Spelling the word.)* . . . s-c-a-l . . .

Hally: Scalars.

Sam: Scalars! *(Shaking his head with a laugh.)* You understand all that?

Hally *(Turning a page.):* No. And I don't intend to try.

Sam: So what happens when the exams come?

Hally: Failing a maths exam isn't the end of the world, Sam. How many times have I told you that examination results don't measure intelligence?

Sam: I would say about as many times as you've failed one of them.

Hally *(Mirthlessly.):* Ha, ha, ha.

Sam *(Simultaneously.):* Ha, ha, ha.

Hally: Just remember Winston Churchill[8] didn't do particularly well at school.

---

[7] French military leader and heroine, later canonized by the Catholic church (1412–31). [8] Prime minister of England during World War II (1940–45) and recipient of the Nobel Prize for Peace in 1953 (1874–1965).

Sam: You've also told me that one many times.

Hally: Well, it just so happens to be the truth.

Sam *(Enjoying the word.):* Magnitude! Magnitude! Show me how to use it.

Hally (*After thought.):* An intrepid social reformer will not be daunted by the magnitude of the task he has undertaken.

Sam *(Impressed.):* Couple of jaw-breakers in there!

Hally: I gave you three for the price of one. Intrepid, daunted and magnitude. I did that once in an exam. Put five of the words I had to explain in one sentence. It was half a page long.

Sam: Well, I'll put my money on you in the English exam.

Hally: Piece of cake. Eighty percent without even trying.

Sam *(Another textbook from Hally's case.):* And history?

Hally: So-so. I'll scrape through. In the fifties if I'm lucky.

Sam: You didn't do too badly last year.

Hally: Because we had World War One. That at least had some action. You try to find that in the South African Parliamentary system.

Sam *(Reading from the history textbook.):* "Napoleon[9] and the principle of equality." Hey! This sounds interesting. "After concluding peace with Britain in 1802, Napoleon used a brief period of calm to in-sti-tute . . ."

Hally: Introduce.

Sam: ". . . many reforms. Napoleon regarded all people as equal before the law and wanted them to have equal opportunities for advancement. All ves-ti-ges of the feu-dal system with its oppression of the poor were abolished. Vestiges, feudal system and abolished." I'm all right on oppression.

Hally: I'm thinking. He swept away . . . abolished . . . the last remains . . . vestiges . . . of the bad old days . . . feudal system.

Sam: Ha! There's the social reformer we're waiting for. He sounds like a man of some magnitude.

Hally: I'm not so sure about that. It's a damn good title for a book, though. A man of magnitude!

Sam: He sounds pretty big to me, Hally.

Hally: Don't confuse historical significance with greatness. But maybe I'm being a bit prejudiced. Have a look in there and you'll see he's two chapters long. And hell! . . . has he only got dates, Sam, all of which you've got to remember! This campaign and that campaign, and then, because of all the fighting, the next thing is we get Peace Treaties all over the place. And what's the end of the story? Battle of Waterloo,[10] which he loses. Wasn't worth it. No, I don't know about him as a man of magnitude.

Sam: Then who would you say was?

Hally: To answer that, we need a definition of greatness, and I suppose that would be somebody who . . . somebody who benefited all mankind.

---

[9] French general who declared himself emperor of France from 1804 to 1814 (1769–1821). [10] Town in Belgium, site of major battle in which Napoleon was defeated in 1815.

Sam: Right. But like who?

Hally *(He speaks with total conviction.):* Charles Darwin.[11] Remember him? That big book from the library. *The Origin of the Species.*

Sam: Him?

Hally: Yes. For his Theory of Evolution.

Sam: You didn't finish it.

Hally: I ran out of time. I didn't finish it because my two weeks was up. But I'm going to take it out again after I've digested what I read. It's safe. I've hidden it away in the Theology section. Nobody ever goes in there. And anyway who are you to talk? You hardly even looked at it.

Sam: I tried. I looked at the chapters in the beginning and I saw one called "The Struggle for an Existence." Ah ha, I thought. At last! But what did I get? Something called the mistletoe which needs the apple tree and there's too many seeds and all are going to die except one . . . ! No, Hally.

Hally *(Intellectually outraged.):* What do you mean, No! The poor man had to start somewhere. For God's sake, Sam, he revolutionized science. Now we know.

Sam: What?

Hally: Where we come from and what it all means.

Sam: And that's a benefit to mankind? Anyway, I still don't believe it.

Hally: God, you're impossible. I showed it to you in black and white.

Sam: Doesn't mean I got to believe it.

Hally: It's the likes of you that kept the Inquisition in business. It's called bigotry. Anyway, that's my man of magnitude. Charles Darwin! Who's yours?

Sam *(Without hesitation.):* Abraham Lincoln.

Hally: I might have guessed as much. Don't get sentimental, Sam. You've never been a slave, you know. And anyway we freed your ancestors here in South Africa long before the Americans. But if you want to thank somebody on their behalf, do it to Mr. William Wilberforce.[12] Come on. Try again. I want a real genius. *(Now enjoying himself, and so is Sam. Hally goes behind the counter and helps himself to a chocolate.)*

Sam: William Shakespeare.[13]

Hally *(No enthusiasm.):* Oh. So you're also one of them, are you? You're basing that opinion on only one play, you know. You've only read my *Julius Caesar* and even I don't understand half of what they're talking about. They should do what they did with the old Bible: bring the language up to date.

Sam: That's all you've got. It's also the only one *you've* read.

Hally: I know. I admit it. That's why I suggest we reserve our judgment until we've checked up on a few others. I've got a feeling, though, that by the

---

[11] Nineteenth-century British scientist and naturalist who developed the theory of evolution. [12] English abolitionist (1759–1833). [13] English poet and dramatist (1564–1616). See chapter 4.

end of this year one is going to be enough for me, and I can give you the names of twenty-nine other chaps in the Standard Nine class of the Port Elizabeth Technical College who feel the same. But if you want him, you can have him. My turn now. *(Pacing.)* This is a damned good exercise, you know! It started off looking like a simple question and here it's got us really probing into the intellectual heritage of our civilization.

Sam: So who is it going to be?

Hally: My next man . . . and he gets the title on two scores: social reform and literary genius . . . is Leo Nikolaevich Tolstoy.[14]

Sam: That Russian.

Hally: Correct. Remember the picture of him I showed you?

Sam: With the long beard.

Hally *(Trying to look like Tolstoy.):* And those burning, visionary eyes. My God, the face of a social prophet if ever I saw one! And remember my words when I showed it to you? Here's a *man,* Sam!

Sam: Those were words, Hally.

Hally: Not many intellectuals are prepared to shovel manure with the peasants and then go home and write a "little book" called *War and Peace.* Incidentally, Sam, he was somebody else who, to quote, ". . . did not distinguish himself scholastically."

Sam: Meaning?

Hally: He was also no good at school.

Sam: Like you and Winston Churchill.

Hally *(Mirthlessly.):* Ha, ha, ha.

Sam *(Simultaneously.):* Ha, ha, ha.

Hally: Don't get clever, Sam. That man freed his serfs of his own free will.

Sam: No argument. He was a somebody, all right. I accept him.

Hally: I'm sure Count Tolstoy will be very pleased to hear that. Your turn. Shoot. *(Another chocolate from behind the counter.)* I'm waiting, Sam.

Sam: I've got him.

Hally: Good. Submit your candidate for examination.

Sam: Jesus.

Hally *(Stopped dead in his tracks.):* Who?

Sam: Jesus Christ.

Hally: Oh, come on, Sam!

Sam: The Messiah.

Hally: Ja, but still . . . No, Sam. Don't let's get started on religion. We'll just spend the whole afternoon arguing again. Suppose I turn around and say Mohammed?

Sam: All right.

Hally: You can't have them both on the same list!

Sam: Why not? You like Mohammed, I like Jesus.

---

[14] Russian novelist, author of *Anna Karenina* and *War and Peace* (1828–1910).

Hally: I *don't* like Mohammed. I never have. I was merely being hypothetical. As far as I'm concerned, the Koran is as bad as the Bible. No. Religion is out! I'm not going to waste my time again arguing with you about the existence of God. You know perfectly well I'm an atheist . . . and I've got homework to do.

Sam: Okay, I take him back.

Hally: You've got time for one more name.

Sam *(After thought.):* I've got one I know we'll agree on. A simple straightforward great Man of Magnitude . . . and no arguments. And *he* really *did* benefit all mankind.

Hally: I wonder. After your last contribution I'm beginning to doubt whether anything in the way of an intellectual agreement is possible between the two of us. Who is he?

Sam: Guess.

Hally: Socrates?[15] Alexandre Dumas?[16] Karl Marx?[17] Dostoevsky?[18] Nietzsche?[19]

(Sam shakes his head after each name.)

Give me a clue.

Sam: The letter P is important . . .

Hally: Plato!

Sam: . . . and his name begins with an F.

Hally: I've got it. Freud and Psychology.[20]

Sam: No. I didn't understand him.

Hally: That makes two of us.

Sam: Think of mouldy apricot jam.

Hally *(After a delighted laugh.):* Penicillin and Sir Alexander Fleming![21] And the title of the book: *The Microbe Hunters. (Delighted.)* Splendid, Sam! Splendid. For once we are in total agreement. The major breakthrough in medical science in the Twentieth Century. If it wasn't for him, we might have lost the Second World War. It's deeply gratifying, Sam, to know that I haven't been wasting my time in talking to you. *(Strutting around proudly.)* Tolstoy may have educated his peasants, but I've educated you.

Sam: Standard Four to Standard Nine.

Hally: Have we been at it as long as that?

Sam: Yep. And my first lesson was geography.

Hally *(Intrigued.):* Really? I don't remember.

---

[15] Greek philosopher (470–399 B.C.). [16] Nineteenth-century French novelist (1824–95). [17] Nineteenth-century German political philosopher and economist whose thought provided the basis of the socialist state. [18] Nineteenth-century Russian novelist, author of *Crime and Punishment* and *The Brothers Karamazov* (1821–81). [19] German philosopher (1844–1900). [20] Founder of modern psychology; physician and psychiatrist (1856–1939). [21] Physician and scientist who with Sir Howard Florey discovered penicillin in 1929 (1881–1955).

Sam: My room there at the back of the old Jubilee Boarding House. I had just started working for your Mom. Little boy in short trousers walks in one afternoon and asks me seriously: "Sam, do you want to see South Africa?" Hey man! Sure I wanted to see South Africa!

Hally: Was that me?

Sam: . . . So the next thing I'm looking at a map you had just done for homework. It was your first one and you were very proud of yourself.

Hally: Go on.

Sam: Then came my first lesson. "Repeat after me, Sam: Gold in the Transvaal, mealies in the Free State, sugar in Natal and grapes in the Cape." I still know it!

Hally: Well, I'll be buggered. So that's how it all started.

Sam: And your next map was one with all the rivers and the mountains they came from. The Orange, the Vaal, the Limpopo, the Zambezi[22] . . .

Hally: You've got a phenomenal memory!

Sam: You should be grateful. That is why you started passing your exams. You tried to be better than me.

(They laugh together. Willie is attracted by the laughter and joins them.)

Hally: The old Jubilee Boarding House. Sixteen rooms with board and lodging, rent in advance and one week's notice. I haven't thought about it for donkey's years . . . and I don't think that's an accident. God, was I glad when we sold it and moved out. Those years are not remembered as the happiest ones of an unhappy childhood.

Willie *(Knocking on the table and trying to imitate a woman's voice.):* "Hally, are you there?"

Hally: Who's that supposed to be?

Willie: "What you doing in there, Hally? Come out at once!"

Hally *(To Sam.):* What's he talking about?

Sam: Don't you remember?

Willie: "Sam, Willie . . . is he in there with you boys?"

Sam: Hiding away in our room when your mother was looking for you.

Hally *(Another good laugh.):* Of course! I used to crawl and hide under your bed! But finish the story, Willie. Then what used to happen? You chaps would give the game away by telling her I was in there with you. So much for friendship.

Sam: We couldn't lie to her. She knew.

Hally: Which meant I got another rowing for hanging around the "servants' quarters." I think I spent more time in there with you chaps than anywhere else in that dump. And do you blame me? Nothing but bloody misery wherever you went. Somebody was always complaining about the food, or my mother was having a fight with Micky Nash because she'd caught her with a petty officer in her room. Maud Meiring was another

[22] Rivers in South Africa.

one. Remember those two? They were prostitutes, you know. Soldiers and sailors from the troopships. Bottom fell out of the business when the war ended. God, the flotsam and jetsam that life washed up on our shores! No joking, if it wasn't for your room, I would have been the first certified ten-year-old in medical history. Ja, the memories are coming back now. Walking home from school and thinking: "What can I do this afternoon?" Try out a few ideas, but sooner or later I'd end up in there with you fellows. I bet you I could still find my way to your room with my eyes closed. *(He does exactly that.)* Down the corridor . . . telephone on the right, which my Mom keeps locked because sombody is using it on the sly and not paying . . . past the kitchen and unappetizing cooking smells . . . around the corner into the backyard, hold my breath again because there are more smells coming when I pass your lavatory, then into that little passageway, first door on the right and into your room. How's that?

Sam: Good. But, as usual, you forgot to knock.

Hally: Like that time I barged in and caught you and Cynthia . . . at it. Remember? God, was I embarrassed! I didn't know what was going on at first.

Sam: Ja, that taught you a lesson.

Hally: And about a lot more than knocking on doors, I'll have you know, and I don't mean geography either. Hell, Sam, couldn't you have waited until it was dark?

Sam: No.

Hally: Was it that urgent?

Sam: Yes, and if you don't believe me, wait until your time comes.

Hally: No, thank you. I am not interested in girls. *(Back to his memories . . . Using a few chairs he recreates the room as he lists the items.)* A gray little room with a cold cement floor. Your bed against that wall . . . and I now know why the mattress sags so much! . . . Willie's bed . . . it's propped up on bricks because one leg is broken . . . that wobbly little table with the washbasin and jug of water . . . Yes! . . . stuck to the wall above it are some pin-up pictures from magazines. Joe Louis . . .

Willie: Brown Bomber.[23] World Title. *(Boxing pose.)* Three rounds and knockout.

Hally: Against who?

Sam: Max Schmeling.

Hally: Correct. I can also remember Fred Astaire and Ginger Rogers, and Rita Hayworth in a bathing costume which always made me hot and bothered when I looked at it. Under Willie's bed is an old suitcase with all his clothes in a mess, which is why I never hide there. Your things are neat and tidy in a trunk next to your bed, and on it there is a picture of you and Cynthia in your ballroom clothes, your first silver cup for third place in a

[23] Nickname of U.S. prizefighter Joseph Louis, (1914–81), who won the heavyweight boxing championship in 1938 against German Max Schmeling.

competition and an old radio which doesn't work anymore. Have I left out anything?

Sam: No.

Hally: Right, so much for the stage directions. Now the characters. *(Sam and Willie move to their appropriate positions in the bedroom.)* Willie is in bed, under his blankets with his clothes on, complaining nonstop about something, but we can't make out a word of what he's saying because he's got his head under the blankets as well. You're on your bed trimming your toenails with a knife—not a very edifying sight—and as for me . . . What am I doing?

Sam: You're sitting on the floor giving Willie a lecture about being a good loser while you get the checker board and pieces ready for a game. Then you go to Willie's bed, pull off the blankets and make him play with you first because you know you're going to win, and that gives you the second game with me.

Hally: And you certainly were a bad loser, Willie!

Willie: Haai!

Hally: Wasn't he, Sam? And so slow! A game with you almost took the whole afternoon. Thank God I gave up trying to teach you how to play chess.

Willie: You and Sam cheated.

Hally: I never saw Sam cheat, and mine were mostly the mistakes of youth.

Willie: Then how is it you two was always winning?

Hally: Have you ever considered the possibility, Willie, that it was because we were better than you?

Willie: Every time better?

Hally: Not every time. There were occasions when we deliberately let you win a game so that you would stop sulking and go on playing with us. Sam used to wink at me when you weren't looking to show me it was time to let you win.

Willie: So then you two didn't play fair.

Hally: It was for your benefit, Mr. Malopo, which is more than being fair. It was an act of self-sacrifice. *(To Sam.)* But you know what my best memory is, don't you?

Sam: No.

Hally: Come on, guess. If your memory is so good, you must remember it as well.

Sam: We got up to a lot of tricks in there, Hally.

Hally: This one was special, Sam.

Sam: I'm listening.

Hally: It started off looking like another of those useless nothing-to-do afternoons. I'd already been down to Main Street looking for adventure, but nothing had happened. I didn't feel like climbing trees in the Donkin Park or pretending I was a private eye and following a stranger . . . so as usual: See what's cooking in Sam's room. This time it was you on the floor. You had two thin pieces of wood and you were smoothing them down with a knife. It didn't look particularly interesting, but when I asked you what you were doing, you just said, "Wait and see, Hally. Wait . . . and see" . . . in that secret sort of way of yours, so I knew there was a surprise coming. You teased me, you bugger, by being deliberately slow and not answering my questions!

(Sam laughs.)

And whistling while you worked away! God, it was infuriating! I could have brained you! It was only when you tied them together in a cross and put that down on the brown paper that I realized what you were doing. "Sam is making a kite?" And when I asked you and you said "Yes . . . !" *(Shaking his head with disbelief.)* The sheer audacity of it took my breath away. I mean, seriously, what the hell does a black man know about flying a kite? I'll be honest with you, Sam, I had no hopes for it. If you think I was excited and happy, you got another guess coming. In fact, I was shit-scared that we were going to make fools of ourselves. When we left the boarding house to go up onto the hill, I was praying quietly that there wouldn't be any other kids around to laugh at us.

Sam *(Enjoying the memory as much as Hally.):* Ja, I could see that.

Hally: I made it obvious, did I?

Sam: Ja. You refused to carry it.

Hally: Do you blame me? Can you remember what the poor thing looked like? Tomato-box wood and brown paper! Flour and water for glue! Two of my mother's old stockings for a tail, and then all those bits and pieces of string you made me tie together so that we could fly it! Hell, no, that was now only asking for a miracle to happen.

Sam: Then the big argument when I told you to hold the string and run with it when I let go.

Hally: I was prepared to run, all right, but straight back to the boarding house.

Sam *(Knowing what's coming.):* So what happened?

Hally: Come on, Sam, you remember as well as I do.

Sam: I want to hear it from you.

(Hally pauses. He wants to be as accurate as possible.)

Hally: You went a little distance from me down the hill, you held it up ready to let it go. . . . "This is it," I thought. "Like everything else in my life, here comes another fiasco." Then you shouted, "Go, Hally!" and I started to run. *(Another pause.)* I don't know how to describe it, Sam. Ja! The miracle happened! I was running, waiting for it to crash to the ground, but instead suddenly there was something alive behind me at the end of the string, tugging at it as if it wanted to be free. I looked back . . . *(Shakes his head.)* . . . I still can't believe my eyes. It was flying! Looping around and trying to climb even higher into the sky. You shouted to me to let it have more string. I did, until there was none left and I was just holding that piece of wood we had tied it to. You came up and joined me. You were laughing.

Sam: So were you. And shouting, "It works, Sam! We've done it!"

Hally: And we had! I was so proud of us! It was the most splendid thing I had ever seen. I wished there were hundreds of kids around to watch us. The part that scared me, though, was when you showed me how to make it dive down to the ground and then just when it was on the point of crashing, swoop up again!

Sam: You didn't want to try yourself.

Hally: Of course not! I would have been suicidal if anything had happened to it. Watching you do it made me nervous enough. I was quite happy just to see it up there with its tail fluttering behind it. You left me after that, didn't you? You explained how to get it down, we tied it to the bench so that I could sit and watch it, and you went away. I wanted you to stay, you know. I was a little scared of having to look after it by myself.

Sam *(Quietly.):* I had work to do, Hally.

Hally: It was sort of sad bringing it down, Sam. And it looked sad again when it was lying there on the ground. Like something that had lost its soul. Just tomato-box wood, brown paper and two of my mother's old stockings! But, hell, I'll never forget that first moment when I saw it up there. I had a stiff neck the next day from looking up so much.

(Sam laughs. Hally turns to him with a question he never thought of asking before.)

Why did you make that kite, Sam?

Sam *(Evenly.):* I can't remember.

Hally: Truly?

Sam: Too long ago, Hally.

Hally: Ja, I suppose it was. It's time for another one, you know.

Sam: Why do you say that?

Hally: Because it feels like that. Wouldn't be a good day to fly it, though.

Sam: No. You can't fly kites on rainy days.

Hally *(He studies Sam. Their memories have made him conscious of the man's presence in his life.):* How old are you, Sam?

Sam: Two score and five.

Hally: Strange, isn't it?

Sam: What?

Hally: Me and you.

Sam: What's strange about it?

Hally: Little white boy in short trousers and a black man old enough to be his father flying a kite. It's not every day you see that.

Sam: But why strange? Because the one is white and the other black?

Hally: I don't know. Would have been just as strange, I suppose, if it had been me and my Dad . . . cripple man and a little boy! Nope! There's no chance of me flying a kite without it being strange. *(Simple statement of fact—no self-pity.)* There's a nice little short story there. "The Kite-Flyers." But we'd have to find a twist in the ending.

Sam: Twist?

Hally: Yes. Something unexpected. The way it ended with us was too straightforward . . . me on the bench and you going back to work. There's no drama in that.

Willie: And me?

Hally: You?

Willie: Yes me.

Hally: You want to get into the story as well, do you? I got it! Change the title: "Afternoons in Sam's Room" . . . expand it and tell all the stories. It's on its way to being a novel. Our days in the old Jubilee. Sad in a way that they're over. I almost wish we were still in that little room.

Sam: We're still together.

Hally: That's true. It's just that life felt the right size in there . . . not too big and not too small. Wasn't so hard to work up a bit of courage. It's got so bloody complicated since then.

(The telephone rings. Sam answers it.)

Sam: St. George's Park Tea Room . . . Hello, Madam . . . Yes, Madam, he's here . . . Hally, it's your mother.

Hally: Where is she phoning from?

Sam: Sounds like the hospital. It's a public telephone.

Hally *(Relieved.):* You see! I told you. *(The telephone.)* Hello, Mom . . . Yes . . . Yes no fine. Everything's under control here. How's things with poor old Dad? . . . Has he had a bad turn? . . . What? . . . Oh, God! . . . Yes, Sam told me, but I was sure he'd made a mistake. But what's this all about, Mom? He didn't look at all good last night. How can he get better so quickly? . . . Then very obviously you must say no. Be firm with him. You're the boss. . . . You know what it's going to be like if he comes home. . . . Well, then, don't blame me when I fail my exams at the end of the year. . . . Yes! How am I expected to be fresh for school when I spend half the night massaging his gammy leg? . . . So am I! . . . So tell him a white lie. Say Dr. Colley wants more X-rays of his stump. Or bribe him. We'll sneak in double tots of brandy in future. . . . What? . . . Order him to get back into bed at once! If he's going to behave like a child, treat him like one. . . . All right, Mom! I was just trying to . . . I'm sorry. . . . I said I'm sorry. . . . Quick, give me your number. I'll phone you back. *(He hangs up and waits a few seconds.)* Here we go again! *(He dials.)* I'm sorry, Mom. . . . Okay . . . But now listen to me carefully. All it needs is for you to put your foot down. Don't take no for an answer. . . . Did you hear me? And whatever you do, don't discuss it with him. . . . Because I'm frightened you'll give in to him. . . . Yes, Sam gave me lunch. . . . I ate all of it! . . . No, Mom not a soul. It's still raining here. . . . Right, I'll tell them. I'll just do some homework and then lock up. . . . But remember now, Mom. Don't listen to anything he says. And phone me back and let me know what happens. . . . Okay. Bye, Mom. *(He hangs up. The men are staring at him.)* My Mom says that when you're finished with the floors you must do the windows. *(Pause.)* Don't misunderstand me, chaps. All I want is for him to get better. And if he was, I'd be the first person to say: "Bring him home." But he's not, and we can't give him the medical care and attention he needs at home. That's what hospitals are there for. *(Brusquely.)* So don't just stand there! Get on with it!

(Sam clears Hally's table.)

You heard right. My Dad wants to go home.

Sam: Is he better?

Hally *(Sharply.):* No! How the hell can he be better when last night he was groaning with pain? This is not an age of miracles!

Sam: Then he should stay in hospital.

Hally *(Seething with irritation and frustration.):* Tell me something I don't know, Sam. What the hell do you think I was saying to my Mom? All I can say is fuck-it-all.

Sam: I'm sure he'll listen to your Mom.

Hally: You don't know what she's up against. He's already packed his shaving kit and pajamas and is sitting on his bed with his crutches, dressed and ready to go. I know him when he gets in that mood. If she tries to reason with him, we've had it. She's no match for him when it comes to a battle of words. He'll tie her up in knots. *(Trying to hide his true feelings.)*

Sam: I suppose it gets lonely for him in there.

Hally: With all the patients and nurses around? Regular visits from the Salvation Army? Balls! It's ten times worse for him at home. I'm at school and my mother is here in the business all day.

Sam: He's at least got you at night.

Hally *(Before he can stop himself.):* And we've got him! Please! I don't want to talk about it anymore. *(Unpacks his school case, slamming down books on the table.)* Life is just a plain bloody mess, that's all. And people are fools.

Sam: Come on, Hally.

Hally: Yes, they are! They bloody well deserve what they get.

Sam: Then don't complain.

Hally: Don't try to be clever, Sam. It doesn't suit you. Anybody who thinks there's nothing wrong with this world needs to have his head examined. Just when things are going along all right, without fail someone or something will come along and spoil everything. Somebody should write that down as a fundamental law of the Universe. The principle of perpetual disappointment. If there is a God who created this world, he should scrap it and try again.

Sam: All right, Hally, all right. What you got for homework?

Hally: Bullshit, as usual. *(Opens an exercise book and reads.)* "Write five hundred words describing an annual event of cultural or historical significance."

Sam: That should be easy enough for you.

Hally: And also plain bloody boring. You know what he wants, don't you? One of their useless old ceremonies. The commemoration of the landing of the 1820 Settlers,[24] or if it's going to be culture, Carols by Candlelight every Christmas.

Sam: It's an impressive sight. Make a good description, Hally. All those candles glowing in the dark and the people singing hymns.

Hally: And it's called religious hysteria. *(Intense irritation.)* Please, Sam! Just leave me alone and let me get on with it. I'm not in the mood for games this afternoon. And remember my Mom's orders . . . you're to help Willie with the windows. Come on now, I don't want any more nonsense in here.

Sam: Okay, Hally, okay.

(Hally settles down to his homework; determined preparations . . . pen, ruler, exercise book, dictionary, another cake . . . all of which will lead to nothing.)

(Sam waltzes over to Willie and starts to replace tables and chairs. He practices a ballroom step while doing so. Willie watches. When Sam is finished, Willie tries.) Good! But just a little bit quicker on the turn and only move in to her after she's crossed over. What about this one?

(Another step. When Sam is finished, Willie again has a go.)

Much better. See what happens when you just relax and enjoy yourself? Remember that in two weeks' time and you'll be all right.

Willie: But I haven't got partner, Boet Sam.

Sam: Maybe Hilda will turn up tonight.

Willie: No, Boet Sam. *(Reluctantly.)* I gave her a good hiding.

Sam: You mean a bad one.

Willie: Good bad one.

Sam: Then you mustn't complain either. Now you pay the price for losing your temper.

Willie: I also pay two pounds ten shilling entrance fee.

Sam: They'll refund you if you withdraw now.

Willie *(Appalled.):* You mean, don't dance?

Sam: Yes.

Willie: No! I wait too long and I practice too hard. If I find me new partner, you think I can be ready in two weeks? I ask Madam for my leave now and we practice every day.

Sam: Quickstep non-stop for two weeks. World record, Willie, but you'll be mad at the end.

Willie: No jokes, Boet Sam.

Sam: I'm not joking.

Willie: So then what?

Sam: Find Hilda. Say you're sorry and promise you won't beat her again.

Willie: No.

Sam: Then withdraw. Try again next year.

---

[24] In 1819–20, the British government paid Britons who moved to South Africa 100 acres of land per family.

Willie: No.

Sam: Then I give up.

Willie: Haaikona, Boet Sam, you can't.

Sam: What do you mean, I can't? I'm telling you: I give up.

Willie *(Adamant.):* No! *(Accusingly.)* It was you who start me ballroom dancing.

Sam: So?

Willie: Before that I use to be happy. And is you and Miriam who bring me to Hilda and say here's partner for you.

Sam: What are you saying, Willie?

Willie: You!

Sam: But me what? To blame?

Willie: Yes.

Sam: Willie . . . ? *(Bursts into laughter.)*

Willie: And now all you do is make jokes at me. You wait. When Miriam leaves you is my turn to laugh. Ha! Ha! Ha!

Sam *(He can't take Willie seriously any longer.):* She can leave me tonight! I know what to do. *(Bowing before an imaginary partner.)* May I have the pleasure? *(He dances and sings.)*

Just a fellow with his pillow . . .
Dancin' like a willow . . .
In an autumn breeze . . ."

Willie: There you go again!

(Sam goes on dancing and singing.)

Boet Sam!

Sam: There's the answer to your problem! Judges' announcement in two weeks' time: "Ladies and gentlemen, the winner in the open section . . . Mr. Willie Malopo and his pillow!"

(This is too much for a now really angry Willie. He goes for Sam, but the latter is too quick for him and puts Hally's table between the two of them.)

Hally *(Exploding.):* For Christ's sake, you two!

Willie *(Still trying to get at Sam.):* I donner you, Sam! Struesgod!

Sam *(Still laughing.):* Sorry, Willie . . . Sorry . . .

Hally: Sam! Willie! *(Grabs his ruler and gives Willie a vicious whack on the bum.)* How the hell am I supposed to concentrate with the two of you behaving like bloody children!

Willie: Hit him too!

Hally: Shut up, Willie.

Willie: He started jokes again.

Hally: Get back to your work. You too, Sam. *(His ruler.)* Do you want another one, Willie?

(Sam and Willie return to their work. Hally uses the opportunity to escape from his unsuccessful attempt at homework. He struts around like a little despot, ruler in hand, giving vent to his anger and frustration.)

Suppose a customer had walked in then? Or the Park Superintendent. And seen the two of you behaving like a pair of hooligans. That would have been the end of my mother's license, you know. And your jobs! Well, this is the end of it. From now on there will be no more of your ballroom nonsense in here. This is a business establishment, not a bloody New Brighton dancing school. I've been far too lenient with the two of you. *(Behind the counter for a green cool drink and a dollop of ice cream. He keeps up his tirade as he prepares it.)* But what really makes me bitter is that I allow you chaps a little freedom in here when business is bad and what do you do with it? The foxtrot![25] Specially you, Sam. There's more to life than trotting around a dance floor and I thought at least you knew it.

Sam: It's a harmless pleasure, Hally. It doesn't hurt anybody.

Hally: It's also a rather simple one, you know.

Sam: You reckon so? Have you ever tried?

Hally: Of course not.

Sam: Why don't you? Now.

Hally: What do you mean? Me dance?

Sam: Yes. I'll show you a simple step—the waltz—then you try it.

Hally: What will that prove?

Sam: That it might not be as easy as you think.

Hally: I didn't say it was easy. I said it was simple—like in simple-minded, meaning mentally retarded. You can't exactly say it challenges the intellect.

Sam: It does other things.

Hally: Such as?

Sam: Make people happy.

Hally *(The glass in his hand.)*: So do American cream sodas with ice cream. For God's sake, Sam, you're not asking me to take ballroom dancing serious, are you?

Sam: Yes.

Hally *(Sigh of defeat.)*: Oh, well, so much for trying to give you a decent education. I've obviously achieved nothing.

Sam: You still haven't told me what's wrong with admiring something that's beautiful and then trying to do it yourself.

Hally: Nothing. But we happen to be talking about a foxtrot, not a thing of beauty.

Sam: But that is just what I'm saying. If you were to see two champions doing, two masters of the art . . . !

Hally: Oh, God, I give up. So now it's also art!

Sam: Ja.

Hally: There's a limit, Sam. Don't confuse art and entertainment.

Sam: So then what is art?

Hally: You want a definition?

---

[25] A dance characterized by slow, quick steps.

Sam: Ja.

Hally *(He realizes he has got to be careful. He gives the matter a lot of thought before answering.):* Philosophers have been trying to do that for centuries. What is Art? What is Life? But basically I suppose it's . . . the giving of meaning to matter.

Sam: Nothing to do with beautiful?

Hally: It goes beyond that. It's the giving of form to the formless.

Sam: Ja, well, maybe it's not art, then. But I still say it's beautiful.

Hally: I'm sure the word you mean to use is "entertaining."

Sam *(Adamant.):* No. Beautiful. And if you want proof, come along to the Centenary Hall in New Brighton in two weeks' time.

(The mention of the Centenary Hall draws Willie over to them.)

Hally: What for? I've seen the two of you prancing around in here often enough.

Sam *(He laughs.):* This isn't the real thing, Hally. We're just playing around in here.

Hally: So? I can use my imagination.

Sam: And what do you get?

Hally: A lot of people dancing around and having a so-called good time.

Sam: That all?

Hally: Well, basically it is that, surely.

Sam: No, it isn't. Your imagination hasn't helped you at all. There's a lot more to it than that. We're getting ready for the championships, Hally, not just another dance. There's going to be a lot of people, all right, and they're going to have a good time, but they'll only be spectators, sitting around and watching. It's just the competitors out there on the dance floor. Party decorations and fancy lights all around the walls! The ladies in beautiful evening dresses!

Hally: My mother's got one of those, Sam, and quite frankly, it's an embarrassment every time she wears it.

Sam *(Undeterred.):* Your imagination left out the excitement.

(Hally scoffs.)

Oh, yes. The finalists are not going to be out there just to have a good time. One of those couples will be the 1950 Eastern Province Champions. And your imagination left out the music.

Willie: Mr. Elijah Gladman Guzana and his Orchestral Jazzonions.

Sam: The sound of the big band, Hally. Trombone, trumpet, tenor and alto sax. And then, finally, your imagination also left out the climax of the evening when the dancing is finished, the judges have stopped whispering among themselves and the Master of Ceremonies collects their scorecards and goes up onto the stage to announce the winners.

Hally: All right. So you make it sound like a bit of a do. It's an occasion. Satisfied?

Sam *(Victory.):* So you admit that!

Hally: Emotionally yes, intellectually no.

Sam: Well, I don't know what you mean by that, all I'm telling you is that it is going to be the event of the year in New Brighton. It's been sold out for two weeks already. There's only standing room left. We've got competitors coming from Kingwilliamstown, East London, Port Alfred.

(Hally starts pacing thoughtfully.)

Hally: Tell me a bit more.

Sam: I thought you weren't interested . . . intellectually.

Hally *(Mysteriously.):* I've got my reasons.

Sam: What do you want to know?

Hally: It takes place every year?

Sam: Yes. But only every third year in New Brighton. It's East London's turn to have the championships next year.

Hally: Which, I suppose, makes it an even more significant event.

Sam: Ah ha! We're getting somewhere. Our "occasion" is now a "significant event."

Hally: I wonder.

Sam: What?

Hally: I wonder if I would get away with it.

Sam: But what?

Hally *(To the table and his exercise book.):* "Write five hundred words describing an annual event of cultural or historical significance." Would I be stretching poetic license a little too far if I called your ballroom championships a cultural event?

Sam: You mean . . . ?

Hally: You think we could get five hundred words out of it, Sam?

Sam: Victor Sylvester has written a whole book on ballroom dancing.

Willie: You going to write about it, Master Hally?

Hally: Yes, gentlemen, that is precisely what I am considering doing. Old Doc Bromely—he's my English teacher—is going to argue with me, of course. He doesn't like natives. But I'll point out to him that in strict anthropological terms the culture of a primitive black society includes its dancing and singing. To put my thesis in a nutshell: The war-dance has been replaced by the waltz. But it still amounts to the same thing: the release of primitive emotions through movement. Shall we give it a go?

Sam: I'm ready.

Willie: Me also.

Hally: Ha! This will teach the old bugger a lesson. *(Decision taken.)* Right. Let's get ourselves organized. *(This means another cake on the table. He sits.)* I think you've given me enough general atmosphere, Sam, but to build the tension and suspense I need facts. *(Pencil poised.)*

Willie: Give him facts, Boet Sam.

Hally: What you called the climax . . . how many finalists?

Sam: Six couples.

Hally *(Making notes.)*: Go on. Give me the picture.

Sam: Spectators seated right around the hall. *(Willie becomes a spectator.)*

Hally: . . . and it's a full house.

Sam: At one end, on the stage, Gladman and his Orchestral Jazzonions. At the other end is a long table with the three judges. The six finalists go onto the dance floor and take up their positions. When they are ready and the spectators have settled down, the Master of Ceremonies goes to the microphone. To start with, he makes some jokes to get the people laughing . . .

Hally: Good touch! *(As he writes.)* ". . . creating a relaxed atmosphere which will change to one of tension and drama as the climax is approached."

Sam *(Onto a chair to act out the M.C.)*: "Ladies and gentlemen, we come now to the great moment you have all been waiting for this evening. . . . The finals of the 1950 Eastern Province Open Ballroom Dancing Championships. But first let me introduce the finalists! Mr. and Mrs. Welcome Tchabalala from Kingwilliamstown . . ."

Willie *(He applauds after every name.)*: Is when the people clap their hands and whistle and make a lot of noise, Master Hally.

Sam: Mr. Mulligan Njikelane and Miss Nomhle Nkonyeni of Grahamstown; Mr. and Mrs. Norman Nchinga from Port Alfred; Mr. Fats Bokolane and Miss Dina Plaatjies from East London; Mr. Sipho Dugu and Mrs. Mable Magada from Peddie; and from New Brighton our very own Mr. Willie Malopo and Miss Hilda Samuels.

(Willie can't believe his ears. He abandons his role as spectator and scrambles into position as a finalist.)

Willie: Relaxed and ready to romance!

Sam: The applause dies down. When everybody is silent, Gladman lifts up his sax, nods at the Orchestral Jazzonions . . .

Willie: Play the jukebox please, Boet Sam!

Sam: I also only got bus fare, Willie.

Hally: Hold it, everybody. *(Heads for the cash register behind the counter.)* How much is in the till, Sam?

Sam: Three shillings. Hally . . . your Mom counted it before she left.

(Hally hesitates.)

Hally: Sorry, Willie. You know how she carried on the last time I did it. We'll just have to pool our combined imaginations and hope for the best. *(Returns to the table.)* Back to work. How are the points scored, Sam?

Sam: Maximum of ten points each for individual style, deportment, rhythm and general appearance.

Willie: Must I start?

Hally: Hold it for a second, Willie. And penalties?

Sam: For what?

Hally: For doing something wrong. Say you stumble or bump into somebody . . . do they take off any points?

Sam *(Aghast.):* Hally . . . !

Hally: When you're dancing. If you and your partner collide into another couple.

(Hally can get no further. Sam has collapsed with laughter. He explains to Willie.)

Sam: If me and Miriam bump into you and Hilda . . .

(Willie joins him in another good laugh.)

Hally, Hally . . . !

Hally *(Perplexed.):* Why? What did I say?

Sam: There's no collisions out there, Hally. Nobody trips or stumbles or bumps into anybody else. That's what that moment is all about. To be one of those finalists on that dance floor is like . . . like being in a dream about a world in which accidents don't happen.

Hally *(Genuinely moved by Sam's image.):* Jesus, Sam! That's beautiful!

Willie *(Can endure waiting no longer.):* I'm starting! *(Willie dances while Sam talks.)*

Sam: Of course it is. That's what I've been trying to say to you all afternoon. And it's beautiful because that is what we want life to be like. But instead, like you said, Hally, we're bumping into each other all the time. Look at the three of us this afternoon: I've bumped into Willie, the two of us have bumped into you, you've bumped into your mother, she bumping into your Dad. . . . None of us knows the steps and there's no music playing. And it doesn't stop with us. The whole world is doing it all the time. Open a newspaper and what do you read? America has bumped into Russia, England is bumping into India, rich man bumps into poor man. Those are big collisions, Hally. They make for a lot of bruises. People get hurt in all that bumping, and we're sick and tired of it now. It's been going on for too long. Are we never going to get it right? . . . Learn to dance life like champions instead of always being just a bunch of beginners at it?

Hally *(Deep and sincere admiration of the man.):* You've got a vision, Sam!

Sam: Not just me. What I'm saying to you is that everybody's got it. That's why there's only standing room left for the Centenary Hall in two weeks' time. For as long as the music lasts, we are going to see six couples get it right, the way we want life to be.

Hally: But is that the best we can do, Sam . . . watch six finalists dreaming about the way it should be?

Sam: I don't know. But it starts with that. Without the dream we won't know what we're going for. And anyway I reckon there are a few people who have got past just dreaming about it and are trying for something real. Remember that thing we read once in the paper about the Mahatma Gandhi?[26] Going without food to stop those riots in India?

---

[26] Indian religious leader and philosopher who developed the idea of *satyagraha,* passive resistance (1869–1948).

Hally: You're right. He certainly was trying to teach people to get the steps right.

Sam: And the Pope.

Hally: Yes, he's another one. Our old General Smuts as well, you know. He's also out there dancing. You know, Sam, when you come to think of it, that's what the United Nations boils down to . . . a dancing school for politicians!

Sam: And let's hope they learn.

Hally *(A little surge of hope.):* You're right. We mustn't despair. Maybe there's some hope for mankind after all. Keep it up, Willie. *(Back to his table with determination.)* This is a lot bigger than I thought. So what have we got? Yes, our title: "A World Without Collisions."

Sam: That sounds good! "A World Without Collisions."

Hally: Subtitle: "Global Politics on the Dance Floor." No. A bit too heavy, hey? What about "Ballroom Dancing as a Political Vision"?

(The telephone rings. Sam answers it.)

Sam: St. George's Park Tea Room . . . Yes, Madam . . . Hally, it's your Mom.

Hally *(Back to reality.):* Oh, God, yes! I'd forgotten all about that. Shit! Remember my words, Sam? Just when you're enjoying yourself, someone or something will come along and wreck everything.

Sam: You haven't heard what she's got to say yet.

Hally: Public telephone?

Sam: No.

Hally: Does she sound happy or unhappy?

Sam: I couldn't tell. *(Pause.)* She's waiting, Hally.

Hally *(To the telephone.):* Hello, Mom . . . No, everything is okay here. Just doing my homework. . . . What's your news? . . . You've what? . . . *(Pause. He takes the receiver away from his ear for a few seconds. In the course of Hally's telephone conversation, Sam and Willie discreetly position the stacked tables and chairs. Hally places the receiver back to his ear.)* Yes, I'm still here. Oh, well, I give up now. Why did you do it, Mom? . . . Well, I just hope you know what you've let us in for. . . . *(Loudly.)* I said I hope you know what you've let us in for! It's the end of the peace and quiet we've been having. *(Softly.)* Where is he? *(Normal voice.)* He can't hear us from in there. But for God's sake, Mom, what happened? I told you to be firm with him. . . . Then you and the nurses should have held him down, taken his crutches away. . . . I know only too well he's my father! . . . I'm not being disrespectful, but I'm sick and tired of emptying stinking chamberpots full of phlegm and piss. . . . Yes, I do! When you're not there, he asks *me* to do it. . . . If you really want to know the truth, that's why I've got no appetite for my food. . . . Yes! There's a lot of things you don't know about. For your information, I still haven't got that science textbook I need. And you know why? He borrowed the money you gave me for it. . . . Because I didn't want to start another fight between you two. . . . He says that every time. . . . All right, Mom! *(Viciously.)* Then just remember to start hiding your bag away again, because he'll be at your purse before long for money for booze. And when he's well enough to come down here, you better keep an eye on the till as well, because that is also going to develop a leak. . . . Then don't complain to me when he starts his old tricks. . . . Yes, you do. I get it from you on one side and from him on the other, and it makes life hell for me. I'm not going to be the peacemaker anymore. I'm warning you now: when the two of you start fighting again, I'm leaving home. . . . Mom, if you start crying, I'm going to put down the receiver. . . . Okay . . . *(Lowering his voice to a vicious whisper.)* Okay, Mom. I heard you. *(Desperate.)* No. . . . Because I don't want to. I'll see him when I get home! Mom! . . . *(Pause. When he speaks again, his tone changes completely. It is not simply pretense. We sense a genuine emotional conflict.)* Welcome home, chum! . . . What's that? . . . Don't be silly, Dad. You being home is just about the best news in the world. . . . I bet you are. Bloody depressing there with everybody going on about their ailments, hey! . . . How you feeling? . . . Good . . . Here as well, pal. Coming down cats and dogs. . . . That's right. Just the day for a kip and a toss in your old Uncle Ned. . . . Everything's just hunky-dory on my side, Dad. . . . Well, to start with, there's a nice pile of comics for you on the counter. . . . Yes, old Kemple brought them in. *Batman and Robin, Submariner* . . . just your cup of tea . . . I will. . . . Yes, we'll spin a few yarns tonight. . . . Okay, chum, see you in a little while. . . . No, I promise. I'll come straight home. . . . *(Pause—his mother comes back on the phone.)* Mom? Okay. I'll lock up now. . . . What? . . . Oh, the brandy . . . Yes, I'll remember! . . . I'll put it in my suitcase now, for God's sake. I know well enough what will happen if he doesn't get it. . . . *(Places a bottle of brandy on the counter.)* I was kind to him, Mom. I didn't say anything nasty! . . . All right. Bye. *(End of telephone conversation. A desolate Hally doesn't move. A strained silence.)*

Sam *(Quietly.):* That sounded like a bad bump, Hally.

Hally *(Having a hard time controlling his emotions. He speaks carefully.):* Mind your own business, Sam.

Sam: Sorry. I wasn't trying to interfere. Shall we carry on? Hally? *(He indicates the exercise book. No response from Hally.)*

Willie *(Also trying.):* Tell him about when they give out the cups, Boet Sam.

Sam: Ja! That's another big moment. The presentation of the cups after the winners have been announced. You've got to put that in.

(Still no response from Hally.)

Willie: A big silver one, Master Hally, called floating trophy for the champions.

Sam: We always invite some big-shot personality to hand them over. Guest of honor this year is going to be His Holiness Bishop Jabulani of the All African Free Zionist Church.

(Hally gets up abruptly, goes to his table and tears up the page he was writing on.)

Hally: So much for a bloody world without collisions.

Sam: Too bad. It was on its way to being a good composition.

Hally: Let's stop bullshitting ourselves, Sam.

Sam: Have we been doing that?

Hally: Yes! That's what all our talk about a decent world has been . . . just so much bullshit.

Sam: We did say it was still only a dream.

Hally: And a bloody useless one at that. Life's a fuck-up and it's never going to change.

Sam: Ja, maybe that's true.

Hally: There's no maybe about it. It's a blunt and brutal fact. All we've done this afternoon is waste our time.

Sam: Not if we'd got your homework done.

Hally: I don't give a shit about my homework, so, for Christ's sake, just shut up about it. *(Slamming books viciously into his school case.)* Hurry up now and finish your work. I want to lock up and get out of here. *(Pause.)* And then go where? Home-sweet-fucking-home. Jesus, I hate that word.

(Hally goes to the counter to put the brandy bottle and comics in his school case. After a moment's hesitation, he smashes the bottle of brandy. He abandons all further attempts to hide his feelings. Sam and Willie work away as unobtrusively as possible.)

Do you want to know what is really wrong with your lovely little dream, Sam? It's not just that we are all bad dancers. That does happen to be perfectly true, but there's more to it than just that. You left out the cripples.

Sam: Hally!

Hally *(Now totally reckless.):* Ja! Can't leave them out, Sam. That's why we always end up on our backsides on the dance floor. They're also out there dancing . . . like a bunch of broken spiders trying to do the quickstep! *(An ugly attempt at laughter.)* When you come to think of it, it's a bloody comical sight. I mean, it's bad enough on two legs . . . but one and a pair of crutches! Hell, no, Sam. That's guaranteed to turn that dance floor into a shambles. Why you shaking your head? Picture it, man. For once this afternoon let's use our imaginations sensibly.

Sam: Be careful, Hally.

Hally: Of what? The truth? I seem to be the only one around here who is prepared to face it. We've had the pretty dream, it's time now to wake up and have a good long look at the way things really are. Nobody knows the steps, there's no music, the cripples are also out there tripping up everybody and trying to get into the act, and it's all called the All-Comers-How-to-Make-a-Fuckup-of-Life Championships. *(Another ugly laugh.)* Hang on, Sam! The best bit is still coming. Do you know what the winner's trophy is? A beautiful big chamber-pot with roses on the side, and it's full to the brim with piss. And guess who I think is going to be this year's winner.

Sam *(Almost shouting.):* Stop now!

Hally *(Suddenly appalled by how far he has gone.):* Why?

Sam: Hally? It's your father you're talking about.

Hally: So?

Sam: Do you know what you've been saying?

(Hally can't answer. He is rigid with shame. Sam speaks to him sternly.)

No, Hally, you mustn't do it. Take back those words and ask for forgiveness! It's a terrible sin for a son to mock his father with jokes like that. You'll be punished if you carry on. Your father is your father, even if he is a . . . cripple man.

Willie: Yes, Master Hally. Is true what Sam say.

Sam: I understand how you are feeling, Hally, but even so . . .

Hally: No, you don't!

Sam: I think I do.

Hally: And I'm telling you you don't. Nobody does. *(Speaking carefully as his shame turns to rage at Sam.)* It's your turn to be careful, Sam. Very careful! You're treading on dangerous ground. Leave me and my father alone.

Sam: I'm not the one who's been saying things about him.

Hally: What goes on between me and my Dad is none of your business!

Sam: Then don't tell me about it. If that's all you've got to say about him, I don't want to hear.

(For a moment Hally is at loss for a response.)

Hally: Just get on with your bloody work and shut up.

Sam: Swearing at me won't help you.

Hally: Yes, it does! Mind your own fucking business and shut up!

Sam: Okay. If that's the way you want it, I'll stop trying.

(He turns away. This infuriates Hally even more.)

Hally: Good. Because what you've been trying to do is meddle in something you know nothing about. All that concerns you in here, Sam, is to try and do what you get paid for—keep the place clean and serve the customers. In plain words, just get on with your job. My mother is right. She's always warning me about allowing you to get too familiar. Well, this time you've gone too far. It's going to stop right now.

(No response from Sam.)

You're only a servant in here, and don't forget it.

(Still no response. Hally is trying hard to get one.)

And as far as my father is concerned, all you need to remember is that he is your boss.

Sam *(Needled at last.)*: No, he isn't. I get paid by your mother.

Hally: Don't argue with me, Sam!

Sam: Then don't say he's my boss.

Hally: He's a white man and that's good enough for you.

Sam: I'll try to forget you said that.

Hally: Don't! Because you won't be doing me a favor if you do. I'm telling you to remember it.

(A pause. Sam pulls himself together and makes one last effort.)

Sam: Hally, Hally . . . ! Come on now. Let's stop before it's too late. You're right. We *are* on dangerous ground. If we're not careful, somebody is going to get hurt.

Hally: It won't be me.

Sam: Don't be so sure.

Hally: I don't know what you're talking about, Sam.

Sam: Yes, you do.

Hally *(Furious.):* Jesus, I wish you would stop trying to tell me what I do and what I don't know.

(Sam gives up. He turns to Willie.)

Sam: Let's finish up.

Hally: Don't turn your back on me! I haven't finished talking.

(He grabs Sam by the arm and tries to make him turn around. Sam reacts with a flash of anger.)

Sam: Don't do that, Hally! *(Facing the boy.)* All right, I'm listening. Well? What do you want to say to me?

Hally *(Pause as Hally looks for something to say.):* To begin with, why don't you also start calling me Master Harold, like Willie.

Sam: Do you mean that?

Hally: Why the hell do you think I said it?

Sam: And if I don't.

Hally: You might just lose your job.

Sam *(Quietly and very carefully.):* If you make me say it once, I'll never call you anything else again.

Hally: So? *(The boy confronts the man.)* Is that meant to be a threat?

Sam: Just telling you what will happen if you make me do that. You must decide what it means to you.

Hally: Well, I have. It's good news. Because that is exactly what Master Harold wants from now on. Think of it as a little lesson in respect, Sam, that's long overdue, and I hope you remember it as well as you do your geography. I can tell you now that somebody who will be glad to hear I've finally given it to you will be my Dad. Yes! He agrees with my Mom. He's always going on about it as well. "You must teach the boys to show you more respect, my son."

Sam: So now you can stop complaining about going home. Everybody is going to be happy tonight.

Hally: That's perfectly correct. You see, you mustn't get the wrong idea about me and my Dad, Sam. We also have our good times together. Some bloody good laughs. He's got a marvelous sense of humor. Want to know what our favorite joke is? He gives out a big groan, you see, and says: "It's not fair, is it, Hally?" Then I have to ask: "What, chum?" And then he says: "A nigger's arse" . . . and we both have a good laugh.

(The men stare at him with disbelief.)

What's the matter, Willie? Don't you catch the joke? You always were a bit slow on the uptake. It's what is called a pun. You see, fair means both light in color and to be just and decent. *(He turns to Sam.)* I thought *you* would catch it, Sam.

Sam: Oh ja, I catch it all right.

Hally: But it doesn't appeal to your sense of humor.

Sam: Do you really laugh?

Hally: Of course.

Sam: To please him? Make him feel good?

Hally: No, for heaven's sake! I laugh because I think it's a bloody good joke.

Sam: You're really trying hard to be ugly, aren't you? And why drag poor old Willie into it? He's done nothing to you except show you the respect you want so badly. That's also not being fair, you know . . . and *I* mean just or decent.

Willie: It's all right, Sam. Leave it now.

Sam: It's me you're after. You should just have said "Sam's arse" . . . because that's the one you're trying to kick. Anyway, how do you know it's not fair? You've never seen it. Do you want to? *(He drops his trousers and underpants and presents his backside for Hally's inspection.)* Have a good look. A real Basuto[27] arse . . . which is about as nigger as they can come. Satisfied? *(Trousers up.)* Now you can make your Dad even happier when you go home tonight. Tell him I showed you my arse and he is quite right. It's not fair. And if it will give him an even better laugh next time, I'll also let *him* have a look. Come, Willie, let's finish up and go.

(Sam and Willie start to tidy up the tea room. Hally doesn't move. He waits for a moment when Sam passes him.)

Hally *(Quietly.):* Sam . . .

(Sam stops and looks expectantly at the boy. Hally spits in his face. A long and heartfelt groan from Willie. For a few seconds Sam doesn't move.)

Sam *(Taking out a handkerchief and wiping his face.):* It's all right, Willie.

(To Hally.)

Ja, well, you've done it . . . Master Harold. Yes, I'll start calling you that from now on. It won't be difficult anymore. You've hurt yourself, Master Harold. I saw it coming. I warned you, but you wouldn't listen. You've just hurt yourself *bad.* And you're a coward, Master Harold. The face you should be spitting in is your father's . . . but you used mine, because you

[27] A person from Basutoland, South Africa.

think you're safe inside your fair skin . . . and this time I don't mean just or decent. *(Pause, then moving violently towards Hally.)* Should I hit him, Willie?

Willie *(Stopping Sam.):* No, Boet Sam.

Sam *(Violently.):* Why not?

Willie: It won't help, Boet Sam.

Sam: I don't want to help! I want to hurt him.

Willie: You also hurt yourself.

Sam: And if he had done it to you, Willie?

Willie: Me? Spit at me like I was a dog? *(A thought that had not occurred to him before. He looks at Hally.)* Ja. Then I want to hit him. I want to hit him hard!

(A dangerous few seconds as the men stand staring at the boy. Willie turns away, shaking his head.)

But maybe all I do is go cry at the back. He's little boy, Boet Sam. Little *white* boy. Long trousers now, but he's still little boy.

Sam *(His violence ebbing away into defeat as quickly as it flooded.):* You're right. So go on, then: groan again, Willie. You do it better than me. *(To Hally.)* You don't know all of what you've just done . . . Master Harold. It's not just that you've made me feel dirtier than I've ever been in my life . . . I mean, how do I wash off yours and your father's filth? . . . I've also failed. A long time ago I promised myself I was going to try and do something, but you've just shown me . . . Master Harold . . . that I've failed. *(Pause.)* I've also got a memory of a little white boy when he was still wearing short trousers and a black man, but they're not flying a kite. It was the old Jubilee days, after dinner one night. I was in my room. You came in and just stood against the wall, looking down at the ground, and only after I'd asked you what you wanted, what was wrong, I don't know how many times, did you speak and even then so softly I almost didn't hear you. "Sam, please help me to go and fetch my Dad." Remember? He was dead drunk on the floor of the Central Hotel Bar. They'd phoned for your Mom, but you were the only one at home. And do you remember how we did it? You went in first by yourself to ask permission for me to go into the bar. Then I loaded him onto my back like a baby and carried him back to the boarding house with you following behind carrying his crutches. *(Shaking his head as he remembers.)* A crowded Main Street with all the people watching a little white boy following his drunk father on a nigger's back! I felt for that little boy . . . Master Harold. I felt for him. After that we still had to clean him up, remember? He'd messed in his trousers, so we had to clean him up and get him into bed.

Hally *(Great pain.):* I love him, Sam.

Sam: I know you do. That's why I tried to stop you from saying these things about him. It would have been so simple if you could have just despised him for being a weak man. But he's your father. You love him and you're ashamed of him. You're ashamed of so much! . . . And now that's going to include yourself. That was the promise I made to myself: to try and stop that happening. *(Pause.)* After we got him to bed you came back with me to my room and sat in a corner and carried on just looking down at the ground. And for days after that! You hadn't done anything wrong, but you went around as if you owed the world an apology for being alive. I didn't like seeing that! That's not the way a boy grows up to be a man! . . . But the one person who should have been teaching you what that means was the cause of your shame. If you really want to know, that's why I made you that kite. I wanted you to look up, be proud of something, of yourself . . . *(Bitter smile at the memory.)* . . . and you certainly were that when I left you with it up there on the hill. Oh, ja . . . something else! . . . If you ever do write it as a short story, there *was* a twist in our ending. I couldn't sit down there and stay with you. It was a "Whites Only" bench. You were too young, too excited to notice then. But not anymore. If you're not careful . . . Master Harold . . . you're going to be sitting up there by yourself for a long time to come, and there won't be a kite in the sky. *(Sam has got nothing more to say. He exits into the kitchen, taking off his waiter's jacket.)*

Willie: Is bad. Is all all bad in here now.

Hally *(Books into his school case, raincoat on.):* Willie . . . *(It is difficult to speak.)* Will you lock up for me and look after the keys?

Willie: Okay.

(Sam returns. Hally goes behind the counter and collects the few coins in the cash register. As he starts to leave . . .)

Sam: Don't forget the comic books.

(Hally returns to the counter and puts them in his case. He starts to leave again.)

Sam *(To the retreating back of the boy.):* Stop . . . Hally . . .

(Hally stops, but doesn't turn to face him.)

Hally . . . I've got no right to tell you what being a man means if I don't behave like one myself, and I'm not doing so well at that this afternoon. Should we try again, Hally?

Hally: Try what?

Sam: Fly another kite, I suppose. It worked once, and this time I need it as much as you do.

Hally: It's still raining, Sam. You can't fly kites on rainy days, remember.

Sam: So what do we do? Hope for better weather tomorrow?

Hally *(Helpless gesture.):* I don't know. I don't know anything anymore.

Sam: You sure of that, Hally? Because it would be pretty hopeless if that was true. It would mean nothing has been learnt in here this afternoon, and there was a hell of a lot of teaching going on . . . one way or the other. But anyway, I don't believe you. I reckon there's one thing you know. You don't *have* to sit up there by yourself. You know what that bench means now, and you can leave it any time you choose. All you've got to do is stand up and walk away from it.

(Hally leaves. Willie goes up quietly to Sam.)

Willie: Is okay, Boet Sam. You see. Is . . . *(He can't find any better words.)* . . . *is* going to be okay tomorrow. *(Changing his tone.)* Hey, Boet Sam! *(He is trying hard.)* You right. I think about it and you right. Tonight I find Hilda and say sorry. And make promise I won't beat her no more. You hear me, Boet Sam?

Sam: I hear you, Willie.

Willie: And when we practice I relax and romance with her from beginning to end. Non-stop! You watch! Two weeks' time: "First prize for promising newcomers: Mr. Willie Malopo and Miss Hilda Samuels." *(Sudden impulse.)* To hell with it! I walk home. *(He goes to the jukebox, puts in a coin and selects a record. The machine comes to life in the gray twilight, blushing its way through a spectrum of soft, romantic colors.)* How did you say it, Boet Sam? Let's dream. *(Willie sways with the music and gestures for Sam to dance.)*

(Sarah Vaughan sings.)

"Little man you're crying,
I know why you're blue,
Someone took your kiddy car away;
Better go to sleep now,
Little man you've had a busy day." *(etc. etc.)*
You lead. I follow.

(The men dance together.)

"Johnny won your marbles,
Tell you what we'll do;
Dad will get you new ones
right away;
Better go to sleep now,
Little man you've had a
busy day."

Explorations of the Text

1. Describe the characters in the initial scene. What does the dancing symbolize? What is the nature of the relationship between Sam and Willie before Hally enters?
2. Describe Hally. How does his relationship with his father affect him? Analyze his attitudes toward Willie and Sam.
3. To what extent are the relationships in this play determined by South African history, culture, economics, and politics?

4. Why is Hally so pessimistic? Explain: "It's a bloody awful world when you come to think of it. People can be real bastards."
5. Explore the discussion of history, "magnitude," and social reformers. What does it reveal about Hally? about Sam?
6. What does the kite symbolize? How does Hally describe the event? Why does Sam not give a true answer to Hally's question, "Why did you make that kite, Sam?"
7. Why does Hally long to be in the Jubilee again? Why did life "[feel] the right size in there"?
8. What can be inferred from the first telephone conversation? What is Hally's attitude toward his father's returning home from the hospital? How does it affect his attitude about life?
9. Why does Sam believe that ballroom dancing is an art? Why does Hally choose to write about the contest? Is the scene **ironic**?
10. Consider the line: "There's no collisions out there, Hally." What are the big collisions?
11. What does dreaming represent to Sam?
12. Why does Hally not finish his composition on "A World Without Collisions"?
13. Examine the second telephone conversation. Why does Hally say, "Life's a fuck-up and it's never going to change"?
14. Why do "the cripples" trip everyone else? Why does Sam warn Hally to be careful about mocking his father? Why does Hally warn Sam?
15. Why does Hally insult Sam and Willie? Why does Hally insist on being called "Master Harold"?
16. Why does Hally spit in Sam's face? Why does Sam retort, "The face you should be spitting in is your father's"?
17. Discuss the incident in the Central Hotel Bar.
18. Why did Sam build the kite? Why did he want Hally or "Master Harold" not to be ashamed?
19. Will Hally leave "the bench" now that he knows what it means?
20. Discuss the relationships of the characters at the end of the play. Look carefully at the title and the punctuation in the title.
21. Fugard wrote in his notebook about a moment in his childhood that led him to spit in Sam's face. After this action, Fugard stated that he was "overwhelmed" with "shame." Consider this personal revelation in relation to the play and to works by Walcott and Gordimer.

The Reading/Writing Connection

1. Write a journal entry in the voice of Hally, Sam, or Willie.
2. Respond to the final incident. Freewrite.

3. "Think" Topic: What is Willie's function in the play? Discuss in a paragraph.

Ideas for Writing

1. Describe Sam as a spiritual father or as a mentor.
2. Discuss power and powerlessness in the play. Refer to Gordimer and to Morrison.
3. Write a character analysis of Sam or Hally.
4. Analyze the structure of the play. Why are there no scenes or acts?

THE NOBEL PRIZE SPEECH

Toni Morrison

Toni Morrison (1931–) was born in Lorain, Ohio, and was educated at Harvard and Cornell Universities. She published her first novel, The Bluest Eye, *in 1970. Subsequent novels include* Sula *(1974);* Song of Solomon *(1977);* Beloved *(1987), which won the Pulitzer Prize; and* Paradise *(1998). In 1993, Morrison was awarded the Nobel Prize for Literature, the first African American woman to receive it. She serves as the Golheen Professor of the Humanities at Princeton University.*

1993

Members of the Swedish Academy, Ladies and Gentlemen:

Narrative has never been merely entertainment for me. It is, I believe, one of the principal ways in which we absorb knowledge. I hope you will understand, then, why I begin these remarks with the opening phrase of what must be the oldest sentence in the world, and the earliest one we remember from childhood: "Once upon a time . . ."

"Once upon a time there was an old woman. Blind but wise." Or was it an old man? A guru, perhaps. Or a *griot*[1] soothing restless children. I have heard this story, or one exactly like it, in the lore of several cultures.

"Once upon a time there was an old woman. Blind. Wise."

5 In the version I know the woman is the daughter of slaves, black, American, and lives alone in a small house outside of town. Her reputation for wisdom is without peer and without question. Among her people she is both the law and its transgression. The honor she is paid and the awe in which she is held reach beyond her neighborhood to places far away; to the city where the intelligence of rural prophets is the source of much amusement.

One day the woman is visited by some young people who seem to be bent on disproving her clairvoyance and showing her up for the fraud they believe she is. Their plan is simple: they enter her house and ask the one question the answer to which rides solely on her difference from them, a difference they

---

[1] A storyteller in western Africa.

regard as a profound disability: her blindness. They stand before her, and one of them says,

"Old woman, I hold in my hand a bird. Tell me whether it is living or dead."

She does not answer, and the question is repeated. "Is the bird I am holding living or dead?"

Still she does not answer. She is blind and cannot see her visitors, let alone what is in their hands. She does not know their color, gender, or homeland. She knows only their motive.

10 The old woman's silence is so long, the young people have trouble holding their laughter.

Finally she speaks, and her voice is soft but stern. "I don't know," she says. "I don't know whether the bird you are holding is dead or alive, but what I do know is that it is in your hands. It is in your hands."

Her answer can be taken to mean: if it is dead, you have either found it that way or you have killed it. If it is alive, you can still kill it. Whether it is to stay alive is your decision. Whatever the case, it is your responsibility.

For parading their power and her helplessness, the young visitors are reprimanded, told they are responsible not only for the act of mockery but also for the small bundle of life sacrificed to achieve its aims. The blind woman shifts attention away from assertions of power to the instrument through which that power is exercised.

Speculation on what (other than its own frail body) that bird in the hand might signify has always been attractive to me, but especially so now, thinking as I have been about the work I do that has brought me to this company. So I choose to read the bird as language and the woman as a practiced writer.

15 She is worried about how the language she dreams in, given to her at birth, is handled, put into service, even withheld from her for certain nefarious purposes. Being a writer, she thinks of language partly as a system, partly as a living thing over which one has control, but mostly as agency—as an act with consequences. So the question the children put to her, "Is it living or dead?," is not unreal, because she thinks of language as susceptible to death, erasure; certainly imperiled and salvageable only by an effort of the will. She believes that if the bird in the hands of her visitors is dead, the custodians are responsible for the corpse. For her a dead language is not only one no longer spoken or written, it is unyielding language content to admire its own paralysis. Like statist language, censored and censoring. Ruthless in its policing duties, it has no desire or purpose other than to maintain the free range of its own narcotic narcissism, its own exclusivity and dominance. However, moribund, it is not without effect, for it actively thwarts the intellect, stalls conscience, suppresses human potential. Unreceptive to interrogation, it cannot form or tolerate new ideas, shape other thoughts, tell another story, fill baffling silences. Official language smitheried to sanction ignorance and preserve privilege is a suit of armor, polished to shocking glitter, a husk from which the knight departed long ago. Yet there it is; dumb, predatory, sentimental. Exciting reverence in schoolchildren, providing shelter for despots, summoning false memories of stability, harmony among the public.

She is convinced that when language dies, out of carelessness, disuse, indifference, and absence of esteem, or killed by fiat, not only she herself but all users and makers are accountable for its demise. In her country children have bitten their tongues off and use bullets instead to iterate the void of speechlessness, of disabled and disabling language, of language adults have abandoned altogether as a device for grappling with meaning, providing guidance, or expressing love. But she knows tongue-suicide is not only the choice of children. It is common among the infantile heads of state and power merchants whose evacuated language leaves them with no access to what is left of their human instincts, for they speak only to those who obey, or in order to force obedience.

The systematic looting of language can be recognized by the tendency of its users to forgo its nuanced, complex, midwifery properties, replacing them with menace and subjugation. Oppressive language does more than represent violence; it is violence; does more than represent the limits of knowledge; it limits knowledge. Whether it is obscuring state language or the faux language of mindless media; whether it is the proud but calcified language of the academy or the commodity-driven language of science; whether it is the malign language of law-without-ethics, or language designed for the estrangement of minorities, hiding its racist plunder in its literary cheek—it must be rejected, altered, and exposed. It is the language that drinks blood, laps vulnerabilities, tucks its fascist boots under crinolines of respectability and patriotism as it moves relentlessly toward the bottom line and the bottomed-out mind. Sexist language, racist language, theistic language—all are typical of the policing languages of mastery, and cannot, do not, permit new knowledge or encourage the mutual exchange of ideas.

The old woman is keenly aware that no intellectual mercenary or insatiable dictator, no paid-for politician or demagogue, no counterfeit journalist would be persuaded by her thoughts. There is and will be rousing language to keep citizens armed and arming; slaughtered and slaughtering in the mauls, courthouses, post offices, playgrounds, bedrooms, and boulevards; stirring, memorializing language to mask the pity and waste of needless death. There will be more diplomatic language to countenance rape, torture, assassination. There is and will be more seductive, mutant language designed to throttle women, to pack their throats like pâté-producing geese with their own unsayable, transgressive words; there will be more of the language of surveillance disguised as research; of politics and history calculated to render the suffering of millions mute; language glamorized to thrill the dissatisfied and bereft into assaulting their neighbors; arrogant pseudo-empirical language crafted to lock creative people into cages of inferiority and hopelessness.

Underneath the eloquence, the glamour, the scholarly associations, however stirring or seductive, the heart of such language is languishing, or perhaps not beating at all—if the bird is already dead.

20 She had thought about what could have been the intellectual history of any discipline if it had not insisted upon, or been forced into, the waste of time and life that rationalizations for and representations of dominance required—

lethal discourses of exclusion blocking access to cognition for both the excluder and the excluded.

The conventional wisdom of the Tower of Babel story is that the collapse was a misfortune. That it was the distraction or the weight of many languages that precipitated the tower's failed architecture. That one monolithic language would have expedited the building, and heaven would have been reached. Whose heaven, she wonders? And what kind? Perhaps the achievement of Paradise was premature, a little hasty if no one could take the time to understand other languages, other views, other narratives. Had they, the heaven they imagined might have been found at their feet. Complicated, demanding, yes, but a view of heaven as life; not heaven as post-life.

She would not want to leave her young visitors with the impression that language should be forced to stay alive merely to be. The vitality of language lies in its ability to limn the actual, imagined, and possible lives of its speakers, readers, writers. Although its poise is sometimes in displacing experience, it is not a substitute for it. It arcs toward the place where meaning may lie. When a president of the United States thought about the graveyard his country had become, and said, "The world will little note nor long remember what we say here. But it will never forget what they did here," his simple words were exhilarating in their life-sustaining properties because they refused to encapsulate the reality of 600,000 dead men in a cataclysmic race war. Refusing to monumentalize, disdaining the "final word," the precise "summing up," acknowledging their "poor power to add or detract," his words signal deference to the uncapturability of the life it mourns. It is deference that moves her, that recognition that language can never live up to life once and for all. Nor should it. Language can never "pin down" slavery, genocide, war. Nor should it yearn for the arrogance to be able to do so. Its force, its felicity, is in its reach toward the ineffable.

Be it grand or slender, burrowing, blasting or refusing to sanctify; whether it laughs out loud or is a cry without an alphabet, the choice word or the chosen silence, unmolested language surges toward knowledge, not its destruction. But who does not know of literature banned because it is interrogative; discredited because it is critical; erased because alternate? And how many are outraged by the thought of a self-ravaged tongue?

Word-work is sublime, she thinks, because it is generative; it makes meaning that secures our difference, our human difference—the way in which we are like no other life.

25 We die. That may be the meaning of life. But we *do* language. That may be the measure of our lives.

"Once upon a time . . ." Visitors ask an old woman a question. Who are they, these children? What did they make of that encounter? What did they hear in those final words: "The bird is in your hands"? A sentence that gestures toward possibility, or one that drops a latch? Perhaps what the children heard was, "It's not my problem. I am old, female, black, blind. What wisdom I have now is in knowing I cannot help you. The future of language is yours."

They stand there. Suppose nothing was in their hands. Suppose the visit was only a ruse, a trick to get to be spoken to, taken seriously as they have not been before. A chance to interrupt, to violate the adult world, its miasma of discourse about them. Urgent questions are at stake, including the one they have asked: "Is the bird we are holding living or dead?" Perhaps the question meant: "Could someone tells us what is life? What is death?" No trick at all; no silliness. A straightforward question worthy of the attention of a wise one. An old one. And if the old and wise who have lived life and faced death cannot describe either, who can?

But she does not; she keeps her secret, her good opinion of herself, her gnomic pronouncements, her art without commitment. She keeps her distance, enforces it and retreats into the singularity of isolation, in sophisticated, privileged space.

Nothing, no word follows her declaration of transfer. That silence is deep, deeper than the meaning available in the words she has spoken. It shivers, this silence, and the children, annoyed, fill it with language invented on the spot.

"Is there no speech," they ask her, "no words you can give us that help us break through your dossier of failures" through the education you have just given us that is no education at all because we are paying close attention to what you have done as well as to what you have said? to the barrier you have erected between generosity and wisdom?

"We have no bird in our hands, living or dead. We have only you and our important question. Is the nothing in our hands something you could not bear to contemplate, to even guess? Don't you remember being young, when language was magic without meaning? When what you could say, could not mean? When the invisible was what imagination strove to see? When questions and demands for answers burned so brightly you trembled with fury at not knowing?

"Do we have to begin consciousness with a battle heroes and heroines like you have already fought and lost, leaving us with nothing in our hands except what you imagined is there? Your answer is artful, but its artfulness embarrasses us and ought to embarrass you. Your answer is indecent in its self-congratulation. A made-for-television script that makes no sense if there is nothing in our hands.

"Why didn't you reach out, touch us with your soft fingers, delay the sound bite, the lesson, until you knew who we were? Did you so despise our trick, our modus operandi, that you could not see that we were baffled about how to get your attention? We are young. Unripe. We have heard all our short lives that we have to be responsible. What could that possibly mean in the catastrophe this world has become; where, as a poet said, 'nothing needs to be exposed since it is already barefaced'? Our inheritance is an affront. You want us to have your old, blank eyes and see only cruelty and mediocrity. Do you think we are stupid enough to perjure ourselves again and again with the fiction of nationhood? How dare you talk to us of duty when we stand waist deep in the toxin of our past?

"You trivialize us and trivialize the bird that is not in our hands. Is there no context for our lives? No song, no literature, no poem full of vitamins, no history connected to experience that you can pass along to help us start strong? You are an adult. The old one, the wise one. Stop thinking about saving your face. Think of our lives and tell us your particularized world. Make up a story. Narrative is radical, creating us at the very moment it is being created. We will not blame you if your reach exceeds your grasp; if love so ignites your words that they go down in flames and nothing is left but their scald. Or if, with the reticence of a surgeon's hands, your words suture only the places where blood might flow. We know you can never do it properly—once and for all. Passion is never enough; neither is skill. But try. For our sake and yours forget your name in the street; tell us what the world has been to you in the dark places and in the light. Don't tell us what to believe, what to fear. Show us belief's wide skirt and the stitch that unravels fear's caul. You, old woman, blessed with blindness, can speak the language that tells us what only language can: how to see without pictures. Language alone protects us from the scariness of things with no names. Language alone is meditation.

"Tell us what it is to be a woman so that we may know what it is to be a man. What moves at the margin. What it is to have no home in this place. To be set adrift from the one you knew. What it is to live at the edge of towns that cannot bear your company.

35 "Tell us about ships turned away from shorelines at Easter, placenta in a field. Tell us about a wagonload of slaves, how they sang so softly their breath was indistinguishable from the falling snow. How they knew from the hunch of the nearest shoulder that the next stop would be their last. How, with hands prayered in their sex, they thought of heat, then sun. Lifting their faces as though it was there for the taking. They stop at an inn. The driver and his mate go in with the lamp, leaving them humming in the dark. The horse's void steams into the snow beneath its hooves and the hiss and melt are the envoy of the freezing slaves.

"The inn door opens: a girl and a boy step away from its light. They climb into the wagon bed. The boy will have a gun in three years, but now he carries a lamp and a jug of warm cider. They pass it from mouth to mouth. The girl offers bread, pieces of meat, and something more: a glance into the eyes of the one she serves. One helping for each man, two for each woman. And a look. They look back. The next stop will be their last. But not this one. This one is warmed."

"It's quiet again when the children finish speaking, until the woman breaks into the silence.

"Finally," she says, "I trust you now. I trust you with the bird that is not in your hands because you have truly caught it. Look. How lovely it is, this thing we have done—together."

Explorations of the Text

1. Consider aspects of audience for this essay including and beyond: "Members of the Swedish Academy, Ladies and Gentlemen."
2. At one point in the essay we read the following: "Narrative is radical, creating us at the very moment it is being created." Analyze and explain

the complex layers of narrative Morrison uses in this essay. What is the function, for example, of the story within a story?

3. Consider the various symbolic references to the bird. How does the symbolism of the bird change? What is the significance of the "bird in . . . [the] hand"?
4. As you interpret the references to the bird, consider the possibility of forms of narrative as a way into symbolic meaning. Is this a parable, a folk story, an allegory, or even a Socratic dialogue? (Refer to chapter 9 on forms of narrative; to the excerpt from *The Symposium* in chapter 6; to "The Allegory of the Cave" in this chapter).
5. Morrison makes numerous powerful, even provocative, statements about language in this essay. Examine and discuss at least three of these statements. Do you agree with her views of language? Possible examples include the following: "The systematic looting of language can be recognized by the tendency of its user to forgo its nuanced, complex, midwifery properties replacing them with menace and subjugation"; or "Official language smitheried to sanction ignorance and preserve privilege is a suit of armor, polished to shocking glitter, a husk from which the knight departed long ago."
6. What does the speech suggest about storytelling, language, and the power of words?
7. Compare her views of the power of words with the treatment of language in *"Master Harold" . . . and the Boys.*

The Reading/Writing Connection

1. Gloss and annotate the text of the speech—concentrate on the symbolism of the bird—in preparation for class discussion of question 3 in Explorations of the Text.
2. Draft a letter from Toni Morrison to Hally in *"Master Harold."* Or imagine that Hally has read Morrison's speech. Write a letter in his voice to Morrison.
3. After reading this speech, list several questions that you have about the work. Then answer one of your questions in the form of a paragraph.

Ideas for Writing

1. Choose one of Morrison's controversial statements about language. Agree or disagree with her. Your response may take the form of a letter to Morrison.
2. Continue exploring question 4 in Explorations of the Text. Is Morrison's essay a parable, allegory, or something else? Defend your choice.
3. Is Morrison's speech effective? Convincing? Evaluate her work. Refer to the student portfolio in chapter 12 for ideas.

FICTION

Harrison Bergeron

Kurt Vonnegut, Jr.

Kurt Vonnegut, Jr. (1922–), born in Indianapolis, Indiana, enlisted in the U.S. Army in World War II and was captured by the Germans in 1944. He survived the Allied firebombing of Dresden, after which he and his fellow prisoners were given the task of searching for corpses. This experience was the source for his best-known novel, Slaughterhouse Five *(1969). His other novels include* The Sirens of Titan *(1959) and* Jailbird *(1979). His short stories are collected in* Canary in a Cathouse *(1961) and* Welcome to the Monkey House *(1968).*

1968

The year was 2081, and everybody was finally equal. They weren't only equal before God and the law. They were equal every which way. Nobody was smarter than anybody else. Nobody was better looking than anybody else. Nobody was stronger or quicker than anybody else. All this equality was due to the 211th, 212th, and 213th Amendments to the Constitution, and to the unceasing vigilance of agents of the United States Handicapper General.

Some things about living still weren't quite right, though. April, for instance, still drove people crazy by not being springtime. And it was in that clammy month that the H-G men took George and Hazel Bergeron's fourteen-year-old son, Harrison, away.

It was tragic, all right, but George and Hazel couldn't think about it very hard. Hazel had a perfectly average intelligence, which meant she couldn't think about anything except in short bursts. And George, while his intelligence was way above normal, had a little mental handicap radio in his ear. He was required by law to wear it at all times. It was tuned to a government transmitter. Every twenty seconds or so, the transmitter would send out some sharp noise to keep people like George from taking unfair advantage of their brains.

George and Hazel were watching television. There were tears on Hazel's cheeks, but she'd forgotten for the moment what they were about.

5 On the television screen were ballerinas.

A buzzer sounded in George's head. His thoughts fled in panic, like bandits from a burglar alarm.

"That was a real pretty dance, that dance they just did," said Hazel.

"Huh?" said George.

"That dance—it was nice," said Hazel.

10 "Yup," said George. He tried to think a little about the ballerinas. They weren't really very good—no better than anybody else would have been, anyway. They were burdened with sashweights and bags of birdshot, and

their faces were masked, so that no one, seeing a free and graceful gesture or a pretty face, would feel like something the cat drug in. George was toying with the vague notion that maybe dancers shouldn't be handicapped. But he didn't get very far with it before another noise in his ear radio scattered his thoughts.

George winced. So did two out of the eight ballerinas.

Hazel saw him wince. Having no mental handicap herself, she had to ask George what the latest sound had been.

"Sounded like somebody hitting a milk bottle with a ball peen hammer," said George.

"I'd think it would be real interesting, hearing all the different sounds," said Hazel, a little envious. "All the things they think up."

"Um," said George.

"Only, if I was Handicapper General, you know what I would do?" said Hazel. Hazel, as a matter of fact, bore a strong resemblance to the Handicapper General, a woman named Diana Moon Glampers. "If I was Diana Moon Glampers," said Hazel, "I'd have chimes on Sunday—just chimes. Kind of in honor of religion."

"I could think, if it was just chimes," said George.

"Well—maybe make 'em real loud," said Hazel. "I think I'd make a good Handicapper General."

"Good as anybody else," said George.

"Who knows better'n I do what normal is?" said Hazel.

"Right," said George. He began to think glimmeringly about his abnormal son who was now in jail, about Harrison, but a twenty-one-gun salute in his head stopped that.

"Boy!" said Hazel, "that was a doozy, wasn't it?"

It was such a doozy that George was white and trembling, and tears stood on the rims of his red eyes. Two of the eight ballerinas had collapsed to the studio floor, were holding their temples.

"All of a sudden you look so tired," said Hazel. "Why don't you stretch out on the sofa, so's you can rest your handicap bag on the pillows, honeybunch." She was referring to the forty-seven pounds of birdshot in a canvas bag, which was padlocked around George's neck. "Go on and rest the bag for a little while," she said. "I don't care if you're not equal to me for a while."

George weighed the bag with his hands. "I don't mind it," he said. "I don't notice it any more. It's just a part of me."

"You been so tired lately—kind of wore out," said Hazel. "If there was just some way we could make a little hole in the bottom of the bag, and just take out a few of them lead balls. Just a few."

"Two years in prison and two thousand dollars fine for every ball I took out," said George. "I don't call that a bargain."

"If you could just take a few out when you came home from work," said Hazel. "I mean—you don't compete with anybody around here. You just set around."

"If I tried to get away with it," said George, "then other people'd get away with it—and pretty soon we'd be right back to the dark ages again, with everybody competing against everybody else. You wouldn't like that, would you?"

"I'd hate it," said Hazel.

"There you are," said George. "The minute people start cheating on laws, what do you think happens to society?"

If Hazel hadn't been able to come up with an answer to this question, George couldn't have supplied one. A siren was going off in his head.

"Reckon it'd fall all apart," said Hazel.

"What would?" said George blankly.

"Society," said Hazel uncertainly. "Wasn't that what you just said?"

"Who knows?" said George.

The television program was suddenly interrupted for a news bulletin. It wasn't clear at first as to what the bulletin was about, since the announcer, like all announcers, had a serious speech impediment. For about half a minute, and in a state of high excitement, the announcer tried to say, "Ladies and gentlemen—"

He finally gave up, handed the bulletin to a ballerina to read.

"That's all right—" Hazel said of the announcer, "he tried. That's the big thing. He tried to do the best he could with what God gave him. He should get a nice raise for trying so hard."

"Ladies and gentlemen—" said the ballerina, reading the bulletin. She must have been extraordinarily beautiful, because the mask she wore was hideous. And it was easy to see that she was the strongest and most graceful of all the dancers, for her handicap bags were as big as those worn by two-hundred-pound men.

And she had to apologize at once for her voice, which was a very unfair voice for a woman to use. Her voice was a warm, luminous, timeless melody. "Excuse me—" she said, and she began again, making her voice absolutely uncompetitive.

"Harrison Bergeron, age fourteen," she said in a grackle squawk, "has just escaped from jail, where he was held on suspicion of plotting to overthrow the government. He is a genius and an athlete, is under-handicapped, and should be regarded as extremely dangerous."

A police photograph of Harrison Bergeron was flashed on the screen upside down, then sideways, upside down again, then right side up. The picture showed the full length of Harrison against a background calibrated in feet and inches. He was exactly seven feet tall.

The rest of Harrison's appearance was Halloween and hardware. Nobody had ever borne heavier handicaps. He had outgrown hindrances faster than the H-G men could think them up. Instead of a little ear radio for a mental handicap, he wore a tremendous pair of earphones, and spectacles with thick wavy lenses. The spectacles were intended to make him not only half blind, but to give him whanging headaches besides.

45 Scrap metal was hung all over him. Ordinarily, there was a certain symmetry, a military neatness to the handicaps issued to strong people, but Harrison looked like a walking junkyard. In the race of life, Harrison carried three hundred pounds.

And to offset his good looks, the H-G men required that he wear at all times a red rubber ball for a nose, keep his eyebrows shaved off, and cover his even white teeth with black caps at snaggle-tooth random.

"If you see this boy," said the ballerina, "do not—I repeat, do not—try to reason with him."

There was the shriek of a door being torn from its hinges.

Screams and barking cries of consternation came from the television set. The photograph of Harrison Bergeron on the screen jumped again and again, as though dancing to the tune of an earthquake.

50 George Bergeron correctly identified the earthquake, and well he might have—for many was the time his own home had danced to the same crashing tune. "My God—" said George, "that must be Harrison!"

The realization was blasted from his mind instantly by the sound of an automobile collision in his head.

When George could open his eyes again, the photograph of Harrison was gone. A living, breathing Harrison filled the screen.

Clanking, clownish, and huge, Harrison stood in the center of the studio. The knob of the uprooted studio door was still in his hand. Ballerinas, technicians, musicians, and announcers cowered on their knees before him, expecting to die.

"I am the Emperor!" cried Harrison. "Do you hear? I am the Emperor! Everybody must do what I say at once!" He stamped his foot and the studio shook.

55 "Even as I stand here—" he bellowed, "crippled, hobbled, sickened—I am a greater ruler than any man who ever lived! Now watch me become what I *can* become!"

Harrison tore the straps of his handicap harness like wet tissue paper, tore straps guaranteed to support five thousand pounds.

Harrison's scrap-iron handicaps crashed to the floor.

Harrison thrust his thumbs under the bar of the padlock that secured his head harness. The bar snapped like celery. Harrison smashed his headphones and spectacles against the wall.

He flung away his rubber-ball nose, revealed a man that would have awed Thor, the god of thunder.

60 "I shall now select my Empress!" he said, looking down on the cowering people. "Let the first woman who dares rise to her feet claim her mate and her throne!"

A moment passed, and then a ballerina arose, swaying like a willow.

Harrison plucked the mental handicap from her ear, snapped off her physical handicaps with marvelous delicacy. Last of all, he removed her mask.

She was blindingly beautiful.

"Now—" said Harrison, taking her hand, "shall we show the people the meaning of the word dance? Music!" he commanded.

The musicians scrambled back into their chairs, and Harrison stripped them of their handicaps, too. "Play your best," he told them, "and I'll make you barons and dukes and earls."

The music began. It was normal at first—cheap, silly, false. But Harrison snatched two musicians from their chairs, waved them like batons as he sang the music as he wanted it played. He slammed them back into their chairs.

The music began again and was much improved.

Harrison and his Empress merely listened to the music for a while—listened gravely, as though synchronizing their heartbeats with it.

They shifted their weights to their toes.

Harrison placed his big hands on the girl's tiny waist, letting her sense the weightlessness that would soon be hers.

And then, in an explosion of joy and grace, into the air they sprang!

Not only were the laws of the land abandoned, but the law of gravity and the laws of motion as well.

They reeled, whirled, swiveled, flounced, capered, gamboled, and spun.

They leaped like deer on the moon.

The studio ceiling was thirty feet high, but each leap brought the dancers nearer to it.

It became their obvious intention to kiss the ceiling.

They kissed it.

And then, neutralizing gravity with love and pure will, they remained suspended in air inches below the ceiling, and they kissed each other for a long, long time.

It was then that Diana Moon Glampers, the Handicapper General, came into the studio with a double-barreled ten-gauge shotgun. She fired twice, and the Emperor and the Empress were dead before they hit the floor.

Diana Moon Glampers loaded the gun again. She aimed it at the musicians and told them they had ten seconds to get their handicaps back on.

It was then that the Bergerons' television tube burned out.

Hazel turned to comment about the blackout to George. But George had gone out into the kitchen for a can of beer.

George came back in with the beer, paused while a handicap signal shook him up. And then he sat down again. "You been crying?" he said to Hazel.

"Yup," she said.

"What about?" he said.

"I forget," she said. "Something real sad on television."

"What was it?" he said.

"It's all kind of mixed up in my mind," said Hazel.

"Forget sad things," said George.

"I always do," said Hazel.

"That's my girl," said George. He winced. There was the sound of a rivetting gun in his head.

"Gee—I could tell that one was a doozy," said Hazel.

"You can say that again," said George.
"Gee—" said Hazel, "I could tell that one was a doozy."

Explorations of the Text

1. React to the first paragraph. What associations does the concept of "equality" evoke?
2. Why do people in the story have "handicaps"?
3. Contrast Hazel and George. Why does George's "mental handicap radio" make noise?
4. Analyze Harrison's appearance, character, behavior, and rebellion. Why is he depicted as a fourteen-year-old? Why is Harrison dangerous?
5. Explain the conclusion of the story. Is it **ironic?**
6. Evaluate the **satire** and humor in the story.
7. Why does Vonnegut create a series of short paragraphs to depict Harrison's and the ballerina's dance? What is the effect of this technique?
8. Discuss the world of 2081. What are its collective values? In what ways does Vonnegut criticize North American society and its values?

The Reading/Writing Connection

1. "Think" Topic: React to Vonnegut's vision of equality.
2. Begin a journal entry: "It was 2081 and. . . ." Freewrite. (Imagine that you are a character in a place.)
3. Write a monologue in Diana Glampers's or in Harrison's voice.

Ideas for Writing

1. What critique of North American society is presented?
2. Compare this story's view of individuality with the view of identity in "To live in the Borderlands means you."

The Imagination of Disaster

Mary Gordon

Mary Gordon (1950–), born on Long Island, has written five novels: including Final Payments *(1978),* Men and Angels *(1985), and* Spending *(1998). Her shorter fiction has been collected in* Temporary Shelter *(1987) and* The Rest of Life *(1993). Her nonfiction writings have been collected in* Good Boys and Dead Girls *(1991) and* Seeing Through Places: Reflections on Geography and Identity *(1999). She has written a memoir,* The Shadow Man *(1996), and a biography of*

Joan of Arc (2000). Winner of the Kafka Prize for fiction, she holds the McIntosh Chair as Professor of English at Barnard College. Her writing is marked by its relentless scrutiny of experience.

1987

I am aware of my own inadequacies, of course, but if this happens, no one will be adequate: to be adequate requires a prior act of the imagination, and this is impossible. We are armed; they are armed; someone will take the terrible, the unimaginable, vengeful step. And so we think in images of all that we have known to be the worst. We think of cold, of heat, of heaviness. But that is not it; that does not begin to be it. A mother thinks: how will I carry my children, what will I feed them? But this is not it, this is not it. There will be no place to carry them, food itself will be dangerous. We cannot prepare ourselves; we have known nothing of the kind.

But some days I think: I should prepare, I should do only what is difficult. I think: I will teach myself to use a gun. I hide behind the curtain, and when the mailman comes I try to imagine his right temple in the gunsight as he goes down the sidewalk. How sure one must be to pull the trigger, even to kill for one's own children, for their food, their water, perhaps even poison. The imagination is of no use.

The imagination is of no use. When I run two miles a day, I make myself run faster, farther, make myself feel nauseated, make myself go on despite my burning ribs. In case this one day will be a helpful memory, a useful sensation. Of endurance and of pain. My daughter comes and asks my help in making clay animals. On days like this, I want to say: no, no clay animals, we'll dig, we'll practice digging, once your father was a soldier, he will teach you to use a gun. But of course I cannot do this; I cannot pervert her life so that she will be ready for the disaster. There is no readiness; there is no death in life.

❋ ❋ ❋

My baby son is crying. Will it be harder for males or females? Will they capture boy children to wander in roving gangs? Will my son, asleep now in his crib, wander the abashed landscape, killing other boys for garbage? Will my daughter root among the grain stalks, glistening with danger, for the one kernel of safe nourishment? Ought I to train them for capitulation? I croon to him; I rock him, watch the gold sun strike a maple, turn it golder. My daughter comes into the room, still in her long nightgown. Half an hour ago, I left her to dress herself. She hasn't succeeded; she's used the time to play with my lipstick. It is all over her face, her hands, her arms. Inside her belly is another tiny belly, empty. Will she have the chance to fill herself with a child, as I have filled myself with her and with her brother? On days like this I worry: if she can't dress herself in half an hour, if she cannot obey me in an instant, like the crack of a whip, will she perish? She can charm anyone. Will there be a place for charm after the disaster? What will be its face?

5 When the babysitter comes, I get into my car. She can make my daughter obey in an instant; she can put my son to sleep without rocking him, or feeding

him, or patting him in his crib. On days like this I think I should leave them to her and never come back, for I will probably not survive and with her they will have a greater chance of surviving.

To calm myself I read poetry. When it comes, will the words of "To His Coy Mistress"[1] comfort me, distract me as I wait to hear the news of the death of everything? I want to memorize long poems in case we must spend months in hiding underground. I will memorize "Lycidas,"[2] although I don't like Milton. I will memorize it because of what Virginia Woolf[3] said: "Milton is a comfort because he is nothing like our life." At that moment, when we are waiting for the news of utter death, what we will need is something that is nothing like our life.

❄ ❄ ❄

I come home, and begin making dinner. I have purposely bought a tough cut of meat; I will simmer it for hours. As if that were an experience that would be helpful; as if that were the nature of it: afterwards only tough cuts of meat. I pretend I am cooking on a paraffin stove in a basement. But I cannot restrain myself from using herbs; my own weakness makes me weep. When it comes, there will be no herbs, or spices, no beautiful vegetables like the vegetables that sit on my table in a wooden bowl: an eggplant, yellow squash, tomatoes, a red pepper and some leeks. The solid innocence of my vegetables! When it comes, there will be no innocence. When it comes, there will be no safety. Even the roots hidden deep in the earth of forests will be the food of danger. There will be nothing whose history will be dear. I could weep for my furniture. The earth will be abashed; the furniture will stand out, balked and shameful in the ruin of everything that was our lives.

We have invited friends to dinner. My friend and I talk about our children. I think of her after the disaster; I try to imagine how she will look. I see her standing with a knife; her legs are knotted and blue veins stick out of them like bruised grapes. She is wearing a filthy shirt; her front teeth are missing; her thick black hair is falling out. I will have to kill her to keep her from entering our shelter. If she enters it she will kill us with her knife or the broken glass in her pocket. Kill us for the food we hide which may, even as we take it in, be killing us. Kill us for the life of her own children.

We are sitting on the floor. I want to turn to my friend and say: I do not want to have to kill you. But they have not had my imagination of disaster, and there can be no death in the midst of life. We talk about the autumn; this year we'll walk more in the country, we agree. We kiss our friends good night. Good night, good night, we say, we love you. Good night, I think, I pray I do not have to kill you for my children's food.

❄ ❄ ❄

[1] Poem by Andrew Marvell. See chapter 6.

[2] Poem by John Milton, English poet (1608–84).

[3] English novelist and essayist (1882–1941).

10 My husband puts on red pajamas. I do not speak of my imagination of disaster. He takes my nightgown off and I see us embracing in the full-length mirror. We are, for now, human, beautiful. We go to bed. He swims above me, digging in. I climb and meet him, strike and fall away. Because we have done this, two more of us breathe in the next room, bathed and perfect as arithmetic.

I think: Perhaps I should kill us all now and save us from the degradation of disaster. Perhaps I should kill us while we are whole and dignified and full of our sane beauty. I do not want to be one of the survivors; I am willing to die with my civilization. I have said to my husband: Let us put aside some pills, so that when the disaster strikes we may lie down together, holding each other's hands and die before the whole earth is abashed. But no, he says, I will not let you do that, we must fight. Someone will survive, he says, why not us? Why not our children?

Because the earth will be abashed, I tell him. Because our furniture will stand out shamed among the glistening poisoned objects. Because we cannot imagine it; because imagination is inadequate; because for this disaster, there is no imagination.

But because of this I may be wrong. We live with death, the stone in the belly, the terror on the road alone. People have lived with it always. But we live knowing not only that we will die, that we may suffer, but that all that we hold dear will finish; that there will be no more familiar. That the death we fear we cannot even imagine, it will not be the distinguished thing, it will not be the face of dream, or even nightmare. For we cannot dream the poisoned earth abashed, empty of all we know.

Explorations of the Text

1. Explain the many references to "when it comes."
2. Why is no one able to be "adequate"? Why is the "imagination . . . of no use"?
3. Discuss: "when we are waiting for the news of utter death, what we will need is something that is nothing like our life."
4. How does the narrator try to prepare for the disaster? Do some of her thoughts about preparation seem foolish? cruel?
5. "I shall have to kill her to keep her from entering our shelter." Would you kill a friend to preserve your own life? your children's lives?
6. Explore the conclusion: "The death we fear we cannot even imagine."
7. The word "imagination" appears frequently. Does the word always have the same meaning?
8. Gordon describes the earth as "abashed" several times. How can the earth be "abashed"?
9. Why will the furniture in her house be "balked and shameful" and "shamed among the glistening poisoned objects"?

10. Contrast this dystopian vision with Vonnegut's story. What is the "unimaginable" in each vision?

The Reading/Writing Connection

1. Imagine your response to this "disaster."
2. What would you do to preserve your life? your children's lives?
3. "Think" Topic: Do you agree: "We live with death, the stone in the belly, the terror on the road alone"? Respond in a paragraph.

Ideas for Writing

1. Discuss the oppositions of life and death in this story. How does imagery create this tension?
2. Analyze the character of the narrator. Concentrate on point of view and tone.
3. Imagine the "unimaginable." Write a descriptive essay. Use question 1 in The Reading/Writing Connection as a beginning.

Girls at War

Chinua Achebe

*"Your personal god fights for you": these words translate the name of Chinua Achebe, born Albert Chinwalumogo Achebe (1930–) in Ogide, Nigeria. In writing about the clash between cultures and the quest for independence, Achebe has celebrated the spirit of Africa by writing essays, children's books, poetry, short stories, and novels. His work includes novels (*Things Fall Apart, *1958, which brought him immediate fame, and* No Longer at Ease, *1960), short stories (*Girls at War, *1972), and poetry (*Beware, Soul Brother and Other Poems, *1971).*

1972

The first time their paths crossed, nothing happened. That was in the first heady days of warlike preparation, when thousands of young men (and sometimes women, too) were daily turned away from enlistment centers because far too many of them were coming forward burning with readiness to bear arms in defense of the exciting new nation.[1]

[1] Nigeria became an independent nation in 1960. Later, civil unrest broke out between the Hausa and Igbo peoples, and the Igbos fled to the east, where they formed the independent nation of Biafra and seceded from Nigeria. The war lasted from 1967 to 1970, when the Biafrans surrendered.

The second time they met was at a checkpoint at Awka. Then the war had started and was slowly moving southwards from the distant northern sector. He was driving from Onitsha to Enugu and was in a hurry. Although intellectually he approved of thorough searches at roadblocks, emotionally he was always offended whenever he had to submit to them. He would probably not admit it but the feeling people got was that if you were put through a search then you could not really be one of the big people. Generally he got away without a search by pronouncing in his deep, authoritative voice: "Reginal Nwankwo, Ministry of Justice." That almost always did it. But sometimes either through ignorance or sheer cussedness the crowd at the odd checkpoint would refuse to be impressed. As happened now at Awka. Two constables carrying heavy Mark 4 rifles were watching distantly from the roadside, leaving the actual searching to local vigilantes.

"I am in a hurry," he said to the girl who now came up to his car. "My name is Reginald Nwankwo, Ministry of Justice."

"Good afternoon, sir. I want to see your boot."

5 "Oh Christ! What do you think is in the boot?"

"I don't know, sir."

He got out of the car in suppressed rage, stalked to the back, opened the boot, and holding the lid up with his left hand he motioned with the right as if to say: After you!

"Are you satisfied?" he demanded.

"Yes, sir. Can I see your pigeonhole?"

10 "Christ Almighty!"

"Sorry to delay you, sir. But you people gave us this job to do."

"Never mind. You are damn right. It's just that I happen to be in a hurry. But never mind. That's the glove box. Nothing there as you can see."

"All right, sir, close it." Then she opened the rear door and bent down to inspect under the seats. It was then he took the first real look at her, starting from behind. She was a beautiful girl in a breasty blue jersey, khaki jeans, and canvas shoes with the new-style hair plait which gave a girl a defiant look and which they called—for reasons of their own—"air force base"; and she looked vaguely familiar.

"I am all right, sir," she said at last, meaning she was through with her task. "You don't recognize me?"

15 "No. Should I?"

"You gave me a lift to Enugu that time I left my school to go and join the militia."

"Ah, yes, you were the girl. I told you, didn't I, to go back to school because girls were not required in the militia. What happened?"

"They told me to go back to my school or join the Red Cross."

"You see, I was right. So, what are you doing now?"

20 "Just patching up with Civil Defense."

"Well, good luck to you. Believe me, you are a great girl."

That was the day he finally believed there might be something in this talk about revolution. He had seen plenty of girls and women marching and demonstrating before now. But somehow he had never been able to give it much thought. He didn't doubt that the girls and the women took themselves seriously, they obviously did. But so did the little kids who marched up and down the streets at the time, drilling with sticks and wearing their mothers' soup bowls for steel helmets. The prime joke of the time among his friends was the contingent of girls from a local secondary school marching behind a banner: WE ARE IMPREGNABLE!

But after that encounter at the Awka checkpoint he simply could not sneer at the girls again, nor at the talk of revolution, for he had seen it in action in that young woman whose devotion had simply and without self-righteousness convicted him of gross levity. What were her words? We are doing the work you asked us to do. She wasn't going to make an exception even for one who once did her a favor. He was sure she would have searched her own father just as rigorously.

When their paths crossed a third time, at least eighteen months later, things had got very bad. Death and starvation, having long chased out the headiness of the early days, now left in some places blank resignation, in others a rock-like, even suicidal, defiance. But surprisingly enough there were many at this time who had no other desire than to corner whatever good things were still going and to enjoy themselves to the limit. For such people a strange normalcy had returned to the world. All those nervous checkpoints disappeared. Girls became girls once more and boys boys. It was a tight, blockaded, and desperate world but nonetheless a world—with some goodness and some badness and plenty of heroism, which, however, happened most times far, far below the eye level of the people in this story—in out-of-the-way refugee camps, in the damp tatters, in the hungry and barehanded courage of the first line of fire.

25 Reginald Nwankwo lived in Owerri then. But that day he had gone to Nkwerri in search of relief. He had got from Caritas in Owerri a few heads of stockfish, some tinned meat, and the dreadful American stuff called Formula Two, which he felt certain was some kind of animal feed. But he always had a vague suspicion that not being a Catholic put one at a disadvantage with Caritas. So he went now to see an old friend who ran the WCC depot at Nkwerri to get other items like rice, beans, and that excellent cereal commonly called *Gabon gari.*[2]

He left Owerri at six in the morning so as to catch his friend at the depot, where he was known never to linger beyond 8:30 for fear of air raids. Nwankwo was very fortunate that day. The depot had received on the previous day large supplies of new stock as a result of an unusual number of plane landings a few nights earlier. As his driver loaded tins and bags and cartons into his car the starved crowds that perpetually hung around relief centers made

[2] **Gari** is a staple made from a starchy root that when cooked has the consistency of grits. During the civil war, when the Nigerian government imposed a food embargo on Biafra, relief supplies were flown in from Gabon. One supply, farina, was used as a substitute for gari, and hence was called Gabon gari.

crude, ungracious remarks like "War Can Continue!" meaning the WCC! Somebody else shouted "*Irevolu!*" and his friends replied "*shum! "Irevolu!*" "*shum!*" "*Isofeli?*" "*shum*" "*Isofeli?*" "*Mba!*"[3]

Nwankwo was deeply embarrassed not by the jeers of this scarecrow crowd of rags and floating ribs but by the independent accusation of their wasted bodies and sunken eyes. Indeed, he would probably have felt much worse had they said nothing, simply looked on in silence, as his boot was loaded with milk, and powdered egg and oats and tinned meat and stockfish. By nature such singular good fortune in the midst of a general desolation was certain to embarrass him. But what could a man do? He had a wife and four children living in the remote village of Ogbu and completely dependent on what relief he could find and send them. He couldn't abandon them to kwashiorkor. The best he could do—and did do, as a matter of fact—was to make sure that whenever he got sizable supplies like now he made over some of it to his driver, Johnson, with a wife and six, or was it seven, children and a salary of ten pounds a month when *gari* in the market was climbing to one pound per cigarette cup. In such a situation one could do nothing at all for crowds; at best one could try to be of some use to one's immediate neighbors. That was all.

On his way back to Owerri, a very attractive girl by the roadside waved for a lift. He ordered the driver to stop. Scores of pedestrians, dusty and exhausted, some military, some civilian, swooped down on the car from all directions.

"No, no, no," said Nwankwo firmly. "It's the young woman I stopped for. I have a bad tire and can only take one person. Sorry."

"My son, please," cried one old woman in despair, gripping the door handle.

"Old woman, you want to be killed?" shouted the driver as he pulled away, shaking her off. Nwankwo had already opened a book and sunk his eyes there.

For at least a mile after that he did not even look at the girl until she, finding, perhaps, the silence too heavy, said: "You've saved me today. Thank you."

"Not at all. Where are you going?"

"To Owerri. You don't recognize me?"

"Oh yes, of course. What a fool I am . . . You are . . ."

"Gladys."

"That's right, the militia girl. You've changed, Gladys. You were always beautiful, of course, but now you are a beauty queen. What do you do these days?"

"I am in the Fuel Directorate."

"That's wonderful."

---

[3] **Irevolu** and **shum** are a variation of *revolution.* **Isofeli** means "are you joining them (the revolutionaries) in the feast?" or are the poor people benefiting from the so-called revolution? The final response, **"Mba!"** means "No."

It was wonderful, he thought, but even more it was tragic. She wore a high-tinted wig and a very expensive skirt and low-cut blouse. Her shoes, obviously from Gabon, must have cost a fortune. In short, thought Nwankwo, she had to be in the keep of some well-placed gentleman, one of those piling up money out of the war.

"I broke my rule today to give you a lift. I never give lifts these days."

"Why?"

"How many people can you carry? It is better not to try at all. Look at that old woman."

"I thought you would take her."

He said nothing to that and after another spell of silence Gladys thought maybe he was offended and so added: "Thank you for breaking your rule for me." She was scanning his face, turned slightly away.

He smiled, turned, and tapped her on the lap. "What are you going to Owerri to do?"

"I am going to visit my girlfriend."

"Girlfriend? You sure?"

"Why not? . . . If you drop me at her house you can see her. Only I pray God she hasn't gone on weekend today; it will be serious."

"Why?"

"Because if she is not at home I will sleep on the road today."

"I pray to God that she is not at home."

"Why?"

"Because if she is not at home I will offer you bed and breakfast . . . What is that? he asked the driver, who had brought the car to an abrupt stop. There was no need for an answer. The small crowd ahead was looking upwards. The three scrambled out of the car and stumbled for the bush, necks twisted in a backward search of the sky. But the alarm was false. The sky was silent and clear except for two high-flying vultures. A humorist in the crowd called them Fighter and Bomber and everyone laughed in relief. The three climbed into their car again and continued their journey.

"It is much too early for raids," he said to Gladys, who had both her palms on her breast as though to still a thumping heart. "They rarely come before ten o'clock."

But she remained tongue-tied from her recent fright. Nwankwo saw an opportunity there and took it at once.

"Where does your friend live?"

"250 Douglas Road."

"Ah; that's the very center of town—a terrible place. No bunkers, nothing. I won't advise you to go there before 6 p.m.; it's not safe. If you don't mind I will take you to my place, where there is a good bunker, and then as soon as it is safe, around six, I shall drive you to your friend. How's that?"

"It's all right," she said lifelessly. "I am so frightened of this thing. That's why I refused to work in Owerri. I don't even know who asked me to come out today."

"You'll be all right. We are used to it."

"But your family is not there with you?"

"No," he said. "Nobody has his family there. We like to say it is because of air raids but I can assure you there is more to it. Owerri is a real swinging place now, and we live the life of gay bachelors."

"That is what I have heard."

"You will not just hear it; you will see it today. I shall take you to a real swinging party. A friend of mine, a lieutenant colonel, is having a birthday party. He's hired the Sound Smashers to play. I'm sure you'll enjoy it."

He was immediately and thoroughly ashamed of himself. He hated the parties and frivolities to which his friends clung like drowning men. And to talk so approvingly of them because he wanted to take a girl home! And this particular girl, too, who had once had such beautiful faith in the struggle and was betrayed (no doubt about it) by some man like him out for a good time. He shook his head sadly.

"What is it?" asked Gladys.

"Nothing. Just my thoughts."

They made the rest of the journey to Owerri practically in silence.

She made herself at home very quickly as if she was a regular girlfriend of his. She changed into a housedress and put away her auburn wig.

"That is a lovely hairdo. Why do you hide it with a wig?"

"Thank you," she said, leaving his question unanswered for a while. Then she said: "Men are funny."

"Why do you say that?"

" 'Now you are a beauty queen,' " she mimicked.

"Oh, that! I meant every word of it." He pulled her to him and kissed her. She neither refused nor yielded fully, which he liked for a start. Too many girls were simply too easy those days. War sickness, some called it.

He drove off a little later to look in at the office and she busied herself in the kitchen helping his boy with lunch. It must have been literally a look-in, for he was back within half an hour, rubbing his hands and saying he could not stay away too long from his beauty queen.

As they sat down to lunch, she said: "You have nothing in your fridge."

"Like what?" he asked, half offended.

"Like meat," she replied, undaunted.

"Do you still eat meat?" he challenged.

"Who am I? But other big men like you eat."

"I don't know which big men you have in mind. But they are not like me. I don't make money trading with the enemy or selling relief or . . ."

"Augusta's boyfriend doesn't do that. He just gets foreign exchange."

"How does he get it? He swindles the government—that's how he gets foreign exchange, whoever he is. Who is Augusta, by the way?"

"My girlfriend."

"I see."

"She gave me three dollars last time which I changed to forty-five pounds. The man gave her fifty dollars."

"Well, my dear girl, I don't traffic in foreign exchange and I don't have meat in my fridge. We are fighting a war and I happen to know that some young boys at the front drink *gari* and water once in three days."

"It is true," she said simply. "Monkey de work, baboon de chop."

"It is not even that; it is worse," he said, his voice beginning to shake. "People are dying every day. As we talk now somebody is dying."

"It is true," she said again.

"Plane!" screamed his boy from the kitchen.

"My mother!" screamed Gladys. As they scuttled toward the bunker of palm stems and red earth, covering their heads with their hands and stooping slightly in their flight, the entire sky was exploding with the clamor of jets and the huge noise of homemade antiaircraft rockets.

Inside the bunker she clung to him even after the plane had gone and the guns, late to start and also to end, had all died down again.

"It was only passing," he told her, his voice a little shaky. "It didn't drop anything. From its direction I should say it was going to the war front. Perhaps our people are pressing them. That's what they always do. Whenever our boys press them, they send an SOS to the Russians and Egyptians to bring the planes." He drew a long breath.

She said nothing, just clung to him. They could hear his boy telling the servant from the next house that there were two of them and one dived like this and the other dived like that.

"I see dem well well," said the other with equal excitement. "If no to say de ting de kill porson e for sweet for eye. To God."

"Imagine!" said Gladys, finding her voice at last. She had a way, he thought, of conveying with a few words or even a single word whole layers of meanings. Now it was at once her astonishment as well as reproof, tinged perhaps with grudging admiration for people who could be so lighthearted about these bringers of death.

"Don't be so scared," he said. She moved closer and he began to kiss her and squeeze her breasts. She yielded more and more and then fully. The bunker was dark and unswept and might harbor crawling things. He thought of bringing a mat from the main house but reluctantly decided against it. Another plane might pass and send a neighbor or simply a chance passerby crashing into them. That would be only slightly better than a certain gentleman in another air raid who was seen in broad daylight fleeing his bedroom for his bunker stark-naked, pursued by a woman in a similar state!

Just as Gladys had feared, her friend was not in town. It would seem her powerful boyfriend had wangled for her a flight to Libreville to shop. So her neighbors thought, anyway.

"Great!" said Nwankwo as they drove away. "She will come back on an arms plane loaded with shoes, wigs, pants, bras, cosmetics, and what have you, which she will then sell and make thousands of pounds. You girls are really at war, aren't you?"

She said nothing and he thought he had got through at last to her. Then suddenly she said, "That is what you men want us to do."

"Well," he said, "here is one man who doesn't want you to do that. Do you remember that girl in khaki jeans who searched me without mercy at the checkpoint?"

She began to laugh.

105 That is the girl I want you to become again. Do you remember her? No wig. I don't even think she had any earrings . . ."

"Ah, na lie-o. I had earrings."

"All right. But you know what I mean."

"That time done pass. Now everybody want survival. They call it number six. You put your number six; I put my number six. Everything all right."

The lieutenant colonel's party turned into something quite unexpected. But before it did, things had been going well enough. There was goat meat, some chicken and rice, and plenty of homemade spirits. There was one fiery brand nicknamed "tracer" which indeed sent a flame down your gullet. The funny things was, looked at in the bottle, it had the innocent appearance of an orange drink. But the thing that caused the greatest stir was the bread—one little roll for each person! It was the size of a golf ball and about the same consistency, too! But it was real bread. The band was good, too, and there were many girls. And to improve matters even further two white Red Cross people soon arrived with a bottle of Courvoisier and a bottle of Scotch! The party gave them a standing ovation and then scrambled to get a drop. It soon turned out from his general behavior, however, that one of the white men had probably drunk too much already. And the reason, it would seem, was that a pilot we knew well had been killed in a crash at the airport the night before, flying in relief in awful weather.

110 Few people at the party had heard of the crash by then. So there was an immediate damping of the air. Some dancing couples went back to their seats and the band stopped. Then for some strange reason the drunken Red Cross man just exploded.

"Why should a man, a decent man, throw away his life. For nothing! Charley didn't need to die. Not for this stinking place. Yes, everything stinks here. Even these girls who come here all dolled up and smiling, what are they worth? Don't I know? A head of stockfish, that's all, or one American dollar and they are ready to tumble into bed."

In the threatening silence following the explosion one of the young officers walked up to him and gave him three thundering slaps—right! left! right!—pulled him up from his seat and (there were things like tears in his eyes) shoved him outside. His friend, who had tried in vain to shut him up, followed him out and the silenced party heard them drive off. The officer who did the job returned, dusting his palms.

"Fucking beast!" said he with an impressive coolness. And all the girls showed with their eyes that they rated him a man and a hero.

"Do you know him?" Gladys asked Nwankwo.

115 He didn't answer her. Instead, he spoke generally to the party. "The fellow was clearly drunk," he said.

"I don't care," said the officer. "It is when a man is drunk that he speaks what is on his mind."

"So you beat him for what was on his mind," said the host. "That is the spirit, Joe."

"Thank you, sir," said Joe, saluting.

"His name is Joe," Gladys and the girl on her left said in unison, turning to each other.

120 At the same time Nwankwo and a friend on the other side of him were saying quietly, very quietly, that although the man had been rude and offensive, what he had said about the girls was unfortunately the bitter truth, only he was the wrong man to say it.

When the dancing resumed Captain Joe came to Gladys for a dance. She sprang to her feet even before the word was out of his mouth. Then she remembered immediately and turned round to take permission from Nwankwo. At the same time the captain also turned to him and said "Excuse me."

"Go ahead," said Nwankwo, looking somewhere between the two.

It was a long dance and he followed them with his eyes without appearing to do so. Occasionally a relief plane passed overhead and somebody immediately switched off the lights, saying it might be the Intruder. But it was only an excuse to dance in the dark and make the girls giggle, for the sound of the Intruder was well known.

Gladys came back feeling very self-conscious and asked Nwankwo to dance with her. But he wouldn't. "Don't bother about me," he said. "I am enjoying myself perfectly sitting here and watching those of you who dance."

125 "Then let's go," she said, "if you won't dance."

"But I never dance, believe me. So please enjoy yourself."

She danced next with the lieutenant colonel and again with Captain Joe, and then Nwankwo agreed to take her home.

"I am sorry I didn't dance," he said as they drove away. "But I swore never to dance as long as this war lasts."

She said nothing.

130 "When I think of somebody like that pilot who got killed last night. And he had no hand whatever in the quarrel. All his concern was to bring us food . . ."

"I hope that his friend is not like him," said Gladys.

"The man was just upset by his friend's death. But what I am saying is that with people like that getting killed and our own boys suffering and dying at the war fronts I don't see why we should sit around throwing parties and dancing."

"You took me there," said she in final revolt. "They are your friends. I don't know them before."

"Look, my dear, I am not blaming you. I am merely telling you why I personally refuse to dance. Anyway, let's change the subject . . . Do you still say you want to go back tomorrow? My driver can take you early enough on Monday morning for you to go to work. No? All right, just as you wish. You are the boss."

135 She gave him a shock by the readiness with which she followed him to bed and by her language.

"You want to shell?" she asked. And without waiting for an answer said, "Go ahead but don't pour in troops!"

He didn't want to pour in troops either and so it was all right. But she wanted visual assurance and so he showed her.

One of the ingenious economies taught by the war was that a rubber condom could be used over and over again. All you had to was wash it out, dry it, and shake a lot of talcum powder over it to prevent its sticking; and it was as good as new. It had to be the real British thing, though, not some of the cheap stuff they brought in from Lisbon, which was about as strong as a dry *cocoyam* leaf in the *harmattan.*

He had his pleasure but wrote the girl off. He might just as well have slept with a prostitute, he thought. It was clear as daylight to him now that she was kept by some army officer. What a terrible transformation in the short period of less than two years! Wasn't it a miracle that she still had memories of the other life, that she even remembered her name? If the affair of the drunken Red Cross man should happen again now, he said to himself, he would stand up beside the fellow and tell the party that here was a man of truth. What terrible fate to befall a whole generation! The mothers of tomorrow!

By morning he was feeling a little better and more generous in his judgments. Gladys, he thought, was just a mirror reflecting a society that had gone completely rotten and maggoty at the center. The mirror itself was intact; a lot of smudge but no more. All that was needed was a clean duster. "I have a duty to her," he told himself, "the little girl that once revealed to me our situation. Now she is in danger, under some terrible influence."

He wanted to get to the bottom of this deadly influence. It was clearly not just her good-time girlfriend, Augusta, or whatever her name was. There must be some man at the center of it, perhaps one of these heartless attack traders who traffic in foreign currencies and make their hundreds of thousands by sending young men to hazard their lives bartering looted goods for cigarettes behind enemy lines, or one of those contractors who receive piles of money daily for food they never deliver to the army. Or perhaps some vulgar and cowardly army officer full of filthy barrack talk and fictitious stories of heroism. He decided he had to find out. Last night he had thought of sending his driver alone to take her home. But no, he must go and see for himself where she lived. Something was bound to reveal itself there. Something on which he could anchor his rescue operation. As he prepared for the trip his feeling toward her softened with every passing minute. He assembled for her half of the food he had received at the relief center the day before. Difficult as things were, he though, a girl who had something to eat would be spared, not all, but some of the temptation. He would arrange with his friend at the WCC to deliver something to her every fortnight.

Tears came to Gladys's eyes when she saw the gifts. Nwankwo didn't have too much cash on him but he got together twenty pounds and handed it over to her.

"I don't have foreign exchange, and I know this won't go far at all, but . . ."

She just came and threw herself at him, sobbing. He kissed her lips and eyes and mumbled something about victims of circumstances, which went over her head. In deference to him, he thought with exultation, she had put away her high-tinted wig in her bag.

"I want you to promise me something," he said.

"What?"

"Never use that expression about shelling again."

She smiled with tears in her eyes. "You don't like it? That's what all the girls call it."

"Well, you are different from all the girls. Will you promise?"

"O.K."

Naturally their departure had become a little delayed. And when they got into the car it refused to start. After poking around the engine the driver decided that the battery was flat. Nwankwo was aghast. He had that very week paid thirty-four pounds to change two of the cells and the mechanic who performed it had promised him six months' service. A new battery, which was then running at two hundred and fifty pounds, was simply out of the question. The driver must have been careless with something, he thought.

"It must be because of last night," said the driver.

"What happened last night?" asked Nwankwo sharply, wondering what insolence was on the way. But none was intended.

"Because we use the headlight."

"Am I supposed not to use my light, then? Go and get some people and try pushing it." He got out again with Gladys and returned to the house while the driver went over to neighboring houses to seek the help of other servants.

After at least half an hour of pushing it up and down the street, and a lot of noisy advice from the pushers, the car finally spluttered to life, shooting out enormous clouds of black smoke from the exhaust.

It was eight-thirty by his watch when they set out. A few miles away a disabled soldier waved for a lift.

"Stop!" screamed Nwankwo. The driver jammed his foot on the brakes and then turned his head toward his master in bewilderment.

"Don't you see the soldier waving? Reverse and pick him up!"

"Sorry, sir," said the driver. "I don't know Master want to pick him."

"If you don't know you should ask. Reverse back."

The soldier, a mere boy, in filthy khaki drenched in sweat, lacked his right leg from the knee down. He seemed not only grateful that a car should stop for him but greatly surprised. He first handed in his crude wooden crutches, which the driver arranged between the two front seats, then painfully he levered himself in.

"Thanks, sir," he said, turning to look at the back and completely out of breath.

"I am very grateful. Madame, thank you."

"The pleasure is ours," said Nwankwo. "Where did you get your wound?"

"At Azumini, sir. On tenth of January."

"Never mind. Everything will be all right. We are proud of you boys and will make sure you receive your due reward when it is all over."

"I pray God, sir."

They drove in silence for the next half hour or so. Then as the car sped down a slope toward a bridge somebody screamed—perhaps the driver, perhaps the solder—"They have come!" The screech of the brakes merged into the scream and the shattering of the sky overhead. The doors flew open even before the car had come to a stop and they were fleeing blindly to the bush. Gladys was a little ahead of Nwankwo when they heard through the drowning tumult the solder's voice crying: "Please come and open for me!" Vaguely he saw Gladys stop; he pushed past her, shouting to her at the same time to come on. Then a high whistle descended like a spear through the chaos and exploded in a vast noise and motion that smashed up everything. A tree he had embraced flung him through the bush. Then another terrible whistle starting high up and ending again in a monumental crash of the world; and then another, and Nwankwo heard no more.

He work up to human noises and weeping and the smell and smoke of a charred world. He dragged himself up and staggered toward the source of the sounds.

From afar he saw his driver running toward him in tears and blood. He saw the remains of his car smoking and the entangled remains of the girl and the soldier. And he let out a piercing cry and fell down again.

Exploration of the Text

1. What view do you gain of Nigeria's civil war (1967–70)?
2. Do you trust the narrator? Is he a reliable narrator? Analyze his character.
3. Analyze Glady's character. How has she changed in the years that the narrator has known her?
4. What is the purpose of the incident of the party? How does the scene reveal aspects of the narrator's and of Glady's characters?
5. Discuss the irony of the phrase, "deadly influence," and the ending.

The Reading/Writing Connection

1. "Think" Topic: Is Gladys a "mirror reflecting a society that had gone completely rotten and maggoty at the center"? Create an argumentative response to this question.
2. Journal Entry: Who is a more sympathetic character—Nwankwo or Gladys? Defend your choice.

Ideas for Writing

1. Discuss the tension between the traditional and the modern in this story.
2. Analyze Nwankwo's or Glady's character.

The Handsomest Drowned Man in the World
A Tale for Children

Gabriel García Márquez Translated by Gregory Rabassa

Gabriel García Márquez (1928–) was born in the coastal village of Aracataca, Colombia. After studying at the University of Colombia at Bogota and the University of Cartagena, he traveled throughout South America, the United States, and Europe as a reporter and began writing short stories. Although he has lived in Mexico City for the past twenty years, García Márquez returns frequently to Colombia, the setting for most of his work. His most famous work is One Hundred Years of Solitude *(1972); other works include* Chronicle of a Death Foretold *(1983) and* Love in the Time of Cholera *(1987). García Márquez is considered one of the leading practitioners of the school of fiction known as Magic Realism, which combines the fantastic with the mundane. He was awarded the Nobel Prize for Literature in 1982.*

1971

The first children who saw the dark and slinky bulge approaching through the sea let themselves think it was an empty ship. Then they saw it had no flags or masts and they thought it was a whale. But when it washed up on the beach, they removed the clumps of seaweed, the jellyfish tentacles, and the remains of fish and flotsam, and only then did they see that it was a drowned man.

They had been playing with him all afternoon, burying him in the sand and digging him up again, when someone chanced to see them and spread the alarm in the village. The men who carried him to the nearest house noticed that he weighed more than any dead man they had ever known, almost as much as a horse, and they said to each other that maybe he'd been floating too long and the water had got into his bones. When they laid him on the floor they said he'd been taller than all other men because there was barely enough room for him in the house, but they thought that maybe the ability to keep on growing after death was part of the nature of certain drowned men. He had the smell of the sea about him and only his shape gave one to suppose that it was the corpse of a human being, because the skin was covered with a crust of mud and scales.

They did not even have to clean off his face to know that the dead man was a stranger. The village was made up of only twenty-odd wooden houses that had stone courtyards with no flowers and which were spread about on the end of a desertlike cape. There was so little land that mothers always went about with the fear that the wind would carry off their children and the few dead that the years had caused among them had to be thrown off the cliffs. But the sea was calm and bountiful and all the men fit into seven boats. So when they found the drowned man they simply had to look at one another to see that they were all there.

That night they did not go out to work at sea. While the men went to find out if anyone was missing in neighboring villages, the women stayed behind to care for the drowned man. They took the mud off with grass swabs, they removed the underwater stones entangled in his hair, and they scraped the crust off with tools used for scaling fish. As they were doing that they noticed that the vegetation on him came from faraway oceans and deep water and that his clothes were in tatters, as if he had sailed through labyrinths of coral. They noticed too that he bore his death with pride, for he did not have the lonely look of other drowned men who came out of the sea or that haggard, needy look of men who drowned in rivers. But only when they finished cleaning him off did they become aware of the kind of man he was and it left them breathless. Not only was he the tallest, strongest, most virile, and best built man they had ever seen, but even though they were looking at him there was no room for him in their imagination.

5 They could not find a bed in the village large enough to lay him on nor was there a table solid enough to use for his wake. The tallest men's holiday pants would not fit him, nor the fattest ones' Sunday shirts, nor the shoes of the one with the biggest feet. Fascinated by his huge size and his beauty, the women then decided to make him some pants from a large piece of sail and a shirt from some bridal Brabant[1] linen so that he could continue through his death with dignity. As they sewed, sitting in a circle and gazing at the corpse between stitches, it seemed to them that the wind had never been so steady nor the sea so restless as on that night and they supposed that the change had something to do with the dead man. They thought that if that magnificent man had lived in the village, his house would have had the widest doors, and highest ceiling, and the strongest floor; his bedstead would have been made from a midship frame held together by iron bolts, and his wife would have been the happiest woman. They thought that he would have had so much authority that he could have drawn fish out of the sea simply by calling their names and that he would have put so much work into his land that springs would have burst forth from among the rocks so that he would have been able to plant flowers on the cliffs. They secretly compared him to their own men, thinking that for all their lives theirs were incapable of doing what he could do in one night, and they ended up dismissing them deep in their hearts as the weakest, meanest, and most useless creatures on earth. They were wandering through that maze of fantasy when the oldest woman, who as the oldest had looked upon the drowned man with more compassion than passion, sighed:

[1] Former region of Western Europe including the current Brabant province of the Netherlands and Brabant and Antwerp regions of Belgium.

"He has the face of someone called Esteban."

It was true. Most of them had only to take another look at him to see that he could not have any other name. The more stubborn among them, who were the youngest, still lived for a few hours with the illusion that when they put his clothes on and he lay among the flowers in patent leather shoes his name might be Lautaro. But it was a vain illusion. There had not been enough canvas, the poorly cut and worse sewn pants were too tight, and the hidden strength of his heart popped the buttons on his shirt. After midnight the whistling of the wind died down and the sea fell into its Wednesday drowsiness. The silence put an end to any last doubts: he was Esteban. The women who had dressed him, who had combed his hair, had cut his nails and shaved him were unable to hold back a shudder of pity when they had to resign themselves to his being dragged along the ground. It was then that they understood how unhappy he must have been with that huge body since it bothered him even after death. They could see him in life, condemned to going through doors sideways cracking his head on crossbeams, remaining on his feet during visits, not knowing what to do with his soft pink, sealion hands while the lady of the house looked for her most resistant chair and begged him, frightened to death, sit here, Esteban, please, and he, leaning against the wall, smiling, don't bother, ma'am, I'm fine where I am, his heels raw and his back roasted from having done the same thing so many times whenever he paid a visit, don't bother, ma'am, I'm fine where I am to avoid the embarrassment of breaking up the chair, and never knowing perhaps that the one who said don't go, Esteban, at least wait till the coffee's ready, were the ones who later on would whisper the big boob finally left, how nice, the handsome fool has gone. That was what the women were thinking beside the body a little before dawn. Later, when they covered his face with a handkerchief so that the light would not bother him, he looked so forever dead, so defenseless, so much like their men that the first furrows of tears opened in their hearts. It was one of the younger ones who began the weeping. The others, coming to, went from sighs to wails, and the more they sobbed the more they felt like weeping, because the drowned man was becoming all the more Esteban for them, and so they wept so much, for he was the most destitute, most peaceful, and most obliging man on earth, poor Esteban. So when the men returned with the news that the drowned man was not from the neighboring villages either, the women felt an opening of jubilation in the midst of their tears.

"Praise the Lord," they sighed, "he's ours!"

The men thought the fuss was only womanish frivolity. Fatigued because of the difficult nighttime inquiries, all they wanted was to get rid of the bother of the newcomer once and for all before the sun grew strong on that arid, windless day. They improvised a litter with the remains of foremasts and gaffs, tying it together with rigging so that it would bear the weight of the body until they reached the cliffs. They wanted to tie the anchor from a cargo ship to him so that he would sink easily into the deepest waves, where the fish are blind and divers die of nostalgia, and bad currents would not bring him back to shore, as had happened with other bodies. But the more they hurried, the more the women thought of ways to waste time. They walked about like startled hens, pecking with the sea charms on their breasts, some interfering on one side to put a scapular of the good wind on the drowned man, some on the other side to put a wrist compass on him, and after a great deal of *get away from there, woman, stay out of the way, look, you almost made me fall on top of the dead man,* the men began to feel mistrust in their livers and started grumbling about why so many main-altar decorations for a stranger, because no matter how many nails and holywater jars he had on him, the sharks would chew him all the same, but the women kept on piling on their junk relics, running back and forth, stumbling, while they released in sighs what they did not in tears, so that the men finally exploded with *since when has there ever been such a fuss over a drifting corpse, a drowned nobody, a piece of cold Wednesday meat.* One of the women, mortified by so much lack of care, then removed the handkerchief from the dead man's face and the men were left breathless too.

10 He was Esteban. It was not necessary to repeat it for them to recognize him. If they had been told Sir Walter Raleigh,[2] even they might have been impressed with his gringo accent, the macaw on his shoulder, his cannibal-killing blunderbuss, but there could be only one Esteban in the world and there he was, stretched out like a sperm whale, shoeless, wearing the pants of an undersized child, and with those stony nails that had to be cut with a knife. They had only to take the handkerchief off his face to see that he was ashamed, that it was not his fault that he was so big or so heavy or so handsome, and if he had known that this was going to happen, he would have looked for a more discreet place to drown in; seriously, I even would have tied the anchor off a galleon around my neck and staggered off a cliff like someone who doesn't like things in order not to be upsetting people now with this Wednesday dead body, as you people say, in order not to be bothering anyone with this filthy piece of cold meat that doesn't have anything to do with me. There was so much truth in his manner that even the most mistrustful men, the ones who felt the bitterness of endless nights at sea fearing that their women would tire of dreaming about them and begin to dream of drowned men, even they and others who were harder still shuddered in the marrow of their bones at Esteban's sincerity.

That was how they came to hold the most splendid funeral they could conceive of for an abandoned drowned man. Some women who had gone to get flowers in the neighboring villages returned with other women who could not believe what they had been told, and those women went back for more flowers when they saw the dead man, and they brought more and more until there were so many flowers and so many people that it was hard to walk about. At the final moment it pained them to return him to the waters as an orphan and they chose a father and mother from among the best people, and aunts and uncles and cousins, so that through him all the inhabitants of the village became

[2] English navigator, courtier, and historian (1554–1618).

kinsmen. Some sailors who heard the weeping from a distance went off course, and people heard of one who had himself tied to the mainmast, remembering ancient fables about sirens. While they fought for the privilege of carrying him on their shoulders along the steep escarpment by the cliffs, men and women became aware for the first time of the desolation of their streets, the dryness of their courtyards, the narrowness of their dreams as they faced the splendor and beauty of their drowned man. They let him go without an anchor so that he could come back if he wished and whenever he wished, and they all held their breath for the fraction of centuries the body took to fall into the abyss. They did not need to look to one another to realize that they were no longer all present, that they would never be. But they also knew that everything would be different from then on, that their houses would have wider doors, higher ceilings, and stronger floors so that Esteban's memory could go everywhere without bumping into beams and so that no one in the future would dare whisper the big boob finally died, too bad, the handsome fool has finally died, because they were going to paint their house fronts gay colors to make Esteban's memory eternal and they were going to break their backs digging for springs among the stones and planting flowers on the cliffs so that in future years at dawn the passengers on great liners would awaken, suffocated by the smell of gardens on the high seas, and the captain would have to come down from the bridge in his dress uniform, with his astrolabe,[3] his pole star, and his row of war medals and, pointing to the promontory of roses on the horizon, he would say in fourteen languages, look there, where the wind is so peaceful now that it's gone to sleep beneath the beds, over there, where the sun's so bright that the sunflowers don't know which way to turn, yes, over there, that's Esteban's village.

Explorations of the Text

1. Why does García Márquez subtitle the story "A Tale for Children"? What expectations does the subtitle create in the reader?
2. Why do the children play with the body? What is their attitude toward death?
3. What is the meaning of the symbolism of the vegetation and mud on the drowned man's body?
4. What are the consequences of the women's comparisons to their own men? What is the importance of identifying him as Esteban?
5. Examine the imaginary conversation about his size. How does he become "the big boob" and "the handsome fool"? Why do the villagers feel "jubilation" when Esteban becomes their drowned man?
6. Explore the men's attitudes, the funeral, and the behavior of the women. How does Esteban win the people with his sincerity?

[3] An instrument used to observe and calculate the positions of stars and planets before the invention of the sextant.

7. Describe the ritual of the "most splendid funeral." How does the experience with the drowned man transform the people and the village?
8. Compare the transformation of the people in this story with the change in the narrator in Wright's "A Blessing."

The Reading/Writing Connection

1. Write a story that imitates both the style and theme of "The Handsomest Drowned Man in the World."
2. Gloss and annotate the story. Consider the use of **hyperbole.**
3. React to the idea of Esteban as "the stranger" who is taken into the community. Write a short essay on this subject.

Ideas for Writing

1. Analyze the transformation of the people and their village.
2. Discuss the symbolism of the drowned man.
3. How do the settings (village and sea) elucidate theme?
4. Look for elements of fairy tales in this story. How are they effective?
5. Contrast García Márquez's view of death with the attitude of Thomas in "Do Not Go Gentle . . . ."
6. Compare the idea of community in García Márquez, Achebe, and Lahiri.
7. Argue: Without imagination, people live constricted, static lives.

The Third and Final Continent

Jhumpa Lahiri

Jhumpa Lahiri (1967–) was born in London to Indian parents and raised in Rhode Island. She was educated at Barnard College and Boston University. Her short stories have appeared in The New Yorker, Story, *and* Salamander. *In 1999, she published her first collection of stories,* The Interpreter of Maladies, *which won a Pulitzer Prize.*

1999

I left India in 1964 with a certificate in commerce and the equivalent, in those days, of ten dollars to my name. For three weeks I sailed on the SS *Roma,* an Italian cargo vessel, in a cabin next to the ship's engine, across the Arabian Sea, the Red Sea, the Mediterranean, and finally to England. I lived in north London, in Finsbury Park, in a house occupied entirely by penniless Bengali bachelors like myself, at least a dozen and sometimes more, all struggling to educate and establish ourselves abroad.

I attended lectures at LSE[1] and worked at the university library to get by. We lived three or four to a room, shared a single, icy toilet, and took turns cooking pots of egg curry, which we ate with our hands on a table covered with newspapers. Apart from our jobs we had few responsibilities. On weekends we lounged barefoot in drawstring pajamas, drinking tea and smoking Rothmans, or set out to watch cricket at Lord's. Some weekends the house was crammed with still more Bengalis, to whom we had introduced ourselves at the greengrocer, or on the Tube, and we made yet more egg curry, and played Mukesh[2] on a Grundig reel-to-reel, and soaked our dirty dishes in the bathtub. Every now and then someone in the house moved out, to live with a woman whom his family back in Calcutta had determined he was to wed. In 1969, when I was thirty-six years old, my own marriage was arranged. Around the same time I was offered a full-time job in America, in the processing department of a library at MIT. The salary was generous enough to support a wife, and I was honored to be hired by a world-famous university, and so I obtained a sixth-preference green card, and prepared to travel farther still.

By now I had enough money to go by plane. I flew first to Calcutta, to attend my wedding, and a week later I flew to Boston, to begin my new job. During the flight I read *The Student Guide to North America,* a paperback volume that I'd bought before leaving London, for seven shillings six pence on Tottenham Court Road, for although I was no longer a student I was on a budget all the same. I learned that Americans drove on the right side of the road, not the left, and that they called a lift an elevator and an engaged phone busy. "The pace of life in North America is different from Britain as you will soon discover," the guidebook informed me. "Everybody feels he must get to the top. Don't expect an English cup of tea." As the plane began its descent over Boston Harbor, the pilot announced the weather and time, and that President Nixon had declared a national holiday: two American men had landed on the moon. Several passengers cheered. "God bless America!" one of them hollered. Across the aisle, I saw a woman praying.

I spent my first night at the YMCA in Central Square, Cambridge, an inexpensive accommodation recommended by my guidebook. It was walking distance from MIT, and steps from the post office and a supermarket called Purity Supreme. The room contained a cot, a desk, and a small wooden cross on one wall. A sign on the door said cooking was strictly forbidden. A bare window overlooked Massachusetts Avenue, a major thoroughfare with traffic in both directions. Car horns, shrill and prolonged, blared one after another. Flashing sirens heralded endless emergencies, and a fleet of buses rumbled past, their doors opening and closing with a powerful hiss, throughout the night. The noise was constantly distracting, at times suffocating. I felt it deep in my ribs, just as I had felt the furious drone of the engine on the SS *Roma.* But there was no ship's deck to escape to, no glittering ocean to thrill my soul, no breeze to cool my face, no one to talk to. I was too tired to pace the gloomy

[1] London School of Economics.

[2] Popular playback singer of popular music and classical music in India.

corridors of the YMCA in my drawstring pajamas. Instead I sat at the desk and stared out the window, at the city hall of Cambridge and a row of small shops. In the morning I reported to my job at the Dewey Library, a beige fort-like building by Memorial Drive. I also opened a bank account, rented a post office box, and bought a plastic bowl and a spoon at Woolworth's, a store whose name I recognized from London. I went to Purity Supreme, wandering up and down the aisles, converting ounces to grams and comparing prices to things in England. In the end I bought a small carton of milk and a box of cornflakes. This was my first meal in America. I ate it at my desk. I preferred it to hamburgers or hot dogs, the only alternative I could afford in the coffee shops on Massachusetts Avenue, and, besides, at the time I had yet to consume any beef. Even the simple chore of buying milk was new to me; in London we'd had bottles delivered each morning to our door.

5 In a week I had adjusted, more or less. I ate cornflakes and milk, morning and night, and bought some bananas for variety, slicing them into the bowl with the edge of my spoon. In addition I bought tea bags and a flask, which the salesman in Woolworth's referred to as a thermos (a flask, he informed me, was used to store whiskey, another thing I had never consumed). For the price of one cup of tea at a coffee shop, I filled the flask with boiling water on my way to work each morning, and brewed the four cups I drank in the course of a day. I bought a larger carton of milk, and learned to leave it on the shaded part of the windowsill, as I had seen another resident at the YMCA do. To pass the time in the evenings I read the *Boston Globe* downstairs, in a spacious room with stained-glass windows. I read every article and advertisement, so that I would grow familiar with things, and when my eyes grew tired I slept. Only I did not sleep well. Each night I had to keep the window wide open; it was the only source of air in the stifling room, and the noise was intolerable. I would lie on the cot with my fingers pressed into my ears, but when I drifted off to sleep my hands fell away, and the noise of the traffic would wake me up again. Pigeon feathers drifted onto the windowsill, and one evening, when I poured milk over my cornflakes, I saw that it had soured. Nevertheless I resolved to stay at the YMCA for six weeks, until my wife's passport and green card were ready. Once she arrived I would have to rent a proper apartment, and from time to time I studied the classified section of the newspaper, or stopped in at the housing office at MIT during my lunch break, to see what was available in my price range. It was in this manner that I discovered a room for immediate occupancy, in a house on a quiet street, the listing said, for eight dollars per week. I copied the number into my guidebook and dialed from a pay telephone, sorting through the coins with which I was still unfamiliar, smaller and lighter than shillings, heavier and brighter than *paisas*.

"Who is speaking?" a woman demanded. Her voice was bold and clamorous.

"Yes, good afternoon, madame. I am calling about the room for rent."

"Harvard or Tech?"

"I beg your pardon?"

10 "Are you from Harvard or Tech?"

Gathering that Tech referred to the Massachusetts Institute of Technology, I replied, "I work at Dewey Library," adding tentatively, "at Tech."

"I only rent rooms to boys from Harvard or Tech!"

"Yes, madame."

I was given an address and an appointment for seven o'clock that evening. Thirty minutes before the hour I set out, my guidebook in my pocket, my breath fresh with Listerine. I turned down a street shaded with trees, perpendicular to Massachusetts Avenue. Stray blades of grass poked between the cracks of the footpath. In spite of the heat I wore a coat and a tie, regarding the event as I would any other interview; I had never lived in the home of a person who was not Indian. The house, surrounded by a chain-link fence, was off-white with dark brown trim. Unlike the stucco row house I'd lived in in London, this house, fully detached, was covered with wooden shingles, with a tangle of forsythia bushes plastered against the front and sides. When I pressed the calling bell, the woman with whom I had spoken on the phone hollered from what seemed to be just the other side of the door, "One minute, please!"

15 Several minutes later the door was opened by a tiny, extremely old woman. A mass of snowy hair was arranged like a small sack on top of her head. As I stepped into the house she sat down on a wooden bench positioned at the bottom of a narrow carpeted staircase. Once she was settled on the bench, in a small pool of light, she peered up at me with undivided attention. She wore a long black skirt that spread like a stiff tent to the floor, and a starched white shirt edged with ruffles at the throat and cuffs. Her hands, folded together in her lap, had long pallid fingers, with swollen knuckles and tough yellow nails. Age had battered her features so that she almost resembled a man, with sharp, shrunken eyes and prominent ceases on either side of her nose. Her lips, chapped and faded, had nearly disappeared, and her eyebrows were missing altogether. Nevertheless she looked fierce.

"Lock up!" she commanded. She shouted even though I stood only a few feet away. "Fasten the chain and firmly press that button on the knob! This is the first thing you shall do when you enter, is that clear?"

I locked the door as directed and examined the house. Next to the bench on which the woman sat was a small round table, its legs fully concealed, much like the woman's, by a skirt of lace. The table held a lamp, a transistor radio, a leather change purse with a silver clasp, and a telephone. A thick wooden cane coated with a layer of dust was propped against one side. There was a parlor to my right, lined with bookcases and filled with shabby claw-footed furniture. In the corner of the parlor I saw a grand piano with its top down, piled with papers. The piano's bench was missing; it seemed to be the one on which the woman was sitting. Somewhere in the house a clock chimed seven times.

"You're punctual!" the woman proclaimed. "I expect you shall be so with the rent!"

"I have a letter, madame." In my jacket pocket was a letter confirming my employment from MIT, which I had brought along to prove that I was indeed from Tech.

20 She stared at the letter, then handed it back to me carefully, gripping it with her fingers as if it were a dinner plate heaped with food instead of a sheet of paper. She did not wear glasses, and I wondered if she'd read a word of it. "The last boy was always late! Still owes me eight dollars! Harvard boys aren't what they used to be! Only Harvard and Tech in this house! How's Tech, boy?"

"It is very well."

"You checked the lock?"

"Yes, madame."

She slapped the space beside her on the bench with one hand, and told me to sit down. For a moment she was silent. Then she intoned as if she alone possessed this knowledge:

25 "There is an American flag on the moon!"

"Yes, madame." Until then I had not thought very much about the moon shot. It was in the newspaper, of course, article upon article. The astronauts had landed on the shores of the Sea of Tranquillity, I had read, traveling farther than anyone in the history of civilization. For a few hours they explored the moon's surface. They gathered rocks in their pockets, described their surroundings (a magnificent desolation, according to one astronaut), spoke by phone to the president, and planted a flag in lunar soil. The voyage was hailed as man's most awesome achievement. I had seen full-page photographs in the *Globe,* of the astronauts in their inflated costumes, and read about what certain people in Boston had been doing at the exact moment the astronauts landed, on a Sunday afternoon. A man said that he was operating a swan boat with a radio pressed to his ear; a woman had been baking rolls for her grandchildren.

The woman bellowed, "A flag on the moon, boy! I heard it on the radio! Isn't that splendid?"

"Yes, madame."

But she was not satisfied with my reply. Instead she commanded, "Say 'splendid'!"

30 I was both baffled and somewhat insulted by the request. It reminded me of the way I was taught multiplication tables as a child, repeating after the master, sitting cross-legged, without shoes or pencils, on the floor of my one-room Tollygunge school. It also reminded me of my wedding, when I had repeated endless Sanskrit verses after the priest, verses I barely understood, which joined me to my wife. I said nothing.

"Say 'splendid'!" the woman bellowed once again.

"Splendid," I murmured. I had to repeat the word a second time at the top of my lungs, so she could hear. I am soft-spoken by nature and was especially reluctant to raise my voice to an elderly woman whom I had met only moments ago, but she did not appear to be offended. If anything the reply pleased her because her next command was:

"Go see the room!"

I rose from the bench and mounted the narrow carpeted staircase. There were five doors, two on either side of an equally narrow hallway, and one at the opposite end. Only one door was partly open. The room contained a twin bed under a sloping ceiling, a brown oval rug, a basin with an exposed pipe, and a chest of drawers. One door, painted white, led to a closet, another to a toilet and a tub. The walls were covered with gray and ivory striped paper. The window was open; net curtains stirred in the breeze. I lifted them away and inspected the view: a small back yard, with a few fruit trees and an empty clothesline. I was satisfied. From the bottom of the stairs I heard the woman demand, "What is your decision?"

When I returned to the foyer and told her, she picked up the leather change purse on the table, opened the clasp, fished about with her fingers, and produced a key on a thin wire hoop. She informed me that there was a kitchen at the back of the house, accessible through the parlor. I was welcome to use the stove as long as I left it as I found it. Sheets and towels were provided, but keeping them clean was my own responsibility. The rent was due Friday mornings on the ledge above the piano keys. "And no lady visitors!"

"I am a married man, madame." It was the first time I had announced this fact to anyone.

But she had not heard. "No lady visitors!" she insisted. She introduced herself as Mrs. Croft.

My wife's name was Mala. The marriage had been arranged by my older brother and his wife. I regarded the proposition with neither objection nor enthusiasm. It was a duty expected of me, as it was expected of every man. She was the daughter of a schoolteacher in Beleghata. I was told that she could cook, knit, embroider, sketch landscapes, and recite poems by Tagore, but these talents could not make up for the fact that she did not possess a fair complexion, and so a string of men had rejected her to her face. She was twenty-seven, an age when her parents had begun to fear that she would never marry, and so they were willing to ship their only child halfway across the world in order to save her from spinsterhood.

For five nights we shared a bed. Each of those nights, after applying cold cream and braiding her hair, which she tied up at the end with a black cotton string, she turned from me and wept; she missed her parents. Although I would be leaving the country in a few days, custom dictated that she was now a part of my household, and for the next six weeks she was to live with my brother and his wife, cooking, cleaning, serving tea and sweets to guests. I did nothing to console her. I lay on my own side of the bed, reading my guidebook by flashlight and anticipating my journey. At times I thought of the tiny room on the other side of the wall which had belonged to my mother. Now the room was practically empty; the wooden pallet on which she'd once slept was piled with trunks and old bedding. Nearly six years ago, before leaving for London, I had watched her die on that bed, had found her playing with her excrement in her final days. Before we cremated her I had cleaned each of her fingernails with a hairpin, and then, because my brother could not bear it, I had assumed the role of eldest son, and had touched the flame to her temple to release her tormented soul to heaven.

40 The next morning I moved into the room in Mrs. Croft's house. When I unlocked the door I saw that she was sitting on the piano bench, on the same side as the previous evening. She wore the same black skirt, the same starched white blouse, and had her hands folded together the same way in her lap. She looked so much the same that I wondered if she'd spent the whole night on the bench. I put my suitcase upstairs, filled my flask with boiling water in the kitchen, and headed off to work. That evening when I came home from the university, she was still there.

"Sit down, boy!" She slapped the space beside her.

I perched beside her on the bench. I had a bag of groceries with me—more milk, more cornflakes, and more bananas, for my inspection of the kitchen earlier in the day had revealed no spare pots, pans, or cooking utensils. There were only two saucepans in the refrigerator, both containing some orange broth, and a copper kettle on the stove.

"Good evening, madame."

She asked me if I had checked the lock. I told her I had.

45 For a moment she was silent. Then suddenly she declared, with the equal measures of disbelief and delight as the night before, "There's an American flag on the moon, boy!"

"Yes, madame."

"A flag on the moon! Isn't that splendid?"

I nodded, dreading what I knew was coming. "Yes, madame."

"Say 'splendid'!"

50 This time I paused, looking to either side in case anyone were there to overhear me, though I knew perfectly well that the house was empty. I felt like an idiot. But it was a small enough thing to ask. "Splendid!" I cried out.

Within days it became our routine. In the mornings when I left for the library Mrs. Croft was either hidden away in her bedroom, on the other side of the staircase, or she was sitting on the bench, oblivious to my presence, listening to the news or classical music on the radio. But each evening when I returned the same thing happened: she slapped the bench, ordered me to sit down, declared that there was a flag on the moon, and declared that it was splendid. I said it was splendid, too, and then we sat in silence. As awkward as it was, and as endless as it felt to me then, the nightly encounter lasted only about ten minutes; inevitably she would drift off to sleep, her head falling abruptly toward her chest, leaving me free to retire to my room. By then, of course, there was no flag standing on the moon. The astronauts, I had read in the paper, had seen it fall before they flew back to Earth. But I did not have the heart to tell her.

Friday morning, when my first week's rent was due, I went to the piano in the parlor to place my money on the ledge. The piano keys were dull and discolored. When I pressed one, it made no sound at all. I had put eight one-dollar bills in an envelope and written Mrs. Croft's name on the front of it. I was not in the habit of leaving money unmarked and unattended. From where I stood I could see the profile of her tent-shaped skirt. She was sitting on the bench, listening to the radio. It seemed unnecessary to make her get up and walk all the way to the piano. I never saw her walking about, and assumed, from the cane always propped against the round table at her side, that she did so with difficulty. When I approached the bench she peered up at me and demanded:

"What is your business?"

"The rent, madame."

"On the ledge above the piano keys!"

"I have it here." I extended the envelope toward her, but her fingers, folded together in her lap, did not budge. I bowed slightly and lowered the envelope, so that it hovered just above her hands. After a moment she accepted, and nodded her head.

That night when I came home, she did not slap the bench, but out of habit I sat beside her as usual. She asked me if I had checked the lock, but she mentioned nothing about the flag on the moon. Instead she said:

"It was very kind of you!"

"I beg your pardon, madame?"

"Very kind of you!"

She was still holding the envelope in her hands.

On Sunday there was a knock on my door. An elderly woman introduced herself: she was Mrs. Croft's daughter, Helen. She walked into the room and looked at each of the walls as if for signs of change, glancing at the shirts that hung in the closet, the neckties draped over the doorknob, the box of cornflakes on the chest of drawers, the dirty bowl and spoon in the basin. She was short and thick-waisted, with cropped silver hair and bright pink lipstick. She wore a sleeveless summer dress, a row of white plastic beads, and spectacles on a chain that hung like a swing against her chest. The backs of her legs were mapped with dark blue veins, and her upper arms sagged like the flesh of a roasted eggplant. She told me she lived in Arlington, a town farther up Massachusetts Avenue. "I come once a week to bring Mother groceries. Has she sent you packing yet?"

"It is very well, madame."

"Some of the boys run screaming. But I think she likes you. You're the first boarder she's ever referred to as a gentleman."

"Not at all, madame."

She looked at me, noticing my bare feet (I still felt strange wearing shoes indoors, and always removed them before entering my room). "Are you new to Boston?"

"New to America, madame."

"From?" She raised her eyebrows.

"I am from Calcutta, India."

"Is that right? We had a Brazilian fellow, about a year ago. You'll find Cambridge a very international city."

I nodded, and began to wonder how long our conversation would last. But at that moment we heard Mrs. Croft's electrifying voice rising up the stairs. When we stepped into the hallway we heard her hollering:

"You are to come downstairs immediately!"

"What is it?" Helen hollered back.

"Immediately!"

I put on my shoes at once. Helen sighed.

We walked down the staircase. It was too narrow for us to descend side by side, so I followed Helen, who seemed to be in no hurry, and complained at one point that she had a bad knee. "Have you been walking without your cane?" Helen called out. "You know you're not supposed to walk without that cane." She paused, resting her hand on the banister, and looked back at me. "She slips sometimes."

For the first time Mrs. Croft seemed vulnerable. I pictured her on the floor in front of the bench, flat on her back, staring at the ceiling, her feet pointing in opposite directions. But when we reached the bottom of the staircase she was sitting there as usual, her hands folded together in her lap. Two grocery bags were at her feet. When we stood before her she did not slap the bench, or ask us to sit down. She glared.

"What is it, Mother?"

"It's improper!"

"What's improper?"

"It is improper for a lady and gentleman who are not married to one another to hold a private conversation without a chaperone!"

Helen said she was sixty-eight years old, old enough to be my mother, but Mrs. Croft insisted that Helen and I speak to each other downstairs, in the parlor. She added that it was also improper for a lady of Helen's station to reveal her age, and to wear a dress so high above the ankle.

"For your information, Mother, it's 1969. What would you do if you actually left the house one day and saw a girl in a miniskirt?"

Mrs. Croft sniffed. "I'd have her arrested."

Helen shook her head and picked up one of the grocery bags. I picked up the other one, and followed her through the parlor and into the kitchen. The bags were filled with cans of soup, which Helen opened up one by one with a few cranks of a can opener. She tossed the old soup in the saucepans into the sink, rinsed the pans under the tap, filled them with soup from the newly opened cans, and put them back in the refrigerator. "A few years ago she could still open the cans herself," Helen said. "She hates that I do it for her now. But the piano killed her hands." She put on her spectacles, glanced at the cupboards, and spotted my tea bags. "Shall we have a cup?"

I filled the kettle on the stove. "I beg your pardon, madame. The piano?"

"She used to give lessons. For forty years. It was how she raised us after my father died." Helen put her hands on her hips, staring at the open refrigerator. She reached into the back, pulled out a wrapped stock of butter, frowned, and tossed it into the garbage. "That ought to do it," she said, and put the unopened cans of soup in the cupboard. I sat at the table and watched as Helen washed the dirty dishes, tied up the garbage bag, watered a spider plant over the sink, and poured boiling water into two cups. She handed one to me without milk, the string of the tea bag trailing over the side, and sat down at the table.

"Excuse me, madame, but is it enough?"

Helen took a sip of her tea. Her lipstick left a smiling pink stain on the inside rim of the cup. "Is what enough?"

90 "The soup in the pans. Is it enough food for Mrs. Croft?"

"She won't eat anything else. She stopped eating solids after she turned one hundred. That was, let's see, three years ago."

I was mortified. I had assumed Mrs. Croft was in her eighties, perhaps as old as ninety. I had never known a person who had lived for over a century. That this person was a widow who lived alone mortified me further still. It was widowhood that had driven my own mother insane. My father, who worked as a clerk at the General Post Office of Calcutta, died of encephalitis when I was sixteen. My mother refused to adjust to life without him; instead she sank deeper into a world of darkness from which neither I, nor my brother, nor concerned relatives, nor psychiatric clinics on Rash Behari Avenue could save her. What pained me most was to see her so unguarded, to hear her burp after meals or expel gas in front of company without the slightest embarrassment. After my father's death my brother abandoned his schooling and began to work in the jute mill he would eventually manage, in order to keep the household running. And so it was my job to sit by my mother's feet and study for my exams as she counted and recounted the bracelets on her arm as if they were the beads of an abacus. We tried to keep an eye on her. Once she had wandered half naked to the tram depot before we were able to bring her inside again.

"I am happy to warm Mrs. Croft's soup in the evenings," I suggested, removing the tea bag from my cup and squeezing out the liquor. "It is no trouble."

Helen looked at her watch, stood up, and poured the rest of her tea into the sink. "I wouldn't if I were you. That's the sort of thing that would kill her altogether."

95 That evening, when Helen had gone back to Arlington and Mrs. Croft and I were alone again, I began to worry. Now that I knew how very old she was, I worried that something would happen to her in the middle of the night, or when I was out during the day. As vigorous as her voice was, and imperious as she seemed, I knew that even a scratch or a cough could kill a person that old; each day she lived, I knew, was something of a miracle. Although Helen had seemed friendly enough, a small part of me worried that she might accuse me of negligence if anything were to happen. Helen didn't seem worried. She came and went, bringing soup for Mrs. Croft, one Sunday after the next.

In this manner the six weeks of that summer passed. I came home each evening, after my hours at the library, and spent a few minutes on the piano bench with Mrs. Croft. I gave her a bit of my company, and assured her that I had checked the lock, and told her that the flag on the moon was splendid. Some evenings I sat beside her long after she had drifted off to sleep, still in awe of how many years she had spent on this earth. At times I tried to picture the world she had been born into, in 1866—a world, I imagined, filled with women in long black skirts, and chaste conversations in the parlor. Now, when I looked at her hands, with their swollen knuckles folded together in her lap, I imagined them smooth and slim, striking the piano keys. At times I came downstairs before going to sleep, to make sure she was sitting upright on the bench, or was safe in her bedroom. On Fridays I made sure to put the rent in her hands. There was nothing I could do for her beyond these simple gestures. I was not her son, and apart from those eight dollars, I owed her nothing.

At the end of August, Mala's passport and green card were ready. I received a telegram with her flight information; my brother's house in Calcutta had no telephone. Around that time I also received a letter from her, written only a few days after we had parted. There was no salutation; addressing me by name would have assumed an intimacy we had not yet discovered. It contained only a few lines. "I write in English in preparation for the journey. Here I am very much lonely. Is it very cold there. Is there snow. Yours, Mala."

I was not touched by her words. We had spent only a handful of days in each other's company. And yet we were bound together; for six weeks she had worn an iron bangle on her wrist, and applied vermilion powder to the part in the hair, to signify to the world that she was a bride. In those six weeks I regarded her arrival as I would the arrival of a coming month, or season—something inevitable, but meaningless at the time. So little did I know her that, while details of her face sometimes rose to my memory, I could not conjure up the whole of it.

A few days after receiving the letter, as I was walking to work in the morning, I saw an Indian woman on the other side of Massachusetts Avenue, wearing a sari with its free end nearly dragging on the footpath, and pushing a child in a stroller. An American woman with a small black dog on a leash was walking to one side of her. Suddenly the dog began barking. From the other side of the street I watched as the Indian woman, startled, stopped in her path, at which point the dog leapt up and seized the end of the sari between its teeth. The American woman scolded the dog, appeared to apologize, and walked quickly away, leaving the Indian woman to fix her sari in the middle of the footpath, and quiet her crying child. She did not see me standing there, and eventually she continued on her way. Such a mishap, I realized that morning, would soon be my concern. It was my duty to take care of Mala, to welcome her and protect her. I would have to buy her her first pair of snow boots, her first winter coat. I would have to tell her which streets to avoid, which way the traffic came, tell her to wear her sari so that the free end did not drag on the footpath. A five-mile separation from her parents, I recalled with some irritation, had caused her to weep.

Unlike Mala, I was used to it all by then: used to cornflakes and milk, used to Helen's visits, used to sitting on the bench with Mrs. Croft. The only thing I was not used to was Mala. Nevertheless I did what I had to do. I went to the housing office at MIT and found a furnished apartment a few blocks away, with a double bed and a private kitchen and bath, for forty dollars a week. One last Friday I handed Mrs. Croft eight one-dollar bills in an envelope, brought my suitcase downstairs, and informed her that I was moving. She put my key into her change purse. The last thing she asked me to do was hand her the cane propped against the table, so that she could walk to the door and lock it behind me. "Good-bye, then," she said, and retreated back into the house. I did not expect any display of emotion, but I was disappointed all the same. I was only a boarder, a man who paid her a bit of money and passed in and out of her home for six weeks. Compared to a century, it was no time at all.

At the airport I recognized Mala immediately. The free end of her sari did not drag on the floor, but was draped in a sign of bridal modesty over her head, just as it had draped my mother until the day my father died. Her thin brown arms were stacked with gold bracelets, a small red circle was pointed on her forehead, and the edges of her feet were tinted with a decorative red dye. I did not embrace her, or kiss her, or take her hand. Instead I asked her, speaking Bengali for the first time in America, if she was hungry.

She hesitated, then nodded yes.

I told her I had prepared some egg curry at home. "What did they give you to eat on the plane?"

"I didn't eat."

105 "All the way from Calcutta?"

"The menu said oxtail soup."

"But surely there were other items."

"The thought of eating an ox's tail made me lose my appetite."

When we arrived home, Mala opened up one of her suitcases, and presented me with two pullover sweaters, both made with bright blue wool, which she had knitted in the course of our separation, one with a V neck, the other covered with cables. I tried them on; both were tight under the arms. She had also brought me two new pairs of drawstring pajamas, a letter from my brother, and a packet of loose Darjeeling tea. I had no present for her apart from the egg curry. We sat at a bare table, each of us staring at our plates. We ate with our hands, another thing I had not yet done in America.

110 "The house is nice," she said. "Also the egg curry." With her left hand she held the end of her sari to her chest, so it would not slip off her head.

"I don't know many recipes."

She nodded, peeling the skin off each of her potatoes before eating them. At one point the sari slipped to her shoulders. She readjusted it at once.

"There is no need to cover your head," I said. "I don't mind. It doesn't matter here."

She kept it covered anyway.

115 I waited to get used to her, to her presence at my side, at my table and in my bed, but a week later we were still strangers. I still was not used to coming home to an apartment that smelled of steamed rice, and finding that the basin in the bathroom was always wiped clean, our two toothbrushes lying side by side, a cake of Pears soap from India resting in the soap dish. I was not used to the fragrance of the coconut oil she rubbed every other night into her scalp, or the delicate sound her bracelets made as she moved about the apartment. In the mornings she was always awake before I was. The first morning when I

came into the kitchen she had heated up the leftovers and set a plate with a spoonful of salt on its edge on the table, assuming I would eat rice for breakfast, as most Bengali husbands did. I told her cereal would do, and the next morning when I came into the kitchen she had already poured the cornflakes into my bowl. One morning she walked with me down Massachusetts Avenue to MIT, where I gave her a short tour of the campus. On the way we stopped at a hardware store and I made a copy of the key, so that she could let herself into the apartment. The next morning before I left for work she asked me for a few dollars. I parted with them reluctantly, but I knew that this, too, was now normal. When I came home from work there was a potato peeler in the kitchen drawer, and a tablecloth on the table, and chicken curry made with fresh garlic and ginger on the stove. We did not have a television in those days. After dinner I read the newspaper, while Mala sat at the kitchen table, working on a cardigan for herself with more of the bright blue wool, or writing letters home.

At the end of our first week, on Friday, I suggested going out. Mala set down her knitting and disappeared into the bathroom. When she emerged I regretted the suggestion; she had put on a clean silk sari and extra bracelets, and coiled her hair with a flattering side part on top of her head. She was prepared as if for a party, or at the very least for the cinema, but I had no such destination in mind. The evening air was balmy. We walked several blocks down Massachusetts Avenue, looking into the windows of restaurants and shops. Then, without thinking, I led her down the quiet street where for so many nights I had walked alone.

"This is where I lived before you came," I said, stopping at Mrs. Croft's chain-link fence.

"In such a big house?"

"I had a small room upstairs. At the back."

"Who else lives there?"

"A very old woman."

"With her family?"

"Alone."

"But who takes care of her?"

I opened the gate. "For the most part she takes care of herself."

I wondered if Mrs. Croft would remember me; I wondered if she had a new boarder to sit with her on the bench each evening. When I pressed the bell I expected the same long wait as that day of our first meeting, when I did not have a key. But this time the door was opened almost immediately, by Helen. Mrs. Croft was not sitting on the bench. The bench was gone.

"Hello there," Helen said, smiling with her bright pink lips at Mala. "Mother's in the parlor. Will you be visiting awhile?"

"As you wish, madame."

"Then I think I'll run to the store, if you don't mind. She had a little accident. We can't leave her alone these days, not even for a minute."

I locked the door after Helen and walked into the parlor. Mrs. Croft was lying flat on her back, her head on a peach-colored cushion, a thin white quilt spread over her body. Her hands were folded together on top of her chest.

When she saw me she pointed at the sofa, and told me to sit down. I took my place as directed, but Mala wandered over to the piano and sat on the bench, which was now positioned where it belonged.

"I broke my hip!" Mrs. Croft announced, as if no time had passed.

"Oh dear, madame."

"I fell off the bench!"

"I am so sorry, madame."

135 "It was the middle of the night! Do you know what I did, boy?"

I shook my head.

"I called the police!"

She stared up at the ceiling and grinned sedately, exposing a crowded row of long gray teeth. Not one was missing. "What do you say to that, boy?"

As stunned as I was, I knew what I had to say. With no hesitation at all, I cried out, "Splendid!"

140 Mala laughed then. Her voice was full of kindness, her eyes bright with amusement. I had never heard her laugh before, and it was loud enough so that Mrs. Croft had heard, too. She turned to Mala and glared.

"Who is she, boy?"

"She is my wife, madame."

Mrs. Croft pressed her head at an angle against the cushion to get a better look. "Can you play the piano?"

"No, madame," Mala replied.

145 "Then stand up!"

Mala rose to her feet, adjusting the end of her sari over her head and holding it to her chest, and, for the first time since her arrival, I felt sympathy. I remembered my first days in London, learning how to take the Tube to Russell Square, riding an escalator for the first time, being unable to understand that when the man cried "piper" it meant "paper," being unable to decipher, for a whole year, that the conductor said "mind the gap" as the train pulled away from each station. Like me, Mala had traveled far from home, not knowing where she was going, or what she would find, for no reason other than to be my wife. As strange as it seemed, I knew in my heart that one day her death would affect me, and stranger still, that mine would affect her. I wanted somehow to explain this to Mrs. Croft, who was still scrutinizing Mala from top to toe with what seemed to be placid disdain. I wondered if Mrs. Croft had ever seen a woman in a sari, with a dot painted on her forehead and bracelets stacked on her wrists. I wondered what she would object to. I wondered if she could see the red dye still vivid on Mala's feet, all but obscured by the bottom edge of her sari. At last Mrs. Croft declared, with the equal measures of disbelief and delight I knew well:

"She is a perfect lady!"

Now it was I who laughed. I did so quietly, and Mrs. Croft did not hear me. But Mala had heard, and, for the first time, we looked at each other and smiled.

I like to think of that moment in Mrs. Croft's parlor as the moment when the distance between Mala and me began to lessen. Although we were not yet fully in love, I like to think of the months that followed as a honeymoon of sorts. Together we explored the city and met other Bengalis, some of whom are still friends today. We discovered that a man named Bill sold fresh fish on Prospect Street, and that a shop in Harvard Square called Cardullo's sold bay leaves and cloves. In the evenings we walked to the Charles River to watch sailboats drift across the water, or had ice cream cones in Harvard Yard. We bought an Instamatic camera with which to document our life together, and I took pictures of her posing in front of the Prudential building, so that she could send them to her parents. At night we kissed, shy at first but quickly bold, and discovered pleasure and solace in each other's arms. I told her about my voyage on the SS *Roma,* and about Finsbury Park and the YMCA, and my evenings on the bench with Mrs. Croft. When I told her stories about my mother, she wept. It was Mala who consoled me when, reading the *Globe* one evening, I came across Mrs. Croft's obituary. I had not thought of her in several months—by then those six weeks of the summer were already a remote interlude in my past—but when I learned of her death I was stricken, so much so that when Mala looked up from her knitting she found me staring at the wall, the newspaper neglected in my lap, unable to speak. Mrs. Croft's was the first death I mourned in America, for hers was the first life I had admired; she had left this world at last, ancient and alone, never to return.

150 As for me, I have not strayed much farther. Mala and I live in a town about twenty miles from Boston, on a tree-lined street much like Mrs. Croft's, in a house we own, with a garden that saves us from buying tomatoes in summer, and room for guests. We are American citizens now, so that we can collect social security when it is time. Though we visit Calcutta every few years, and bring back more drawstring pajamas and Darjeeling tea, we have decided to grow old here. I work in a small college library. We have a son who attends Harvard University. Mala no longer drapes the end of her sari over her head, or weeps at night for her parents, but occasionally she weeps for our son. So we drive to Cambridge to visit him, or bring him home for a weekend, so that he can eat rice with us with his hands, and speak in Bengali, things we sometimes worry he will no longer do after we die.

Whenever we make that drive, I always make it a point to take Massachusetts Avenue, in spite of the traffic. I barely recognize the buildings now, but each time I am there I return instantly to those six weeks as if they were only the other day, and I slow down and point to Mrs. Croft's street, saying to my son, here was my first home in America, where I lived with a woman who was 103. "Remember?" Mala says, and smiles, amazed, as I am, that there was ever a time that we were strangers. My son always expresses his astonishment, not at Mrs. Croft's age, but at how little I paid in rent, a fact nearly as inconceivable to him as a flag on the moon was to a woman born in 1866. In my son's eyes I see the ambition that had first hurled me across the world. In a few years he will graduate and pave his way, alone and unprotected. But I remind myself that he has a father who is still living, a mother who is happy and strong. Whenever he is discouraged, I tell him that if I can survive on three continents, then there is no obstacle he cannot conquer. While the astronauts, heroes forever, spent mere hours on the moon, I have remained in this new world for nearly thirty years. I know that my achievement is quite ordinary. I am not the only man to seek his fortune far from home, and certainly I am not the first. Still, there are times I am bewildered by each mile I have traveled, each meal I have eaten, each person I have known, each room in which I have slept. As ordinary as it all appears, there are times when it is beyond my imagination.

Explorations of the Text

1. Describe the point of view of the narrator. What impact does this narrative perspective have?
2. What main impression do you gain of the narrator at the beginning of the story? Does your view of him change as the story progresses?
3. Discuss the narrator's interactions with Mrs. Croft. In what ways are they both outsiders in North American society?
4. What does he learn from his experiences with Mrs. Croft? How does his relationship with her prepare him for his marriage? How does the narrator change as the story progresses?
5. What possible interpretations exist for the phrase "the third and final continent"? What views do you gain of the immigrant experience in North America?
6. Explore the significance of the moon landing. How does the symbol develop themes of the story?
7. Compare the vision of exile in this story with Said's views in "Reflections on Exile." What characterizes the state of exile (the physical, emotional, social conditions of exile)?

The Reading/Writing Connection

1. Do a freewrite on the topic of exile.
2. "Think" Topic: Argue for or against arranged marriage.

Ideas for Writing

1. Explore the symbolism of the "third and final continent." How many different "third . . . continents" are there in this story? How do they intersect?
2. Compare the idea of the "new world" in this story with several works in this chapter. Or compare the treatment of the theme in this story with its depiction in *The Tempest.*

POETRY

THE SECOND COMING[1]

William Butler Yeats

William Butler Yeats (1865–1939) was born in Dublin, Ireland. The leader of the Irish Renaissance, he helped found the Abbey Theater in 1904. In 1922, he was elected to a six-year term as senator after the Irish Free State was formed. Yeats's writing displays an imaginative, skillful blend of Eastern and Western cultures and ancient and modern thought. Despite this impressive eclecticism, Yeats always remains an Irish poet. His works include the prose volumes A Vision *(1925) and* Autobiographies *(1926) and the poetic volumes* The Tower *(1928),* The Winding Stair *(1929), and* The Collected Poems *(1933). Yeats was awarded the Nobel Prize for Literature in 1923.*

1919

Turning and turning in the widening gyre
The falcon cannot hear the falconer;
Things fall apart; the center cannot hold;
Mere anarchy is loosed upon the world,
The blood-dimmed tide is loosed, and everywhere
The ceremony of innocence is drowned;
The best lack all conviction, while the worst
Are full of passionate intensity.
Surely some revelation is at hand.
Surely the Second Coming is at hand.
The Second Coming! Hardly are those words out
When a vast image out of *Spiritus Mundi*[2]
Troubles my sight: somewhere in sands of the desert
A shape with lion body and the head of a man,[3]
A gaze blank and pitiless as the sun,
Is moving its slow thighs, while all about it
Reel shadows of the indignant desert birds.
The darkness drops again; but now I know
That twenty centuries[4] of stony sleep

---

[1] Allusion to Jesus's prediction of his second coming. Written in 1919, the poem refers to the Black and Tan War in Ireland when British soldiers were sent to quell the republicans.

[2] The author's term for divine inspiration or for a place from which images are received, never invented.

[3] The Egyptian sphinx.

[4] Reference to twenty centuries of Christianity.

Were vexed to nightmare[5] by a rocking cradle,
And what rough beast, its hour come round at last,
Slouches towards Bethlehem[6] to be born?

Explorations of the Text

1. What do the symbols of the "gyre," "the falcon," and "the falconer" suggest about the speaker's view of the state of the world?
2. Why do "Things fall apart"? Why is it that "the center cannot hold"?
3. Explore the significance of the images of the Egyptian sphinx, the "blank and pitiless" gaze, and the "shadows of the indignant desert birds."
4. Why does Yeats choose the word "reel" in line 17? What is the effect of this word choice?
5. What is the speaker's view of the millennium? of the Apocalypse? What will be "born"?
6. Examine the rhyme scheme of the poem. Why do you think Yeats rhymes only certain lines?
7. Discuss the meaning and **irony** of the title and of the ending.

The Reading/Writing Connection

1. Freewrite. React to the view of the future expressed in the poem.
2. "Think" Topic: Do you agree with Yeats' view of the decline of civilization?

Ideas for Writing

1. Does Yeats's vision seem relevant today? What world events may be evoked by references in the poem?
2. Contrast Yeats's view of the future with the ideas in two other works in this chapter.

STONE OLIVES

Judith Emlyn Johnson

Judith Emlyn Johnson (1936–) is Professor of English at the State University of New York at Albany. Educated at Radcliffe, Barnard, and

[5] Implication that Christianity created its opposite.
[6] Birthplace of Jesus.

Columbia, Johnson has been recipient of many awards, including the Yale University Younger Poets Award. She served as President of the Poetry Society of America, 1975–78. Her works include How the Dead Count *(1978) and* The Ice Lizard *(1992). She is editor-in-chief of* 13th Moon: A Feminist Literary Journal. *Commenting on poetry, Johnson says, "Before poetry was anything else, it was a physical act: the act of making sounds in the throat." About fiction she says there was "the current of concentration uniting the storyteller with his or her listeners around the campfire or in the workplace, when the hands moved and the minds moved, and the dancer and the dance were one moving creature." In "Stone Olives," the speaker mourns the death of a student on Pan Am Flight 103, a plane destroyed by a terrorist bomb over Lockerbie, Scotland, in December 1988.*

1992

(in memoriam Melina Hudson, of Albany,
Pan Am Flight 103, December 1988)

Tulip-flowered wind, night-smelling sea,
long swell of desert sands, and the roar of tractors
crawling up from the Hudson,[1] from under water
into Albany's Washington Park:[2] what is that ploughing?

It is the sound
of olive trees.
First one, then two, then the whole grove, they drop
their small, hard fruits,
and their tears are gathered up,
packed into baskets, then carried
to the earth-floored rooms.
Some go into jars.
Some have their centers plucked out
to be filled with slivered almonds or roasted
red peppers. Some go to the press
where they're crushed. From their pulp
oozes the purest gold,
to be strained into jars and sold.
Little dead ones, they sing, *blink blink,*
as they fall, *little dead ones, blink blink*
la muerte, ay, los niños, ay, la muerte.[3]
Take my hand, come down, dance with me, take my hand.

---

[1] A major river in New York.

[2] Reference to a park where Melina Hudson enjoyed leisure time with her friends, among them the poet's daughter.

[3] "Death, oh, the children, oh, death" (from the Spanish).

Tulip-fluttered wind, night-swelling sea:
in the smell of desert sands, before we were born,
the tractors ploughed back time from under Mount Sinai[4]
into Washington Park. There, carved stone
Moses[5] watches his wise God stand hard by
as the father prepares to spill on the quickening sand
his son. No olive trees whisper here. Does Abraham[6]
see that no scapegoat waits at hand? His son
    and his son's sons and daughters,
sucked down, will sweeten that sand, no matter how many
small, innocent, wordless furs squeak out their lives.
What is dying now, even as we speak, to save us?

            It is the stand
        of apple trees behind the barbed wire.
        First one, then two, then the whole grove, the sun
            flattens them. Gravid, they droop,
            ripen, and men lean ladders,
        and their treasures are gathered, packed,
            into baskets, then ferried out
            from the earth-walled rooms.
              Some are rendered down,
            some peeled of their skins, grated
        with almonds, and mixed to haroseth that makes sweet
        the bitter herbs. Some have their teeth plucked out
        for the fillings. Some go to the press.
                From their pulped flesh oozes the purest gold,
        sweeter, oh Lord their God, than the fruit of the vine
        to be filtered through cheesecloth and sold.
    Little dead ones, they sing, *shalom,*[7]
    as they drop, *little dead ones, shalom*
    ich sterbe hier,[8] *nicht versteh,*[9] *je crêve,*[10] *nou verbeshti,*[11] *mamaye.*[12]
Take my hand, come down, dance with me, take my hand.

---

[4] Mountain of northeastern Egypt on the Sinai Peninsula.

[5] Hebrew prophet who led the Israelites out of Egyptian slavery. He delivered to them the commandments of their God's covenant at Mount Sinai.

[6] Allusion to patriarch of the Jews regarded as the founder of the Hebrew people through his son Isaac. This passage refers to God's commanding Abraham to sacrifice Isaac.

[7] Hebrew for "peace."

[8] "I'm dying here." (German).

[9] "I don't understand" (German).

[10] "I'm collapsing"; "I'm being slaughtered"; "I'm dying like a dog." (French)

[11] "Shut up"; "don't talk"; literally "no more words." (Rumanian).

[12] "Mommy." (Rumanian).

Tulip-sequined wind, night-shimmying sea,
long bloom of desert sands, and the roar of the spring
festival onto the grass: tell me the mother,
before our history sprouted, should have thrown
herself under the blades to save her child. Yes, tell me
the father should have given to God the Father
his own life, not his son's. Tell me, if all,
man, woman, child, had thrown their lives away
rather than take that dumb, furred sacrifice
still squeaking its lives out under our knives
would all our history have borne different fruits?
We planted no orchard here next to City Hall[13]
but the walls still shake. What are we ploughing under
when we do that prime time shimmy?

It is the sands
of the pyramids.
One grain, then two, then whole stones, they melt.
Their sharp, unlanded granules
drill from their homeless camps the far away dam.
The wind lifts them, gathers them in, and they ride
the red tide's maternal breast
from their hulled earth rooms to their ghost of a promised land.
Stones fall, whole shoulders drop
from the Sphinx[14] who was raised
by forced labor. Eyes run
from their heads. Scalps, halves of scalps rain down.
Melina, who once danced
at proms far from Beirut,[15] laughed with my daughter
years after Hiroshima[16] broke into flower, told
her beads in a church the Gulag[17] never touched,
now pours down through our air
her young hands full with the seventeen pressed years
that are all she can hold
of spring: will the Dead Sea[18]
grow fat with these fragments? Our mouths are being stuffed

[13] In Albany, New York.

[14] Egyptian statue in the form of a lion, having a man's head.

[15] Capital city of Lebanon.

[16] City in Japan. In this case, an allusion to the United States dropping an atomic bomb during World War II, an action that destroyed the city and ended the war in the Pacific.

[17] Network of labor camps in the former USSR.

[18] Salt lake on the boundary between Israel and Jordan.

with our sons and daughters, our centers plucked out
with tongs. From our poor,
pressed through heat, through cold
over vents and gratings, flow simples, poultices, tinctures
to be forced into jars and sold.
Little dead ones, they sing, *ushh, ushh,*
as they drop, *little dead ones, ushh, ushh.*
d d d kkkkk d d d kkkkk aaaaaaah heart
Take my hand, come down, dance with me, take my hand.

Tulip-grinning wind, night-crying sea,
long shudder of desert sands, and the drowned tractors
bubbling up from our bodies, cut from our tongues
deep into Washington Park where Moses holds
his law in his hands: they told me God Himself
gave His Son's life to stop it as Abraham
gave Isaac. But what if each father
should give himself? What if we all stand up,
we, who are old enough to have held our lives,
and empty out, not our children, but ourselves?
Why do I hear no such ploughing?

Instead, I hear the bend
beyond the asteroids bleed.
First one, then two, then whole planets they fall
and their milk will be pressed out,
their hulled tears, neither water or salt, hold elements
we can neither measure nor read
their red shift to name. They carry
no life we know as life in their milled earths.
Their centaurs[19] are long gone
replaced by an airless patience,
their languages hot ores,
or frozen metals.
Of their forgiveness nothing remains, not even Aztec
gold to be ferried away
to the galaxies and sold. We know what their silence says.
Little dead ones, they sing as they shimmy, *aaah nnnnn,*
as they drop, *little dead ones, aaah nnnnnnnn*
eiaa mohsrden, aiee, eiaa khilsderin, aiee, eiaaaa mohsdenn
nnnnhh aaaaaqaaaaahhhhh.[20]
Take my hand, come down, dance with me, take my hand.

[19] Creature fabled to be half man and half horse.

[20] Invented language intended to convey the cries of the children; equivalent to "ay, los niños," or "Ick sterbe hier."

Explorations of the Text

1. What worlds converge in stanza 1? What does the "ploughing" signify?
2. How does the symbolism of the "olive trees" change throughout the poem. With what are the olives connected?
3. With whom does the speaker identify at the end of stanza 2?
4. Explain the references to Abraham and Isaac. (See Genesis 22.)
5. Analyze the following: "What is dying now, even as we speak, to save us?"
6. What historical allusions are suggested in stanzas 3, 4, and 6?
7. What does the speaker present as the alternative to the sacrifice of "our children"?
8. In the last stanza, why does Johnson enlarge her vision to include the "fall" of the "planets"? What poetic device is used?
9. Discuss the contrasting images of "gold," pressed blood and flesh, and the pressed pulp of fruit.
10. What is the significance of the repetition and variation of the lines: "Tulip-flowered wind, night-smelling sea,/long swell of desert sands"?
11. What is the significance of the repetition of "Little dead ones" and "Take my hand, come down, dance with me, take my hand"?
12. Who is the speaker? What is the speaker's role in the poem?
13. Why does Johnson include lines in different languages?
14. Compare the speaker's view of global issues with Gordon's. What futures do these writers imagine?

The Reading/Writing Connection

1. Read this poem aloud, and react to it.
2. Paraphrase the message of each stanza. How does the argument progress?
3. In a short essay, react to the visions of the past, of the present, and of the future. Do you agree with those visions?

Ideas for Writing

1. Gloss and annotate the text. Analyze the symbolism of the "stone olives."
2. Discuss the theme of sacrifice.
3. Who is the speaker? What is the speaker's role?

Gitanjali: Songs I and II

Rabindranath Tagore

Rabindranath Tagore (1861–1941) was born in Calcutta, India. A mystical experience in 1883 led him to a conception of god as intimate, a wellspring of inspiration that greatly influenced his work. He wrote nearly sixty volumes of verse, more than forty plays, fourteen novels, two hundred short stories, and thousands of songs, in addition to numerous essays, journals, and religious and philosophical tracts. In 1913, shortly after he wrote Gitanjali *(1910, "Song Offerings"), a collection of serenely mystical poems inspired by the deaths of his father, wife, two daughters, and youngest son, Tagore became the first Indian writer to win the Nobel Prize for Literature.*

1910

I

Thou hast made me endless, such is thy pleasure. This frail vessel thou emptiest again and again, and fillest it ever with fresh life.

This little flute of a reed thou hast carried over hills and dales, and has breathed through it melodies eternally new.

At the immortal touch of thy hands my little heart loses its limits in joy, and gives birth to utterance ineffable.

Thy infinite gifts come to me only on these very small hands of mine. Ages pass, and still thou pourest, and still there is room to fill.

II

When thou commandest me to sing, it seems that my heart would break with pride; and I look to thy face, and tears come to my eyes.

All that is harsh and dissonant in my life melts into one sweet harmony—and my adoration spreads wings like a glad bird on its flight across the sea.

I know thou takest pleasure in my singing. I know that only as a singer I come before thy presence.

Explorations of the Text

Song I

1. What does the speaker experience? Examine the images of the "vessel," the "flute," and the "heart."
2. What does the speaker mean when he describes "utterance ineffable"?
3. Interpret the last line. Explain the **paradox.**

Song II

1. What is the commandment "to sing"?
2. Why does "all that is harsh and dissonant" melt? Describe the speaker's version of harmony.
3. Explain the bird **simile.**
4. Why can the speaker come into the presence of divinity only as a singer? What does the joy of "singing" suggest?
5. Compare Tagore's and Rilke's views of spirit and divinity.

The Reading/Writing Connection

1. Describe the voice in these lyrics.
2. Create your own version of a third song in this sequence. Consider speaker, tone, imagery, and theme.
3. "Think" Topic: What is the source of joy in these works?

Ideas for Writing

1. Write about the concept of divinity in these poems.
2. Characterize the speaker.
3. How does Tagore's poetry differ from other poets?

SONNET I

Rainer Maria Rilke

Born in Czechoslovakia, Rainer Maria Rilke (1875–1926) went to military school as a child and attended university in his native Prague, in Berlin, and in Munich. The work that first gained him recognition as a poet was The Book of Images *(1902). Rilke wrote intermittently, in great prolific bursts that he believed were periods of grace when the poems were "dictated" to him. He composed the* Sonnets to Orpheus *in 1923 while he lived alone in a tower in Switzerland, but they were not published until eight years after his death from blood poisoning. With Rilke's* Duino Elegies, *the* Sonnets *are considered the greatest poems in modern German literature.*

1923

There arose a tree. Oh, pure transcension!
Oh, Orpheus sings[1]! Oh, tall tree in the ear!

[1] According to Greek mythology, Orpheus was the son of Oeagrus, a river god, and one of the Muses (Polyhymnia, Clio, or Calliope). Born in Thrace, Orpheus may have been king of some Thracian tribes and was famous as a great singer, musician,

And all was still. But even in this suspension
new beginnings, signs, and changes were.

Animals from the silence, from the clear
now opened wood came forth from nest and den;
and it so came to pass that not from fear
or craftiness were they so quiet then,

but to be listening. Howling, cry, roar
seemed little to their hearts. Where scarce a
humble
hut for such reception was before,

a hiding-place of the obscurest yearning,
with entrance shaft whose underpinnings tremble,
you made for the beasts temples in the hearing.

Explorations of the Text

1. What is the "transcension" in the first **quatrain?** What does the tree symbolize? What is the "tall tree in the ear"?
2. Why do the animals come forth? Why is the silence significant?
3. Explicate: "Howling, cry, roar/seemed little to their hearts."
4. Explain the last line. Who is "you"? Interpret "temples in the hearing."
5. What has Orpheus accomplished?
6. Explore the form of the poem as a version of the **Petrarchan sonnet,** with two **quatrains** (an **octave**) and two **tercets** (a **sestet**). What other formal elements are noteworthy?
7. Compare the tone of this sonnet to the tone in Rich's "Diving into the Wreck" and in Tagore's lyrics.

---

and poet. In some legends, he supposedly invented the lyre. Because of the magic of his songs, all of nature responded to his music. Wild animals followed him, trees and plants leaned in his direction, and he tamed the souls of the wildest men.

The most famous exploit of Orpheus concerns his descent into the underworld to save his wife, Eurydice, who died when a serpent bit her. Inconsolable, he charmed monsters guarding the gates of hell and the gods of the dead in order to rescue her. For a brief moment, even the damned were relieved of pain by his music. The underworld deities, Hades and Persephone, agreed to allow Eurydice to return to earth with one stipulation: that Orpheus, followed by Eurydice, leave and that he not look back at her. When he could not resist temptation, he turned around, and she disappeared—lost to him forever.

The Reading/Writing Connection

1. Gloss, annotate, and comment on this sonnet.
2. Create a scene in which music or art transforms animals and/or people.
3. Analyze the **paradoxes** in the poem.
4. Freewrite about silence in this sonnet.

Ideas for Writing

1. Write about the figure of Orpheus. What are his powers?
2. Explicate and evaluate this sonnet. Use Reading/Writing Connection 1 as a beginning. Focus on imagery and form. (See chapter 10.)
3. Explore the theme of transformation in this poem, in "Diving into the Wreck," and in "My Name Is 'I Am Living.' "

Sonnet 29

1923

Still friend of many distances, feel yet
how your breathing is augmenting space.
From the beamwork of gloomy belfries let
yourself ring. What devours you will increase

more strongly from this food. Explore and win
knowledge of transformation through and
 through.
What experience was the worst for you?
Is drinking bitter, you must turn to wine.

Be the magic power of this immense
midnight at the crossroads of your senses,
be the purport of their strange meeting.
 Though

earth itself forgot your very name,
say unto the tranquil earth: I flow.
To the fleeting water speak: I am.

Explorations of the Text

1. Who is the "friend"?
2. How does the poet "win" "transformation"? What is the value of the "worst" "experience"?

3. Why does the speaker mean: "Be the magic power of this immense/ midnight at the crossroads of your senses"?
4. Interpret the last three lines. What is the meaning of the declarations "I flow" and "I am"?
5. Compare the form of this sonnet with Sonnet 1.

The Reading/Writing Connection

1. Does a person or poet learn from bitter experiences? Respond to this question in a journal entry.
2. "Think" Topic: Discuss transformation in Rilke's sonnets.

Ideas for Writing

1. Analyze the form of the poem. Is it effective?
2. Write a **parody** of this sonnet. Analyze your parody. Focus on point of view, tone, imagery, and form.
3. Can the poet or his or her art change the world?

Diving into the Wreck

Adrienne Rich

Adrienne Rich (1929–), born in Baltimore, Maryland, is one of America's finest poets and most influential feminists. She is also an essayist and teacher. Her works include the poetry collections A Change of World *(1951), selected by W. H. Auden for the Yale Younger Poets Award;* Snapshots of a Daughter-in-Law *(1963);* Facts of a Doorframe *(1984), as well as* On Lies, Secrets, and Silence—Selected Prose 1966–1978 *(1979) and* What Is Found There: Notebooks on Poetry and Politics *(1993). Her awards include the 1974 National Book Award for* Diving into the Wreck.

1972

First having read the book of myths,
and loaded the camera,
and checked the edge of the knife-blade,
I put on
the body-armor of black rubber
the absurd flippers
the grave and awkward mask.
I am having to do this
not like Cousteau[1] with his

[1] French underwater explorer and film maker (1910–97).

assiduous team
aboard the sun-flooded schooner
but here alone.

There is a ladder.
The ladder is always there
hanging innocently
close to the side of the schooner.
We know what it is for,
we who have used it.
Otherwise
it's a piece of maritime floss
some sundry equipment.

I go down.
Rung after rung and still
the oxygen immerses me
the blue light
the clear atoms
of our human air.
I go down.
My flippers cripple me,
I crawl like an insect down the ladder
and there is no one
to tell me when the ocean
will begin.

First the air is blue and then
it is bluer and then green and then
black I am blacking out and yet
my mask is powerful
it pumps my blood with power
the sea is another story
the sea is not a question of power
I have to learn alone
to turn my body without force
in the deep element.

And now: it is easy to forget
what I came for
among so many who have always
lived here
swaying their crenellated[2] fans

[2] Having notched or scalloped projections.

between the reefs
and besides
you breathe differently down here.

I came to explore the wreck.
The words are purposes.
The words are maps.
I came to see the damage that was done
and the treasures that prevail.
I stroke the beam of my lamp
slowly along the flank
of something more permanent
than fish or weed

the thing I came for:
the wreck and not the story of the wreck
the thing itself and not the myth
the drowned face always staring
toward the sun
the evidence of damage
worn by salt and sway into this threadbare beauty
the ribs of the disaster
curving their assertion
among the tentative haunters.

This is the place.
And I am here, the mermaid whose dark hair
streams black, the merman in his armored body
We circle silently
about the wreck
we dive into the hold.
I am she: I am he

whose drowned face sleeps with open eyes
whose breasts still bear the stress
whose silver, copper, vermeil[3] cargo lies
obscurely inside barrels
half-wedged and left to rot
we are the half-destroyed instruments
that once held to a course
the water-eaten log
the fouled compass

[3] Metal that is gilded.

We are, I am, you are
by cowardice or courage
the one who find our way
back to this scene
carrying a knife, a camera
a book of myths
in which
our names do not appear.

Explorations of the Text

1. Trace and paraphrase the stages of this journey. What is your reaction to the metaphor of diving? Why does Rich choose the metaphor of "diving into the wreck"?
2. Why does the speaker switch from "I" to "we" to "you"?
3. What does the "book of myths" represent?
4. Why does the speaker refer to Cousteau in line 9?
5. Explore the water imagery. What do the "sea" and "the deep element" symbolize (stanzas 3, 4, 5)?
6. Explain stanza 6. What does "the wreck" signify? Why are the words "purposes" and "maps"? What are "the damage" and "the treasures"?
7. Interpret: "the wreck and not the story of the wreck/the thing itself and not the myth" (lines 62–63).
8. Why is the speaker "the mermaid"? Why is she androgynous ("I am she: I am he")? With whom does she merge?
9. Examine the symbolism of the "cargo" and the drowned remnants of the captain's quarters: "instruments," "log," and "compass."
10. Consider the conclusion of the poem. What revelation does the speaker experience? Is the ending hopeful? pessimistic?

The Reading/Writing Connection

1. Write about a time in your life when you searched "the wreck." What "damage" and "treasures" did you discover?
2. Write about a person who guided you when your own "instruments" became "half-destroyed."
3. Write a double-entry notebook for this poem.

Ideas for Writing

1. Explore the symbolism of "diving into the wreck." Interpret the images and the symbolism of each stage of the journey.

2. What new mythology for men and for women emerges in the poem?
3. Create an alternative mythology for the relation of men and of women.
4. In an essay, "When We Dead Awaken: Writing as Re-Vision," Rich asserts that "re-vision—the act of looking back, of seeing with fresh eyes . . . —is for women more than a chapter in cultural history; it is an act of survival." Is this poem a model of the process of "re-vision"? Argue.

A Far Cry from Africa

Derek Walcott

The first Caribbean writer to win the Nobel Prize for Literature (1992), Derek Walcott (1930–) was born on the island of St. Lucia. His first book appeared in 1948 when his mother gave him two hundred dollars to have Twenty-Five Poems *published. His volumes of poetry include* Sea Grapes *(1976),* Midsummer *(1984), and the epic* Omeros *(1990). Walcott's poetry celebrates the diversity of modern English, Creole pidgin, and slang; he writes, "I had a sound colonial education. / I have Dutch, nigger and English in me, / and either I'm nobody or I'm a nation."*

1962

A wind is ruffling the tawny pelt
Of Africa. Kikuyu,[1] quick as flies,
Batten upon the bloodstreams of the veldt.[2]
Corpses are scattered through a paradise.
Only the worm, colonel of carrion, cries:
"Waste no compassion on these separate dead!"
Statistics justify and scholars seize
The salients of colonial policy.
What is that to the white child hacked in bed?
To savages, expendable as Jews?
Threshed out by beaters,[3] the long rushes break
In a white dust of ibises whose cries
Have wheeled since civilization's dawn
From the parched river or beast-teeming plain.
The violence of beast on beast is read
As natural law, but upright man
Seeks his divinity by inflicting pain.
Delirious as these worried beasts, his wars

---

[1] African tribe who conducted an eight-year fight against British colonial settlers. They were known as Mau Mau.

[2] Grassland in southern Africa with sparsely growing trees and shrubs.

[3] People hired by game hunters to beat the bush in order to chase wild animals.

Dance to the tightened carcass of a drum,
While he calls courage still that native dread
Of the white peace contracted by the dead.

Again brutish necessity wipes its hands
Upon the napkins of a dirty cause, again
A waste of our compassion, as with Spain,[4]
The gorilla wrestles with the superman.

I who am poisoned with the blood of both,
Where shall I turn, divided to the vein?
I who have cursed
The drunken officer of British rule, how choose
Between this Africa and the English tongue I love?
Betray them both, or give back what they give?
How can I face such slaughter and be cool?
How can I turn from Africa and live?

Explorations of the Text

1. What are the double meanings of the title?
2. Analyze the depiction and **personification** of Africa in stanza 1. Examine the questions in lines 9–10. Why does the speaker allude to the Jews?
3. Explain the image of the ibises. How does this scene function?
4. How does the violence of "beast on beast" contrast with that of "upright man"?
5. Why does the speaker mention "a dirty cause"? Interpret the reference to Spain.
6. Explain: "The gorilla wrestles with the superman."
7. Examine the divided loyalties of the speaker. Will he choose?
8. Compare the view of Africa in this poem to that of *"Master Harold" . . . and the Boys.*

The Reading/Writing Connection

1. Describe a conflict, "divided to the vein," that represents your background.
2. Characterize the speaker. Respond to him. Is he "a far cry from Africa"?
3. Explicate a powerful image in the poem.
4. Relate the title of the poem to the effects of "colonial policy."

[4] Allusion to the Spanish Civil War (1936–39).

Ideas for Writing

1. Explicate this poem. Focus on persona, imagery, and formal elements.
2. What are themes of this poem?
3. Create a prose version of the poem. What is lost? What is gained?
4. Explore the image of Africa in this poem and in another work in this chapter.
5. Compare this poem with W. B. Yeats's "The Second Coming."

To Live in the Borderlands Means You

Gloria Anzaldúa

In this poem, the speaker begins by reflecting on being a "mulata"[1]*—Hispanic, Indian, black, Spanish, and white.*

1986

To live in the Borderlands means you
are neither *hispana india negra española*[2]
ni[3] *gabacha,*[4] *eres mestiza,*[5] *mulata,* half-breed
caught in the crossfire between camps
while carrying all five races on your back
not knowing which side to turn to, run from;

To live in the Borderlands means knowing
that the *india* in you, betrayed for 500 years,
is no longer speaking to you,
that *mexicanas* call you *rajetas,*[6]
that denying the Anglo inside you
is as bad as having denied the Indian or Black;

Cuando vives en la frontera[7]
people walk through you, the wind steals your voice,
you're a *burra,*[8] *buey,*[9] scapegoat,
forerunner of a new race,
half and half—both woman and man, neither—
a new gender;

[1] A person of mixed racial ancestry.
[2] Spanish, Indian, black, black Spanish woman.
[3] Neither (nor).
[4] A Chicano term for a white woman [Author's note].
[5] You are of mixed blood.
[6] Literally, "Split," that is, having betrayed your word [Author's note].
[7] When you live in the borderlands.
[8] Donkey [Author's note].
[9] Ox [Author's note].

To live in the Borderlands means to
put *chile* in the borscht,
eat whole wheat *tortillas,*
speak Tex-Mex with a Brooklyn accent;
be stopped by *la migra* at the border checkpoints;

Living in the Borderlands means you fight hard to
resist the gold elixer beckoning from the bottle,
the pull of the gun barrel,
the rope crushing the hollow of your throat;

In the Borderlands
you are the battleground
where enemies are kin to each other;
you are at home, a stranger,
the border disputes have been settled
the volley of shots have shattered the truce
you are wounded, lost in action
dead, fighting back;

To live in the Borderlands means
the mill with the razor white teeth wants to shred off
your olive-red skin, crush out the kernel, your heart
pound you pinch you roll you out
smelling like white bread but dead;

To survive the Borderlands
you must live *sin fronteras*[10]
be a crossroads.

Explorations of the Text

1. Who is "you"? How does the speaker characterize "you"?
2. In the Borderlands, "people walk through you, the wind steals your voice"—why?
3. How does the speaker extend her vision beyond the "mestiza"? Whom does her vision include? What are the other borders?
4. Analyze stanzas 5–8. To what specific historical contexts does Anzaldúa refer in stanzas 5 and 6?
5. Explain the symbolism of "the mill" in stanza 7. What is the central metaphor?

[10] Without borders [Author's note].

6. Examine the speaker's conclusion. What **paradox** is apparent?
7. Analyze the impact of the Spanish words. What do they add to the poem's effect?
8. Compare views of language, heritage, and naming in this poem with those in Walcott's "A Far Cry from Africa" or Rich's "Diving into the Wreck."

The Reading/Writing Connection

1. Freewrite. Respond to this poem. How do you react to the violent images?
2. Choose one stanza, and write a reader response. Do you agree with the persona's views?
3. "Think" Topic: Analyze the poem's structure as if it were an expository essay. What modes of development does Anzaldúa employ?

Ideas for Writing

1. Compare processes of awakening and revelation in this poem and in "Diving into the Wreck."
2. How does Anzaldúa envision/re-envision North American ethnic identity? Do you agree?
3. Paraphrase and analyze the political argument of this poem.
4. Compare the clash of traditions in this poem with the conflicts in *"Master Harold" . . . and the Boys,* "Girls at War," and *The Tempest.*
5. Contrast Anzaldúa's view of "living in the borderlands" with Tagore's view of a limitless world.

POSTCARD FROM KASHMIR

Agha Shahid Ali

Agha Shahid Ali (1949–) was born in New Delhi, India. He attended the University of Kashmir, the University of Delhi, the University of Arizona, and Penn State University. His volumes of poetry include A Walk Through the Yellow Pages *(1986),* The Half-Inch Himalayas *(1987), and* The Country Without a Post Office *(1997). Ali has received Guggenheim and Ingram-Marshall Fellowships. Currently, he teaches at the University of Massachusetts, Amherst.*

1987

(for Pavan Sahgal)

Kashmir shrinks into my mailbox,
my home a neat four by six inches.

I always loved neatness. Now I hold
the half-inch Himalayas[1] in my hand.
This is home. And this the closest
I'll ever be to home. When I return,
the colors won't be so brilliant,
the Jhelum's waters[2] so clean,
so ultramarine. My love
so overexposed.

And my memory will be a little
out of focus, in it
a giant negative, black
and white, still undeveloped.

Explorations of the Text

1. What is the speaker's attitude toward home? How does the poet use size to suggest the speaker's memories of home and state of exile?
2. Discuss the imagery of the postcard. What does it suggest about the persona's memory of home?
3. Explore the symbolism of the photograph (e.g., colors, lack of "focus," status as a negative), and connect it with the process of remembering home. How have the speaker's views of Kashmir, of home, changed?
4. Why is the "negative" still undeveloped"?
5. Compare the persona's situation in this poem with the speaker in "To Live in the Borderlands Means You."

The Reading/Writing Connection

1. "Think" Topic: In a mini-essay, compare the speaker's process of reminiscing with your own process of autobiographical writing and remembrance. Does the poem present "truths" about autobiographical writing and remembrance?
2. Journal Entry: Discuss visions of displacement and alienation in this work, and compare the treatment of this theme with that of another work in this chapter.

[1] Mountain range along the border between India and Tibet.

[2] A river that runs through Kashmir and Pakistan.

Ideas for Writing

1. The persona in this poem is caught between worlds. Compare his situation with that of the speaker in "To Live in the Borderlands . . ." and in "Persimmons" (chapter 4).
2. Create a dialogue between two speakers on the subject of home.
3. Create the speaker's imaginary return home to Kashmir. Have the speaker describe his homecoming in a letter to a relative in North America.

My Name Is "I Am Living"

Anna Lee Walters

Anna Lee Walters (1946–), a member of the Pawnee and Otoe-Missouria tribes of Oklahoma, is a technical writer, an author of textbooks, and a poet. Her volumes of poetry include The Man to Send Rain Clouds *(1974),* Warriors of the Rainbow *(1975), and* The Third Woman *(1978). She is director of the Navajo Community College Press, which publishes books about Native Americans, past and present.*

1975

My name is "I am living."
My home is all directions and is everlasting.
Instructed and carried to you by the wind,
I have felt the feathers in pale clouds and bowed before the Sun
who watches me from a blanket of faded blue.
In a gentle whirlwind I was shaken,
made to see on earth in many ways,
And when in awe my mouth fell open,
I tasted a fine red clay.
Its flavor has remained after uncounted days.
This gave me cause to drink from a crystal stream
that only I have seen.
So I listened to all its flowing wisdom
and learned from it a Song—
This song the wind and I
have since sung together.
Unknowing, I was encircled by its water and cleansed.
Naked and damp, I was embraced and dried
by the warmth of your presence.
Dressed forever in the scent of dry cedar,
I am purified and free.
And I will not allow you to ignore me.
I have brought to you a gift.

It is all I have but it is yours.
You may reach out and enfold it.
It is only the strength in the caress of a gentle breeze,
But it will carry you to meet the eagle in the sky.
My name is "I am living." I am here.
My name is "I am living." I am here.

Explorations of the Text

1. Who is the "I" in the poem? Characterize the voice of the speaker. Is she real? mythic?
2. Explain: "My home is all directions and is everlasting."
3. Why is the speaker "purified and free"?
4. Who is the "you"? What does the speaker give to the "you"?
5. What is the symbolism of "the eagle in the sky"?
6. Why does line 29 repeat line 28 in the closing refrain?
7. Discuss the poem's chanting rhythm.
8. Contrast the theme of this poem with "Diving into the Wreck," "The Second Coming," or "Stone Olives."

The Reading/Writing Connection

1. "Think" Topic: Characterize the speaker. Whom does the speaker address? What is the speaker's purpose?
2. Write a reader-response journal entry for this poem.
3. Write your own poem or chant. You may begin with "I am living. . . ."

Ideas for Writing

1. Analyze this poem as a chant, not as a written expression. Examine the role of the speaker and the presentation of the message. You may use Reading/Writing Connection 1 as a beginning.
2. Explain the imagery in this poem.
3. Compare the speaker and themes in this poem with those in Johnson's "Stone Olives"; Szymborska's "Could Have"; and Walker's "Am I Blue?"

Ghosts

Mary Oliver

Mary Oliver (1935–) was born in Maple Heights, Ohio, and educated at Vassar College. Her first book of poems, No Voyage and Other Poems, *was published in 1963. Subsequent volumes include* Twelve Moons *(1979);* American Primitive *(1983), which won a Pulitzer Prize;* New and Selected Poems *(1992), which won the National Book Award; and* West Wind *(1997). Oliver teaches at Bennington College; she has received fellowships from the Guggenheim Foundation and the National Endowment for the Arts.*

1983

1

Have you noticed?

2

Where so many millions of powerful bawling beasts
lay down on the earth and died
it's hard to tell now
what's bone, and what merely
was once.

The golden eagle, for instance,
has a bit of heaviness in him;
moreover the huge barns
seem ready, sometimes, to ramble off
toward deeper grass.

3

1805
near the Bitterroot Mountains:
a man named Lewis kneels down
on the prairie watching

a sparrow's nest cleverly concealed in the wild hyssop
and lined with buffalo hair. The chicks,
not more than a day hatched, lean
quietly into the thick wool as if
content, after all,
to have left the perfect world and fallen
helpless and blind
into the flowered fields and the perils
of this one.

4

In the book of the earth it is written:
nothing can die.

In the book of the Sioux it is written:
they have gone away into the earth to hide.
Nothing will coax them out again
but the people dancing.

5

Said the old-timers:
the tongue
is the sweetest meat.

Passengers shooting from train windows
could hardly miss, they were
that many.

Afterward the carcasses
stank unbelievably, and sang with flies, ribboned
with slopes of white fat,
black ropes of blood—hellhunks
in the prairie heat.

6

Have you noticed? how the rain
falls soft as the fall
of moccasins. *Have you noticed?*
how the immense circles still,
stubbornly, after a hundred years,
mark the grass where the rich droppings
from the roaring bulls
fell to the earth as the herd stood
day after day, moon after moon
in the tribal circle, outwaiting
the packs of yellow-eyed wolves that are also
have you noticed? gone now.

7

Once only, and then in a dream,
I watched while, secretly
and with the tenderness of any caring woman,
a cow gave birth
to a red calf, tongued him dry and nursed him
in a warm corner

of the clear night
in the fragrant grass
in the wild domains
of the prairie spring, and I asked them,
in my dream I knelt down and asked them
to make room for me.

Explorations of the Text

1. Characterize the voice of the speaker.
2. Whom is she addressing? Why does the poet repeat the line, "Have you noticed?"
3. Paraphrase the situation and action in each stanza. What contrasting patterns of imagery emerge? What themes are implied?
4. Explicate the following lines: "It's hard to tell now/what's bone, and what merely/was once" and "in the book of the earth it is written:/nothing can die."
5. What view of the universe emerges in the poem? Compare Oliver's view of the world with Walter's in "My Name Is 'I am Living' or with Yeats's in "The Second Coming."

The Reading/Writing Connection

1. List questions that you have about this poem as a prelude to class discussion.
2. Choose one stanza for analysis. Respond in a double-entry notebook.
3. "Think" Topic: Why does she repeat the line: *"Have you noticed?"*

Ideas for Writing

1. Discuss Oliver's conception of nature and of humankind.

The Century's Decline, Could Have, Hatred

Wislawa Szymborska

Wislawa Szymborska (1923–) was born in Kornik, Poland, and educated at Jagiellonian University, where she studied Polish literature and sociology. From 1953 to 1981, she was poetry editor and a columnist for a literary weekly. She has published sixteen volumes of poetry, including Calling Out to Yeti *(1957),* No End of Fun *(1967), and* The People on the Bridge *(1986). In 1996, Szymborska was awarded the Nobel Prize for Literature.*

The Century's Decline

1986

Our twentieth century was going to improve on the others.
It will never prove it now,
now that its years are numbered,
its gait is shaky,
its breath is short.

Too many things have happened
that weren't supposed to happen,
and what was supposed to come about
has not.

Happiness and spring, among other things,
were supposed to be getting closer.

Fear was expected to leave the mountains and the valleys.
Truth was supposed to hit home
before a lie.

A couple of problems weren't going
to come up anymore:
hunger, for example,
and war, and so forth.

There was going to be respect
for helpless people's helplessness,
trust, that kind of stuff.

Anyone who planned to enjoy the world
is now faced
with a hopeless task.

Stupidity isn't funny.
Wisdom isn't gay.
Hope
isn't that young girl anymore,
et cetera, alas.

God was finally going to believe
in a man both good and strong,
but good and strong
are still two different men.

"How should we live?" someone asked me in a letter.
I had meant to ask him
the same question.

Again, and as ever,
as may be seen above,
the most pressing questions
are naïve ones.

Could Have

1972

It could have happened.
It had to happen.
It happened earlier. Later.
Nearer. Farther off.
It happened, but not to you.

You were saved because you were the first.
You were saved because you were the last.
Alone. With others.
On the right. The left.
Because it was raining. Because of the shade.
Because the day was sunny.

You were in luck—there was a forest.
You were in luck—there were no trees.
You were in luck—a rake, a hook, a beam, a brake,
a jamb, a turn, a quarter inch, an instant.
You were in luck—just then a straw went floating by.

As a result, because, although, despite.
What would have happened if a hand, a foot,
within an inch, a hairsbreadth from
an unfortunate coincidence.

So you're here? Still dizzy from another dodge, close shave,
    reprieve?
One hole in the net and you slipped through?
I couldn't be more shocked or speechless.
Listen,
how your heart pounds inside me.

Hatred

1993

See how efficient it still is,
how it keeps itself in shape—
our century's hatred.
How easily it vaults the tallest obstacles.
How rapidly it pounces, tracks us down.

It's not like other feelings.
At once both older and younger.
It gives birth itself to the reasons
that give it life.
When it sleeps, it's never eternal rest.
And sleeplessness won't sap its strength; it feeds it.

One religion or another—
whatever gets it ready, in position.
One fatherland or another—
whatever helps it get a running start.
Justice also works well at the outset
until hate gets its own momentum going.
Hatred. Hatred.
Its face twisted in a grimace
of erotic ecstasy.

Oh these other feelings,
listless weaklings.
Since when does brotherhood
draw crowds?
Has compassion
ever finished first?
Does doubt ever really rouse the rabble?
Only hatred has just what it takes.

Gifted, diligent, hardworking.
Need we mention all the songs it has composed?
All the pages it has added to our history books?
All the human carpets it has spread
over countless city squares and football fields?

Let's face it:
it knows how to make beauty.
The splendid fire-glow in midnight skies.
Magnificent bursting bombs in rosy dawns.
You can't deny the inspiring pathos of ruins
and a certain bawdy humor to be found
in the sturdy column jutting from their midst.

Hatred is a master of contrast—
between explosions and dead quiet,
red blood and white snow.
Above all, it never tires
of its leitmotif—the impeccable executioner
towering over its soiled victim.

It's always ready for new challenges.
If it has to wait awhile, it will.
They say it's blind. Blind?
It has a sniper's keen sight
and gazes unflinchingly at the future
as only it can.

Explorations of the Text

1. In "Century's Decline," characterize the voice and tone of the speaker. Discuss the poet's use of irony.
2. Discuss the last two stanzas of the poem. What is the significance of the lines "the most pressing questions / are naïve ones"? Does the poem answer the question "How should we live"?
3. Discuss the form and diction of the poem. How do these elements contribute to the development of the themes of the work?
4. What vision of the twentieth century is represented in the work?
5. In "Could Have," what "could have" happened? Who is the "you"? To whom is the persona speaking? Theorize as to the events to which the speaker is alluding. Are they necessarily specific? What does the poet accomplish by using abstract language?
6. Interpret the closing lines: "Listen, / how your heart pounds inside me."
7. What view of fate is suggested in the work?
8. In "Hatred" what poetic devices—forms of figurative language—does she use? Discuss the effect of this technique.
9. Does "hatred" have the power the speaker ascribes to it?
10. Discuss Szymborska's use of irony. Choose several examples and explicate them.
11. Is her use of questions effective?
12. What views of the twentieth century, of human nature, of civilization do these poems suggest?

The Reading/Writing Connection

1. Journal Entry: Choose a line or several lines from one of these poems. Agree or disagree with the positions expressed or use the line(s) as the beginning of your own poem.
2. "Think" Topic: In a mini-essay, analyze the voice of the speakers and poetic technique in these poems. What seems characteristic of her style as a poet?
3. Write a poem in response to one of these poems. You may choose to imitate her style.

Ideas for Writing

1. Write an essay on Szymborska's view of the millennium.
2. Compare the poet's views of events in the twentieth century with those expressed in one of the fictional works in this chapter.
3. Write a letter to Szymborska, expressing your reactions to her work.
4. Critique your own poem.

Poems for Further Reading

My Heart Leaps Up When I Behold

William Wordsworth (1770–1850)

1802

My heart leaps up when I behold
A rainbow in the sky:
So was it when my life began;
So is it now I am a man;
So be it when I shall grow old,
Or let me die!
The Child is father of the Man;
And I could wish my days to be
Bound each to each by natural piety.

Kubla Khan: or, a Vision in a Dream[1]

Samuel Taylor Coleridge (1772–1834)

1816

In Xanadu[2] did Kubla Khan[3]
A stately pleasure-dome decree:
Where Alph, the sacred river, ran
Through caverns measureless to man
Down to a sunless sea.
So twice five miles of fertile ground
With walls and towers were girdled round:
And here were gardens bright with sinuous rills
Where blossomed many an incense-bearing tree;

[1] The poem resulted from a dream induced by opium. Because he was interrupted, Coleridge remembered only a fragment.

[2] Summer capital of Kubla Khan.

[3] Kubla Khan (1216–1294), grandson of Genghis Khan and founder of the Mongol Empire in China.

And there were forests ancient as the hills,
Enfolding sunny spots of greenery.
But oh! that deep romantic chasm which slanted
Down the green hill athwart a cedarn cover![4]
A savage place! as holy and enchanted
As e'er beneath a waning moon was haunted
By woman wailing for her demon-lover!
And from this chasm, with ceaseless turmoil seething,
As if this earth in fast thick pants were breathing,
A mighty fountain momently was forced,
Amid whose swift half-intermitted burst
Huge fragments vaulted like rebounding hail,
Or chaffy grain beneath the thresher's flail:
And 'mid these dancing rocks at once and ever
It flung up momently the sacred river.
Five miles meandering with a mazy motion
Through wood and dale the sacred river ran,
Then reached the caverns measureless to man,
And sank in tumult to a lifeless ocean:
And 'mid this tumult Kubla heard from far
Ancestral voices prophesying war!

The shadow of the dome of pleasure
Floated midway on the waves;
Where was heard the mingled measure
From the fountain and the caves.
It was a miracle of rare device,
A sunny pleasure-dome with caves of ice!

A damsel with a dulcimer
In a vision once I saw;
It was an Abyssinian[5] maid,
And on her dulcimer she played,
Singing of Mount Abora.[6]
Could I revive within me
Her symphony and song,
To such a deep delight 'twould win me,
That with music loud and long,
I would build that dome in air,
That sunny dome! those caves of ice!
And all who heard should see them there,

---

[4] Spanning a grove of cedars.

[5] Ethiopian.

[6] Mount Abora in Abyssinia, referred to by Milton, *Paradise Lost* 4:28.

And all should cry, Beware! Beware!
His flashing eyes, his floating hair!
Weave a circle round him thrice,
And close your eyes with holy dread,
For he on honey-dew hath fed,
And drunk the milk of Paradise.

Ode on a Grecian Urn

John Keats (1795–1821)

1820

I

Thou still unravished bride of quietness,
Thou foster child of silence and slow time,
Sylvan[1] historian, who canst thus express
A flowery tale more sweetly than our rhyme:
What leaf-fringed legend haunts about thy shape
Of deities or mortals, or of both,
In Tempe[2] or the dales of Arcady?[3]
What men or gods are these? What maidens loath?
What mad pursuit? What struggle to escape?
What pipes and timbrels? What wild ecstasy?

II

Heard melodies are sweet, but those unheard
Are sweeter; therefore, ye soft pipes, play on;
Not to the sensual ear, but, more endeared,
Pipe to the spirit ditties of no tone:
Fair youth, beneath the trees, thou canst not leave
Thy song, nor ever can those trees be bare;
Bold Lover, never, never canst thou kiss,
Though winning near the goal—yet, do not grieve;
She cannot fade, though thou hast not thy bliss,
Forever wilt thou love, and she be fair!

III

Ah, happy, happy boughs! that cannot shed
Your leaves, nor ever bid the Spring adieu;
And, happy melodist, unweariéd,

[1] Referring to woods or forest.
[2] Valley in Greece.
[3] Valleys of Arcadia, symbolic of pastoral life and beauty.

Forever piping songs forever new;
More happy love! more happy, happy love!
Forever warm and still to be enjoyed,
Forever panting, and forever young;
All breathing human passion far above,
That leaves a heart high-sorrowful and cloyed,
A burning forehead, and a parching tongue.

IV

Who are these coming to the sacrifice?
To what green altar, O mysterious priest,
Lead'st thou that heifer lowing at the skies,
And all her silken flanks with garlands dressed?
What little town by river or sea shore,
Or mountain-built with peaceful citadel,
Is emptied of this folk, this pious morn?
And, little town, thy streets forevermore
Will silent be; and not a soul to tell
Why thou art desolate, can e'er return.

V

O Attic[4] shape! Fair attitude! with brede[5]
Of marble men and maidens overwrought,[6]
With forest branches and the trodden weed;
Thou, silent form, dost tease us out of thought
As doth eternity: Cold Pastoral![7]
When old age shall this generation waste,
Thou shalt remain, in midst of other woe
Than ours, a friend to man, to whom thou say'st,
"Beauty is truth, truth beauty,—that is all
Ye know on earth, and all ye need to know."

The Haunted Palace

Edgar Allan Poe (1809–49)

1832

I

In the greenest of our valleys,
By good angels tenanted,

[4] Referring to Athens or Athenians.

[5] Braid.

[6] Elaborate; highly decorated.

[7] An idealized vision of country or rural life.

Once a fair and stately palace—
Radiant palace—reared its head.
In the monarch Thought's dominion—
It stood there!
Never seraph spread a pinion
Over fabric half so fair.

II

Banners yellow, glorious, golden,
On its roof did float and flow;
(This—all this—was in the olden
Time long ago)
And every gentle air that dallied,
In that sweet day,
Along the ramparts plumed and pallid,
A winged odor went away.

III

Wanderers in that happy valley
Through two luminous windows saw
Spirits moving musically
To a lute's well-tunèd law,
Round about a throne, where sitting
(Porphyrogene!)[1]
In state his glory well befitting,
The ruler of the realm was seen.

IV

And all with pearl and ruby glowing
Was the fair palace door,
Through which came flowing, flowing, flowing
And sparkling evermore,
A troop of Echoes whose sweet duty
Was but to sing,
In voices of surpassing beauty,
The wit and wisdom of their king.

V

But evil things, in robes of sorrow,
Assailed the monarch's high estate;

[1] Born to purple, in royal demeanor.

(Ah, let us mourn, for never morrow
Shall dawn upon him, desolate!)
And, round about his home, the glory
That blushed and bloomed
Is but a dim-remembered story
Of the old time entombed.

VI

And travelers now within that valley,
Through the red-litten windows see
Vast forms that move fantastically
To a discordant melody;
While, like a rapid ghastly river,
Through the pale door,
A hideous throng rush out forever,
And laugh—but smile no more.

Facing West from California's Shores

Walt Whitman (1819–92)

1860

Facing west from California's shores,
Inquiring, tireless, seeking what is yet unfound,
I, a child, very old, over waves, towards the house of maternity, the land of migrations, look afar,
Look off the shores of my Western sea, the circle almost circled;
For starting westward from Hindustan, from the vales of Kashmere,
From Asia, from the north, from the God, the sage, and the hero,
From the south, from the flowery peninsulas and the spice islands,
Long having wander'd since, round the earth having wander'd,
Now I face home again, very pleas'd and joyous,
(But where is what I started for so long ago?
And why is it yet unfound?)

I Heard a Fly Buzz—When I Died

Emily Dickinson

1862

I heard a Fly buzz—when I died—
The Stillness in the Room
Was like the Stillness in the Air—
Between the Heaves of Storm—

The Eyes around—had wrung them dry—
And Breaths were gathering firm
For that last Onset—when the King
Be witnessed—in the Room—

I willed my Keepsakes—Signed away
What portion of me be
Assignable—and then it was
There interposed a Fly—

With Blue—uncertain stumbling Buzz—
Between the light—and me—
And then the Windows failed—and then
I could not see to see—

Sailing to Byzantium[1]

William Butler Yeats (1865–1939)

1926

I

That is no country[2] for old men. The young
In one another's arms, birds in the trees
—Those dying generations—at their song,
The salmon-falls, the mackerel-crowded seas,
Fish, flesh, or fowl, commend all summer long
Whatever is begotten, born, and dies.
Caught in that sensual music all neglect
Monuments of unageing intellect.

II

An aged man is but a paltry thing,
A tattered coat upon a stick, unless
Soul clap its hands and sing, and louder sing
For every tatter in its mortal dress,
Nor is there singing school but studying
Monuments of its own magnificence;
And therefore I have sailed the seas and come
To the holy city of Byzantium.

[1] Capital of the Byzantine Empire; revered by Yeats as a place where artistry reached its apex. Now called Istanbul, "Byzantium was the center of European civilization and the source of its spiritual philosophy, so I symbolize the search for spiritual life by a journey to that city." (Yeats, BBC, 1931)

[2] Ireland.

III

O sages standing in God's holy fire
As in the gold mosaic of a wall,
Come from the holy fire, perne in a gyre[3]
And be the singing-masters of my soul.
Consume my heart away; sick with desire
And fastened to a dying animal
It knows not what it is; and gather me
Into the artifice of eternity.

IV

Once out of nature I shall never take
My bodily form from any natural thing,
But such a form as Grecian goldsmiths make
Of hammered gold and gold enamelling[4]
To keep a drowsy Emperor awake;
Or set upon a golden bough to sing
To lords and ladies of Byzantium
Of what is past, or passing, or to come.

The Waking

Theodore Roethke (1908–63)

1953

I wake to sleep, and take my waking slow.
I feel my fate in what I cannot fear.
I learn by going where I have to go.

We think by feeling. What is there to know?
I hear my being dance from ear to ear.
I wake to sleep, and take my waking slow.

Of those so close beside me, which are you?
God bless the Ground! I shall walk softly there,
And learn by going where I have to go.

Light takes the Tree; but who can tell us how?
The lowly worm climbs up a winding stair;
I wake to sleep, and take my waking slow.

---

[3] Whirl in spirals. The gyre or cone represented cycles of history and the fate of the individual. The speaker asks the sages in the mosaic to take him from the ordinary world and to the eternal world of art.

[4] Yeats read that the emperor's palace contained a tree of gold and silver and artificial birds that could sing.

Great Nature has another thing to do
To you and me; so take the lively air,
And, lovely, learn by going where to go.

This shaking keeps me steady. I should know.
What falls away is always. And is near.
I wake to sleep, and take my waking slow.
I learn by going where I have to go.

Do Not Go Gentle into That Good Night

Dylan Thomas (1914–53)

1951

Do not go gentle into that good night,
Old age should burn and rave at close of day;
Rage, rage against the dying of the light.

Though wise men at their end know dark is right,
Because their words had forked no lightning they
Do not go gentle into that good night.

Good men, the last wave by, crying how bright
Their frail deeds might have danced in a green bay,
Rage, rage against the dying of the light.

Wild men who caught and sang the sun in flight,
And learn, too late, they grieved it on its way,
Do not go gentle into that good night.

Grave men, near death, who see with blinding sight
Blind eyes could blaze like meteors and be gay,
Rage, rage against the dying of the light.

And you, my father, there on the sad height,
Curse, bless, me now with your fierce tears, I pray.
Do not go gentle into that good night.
Rage, rage against the dying of the light.

A Blessing

James Wright (1927–80)

1963

Just off the highway to Rochester, Minnesota,
Twilight bounds softly forth on the grass.

And the eyes of those two Indian ponies
Darken with kindness.
They have come gladly out of the willows
To welcome my friend and me.
We step over the barbed wire into the pasture
Where they have been grazing all day, alone.
They ripple tensely, they can hardly contain their happiness
That we have come.
They bow shyly as wet swans. They love each other.
There is no loneliness like theirs.
At home once more,
They begin munching the young tufts of spring in the darkness.
I would like to hold the slenderer one in my arms.
For she has walked over to me
And nuzzled my left hand.
She is black and white,
Her mane falls wild on her forehead,
And the light breeze moves me to caress her long ear
That is delicate as the skin over a girl's wrist.
Suddenly I realize
That if I stepped out of my body I would break
Into blossom.

The Idea of Order at Key West

Wallace Stevens

1935

She sang beyond the genius of the sea.
The water never formed to mind or voice,
Like a body wholly body, fluttering
Its empty sleeves; and yet its mimic motion
Made constant cry, caused constantly a cry,
That was not ours although we understood,
Inhuman, of the veritable ocean.

The sea was not a mask. No more was she.
The song and water were not medleyed sound
Even if what she sang was what she heard,
Since what she sang was uttered word by word.
It may be that in all her phrases stirred
The grinding water and the gasping wind;
But it was she and not the sea we heard.

For she was the maker of the song she sang.
The ever-hooded, tragic-gestured sea

Was merely a place by which she walked to sing.
Whose spirit is this? we said, because we knew
It was the spirit that we sought and knew
That we should ask this often as she sang.

If it was only the dark voice of the sea
That rose, or even colored by many waves;
If it was only the outer voice of sky
And cloud, of the sunken coral water-walled,
However clear, it would have been deep air,
The heaving speech of air, a summer sound
Repeated in a summer without end
And sound alone. But it was more than that,
More even than her voice, and ours, among
The meaningless plungings of water and the wind,
Theatrical distances, bronze shadows heaped
On high horizons, mountainous atmospheres
Of sky and sea.
                          It was her voice that made
The sky acutest at its vanishing.
She measured to the hour its solitude.
She was the single artificer of the world
In which she sang. And when she sang, the sea,
Whatever self it had, because the self
That was her song, for she was the maker. Then we,
As we beheld her striding there alone,
Knew that there never was a world for her
Except the one she sang and, singing, made.

Ramon Fernandez,[1] tell me, if you know,
Why, when the singing ended and we turned
Toward the town, tell why the glass lights,
The lights in the fishing boats at anchor there,
As the night descended, tilting in the air,
Mastered the night and portioned out the sea,
Fixing emblazoned zones and fiery poles,
Arranging, deepening, enchanting night.

Oh! Blessed rage for order, pale Ramon,
The maker's rage to order words of the sea,
Words of the fragrant portals, dimly-starred,
And of ourselves and of our origins,
In ghostlier demarcations, keener sounds.

[1] According to information contained in one of his letters, Stevens combined two Spanish names to form this figure's presence in the poem, and he did not mean to refer to French critic Ramon Fernandez.

Heaven

Cathy Song

1988

He thinks when we die we'll go to China.
Think of it—a Chinese heaven
where, except for his blond hair,
the part that belongs to his father,
everyone will look like him.
China, that blue flower on the map,
bluer than the sea
his hand must span like a bridge
to reach it.
An octave away.

I've never seen it.
It's as if I can't sing that far.
But look—
on the map, this black dot.
Here is where we live,
on the pancake plains
just east of the Rockies,
on the other side of the clouds.
A mile above the sea,
the air is so thin, you can starve on it.
No bamboo trees
But the alpine equivalent,
reedy aspen with light, fluttering leaves.
Did a boy in Guangzhou[1] dream of this
as his last stop?

I've heard the trains at night
whistling past our yards,
what we've come to own,
the broken fences, the whiny dog, the rattletrap cars.
It's still the wild west,
mean and grubby,
the shootouts and fistfights in the back alley.
With my son the dreamer
and my daughter, who is too young to walk,
I've sat in this spot
and wondered why here?
Why in this short life,
this town, this creek they call a river?

[1] Canton, a seaport in southeastern China.

He had never planned to stay,
the boy who helped to build
the railroads for a dollar a day.[2]
He had always meant to go back.
When did he finally know
that each mile of track led him further away,
that he would die in his sleep,
dispossessed,
having seen Gold Mountain,
the icy wind tunneling through it,
these landlocked, makeshift ghost towns?

It must be in the blood,
this notion of returning.
It skipped two generations, lay fallow,
the garden an unmarked grave.
On a spring sweater day
it's as if we remember him.
I call to the children.
We can see the mountains
shimmering blue above the air.
If you look really hard
says my son the dreamer,
leaning out from the laundry's rigging,
the work shirts fluttering like sails
you can see all the way to heaven.

[2] In the nineteenth century Chinese laborers and other immigrants laid the railroad tracks.

DRAMA

The Tempest

William Shakespeare

The Tempest *(1611), the last play William Shakespeare wrote before retiring to Stratford-on-Avon, is considered a romance, which is to say, a play that mixes elements of tragedy and comedy and in which magic and fantastic creatures and events play a conspicuous part.*

1611

Names of the Actors

Alonso, *King of Naples*[1]
Sebastian, *his brother*
Prospero, *the right Duke of Milan*[2]
Antonio, *his brother, the usurping Duke of Milan*
Ferdinand, *son to the King of Naples*
Gonzalo, *an honest old councillor*
Adrian and Francisco, *lords*
Caliban, *a savage and deformed slave*
Trinculo, *a jester*
Stephano, *a drunken butler*
Master of a Ship
Boatswain
Mariners
Miranda, *daughter to Prospero*
Ariel, *an airy spirit*
Iris, Ceres, Juno, Nymphs, Reapers } spirits
[Other Spirits attending on Prospero]

The Scene:

[A ship at sea;] an uninhabited island

Act I

Scene I

(A tempestuous noise of thunder and lightning heard. Enter a Ship-Master and a Boatswain.)

---

[1]**Naples:** City on southwest coast of Italy.
[2]**Milan:** City in northwest Italy

Master: Boatswain!

Boatswain: Here, master; what cheer?

Master: Good;[3] speak to th' mariners. Fall to't, yarely,[4] or we run ourselves aground. Bestir, bestir.

(Exit.)

(Enter Mariners.)

Boatswain: Heigh, my hearts! cheerly, cheerly, my hearts! yare, yare! Take in the topsail. Tend[5] to th' master's whistle.—Blow till thou burst thy wind, if room enough![6]

(Enter Alonso, Sebastian, Antonio, Ferdinand, Gonzalo, and others.)

Alonso: Good boatswain, have care. Where's the master? Play the men.[7]

Boatswain: I pray now keep below.

Antonio: Where is the master, bos'n?

Boatswain: Do you not hear him? You mar our labor. Keep your cabins; you do assist the storm.

Gonzalo: Nay, good, be patient.

Boatswain: When the sea is. Hence! What cares these roarers[8] for the name of king? To cabin! silence! trouble us not.

Gonzalo: Good, yet remember whom thou hast aboard.

Boatswain: None that I love more than myself. You are a councillor;[9] if you can command these elements to silence, and work the peace of the present,[10] we will not hand a rope more. Use your authority. If you cannot, give thanks you have liv'd so long, and make yourself ready in your cabin for the mischance of the hour, if it so hap.—Cheerly, good hearts!—Out of our way, I say. *(Exit.)*

Gonzalo: I have great comfort from this fellow. Methinks[11] he hath no drowning mark upon him, his complexion[12] is perfect gallows. Stand fast, good Fate, to his hanging, make the rope of his destiny our cable, for our own doth little advantage.[13] If he be not born to be hang'd, our case is miserable. *(Exeunt.)*

(Enter Boatswain.)

---

[3] **Good:** An acknowledgment of the boatswain's reply. The punctuation differentiates this from the *good* in line 15, which means "good fellow." [4] **yarely:** smartly, nimbly. [5] **Tend:** attend. [6] **Blow . . . enough:** He addresses the storm. **if room enough:** so long as we have sea-room, i.e., space in which to maneuver without going aground. [7] **Play:** ply, urge on (?). [8] **roarers:** (1) turbulent waves: (2) rowdies. [9] **councillor:** member of the King's council. [10] **the present:** the present occasion; but *present* may be a mistake for *presence,* i.e., the King's presence or presence chamber. [11] **Methinks . . . gallows:** Alluding to the proverb "He that is born to be hanged need fear no drowning." [12] **complexion:** appearance (as reflecting his temperament). [13] **make . . . advantage:** make the rope that will hang him our anchor chain, since our actual one now does us little good.

Boatswain: Down with the topmast! yare! lower, lower! Bring her to try with main-course.[14] *(A cry within.)* A plague upon this howling! they are louder than the weather, or our office.[15]

(Enter Sebastian, Antonio, and Gonzalo.)

Yet again? What do you here? Shall we give o'er[16] and drown? Have you a mind to sink?

Sebastian: A pox o' your throat, you bawling, blasphemous, incharitable dog!

Boatswain: Work you then.

Antonio: Hang, cur! hang, you whoreson, insolent noisemaker! We are less afraid to be drown'd than thou art.

Gonzalo: I'll warrant him for[17] drowning, though the ship were no stronger than a nutshell, and as leaky as an unstanch'd wench.

Boatswain: Lay her a-hold, a-hold![18] Set her two courses off to sea[19] again! Lay her off.

(Enter Mariners wet.)

Mariners: All lost! To prayers, to prayers! All lost! *(Exeunt.)*

Boatswain: What, must our mouths be cold?

Gonzalo: The King and Prince at prayers, let's assist them,
For our case is as theirs.

Sebastian: I am out of patience.

Antonio: We are merely[20] cheated of our lives by drunkards.
This wide-chopp'd[21] rascal—would thou mightst lie drowning
The washing of ten tides![22]

Gonzalo: He'll be hang'd yet,
Though every drop of water swear against it,
And gape at wid'st to glut him.[23]
(A confused noise within.) "Mercy on us!"—
"We split, we split!"—"Farewell, my wife and children!"—
"Farewell, brother!"—"We split! we split! we split!"

(Exit Boatswain.)

Antonio: Let's all sink wi' th' King.

Sebastian: Let's take leave of him. *(Exit [with Antonio].)*

Gonzalo: Now would I give a thousand furlongs of sea for an acre of barren ground, long heath, brown [furze],[24] any thing. The wills above be done! but I would fain[25] die a dry death. *(Exit.)*

---

[14] **bring . . . main-course:** keep her close to the wind by means of the mainsail. [15] **office:** duties [16] **give o'er:** give up. [17] **warrant him for:** guarantee him against. [18] **a-hold:** a-hull, close to the wind. [19] **Set . . . sea:** i.e., set her mainsail and foresail so as to get her out to sea. [20] **merely:** utterly. [21] **wide-chopp'd:** wide-jawed. [22] **ten tides:** Pirates were hanged on shore and left until three tides had washed over them. [23] **gape . . . him:** open its mouth to the widest to gulp him down. [24] **heath . . . furze:** heather . . . gorse (plants that grow in poor soil). [25] **fain:** gladly.

Scene II

(Enter Prospero and Miranda.)[26]

Miranda: If by your art,[27] my dearest father, you have
Put the wild waters in this roar, allay them.
The sky, it seems, would pour down stinking pitch,
But that the sea, mounting to th' welkin's[28] cheek,[29]
Dashes the fire out. O! I have suffered
With those that I saw suffer. A brave[30] vessel
(Who had, no doubt, some noble creature in her)
Dash'd all to pieces! O, the cry did knock
Against my very heart. Poor souls, they perish'd.
Had I been any God of power, I would
Have sunk the sea within the earth or ere[31]
It should the good ship so have swallow'd, and
The fraughting[32] souls within her.
Prospero: Be collected.[33]
No more amazement.[34] Tell your piteous[35] heart
There's no harm done.
Miranda: O woe the day!
Prospero: No harm:
I have done nothing, but in care of thee
(Of thee my dear one, thee my daughter), who
Art ignorant of what thou art, nought knowing
Of whence I am, nor that I am more better[36]
Than Prospero, master of a full[37] poor cell,
And thy no greater[38] father.
Miranda: More to know
Did never meddle with[39] my thoughts.
Prospero: 'Tis time
I should inform thee farther. Lend thy hand,
And pluck my magic garment from me. So,

(Lays down his mantle.)

Lie there, my art. Wipe thou thine eyes; have comfort.
The direful spectacle of the wrack,[40] which touch'd
The very virtue[41] of compassion in thee,
I have with such provision[42] in mine art

---

[26] **Location:** An island. Before Prospero's cell. [27] **art:** magic. [28] **welkin's:** sky's. [29] **cheek:** (1) face; (2) side of a grate. [30] **brave:** splendid. [31] **or ere:** before. [32] **fraughting:** forming the cargo. [33] **collected:** composed. [34] **amazement:** terror. [35] **piteous:** pitying. [36] **more better:** of higher rank (common Elizabethan double comparative). [37] **full:** very. [38] **no greater:** i.e., of no loftier position than is implied by his "full poor cell." [39] **meddle with:** mingle with, enter. [40] **wrack:** shipwreck. [41] **virtue:** essence. [42] **provision:** foresight.

So safely ordered that there is no soul—[43]
No, not so much perdition[44] as an hair
Betid[45] to any creature in the vessel
Which thou heardst cry, which thou saw'st sink. Sit down,
For thou must now know farther.
Miranda: You have often
Begun to tell me what I am, but stopp'd
And left me to a bootless inquisition,[46]
Concluding, "Stay, not yet."
Prospero: The hour's now come,
The very minute bids thee ope thine ear.
Obey,[47] and be attentive. Canst thou remember
A time before we came unto this cell?
I do not think thou canst, for then thou wast not
Out[48] three years old.
Miranda: Certainly, sir, I can.
Prospero: By what? by any other house, or person?
Of any thing the image, tell me, that
Hath kept with thy remembrance.
Miranda: 'Tis far off;
And rather like a dream than an assurance[49]
That my remembrance warrants.[50] Had I not
Four, or five, women once that tended me?
Prospero: Thou hadst; and more, Miranda. But how is it
That this lives in thy mind? What seest thou else
In the dark backward and abysm of time?[51]
If thou rememb'rest aught ere thou cam'st here,
How thou cam'st here thou mayst.
Miranda: But that I do not.
Prospero: Twelve year since, Miranda, twelve year since,
Thy father was the Duke of Milan and
A prince of power.
Miranda: Sir, are not you my father?
Prospero: Thy mother was a piece[52] of virtue,[53] and
She said thou wast my daughter; and thy father
Was Duke of Milan, and his only heir
And princess no worse issued.[54]
Miranda: O the heavens,
What foul play had we, that we came from thence?
Or blessed was't we did?

---

[43] **soul—:** The sentence changes its course in what follows, but the sense is plain. [44] **perdition:** loss. [45] **Betid:** happened. [46] **bootless inquisition:** useless inquiry. [47] **Obey:** i.e., listen. [48] **Out:** fully. [49] **assurance:** certainty. [50] **remembrance warrants:** memory guarantees. [51] **backward . . . time:** abyss of the past. [52] **piece:** masterpiece. [53] **virtue:** chastity. [54] **no worse issued:** no less noble in birth.

Prospero: Both, both, my girl.
By foul play (as thou say'st) were we heav'd thence,
But blessedly holp[55] hither.
Miranda: O, my heart bleeds
To think o' th' teen[56] that I have turn'd you to,[57]
Which is from[58] my remembrance! Please you, farther.
Prospero: My brother and thy uncle, call'd Antonio—
I pray thee mark me—that a brother should
Be so perfidious!—he whom next thyself
Of all the world I lov'd, and to him put
The manage of my state, as at that time
Through all the signories[59] it was the first,
And Prospero the prime[60] duke, being so reputed
In dignity, and for the liberal arts
Without a parallel; those being all my study,
The government I cast upon my brother,
And to my state grew stranger, being transported
And rapt in secret studies. Thy false uncle—
Dost thou attend me?
Miranda: Sir, most heedfully.
Prospero: Being once perfected[61] how to grant suits,
How to deny them, who t' advance, and who
To trash for overtopping,[62] new created
The creatures that were mine, I say, or[63] chang'd 'em,
Or else new form'd 'em; having both the key[64]
Of officer and office, set all hearts i' th' state
To what tune pleas'd his ear, that now he was
The ivy which had hid my princely trunk,
And suck'd my verdure[65] out on't. Thou attend'st not!
Miranda: O, good sir, I do.
Prospero: I pray thee mark me.
I, thus neglecting worldly ends, all dedicated
To closeness[66] and the bettering of my mind
With that which, but by being so retir'd,
O'er-priz'd all popular rate,[67] in my false brother
Awak'd an evil nature, and my trust,

---

[55] **blessedly holp:** providentially helped. [56] **teen:** sorrow, trouble. [57] **turn'd you to:** reminded you of. [58] **from:** out of. [59] **signories:** city states. [60] **prime:** chief, first in rank. [61] **perfected:** expert in. [62] **trash for overtopping:** restrain from becoming too powerful. Two images are combined here: *trash* = check a hunting dog from going too fast; *overtopping* = growing too high. [63] **or:** either. [64] **key:** (1) key to office; (2) tuning key. [65] **verdure:** vigor, vitality. [66] **closeness:** seclusion. [67] **O'er-priz'd . . . rate:** had greater worth than any vulgar evaluation would place upon it.

Like a good parent,[68] did beget of him
A falsehood in its contrary, as great
As my trust was, which had indeed no limit,
A confidence sans[69] bound. He being thus lorded,[70]
Not only with what my revenue yielded,
But what my power might else exact—like one
Who having into[71] truth, by telling of it,
Made such a sinner of his memory
To[72] credit his own lie—he did believe
He was indeed the Duke, out[73] o' th' substitution,
And executing th' outward face of royalty
With all prerogative. Hence his ambition growing—
Dost thou hear?

Miranda: Your tale, sir, would cure deafness.

Prospero: To have no screen between this part he play'd
And him he play'd it for,[74] he needs will be
Absolute Milan[75]—me (poor man) my library
Was dukedom large enough: of temporal royalties[76]
He thinks me now incapable; confederates[77]
(So dry[78] he was for sway) wi' th' King of Naples
To give him annual tribute, do him homage,
Subject his coronet to his crown, and bend
The dukedom yet unbow'd (alas, poor Milan!)
To most ignoble stooping.

Miranda: O the heavens!

Prospero: Mark his condition,[79] and th' event,[80] then tell me
If this might be a brother.

Miranda: I should sin
To think but nobly of my grandmother.
Good wombs have borne bad sons.

Prospero: Now the condition.
This King of Naples, being an enemy
To me inveterate, hearkens my brother's suit,
Which was, that he in lieu o' th' premises,[81]
Of homage, and I know not how much tribute,
Should presently extirpate[82] me and mine

---

[68] **good parent:** That a good parent often bred a bad child was proverbial. [69] **sans:** without. [70] **lorded:** i.e., established in a position of power. [71] **into:** unto, against (*into truth* modifies *sinner*). [72] **To:** as to. [73] **out:** as a result. [74] **no . . . for:** i.e., no separation between acting as Duke and being Duke. [75] **Absolute Milan:** actual Duke of Milan. [76] **temporal royalties:** practical administration. [77] **confederates:** makes alliance. [78] **dry:** thirsty. **condition:** compact. [80] **event:** outcome. [81] **lieu . . . premises:** return for the pledge. [82] **presently extirpate:** immediately remove.

Out of the dukedom, and confer fair Milan
With all the honors on my brother; whereon,
A treacherous army levied, one midnight
Fated to th' purpose, did Antonio open
The gates of Milan, and i' th' dead of darkness
The ministers[83] for th' purpose hurried thence
Me and thy crying self.

Miranda: Alack,[84] for pity!
I, not rememb'ring how I cried out then,
Will cry it o'er again. It is a hint[85]
That wrings[86] mine eyes to't.

Prospero: Hear a little further,
And then I'll bring thee to the present business
Which now's upon's; without the which this story
Were most impertinent.[87]

Miranda: Wherefore did they not
That hour destroy us?

Prospero: Well demanded, wench;
My tale provokes that question. Dear, they durst not,
So dear the love my people bore me; nor set
A mark so bloody on the business; but
With colors fairer painted their foul ends.[88]
In few,[89] they hurried us aboard a bark,
Bore us some leagues to sea, where they prepared
A rotten carcass of a butt,[90] not rigg'd,
Nor tackle, sail, nor mast, the very rats
Instinctively have quit it. There they hoist us,
To cry to th' sea, that roar'd to us; to sigh
To th' winds, whose pity, sighing back again,
Did us but loving wrong.[91]

Miranda: Alack, what trouble
Was I then to you!

Prospero: O, a cherubin
Thou wast that did preserve me. Thou didst smile,
Infused with a fortitude from heaven,
When I have deck'd[92] the sea with drops full salt,
Under my burden groan'd, which[93] rais'd in me
An undergoing stomach,[94] to bear up
Against what should ensue.

---

[83] **ministers:** agents. [84] **Alack:** Expression of sorrow or regret. [85] **hint:** occasion. [86] **wrings:** (1) constrains; (2) extracts moisture from. [87] **impertinent:** irrelevant. [88] **With . . . ends:** i.e., undertook to accomplish the same end by less violent means. [89] **In few:** in short. [90] **butt:** tub. [91] **Did . . . wrong:** i.e., only added to our discomfort. [92] **deck'd:** (1) adorned; (2) covered. [93] **which:** i.e., Miranda's smile. [94] **undergoing stomach:** courage to endure.

65 **Miranda:** How came we ashore?
Prospero: By Providence divine.
Some food we had, and some fresh water, that
A noble Neapolitan, Gonzalo,
Out of his charity, who being then appointed
Master of this design, did give us, with
Rich garments, linens, stuffs, and necessaries,
Which since have steaded[95] much; so of his gentleness,[96]
Knowing I lov'd my books, he furnish'd me
From mine own library with volumes[97] that
I prize above my dukedom.
Miranda: Would I might
But ever see that man!
Prospero: Now I arise. *(Puts on his robe.)*
Sit still, and hear the last of our sea-sorrow:
Here in this island we arriv'd, and here
Have I, thy schoolmaster, made thee more profit[98]
Than other princess'[99] can, that have more time
For vainer hours, and tutors not so careful.
Miranda: Heavens thank you for't! And now I pray you, sir,
For still 'tis beating[100] in my mind, your reason
For raising this sea-storm?
70 **Prospero:** Know thus far forth:
By accident most strange, bountiful Fortune
(Now my dear lady)[101] hath mine enemies
Brought to this shore; and by my prescience
I find my zenith[102] doth depend upon
A most auspicious star, whose influence[103]
If now I court not, but omit,[104] my fortunes
Will ever after droop. Here cease more questions.
Thou art inclin'd to sleep; 'tis a good dullness,[105]
And give it way. I know thou canst not choose.

(Miranda sleeps.)

Come away,[106] servant, come; I am ready now.
Approach, my Ariel. Come.

(Enter Ariel.)

[95] **steaded:** been of use. [96] **gentleness:** character proper to one of high birth and cultivation. [97] **volumes:** i.e., books of magic. [98] **more profit:** profit more. [99] **princess':** princesses. [100] **beating:** working violently. [101] **my dear lady:** i.e., favorable to me. [102] **zenith:** height of fortune. [103] **influence:** power (astrological term). [104] **omit:** ignore. [105] **good dullness:** timely sleepiness. [106] **Come away:** come here.

Ariel: All hail, great master, grave sir, hail! I come
To answer thy best pleasure, be't to fly,
To swim, to dive into the fire, to ride
On the curl'd clouds. To thy strong bidding, task
Ariel, and all his quality.[107]
Prospero: Hast thou, spirit,
Perform'd to point[108] the tempest that I bade thee?
Ariel: To every article.
I boarded the King's ship; now on the beak,[109]
Now in the waist, the deck, in every cabin,
I flam'd amazement.[110] Sometime I'ld divide,
And burn in many places; on the topmast,
The yards and boresprit,[111] would I flame distinctly,[112]
Then meet and join. Jove's lightning, the precursors
O' th' dreadful thunder-claps, more momentary
And sight-outrunning were not; the fire and cracks
Of sulphurous roaring the most mighty Neptune
Seem to besiege, and make his bold waves tremble,
Yea, his dread trident shake.
Prospero: My brave[113] spirit!
Who was so firm, so constant, that this coil[114]
Would not infect his reason?
Ariel: Not a soul
But felt a fever of the mad,[115] and play'd
Some tricks of desperation. All but mariners
Plung'd in the foaming brine, and quit the vessel;
Then all afire with me,[116] the King's son, Ferdinand,
With hair up-staring[117] (then like reeds, not hair),
Was the first man that leapt; cried, "Hell is empty,
And all the devils are here."
Prospero: Why, that's my spirit!
But was not this nigh shore?
Ariel: Close by, my master.
Prospero: But are they, Ariel, safe?
Ariel: Not a hair perish'd.
On their sustaining garments[118] not a blemish,
But fresher than before; and as thou badst me,

---

[107] **quality:** (1) skill; (2) cohorts, minor spirits under him. [108] **to point:** in detail. [109] **beak:** prow. [110] **flam'd amazement:** struck terror by appearing as the flamelike phenomenon called St. Elmo's fire or the corposant.
[111] **boresprit:** bowsprit. [112] **distinctly:** in separate places. [113] **brave:** splendid. [114] **coil:** uproar. [115] **of the mad:** such as madmen have.
[116] **Then . . .me:** Many editors repunctuate to make this phrase modify *vessel* rather than *son.* [117] **up-staring:** standing on end. [118] **sustaining garments:** garments that bore them up in the water.

In troops I have dispers'd them 'bout the isle.
The King's son have I landed by himself,
Whom I left cooling of the air with sighs,
In an odd angle of the isle, and sitting,
His arms in this sad knot.[119]

Prospero: Of the King's ship,
The mariners, say how thou hast dispos'd,
And all the rest o' th' fleet.

Ariel: Safely in harbor
Is the King's ship, in the deep nook,[120] where once
Thou call'dst me up at midnight to fetch dew
From the still-vex'd Bermoothes,[121] there she's hid;
The mariners all under hatches stowed,
Who, with a charm[122] join'd to their suff'red labor,[123]
I have left asleep; and for the rest o' th' fleet
(Which I dispers'd), they all have met again,
And are upon the Mediterranean float[124]
Bound sadly home for Naples,
Supposing that they saw the King's ship wrack'd,
And his great person perish.

Prospero: Ariel, thy charge
Exactly is perform'd; but there's more work.
What is the time o' th' day?

Ariel: Past the midseason.[125]

Prospero: At least two glasses.[126] The time 'twixt six and now
Must by us both be spent most preciously.

Ariel: Is there more toil? Since thou dost give me pains,[127]
Let me remember[128] thee what thou hast promis'd,
Which is not yet perform'd me.

Prospero: How now? moody?
What is't thou canst demand?

Ariel: My liberty.

Prospero: Before the time be out? No more!

Ariel: I prithee,
Remember I have done thee worthy service,
Told thee no lies, made thee no mistakings, serv'd
Without or grudge or grumblings. Thou did promise
To bate[129] me a full year.

---

[119] **in . . . knot:** i.e., crossed thus (Ariel illustrates with a gesture). Crossed arms indicated melancholy. [120] **nook:** inlet, small bay. [121] **still-vex'd Bermoothes:** always stormy Bermuda islands. [122] **with a charm:** by means of a magic spell. [123] **their suff'red labor:** the labor they have endured. [124] **float:** flood, sea. [125] **mid season:** noon. [126] **glasses:** hourglasses. [127] **pains:** duties, chores. [128] **remember:** remind. [129] **bate:** remit.

Prospero: Dost thou forget
From what a torment I did free thee?
Ariel: No.
Prospero: Thou dost; and think'st it much to tread the ooze[130]
Of the salt deep,
To run upon the sharp wind of the north,
To do me business in the veins[131] o' th' earth
When it is bak'd[132] with frost.
Ariel: I do not, sir.
Prospero: Thou liest, malignant thing! Hast thou forgot
The foul witch Sycorax, who with age and envy[133]
Was grown into a hoop? Hast thou forgot her?
Ariel: No, sir.
Prospero: Thou hast. Where was she born? Speak. Tell me.
Ariel: Sir, in Argier.[134]
Prospero: O, was she so? I must
Once in a month recount what thou hast been,
Which thou forget'st. This damn'd witch Sycorax,
For mischiefs manifold, and sorceries terrible
To enter human hearing, from Argier
Thou know'st was banish'd; for one thing she did
They would not take her life. Is not this true?
Ariel: Ay, sir.
Prospero: This blue-ey'd[135] hag was hither brought with child,
And here was left by th' sailors. Thou, my slave,
As thou report'st thyself, was then her servant,
And for[136] thou wast a spirit too delicate
To act her earthy and abhorr'd commands,
Refusing her grand hests,[137] she did confine thee,
By help of her more potent ministers.
And in her most unmitigable rage,
Into a cloven pine, within which rift
Imprison'd, thou didst painfully remain
A dozen years; within which space she died,
And left thee there, where thou didst vent thy groans
As fast as mill-wheels[138] strike. Then was this island
(Save for the son that [she] did litter here,
A freckled whelp, hag-born) not honor'd with
A human shape.
Ariel: Yes—Caliban her son.

---

[130] **ooze:** mud at sea-bottom. [131] **veins:** underground streams, which were thought to correspond to veins of the body. [132] **bak'd:** hardened. [133] **envy:** malice. [134] Argier: Algiers. [135] **blue-ey'd:** with dark circles around the eyes. [136] **for:** because. [137] **hests:** commands. [138] **mill-wheels:** i.e., the clappers on mill-wheels.

Prospero: Dull thing, I say so; he, that Caliban
Whom now I keep in service. Thou best know'st
What torment I did find thee in; thy groans
Did make wolves howl, and penetrate the breasts
Of ever-angry bears. It was a torment
To lay upon the damn'd, which Sycorax
Could not again undo. It was mine art,
When I arriv'd and heard thee, that made gape[139]
The pine, and let thee out.
Ariel: I thank thee, master.
Prospero: If thou more murmur'st, I will rend an oak
And peg thee in his[140] knotty entrails till
Thou hast howl'd away twelve winters.
Ariel: Pardon, master,
I will be correspondent[141] to command
And do my spriting gently.[142]
Prospero: Do so; and after two days
I will discharge thee.
Ariel: That's my noble master!
What shall I do? say what? what shall I do?
Prospero: Go make thyself like a nymph o' th'sea; be subject
To no sight but thine and mine, invisible
To every eyeball else. Go take this shape
And hither come in't. Go. Hence with diligence!

(Exit Ariel.)

Awake, dear heart, awake! Thou hast slept well,
Awake!
Miranda: The strangeness of your story put
Heaviness[143] in me.
Prospero: Shake it off. Come on,
We'll visit Caliban my slave, who never
Yields us kind answer.
Miranda: 'Tis a villain, sir,
I do not love to look on.
Prospero: But as 'tis,
We cannot miss[144] him. He does make our fire,
Fetch in our wood, and serves in offices
That profit us. What ho! slave! Caliban!
Thou earth, thou! speak.
Caliban: *(Within.):* There's wood enough within.

---

[139] **gape:** open wide. [140] **his:** its. [141] **correspondent:** obedient.
[142] **do . . . gently:** perform my tasks as a spirit ungrudgingly. [143] **Heaviness:** drowsiness. [144] **miss:** do without.

Prospero: Come forth, I say, there's other business for thee.
Come, thou tortoise, when?[145]

(Enter Ariel like[146] a water-nymph.)

Fine apparition! My quaint[147] Ariel,
Hark in thine ear.
Ariel: My lord, it shall be done. *(Exit.)*
Prospero: Thou poisonous slave, got by the devil himself
Upon thy wicked dam, come forth!

(Enter Caliban.)

Caliban: As wicked[148] dew as e'er my mother brush'd
With raven's feather from unwholesome fen
Drop on you both! A south-west[149] blow on ye,
And blister you all o'er!
Prospero: For this, be sure, to-night thou shalt have cramps,
Side-stitches, that shall pen thy breath up; urchins[150]
Shall, for that vast of night that they may work,[151]
All exercise on thee; thou shalt be pinch'd
As thick as honeycomb, each pinch more stinging
Than bees that made 'em.[152]
Caliban: I must eat my dinner.
This island's mine by Sycorax my mother,
Which thou tak'st from me. When thou cam'st first,
Thou strok'st me and made much of me, wouldst give me
Water with berries in't, and teach me how
To name the bigger light, and how the less,
That burn by day and night; and then I lov'd thee
And show'd thee all the qualities o' th' isle,
The fresh springs, brine-pits, barren place and fertile.
Curs'd be I that did so! All the charms
Of Sycorax, toads, beetles, bats, light on you!
For I am all the subjects that you have,
Which first was mine own king; and here you sty me
In this hard rock, whiles you do keep from me
The rest o' th' island.
Prospero: Thou most lying slave,
Whom stripes[153] may move, not kindness, I have us'd thee

---

[145] **when:** a common expression of impatience. [146] s.d. **like:** in the shape of. [147] **quaint:** clever, ingenious. [148] **wicked:** harmful. [149] **south-west:** southwest wind, thought to bring pestilence. [150] **urchins:** hedgehogs; here, goblins in the shape of hedgehogs. [151] **for . . . work:** during that long and desolate period of darkness during which they are permitted to perform their mischief. It was thought that malignant spirits lost their power with the coming of day. [152] **'em:** i.e., cells of the honeycomb. [153] **stripes:** lashes.

(Filth as thou art) with human[154] care, and lodg'd thee
In mine own cell, till thou didst seek to violate
The honour of my child.

Caliban: O ho, O ho, would't had been done!
Thou didst prevent me; I had peopled else
This isle with Calibans.

Miranda:[155] Abhorred slave,
Which any print of goodness wilt not take,
Being capable of all ill! I pitied thee,
Took pains to make thee speak, taught thee each hour
One thing or other. When thou didst not, savage,
Know thine own meaning, but wouldst gabble like
A thing most brutish, I endow'd thy purposes
With words that made them known. But thy vild[156] race[157]
(Though thou didst learn) had that in't which good natures
Could not abide to be with; therefore wast thou
Deservedly confin'd into this rock,
Who hadst deserv'd more than a prison.

Caliban: You taught me language, and my profit on't
Is, I know how to curse. The red-plague[158] rid[159] you
For learning[160] me your language!

Prospero: Hag-seed, hence!
Fetch us in fuel, and be quick, thou'rt best,[161]
To answer other business. Shrug'st thou, malice?
If thou neglect'st, or dost unwillingly
What I command, I'll rack thee with old[162] cramps,
Fill all thy bones with aches,[163] make thee roar
That beasts shall tremble at thy din.

Caliban: No, pray thee.
(Aside.) I must obey. His art is of such pow'r,
It would control my dam's god, Setebos,
And make a vassal of him.

Prospero: So, slave, hence! *(Exit Caliban.)*

(Enter Ferdinand; and Ariel, invisible,[164] playing and singing.)

(Ariel['s] Song.)

Come unto these yellow sands,
And then take hands:

---

[154] **human:** humane. [155] **Miranda:** Some editors make Prospero the speaker. [156] **vild:** vile. [157] **race:** nature. [158] **red-plague:** plague that produces red sores. [159] **rid:** destroy. [160] **learning:** teaching. [161] **thou'rt best:** you had better. [162] **old:** i.e., such as old people have. [163] **aches:** Pronounced *aitches.* [164] s.d. **invisible:** Ariel is of course visible to the audience but he wears a costume that by convention makes him invisible to other persons on the stage, except Prospero.

Curtsied when you have, and kiss'd,
The wild waves whist:[165]
Foot it featly[166] here and there,
And, sweet sprites, [the burthen bear].[167]
Hark, hark!
Burthen, dispersedly,[168] *[within].* Bow-wow.
The watch-dogs bark!
[Burthen, dispersedly, within.] Bow-wow.
Hark, hark, I hear
The strain of strutting chanticleer:
Cry *[within].* Cock-a-diddle-dow.

Ferdinand: Where should this music be? I' th' air, or th' earth?
It sounds no more; and sure it waits upon
Some god o' th' island. Sitting on a bank,
Weeping again the King my father's wrack,
This music crept by me upon the waters,
Allaying both their fury and my passion[169]
With its sweet air; thence I have follow'd it,
Or it hath drawn me rather. But 'tis gone.
No, it begins again.

(Ariel[s] Song)

Full fadom[170] five thy father lies,
Of his bones are coral made:
Those are pearls that were his eyes:
Nothing of him that doth fade,
But doth suffer a sea-change
Into something rich and strange.
Sea-nymphs hourly ring his knell:
(Burthen [within]. Ding-dong.
Hark, now I hear them—ding-dong bell.

Ferdinand: The ditty[171] does remember[172] my drown'd father.
This is no mortal business, nor no sound
That the earth owes.[173] I hear it now above me.

Prospero: The fringed curtains of thine eye advance,[174]
And say what thou seest yond.

Miranda: What, is't a spirit?
Lord, how it looks about! Believe me, sir,
It carries a brave[175] form. But 'tis a spirit.

---

[165] **whist:** being hushed. [166] **featly:** nimbly. [167] **the burthen bear:** bear the burden, i.e., the bass undersong. [168] **dispersedly:** from several directions. [169] **passion:** sorrow. [170] **fadom:** fathom. [171] **ditty:** words of the song. [172] **remember:** commemorate. [173] **owes:** owns. [174] **advance:** raise. [175] **brave:** excellent, splendid.

Prospero: No, wench, it eats, and sleeps, and hath such senses
As we have—such. This gallant which thou seest
Was in the wrack; and but[176] he's something stain'd[177]
With grief (that's beauty's canker),[178] thou mightst call him
A goodly person. He hath lost his fellows,
And strays about to find 'em.
Miranda: I might call him
A thing divine, for nothing natural
I ever saw so noble.
Prospero *(Aside.):* It[179] goes on, I see,
As my soul prompts it. Spirit, fine spirit, I'll free thee
Within two days for this.
Ferdinand: Most sure, the goddess
On whom these airs[180] attend! Vouchsafe my pray'r
May know if you remain upon this island,
And that you will some good instruction give
How I may bear me here. My prime[181] request,
Which I do last pronounce, is (O you wonder!)
If you be maid, or no?
Miranda: No wonder, sir,
But certainly a maid.[182]
Ferdinand: My language? heavens!
I am the best[183] of them that speak this speech,
Were I but where 'tis spoken.
Prospero: How? the best?
What wert thou, if the King of Naples heard thee?
Ferdinand: A single[184] thing, as I am now, that wonders
To hear thee speak of Naples. He does hear me,
And that he does I weep. Myself am Naples,[185]
Who with mine eyes (never since at ebb)[186] beheld
The King my father wrack'd.
Miranda: Alack, for mercy!
Ferdinand: Yes, faith, and all his lords, the Duke of Milan
And his brave son[187] being twain.
Prospero *(Aside.):* The Duke of Milan
And his more braver daughter could control[188] thee,
If now 'twere fit to do't. At the first sight

[176] **but:** except that. [177] **something stain'd:** somewhat disfigured. [178] **canker:** worm that eats blossoms. [179] **It:** i.e., the charm. [180] **airs:** i.e., the music he has heard. [181] **prime:** first, most important. [182] **maid:** i.e., a human maiden, not a goddess. [183] **best:** first in rank. [184] **single:** solitary (because he thinks that he and the King are one and the same), but he probably has in mind also the senses "deserted" and "helpless." [185] **Naples:** King of Naples. [186] **at ebb:** dry (a part of the continued sea-imagery in the play). [187] **his brave son:** Not mentioned elsewhere in the play. [188] **control:** refute.

They have chang'd eyes.[189] Delicate Ariel,
I'll set thee free for this.—A word, good sir,
I fear you have done yourself some wrong;[190] a word.

Miranda: Why speaks my father so ungently? This
Is the third man that e'er I saw; the first
That e'er I sigh'd for. Pity move my father
To be inclin'd my way!

Ferdinand: O, if a virgin,
And your affection not gone forth, I'll make you
The Queen of Naples.

Prospero: Soft, sir, one word more.
(Aside.) They are both in either's pow'rs; but this swift business
I must uneasy[191] make, lest too light winning
Make the prize light.[192]—One word more: I charge thee
That thou attend me. Thou dost here usurp
The name thou ow'st not, and hast put thyself
Upon this island as a spy, to win it
From me, the lord on't.[193]

Ferdinand: No, as I am a man.

Miranda: There's nothing ill can dwell in such a temple.
If the ill spirit have so fair a house,
Good things will strive to dwell with't.

Prospero: Follow me.—
Speak not you for him; he's a traitor.—Come,
I'll manacle thy neck and feet together.
Sea-water shall thou drink; thy food shall be
The fresh-brook mussels, wither'd roots, and husks
Wherein the acorn cradled. Follow.

Ferdinand: No,
I will resist such entertainment[194] till
Mine enemy has more pow'r.

(He draws, and is charmed[195] from moving.)

Miranda: O dear father,
Make not too rash a trial of him, for
He's gentle,[196] and not fearful.[197]

Prospero: What, I say,
My foot[198] my tutor? Put thy sword up, traitor,
Who mak'st a show but dar'st not strike, thy conscience

---

[189] **chang'd eyes:** exchanged loving looks. [190] **done . . . wrong:** An ironically polite way of charging him with lying. [191] **uneasy:** difficult. [192] **light . . . light:** easy . . . lightly esteemed. [193] **on't:** of it. [194] **entertainment:** treatment. [195] s.d. **charmed:** magically prevented. [196] **gentle:** of high birth. [197] **fearful:** cowardly. [198] **foot:** i.e., subordinate (Miranda).

Is so possess'd with guilt. Come, from thy ward,[199]
For I can here disarm thee with this stick,[200]
And make thy weapon drop.

Miranda: Beseech you, father.

Prospero: Hence! Hang not on my garments.

Miranda: Sir, have pity,
I'll be his surety.

Prospero: Silence! one word more
Shall make me chide thee, if not hate thee. What,
An advocate for an imposter? Hush!
Thou think'st there is no more such shapes as he,
Having seen but him and Caliban. Foolish wench,
To[201] th' most of men this is a Caliban,
And they to him are angels.

Miranda: My affections[202]
Are then most humble; I have no ambition
To see a goodlier man.

Prospero *(To Ferdinand.):* Come on, obey:
Thy nerves[208] are in their infancy again
And have no vigor in them.

Ferdinand: So they are.
My spirits,[209] as in a dream, are all bound up.
My father's loss, the weakness which I feel,
The wrack of all my friends, nor this man's threats
To whom I am subdu'd, are but light to me,
Might I but through my prison once a day
Behold this maid. All corners else o' th' earth
Let liberty make use of; space enough
Have I in such a prison.

Prospero *(Aside.):* It works. *(To Ferdinand.)* Come on.—
Thou hast done well, fine Ariel! *(To Ferdinand.)* Follow me.
(To Ariel.) Hark what thou else shalt do me.[205]

Miranda *(To Ferdinand.):* Be of comfort.
My father's of a better nature, sir,
Than he appears by speech. This is unwonted
Which now came from him.

Prospero *(To Ariel.):* Thou shalt be as free
As mountain winds; but then exactly do
All points of my command.

Ariel: To th' syllable.

Prospero *(To Ferdinand.):* Come, follow. *(To Miranda.)*
Speak not for him. *(Exeunt.)*

---

[199] **ward:** position of defense. [200] **stick:** staff. [201] **To:** in comparison with.
[202] **affections:** inclinations. [203] **nerves:** sinews. [204] **spirits:** vital powers.
[205] **do me:** do for me.

Act II

Scene I[1]

(Enter Alonso, Sebastian, Antonio, Gonzalo, Adrian, Francisco, and others.)

Gonzalo: Beseech you, sir, be merry; you have cause
(So have we all) of joy; for our escape
Is much beyond our loss. Our hint[2] of woe
Is common: every day some sailor's wife,
The masters[3] of some merchant, and the merchant
Have just our theme of woe; but for the miracle
(I mean our preservation), few in millions
Can speak like us. Then wisely, good sir, weigh
Our sorrow with[4] our comfort.
Alonso: Prithee, peace.
Sebastian: He receives comfort like cold porridge.[5]
Antonio: The visitor[6] will not give him o'er so.
Sebastian: Look, he's winding up the watch of his wit, by and by it will strike.
Gonzalo: Sir,—
Sebastian: One. Tell.[7]
Gonzalo: When every grief is entertain'd that's offer'd
Comes to th' entertainer—[8]
Sebastian: A dollar.[9]
Gonzalo: Dolor[10] comes to him indeed, you have spoken truer than you purpos'd.
Sebastian: You have taken it wiselier than I meant you should.
Gonzalo: Therefore, my lord—
Antonio: Fie, what a spendthrift is he of his tongue!
Alonso: I prithee spare.
Gonzalo: Well, I have done. But yet—
Sebastian: He will be talking.
Antonio: Which, of he or Adrian, for a good wager, first begins to crow?
Sebastian: The old cock.[11]
Antonio: The cock'rel.[12]
Sebastian: Done. The wager?
Antonio: A laughter.[13]

---

[1] **Location:** Another part of the island. [2] **hint:** occasion. [3] **masters . . . the merchant:** chief officers of some merchant vessel, and the owner of it. [4] **with:** against. [5] **porridge:** broth. There is an underlying pun on *peace* and *pease,* i.e., peas, a common ingredient of porridge. [6] **visitor:** minister who visits the sick and bereaved, i.e., would-be comforter. [7] **Tell:** count. [8] **entertainer:** sufferer. Sebastian puns on the sense "innkeeper." [9] **dollar:** a continental coin. [10] **Dolor:** sorrow. [11] **old cock:** i.e., Gonzalo. [12] **cock'rel:** i.e., Adrian. [13] **laughter:** a laugh (perhaps with pun on the sense "a sitting of eggs," consistent with the poultry imagery).

Sebastian: A match!

Adrian: Though this island seem to be desert—[14]

Sebastian: Ha, ha, ha![15]

Antonio: So: you're paid!

Adrian: Uninhabitable, and almost inaccessible—

Sebastian: Yet—

Adrian: Yet—

Antonio: He could not miss't.[16]

Adrian: It must needs be of subtle, tender, and delicate temperance.[17]

Antonio: Temperance was a delicate wench.

Sebastian: Ay, and a subtle, as he most learnedly deliver'd.

Adrian: The air breathes upon us here most sweetly.

Sebastian: As if it had lungs, and rotten ones.

Antonio: Or, as 'twere perfum'd by a fen.

Gonzalo: Here is everything advantageous to life.

Antonio: True, save means to live.

Sebastian: Of that there's none, or little.

Gonzalo: How lush and lusty the grass looks! How green!

Antonio: The ground indeed is tawny.[18]

Sebastian: With an eye[19] of green in't.

Antonio: He misses not much.

Sebastian: No; he doth but mistake the truth totally.

Gonzalo: But the rariety[20] of it is—which is indeed almost beyond credit—

Sebastian: As many vouch'd[21] rarieties are.

Gonzalo: That our garments, being (as they were) drench'd in the sea, hold notwithstanding their freshness and glosses, being rather new dy'd than stain'd with salt water.

Antonio: If but one of his pockets could speak, would it not say he lies?

Sebastian: Ay, or very falsely pocket up[22] his report.

Gonzalo: Methinks our garments are now as fresh as when we put them on first in Afric, at the marriage of the King's fair daughter Claribel to the King of Tunis.

Sebastian: 'Twas a sweet marriage, and we prosper well in our return.

Adrian: Tunis was never grac'd before with such a paragon to[23] their queen.

Gonzalo: Not since widow Dido's time.

---

[14] **desert:** uninhabited. [15] **Ha, ha, ha:** Antonio wins the bet, since Adrian spoke first. The winner was entitled to laugh. Accordingly most editors reverse the speech prefixes for paragraphs 24 and 25. [16] **miss't:** (1) escape saying "yet"; (2) avoid the island. [17] **temperance:** climate. Antonio puns on the word as a girl's name. [18] **tawny:** parched tan or yellow. [19] **eye:** spot. [20] **rariety:** Perhaps this spelling indicates an unusual pronunciation of the word by Gonzalo, which Sebastian mimics. [21] **vouch'd:** guaranteed true. [22] **pocket up:** conceal, suppress. One who failed to challenge a lie or an insult was said to "pocket up" the injury. [23] **to:** for.

Antonio: Widow? a pox o' that! How came that widow in? Widow Dido![24]
Sebastian: What if he had said "widower Aeneas" too? Good Lord, how you take it!
Adrian: "Widow Dido," said you? You make me study of that. She was of Carthage, not of Tunis.
Gonzalo: This Tunis, sir, was Carthage.[25]
Adrian: Carthage?
Gonzalo: I assure you, Carthage.
Antonio: His word is more than the miraculous harp.[26]
Sebastian: He hath rais'd the wall, and houses too.
Antonio: What impossible matter will he make easy next?
Sebastian: I think he will carry this island home in his pocket, and give it his son for an apple.
Antonio: And sowing the kernels[27] of it in the sea, bring forth more islands.
Gonzalo: Ay.[28]
Antonio: Why, in good time.
Gonzalo *(to Alonso.):* Sir, we were talking that our garments seem now as fresh as when we were at Tunis at the marriage of your daughter, who is now queen.
Antonio: And the rarest that e'er came there.
Sebastian: Bate,[29] I beseech you, widow Dido.
Antonio: O, widow Dido? Ay, widow Dido.
Gonzalo: Is not, sir, my doublet as fresh as the first day I wore it? I mean, in a sort.[30]
Antonio: That "sort" was well fish'd for.
Gonzalo: When I wore it at your daughter's marriage?
Alonso: You cram these words into mine ears against
The stomach of my sense.[31] Would I had never
Married my daughter there! for coming thence,
My son is lost and (in my rate)[32] she too,
Who is so far from Italy removed
I ne'er again shall see her. O thou mine heir

[24] **Widow . . . Dido:** Antonio's vigorous reaction has been variously explained. Dido was indeed a widow, and Aeneas a widower, when they met, and perhaps Antonio is laughing at what he considers Gonzalo's prudery in referring to her as widow rather than as Aeneas' mistress. *Widow* could also be used of a wife separated from or deserted by her husband, and Antonio may be laughing at Gonzalo for prudish evasion of the fact that the deserted Dido was not Aeneas' wife.
[25] **This . . . Carthage:** Tunis and Carthage were separate cities, though not far apart. [26] **miraculous harp:** the legendary harp of Amphion, which raised the walls of Thebes. Gonzalo's error has created a whole new city. [27] **kernels:** seeds. [28] **Ay:** Probably a reassertion of the identity of the two cities. Antonio responds with a sarcastic expression of approbation. [29] **Bate:** except.
[30] **in a sort:** comparatively. [31] **You . . . sense:** The image is of someone being fed against his will; *stomach* = appetite. [32] **rate:** opinion.

Of Naples and of Milan, what strange fish
Hath made his meal on thee?
Francisco: Sir, he may live.
I saw him beat the surges under him,
And ride upon their backs. He trod the water,
Whose enmity he flung aside, and breasted
The surge most swoll'n that met him. His bold head
'Bove the contentious waves he kept, and oared
Himself with his good arms in lusty stroke
To th' shore, that o'er his wave-worn basis[33] bowed,
As stooping to relieve him. I not doubt
He came alive to land.
Alonso: No, no, he's gone.
Sebastian: Sir, you may thank yourself for this great loss,
That[34] would not bless our Europe with your daughter,
But rather loose[35] her to an African,
Where she, at least, is banish'd from your eye,
Who hath cause to wet the grief on't.
Alonso: Prithee, peace.
Sebastian: You were kneel'd to, and importun'd otherwise
By all of us, and the fair soul herself
Weigh'd between loathness and obedience, at
Which end o' th' beam should bow.[36] We have lost your son,
I fear for ever. Milan and Naples have
Moe[37] widows in them of this business' making
Than we bring men to comfort them.
The fault's your own.
Alonso: So is the dear'st[38] o' th' loss.
Gonzalo: My lord Sebastian,
The truth you speak doth lack some gentleness,
And time[39] to speak it in. You rub the sore,
When you should bring the plaster.
Sebastian: Very well.
Antonio: And most chirurgeonly.[40]
Gonzalo It is foul weather in us all, good sir,
When you are cloudy.
Sebastian: Fowl[41] weather?
Antonio: Very foul.

---

[33] **his wave-worn basis:** its foundation hollowed by the action of the sea.
[34] **That:** you who. [35] **loose:** With second (perhaps primary) sense "lose," often spelled *loose*. [36] **Weigh'd . . . bow:** weighed in the scale her unwillingness to marry and her duty of obedience to her father, to see which would prevail.
[37] **Moe:** more. [38] **dear'st:** most heartfelt. [39] **time:** appropriate occasion.
[40] **chirurgeonly:** like a surgeon. [41] **Fowl:** Sebastian's pun returns to the imagery of paragraphs 17–19.

Gonzalo: Had I plantation[42] of this isle, my lord—
Antonio: He'd sow't with nettle-seed.
Sebastian: Or docks, or mallows.
Gonzalo: And were the king on't, what would I do?
Sebastian: Scape being drunk, for want of wine.
Gonzalo: I' th' commonwealth I would by contraries,[43]
Execute all things; for no kind of traffic[44]
Would I admit; no name of magistrate;
Letters[45] should not be known; riches, poverty,
And use of service,[46] none; contract, succession,[47]
Bourn,[48] bound of land, tilth,[49] vineyard, none;
No use of metal, corn,[50] or wine, or oil;
No occupation, all men idle, all;
And women too, but innocent and pure;
No sovereignty—
Sebastian: Yet he would be king on't.
Antonio: The latter end of his commonwealth forgets the beginning.
Gonzalo: All things in common nature should produce
Without sweat or endeavor: Treason, felony,
Sword, pike,[51] knife, gun, or need of any engine,[52]
Would I not have; but nature should bring forth,
Of it[53] own kind, all foison,[54] all abundance,
To feed my innocent people.
Sebastian: No marrying 'mong his subjects?
Antonio: None, man, all idle—whores and knaves.
Gonzalo: I would with such perfection govern, sir,
T' excel the golden age.
Sebastian: 'Save[55] his Majesty!
Antonio: Long live Gonzalo!
Gonzalo: And—do you mark me, sir?
Alonso: Prithee no more; thou dost talk nothing to me.
Gonzalo: I do well believe your Highness, and did it to minister occasion[56] to these gentlemen, who are of such sensible and nimble[57] lungs that they always use to laugh at nothing.
Antonio: 'Twas you we laugh'd at.
Gonzalo: Who, in this kind of merry fooling, am nothing to you; so you may continue, and laugh at nothing still.
Antonio: What a blow was there given!

---

[42] **plantation:** colonization, but the following speakers take up the word in the sense "planting." [43] **contraries:** the opposite of what is customary. [44] **traffic:** business, trade. [45] **Letters:** learning, literacy. [46] **service:** servanthood, serving of some by others. [47] **succession:** inheritance, hereditary privilege. [48] **Bourn:** boundary, i.e., division of land among individual owners. [49] **tilth:** tillage. [50] **corn:** grain. [51] **pike:** spear. [52] **engine:** instrument of war. [53] **it:** its. [54] **foison:** plenty. [55] **'Save:** God save. [56] **minister occasion:** give opportunity. [57] **sensible and nimble:** sensitive and lively.

Sebastian: And[58] it had not fall'n flat-long.[59]
Gonzalo: You are gentlemen of brave mettle; you would lift the moon out of her sphere, if she would continue in it five weeks without changing.

(Enter Ariel (invisible), playing solemn music.)

Sebastian: We would so, and then go a-batfowling.[60]
Antonio: Nay, good my lord, be not angry.
Gonzalo: No, I warrant you, I will not adventure[61] my discretion so weakly. Will you laugh me asleep, for I am very heavy?[62]
Antonio: Go sleep, and hear us.[63]

(All sleep except Alonso, Sebastian, and Antonio.)

Alonso: What, all so soon asleep? I wish mine eyes
Would, with themselves, shut up my thoughts. I find
They are inclin'd to do so.
Sebastian: Please you, sir,
Do not omit[64] the heavy offer of it.
It seldom visits[65] sorrow; when it doth,
It is a comforter.
Antonio: We two, my lord,
Will guard your person while you take your rest,
And watch your safety.
Alonso: Thank you. Wondrous heavy.

(Alonso sleeps. Exit Ariel.)

Sebastian: What a strange drowsiness possesses them!
Antonio: It is the quality o' th' climate.
Sebastian: Why
Doth it not then our eyelids sink? I find not
Myself dispos'd to sleep.
Antonio: Nor I, my spirits are nimble.
They fell together all, as by consent;
They dropp'd, as by a thunder-stroke. What might,
Worthy Sebastian, O, what might—? No more—
And yet methinks I see it in thy face,
What thou shouldst be. Th' occasion speaks thee,[66] and
My strong imagination sees a crown
Dropping upon thy head.

---

[58] **And:** if. [59] **flat-long:** with the sword blade flat, not on edge.
[60] **a-batfowling:** bird-hunting with sticks (*bats*) at night. He suggests that they would use the moon as their lantern. [61] **adventure . . . weakly:** risk my reputation for good sense by getting angry at such superficial fellows. [62] **heavy:** drowsy. [63] **hear us:** i.e., listen to our laughter. [64] **omit . . . offer:** neglect the opportunity sleepiness provides. [65] **visits:** See note to II.i paragraph 6.
[66] **speaks thee:** calls upon you (to seize the opportunity).

Sebastian: What? art thou waking?
Antonio: Do you not hear me speak?
Sebastian: I do, and surely
It is a sleepy language, and thou speak'st
Out of thy sleep. What is it thou didst say?
This is a strange repose, to be asleep
With eyes wide open—standing, speaking, moving—
And yet so fast asleep.
Antonio: Noble Sebastian,
Thou let'st thy fortune sleep—die, rather; wink'st[67]
Whiles thou art waking.
Sebastian: Thou dost snore distinctly,
There's meaning in thy snores.
Antonio: I am more serious than my custom; you
Must be so too, if heed me; which to do,
Trebles[68] thee o'er.
Sebastian: Well; I am standing water.[69]
Antonio: I'll teach you how to flow.
Sebastian: Do so. To ebb
Hereditary sloth[70] instructs me.
Antonio: O!
If you but knew how you the purpose cherish[71]
Whiles thus you mock it! how, in stripping it,
You more invest[72] it! Ebbing men, indeed,
Most often do so near the bottom run
By their own fear or sloth.
Sebastian: Prithee say on.
The setting[73] of thine eye and cheek proclaim
A matter from thee; and a birth, indeed,
Which throes[74] thee much to yield.
Antonio: Thus, sir:
Although this lord[75] of weak remembrance,[76] this
Who shall be of as little memory
When he is earth'd,[77] hath here almost persuaded
(For he's a spirit of persuasion, only
Professes to persuade)[78] the King his son's alive,
'Tis as impossible that he's undrown'd
As he that sleeps here swims.

---

[67] **wink'st:** keep your eyes shut. [68] **Trebles thee o'er:** triples your fortune. [69] **standing water:** i.e., indecisive, going neither forward nor back. [70] **Hereditary sloth:** natural laziness. [71] **cherish:** enrich. [72] **invest:** dress up. [73] **setting:** fixed look. [74] **throes:** causes labor pains. [75] **this lord:** i.e., Gonzalo. [76] **of weak remembrance:** having a short memory (perhaps alluding to Gonzalo's lapse in identifying Tunis with Carthage); with following shift to the sense "remembered only briefly after death." [77] **earth'd:** buried. [78] **only . . . persuade:** has no function except to persuade. Gonzalo is a privy councillor.

Sebastian: I have no hope
That he's undrown'd.
Antonio: O, out of that no hope
What great hope have you! No hope, that way,[79] is
Another way so high a hope that even
Ambition cannot pierce a wink[80] beyond,
But doubt discovery there.[81] Will you grant with me
That Ferdinand is drown'd?
Sebastian: He's gone.
Antonio: Then tell me,
Who's the next heir of Naples?
Sebastian: Claribel.
Antonio: She that is Queen of Tunis; she that dwells
Ten leagues beyond man's life;[82] she that from Naples
Can have no note,[83] unless the sun were post—[84]
The Man i' th' Moon's too slow—till new-born chins
Be rough and razorable; she that from[85] whom
We all were sea-swallow'd, though some cast[86] again
(And by that destiny) to perform an act
Whereof what's past is prologue, what to come
In yours and my discharge.[87]
Sebastian: What stuff is this? How say you?
'Tis true, my brother's daughter's Queen of Tunis,
So is she heir of Naples; 'twixt which regions
There is some space.
Antonio: A space whose ev'ry cubit[88]
Seems to cry out, "How shall that Claribel
Measure us[89] back to Naples? Keep in Tunis,
And let Sebastian wake."[90] Say this were death
That now hath seiz'd them, why, they were no worse
Than now they are. There be that can rule Naples
As well as he that sleeps; lords that can prate
As amply and unnecessarily
As this Gonzalo; I myself could make
A chough of as deep chat.[91] O that you bore
The mind that I do! what a sleep were this
For your advancement! Do you understand me?

---

[79] **that way:** i.e., with respect to Ferdinand's being undrowned. [80] **wink:** glimpse. [81] **doubt discovery there:** is uncertain of seeing clearly even there. [82] **Ten . . . life:** thirty miles farther than a lifetime's journey. [83] **note:** news. [84] **post:** messenger. [85] **from:** coming from. [86] **cast:** (1) cast up; (2) cast as actors. [87] **discharge:** performance. [88] **cubit:** measure of about 20 inches. [89] **Measure us:** i.e., travel over the cubits. [90] **wake:** i.e., awake to fortune. [91] **make . . . chat:** train a jackdaw to speak as wisely as he. Jackdaws were taught to speak.

Sebastian: Methinks I do.
Antonio: And how does your content[92]
Tender[93] your own good fortune?
Sebastian: I remember
You did supplant your brother Prospero.
Antonio: True.
And look how well my garments sit upon me,
Much feater[94] than before. My brother's servants
Were then my fellows, now they are my men.
Sebastian: But, for your conscience?
Antonio: Ay, sir; where lies that? If 'twere a kibe,[95]
'Twould put me to[96] my slipper; but I feel not
This deity in my bosom. Twenty consciences,
That stand 'twixt me and Milan,[97] candied[98] be they,
And melt ere they molest! Here lies your brother,
No better than the earth he lies upon,
If he were that which now he's like—that's dead,
Whom I with this obedient steel, three inches of it,
Can lay to bed for ever; whiles you, doing thus,
To the perpetual wink[99] for aye might put
This ancient morsel, this Sir Prudence, who
Should not upbraid our course. For all the rest,
They'll take suggestion[100] as a cat laps milk;
They'll tell the clock to[101] any business that
We say befits the hour.
Sebastian: Thy case, dear friend,
Shall be my president:[102] as thou got'st Milan,
I'll come by Naples. Draw thy sword. One stroke
Shall free thee from the tribute which thou payest,
And I the King shall love thee.
Antonio: Draw together,
And when I rear my hand, do you the like,
To fall it[103] on Gonzalo.
Sebastian: O, but one word. *(They talk apart.)*

(Enter Ariel, [invisible], with music and song.)

Ariel: My master through his art foresees the danger
That you, his friend, are in, and sends me forth
(For else his project dies) to keep them living.

(Sings in Gonzalo's ear.)

---

[92] **content:** inclination. [93] **Tender:** regard. [94] **feater:** more gracefully. [95] **kibe:** chilblain. [96] **put me to:** make me wear. [97] **Milan:** the dukedom of Milan. [98] **candied:** sugared. [99] **wink:** sleep. [100] **suggestion:** evil prompting. [101] **tell . . . to:** i.e., agree that the time sorts with. [102] **president:** precedent. [103] **fall it:** let it fall.

While you here do snoring lie,
Open-ey'd conspiracy
His time[104] doth take.
If of life you keep a care,
Shake off slumber, and beware.
Awake, awake!

Antonio: Then let us both be sudden.
Gonzalo *(Waking.):* Now, good angels
Preserve the King! *(Wakes Alonso.)*
Alonso: Why, how now, ho! Awake? Why are you drawn?
Wherefore this ghastly looking?
Gonzalo: What's the matter?
Sebastian: Whiles we stood here securing[105] your repose,
Even now, we heard a hollow burst of bellowing
Like bulls, or rather lions. Did't not wake you?
It strook[106] mine ear most terribly.
Alonso: I heard nothing.
Antonio: O, 'twas a din to fright a monster's ear,
To make an earthquake; sure, it was the roar
Of a whole herd of lions.
Alonso: Heard you this, Gonzalo?
Gonzalo: Upon mine honour, sir, I heard a humming,
(And that a strange one too) which did awake me.
I shak'd you, sir, and cried.[107] As mine eyes open'd
I saw their weapons drawn. There was a noise,
That's verily. 'Tis best we stand upon our guard,
Or that we quit this place. Let's draw our weapons.
Alonso: Lead off this ground, and let's make further search
For my poor son.
Gonzalo: Heavens keep him from these beasts!
For he is sure i' th' island.
Alonso: Lead away.
Ariel: Prospero my lord shall know what I have done.
So, King, go safely on to seek thy son. *(Exeunt.)*

Scene II[108]

(Enter Caliban with a burden of wood. A noise of thunder heard.)

Caliban: All the infections that the sun sucks up
From bogs, fens, flats, on Prosper fall, and make him
By inch-meal[109] a disease! His spirits hear me,
And yet I needs must curse. But they'll nor pinch,

[104] **time:** opportunity. [105] **securing:** guarding. [106] **strook:** struck. [107] **cried:** called out. [108] **Location:** any part of the island. [109] **By inch-meal:** inch by inch. Cf. *piecemeal.*

Fright me with urchin-shows,[110] pitch me i' th' mire,
Nor lead me, like a fire-brand,[111] in the dark
Out of my way, unless he bid 'em; but
For every trifle are they set upon me,
Sometime like apes that mow[112] and chatter at me,
And after bite me; then like hedgehogs which
Lie tumbling in my barefoot way, and mount
Their pricks at my footfall; sometime am I
All wound[113] with adders, who with cloven tongues
Do hiss me into madness.

(Enter Trinculo.)

Lo, now, lo,
Here comes a spirit of his, and to torment me
For bringing wood in slowly. I'll fall flat.
Perchance he will not mind[114] me.

Trinculo: Here's neither bush nor shrub to bear off[115] any weather at all. And another storm brewing, I hear it sing i' th' wind. Yond same black cloud, yond huge one, looks like a foul bumbard[116] that would shed his[117] liquor. If it should thunder as it did before, I know not where to hide my head. Yond same cloud cannot choose but fall by pailfuls. What have we here? a man or a fish? dead or alive? A fish, he smells like a fish; a very ancient and fish-like smell; a kind of, not-of-the-newest poor-John.[118] A strange fish! Were I in England now (as once I was) and had but this fish painted,[119] not a holiday fool there but would give a piece of silver. There would this monster make a man;[120] any strange beast there makes a man. When they will not give a doit[121] to relieve a lame beggar, they will lay out ten to see a dead Indian. Legg'd like a man; and his fins like arms! Warm, o' my troth![122] I do now let loose my opinion, hold it[123] no longer: this is no fish, but an islander, that hath lately suffer'd by a thunderbolt. *(Thunder.)* Alas, the storm is come again! My best way is to creep under his gaberdine;[124] there is no other shelter hereabout. Misery acquaints a man with strange bedfellows. I will here shroud till the dregs[125] of the storm be past.

(Enter Stephano, singing, [a bottle in his hand].)

---

[110] **urchin-shows:** sights of goblins in the shape of hedgehogs. [111] **like a fire-brand:** in the shape of a will-o'-the wisp. [112] **mow:** make faces. [113] **wound:** twined about. [114] **mind:** notice. [115] **bear off:** ward off. [116] **bumbard:** bombard, leather bottle. [117] **his:** its. [118] **poor-John:** cheap dried fish. [119] **painted:** i.e., on a sign hung outside a booth at a fair to attract customers, with the monster exhibited within. [120] **make a man:** make a man's fortune, with obvious punning sense "be indistinguishable from an Englishman." [121] **doit:** coin of trifling value. [122] **o' my troth:** by my faith. [123] **hold it:** hold it back. [124] **gaberdine:** cloak. [125] **dregs:** lees (recurring to the image of the rain as liquor poured from a jug).

Stephano: "I shall no more to sea, to sea,
Here shall I die ashore—"
This is a very scurvy tune to sing at a man's funeral.
Well, here's my comfort. *(Drinks.)*
(Sings.) "The master, the swabber, the boatswain, and I,
The gunner, and his mate,
Lov'd Mall, Meg, and Marian, and Margery,
But none of us car'd for Kate;
For she had a tongue with a tang,
Would cry to a sailor, 'Go hang!'
She lov'd not the savor of tar nor of pitch,
Yet a tailor might scratch her where e'er she did itch.
Then to sea, boys, and let her go hang!"
This is a scurvy tune too; but here's my comfort. *(Drinks.)*

Caliban: Do not torment me! O![126]

Stephano: What's the matter? Have we devils here? Do you put tricks upon 's[127] with salvages[128] and men of Inde?[129] Ha? I have not scap'd drowning to be afeard now of your four legs; for it hath been said, "As proper a man as ever went on four legs[130] cannot make him give ground"; and it shall be said so again while Stephano breathes at'[131] nostrils.

Caliban: The spirit torments me! O!

Stephano: This is some monster of the isle with four legs, who hath got (as I take it) an ague. Where the devil should he learn our language? I will give him some relief, if it be but for that.[132] If I can recover[133] him, and keep him tame, and get to Naples with him, he's a present for any emperor that ever trod on neat's-leather.[134]

Caliban: Do not torment me, prithee. I'll bring my wood home faster.

Stephano: He's in his fit now, and does not talk after the wisest. He shall taste of my bottle; if he have never drunk wine afore, it will go near to remove his fit. If I can recover him, and keep him tame, I will not take too much[135] for him; he shall pay for him that hath[136] him, and that soundly.

Caliban: Thou dost me yet but little hurt; thou wilt anon,[137] I know it by thy trembling. Now Prosper works upon thee.

Stephano: Come on your ways. Open your mouth; here is that which will give language to you, cat.[138] Open your mouth; this will shake your shaking, I

---

[126] **Do . . . me:** Caliban takes Stephano for a spirit sent by Prospero to plague him. [127] **put tricks upon 's:** delude us with a conjuror's or showman's devices. [128] **salvages:** savages. [129] **Inde:** India. [130] **As . . . legs:** Stephano adapts a proverbial expression by substituting *four* for *two. Proper* = handsome. [131] **at':** at the. [132] **for that:** i.e., because he knows our language. [133] **recover:** restore. [134] **neat's-leather:** cowhide. [135] **I will . . . much:** whatever I can take for him won't be too much. [136] **hath:** gets. [137] **thou wilt anon:** i.e., you will hurt me more very soon. [138] **here . . . cat:** Alluding to the proverb "Liquor will make a cat talk."

can tell you, and that soundly. You cannot tell who's your friend. Open your chaps[139] again. *(Caliban drinks.)*

Trinculo: I should know that voice; it should be—but he is drown'd; and these are devils. O, defend me!

Stephano: Four legs and two voices; a most delicate[140] monster! His forward voice now is to speak well of his friend; his backward voice is to utter foul speeches and to detract. If all the wine in my bottle will recover him, I will help his ague. Come. *(Caliban drinks again.)* Amen! I will pour some in thy other mouth.

Trinculo: Stephano!

Stephano: Doth thy other mouth call me? Mercy, mercy! This is a devil, and no monster. I will leave him, I have no long spoon.[141]

Trinculo: Stephano! If thou beest Stephano, touch me, and speak to me; for I am Trinculo—be not afeard—thy good friend Trinculo.

Stephano: If thou beest Trinculo, come forth. I'll pull thee by the lesser legs. If any be Trinculo's legs, these are they. Thou art very Trinculo indeed! How cam'st thou to be the siege[142] of this moon-calf?[143] Can he vent[144] Trinculos?

Trinculo: I took him to be kill'd with a thunder-stroke. But art thou not drown'd, Stephano? I hope now thou art not drown'd. Is the storm overblown? I hid me under the dead moon-calf's gaberdine for fear of the storm. And art thou living, Stephano? O Stephano, two Neapolitans scap'd!

Stephano: Prithee do not turn me about, my stomach is not constant.

Caliban *(Aside.):* These be fine things, and if[145] they be not sprites.
That's a brave god, and bears celestial liquor.
I will kneel to him.

Stephano: How didst thou scape? How cam'st thou hither? Swear by this bottle how thou cam'st hither—I escap'd upon a butt of sack[146] which the sailors heav'd o'erboard—by this bottle, which I made of the bark of a tree with mine own hands since I was cast ashore.

Caliban: I'll swear upon that bottle to be thy true subject, for the liquor is not earthly.

Stephano: Here; swear then how thou escap'dst.

Trinculo: Swom[147] ashore, man, like a duck. I can swim like a duck, I'll be sworn.

Stephano: Here, kiss the book.[148] *(Passing the bottle.)* Though thou canst swim like a duck, thou art made like a goose.

Trinculo: O Stephano, hast any more of this?

---

[139] **chaps:** jaws. [140] **delicate:** ingenious. [141] **long spoon:** Alluding to the proverb "He must have a long spoon that will eat with the devil." [142] **siege:** excrement. [143] **moon-calf:** monstrosity, creature born misshapen because of lunar influence. [144] **vent:** emit. [145] **and if:** if. [146] **butt of sack:** barrel of Spanish wine. [147] **Swom:** swam. [148] **kiss the book:** Trinculo has taken his oath on the bottle, not on the customary Bible. Stephano means "Take a drink."

Stephano: The whole butt, man. My cellar is in a rock by th' sea-side, where my wine is hid. How now, moon-calf, how does thine ague?

Caliban: Hast thou not dropp'd from heaven?

Stephano: Out o' th' moon, I do assure thee. I was the Man i' th' Moon, when time was.[149]

Caliban: I have seen thee in her, and I do adore thee. My mistress show'd me thee, and thy dog, and thy bush.[150]

Stephano: Come, swear to that; kiss the book. I will furnish it anon with new contents. Swear.

(Caliban drinks.)

Trinculo: By this good light, this is a very shallow monster! I afeard of him? A very weak monster! The Man i' th' Moon? A most poor, credulous monster! Well drawn,[151] monster, in good sooth![152]

Caliban: I'll show thee every fertile inch o' th' island; And I will kiss thy foot. I prithee be my god.

Trinculo: By this light, a most perfidious and drunken monster! When's god's asleep, he'll rob his bottle.

Caliban: I'll kiss thy foot. I'll swear myself thy subject.

Stephano: Come on, then; down, and swear.

Trinculo: I shall laugh myself to death at this puppy-headed monster. A most scurvy monster! I could find in my heart to beat him—

Stephano: Come, kiss.

Trinculo: But that the poor monster's in drink. An abominable monster!

Caliban: I'll show thee the best springs; I'll pluck thee berries;
I'll fish for thee, and get thee wood enough.
A plague upon the tyrant that I serve!
I'll bear him no more sticks, but follow thee,
Thou wondrous man.

Trinculo: A most ridiculous monster, to make a wonder of a poor drunkard!

Caliban: I prithee let me bring thee where crabs[153] grow;
And I with my long nails will dig thee pig-nuts,[154]
Show thee a jay's nest, and instruct thee how
To snare the nimble marmazet.[155] I'll bring thee
To clust'ring filberts, and sometimes I'll get thee
Young scamels[156] from the rock. Wilt thou go with me?

Stephano: I prithee now lead the way without any more talking. Trinculo, the King and all our company else being drown'd, we will inherit here. Here! bear my bottle. Fellow Trinculo, we'll fill him by and by again.

---

[149] **when time was:** once upon a time. [150] **dog . . . bush:** The man in the moon was placed there in punishment for gathering firewood on Sunday. [151] **Well drawn:** that's a good long draught you've taken. [152] **sooth:** truth. [153] **crabs:** crab apples. [154] **pig-nuts:** peanuts. [155] **marmazet:** marmoset (a small monkey). [156] **scamels:** Meaning unknown, but apparently either shellfish or rock-inhabiting birds. Some editors emend to *sea-mels,* i.e., sea-mews.

Caliban *(Sings drunkenly.)*: Farewell, master; farewell, farewell!
Trinculo: A howling monster; a drunken monster!
Caliban: No more dams I'll make for fish,
Nor fetch in firing
At requiring,
Nor scrape trenchering,[157] nor wash dish.
'Ban, 'Ban, Ca-Caliban
Has a new master, get a new man.
Freedom, high-day! high-day, freedom! freedom, high-day, freedom!
Stephano: O brave monster! lead the way. *(Exeunt.)*

Act III

Scene I[1]

(Enter Ferdinand bearing a log.)

Ferdinand: There be some sports are painful,[2] and their labor
Delight in them [sets] off;[3] some kinds of baseness[4]
Are nobly undergone; and most poor matters
Point to rich ends. This my mean task
Would be as heavy to me as odious, but
The mistress which I serve quickens[5] what's dead,
And makes my labors pleasures. O, she is
Ten times more gentle than her father's crabbed;
And he's compos'd of harshness. I must remove
Some thousands of these logs, and pile them up,
Upon a sore injunction.[6] My sweet mistress
Weeps when she sees me work, and says such baseness
Had never like[7] executor. I forget;
But these sweet thoughts do even refresh my labors,
Most [busil'est] when I do it.[8]

(Enter Miranda, and Prospero [at a distance, unseen].)

Miranda: Alas, now pray you
Work not so hard. I would the lightning had
Burnt up those logs that you are enjoin'd to pile!
Pray set it down, and rest you. When this burns,
'Twill weep[9] for having wearied you. My father

---

[157] **trenchering:** trenchers, wooden plates.
[1] **Location:** Before Prospero's cell. [2] **are painful:** that are laborious.
[3] **their . . . off:** their laboriousness increases our pleasure in them (?) or our pleasure in them offsets their laboriousness (?). [4] **baseness:** menial activity.
[5] **quickens:** brings to life. [6] **sore injunction:** harsh command. [7] **like:** such, i.e., such a noble. [8] **Most . . . it:** when I am working hardest. [9] **weep:** i.e., exude resin.

Is hard at study; pray now rest yourself,
He's safe for these three hours.

Ferdinand: O most dear mistress,
The sun will set before I shall discharge
What I must strive to do.

Miranda: If you'll sit down,
I'll bear your logs the while. Pray give me that,
I'll carry it to the pile.

Ferdinand: No, precious creature,
I had rather crack my sinews, break my back,
Than you should such dishonor undergo,
While I sit lazy by.

Miranda: It would become me
As well as it does you; and I should do it
With much more ease, for my good will is to it,
And yours it is against.

Prospero *(Aside.):* Poor worm, thou art infected!
This visitation[10] shows it.

Miranda: You look wearily.

Ferdinand: No, noble mistress, 'tis fresh morning with me
When you are by at night. I do beseech you—
Chiefly that I might set it in my prayers—
What is your name?

Miranda: Miranda.—O my father,
I have broke your hest[11] to say so.

Ferdinand: Admir'd Miranda,[12]
Indeed the top of admiration! worth
What's dearest to the world! Full many a lady
I have ey'd with best regard,[13] and many a time
Th' harmony of their tongues hath into bondage
Brought my too diligent ear. For several[14] virtues
Have I lik'd several women, never any
With so full soul but some defect in her
Did quarrel with the noblest grace she ow'd,[15]
And put it to the foil.[16] But you, O you,
So perfect and so peerless, are created
Of every creature's best!

Miranda: I do not know
One of my sex; no woman's face remember,
Save, from my glass, mine own; nor have I seen
More that I may call men than you, good friend,

---

[10] **visitation:** (1) visit; (2) attack of plague (carrying on the medical figure in *infected*). [11] **hest:** command. [12] **Admir'd Miranda:** A pun, since *Miranda* admired, i.e., wondered at. [13] **best regard:** highest approval. [14] **several:** particular. [15] **ow'd:** owned. [16] **foil:** (1) contrast; (2) defeat.

And my dear father. How features are abroad[17]
I am skilless[18] of; but by my modesty
(The jewel in my dower), I would not wish
Any companion in the world but you;
Nor can imagination form a shape,
Besides yourself, to like of. But I prattle
Something too wildly, and my father's precepts
I therein do forget.
Ferdinand: I am, in my condition,[19]
A prince, Miranda; I do think, a king
(I would, not so!), and would no more endure
This wooden slavery[20] than to suffer
The flesh-fly blow[21] my mouth. Hear my soul speak:
The very instant that I saw you, did
My heart fly to your service, there resides,
To make me slave to it, and for your sake
Am I this patient log-man.
Miranda: Do you love me?
Ferdinand: O heaven, O earth, bear witness to this sound,
And crown what I profess with kind event[22]
If I speak true! if hollowly,[23] invert[24]
What best is boded[25] me to mischief! I,
Beyond all limit of what else i' th' world,
Do love, prize, honor you.
Miranda: I am a fool
To weep at what I am glad of.
Prospero: *(Aside.)* Fair encounter
Of two most rare affections! Heavens rain grace
On that which breeds between 'em!
Ferdinand: Wherefore weep you?
Miranda: At mine unworthiness, that dare not offer
What I desire to give; and much less take
What I shall die to want.[26] But this is trifling,
And all the more it seeks to hide itself,
The bigger bulk it shows. Hence, bashful cunning,[27]
And prompt me, plain and holy innocence!
I am your wife, if you will marry me;
If not, I'll die your maid.[28] To be your fellow[29]
You may deny me, but I'll be your servant,
Whether you will or no.

---

[17] **abroad:** elsewhere. [18] **skilless:** ignorant. [19] **condition:** rank. [20] **wooden slavery:** being compelled to carry wood. [21] **blow:** defile. [22] **kind event:** favorable outcome. [23] **hollowly:** insincerely. [24] **invert . . . to mischief:** turn . . . to ill fortune. [25] **boded:** destined. [26] **want:** be without. [27] **bashful cunning:** coyness. [28] **maid:** handmaiden. [29] **fellow:** mate.

Ferdinand: My mistress, dearest,
And I thus humble ever.
Miranda: My husband then?
Ferdinand: Ay, with a heart as willing
As bondage e'er of freedom. Here's my hand.
Miranda: And mine, with my heart in't. And now farewell
Till half an hour hence.
Ferdinand: A thousand, thousand![30]

(Exeunt [Ferdinand and Miranda severally].)

Prospero: So glad of this as they I cannot be,
Who are surpris'd [withal];[31] but my rejoicing
At nothing can be more. I'll to my book,
For yet ere supper-time must I perform
Much business appertaining. *(Exit.)*

Scene II[32]

(Enter Caliban, Stephano, and Trinculo.)

Stephano: Tell not me. When the butt is out,[33] we will drink water—not a drop before; therefore bear up and board 'em.[34] Servant-monster, drink to me.

Trinculo: Servant-monster? the folly[35] of this island! They say there's but five upon this isle: we are three of them; if th' other two be brain'd like us, the state totters.

Stephano: Drink, servant-monster, when I bid thee. Thy eyes are almost set[36] in thy head.

Trinculo: Where should they be set else? He were a brave monster indeed if they were set in his tail.

Stephano: My man-monster hath drown'd his tongue in sack. For my part, the sea cannot drown me: I swam, ere I could recover the shore, five and thirty leagues off and on. By this light, thou shalt be my lieutenant, monster, or my standard.[37]

Trinculo: Your lieutenant if you list, he's no standard.[38]

Stephano: We'll not run,[39] Monsieur Monster.

Trinculo: Nor go[40] neither; but you'll lie[41] like dogs, and yet say nothing neither.

---

[30] **thousand:** i.e., thousand farewells. [31] **withal:** with it, i.e., by it.
[32] **Location:** Another part of the island. [33] **out:** empty.
[34] **bear . . . 'em:** stand firm and attack. Stephano uses naval jargon as an encouragement to drink. [35] **folly of:** low level of intellect on. [36] **set:** sunk out of sight. Trinculo puns on the sense "placed." [37] **standard:** standard-bearer. [38] **no standard:** i.e., unable to stand. [39] **run:** run from the enemy. [40] **go:** walk. [41] **lie:** (1) lie down; (2) tell lies; (3) excrete (with a backward glance at *run* in the sense "urinate" and perhaps at *standard* in the sense "conduit").

Stephano: Moon-calf, speak once in thy life, if thou beest a good moon-calf.

Caliban: How does thy honor? Let me lick thy shoe. I'll not serve him, he is not valiant.

Trinculo: Thou liest, most ignorant monster, I am in case[42] to justle a constable. Why, thou debosh'd[43] fish thou, was there ever man a coward that hath drunk so much sack as I to-day? Wilt thou tell a monstrous lie, being but half a fish and half a monster?

Caliban: Lo, how he mocks me! Wilt thou let him, my lord?

Trinculo: "Lord," quoth he? That a monster should be such a natural![44]

Caliban: Lo, lo again. Bite him to death, I prithee.

Stephano: Trinculo, keep a good tongue in your head. If you prove a mutineer—the next tree! The poor monster's my subject, and he shall not suffer indignity.

Caliban: I thank my noble lord. Wilt thou be pleas'd to hearken once again to the suit I made to thee?

Stephano: Marry,[45] will I; kneel, and repeat it. I will stand, and so shall Trinculo.

(Enter Ariel, invisible.)

Caliban: As I told thee before, I am subject to a tyrant,
A sorcerer that by his cunning hath
Cheated me of the island.

Ariel: Thou liest.

Caliban *(To Trinculo.):* Thou liest, thou jesting monkey, thou!
I would my valiant master would destroy thee!
I do not lie.

Stephano: Trinculo, if you trouble him any more in 's tale, by this hand, I will supplant some of your teeth.

Trinculo: Why, I said nothing.

Stephano: Mum then, and no more.—Proceed.

Caliban: I say by sorcery he got this isle;
From me he got it. If thy greatness will
Revenge it on him—for I know thou dar'st,
But this thing[46] dare not—

Stephano: That's most certain.

Caliban: Thou shalt be lord of it, and I'll serve thee.

Stephano: How now shall this be compass'd? Canst thou bring me to the party?

Caliban: Yea, yea, my lord. I'll yield him thee asleep,
Where thou mayst knock a nail into his head.

Ariel: Thou liest, thou canst not.

---

[42] **case:** fit condition. [43] **debosh'd:** debauched. [44] **natural:** idiot. The point is that a monster is by definition "unnatural." [45] **Marry:** indeed (originally the name of the Virgin Mary used as an oath). [46] **this thing:** i.e., Trinculo.

Caliban: What a pied ninny's this! Thou scurvy patch![47]
I do beseech thy greatness, give him blows,
And take his bottle from him. When that's gone,
He shall drink nought but brine, for I'll not show him
Where the quick freshes[48] are.

Stephano: Trinculo, run into no further danger; interrupt the monster one word further, and by this hand, I'll turn my mercy out o' doors, and make a stock-fish[49] of thee.

Trinculo: Why, what did I? I did nothing. I'll go farther off.

Stephano: Didst thou not say he lied?

Ariel: Thou liest.

Stephano: Do I so? Take thou that. *(Beats Trinculo.)* As you like this, give me the lie another time.

Trinculo: I did not give the lie. Out o' your wits, and hearing too? A pox o' your bottle! this can sack and drinking do. A murrain[50] on your monster, and the devil take your fingers!

Caliban: Ha, ha, ha!

Stephano: Now forward with your tale.—Prithee, stand further off.

Caliban: Beat him enough. After a little time
I'll beat him too.

Stephano: Stand farther.—Come, proceed.

Caliban: Why, as I told thee, 'tis a custom with him
I' th' afternoon to sleep. There thou mayst brain him,
Having first seiz'd his books; or with a log
Batter his skull, or paunch[51] him with a stake,
Or cut his wezand[52] with thy knife. Remember
First to possess his books; for without them
He's but a sot,[53] as I am; nor hath not
One spirit to command: they all do hate him
As rootedly as I. Burn but his books.
He has brave utensils[54] (for so he calls them)
Which when he has a house, he'll deck withal.[55]
And that most deeply to consider is
The beauty of his daughter. He himself
Calls her a nonpareil. I never saw a woman
But only Sycorax, my dam and she;
But she as far surpasseth Sycorax
As great'st does least.

Stephano: Is it so brave a lass?

---

[47] **pied . . . patch:** foolish . . . fool (from the multicolored garb of the professional fool). [48] **quick freshes:** fresh-water springs. [49] **stock-fish:** dried cod, so stiff it had to be beaten before cooking. [50] **murrain:** a disease of cattle. [51] **paunch:** stab in the belly. [52] **wezand:** windpipe. [53] **sot:** fool. [54] **utensils:** furnishings. [55] **withal:** with.

Caliban: Ay, lord, she will become thy bed, I warrant,
And bring thee forth brave brood.

Stephano: Monster, I will kill this man. His daughter and I will be king and queen—'save our Graces! and Trinculo and thyself shall be viceroys. Dost thou like the plot, Trinculo?

Trinculo: Excellent.

Stephano: Give me thy hand. I am sorry I beat thee; but while thou liv'st keep a good tongue in thy head.

Caliban: Within this half hour will he be asleep.
Wilt thou destroy him then?

Stephano: Ay, on mine honor.

Ariel: This will I tell my master.

Caliban: Thou mak'st me merry; I am full of pleasure,
Let us be jocund. Will you troll the catch[56]
You taught me but while-ere?[57]

Stephano: At thy request, monster, I will do reason, any reason. Come on, Trinculo, let us sing. *(Sings.)*

"Flout 'em[58] and [scout] 'em,
And scout[59] 'em and flout 'em!
Thought is free."

Caliban: That's not the tune.

(Ariel plays the tune on a tabor[60] and pipe.)

Stephano: What is this same?

Trinculo: This is the tune of our catch, play'd by the picture of Nobody.[61]

Stephano: If thou beest a man, show thyself in thy likeness. If thou beest a devil, take't as thou list.[62]

Trinculo: O, forgive me my sins!

Stephano: He that dies pays all debts. I defy thee. Mercy upon us!

Caliban: Art thou afeard?

Stephano: No, monster, not I.

Caliban: Be not afeard, the isle is full of noises,[63]
Sounds, and sweet airs, that give delight and hurt not.
Sometimes a thousand twangling[64] instruments
Will hum about mine ears; and sometime voices,
That if I then had wak'd after long sleep,
Will make me sleep again, and then in dreaming,
The clouds methought would open, and show riches
Ready to drop upon me, that when I wak'd
I cried to dream again.

---

[56] **troll the catch:** sing the round. [57] **but while-ere:** a short time ago. [58] **Flout:** deride. [59] **scout:** jeer at. [60] **tabor:** small drum. [61] **picture of Nobody:** traditional image of a man with arms and legs but no torso; but Trinculo means an invisible agency. [62] **take't . . . list:** do as you please (a challenge). [63] **noises:** musical sounds. [64] **twangling:** An invented word.

Stephano: This will prove a brave kingdom to me, where I shall have my music for nothing.

Caliban: When Prospero is destroy'd.

Stephano: That shall be by and by.[65] I remember the story.

Trinculo: The sound is going away. Let's follow it, and after do our work.

Stephano: Lead, monster, we'll follow. I would I could see this taborer; he lays it on.

Trinculo: Wilt come? I'll follow Stephano. *(Exeunt.)*

Scene III[66]

(Enter Alonso, Sebastian, Antonio, Gonzalo, Adrian, Francisco, etc.)

Gonzalo: By'r lakin,[67] I can go no further, sir,
My old bones aches. Here's a maze trod indeed
Through forth-rights[68] and meanders! By your patience,
I needs must rest me.

Alonso: Old lord, I cannot blame thee,
Who am myself attach'd[69] with weariness
To th' dulling of my spirits. Sit down, and rest.
Even here I will put off my hope, and keep it
No longer for[70] my flatterer. He is drown'd
Whom thus we stray to find, and the sea mocks
Our frustrate search on land. Well, let him go.

Antonio *(Aside to Sebastian.):* I am right glad that he's so out of hope.
Do not for[71] one repulse forgo the purpose
That you resolv'd t' effect.

Sebastian *(Aside to Antonio.):* The next advantage
Will we take throughly.[72]

Antonio *(Aside to Sebastian.):* Let it be to-night,
For now they are oppress'd with travail, they
Will not, nor cannot, use such vigilance
As when they are fresh.

Sebastian *(Aside to Antonio.):* I say to-night. No more.

(Solemn and strange music; and Prospero on the top,[73] invisible.)

Alonso: What harmony is this? My good friends, hark!

Gonzalo: Marvellous sweet music!

(Enter several strange Shapes, bringing in a banket;[74] and dance about it with gentle actions of salutations; and inviting the King, etc., to eat, they depart.)

---

[65] **by and by:** immediately. [66] **Location:** Another part of the island. [67] **By'r lakin:** by our Ladykin, i.e., the Virgin Mary. [68] **forth-rights:** straight paths. [69] **attach'd:** seized. [70] **for:** as. [71] **for:** because of. [72] **throughly:** thoroughly. [73] s.d. **top:** Probably the third level of the tiring-house. [74] s.d. **banket:** banquet, i.e., light repast.

Alonso: Give us kind keepers,[75] heavens! What were these?
Sebastian: A living drollery.[76] Now I will believe
That there are unicorns; that in Arabia
There is one tree, the phoenix' throne, one phoenix
At this hour reigning there.
Antonio: I'll believe both;
And what does else want credit,[77] come to me,
And I'll be sworn 'tis true. Travellers ne'er did lie,
Though fools at home condemn 'em.
Gonzalo: If in Naples
I should report this now, would they believe me?
If I should say I saw such [islanders]
(For, certes,[78] these are people of the island),
Who though they are of monstrous[79] shape, yet note
Their manners are more gentle, kind, than of
Our human generation you shall find
Many, nay, almost any.
Prospero *(Aside.):* Honest lord,
Thou hast said well; for some of you there present
Are worse than devils.
Alonso: I cannot too much muse[80]
Such shapes, such gesture, and such sound expressing
(Although they want the use of tongue) a kind
Of excellent dumb discourse.
Prospero *(Aside.):* Praise in departing.[81]
Francisco: They vanished strangely.
Sebastian: No matter, since
They have left their viands behind; for we have stomachs.[82]
Will't please you taste of what is here?
Alonso: Not I.
Gonzalo: Faith, sir, you need not fear. When we were boys,
Who would believe that there were mountaineers,
Dew-lapp'd,[83] like bulls, whose throats had hanging at 'em
Wallets of flesh? or that there were such men
Whose heads stood in their breasts?[84] which now we find
Each putter-out of five for one[85] will bring us
Good warrant of.

---

[75] **kind keepers:** guardian angels. [76] **living drollery:** puppet show with live actors. [77] **want credit:** lack credence. [78] **certes:** certainly.
[79] **monstrous:** abnormal, unnatural. [80] **muse:** wonder at. [81] **Praise in departing:** i.e., don't judge until you see the conclusion (proverbial).
[82] **stomachs:** appetites. [83] **Dew-lapp'd:** with pouches of skin hanging from the neck (probably alluding to travelers' tales about goiter among Swiss mountaineers).
[84] **men . . . breasts:** A common travelers' tale. See *Othello,* I.iii.144–45.
[85] **Each . . . one:** Travelers deposited a sum of money at home to be repaid fivefold if they returned, forfeited if they did not.

Alonso: I will stand to,[86] and feed,
Although my last, no matter, since I feel
The best[87] is past. Brother, my lord the Duke,
Stand to, and do as we.

(Thunder and lightning. Enter Ariel, like a harpy,[88] claps his wings upon the table, and with a quaint device[89] the banquet vanishes.)

Ariel: You are three men of sin, whom Destiny,
That hath to[90] instrument this lower world
And what is in't, the never-surfeited sea
Hath caus'd to belch up you; and on this island
Where man doth not inhabit—you 'mongst men
Being most unfit to live. I have made you mad;
And even with such-like valor[91] men hang and drown
Their proper[92] selves.

(Alonso, Sebastian, etc. draw their swords.)

You fools! I and my fellows
Are ministers of Fate. The elements,
Of whom[93] your swords are temper'd, may as well
Wound the loud winds, or with bemock'd-at stabs
Kill the still-closing[94] waters, as diminish
One dowle[95] that's in my plume. My fellow ministers
Are like[96] invulnerable. If you could hurt,
Your swords are now too massy for your strengths,
And will not be uplifted. But remember
(For that's my business to you) that you three
From Milan did supplant good Prospero,
Expos'd unto the sea (which hath requit it)[97]
Him, and his innocent child; for which foul deed
The pow'rs, delaying (not forgetting), have
Incens'd the seas and shores—yea, all the creatures,
Against your peace. Thee of thy son, Alonso,
They have bereft; and do pronounce by me
Ling'ring perdition[98] (worse than any death
Can be at once) shall step by step attend
You and your ways, whose[99] wraths to guard you from—

[86] **stand to:** take the risk. [87] **best:** i.e., best part of life. [88] s.d. **like a harpy:** in the shape of a harpy, a rapacious monster with the face of a woman and the wings and claws of a bird of prey. [89] **with . . . device:** by means of an ingenious stage mechanism. [90] **to:** for. [91] **such-like valor:** i.e., the valor of madness, very different from true courage. [92] **proper:** own. [93] **whom:** which. [94] **still-closing:** always closing as soon as parted. [95] **dowle:** small feather. [96] **like:** similarly. [97] **requit it:** repaid the act (by casting you up here). [98] **perdition:** ruin. [99] **whose:** i.e., those of the "pow'rs" mentioned in line 21 of this speech.

Which here, in this most desolate isle, else falls
Upon your heads—is nothing but heart's sorrow,[100]
And a clear[101] life ensuing.

(He vanishes in thunder; then, to soft music, enter the Shapes again, and dance, with mocks and mows,[102] and carrying out the table.)

Prospero: Bravely the figure of this harpy hast thou
Perform'd, my Ariel; a grace it had, devouring.[103]
Of my instruction hast thou nothing bated[104]
In what thou hadst to say; so with good life,[105]
And observation strange,[106] my meaner[107] ministers
Their several kinds[108] have done. My high charms work,
And these, mine enemies, are all knit up
In their distractions.[109] They now are in my pow'r;
And in these fits I leave them, while I visit
Young Ferdinand, whom they suppose is drown'd,
And his and mine lov'd darling. *(Exit above.)*
Gonzalo: I' th' name of something holy, sir, why stand you
In this strange stare?[110]
Alonso: O, it is monstrous! monstrous!
Methought the billows spoke, and told me of it;[111]
The winds did sing it to me, and the thunder,
That deep and dreadful organ-pipe, pronounc'd
The name of Prosper; it did base[112] my trespass.
Therefore[113] my son i' th' ooze is bedded; and
I'll seek him deeper than e'er plummet sounded,
And with him there lie mudded. *(Exit.)*
Sebastian: But one fiend at a time,
I'll fight their legions o'er.[114]
Antonio: I'll be thy second.

(Exeunt [Sebastian and Antonio].)

Gonzalo: All three of them are desperate: their great guilt
(Like poison given to work a great time after)
Now gins to bite the spirits.[115] I do beseech you
(That are of suppler joints) follow them swiftly,

---

[100] **is . . . sorrow:** there is no means except repentance. [101] **clear:** sinless. [102] s.d. **mocks and mows:** mocking gestures and grimaces. [103] **devouring:** i.e., making the banquet disappear. [104] **bated:** omitted. [105] **life:** realism. [106] **observation strange:** exceptional care. [107] **meaner:** i.e., inferior to Ariel. [108] **several kinds:** individual parts. [109] **knit . . . distractions:** entangled in their madness. [110] **why . . . stare:** Gonzalo has not heard Ariel's speech. [111] **it:** i.e., my sin. [112] **base:** bass, i.e., utter in a deep voice. [113] **Therefore:** therefor, i.e., in consequence of his trespass. [114] **o'er:** one after another. [115] **gins . . . spirits:** begins to cause mental anguish.

And hinder them from what this ecstasy[116]
May now provoke them to.
Adrian: Follow, I pray you. *(Exeunt omnes.)*

Act IV[1]

Scene I

(Enter Prospero, Ferdinand, and Miranda.)

Prospero: If I have too austerely punish'd you,
Your compensation makes amends, for I
Have given you here a third of mine own life,[2]
Or that for which I live; who once again
I tender to thy hand. All thy vexations
Were but my trials of thy love, and thou
Hast strangely[3] stood the test. Here, afore heaven,
I ratify this my rich gift. O Ferdinand,
Do not smile at me that I boast her [off],[4]
For thou shalt find she will outstrip all praise
And make it halt[5] behind her.
Ferdinand: I do believe it
Against an oracle.[6]
Prospero: Then as my [gift], and thine own acquisition
Worthily purchas'd, take my daughter. But
If thou dost break her virgin-knot before
All sanctimonious[7] ceremonies may
With full and holy rite be minist'red,
No sweet aspersion[8] shall the heavens let fall
To make this contract grow;[9] but barren hate,
Sour-ey'd disdain, and discord shall bestrew
The union of your bed with weeds[10] so loathly
That you shall hate it both. Therefore take heed,
As Hymen's lamps shall light you.[11]

---

[116] **ecstasy:** fit of madness.
[1] **Location:** Before Prospero's cell. [2] **a third . . . life:** Various explanations have been put forward: for example, that the other two parts have been his dukedom and his books, or his late wife and his personal interests; or that Miranda represents his future, the other two parts being his past and his present; or that he has spent a third of his life on Miranda's education. [3] **strangely:** wonderfully well.
[4] **boast her off:** i.e., praise her so highly. [5] **halt:** limp. [6] **Against an oracle:** even if an oracle should declare otherwise. [7] **sanctimonious:** sacred, holy.
[8] **aspersion:** i.e., blessing; literally, sprinkling, as of rain that promotes fertility and growth. [9] **grow:** be fruitful (as contrasted with *barren*). [10] **weeds:** Instead of the flowers with which the marriage bed was customarily strewn. [11] **As . . . you:** i.e., as you desire happiness in your marriage. The symbolic torch of Hymen, god of marriage, was supposed to promise happiness if it burned with a clear flame, the opposite if it smoked.

Ferdinand: As I hope
For quiet days, fair issue, and long life,
With such love as 'tis now, the murkiest den,
The most opportune place, the strong'st suggestion[12]
Our worser genius can,[13] shall never melt
Mine honor into lust, to take away
The edge of that day's celebration,
When I shall think or Phoebus' steeds are founder'd,[14]
Or night kept chain'd below.
Prospero: Fairly spoke.
Sit then and talk with her, she is thine own.
What, Ariel! My industrious servant, Ariel!

(Enter Ariel.)

Ariel: What would my potent master? here I am.
Prospero: Thou and thy meaner fellows your last service
Did worthily perform; and I must use you
In such another trick.[15] Go bring the rabble[16]
(O'er whom I give thee pow'r) here to this place.
Incite them to quick motion, for I must
Bestow upon the eyes of this young couple
Some vanity[17] of mine art. It is my promise,
And they expect it from me.
Ariel: Presently?[18]
Prospero: Ay, with a twink.[19]
Ariel: Before you can say "come" and "go,"
And breathe twice, and cry "so, so,"
Each one, tripping on his toe,
Will be here with mop and mow.[20]
Do you love me, master? no?
Prospero: Dearly, my delicate Ariel. Do not approach
Till thou dost hear me call.
Ariel: Well, I conceive.[21] *(Exit.)*
Prospero: Look thou be true; do not give dalliance
Too much the rein. The strongest oaths are straw
To th' fire i' th' blood. Be more abstenious,[22]
Or else good night your vow!

---

[12] **suggestion:** temptation. [13] **Our . . . can:** our bad angel is capable of. [14] **or . . . founder'd:** either the sun-god's horses have gone lame (because the day is so long). [15] **trick:** ingenious device (technical term in pageantry). [16] **rabble:** troop of interior spirits. [17] **vanity:** show, delusive appearance. [18] **Presently:** immediately. [19] **with a twink:** in a twinkling. [20] **mop and mow:** gesture and grimace. [21] **conceive:** understand. [22] **abstenious:** abstemious.

Ferdinand: I warrant you, sir,
The white cold virgin snow upon my heart
Abates the ardor of my liver.[23]

Prospero: Well.
Now come, my Ariel, bring a corollary,[24]
Rather than want[25] a spirit. Appear, and pertly![26]
No tongue![27] all eyes! Be silent. *(Soft music.)*

(Enter Iris.)[28]

Iris: Ceres,[29] most bounteous lady, thy rich leas[30]
Of wheat, rye, barley, fetches,[31] oats, and pease;
Thy turfy mountains, where live nibbling sheep,
And flat meads thatch'd with stover,[32] them to keep;
Thy banks with pioned and twilled[33] brims,
Which spungy[34] April at thy hest betrims,
To make cold[35] nymphs chaste crowns; and thy broom-groves,[36]
Whose shadow the dismissed bachelor[37] loves,
Being lass-lorn; thy pole-clipt[38] vineyard,
And thy sea-marge, sterile and rocky-hard,
Where thou thyself dost air—the Queen o' th' sky,[39]
Whose wat'ry arch and messenger am I,
Bids thee leave these, and with her sovereign Grace,
Here on this grass-plot, in this very place,
To come and sport. [Her] peacocks[40] fly amain.[41]

(Juno descends [slowly in her car].)

Approach, rich Ceres, her to entertain.[42]

(Enter Ceres.)

Ceres: Hail, many-colored messenger, that ne'er
Dost disobey the wife of Jupiter;
Who with thy saffron wings upon my flow'rs
Diffusest honey-drops, refreshing show'rs,

---

[23] **liver:** Supposed seat of the passions. [24] **corollary:** extra. [25] **want:** lack. [26] **pertly:** briskly. [27] **No tongue:** Any speech from the spectators would make the spirits vanish. [28] s.d. **Iris:** goddess of the rainbow and Juno's messenger. [29] **Ceres:** goddess of agriculture. [30] **leas:** meadows, cultivated land. [31] **fetches:** vetch, a fodder plant. [32] **stover:** hay for winter use. [33] **pioned and twilled:** undercut by the stream and retained by interwoven branches. [34] **spungy:** spongy, i.e., wet. [35] **cold:** chaste. [36] **broom:** a kind of shrub bearing yellow flowers. [37] **dismissed bachelor:** rejected suitor. [38] **pole-clipt:** poll-clipped, i.e., with top growth pruned back (?). If *clipt* means (as often) "embraced," the sense could be "enclosed by a fence of poles" or "with poles entwined by the vines." [39] **Queen . . . sky:** Juno. [40] **peacocks:** Juno's sacred birds, which drew her chariot. [41] **amain:** swiftly. [42] **entertain:** receive.

And with each end of thy blue bow dost crown
My bosky[43] acres and my unshrubb'd down,[44]
Rich scarf to my proud earth—why hath thy Queen
Summon'd me hither, to this short-grassed green?

Iris: A contract of true love to celebrate,
And some donation freely to estate[45]
On the bless'd lovers.

Ceres: Tell me, heavenly bow,
If Venus or her son,[46] as thou dost know,
Do now attend the Queen? Since they did plot
The means that dusky Dis[47] my daughter got,
Her and her blind boy's scandall'd[48] company
I have forsworn.

Iris: Of her society
Be not afraid. I met her Deity
Cutting the clouds towards Paphos;[49] and her son
Dove-drawn[50] with her. Here thought they to have done
Some wanton charm[51] upon this man and maid,
Whose vows are, that no bed-right shall be paid
Till Hymen's torch be lighted; but in vain,
Mars's hot minion[52] is return'd[53] again;
Her waspish-headed[54] son has broke his arrows,
Swears he will shoot no more, but play with sparrows,[55]
And be a boy right out.[56]

(Juno alights.)

Ceres: Highest Queen of state.[57]
Great Juno, comes, I know her by her gait.[58]

Juno: How does my bounteous sister? Go with me
To bless this twain, that they may prosperous be,
And honor'd in their issue. *(They sing.)*

Juno: Honor, riches, marriage-blessing,
Long continuance, and increasing,
Hourly joys be still[59] upon you!
Juno sings her blessings on you.

---

[43] **bosky:** wooded. [44] **down:** upland. [45] **estate:** bestow. [46] **son:** Cupid, the "blind boy" mentioned later. [47] **Dis:** Pluto, ruler of the underworld (hence *dusky*), who carried off Ceres's daughter Proserpine to be his queen.
[48] **scandall'd:** scandalous. [49] **Paphos:** place in Cyprus sacred to Venus.
[50] **Dove-drawn:** Venus's chariot was drawn by her sacred doves. [51] **done . . . charm:** cast some unchaste spell. [52] **hot minion:** lustful mistress. Venus and Mars were lovers. [53] **return'd:** i.e., to Paphos. [54] **waspish-headed:** peevish.
[55] **sparrows:** Like doves, sacred to Venus. Sparrows were proverbially lecherous.
[56] **right out:** outright. [57] **Highest . . . state:** most majestic queen. [58] **gait:** i.e., regal bearing. [59] **still:** always.

Ceres: Earth's increase, foison plenty,[60]
Barns and garners never empty;
Vines with clust'ring bunches growing,
Plants with goodly burthen bowing;
Spring come to you at the farthest
In the very end of harvest![61]
Scarcity and want shall shun you,
Ceres' blessing so is on you.

Ferdinand: This is a most majestic vision, and
Harmonious charmingly.[62] May I be bold
To think these spirits?

Prospero: Spirits, which by mine art
I have from their confines called to enact
My present fancies.

Ferdinand: Let me live here ever;
So rare a wond'red[63] father and a wise
Makes this place Paradise.

(Juno and Ceres whisper, and send Iris on employment.)

Prospero: Sweet now, silence![64]
Juno and Ceres whisper seriously;
There's something else to do. Hush, and be mute,
Or else our spell is marr'd.

Iris: You nymphs, call'd Naiades of the windring[65] brooks,
With your sedg'd crowns and ever-harmless[66] looks,
Leave your crisp[67] channels, and on this green land
Answer your summons; Juno does command.
Come, temperate[68] nymphs, and help to celebrate
A contract of true love; be not too late.

(Enter certain Nymphs.)

You sunburn'd sicklemen, of August weary,
Come hither from the furrow and be merry.
Make holiday; your rye-straw hats put on,
And these fresh[69] nymphs encounter[70] every one
In country footing.[71]

---

[60] **foison plenty:** plentiful abundance. [61] **In . . . harvest:** i.e., without intervening winter. [62] **charmingly:** enchantingly, magically.
[63] **wond'red:** (1) to be wondered at; (2) able to perform wonders; (3) possessed of that wonder, Miranda. [64] **Sweet now, silence:** Addressed to Miranda, who is about to speak. [65] **windring:** winding and wandering (apparently a coinage of Shakespeare's). [66] **ever-harmless:** ever-innocent. [67] **crisp:** rippling.
[68] **temperate:** chaste. [69] **fresh:** young and beautiful. [70] **encounter:** meet.
[71] **footing:** dance.

(Enter certain Reapers, properly habited: they join with the Nymphs in a graceful dance, towards the end whereof Prospero starts suddenly, and speaks; after which, to a strange, hollow, and confused noise, they heavily[72] vanish.)

Prospero *(Aside.)*: I had forgot that foul conspiracy
Of the beast Caliban and his confederates
Against my life. The minute of their plot
Is almost come. *(To the Spirits.)* Well done, avoid;[73] No more.
Ferdinand: This is strange. Your father's in some passion
That works[74] him strongly.
Miranda: Never till this day
Saw I him touch'd with anger, so distemper'd.
Prospero: You do look, my son, in a mov'd sort,[75]
As if you were dismay'd; be cheerful, sir.
Our revels[76] now are ended. These our actors
(As I foretold you) were all spirits, and
Are melted into air, into thin air,
And like the baseless fabric[77] of this vision,
The cloud-capp'd tow'rs, the gorgeous palaces,
The solemn temples, the great globe itself,
Yea, all which it inherit,[78] shall dissolve,
And like this insubstantial[79] pageant faded
Leave not a rack[80] behind. We are such stuff
As dreams are made on;[81] and our little life
Is rounded[82] with a sleep. Sir, I am vex'd;
Bear with my weakness, my old brain is troubled.
Be not disturb'd with my infirmity.
If you be pleas'd, retire into my cell,
And there repose. A turn or two I'll walk
To still my beating mind.
Ferdinand, Miranda: We wish your peace.
Prospero *(To Ariel.)*: Come with[83] a thought. *(To Ferdinand and Miranda.)* I thank thee.

(Exeunt Ferdinand and Miranda.)

Ariel! come.

(Enter Ariel.)

Ariel: Thy thoughts I cleave to. What's thy pleasure?
Prospero: Spirit,
We must prepare to meet with Caliban.

---

[72] s.d. **heavily:** reluctantly. [73] **avoid:** be gone. [74] **works:** agitates. [75] **mov'd sort:** troubled state. [76] **revels:** festivity, entertainment. [77] **baseless fabric:** structure without physical foundation. [78] **which it inherit:** who occupy it. [79] **insubstantial:** without material substance. [80] **rack:** wisp of cloud. [81] **on:** of. [82] **rounded:** surrounded. [83] **with:** at the summons of.

Ariel: Ay, my commander. When I presented[84] Ceres,
I thought to have told thee of it, but I fear'd
Lest I might anger thee.
Prospero: Say again, where didst thou leave these varlots?[85]
Ariel: I told you, sir, they were red-hot with drinking,
So full of valor that they smote the air
For breathing in their faces; beat the ground
For kissing of their feet; yet always bending
Towards their project.[86] Then I beat my tabor,
At which like unback'd[87] colts they prick'd their ears,
Advanc'd[88] their eyelids, lifted up their noses
As[89] they smelt music. So I charm'd their ears
That calf-like they my lowing follow'd through
Tooth'd briers, sharp furzes, pricking goss,[90] and thorns,
Which ent'red their frail shins. At last I left them
I' th' filthy-mantled[91] pool beyond your cell,
There dancing up to th' chins, that the foul lake
O'erstunk their feet.
Prospero: This was well done, my bird.
Thy shape invisible retain thou still.
The trumpery[92] in my house, go bring it hither,
For stale[93] to catch these thieves.
Ariel: I go, I go. *(Exit.)*
Prospero: A devil, a born devil, on whose nature
Nurture can never stick; on whom my pains,
Humanely taken, all, all lost, quite lost;
And as with age his body uglier grows,
So his mind cankers.[94] I will plague them all,
Even to roaring.

(Enter Ariel, loaden with glistering apparel, etc.)

Come, hang [them on] this line.[95]

(Prospero and Ariel remain, invisible. Enter Caliban, Stephano, and Trinculo, all wet.)

Caliban: Pray you tread softly, that the blind mole[96] may not
Hear a foot fall; we now are near his cell.

---

[84] **presented:** represented, took the part of (?). [85] **varlots:** varlets, ruffians. [86] **bending . . . project:** pursuing their purpose—the murder of Prospero. [87] **unback'd:** never ridden, unbroken. [88] **Advanc'd:** raised. [89] **As:** as if. [90] **goss:** gorse. [91] **filthy-mantled:** covered with dirty scum. [92] **trumpery:** showy finery (the "glistering apparel" of paragraph 161 s.d. 1). [93] **stale:** bait. [94] **cankers:** becomes malignant. [95] **line:** lime tree, linden. [96] **mole:** Thought to have sensitive hearing.

Stephano: Monster, your fairy, which you say is a harmless fairy, has done little better than play'd the Jack[97] with us.

Trinculo: Monster, I do smell all horse-piss, at which my nose is in great indignation.

Stephano: So is mine. Do you hear, monster? If I should take a displeasure against you, look you—

Trinculo: Thou wert but a lost monster.

Caliban: Good my lord, give me thy favor still.
Be patient, for the prize I'll bring thee to
Shall hoodwink[98] this mischance; therefore speak softly,
All's hush'd as midnight yet.

Trinculo: Ay, but to lose our bottles in the pool—

Stephano: There is not only disgrace and dishonor in that, monster, but an infinite loss.

Trinculo: That's more to me than my wetting; yet this is your harmless fairy, monster!

Stephano: I will fetch off my bottle, though I be o'er ears for my labor.

Caliban: Prithee, my king, be quiet. Seest thou here,
This is the mouth o' th' cell. No noise, and enter.
Do that good mischief which may make this island
Thine own for ever, and I, thy Caliban,
For aye thy foot-licker.

Stephano: Give me thy hand. I do begin to have bloody thoughts.

Trinculo: O King Stephano! O peer![99] O worthy Stephano! look what a wardrobe here is for thee!

Caliban: Let it alone, thou fool, it is but trash.

Trinculo: O, ho, monster! we know what belongs to a frippery.[100] O King Stephano!

Stephano: Put off that gown, Trinculo. By this hand, I'll have that gown.

Trinculo: Thy Grace shall have it.

Caliban: The dropsy drown[101] this fool! what do you mean
To dote thus on such luggage?[102] Let['t] alone
And do the murther first. If he awake,
From toe to crown he'll fill our skins with pinches,
Make us strange stuff.

Stephano: Be you quiet, monster. Mistress line, is not this my jerkin? Now is the jerkin[103] under the line.[104] Now, jerkin, you are like to lose your hair, and prove a bald jerkin.

---

[97] **Jack:** (1) knave; (2) jack-o'-lantern, i.e., will-o'the-wisp. [98] **hoodwink:** make you blind to. [99] **peer:** Referring to the old ballad "King Stephen was a worthy peer," quoted in *Othello,* II.iii.89–96. [100] **frippery:** secondhand-clothes shop. [101] **drown:** suffocate. [102] **luggage:** encumbering trash. [103] **jerkin:** a kind of jacket. [104] **under the line:** With pun on the sense "south of the equator." The joke involves the popular idea that travelers to tropical countries lost their hair through fevers, or from scurvy resulting from lack of fresh food on the long voyage.

Trinculo: Do, do;[105] we steal by line and level,[106] and't like[107] your Grace.

Stephano: I thank thee for that jest; here's a garment for't. Wit shall not go unrewarded while I am king of this country. "Steal by line and level" is an excellent pass[108] of pate;[109] there's another garment for't.

Trinculo: Monster, come put some lime[110] on your fingers, and away with the rest.

Caliban: I will have none on't. We shall lose our time,
And all be turn'd to barnacles,[111] or to apes
With foreheads villainous[112] low.

Stephano: Monster, lay-to your fingers. Help to bear this away where my hogshead of wine is, or I'll turn you out of my kingdom. Go to,[113] carry this.

Trinculo: And this.

Stephano: Ay, and this.

(A noise of hunters heard. Enter divers Spirits in shape of dogs and hounds, hunting them about; Prospero and Ariel setting them on.)

Prospero: Hey, Mountain, hey!

Ariel: Silver! There it goes, Silver!

Prospero: Fury, Fury! there, Tyrant, there! hark, hark![114]

(Caliban, Stephano, and Trinculo are driven out.)

Go, charge my goblins that they grind their joints
With dry convulsions,[115] shorten up their sinews
With aged[116] cramps, and more pinch-spotted make them
Than pard[117] or cat o' mountain.[118]

Ariel: Hark, they roar!

Prospero: Let them be hunted soundly. At this hour
Lies at my mercy all mine enemies.
Shortly shall all my labors end, and thou
Shalt have the air at freedom. For a little.
Follow, and do me service. *(Exeunt.)*

---

[105] **Do, do:** an expression of approval, equivalent to "bravo." [106] **by . . . level:** with plumb-line and carpenter's level, i.e., with professional skill (continuing the puns on *line*). [107] **and't like:** if it please. [108] **pass:** thrust (a fencing term). [109] **pate:** i.e., wit. [110] **lime:** sticky substance; thieves were jokingly said to have lime on their fingers. [111] **barnacles:** a kind of geese traditionally supposed to develop from the shellfish so named. [112] **villainous:** wretchedly. [113] **Go to:** expression of exhortation or reproof, equivalent to "come, come!" [114] **hark:** "sic 'em!" [115] **dry convulsions:** Precisely what sort of painful seizure is meant here is uncertain. [116] **aged:** such as old people have. [117] **pard:** leopard. [118] **cat o' mountain:** catamount, wildcat.

Act V

Scene I[1]

(Enter Prospero in his magic robes, and Ariel.)

Prospero: Now does my project gather to a head:
My charms crack not; my spirits obey; and Time
Goes upright with his carriage.[2] How's the day?
Ariel: On[3] the sixt[4] hour, at which time, my lord,
You said our work should cease.
Prospero: I did say so,
When first I raised the tempest. Say, my spirit,
How fares the King and 's followers?
Ariel: Confin'd together
In the same fashion as you gave in charge,
Just as you left them; all prisoners, sir,
In the line-grove which weather-fends[5] your cell;
They cannot boudge[6] till your release.[7] The King,
His brother, and yours, abide all three distracted,[8]
And the remainder mourning over them,
Brimful of sorrow and dismay; but chiefly
Him that you term'd, sir, "the good old Lord Gonzalo,"
His tears runs down his beard like winter's drops
From eaves of reeds.[9] Your charm so strongly works 'em
That if you now beheld them, your affections[10]
Would become tender.
5 **Prospero:** Dost thou think so, spirit?
Ariel: Mine would, sir, were I human.
Prospero: And mine shall.
Hast thou, which art but air, a touch,[11] a feeling
Of their afflictions, and shall not myself,
One of their kind, that relish[12] all[13] as sharply
Passion as they, be kindlier[14] mov'd than thou art?
Though with their high wrongs I am struck to th' quick,
Yet with my nobler reason, 'gainst my fury
Do I take part.[15] The rarer[16] action is
In virtue than in vengeance. They being penitent,
The sole drift of my purpose doth extend

---

[1] **Location:** Before Prospero's cell. [2] **Goes . . . carriage:** walks upright under what he is carrying (because his burden of coming events has been greatly lightened). [3] **On:** approaching. [4] **sixt:** sixth. On the time, see I.ii, paragraphs 84–85. [5] **weather-fends:** serves as windbreak for. [6] **boudge:** budge, stir. [7] **your release:** i.e., their release by you. [8] **distracted:** out of their wits. [9] **eaves of reeds:** thatched roofs. [10] **affections:** inclinations, bent of mind. [11] **touch:** Synonymous with *feeling*. [12] **relish:** experience. [13] **all:** quite. [14] **kindlier:** (1) more sympathetically; (2) more naturally (as "one of their kind"). [15] **take part:** side. [16] **rarer:** finer, nobler.

Not a frown further. Go, release them, Ariel.
My charms I'll break, their senses I'll restore,
And they shall be themselves.

Ariel: I'll fetch them, sir.

(Exit.) (Prospero traces a magic circle with his staff.)

Prospero: Ye elves of hills, brooks, standing lakes, and groves,
And ye that on the sands with printless foot
Do chase the ebbing Neptune, and do fly him
When he comes back; you demi-puppets[17] that
By moonshine do the green sour ringlets[18] make,
Whereof the ewe not bites; and you whose pastime
Is to make midnight mushrumps,[19] that rejoice
To hear the solemn curfew:[20] by whose aid
(Weak[21] masters though ye be) I have bedimm'd
The noontide sun, call'd forth the mutinous winds,
And 'twixt the green sea and the azur'd vault
Set roaring war; to the dread rattling thunder
Have I given fire, and rifted[22] Jove's stout oak
With his own bolt; the strong-bas'd promontory
Have I made shake, and by the spurs[23] pluck'd up
The pine and cedar. Graves at my command
Have wak'd their sleepers, op'd, and let 'em forth
By my so potent art. But this rough[24] magic
I here abjure; and when I have requir'd[25]
Some heavenly music (which even now I do)
To work mine end upon their senses[26] that
This airy charm[27] is for, I'll break my staff,
Bury it certain fathoms in the earth,
And deeper than did ever plummet sound
I'll drown my book. *(Solemn music.)*

(Here enters Ariel before; then Alonso, with a frantic gesture,[28] attended by Gonzalo; Sebastian and Antonio in like manner, attended by Adrian and Francisco. They all enter the circle which Prospero has made, and there stand charm'd; which Prospero observing, speaks.)

---

[17] **demi-puppets:** quasi-puppets, i.e. creatures of small size. [18] **green sour ringlets:** so-called "fairy rings" in grass, actually caused by mushrooms. [19] **mushrumps:** mushrooms, supposed because of their rapid growth to be made by elves during the night. [20] **curfew:** Supposedly spirits could be abroad only between curfew (9 P.M.) and the first cockcrow; cf. I.ii.118. [21] **Weak:** i.e., as compared with the powerful demons summoned up by black magic. [22] **rifted:** split. [23] **spurs:** roots. [24] **rough:** i.e., capable of producing the violent effects just described (?). [25] **requir'd:** requested. [26] **their senses that:** the senses of those whom. [27] **airy charm:** i.e., the music. [28] s.d. **frantic gesture:** insane demeanor.

A solemn air, and[29] the best comforter
To an unsettled fancy, cure thy brains,[30]
Now useless, [boil'd][31] within thy skull! There stand,
For you are spell-stopp'd.
Holy Gonzalo, honorable man,
Mine eyes, ev'n sociable[32] to the show[33] of thine,
Fall[34] fellowly drops. The charm dissolves apace,
And as the morning steals upon the night,
Melting the darkness, so their rising senses
Begin to chase the ignorant fumes[35] that mantle
Their clearer reason. O good Gonzalo,
My true preserver, and a loyal sir
To him thou follow'st! I will pay thy graces
Home[36] both in word and deed. Most cruelly
Didst thou, Alonso, use me and my daughter;
Thy brother was a furtherer in the act.
Thou art pinch'd for't now, Sebastian. Flesh and blood,
You, brother mine, that [entertain'd] ambition,
Expell'd remorse[37] and nature,[38] whom, with Sebastian
(Whose inward pinches therefore[39] are most strong),
Would here have kill'd your king, I do forgive thee,
Unnatural though thou art.—Their understanding
Begins to swell, and the approaching tide
Will shortly fill the reasonable [shores][40]
That now lie foul and muddy. Not one of them
That yet looks on me, or would know me! Ariel,
Fetch me the hat and rapier in my cell.

(Exit Ariel, and returns immediately.)

I will discase me,[41] and myself present
As I was sometime Milan.[42] Quickly, spirit,
Thou shalt ere long be free.

(Ariel sings and helps to attire him.)

Ariel: Where the bee sucks, there suck I,
In a cowslip's bell I lie;
There I couch when owls do cry.

[29] **and:** i.e., which is. [30] **thy brains:** The first sentence is addressed to Alonso, the next to all six now within the circle. [31] **boil'd:** i.e., made useless by passion. [32] **sociable:** sympathetic. [33] **show:** appearance. [34] **Fall:** let fall. [35] **ignorant fumes:** fumes that make them uncomprehending. [36] **pay . . . Home:** reward your favors fully. [37] **remorse:** pity. [38] **nature:** natural feeling. [39] **therefore:** therefor, to that end. [40] **reasonable shores:** shores of reason, i.e., minds. [41] **discase me:** take off my magician's robe. [42] **As . . . Milan:** dressed as I formerly was as Duke of Milan.

On the bat's back I do fly
After summer merrily.
Merrily, merrily shall I live now,
Under the blossom that hangs on the bough.

Prospero: Why, that's my dainty Ariel! I shall miss thee,
But yet thou shalt have freedom. So, so, so.[43]
To the King's ship, invisible as thou art;
There shalt thou find the mariners asleep
Under the hatches. The master and the boatswain
Being awake, enforce them to this place;
And presently,[44] I prithee.

Ariel: I drink the air before me, and return
Or ere your pulse twice beat. *(Exit.)*

Gonzalo: All torment, trouble, wonder, and amazement
Inhabits here. Some heavenly power guide us
Out of this fearful country!

Prospero: Behold, sir King,
The wronged Duke of Milan, Prospero.
For more assurance that a living prince[45]
Does now speak to thee, I embrace thy body,
And to thee and thy company I bid
A hearty welcome.

Alonso: Whe'er thou beest he or no,
Or some enchanted trifle[46] to abuse[47] me
(As late I have been), I not know. Thy pulse
Beats as of flesh and blood; and since I saw thee,
Th' affliction of my mind amends, with which
I fear a madness held me. This must crave
(And if this be at all) a most strange story.[48]
Thy dukedom I resign, and do entreat
Thou pardon me my wrongs. But how should Prospero
Be living, and be here?

Prospero: *(To Gonzalo.)* First, noble friend,
Let me embrace thine age,[49] whose honor cannot
Be measur'd or confin'd.[50]

Gonzalo: Whether this be,
Or be not, I'll not swear.

Prospero: You do yet taste
Some subtleties[51] o' th' isle, that will [not] let you

---

[43] **So, so, so:** Probably an expression of approval as Ariel finishes attiring him. [44] **presently:** at once. [45] **a living prince:** i.e., not a spirit. [46] **enchanted trifle:** trick of magic. [47] **abuse:** deceive. [48] **This . . . story:** this demands, if it is really taking place, an extraordinary explanation. [49] **thine age:** i.e., thy reverend self. [50] **cannot . . . confin'd:** i.e., is immeasurable and boundless. [51] **subtleties:** illusions, with play (as *taste* suggests) on the word as applied to fancy confections representing actual objects or allegorical figures.

Believe things certain. Welcome, my friends all!
(Aside to Sebastian and Antonio.) But you, my brace of lords, were I so minded,
I here could pluck his Highness' frown upon you
And justify[52] you traitors. At this time
I will tell no tales.

Sebastian: *(Aside.)* The devil speaks in him.

Prospero: No.
For you, most wicked sir, whom to call brother
Would even infect my mouth, I do forgive
Thy rankest fault—all of them; and require
My dukedom of thee, which perforce, I know
Thou must restore.

Alonso: If thou beest Prospero,
Give us particulars of thy preservation,
How thou hast met us here, whom three hours since
Were wrack'd upon this shore; where I have lost
(How sharp the point of this remembrance is!)
My dear son Ferdinand.

Prospero: I am woe for't, sir.

Alonso: Irreparable is the loss, and patience
Says, it is past her cure.

Prospero: I rather think
You have not sought her help, of whose soft grace[53]
For the like loss I have her sovereign aid,
And rest myself content.

Alonso: You the like loss?

Prospero: As great to me, as late,[54] and supportable
To make the dear[55] loss, have I means much weaker
Than you may call to comfort you, for I
Have lost my daughter.

Alonso: A daughter?
O heavens, that they were living both in Naples,
The King and Queen there! That[56] they were, I wish
Myself were mudded in that oozy bed
Where my son lies. When did you lose your daughter?

Prospero: In this last tempest. I perceive these lords
At this encounter do so much admire[57]
That they devour their reason,[58] and scarce think
Their eyes do offices of truth,[59] their words

---

[52] **justify:** prove. [53] **of . . . grace:** by whose mercy. [54] **late:** recent.
[55] **dear:** deeply felt. [56] **That:** provided that. [57] **admire:** marvel.
[58] **devour their reason:** Presumably referring to the open-mouthed astonishment in which their rational powers are lost. [59] **do . . . truth:** function accurately.

Are natural breath; but howsoev'r you have
Been justled from your senses, know for certain
That I am Prospero, and that very duke
Which was thrust forth of[60] Milan, who most strangely
Upon this shore (where you were wrack'd) was landed,
To be the lord on't. No more yet of this,
For 'tis a chronicle of day by day,
Not a relation for a breakfast, nor
Befitting this first meeting. Welcome, sir;
This cell's my court. Here have I few attendants,
And subjects none abroad.[61] Pray you look in.
My dukedom since you have given me again,
I will requite you with as good a thing,
At least bring forth a wonder, to content ye
As much as me my dukedom.

(Here Prospero discovers[62] Ferdinand and Miranda playing at chess.)

Miranda: Sweet lord, you play me false.
Ferdinand: No, my dearest love,
I would not for the world.
Miranda: Yes, for a score of kingdoms you should wrangle,[63]
And I would call it fair play.
Alonso: If this prove
A vision[64] of the island, one dear son
Shall I twice lose.
Sebastian: A most high miracle!
Ferdinand: Though the seas threaten, they are merciful; I have cursed them without cause. *(Kneels.)*
Alonso: Now all the blessings
Of a glad father compass thee about!
Arise, and say how thou cam'st here.
Miranda: O wonder!
How many goodly creatures are there here!
How beauteous mankind is! O brave new world
That has such people in't!
Prospero: 'Tis new to thee.
Alonso: What is this maid with whom thou wast at play?
Your eld'st[65] acquaintance cannot be three hours.
Is she the goddess that hath sever'd us,
And brought us thus together?

---

[60] **of:** from. [61] **abroad:** i.e., elsewhere on the island. [62] s.d. **discovers:** discloses (by pulling aside a curtain). [63] **Yes . . . wrangle:** i.e., certainly you should do so for the world; in fact, for less than the world—for twenty kingdoms you ought to do your utmost against me. [64] **vision:** i.e., illusion. [65] **eld'st:** longest possible.

Ferdinand: Sir, she is mortal;
But by immortal Providence she's mine.
I chose her when I could not ask my father
For his advice, nor thought I had one. She
Is daughter to this famous Duke of Milan,
Of whom so often I have heard renown,
But never saw before; of whom I have
Receiv'd a second life; and second father
This lady makes him to me.
Alonso: I am hers.
But O, how oddly will it sound that I
Must ask my child forgiveness!
Prospero: There, sir, stop.
Let us not burthen our remembrances with
A heaviness[66] that's gone.
Gonzalo: I have inly wept,
Or should have spoke ere this. Look down, you gods,
And on this couple drop a blessed crown!
For it is you that have chalk'd forth the way
Which brought us hither.
Alonso: I say amen, Gonzalo!
Gonzalo: Was Milan thrust from Milan,[67] that his issue
Should become kings of Naples? O, rejoice
Beyond a common joy, and set it down
With gold on lasting pillars: in one voyage
Did Claribel her husband find at Tunis,
And Ferdinand, her brother, found a wife
Where he himself was lost; Prospero, his dukedom
In a poor isle; and all of us, ourselves,
When no man was his own.[68]
Alonso: *(To Ferdinand and Miranda.)* Give me your hands.
Let grief and sorrow still[69] embrace his heart
That[70] doth not wish you joy!
Gonzalo: Be it so, amen!

(Enter Ariel, with the Master and Boatswain amazedly[71] following.)

O, look, sir, look, sir, here is more of us.
I prophesied, if a gallows were on land,
This fellow could not drown. Now, blasphemy,[72]

[66] **heaviness:** grief. [67] **Milan . . . Milan:** the Duke . . . the city. [68] **all . . . own:** we all found ourselves when every man was deluded. [69] **still:** ever. [70] **his heart That:** the heart of anyone who. [71] s.d. **amazedly:** as in a maze, in bewilderment. [72] **blasphemy:** blasphemous fellow. Cf. *diligence* (= diligent creature) in paragraph 53.

That swear'st grace o'erboard,[73] not an oath on shore?
Hast thou no mouth by land? What is the news?
Boatswain: The best news is, that we have safely found
Our king and company; the next, our ship—
Which, but three glasses[74] since, we gave out[75] split—
Is tight and yare,[76] and bravely rigg'd as when
We first put out to sea.
Ariel *(Aside to Prospero.):* Sir, all this service
Have I done since I went.
Prospero *(Aside to Ariel.):* My tricksy[77] spirit!
Alonso: These are not natural events, they strengthen
From strange to stranger.[78] Say, how came you hither?
Boatswain: If I did think, sir, I were well awake,
I'ld strive to tell you. We were dead of sleep,[79]
And (how we know not) all clapp'd under hatches,
Where, but even now, with strange and several noises
Of roaring, shrieking, howling, jingling chains,
And moe[80] diversity of sounds, all horrible,
We were awak'd; straightway, at liberty;[81]
Where we, in all our trim, freshly beheld
Our royal, good, and gallant ship; our master
Cap'ring to eye her. On[82] a trice, so please you,
Even in a dream, were we divided from them,
And were brought moping[83] hither.
Ariel *(Aside to Prospero.):* Was't well done?
Prospero *(Aside to Ariel.):* Bravely, my diligence.
Thou shalt be free.
Alonso: This is as strange a maze as e'er men trod,
And there is in this business more than nature
Was ever conduct[84] of. Some oracle
Must rectify our knowledge.
Prospero: Sir, my liege,[85]
Do not infest[86] your mind with beating on
The strangeness of this business. At pick'd[87] leisure,
Which shall be shortly, single[88] I'll resolve you,
(Which to you shall seem probable)[89] of every
These happen'd accidents;[90] till when, be cheerful

[73] **That . . . o'erboard:** who are profane enough to make heavenly grace forsake the ship. [74] **glasses:** i.e., hours. [75] **gave out:** reported. [76] **yare:** shipshape. [77] **tricksy:** ingenious, adroit. [78] **strengthen . . . stranger:** increase in strangeness. [79] **of sleep:** asleep. [80] **moe:** more. [81] **at liberty:** i.e., no longer under hatches. [82] **On:** in. [83] **moping:** in a daze. [84] **conduct:** conductor. [85] **liege:** sovereign. [86] **infest:** annoy. [87] **pick'd:** i.e., convenient. [88] **single:** by myself (without an oracle). [89] **probable:** satisfactory. [90] **accidents:** occurrences.

And think of each thing well. *(Aside to Ariel.)* Come hither, spirit.
Set Caliban and his companions free;
Untie the spell. *(Exit Ariel.)* How fares my gracious sir?
There are yet missing of your company
Some few odd[91] lads that you remember not.

(Enter Ariel, driving in Caliban, Stephano, and Trinculo in their stol'n apparel.)

Stephano: Every man shift for all the rest,[92] and let no man take care of himself; for all is but fortune. *Coraggio,*[93] bully-monster, *coraggio!*

Trinculo: If these be true spies[94] which I wear in my head, here's a goodly sight.

Caliban: O Setebos, these be brave spirits indeed!
How fine[95] my master is! I am afraid
He will chastise me.

Sebastian: Ha, ha!
What things are these, my Lord Antonio?
Will money buy 'em?

Antonio: Very like; one of them
Is a plain fish, and no doubt marketable.

Prospero: Mark but the badges[96] of these men, my lords,
Then say if they be true.[97] This misshapen knave—
His mother was a witch, and one so strong
That could control the moon, make flows and ebbs,
And deal in her command[98] without her power.[99]
These three have robb'd me, and this demi-devil
(For he's a bastard one) had plotted with them
To take my life. Two of these fellows you
Must know and own, this thing of darkness I
Acknowledge mine.

Caliban: I shall be pinch'd to death.

Alonso: Is not this Stephano, my drunken butler?

Sebastian: He is drunk now. Where had he wine?

Alonso: And Trinculo is reeling-ripe. Where should they
Find this grand liquor that hath gilded 'em?[100]
How cam'st thou in this pickle?[101]

---

[91] **odd:** unaccounted for. [92] **Every . . . rest:** Stephano drunkenly inverts the proverbial "Every man for himself." [93] **Coraggio:** courage (Italian). [94] **true spies:** reliable observers (eyes). [95] **fine:** splendidly dressed (in his ducal robes). [96] **badges:** insignia for servants, indicating what master they served. Stephano and Trinculo are of course dressed in stolen garments. [97] **true:** honest. [98] **her command:** i.e., the moon's authority. [99] **without her power:** beyond the moon's influence. [100] **gilded 'em:** flushed their faces (a common connection between blood and gold). Possibly *grand liquor* contains an alchemical allusion to the long-sought elixir that could transform base substances to gold. [101] **pickle:** predicament.

Trinculo: I have been in such a pickle[102] since I saw you last that I fear me will never out of my bones. I shall not fear fly-blowing.[103]
Sebastian: Why, how now, Stephano?
Stephano: O, touch me not, I am not Stephano, but a cramp.
Prospero: You'd be king o' the isle, sirrah?[104]
Stephano: I should have been a sore[105] one then.
Alonso: This is a strange thing as e'er I look'd on.

(Pointing to Caliban.)

Prospero: He is as disproportion'd in his manners
As in his shape. Go, sirrah, to my cell;
Take with you your companions. As you look
To have my pardon, trim it handsomely.
Caliban: Ay, that I will; and I'll be wise hereafter,
And seek for grace. What a thrice-double ass
Was I to take this drunkard for a god,
And worship this dull fool!
Prospero: Go to, away!
Alonso: Hence, and bestow your luggage where you found it.
Sebastian: Or stole it, rather.

(Exeunt Caliban, Stephano, and Trinculo.)

Prospero: Sir, I invite your Highness and your train
To my poor cell, where you shall take your rest
For this one night; which part of it, I'll waste[106]
With such discourse as, I not doubt, shall make it
Go quick away—the story of my life,
And the particular accidents gone by
Since I came to this isle. And in the morn
I'll bring you to your ship, and so to Naples,
Where I have hope to see the nuptial
Of these our dear-belov'd solemnized,
And thence retire me to my Milan, where
Every third thought shall be my grave.
Alonso: I long
To hear the story of your life, which must
Take[107] the ear strangely.
Prospero: I'll deliver[108] all,
And promise you calm seas, auspicious gales,
And sail[109] so expeditious, that shall catch

[102] **pickle:** preservative (the horse urine of the pool being equivalent to vinegar).
[103] **fly-blowing:** infestation by maggots (to which unpickled meat would be subject).
[104] **sirrah:** form of address to an inferior. [105] **sore:** (1) harsh; (2) pain-wracked.
[106] **waste:** use up. [107] **Take:** enchant. [108] **deliver:** report. [109] **sail:** voyage.

Your royal fleet far off. *(Aside to Ariel.)* My Ariel, chick,
That is thy charge. Then to the elements
Be free, and fare thou well!—Please you draw near.[110]

(Exeunt omnes.)

Epilogue

(Spoken by Prospero.)

Now my charms are all o'erthrown,
And what strength I have's mine own,
Which is most faint. Now 'tis true,
I must be here confin'd by you,
Or sent to Naples. Let me not,
Since I have my dukedom got,
And pardon'd the deceiver, dwell
In this bare island by your spell,
But release me from my bands[1]
With the help of your good hands.[2]
Gentle breath[3] of yours my sails
Must fill, or else my project fails,
Which was to please. Now I want[4]
Spirits to enforce, art to enchant,
And my ending is despair,
Unless I be reliev'd by prayer,[5]
Which pierces so, that it assaults[6]
Mercy itself, and frees[7] all faults.
As you from crimes[8] would pardon'd be,
Let your indulgence set me free. *(Exit.)*

Explorations of the Text

Act I

1. Look closely at Act I, Scene ii, paragraphs 29–70. How do Prospero's revelations to Miranda serve to set up the story and to help you understand what is at stake in terms of the conflicts and human relationships?
2. Ariel enters the play at Act I, Scene ii, paragraph 71, speaking the lines, "All hail, great master, grave sir, hail. I come/To answer thy pleasure. . . ." What qualities of Prospero and Ariel emerge in this exchange?

[110] **draw near:** i.e., enter the cell.
[1] **bands:** bonds. [2] **hands:** i.e., applause. The noise of clapping would break the charm. [3] **Gentle breath:** a favorable breeze (produced by hands clapping). [4] **want:** lack. [5] **prayer:** i.e., this petition. [6] **assaults:** storms the ear of. [7] **frees:** remits. [8] **crimes:** sins.

3. Caliban is introduced immediately after Ariel is. How would you characterize Caliban?
4. Why did Prospero lose his dukedom? Was he merely a victim of political intrigue or is the problem more complex?

Act II

1. Look closely at Gonzalo's speech in Act II, Scene i, paragraphs 89–110. What is revealed about him in this scene? What is your overall assessment of his character as a whole?
2. "What's past is prologue. . . ." (Act II, Scene i, paragraph 37). How does the quotation by Antonio reveal past events and possibly foreshadow forthcoming ones?
3. What do you think the dramatic or thematic value might be of showing Antonio and Sebastian's attempt on the life of Alonso?
4. In Act II, Scene ii, Caliban expresses his great eagerness to join with Trinculo and Stefano. How do you react to his decision to band together with them? Is there a political or cultural subtext at work here?

Act III

1. What is your assessment of the relationship between Miranda and Ferdinand in Act III, Scene i? How are we to take this part of the story?
2. How does Ariel serve as Prospero's agent in Act III, Scene iii? Are we to understand Ariel in terms of some larger purpose or principle here?

Act IV

1. Act IV, Scene i contains a spectacle, called a masque, in which the figures of Iris, Ceres, and Juno appear. What seems to be their purpose at this particular stage in the story?
2. When Prospero hears more of the plot against his life, he calls Caliban "a devil, a born devil, on whose nature/Nurture can never stick" (Act IV, Scene i, paragraph 161). How does the age-old human problem of environment versus psychology apply to Caliban?

Act V

1. Now that you've read the ending, would you classify the work as a tragedy or as a comedy? Why?
2. Prospero claims in Act V, Scene i, paragraph 61, that he acknowledges Caliban, "this thing of darkness," as his own. What do you think these lines are intended to mean? Why?
3. What do you expect will happen to these main characters after they leave the island?

General Discussion Questions

1. Analyze Prospero's relationship with his daughter, Miranda. What are the essential qualities of this father-daughter dynamic?
2. What do you think is gained by setting this story on an island? What does the island symbolize?
3. Critics over the years have been sharply divided on the character of Prospero. To some, he is a benevolent magician who makes everything work out, creating good out of evil, amity out of discord, harmony out of disharmony. To others, however, he is anything but benevolent—an irresponsible, manipulative, and oppressive tyrant. What is your view? What textual evidence supports your view?
4. How do Stefano and Trinculo contribute to the action, the themes, or meanings of *The Tempest?*
5. How important is the promised marriage of Miranda and Ferdinand? How does it fit into or connect to other parts of the play? What might it say about noble marriages in the age of Shakespeare—or in our own, for that matter? In what ways does the love affair between Miranda and Ferdinand differ from our modern notions of romance?
6. Discuss Prospero's view of life. Is it optimistic? pessimistic? Discuss this question with reference to his utterances in the play.

The Reading/Writing Connection

1. Imagine a meeting between Ariel and Caliban one morning to discuss their master Prospero. Write a short scene of this encounter.
2. Miranda at age fourteen writes a message to the outside world of passing mariners asking for help for her father and herself. In a journal entry compose Miranda's message.
3. Prepare a secret journal entry of Prospero's in which he raises suspicion about his brother's growing power in the administration of the dukedom and his own secret pursuits and studies.
4. Magic abounds in the play. If you were a movie director getting ready to create a movie based upon *The Tempest,* what additional stage directions would you prepare for the scripted scenes of the play to take advantage of cinematic approaches?
5. "Think" Topic: The four elements—air, fire, earth, and water—are referred to in the play. Which ones are associated with Ariel? with Caliban? Isolate one excerpt from the drama in which either Ariel or Caliban is portrayed through these elements and do a double-entry notebook response to the passage; then create a paragraph based upon your entry. How do the image patterns of develop the portrayal of the character?

6. Imagine a conversation between Prospero and one of the speakers in Szymborska's poems. Would they agree on the state of their worlds? the possibility of creating harmony in society?

Ideas for Writing

1. Create a feminist interpretation of Miranda's character.
2. The play was written during the early years of the European exploration of the New World. Does the play critique colonialism?
3. Discuss the clash between the old and the new worlds presented in the drama and in Gloria Anzaldúa's poem, "The Borderlands."
4. Discuss how Shakespeare developed the theme of servitude versus freedom.
5. What follows are several questions and responses that were part of an online dialogue about the play in Professor Thomas Olsen's Shakespeare class at the State University of New York New Paltz. Add your voice to this exchange of ideas.

TOP | Post | Reply | Reply/Quote | Email Reply | Delete | Edit | Move
Previous | Next | Previous Tool | Next Topic | Entire Topic

Topic: Discussion/Guidance Question 1 (1 of 12), Read 74 times
Conf: Unit 6: THE TEMPEST
From: Thomas Olsen
Date: Monday, July 03, 2000 02:53 PM

Discussion/Guidance Question 1
This play has a remarkable simplicity to it: it takes place in under one day, in one isolated location, with a fairly reduced cast (especially compared to earlier works such as, let us say, "Richard III"), and it concerns basically one action. What do you see as the principal action of The Tempest? Why do you say so? What key events make up this one central action?

TGO

TOP | Post | Reply | Reply/Quote | Email Reply | Delete | Edit | Move
Previous | Next | Previous Tool | Next Topic | Entire Topic

Topic: Discussion/Guidance Question 1 (2 of 12), Read 73 times
Conf: Unit 6: THE TEMPEST
From: Carly Klein
Date: Wednesday, July 05, 2000 12:16 AM

I didn't think that the play had much of a plot. There was the Miranda-Ferdinand love story and the possible assassinations of Prospero and Alonso, but these plots aren't really developed. The one thing that unifies the play, at least for me, was the way that all of the conspiracies reflected one another. Originally, Prospero is deposed by Antonio; that is why Prospero is living in banishment. Once the others land on the island, the original crime is re-enacted twice. The first instance is when Antonio suggests murdering Alonso so that Sebastian can gain the kingship. Shortly after, Caliban suggests killing Prospero so that he, Stephano and Trinculo can rule the island. These conspiracies are all resolved in the final scene by Prospero; they just seem to give a unifying feeling to the play.

TOP |Post | Reply | Reply/Quote |Email Reply | Delete | Edit | Move
Previous | Next | Previous Tool | Next Topic | Entire Topic

Topic: Discussion/Guidance Question 1 (3 of 12), Read 78 times
Conf: Unit 6: THE TEMPEST
From: Thomas Olsen
Date: Wednesday, July 05, 2000 07:33 AM

That is an excellent comment, Carly. What would you say, then, is the main action of this play? Where does it all come together in terms of the basics of plot conflict and plot resolution?

TOP |Post | Reply | Reply/Quote |Email Reply | Delete | Edit | Move
Previous | Next | Previous Tool | Next Topic | Entire Topic

Topic: Discussion/Guidance Question 1 (4 of 12), Read 68 times
Conf: Unit 6: THE TEMPEST
From: Alisa Liuni
Date: Wednesday, July 05, 2000 04:58 PM

I think the one principle action of "The Tempest" is for Prospero to regain his dukedom from Antonio. I think this is the main focus of the play and the other conflicts and love interests result because of this. There is one key event that occurs to make all of this possible. If it weren't for the big storm, Antonio and the other men wouldn't have become stranded on this island to find Prospero and Miranda, and Prospero wouldn't have been give the opportunity to reclaim what is rightfully his. If it weren't for the storm, none of the other events would have been possible.

TOP |Post | Reply | Reply/Quote |Email Reply | Delete | Edit | Move
Previous | Next | Previous Tool | Next Topic | Entire Topic

Topic: Discussion/Guidance Question 1 (5 of 12), Read 69 times
Conf: Unit 6: THE TEMPEST
From: Patricia Norden
Date: Wednesday, July 05, 2000 06:35 PM

I agree, the central action revolves around Prospero's struggle to usurp control of this former kingdom from his brother, but I think that the storm only acts as a unifying element on a symbolic level. The conflict is definitely symbolized by the storm, but it falls short because it is never fully carried out unless you consider Iris, the goddess of the Rainbow who appears at the end of the play, to be a part of the symbolism. Although the events that occur on the island are a result of the storm, the storm was simply a part of Prospero's master plan. In 1.2, Prospero assures Miranda that he had nothing to do with the storm, but after she leaves he asks Ariel, "Hast thou, spirit, performed to point the tempest that I bade thee?" From this point on the action is continually manipulated by Prospero until the conflict is resolved and he achieves his desired result—namely the return of his dukedom, a request for forgiveness from Alonso, and the political romantic alliance between his daughter and Ferdinand.

TOP | Post | Reply | Reply/Quote | Email Reply | Delete | Edit | Move
Previous | Next | Previous Tool | Next Topic | Entire Topic

Topic: Discussion/Guidance Question 1 (7 of 12), Read 69 times
Conf: Unit 6: THE TEMPEST
From: Thomas Olsen
Date: Wednesday, July 05, 2000 10:18 PM

These are all great comments, everyone. I would underscore the "forgiveness" theme . . . this is a play in which Prospero is allowed a kind of simple Christian forgiveness. Is there some biblical story (or stories) lurking behind this tale? Anyone apply a biblical parallel or parallels?

TOP | Post | Reply | Reply/Quote | Email Reply | Delete | Edit | Move
Previous | Next | Previous Tool | Next Topic | Entire Topic

Topic: Discussion/Guidance Question 1 (9 of 12), Read 21 times
Conf: Unit 6: THE TEMPEST
From: Emily Margolis
Date: Monday, July 10, 2000 12:25 PM

As to a biblical parallel, I was thinking along the lines of the Prodigal Son. Even though "The Tempest" involves brothers rather than father and son, the element of forgiveness is still rather pervasive and the stories bear some similarities. Also, it is interesting that in the biblical story, the son returns home to the father. In "The Tempest," however, Prospero brings Alonso and (more importantly) Antonio to him. This seems to be the central action of the play from my view—the Miranda/Ferdinand love story is peripheral.

TOP | Post | Reply | Reply/Quote | Email Reply | Delete | Edit | Move
Previous | Next | Previous Tool | Next Topic | Entire Topic

Topic: Discussion/Guidance Question 1 (10 of 12), Read 17 times
Conf: Unit 6: THE TEMPEST
From: Thomas Olsen
Date: Monday, July 10, 2000 11:19 PM

The Prodigal Son story does seem to fit, but what about Cain and Abel? What begins the action is fratricide—as old as Genesis.

TGO

TOP | Post | Reply | Reply/Quote | Email Reply | Delete | Edit | Move
Previous | Next | Previous Tool | Next Topic | Entire Topic

Topic: Discussion/Guidance Question 1 (11 of 12), Read 12 times
Conf: Unit 6: THE TEMPEST
From: Gail Sprague
Date: Wednesday, July 12, 2000 02:03 AM

I believe that the principal action of the play is the atonement of sin. Prospero, through the use of magic, creates a storm, and whisks the royal entourage off the ship to the island. He then sets in motion the atonement, using Ariel and magic to manipulate the others, forcing them to come to terms with their past behaviors. The brothers and the King of Naples are then reconciled. Prospero is restored to the ducal court, and Miranda is to marry Ferdinand.

TOP | Post | Reply | Reply/Quote | Email Reply | Delete | Edit | Move
Previous | Next | Previous Tool | Next Topic | Entire Topic

Topic: Discussion/Guidance Question 1 (12 of 12), Read 8 times
Conf: Unit 6: THE TEMPEST
From: Kendra Fagan
Date: Wednesday, July 12, 2000 11:29 PM

I do not know of any biblical parallels to incorporate into the play's story line. I do think, as do my classmates, that the main action in the play is for Prospero to regain power. His attempt to regain power is so important that he will do it by any means necessary. Creating the storm and setting up Ferdinand and Miranda for marriage are perfect examples of how he would do anything he possibly could to regain his power and titles. If he did not want to get revenge on his brother, or if he didn't care about his dukedom then he would not have bothered marrying his daughter off to Ferdinand nor would he have shipwrecked all of those men onto the island.

Research Projects

1. Read Montaigne's essay, "Of the Cannibals" (which Shakespeare allegedly read before he wrote *The Tempest*). What did Shakespeare borrow from Montaigne?
2. Read about the shipwreck that occurred in 1609 near what is presently called Bermuda from William Strachey's *True Repertory of the Wreck*. How did Shakespeare use this information?
3. According to Harold Bloom, the noted Shakespearean scholar, the name Prospero is the Italian name for Faustus. Marlowe's *Dr. Faustus* was played prior to the writing of *The Tempest.* Read the Marlowe play and compare Prospero with Dr. Faustus.
4. There is much music in the play. A research project might develop suitable musical selections (classical and modern) to use at intervals of the

drama. Several scenes—with music—could be dramatically presented to the class.

5. Traditionally critics have viewed this play as Shakespeare's farewell to the theater. Research the biographical and textual information that would lead one to form this opinion.
6. Watch the BBC version of *The Tempest,* produced by Cedric Messina (1979). How does the movie's interpretation differ from your reading of the play? Or look at one of the adaptations of the play: Aime´ Ce´saire's *A Tempest* (New York: Ubu Repertory Theater, 1992); Paul Mazursky's *Tempest* (1982); or *Forbidden Planet,* directed by Fred McLeod Wilcox (1956). How does one of these versions differ from your interpretation of the play?
7. Does the play critique colonialism? Is Caliban African American? Examine the research and create a debate for the class.

NONFICTION

Reflections on Exile

Edward Said

Edward Said (1935–), born in Jerusalem, is a professor of English and comparative literature at Columbia University. In 1966, he published a critical biography, Joseph Conrad and the Fiction of Autobiography. *His other works include the influential* Orientalism *(1979) and* Culture and Imperialism *(1993). Said, a past president of the Modern Language Association, has published a memoir,* Out of Place *(1999).*

1984

Exile is strangely compelling to think about but terrible to experience. It is the unhealable rift forced between a human being and a native place, between the self and its true home: its essential sadness can never be surmounted. And while it is true that literature and history contain heroic, romantic, glorious, even triumphant episodes in an exile's life, these are no more than efforts meant to overcome the crippling sorrow of estrangement. The achievements of exile are permanently undermined by the loss of something left behind for ever.

But if true exile is a condition of terminal loss, why has it been transformed so easily into a potent, even enriching, motif of modern culture? We have become accustomed to thinking of the modern period itself as spiritually orphaned and alienated, the age of anxiety and estrangement. Nietzsche taught us to feel uncomfortable with tradition, and Freud to regard domestic intimacy as the polite face painted on patricidal and incestuous rage. Modern Western culture is in large part the work of exiles, émigrés, refugees. In the United States, academic, intellectual and aesthetic thought is what it is today because of refugees from fascism, communism and other regimes given to the oppression and expulsion of dissidents. The critic George Steiner has even proposed the perceptive thesis that a whole genre of twentieth-century Western literature is "extraterritorial," a literature by and about exiles, symbolizing the age of the refugee. Thus Steiner suggests

> *It seems proper that those who create art in a civilization of quasi-barbarism, which has made so many homeless, should themselves be poets unhoused and wanderers across language. Eccentric, aloof, nostalgic, deliberately untimely . . .*

In other ages, exiles had similar cross-cultural and transnational visions, suffered the same frustrations and miseries, performed the same elucidating and critical tasks—brilliantly affirmed, for instance, in E. H. Carr's classic study of the nineteenth-century Russian intellectuals clustered around Herzen,

The Romantic Exiles. But the difference between earlier exiles and those of our own time is, it bears stressing, scale: our age—with its modern warfare, imperialism and the quasi-theological ambitions of totalitarian rulers—is indeed the age of the refugee, the displaced person, mass immigration.

Against this large, impersonal setting, exile cannot be made to serve notions of humanism. On the twentieth-century scale, exile is neither aesthetically nor humanistically comprehensible: at most the literature about exile objectifies an anguish and a predicament most people rarely experience at first hand; but to think of the exile informing this literature as beneficially humanistic is to banalize its mutilations, the losses it inflicts on those who suffer them, the muteness with which it responds to any attempt to understand it as "good for us." Is it not true that the views of exile in literature and, moreover, in religion obscure what is truly horrendous: that exile is irremediably secular and unbearably historical; that it is produced by human beings for other human beings; and that, like death but without death's ultimate mercy, it has torn millions of people from the nourishment of tradition, family and geography?

* * *

5 To see a poet in exile—as opposed to reading the poetry of exile—is to see exile's antinomies embodied and endured with a unique intensity. Several years ago I spent some time with Faiz Ahmad Faiz, the greatest of contemporary Urdu[1] poets. He was exiled from his native Pakistan[2] by Zia's military regime, and found a welcome of sorts in strife-torn Beirut.[3] Naturally his closest friends were Palestinian, but I sensed that, although there was an affinity of spirit between them, nothing quite matched—language, poetic convention, or life-history. Only once, when Eqbal Ahmad, a Pakistani friend and a fellow-exile, came to Beirut, did Faiz seem to overcome his sense of constant estrangement. The three of us sat in a dingy Beirut restaurant late one night, while Faiz recited poems. After a time, he and Eqbal stopped translating his verses for my benefit, but as the night wore on it did not matter. What I watched required no translation: it was an enactment of a homecoming expressed through defiance and loss, as if to say, "Zia, we are here." Of course Zia was the one who was really at home and who would not hear their exultant voices.

Rashid Hussein was a Palestinian. He translated Bialik, one of the great modern Hebrew poets, into Arabic, and Hussein's eloquence established him in the post-1948 period as an orator and nationalist without peer. He first worked as a Hebrew language journalist in Tel Aviv, and succeeded in establishing a dialogue between Jewish and Arab writers, even as he espoused the cause of Nasserism[4] and Arab nationalism. In time, he could no longer endure the pressure, and he left for New York. He married a Jewish woman, and began

---

[1] Official language of Pakistan; language used by Muslims in India.

[2] Country in Southern Asia.

[3] City and port of Lebanon.

[4] Gamal Nasser (1918–70), president of Egypt 1956–70.

working in the PLO office at the United Nations, but regularly outraged his superiors with unconventional ideas and utopian rhetoric. In 1972 he left for the Arab world, but a few months later he was back in the United States: he had felt out of place in Syria and Lebanon, unhappy in Cairo. New York sheltered him anew, but so did endless bouts of drinking and idleness. His life was in ruins, but he remained the most hospitable of men. He died after a night of heavy drinking when, smoking in bed, his cigarette started a fire that spread to a small library of audio cassettes, consisting mostly of poets reading their verse. The fumes from the tapes asphyxiated him. His body was repatriated for burial in Musmus, the small village in Israel where his family still resided.

These and so many other exiled poets and writers lend dignity to a condition legislated to deny dignity—to deny an identity to people. From them, it is apparent that, to concentrate on exile as a contemporary political punishment, you must therefore map territories of experience beyond those mapped by the literature of exile itself. You must first set aside Joyce and Nabokov[5] and think instead of the uncountable masses for whom UN agencies have been created. You must think of the refugee-peasants with no prospect of ever returning home, armed only with a ration card and an agency number. Paris may be a capital famous for cosmopolitan exiles, but it is also a city where unknown men and women have spent years of miserable loneliness: Vietnamese, Algerians, Cambodians, Lebanese, Senegalese, Peruvians. You must think also of Cairo, Beirut, Madagascar, Bangkok, Mexico City. As you move further from the Atlantic world, the awful forlorn waste increases: the hopelessly large numbers, the compounded misery of "undocumented" people suddenly lost, without a tellable history. To reflect on exiled Muslims from India, or Haitians in America, or Bikinians in Oceania, or Palestinians throughout the Arab world means that you must leave the modest refuge provided by subjectivity and resort instead to the abstractions of mass politics. Negotiations, wars of national liberation, people bundled out of their homes and prodded, bussed or walked to enclaves in other regions: what do these experiences add up to? Are they not manifestly and almost by design irrecoverable?

❄ ❄ ❄

We come to nationalism and its essential association with exile. Nationalism is an assertion of belonging in and to a place, a people, a heritage. It affirms the home created by a community of language, culture and customs; and, by so doing, it fends off exile, fights to prevent its ravages. Indeed, the interplay between nationalism and exile is like Hegel's[6] dialectic of servant and master, opposites informing and constituting each other. All nationalisms in their early stages develop from a condition of estrangement. The struggles to win American independence, to unify Germany or Italy, to liberate Algeria were those of national groups separated—exiled—from what was construed to be

---

[5] James Joyce, twentieth-century English novelist (1882–1941). See chapter 6. Vladimir Nabokov, Russian novelist and poet who spent most of his life in the United States (1899–1977).

[6] German philosopher (1770–1831).

their rightful way of life. Triumphant, achieved nationalism then justifies, retrospectively as well as prospectively, a history selectively strung together in a narrative form: thus all nationalisms have their founding fathers, their basic, quasi-religious texts, their rhetoric of belonging, their historical and geographical landmarks, their official enemies and heroes. This collective ethos forms what Pierre Bourdieu, the French sociologist, calls the *habitus,* the coherent amalgam of practices linking habit with inhabitance. In time, successful nationalisms consign truth exclusively to themselves and relegate falsehood and inferiority to outsiders (as in the rhetoric of capitalist versus communist, or the European versus the Asiatic).

And just beyond the frontier between "us" and the "outsiders" is the perilous territory of not-belonging: this is to where in a primitive time peoples were banished, and where in the modern era immense aggregates of humanity loiter as refugees and displaced persons.

10 Nationalisms are about groups, but in a very acute sense exile is a solitude experienced outside the group: the deprivations felt at not being with others in the communal habitation. How, then, does one surmount the loneliness of exile without falling into the encompassing and thumping language of national pride, collective sentiments, group passions? What is there worth saving and holding on to between the extremes of exile on the one hand, and the often bloody-minded affirmations of nationalism on the other? Do nationalism and exile have any intrinsic attributes? Are they simply two conflicting varieties of paranoia?

These are questions that cannot ever be fully answered because each assumes that exile and nationalism can be discussed neutrally, without reference to each other. They cannot be. Because both terms include everything from the most collective of collective sentiments to the most private of private emotions, there is hardly language adequate for both. But there is certainly nothing about nationalism's public and all-inclusive ambitions that touches the core of the exile's predicament.

Because exile, unlike nationalism, is fundamentally a discontinuous state of being. Exiles are cut off from their roots, their land, their past. They generally do not have armies or states, although they are often in search of them. Exiles feel, therefore, an urgent need to reconstitute their broken lives, usually by choosing to see themselves as part of a triumphant ideology or a restored people. The crucial thing is that a state of exile free from this triumphant ideology—designed to reassemble an exile's broken history into a new whole—is virtually unbearable, and virtually impossible in today's world. Look at the fate of the Jews, the Palestinians and the Armenians.

* * *

Noubar is a solitary Armenian, and a friend. His parents had to leave Eastern Turkey in 1915, after their families were massacred: his maternal grandfather was beheaded. Noubar's mother and father went to Aleppo,[7] then to Cairo. In the middle-sixties, life in Egypt became difficult for non-Egyptians, and his

[7] City of northwest Syria near the Turkish border.

parents, along with four children, were taken to Beirut by an international relief organization. In Beirut, they lived briefly in a pension and then were bundled into two rooms of a little house outside the city. In Lebanon, they had no money and they waited: eight months later, a relief agency got them a flight to Glasgow.[8] And then to Gander.[9] And then to New York. They rode by Greyhound bus from New York to Seattle: Seattle was the city designated by the agency for their American residence. When I asked: "Seattle?," Noubar smiled resignedly, as if to say better Seattle than Armenia—which he never knew, or Turkey where so many were slaughtered, or Lebanon where he and his family would certainly have risked their lives. Exile is sometimes better than staying behind or not getting out: but only sometimes.

Because *nothing* is secure. Exile is a jealous state. What you achieve is precisely what you have no wish to share, and it is in the drawing of lines around you and your compatriots that the least attractive aspects of being in exile emerge: an exaggerated sense of group solidarity, and a passionate hostility to outsiders, even those who may in fact be in the same predicament as you. What could be more intransigent than the conflict between Zionist Jews and Arab Palestinians? Palestinians feel that they have been turned into exiles by the proverbial people of exile, the Jews. But the Palestinians also know that their own sense of national identity has been nourished in the exile milieu, where everyone not a blood-brother or sister is an enemy, where every sympathizer is an agent of some unfriendly power, and where the slightest deviation from the accepted group line is an act of the rankest treachery and disloyalty.

15 Perhaps this is the most extraordinary of exile's fates: to have been exiled by exiles: to relive the actual process of up-rooting at the hands of exiles. All Palestinians during the summer of 1982 asked themselves what inarticulate urge drove Israel, having displaced Palestinians in 1948, to expel them continuously from their refugee homes and camps in Lebanon. It is as if the reconstructed Jewish collective experience, as represented by Israel and modern Zionism,[10] could not tolerate another story of dispossession and loss to exist alongside it—an intolerance constantly reinforced by the Israeli hostility to the nationalism of the Palestinians, who for forty-six years have been painfully reassembling a national identity in exile.

This need to reassemble an identity out of the refractions and discontinuities of exile is found in the earlier poems of Mahmud Darwish, whose considerable work amounts to an epic effort to transform the lyrics of loss into the indefinitely postponed drama of return. Thus he depicts his sense of homelessness in the form of a list of unfinished and incomplete things:

> But I am the exile.
> Seal me with your eyes.

---

[8] City in Scotland.

[9] Town in northeast Newfoundland.

[10] International movement for the establishment and continued support of the State of Israel.

Take me wherever you are—
Take me whatever you are.
Restore to me the color of face
And the warmth of body
The light of heart and eye,
The salt of bread and rhythm,
The taste of earth . . . the Motherland.
Shield me with your eyes.
Take me as a relic from the mansion of sorrow.
Take me as a verse from my tragedy;
Take me as a toy, a brick from the house
So that our children will remember to return.

The pathos of exile is in the loss of contact with the solidity and the satisfaction of earth: homecoming is out of the question.

Joseph Conrad's[11] tale "Amy Foster" is perhaps the most uncompromising representation of exile ever written. Conrad thought of himself as an exile from Poland, and nearly all his work (as well as his life) carries the unmistakable mark of the sensitive émigré's obsession with his own fate and with his hopeless attempts to make satisfying contact with new surroundings. "Amy Foster" is in a sense confined to the problems of exile, perhaps so confined that it is not one of Conrad's best-known stories. This, for example, is the description of the agony of its central character, Yanko Goorall, an Eastern European peasant who, en route to America, is shipwrecked off the British coast:

> *It is indeed hard upon a man to find himself a lost stranger helpless, incomprehensible, and of a mysterious origin, in some obscure corner of the earth. Yet amongst all the adventurers shipwrecked in all the wild parts of the world, there is not one, it seems to me, that ever had to suffer a fate so simply tragic as the man I am speaking of, the most innocent of adventurers cast out by the sea. . . .*

Yanko has left home because the pressures were too great for him to go on living there. America lures him with its promise, though England is where he ends up. He endures in England, where he cannot speak the language and is feared and misunderstood. Only Amy Foster, a plodding, unattractive peasant girl, tries to communicate with him. They marry, have a child, but when Yanko falls ill, Amy, afraid and alienated, refuses to nurse him; snatching their child, she leaves. The desertion hastens Yanko's miserable death, which like the deaths of several Conradian heroes is depicted as the result of a combination of crushing isolation and the world's indifference. Yanko's fate is described as "the supreme disaster of loneliness and despair."

20 Yanko's predicament is affecting: a foreigner perpetually haunted and alone in an uncomprehending society. But Conrad's own exile causes him to

[11] Novelist, born in Ukraine of Polish parents, who wrote primarily in English (1857–1924).

exaggerate the differences between Yanko and Amy. Yanko is dashing, light and bright-eyed, whereas Amy is heavy, dull, bovine; when he dies, it is as if her earlier kindness to him was a snare to lure and then trap him fatally. Yanko's death is romantic: the world is coarse, unappreciative; no one understands him, not even Amy, the one person close to him. Conrad took this neurotic exile's fear and created an aesthetic principle out of it. No one can understand or communicate in Conrad's world, but paradoxically this radical limitation on the possibilities of language doesn't inhibit elaborate efforts to communicate. All of Conrad's stories are about lonely people who talk a great deal (for indeed who of the great modernists was more voluble and "adjectival" than Conrad himself?) and whose attempts to *impress* others compound, rather than reduce, the original sense of isolation. Each Conradian exile fears, and is condemned endlessly to imagine, the spectacle of a solitary death illuminated, so to speak, by unresponsive, uncommunicating eyes.

Exiles look at non-exiles with resentment. *They* belong in their surroundings, you feel, whereas an exile is always out of place. What is it like to be born in a place, to stay and live there, to know that you are of it, more or less for ever?

❄ ❄ ❄

Although it is true that anyone prevented from returning home is an exile, some distinctions can be made between exiles, refugees, expatriates and émigrés. Exile originated in the age-old practice of banishment. Once banished, the exile lives an anomalous and miserable life, with the stigma of being an outsider. Refugees, on the other hand, are a creation of the twentieth-century state. The word "refugee" has become a political one, suggesting large herds of innocents and bewildered people requiring urgent international assistance, whereas "exile" carries with it, I think, a touch of solitude and spirituality.

Expatriates voluntarily live in an alien country, usually for personal or social reasons. Hemingway and Fitzgerald[12] were not forced to live in France. Expatriates may share in the solitude and estrangement of exile, but they do not suffer under its rigid proscriptions. Émigrés enjoy an ambiguous status. Technically, an émigré is anyone who emigrates to a new country. Choice in the matter is certainly a possibility. Colonial officials, missionaries, technical experts, mercenaries and military advisers on loan may in a sense live in exile, but they have not been banished. White settlers in Africa, parts of Asia and Australia may once have been exiles, but as pioneers and nation-builders the label "exile" dropped away from them.

Much of the exile's life is taken up with compensating for disorienting loss by creating a new world to rule. It is not surprising that so many exiles seem to be novelists, chess players, political activists, and intellectuals. Each of these occupations requires a minimal investment in objects and places a

[12] Ernest Hemingway, North American novelist and fiction writer (1899–1961). See chapter 6. Francis Scott Key Fitzgerald, North American fiction writer and novelist (1896–1940).

great premium on mobility and skill. The exile's new world, logically enough, is unnatural and its unreality resembles fiction. Georg Lukács, in *Theory of the Novel,* argued with compelling force that the novel, a literary form created out of the unreality of ambition and fantasy, is *the* form of "transcendental homelessness." Classical epics, Lukács wrote, emanate from settled cultures in which values are clear, identities stable, life unchanging. The European novel is grounded in precisely the opposite experience, that of a changing society in which an itinerant and disinherited middle-class hero or heroine seeks to construct a new world that somewhat resembles an old one left behind for ever. In the epic there is no *other* world, only the finality of *this* one. Odysseus returns to Ithaca after years of wandering; Achilles will die because he cannot escape his fate.[13] The novel, however, exists because other worlds *may* exist, alternatives for bourgeois speculators, wanderers, exiles.

No matter how well they may do, exiles are always eccentrics who *feel* their difference (even as they frequently exploit it) as a kind of orphanhood. Anyone who is really homeless regards the habit of seeing estrangement in everything modern as an affectation, a display of modish attitudes. Clutching difference like a weapon to be used with stiffened will, the exile jealously insists on his or her right to refuse to belong.

This usually translates into an intransigence that is not easily ignored. Wilfulness, exaggeration, overstatement: these are characteristic styles of being an exile, methods for compelling the world to accept your vision—which you make more unacceptable because you are in fact unwilling to have it accepted. It is yours, after all. Composure and serenity are the last things associated with the work of exiles. Artists in exile are decidedly unpleasant, and their stubbornness insinuates itself into even their exalted works. Dante's[14] vision in *The Divine Comedy* is tremendously powerful in its universality and detail, but even the beatific peace achieved in the *Paradiso* bears traces of the vindictiveness and severity of judgment embodied in the *Inferno.* Who but an exile like Dante, banished from Florence, would use eternity as a place for settling old scores?

James Joyce *chose* to be in exile: to give force to his artistic vocation. In an uncannily effective way—as Richard Ellmann has shown in his biography—Joyce picked a quarrel with Ireland and kept it alive so as to sustain the strictest opposition to what was familiar. Ellmann says that "whenever his relations with his native land were in danger of improving, [Joyce] was to find a new incident to solidify his intransigence and to reaffirm the rightness of his voluntary absence." Joyce's fiction concerns what in a letter he once described as the state of being "alone and friendless." And although it is rare to pick banishment as a way of life, Joyce perfectly understood its trials.

* * *

[13] Allusion to the odyssey and the Iliad of Homer; Greek epic poet (ninth–eighth centuries B.C.E.).

[14] Dante Alighieri, Italian poet (1265–1321).

But Joyce's success as an exile stresses the question lodged at its very heart: is exile so extreme and private that any instrumental use of it is ultimately a trivialization? How is it that the literature of exile has taken its place as a *topos* of human experience alongside the literature of adventure, education or discovery? Is this the *same* exile that quite literally kills Yanko Goorall and has bred the expensive, often dehumanizing relationship between twentieth-century exile and nationalism? Or is it some more benign variety?

Much of the contemporary interest in exile can be traced to the somewhat pallid notion that non-exiles can share in the benefits of exile as a redemptive motif. There is, admittedly, a certain plausibility and truth to this idea. Like medieval itinerant scholars or learned Greek slaves in the Roman Empire, exiles—the exceptional ones among them—do leaven their environments. And naturally "we" concentrate on that enlightening aspect of "their" presence among us, not on their misery or their demands. But looked at from the bleak political perspective of modern mass dislocations, individual exiles force us to recognize the tragic fate of homelessness in a necessarily heartless world.

A generation ago, Simone Weil[15] posed the dilemma of exile as concisely as it has ever been expressed. "To be rooted," she said, "is perhaps the most important and least recognized need of the human soul." Yet Weil also saw that most remedies for uprootedness in this era of world wars, deportations and mass exterminations are almost as dangerous as what they purportedly remedy. Of these, the state—or, more accurately, statism—is one of the most insidious, since worship of the state tends to supplant all other human bonds.

Weil exposes us anew to that whole complex of pressures and constraints that lie at the center of the exile's predicament, which, as I have suggested, is as close as we come in the modern era to tragedy. There is the sheer fact of isolation and displacement, which produces the kind of narcissistic masochism that resists all efforts at amelioration, acculturation and community. At this extreme the exile can make a fetish of exile, a practice that distances him or her from all connections and commitments. To live as if everything around you were temporary and perhaps trivial is to fall prey to petulant cynicism as well as to querulous lovelessness. More common is the pressure on the exile to join—parties, national movements, the state. The exile is offered a new set of affiliations and develops new loyalties. But there is also a loss—of critical perspective, of intellectual reserve, of moral courage.

It must also be recognized that the defensive nationalism of exiles often fosters self-awareness as much as it does the less attractive forms of self-assertion. Such reconstitutive projects as assembling a nation out of exile (and this is true in this century for Jews and Palestinians) involve constructing a national history, reviving an ancient language, founding national institutions like libraries and universities. And these, while they sometimes promote strident ethnocentrism, also give rise to investigations of self that inevitably go far beyond such simple and positive facts as "ethnicity." For example, there is the

[15] French mathematician and philosopher who became an exile in England during World War II.

self-consciousness of an individual trying to understand why the histories of the Palestinians and the Jews have certain patterns to them, why in spite of oppression and the threat of extinction a particular ethos remains alive in exile.

Necessarily, then, I speak of exile not as a privilege, but as an *alternative* to the mass institutions that dominate modern life. Exile is not, after all, a matter of choice: you are born into it, or it happens to you. But, provided that the exile refuses to sit on the sidelines nursing a wound, there are things to be learned: he or she must cultivate a scrupulous (not indulgent or sulky) subjectivity.

Perhaps the most rigorous example of such subjectivity is to be found in the writing of Theodor Adorno, the German-Jewish philosopher and critic. Adorno's masterwork, *Minima Moralia,* is an autobiography written while in exile; it is subtitled *Reflexionen aus dem beschädigten Leben (Reflections from a Mutilated Life).* Ruthlessly opposed to what he called the "administered" world, Adorno saw all life as pressed into ready-made forms, prefabricated "homes." He argued that everything that one says or thinks, as well as every object one possesses, is ultimately a mere commodity. Language is jargon, objects are for sale. To refuse this state of affairs is the exile's intellectual mission.

35 Adorno's reflections are informed by the belief that the only home truly available now, though fragile and vulnerable, is in writing. Elsewhere, "the house is past. The bombings of European cities, as well as the labor and concentration camps, merely precede as executors, with what the immanent development of technology had long decided was to be the fate of houses. These are now good only to be thrown away like old food cans." In short, Adorno says with a grave irony, "it is part of morality not to be at home in one's home."

To follow Adorno is to stand away from "home" in order to look at it with the exile's detachment. For there is considerable merit in the practice of noting the discrepancies between various concepts and ideas and what they actually produce. We take home and language for granted; they become nature, and their underlying assumptions recede into dogma and orthodoxy.

The exile knows that in a secular and contingent world, homes are always provisional. Borders and barriers, which enclose us within the safety of familiar territory, can also become prisons, and are often defended beyond reason or necessity. Exiles cross borders, break barriers of thought and experience.

Hugo of St. Victor, a twelfth-century monk from Saxony, wrote these hauntingly beautiful lines:

> *It is, therefore, a source of great virtue for the practiced mind to learn, bit by bit, first to change about invisible and transitory things, so that afterwards it may be able to leave them behind altogether. The man who finds his homeland sweet is still a tender beginner; he to whom every soil is as his native one is already strong; but he is perfect to whom the entire world is as a foreign land. The tender soul has fixed his love on one spot in the world; the strong man has extended his love to all places; the perfect man has extinguished his.*

Erich Auerbach, the great twentieth-century literary scholar who spent the war years as an exile in Turkey, has cited this passage as a model for anyone wishing to transcend national or provincial limits. Only by embracing this attitude can a historian begin to grasp human experience and its written records in their diversity and particularity; otherwise he or she will remain committed more to the exclusions and reactions of prejudice than to the freedom that accompanies knowledge. But note that Hugo twice makes it clear that the "strong" or "perfect" man achieves independence and detachment by *working through* attachments, not by rejecting them. Exile is predicated on the existence of, love for, and bond with, one's native place; what is true of all exile is not that home and love of home are lost, but that loss is inherent in the very existence of both.

40 Regard experiences as if they were about to disappear. What is it that anchors them in reality? What would you save of them? What would you give up? Only someone who has achieved independence and detachment, someone whose homeland is "sweet" but whose circumstances makes it impossible to recapture that sweetness, can answer those questions. (Such a person would also find it impossible to derive satisfaction from substitutes furnished by illusion or dogma.)

This may seem like a prescription for an unrelieved grimness of outlook and, with it, a permanently sullen disapproval of all enthusiasm or buoyancy of spirit. Not necessarily. While it perhaps seems peculiar to speak of the pleasures of exile, there are some positive things to be said for a few of its conditions. Seeing "the entire world as a foreign land" makes possible originality of vision. Most people are principally aware of one culture, one setting, one home; exiles are aware of at least two, and this plurality of vision gives rise to an awareness of simultaneous dimensions, an awareness that—to borrow a phrase from music—is *contrapuntal.*

For an exile, habits of life, expression or activity in the new environment inevitably occur against the memory of these things in another environment. Thus both the new and the old environments are vivid, actual, occurring together contrapuntally. There is a unique pleasure in this sort of apprehension, especially if the exile is conscious of other contrapuntal juxtapositions that diminish orthodox judgment and elevate appreciative sympathy. There is also a particular sense of achievement in acting as if one were at home wherever one happens to be.

This remains risky, however: the habit of dissimulation is both wearying and nerveracking. Exile is never the state of being satisfied, placid, or secure. Exile, in the words of Wallace Stevens,[16] is "a mind of winter" in which the pathos of summer and autumn as much as the potential of spring are nearby but unobtainable. Perhaps this is another way of saying that a life of exile moves according to a different calendar, and is less seasonal and settled than life at home. Exile is life led outside habitual order. It is nomadic, decentered, contrapuntal; but no sooner does one get accustomed to it than its unsettling force erupts anew.

[16] American poet (1879–1955).

Explorations of the Text

1. How does Said define exile? (See paragraph 1.)
2. Is "Modern Western culture . . . the work of exiles"? Why is this century different from the nineteenth century?
3. Why does Said find exile to be "horrendous"? Consider the examples of Faiz and Hussein.
4. Why does reflection on exile require consideration of "mass politics"?
5. What is the "interplay between nationalism and exile"? Examine both terms. Consider Noubar and his family.
6. Interpret Darwish's poem and Said's analysis of Conrad's "Amy Foster." How do these works extend the meaning of "exile"?
7. Consider: "To be rooted in perhaps the most important and least recognized need of the human soul." Is uprootedness "as close as we come in the modern era to tragedy"?
8. Explore the state of exile as a way "to transcend national or provincial limits," as a "contrapuntal" stance, as a "mind of winter."
9. Compare this essay with "To Live in the Borderlands. . . ."

The Reading/Writing Connection

1. "Think" Topic: Define "exile."
2. Describe an exiled person whom you know.
3. Summarize Said's essay.
4. Respond to one of Said's arguments or examples in your journal.

Ideas for Writing

1. Evaluate this essay. Examine purpose, audience, organization, arguments, examples, details, language, and effect.
2. Explore themes of exile and return. Refer to "The Third and Final Continent" and to *The Tempest.*
3. Agree or disagree with Said's essay. Begin with question 4 from The Reading/Writing Connection.

Am I Blue?

"Ain't these tears in these eyes tellin' you?"

Alice Walker

Alice Walker (1944–) was born in Eatonville, Georgia. After attending Spelman College and Sarah Lawrence College, Walker, influenced by her involvement in voter registration in Georgia and in welfare programs in Mississippi, began to write. Her first volume of poetry, Once: Poems *(1968), contains accounts of her work and her travels to Africa. In 1979, she edited* I Love Myself When I Am Laughing, *a selection from the writings of Zora Neale Hurston that was responsible for new interest in and appreciation of Hurston's work. In 1982, Walker was awarded the Pulitzer Prize and the National Book Award for her novel,* The Color Purple. *Her essays have been collected in* In Search of Our Mother's Gardens *(1983) and* Living by the Word: Selected Writings 1973–1987 *(1988).*

1986

For about three years my companion and I rented a small house in the country that stood on the edge of a large meadow that appeared to run from the end of our deck straight into the mountains. The mountains, however, were quite far away, and between us and them there was, in fact, a town. It was one of the many pleasant aspects of the house that you never really were aware of this.

It was a house of many windows, low, wide, nearly floor to ceiling in the living room, which faced the meadow, and it was from one of these that I first saw our closest neighbor, a large white horse, cropping grass, flipping its mane, and ambling about—not over the entire meadow, which stretched well out of sight of the house, but over the five or so fenced-in acres that were next to the twenty-odd that we had rented. I soon learned that the horse, whose name was Blue, belonged to a man who lived in another town, but was boarded by our neighbors next door. Occasionally, one of the children, usually a stocky teen-ager, but sometimes a much younger girl or boy, could be seen riding Blue. They would appear in the meadow, climb up on his back, ride furiously for ten or fifteen minutes, then get off, slap Blue on the flanks, and not be seen again for a month or more.

There were many apple trees in our yard, and one by the fence Blue could almost reach. We were soon in the habit of feeding him apples, which he relished, especially because by the middle of summer the meadow grasses—so green and succulent since January—had dried out from lack of rain, and Blue stumbled about munching the dried stalks half-heartedly. Sometimes he would stand very still just by the apple tree, and when one of us came out he would whinny, snort loudly, or stamp the ground. This meant, of course: I want an apple.

It was quite wonderful to pick a few apples, or collect those that had fallen to the ground overnight, and patiently hold them, one by one, up to his large, toothy mouth. I remained as thrilled as a child by his flexible dark lips, huge, cubelike teeth that crunched the apples, core and all, with such finality, and his high, broad-breasted *enormity;* beside which, I felt small indeed. When I was a child, I used to ride horses, and was especially friendly with one named Nan until the day I was riding and my brother deliberately spooked her and I was thrown, head first, against the trunk of a tree. When I came to, I was in bed and my mother was bending worriedly over me; we silently agreed that perhaps horseback riding was not the safest sport for me. Since then I have walked, and prefer walking to horseback riding—but I had forgotten the depth of feeling one could see in horses' eyes.

5 I was therefore unprepared for the expression in Blue's. Blue was lonely. Blue was horribly lonely and bored. I was not shocked that this should be the case; five acres to tramp by yourself, endlessly, even in the most beautiful of meadows—and his was—cannot provide many interesting events, and once rainy season turned to dry that was about it. No, I was shocked that I had forgotten that human animals and nonhuman animals can communicate quite well; if we are brought up around animals as children we take this for granted. By the time we are adults we no longer remember. However, the animals have not changed. They are in fact *completed* creations (at least they seem to be, so much more than we) who are not likely to change; it is their nature to express themselves; What else are they going to express? And they do. And, generally speaking, they are ignored.

After giving Blue the apples, I would wander back to the house, aware that he was observing me. Were more apples not forthcoming then? Was that to be his sole entertainment for the day? My partner's small son had decided he wanted to learn how to piece a quilt; we worked in silence on our respective squares as I thought . . .

Well, about slavery: about white children, who were raised by black people, who knew their first all-accepting love from black women, and then, when they were twelve or so, were told they must "forget" the deep levels of communication between themselves and "mammy" that they knew. Later they would be able to relate quite calmly, "My old mammy was sold to another good family." "My old mammy was ____________." Fill in the blank. Many more years later a white woman would say: "I can't understand these Negroes, these blacks. What do they want? They're so different from us."

And about the Indians, considered to be "like animals" by the "settlers" (a very benign euphemism for what they actually were), who did not understand their description as a compliment.

And about the thousands of American men who marry Japanese, Korean, Filipina, and other non–English-speaking women and of how happy they report they are, "*blissfully,*" until their brides learn to speak English, at which point the marriages tend to fall apart. What then did the men see, when they looked into the eyes of the women they married, before they could speak English? Apparently only their own reflections.

10 I thought of society's impatience with the young. "Why are they playing the music so loud?" Perhaps the children have listened to much of the music of oppressed people their parents danced to before they were born, with its passionate but soft cries for acceptance and love, and they have wondered why their parents failed to hear.

I do not know how long Blue had inhabited his five beautiful, boring acres before we moved into our house; a year after we had arrived—and had also traveled to other valleys, other cities, other worlds—he was still there.

But then, in our second year at the house, something happened in Blue's life. One morning, looking out the window at the fog that lay like a ribbon over the meadow, I saw another horse, a brown one, at the other end of Blue's field. Blue appeared to be afraid of it, and for several days made no attempt to go near. We went away for a week. When we returned, Blue had decided to make friends and the two horses ambled or galloped along together, and Blue did not come nearly as often to the fence underneath the apple tree.

When he did, bringing his new friend with him, there was a different look in his eyes. A look of independence, of self-possession, of inalienable *horseness*. His friend eventually became pregnant. For months and months there was, it seemed to me, a mutual feeling between me and the horses of justice, of peace. I fed apples to them both. The look in Blue's eyes was one of unabashed "this is *it*ness."

It did not, however, last forever. One day, after a visit to the city, I went out to give Blue some apples. He stood waiting, or so I thought, though not beneath the tree. When I shook the tree and jumped back from the shower of apples, he made no move. I carried some over to him. He managed to half-crunch one. The rest he let fall to the ground. I dreaded looking into his eyes—because I had of course noticed that Brown, his partner, had gone—but I did look. If I had been born into slavery, and my partner had been sold or killed, my eyes would have looked like that. The children next door explained that Blue's partner had been "put with him" (the same expression that old people used, I had noticed, when speaking of an ancestor during slavery who had been impregnated by her owner) so that they could mate and she conceive. Since that was accomplished, she had been taken back by her owner, who lived somewhere else.

15 Will she be back? I asked.

They didn't know.

Blue was like a crazed person. Blue *was,* to me, a crazed person. He galloped furiously, as if he were being ridden, around and around his five beautiful acres. He whinnied until he couldn't. He tore at the ground with his hooves. He butted himself against his single shade tree. He looked always and always toward the road down which his partner had gone. And then, occasionally, when he came up for apples, or I took apples to him, he looked at me. It was a look so piercing, so full of grief, a look so *human,* I almost laughed (I felt too sad to cry) to think there are people who do not know that animals suffer. People like me who have forgotten, and daily forget, all that animals try to tell us. "Everything you do to us will happen to you; we are your teachers, as you are ours. We are one lesson" is essentially it, I think. There are those who never once have even considered animals' rights: those who have been taught that animals actually want to be used and abused by us, as small children "love" to be frightened, or women "love" to be mutilated and raped. . . . They are the great-grandchildren of those who honestly thought, because someone taught them this: "Women can't think," and "niggers can't faint." But most disturbing of all, in Blue's large brown eyes was a new look, more painful than the look of hatred: the look of disgust with human beings, with life; the look of hatred. And it was odd what the look of hatred did. It gave him, for the first time, the look of a beast. And what that meant was that he had put up a barrier within to protect himself from further violence; all the apples in the world wouldn't change that fact.

And so Blue remained, a beautiful part of our landscape, very peaceful to look at from the window, white against the grass. Once a friend came to visit and said, looking out on the soothing view: "And it *would* have to be a *white* horse; the very image of freedom." And I thought, yes, the animals are forced to become for us merely "images" of what they once so beautifully expressed. And we are used to drinking milk from containers showing "contented" cows, whose real lives we want to hear nothing about, eating eggs and drumsticks from "happy" hens, and munching hamburgers advertised by bulls of integrity who seem to command their fate.

As we talked of freedom and justice one day for all, we sat down to steaks. I am eating misery, I thought, as I took the first bite. And spit it out.

Explorations of the Text

1. React to the opening paragraph. Why does Walker describe the setting? What does the setting reveal about her psyche? Her place in the world?
2. How does Walker characterize "Blue"? Discuss the significance of his name. Why does she refer to his "companion"—"Blue's friend"?
3. What is the relationship of the examples given in paragraphs 7–10 to the main story line? Are these paragraphs tangential or relevant to her argument?
4. Is Walker projecting her own feelings onto the horse?
5. Walker's essay uses an extended analogy as the basis of her argument. Summarize her argument. Is this strategy effective?
6. Discuss the significance of the concluding sentence: "I am eating misery. . . ." Why is she upset?
7. Compare Walker's essay with Anna Lee Walter's poem, "My Name Is 'I Am Living.' "

The Reading/Writing Connection

1. Do you believe that animals "suffer"? Are you an animal rights activist? Respond in a freewrite.
2. "Think" Topic: Interpret the title of the essay. Connect the title with themes of the poem.

Ideas for Writing

1. Create an argument based on an analogy. Use Walker's essay as a model.
2. Discuss Walker's and Williams's essays as Utopian visions.

The Wild Card

Terry Tempest Williams

Terry Tempest Williams (1959–) was born in Nevada and educated at the University of Utah, where she studied English and environmental education. She is an essayist known for her concern with environmental issues. Her works include Pieces of White Shell: A Journey to Navajo Land *(1984), which received the Southwest Book Award;* Refuge: An Unnatural History of Family and Place *(1992); and* An Unspoken Hunger: Stories from the Field *(1994). In 1993, Williams was one of ten recipients of the Lannan Literary Award.*

1994

Where do our preoccupations lie as women?

Our home is being held in the arms of angels as it snows and snows, and throughout these winter days I hold the questions of a woman's life in my bones. Quiet days. Days sitting by the fire. Days walking, sleeping, and dreaming. I see myself slowing down and moving away from a darkened state. The Winter Solstice becomes my own. I allow myself to struggle with the obligations of a public life and the spiritual necessity for a private one.

Am I an activist or an artist?

Do I stay home or do I speak out?

5 When Edward Abbey[1] calls for the artist to be a critic of his or her society, do we live on the page or do we live in the world?

It just may be that the most radical act we can commit is to stay home. Otherwise, who will be there to chart the changes? Who will be able to tell us if the long-billed curlews have returned to the grassy vales of Promontory, Utah? Who will be there to utter the cry of loss when the salmon of the McKenzie River in Oregon are nowhere to be seen?

Claudine Herrmann writes in *The Tongue Snatchers:* "The beauty of the world, the health of its creatures, the emotion of love, and the thirst for justice are sacrificed every day to the will of power, and it astonishes me that all political systems, no matter how different they appear, end up with the same singular result: that of placing life last among all their preoccupations."

Where are our preoccupations as women?

Perhaps here: It would begin with each woman carrying a deck of cards—wild cards—cards that could not only portend the future but create it. If a woman saw an act that violated the health and integrity of her community, she would leave a card on-site. If she was moved by a particular piece of legislation on behalf of or against the land, she would dash a card off to her senator or representative. And if she found herself in a board of directors meeting and the truth as she felt it was not being told, she would place all her cards on the table as a sign that the games of men are not the games of women.

---

[1] Edward Abbey (1927–89) was a prominent environmental activist and nature writer. His love of the land and of the West led him to work as a park ranger in Moab, Utah.

10 And here: As Americans, we have always left when the land became degraded, moved on to the next best place. Walked west. Now, our continent is inhabited. There is no place left to go. What would happen, then, if we took the Homestead Act of 1862, designed to open the West to settlement by small family farms in 160-acre parcels, and turned it inside out, reimagined and reshaped it to meet the needs of our own time? We could call it the Home Stand Act of 1994, designed to inspire and initiate a community of vigilance and care toward the lands we inhabit. It would give us courage to honor "the stay option" and dig in, set down roots. A Home Stand Act placed in the hands of women and their families could activate a local force so brilliant and full-spirited it could bypass traditional forms of government altogether. The artistry, intelligence, and compassion of women would flow through our communities like water.

Within Mormon culture, there is an organization of women known as the Relief Society. Organized in 1852, its charge is to attend to the needs of the community. The Relief Society, like other church auxiliaries, provides opportunities for association, leadership, compassionate service, and education. Its motto, "Charity Never Faileth," expresses the commitment of members to love and nurture one another, neighbor to neighbor, household to household, ministering graciously to the needs of others.

The Relief Society was a constant source of comfort in our home as I was growing up in Salt Lake City. Two Mormon sisters were "called" to watch over our family. They visited us monthly, anticipating whatever needs we might have. And when our mother became ill, they not only stayed with us while she was in the hospital but provided meals for us, talked to us, and held us in their prayers. They rendered peace throughout our lives. Again, as I was growing up, I often witnessed casserole diplomacy being exercised in our neighborhood. Food was brought into homes to heal the sick, mend a feud, or welcome a new baby into the world. Personal offerings dissolved political boundaries. I believe the idea of the Home Stand Act could incorporate this kind of community care and awareness, because it has everything to do with home rule: standing our ground in the places we love. This is the wild card we hold, and if we choose to adopt a Home Stand Act, nothing will escape our green eyes.

There are role models among us. Wangari Maathai founded the Green Belt Movement in Kenya, Africa, by planting seven trees on June 5, 1977. "The Green Belt Movement started in my backyard," she writes in her essay "Foresters Without Diplomas." "I became exposed to many of the problems women were facing—problems of firewood, malnutrition, lack of food and adequate water, unemployment, soil erosion . . . so we went to the women and talked about planting trees and overcoming, for example, such problems as the lack of firewood and building and fencing materials, stopping soil erosion, protecting water systems. . . . The women agreed."

It was an arduous, labor-intensive process. "To initiate the campaign," Aubrey Wallace writes in *Eco-Heroes,* "Maathai went into the schools." The children were involved directly: they dug holes, walked to the tree nursery to collect trees, planted them, and took care of them as long as they were in school. "It was the children who took the message home to their parents and eventually got women's groups interested," says Maathai.

15 Sixteen years later, more than three thousand schools have responded to the Green Belt campaign, with over 1 million children involved. More than 10 million trees stand throughout Kenya, with over 1,500 nurseries, virtually all of them operated by women.

I met Wangari Maathai in Nairobi in August 1985, at the United Nations Decade for Women. She took me into the countryside to see for myself how rural women in Africa were gathering indigenous seeds in the folds of their skirts. I remember her picking up a handful of red soil. "The weight of the environmental crisis that rural women have been carrying on their backs is being lessened," she said, "one seed at a time."

In our own country, we only have to look to Rachel Carson to see the impact one woman can have. Carson received a burning letter from her friend Olga Owens Huckins, a journalist, who asked her for help in finding people who could elucidate and speak to the dangers of pesticides. The Huckinses had a small place in Duxbury, Massachusetts, just north of Cape Cod, which they had transformed into a bird sanctuary. Without any thought of the effects on birds and wildlife, the state had sprayed the entire area for mosquito control.

Huckins sent a letter of outrage to the *Boston Herald* in January 1958. An excerpt:

> *The mosquito control plane flew over our small town last summer. Since we live close to the marshes, we were treated to several lethal doses as the pilot crisscrossed our place. And we consider the spraying of active poison over private land to be a serious aerial intrusion.*
>
> 20 *The "harmless" shower bath killed seven of our lovely songbirds outright. We picked up three dead bodies the next morning right by the door. They were birds that lived close to us, trusted us, and built their nests in our trees year after year. The next day three were scattered around the bird bath. (I had emptied it and scrubbed it after the spraying but YOU CAN NEVER KILL D.D.T.). . . . All of these birds died horribly and in the same way. Their bills were gaping open, and their splayed claws were drawn up to their breasts in agony.*

Olga Owens Huckins bore witness. Rachel Carson responded. A correspondence between friends. Two women. Carson wrote to Huckins that it was her letter that had "started it all" and had led her to realize that "I must write the book."

Four and a half years later, *Silent Spring* was published and alerted the world of 1962 to the dangers of pesticides when they enter the food chain. Nothing exists in isolation. The metaphor of silence—birdsong lost forever as a result of chemical pollutants—shot through the conservation community like a wave of electricity. Letters were written. Commissions were formed. Laws were enacted. A new wave of environmentalism began.

And then in 1975, Lois Gibbs brought the issue of toxic wastes into the mainstream of American culture, when she began to speak out against the twenty-two thousand tons of poison that were "bubbling underground" in the

Love Canal neighborhood of Niagara Falls, New York. Cancers, miscarriages, illnesses, and death among the children and adults of the Niagara River valley were being linked to the poisons. Lois Gibbs responded with a community program, the Citizens' Clearing House for Hazardous Wastes. "If they didn't have a sense of community prior to our proposal, they developed it as a result," she said of her neighbors. "It's one issue that can bring all different people together."

Women, health, and the environment. Home rule. The Home Stand Act. We can create beauty through the dailiness of our lives, standing our ground in the places we love. "There is a real world that is really dying," Marilynne Robinson writes in *Mother Country,* "and we had better think about that. My greatest hope, which is a very slender one, is that we will at last find the courage to make ourselves rational and morally autonomous adults, secure enough in the faith that life is good and to be preserved, to recognize the grosser forms of evil and name them and confront them. Who will do it for us?"

25 We must do it for ourselves.

As women wedded to wilderness, we must realize that we do carry the wild card, that our individual voices matter and our collective voice can shatter the status quo that for too long has legislated on behalf of power and far too little on behalf of life. We can flood Congress with our wild cards (imagine hundreds of thousands of brightly colored cards covering the desks of our representatives), demanding that women's issues be recognized as health issues, as environmental issues, as issues centered around a quality of life that touches all of us, deeply. This is the kind of politics we must be engaged in—nothing marginal, nothing peripheral, nothing inessential, not anymore.

As women within the conservation community, we must work tirelessly to see that the staffs, boards of directors, and governing councils of environmental organizations in this country carry a fair representation of women and minorities. We must call for the abandonment of hierarchies that contribute to the vertical power that has compromise the earth. And we must begin to build broad coalitions and alliances, just as Elaine R. Jones, leaders of the NAACP Legal Defense and Educational Fund, has promised to do by expanding its civil rights agenda to include more cases of environmental and health-care discrimination.

"We, as women," Chantal Chawaf writes in *Shifting Scenes: Interviews on Women, Writing, and Politics in Post–'68 France,* "today, in our logos and discourse, have to articulate the excess desire, the uncensored body, and life—not an idealized life, but life just as it is, with its problems, anxieties, and frightening aspects. We must do so because it is precisely this fear of life that has kept life outside culture."

It will not be simple.

30 It will not be fast.

It will be a slow, steady river that braids our communities together.

Home. It continues to snow. My dreams of angels disappear and I think about the wild cards we carry, one by one, flashing the face of Eve on this creation.

Exploration of the Text

1. Describe the point of view, voice, and tone of the speaker (See paragraphs 1–3). How does the use of figurative language develop the speaker's voice?
2. Interpret the following: "It may be that the most radical act we can commit is to stay home."
3. Analyze the imagery of "the wild card." What is her view of the artist's or the writer's role in society?
4. Discuss the play on words: "wild" and "wilderness." Relate this wordplay to themes of the essay.
5. How does Williams develop her argument? What forms of evidence does she use? Are they effective?
6. How does she redefine "home" by the end of the essay?

The Reading/Writing Connection

1. Journal Entry: What is your "wild card"?
2. Gloss and annotate the essay; note her thesis, topics, and forms of evidence. Is the essay persuasive?

Ideas for Writing

1. Research one of the environmental activists she mentions. What impact did her work have?
2. Compare Williams's style as an essayist with Toni Morrison's in her "Nobel Prize Speech." (Consider such elements as rhetorical situation, audience, point of view, structure, and forms of evidence.)
3. How would Williams respond to Szymborska's view of the century? Create a dialogue between the two writers.

The Allegory of the Cave

Plato Translated by Benjamin Jowett

The "Allegory of the Cave" appears in Plato's Republic.

c. 387–367 B.C.

And now, I[1] said, let me show in a figure how far our nature is enlightened or unenlightened:[2]—Behold! human beings housed in an underground cave,

[1] From *The Republic,* Book 7. Socrates speaks to Glaucon.

[2] In the original Greek, the words for enlightened and unenlightened are *paideia* and *apaideusia.* The former, depending on context, also may be understood as "education," "culture," or "knowledge." [Translator's note.]

which has a long entrance open towards the light and as wide as the interior of the cave; here they have been from their childhood, and have their legs and necks chained, so that they cannot move and can only see before them, being prevented by the chains from turning round their heads. Above and behind them a fire is blazing at a distance, and between the fire and the prisoners there is a raised way; and you will see, if you look, a low wall built along the way, like the screen which marionette players have in front of them, over which they show the puppets.

I see.

And do you see, I said, men passing along the wall carrying all sorts of vessels, and statues and figures of animals made of wood and stone and various materials, which appear over the wall? While carrying their burdens, some of them, as you would expect, are talking, others silent.

You have shown me a strange image, and they are strange prisoners.

5 Like ourselves, I replied; for in the first place do you think they have seen anything of themselves, and of one another, except the shadows which the fire throws on the opposite wall of the cave?

How could they do so, he asked, if throughout their lives they were never allowed to move their heads?

And of the objects which are being carried in like manner they would only see the shadows?

Yes, he said.

And if they were able to converse with one another, would they not suppose that the things they saw were the real things?

10 Very true.

And suppose further that the prison had an echo which came from the other side, would they not be sure to fancy when one of the passers-by spoke that the voice which they heard came from the passing shadow?

No question, he replied.

To them, I said, the truth would be literally nothing but the shadows of the images.

That is certain.

15 And now look again, and see in what manner they would be released from their bonds, and cured of their error, whether the process would naturally be as follows. At first, when any of them is liberated and compelled suddenly to stand up and turn his neck round and walk and look towards the light, he will suffer sharp pains; the glare will distress him, and he will be unable to see the realities of which in his former state he had seen the shadows; and then conceive someone saying to him that what he saw before was an illusion, but that now, when he is approaching nearer to being and his eye is turned towards more real existence, he has a clearer vision,—what will be his reply? And you may further imagine that his instructor is pointing to the objects as they pass and requiring him to name them,—will he not be perplexed? Will he not fancy that the shadows which he formerly saw are truer than the objects which are now shown to him?

Far truer.

And if he is compelled to look straight at the light, will he not have a pain in his eyes which will make him turn away to take refuge in the objects of vision which he can see, and which he will conceive to be in reality clearer than the things which are now being shown to him?

True, he said.

And suppose once more, that he is reluctantly dragged up that steep and rugged ascent, and held fast until he is forced into the presence of the sun himself, is he not likely to be pained and irritated? When he approaches the light his eyes will be dazzled, and he will not be able to see anything at all of what are now called realities.

Not all in a moment, he said.

He will require to grow accustomed to the sight of the upper world. And first he will see the shadows best, next the reflections of men and other objects in the water, and then the objects themselves; and, when he turned to the heavenly bodies and the heaven itself, he would find it easier to gaze upon the light of the moon and the stars at night than to see the sun or the light of the sun by day?

Certainly.

Last of all he will be able to see the sun, not turning aside to the illusory reflections of him in the water, but gazing directly at him in his own proper place, and contemplating him as he is.

Certainly.

He will then proceed to argue that this is he who gives the seasons and the years, and is the guardian of all that is in the visible world, and in a certain way the cause of all things which he and his fellows have been accustomed to behold?

Clearly, he said, he would arrive at this conclusion after what he had seen.

And when he remembered his old habitation, and the wisdom of the cave and his fellow-prisoners, do you not suppose that he would felicitate himself on the change, and pity them?

Certainly, he would.

And if they were in the habit of conferring honours among themselves on those who were quickest to observe the passing shadows and to remark which of them went before and which followed after and which were together, and who were best able from these observations to divine the future do you think that he would be eager for such honours and glories, or envy those who attained honour and sovereignty among those men? Would he not say with Homer,[3]

> *"Better to be a serf, labouring for a landless master,"*

and to endure anything, rather than think as they do and live after their manner?

---

[3] Greek epic poet (c. ninth–eighth centuries B.C.).

30 Yes, he said, I think that he would consent to suffer anything rather than live in this miserable manner.

Imagine once more, I said, such a one coming down suddenly out of the sunlight, and being replaced in his old seat; would he not be certain to have his eyes full of darkness?

To be sure, he said.

And if there were a contest, and he had to compete in measuring the shadows with the prisoners who had never moved out of the cave, while his sight was still weak, and before his eyes had become steady (and the time which would be needed to acquire this new habit of sight might be very considerable), would he not make himself ridiculous? Men would say of him that he had returned from the place above with his eyes ruined; and that it was better not even to think of ascending; and if anyone tried to loose another and lead him up to the light, let them only catch the offender, and they would put him to death.

No question, he said.

35 This entire allegory, I said, you may now append, dear Glaucon, to the previous argument; the prison-house is the world of sight, the light of the fire is the power of the sun, and you will not misapprehend me if you interpret the journey upwards to be the ascent of the soul into the intellectual world according to my surmise, which, at your desire, I have expressed—whether rightly or wrongly God knows. But, whether true or false, my opinion is that in the world of knowledge the Idea of good appears last of all, and is seen only with an effort; although, when seen, it is inferred to be the universal author of all things beautiful and right, parent of light and of the lord of light in the visible world, and the immediate and supreme source of reason and truth in the intellectual; and that this is the power upon which he who would act rationally either in public or private life must have his eye fixed.

I agree, he said, as far as I am able to understand you.

Moreover, I said, you must agree once more, and not wonder that those who attain to this vision are unwilling to take any part in human affairs; for their souls are ever hastening into the upper world where they desire to dwell; which desire of theirs is very natural, if our allegory may be trusted.

Yes, very natural.

Then, I said, the business of us who are the founders of the State will be to compel the best minds to attain that knowledge which we have already shown to be the greatest of all, namely, the vision of the good; they must make the ascent which we have described; but when they have ascended and seen enough we must now allow them to do as they do now.

40 What do you mean?

They are permitted to remain in the upper world, refusing to descend again among the prisoners in the cave, and partake of their labours and honours, whether they are worth having or not.

But is not this unjust? he said; ought we to give them a worse life, when they might have a better?

You have again forgotten, my friend, I said, the intention of our law, which does not aim at making any one class in the State happy above the rest; it seeks rather to spread happiness over the whole State, and to hold the citizens together by persuasion and necessity, making each share with others any benefit which he can confer upon the State; and the law aims at producing such citizens, not that they may be left to please themselves, but that they may serve in binding the State together.

True, he said, I had forgotten.

Observe, Glaucon, that we shall do no wrong to our philosophers but rather make a just demand, when we oblige them to have a care and providence of others; we shall explain to them that in other States, men of their class are not obliged to share in the toils of politics; and this is reasonable, for they grow up spontaneously, against the will of the governments in their several States; and things which grow up of themselves, and are indebted to no one for their nurture, cannot fairly be expected to pay dues for a culture which they have never received. But we have brought you into the world to be rulers of the hive, kings of yourselves and of the other citizens, and have educated you far better and more perfectly than they have been educated, and you are better able to share in the double duty. Wherefore each of you, when his turn comes, must go down to rejoin his companions, and acquire with them the habit of seeing things in the dark. As you acquire that habit, you will see ten thousand times better than the inhabitants of the cave, and you will know what the several images are and what they represent, because you have seen the beautiful and just and good in their truth. And thus our State, which is also yours, will be a reality and not a dream only, and will be administered in a spirit unlike that of other States, in which men fight with one another about shadows only and are distracted in the struggle for power, which in their eyes is a great good. Whereas the truth is that the State in which those who are to govern have least ambition to do so is always the best and most quietly governed, and the State in which they are most eager, the worst.

Quite true, he replied.

And will our pupils, when they hear this, refuse to take their turn at the toils of State, when they are allowed to spend the greater part of their time with one another in the heavenly light?

Impossible, he answered; for they are just men, and the commands which we impose upon them are just. But there can be no doubt that every one of them will take office as a stern necessity, contrary to the spirit of our present rulers of State.

Yes, my friend, I said; and there lies the point. You must contrive for your future rulers another and a better life than that of a ruler, and then you may have a well-ordered State; for only in the State which offers this, will they rule who are truly rich, not in gold, but in virtue and wisdom, which are the true blessings of life. Whereas if men who are destitute and starved of such personal goods go to the administration of public affairs, thinking to enrich themselves at the public expense, order there can never be; for they will be fighting about office, and the civil and domestic broils which thus arise will be the ruin of the rulers themselves and of the whole State.

Most true, he replied.

And the only life which looks down upon the life of political ambition is that of true philosophy. Do you know of any other?

Indeed, I do not, he said.

And those who govern should not "make love to their employment?" For, if they do there will be rival lovers, and they will fight.

No question.

Whom, then, will you compel to become guardians of the State? Surely those who excel in judgement of the means by which a State is administered, and who at the same time have other honours and another and a better life than that of politics?

None but these, he replied.

Explorations of the Text

1. Describe or sketch the scene in the cave. Where are the "prisoners," "fire," and "screen"? What do the elements of the allegory represent?
2. What does the "light" signify? Why is it difficult for the prisoners to adjust to the "light"?
3. Describe the stages of illumination presented by Socrates.
4. According to Socrates, how can the "uneducated" and the unenlightened become enlightened?
5. What is the role of the "best minds" of the State? Who are the true rulers? What is the goal of the State? Do you agree to Plato's views?
6. Plato creates a dialogue that is supposed to instruct. Does it? What are the effects of this technique?

The Reading/Writing Connection

1. "Think" Topic: Agree or disagree: "The state in which rulers are most reluctant to govern is always the best . . . and the State in which they are most eager, the worst."
2. Does learning something or changing one's mind cause pain? Cite an incident or experience from your own life.
3. List your own examples and descriptions of Plato's worlds of "shadows" and "light."
4. Create a list of questions you have about this work.

Ideas for Writing

1. Connect Plato's concept of conversion with another experience of awakening, of knowledge, or of faith (for instance, Carver's "Cathedral" in chapter 4).

2. Argue for or against Plato's view of the ideal ruler and the nature of politics.
3. Explore the definitions of the word "see" or "light" in this essay. How do they advance Plato's argument?
4. Write an allegory or a fable to explain an abstraction (death, love, faith).

THE MYTH OF SISYPHUS

Albert Camus

Albert Camus (1913–60) was born in Algeria when it was still a French colony. While studying philosophy at the University of Algiers, he organized and directed a small theater company and became involved in political causes. During World War II, he was active in the French Resistance and also wrote The Stranger *(1942), a novel, and* The Myth of Sisyphus *(1942), a philosophical essay, both important works in existential thought and the literature of the absurd. His other works include a novel,* The Plague *(1948), a short story collection,* Exile and the Kingdom *(1958), and a collection of plays,* Caligula and Three Other Plays *(1958). Camus's work earned him the Nobel Prize for Literature in 1957.*

1942

The gods had condemned Sisyphus to ceaselessly rolling a rock to the top of a mountain, whence the stone would fall back of its own weight. They had thought with some reason that there is no more dreadful punishment than futile and hopeless labor.

If one believes Homer,[1] Sisyphus was the wisest and most prudent of mortals. According to another tradition, however, he was disposed to practice the profession of highwayman. I see no contradiction in this. Opinions differ as to the reasons why he became the futile laborer of the underworld. To begin with, he is accused of a certain levity in regard to the gods. He stole their secrets. Ægina,[2] the daughter of Æsopus, was carried off by Jupiter. The father was shocked by that disappearance and complained to Sisyphus. He, who knew of the abduction, offered to tell about it on condition that Æsopus would give water to the citadel of Corinth. To the celestial thunderbolts he preferred the benediction of water. He was punished for this in the underworld. Homer tells us also that Sisyphus had put Death in chains. Pluto[3] could not endure the

[1] Greek epic poet (c. ninth to eighth centuries B.C.) who wrote about Sisyphus in *The Iliad.*

[2] A story from Greek mythology.

[3] Greek god of the underworld.

sight of his deserted, silent empire. He dispatched the god of war, who liberated Death from the hands of her conqueror.

It is said also that Sisyphus, being near to death, rashly wanted to test his wife's love. He ordered her to cast his unburied body into the middle of the public square. Sisyphus woke up in the underworld. And there, annoyed by an obedience so contrary to human love, he obtained from Pluto permission to return to earth in order to chastise his wife. But when he had seen again the face of this world, enjoyed water and sun, warm stones and the sea, he no longer wanted to go back to the infernal darkness. Recalls, signs of anger, warnings were of no avail. Many years more he lived facing the curve of the gulf, the sparkling sea, and the smiles of earth. A decree of the gods was necessary. Mercury[4] came and seized the impudent man by the collar and, snatching him from his joys, led him forcibly back to the underworld, where his rock was ready for him.

You have already grasped that Sisyphus is the absurd hero. He *is,* as much through his passions as through his torture. His scorn of the gods, his hatred of death, and his passion for life won him that unspeakable penalty in which the whole being is exerted toward accomplishing nothing. This is the price that must be paid for the passions of this earth. Nothing is told us about Sisyphus in the underworld. Myths are made for the imagination to breathe life into them. As for this myth, one sees merely the whole effort of a body straining to raise the huge stone, to roll it and push it up a slope a hundred times over; one sees the face screwed up, the cheek tight against the stone, the shoulder bracing the clay-covered mass, the foot wedging it, the fresh start with arms outstretched, the wholly human security of two earth-clotted hands. At the very end of his long effort measured by skyless space and time without depth, the purpose is achieved. Then Sisyphus watches the stone rush down in a few moments toward that lower world whence he will have to push it up again toward the summit. He goes back down to the plain.

5 It is during that return, that pause, that Sisyphus interests me. A face that toils so close to stones is already stone itself! I see that man going back down with a heavy yet measured step toward the torment of which he will never know the end. That hour like a breathing space which returns as surely as his suffering, that is the hour of consciousness. At each of those moments when he leaves the heights and gradually sinks toward the lairs of the gods, he is superior to his fate. He is stronger than his rock.

If this myth is tragic, that is because its hero is conscious. Where would his torture be, indeed, if at every step the hope of succeeding upheld him? The workman of today works every day in his life at the same tasks, and this fate is no less absurd. But it is tragic only at the rare moments when it becomes conscious. Sisyphus, proletarian of the gods, powerless and rebellious, knows the whole extent of his wretched condition: it is what he thinks of during his descent. The lucidity that was to constitute his torture at the same time crowns his victory. There is no fate that cannot be surmounted by scorn.

[4] Roman god; messenger to the other gods.

If the descent is thus sometimes performed in sorrow, it can also take place in joy. This word is not too much. Again I fancy Sisyphus returning toward his rock, and the sorrow was in the beginning. When the images of earth cling too tightly to memory, when the call of happiness becomes too insistent, it happens that melancholy rises in man's heart: this is the rock's victory, this is the rock itself. The boundless grief is too heavy to bear. These are our nights of Gethsemane.[5] But crushing truths perish from being acknowledged. Thus, Oedipus[6] at the outset obeys fate without knowing it. But from the moment he knows, his tragedy begins. Yet at the same moment, blind and desperate, he realizes that the only bond linking him to the world is the cool hand of a girl. Then a tremendous remark rings out: "Despite so many ordeals, my advanced age and the nobility of my soul make me conclude that all is well." Sophocles' Oedipus, like Dostoevsky's Kirilov,[7] thus gives the recipe for the absurd victory. Ancient wisdom confirms modern heroism.

One does not discover the absurd without being tempted to write a manual of happiness. "What! by such narrow ways—?" There is but one world, however. Happiness and the absurd are two sons of the same earth. They are inseparable. It would be a mistake to say that happiness necessarily springs from the absurd discovery. It happens as well that the feeling of the absurd springs from happiness. "I conclude that all is well," says Oedipus, and that remark is sacred. It echoes in the wild and limited universe of man. It teaches that all is not, has not been, exhausted. It drives out of this world a god who had come into it with dissatisfaction and a preference for futile sufferings. It makes a fate a human matter, which must be settled among men.

All Sisyphus' silent joy is contained therein. His fate belongs to him. His rock is his thing. Likewise, the absurd man, when he contemplates his torment, silences all the idols. In the universe suddenly restored to its silence, the myriad wondering little voices of the earth rise up. Unconscious, secret calls, invitations from all the faces, they are the necessary reverse and price of victory. There is no sun without shadow, and it is essential to know the night. The absurd man says yes and his effort will henceforth be unceasing. If there is a personal fate, there is no higher destiny, or at least there is but one which he concludes is inevitable and despicable. For the rest, he knows himself to be the master of his days. At that subtle moment when man glances backward over his life, Sisyphus returning toward his rock, in that slight pivoting he contemplates that series of unrelated actions which becomes his fate, created by him, combined under his memory's eye and soon sealed by his death. Thus, convinced of the wholly human origin of all that is human, a blind man eager to see who knows that the night has no end, he is still on the go. The rock is still rolling.

---

[5] Garden outside Jerusalem. A reference to Jesus's discussion with his disciples the night before his crucifixion.

[6] See chapter 7.

[7] Character who kills himself in Dostoevsky's novel, *The Possessed* (1871).

10 I leave Sisyphus at the foot of the mountain! One always finds one's burden again. But Sisyphus teaches the higher fidelity that negates the gods and raises rocks. He too concludes that all is well. This universe henceforth without a master seems to him neither sterile nor futile. Each atom of that stone, each mineral flake of that night-filled mountain, in itself forms a world. The struggle itself toward the heights is enough to fill a man's heart. One must imagine Sisyphus happy.

Explorations of the Text

1. Why does Camus include two different versions of Sisyphus's fate? What common thread connects them? What does Sisyphus represent to Camus?
2. Explain: "When he leaves the heights and gradually sinks toward the lairs of the gods, he is superior to his fate."
3. What does Camus mean by consciousness? Why does the "tragic" occur at the point of being "conscious"?
4. What does Camus mean by the "absurd"? Why is Sisyphus "the absurd hero"? What is the "absurd" man's fate?
5. This excerpt is part of Camus's longer essay considered by critics to be a meditation on suicide. What arguments does Camus offer to oppose suicide?
6. Characterize the voice of the persona in the essay and his approach to the audience.
7. Compare Camus's and Plato's views of enlightenment.

The Reading/Writing Connection

1. In a paragraph explore contemporary parallels for each aspect of the allegory (Sisyphus, his meaningless labor, his act of defiance, the gods).
2. "Think" Topic: Do you agree with Camus's view of the absurd universe? his vision of people's fates in such a world?

Ideas for Writing

1. How does Camus define tragedy?
2. Compare Camus's presentation of Oedipus's fate with that in Sophocle's drama in chapter 7.
3. Write an essay discussing Camus's concept of the absurd.
4. Do you agree with Camus's statement: "The absurd man says yes, and his effort will henceforth be unceasing. If there is a personal fate, there is no higher destiny"?

Student Essay: Critical Thematic Analysis

ABOUT "HERITAGE"

Yvette Ho

Yvette Ho, eighteen when she wrote this essay, hails from Queens, New York, where she has ample access to Manhattan's sociocultural milieu. In this essay, Ho compares her Chinese American background with the view discussed in Linda Hogan's "Heritage."

In the poem "Heritage," Linda Hogan expresses the confusion that results from having a diversified ancestry and the obligation she feels toward preserving it. The rich culture of her father's Native-American "red" blood, however, could never quite mix with her mother's American "pale-skinned" culture, and she resents this conflict that led her to view her "whiteness [as] a shame." Pressured by the beliefs and rituals taught to her by her ancestors, she feels a resentment toward them because of "learning the secrets/of never having a home."

I am both Chinese and American and can identify with the speaker's mixed beliefs and confusion of identity as the result of her dual "heritage." I was born and raised here in the United States by traditional Chinese parents and have experienced the difficulties in differentiating which Chinese customs should be kept and which American ones should be adopted. The Chinese, one of thousands of foreign cultures to emigrate here, feel obligated, like Hogan, to defend and preserve our race and customs. At the same time, they must adapt to the diverse, yet racist society of America.

I consider my heritage to be Chinese American—not solely Chinese due to my rearing here, and not completely American since through my blood runs thousands of years of my Chinese ancestry. My parents raised me to believe in myself and to take advantage of the opportunities here since my ancestors were never provided with such opportunities and most back in Communist China never will be. But, I was also told never forget who I am; I am Chinese and proud of my heritage. I will always have Chinese physicalities and view things through the mind of a Chinese person regardless of whatever changes occur in the universe—my identity will follow me to my death.

My parents have taught me to respect others and, in turn, respect will be reciprocated. The Chinese are taught to honor their superiors, whether they be leaders or parents, and not to question authority, as honor is a principal belief in most Asian cultures. "Do what you are supposed to do," "Your teachers are always right," "Education is the key to your future," they would repeat in their broken English. I respected and followed these requests, but as I got older, I began to question their validity.

5 I realized that my parents' experiences were very different from my own. They no longer live in a Communist country fearing the government's authority. It was then that, like Hogan, I began to differentiate the positive and negative aspects of my heritage, and I understood that my beliefs opposed the beliefs my parents imposed on me.

The Chinese, for the most part, are relatively passive individuals. We are taught to avoid hassles whenever possible, and to laugh and smile whenever we deem it necessary to divert attention away from troublesome situations. The passivity has led to racism and stereotypes that will never be broken, stereotypes that are immediately mentally retrieved when one sees a Chinese person, or for that matter any Asian person. This stereotype is a scar, not unlike Linda Hogan's "brown stain/that covered her white shirt." It stands out often overcoming rational thought and is nearly impossible to be rid of it.

Most adults believe that the only way to acquire knowledge is through the teachings of our educators. This example is only one of the negative aspects of my heritage. We do not have to follow what our "superiors" have taught us. Our authority figures here are not necessarily doing what is best for the people, so it is up to us to question these figures and retain knowledge that we find appropriate to believe. This trait was not passed on to me, but *will* be passed on to my children who shall be raised with ideas of equality and self-belief. My parents will continue to believe their views that reinforce the "slitty-eyed, unquestioning" stereotype. For this reason, they feel that I have forgotten my culture, that I have been "Americanized." My refusal to accept stereotypes has created a naïve image of me within them. "Don't be so stupid. You know how those White people are. Be careful," they ignorantly state. They stubbornly hold on to their beliefs—another negative aspect of many of the Chinese. They are headstrong, somewhat racist individuals. Being the victims of oppression by Koreans and the English in history, they continue to hold the "grudges" of the past. These racist ideas are reflected in the language. Within the Chinese language exist colloquialisms for nationalities other than the Chinese, labelling them "ghosts"—as threatening, evil spirits. These slang words are widely accepted and commonly used. The ignorance and rigid ways of the Chinese prevent them from exploring the diversity of the United States, the beauty of the different interacting cultures and not just the hate and corruption.

There are many negative aspects of the typical Chinese person, but despite these beliefs, there is a rich history that should never be forgotten. This history is the positive trait that I *will* pass on to my children—the thousands of years of tradition, culture, and language, the oppression my ancestors and family overcame to obtain freedom, providing for me the different opportunities and freedoms I have here in America. My children will be taught to recognize these ancestors, their past and their history, and not to forget where they are originally from or who their ancestors were. Their cultural history will show them their true heritage. From there on, their identity will be based on their experiences, education, and decisions.

Despite Linda Hogan's childhood confusion about her dual "heritage," she was able to attain her identity. Now an avid author and educator supporting the Native-American movement, she differentiates between the negative and positive aspects of her heritage and retains certain beliefs she chooses to pass on to others. Her grandfather's "silence" and grandmother's "tobacco" will remain a part of her. Her Native-American heritage will forever exist in those images as her dual cultures unify.

HERITAGE

Linda Hogan (1947–)

1979

From my mother, the antique mirror
where I watch my face take on her lines.
She left me the smell of baking bread
to warm fine hairs in my nostrils,
she left the large white breasts that weigh down
my body.

From my father I take his brown eyes,
the plague of locusts that leveled our crops,
they flew in formation like buzzards.

From my uncle the whittled wood
that rattles like bones
and is white
and smells like all our old houses

that are no longer there. He was the man
who sang old chants to me, the words
my father was told not to remember.

From my grandfather who never spoke
I learned to fear silence.
I learned to kill a snake
when you're begging for rain.

And grandmother, blue-eyed woman
whose skin was brown,
she used snuff.[1]
When her coffee can full of black saliva
spilled on me
it was like the brown cloud of grasshoppers
that leveled her fields.
It was the brown stain
that covered my white shirt,
my whiteness a shame.
That sweet black liquid like the food
she chewed up and spit into my father's mouth
when he was an infant.
It was the brown earth of Oklahoma
stained with oil.
She said tobacco would purge your body of poisons.
It has more medicine than stones and knives
against your enemies.

That tobacco is the dark night that covers me.
She said it is wise to eat the flesh of deer
so you will be swift and travel over many miles.
She told me how our tribe has always followed a stick
that pointed west
that pointed east.

From my family I have learned the secrets
of never having a home.

Writing Assignments

1. Compare views of the future in "The Imagination of Disaster," "Harrison Bergeron," and "The Handsomest Drowned Man in the World."
2. Compare views of obedience and conformity suggested in Vonnegut's "Harrison Bergeron," in Griffin's "I Like to Think of Harriet Tubman" (chapter 7), and in Terry Tempest Williams's "The Wild Card."

[1] Finely ground tobacco that can be inhaled through the nose.

3. Examine the views of global and environmental issues presented in the following: "Stone Olives"; "My Name Is 'I Am Living' "; and "Ghosts."
4. a. What were your preconceptions of Africa before you read the works in this chapter? What did you know about Africa? About apartheid?
   b. Explore conceptions of Africa presented in the Thematic Preview.
   c. Compare your original ideas with your observations after the reading.
   d. In several works about Africa, trace one theme, such as apartheid, sense of exile, or the tension between the traditional and the modern.
5. a. What does Anzaldúa mean by "borderland"?
   b. Describe a "borderland" in which you live.
   c. Compare your "borderland" with a work in this chapter that presents a borderland.
   d. Compare Anzaldúa's view of "the borderland" with the representation of the "New World" in *The Tempest.*
6. Discuss the concept of exile presented in three works in this chapter.
7. a. Explain the concept of renewal in one work in this chapter.
   b. The possibility and impossibility of renewal and rebirth in a global world are recurring themes in this chapter. Compare and contrast three visions of renewal.
   c. Which works present the most convincing and/or believable visions?
8. Explicate "Diving into the Wreck" or one of Rilke's sonnets. Focus on point of view, imagery, figurative language, and form. (See chapter 10.)
9. a. Explore the water or natural imagery in three works in this chapter.
   b. Explain kite imagery in *"Master Harold" . . . and the Boys.*
10. Compare the points of view of three speakers in three poems. How does point of view relate to tone, imagery, and theme?
11. a. What new myths of the future emerge in "Diving into the Wreck" and "The Second Coming"?
    b. Create your own myth or allegory for a view of the future.
12. Contrast Walker's vision in "Am I Blue?" with the themes of Szymborska's poems.
13. a. Ask several people to envision the world in 2102. What do they fear about the future, and what do they wish for the future?
    b. Analyze your results. What patterns do you perceive?
    c. Use one interview as the basis for an essay.
    d. Compare one of your interviewee's views of the future with a work in this chapter.
14. Create a science fiction short story. Develop a view of a utopian or dystopian society.

15. Choose one of the following topics as the basis for research: apartheid, Nelson Mandela, world hunger, world drought, ecological issues (the destruction of the Brazilian rain forest, acid rain, oil spills), nuclear holocaust–nuclear winter, Hiroshima and Nagasaki, genetic engineering, a contemporary African novelist or poet, Utopian literature, or existentialism.
16. Write a character analysis of Hally or Sam from *"Master Harold" . . . and the Boys.* (Refer to the model in chapter 11.)
17. Compare two works that present hopeful views of the future.
18. a. Evaluate your favorite work in this chapter. Argue for its inclusion in the next edition of this text. Write a letter to the authors.
    b. Evaluate your favorite work in this book. Assume that your audience is the publisher of this anthology.
    c. Select one work from *Legacies* that has changed your views. Explain your reaction to it. How did it change your perspective?
19. Write an argument, agreeing or disagreeing with Yeats's "The Second Coming." You may refer to other works in this chapter.
20. a. Summarize Said's arguments in "Reflections on Exile."
    b. Agree or disagree with Said's contention that exile is the nature of the human condition in the global village.
    c. Posit an alternative to Said's view of the human condition in the global village.
    d. Compare Said's views with the speaker's ideas in Anzaldúa's poem.
    e. Evaluate Said's essay. (Refer to chapter 12.)
21. Create comments for several characters from works in this chapter about the following: "the secrets/of never having a home" (Linda Hogan, "Heritage").
22. Discuss the ideal versus the reality of harmony among people of different races and/or cultures in the works in this chapter's Thematic Preview. You also may refer to "The Handsomest Drowned Man in the World."
23. Compare the views of Plato, Camus, and Márquez on the cosmos and on human beings and their destinies. Compare the philosophies of life depicted in the works.
24. Discuss the collision of the Old and the New Worlds presented in *The Tempest.*
25. a. What is your view of the relationship between the individual and the community?
    b. Discuss the sense of community represented in three works in this chapter.
    c. Which work exemplifies your view of the interrelationship between the individual and the community?

PART THREE

Reading and Writing about the Genres

CHAPTER 9

FICTION

Fiction is the imagined creation of character and action for the purpose of conveying a vision of life. Like forms of nonfictional narration (storytelling), fiction depends on a recording of a sequence of events (as in historical rendering) and on an organization of incident and action (as in reporting). Fiction also requires a colorful, vivid depiction of characters and action (as in oral storytelling).

Fundamental to short fiction are a concentration on characters and the changes in characters brought about by events. Discussing the components of plot in *Aspects of the Novel,* E. M. Forster differentiates between an account of incidents and plot. He states that "The king died, and then the queen died" does not form a story line for fiction; however, the following presents the kernel of a tale, "The king died, and the queen died of grief." In the second version, the fiction emerges from the effect of the husband's death on the wife; a vision of mourning and loss is implied.

FORMS OF NARRATIVE

The earliest forms of narrative stories are the **myths** that ancient people conceived to explain their worlds—natural phenomena, human behavior, beliefs, and values—and to satisfy their need for transcendent experiences and meanings. Creation myths appear in the Old Testament, in Norse legends, and in Native American tribal lore. Greek and Roman myths of gods and goddesses and the creation of the world are written in such works as Thesiod's *Theogeny* and Ovid's *Metamorphoses.* The *Vedas,* the sacred Sanskrit texts of the Hindus, explore the origins of the gods of India.

Many myths explain facts of life, death, and immortality. "Coyote and the Shadow People," a Nez Percé myth, for example, relates the story of Coyote, who longs for his wife's return from the dead. The Death Spirit permits Coyote's wife to live in the world as a shadow for a three-day trial, but, because Coyote touches his wife's shadow, he loses the opportunity to regain his wife permanently. In "This Is What It Mean to Say Phoenix, Arizona," Sherman Alexie intertwines Native American myth and legend in the story of two young men's journey of self-discovery.

Some stories, called **parables,** provide moral instruction or convey moral, religious, or spiritual truths. Consider the story of the prodigal son in the New Testament, a story in which the younger son squanders his share of his father's wealth in riotous living, while his older brother stays and works with the father. The prodigal son endures hard times and returns to his father to ask for mercy, and the father joyously welcomes him and celebrates his homecoming. When the elder son protests, the father replies, "Be glad: for this thy brother was dead and is alive again and was lost and is found." This tale teaches the need for charity, compassion, and forgiveness. Luisa Valenzuela in "The Verb to Kill" (chapter 4) creates a short story in parabolic language to suggest the effects of violence on children who live under a militaristic regime.

A **fable,** another kind of moralizing story, commonly features animals or inanimate objects endowed with human qualities. Their experiences and behavior teach a lesson, stated explicitly at the conclusion of the tale. Some of the oldest fables may be traced to Aesop, a sixth-century Roman. In his story, "The Tortoise and the Hare," for instance, the hare, conceited and overly confident, falls asleep during a race while the slower tortoise plods ahead and wins. The moral of the tale is "slow but steady wins the race." In "My Life with the Wave," Octavio Paz, working out of the tradition of the fable, creates a male character who falls in love with a wave, a female lover (chapter 6). The lesson of the story concerns the power and consequences of romantic love.

Every culture also has its epics—stories of the exploits of heroes and mythical creatures—and folk tales that provide entertainment and present moral truths. Like myths, **epic poems** were passed from generation to generation as strictly oral entertainment before being written down and read as literature. *The Iliad* and *The Odyssey,* the oldest known Western epics, recount the exploits of the warriors of the Trojan War and the wanderings of the Greek hero Odysseus after the war. The *Mahabharata,* a monumental Hindu epic, depicts the strife of two Indian royal families and the spiritual development of the Indian hero, Krishna.

Each culture enjoys folk tales. The fairy tales we learned as children from Hans Christian Andersen or from the Brothers Grimm were actually Danish and German stories. *Cinderella,* for example, has many incarnations as a French folk tale transcribed by Perrault; as a German story recorded by the Brothers Grimm; as Algonquin Indian and Chinese tales. Although each version transmits different cultural values, fairy tales around the world convey recurring and familiar motifs: they portray the struggle between parents and children, between innocence and corruption, between good and evil, and between life and death. Short story writers often draw on folk and fairy tales in the development of character, plot, and theme. Gabriel Garciá Márquez deliberately titles "The Handsomest Drowned Man in the World" (chapter 8) a "Tale for Children" to highlight its fairy tale elements.

Other forms of narrative emerged in the Middle Ages and the Renaissance. The epic, the tale of the hero, became transformed into romances in which knights fought battles for the love of their ladies. Sometimes the quest for romance also became a quest for spiritual salvation, as in many of the stories of King Arthur, his knights of the Round Table, and their search for the Holy Grail, as in the poem, *Sir Gawain and the Green Knight.*

The word **novella** came into existence to describe the short tales of Boccacio written in the fourteenth century. Now the term signifies a work of fiction longer than and more expansive than a short story but less complex than a novel. They were stories of love, designed as courtly entertainment. Boccacio's *The Decameron* is a collection of one hundred short stories told by ten residents of Florence who attempted to escape the plague.

Lady Murasaki of Japan wrote the first **novel,** *The Tale of Genji,* in 1022. The novel emerged as a form of fictional prose narrative in the seventeenth century in England with the advent of a middle class that had both the leisure and a level of literacy to read and to support magazines. The first English protonovels were Aphra Behn's *Oroonoko* (1688) and Daniel Defoe's *Robinson Crusoe* (1719), a tale of a man abandoned on an island. The reading public and the demand for novels grew in the eighteenth century. The nineteenth century, however, became the great age of the British novel. The fullest representation of a story line, the novel captures a moment in time, a moment in a culture. This form incorporates the breadth and depth created by development of many characters, plots, subplots, and themes.

The invention of the modern **short story** is often attributed to Edgar Allen Poe. His most famous works include "The Masque of the Red Death," "The Pit and the Pendulum," and "The Telltale Heart." Poe suggested that a reader should be able complete a story in a single sitting. In the nineteenth century, the tradition of the American short story began with the publication of works by Poe, Nathaniel Hawthorne, Herman Melville, Mary Wilkins Freeman, Sarah Orne Jewett, and Kate Chopin. See, for example, Jewett's "A White Heron" (chapter 4).

A single concentrated story line, a single plot that involves a conflict or crisis that leads to a climax and to a resolution, and a limited number of characters distinguish the short story. Another usual feature of the genre is that it, like poetry, is compressed so that all elements may develop character, plot, and theme.

The modern short story was influenced by James Joyce's conception that a central character should be involved in a conflict or momentary experience that leads to discovery or to an awakening—in Joyce's term—an epiphany. However, contemporary short stories portray characters caught in experiences that may not lead to a climax, resolution, or realization. The stories conclude without the characters undergoing any change or gaining any great insight. The characters—in stasis—remain in a cycle of sterility. According to its creators, this form of development mirrors the absurdity and lack of meaning in the modern world. Finally, many fiction writers today, aware of the history of the genre, mix narrative techniques and modes to create new forms of the short story.

ELEMENTS OF FICTION

Point of View

Many elements of fiction—**point of view, setting, plot, characters, conflict, symbolism,** and **theme**—combine to create a work. We use these elements when we create even a simple, informal narrative, as when we recount a tragedy reported in the news or describe the previous night's party. Read this ghost story:

> I woke up in the middle of the night because I thought someone was watching me. When I awakened, a girl, dressed in a white nightgown, stood at the foot of my bed. She had long, yellow hair and large, luminous eyes, staring at me. I was petrified. I freaked. I closed my eyes. She was still there. I pulled the pillow over my head. When I lifted the pillow, she had disappeared. Only later, much later, did I tell my husband this story. He told me that he had shared the same experience. Later, much later, I learned that a little girl had died in our house in Kentucky, in the house where we experienced those nightmares.

Many elements of fiction are prevalent in this short tale, including a certain **point of view,** a narrative perspective. The choice of narrative perspective shapes the direction of the tale and is intertwined with plot, character, and theme. In this case, the story presents a first-person, singular point of view—"I." Writers create a sense of immediacy and personal involvement with first-person narrators.

An alternative to the first-person point of view is third-person narrative. To recognize the third-person point of view, look for the use of "he," "she," and "they." In third-person, the narrative perspective presents the characters and action and tells the tale from a certain distance. Recast the ghost story into third-person, using *she* and *her* in place of *I* and *me.* Such a change may result in a loss of intimacy, immediacy, and urgency.

There are several forms of third-person narration. An omniscient narrator assumes the vantage point of knowing everything in his or her characters' minds. Readers gain insights into the consciousness of all characters in the story. A narrator with limited knowledge discloses information about one or several, but not all, of the narrative points of view. In detached or dramatic narrative point of view, the speaker describes the characters and actions with no insight into characters' feelings. If the ghost story appeared in third-person, the narrator could develop his or her perspective, or possibly the husband's, or even the ghost's point of view. The story would progress differently. Consider this excerpt from Joyce Carol Oates' "Where Are You Going, Where Have You Been?" (chapter 4):

> Her name was Connie. She was fifteen and she had a quick nervous giggling habit of craning her neck to glance into mirrors, or checking other people's faces to make sure her own was all right. Her mother, who noticed everything and knew everything and who hadn't much reason any longer to look at her own face, always scolded Connie about it. "Stop gawking at yourself, who are you? You think you're so pretty?" she would say. Connie would raise her eyebrows at these familiar complaints and look right through her mother, into a shadowy

> vision of herself as she was right at that moment: she knew she was pretty and that was everything. Her mother had been pretty once too, if you could believe those old snapshots in the album, but now her looks were gone and that was why she was always after Connie.

Oates creates a limited third-person narrative perspective to depict her main character's struggles in adolescence. The reader gains insight into Connie's feelings about her appearance and about her disdainful attitudes toward her mother, but does not learn anything about Connie from the mother's point of view.

We also may characterize a narrator as participant or as nonparticipant. A participant narrator is a presence within the story who creates and engages in the action. A nonparticipant narrator observes the action. In the ghost story, a participant first-person narrator tells her own tale. Imagine this first-person narrator as a nonparticipant in the action, a woman who recounts a tale she heard from her friend. The story would have a different dramatic impact.

A participant narrator also may be trustworthy or untrustworthy. We consider a narrator trustworthy when we accept his or her view of the situation, when we think it is credible or, perhaps, represents the position of the author. In a story with an untrustworthy narrator, we question the narrative's stance and ask if it is credible, biased, or even, perhaps, delusional or hysterical. We question the validity of the point of view and realize that a distinction exists between the narrative and authorial point of view. In the ghost story, the narrator is trustworthy because her responses seem skeptical and because she qualifies her discussion. We accept her version of the truth. Imagine an untrustworthy narrator, extremely overwrought, talking to the ghost—we would not believe her version.

Setting

Setting is the location, time, place, and/or environment in which the story takes place. In the ghost story, the location is the bedroom of a house, the time is night and the present; and the environment is a middle-class household in the 1980s in Kentucky. The setting creates a particular mood, sense of place, and context. The ghost story would have little impact if the event occurred in broad daylight, in a city, and in a less scientific and skeptical age.

Plot

A **plot** presents the sequence of events in a story. In a short story the sequence of events is concentrated and does not necessarily represent actual time. Events in daily life, perhaps having taken place over a period of time, or events that appear random or fragmentary are often shaped, developed, and given cohesive form. For example, routine trips to work on the bus may become the basis for a central episode in a story, or a chance encounter with an old friend may be transformed into the central action of a tale. In the case of the ghost story, the sighting may represent many nights of uneasy feelings or partial glimpses.

Since a short story is so compressed, usually the sequence of events narrows to a single moment, a series of moments, or action that reveals a larger truth of character and life. The sequence builds to a **climax,** a high point of action. In an adventure or horror short story, the climax may be an apex of suspense; in a short story focused on character, the climactic point may be a moment of discovery, awakening, or revelation. For example, in the ghost story, the most important event is not the appearance of the spirit, but the discovery that a child had died in the house, and, indeed, that the apparition could be a real ghost; in short, the narrator begins to recognize the possibility of supernatural occurrences.

Short story writers also manipulate the sequence of events in a story; they may not present the events in chronological (time) order. For example, the story may begin in the middle of the action or at the end of the sequence, and then the narrator may *flash back*—move back in time—to the beginning of the action. The ghost story, for instance, could have begun with the sighting of the ghost and then could have returned to the beginning of the night's sleep. Flashback techniques add dramatic impact and meaning to the unfolding events since the reader already knows what will transpire; the technique also may shift the focus from the plot to character development since attention moves away from the rendering of the action. *Flash forward* is another method of manipulating time in which the narrator relates the beginning of the tale, then moves quickly to the ending, and then returns to the beginning of the story. This technique adds dramatic impact and irony (double meanings) to each stage of the action since the reader is aware of the contribution of each moment to the unfolding of the action. In a rendering of the ghost story, the narrator could have quickly moved to the sighting, then returned to see partial, mysterious glimpses of the face, hair, clothes, and eyes of a figure—these glimpses would have dramatic impact for a reader. Short stories also may unfold through associations and may move backward and forward in time.

Conflict

Conflict is the tension between two forces; the exposition of a problem; an internal battle between two forces, psychic or external. Major conflicts in fiction arise between people and nature, between people and their environments, among people, or within a person. In the ghost story, the conflict, an internal struggle, centers on whether the narrator believes that she has seen a ghost. The plot of the short story concentrates on and develops such a conflict until it is resolved after a moment of crisis. In conventional short stories, the climax prompts the resolution through a moment of reckoning, recognition, awakening, or discovery. However, many contemporary short stories do not present resolutions of conflict. Again in the ghost story, no answers exist to test the validity of the reported sighting of the apparition. The story leaves questions open. The story ends in an ambivalent, mysterious way.

Character

The short story primarily concentrates on the presentation of **characters:** the people in the story and their conflicts. In the ghost story, the characters are the first-person narrator, the apparition, and the husband. The conflict concerns the tension within the narrator between believing and negating the presence of the little girl. We learn about characters through action, dialogue, and physical appearance. Their personalities evolve through events and through interaction with others.

In fiction, E. M. Forster has distinguished between **round** and **flat** characters. Round characters are multidimensional, capable of growth and change. Flat characters, according to Forster, are one-dimensional and often stereotypical. The effective short story concentrates on presenting at least one round character in conflict with others. Because of the length and complicated texture of a short story, the writer of this genre cannot develop as many characters in depth as can writers of such longer forms as the novella or novel. In a further draft of the ghost story, the narrator could become the round character and the ghost of the little girl, the flat, one-dimensional character.

Language

The **language** in a short story is compressed. Each word is well chosen and contributes to the impact of the whole. Sharp, vivid sensory details involve the reader in the world of the narrator, in setting, in characters, in the unfolding drama of the plot. In addition, short story writers often choose elements of poetic diction: images, figurative language, symbolism, allusion, and irony to create their worlds (see chapter 3).

Short story writers also work with the **denotations** (dictionary definitions) and **connotations** (associations) of words to create effect. Because the form is concentrated, each word must have impact and add to the presentation of theme (messages of the work). Think of the word "luminous" in the ghost story as it alludes to the physical presence of the ghost as transparent and also refers to the girl's wide-eyed stare. The connotations lead readers to form a picture of a ghost: mysterious, innocent, and yet scary.

Another element of language is the texture of the prose: the sounds and the rhythms of the language. Storytelling, originally oral entertainment, does exist as "music." Think of the tension between the liquid "l" sounds and the staccato "e" words, which reflects the narrator's state of mind. The repetition of the "s" and the "d" sounds evoke feelings of sharpness and of hardness, appropriate to a confrontation with the supernatural.

In addition, aspects of style that create the rhythm of language are repetition and parallelism (repeated and balanced wording). The short, simple sentences evoke the fear felt by the narrator.

For stories to be powerful, writers also avoid **clichés** (hackneyed or overused expressions and figures of speech). Clichés detract from impact because they belong to everyday conversational speech, not to the heightened language of fiction; and, therefore, they are jarring and destructive to the mood. They also do not add descriptive detail or image because they cannot evoke word pictures since their meanings are predictable and often taken for granted. In the ghost story, the narrator reverts to a level of colloquial language: "freaked." This shift is jarring. She could have used a stronger verb to convey both her fear and astonishment.

Tone

Tone, the sense of the narrator, emerges from the connotations, the inferences, of every word. Tone also conveys the attitude of the narrator toward his or her subject, for example, characters and events in the work. Apparent from the first word, tone colors every detail of the work—dialogue, imagery, symbol, and setting. In the ghost story, the tone shifts from fear to puzzlement to mystery as the narrator learns about the death of the child.

Symbolism

A **symbol** is a person, place, object, thing, name, title, aspect of setting that suggests something beyond itself and has a range of meanings. Since a short story, like poetry, is compressed, all aspects of the story—title, setting, characters' names, appearance, dialogue, and events of the plot—may contain symbolic meanings and create the theme. For example, even in the informal telling of the ghost story, the girl's yellow hair and white dress suggest her innocence; the head under the pillow, the denial of truth.

Theme

The **theme** of the short story is the message presented by the work. No story has a single central idea; there may be several themes. As he or she is crafting the story, the writer may be conscious of several themes of the work and may shape it with these ideas in mind. In addition, readers may discover other messages from careful analyses of the text. In the ghost story, one theme certainly is the mystery of supernatural occurrences. Another theme concerns the omnipresence of death and the human drive to negate that reality.

All aspects of an effective short story may create themes: point of view, setting, plot, character, conflict, tone, and symbolism. In the narrator's story one theme centers on the impossibility of escaping death. The point of view—first person—gives the reader the thoughts of the woman facing the appearance of the ghost and the fact of death itself. The setting also develops this theme: it is the "middle of the night," a time of dream and unreality that contrasts with the stark presence of the apparition. The tension and conflict in the plot center on the narrator's vision of the ghost—is she real? The stark, simple language builds the confrontation and mood of the work. The gesture of "[pulling] the pillow over [her] head" symbolically suggests the narrator's need for denial. This short story then becomes a tightly woven anecdote about facing the supernatural and the irrefutable fact of death.

THE READING/WRITING PROCESS: FICTION

In addition to critical reading responses, we recommend a process for understanding fiction. First, read the story. Involve yourself on the level of point of view and plot. Ask yourself who is telling the story, and explore your reactions to the narrative point of view. Is the narrator part of the story? Is the narrator objective about the events? Is the narrator trustworthy? As you read, remember the main events and follow the sequence of action. Who are the main characters? With whom do you sympathize? Locate the problems and conflicts. As you read, notice the shifts in conflict and the development of crisis. At the story's conclusion, ask yourself if the conflicts are resolved. Ask if any of the characters have changed. How have they developed? Ask if your sympathies and involvement with certain characters have shifted. What messages have you discovered in the text? Explore the emotional impact of the work. Ask how you felt after finishing the story. In a second or third reading, analyze the function of point of view, setting, tone, symbolism, word choice, detail, imagery, and figurative language used by the writer in building the story. Throughout your reading, explore your own reactions and associations with the story. Assess your reactions to the themes of the narrative.

CHECKLIST FOR READING SHORT FICTION

1. What point of view is apparent? First person? Third person? Omniscient? Limited? Detached? What is the impact of this choice of narrative perspective? participant or nonparticipant narrative point of view?
2. What is the setting of the story? Time? Place? Environment? What moods are created by the setting in the story? What social, cultural, historical contexts are established by setting?
3. What are the key events of the plot? Does the plot build to a climax? What are the conflicts in the story? Are the conflicts resolved? Is there a moment of awakening or discovery?
4. Who are the main characters? Are they round? flat? With whom do you relate? sympathize? How are they related to each other? What is the role of minor characters?
5. What is the tone of the story? What can you tell about the tone from the opening? Why? From key descriptions and details?
6. Characterize word choice. Is there vivid detail? Figurative language? Irony?
7. What are the symbolic details (title, names, setting, gesture, objects, events)? How does symbolism create theme?

8. What are the themes of the work? Do all elements of the story contribute to the theme?

Student Portfolio:
Response to Kate Chopin's "The Story of an Hour"

The Story of an Hour

Kate Chopin

Knowing that Mrs. Mallard was afflicted with a heart trouble, great care was taken to break to her as gently as possible the news of her husband's death.

It was her sister Josephine who told her, in broken sentences; veiled hints that revealed in half concealing. Her husband's friend Richards was there, too, near her. It was he who had been in the newspaper office when intelligence of the railroad disaster was received, with Brently Mallard's name leading the list of "killed." He had only taken the time to assure himself of its truth by a second telegram, and had hastened to forestall any less careful, less tender friend in bearing the sad message.

She did not hear the story as many women have heard the same, with a paralyzed inability to accept its significance. She wept at once, with sudden, wild abandonment, in her sister's arms. When the storm of grief had spent itself she went away to her room alone. She would have no one follow her.

There stood, facing the open window, a comfortable, roomy armchair. Into this she sank, pressed down by a physical exhaustion that haunted her body and seemed to reach into her soul.

5 She could see in the open square before her house the tops of trees that were all aquiver with the new spring life. The delicious breath of rain was in the air. In the street below a peddler was crying his wares. The notes of a distant song which some one was singing reached her faintly, and countless sparrows were twittering in the eaves.

There were patches of blue sky showing here and there through the clouds that had met and piled one above the other in the west facing her window.

She sat with her head thrown back upon the cushion of the chair, quite motionless, except when a sob came up into her throat and shook her, as a child who had cried itself to sleep continues to sob in its dreams.

She was young, with a fair, calm face, whose lines bespoke repression and even a certain strength. But now there was a dull stare in her eyes, whose gaze was fixed away off yonder on one of those patches of blue sky. It was not a glance of reflection, but rather indicated a suspension of intelligent thought.

There was something coming to her and she was waiting for it, fearfully. What was it? She did not know; it was too subtle and elusive to name. But she felt it, creeping out of the sky, reaching toward her through the sounds, the scents, the color that filled the air.

10 Now her bosom rose and fell tumultuously. She was beginning to recognize this thing that was approaching to possess her, and she was striving to beat it back with her will—as powerless as her two white slender hands would have been.

When she abandoned herself a little whispered word escaped her slightly parted lips. She said it over and over under her breath: "free, free, free!" The vacant stare and the look of terror that had followed it went from her eyes. They stayed keen and bright. Her pulses beat fast, and the cursing blood warmed and relaxed every inch of her body.

She did not stop to ask if it were or were not a monstrous joy that held her. A clear and exalted perception enabled her to dismiss the suggestion as trivial.

She knew that she would weep again when she saw the kind, tender hands folded in death; the face that had never looked save with love upon her, fixed and gray and dead. But she saw beyond that bitter moment a long procession of years to come that would belong to her absolutely. And she opened and spread her arms out to them in welcome.

There would be no one to live for her during those coming years; she would live for herself. There would be no powerful will bending hers in that blind persistence with which men and women believe they have a right to impose a private will upon a fellow-creature. A kind intention or a cruel intention made the act seem no less a crime as she looked upon it in that brief moment of illumination.

15 And yet she had loved him—sometimes. Often she had not. What did it matter! What could love, the unsolved mystery, count for in face of this possession of self-assertion which she suddenly recognized as the strongest impulse of her being!

"Free! Body and soul free!" she kept whispering.

Josephine was kneeling before the closed door with her lips to the keyhole, imploring for admission. "Louise, open the door! I beg; open the door—you will make yourself ill. What are you doing, Louise? For heaven's sake open the door."

"Go away. I am not making myself ill." No; she was drinking in a very elixir of life through that open window.

Her fancy was running riot along those days ahead of her. Spring days, and summer days, and all sorts of days that would be her own. She breathed a quick prayer that life might be long. It was only yesterday she had thought with a shudder that life might be long.

20 She arose at length and opened the door to her sister's importunities. There was a feverish triumph in her eyes, and she carried herself unwittingly like a goddess of Victory. She clasped her sister's waist, and together they descended the stairs. Richards stood waiting for them at the bottom.

Someone was opening the front door with a latchkey. It was Brently Mallard who entered, a little travel-stained, composedly carrying his grip-sack and umbrella. He had been far from the scene of the accident, and did not even know there had been one. He stood amazed at Josephine's piercing cry; at Richards' quick motion to screen him from the view of his wife.

But Richards was too late.

When the doctors came they said she had died of heart disease—of joy that kills.

❄ ❄ ❄

The following works present a student's reaction responses to Kate Chopin's "The Story of an Hour." To demonstrate the process of constructing a response essay to a work, we include Maria Taylor's initial journal entry and three drafts of her essay.

The thesis of the essay evolved from Taylor's freewrite (composed in her journal), designed to spur personal connections with the work. Students in the class were asked to write a monologue in the voice of Mrs. Mallard. After the completion of her assignment, Taylor discovered that she empathized with Mrs. Mallard and shared her feelings of imprisonment. Taylor's position is voiced in the lines: "I want to be free to be for me, only me." She begins with Mrs. Mallard's exclamations (" 'free, free, free. . . . ' ") and moves to her own: "I never really felt free," and "It was the only house I knew as woman." She shifts from speaking in Mrs. Mallard's voice to voicing her own ideas and experiences. The discovery gained from the freewrite became the kernel of the first draft of the reaction essay. In this version, she expresses her yearning.

A collage writer, Taylor jumps from association to association: household duties, her relationship with her husband, the memories of his goodness and his abuse, her need for "balance," her panic, eating disorder, and fear. In her next two drafts, she more freely articulates her connections with Mrs. Mallard, organizes her thoughts, treats her responses in a systematic manner, and arranges them in stages that follow Mrs. Mallard's process of discovering her desire to be free. She also includes the quotations from the work that spark her insights.

Journal Entry

Freewrite: A Monologue Spoken by Mrs. Mallard
By Maria Taylor

I've said it over and over under my breath, "I want to be free, free, free." I want to be free to be for me, only me. To be no-one's mother, daughter, wife. I want to be free to come and go as I please, when I please, how I please. The words "free, free, free" speak to my longing soul.

I never really felt free. I went from Dad's household to my husband's control. The transition was easy for me; it was a role I always wanted. It was expected of me. It was the only role I knew as woman.

As a female, I was to be wife, mother, daughter, depending on "man" in all roles. I never realized then, in playing out my role I was always depending on a man for my well being. If I needed nurturing, I went to him. If I needed money, I went to him.

Note following reading of the story:

I could see so clearly the truth in the quotation "free." I see the dichotomy in her.

Taylor's First Draft

I want to enjoy a relationship based on equality. Do I sound selfish? Well—it may be—but maybe it's my time, huh? I don't want to cook, clean, do laundry, shop, have to be home, say when I'll be home, where I'll be etc., be questioned about anything—anymore. I want to be free, and yet, I want to be connected. I suppose that would be with and to him. He is my husband, and he has been a good one. He is the father of my four incredible children, and he has been a good father. But there are the horrendous memories of his drinking and emotional and psychological abuse, all of which he denies to this day. He's demeaning of me and my role as woman, wife, person. I want out. I feel selfish and wrong and guilty, but I cannot continue to be a wife anymore. I want a balance in my life. No, this isn't even true. I want it all to be for me now. I know I cannot fulfill my roles anymore because my own health is beginning to fail. I have "panic attacks" regularly, and they are the most painful, terrorizing feelings I have ever experienced. I cannot control my food intake, anymore. Food has become my friend, lover, consoler, comforter. All things except what it truly is—I feel my own life has been fused to others for so long, and in that fusion, I've become lost. I am so frightened. I wonder how I can go on and on and what is left for me? Would I have been better off never knowing him or any man and just be for me?

Conclusion?

Is there ever a relationship between man and woman that is based on true equality and true freedom? Isn't love supposed to give these gifts? Will I, like Mrs. Mallard, have to die before I am truly free?

In the next draft, Taylor creates paragraphs to explore each topic.

Taylor's Second Draft

It's almost too difficult to write, to express on paper, but I know this story. I have in many ways lived it.

I suppose you would have to be married for a while to understand Mrs. Mallard. I have been married for thirty-one years, so I understand her. (We can only really understand someone when we have walked in her shoes.)

I like Chopin's Mrs. Mallard's wish to be free. Free to be, for me—only me, no-one else. Free to sleep and eat, come and go—do, not do, whatever I want, when I want, for a while.

And yet am I afraid of this? Yes, for I have never lived for myself, lived by myself. I have never taken care of myself financially. I always took care of others and was taken care of financially by others.

I went from Dad's home living under his jurisdiction to my husband's home living under his jurisdiction. This sounds so cynical; doesn't it? But this is how I feel and how it was.

I never felt "free." Their control was always so subtle and elusive, but I knew it was there like Mr. Mallard and that I had to walk within the lines of their boundaries. If not, I would be abandoned, emotionally, physically and financially. Then how would I exist? I was programmed to believe I could not live without them.

And yet I love him. I believe I do anyway. But I so want to be free. I want to be like Mrs. Mallard looking out the window. I want to continue to love him, but I do not want to live within the confines of what he believes that love should be.

In the final draft, Taylor develops substantial responses and connection to the work.

Taylor's Final Draft
"Free, Free, Free": Chopin's
"The Story of an Hour"

Under her breath, Mrs. Mallard says, "free, free, free!" Over and over again. I have said the same words over and over again under my breath. I want to be free. Free to be for me, only me, to be no one's daughter, wife, or mother. I do not want to be caregiver, support, keeper. I want to live only for myself. I want to be free to come and go as I please, when I please, how I please.

The adjectives, "free, free, free," speak to my longing soul. And yet I am afraid. Yes, for I have never lived for myself, lived by myself. I have never taken care of myself financially. In many ways, I am like Mrs. Mallard's sobbing child. I always took care of others and was taken care of financially by others. I took care of both my parents when they were ill. Then I became a wife and mother. Emotionally, all of my energies were out there, caring for others all my life, leaving very little energy for nurturing myself. Consequently, I feel uncomfortable and I question whether or not I can be free. At fifty-one, this is a sorry commentary. Like Mrs. Mallard, I have never lived for myself.

I went from Dad's house, living under his jurisdiction, to my husband's home, living under his jurisdiction. Coming from a patriarchal home and environment, I thought that this simply was the way that it was for all women. I thought that the "powerful will bending [mine] in that blind persistence with which men and women believe they have a right to impose a private will upon a fellow-creature" was to be expected and the way it should be.

I never felt free. Their control was always so subtle and elusive, but I knew it was there and that I had to walk within the lines of their boundaries. If not, I would be abandoned, emotionally, physically and financially. Then how would I exist, survive? I was programmed to believe I could not live without them. As a result, I felt as if I danced around this big bear that lived in the center of the living room for most of my life. I do not want to dance anymore. Like Mrs. Mallard, who said "she would live for herself," I too wish for autonomy.

5 I want to continue a relationship with him, but I do not want to live within the confines of what he believes that love should be. I want to feel "spring days, and summer days . . . that would be [my] own."

My husband is a domineering man. He often treats me in a way that suffocates me. His constant questions, his lack of trust, his knee-jerk anger oppress and fatigue me. I understand his fear, that he will lose me, that he doesn't understand me any more, and I empathize with him. But I no longer can claim this shattering as my own. When I do, I become shattered myself. I love my husband, and yet I want to be free.

I want to enjoy a relationship based on equality and freedom. Can a relationship between a man and a woman be based on these things? Is it possible? Is it possible with my relationship with him? Has he snatched that away from me, too? Would I have been happier never knowing my love or any man and just be, for me? Will I, like Mrs. Mallard, have to die before I feel free, before I feel that "monstrous joy"—the "joy that kills?"

In the introduction to this last draft, Taylor states her thesis, the yearning "to be free" that she shares with Mrs. Mallard. In the middle paragraphs, she explains the origins of that desire, tracing her need for autonomy to her family background (paragraph 2), and to her marriage, an extension of that "patriarchal home and environment" (paragraph 3). She next presents (in paragraphs 5 and 6) her desire for autonomy; finally, she articulates her dilemma: the conflict between her love and loyalty to her husband and her need to find a "relationship based on equality and freedom." Her conclusion contains her pessimistic assessment: "Will I, like Mrs. Mallard, have to die before I feel free, before I feel that 'monstrous joy'—the 'joy that kills'?" She builds the essay to its dramatic conclusion.

Taylor also strives to include more quotations from the story so that the progression in her thinking mirrors, in some ways, the logic and progression of the plot of "Story of An Hour." She begins by citing Mrs. Mallard's wish to be "free, free, free," which appears midway in Chopin's story. In the description of her relationship to her husband, she includes Mrs. Mallard's realization that after her husband's death, there will be no "powerful will bending [her]" into submission. By following the pattern of Mrs. Mallard's recognition, Taylor makes their situations analogous and strengthens the comparison of her situation with the character's plight. They both came to similar despairing assessments of the possibility of "true equality" in the relation of men and women. Chopin's character dies . . . death is her only release. Taylor despairs of the possibility of finding relationships based on a "true balance" between the sexes.

Taylor's connections with "The Story of an Hour" are made explicit: her understanding of Mrs. Mallard's imprisonment caused by her social role; Mrs. Mallard's inability to change her circumstances; the protagonist's inhibited desire for freedom and her ambivalent feelings toward her husband; her desire for release from a marriage that denies her autonomy.

CHAPTER 10

Poetry

When asked to define poetry, a student responded, "Poems make words dance." This brief reply stimulates many provocative ideas and images concerning a difficult question. The excellent answer implies that poems are metaphorical, paradoxical, and dynamic. In poetry the images do not work if they do not inspire sudden connection and insight. The words must "dance," or they cannot create effective and astonishing meanings. This definition also suggests the necessity of rhythm, beat, and accent. If the work lacks these intrinsic qualities, it is not poetry.

What else does this definition signify? It indicates that poems create themes, character, and contexts through compressed language, through figures of speech, through economy of form, and through sound. If academic definitions always require appropriate language, then the student's answer insists upon such words. If academic definitions insist upon rhythm or meter, then the student's answer alludes to rhythm through the word "dance." If academic definitions require that poetry elicit feelings and imagination, the student's answer implies that poetry creates these responses in the reader or the listener.

The word "make," above all, connotes *art* and insists that words have the power of the visual to imitate, signify, please, mean, and construct new realities and truths. In ancient cultures, chants and religious rituals were poetry; epics and dramas were poetry. We appreciate the enduring value of the genre as an accessible source of wisdom and pleasure, a significant form of enrichment and of redemption, and an expression of the deepest experiences and truths of human existence.

KINDS OF POETRY

In general, every poem falls into one of three broad categories: **narrative poetry** tells a story, **lyric poetry** gives a brief account of the person's feelings, ideas, or moods, and **dramatic poetry** presents monologues and soliloquies.

Narrative Poetry

Any poem that spins a tale may be defined as a *narrative* work. In Gwendolyn Brooks' "The Chicago Defender Sends a Man to Little Rock" (chapter 7), the speaker catalogues the daily actions of citizens who bear children, celebrate holidays, play baseball, attend concerts, and love each other. The persona wants to report that "they are like people everywhere." Another story, however, exists in Little Rock; people are "hurling spittle, rocks, garbage, and fruit." The speaker must recount this conflict. Why? The Supreme Court had ordered desegregation of the schools in an historic decision in the case of *Brown* vs. *The Board of Education,* a case never directly mentioned in Brooks' narrative. Because of its political context, "The Chicago Defender Sends a Man to Little Rock" may be called a *protest poem.*

Other forms of narrative poetry include the epic and the ballad. **Epics,** written in many eras and in many cultures, derive from oral tradition and describe the adventures and accomplishments of great heroes. The story assumes grand proportions and often includes supernatural beings and their actions that create monumental consequences. The language of epics is formal and figurative, and almost all epics share similar conventions. *The Iliad* and *The Odyssey* by Homer (Greek), *The Epic of Gilgamesh* (Babylonian), *Sundiata* (Mali), and *Beowulf* (Anglo-Saxon) represent works in this tradition.

Ballads, another form of narrative poetry, also derive from oral tradition since originally they were songs. Literary ballads include most features of the oral form: repetition and refrain—phrases or lines reappearing at certain places in the poem. Ballads alternate lines of eight and six syllables, with rhymes in the second and fourth lines. Not every ballad must be written in the standard stanzaic pattern. Not every ballad contains a refrain. The Beatles, for example, wrote a humorous song about "Rocky Raccoon" that mimics "Frankie and Johnny"; both are ballads. More serious works tell stories of young women such as Thomas Hardy's "The Ruined Maid."

Lyric Poetry

Lyrics are short and subjective; in these poems, the speakers describe their thoughts or feelings. The original definition of the lyric meant a song accompanied by a lyre. This category includes the following forms:

1. An **elegy** mourns the death of a particular person, or sometimes, the inexorable fate of humans, their mortality. Ben Jonson's "On My First Son" presents a father's grief, a sorrow so deep that it renders his identity as a poet meaningless (see chapter 5).
2. A **meditation** centers on a particular object as a method for consideration of metaphysical ideas. (see "Dover Beach" by Mathew Arnold in chapter 6.)
3. An **ode,** a song of praise, is long, serious, and formal in all of its aspects. It always has a complex stanzaic pattern. Keats' "Ode on a Grecian Urn" is an example of this form (see chapter 8).
4. A **pastoral** celebrates the idyllic nature of country life. James Wright's "A Blessing" represents a modern version of the pastoral (see chapter 8).

Matsuo Bashō, a Japanese poet who lived in the seventeenth century, wrote haiku, unrhymed three-line poems with seventeen syllables. Haiku also may be considered lyrical in nature:

Sleeping at noon
the body of the blue heron
poised in nobility
(hiru neburu / aosagi no mi no / tōtosayo)
(translated by Earl Miner)

Notice that Bashō has compressed a strong image into three lines. The meaning depends on sudden insight and a connection between the heron's pose and a spiritual stance. At first glance, the poem seems to celebrate the serene immobility of the heron, "sleeping at noon." The closing line, however, implies a moment of spiritual awareness that transcends the physical.

Dramatic Poetry

In **dramatic poetry,** the speaker becomes an actor. In "Girl," (see chapter 5), for example, Jamaica Kincaid creates a **monologue** for a mother who is attempting to inculcate gender roles into her young daughter.

Other forms of dramatic poems include epistolary monologues—letters written as poems. In the most familiar example of this kind of work, Ezra Pound's "The River Merchant's Wife: A Letter," loosely translated from a poem in Chinese written by Rihaku (also known as Li Po), the speaker has loved her husband deeply since childhood. The young Chinese wife waits patiently for his return and expresses her loneliness and longing in the letter. Admired as a model of dignity and of marital love, this eighth-century poem by Li Po presents great autobiographical detail in highly controlled and terse language.

Although readers wish to designate strict categories for poems, some works defy such classification. Contemporary poetry often combines narrative and lyric modes; poets often extend the limits of traditional forms; and in their experiments, they create new language and images; they step into the borderland between narration and lyric, a place where new voices may sing and be heard.

ELEMENTS OF POETRY

Voice

Poems, like fiction, present speakers who tell about events, experiences, emotions, or ideas. The poet remains separate from the persona or speaker, although in some works little distance exists between the two. In all cases, however, the reader should assume that poet and speaker have distinct identities. Often the poet creates a voice exceedingly different from him or herself. The speaker may even be anonymous.

One of the best methods of interpreting poetry is to define the voice, to discover as much as possible about its quality, mood, and concerns. In "Danaë," a voice poem based on Greek myth, the anonymous poet alludes to the imprisonment of the virgin, Danaë, by her father, a crime that he committed to circumvent the fulfillment of a prophecy that predicted the death of Acrisius at the hands of his grandson. Zeus, however, seduced Danaë in a shower of gold; and from this magical union, Perseus was born. Eventually the curse was fulfilled. Listen to the voice of Danaë. Consider the poem, and answer the following questions:

1. Who is the speaker?
2. What is the point of view?
3. What can you tell about the speaker? What is the situation of the speaker?
4. How is the story told? What story is being told?
5. What details and words characterize the speaker?
6. To whom does the speaker talk? Who is the audience?

Danaë

to be born to a curse
is all of history
that dark will
is all I knew
in the dark cavern
I lived
I saw just the
immediate edge of my body
the dark shadings and contours
of that shell
and you live in it
as if it were light
as if it gave you light
then one day
a rain came
a gold rain
a sheen of rain
a cool yellow breeze
a shimmer of gold
a sift of gold all over my skin
a wash of yellow light
and in this way
he came
my child
came as rain fell
came as silently

to life
came to me
a rinse of yellow gold
that boy child
my words
my history
my unsaid self
a blessing
too fragile
to be dreamt

The poet retells the story of Danaë with a first-person point of view and adds some new details to the ancient Greek myth. The persona expresses her sadness and loneliness as she considers her body as something to "live in." Subject to "the dark will," she exists in shadow "as if it were light." She seems concerned about the body, its history; and she feels resignation. She does not speak in anger, but she acknowledges indirectly that men and gods have power over her body. Yet the men are completely absent from the speaker's story.

The poet devotes half of the poem to the gold rain that impregnates Danaë and gives her a son. The repetition of "rain," "gold," "yellow," and "light" introduces a sense of quiet joy into the poem. These details about the conception of the child allow the speaker to claim herself, her history, and her child through words. In this connection between language and the body, the poet transforms Danaë into a contemporary woman.

Tone

The **tone** of a poem establishes the mood of the piece, the changing emotions of the speaker, or the attitude of the persona toward the subject. The poem may be sad, angry, shocking, nostalgic, or humorous. In "Daddy" by Sylvia Plath, the speaker begins with a mildly angry tone as she announces her rejection of her father, but the voice quickly becomes sad as she admits, "you died before I had time" (chapter 5). In the monologue, the young woman, the persona, calls her father a god, a Nazi, and the devil. At the end, she attempts to exorcise him through a darkly humorous allusion to Dracula in vampire movies:

There's a stake in your fat black heart
And the villagers never liked you.
They are dancing and stamping on you.
They always knew it was you.
Daddy, daddy, you bastard, I'm through.

Here the speaker refers to the only method that kills a vampire: a stake in the heart. She indicates that the villagers in Transylvania always knew that the vampire really was Count Dracula who lived in the eerie castle above the town. As a final shock, the speaker calls "Daddy" a "bastard" and declares wildly that she is "through." Some critics find the tone too exaggerated and do not believe that the ending convinces; others praise the poem for its devastating truth about the impact of the death of a parent and about the overwhelming anger of the betrayed and bereaved child.

Theme

Poems can explore any **theme,** any central idea. The poet can write about the terror of war, the ecstasy of love or religion, the mysteries or certainties of life or ideas. A poem may protest injustice, define itself, or mourn the death of a particular person. Many of these themes recur frequently. In every culture, poets write about time, death, love, and art. They celebrate achievements and laugh at and satirize human error and folly.

In order to determine the theme of a poem, look at images, voice, symbols, form, and sound. Combined, these aspects create the conceptions central to meaning. Because poetry is allusive and highly compressed, however, many interpretations become possible. Each reader may discover a different theme; but most of the time, a poem, rich in language and content, leads to certain agreements about thematic intent.

Chasing Fire Engines

The women in my family
always chase fire engines,
sirens wailing in their ears,
long funnels down and in,
a throb in their arms—
the urge to touch men,
the big hoses, eyes on the stream
arching toward smoke.
I was born with arson
in my heart, the desire
to light fires, to set
aflame every hand
that brushes my wrist,
to incinerate.

Now I dream of a stranger,
incendiary fingers on my breast.
I rise toward shadow,
light a match to identify
the face, to reach
the tender place;
and I smell ashes,
push the hand aside,
heat cooling

as I wake, women
in my family running
after fire engines, watching
men dowse flames,
water arching and arching:
the spray, the spray.

Then you turn to me in sleep,
move your leg over mine,
easy in your skin,
and I slide under you,
old luminations surround us,
the longing for arson
rising in my throat,
a moan subsides
as I chase the engines.
Fires, burning everywhere,
light the pillow where
your head circles mine.

In "Chasing Fire Engines," the persona speaks of natural curiosity and obsessions about sexuality; she feels the "heat cooling" and fantasizes about strangers; finally, she embraces her lover, familiar fires circling their heads on the pillow. Traditional themes about love and loss are deflated, but they remain relevant. The themes in this work center on the highly sexual nature of men and women, represented by the fire, the hoses, the spray. The heat cools in relationships, but every person eventually discovers that familiarity and "old luminations" in love remain more important than initial and easy incendiary impulses.

Setting

Every poem presents a persona and a theme or themes; every poem takes place in a **setting**—the place, location, or atmosphere. Consider the various places in "Chasing Fire Engines." At first, the persona remembers the world of her childhood, a time when all of the men in the family served in the volunteer fire department and when the women and children hurried to watch the men in action. Of necessity, the town must have been small—perhaps, a village located in the South or Midwest. The setting also becomes a dream where a stranger touches the speaker, and the place seems shadowy and dark. As the third setting, the speaker alludes to a bed where she and her lover sleep; and, as they awaken, fire circles their heads on a pillow. Through an examination of setting, you can discover new aspects of meaning in every poem. By carefully describing locations in "Chasing Fire Engines," for example, you learn that the shifts in settings create important complications in the poem, complications that enrich its texture and significance.

Imagery

Everyone's first experience with reality begins with an **image**—a message from the world that comes to consciousness through the senses. It may enter through the eye as shape and shade; it may enter the nose as odor; it may enter the ear as sound; it may tingle the tongue as taste; it may caress the skin as touch. Every strong memory exists as an image or as a series or composite of images. Every dream emerges as vivid, often surreal, imagery. Scientists and poets confirm the inextricable relationship between ideas and images. Einstein arrived at his theory of relativity by picturing a man traveling on a wave of light. Goethe complained that he no sooner had an idea before "it [turned] into an image."

Certainly poetry cannot exist without **imagery.** Those things that appear as physical sensation are called **concrete images**; those that represent ideas may be **abstract images.** Consider this short poem by Margaret Atwood:

You Fit into Me

you fit into me
like a hook into an eye.

a fish hook
an open eye

The first two lines create the picture of the fitting together of the two parts of a familiar household fastener to connote a couple's embracing, caressing, or making love. The next two images twist the meaning—the hook becomes a fish hook penetrating a literal, not a metaphorical, eye—and they shock the reader with the deliberate announcement of pain. The relationship is an agonizing, not a loving, one.

Economy and brevity represent the advantages of images in poetry. They suggest; they enable readers to imagine experiences or sensations. They provide emotional connotations that color responses and evoke feelings in readers. William Carlos Williams's poem, "The Red Wheelbarrow," represents the compressed nature of poetry:

so much depends
upon
a red wheel
barrow

glazed with rain
water

beside the white
chickens.

What does the picture suggest? For a moment, the wet wheelbarrow beside the white chickens composes the world in a particular order, one that ascribes harmony and beauty to an ordinary scene. Through the first two lines Williams takes his representation of a bucolic scene and transforms it into a vision of the pleasures and purposes of perception. Williams suggests that the ability to perceive the relationship of images gives meaning to life. This poem exemplifies the tenets of the Imagist movement of the early twentieth century. Ezra Pound, who created such poetry, stated, "In a poem of this sort, one is trying to record the precise instant when a thing outward and objective transforms itself, or darts into a thing inward and subjective."

Poems often present highly complicated series of images that are woven through the entire work, strands that become a fabric of meaning. In this extension of imagery lies much of the pleasure of poetic form. In Walt Whitman's "When I Heard the Learn'd Astronomer," the speaker sits in a classroom and listens to a lecture. The first six lines of the poem introduce the astronomer and extend the images associated with him: "proofs," "figures," "charts and diagrams." The speaker, "sick" from the aridity of technical explanations, glides outside to enjoy the "mystical" experience of looking at the stars. The final lines emphasize and elaborate images of freedom in the natural world.

When I heard the learn'd astronomer,
When the proofs, the figures, were 'ranged in columns
  before me,
When I was shown the charts and diagrams, to add,
  divide and measure them,
When I sitting heard the astronomer where he lectured
  with much applause in the lecture-room,
How soon unaccountable I became tired and sick
Till rising and gliding out I wander'd off by myself,
In the mystical moist night-air, and from time to time,
Look'd up in perfect silence at the stars.

Note the passivity of the persona who listens, who "heard," and who "was shown," as the astronomer teaches in a "lecture-room." The speaker must perform calculations—"add/divide and measure"—in order to understand the "columns" placed before him. The proliferation and repetition ("when") of images denigrate the concrete, scientific atmosphere of the academy. The beautiful, abstract, active quality of the imagery that evokes the natural world, the world of "mystical moist night-air" and "stars," creates a "perfect" and silent contrast to the confinement of the lecture and the lecture-room. Whitman demonstrates the value of human experience and his view of the dangers of science by weaving images of a boring, sickening astronomy lecture and active perception of a starry night as threads through his work.

Figures of Speech

Figures of speech, expressions that suggest more than their literal meanings, present implied or direct comparisons that give readers the experience of an abstraction or of an emotion. Some figures are **metaphor, simile, personification,**

synecdoche, metonymy, and **hyperbole.** In this famous section from Keats' "Endymion," the first line contains a metaphor:

A thing of beauty is a joy for ever.
Its loveliness increases; it will never
Pass into nothingness; but still will keep
A bower quiet for us, and a sleep
Full of sweet dreams, and health, and quiet breathing.
Therefore, on the morrow, are we wreathing
A flowery band to bind us to the earth,
Spite of despondence, of the inhuman death
Of noble natures, of the gloomy days,
Of all the unhealthy and o'er-darkened ways
Made for our searching; yes, in spite of all,
Some shape of beauty moves away the pall
From our dark spirits.

Metaphor and Simile

The **metaphor** equates "A thing of beauty" with eternal joy and expresses Keats' belief that beauty transcends time, space, and matter, that beauty redeems the darkness in human life. A metaphor pictures a thing or an idea, "thing of beauty," and juxtaposes it with something different, "a joy forever," and implies an analogy between them. Look at the passage, and notice the additional comparisons that Keats creates. The "thing of beauty" becomes a "flowery band" and "some shape" that "moves away the pall." In fact, Keats extends the metaphor of beauty beyond the first line and elaborates the idea with numerous images. **Extended metaphors,** sometimes called conceits, often appear in poetry and serve to complicate its form and meaning, to create depth. In "The Love Song of J. Alfred Prufrock," T. S. Eliot describes the fog as a cat in stanzas two and three (chapter 6). This extraordinary extended metaphor presents the fog in such a catlike manner that the comparison becomes obvious—even though Eliot never mentions the word *cat.*

Similes make a direct comparison of one thing to another; usually the words "like" or "as" serve to create connections. Keats, for example, could have written the first line of the passage from "Endymion" as a simile, "A thing of beauty is [like] a joy for ever." Think of William Wordsworth's "I Wandered Lonely *as* a Cloud." In this title, Wordsworth's speaker convinces the reader of his loneliness through a concrete object, a cloud. Its solitary movement in the sky suddenly illuminates the emotional state of the persona.

Personification, Synecdoche, Metonymy, and Hyperbole

These figures of speech appear frequently in poetry:

Personification is the attribution of human traits to objects, ideas, or creatures. In Keats's "Endymion" beauty possesses human powers to "keep" and to "move." Keats endows beautiful things with noble human qualities that can negate the dark nature of life.

Synecdoche, sometimes considered a special type of metonymy, is a figure of speech in which part of a thing is used to represent the whole. References to a monarch as the crown and to sailors as hands provide familiar samples of this technique.

Metonymy is a figure of speech in which a single name of a person, place, or thing stands for a more complex situation or experience with which the name is associated. Washington sometimes represents all branches of the government of the United States.

Hyperbole or **exaggeration** is overstatement of the situation, idea, person in order to shock, to create humor, to command attention. In Nikki Giovanni's "Ego Tripping," the entire poem becomes an exercise in hyperbole (chapter 4). The speaker makes wild claims that she "gives oil to the Arab World," that her son is Hannibal, that she "cannot be comprehended."

Symbol, Myth, Allusion

Symbol

A **symbol** is an object or event that represents something else or that has meaning beyond itself. Everyday objects become symbols when a red cross signifies an international relief organization, when ram's horns symbolize a football team, or when a swastika stands as a Nazi emblem.

In many cultures, poetic symbols have conventional meanings: cherry blossoms, jade, birds, and roses all have well-established significance in Japanese, Chinese, or English poetry. Many contemporary poets, however, create private symbols that readers may interpret from a close reading of the work. This development can make symbols more difficult to discover and to comprehend. Adrienne Rich's "Diving into the Wreck" presents a complex system of symbols that can be read simply as a dive to a sunken ship for treasure and as a personal search through the wreckage of a life (chapter 8). In the end, however, the poet shifts from the first-person singular "I" to plural and multiple points of view:

> We are, I am, you are
> by cowardice or courage
> the one who finds our way
> back to this scene
> carrying a knife, a camera
> a book of myths
> in which our names do not appear

The "we" who dive into the wreck become an androgynous "one who finds our way/back" to a place where "a book of myths" denies existence through the absence of names. Rich seems to proclaim that none can have identity if the "book of myths" is not replaced by the recognition of personhood and autonomy for women as well as for men, for the oppressed as well as for the oppressors, by a merging, in fact, of these categories.

Myth

A **myth** is similar to a symbol, but it includes a story that stands for something else. In many cultures and traditions, myths explain the inexplicable and the mysterious; they preserve history, culture, customs; they describe the actions of supernatural beings. Some of these beings symbolize natural forces—fertility, harvest, the sea. Some of them represent abstract qualities—love, wisdom, cunning, evil. A **mythology,** a system or collection of myths, represents the beliefs of a culture or a particular group; these myths often originated in religious belief and ritual. Among the mythologies most commonly found in poetry are Greek, Roman, Germanic, Native American, and Egyptian.

In Audre Lorde's "The House of Yemanjá," the reference to the great African mother from whose breasts all rivers flow augments the power of the mother of the speaker of the poem (chapter 5). In one legend, Lorde notes that Yemanjá's husband insulted her long breasts. She escaped with her pots, and he followed her and beat her. Rivers flowed from her breasts, and all of the other Yoruban gods were born from her body. Therefore, when the speaker claims twice that her "mother had two faces and a broken pot," she implies that her mother is Yemanjá or, at least, resembles her. When she claims that her mother's breasts are "huge exciting anchors/in the midnight storm," she also suggests that Yemanjá represents her good mother. The myth enlarges and complicates the meaning of the poem.

Allusion

An **allusion** refers to a well-known literary work, person, event, or place. Whether it is implicit or explicit, the allusion enlarges the world of the poem. In "Sailing to Byzantium," for example, Yeats refers to the city where the beauty and culture of the Byzantine empire reached its height in the fifth and sixth centuries (chapter 8). Judith Johnson writes about Abraham and Isaac and the divine command that Abraham sacrifice his son in her poem, "Stone Olives" (chapter 8). She also alludes to the terrorists who killed the passengers on Pan Am Flight 103, the plane that exploded near Lockerbie, Scotland, in December 1988. In particular, the speaker mourns the death of Melina Hudson of Albany, New York:

> Melina, who once danced
> at proms far from Beirut, laughed with my daughter
> years after Hiroshima broke into flower, told
> her beads in a church the Gulag never touched
> now pours down through our air.

Johnson traces the senseless deaths of children in Beirut, Lebanon, in the atomic bomb blast in Hiroshima, in the Soviet Gulag camps as she pictures the fragments of Melina's body raining to the ground. In "Stone Olives," the persona suggests that fathers allow and cause the sacrifice of children.

STRUCTURE

Stanzas

Historically poems originated as oral expression. Poets accompanied their songs with instruments, or they performed with choral or instrumental groups. The first aspect of the poem in any analysis of sound should be the visual picture of lines arranged on a page. The lines of a poem may be divided into separate groups or units called **stanzas** that function like paragraphs in fiction and in essays. Some questions to pose about stanzaic patterns include: How are the poetic groups or stanzas divided? Where do they begin and end? How does the punctuation provide cues for reading? The strong marks of punctuation—periods, semicolons, dashes, question marks, colons, exclamation points—require longer pauses than a comma. Examine Gwendolyn Brooks's poem:

We Real Cool
The Pool Players
Seven at the Golden Shovel

We real cool. We
Left school. We

Lurk late. We
Strike straight. We

Sing sin. We
Thin gin. We

Jazz June. We
Die soon.

The short sentences, each three words long, require a fast pace and regular beat. The two-line stanzas, called **couplets,** are open because each line and each couplet ends with "we." A line of poetry that ends without punctuation or pause is known as a run-on line, also as an **enjambment.** The internal periods command pauses, and the repetitions and positions of the pronoun "we" also demand emphasis. Read the poem as eight short sentences, and then read it according to stanzaic and line arrangements. What is the connection between sound and meaning?

Rhyme and Sound

Rhyme, the repetition of sounds usually at the ends of lines in regular patterns, represents a traditional technique that pleases the ear and enhances the effects of images and symbols. In Brooks's poem, each line rhymes because all except the last line end with the same word. In each couplet, Brooks has used internal rhyme: cool, school; late, straight; sin, gin; June, soon. If these rhymes were **end rhymes,** the **rhyme scheme** would read aa, bb, cc, dd. To determine the scheme of any rhymed poem, simply assign letters of the alphabet to each new rhyming sound, and begin with *a.*

Another good example of rhyme is Shakespeare's "Shall I Compare Thee to a Summer's Day?" (See page 534.) Its form, called a **Shakespearean** or **Elizabethan sonnet,** divides the traditional fourteen lines into three four-line verses or quatrains and a final couplet. The rhyme scheme reads abab, cdcd, efef, gg. Sonnets also may take **Petrarchan** form, named for the famous Italian poet, Petrarch. In this kind of sonnet, the poet writes two **quatrains,** called the **octave** (eight lines), and two **tercets,** three-line verses, called the **sestet** (six lines). The theme shifts radically at the ninth line in Petrarchan sonnets; this turn is known as the volta. The rhyme scheme in the octave usually reads abba abba. The sestet may rhyme in a number of ways: cdecde, cdccdc, cdedce. Another technique for rhyming in free verse or formal poetry includes slant or half rhyme, one in which words almost rhyme.

The sounds of the words contribute to the meaning of the poem. The repetition of the initial sounds of accented consonant syllables at close intervals, called **alliteration,** may create effects that enlarge, reinforce, or contradict the ideas and mood of the poem. In Brooks's work, for example, the alliteration begins with the identification of the speakers as *p*ool *p*layers, and she continues this pattern in *l*urk *l*ate, in *str*ike *str*aight, in *s*ing *s*in, in *j*azz *J*une. This frequent use of alliteration in such a short poem heightens the sense of jazz and music. Brooks also employs **assonance,** the repetition of vowel sounds of stressed syllables or important words at close intervals: c*oo*l sch*oo*l. Notice that this poem relies heavily on sound for meaning. Notice that the long, sighing vowel in d*ie* in the last line stands alone, a jarring conclusion.

Rhythm

One of the indispensable elements distinguishing poetry is **rhythm.** Like song or dance, no poem can exist without a beat that augments its meaning and beauty or contradicts and conflicts with its themes and images to create tension. Poets choose rhythms from four basic categories: *traditional meters, strong stress rhythms, syllabic counts,* and *free verse.*

Meter

Meter is a rhythmic pattern of stressed (/) and unstressed (◡) syllables in a poem. Each unit, called a *foot,* has either two or three syllables. The most common feet in poetry follow:

Foot	*Designation*	*Example*
iamb or iambic	(◡ /)	◡ / delight
trochee or trochaic	(/ ◡)	/ ◡ coral

spondee or spondaic	(/ /)	/ / ho hum
pyrrhus or pyrrhic	(˘ ˘)	˘ ˘ advantage of
anapest or anapestic	(˘ ˘ /)	˘ ˘ / in a flash
dactyl or dactylic	(/ ˘ ˘)	/ ˘ ˘ night coming

Line lengths can be measured in number of feet.

Line Length	*Number of Feet*
monometer	one foot
dimeter	two feet
trimeter	three feet
tetrameter	four feet
pentameter	five feet
hexameter	six feet
heptameter	seven feet
octometer	eight feet

Scansion

In order to discover the meter of a poem, each line is scanned for accented and unaccented syllables. This process, called **scansion,** enables you to examine the effects of rhythm in the work. Look at this scansion of Shakespeare's parody of the conceits in the sonnet tradition. Note that each syllable is marked to indicate stressed or unstressed pronunciations.

> ˘ / ˘ / ˘ / ˘ / ˘ /
> My mistress' eyes, are nothing like the Sun;
> / ˘ ˘ / ˘ / ˘ / ˘ /
> Coral is far more red, than her lips' red:
> ˘ / ˘ / ˘ / ˘ / ˘ /
> If snow be white, why then her breasts are dun;
> ˘ / ˘ / ˘ / / ˘ ˘ /
> If hairs be wires, black wires grow on her head.
> ˘ / ˘ / ˘ / ˘ / ˘ /
> I have seen Roses damasked, red and white,
> ˘ / ˘ / ˘ / / ˘ ˘ /
> But no such Roses see I in her cheeks;
> ˘ / ˘ / ˘ / ˘ / ˘ /
> And in some perfumes is there more delight
> ˘ / ˘ / ˘ / ˘ / ˘ /
> Than in the breath that from my Mistress reeks.
> ˘ / ˘ / ˘ / ˘ / ˘ /
> I love to hear her speak, yet well I know
> ˘ / ˘ / ˘ / ˘ / ˘ /
> That music hath a far more pleasing sound:

˘ / ˘ / ˘ / ˘ / ˘ /
I grant I never saw a goddess go,
/ ˘ ˘ / ˘ / / ˘ ˘ /
My Mistress, when she walks treads on the ground.
˘ / ˘ / ˘ ˘ / ˘ / ˘ /
And yet, by heaven, I think my love as rare
˘ /˘ / ˘ / ˘ / ˘ /
As any she belied with false compare.

With very little variation, this poem's meter is iambic pentameter (five iambic feet), the most frequent and natural rhythm in English. Line 2 contains a trochee (coră), as does line 6 (Í in). Such variety prevents boredom, a sing-song quality, and commands attention. In this sonnet, Shakespeare makes little attempt to provide alternate rhythm. The boring regularity suits the purposes of his parody.

Strong Stress Meter

Early Anglo-Saxon and Germanic rhythms featured only strong stresses or **accents,** each line containing four stressed syllables. *Beowulf* and some Middle English poetry exemplify accentual meter. Strong stress rhythms still appear in such children's rhymes as "Hickory Dickory Dock." Gerard Manley Hopkins, an English poet, developed sprung rhythm, a variant of accentual meter, in the nineteenth century. In his poems, each line begins with a stressed syllable that may be followed by one, two, or three unaccented syllables or that may stand alone.

Syllabic Rhythm

Poetry also may receive its beat from patterns of **counted syllables,** a method that disregards accentual feet. In this mode, the poet chooses any combination of syllables and repeats the pattern. In Sylvia Plath's "Metaphors," she writes a riddle in nine lines, each containing nine syllables:

1 2 3 4 5 6 7 8 9
I'm a riddle in nine syllables

1 23 4 5 6 7 8 9
An elephant, a ponderous house

This clever poem catalogues metaphors about pregnancy. Japanese haiku also represents a form in which syllabic count is fixed and traditional: five syllables; seven; five syllables. Remember Bashō's lyric, "On New Year's Day."

Free Verse

More than eighty years ago, Ezra Pound theorized about composing "in the sequence of the metrical phrase, not in the sequence of a metronome. . . ."

Pound noted that some poets had abandoned traditional meters and explored natural rhythms, and he advocated **free verse** as an exciting alternative to traditional meters. Pound was not the first poet to recognize the value of this approach, but his description certainly provides an apt definition.

Free verse has no strict meter or line length. Traditional feet appear but in natural order. Such rising feet as iambs and anapests may occur together; such falling feet as trochees and dactyls may occur together. One of the most famous examples of free verse is Walt Whitman's great poem of love and death, "Out of the Cradle Endlessly Rocking" (chapter 4). Read the first few lines without any attempt at analysis; follow the surge of the sea.

> Out of the cradle endlessly rocking,
> Out of the mocking-bird's throat, the musical shuttle,
> Out of the Ninth-month midnight,
> Over the sterile sands and the fields beyond, where the child
>   leaving his bed wander'd alone, bareheaded, barefoot,
> Down from the shower'd halo, ...

Anaphora—the repetition of phrases—in this case, adverbial phrases as "Out of" and biblical rhythm characterize this poem.

Needless to say, poets change and combine all of these categories. Every culture's poetic tradition recognizes rhythm as essential to the enjoyment and meaning of poetry because rhythm remains central to all natural movement: the beating of the heart, the rocking of the cradle, the swaying of the sea.

THE READING/WRITING PROCESS: POETRY

A poem requires more than one reading. Several examinations of the text may be necessary simply to understand the general idea of the piece. Any work of art worth attention—a Verdi opera, a Rembrandt painting, Lady Murasaki's *The Tale of Genji*—becomes more exciting and more valuable after careful examination.

The second task in understanding poetry should become the constant use of a dictionary. The multiple meanings of words in each poem result from the compression that characterizes this form. Any dictionary will suffice, but the *Oxford English Dictionary* presents the most comprehensive history of the meanings of words in English. A reader also should have access to other reference books on world mythology and to religious texts.

Listen to the sounds of poetry. Since poems originated in song and in oral tradition, the meaning resides in the sounds as well as in the words. Read poems aloud, and begin with your favorites. In your interpretation, be animated. Muriel Rukeyser once stated that fear of poetry is a fear of emotion. The feelings and meaning already exist in a poem; they will express themselves. In any attempt to render the work as an oral interpretation, find the patterns of rhythm, grammar, and punctuation. Try not to swallow the last lines or important words.

The central purpose of the poem becomes the next question. To comprehend the poem's purpose, characterize the voice of the speaker and paraphrase the action of the poem. Ask yourself: Who is speaking? What is happening in the poem? The speaker in "Daddy" feels angry and concludes: "Daddy, you bastard, I'm through." Victimized like the Jews in Nazi concentration camps, she transforms her father from God into a devil and later into a vampire. The purpose of the poem appears to reside in the speaker's desire to resolve her feelings about her father's death.

Ask, then, about the achievement of purpose. How is it achieved? Find the answer by describing the organization of ideas in the poem. In Plath's soliloquy, she begins with fairy tale; then she describes Daddy as "a bag full of God." Her speaker relates his roots, his language, to German history; and she contends that every woman wants a brutal father and that her speaker marries a "man in black with a Meinkampf look" (like Hitler) in order to recover her father. Finally, both men are symbolically killed, and Daddy becomes the villain in a Dracula movie. The purpose is achieved. Readers find the poem powerful; not everyone likes it or believes that the speaker has resolved her losses.

When reading a poem, give it what Shakespeare called "passionate attention." Consider voice, tone, theme, setting, imagery, figures of speech, symbols, sounds, and rhythm. These elements of poetry will reveal the richness of meaning and evoke responses and evaluation.

CHECKLIST FOR WRITING ABOUT POETRY

1. What is the category for the poem? Is it lyrical, narrative, or dramatic?
2. Who is the speaker? What is the point of view? What is the speaker's attitude toward the subject? What details, images, and uses of language give information about the persona?
3. What is the tone, and does it change? Why?
4. What is happening in the poem?
5. What are the significant figures of speech? How do they function?
6. Describe the setting.
7. Which senses do the images evoke? Does the poem have one image or a series of images? Are the images related? Is there a pattern? What concepts do the images represent? How do the images support the theme? How effective is the use of imagery?
8. What is the central symbol? Are the symbols universal or private? How does symbolism function in the poem?
9. Does the poem refer to mythological figures? Does the poet change the myth?
10. Are there any allusions? What are the specific historical events, names, and/or literary references in the poem? How do the allusions work? Are they effective?

11. What sounds are important? Does the poem contain alliteration or assonance? How does the poet arrange the lines?
12. What is the rhythm of the poem? How does rhythm function?
13. Does the poem have a conventional form? Is the poem a sonnet, villanelle, or sestina? Is the poem an open form?
14. Is the poem effective? What is best about this work? What are its flaws? What is the final evaluation of this work?

Student Portfolio:
Response to Wilfred Owen's "Arms and the Boy"

Ursula Lebris's work presents a model of an explication of Wilfred Owen's "Arms and the Boy" and evolves from a gloss of the text, from notes, from freewriting, and from several drafts. An explication offers a careful analysis of a poem. The methodology requires an examination of the work to gain knowledge of each of its aspects and parts, and it attempts to determine the relation of all of the elements in the poem to the meaning of the whole. Note that the first draft of "Let the Boy Try" is articulate and structured but also seriously underdeveloped and lacking in precision. The final draft overcomes these deficiencies and demonstrates outstanding mastery of this poem.

Title refers to weapons, but also to physical arms, protection. Why?

allusion? Arms and the Boy

Lebris's Gloss of Wilfred Owen's "Arms and the Boy"

(imperative)

Is the speaker cruel?

Let the boy try along this bayonet-blade
How cold steel is, and keen with hunger of blood;
Blue with all malice, like a madman's flash;
And thinly drawn with famishing for flesh.

alliteration (effect?)

?

Tone serious or ironic?

Why? (Again imperatives)

Lend him to stroke these blind, blunt bullet-heads
Which long to nuzzle in the hearts of lads,
Or give him cartridges of fine zinc teeth,
Sharp with the sharpness of grief and death.

repetition—good!

For his teeth seem for laughing round an apple.
There lurk no claws behind his fingers supple;
And God will grow no talons at his heels,
Nor antlers through the thickness of his curls.

Why animal imagery?

Can't or won't?

Does speaker believe in God?

Consonants used throughout poem. (effect?)

Notes

bayonet—a weapon attached to the muzzle of a rifle
keen—eager and sharp
malice—intention to injure others
thinly drawn—a sword is "drawn" in order to fight; the shape of the bayonet is like a thin line; also can mean drawn in (i.e., with hunger)
famishing—suffering extreme hunger
zinc—bluish white metallic element
talons—claws, esp. of a bird of prey
antlers—the horns of a stag or deer

Personification—the bayonet is starving to death ("famishing for flesh") and capable of emotion ("blue with all malice."). The bullets "long to nuzzle" and the cartridges feel "grief and death." The poem is divided into three quatrains; the first two discuss human weapons; the third introduces "natural" (animal) weapons. I don't think the poem uses a particular meter, but in the first two quatrains each line ends with a heavily stressed syllable. I really hear this when I read the poem aloud. The emphasis (e.g., on "blade" and "blood") makes the weapons seem more threatening.
Alliteration—the hard "b" sounds are like explosions and the "sh" sounds are like the hiss of bullets through the air.
What about consonance (half-rhyme)? The words seem to rhyme at first but there is a jarring effect. Is this significant?
Simile—"like a madman's flash." This is weird. Is a flash a kind of fit? I suppose like a flash of anger (malice). Why *blue?* Metal can look bluish. Ok. Also the blue flash of gunfire.
Metaphor—"blind, blunt bullet-heads." They are blunt but they are not literally *blind.* The bullets are made to seem vulnerable like newly born animals, but all they want to do is kill young "lads." They do not see their targets; they are not meant to see.

Freewrite

I remember years ago taking my father's gun out of its case, even though I was forbidden to touch it. I wanted to see what all the fuss was about. So I can understand why a young boy would want to test the sharpness of a blade or play with bullets and cartridges. But I don't understand why the speaker in the poem wants him to. I feel frustrated by the poem overall. I like the way the weapons are described as being alive because it makes them seem even more threatening. But allowing a kid to play with things which intend to kill him is pretty sadistic. I suppose it's the final verse which really throws me. Ok, the boy's teeth are innocent compared to the "grief and death" of the cartridge teeth, but why does the poet then go on to talk about claws and talons and antlers? Maybe the claw is meant to represent the trigger of a gun. "And God will grow no talons at his heels"—is it that God can protect the boy, but won't? Why "talons"? I suppose that unlike animals the boy has no natural defenses. So "give him cartridges of fine zinc teeth" so that he can protect himself. But I think the poet is implying that to fight is to go against God—human beings are not naturally equipped for battle ("Thou shalt not kill"). Anyway the poem is deliberately shocking because Owen wants to show how vulnerable the young boy is. Let him touch these weapons, and maybe he will realize how sick war is before it is too late.

Essay: First Draft: "Let the Boy Try"

At first "Arms and the Boy" may seem to be a cruel, even sadistic, poem, for in the first two stanzas a young boy is encouraged to play with potentially lethal weapons. However, in the final stanza the poet's compassion for the young lives lost in World War I is revealed. Although the poem is only twelve lines long, Owen makes the reader vividly aware of the vulnerability of youth by using several techniques to emphasize the horror of war.

The technique of personification is perhaps the most important. The bayonet is not only some starving animal "famishing for flesh." This simile likens the blue flash of gunfire to the indiscriminate malice of a madman. The bullets are also personified but in a different way. Far from being evil madmen, they are like the new-born young of some animal which "long to nuzzle in the hearts of lads." This perverse image is intended to shock: Owen wants the reader to realize how sick and unnatural war is.

The disturbing images of the first two quatrains are intensified through alliteration. The repetition of consonants in "blade," "blood," "blind," and "blunt" creates a hard, explosive effect like that of gunfire, while the "s," "f," and "sh" sounds suggest the hiss of blades or bullets through the air. These sounds, along with the strongly stressed syllables at the end of each line, give the poem a threatening tone, as though the speaker is talking through clenched teeth. The use of half-rhyme combines certain key images in the reader's mind while giving a jarring effect that adds to the tension in these first two quatrains.

The sinister effects created by personification, alliteration, and meter disappear in the final quatrain. The boy's youthful innocence is shown in the comparison between his laughing teeth and the "grief and death" of the cartridge teeth and by references to "his fingers supple" and "the thickness of his curls." These images emphasize how vulnerable he is. The boy has no natural defenses, and since "God will grow no talons at his heels" perhaps it is necessary to "give him cartridges of fine zinc teeth" so that he may survive. However, this is no answer because the weapons intended to protect him are bent on his destruction.

The figurative language and the several possible readings of the final quatrain make "Arms and the Boy" a somewhat difficult poem. But despite this the reader cannot help but share the poet's compassion for the young victims of armed conflict. And there is a more hopeful interpretation—perhaps if the boy experiences the 'grief and death' of the weapons now, he will decide against becoming part of the horror and insanity that is war.

Lebris' Final Draft: "Let the Boy Try"

"Arms and the Boy" is a short lyric poem of great power, comprising three quatrains and employing the rhyme scheme AABB CCDD EEFF. The alliteration used throughout is an important feature, as it creates a tension appropriate to the subject matter. At first "Arms and the Boy" may seem to be a cruel, even sadistic, poem, for in the initial two stanzas, the speaker encourages another to give potentially lethal weapons to a young boy. The final stanza, however, reveals the deep compassion felt for the young lives lost on the battlefield. As an officer in the First World War, Wilfred Owen witnessed firsthand the atrocities inflicted by men upon other men. Although the poem is only twelve lines long, he succeeds in making the reader vividly aware of the vulnerability of youth and of the horror and perversity of war.

It is significant that the poem begins with an imperative statement: "Let the boy try along this bayonet-blade/ How cold steel is, and keen with hunger of blood." The note of challenge introduced here quickly becomes one of menace as the description of the bayonet shifts rapidly from the literal "cold steel" to the figurative "keen with hunger of blood." This personification of the weaponry is one of the most important devices used in the poem, as it transforms them from inanimate objects into evil personalities with conscious intentions. The bayonet, "keen" in the sense of both eager *and* sharp, is not only like a starving animal but also

"Blue with all malice, like a madman's flash." This startling simile takes the blue flash of gunfire and likens it to the indiscriminate malice of a psychopath, a telling indication of how Owen himself had come to view military action. Note that "blue" also suggests the hue of cold steel and the pallor of death.

The second quatrain continues the menacing tone with another imperative statement: "Led him to stroke these blind, blunt bullet-heads/Which long to nuzzle in the hearts of lads." Again personification is used, but this time in a slightly different way. Far from being like evil madmen, the bullets are described as being like the new-born young of some animal. Paradoxically, it is they who seem vulnerable rather than the young boy who is being allowed to play with them. The use of the casual, inoffensive "lads" here is also significant; it strikes an even more chilling note into the metaphor. The sexual connotations of "stroke" and "nuzzle," in conjunction with the phallic symbolism of the bayonet and the bullets, create a very unsettling undercurrent in an already disturbing poem. That instruments of death should be described in sexual, hence creative, terms does, however, highlight the poem's main theme—that war is something perverse and unnatural.

The second quatrain concludes with the third imperative statement: "Or give him cartridges of fine zinc teeth,/Sharp with the sharpness of grief and death." There is an important progression here in the level of involvement implied: the boy was initially allowed to touch the bayonet, was then lent bullets, and is now *given* cartridges. Although it is never made clear whom the speaker in the poem is addressing, there is a note of accusation here which implicates a far wider group of people than just a few soldiers on sentry duty. That the boy should be encouraged to play with weapons which actively seek to harm him is the key paradox in the poem, and it is this action which gives the final quatrain its power.

5 The sinister mood of the first two quatrains is intensified through a variety of poetic devices. The alliteration in "blood," "blade," "blind," and "blunt" creates a hard, exploding effect like that of gunfire, while the softer "s," "f," and "sh" sounds suggest the hiss of blades or bullets through the air. These sounds, along with the strongly stressed syllables at the end of each line, further contribute to the threatening tone, as though the speaker is talking through clenched teeth. Although the poem does not employ any fixed metrical pattern, the groups of unstressed

syllables followed by several stressed syllables ("Blue with all malice, like a madman's flash") seem to mimic the stabbing motion of a bayonet. Certain key images are combined in the reader's mind through consonance ("blade"/"blood"), while the jarring effect of the half-rhyme adds an appropriate air of tension to the first eight lines.

In the final quatrain, however, the tone changes, and the sinister effects created by personification, alliteration, and meter disappear. Consonance is still used, but weak rhyme replaces the strong, heavily stressed rhyme of the first two quatrains, giving the last four lines a much more gentle mood. The boy's youthful innocence is shown in the comparison between his teeth "laughing round an apple" and the "grief and death" of the cartridge teeth. It is at this point that the disturbing images of the first two quatrains are justified, and the apparent sadism of the speaker is now revealed as compassion. The poet emphasizes the boy's vulnerability through references to "his finger supple" and "the thickness of his curls," while his complete lack of aggression is expressed through a series of negative statements ("no claws," "no talons," "nor antlers"). The boy, unlike animals, has no natural defenses, and since "God will grow no talons at his heels," perhaps it is necessary to "give him cartridges of fine zinc teeth" so that he may survive. But the meaning of the poem cannot be quite as straightforward as this, because the implication is that for any human being to fight, whether boy or man, is to go against God. The poem's power comes from its tragic irony—that the weapons meant to protect the boy are intent only on his destruction.

The several possible readings of the final quatrain, along with the figurative language used throughout, make "Arms and the Boy" a somewhat difficult poem. It is also a shocking poem, and intentionally so, for Owen seems to have had in mind an audience of complacent armchair patriots. The poem's message is, of course, not limited to his contemporaries of the First World War but is, regrettably, still very relevant today. The knowledge that Owen himself was killed on the front lines at the age of twenty-five adds another dimension to the poem, but even without this fact, the reader cannot help but feel sadness and anger at the young lives which were, and still are, wasted on the battlefield. But there is a more hopeful interpretation—perhaps if the boy experiences the "grief and death" of weaponry secondhand, he will decide against becoming involved in the horror and insanity that is war.

❋ ❋ ❋

The gloss and notes identify and explore the grammar, figurative language, sounds, and meaning of Owen's poem. The writer focuses on the formal elements of "Arms and the Boy" and on the connection between form and meaning. The journal entry describes a personal experience of touching a weapon and reveals the writer's attitudes toward violence, toward the poem, and toward war. In the journal the initial ideas for the essay are formulated.

The first draft contains an excellent introduction. The explication analyzes personification and alliteration in the first two stanzas or quatrains. The third paragraph discusses the meaning of the last verse, and the conclusion is excellent.

In the final version of "Let the Boy Try," the writer enlarges the vision of the poem and announces her view in the introduction that seems slightly cluttered with the rhyme scheme and with a comment concerning alliteration. Although the paper is well organized, the introduction fails to focus exclusively on the writer's plan. The beginning, however, engages the reader's interest and expresses the major ideas. The paragraphs on the three quatrains are brilliantly conceived and brilliantly illustrated. The careful reading of imagery, significant figures of speech, grammatical constructions (imperative statements), sounds, tone, speaker, and theme result in an exemplary performance. The introduction of biographical details about Wilfred Owen emphasizes the dramatic conclusion about the "insanity that is war."

CHAPTER 11

DRAMA

In *As You Like It,* Shakespeare claims that "all the world's a stage." His declaration captures the deep connection between dramatic literature and life; and, by extension, Shakespeare captures the human fascination with all of the imaginative arts. Every person views his or her experience as dramatic; each views the world as a setting for personal and public actions and ideas, for triumphs and crises, for the ordinary and the sublime. Plays and other forms of literature, therefore, are not simply imitations of life; they represent much more. They order, concentrate, and elevate acts of interpretation that may be crucial to daily life.

Theater existed in human cultures long before recorded history. Societies developed dramatic rituals with characters, costumes, makeup, masks, settings, and special effects to inspire, educate, entertain, initiate, worship the gods, and control the environment. Music became the universal accompaniment. In the rain dance of the Dieri in Australia, for instance, a lodge was constructed; and then, at the end of the ritual, it was destroyed by dancers who knocked it down with their heads. This ceremony signified the elimination of clouds so that rain could fall. In the drama of the Great Serpent held to celebrate the March moon, the Hopis burned fires in the kivas (ceremonial chambers) that they built; a prop person smothered the blazes to produce smoke curtains at certain intervals to facilitate changes in scenes and actors. They also devised sets with painted backdrops containing holes through which symbols of dancing serpents appeared. These performances exemplify the complexity of the drama before the practice of writing scripts. Some early comedies appeared as animal impersonations. For entertainment, one society in the Philippines created a comic play in which a searcher for honey experienced many outrageous indignations. Religious expression was central to many of these productions, but secular concerns also provided subject matter and impetus for public spectacles. Except for written scripts, the elements of modern drama—setting, character, action, plot—existed in prototype in these ceremonies.

The oldest evidences of scripts for drama are the fifty-five Pyramid Texts (3000 B.C.) of Egypt. Written on the walls of tombs and pyramids, they contain stage directions and lines for different characters. The major theme of these dramas was resurrection. Scholars estimate that more than four thousand texts once existed, developed, perhaps, from rituals celebrating the return of spring. The Egyptians also performed coronation festival plays that hailed the crowning of a new monarch.

FORMS OF DRAMA

Much of the theater, as it exists today, originated in Greece. Performances to honor gods or to commemorate rites of spring developed into formal productions. The most famous playwrights, Aeschylus (525–426 B.C.), Sophocles (496–406 B.C.), and Euripedes (c. 480–406 B.C.) composed plays for the annual Dionysian festivals. Presented to a selection group and later evaluated by judges, the plays—three tragedies and one comedy by each playwright—were performed in a semicircular theater.

Tragedy is a form of drama about fortunes and misfortunes, about disaster. Broadly defined, tragedy refers to dramatic representations of serious and significant actions that result in disaster for the protagonist or main character. In classical plays, these disasters happened to human beings with high position and great power such as Oedipus, Agamemnon, and Antigone. These characters possessed noble qualities and high passion. In tragedy, these attributes could not, however, save them from self-destruction or from fate.

Aristotle's classic theory in the *Poetics* (fourth century B.C.) describes tragedy as "the imitation of an action that is serious and also, as having magnitude, complete in itself," written in dramatic form and in poetic language. The tragic drama features "incidents arousing pity and fear, wherewith to accomplish the catharsis of such emotion." This **catharsis,** or purging of emotion, implies that the play will leave the audience or reader with feelings of relief or even exaltation. According to Aristotle, the play focuses on a **tragic hero** who has higher than ordinary moral values. This hero suffers a change or reversal of fortune, caused by his or her **tragic flaw, hamartia,** an "error in judgment." One common expression of hamartia in Greek drama is **hubris** or excessive pride.

Greek **comedy** first appeared in fertility rites and in the worship of Dionysus. From the time of Aristophanes (c. 448–c. 380 B.C.), the greatest Greek comic playwright, the form has been associated primarily with drama. Aristophanes wrote a variety of comedies combining lyrics, dance, satire, social comment, fantasy, and buffoonery. He attempted to reveal truth by exposing political deceit and pretense in such plays as *Lysistrata, The Wasps,* and *The Peace.* His more philosophical works include *The Clouds, The Frogs,* and *The Birds.* Aristotle distinguished comedy from tragedy by suggesting that it features ordinary people in amusing, everyday situations. It derives from the word **komos** or revel.

Few of the early tragedies or comedies still exist, but those that have survived convey the beauty and wisdom, the bawdy humor, the awe and wonder of classical Greece. They establish without a doubt the incredible influence of the Greek theater on world drama during the past two thousand years.

Fifteen years after the death of Aristophanes, scenic entertainments to appease the gods began in Rome (364 B.C.). Like Greek theater, Roman drama also originated in ritual ceremonies and secular entertainment. The most famous Roman dramatist was Seneca (3 B.C.–A.D. 65), although his tragedies may never have been performed in public.

During the Roman Empire, comedy employed two kinds of subjects: one derived from Greek dramas and the other concerned Roman materials. Seventy works from the Roman-based comedies are recorded, but the two best known Roman dramatists who wrote comedies depended on Greek plays. They are Maccius Plautus and Publius Terentius Afer, known as Terence. Plautus created the form known as **tragicomedy** by referring to the unconventional mixture of kings and servants in his play *Amphitrus,* as *tragico-comedia.* Choosing elements of both comedy and tragedy, the playwright attempted to balance a conflict of vision. The extant plays of both Plautus and Terence greatly influenced Elizabethan theater and, in turn, modern theater. Mime and pantomime, which developed as elaborate performances separate from dramas, also represent an original contribution of the Romans to the art.

The theater did not die with the fall of Rome. Until the twelfth century, it survived in public entertainment and in religious performances, in particular, in cycles and in noncyclical plays. In England, Elizabethan drama developed from religious plays performed at medieval festivals during the twelfth and thirteenth centuries. These **mystery plays,** as they were called, presented Biblical stories—Noah and the ark, Jonah and the whale, the passion of Jesus—in town squares or in churches. As the dramas grew in popularity, platforms, called **pageants,** were wheeled from city to city; and the plays often expanded into a series that was enacted over a period of several days.

The **miracle play,** another dramatic genre related to the mystery play, presented saints' lives and miracles. It often centered on the divine acts of the Virgin Mary. A famous cycle of forty-two plays, the *Miracles de Notre Dame,* is extant in France. Other European examples are the German *Marienklage* (*The Complaint of Mary*), and the Dutch *Mariken Van Nieumaghen* (*Mary of Nieumaghen*). In England, where the cult of the Virgin Mary did not flourish, most miracle plays dramatized the lives of saints.

During the fourteenth and fifteenth centuries, **morality plays** allegorized Christian values. Characters symbolized Christian virtues and vices. The most famous play, *Everyman* (1500), presented positive and negative human qualities in a single representative figure whose conflicts mirrored all life processes.

In the sixteenth century, Greek and Roman drama began to influence English theater. Secular plays became popular as interest in religious dramatizations waned. At first the new plays, based on classic Greek models, focused on murder and revenge. Roman dramatists, Seneca and Menander, also influenced the writers of these plays. Professional actors performed plays in courtyards and later in theaters. Audiences were composed of both educated and illiterate spectators.

From the defeat of the Spanish Armada in 1588 until 1642 when all theaters were closed during the Civil War, the English theater reached its highest development through the genius of such playwrights as Christopher Marlowe, Ben Jonson, Thomas Kyd, Thomas Dekker, John Webster, and William Shakespeare. In *Tamburlaine* and *Dr. Faustus,* Marlowe (1564–93) invented blank verse, or unrhymed iambic pentameter, a rhythm that became the dominant meter of Elizabethan drama.

The greatest genius of the reigns of Queen Elizabeth I and James I was William Shakespeare. A writer of comedies, tragedies, and histories, Shakespeare was the best of many astonishingly fine dramatists. A member of the Lord Chamberlain's company (1594), he joined a group that constructed the Globe Theater (1599), a most successful structure, small enough to fit into the orchestra area of the Greek Theater of Dionysius. At most, the Globe could have accommodated two thousand people.

The stage was a platform that projected into the audience. In the rear was an area with a curtain for intimate scenes; above was a balcony. There was a trap door for such purposes as the gravedigger scene in *Hamlet,* and ghosts descended on ropes from a canopy. The theater had no painted sets, and props were minimal. As in Greek drama, all actors were male. Elizabethan theaters were designed like courtyards. Six hundred "groundlings" sat or stood in the open yards. More privileged spectators occupied tiers of covered balconies.

In *Hamlet,* the prince lectures the actors who perform the play-within-the-play and defines the purpose of drama: "to hold, as 'twere, the mirror up to nature." This blossoming of dramas in England focused on imitation of reality. At the same time, the performances of plays in the open theaters created a wonderful and wild public life—real entertainment.

The excitement of the Renaissance renewed interest in drama in Italy, France, and Germany; and audiences enjoyed many kinds of theater. No great dramatic literature emerged during the Renaissance in these countries. However, innovations in theater architecture influenced the development and form of modern drama: horseshoe seating, the **proscenium arch** (a frame enclosing the stage area behind which the front curtain hangs), painted sets, indoor lighting, and spectacular costumes.

In Spain, Lope de Vega and Calderón wrote spectacular plays, the most famous in Spanish literature. More than two thousand actors are listed in public records, and public playhouses in Spain developed in the same patterns as English theaters. They accommodated the same kind of enthusiastic audiences. Complete professionalization of theater and establishment of repertory groups represent significant accomplishments during this period.

In the seventeenth century, French theater was greatly influenced by Greek and Roman drama. During this time, the most significant drama was written by Molière, Racine, and Corneille. The actors developed revolutionary performing styles, and the first national European theater, the Comèdie Francaise, began.

During the Restoration in England (after 1688), the great achievement became the comedy of manners—hard, brilliant, accomplished. The major playwrights were George Etherege, William Wycherley, and William Congreve. In the eighteenth century in England, theater did not occupy a primary place. Oliver Goldsmith and Richard Brinsley Sheridan are notable exceptions. The art of acting, however, reached new heights; the best performer was the legendary David Garrick. This period also produced the **picture frame stage** and very large theaters.

On the European continent, Voltaire and Diderot in France and Goethe and Lessing in Germany wrote memorable and classic works. Dramatic theory and criticism received great attention. Many great actors emerged, and the number of theaters increased. Spectacular effects appeared in stage design. All of these developments received more attention in the nineteenth and twentieth centuries.

NINETEENTH AND TWENTIETH CENTURY DRAMA

In Europe and in North America, three major movements in drama have developed in the last century: realism, Theater of the Absurd, Symbolist Drama.

Realism

At the end of the nineteenth century, writers began to create realistic dramas that presented accurate versions of the world and of human nature, of ordinary people leading ordinary lives. In dramatic literature, realism avoided all that was visionary and unbelievable. These dramatists chose serious, often tragic themes and well-developed characters who did not possess special status. They reacted against the spirit of Romanticism in England and in Europe, which emphasized the emotions and imagination above reason and intellect. They also reacted against melodrama, plays that depend on spectacle, action, and extravagant emotional appeal.

Realism, as it is defined and recognized today, is primarily the invention of Henrik Ibsen, a nineteenth century Norwegian playwright. This dramatic movement corresponded to great cultural upheavals—the Napoleonic Wars, the Industrial Revolution, the rise of the middle class. People longed for critical analysis of social institutions.

In Russia, Anton Chekhov, Leo Tolstoy, and Maxim Gorki wrote realistic plays and fiction. In France, Émile Zola and Guy de Maupassant provided analysis of a movement that they called naturalism. The bases for this theory were Charles Darwin's idea of the survival of the fittest and Karl Marx's contention that economic conditions shape human life.

Ibsen influenced George Bernard Shaw, August Strindberg, and, subsequently, an entire generation of famous dramatists. Ibsen's work deeply affected Stanislavsky's teaching of method acting. Many North American playwrights—Eugene O'Neill, Arthur Miller, and Tennessee Williams—adopted fundamental tenets of realism. Lorraine Hansberry's *A Raisin in the Sun* (chapter 5) is an example of realist drama.

Theater of the Absurd

The notion that life is absurd is not new, but it has acquired more specific meaning in the past century. Philosophers have defined the purposeless role of humans in a purposeless universe as absurd—mathematically, a *surd* is that which cannot be expressed in finite terms of ordinary numbers or quantities. It is in this mathematical sense that the philosophy of the absurd has been defined. (See Camus' "The Myth of Sisyphus" in chapter 8.). The theatrical phrase was coined by Martin Esslin, who wrote *The Theatre of the Absurd* in

1961. Scholars trace the lineage of this form from Roman mime plays to the comic techniques of medieval and Renaissance drama, especially commedia dell'arte, comedy originating in the Italian Renaissance that featured improvisation, stock characters, and masks. Finally, Esslin cites the influence of August Strindberg and of Bertolt Brecht.

In the 1950s, this concept was expressed in a number of plays that focus on characters struggling with existential angst, anxiety, and anguish. The human condition is presented as essentially meaningless. The plays have no formal logic and lack conventional structure. The following dramatists and works represent this tradition: Samuel Beckett, *Waiting for Godot, Endgame;* Jean Genet, *Les Negres* (The Blacks), *Le Balcon* (The Balcony); Eugene Ionesco, *La Leçon* (The Lesson), *La Cantatrice Chauve* (The Bald Soprano), *Rhinoceros;* Harold Pinter, *The Birthday Party, The Homecoming;* Edward Albee, *The Zoo Story* and *The Sandbox.* David Ives's *Sure Thing* (see chapter 6) is a comic representation of Theater of the Absurd.

Symbolist Drama

With the advent of realism, twentieth-century theater relinquished many traditional sources of dramatic tension—poetic language, symbols, illusions, such as the ghost in *Hamlet.* Like symbols in poetry and fiction, the actions and characters in symbolist drama refer to eternal ideas, abstract concepts. In such a play, a woman might encounter an abandoned child. The situation would not be presented as criticism of a particular society. Instead, the event might indicate the woman's discovery of her real and autonomous self; it might mean that humans are always abandoned in life.

Most plays contain symbols, but most dramatists do not intend that all action be interpreted as symbolic. **Symbolist dramas,** however, may feature many traditional poetic symbols and allegorical names, and they employ dreamlike atmospheres. This mode traces its roots to Kabuki theater, to Nō plays, to morality plays, and to the folk dramas of William Butler Yeats and of John Millington Synge. (See *Riders to the Sea* in chapter 5.) Contemporary Chinese American playwright David Henry Hwang has written such symbolist dramas as *The Sound of a Voice* and *M. Butterfly.*

Performance Drama

Performance drama has its roots in such diverse traditions as the oral narratives told by African griots and Native American seers; as the soliloquies of Shakespearean drama; as the surreal cabaret performances of the Dadaists and Surrealists of the 1920s (e.g., Andre Breton); as the monologues of stand-up comics; and as the performance art of the 1970s, which drew on forms of different media and often incorporated lighting, music, visuals, dance, and written text.

Performance drama combines elements of drama, poetry, and the short story as the genre also breaks down the boundaries between art forms. The central figure is a speaker, a solo artist who often creates an autobiographical persona or impersonates a collection of characters. The speaker presents interior monologues—a combination of inner thoughts, remembrance, and, often, social commentary. The approach is open and personal; the audience feels as if the persona is conversing in an intimate way with the public or letting the audience overhear his/her inner thoughts. The structure of the drama is open-ended and fluid. The script does not adhere to traditional forms of narrative or of dramatic structure, often following a stream-of-consciousness logic and using symbolism, dream, and anecdote to convey state of mind, character, and theme. The script, sometimes spontaneously improvised, also may draw on such poetic techniques as imagery, symbolism, and figurative language. One element of the form resembles the structure of the modern short story, created by James Joyce. The speaker often experiences a realization—an epiphany—by the end of the monologue, as does a protagonist in Joyce-ian short fiction. The performance also may include décor, costumes, settings, music, art, graphics, lighting, video—elements of other art forms. Finally, performance texts challenge orthodox notions of drama because they may be performed in such alternative spaces as cafes, coffeehouses, or art galleries instead of theaters, and therefore, attract public audiences who may not attend theatrical performances.

Like other forms of literature, the work also conveys a message—oftentimes a critique of everyday life or a vision of social protest. Some performance artists are noted for their comic, outrageous, or iconoclastic productions that challenge societal norms of appropriate behavior and North American cultural and social values. For example, in 1981, Laurie Anderson, combining elements of music, narrative, and visuals, created an eight-hour montage of song, story, and spectacle that critiqued the media culture of North America. In another performance scenario, "Constant State of Desire (1986)," Karen Finlay rebels quite vividly against the constraints of urban domesticity. Two important performance artists whose work expands the narrative and dramatic possibilities of the form are Spalding Gray, who in "Swimming to Cambodia" explores autobiographical landscapes of his life, and Eric Bogosian, who in several performance pieces critiques the character of men in America and what he views as an apathetic American society.

Anna Deavere Smith's *Twilight Los Angeles: 1992* portrays many characters who witnessed the Los Angeles riots. Her monologues, based on interviews, give readers multiple perspectives and visions of this moment in history. Her monologue, based on a interview with gang leader, Twilight Bey, is included in chapter 7.

Film and Television

An important twentieth-century development that influences public interest in theater is the moving image—film. The advent of moving pictures and of television has changed the viewing habits of human beings forever. As laser disc technology becomes available for computers and interactive television becomes more sophisticated, a revolution will occur, a revolution that will make knowledge and images of all kinds immediately available. What will these innovations mean to writers and readers, to public and commercial theaters? Hopefully, they will mean a multiplicity of choices for everyone. They will mean a heightening of imaginative power, of creativity, and of artistic vision for every society—a positive transformation.

Film shares many characteristics with literature: setting, character, conflict, dialogue, images, symbolism, and theme. The image adds new dimensions to language on screen; in drama, the work retains a more powerful position. Films, like drama, require conventions. For example, movies generally have music in the background—a score that helps to determine tone or mood.

One advantage of film is the capacity to change settings and locations. Since movies are shot in small scenes and out of sequence, the screenwriter can defy all of the dramatic unities. A film can span centuries and continents. Special effects and computers can create new worlds that stage sets can only suggest.

Like fiction writers, screenwriters have enormous freedom with point of view. Cameras can determine viewer response by the angle of the shot. A close-up can create the illusion of intimacy just as a first-person narrator in a novel may achieve the same effect. A long shot provides distance, objectivity, and a sweeping view. A zoom can accomplish both purposes. A wide-angle shot of helicopters in the air with Richard Wagner's "Ride of the Valkyries" playing in the background in Francis Ford Coppola's *Apocalypse Now* gives the viewer an idea of the idiocy of war and of the powerful exhilaration of battle before it subsides inescapably into horror. A close-up of Martin Sheen's face as he witnesses his friend's severed head renders the terror personal and human.

Television shares many techniques with film; the great difference, of course, is the size of the screen. Because the viewing area is confined, television employs more close-up shots. Programs are shaped by segments and by commercials, and series require twenty-six episodes each season. These constraints determine character, theme, conflict, and quality.

With the expansion of cable and pay per view television, specialty networks—news, music, science fiction, cartoons, movie, sports—make the possibilities endless. At the same time, Bruce Springsteen still sings that he has "fifty-seven channels and nothing to watch." Surely, more exciting productions will come from artists in the future as they explore the full potential of television.

ELEMENTS OF DRAMA

Character

Imagined people stand at the center of almost all of the forms of literature. Anyone who appears in a work is called a **character,** a term chosen carefully for its meaning—those innate faculties that give a person identity and that distinguish him or her from others. Plays present a special framework for characters because the genre differs from fiction and from poetry since most dramas function without narration and narrators.

The *major* characters tend to be round, dynamic, and well-developed, whereas *minor* characters remain flat, static, and slightly developed. Often a character appears in order to illuminate, double, or contradict a main character—a foil. Because they are easily recognized types, some characters are known as **stereotypes** or **stock** characters. In commedia dell'arte, for example, the harlequin always plays the same part—always acts in a predictable manner. All of the characters in this kind of drama are stereotypes by definition. This comfortable recognition allows the playwright to create characters easily.

The personae in most plays, however, grow and change; the development of the characters leads to important knowledge concerning the meaning of the drama. For example, at the end of *Oedipus Rex,* Oedipus recognizes his responsibility for the tragedy that has ruined both his life and the city of Thebes. Characterization, then, represents the most important element in drama. Through the personae, the playwright creates everything else.

Soliloquy, Monologue, Dialogue

A character's language reveals his or her feelings, values, situation, and/or beliefs. In a **soliloquy**—a long speech by one character, the speaker communicates special information to the audience. Think of Hamlet's famous words on suicide, "To be or not to be." Through this eloquent aside, the audience learns of Hamlet's pain as he contemplates his duty to exact revenge for his father's death, a pain that makes life unbearable. Hamlet resents his situation, his mother, his uncle; he feels increasingly angry, desperate, sad, and suicidal. Indeed, he cannot decide on an adequate response to the unreasonable demands of life (chapter 4). Unlike a soliloquy, a **monologue** may be addressed to other characters as well as to the audience. It serves the same function; it permits an extended discussion of information, attitudes, or ideas by one character.

Most words in a play, however, are spoken between two characters. This exchange, called **dialogue,** demonstrates agreements, conflicts, relationships, differing or similar beliefs and motives between personae. Dialogue becomes the main element in the play for the development of character, plot, and theme. Consider the following lines from Synge's *Riders to the Sea* (chapter 5), in which Synge writes about the power of family ties and about the power of the sea. The mother, Maurya, fears that her son, Michael, is dead; and she awaits news of his being washed ashore after buying wood to build a coffin for his burial. She entreats Bartley, her remaining son, not to leave the island. Examine the language:

Bartley *(Beginning to work with the rope.):* I've no halter the way I can ride down on the mare, and I must go now quickly. This is the one boat going for two weeks or beyond it, and the fair will be a good fair for horses I heard them saying below.

Maurya: It's a hard thing they'll be saying below if the body is washed up and there's no man in it[1] to make the coffin, and I after giving a big price for the finest white boards you'd find in Connemara.

Bartley: How would it be washed up, and we after looking[2] each day for nine days, and a strong wind blowing a while back from the west and south?

Maurya: If it isn't found itself,[3] that wind is raising the sea, and there was a star up against the moon, and it rising in the night. If it was a hundred horses, or a thousand horses you had itself, what is the price of a thousand horses against a son where there is one son only?

The poetry of Maurya's language, the persuasive quality of her description of the landscape and of the horses, and the value that she places on her love for and need of her sons make the difference. Bartley leaves wishing "the Blessing of God" on his family. Ironically, the audience knows at the moment of Bartley's departure that he, too, will ride to the sea and drown. Synge's use of accent, dialect, ungrammatical constructions, figurative language, and poetic style are examples of effective use of dialogue to create meaning.

Action

Every character, played by an actor, not only speaks, but also acts and reacts to others and to events. A character may portray motivation through action. In *"Master Harold" . . . and the Boys,* Hally's action of spitting on Sam reveals his motive. Sam is African, but Sam represents Hally's spiritual father. Hally's action, in many ways, is unexplicable and unforgivable. His motives, however, arise from a lifetime of subtle bigotry and personal frustration.

The audience also can learn about characters when they refuse to act according to normal expectations. Mrs. Hale and Mrs. Peters do not reveal their knowledge about the Wright murder to the sheriff. They realize that Mrs. Wright was motivated to commit such violence by actions which the men would consider *Trifles* (chapter 6). In this play, Susan Glaspell artfully portrays character through *in*action.

Much of the interaction in drama becomes quite complicated. Hamlet kills Polonius by mistake; Ophelia kills herself because she erroneously believes that Hamlet does not love her; Laertes agrees to kill Hamlet with a foil dipped in poison because he thinks that Hamlet has deliberately caused the deaths of his father and sister. All of these actions involve misunderstandings, and they represent only a small proportion of the intricate events in the play. Such complexity in relationships among characters deepens the texture and meaning of drama.

Plot

The **plot** in a dramatic or narrative work is the structure of its actions, ordered to achieve emotional and aesthetic effects. This definition becomes

[1]i.e., the house. [2]when we have been looking. [3]even if it isn't found.

complicated by the relationship between plot and character. The actions, both verbal and physical, are performed by characters; they provide the vehicle through which characters reveal their moral and personal traits. Plot is more, much more, than the "story" of a play, which is a simple synopsis of the temporal events. Only when the story becomes related to discussions of relationships and organization of actions in order to produce meaning does it become part of the definition of plot.

Numerous patterns for plots exist; each depends on the mode of drama and its purposes. Is it tragedy? comedy? romance? satire? ritual? melodrama? Whatever the genre, all plots share certain elements in traditional forms of dramatic literature.

In any play, the interest centers on the **protagonist,** the hero or heroine. Usually this character struggles against an opponent or enemy, the character designated as the **antagonist.** The relation between them becomes the **conflict.** Many, but not all, plays contain one or more conflicts. In Shakespeare's *Hamlet,* the prince is the protagonist, and King Claudius, the antagonist. As Hamlet seeks revenge for his father's murder, a conflict between them escalates and complicates until both men die. Often the protagonist struggles in conflict with fate or circumstance; often the conflict resides within the main character.

Sometimes a character concocts a scheme that entraps another person, one who is naïve, trusting, and vulnerable. This scheme is called **intrigue.** Rosencrantz and Guildenstern agree to assist Claudius in his plans against Hamlet; this intrigue fails. Many comedies also depend upon this device.

As the audience or reader begins to follow and to sympathize with characters, the plot builds **suspense** about its events and resolutions. If the action contradicts readers' expectations, the result becomes **surprise.** The relationship of suspense and surprise provides the essential dynamism in a play and must be predicated on the effectiveness of motive and of previous action.

A traditional plot has what Aristotle called **unity of action,** by which he meant that every part or event becomes necessary and integral to the whole and that the loss of any part destroys the whole. Aristotle considered *Oedipus Rex* as a perfect example of unity of action in plot. The slow unraveling of Oedipus as the murderer of Laius, as the scourge of Thebes, incident by incident, clue by clue, exemplifies this quality (chapter 7).

Other plays include **double plots,** as in Elizabethan drama. Such plays involve a second story that becomes fascinating on its own merits and that enlarges understanding of the main plot. Such a **subplot** exists in *Hamlet* in the relationship between Hamlet and Ophelia. Plays may have multiple subplots.

In this traditional definition of plot, a sequence of events provides a *beginning* that establishes the situation and introduces characters, a *middle* that complicates the actions and develops character and an *end* that completes the action. The beginning of Hamlet captures attention with the appearance of the ghost and an exposition that implies that "something is rotten in the state of Denmark." The middle reveals Claudius as murderer, Hamlet as a pretended madman with a plan "to capture the conscience of a king." At this moment, the conflict reaches its highest point of tension for the protagonist, a point called the **apex.** By the end, Claudius has plotted the death of Hamlet;

Ophelia has committed suicide; Hamlet has killed Polonius; Gertrude has swallowed poison; Laertes has killed Hamlet. Only Horatio remains to mourn the death of his "sweet prince" and to welcome Fortinbras.

In *Technique of the Drama* (1863), Gustav Freytag described plot in a configuration known as **Freytag's Pyramid.** According to this schema, a plot begins with rising action. In *Hamlet* this complication includes the appearance of the ghost; it includes the conflict between Claudius and Hamlet and events that eventually lead to Hamlet's success in achieving control. This rising action reaches a **climax** or **apex** for the hero. In *Hamlet* it becomes the proof of Claudius's crime through the play-within-the-play. Then comes the crisis where Hamlet fails to kill Claudius because the latter is praying. Then the **falling action** leads to the ascendance of Claudius until a **catastrophe** happens, as in the deaths of the main characters. This catastrophe may also be called the **denouement,** for not all plays end in tragic circumstances. Contemporary dramas often deliberately defy expectations of conventional plots, and some attempt to eliminate plot entirely.

Setting

In drama, **setting** differs greatly from other forms of literature because of the imperative for performance. In stage directions and in dialogue, the dramatist describes the place and time for the play. A designer creates stage sets that suggest the background for each scene. Shakespeare, for example, places Hamlet in Denmark; yet the stage can be transformed only into semblances of rooms in a castle, a graveyard, or a ship. The audience or reader must imagine the drowning of Ophelia and the battle won by Fortinbras. Still, the stage adds a dimension to drama that other forms of literature lack—visual and auditory images, live action, and spatial and temporal realities.

Props, scenery, costumes, and lights can change as the play progresses; but the setting on stage remains both limited and central to all productions. For instance, the set for *Riders to the Sea* should indicate the poverty of the modest cottage. One entrance must lead to the external world, to the sea that gives each family work and that claims each family's sons. Setting in drama may reveal economic status, geographic location, time period, and personal taste. Unlike fiction writers and poets, the playwright does not describe place in great detail, and he or she leaves much more to the imagination or to the stage.

Symbolism

In dramatic literature, **symbols** often are not subtle. They appear on stage as visual reminders of their central place in the meaning of the play. In Yamauchi's *And the Soul Shall Dance* (chapter 6), one of the symbols takes the form of a song about a caged bird. In the lyrics to this popular Japanese song, separated lovers express their loneliness. The woman describes herself as a "caged bird, unable to leave" in the third stanza. This bird represents Emiko who is lost in the past, who is lost in exile, who is lost in the desert, and who is finally lost in madness. She, like the bird, is "unable to leave."

Irony

Dramatic irony appears in a play or in fiction when a situation or action becomes apparent to the audience but remains unknown to a character or to characters. Consequently, the persona acts in ignorance and often inappropriately. The Greek tragedians, whose conflicts and stories were already known to their audiences, based their works on a constant use of this technique. In Sophocles's *Oedipus Rex* the irony is **tragic** since the king searches for a murderer whose deeds have caused the plague in Thebes. The audience knows that Oedipus will find himself guilty of the crimes he decries.

Other kinds of irony:

- **Verbal irony** is a statement in which the meaning is different from the message that is expressed. Jonathan Swift's "A Modest Proposal" for eating children as a solution to the problem caused by the potato famine in Ireland depends greatly on this device.
- **Structural irony** sustains double meaning throughout the work. In drama, this technique requires a naïve protagonist; in fiction an unreliable narrator often serves this purpose.

Theme

The **themes** of a play are not its subjects, but rather its central idea or ideas. One theme of *Oedipus Rex* concerns the protagonist's search for vision and for truth. Oedipus reluctantly discovers the secrets of his identity and the meaning of his past actions. Knowledge of his personal guilt forces him into exile. The unbearable consequences of his pride result in patricide, suicide, and blindness—the fulfillment of a hideous destiny. Because Oedipus solves the riddle of the Sphinx, he saves Thebes and becomes king. Because he unknowingly murders his father, he then brings a new plague upon the city. Therefore, another theme in this drama focuses on the political importance of the personal tragedy of the king. His errors not only ruin him and his family, they also destabilize the state. Like Shakespeare's *Hamlet,* the fall of the hero creates a political tragedy. Surely Sophocles intended these two intertwined thematic threads; surely these related themes contribute to the play's greatness.

THE READING/WRITING PROCESS: DRAMA

Interpreting drama begins with impressions about a play. Feelings often provide guidelines to intellectual analysis and responses. Reread the drama and examine its parts—character, plot, theme—to determine their relationship to the whole. Grasping the wholeness in a drama depends on looking carefully at all of its elements. Consider characters and their development; consider the conflicts and their complications and possible resolutions. Consider how themes emerge. Evaluate how well the play comes together.

Take notes, and be careful to pay close attention to stage directions, prologues, epilogues, and important quotations. Determine the play's meaning, and assess its ability to force a reader or audience to face matters of enduring value.

CHECKLIST FOR WRITING ABOUT DRAMA

1. Does the play have a **narrator**? How does this character function? Is he or she reliable?
2. Are the main characters fully developed? How do they change? What actions or words demonstrate such change? How do minor characters function in the play? What do you learn about characters from the dialogue of others? Is the character sympathetic? How would an audience react? What different interpretations of these characters are possible?
3. What is the central conflict? How is it resolved? Are there subplots? Which acts or scenes represent the **rising action?** Identify the **climax.** Is there suspense? Which acts or scenes represent the falling action? How are the **subplots** resolved?
4. How does the **dialogue** contribute to the **plot?** How do characters advance the plot or plots? How does **setting** function in relation to plot? Does offstage action contribute to the development of conflict? How?
5. Does the play contain **irony?** What kinds of irony are present? Is the irony effective?
6. Are there symbols that suggest the theme?
7. What information about production is included in the stage directions? What information does the play give about costume, set, lighting, sound effects?
8. What are central themes? What are other significant issues? How do characters and conflicts illuminate themes?
9. Discuss conflict, character, language, theme in relation to the total effect of the play. Does it work? What does it mean?
10. What is the best feature of the play? What is the weakest feature of the play? What is the final evaluation?

Student Portfolio:
Response to Wakako Yamauchi's *And the Soul Shall Dance*

The assignment for this essay—analysis of one or more of the characters in Yamauchi's play, *And the Soul Shall Dance*—required a number of writing responses, a series of drafts, and a final draft. Vicky Hayes began with the purpose of analyzing both Emiko and Masako, the central protagonists. However, after doing a reader response journal entry and a first draft, she realized that she was more interested in analyzing Emiko's character; in her second draft, she eliminated treatment of Masako and concentrated on Emiko's character and fate. Hayes progressed through several stages of responding and writing: an initial reader response journal entry; three successive drafts of work; and a final revision.

Her work reveals her personal exploratory response to literature, her involvement in the text, her questioning, and her acute and in-depth examination of character. Instead of writing an outline, Hayes reveals that she needed to write several drafts to discover her thesis (main impression of character), subtopics, and evidence. Her final conclusion came out of an extended discussion with her peer mentor during a conference about the first draft. Her peer critic also offered an alternative to creating an outline as a mode of planning: a method of glossing a draft, identifying subtopics, and then reorganizing and revising the writing. What emerges in the final draft is a powerful treatment of a woman caught between worlds whose tragic situation leads to madness. Note that the final version of the essay contains a clear focus and thesis in the introduction; extensive character analysis (focusing on Emiko's gestures, actions, and words); development of points with sufficient evidence (specific details and quotations from the play); and an effective conclusion. Hayes's assessment of her process ends the portfolio.

Stage One: Reader Response

Journal Entry

Plays are more difficult for me to read in some ways. The voices are constantly changing. The glimpses into their characters are brief. But the scenes are concentrated, so that what you get is the real mood that prevails in the room, not just a glimpse into one character but how they all relate to one another. Sometimes the stage directions divert me, like when they say a character gestures. I have read very few plays. Plays are very different, I think, because dialogue, real dialogue is the way people talk. They don't finish sentences. Sometimes they don't say complete words. Sometimes they just stand there and we can't see them because plays are more meant to be visual, like when the two young girls meet (569), not read from the page. I have to put myself in the place of an actor. How would I begin to interpret my character if I were . . . I don't know who I would want to be in this play. I could do Masako because I like the way the playwright has captured her place in adolescence. I like Masako and her dad because Masako is not a fixed character. I know she can change. And her father, her father is not a worrier like her mother. He does not give in easily to defeat. In this desperate situation, is anyone going to win?

If I were playing Masako, I guess I'd be ashamed about burning down the bathhouse, and maybe angry at my mother because she scolds me. My mother worries about everything constantly. No let up. She was all out of shape about the bathhouse. Dad said we could rebuild it or take a bath outside in the dark, but she wouldn't have that. She told everyone I was careless (line 21, 545) They always say I have no manners (line 33, 565) also about how "in this country they don't make too much to-do about manners) and my mother says I'm sulking. I'm tired of doing everything they tell me to do. I don't want to make friends with Kiyoko (Begins on bottom of 568). She's too old. Besides, she acts like a baby. Here goes Hana—the manners thing again.

Masako is drawn more toward Emiko than to her mother or to Kiyoko. Hana has sympathy for Emiko when she is trying to sell her the kimonos, but I don't think she likes her. At the top of 559 she does say Emiko is not crazy. "She just can't adjust to this like. She can't get over the good times she had in Japan" (around like 163) Hana says she tries to be friendly (around 170) but that Emiko is going on about the past, just living in her memories of dancing and music, and old lovers. The thing is, Hana is infinitely practical and she wants to pass this on to Masako, while Emiko lives in a dream world, and she conveys this to Masako too. Does this writer use Masako as a plot device to hear both women's stories?

Hana warns Masako about her reading American books and "dreaming." Masako says she wants to read and her mother replies "Some of the things you read, you're never going to know (experience?)." "I can dream though," Masako says. Then Hana replies, "Sometimes the dreaming makes the living harder. Better to keep your head out of the clouds."

Emiko, the dreamer, we all love a dreamer don't we? She gives a body and a life and a voice to the words of the song that Masako likes so much, *And the Soul Shall Dance* (lyrics on 584) "Red lips press against a glass/Drink the green wine/and the soul shall dance." Masako hears the music and this song about the tension between what really happens to us in this life, and what we want to happen. Is this a real central theme to this play? Emiko said she was almost an artist? Top of page 558, "I was almost a natori." Masako, as an adolescent floats between her mother's world and Emiko's dream world. She is like a voyeur, always watching at windows, listening, even in the last scene she watches Emiko from behind a bush. The child as a voyeur is a striking image. Not yet fully engaged in life, just watching. Emiko tells her, someday she will fall in love. I need to look up that passage. What does it mean to fall in love in Emiko's world?

I keep coming back to Emiko. Her character has the strongest pull on me. I will focus on Emiko for my character sketch because we know so much about how Emiko's past and how she feels as a homeless, compromised woman, living in the shadow of her dead sister with a husband who calls her a whore.

First Draft of Character Analysis [Blocked in Terms of Topics]

Where do we find beauty in this life? Where do we begin to look for it? When I think of Emiko I see a solitary dancer in tattered clothes moving to music in her head, moving to notes that have long faded from the ears of those around her. Masako awakens music in Emiko when she brings the phonograph to her home. Emiko, uncommunicative till now, begins to dance for her guests, weeping when she hears the music. Masako has played her favorite song, and Emiko responds by asking the little girl if she likes it, understands it. Together, as they interpret the song, Emiko begins to talk about her former life in Japan (556)

> My home, Japan, my real home. I'm planning to go back.
> By yourself?
> Oh, yes. It's a secret. Can you keep a secret?

Music

Emiko has no secrets. Like all the characters, she is fallen, in that they have all been forced to leave their native land. But Emiko is a fallen woman. Groomed to be a rich man's wife, some indiscretion she committed led to her fall from her family's grace, all the way from the top of the world to Oka's lap. All her cultured activities, the pursuits of a lady, are lost to her. Her husband addresses her as a secondhand woman.

> "you don't know what I'm talking about. I know the whole village knows. They are all laughing at you. At me! Stupid Oka got stuck with a secondhand woman." (550, line 12)

Secrets

Growing angrier at her lack of compliance, Oka calls her a whore.

> "I'm not a whore, I'm true . . . he knows I'm true." (561, line 20)

Emiko has managed to keep a secret part of her soul protected from the tyranny of a patriarchal society, even from a husband who uses her body. Oka cannot possess her soul. She declares that her lover is waiting for her in Japan as Oka ridicules her. "All I wanted was a little comfort" he pleads (562, line 45)

But she cannot give him this, anymore than she could deny her "saru shibai" in order to wed a rich man. At the close of their argument, Emiko utters the words that are her truth, the words that echoed in the song "And the Soul Shall Dance".

Secret Self

> "Because I must keep the dream alive . . . the dream is all I live for. I am only in exile now. Because if I give in, all I've lived for before will mean nothing." (563, top)

Even after Oka takes the money she has been saving for her return to Japan and spends it on his daughter, Emiko does not give in. She tries to sell the last relic of her life in Japan, the ceremonial robes, in order to finance her trip home.

Masako has great desire to possess these robes. Masako is drawn to Emiko all along. Emiko lives in a dream world and she conveys her life to the young girl who drawn her out. But Hana's world is a practical world, and she wants to teach her daughter practicality. Hana warns Masako about her reading American books and "dreaming." Masako says she wants to read and her mother replies "Some of the things you read, you're never going to know (experience?)." "I can dream though," Masako says. Then Hana replies, "Sometimes the dreaming makes the living harder. Better to keep your head out of the clouds."

Resolution

Emiko is the dreamer; she give a body and a life and a voice to the words of the song that Masako likes "And the Soul Shall Dance (lyrics on 584). "Red lips press against a glass/Drink the green wine/and the soul shall dance. Masako hears the music and this song about the tension between what really happens to us in this life (morning's reality scatters the dreams, [584], and what we want to happen.) Masako, as an adolescent floats between her mother's world and Emiko's dream world. She is like a voyeur, always watching at windows, listening; even in the last scene she watched Emiko from behind a bush. The child as a voyeur is a striking image. She is privy to Emiko's private life, and to her last moment on stage.

Role of Masako

Stripped of everything tangible save her ceremonial robe, Emiko, her hair free, and singing, dances into the desert while Masako looks on. The metaphor of the dance, and Emiko's dilemma combine to play out the tension between reality and dream world, between what we desire and what we attain in this life. Emiko will live in her dream world.

Dream World

Final Draft—Emiko: Dancing Alone

In *And the Soul Shall Dance* Emiko is, in her way, an invincible character. She bows to no one in a society that values humility and service as desirable feminine traits. Her refusal to assimilate into a culture or a lifestyle that she finds unacceptable sets her apart from the others. Emiko is an exile. When we first hear about Emiko through her neighbors, she does not seem like one of the immigrants. Hana describes her as being "not just shy . . . she's strange" (I, i). Emiko does not seem to be concerned with manners (societal expectations) as Hana is and does not even offer a cup of tea to her guests. Unlike Hana, the practical and dutiful wife, Emiko does not rush to fill her husband's sake bowl (I, ii). There is something unsettling and different about Emiko. Oka ridicules her and punishes her. Hana both criticizes and excuses her.

Emiko appears as an outsider. She lives in memory of her past life as a "natori," a beautiful, cultured woman trained to be a wife to a wealthy patron. We see Emiko through a window, neighbors looking on as she begins to dance (I, ii).

> From the side of the house Emiko appears. Her hair is down, she wears an old straw hat. She dances in front of the Muratas. They're startled. After the first shock they watch with frozen smiles. They try to join Emiko's mood but something of the mood is missing. Oka is grieved. He finally stands as though he's had enough." (I, ii) [Later we learn Oka slaps her for her performance.]

The dance represents Emiko's tie to the past, a link that she refuses to give up. Emiko and Masako translate the lines of the song, which expresses the theme of the play, "And the Soul Shall Dance." Emiko confides that she will go home soon, and alone. "Oh yes," she cautions the child, "it's a secret. You can keep a secret?" (I, ii).

Emiko has no secrets; she only has a dream. Her husband tells us about her "questionable past," taking away from her all her mystery as he chides and accuses her. Like all the characters, she is fallen, in that they have all been forced to leave their native land. But Emiko is a fallen woman. Groomed to be a rich man's wife, she fell from her family's grace because of a sexual indiscretion. She fell in love with the wrong man and loves him still. She plunged from the life of an artist to Oka's lap. All her cultured activities, the pursuits of a lady, are lost to her. Her husband addresses her as a "secondhand woman." He states:

> You don't know what I'm talking about. I know. The whole village knows. They are all laughing at you. At me! Stupid Oka got stuck with a secondhand woman. (I, iii)

Growing angrier at her lack of compliance, Oka calls her a whore. And Emiko replies, "I'm not a whore, I'm true . . . he knows I'm true" (I, iii).

5 Emiko has managed to keep a secret part of her soul protected from the tyranny of a patriarchal society, even from a husband who uses her body. Oka cannot possess her soul. She declares that her lover is waiting for her. But she cannot give him this, anymore than she could deny her "saru shibai" in order to wed a rich man. At the close of their argument,

Emiko utters the words that are her truth, the words that are echoed in the song "And the Soul Shall Dance":

> "Because I must keep the dream alive . . . the dream is all I live for. I am only in exile now. Because if I give in, all I've lived for before will mean nothing." (I, iii)

Even after the emotional scene where Oka takes the money she has been saving for her return to Japan and spends it on his daughter, Emiko does not give in. she tries to sell the last relic of her life in Japan, the ceremonial robes, in order to finance her trip home. She refuses to do what Hana tells Masako we must do in order to survive:

> "Emiko San isn't crazy. She just likes her drinks. . . . She can't adjust to this life She can't get over the good times she had in Japan. Well, it's not easy . . . but one has to know when to bend . . . like the bamboo. When the wind blows, bamboo bends. You bend or crack. Remember that, Masako." (I, iii)

Emiko refuses to "[bend]" to her new life. She will dream of Japan. Emiko, the dreamer, we all love a dreamer don't we? How does Emiko find beauty in her brutal life? She gives a body and a voice to the words of the song that Masako likes so much, "Red lips / Press against a glass / Drink the green wine / and the soul shall dance" (II, vi). Masako hears the music and this song about the tension between what really happens to us in this life (morning's reality scatters the dreams) and what we want to happen. Stripped of everything tangible save her ceremonial robe, Emiko, her hair free, singing, dances into the desert while Masako looks on. The metaphor of the dance and Emiko's dilemma combine to play out the tension between reality and dream world, between what we desire and what we attain in this life.

Emiko becomes a solitary dancer moving to the music in her own head, moving to notes that have long faded from ears around her. Her refusal to engage in the world of relationships with the people around her seals her life of exile and drives her to madness.

Reflective Letter (Written by Hayes About Her Process of Writing)

Like most students who have spent a few years in college, I developed a method for writing academic papers. I read the text with an underliner in one hand and a pen in the other. I yellow line passages that reveal meaning or give me clues; then when I finish each page, I write a sentence in the margin so I can easily relocate key passages. Then I sit down and write a page or so of wondering. I get it out of my system this way, and usually this leads me to a tentative thesis. This time it helped me to identify the most developed character in the text, Emiko, and it gave me an idea on what I might say about her as a character.

In the freewrite, I wrote a few sentences about most of the characters. It was very hard to give up writing about Masako because I was drawn to her. She kept coming into my focus. You will see that even in the third draft, in which Masako comes into the conclusion of the paper. Each draft brings Emiko more clearly into my sight and utilizes the voice of the other characters to reveal important facets of Emiko's character.

When I finished the exercise, I was just as surprised as I always am, at the fact that each revision builds on the freewrite, yet eliminates everything that is not necessary for the character sketch. My assignment after all was to do a character analysis. A writer is known more by what he throws away than by what he keeps, according to one famous writer, Gabriel García Márquez. It's my willingness to eliminate ideas from a tangle of thought and slim down the paper that helps me to write without so much apprehension. I have seen Emiko both through the eyes of the other characters and through her own words in order to understand who she is, but I must make the characters speak only for her.

Finally, a consultation with my peer critic allowed me to reach the conclusion in my paper. This allows me to utilize a wider thought pattern than just my own. I always reach a point in a paper where I get stuck. Sometimes it's early on, but this time it was toward the conclusion. I couldn't decide whether Emiko was choosing life over despair, so we sat down and talked it out. I found that paradoxically she chose life—her dream world—but that choice led to despair and self-destruction—her descent into madness. I also worked through several drafts by blocking them in term of topics and redrafting the essay. I naturally write in several drafts. I know students who do not find this necessary. The magic paper fairy must sit on their shoulder while they stare at a screen. My muse is more like an elephant that gets lighter and lighter during each draft until, finally, I can't feel him at all.

CHAPTER 12

NONFICTION

When we think of nonfiction prose, we envision objective **expository** writing designed to convey information to an audience: newswriting, for example, or scientific and business communications. Nonfiction also may be creative, evocative essays replete with a sense of voice and power. Imaginative reaction, passionate commitment, and the urgency of personal perspective play a role in some kinds of nonfiction. Many forms have features of fiction, poetry, and drama: vivid, descriptive detail, narrative example, metaphoric language, and dialogue.

In nonfiction, we may be drawn into the world of the writing just as we are in fiction, in poetry, or in drama. However, we become involved in different ways. We read to absorb, to react, perhaps to be moved and enlightened by facts, arguments, issues, and ideas. As Susan Sontag suggests, "an essay could be as much an event, a transforming event, as a novel or a poem."

FORMS OF NONFICTION

Speech

As major civilizations and communal life flourished, public discourse evolved. The **speech,** oral communication designed to be delivered to an audience, became a popular form of public communication in Greek times, particularly during the fifth century B.C., the age of Pericles, at the height of Athenian democracy. In his treatise, *The Rhetoric,* Aristotle (384–322 B.C.), a Greek philosopher, categorized the three kinds of speeches prevalent in his society: orations delivered in the law courts, in the political arena, at ceremonial occasions. Many examples of these declamations, of course, did not survive because they were not transcribed. One famous speech is Pericles's funeral oration for the Athenian dead (430 B.C.), which appears in Thucydides's *History of the Peloponnesian Wars.* Among other arguments, Pericles praises the Athenian democratic "system of government" as a "model to others." Many famous Greek orators and teachers developed the form of the speech between the fifth and fourth centuries B.C., including Isocrates and Demosthenes whose political works are notable examples. Roman rhetoric was patterned after Greek models. Cicero (106–43 B.C.), a Roman statesman, politician, and rhetorician, excelled at oratory and published his own speeches, which still serve as exemplars of classical argument. (See chapter 3.) Examples of speeches in *Legacies* include Sojourner Truth's "Ain't I a

Woman?" (chapter 7) and Martin Luther King's "Letter from Birmingham Jail" (chapter 12).

Philosophical Treatise

Another human imperative has been to speculate on the state of the world and on human nature. One of the earliest forms of nonfiction has been the **philosophical treatise,** an extended formal meditation on a philosophical, religious, or political subject. Such treatises convey the central ideas, beliefs, and values of many Western and Eastern societies. Interestingly, at approximately the same time (c. 600 B.C.), Pythagoras wrote about mathematics in ancient Greece, Confucius was a teacher in China, and Hindu sages created the *Upanishads,* the central documents of Hindu thought in India.

Plato (428–347 B.C.), one of the foremost Greek philosophers, wrote tracts on such subjects as the nature of love, "The Symposium" (chapter 6) and the ideal state, *The Republic* (chapter 8). The wisdom of Confucius (551–479(?) B.C.), a Chinese scholar and teacher, instructed people to live a good life in harmony with others. Confucius suggests, for example, that a ruler must "govern by virtue. . . .": "Govern the people by virtue . . . and the people . . . will be reformed of themselves." Another Chinese philosopher, known as Lao-tzu (575–485(?) B.C.), assumes a different religious stance: withdrawal from the world, meditation, mysticism, and the cultivation of silence as the way of the spirit. Lao-tzu is considered responsible for the *Tao te Ching,* the opening line of which states, "The way that can be spoken of is not the way. . . ."

Examples of political, philosophical, and or religious treatises abound in world history. Think of the documents of the American or the French revolution; the Communist Manifesto; Chairman Mao's sayings; the sacred texts of world religions. The poem of Lao-tzu (chapter 7) and the reflections of Albert Camus (chapter 8) also exemplify this form of nonfiction.

Autobiography

One structured type of personal writing is **autobiography,** defined as writing about one's life. Autobiography became prevalent with the rise of Christianity as people had the urge to document their spiritual conversions. One of the earliest stories of such a conversion, St. Augustine's *Confessions,* written between A.D. 397 and 400, describes the author's childhood, his conversion to Christianity at thirty-two, and his transformation from sinner to Christian.

The desires to fashion a story of one's life, to create from memories—from inchoate reminiscences—an ordered vision of one's past, and to seek personal meaning from one's past are deep needs in human beings. The autobiographical impulse has taken hold of writers throughout the ages as diverse as Machiavelli, Helen Keller, and Maya Angelou. Autobiography becomes a particularly powerful means of expression for those groups who feel disenfranchised because this form of writing defines and asserts selfhood in response to the lack of recognition of ethnic identity. Alice Walker has written many autobiographical essays that explore her stance as an African American woman, for example, "Am I Blue?" (chapter 8). One particularly North American form of autobiography is the *slave narrative,* a story that portrays the slave's efforts to secure release from bondage and to gain freedom. Read Harriet Jacobs's autobiography, *Incidents in the Life of a Slave Girl* in chapter 7.

Memoir

As eras of conquest and travel progressed during the Middle Ages and the Renaissance, another autobiographical form emerged. **Memoir** presents the remembrances of a public figure and the events of an historical era. Perhaps, one of the earliest examples of such a document is Julius Caesar's record of his military campaigns in Gaul 102–44 B.C. Other examples of memoir include Marco Polo's travels in China and India (*The Travels of Marco Polo,* 1293), Leo Africanus's account of Africa written when he was taken captive and held as a slave by pirates (1526), and Babur's (Zahir Ud-Din Mohammed's) recounting of his battles in India (1526). Contemporary memoirists include Winston Churchill and Richard Nixon.

Journal

The **journal,** another form of personal writing, concerns the self exclusively, and the presumed audience is the author. Some of the earliest examples include the lists of Sei Shonogan—a form of a diary kept by a woman in the court of the emperor in tenth-century Japan. Titles from Shonogan's diary reveal "Things That Make One's Heart Beat Faster"; "Things That Arouse a Fond Memory of the Past"; "Hateful Things"; and "Depressing Things."

As journals developed, many types emerged: travel diaries, diaries of spiritual life, journals kept during the settlement of the frontier by the pioneers in North America, and diaries kept by women during the Civil War. Throughout literary history, numerous artists and writers were inveterate journal keepers: Leonardo da Vinci wrote and drew in sketchbooks; Henry David Thoreau composed more than 60,000 pages of journals; Anaïs Nin had at least sixteen volumes of journals.

Letter writing represents another form of personal expression; often in letter writing, the assumption of a public as well as a private audience exists. Benjamin Franklin composed letters to his son; F. Scott Fitzgerald communicated by letter with his daughter, Scottie. Martin Luther King's "Letter from Birmingham Jail" presents a complex political argument that suggests the fusion of both the public and the private self and the impossibility of separating these selves in the response to political oppression.

Essay

During the Renaissance, with its emphasis on individual will and consciousness, the **essay** developed, a form of prose that presented a person's reflections and ideas on a specific topic. The essay (derived from the French verb *assayer*—meaning to try, to attempt) presents a concise, prose discussion of a limited topic and of limited length, designed for a general audience. Although the origin of the essay can be traced to ancient Rome—to Seneca and to Plutarch who wrote works with such titles as "On Envy and Hate," "On the Control of Anger," and "On Having Many Friends,"—Francis Bacon, the English scientist and philosopher (1561–1628), often receives credit for inventing the modern form of the genre. He wrote volumes of essays on subjects as varied as the relation of parents and children, death, truth, adversity, anger, revenge, atheism, suspicion, and cunning. During the 1600s and 1700s, many writers experimented with this form, including Blaise Pascal, who produced his *Pensées* (Thoughts, 1670), a collection of his thoughts; Montaigne, who penned his *Essais* (1580), his meditations; and in England in the 1700s Joseph Addison and Richard Steele, who wrote essays for their literary journal, *The Spectator.* The essay flourished in the hands of such eighteenth-century British writers as Jonathan Swift, Samuel Johnson, and William Hazlitt and such nineteenth-century North American writers as Henry David Thoreau and Ralph Waldo Emerson who wrote "Civil Disobedience" and "The American Scholar," respectively. Essay writing reached its apex in Britain and in North America in the eighteenth and nineteenth centuries.

Kinds of Essays

Exposition

Exposition, the main form of nonfiction, explains or conveys information to a particular audience. Exposition may have a range of approaches—objective, subjective, factual, or reflective. An expository essay may describe, explain, give examples, compare, define, analyze, or demonstrate cause and effect. Lewis Thomas's essay, "The Medusa and the Snail" (in chapter 4), takes the example of the symbiosis between the Medusa jellyfish and the snail and transforms it into a frightening analogy to explore growth of identity. His examination prompts us to evaluate our own concepts of selfhood.

Expository essays may fall into two classes: *formal* and *informal* writing. In a formal expository essay, the writing may be organized with an introduction, middle paragraphs, and conclusion. The essay is carefully and tightly developed: a thesis and subtopics exist; the writer orders ideas into supporting paragraphs with clear topic sentences and supporting evidence; a direct and logical progression of points moves toward the conclusion. The point of view and tone may be more objective and less personal. "The Medusa and the Snail" (chapter 4) represents a superb example of a tightly and formally organized essay. The informal essay may be organized by associations and may use techniques of fiction (personal, symbolic detail, dialogue, narrative excerpts) and of poetry (imagery, figurative language, repetition). Witness Maxine Hong Kingston's mix of description, reminiscence, narration, character sketch, and reflection in "No Name Woman" (chapter 6).

ARGUMENTATION

In **argumentation,** one of the primary forms of nonfiction prose, the writer presents a personal opinion with the intention of convincing an audience about his or her point of view, constructs reasons for that position, and develops supporting evidence. Informal and formal modes of structuring argument exist. Informal argument may take the form of persuasive writing in which emotional appeals, detail, narrative and personal examples provide the proof designed to convince a reader. For instance, if a writer composed an essay for a local paper to convince the audience that eighteen-year-olds' drunken driving poses a serious threat to others, he or she refers to the experience of witnessing a violent and fatal accident caused by an eighteen-year-old. Or the writer may recount a tale about his or her child or another teenager in order to persuade readers. The intent is to convince an audience of the validity of the position or to persuade people to take some action.

In formal argument, the writer also will develop an argumentative thesis (a position) and reason with his or her audience in mind. However, the position and the thesis will be more objectively stated; the reasons supported with proofs, data, statistics, examples. One option is to shape an argument in classic, Aristotelian style (see chapter 3). Martin Luther King's "Letter from Birmingham Jail" (chapter 12) is an excellent example of a formally structured, complex argumentative essay.

At the heart of argumentative writing remains a solid statement of thesis (position), development of reasons and supporting evidence, and sound, logical reasoning. Compare Marjorie Agosin's exploratory, allusive, lyrical, personal political argument against oppression in "A Visit to the Mothers of the Plaza de Mayo" (chapter 7) with Simone de Beauvoir's logically structured presentation of women's position as "object" in "Woman as Other" (chapter 6).

ELEMENTS OF NONFICTION

All forms of nonfiction share some similarities. A writer thinks of the audience, of the occasion for writing, of the reasons for the writing; he or she then shapes the writing with audience in mind. The writer becomes aware of purposes, intentions and overall goals and chooses relevant details, examples, facts, and reasons. Furthermore, he or she considers **point of view,** voice, the attitude and relationship to material and to audience, and thinks about the relationship between point of view and the persona in the work. This relationship provides readers with a sense of the writer as the character, the person behind the writing. Is the person honest? Does the voice sound real? truthful? distant? impassioned? angry? The persona and point of view of the writer influence the slant of the piece, the main idea, the thesis, the organization, the details, and the word choice. Rhetoricians label this consciousness of audience, occasion, purpose, goals, intent, and point of view the *rhetorical situation.*

Tone involves the feeling, mood, and attitude that readers infer from the content of the essay. In Terry Tempest Williams' "The Wild Card," part of the tone emanates from a sense of righteous anger at the ways in which people are threatening the environment.

The crux of effective nonfiction prose, detail and specific example, makes the piece come alive. The power of nonfiction rests in the interplay of the general and of the specific, of the abstract and of the concrete. Return to the drunken driving example. Just saying eighteen-year-olds should not drive when they are drunk will not convince a reader. An example of a car accident or a statistic regarding the number of eighteen-year-olds involved in drunken-driving accidents and the consequence for others—death, injury of passengers—is much more persuasive.

A college freshman, Jody Levy, wrote the following paragraph. The sensory details, including "as a calm river, soon interrupted by rapids," intensify the description of a commonplace object.

Incense

I watched a stick of incense burn. It was a pale brown colored stick of musk incense, with a red hot tip that slowly smoldered downward. A stream of smoke rose from it, and moved with the wind. It was relaxing to watch the dreamy mist. It was calm and controlled, mesmerizing and hypnotic. The smoke ascended straight towards the ceiling, and, then broke its flow; it spurt, swirled, waved, and curled. It started as a calm river, soon interrupted by rapids. Ashes fell, and, crumbled on the tissue underneath, creating a pile of dirt. Dead and used. I let out a deep breath, and, the smoke scrambled. More ashes formed on the top as the red dot moved down. The ashes bent, and then broke, but they did not fall. They hung like a dead leaf on a tree. I followed the smoke with my eyes—thin, thick, straight, smooth, wavy, curly, spiral, fast, slow, short, long,—always moving and changing—floating lines and forms. A continuous flow of greyish, whitish, bluish smoke. Beautiful, like silk thread. . . . As the stick became shorter, the room smelled nicer; the smoke spiraled off with its musk scent. I liked the smell. The scent obscured the smell of my roommate's fat and odorous boyfriend. My roommate walked in; she hates the smell of incense. And the smoke rose in circles, like a horn shouting out scent. Two lines streamed from the stick, sometimes synchronized, cooperating to make forms. Other times, they crossed

> and waved in opposition, independently creating their own design, and then coming together again. The smoke formed a tunnel, and, then a spiral shell. . . . The incense neared its end, and spurted its last breaths of smoke that slowly floated away and disappeared; but they wafted somewhere in the air. For hours after the final stream of smoke was gone. The red glow faded and left the stick, solitary and lifeless, with a head of ashes. It died and left a lasting memory.

In this piece, the reader senses the persona of the observer: her awe as the stick of incense assumes a life of its own as a "river," as "dirt," as "a dead leaf," then as smoke "like silk thread." The details—color, shape, texture, and smell—of the concrete comparisons and figurative language give this vision of incense its "lasting" place in our minds.

The **organization** of an essay remains crucial. The introduction attracts readers and involves them in the world of the writing and the main idea (the thesis); the middle paragraphs compel through their treatment of evidence (the interplay of generalization and specifics, details and example); and the conclusion reinforces the thesis and leaves the reader with a view to contemplate, feeling enriched, enlivened, convinced, and intellectually aware.

Word choice and *style* are crucial in nonfiction. The writer selects words as carefully as a novelist, poet, or dramatist. He or she plays with words: ironic, witty, comic, lyrical; evocative wordplay and figurative language become crucial to nonfiction. Inexact or diffuse wording leads readers astray; and the work loses its impact. In "Incense" Jody Levy occasionally undermines vivid descriptions by the use of vague words and clichés. For example, after describing the "smoke" as "silk thread," Levy then depicts the room, which "smelled nicer." The "nicer" smell, vague, not at all suggestive of any odor, causes the piece to lose some of its power. The work also loses impact at the end because "lasting memory" is a cliché, a hackneyed means of stating the effect of a moment. Levy easily could have omitted the last sentence.

The total effect of a piece of nonfiction prose is its message: the total meaning of a work. As parts of a short story, drama, poem, build themes, so parts of a nonfiction essay build the message or thesis.

THE READING/WRITING RESPONSE: NONFICTION

When you read nonfiction prose, a checklist of questions will help you analyze the text.

CHECKLIST OF QUESTIONS FOR NONFICTION PROSE

1. What form of nonfiction prose am I reading: speech, treatise, autobiography, memoir, journal, essay?

2. Is it exposition or argument?
3. What is the rhetorical situation (purpose, occasion, audience)?
4. What is the writer's point of view? persona?
5. What is the writer's tone?
6. How do I, as a reader, respond to the point of view and tone?
7. What is the thesis? supporting points?
8. What are significant details? examples?
9. How is the essay organized? formally? informally?
10. What do I notice about style, word choice?
11. What have I learned from reading this work?

Student Portfolio:
Response to King's "Letter from Birmingham Jail"[1]

The portfolio presents a model that demonstrates the stages in the process of writing an evaluation essay. Because King's work is so complex, Jack Ferguson created both a gloss and an outline of the essay to make sure that he grasped the structure of the argument. He next wrote a double-entry notebook. Finally, he composed first and final drafts of his essay. In the final draft, the writer tightened the introduction, clarified King's use of appeals, and analyzed his style.

[1] This response to a published statement by eight fellow clergymen from Alabama (Bishop C. C. J. Carpenter, Bishop Joseph A. Durick, Rabbi Hilton L. Grafman, Bishop Paul Hardin, Bishop Holan B. Harmon, the Reverend George M. Murray, the Reverend Edward V. Ramage and the Reverend Earl Stallings) was composed under somewhat constricting circumstances. Begun on the margins of the newspaper in which the statement appeared while I was in jail, the letter was continued on scraps of writing paper supplied by a friendly Negro trusty, and concluded on a pad my attorneys were eventually permitted to leave me. Although the text remains in substance unaltered, I have indulged in the author's prerogative of polishing it for publication. [King's note.]

Ferguson's Gloss

My Dear Fellow Clergymen:

While confined here in the Birmingham city jail, I came across your recent statement calling my present activities "unwise and untimely." Seldom do I pause to answer criticism of my work and ideas. If I sought to answer all the criticisms that cross my desk, my secretaries would have little time for anything other than such correspondence in the course of the day, and I would have no time for constructive work. But since I feel that you are men of genuine good will and that your criticisms are sincerely set forth, I want to try to answer your statement in what I hope will be patient and reasonable terms.

King adopts a non-confrontational "Rogerian" stance.

Appeal to character— King wants to appear trustworthy.

opposing argument # 1

Refutation a)

I think I should indicate why I am here in Birmingham, since you have been influenced by the view which argues against "outsiders coming in." I have the honor of serving as president of the Southern Christian Leadership Conference, an organization operating in every southern state, with headquarters in Atlanta, Georgia. We have some eighty-five affiliated organizations across the South, and one of them is the Alabama Christian Movement for Human Rights. Frequently we share staff, educational, and financial resources with our affiliates. Several months ago the affiliate here in Birmingham asked us to be on call to engage in a nonviolent direct-action program if such were deemed necessary. We readily consented, and when the hour came we lived up to our promise. So I, along with several members of my staff, am here because I was invited here. I am here because I have organizational ties here.

Appeal to character— establishes credibility.

b)

But more basically, I am in Birmingham because injustice is here. Just as the prophets of the eighth century B.C. left their villages and carried their "thus saith the Lord" far beyond the boundaries of their home towns, and just as the Apostle Paul left his village of Tarsus and carried the gospel of Jesus Christ to the far corners of the Greco-Roman world, so am I compelled to carry the gospel of freedom beyond my own home town. Like Paul, I must constantly respond to the Macedonian call for aid.

Biblical allusions indicate his audience.

c)

Moreover, I am cognizant of the interrelatedness of all communities and states. I cannot sit idly by in Atlanta and not be concerned about what happens in Birmingham. Injustice anywhere is a threat to justice everywhere. We are caught in an inescapable network of mutuality, tied in a single garment of destiny. Whatever affects one directly, affects all indirectly. Never again can we afford to live with the narrow, provincial "outside agitator" idea. Anyone who lives inside the United States can never be considered an outsider anywhere within its bounds.

opposing argument #2

You deplore the demonstrations taking place in Birmingham. But your statement, I am sorry to say, fails to express a similar concern for the conditions that brought about the demonstrations. I am sure that none of you would want to rest content with the superficial kind of social analysis that deals merely with effects and does not grapple with underlying causes. It is unfortunate that demonstrations are taking place in Birmingham, but it is even more unfortunate that the city's white power structure left the Negro community with no alternative.

Rogerian approach to opponents.

Refutation

a)

In any nonviolent campaign there are four basic steps: collection of the facts to determine whether injustices exist; negotiation; self-purification; and direct action. We have gone through all these steps in Birmingham. There can be no gainsaying the fact that racial injustice engulfs this community. Birmingham is probably the most thoroughly segregated city in the United States. Its ugly record of brutality is widely known. Negroes have experienced grossly unjust treatment in the courts. There have been more unsolved bombings of Negro homes and churches in Birmingham than in any other city in the nation. These are the hard, brutal facts of the case. On the basis of these conditions, Negro leaders sought to negotiate with the city fathers. But the latter consistently refused to engage in good-faith negotiation.

Evidence—but maybe this could have been more specific.

b)

Then, last September, came the opportunity to talk with leaders of Birmingham's economic community. In the course of the negotiations, certain promises were made by the merchants—for example, to remove the stores' humiliating racial signs. On the basis of these promises, the Reverend Fred Shuttlesworth and the leaders of the Alabama Christian Movement for Human Rights agreed to a moratorium on all demonstrations. As the weeks and months went by, we realized that we were the victims of a broken promise. A few signs, briefly removed, returned; the others remained.

c) As in so many past experiences, our hopes had been blasted, and the shadow of deep disappointment settled upon us. We had no alternative except to prepare for direct action, whereby we would present our very bodies as a means of laying our case before the conscience of the local and the national community. Mindful of the difficulties involved, we decided to undertake a process of self-purification. We began a series of workshops on nonviolence, and we repeatedly asked ourselves: "Are you able to accept blows without retaliating?" "Are you able to endure the ordeal of jail?" We decided to schedule our direct-action program for the Easter season, realizing that except for Christmas, this is the main shopping period of the year. Knowing that a strong economic-withdrawal program would be the by-product of direct action, we felt that this would be the best time to bring pressure to bear on the merchants for the needed change.

Then it occurred to us that Birmingham's mayoral election was coming up in March, and we speedily decided to postpone action until after election day. When we discovered that the Commissioner of Public Safety, Eugene "Bull" Connor, had piled up enough votes to be in the run-off, we decided again to postpone action until the day after the run-off so that the demonstrations could not be used to cloud the issues. Like many others, we wanted to see Mr. Connor defeated, and to this end we endured postponement after postponement. Having aided in this community need, we felt that our direct-action program could be delayed no longer.

Appeal to character.

d) You may well ask, "Why direct action? Why sit-ins, marches, and so forth? Isn't negotiation a better path?" You are quite right in calling for negotiation. Indeed, this is the very purpose of direct action. Nonviolent direct action seeks to create such a crisis and foster such a tension that a community which has constantly refused to negotiate is forced to confront the issue. It seeks so to dramatize the issue that it can no longer be ignored. My citing the creation of tension as part of the work of the nonviolent-resister may sound rather shocking. But I must confess that I am not afraid of the word "tension." I have earnestly opposed violent tension, but there is a type of constructive, nonviolent tension which is necessary for growth. Just as Socrates felt that it was necessary to create a tension in the mind so that individuals could rise from the bondage of

Appeal to reason.

Interesting!

myths and half-truths to the unfettered realm of creative analysis and objective appraisal, so must we see the need for nonviolent gadflies to create the kind of tension in society that will help men rise from the dark depths of prejudice and racism to the majestic heights of understanding and brotherhood.

King seeks to establish common ground.

The purpose of our direct-action program is to create a situation so crisis-packed that it will inevitably open the door to negotiation. I therefore concur with you in your call for negotiation. Too long has our beloved Southland been bogged down in a tragic effort to live in monologue rather than dialogue.

*

"Our" implies unity.

opposing argument #3

Refutation

Appeal to reason.

One of the basic points in your statement is that the action that I and my associates have taken in Birmingham is untimely. Some have asked: "Why didn't you give the new city administration time to act?" The only answer that I can give to this query is that the new Birmingham administration must be prodded about as much as the outgoing one, before it will act. We are sadly mistaken if we feel that the election of Albert Boutwell as mayor will bring the millennium to Birmingham. While Mr. Boutwell is a much more gentle person than Mr. Connor, they are both segregationists, dedicated to maintenance of the status quo. I have hoped that Mr. Boutwell will be reasonable enough to see the futility of massive resistance to desegregation. But he will not see this without pressure from devotees of civil rights. My friends, I must say to you that we have not made a single gain in civil rights without determined legal and nonviolent pressure. Lamentably, it is an historical fact that privileged groups seldom give up their privileges voluntarily. Individuals may see the moral light and voluntarily give up their unjust posture; but, as Reinhold Niebuhr has reminded us, groups tend to be more immoral than individuals.

Uses outside authority to support his argument.

We know through painful experience that freedom is never voluntarily given by the oppressor; it must be demanded by the oppressed. Frankly, I have yet to engage in a direct-action campaign that was "well timed" in the view of those who have not suffered unduly from the disease of segregation. For years now I have heard the word "Wait!" It rings in the ear of every Negro with piercing familiarity. This "Wait" has almost always meant "Never." We must come to see, with one of our distinguished jurists, that "justice too long delayed is justice denied." ✓

We have waited for more than 340 years for our constitutional and God-given rights. The nations of Asia and Africa are moving with jetlike speed toward gaining political independence, but we still creep at horse-and-buggy pace toward gaining a cup of coffee at a lunch counter. Perhaps it is easy for those who have never felt the stinging darts of segregation to say, "Wait." But when you have seen vicious mobs lynch your mothers and fathers at will and drown your sisters and brothers at whim; when you have seen hate-filled policemen curse, kick, and even kill your black brothers and sisters; when you see the vast majority of your twenty million Negro brothers smothering in an airtight cage of poverty in the midst of an affluent society; when you suddenly find your tongue twisted and your speech stammering as you seek to explain to your six-year-old daughter why she can't go to the public amusement park that has just been advertised on television, and see tears welling up in her eyes when she is told that Funtown is closed to colored children, and see ominous clouds of inferiority beginning to form in her little mental sky, and see her beginning to distort her personality by developing an unconscious bitterness toward white people; when you have to concoct an answer for a five-year-old son who is asking, "Daddy, why do white people treat colored people so mean?"; when you take a cross-country drive and find it necessary to sleep night after night in the uncomfortable corners of your automobile because no motel will accept you; when you are humiliated day in and day out by nagging signs reading "white" and "colored"; when your first name becomes "nigger," your middle name becomes "boy" (however old you are) and your last name becomes "John," and your wife and mother are never given the respected title "Mrs."; when you are harried by day and haunted by night by the fact that you are a Negro, living constantly at tiptoe stance, never quite knowing what to expect next, and are plagued with inner fears and outer resentments; when you are forever fighting a degenerating sense of "nobodiness"—then you will understand why we find it difficult to wait. There comes a time when the cup of endurance runs over, and men are no longer willing to be plunged into the abyss of despair. I hope, sirs, you can understand our legitimate and unavoidable impatience.

good contrast

Appeal to emotion.

parallelism and repetition

Personal examples—very persuasive

"Sirs" indicates respect—King does not want to alienate his audience.

You express a great deal of anxiety over our willingness to break laws. This is certainly a legitimate concern. Since we so diligently urge people to obey the Supreme Court's decision of 1954 outlawing segregation in the public schools, at first glance it may seem rather paradoxical for us consciously to break laws. One may well ask: "How can you advocate breaking some laws and obeying others?" The answer lies in the fact that there are two types of laws: just and unjust. I would be the first to advocate obeying just laws. One has not only a legal but a moral responsibility to obey just laws. Conversely, one has a moral responsibility to disobey unjust laws. I would agree with St. Augustine that "an unjust law is no law at all."

opposing argument #4

Refutation

Appeal to reason.

Now, what is the difference between the two? How does one determine whether a law is just or unjust? A law is a man-made code that squares with the moral law or the law of God. An unjust law is a code that is out of harmony with the moral law. To put it in the terms of St. Thomas Aquinas: An unjust law is a human law that is not rooted in eternal law and natural law. Any law that uplifts human personality is just. Any law that degrades human personality is unjust. All segregation statutes are unjust because segregation distorts the soul and damages the personality. It gives the segregator a false sense of superiority and the segregated a false sense of inferiority. Segregation, to use the terminology of the Jewish philosopher Martin Buber, substitutes an "I-it" relationship for an "I-thou" relationship and ends up relegating persons to the status of things. Hence segregation is not only politically, economically, and sociologically unsound, it is morally wrong and sinful. Paul Tillich has said that sin is separation. Is not segregation an existential expression of man's tragic separation, his awful estrangement, his terrible sinfulness? Thus it is that I can urge men to obey the 1954 decision of the Supreme Court, for it is morally right; and I can urge them to disobey segregation ordinances, for they are morally wrong.

Again King refers to a respected authority to support his argument.

Let us consider a more concrete example of just and unjust laws. An unjust law is a code that a numerical or power majority group compels a minority group to obey but does not make binding on itself. This is difference made legal. By the same token, a just law is a code that a majority compels a minority to follow and that it is willing to follow itself. This is sameness made legal.

Let me give another explanation. A law is unjust if it is inflicted on a minority that, as a result of being denied the right to vote, had no part in enacting or devising the law. Who can say that the legislature of Alabama which set up that state's segregation laws was democratically elected? Throughout Alabama all sorts of devious methods are used to prevent Negroes from becoming registered voters, and there are some counties in which, even though Negroes constitute a majority of the population, not a single Negro is registered. Can any law enacted under such circumstances be considered democratically structured?

Again I think his evidence could be more specific —what methods?

Sometimes a law is just on its face and unjust in its application. For instance, I have been arrested on a charge of parading without a permit. Now, there is nothing wrong in having an ordinance which requires a permit for a parade. But such an ordinance becomes unjust when it is used to maintain segregation and to deny citizens the First-Amendment privilege of peaceful assembly and protest.

I hope you are able to see the distinction I am trying to point out. In no sense do I advocate evading or defying the law, as would the rabid segregationist. That would lead to anarchy. One who breaks an unjust law must do so openly, lovingly, and with a willingness to accept the penalty. I submit that an individual who breaks a law that conscience tells him is unjust, and who willingly accepts the penalty of imprisonment in order to arouse the conscience of the community over its injustice, is in reality expressing the highest respect for law.

These biblical allusions create a common ground between King and his audience.

Of course, there is nothing new about this kind of civil disobedience. It was evidenced sublimely in the refusal of Shadrach, Meshach, and Abednego to obey the laws of Nebuchadnezzar, on the ground that a higher moral law was at stake. It was practiced superbly by the early Christians, who were willing to face hungry lions and the excruciating pain of chopping blocks rather than submit to certain unjust laws of the Roman empire. To a degree, academic freedom is a reality today because Socrates practiced civil disobedience. In our own nation, the Boston Tea Party represented a massive act of civil disobedience.

Wasn't Thoreau a big influence on M. L. King?

This is a pretty challenging parallel to draw.

We should never forget that everything Adolph Hitler did in Germany was "legal" and everything the Hungarian fighters did in Hungary was "illegal." It was "illegal" to aid and comfort a Jew in Hitler's Germany. Even so, I am sure that, had I lived in Germany at the time, I would have aided and comforted my Jewish brothers. If today I lived in a Communist country where certain principles dear to the Christian faith are suppressed, I would openly advocate disobeying that country's antireligious laws.

parallelism

I must make two honest confessions to you, my Christian and Jewish brothers. First, I must confess that over the past few years I have been gravely disappointed with the white moderate. I have almost reached the regrettable conclusion that the Negro's great stumbling block in his stride toward freedom is not the White Citizen's Counciler or the Ku Klux Klanner, but the white moderate who is more devoted to "order" than to justice; who prefers a negative peace which is the absence of tension to a positive peace which is the presence of justice; who constantly says, "I agree with you in the goal you seek, but I cannot agree with your methods of direct action"; who paternalistically believes he can set the timetable for another man's freedom; who lives by a mythical concept of time and who constantly advises the Negro to wait for a "more convenient season." Shallow understanding from people of good will is more frustrating than absolute misunderstanding from people of ill will. Lukewarm acceptance is much more bewildering than outright rejection.

strong metaphor

I had hoped that the white moderate would understand that law and order exist for the purpose of establishing justice and that when they fail in this purpose they become the dangerously structured dams that block the flow of social progress. I had hoped that the white moderate would understand that the present tension in the South is a necessary phase of the transition from an obnoxious negative peace, in which the Negro passively accepted his unjust plight, to a substantive and positive peace, in which all men will respect the dignity and worth of human personality. Actually, we who engage in nonviolent direct action are not the creators of tension. We merely bring to the surface the hidden tension that is already alive. We bring it out in the open, where it can be seen and dealt with. Like a boil that can never be cured so long as it is covered up but must be opened with all its ugliness to the natural medicines of air and light, injustice must be exposed, with all the tension its exposure creates, to the light of human conscience and the air of national opinion, before it can be cured.

This is a great analogy—racism is something that festers beneath the surface.

opposing argument #5

In your statement you assert that our actions, even though peaceful, must be condemned because they precipitate violence. But is this a logical assertion? Isn't this like condemning a robbed man because his possession of money precipitated the evil act of robbery? Isn't this like condemning Socrates because his unswerving commitment to truth and his philosophical inquiries precipitated the act by the misguided populace in which they made him drink hemlock? Isn't this like condemning Jesus because his unique God-consciousness and never-ceasing devotion to God's will precipitated the evil act of crucifixion? We must come to see that, as the federal courts have consistently affirmed, it is wrong to urge an individual to cease his efforts to gain his basic constitutional rights because the quest may precipitate violence. Society must protect the robbed and punish the robber.

False analogy maybe?

Isn't this a little weak? He uses rhetorical questions instead of specific evidence.

I had hoped that the white moderate would reject the myth concerning time in relation to the struggle for freedom. I have just received a letter from a white brother in Texas. He writes: "All Christians know that the colored people will receive equal rights eventually, but it is possible that you are in too great a religious hurry. It has taken Christianity almost two thousand years to accomplish what it has. The teachings of Christ take time to come to earth." Such an attitude stems from a tragic misconception of time, from the strangely irrational notion that there is something in the very flow of time that will inevitably cure all ills. Actually, time itself is neutral; it can be used either destructively or constructively. More and more I feel that the people of ill will have used time much more effectively than have the people of good will. We will have to repent in this generation not merely for the hateful words and actions of the bad people, but for the appalling silence of the good people. Human progress never rolls in on wheels of inevitability; it comes through the tireless efforts of men willing to be coworkers with God, and without this hard work, time itself becomes an ally of the forces of social stagnation.

✓

We must use time creatively, in the knowledge that the time is always ripe to do right. Now is the time to make real the promise of democracy and transform our pending national elegy into a creative psalm of brotherhood. Now is the time to lift our national policy from the quicksand of racial injustice to the solid rock of human dignity.

opposing argument #6

Refutation

You speak of our activity in Birmingham as extreme. At first I was rather disappointed that fellow clergymen would see my nonviolent efforts as those of an extremist. I began thinking about the fact that I stand in the middle of two opposing forces in the Negro community. One is a force of complacency, made up in part of Negroes who, as a result of long years of oppression, are so drained of self-respect and a sense of "somebodiness" that they have adjusted to segregation; and in part of a few middle-class Negroes who, because of a degree of academic and economic security and because in some ways they profit by segregation, have become insensitive to the problems of the masses. The other force is one of bitterness and hatred, and it comes perilously close to advocating violence. It is expressed in the various black nationalist groups that are springing up across the nation, the largest and best-known being Elijah Muhammad's Muslim movement. Nourished by the Negro's frustration over the continued existence of racial discrimination, this movement is made up of people who have lost faith in America, who have absolutely repudiated Christianity, and who have concluded that the white man is an incorrigible "devil."

I have tried to stand between these two forces, saying that we need emulate neither the "donothingism" of the complacent nor the hatred and despair of the black nationalist. For there is the more excellent way of love and nonviolent protest. I am grateful to God that, through the influence of the Negro church, the way of nonviolence became an integral part of our struggle.

He constantly reminds his audience of this.

If this philosophy had not emerged, by now many streets of the South would, I am convinced, be flowing with blood. And I am further convinced that if our white brothers dismiss as "rabble-rousers" and "outside agitators" those of us who employ nonviolent direct action, and if they refuse to support our nonviolent efforts, millions of Negroes will, out of frustration and

✓ despair, seek solace and security in black-nationalist ideologies—a development that would inevitably lead to a frightening racial nightmare.

Oppressed people cannot remain oppressed forever. The yearning for freedom eventually manifests itself, and that is what has happened to the American Negro. Something within has reminded him of his birthright of freedom, and something without has reminded him that it can be gained. Consciously or unconsciously, he has been caught up by the Zeitgeist, and with his black brothers of Africa and his brown and yellow brothers of Asia, South America, and the Caribbean, the United States Negro is moving with a sense of great urgency toward the promised land of racial justice. If one recognizes this vital urge that has engulfed the Negro community, one should readily understand why public demonstrations are taking place. The Negro has many pent-up resentments and latent frustrations, and he must release them. So let him march; let him make prayer pilgrimages to the city hall; let him go on freedom rides—and try to understand why he must do so. If his repressed emotions are not released in nonviolent ways, they will seek expression through violence; this is not a threat but a fact of history. So I have not said to my people, "Get rid of your discontent." Rather, I have tried to say that this normal and healthy discontent can be channeled into the creative outlet of nonviolent direct action. And now this approach is being termed extremist.

Rhetorical questions create strong tone.

Again parallism is used for emotional emphasis.

King wants to connect Christian tradition with American history.

But though I was initially disappointed at being categorized as an extremist, as I continued to think about the matter I gradually gained a measure of satisfaction from the label. Was not Jesus an extremist for love: "Love your enemies, bless them that curse you, do good to them that hate you, and pray for them which despitefully use you, and persecute you." Was not Amos an extremist for justice: "Let justice roll down like waters and righteousness like an everflowing stream." Was not Paul an extremist for the Christian gospel: "I bear in my body the marks of the Lord Jesus." Was not Martin Luther an extremist: "Here I stand; I cannot do otherwise, so help me God." And John Bunyan: "I will stay in jail to the end of my days before I make a butchery of my conscience." And Abraham Lincoln: "This nation cannot survive half slave and half free." And Thomas Jefferson: "We hold these truths to be self-evident, that all men are created equal. . . ." So the question is not whether we will be extremists, but what kind of extremists we will be. Will we be extremists for hate or for love? Will we be extremists for the preservation of injustice or for the extension of justice? In that dramatic scene on Calvary's hill three men were crucified. We must never forget that all three were crucified for the same crime—the crime of extremism. Two were extremists for immorality, and thus fell below their environment. The other, Jesus Christ, was an extremist for love, truth, and goodness, and thereby rose above his environment. Perhaps the South, the nation, and the world are in dire need of creative extremists. ✓

I had hoped that the white moderate would see this need. Perhaps I was too optimistic; perhaps I expected too much. I suppose I should have realized that few members of the oppressor race can understand the deep groans and passionate yearnings of the oppressed race, and still fewer have the vision to see that injustice must be rooted out by strong, persistent, and determined action. I am thankful, however, that some of our white brothers in the South have grasped the meaning of this social revolution and committed themselves to it. They are still all too few in quantity, but they are big in quality. Some—such as Ralph McGill, Lillian Smith, Harry Golden, James McBridge Dabbs, Ann Braden, and Sarah Patton Boyle—have written about our struggle in eloquent and prophetic terms. Others have marched with us down nameless streets of the South. They have languished in filthy, roach-infested jails, suffering the abuse and brutality of policemen who view them as "dirty nigger-lovers." Unlike so many of their moderate brothers and sisters, they have recognized the urgency of the moment and sensed the need for powerful "action" antidotes to combat the disease of segregation.

Let me take note of my other major disappointment. I have been so greatly disappointed with the white church and its leadership. Of course, there are some notable exceptions. I am not unmindful of the fact that each of you has taken some significant stands on this issue. I commend you, Reverend Stallings, for your Christian stand on this past Sunday, in welcoming Negroes to your worship service on a nonsegregational basis. I commend the Catholic leaders of this state for integrating Spring Hill College several years ago.

But despite these notable exceptions, I must honestly reiterate that I have been disappointed with the church. I do not say this as one of those negative critics who can always find something wrong with the church. I say this as a minister of the gospel, who loves the church; who was nurtured in its bosom; who has been sustained by its spiritual blessings and who will remain true to it as long as the cord of life shall lengthen.

When I was suddenly catapulted into the leadership of the bus protest in Montgomery, Alabama, a few years ago, I felt we would be supported by the white church. I felt that the white ministers, priests, and rabbis of the South would be among our strongest allies. Instead, some have been outright opponents, refusing to understand the freedom movement and misrepresenting its leaders; all too many others have been * more cautious than courageous and have remained silent behind the anesthetizing security of stained-glass windows.

In spite of my shattered dreams, I came to Birmingham with the hope that the white religious leadership of this community would see the justice of our cause and, with deep moral concern, would serve as the channel through which our just grievances could reach the power structure. I had hoped that each of you would understand. But again I have been disappointed.

I have heard numerous southern religious leaders admonish their worshipers to comply with a desegregation decision because it is the law, but I have longed to hear white ministers declare: "Follow this decree because integration is morally right and because the Negro is your brother." In the midst of blatant injustices inflicted upon the Negro, I have watched white churchmen stand on the sideline and mouth pious irrelevancies and sanctimonious trivialities. In the midst of a mighty struggle to rid our nation of racial and economic injustice, I have heard many ministers say: "Those are social issues, with which the gospel has no real concern." And I have watched many churches commit themselves to a completely otherworldly religion which makes a strange, un-Biblical distinction between body and soul, between the sacred and the secular.

I have traveled the length and breadth of Alabama, Mississippi, and all the other southern states. On sweltering summer days and crisp autumn mornings I have looked at the South's beautiful churches with their lofty spires pointing heavenward. I have beheld the impressive outlines of her massive religious-education buildings. Over and over I have found myself asking: "What kind of people worship here? Who is their God? Where were their voices when the lips of Governor Barnett dripped with words of interposition and nullification? Where were they when Governor Wallace gave a clarion call for defiance and hatred? Where were their voices of support when bruised and weary Negro men and women decided to rise from the dark dungeons of complacency to the bright hills of creative protest?"

Again, series of questions creates strong tone.

opposition

Yes, these questions are still in my mind. In deep disappointment I have wept over the laxity of the church. But be assured that my tears have been tears of love. There can be no deep disappointment where there is not deep love. Yes, I love the church. How could I do otherwise? I am in the rather unique position of being the son, the grandson, and the great-grandson of preachers. Yes, I see the church as the body of Christ. But, oh! How we have blemished and scarred that body through social neglect and through fear of being nonconformists.

Note use of 'we' here—King wants to create an impression of unity, rather than one of alienation.

There was a time when the church was very powerful—in the time when the early Christians rejoiced at being deemed worthy to suffer for what they believed. In those days the church was not merely a thermometer that recorded the ideas and principles of popular opinion; it was a thermostat that transformed the mores of society. Whenever the early Christians entered a town, the people in power became disturbed and immediately sought to convict the Christians for being "disturbers of the peace" and "outside agitators." But the Christians pressed on, in the conviction that they were "a colony of heaven," called to obey God rather than man. Small in number, they were big in commitment. They were too God-intoxicated to be "astronomically intimidated." By their effort and example they brought an end to such ancient evils as infanticide and gladiatorial contests.

Things are different now. So often the contemporary church is a weak, ineffectual voice with an uncertain sound. So often it is an archdefender of the status quo. Far from being disturbed by the presence of the church, the power structure of the average community is consoled by the church's silent—and often even vocal—sanction of things as they are.

But the judgment of God is upon the church as never before. If today's church does not recapture the sacrificial spirit of the early church, it will lose its authenticity, forfeit the loyalty of millions, and be dismissed as an irrelevant social club with no meaning for the twentieth century. Every day I meet young people whose disappointment with the church has turned into outright disgust.

Perhaps I have once again been too optimistic. Is organized religion too inextricably bound to the status quo to save our nation and the world? Perhaps I must turn my faith to the inner spiritual church, the church within the church, as the true ekklesia and the hope of the world. But again I am thankful to God that some noble souls from the ranks of organized religion have broken loose from the paralyzing chains of conformity and joined us as active partners in the struggle for freedom. They have left their secure congregations and walked the streets of Albany, Georgia, with us. They have gone down the highways of the South on tortuous rides for freedom. Yes, they have gone to jail with us. Some have been dismissed from their churches, have lost the support of their bishops and fellow ministers. But they have acted in the faith that right defeated is stronger than evil triumphant. Their witness has been the spiritual salt that has preserved the true meaning of the gospel in these troubled times. They have carved a tunnel of hope through the dark mountain of disappointment.

I hope the church as a whole will meet the challenge of this decisive hour. But even if the church does not come to the aid of justice, I have no despair about the future. I have no fear about the outcome of our struggle in Birmingham, even if our motives are at present misunderstood. We will reach the goal of freedom in Birmingham and all over the nation, because the goal of America is freedom. Abused and scorned though we may be, our destiny is tied up with America's destiny. Before the pilgrims landed at Plymouth we were here. Before the pen of Jefferson etched the majestic words of the Declaration of Independence across the pages of history, we were here. For more than two centuries our forebears labored in this country without wages; they made cotton king; they built *

This is an important aspect of his argument—the fate of the black Americans is linked with the fate of the nation as a whole.

the homes of their masters while suffering gross injustice and shameful humiliation—and yet out of a bottomless vitality they continued to thrive and develop. If the inexpressible cruelties of slavery could not stop us, the opposition we now face will surely fail. We will win our freedom because the sacred heritage of our nation and the eternal will of God are embodied in our echoing demands.

Before closing I feel impelled to mention one other point in your statement that has troubled me profoundly. You warmly commended the Birmingham police force for keeping "order" and "preventing violence." I doubt that you would have so warmly commended the police force if you had seen its dogs sinking their teeth into unarmed, nonviolent Negroes. I doubt that you would so quickly commend the policemen if you were to observe their ugly and inhumane treatment of Negroes here in the city jail; if you were to watch them push and curse old Negro women and young Negro girls; if you were to see them slap and kick old Negro men and young boys; if you were to observe them, as they did on two occasions, refuse to give us food because we wanted to sing our grace together. I cannot join you in your praise of the Birmingham police department.

more parallelism

emotional language

It is true that the police have exercised a degree of discipline in handling the demonstrators. In this sense they have conducted themselves rather "nonviolently" in public. But for what purpose? To preserve the evil system of segregation. Over the past few years I have consistently preached that nonviolence demands that the means we use must be as pure as the ends we seek. I have tried to make clear that it is wrong to use immoral means to attain moral ends. But now I must affirm that it is just as wrong, or perhaps even more so, to use moral means to preserve immoral ends. Perhaps Mr. Connor and his policemen have been rather nonviolent in public, as was Chief Pritchett in Albany, Georgia, but they have used the moral means of nonviolence to maintain the immoral end of racial injustice. As T. S. Eliot has said, "The last temptation is the greatest treason: To do the right deed for the wrong reason."

Concedes opposing point of view but immediately modifies it.

I wish you had commended the Negro sit-inners and demonstrators of Birmingham for their sublime courage, their willingness to suffer, and their amazing discipline in the midst of great provocation. One day the South will recognize its real heroes. They will be the James Merediths, with the noble sense of purpose that enables them to face jeering and hostile mobs, and with the agonizing loneliness that characterizes the life of the pioneer. They will be old, oppressed, battered Negro women, symbolized in a seventy-two-year-old woman in Montgomery, Alabama, who rose up with a sense of dignity and with her people decided not to ride segregated buses, and who responded with ungrammatical profundity to one who inquired about her weariness: "My feets is tired, but my soul is at rest." They will be the young high school and college students, the young ministers of the gospel and a host of their elders, courageously and nonviolently sitting in at lunch counters and willingly going to jail for conscience' sake. One day the South will know that when these disinherited children of God sat down at lunch counters, they were in reality standing up for what is best in the American dream and for the most sacred values in our Judaeo-Christian heritage, thereby bringing our nation back to those great wells of democracy which were dug deep by the founding fathers in their formulation of the Constitution and the Declaration of Independence. *

Never before have I written so long a letter. I'm afraid it is much too long to take your precious time. I can assure you that it would have been much shorter if I had been writing from a comfortable desk, but what else can one do when he is alone in a narrow jail cell, other than write long letters, think long thoughts, and pray long prayers?

appeal to emotion

If I have said anything in this letter that overstates the truth and indicates an unreasonable impatience, I beg you to forgive me. If I have said anything that understates the truth and indicates my having a patience that allows me to settle for anything less than brotherhood, I beg God to forgive me.

appeal to character

I hope this letter finds you strong in the faith. I also hope that circumstances will soon make it possible for me to meet each of you, not as an integrationist or a civil-rights leader but as a fellow clergyman and a Christian brother. Let us all hope that the dark clouds of racial prejudice will soon pass away and the deep fog of misunderstanding will be lifted from our fear-drenched communities, and in some not too distant tomorrow the radiant stars of love and brotherhood will shine over our great nation with all their scintillating beauty.

King addresses his audience directly to establish personal tone.

Figurative language here—to stir his readers' imaginations by reminding his audience of their common national identity.

Yours for the cause of Peace and Brotherhood,
MARTIN LUTHER KING, JR.

Ferguson's Outline of Argument

This letter was written by King as a direct answer to the criticisms made by eight clergymen that his involvement in the Birmingham demonstrations was "unwise and untimely." For the most part, the essay consists of a point-by-point refutation of his opponents' arguments.

POINT 1: As an "outsider," King has no right to be in Birmingham.

Refutation:

(a) As president of the Southern Christian Leadership Conference, King was invited by the Birmingham affiliate to take part in the demonstrations.

(b) As a Christian, King cannot ignore injustice, but must respond to any "call for aid" no matter where it comes from.

(c) The term "outside agitator" is dated and narrow-minded. "Injustice anywhere is a threat to justice everywhere."

POINT 2: The demonstrations in Birmingham were deplorable and cannot be justified.

Refutation:

(a) The Negro community had no choice. Birmingham is one of the most segregated cities in the country.

(b) Previous attempts at negotiation had failed.

(c) Self-purification workshops were held to ensure that the demonstrations were peaceful.

(d) Direct action is the only way to force a complacent system to face the issue.

POINT 3: The new Boutwell administration should have been given time to act.

Refutation:

The new administration is also segregationist and will not act without direct pressure from the Negro community.

POINT 4: The civil rights movement is hypocritical in its willingness to break certain laws while upholding others.

Refutation:

Only just laws should be obeyed.

POINT 5: Direct action leads to violence.

Refutation:

It is illogical to condemn peaceful protestors for precipitating violence. The fault lies with those who seek to disrupt the demonstrations. Those seeking their constitutional rights should be protected from violence by law.

POINT 6: King's activity in Birmingham has been extreme.
Refutation:
King does, in fact, occupy a moderate position between the two extremes of violence and passivity. Without this moderate position, the streets of the South would be "flowing with blood."

King then expresses his disappointment with both the white moderates and the white church. He criticizes the church in particular for its lack of moral initiative, its lack of strong leadership, and its failure to support the civil rights movement.

King's last main point is that it is the demonstrators who should be commended for their self-control, not the police. He calls for the recognition of the "real heroes" of the civil rights movement, such as the "James Merediths."

The essay concludes on a uplifting note as King expresses his hope that "the dark clouds of racial prejudice will soon pass away . . . and in some not too distant tomorrow the radiant stars of love and brotherhood will shine over our great nation with all their scintillating beauty."

Excerpt from Ferguson's Double-Entry Notebook

Quotes and Summaries	Reactions
"I doubt you would have so warmly commended the police force if you had seen its dogs sinking their teeth into unarmed, nonviolent Negroes."	King really knows how to use language to involve the reader emotionally. His reasonable tone allows him to do this without losing his reader's trust. So rather than just saying 'dogs attacking Negroes' he says "dogs *sinking* their teeth into *unarmed, nonviolent* Negroes." He's making an appeal to emotion here and uses parallelism to increase the effect ("if you were to watch," "if you were to see" etc.). His use of the word "Negro" makes me kind of uncomfortable. It seems so dated now. At first it makes it seem as though a lot has changed since King wrote this essay. But how

Quotes and Summaries	Reactions
	much is different, really? We hardly live in an equitable society. Maybe that's why "Negro" bothers me so much. We've made the terminology "politically correct" but the injustices remain.
King concedes that the police officers may have appeared restrained in public, but argued that their behavior is still indefensible. No actions can be considered moral if they are used for immoral purposes.	King doesn't want to antagonize his audience, so he sometimes concedes the opposing point of view. Here he quickly turns the point around so that his own argument doesn't lose any ground. Nonviolent law enforcement cannot be commended if it is used to enforce unjust laws. It's important that King addresses this point because otherwise he might seem to be avoiding the issue. I mean, ignoring evidence in favor of the police would make him look biased. Instead, he makes this possible weakness into one of his strengths.
As T. S. Eliot has said, "The last temptation is the greatest treason: To do the right deed for the wrong reason."	King does this a lot—brings in some respected individual to support his argument. It shows that he is writing for a literate audience, and also that King himself is well educated (appeal to character again).
King suggests that his fellow clergymen commend the demonstrators for their self-control, not the police.	I admire King for his forthright criticisms of the white church. He's not afraid to say what he really thinks, despite his

Quotes and Summaries	Reactions
	non-confrontational approach. I wonder how these clergymen reacted to the letter. I imagine it made them pretty uncomfortable. I hope so.
"One day the South will recognize its real heroes."	I've come to realize through studying this essay that there is a reason for everything King does. Here I think he is deliberately bringing the focus back to ordinary people after a lot of fairly abstract discussion. The "My feets is tired but my soul is at rest" quote suddenly makes it all real. You can feel the struggle and frustration. Again King uses parallelism for emphasis.
One day the South will know that when these disinherited children of God sat down at lunch counters, they were in reality standing up for what is best in the American dream and for the most sacred values in our Judaeo-Christian heritage, thereby bringing our nation back to those great wells of democracy which were dug deep by the founding fathers in their formulations of the Constitution and the Declaration of Independence.	I've quoted this whole passage because I think it's one of the most important in the whole essay. It gives the civil rights movement an historical context—this is not just about one town in the South; it's about American and Christian traditions. This prevents people from seeing the protest movement as "outside agitation." In referring to the Constitution, etc. King is playing on his audience's patriotic feelings and trying to stir their emotions. I think this is a legitimate tactic. He's not distorting anything—the American dream is meant to be about freedom and equality for all. But he is being quite clever here—

Quotes and Summaries	Reactions
	these patriotic references ensure that no one can accuse him of being "un-American." I like the opposition between "sat down" and "standing up."
"Let us all hope that the dark clouds of racial prejudice will soon pass away and the deep fog of misunderstanding will be lifted from our fear-drenched communities, and in some not too distant tomorrow the radiant stars of love and brotherhood will shine over our great nation with all their scintillating beauty."	King really likes long sentences. The repetition of "hope" is important—King wants to lift the tone of the essay and end on a positive note. He wants to involve the reader emotionally so he uses a lot of figurative language. The "dark clouds" and "deep fog" are contrasted with the "radiant stars." (Religious imagery here? Dark vs light etc.) The reference to "our great nation" reminds the audience again of common national identity. These final sentences are uplifting and inspiring, but they rather depress me, too. We are still waiting for those "radiant stars of love and brotherhood" to shine. Has King's "not too distant tomorrow" come much closer in the past forty years, or not?

Ferguson's First Draft

"Letter from Birmingham Jail" is a powerful, persuasive essay which argues for the necessity of direct, nonviolent action to end racial segregation in the city of Birmingham in 1963. King wrote it while in solitary confinement, in response to the published criticisms of eight white clergymen, but its scope goes far beyond that of a personal letter. In the course of the essay's pages, King demonstrates the most important aspects of argument, such as the use of appeals to character, emotion, and reason, logical structure and development, and the effective refutation of the opposition. Through reading "Letter from Birmingham Jail" I have a greater appreciation of persuasive writing and also of Martin Luther King himself.

King begins by establishing his own credibility—as the president of the Southern Christian Leadership Conference, he has a great deal of experience in the civil rights movement. This is part of the appeal to character which King maintains all the way through the essay. Aware that his audience is not sympathetic to his position, King also seeks to establish common ground between them by emphasizing their mutual involvement in the church. Himself a preacher, King draws attention to his thoroughly respectable background, "I am in the rather unique position of being the son, the grandson, and the great-grandson of preachers." By making a great many Biblical allusions, King hopes to win the trust of his opponents and so lead them towards his way of thinking. For the same reason, he presents their point of view in a calm and reasonable manner, "It is true that the police have exercised a degree of discipline in handling the demonstrators. In this sense, they have conducted themselves nonviolently in public. But for what purpose? To preserve the vile system of segregation." By fairly presenting the opposing point of view, which King does through the essay, he shows that he is unbiased and objective and, therefore, trustworthy.

The reasonable tone and the strong appeal to character allow King to manipulate his audience emotionally without losing his own credibility. He does this through the skillful use of such devices as vivid detail, metaphorical language, parallelism, and repetition. For instance, in response to the criticism that the campaign was "untimely," King creates a sharp metaphorical contrast to emphasize the natural impatience of the African American community,

> We have waited more than 340 years for our constitutional and God-given rights. The nations of Africa and Asia are moving with jetlike speed toward gaining political independence, but we still creep at horse-and-buggy pace toward gaining a cup of coffee at a lunch counter." King builds on this point by using a great deal of vivid detail, as in "when you have seen hate-filled policemen curse, kick, and even kill your Negro brothers and sisters; when you see the vast majority of your Negro brothers smothering in an airtight cage of poverty in the midst of an affluent society . . .

This appeal to emotion is further strengthened through parallelism and repetition as King lists examples of his own personal humiliations. The reader cannot help but feel shocked and disgusted by these many injustices and must agree with

King's final comment, "I hope, sirs, you can understand our legitimate and unavoidable impatience."

King also makes constant appeals to reason when refuting the opposing point of view, most notably when answering the criticism that the movement was too ready to break the law. While King agrees that this is "certainly a legitimate concern," he points out that "there are two types of law—just and unjust." In an extended appeal to reason, King argues that "An unjust law is a code that a numerical or power majority group compels a minority group to obey but does not make binding on itself." He then illustrates this by referring to the segregation laws of Alabama and further supports his argument by bringing in the opinions of respected individuals such as Paul Tillich and Martin Buber. King deliberately and methodically makes the distinction between just and unjust laws, and again draws on the Bible to remind his audience of the common ground between them.

In his powerful and moving conclusion, King expresses his hope that "the dark clouds of racial prejudice will soon pass away." A great deal may have changed in the forty years since King wrote "Letter from Birmingham Jail," but we are still waiting for "the radiant stars of love and brotherhood" to shine over "our great nation." Racism is still a "hidden tension" in our society, and we desperately need "creative extremists" such as Martin Luther King to bring it to the surface and cure it. The value of this essay is not just that it demonstrates the most important features of persuasive writing, but that it reminds us that racism is something that affects us all in our common identity as American citizens. As King said of himself and his followers, "our destiny is tied up with America's destiny."

An Analysis of "Letter from Birmingham Jail"

Ferguson's Final Draft

"Letter from Birmingham Jail" was written by Martin Luther King in 1963 while he was being held in solitary confinement for daring to lead a protest march against the city's segregationist policies. It is a direct response to the statement published by eight white clergymen criticizing King's direct action campaign, but its scope goes far beyond that of a personal letter. Rather than being simply a justification of his own actions, King's carefully constructed and eloquently worded argument is a justification of the civil rights movement itself. In his lengthy essay, King systematically addresses each of his opponents' points, refutes them in turn, and concludes with a series of his own criticisms of white moderates and church leaders. "Letter from Birmingham Jail" is a remarkable piece of persuasive writing which demonstrates both the principal features of argument and those individual aspects of King's style which made him such a powerful preacher and political activist.

Perhaps, the essay's greatest strength is King's non-confrontational or Rogerian approach to the argument. To avoid antagonizing an unsympathetic audience, King must appear to be a reasonable, well-informed individual whose views on this sensitive issue can be trusted. This is done very effectively in a number of ways. For instance, at the start of the essay he establishes his own credibility by describing his involvement in the Southern Christian Leadership Conference. As the president of this respected organization, it can be assumed that he has a great deal of experience in the civil rights movement. Furthermore, King constantly emphasizes his own involvement in the Church, pointing out that he is "the son, the grandson, and the great-grandson of preachers." He also compares himself with famous Christian figures, "Like Paul, I must constantly respond to the Macedonian call for aid." These somewhat obscure Biblical allusions not only show that King is thoroughly familiar with the Scriptures, but also establish a common ground between two adversaries who have little else in common but the Church. To further lessen any sense of conflict King refers to his fellow clergymen as "my friends" and "my Christian and Jewish brothers" and calls them "men of genuine good faith." Finally, King presents the opposing point of view in a calm and reasonable manner, often conceding its validity before presenting his own case: "It is true that the police have exercised a degree of discipline in handling the demonstrators. In this sense they have conducted themselves "nonviolently" in public. But for what purpose? To preserve the vile system of segregation." By fairly addressing the opposition, King shows that he is unbiased and capable of viewing the situation objectively. Therefore, when he attacks the white church for its lack of leadership and moral initiative, his criticisms carry real weight.

This strong appeal to character is maintained throughout and allows King to play on his audience's emotions without losing his own credibility. He proceeds through the constant use of metaphorical language, vivid detail, parallelism, and repetition, all of which combine to create his own unique style. For instance, in response to the criticism that the direct action campaign was "untimely" King stresses the natural impatience of his people:

> We have waited more than 340 years for our constitutional and God-given rights. The nations of Africa and Asia are moving with jetlike speed toward gaining political independence, but we still creep at horse-and-buggy pace toward gaining a cup of coffee at a lunch counter.

The contrast of these metaphors causes the reader to feel the frustration and humiliation of segregation. King builds on this by combining further metaphor with vivid detail, as in "when you have seen hate-filled policemen curse, kick, and even kill your Negro brothers and sisters; when you see the vast majority of your Negro brothers smothering in an airtight cage of poverty in the midst of an affluent society. . . ." This appeal to emotion is given even more impact through the skillful parallelism and repetition of "when you have seen . . . when you see . . . when you suddenly find . . . when you have to concoct . . ." The effect on the reader of this catalog of social injustice is one of shock and disgust, so that even the most conservative individual would have to concur with King's final comment, "I hope, sirs, you can understand our legitimate and unavoidable impatience." It is noteworthy that, despite the emotional intensity of this long passage, King never loses his self-control. With the simple insertion of "sirs" he maintains the modest and respectful tone which characterizes the whole essay.

While the appeals to character and emotion are arguably the most memorable aspects of the essay, King also makes constant appeals to reason in his defense of the direct action campaign in Birmingham. One of the best examples of his use of logic is his refutation of one of the most damaging criticisms of the movement—its "willingness to break laws." King concedes that this is "certainly a legitimate concern" but points out that "there are two types of law: just and unjust." In an extended appeal to reason, King argues that "An unjust law is a code that a numerical or power majority group compels a minority group to obey but does not make binding on itself." He then illustrates this general statement with a specific example:

> Who can say that the legislature of Alabama which set up that state's segregation laws was democratically

> elected? Throughout Alabama all sorts of devious methods are used to prevent Negroes from becoming registered voters, and there are even some counties in which, even though Negroes constitute a majority of the population, not a single Negro is registered.

Perhaps King could have given more detailed evidence here, by describing the "devious methods" used and identifying the counties in question. He does, however, refer repeatedly to respected intellectuals such as Paul Tillich and Martin Buber to support his points, and it must be remembered that his essay was composed in a jail cell where there were no reference books.

In his powerful and moving conclusion, King expresses his hope that "the dark clouds of racial prejudice will soon pass away." The highly figurative language in this final paragraph creates another strong appeal to emotion, but this time the effect is one of promise and elation rather than shock and disgust. Throughout the letter, King has made references to the American Dream, the Constitution, and symbolic figures such as Thomas Jefferson and Abraham Lincoln, and this is continued in "our great nation." These references not only stir positive, patriotic feelings in his audience but also create a feeling of a shared national identity. For me, the value of this essay is not just in its tone, its skillful use of appeals, or its powerful language, but in its reminder that racism is something which affects us all in our common cultural identity. As King said of himself and of his followers, "our destiny is tied up with America's destiny." This is something none of us should forget. A great deal may have changed in the forty years since King wrote "Letter from Birmingham Jail," but we are still waiting for "the radiant stars of love and brotherhood" to shine. Racism is still a "hidden tension" in our society, and more than ever we need "creative extremists" such as Martin Luther King to bring it to the surface and to cure it.

In the final draft, the writer moves from a diffuse focus on imagery to a concentration on the three forms of appeal and the stylistic devices that create the appeals and that make them persuasive.

PART FOUR

Appendixes

APPENDIX A

The Research Process and MLA Documentation

The reason for doing research is to attain information that will enlarge your understanding and analysis of a subject or topic. In your research, you may conceive of yourself as a detective, posing problems, deciphering the mysteries in the text or texts that need to be solved. You begin with clues, the words on a page; the clues reveal patterns. You discard false leads, red herrings, and develop a vision of a work or topic—your interpretation—expanded by information that you have gained from reading sources other than the work itself (if your subject concerns one particular text). The technical term in the research process for the work itself is the primary source. Other primary or original sources include autobiography, letters, journals, documents, and manuscripts. After you examine primary documents, then you study secondary sources that give you commentary about the topic. These materials may be biographical, historical, or critical.

An instructor may assign a specific subject for the research paper, for example, the role of the ghost or the play within the play in *Hamlet.* Other instructors may offer you the opportunity to determine the topic. If no particular assignment is given, you may want to concentrate on one of these areas:

- The biography of the author.
- The relationship between the writer's life and works.
- The artistic influences upon the writer.
- Analysis of the process of the writer through examination of drafts.
- Features of a particular work, characteristics of the genre, such as point of view and symbolism in a short story, imagery and tone in a poem, character and conflict in a play.
- The social, historical, and political contexts of a work.
- A particular critical approach, such as a formalist analysis of Keats's "Ode on a Grecian Urn"; a feminist reading of "The Yellow Wallpaper."

These key topic areas may be posed as beginning questions for research:

- What biographical facts do I need to know about the writer that will help me understand the topic?

- What are the connections between the life and works?
- How did the writer develop his or her work? What can I learn by examining successive drafts of a work or by reading about the writer's artistic techniques?
- What features of the genre do I want to explore? Refer to the checklists for the evaluation of short fiction, poetry, drama, and nonfiction in chapters 9 through 12.
- What themes seem most important?
- How did the historical, social, political, and cultural realities of the time influence the writer?
- How are the intellectual movements of the writer's time evident in his or her work?
- How will my reading of criticism enlarge my vision of the topic?
- What aspects of the subject do I find most puzzling?
- What interpretations of the topic do I find most debatable?
- What schools of thought will enlarge my understanding and provide new intellectual contexts and directions for further analysis?

Any one of these questions may provide a starting point.

THE RESEARCH PROCESS

For the sake of discussion, assume that you have chosen a particular work that interests or intrigues you. Before you begin your research project, you need to develop an understanding of the work. Perhaps you have discussed it in class. Perhaps you have talked about the reading in collaborative learning groups or with friends. Perhaps you have determined your own topic and have selected and studied a work not assigned or discussed in the course. After you analyze the text, you are ready to begin your research. Some suggested stages of the process follow. As you become more comfortable with the process, you may adapt or modify these stages to fit your needs.

Begin with a full exploration of the work. Engage in forms of reader response: annotate the text, brainstorm, freewrite, compose a double-entry notebook, and write several journal entries. Determine your interpretation, analyze your interpretation, and identify questions that remain. Discover the most puzzling areas concerning the topic. Then formulate a list of research questions. Check the most interesting queries. Have potential directions for research before you go to the library.

Next, explore other primary and secondary sources that will provide you with further information about the work. In the library, you may want to consult a general encyclopedia for information on the writer and his or her work. Often the encyclopedia will have a signed entry by an expert and additional bibliographic sources. You may assume that the author of the encyclopedia entry is a reliable expert on the topic as are the other writers of cited secondary references. You now have a beginning point for research. After you complete this overview of a writer's life and works, you may choose a specialized biographical source, including the *Dictionary of National Biography, Dictionary of American Biography, Contemporary Authors, Twentieth-Century Authors,* the *Oxford Companion to American Literature,* and the *Oxford Companion to English Literature.* The Oxford Companion series also includes guides to other areas of literary study besides British and American literature (e.g., *The Oxford Companion to African American Literature, to American Theater,* etc). Cambridge University Press also publishes literary reference guides. One title, for example, is *The Cambridge Guide to Asian Theatre* (1993). Other values resources for background information include the following: *The Bloomsbury Guide to Women's Literature, The Feminist Companion to Literature in English: Women Writers from the Middle Ages to the Present,* and *The Penguin Companion to World Literature.* These works are found in the reference room of your library. These reference books will give you a more comprehensive view of the writer and his or her work and additional sources for research.

After you gather information about a writer's life and works, you may narrow your focus to a single research area. At this point, you also will consult the card catalog, the computerized catalog, or computer indices of information to discover and gain additional secondary sources concerning biography and criticism. Other specialized indices in print form for research in journals and periodicals include the *Arts and Humanities Citation Index, Biography Index, Book Review Index, and Essay and General Literature Index.* Online indices include the Academic Index and Expanded Humanities Index. Note: First Search, a commercial database service to which many schools subscribe, allows you to find information on a broad range of subject areas. In many cases, collections of essays on the author and substantial critical treatments of the writer's life and works exist. You then survey and skim your materials with a slant or idea in mind. Before writing in order to determine a focus, review biographical and critical materials so that you do not take too many preliminary notes.

As you consult sources, you write bibliographic entries. Each source may appear on a separate card, or you may devise some other system. The entry should contain the following information for a book: Author, Title, Publication Information (Place Published, Publisher, Date), and Library of Congress reference number so that you can find the book again without searching for it in the catalog. A bibliographic entry for a journal should contain the following: Author, Title of the Article, Journal, Publication Source, Volume, Year, Date, and Page. Include a brief evaluation of the source.

BOOK

Bundtzen, Lynda K.	PS 3566 .L27 Z588 1983
Plath's Incarnations: A Woman and the Creative Process	
Ann Arbor: University of Michigan Press, 1983	
Good evidence and analysis of theme of transcendence.	

JOURNAL

Pollitt, Katha	PMLA Bibliography
"A Note of Triumph" *Nation.*	
16 January 1982: 52–55.	
Excellent review of *Collected Poems* by Plath	

Both biographical and critical treatments of the author and collections of essays may provide additional reference materials. You also may want to consult such general indices as *The Reader's Guide to Periodical Literature* (for information on current writers), *The New York Times Index,* and *The Book Review Digest* as well as computerized general subject indices for information in periodicals, magazines, journals, and newspapers and for reviews of current authors. The reference room also contains specialized bibliographies. For example, there are several bibliographies of women's studies materials (e.g., see *American Women Writers: A Critical Reference Guide from Colonial Times to the Present*). A standard bibliography for information on literature is the *Modern Language Association International Bibliography of Books and Articles on Modern Language and Literature.* This bibliography indexes the major scholarship in the discipline and lists entries for authors according to field of literature, nationality, and time period. For example, Ernest Hemingway's name would appear in the Twentieth Century American Literature section. Other specialized bibliographies include *American Literary Scholarship, American Literature and Language: A Guide to Information Sources, The New Cambridge Bibliography of English Literature,* and *The Oxford History of English*

Literature. Also particularly helpful reference sources are the *Literary Criticism Index, Contemporary Literary Criticism, Contemporary Authors,* and *Gale Literary Criticism Series.*

After you have decided on a research question and after you have narrowed your focus and established a preliminary direction for research, isolate the materials that you plan to study. At this point, you have an initial list of "works consulted" and a working bibliography of those books and articles from which you genuinely intend to gather information. Your instructor may want to check your bibliography and to offer further directions for research. As you shape your bibliography, examine your sources of information. You want to be aware of the publication date of your secondary sources so that you do not rely on outdated materials or interpretations of works.

Now, the notetaking phase of the research process begins. Before you start taking notes, however, keep your research questions and possible subtopics or subheadings for analysis on a separate sheet of paper so that they are foremost in your mind. You also may draft a potential thesis and determine a tentative purpose and audience for your essay. The purposes of research essays about literature are informative, argumentative, or evaluative; that is, the writer explains an interpretation, argues a point of view, or evaluates the effectiveness of a work or a writer's use of a particular technique. You may assume that your audience is your instructor and a community of knowledgeable peers. Having a beginning idea of questions, of topics, of thesis, of purpose, and of audience will direct your thinking and notetaking and will help you to assess the information from your sources. As you take notes, be aware that you may change your approach, thesis, topics, purpose, and audience.

Read and review your secondary sources carefully. Some people prefer to take notes on index cards; others use sheets of paper; others take minimal notes on cards or paper and create a system of notes that refers to photocopied information. You may put notes in the margins of duplicated information. In addition, you may wish to enter data into a computer. Whatever method you use, as you take notes, you engage in a combination of summarizing, paraphrasing, and quoting. When you summarize, you compress the central idea and main points in a work. When you paraphrase, you "translate" a passage from a work into your own words. Paraphrasing keeps the length, spirit, tone, logic, and ideas of the original passage, but the wording is different. When you quote, you are recording the author's statement exactly. Be certain not to include any words from the original work within your summary or paraphrase without using quotation marks. Any material from a source in the words of the author *must* be quoted. For this reason, take notes meticulously. Summarize, paraphrase, and quote accurately on the front of a note card or page. Then write your reaction and comments on the back of the card or paper or photocopy so that you have carefully documented and differentiated between your words and the language in the source, between your view and the critic's interpretations.

Each note also should contain an abbreviated annotation for source and page and a heading so that you may arrange your notes into categories of discussion and reshuffle them as your thesis and topics evolve.

THE RESEARCH PROCESS ONLINE

The stages of researching online are similar to traditional research methods: gain an overview of your topic by using an online encyclopedia (e.g., Encyclopedia Britannica on CD-ROM); develop a search strategy—narrow your topic; define and then refine your search terms and key words; and then limit your search and isolate appropriate online resources (CD-ROM; databases; indices; works online; other World Wide Web resources—public posting, home pages, etc).

Consider carefully the search engine. Some search engines index general information according to subject areas (e.g., Yahoo!) and compile information from other search engines, while others are more appropriate for literary research (e.g., AltaVista). What follows are some important procedures for doing research online once you have chosen a search engine:

- Define the terms of your search (author, title, work, phrase).
- Identify a phrase or subject area by using parentheses or quotation marks.
- Limit your search by combining key words with Boolean operators. Remember that "and" narrows your search, "or" widens the search, and "not" excludes information.
- Check each search engine for appropriate field indicators and for directions as to how to search.
- Once you find sources, bookmark them.
- Create a list of viable sources. You may create a hyperlinked bibliography.
- Print out the most important information.

It is especially important when you are doing research on the Web that you evaluate your sources carefully and that you verify your information by using print sources. To assess Web sources, consider these important questions about a Web site:

- Who is the author? What is the intended audience? Do you detect bias on the part of the authors?
- In what format is the site? A personal home page? Newsgroup? Article online? (Be aware that information from online dialogues and online forums may not be useful. The people are not likely to be authorities on a subject, so the information may be inaccurate.)
- What organization is sponsoring the Web site? These abbreviations commonly indicate the kind of group sponsoring the site: .com = commercial site; .org = organization; .edu = educational institution; .gov = government site. (Be careful to distinguish between a personal home page and authorized sites for authors or for organizations.)

- Is the information accurate? Current? Verifiable?
- Is the treatment of subject comprehensive? Balanced?
- What is the date of the entry?

As you download material, be selective. Note the date that you accessed the material as well as the URL and information about the site.

Here is a list of selected search engines and helpful web sites for literary research:

- Yahoo!—http://www.yahoo.com (a subject guide to the Web with links to other sites and search engines).
- Google—http://www.google.com (a comprehensive search engine with links to more than a billion Web pages).
- Ask Jeeves—http://www.ask.com (a resource for general information).
- Galaxy—http://www.galaxy.com (a resource for humanities and literature research).
- AltaVista—http://www.altavista.com (a search engine for humanities and literature topics).
- Lycos—http://www.lycos.com (another useful search engine).
- The Argus Clearinghouse—http://www.clearinghouse.net (a directory of subject guides, helpful to scholars).
- MLA on the Web—http://www.mla.org (the site of the Modern Language Association with a link to guidelines for documenting sources in MLA format).
- The Voice of the Shuttle: Web Pages for Humanities Research—http://www.vos.ucsb.edu/ (guide to Web sites on literary studies).
- The EServer (University of Washington)—http://eserver.org.

PRINCIPLES OF DOCUMENTATION

You need to follow principles of documentation in your research process. Documentation indicates the sources of your information to a reader and demonstrates that you have absorbed and synthesized the materials from your secondary sources. Information that you should document in the text of your research paper includes the following:

- Facts that are not common knowledge (that could not be verified in several sources).
- Paraphrased information from a source (information from a source that you have put into your own words).
- Quoted material.
- Other people's views—even when they are paraphrased, not quoted—interviews, and other sources of information.

All of the above forms of information must be documented. If you do not document thoroughly or if you inadequately paraphrase the source, you will be plagiarizing. **Plagiarism** is the taking of someone else's ideas or words and representing them as your own. This act, which constitutes academic "theft," is a serious matter.

Once you have refined your research question, decided upon a focus for your research, a preliminary approach, thesis, and subtopics, and conducted research, you are ready to revise your thesis, to create an outline, and to draft your essay. The final stage in the research process is actually composing the essay. During this phase, you may repeat the acts of the writing process although you already have done considerable prewriting and planning: brainstorming, shaping, drafting, revising, and writing several versions of your paper. In this research-writing process, however, you must document carefully from all your sources.

For students, another issue in the research process becomes the value of their own opinions and thinking. During the drafting of a research essay, you focus on an original thesis and idea. Your thesis emerges from your thinking, reading, and research. The exploration, evaluation, and synthesis of evidence from sources also emanate from your own thinking. When you piece together your opinions, analysis, and information from primary and secondary sources, you may discover that you may experience the satisfaction of exploring and validating your thesis and of sharing your findings with others.

FORM OF MLA DOCUMENTATION—CITATION WITHIN THE TEXT

All sources must be cited; that is, you must give the reader information about the material to which you refer. The accepted method of documenting information in research is MLA citation form that requires three steps: (1) use parenthetical references within your research essay; (2) include a "Works Cited" page that contains an alphabetized list of all of the primary and secondary sources that you have used in the development of your essay; and (3) include explanatory endnotes, if necessary.

The parenthetical reference involves two parts: an indication of author and of page. If the author's name is mentioned in the discussion, then you only need to indicate page number. If the author has written two books and if the title of the book is not given, then you should include an abbreviated title in the citation.

The common forms of parenthetical citation for papers about literature appear in the following examples. Examine these manuscript and punctuation forms—the conventions for citations:

1. Discussion (author and page)
   (Alexander 200).
2. Discussion—author already mentioned
   (79).

3. Two Works by Same Author whose name is mentioned
("Hope" 265) (*Ariel* 54).
4. Paraphrased and Summarized Material—author not mentioned
(Alexander 302).
5. Direct Quotation—author mentioned
Kroll states that "it is uncertain how seriously the speaker will entertain the theme of purity, and its related theme of transcendence" (178).
Note: Citation appears after quotation mark and before final punctuation.
6. Indented quotation—more than two lines of poetry and four lines of prose:
This poem is about two kinds of fire—
the fires of hell, which merely
agonize, and the fires of hell which
purify. During the poem, the first
suffers into the second. (Newman 62)

If you interpret only one literary work, you may indicate the paragraphs or pages of a short story, the lines of a poem, or the acts and scenes of a drama in a citation rather than the author and title since they previously have appeared in the introduction to the essay.

"WORKS CITED" PAGE

The "Works Cited" page also has a specific format, a particular pattern for each form of reference, dictated by the conventions of the MLA documentation system. The following are the most common bibliographic forms for the "Works Cited" page. Consult the handbook used in your school's freshman composition program for further information.

Common Forms of Bibliographic Entries for the "Works Cited" Page

FOR A BOOK

Gilligan, Carol. *In a Different Voice: Psychological Theory and Women's Development.* Cambridge; Harvard University Press, 1982.

Kincaid, Jamaica. *Annie John.* New York: Farrar, Straus, Giroux, 1985.

Morrison, Toni. *Beloved.* New York: Knopf, 1987.

The citation is double-spaced, the author's name is placed at the margin, and the second line indented (five spaces). There are periods between parts of the entry. The citation includes author's name, the title of the work and publication information—place published, publisher, and date.

For a Book with Two Authors

Flynn, Elizabeth A. and Patrocino Schweickart, eds. *Gender and Reading: Essays on Readers, Texts and Contexts.* Baltimore: John Hopkins Press, 1986.

When there are two authors, the second author's name is presented first name and then last name.

For an Author with Two Works

Rich, Adrienne. *An Atlas of a Difficult World: Poems 1988–1991.* New York: W.W. Norton, 1991.

—.*On Lies, Secrets and Silence: Selected Prose 1966–1978.* New York: W.W. Norton, 1979.

Note the alphabetical order of books for the author and a long (em) dash or three hyphens with a period to indicate the repeated name.

For Three or More Authors

Belenky, Mary Field, et al. *Women's Ways of Knowing: The Development of Self, Voice, and Mind.* New York: Basic Books, 1986.

Notice the use of "et al." to indicate the additional authors.

Translation

Wolf, Christa. *The Quest for Christa T.* Trans. Christopher Middletown. New York: Farrar, Straus, and Giroux, 1970.

Note that the translator's name appears after title and before publication information.

A Work Within an Anthology of Works

Mukherjee, Bharati. "Courtly Vision." *Sudden Fiction International: Sixty Short-Short Stories.* Eds. Robert Shapard and James Thomas. New York: W.W. Norton, 1989. 215–219.

The author's name and work appear before the title of the anthology. The names of the authors of the anthology are acknowledged, with the abbreviation indicating that they are the editors. Finally, the publication information is given.

Additional Entries for Works in an Anthology

Bogarad, Carley and Jan Zlotnik Schmidt, eds. *Legacies.* Fort Worth: Harcourt Brace, 1995.

Shakespeare, William. *Hamlet.* Bogarad and Schmidt, eds. 174–261.

Keats, John. "Ode on a Grecian Urn." Bogarad and Schmidt, eds. 1094–1095.

If you cite more than one selection from the same anthology, list the anthology as a separate entry with all publication information. If you use more than one work from the same anthology, also list each selection. Give the author's name and title of the selection, but mention only the name(s) of the editor(s) of the anthology and the page numbers.

Other Examples of a Short Story, Poem, or Play in an Edited Anthology

Borowski, Tadeusz. "Silence." *Literature: Reading, Reacting, Writing.* Eds. Laurie G. Kirzner and Stephen R. Mandell. Fort Worth: Harcourt Brace, 1993. 315–316.

Note the indication of page numbers.

Kumin, Maxine. "The Envelope." *Tangled Vines: A Collection of Mother and Daughter Poems.* Ed. Lyn Lifshin. New York: Harcourt, Brace, Jovanovich, 1992. 143.

Childress, Alice. *Wedding Band. 9 Plays by Black Women.* Ed. Margaret B. Wilkerson. New York: New American Library, 1986. 69–133.

Note that titles of short stories, poems, and essays require quotation marks and that titles of plays are underlined or italicized. As a general rule, complete works are underlined, and shorter works appear in quotation marks.

Work in Several Volumes

Eagleton, T. Allston. *A History of the New York Stage.* 3 vols. New York: Prentice Hall, 1987.

Note the indication of volumes.

One Work in a Several Volume Work

Eagleton, T. Allston. *A History of the New York Stage.* New York: Prentice Hall, 1987. Vol. 2.

Note the indication of the particular volume cited in the essay at the end of the note.

An Edited Anthology Cited as a Whole Work, Not as a Single Citation of a Particular Selection

Halpern, Daniel, ed. *The American Poetry Anthology.* New York: Avon, 1975.

Note the indication that Halpern is the editor.

An Article in a Critical Anthology

Volpe, Edmond L. "The Wasteland of Nathanael West." *Nathanael West: A Collection of Critical Essays.* Ed. Jay Martin. Englewood Cliffs, NJ: Prentice Hall, 1971. 91–101.

An Article or Selection in a Weekly Magazine for General Audiences, Paginated Anew in Each Issue

Barthelme, Frederick. "Law of Averages." *The New Yorker,* 5 October 1987: 36–39.

Notice the format for presentation of articles: Author, Title of Work, Name of Magazine, Date, a colon, and then pages.

An Article in an Academic Journal Paginated Continuously Throughout the Volume Year

Wilentz, Gay. "Toward a Diaspora Literature: Black Women Writers from Africa, the Caribbean and the United States." *College English* 54 (1992): 385–445.

Note the addition of volume number after the title of the journal and the placement of year within parentheses.

An Article in a Journal That Comes Out Once a Month, That Is Paginated Anew Each Month, and That Has a Volume and Issue Number

Muscatine, Charles. "Faculty Responsibility for the Curriculum." *Academe* 71.5 (1985): 18–21.

Notice that 71 is the volume number and that 5 is the issue number.

An Encyclopedia

Blotner, Joseph L. "James Joyce." *The Webster Family Encyclopedia,* 1984 ed.

You do not need to include publication information for well-known reference sources.

An Article in a Newspaper

Sontag, Deborah. "Making 'Refugee Experience' Less Daunting." *New York Times* 27 September 1992: Sec.1:1,35.

A Film or Book Review

Rafferty, Terrence. "Closing Time." Rev. of *Leaving Las Vegas,* dir. Mike Figgis with Nicholas Cage and Elizabeth Shue. *The New Yorker.* 6 Nov. 1995: 176–178.

Note: The reviewer's name and the title of the review precede the film or publication information.

INTERVIEW

Dove, Rita. "An Interview with Helen Vendler." The National Humanities Center, January 16, 1989.

Bogarad, Carley. "Sylvia Plath's and Ted Hughes' Poetry." Talk given at State University of New York College at New Paltz. New Paltz, October 24, 1990.

PRINCIPLES OF ONLINE DOCUMENTATION

When you document online sources, follow these general guidelines. Begin with the author's name, title of the work, and publication information as you would for a print source. Next list the electronic publication date and then the date you accessed the information. Finally, include the URL (uniform resource locator). If the URL takes more than one line of text, split the citation following a slash. Do not break the URL with a hyphen.

What follows is a list of online resources for teaching Sherman Alexie's "This Is What It Means to Say Phoenix, Arizona" that Vika Shock, an ESL instructor at the State University of New York at New Paltz, compiled as background material for teaching the story.

Common Forms of Bibliographic Entries for Internet Sources on the "Works Cited" Page

ONLINE NEWSPAPER

"Sherman Alexie, Indian Country's Favorite Writer." *Oklahoma Indian Times Online: The Native American Resources.* 5 July 2000. <http://www.okit.com/news/2000/September/Best/shermanalexie.htm>

ONLINE NOT-FOR-PROFIT ORGANIZATION

Soneda, Brian. "Sherman and the Heavy Hitters." *ALKI: The Washington Library Association Journal* December 1998. WLA Online. 5 July 2000. <http://www.wla.org/alki/dec98/soneda.html>

ONLINE ARTICLE FROM AN EDUCATION SOURCE

Luscher, Robert M. *Anthology of Modern American Poetry.* Book. *Modern American Poetry: Sherman Alexie (1966–)* Multimedia Companion Online. University of Illinois at Urbana-Champaign. 1999. <http://www.english.uiuc.edu/maps/poets/a-f/alexie/alexie.htm>

HOME PAGE

Rani. "The Official Sherman Alexie Site." Home page. January 1999. <http://www.fallsapart.com/>

ONLINE INTERVIEW

West, Dennis and Joan M. West. Interview. "Sending Cinematic Smoke Signals: An Interview with Sherman Alexie." *Cineaste* v23, n4 (Fall, 1998) :28 (5 pages) <http://www.lib.berkeley.edu/MRC/alexie.html>

ENDNOTES

When you use parenthetical citation form, you may create endnotes to include explanatory information that is not necessary to the text. This information may be additional sources, added biographical data, or an opposing critical view. Endnotes are numbered, follow in numerical order in the essay, and are indicated by a number in superscript above the line:[1] The "Endnote" page, labeled "Notes," is doubled-spaced, appears after the last page of your paper, and is your last numbered page. The "Works Cited" page is the last page of your research essay.

Here is an example of an endnote designed to provide additional bibliographic information:

Text of Essay

In recent years, there have been many attempts to define women's separate ways of knowing and developing moral consciousness.[1]

Notes

[1] See, for example, Belenky et al. and Gilligan.

Here is an endnote designed to provide a differing critical view:

Text of Essay

House on Mango Street is considered by many critics to be Cisneros' best work. This first, autobiographical work brought her critical acclaim.[1]

Notes

[1] Although *House on Mango Street* brought Cisneros acclaim, I would contend that *Woman Hollering Creek* is a more complex and subtle work.

AN EXAMPLE OF THE RESEARCH PROCESS—MLA DOCUMENTATION

This case study presents the research and writing process of a student, Kevin Stoffel. It includes a journal entry, an outline, and the final version of the essay with annotations by the editors. The assignment for the research paper offered the option of literary analysis, and Stoffel immediately chose to write about Sylvia Plath. The instructor required eight typewritten pages and a variety of sources. The paper was due in six weeks. In order to ensure success, the instructor established deadlines for parts of the work. She encouraged her students to conduct research and writing according to the processes described in this chapter. Stoffel created a work schedule, chose and defined a topic, thought about the rhetorical situation, took notes, kept a journal, and made careful copies of sources to avoid plagiarism. When he submitted his complete portfolio, it contained far more work than the instructor had assigned. In the folder, he placed copies of original drafts of Plath's poems, an essay on "Lady Lazarus," several handwritten versions of the paper, many articles on the topic, note cards, and copious written notes and summaries of articles and of books, and his final research project.

In many ways, Kevin Stoffel began his college composition research project in high school when he watched a segment of the PBS series on American poets, *Voices and Visions.* The program on Sylvia Plath sparked his interest in her poetry and impelled him to purchase, to read, and to memorize *Ariel,* her most famous single volume. In the first conference with his composition professor, he discussed his desire to write about Plath; and he presented a number of ideas in order to choose an original thesis for his research paper. Possible ideas included Plath's marriage and her poetry; *The Bell Jar;* Plath's suicide; her obsession with death. As he prepared his bibliography, read primary and secondary sources, and took notes, he received critiques and suggestions from other students in the class.

His instructor then encouraged him to consult a member of the English department faculty whose research focused on Plath; and she, in turn, called Ruth Mortimer, curator of the Rare Book Room of the Neilson Library at Smith College which owns the manuscripts of sixty-six of the lyrics known as the "Ariel Poems" by Sylvia Plath. At this point, Stoffel's term paper became an adventure. He drove to Smith College, a long journey, and worked extensively in the Sylvia Plath Collection.

He began with three research questions:

1. What is the relation between Plath's life and her poems?
2. Is the poetry totally personal, depressing, and suicidal?
3. What is the connection between death and transformation?

These questions led him to a thematic consideration of several poems in *Ariel,* and he began to focus on the theme of transcendence in Plath's draft versions. His research in the original manuscripts clarified some of his questions and suggested a new problem: What do the draft versions reveal about themes of the works? He wanted to answer these questions, and he wanted to explore Plath's revisions.

During his visit to Smith, he copied by hand all drafts of "Lady Lazarus," "Stings," "Edge," "Fever 103°," and "Ariel" since the Plath estate permitted no duplication of manuscripts. He also wrote all significant emendations in pencil (no pens permitted) in the margins and between the lines of his battered copy of *Ariel.* In the following journal entry, he records his responses to his encounter with the original drafts of these poems:

> I have just returned from Smith College where I worked in the Sylvia Plath Collection. For such a long time, I have admired Plath's poems, and I can hardly believe that the facsimiles of the manuscript lay in my hands, that I touched her books, that I scrutinized her list of submissions. I am in awe of Plath's poetic powers, and I feel exhilarated, happy, great.
>
> In high school, I became fascinated by her poems when I watched the Plath segment of PBS' *Voices and Visions* on American poets. I began reading her books over and over, and eventually my interest resulted in a paper on "Daddy" that my teacher really liked. He encouraged me to continue my research. When I took the Regents examination in English, Plath's poem "Mirror" appeared in a major question. My passion for Plath paid off in a truly unexpected moment.
>
> Now after studying the manuscripts of "Lady Lazarus," "Edge," "Ariel," and "Fever 103°" closely, I believe that my idea about her search for transcendence holds validity and that the drafts have exciting new information in them, information that seems, at first glance, to support my thesis. I feel certain that I can write an original paper because no one has published any materials from these drafts and all important scholars seem to have divided opinions on the question of transcendence.

After a number of drafts of his essay, Stoffel submitted a version to the class and to his professor. In order to assist him with his revisions, they asked these questions about his tentative paper:

> Do you want to include the texts of the poems so that readers may refer to them?
>
> Where is your thesis?
>
> What is the connection between the biographical details and your paper?
>
> How does the theme of transcendence connect to the draft versions of the poems?
>
> What is the organizing principle (the thesis) of the paper? of the paragraphs?
>
> How does "Edge" become transcendent?

Why does the analysis of "Edge" focus on the drafts and *not* on the theme?

Who is your audience?

They praised Stoffel's intention and passion for his subject, his command of the research process, and his enormous portfolio. Everyone expressed a sense of enrichment and excitement that he or she attributed to Stoffel's conception of himself as a scholar.

Stoffel then reorganized and revised his essay according to the suggestions given by his instructor and his peers. On the basis of their critiques, he clarified his thesis and decided to limit his interpretations to "Fever 103°" and to "Ariel." He realized that he could not complete his ambitious project successfully unless he concentrated more fully on his two best examples. He eliminated "Lady Lazarus" because of the length of the poem and because of the number of draft versions. Since he believed that the analysis of the manuscripts of "Edge" in his rough draft included new material about Plath's attitude toward the dead children in the poem, he reluctantly chose to omit that section. A careful reading of his first essay, however, convinced him that he had lost the thematic emphasis in his interpretation of "Edge" and that his description of the drafts lacked specificity. He concluded that his paper changed focus at that point and that the analysis was not necessary for the final revision of his paper.

His instructor asked him to review MLA notation form since his draft contained inaccurate citations and to revise his "Works Cited" list to include his primary sources, *Ariel* and the Sylvia Plath Collection at Smith College. She requested that he include copies of the poems with his essay. His outline and final research paper, which follow, offer clarity of organization, a revised thesis, and expanded interpretations of the theme of transcendence in "Fever 103°" and "Ariel." Notice the inclusion of secondary sources and of interesting examples from the manuscripts of the drafts. The citations, the Notes, and the "Works Cited" list now are correct, and they provide models for MLA documentation. Kevin Stoffel selected an extremely difficult topic, and he received high praise for his original project. His paper represents an excellent example of the value of research and of writing.

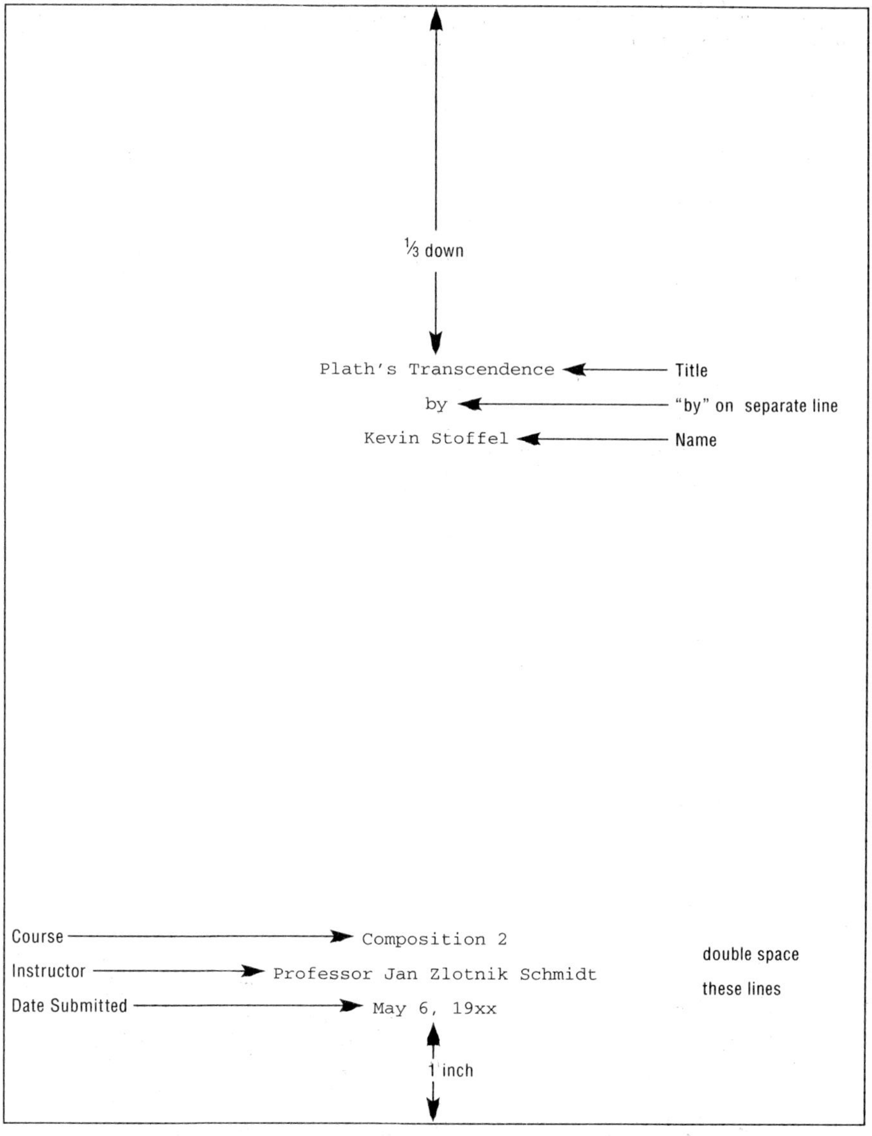
⅓ down
Plath's Transcendence
Title
by
"by" on separate line
Kevin Stoffel
Name
Course
Composition 2
Instructor
Professor Jan Zlotnik Schmidt
Date Submitted
May 6, 19xx
double space
these lines
1 inch

½ inch

Stoffel i

Name, number. (Number appears in lowercase Roman numerals.) Center the word "Outline." Place one inch from top of page. Double space outline.

OUTLINE

I. Introduction

A. Critics interpret Plath's poems as autobiography.

B. Theme of transcendence is central to Plath's poems, and draft versions reveal Plath's movement away from autobiography toward universal experience of transcendence.

C. "Fever 103°" and "Ariel" are two versions of transcendence and prove hypothesis about revisions.

Thesis statement

Stoffel writes a topic outline.

II. Autobiography in "Fever 103°" and in "Ariel":

A. "Fever 103°" versions show omission of materials on Ted Hughes in order to focus on transformation.

B. "Ariel" recounts a real event on a runaway horse, but experience becomes transcendent.

Divide major sections with Roman numerals.

Each part in a major section of the outline should be numbered A, B, C, etc.

III. Interpretation of "Fever 103°"

A. Plath's statement on two kinds of fire.

B. Purity defined by opposite images of hell, sexual sin.

C. Universal death from radiation (Hiroshima) caused by adultery.

D. Purgation by retching.

Strive for parallel constructions.

All verbs should be in the present tense.

Stoffel ii

E. Transformations:

1. lantern.

2. camellia.

3. acetylene virgin.

F. Draft versions.

IV. Transition

A. Use of sexual imagery in "Fever 103°"–it is the sin.

B. Use of sexual imagery as metaphor for ecstatic transformation in "Ariel."

V. Interpretation of "Ariel"

A. The ride on the horse:

1. sexual imagery

2. out-of-control

3. the hooks

B. "Something else hauls me through air"–the beginning of merging, of transformation.

C. White Godiva:

1. She "unpeels"

2. "Dead hands, dead stringencies."

D. Arrow and dew–evaporated into the sun/annihilation:

1. Creative energy.

2. Unification with sun.

E. Draft versions.

Stoffel iii

VI. Conclusion

A. Summary of thesis and proofs.

B. Quote from Katha Pollitt.

ARIEL

Sylvia Plath

Stasis in darkness.
Then the substanceless blue
Pour of tor and distances.

God's lioness,
How one we grow,
Pivot of heels and knees!—The furrow

Splits and passes, sister to
The brown arc
Of the neck I cannot catch,

Nigger-eye
Berries cast dark
Hooks—

Black sweet blood mouthfuls,
Shadows,
Something else

Hauls me through air—
Thighs, hair;
Flakes from my heels.

Stoffel iv

White
Godiva, I unpeel—
Dead hands, dead stringencies

And now I
Foam to wheat, a glitter of seas.
The child's cry

Melts in the wall,
And I
Am the arrow,

The dew that flies
Suicidal, at one with the drive
Into the red

Eye, the cauldron of morning.

(27 October 1962)

FEVER 103°

Sylvia Plath

Pure? What does it mean?
The tongues of hell
Are dull, dull as the triple

Tongues of dull, fat Cerberus
Who wheezes at the gate. Incapable
Of licking clean

Stoffel v

The aguey tendon, the sin, the sin.
The tinder cries.
The indelible smell

Of a snuffed candle!
Love, Love, the low smokes roll
From me like Isadora's scarves, I'm in a
fright

One scarf will catch and anchor in the wheel
Such yellow sullen smokes
Make their own element. They will not rise,

But trundle round the globe
Choking the aged and the meek,
The weak

Hothouse baby in its crib,
The ghastly orchid
Hanging its hanging garden in the air,

Devilish leopard!
Radiation turned it white
And killed it in an hour.

Greasing the bodies of adulterers
Like Hiroshima ash and eating in.
The sin. The sin.

Stoffel vi

Darling, all night
I have been flickering, off, on, off, on.
The sheets grow heavy as a lecher's kiss.

Three days. Three nights.
Lemon water, chicken
Water, water make me retch.

I am too pure for you or anyone.
Your body
Hurts me as the world hurts God. I am a
lantern—

My head a moon
Of Japanese paper, my gold beaten skin
Infinitely delicate and infinitely expensive.

Does not my heat astound you. And my light.
All by myself I am a huge camellia
Glowing and coming and going, flush on flush.

I think I am going up,
I think I may rise—
The beads of hot metal fly, and I, love, I

Am a pure acetylene
Virgin
Attended by roses,

By kisses, by cherubim,
By whatever these pink things mean.
Not you, nor him

Not him, nor him
(My selves dissolving, old whore petticoats)—
To Paradise.

(20 October 1962)

½ inch

1

PLATH'S TRANSCENDENCE

Sylvia Plath's suicide in 1963 casts a shadow over her poems, a long shadow which seems to encourage readers and critics to interpret her work as autobiography. Her writing certainly includes details from her life, and no one can challenge M. L. Rosenthal's definition of her poetry as "confessional" in *The New Poets* (79). However, strong evidence of Plath's emphasis on transformation and of her control of both form and content which consistently made her poems less personal appears in her late poetry[1] and in the draft versions of the poems from *Ariel* in the Sylvia Plath Collection in the Neilson Library at Smith College.[2]

In "Fever 103°" and in "Ariel," Plath creates two kinds of transcendent visions, and drafts of both poems reveal her careful revisions through handwritten and typed versions—each draft a movement away from personal anger and outrage, from desire for revenge, and from confession.

Both poems begin in personal suffering, and both poems refer to events in her life. "Fever 103°" alludes to Plath's separation from her husband, Ted Hughes, former Poet Laureate of England, and to his affair with Assia Wevill which ended their marriage in 1962 (Alexander 290). The poem's preoccupation with sexuality and with sin and its emphasis on "adulterers" may stem from

PAGE NUMBER—Because Stoffel uses a cover page, he typed the number 1 in the right-hand corner, placed one half inch from the top.

TITLE—Stoffel's title is required, and it indicates the thematic emphasis of his paper.

INTRODUCTORY MATERIAL—Stoffel mentions Plath's suicide and autobiographical interpretations as a way of gaining the reader's attention and of giving background information. He attempts to show that Plath "transcends" her personal history.

ENDNOTES—Endnotes give information not necessary in text.

THESIS STATEMENT

EXPLANATION OF THESIS

Stoffel 2

On every sheet, except page 1, Stoffel types his name before the number.

Plath's experience with Hughes, but the drafts demonstrate repeated efforts to eliminate direct references to him. "Ariel" recounts a wild ride on a horse, Sam, which galloped out of control (Alexander 302), but the drafts transform the incident into "something else." Sylvia Plath begins with her own pain and despair, with the concrete details of her daily life, but she often focuses on transcendence, and she often revises autobiography into stunning and symbolic figures including the "pure acetylene/virgin" (*Ariel* 54)[3] of "Fever 103°" and the "White/Godiva" (*Ariel* 26) of "Ariel."

PARENTHETICAL REFERENCE TO SOURCE.

PARAPHRASE OF SOURCE—To avoid too many quotations, Stoffel paraphrases central events from Alexander's biography of Plath.

In a statement prepared for a BBC reading, Plath describes "Fever 103°": "This poem is about two kinds of fire—the fires of hell, which merely agonize, and the fires of heaven which purify. During the poem, the first sort suffers into the second" (Newman 62). "Fever 103°" is one of several poems by Plath in which fire serves to create a sense of purity equivalent to a type of transcendence, a movement to a higher plane. However, in the beginning of the poem, Judith Kroll suggests that "it is uncertain how seriously the speaker will entertain the theme of purity, and its related theme of transcendence" (178). The speaker inquires about the meaning of the term "pure," but she defines it through descriptions of its opposite, images of hell—all evil, impure images. The speaker, in her feverish state, descends into the classical underworld. In order for

Parenthetical reference to author not named in the text. The source (author and page) is added in parentheses.

TOPIC SENTENCE—Stoffel analyzes theme in "Fever 103°."

Stoffel 3

its fires to purify and for death, rebirth, and transcendence to occur, she must confront sexual sins, lust, and the "full images of hell" (Bassnett 127). These depths include Cerberus, the mythological three-headed dog that guards the gates of Hades. His disgusting tongues cannot ". . . clean/The aguey tendon, the sin, the sin" (*Ariel* 53). Nothing can clean the sin. This image blends into the sulfurous smell of a "snuffed candle" (Ariel 53) and into the speaker's illness rolling from her like the scarves of Isadora Duncan, scarves that can choke and kill. The smokes "will not rise" (*Ariel* 53). Instead, they reach a universal level as they "trundle round the globe" (*Ariel* 53). This sexual circle of hell with the smell and smoke and taste of sin engulfs the world and seems "dull" and "sullen" (*Ariel* 53), a parody of its Biblical and classical counterparts.

Evidence of purifying fires in poem. Quotation within sentence. Stoffel quotes Bassnett and fits her description into his sentence.

The smoke of hell murders the old and the young. The speaker ceases her concern for her own plight and for the sins committed against her which render her impure, and she moves to a global level as the smokes choke "The weak/ Hothouse baby in its crib" (*Ariel* 53), and "The ghastly orchid" (*Ariel* 53). The smokes transform into radiation which kills the "Devilish leopard" (*Ariel* 53). The nuclear fall-out from the destruction of Hiroshima—a version of hell on earth—greases ". . . the bodies of adulterers/ Like Hiroshima ash. . ." (*Ariel* 54). Even

Evidence of sexual sin, impurity.

Stoffel 4

in this form, the radiation becomes a punishment for adultery and for sexual sin. Some of its victims are not innocent like those upon whom the atomic bomb was dropped.

Thus, the speaker, by being impure, takes on the role of a Hiroshima radiation victim:

> Darling, all night
> I have been flickering, off,
>   on, off, on,
> The sheets grow heavy as a
>   lecher's kiss
>
> Three days. Three nights.
> Lemon water, chicken
> Water, water makes me retch. (*Ariel* 54)

An apt and accurate description of a feverish state, the flickering clearly connotes sexuality—the rhythm of the lines, the lecher. The speaker begins to experience purgation through retching.

After being a victim of the bombing of Hiroshima, the speaker becomes ". . . a huge camellia/Glowing and coming and going, flush on flush" (*Ariel* 54). This orgasmic blossom creates its own metamorphosis, "all by [it]self" (*Ariel* 54). Then the speaker enters a state of purity. The first fire "suffers into the second." Plath alludes to the Ascension of Mary: "I think I am going

LONG QUOTATION—A quotation of more than four typewritten lines is separated from the rest of the text.

Stoffel indents ten spaces and double spaces the quotation.

The reference for the quotation is given in parentheses after the quotation. Since Stoffel uses two Plath references in his paper, he gives the name of the volume to indicate which primary source by Plath serves as the text.

Stoffel 5

up,/I think I may rise" (*Ariel* 54). (Note the sexual implications of her language.) The speaker transforms herself into a virgin, not because she wants this persona, but because she still retains the "glow" and the "heat" of the radiation. She "emerges from her suffering as an infinitely desirable, but untouchable virgin" (Bundtzen 199)—too hot for any man to touch or to enjoy. All men are pushed aside as she rises. She needs no one as she ascends to heaven, as she overflows with purity. She turns all men away from her "unquenchable fire" (Bundtzen 199). All of the sins, "old whore petticoats" (*Ariel* 54), dissolve as she ascends, through purification, into Paradise.

This transcendence becomes a kind of purification of the fiery "acetylene/Virgin" (*Ariel* 54) in three draft versions of this poem written on October 20, 1962. In the first two drafts of this poem, Plath refers to the devilish leopard as "you": "Oh that devilish leopard!/ Radiation turned you white/And killed you in an hour" (Plath Collection, Smith College). Here she reveals her anger about Hughes' affair with Assia Wevill. However, in the third and final version, she changes the "you" to "it" in order to depersonalize the image and to move the poem from a personal to a general level. The lover, the man, the darling is not killed, simply left behind.

QUOTATION FROM DRAFT VERSIONS—Stoffel indicates the source of the quotation from Plath because he has used two entries for Plath: *Ariel* and the Sylvia Plath Collection.

Movement to more general level of interpretation.

Paraphrase of third draft.

In both poems, Plath creates sexual imagery, but the imagery serves different purposes. In "Fever 103°," the illness clearly serves as metaphor for the speaker's pain, for her descent into hell because of adultery and because of sexual sin. "Your Body/Hurts me as the world hurts God. . . ." (*Ariel* 54). The purgation of illness leads to transcendence, even though the virgin in this case rises to Paradise from "hot beads" and from fire. She is not the image of a Renaissance madonna. Still, she transcends her experience of impurity and suffering; and she reaches Paradise, the ultimate state of blessedness. In "Ariel," however, the sexual imagery stands for transformation of the speaker into a bare, "White Godiva" from whom things drop away, and the speaker's annihilation becomes a unification of personal and artistic energy through evaporation into the source of all human life, the sun, ". . . the red/eye, the cauldron of morning" (*Ariel* 27). The sexual ride and the connotations represent "something else" which "hauls [her] through air" (*Ariel* 26). The sexual imagery is *not* the subject matter here as it is in "Fever 103°." The subject matter is "something else" (*Ariel* 26).

TRANSITION—Sexual imagery in both poems.

Transition to interpretation of theme in "Ariel."

"Ariel" begins in a motionless and black state—"Stasis in darkness" (Ariel 26)—as the persona describes the commencement of a ride on a horse that gallops out of control. The name, Ariel, refers to a favorite horse that Plath rode in Devonshire (Butscher 377). The name

Paraphrase of numerous primary and secondary sources. Plath, the *Bible*, and Shakespeare represent primary sources. Kroll is a secondary source.

Stoffel 7

also conveys a key to the poem. It refers to Jerusalem (Isaiah 29:1-3). The derivation may be either "lioness of God," which was underlined in her dictionary and which was written at the top of the first page of the first draft of the poem (Plath Collection, Smith College), or "altar of God" (Isaiah 29:1-3). In forming a connection between the horse and the Biblical allusions, Plath also infers that the horse is an altar upon which the speaker can be consumed. The horse is the "scrobis" upon which the speaker can shed all of the "inessentials of life, thus becoming free and pure" (Kroll 181). Plath also invokes the air spirit, Ariel, from Shakespeare's *The Tempest,* the spirit who seeks only to be free.

In the first two tercets of the poem, the speaker becomes one with the runaway horse, God's lioness. The violent ride itself merges woman and horse, female and male. In every image, the reader discovers sexual connotations: "Pivot of heels and knees!—The furrow/Splits and passes. . ." (*Ariel* 26). Yet the concrete details of the "brown arc/of the neck. . ." (*Ariel* 26) and of the "Black sweet blood mouthfuls" (*Ariel* 26) of the berries eventually become "Shadows" (*Ariel* 26). The wild galloping ends, and the speaker is "Haul[ed]. . . through air" (Ariel 26) by "Something else" (Ariel 26) as she transforms into a symbolic figure like Lady Godiva as she sheds her body and her past:

Paraphrase of action of the poem. The horse and woman merge. The speaker becomes one with the horse.

Stoffel 8

White
Godiva, I unpeel—
Dead hands, dead stringencies. (*Ariel* 27)

When she experiences the orgasmic "foam[ing] to wheat" (*Ariel* 26), she transforms again. "Thus the identity not only of the rider but also of the horse is dissolved: the newly created self is an 'arrow'. . ." (Wagner 116). After this merging with the landscape, "seas" of "wheat" (*Ariel* 26), the speaker becomes one with the horse, even though, at the beginning of the poem, she is restrained from this unity. The berries "still tried to catch her with their hooks" (Kroll 182). Thus, just as "the child's cry/Melts in the wall" (Ariel 26-27), the speaker blends with the horse and the landscape, escapes her body and her suffering (the "White/Godiva" (*Ariel* 26)), and "flies" as the "arrow" and "the dew" (*Ariel* 27)—pure energy—into the sun. The flight is both suicidal and ecstatic since the transcendence leads to the creative source. The poem, which begins in motionless darkness, ends in infinite motion and light. The speaker enters a "revelation of a new world. It is a transcendence into a new world written at no one's expense but her own. . . . 'Ariel' is Plath's most triumphant assertion of her poetic powers. . ." (Bundtzen 256).[4]

Endnote acknowledges alternative interpretations of the ending.

How does Plath create the amazing transformations in "Ariel"? To what degree does she control autobiographical

Stoffel 9

detail for artistic and thematic purposes? She writes about a real event and a real horse. She changes the name of the horse for symbolic reasons. (Sam becomes Ariel.) She invents an extended sexual metaphor for the experience, and an examination of draft versions reveals that she controls the erotic imagery through revision. In the first three drafts of "Ariel," Plath calls the horse "crude mover whom I move/And burn to love," "oh, bright beast," "lover," "the plunging/Hooves" (Plath Collection, Smith College). The fourth draft consists mainly of versions of one tercet, the pivotal stanza about the unpeeling Godiva. Here she presents the same tendency to kill the lover (Hughes) that appears in the drafts of "Fever 103°."

Evidence of control of personal materials for thematic purposes.

> Hands, hearts, dead men,
> Dead men,
> Hands, heads, peel off. (Plath
> Collection, Smith College)

Use of primary source. Draft versions of poems.

Plath attempts six different revisions of the above stanza before she writes:

> White
> Godiva, I unpeel—
> Dead hands, dead stringencies. (Plath
> Collection, Smith College)

Stoffel 10

Note that she eliminates the desire for revenge, the thinly veiled details of her life. She had written the same lines which appear in the above stanza in the first three versions, but she had not ordered them as a separate tercet. In the fourth draft, she attempts numerous revisions of the idea before she returns to her original language and rearranges it as a distinct stanza. Once again, the reader discovers that Plath controls her personal anger in order to enhance the effect of her poem and to attain a larger meaning. These draft versions reveal a tightening of the language which creates a fast tempo and an ecstatic tone, the idea of transcending, of changing to another form, of merging with the sun.

Analysis of theme in draft of "Ariel."

Plath fully develops the theme of transcendence in "Fever 103°" and in "Ariel." Through revision, she crafts great poems and often eliminates her private angers and desire for revenge in order to create deeply human themes. Through rising and blending images, the ideas of rebirth and of transcendence to a higher plane are expressed with great intensity. The strength of her poetic vision emerges and begins to balance the widely held conception of her negativity. These poems—wonderfully controlled, brilliantly worded, deeply felt, wisely conceived—earn her an important place in twentieth century poetry. As Katha Pollitt writes in the

CONCLUSION

Stoffel 11

Nation: "She was always becoming more distinctly herself, and by the time she came to write her last seventy or eighty poems, there was no other voice like hers on earth" (53).

Quotation with author and source named in the text.

Stoffel 12

NOTES

[1]See Susan R. Van Dyne's essay, "'More Terrible Than She Ever Was': The Manuscripts of Sylvia Plath's Bee Poems" in Wagner's Collection for confirmation of this thesis.

[2]I wish to acknowledge the assistance of Ruth Mortimer and her staff at the Rare Book Room of Neilson Library at Smith College and to express my gratitude for permission to quote from the manuscripts to the library and to the Plath Estate through Faber and Faber.

[3]All future references to the two poems are taken from Sylvia Plath. *Ariel*. New York: Harper and Row, 1973 or from draft versions in the Plath Collection at Smith College.

[4]Such critics as Alvarez and Rosenthal interpret this poem pessimistically.

"Notes" appear on separate numbered page, the last numbered page of the essay. The endnotes give material that does not fit into the text. The note begins with number in superscript and is indented five spaces for the first line. All notes are double spaced. Stoffel offers comparison with his thesis. Stoffel acknowledges the assistance of Ruth Mortimer at Smith College and permission to quote from Plath material.

Stoffel acknowledges alternatives to his interpretations.

Stoffel 12

WORKS CITED

Alexander, Paul. *Rough Magic: A Biography of Sylvia Plath.* New York: Viking Press, 1991.

Alvarez, A., *The Savage God.* New York: Random House, 1972.

Bassnett, Susan. *Sylvia Plath.* Totowa, New Jersey: Barnes and Noble Books, 1987.

Bundtzen, Lynda K. *Plath's Incarnations: A Woman and the Creative Process.* Ann Arbor: University of Michigan Press, 1983.

Butscher, Edward. *Sylvia Plath: Method and Madness.* New York: Simon and Schuster, 1977.

Kroll, Judith. *Chapters in a Mythology: The Poetry of Sylvia Plath.* New York: Harper and Row, 1976.

Newman, Charles. *The Art of Sylvia Plath.* Bloomington: Indiana University Press, 1970.

Perloff, Marjorie. "Angst and Animism in the Poetry of Sylvia Plath." *Critical Essays on Sylvia Plath.* Ed. Linda W. Wagner. Boston: G. K. Hall and Company, 1984. 109-124.

Plath, Sylvia. *Ariel.* New York: Harper and Row, 1973.

---. Unpublished Manuscripts. Sylvia Plath Collection. Rare Book Room, Neilson Library, Smith College.

Pollitt, Katha. "A Note of Triumph." Nation 16 January 1982:52-55.

Rosenthal, M. L. *The New Poets.* New York: Oxford University Press, 1967.

Bibliography, named "Works Cited," appears at the end of the paper. Entries are alphabetized by author's last name, with a five-space indentation after the first line of each citation. Double space entries, and double space between entries.

Entry for a book by a single author.

Essay in an edited book.

Second work by the same author. Three hyphens and a period represent the author's name. Works are listed in alphabetical order by title.

Entry for an essay in a journal. Essay title is in quotation marks; the journal, date, and year appear, and page numbers are denoted without pp. designation.

Please note: Another example of research writing, Anne Cilia's essay—"Sylvia Plath's 'Daddy' and an Analysis of Poetic Language"—is included in chapter 5.

APPENDIX B

Critical Approaches to Literature

We approach literary texts with presuppositions, often undefined, about what literature is, about what it means, and about what determines its worth. Critical theories enable us to articulate assumptions and to devise methodologies for reading, for analyzing, for interpreting, for evaluating, and for writing about literary works. A number of theories offer sometimes complementary, often competing, views of the literary text, of language itself, of the meaning or meanings of the text, of the process of creating meaning, and of the question concerning who or what creates meaning—the work, the writer, the reader, the culture.

Some critics think of a work of literature as fixed—a thing in itself with little if any relationship to the author or to his or her purpose or experiences, with no relationship to the reader, or with no relationship to the culture of the writer. The work, according to such a view, is objective and, consequently, free from the subjectivity of the writer or the reader. We begin with these theories that focus on the text; then we move to critical approaches that center on the writer, the reader, or the culture.

FORMALISM/NEW CRITICISM

Formalism in English language literary criticism began with I. A. Richards's *Practical Criticism* (1929) in England. It was picked up and developed in the 1940s by a group of American literary critics including Cleanth Brooks, Robert Penn Warren, and Rene Wellek, who came to be known as the New Critics. Formalist criticism considers formal elements of literature (organization, structure, language, etc.) in order to determine meaning. Each work is independent, complete in itself, and everything external to the work is of secondary importance. The formalist is less concerned with the state of mind of the writer, with any biographical, economic, political, or social information than with such intrinsic features as plot, character, narrative technique, irony, and paradox.

Both the underlying assumptions and something of the methodology of formalism can be glimpsed in a quotation from Cleanth Brooks: "The language of poetry is the language of paradox." Brooks's use of the word "paradox" is key: a paradox is an apparent contradiction that is resolved on a deeper level. Perhaps the simplest example of this is the metaphor. Consider the statement, "my love is a red rose." Taken literally, such a statement is nonsensical: unless the speaker actually is in love with a flower, there is no way for it to be factually true. Taken nonliterally (as of course we do take it), the statement is easily understood: the speaker is comparing his beloved to a particular kind of flower. What seems contradiction is revealed to be coherent meaning. We find similar examples of such conflict and tension at the level of character and plot: consider the character of Hamlet, whose attitudes toward Ophelia include both callous indifference to her love for him and overwhelming grief at her death; or the conclusion of "The Story of an Hour," where we are told that Mrs. Mallard, who has spent the story awakening to the freedom her husband's death brings her, has died of "joy" at the sight of him still alive. For this reason, formalist critics are interested in irony, since irony is another means to reconcile seemingly contradictory meanings.

Formalist critics judge the use of language in a literary work as a special situation in which the way the substance of a work is conveyed is as important as the substance itself. For this reason, Cleanth Brooks writes of "the heresy of paraphrase," the mistaken belief that a summary of the literary work could be equivalent to the work itself. For the formalist, method and message are intimately connected—another example of Formalism's concern with textual unity—and so there is no substitute for the literary text itself.

For the formalist critic, then, literature is an art form that always appears to be in tension with itself, but that ultimately resolves into a unified whole. It is the task of the formalist critic to demonstrate how that resolution is achieved, to identify the move from contradiction to coherence. To do so, the critic employs a strategy of "close reading," in which the work is subjected to close, even minute consideration and analysis, its moments of tension studied to reveal its underlying unity. A formalist reading of a literary work will attempt to demonstrate how its seemingly diverse components add up to a coherent whole.

In formalist criticism, the reader can make assumptions about the validity of interpretation and about the worth of the work of art; that is, some interpretations, based on evidence from the text, are better than others, while some works of art, based on their complexity, beauty, and depth, may be considered greater than others.

A formalist reading of "The Story of an Hour" by Kate Chopin (chapter 9) might begin by focusing on the story's last line: "When the doctors came they said she had died of heart disease—of joy that kills." From having read the story, which has given us access to Mrs. Mallard's inner experience, we know that the doctors' assessment is incorrect. Mrs. Mallard has experienced "joy," but not the "joy" the doctors assume. Why, then, does the story conclude with their diagnosis? Is this ending a carefully planned, unifying culmination of the story's events, or is it merely a trick, a simple surprise? To answer this question, the formalist critic would seek to resolve the tension between what we know of Mrs. Mallard and the doctors' diagnosis. The critic would ask if there is a level of meaning on which the doctors' assessment could be true, if Mrs. Mallard could be described accurately as the victim "of joy that kills"? The critic might consider the descriptions of Mrs. Mallard's happiness at the freedom her husband's death brings her, of the way her "fancy . . . [runs] riot along those days ahead of her." The critic might hypothesize that it is this joy at her liberation from the constraints of marriage that stops her heart, as it turns to despair that she will not be free from marriage after all. Mrs. Mallard must be free, and if she cannot be free in life, then she will be free in death. Thus, the formalist critic would argue, the doctors are correct in their diagnosis, but they are so ironically. Through such an exploration, the formalist critic would begin to determine the unifying principle of the story's ending.

Although formalism has been superceded by more recent theories of literary criticism, its methodology of close reading remains the bedrock for beginning students of literary criticism and for most of the critical schools that come after it. If formalism has taught and continues to teach anything, it is that nothing substitutes for close attention to the literary text.

STRUCTURALISM

Like formalism, *structuralism* attempts to offer objective analysis of the meaning of literature. The structuralist critic also seeks to minimize considerations of history, economics, and politics. The theory aspires to scientific inquiry through ideas and methods borrowed from linguistics and from anthropology. Each work becomes a system, and the critic's task becomes the discovery of the laws that pertain to the interaction of elements in the system. The structuralist examines surface phenomena in order to uncover "a deep structure." For example, the structuralist attempts to define conventions of literary form, perhaps aspiring to understand the features or elements that identify a text as a poem or drama.

Because structuralism developed from linguistics, some critics apply linguistic approaches to literature. In *Course in General Linguistics* (1915), Ferdinand de Saussure, a French linguist, called the relationship between an object and the name by which the object is designated (i.e., a sign) arbitrary. A word makes sense only within the system of an entire language, and it signifies meaning only to those who know that particular language system. Saussure further assumes that signs or words are useful when they emphasize difference: a hand and a foot are both appendages, but a hand has fingers and a foot has toes. A hand is attached to an arm, a foot to a leg, and so on.

Saussure theorized about the rules that govern the complex system of signs in language. He claimed that a *semiotic* (a science of signs) principle, which enables humans to communicate through a system of signs, governs the structure of language. Literary critics who apply linguistics to texts assume that poems, fiction, and drama are part of a larger system. Any analysis of a work requires the comprehension of the system in which the work operates and of the difference between that system and other systems. Structuralism also requires readers to discover the way in which sign systems create meaning.

A structuralist approach, then, requires the critic to think about the way that a story functions as a story, as opposed to a poem or drama. Structuralism looks to establish categories: for kinds of plot, for occurrences within plots, for kinds of characters, and so on. In the case of "The Story of an Hour," a structuralist would seek to reduce the story to its essentials in order to understand how it functions. It begins with Mrs. Mallard's learning of the death of her husband. It has a middle that complicates the action—she uncharacteristically finds herself joyful because of her newly acquired freedom. The end, which has a surprising twist, is also Mrs. Mallard's end since she suffers a fatal coronary when she learns that her husband still lives. The structuralist would recognize conventions of plot, theme, and character that appear in similar stories: the surprise O. Henry ending, for example, which began as a device in mystery stories and remains a recognizable feature in short fiction. The structuralist would compare the story to others in which characters gain autonomy and happiness only to suffer a tragic reversal of fortune, a reversal both surprising and ironic. The structuralist would note that Mrs. Mallard is made happy by an event that should make her unhappy and made unhappy by an event that should make her happy. A scheme for the structure of this story, then, might be that a character undergoes a pair of reversals, each of which is received in a manner the reverse of what one might expect.

Structuralist criticism lost favor in the 1970s, and many new theories that borrowed from Saussure or that contradicted the objectivist approach appeared. Scholars often consider contemporary criticism to be "poststructuralism."

DECONSTRUCTION

Deconstruction contends that literary works do not contain unified or stable meanings. Unlike formalist critics, who seek to reconcile tensions in a text in order to establish the relation of the parts to the whole work, deconstructionists argue that any close reading of a text uncovers contradictions that inevitably "deconstruct" or dissolve the possibility of unity. Underlying and motivating deconstructive criticism is a belief that what we accept as truth, especially as it is conveyed through language, is nothing of the kind. Because they believe that language can never truly convey single, fixed messages, deconstructionists postulate that language creates endless meanings that destabilize a text and that create contradictions that cannot be reconciled.

Deconstruction begins with the assertion that there is nothing outside language, that language shapes and orders our perceptions. As described by its most prominent theorist, philosopher Jacques Derrida, language (and all linguistic constructions) operates through *différance,* a term that contains two meanings: "to be different" and "to defer." We do not understand a word, Derrida argues, because of any inherent qualities in it. Rather, we understand a word because of its difference from other words (e.g., "cat" is not the same as "cut" or "cap"). We also understand it in terms of other words (i.e., its dictionary definition), which we in turn understand in terms of other words (i.e., the dictionary definitions of the words that make up the dictionary definitions), and so on. Thus, meaning in language is always provisional and endlessly deferred. Deconstruction assumes that since the word that signifies an object is separate from that object, the word stands for the object in a metaphorical way, and so all language is metaphorical. Because words can only signify, they cannot serve as reality or truth. Because they cannot serve as truth, there is nothing to stop them from tangling and/or contradicting. If we read a text attentively, Derrida argues, we will see that this is exactly what happens. Every written text contains elements that will destabilize it. The appearance of stable, unitary meaning in a literary work is just that, an appearance: every work contains a multiplicity of meaning that undermines any notion of a stable, unitary literary text. Literary criticism that claims to find a single meaning in a text, deconstructionists argue, is, in fact, imposing that meaning onto it, choosing one of its competing meanings and focusing on it to the exclusion of all others.

Like formalists and structuralists, deconstructionists focus on the text. In deconstructing a work, however, the reader examines ambiguities, wordplay, competing meanings. The task of the critic becomes to expose the text's contradictions, to show the way that it does not add up to a unified achievement. One of deconstruction's favorite techniques is to take a text that has been understood as saying one thing and then to demonstrate how it can be read as saying exactly the opposite. The critic does so by examining the elements in the story that seem to be encouraging us to interpret it in one way and then demonstrating how those elements could as easily be understood as asking us to interpret it in exactly the opposite way. The purpose of such an interpretation is not to replace the old reading with the new, but to show how both readings exist within the text simultaneously, thus foreclosing any chance of achieving a unitary interpretation of it.

A deconstructive reading of "The Story of an Hour" might begin by considering the opposition the story appears to set up between freedom and captivity. Mrs. Mallard, it seems, moves from the captivity of marriage to the freedom of widowhood. The deconstructive critic might focus on the language the story uses to present that movement. After hearing the news of her husband's death, brought by "her sister Josephine," Mrs. Mallard sits facing an "open window." She is "reached" by the "notes of a distant song." She is "motionless, except when a sob . . . [shakes] her." Gradually, "something . . . [approaches] to possess her." Accepting her joy at her new freedom, Mrs. Mallard "[drinks] in a very elixir of life through that open window." The deconstructive critic would note that although these images ostensibly refer to Mrs. Mallard's becoming free, they do so using language that relentlessly emphasizes freedom as external to Mrs. Mallard. Freedom is something that is visited upon her, as much outside her control as was her marriage. Such language suggests that Mrs. Mallard still is not acting as an autonomous being and that she remains under the sway of external forces. Although, pragmatically speaking, Mrs. Mallard may be free of her marriage, at the level at which she experiences life she remains passive. Thus, the critic would argue, while the story appears to be telling us about Mrs. Mallard's moment of liberation, it does so in language that emphasizes her subjection. Mrs. Mallard is at once free and not free. The deconstructive critic would find another level of irony to the story's ending: namely, that Mrs. Mallard is killed by external forces, just as her entire life—even what has appeared to be her one moment of liberation—has been dominated by external forces.

Although not all critics accept deconstruction's insistence on the ultimate indeterminacy of meaning, a number of critical schools have employed deconstructive techniques in order to advance their own concerns. Feminist, gender, and postcolonial theorists, to name a few, have used deconstructive techniques to destabilize prevailing assumptions about sexuality and race.

PSYCHOLOGICAL CRITICISM

Psychological criticism applies the insights offered by such psychologists as Sigmund Freud, Jacques Lacan, and Julia Kristeva to the interpretation of literary works. Most psychological criticism has drawn on Freud's writing; although many of his insights into and assertions concerning consciousness have been superceded by more recent developments within the field, his ideas remain fruitful for the interpretation of literary works. A number of Freud's ideas—the Oedipus complex, the concept of repression, the significance of dreams—have entered popular discourse to the extent that we employ them unaware that they originated with him. We might find ourselves discussing the significance of Hamlet's attachment to his mother without being fully aware that our interpretation is informed by Freud's notion of the Oedipus complex. The responsible psychological critic makes an effort to understand Freud's (or Lacan's or Kristeva's) theories before attempting to apply them to a literary work. This is not to say that the psychological critic must be a practicing psychologist, only that a certain level of competency with the psychological concepts is necessary.

Psychological criticism tends to fall into one of three categories: the *biographical,* the *character oriented,* and the *structural.* In *biographical* criticism, the critic assumes a reasonably straightforward connection between events and forces in the author's personal life and the concerns, subject matter, and themes of her/his art. The artwork becomes a rather complex symptom through which the critic attempts to diagnose the writer. Such "psychobiographical" critics consider the connections they explore as being central to an understanding of the work.

Thus, in Kate Chopin's "Story of an Hour," the critic might assert similarities between Chopin's life and her heroine' existence: Chopin represented her own traditional marriage in which her role as a woman was restricted in her depiction of Mrs. Mallard's relationship to Brently. She recreated her genteel, bourgeois existence as the wife of a Creole cotton trader in her portrayal of Mrs. Mallard's domestic situation. The biographical critic might note that Chopin suppressed her own needs and desires until her husband died, as does Mrs. Mallard. Chopin subsequently chose to pursue a career as a writer to support her six children; a choice Mrs. Mallard never has. The biographical critic might suggest that Chopin created versions of her own life not only in this story, but again and again in her fiction.

Beyond psychobiography, the psychological critic may choose to *analyze the behavior of a character or characters in a literary work.* Such a critical approach assumes that since literary characters are meant to be representations of real people, they may be analyzed in the same manner as real people. The psychological critic approaching "The Story of an Hour" might notice the description of the "repression" in Mrs. Mallard's face. That same term is used in Freudian psychology to indicate the mechanism whereby the conscious mind suppresses unacceptable desires into the unconscious, whence they cannot arise directly without great trauma. Equipped with this definition, the critic might see that it describes Mrs. Mallard's character quite accurately: in order to fulfill her own expectations of what a good wife should be, Mrs. Mallard has repressed any feelings of dissatisfaction with her husband in particular and marriage in general. It is only through the unexpected shock of her husband's death that Mrs. Mallard's repressed feelings can surface, and their appearance is traumatic, heralded by "her bosom . . . [rising and falling] . . . tumultuously." The critic might note that Mrs. Mallard experiences the return of these repressed feelings as if they come from outside herself, as "something coming to her," as "this thing that was approaching to posses her," and that she struggles "to beat it back with her will." Her feelings are so unacceptable to Mrs. Mallard that she projects them outside herself and contests them to the end. The critic might note that it is not until Mrs. Mallard has accepted her feelings (or been overwhelmed by them) that she can articulate them: "free, free, free!" Having accepted what she had repressed, Mrs. Mallard achieves a new level of personal wholeness, indicated by her speaking of herself as free in "[b]ody and soul," that is, in a manner that emphasizes her integration physically and mentally. Like other critics, the psychological critic would recognize the irony of the story's ending: Mrs. Mallard integrates what she has so long repressed, and in so doing makes herself susceptible to the fatal shock of her husband's reappearance.

Finally, the psychological critic may choose to examine the way in which the literary work itself enacts psychological concepts. Such *structuralist psychological criticism* attempts to psychologize the literary text, treating it as a psychologist might treat a patient. The psychological critic looks to find the psychological principles at work in the construction of a given work. The critic approaching "The Story of an Hour" might find that, in addition to presenting a protagonist who represses information from herself, the story itself represses information from the reader. While the story wants to be about Mrs. Mallard's dawning realization of freedom, its language indicates that she is not free, that she is still acted upon by outside forces. It, therefore, contains a series of rhetorical Freudian slips. Mrs. Mallard is not in control of her own body: she sits "motionless, except when a sob . . . [shakes] her." Her awareness of her own freedom is "something . . . [approaching] to possess her." Even when she accepts her joy at her new freedom, Mrs. Mallard "[drinks] in a very elixir of life through that open window," taking it into herself from the outside. Such an interpretation has much in common with that offered by deconstruction; both critical approaches look to discover what other meanings may be present in the literary text than the seemingly obvious one.

The examples we have considered have employed principles drawn from Freudian psychology. They need not have: we could as easily have used the work of Lacan, Kristeva, or any number of other psychologists (and psychological critics) to analyze "The Story of an Hour." The benefit to psychological criticism is that it allows us to speak of dimensions of the work neglected by the critical schools we have considered thus far. As is always the case with literary criticism, however, the best psychological criticism is that which remains rooted in the text, drawing its insights from the words on the page.

READER RESPONSE CRITICISM

Reader response criticism is grounded in certain assumptions about literary texts and their readers. The first is that texts have their existence in the reading: until a reader is engaged with the words on the page, we cannot speak of them as having meaning. Therefore, literary texts must be understood rhetorically, which is to say, for the effect they have on an audience. As Stanley Fish, one of the leading proponents of this school, has claimed, the critic should describe not what a poem is, but what it does. The reader response critic seeks to analyze the ways in which a given text arouses expectations that it then fulfills or frustrates. The emphasis is on understanding the text as a site where readers may produce meaning. Reader response critics differ in terms of how much independence they give to the text as a separate object of study. Louise Rosenblatt, for example, views the reading process as interactive, as "transitive," as an interaction between the world of the reader and the world of the text. Norman Holland envisions the reading process as a re-creation based on a dynamic interaction between a reader who has a particular "identity theme," a particular personality pattern, and a text that is re-created and shaped by the demands of the reader's identity theme. Holland theorizes that identity replicates itself—in all acts of living and of reading. David Bleich, another reader response theorist, contends in his early works, *Reading and Feeling* (1975) and *Subjective Criticism* (1978), that the reader response process primarily is individual and subjective and that the interpretation of a work is based on the reader's subjective response to it: the reader's "resymbolization" of that work. In his more recent work, *The Double Perspective: Language, Literacy, and Social Relations* (1988), Bleich acknowledges the role of gender and social context in shaping the reader's "resymbolization" of a work. What finally accounts for and governs response? Are there only totally idiosyncratic, subjective individual responses to works? For reader response critics, the reading process always will be personal; this is not to say, however, that such an approach must lapse into hopeless relativism and subjectivism. Reader response criticism is, as its name indicates, not only about the reader, but also about the response to a specific text. The best reader response criticism describes the reactions evoked by specific features of the text. In addition, the totality of response depends on what Stanley Fish labels "the interpretive community of readers." That is, part of the process is influenced by the intellectual community and concerns of readers. The community helps shape the intellectual background—the approach, views, and values—of the reader. Reader response critics also maintain that interpretation of a text may change depending on when a person reads a work. People read differently at different phases of their lives. Part of this process is determined by cultural context. The world of the 2000s in the United States, for example, contrasts drastically with the world of the 1950s in the United States.

The student's essay in chapter 9 is a reader response to "The Story of an Hour." The writer compares Mrs. Mallard's entrapment and desire for freedom with her own situation: her own marriage and yearning for autonomy. Reader response criticism may begin with highly personal responses, as the freewrites that follow demonstrate. In them, the writer reflects on the changes in her view of "The Story of an Hour" at varying stages of her life.

> When I first read "The Story of an Hour," I thought about how entrapped Mrs. Mallard was and how limited her life and her options were. She seemed totally cowed by the authority figures in her life: her sister, her husband. She seemed spineless.
>
> I tasted her single delightful moment of freedom and felt sorry for her. I truly felt pity. As a young twenty-two year old, I couldn't imagine a life without infinite possibility.
>
> I reread the story in my thirties when I taught it in a creative writing class to a group of older, returning women students. I saw it as a story of awakenings. I saw it as a reflection of changing values. She recognized her own oppression. She realized a possibility for freedom. That opening up was vividly depicted in her looking out the window.
>
> That view of the story very much seemed to go with the times, with the burgeoning of the women's movement in the mid 1970s, with the faith that roles for women could be, as Adrienne Rich said, "reenvision(ed)." It was all in the recognition of oppression and the opening up. Writing was an act of consciousness. Mrs. Mallard's opening up of consciousness seemed the center of the work and her death—just at the point of dawning awareness—seemed tragic.
>
> As I reread the work to teach it again in my forties, what strikes me anew is imprisonment. Roles are still being redefined—but not as quickly or as easily. Women are still trapped. Women are still not able to let go of traditional roles. Many women are still caught in the same bind: the struggle between duty and responsibility and self-fulfillment.
>
> Mrs. Mallard's imprisonment and her only way out—death—seem more poignant—and even more realistic—now.

These responses represent the reader exploring her own changing response to the story. The next step in developing a critical essay would be for the writer to establish how her feelings are grounded in specific features of the text.

As criticism moves away from concentrating solely on the text and toward embracing both the writer and the reader, it also moves toward suggesting the place of the text within the larger social order. Sociological critics analyze the work within its cultural context. Treatment is given to the ways in which the text both mirrors and is defined by the social and cultural concerns of the age.

FEMINIST CRITICISM

One important form of sociological criticism is *feminist theory,* which views the work in terms of sexual politics. To talk about "sexual politics" is to talk about how the unequal distribution of power operates in male/female relationships and how this imbalance structures many unspoken assumptions about the roles that men and women are expected to play within society. That these roles have traditionally been oppressive for women is the basic foundation of feminist thought. Feminist critics assert that throughout history, men have exercised political, social, and economic authority in ways that have privileged their own needs and interests while making the needs and interests of women secondary. Women's roles have been defined in ways that tend to support the patriarchal system; moreover, the male perspective is presented as the norm for humankind while the female perspective is presented as being somehow intrinsically "feminine" rather than simply "human." Simone de Beauvior describes this eloquently in "Woman as Other," where she says, "Thus humanity is male and man defines woman not in herself but as relative to him; she is not regarded as an autonomous being." Taking this unequal power dynamic as their basic starting point, feminist critics have raised many challenging questions about the ways in which literature is both written and read.

In the 1960s, feminist criticism sought to expose the patriarchal assumptions embedded in society by analyzing the representation of women in literary works written by men. In *Sexual Politics* (1970), Kate Millet took on the literary establishment by critiquing a number of canonical male novelists for the chauvinist assumptions underlying their characters. For instance, Millet claims that D. H. Lawrence associates activity and intellect with the masculine realm and sees any attempt by women to enter that realm as both unnatural and threatening to men. For Millet, literary criticism must address such chauvinism, because "sexual distinctions are political definitions." In *Thinking About Women* (1968), Mary Ellman considered the reader as well as the writer, noting that "the working rule is simple, basic: there must always be two literatures like two public toilets, one for Men and one for Women." The underlying claim in much feminist criticism of this period was that literature, no matter how "great" it might be, implicitly socializes men and women according to established categories of masculine and feminine.

In the 1970s, much feminist criticism was concerned with rediscovering and reevaluating women writers who had previously been excluded from the predominantly male canon of "great works." The Feminist Press in the United States and the Women's Press in Britain were committed to reprinting neglected works by women (for example, Rebecca Harding Davis's 1861 novel *Life in the Iron Mills*) and were instrumental in furthering feminist scholarship. One landmark study from this period is *A Literature of Their Own:*

British Women Novelists from Brontë to Lessing (1977) by Elaine Showalter. Showalter charts the struggle of female writers to establish themselves in a predominantly male tradition. Bringing together famous and less well-known writers, Showalter describes an alternative female tradition that first imitated male models, then challenged them, and finally established its own agenda. Showalter also coined the term "gynocriticism," a new approach that would specifically address "the psychodynamics of female creativity; linguistics and the problem of a female language; the trajectory of the individual or collective female literary career; literary history; and, of course, studies of particular writers and works." By focusing on issues such as female creativity and female language, Showalter raised a question that preoccupied feminist critics of the 1980s: Is there a particularly female mode of writing?

In the 1980s, a number of poststructuralist feminists came to the forefront of literary theory. Influenced, like other poststructuralists, by the French philosopher Michel Foucault, these critics saw language not as a transparent medium that reflects reality, but at a system of meanings that partially construct what we understand as reality. And, like Foucault, these critics saw language as one of the fundamental means by which power relations are maintained in a society. Therefore, challenging the accepted ways of speaking and writing can be a means of challenging inequitable power relations. According to Luce Irigaray, feminists have to work within patriarchal discourses, whether literary, philosophical, or scientific, and challenge the assumptions of those discourses, in the process "leaving open the possibility of a different language." Similarly, Hélène Cixous advocated an *écriture féminine,* or "feminine writing," that would provide an alternative to the "phallocentric" language of Western culture—language that, in privileging reason and logic, privileged principles associated with the masculine intellect. Cixous sought a nonlinear, fluid form of writing that allowed for instability and excess of meaning; she also insisted on the connection between women's creativity and their sexuality: "Write your self. Your body must be heard." Other feminists, however, have critiqued this strong identification between feminine writing and the female body. For some, to define female writing as unstructured and diffuse is to revert to the biological essentialism that for so many centuries has categorized women as not intellectual, not logical, not coherent.

Current feminism continues to work with all of the preceding issues, but has also become more interested in race and class in relation to gender, resisting the idea of a universal female nature or experience. Postcolonial feminism, for instance, considers the assumptions at work within a predominantly white, middle-class, and academic feminist tradition, and whether the terms and concepts used by such feminists are relevant to those in minority or non-Western cultures. A woman can have multiple identities in terms of race, class, and sexual preference, and the tendency now is to talk about "feminisms" rather than simply "feminism."

A basic feminist reading of "The Story of an Hour" would foreground the tragedy inherent in the plot: that in order to feel empowered and emotionally connected, a woman must suffer the death of her husband. This is a harsh statement to make, but a feminist critic would argue that for the Victorian woman, marriage was such an oppressive institution that most women had to sacrifice their own needs and ambitions, even their identities as autonomous individuals. The pain of such sacrifice could be so acute that the death of a husband, while traumatic, could also represent tremendous freedom—the kind of freedom that would not be available to a young single woman whose sole purpose in life, in this era, was to marry and have children. By analyzing the process of change in Mrs. Mallard, the feminist critic might note the initial negativity of her portrayal: she is weak, emotionally and physically, even before the news of her husband's death. She sinks into a "comfortable, roomy armchair"—the symbol of her domestic entrapment—and is "pressed down by a physical exhaustion that seemed haunted her body and seemed to reach into her soul." Her dawning consciousness, however, is expressed positively in terms of the natural world, with images of spring and renewal: "the tops of the trees that were all aquiver with the new spring life." In this way, the text affirms Mrs. Mallard's process of self-empowerment, which becomes fully realized when she whispers, "Free! Body and soul free!" By encouraging the reader to empathize with Mrs. Mallard, this text communicates a powerful feminist message. But the feminist critic might also question the text's underlying assumption: that Mrs. Mallard is so much the victim of social institutions that only the death of her husband can free her. This is not, perhaps, such an inspiring message for women seeking to challenge those institutions.

GENDER CRITICISM

Gender criticism is related to feminist criticism in that both are interested in how sexual difference functions socially and politically. However, gender criticism has several important differences. Firstly, gender criticism is not as woman-centered as feminist criticism. As Myra Jehlen puts it, "*The Adventures of Huckleberry Finn* is a man's book about a boy, and just as likely an object of gender criticism as writing by or about women." Jehlen focuses on the scene in which Huck, disguised as a girl, is discovered by the motherly Judith Loftus, who contrives a series of tests to prove that Huck is (as she suspects) actually a boy. By performing the tests of throwing, catching, and threading a needle like a boy, Huck shows that being a boy *is* largely a matter of performance—of playing a role according to certain learned behaviors. Jehlen describes this scene as "the reversal of feminity from nature to nurture—from sex to gender" and relates it to the broader themes of the novel: Huck learns through Jim that racial categories are also socially constructed, and he comes (however imperfectly) to learn another way of relating to Jim—as another person rather than as a black slave.

Secondly, gender criticism is also specifically interested in gay and lesbian issues, and many critics have adopted the term *queer theory* to describe their approach. Some of the issues they address are similar to those of feminist critics, but with a different emphasis. If there is a female tradition in literature, is there also a gay tradition? What happens when one rereads canonical authors from a perspective outside the category of heterosexual love? Are there identifiably gay strategies for reading and writing? How should a critic address homophobia in a literary text? How do we talk about these issues in the classroom? Such questions have motivated gender critics to reread such authors as Herman Melville, Emily Dickinson, Henry James, Willa Cather, and Virginia Woolf, writers whose conservative social contexts did not allow them to explore their sexual identities openly in their work. Other writers who were more open can now be appreciated for this openness. Walt Whitman, for instance, whose celebrations of male love were previously interpreted as asexual comradeship, can now be recognized as a great poet who was also a gay poet.

Within gender criticism there are those who wish to distinguish between male and female homosexuality. Some see women and men as essentially different regardless of their sexual preference. Some argue that society marginalizes the male homosexual differently from the female lesbian, and that, therefore, their lived experiences are different. Important questions are raised by this division. Is sexual preference or physiology the primary factor in identity formation? Are gay men psychologically more like women than other men? Does the biological fact of maternity create a distinctively feminine sensibility, regardless of whether the woman is straight or gay? Some critics, however, completely eschew the notion of innate male/female essences. According to Teresa de Lauretis, "sexuality, commonly thought to be a natural as well as a private matter, is in fact completely constructed in culture according to the political aims of the society's dominant class." But for all gender critics, the process of literary analysis is conceived of as a liberating project that can open up scholarly and classroom discussion to issues that have serious implications from all individuals and their communities. A readiness to explore the intersection of personal and social realities from the perspective of gender not only enriches the reading of literature, but also builds an understanding of the ways in which all cultures create categories of identification and difference that often need to be interrogated.

A gender critic would consider how individual characters in "The Story of an Hour" suggest particular things about the categories of "female" and "male" in Chopin's own social milieu. Several patterns emerge quite clearly: women are associated with the domestic sphere, with fragility and passivity, while men are associated with the public sphere, with control and activity. Thus, it is Richards who first learns about Brently Mallard's death in the newspaper office and brings that information back to Mrs. Mallard at home. She shuts herself away in her room and sinks into her "comfortable, roomy armchair," where, through the open window, she hears a peddler "crying his wares in the street below." The world through the open window is not one in which Mrs. Mallard can actively participate, but it calls to her powerfully as the implications of her husband's death begin to sink in: "she was drinking in a very elixir of life through that open window." When her husband appears at the end of the story, his entrance into the domestic sphere of the house is described so as to emphasize both his masculine activity and his self-control: "Somebody was opening the front door with a latchkey. It was Brently Mallard who entered, a little travel-stained, composedly carrying his gripsack and umbrella." The other male character, Richards, automatically moves to protect Mrs. Mallard—unsuccessfully, of course, but nonetheless reinforcing the role of men as active and women as passive. Such a reading need not undermine the effectiveness of the story, but would simply emphasize the extent to which all art, regardless of its aesthetic achievements, inevitably carries with it a sociological dimension.

NEW HISTORICISM

The *new historicism* represents another variant of sociological criticism. By reading a literary work through its historical and social context, the new historicist seeks to reconnect the text with the complexity of lived experience during its own time. In doing so, the new historicist emphasizes issues of social power and considers how a particular text dramatizes the social and political struggles of certain groups. In this way new historicism is quite different from "old" or traditional historicism, which tended to explored the thematic unity of a work against the backdrop of "official" history—that is, the broad sweep of famous personages and noteworthy events. In contrast, new historicism is concerned less with thematic unity and more with the contesting voices in a work, voices that, when we allow ourselves to hear them, may destabilize thematic unity rather than reinforce it. The new historicist considers how a literary work speaks to the power struggles of its own time, struggles that often involve the ordinary people that traditional historicism had marginalized or silenced. This impulse to make the marginal the center of study arises from the assumption that all forms of writing embody cultural realities. The new historicist considers newspaper articles, legal documents, letters, advertisements, and popular entertainment in relation to literary texts, arguing that all are equally important as representations of social reality.

New historicism has been significantly influenced by French philosopher Michel Foucault and his ideas about power and language. For Foucault (and many other poststructural theorists), language and meaning are unstable and constantly being contested. When we learn language, we also learn the complex network of values and codes that maintain our culture. For although every society has concrete ways of maintaining order—such as police and prison systems—every society also uses religious, educational, and mass media systems to maintain its status quo. In this way, power is dispersed through a culture in innumerable subtle ways. One might ask, how is it that we don't all see the world in exactly the same way? Certain charismatic dictators have indeed striven for such uniformity. But in democracies, where freedom of speech is upheld, surely language cannot work to control us in the same way? Foucault would argue that the diversity in democratic systems often conceals the operations of power. For instance, advertising teaches us from an early age that material possessions equal social status, and hence we grow up into earning and spending citizens who participate in and support the capitalist economy. We might even say that the mass media produce desires in us that we satisfy through consumer goods. In this way, power is productive as well as repressive and says, "Yes, do this" as well as "No, don't do that." New historicists are interested in Foucault's claim that "Power is everywhere; not because it embraces everything, but because it comes from everywhere." Power is everywhere because language is everywhere, and new historicists want to read literary texts as cultural sites where meaning, and hence power, is contested. And like Foucault, new historicists favor an interdisciplinary approach that combines a variety of cultural documents in order to explore how a particular period constructs its own versions of "truth" and "reality."

Interpretations of *The Tempest* by William Shakespeare illustrate some basic differences between traditional historicism and new historicism. Critics have always connected the play to the 1609 voyage of the English ship *Sea Venture,* which was wrecked on the Bermuda coast on the way to the Jamestown colony in Virginia. But "old" historicist readings have tended to emphasize the romance and adventure of discovery, celebrating this "brave new world" in which conflicts and confusions are resolved through the healing power of Prospero's magic. The play would be discussed according to its internal unities and Shakespeare's genius celebrated by showing how the play resolves structural and thematic tensions. *The Tempest* would be read as a timeless allegory of human endeavor in which benevolent power triumphs over disorder and darkness. And the historical background would be integrated into this vision of positive resolution. Thus, in 1947, G. Wilson Knight interpreted *The Tempest* as a celebration of England's colonial expansion, "especially her will to raise savage peoples from superstition and blood-sacrifice, taboos and witchcraft and the attendant fears and slaveries, to a more enlightened existence."

New historicism, rather than treating English colonialism as background material, would make it the focus of discussion. Shakespeare's construction of Caliban as incorrigibly violent, traitorous, and bestial is seen as emblematic of the European construction of the Native American, a construction that allowed Europeans to conquer and exploit these peoples with a minimum of moral discomfort. According to new historicism, *The Tempest* should be read alongside other cultural documents of the time and its political dimensions interrogated. But does *The Tempest* then romanticize and justify colonial expansion? New historicists tend to avoid such simplifications of complex works. For instance, Stephen Greenblatt, perhaps the most influential new historicist, while acknowledging that the play supports colonialist attitudes, also claims that "even within the powerful constraints of Shakespeare's Jacobean culture, the artist's imaginative mobility enables him to display cracks in the glacial front of princely power and to record a voice, the voice of the displaced and the oppressed, that is heard scarcely anywhere else in his own time. If it is the task of cultural criticism to decipher the power of Prospero, it is equally its task to hear the accents of Caliban."

The new historicist would read "The Story of an Hour," written in 1894, as articulating women's growing anger at their imprisonment within rigid social roles. Contemporaneous documents, such as articles from *Ladies Home Journal* or *Revolution,* the newspaper of the National Woman Suffrage Association, would be read alongside Chopin's story in order to illustrate the conflict for women of that time between a traditional marriage, in which the women belonged both sexually and economically to their husbands, and the independence advocated by such activists as Matilda Gage and Elizabeth Cady Stanton. In 1892 Stanton had given a speech, "The Solitude of Self," which argued for full civil rights for women, and other feminists of the time likewise argued that women should enjoy the privilege of "self-ownership" even within marriage, with the power to control their own reproductive destinies regardless of the marital "rights" of the husband. The new historicist might also look at the many medical documents of the time on the subject of female hysteria, at the dress and behavior codes that rendered women both fragile and nervous, and from such connections argue that Mrs. Mallard's "heart trouble" is a socially produced condition that manifests physically her mental suffering. In interpreting the text, a new historicist would consider how "The Story of an Hour" intersects with other cultural discourses on women and marriage, and how, in exposing the tyranny of a patriarchal social system, the story also demonstrates the seeming invincibility of that system. A new historicist might also be interested in the way that the medical discourse of the (undoubtedly) male doctors at the end fixes the meaning of Mrs. Mallard's death in a way that implicitly supports the existing patriarchy—she has died "of joy" at her husband's return.

POSTCOLONIAL CRITICISM

Postcolonial criticism considers the legacy of European colonialism as it is represented in literature. Drawing its inspiration and methodologies from other schools of literary criticism including deconstruction, psychological criticism, feminism, and new historicism, postcolonial criticism focuses its attention in two directions: at literary texts currently being produced in former colonial regions, to discover the ways in which they respond to the impact of colonialism and its aftermath on their cultures, and at canonical texts to discover evidence of colonial themes. Postcolonial critics consider the ways in which such contemporary writers as Chinua Achebe, Gabriel García Márquez, and Nadine Gordimer represent the legacy of colonialism in their work; they also consider the ways in which such canonical texts as Defoe's *Robinson Crusoe* and Shakespeare's *The Tempest* represent colonial situations. Although the work of such writers as Aime Cesaire and Franz Fanon is important to the establishment of postcolonial criticism, probably the most important text to the movement is Edward Said's *Orientalism* (1978). Said extensively explores the link between English and French colonialism in the Middle East and the representation of the Middle East in scholarly and creative literature. Sometimes intentionally, sometimes unintentionally, Said concludes, scholarly and creative writers worked in collusion with colonial powers to construct an image of the Middle East as "the Orient," a decadent, culturally backward region in need of the steadying hand of European rule. Subsequent critics have built on Said's work, developing the connection between history and literature. Homi Bhabha, in particular, has sought to develop a critical language adequate to describing postcolonial literature. In *The Location of Culture* (1994), Bhabha offers a number of terms to describe postcolonial works, among them mimicry and hybridity. By mimicry, Bhabha refers to postcolonial writers' retelling of such canonical narratives as *Robinson Crusoe* and *The Tempest,* through their mimicry of those sources causing us to understand them in new ways. By hybridity, Bhabha refers to postcolonial literature's drawing on sources from both the indigenous culture and the culture of its former colonizers. Postcolonial critics might apply Bhabha's ideas to a poem such as Derek Walcott's "Far Cry from Africa," finding in the poem a combination of poetic techniques drawn from European (and especially English-language) sources, and subject matter drawn from the colonial history of Africa and the Caribbean. In addition, the interpretation of *The Tempest* offered above as an example of new historicist criticism is the kind of work one might also as easily find being done by a postcolonial critic.

CONCLUSION

If one views a work through the lenses of many critical interpretations, the work becomes kaleidoscopic. The fear may arise that the text will disintegrate and not bear the pressure of so many critical approaches. The work, however, is a pattern of many layers, and one may focus on one layer without hopelessly smearing the whole design.

Moreover, not all works yield themselves to particular interpretations, and each framework for critical interpretation is not equally justified. In one class some years ago, for example, a student suggested that William Carlos Williams's "The Red Wheelbarrow" reveals the pervasive influence of a communist threat, foreshadowing the eventual takeover of the United States by communist forces. After all, the student contended, "the red wheelbarrow" was next to "the white chickens." This assertion was challenged by the other students, who argued that a political interpretation of the bucolic country scene seemed implausible, given what they knew of Williams's poetry, his motivations for writing, his artistic technique, and the relationship of that section of the poem to the themes of the work. In other words, this intellectual community of readers cited biographical, historical, and new critical bases for their response to the first student's interpretation. The community of readers pointed out more applicable interpretations of the poem. For this reason, it is also worth pointing out that the best critics tend to be eclectic, drawing on a variety of critical approaches in whatever combination seems most appropriate to the work at hand.

Critical interpretation leads ultimately to an enriched vision of the text: a pluralistic one in which many meanings coexist. Each interpretation must be contextualized. Each literary work is a particular confluence of linguistic, biographical, cultural realities—a single artifact of language that exhibits and represents those realities. This artifact has the power to sensitize a reader to the forces shaping values, to the ways in which interpretations of the world are based on these systems of values, and to prompt investigations of both the texts and the world in new and expansive ways.

GLOSSARY OF TERMS

abstract and concrete abstract language uses a high proportion of abstract nouns, which refer to concepts, qualities, or general conditions ("truth," "honesty," "poverty"). Concrete language, on the other hand, uses more concrete nouns, which refer to things perceptible through the senses ("house," "rain," "tree"). Effective writing balances the two, using specific details to illustrate abstract ideas.

act a major division in a play; each act normally is composed of several scenes.

aesthetic distance the emotional closeness of either writer or reader to a work of art.

affective responses the emotional responses, including feeling, remembering, and associating.

allegory a story in verse or prose that can be understood on both a literal and symbolic level. In *The Pilgrim's Progress* by John Bunyan (1678), Christian, the hero, embarks on a pilgrimage that takes him through the Slough of Despond, the Valley of the Shadow of Death, and so forth, until finally he reaches the Celestial City. Christian represents everyman, and his journey is an allegory of Christian salvation.

alliteration the repetition of consonant sounds for poetic effect, particularly at the beginnings of words. A famous example is Coleridge's description of the River Alph in "Kubla Khan": "Five miles meandering with a mazy motion" (chapter 8).

allusion a reference to historical events or figures, used to develop and deepen the meaning of a work (e.g., Plath's "Daddy").

ambiguity the state that exists when there are several legitimate interpretations of a literary work.

anaphora repetition of a word at the beginning of successive clauses or verses (e.g., Whitman's "Out of the Cradle").

anecdote a brief account of a story about an individual or an incident.

antagonist the character or force opposing the protagonist in a play.

anthropomorphism the endowment of animals with human thoughts and feelings.

anticlimax a move—in a sentence, stanza, paragraph, or literary work—from a noble tone to a less elevated one.

antihero a protagonist who is deliberately unheroic, i.e., often passive, ineffectual, or self-interested.

apex the height of the action in a drama.

archetype a theme, emblem, or character that reoccurs so frequently in all literature that it is accepted as universal. Examples include the theme of the quest, in which the protagonist sets out on a journey of self-discovery; the character of the femme fatale, or deadly woman; and the emblem of the rose, the symbol for romantic love.

argument a basic rhetorical mode that seeks, through logic and reason, to convince an audience by providing factual evidence to support a certain point of view.

aside in drama, words spoken in an undertone to the audience that are assumed to be inaudible to the other characters on stage.

assonance the repetition of similar vowel sounds, usually close together, for poetic effect. The first lines of Keats's "Ode on a Grecian Urn" contain a number of long /i/ sounds, creating a sensual, unhurried effect: "Thou still unravished br*i*de of qu*i*etness,/ Thou foster ch*i*ld of s*i*lence and slow t*i*me."

atmosphere the emotional ambience created by a writer through setting, action, and word choice. The opening scene of *Hamlet,* in which the ghost appears, has a forbidding, fearful atmosphere.

authorial intrusion when the author of a narrative seems to step out of the story and address the reader directly.

autobiography a biography written by the subject about herself or himself.

ballad a narrative poem, usually arranged in quatrains, that employs the rhyme scheme ABCB. There are two types. The folk ballad, a form of great antiquity, is composed and transmitted orally. It tells a dramatic story vividly and is anonymous. A literary ballad is a conscious imitation of this form by a poet. Many of the most famous literary ballads were written during the Romantic period, such as Coleridge's *Rime of the Ancient Mariner* and Keats's "La Belle Dame sans Merci."

bathos a pejorative term that describes what happens when a writer describes an honestly tragic situation in such an overblown way that the situation becomes unintentionally comic.

Beat movement a literary movement centered in the United States in the 1950s and distinguished by its attempt to combine socially marginal behavior with the quest for spiritual enlightenment (e.g., Ginsberg's "America").

Bildungsroman a German term meaning "novel of education," in which the fortunes of the protagonist are traced from early years to adulthood.

blank verse unrhymed iambic pentameter.

canon the group of literary works a given culture judges to possess special merit.

caricature the exaggeration of aspects or features of a character, usually for humorous or satiric purposes.

catastrophe the tragic conclusion of action in a play.

catharsis Aristotle's term for the therapeutic sense of emotional release supposedly felt by an audience that witnesses the tragic or terrifying onstage.

cause and effect a form of process analysis that explains the factors creating a certain situation or the consequences of a particular event. The downfall of Oedipus, for example, can be analyzed in terms of cause and effect.

character any person represented in a literary work. Characters are commonly described as being *round* (psychologically complex and convincing), *flat* (simplistic and often stereotypical), or *foils* (existing only to highlight certain aspects of the protagonist). It is also useful to distinguish between *dynamic* characters (those undergoing change) and *static* characters (those remaining unchanged).

chorus a group of players in Greek drama who provide a collective commentary on the action and the main characters. Although an essential part of Greek tragedy, a full chorus has rarely been used in English or American drama; two notable exceptions to this are Milton's *Samson Agonistes* (1671) and T. S. Eliot's *Murder in the Cathedral* (1935).

classification the process of grouping items together based on their similarities. Thus, poetry can be classified according to such categories as the sonnet, the ballad, or the ode.

cliché an overused, and hence ineffective, figure of speech such as "pretty as a picture" or "white as snow." Since the purpose of figurative language is to surprise the reader into a new way of seeing, writers should avoid clichés.

climax the point in a narrative or play at which a crisis is reached and resolution achieved.

colloquial expressions informal words and phrases that are a normal part of everyday speech but that are inappropriate in formal writing.

comedy a term usually applied to drama, although any work may have comic elements. There are many types of comedy (high, low, romantic, satiric, etc.), but overall the genre is characterized by its use of humor and the "happy ending." The comedy moves from complication to resolution, frequently resolving individual and social problems through marriage.

comic relief the insertion of a comic scene or character into a serious or tragic work in order to temporarily release some of the work's tension.

commedia dell'arte a sixteenth-century form of drama with mimes, skits, buffoonery, and such stereotypical characters as the harlequin and the young lover.

comparison-contrast the process of analyzing and determining similarities and differences in objects, phenomena, literary works, and so forth; often essays on literature compare character, theme, style. For organization of essays, see chapter 3.

conceit a figure of speech comparing two dissimilar things or states; an elaborate and extended metaphor. See chapter 10.

Confessional poets a group of American poets of the 1950s and 1960s distinguished by their concern with intensely personal subject matter (e.g., Sexton's "My Little Girl").

conflict an aspect of plot that concerns the tensions between opposing forces. Conflicts exist within characters, between or among characters, and between characters and such forces as nature, society, and the cosmos.

connotation the meanings or emotional associations evoked by a word.

couplets in poetry, two-line stanzas.

denotation the dictionary definition(s) of a word.

denouement the part of a narrative that follows the climax, in which any remaining unresolved plot elements are resolved.

deus ex machina literally "god from the machine," this term from classical Greek drama is applied to plot complications that are resolved through unnatural or strained means.

dialect a manner of speaking peculiar to an individual, class, or region that may differ considerably from the standard language of the country. While perfectly acceptable within its own context, dialect should be avoided in most formal writing, as the writer cannot assume a knowing audience. Dialect is most frequently found in fiction or drama, where it is used to make individual characters more realistic.

dialogue the direct speech of characters in any literary context.

Dirty Realism an American school of fiction of the 1970s and 1980s that focused on the minute, and frequently unpleasant, details of people's daily lives (e.g., Carver's "Cathedral").

double plot a second story that becomes fascinating on its own merits and enlarges the meaning of the main plot.

drafting composing and concentrating on organization, development, and fluency in the early stages of the writing process.

drama any work meant to be performed on a stage by actors. Usually, the work is divided into acts and scenes.

dramatic irony See *irony.*

dramatic poetry poetry in which the speaker becomes an actor, as in a monologue or a soliloquy.

editing the stage of the writing process concerned with sharpening word choice and style to clarify meaning and to strengthen presentation of message.

elegy a poem that expresses mourning for the death of a particular person and/or for mortality in general.

Elizabethan or Shakespearean sonnet a fourteen-line poem comprising three quatrains and a final couplet. The quatrains express and develop a dilemma or proposition to which the couplet offers a response (e.g., Shakespeare's "Let Me Not to the Marriage of True Minds").

end rhymes rhymes that occur at the end of verse lines.

enjambment in poetry, a statement that runs on into the next line.

epic poetry poems derived from oral tradition that describe the adventures and accomplishments of great heroes.

epigram a short, pithy, generally humorous observation presented as a general truth.

epigraph the inscription on the title page of a book, which may be a quotation from another literary work or an original remark by the author and which calls attention to the book's theme.

epiphany in a short story, a sudden moment of insight when a character discovers a truth important to the story (e.g., Joyce's "Eveline").

essay a concise prose discussion of a limited topic for a general audience.

evidence the use of facts, statistics, personal experiences, or the opinions of authorities to support a writer's claims or conclusions.

explication the close reading of a text, usually involving line-by-line analysis.

exposition intended primarily to inform, this rhetorical mode can take a variety of forms, such as classification, definition, process analysis, comparison/contrast, and cause and effect.

extended metaphor see *conceit.*

fable a short tale told to illustrate a moral, in which the characters are animals whose character traits represent human traits.

figurative language language that includes figures of speech.

figures of speech expressions that are based on comparisons, either explicit or implied, and that are intended to be interpreted imaginatively rather than literally. Their purpose is to surprise the reader into a new way of seeing. Among the most common are *simile, metaphor, personification, hyperbole,* and *litotes.*

first person narrative point of view in which the narrator speaks as "I" and is a participant in the narrative (e.g., Baldwin's "Sonny's Blues").

flashback a term derived from cinema, referring to any scene inserted into a literary work in order to show an earlier event.

foreshadowing using the current action in a literary work to anticipate later events.

free verse verse with no regular meter or line length. Although it may appear haphazard at first, free verse can acquire rhythms and melodies of its own.

Freytag's Pyramid Gustav Freytag conceived of plot in drama as rising action, climax, and falling action that leads to a dénouement. His conception took the shape of a pyramid.

generalization a broad statement that may well be true but that is not supported by concrete evidence. Generalizations lack substance, and so essays should not rely on them.

genre a literary type or class. The major classical genres are *tragedy, comedy, satire, epic,* and *lyric.*

hamartia a tragic error in judgment in classical Greek drama (e.g., Sophocles's *Oedipus Rex*).

Harlem Renaissance a cultural movement of the 1920s centered in Harlem, New York, which celebrated African American experience and attempted to find literary forms suited to it (e.g., Hughes's "Let America Be America Again").

hubris in classical Greek drama, overweening pride (e.g., Sophocles's *Oedipus Rex*).

hyperbole a figure of speech that uses deliberate exaggeration, usually for comic effect.

iamb a poetic foot consisting of an unstressed syllable followed by a stressed syllable, as in "bĕhóld."

illustration the use of concrete examples to support a generalization.

imagery concrete language that appeals to the senses. An image does not have to be interpreted literally; indeed, many are conveyed by figurative language. (See *figures of speech.*)

in media res literally "in the middle of things," beginning a story in the midst of the action.

inductive and deductive reasoning two forms of everyday thinking. Inductive reasoning uses specific examples to formulate a general truth; deductive reasoning takes a general truth and seeks to demonstrate it through examples.

interior monologue in a work of fiction, an extended passage relating a character's thoughts (e.g., Busch's "Ralph the Duck").

intrigue scheme in a drama in which a character entraps another person who is naïve, trusting, and vulnerable.

introduction the first section of a paper, which should get the reader's attention, state the thesis, and establish the tone and point of view. In most college writing assignments, one paragraph will be sufficient. In longer papers, the introductory material may consist of several paragraphs.

irony a complex attitude that relies on contrast for its effect. There are three basic types. *Verbal irony* occurs when what is said contrasts with what is meant (e.g., "You are really too kind" said with great bitterness). *Dramatic irony* contrasts what is expected with what actually happens (e.g., a character laughs at another's misfortune, unaware that the same misfortune is happening to her). *Structural irony* used a particular device to sustain irony throughout the entire work, i.e., the naïve hero who constantly misinterprets events.

jargon the specialized vocabulary of a particular field or trade, which the general reader is unlikely to understand.

journal a form of personal writing concerning the self. The presumed audience is the author.

Kmart Realism a school of American fiction during the 1980s distinguished by its use of the icons of popular culture to make serious points (e.g., Mason's "Shiloh").

komos revel in classical Greek drama, from which we derive the word *comedy.*

literary theory/criticism a conceptual framework for understanding and interpreting a work of art. (See Appendix A.)

litotes the opposite of *hyperbole,* this figure of speech uses understatement for humorous effect.

lyric any short, non-narrative poem that deals subjectively with the thoughts and feelings of a single speaker. Although written in the first person, its sentiments are not necessarily those of the poet, but may be those of an adopted *persona.*

Magical Realism a twentieth-century literary movement associated with Central and South America in which the fantastical and the everyday are presented as equally "real" (e.g., Garcia Marquez, "The Handsomest Drowned Man in the World").

meditation a reflection on a scene that moves from observation of the object to consideration of metaphysical ideas.

memoir the remembrances of a public figure and/or of an historical era; an autobiographical form.

metafiction fiction that reflects on the subject and writing of fiction.

metaphor an implied comparison that brings together two dissimilar things without the use of "like" or "as." For instance, the metaphorical equivalent of Burns's famous simile "My love is like a red, red rose" would be "My love is a red, red rose."

Metaphysical poets a seventeenth-century English literary movement, whose poetry combined passion and reason through highly innovative conceits (e.g., Donne's "The Flea"). (See *conceit.*)

meter the pattern of stressed and unstressed syllables in lines of verse, each unit being termed a *foot.* / denotes a long or *stressed* syllable; ˘ denotes a short or *unstressed* syllable. The most common feet in English verse are:

iamb:	˘/	e.g., desire (˘ /)
trochee:	/˘	e.g., women (/ ˘)
anapest:	˘˘/	e.g., in a flash (˘ ˘ /)
dactyl:	/˘˘	e.g., yesterday (/ ˘ ˘)
spondee:	//	e.g., outwith (/ /)

In addition, lines are named according to the number of feet they contain:

monometer: one foot
dimeter: two feet
trimeter: three feet
tetrameter: four feet
pentameter: five feet
hexameter: six feet
heptameter: seven feet
octameter: eight feet

metonymy the substitution of one thing for another with which it is closely associated, such as using "the White House" to refer to the president.

mimesis the literary process of attempting to create a convincing and uninterrupted illusion of real life.

miracle plays a dramatic genre presenting Christian saints' lives and miracles.

modernism A European and American literary movement of the first half of the twentieth century, distinguished by its use of experimental techniques, its concern with individual psychology, and its concern with the decay of civilization (e.g., Eliot's "Love Song of J. Alfred Prufrock").

monologue a sustained speech by a single character, either with or without a direct audience (e.g., Shakespeare's *Hamlet,* III, ii, 46–76).

mood the atmosphere or tone of a literary work, created not only by the characters and events but also by the author's style and choice of language.

morality plays a dramatic genre that allegorized Christian values.

motif a theme or image that occurs repeatedly within a literary work and thus acquires symbolic value.

motivation the reason a character performs an action.

multiculturalism the increasing emphasis on race, class, and gender in education. In recognition of the diversity of most classrooms, the traditional curriculum is being modified to encompass the achievements and experiences of many groups.

mystery plays dramas presenting biblical stories.

myth a story involving supernatural beings that usually explains the cosmos and the mysteries of life and death.

narration essay form that seeks to recreate a series of events (i.e., a "story") as vividly as possible using descriptive detail.

narrative poetry form of poetry that tells a story.

narrator person telling a story.

novel an extended work of prose fiction that, although traditionally realistic, can be highly experimental.

novella an extended work of fiction, longer and more expansive than a short story, but shorter than a novel.

objective and subjective terms used to describe the extent and type of the author's involvement with her or his work. *Objective* writing is primarily factual and maintains a detached, impersonal tone. *Subjective* writing reveals the author's feelings and attitudes and often seeks to involve the reader emotionally.

octave see *Petrarchan sonnet.*

ode a formal and elaborate lyric poem that praises either a person or a thing. The *Pindaric Ode,* named after the classical Greek poet Pindar, traditionally celebrates a noteworthy individual upon some public occasion. The *Horatian Ode,* named after the classical Roman poet Horace, is in contrast private and personal (e.g., Keats's "Ode on a Grecian Urn").

onomatopoeia the use of words that imitate the sounds they represent, such as "crash" and "buzz."

organization the way a writer chooses to develop ideas in both paragraphs and essays, according to the purpose and audience. The five main methods are: (1) *deductive,* from general statement to specific example, (2) *inductive,* from specific example to general statement, (3) *climactic,* from least to most important, (4) *chronological,* according to time sequence, (5) *spatial,* according to physical organization.

oxymoron a word or phrase composed of two words that apparently contradict each other, such as "bittersweet."

pageants the platforms used in productions of mystery, miracle, and morality plays.

parable a story with a moral, often religious, the purpose of which is instruction. See discussion of the prodigal son in chapter 9.

paradox an apparent contradiction that resolves itself on a deeper level.

paragraph a group of logically related sentences that together develop a central idea. This idea is stated broadly in a topic sentence and illustrated with supporting detail. Paragraphs break information down into smaller units, which the reader can assimilate more easily.

paraphrase a detailed restatement of information in words other than those of the original source.

parody the imitation of a certain author's style, tone, or attitude with the intent to ridicule. The technique is one of exaggeration.

pastoral a poem celebrating the idyllic nature of country life.

pathetic fallacy the attribution of human emotions to the nonhuman, used particularly when the writing is clichéd or melodramatic.

pathos the aspect of a narrative that causes its reader to feel pity or sorrow for the various characters.

performance art a form of American art of the 1980s and 1990s, distinguished by its combination of aspects of drama and improvisation (e.g., Smith's "Twilight Los Angeles").

persona from the Latin for "mask," this term originally referred to the false face of clay worn by actors. It now denotes the identity adopted by an author for any literary work.

personification the attribution of human qualities to inanimate things for poetic effect.

Petrarchan sonnet named for a famous Italian poet, Petrarch, this sonnet is composed of an eight-line *octave* (composed of two *quatrains*) and a six-line *sestet* (composed of two *tercets*). The octave states a problem or proposition to which the sestet replies; the shift from octave to sestet in the ninth line is called the *volta.*

philosophical treatise an extended formal meditation on a philosophical, religious, or political subject (see chapter 12).

picture frame stage an innovation in European drama that created the effect of framing the stage.

plagiarism the representation of another's words or ideas as though they were the writer's own. This academic theft, whether conscious or unconscious, is a serious offense. To avoid plagiarism, document all outside information.

plot the arrangement of events in a narrative or dramatic work. When two story lines are developed in equal length, the work is said to have a *double plot.* When one story line dominates the other, the latter is said to be the *subplot.*

point of view the perspective from which a story is told. Events can be narrated in the *first person* (the narrator is part of the action), or the *third person* (the narrator is outside the action). Narration in the *second person* is rare. An *omniscient narrator* uses the third person and is all-knowing.

postmodernism A European and American literary movement of the second half of the twentieth century distinguished by its conspicuous irony and its self-conscious concern with the nature of art (e.g., Busch's "Ralph the Duck").

premises supporting statements.

prewriting the generating of ideas prior to the initial drafting of a paper. The common strategies are *freewriting* and *brainstorming.* Freewriting involves writing nonstop for a short period of time. The writer is not concerned with grammar or spelling but with the free association of ideas. Brainstorming involves quickly listing anything and everything related to the topic. Ideas can then be grouped or subdivided to establish what is relevant.

primary and secondary sources *primary sources* are original materials, whether novels, speeches, scientific reports, or government documents. *Secondary sources* are studies of those materials. Thus, Wilfred Owen's poem "Arms and the Boy" is a primary source; a critical analysis of its themes is a secondary source.

proofreading the final stage of the writing process, in which the writer rereads the finished draft carefully for grammatical, spelling, or mechanical errors.

proscenium arch a frame enclosing the stage area behind which the front curtain hangs.

protagonist the principal character in a work of drama or fiction.

purpose and audience a writer's purpose, generally speaking, can be *to entertain, to explain, to explore,* or *to persuade.* Often several purposes will overlap, but the writer's overall intention will be closely tied to the audience being addressed. This can be any individual or group, whether the self, as in a journal entry, or the general public, as in a newspaper article.

quatrains in poetry, four-line stanzas.

realism although all literature is clearly artificial, certain works can be said to represent life more accurately than others. Such works attend to the minutiae of everyday experience and present characters and events realistically rather than romantically.

revision this stage of the writing process involves rewriting a rough draft to improve both form and content. *Purpose* and *audience* should be reconsidered, as should the overall focus and development of the paper. Material may be cut, expanded, or moved around, while the language itself should be reworked for clarity and conciseness.

rhetorical question a question to which no answer is expected, or to which the answer is assumed to be self-evident. Used primarily for stylistic effect, this device encourages an emotional response from the reader and, thus, is often used in persuasive writing.

rhetorical situation purpose, audience, occasion, and point of view for the generation of a piece of writing. It is mainly a term used for the analysis of nonfiction. See, for example, the speech by Sojourner Truth (chapter 7).

rhyme in English poetry, the repetition of the last accented vowel and all succeeding sounds (e.g., boy–joy).

rhyme scheme fixed pattern of rhymes characterizing a poem or its stanzas.

rhythm in poetry or prose, the patterns of beats that establish the rise and fall of sounds; cadence. See the analysis of rhythm in Shakespeare's sonnet, "My Mistress' Eyes Are Nothing Like the Sun" in chapter 10 and the chanting patterns in Anna Lee Walters's "My Name Is 'I Am Living' " in chapter 8.

Romanticism a European literary movement of the late eighteenth and early nineteenth centuries distinguished by its concern with the free and subjective expression of passion, pathos, and personal feelings (e.g., Coleridge's "Kubla Khan").

satire literature that exposes folly and seeks to correct it through ridicule. While the irony employed in satire may be amusing, the intent is not simply to entertain but to enlighten an audience. Swift's essay "A Modest Proposal" is a classic example.

scansion the process of measuring poetry, of marking accented and unaccented syllables, and of dividing lines into feet in order to discern the metrical pattern of the poem and to notice deviations from the pattern.

scene a unit of continuous action in a play in which the setting remains unchanged. Groups of interrelated scenes comprise larger units of the work, known as *acts.*

sestet See *Petrarchan sonnet.*

setting the time, place, and/or environment in which a literary work occurs.

sexist language the misrepresentation or exclusion of either sex. One of the most common forms of sexist language is the use of the male pronoun "he" for an individual of unknown gender.

Shakespearean sonnet see *Elizabethan sonnet.*

short story a fictional narrative of more limited scope than the novel, often focusing on a single incident or character. It is a challenging medium, as the theme must be developed and brought to a satisfactory conclusion within approximately thirty pages.

simile a figure of speech that compares two unlike things using "like" or "as." See *metaphor.*

slave narrative a form of nineteenth century autobiography that documents a slave's journey from bondage to freedom.

soliloquy a dramatic convention in which a character, alone on the stage, voices her or his private thoughts. It is generally assumed that the feelings expressed are sincere (e.g., *Hamlet,* III, i, 56–88).

sonnet a lyric poem of fourteen lines, usually in iambic pentameter, that employs a highly formal pattern of organization. Although there are a great number of possible rhyme schemes, the two most common are the *English* (also known as the *Elizabethan* and the *Shakespearean*) and the *Italian* (also known as the *Petrarchan*). The English consists of three quatrains and a concluding couplet and deploys the rhyme scheme ABAB/CDCD/EFEF/GG. The Italian consists of an octave and a setset and deploys the rhyme scheme ABBA/ABBA/CDC/CDC.

stanza the basic unit of structure in a poem. Each unit consists of a group of interrelated lines arranged in a pattern that is usually repeated throughout the poem.

stereotypes easily recognized types of characters, such as the fool.

stock characters see *stereotypes.*

subplots secondary plot or plots in drama or fiction.

summary a concise restatement of a longer piece of writing, containing only the essential information.

surprise essential element of plot that contradicts the audience's or reader's expectations.

Surrealism a European literary movement of the 1920s and 1930s that emphasizes the author's imaginative expression of dreams and other psychic states reached through the unconscious mind (e.g., Valenzuela's "The Verb To Kill").

suspense element of plot that builds excitement and uncertainty about the resolution of events.

syllabic verse a method of composing poetry that disregards accentual feet and creates rhythm through a regularized pattern of counted syllables.

syllogism a deductive argument in three parts that moves from a major and minor premise to a logical conclusion. For example: a) water is wet; b) rain is water; therefore c) rain is wet.

symbol an object, character, or action that stands for something more than itself. In *"Master Harold" . . . and the Boys,* ballroom dancing symbolizes social harmony.

symbolist dramas form of drama that features many traditional poetic symbols, allegorical names, and a dreamlike atmosphere. All of the action would be interpreted symbolically.

synecdoche the use of a part of something to stand for its whole, i.e., saying "My heart belongs to you" to indicate that the entire self belongs to the beloved.

synonyms words that are close enough in meaning to be interchangeable. Exact synonyms are rare, however, since all words have slightly different connotations.

syntax the arrangement of words within a sentence and the way this arrangement can affect meaning.

tercets three-line stanzas.

Theater of the Absurd a form of drama prevalent in the 1950s and associated with such playwrights as Pinter, Ionesco, and Beckett. Although literature has always explored the potentially comic aspects of humankind, the Theater of the Absurd reflects explicitly the twentieth-century philosophical view of a meaningless universe in which there is no coherence and little dignity. The plays themselves are, therefore, intentionally meaningless.

theme the central idea or message in a work. It can be expressed either directly or indirectly.

thesis statement usually contained in the introduction, the thesis statement establishes the focus of the essay—what it is about—in one or two sentences. Experienced writers sometimes use an *implied thesis statement,* where the purpose of the essay is clear without being directly stated. Student writers, however, should ensure that the thesis statement is identifiable.

tone created by both word choice and syntax, tone reflects the author's attitude toward the subject matter, which can be humorous, sarcastic, and so forth.

topic sentence the concise statement of the idea being developed within a paragraph. The topic sentence focuses the paragraph in the same way that the thesis statement focuses the essay.

tragedy a term usually applied to drama, tragedy traditionally traces the downfall of an initially noble character in a serious and elevated manner. In classical Greek drama, this downfall is invariably attributed to some tragic flaw in the protagonist, a device also seen frequently in Shakespearean tragedy (e.g., *Hamlet*). Modern tragedy is often said to lack the grandeur of classical tragedy, perhaps because it aims at broader social commentary and deals more with ordinary people in everyday situations.

tragic flaw see *hamartia.*

tragic hero protagonist in a tragedy; a person of high moral stature whose downfall is, nonetheless, the result of some tragic flaw (e.g., Shakespeare's Hamlet).

tragicomedy a mixture of tragedy and comedy created by the classical Roman dramatist Plautus.

transitional expressions essential to effective writing, these signal connections between ideas, thus allowing fluency between sentences and paragraphs. Some common transitional expressions are *however, therefore, consequently,* and *on the other hand.*

triplets in poetry, three-line stanzas.

unity of action in the *Poetics,* the classical Greek philosopher Aristotle wrote that every part of the action in a play must be integral to the whole. Any missing or extraneous part destroys the play's integrity.

vignette a sketch or a short scene in a larger work written with great skill for the purpose of either creating a vivid, resonant picture or illuminating some larger aspect of a work's theme.

villanelle a poem consisting of five *tercets* and a *quatrain,* based on two rhymes and with systematic repetitions of lines one and three of the first tercet (e.g., Thomas's "Do Not Go Gentle into That Good Night").

voice the individual personality of the author. Although a work may have many characters and may shift in tone according to the subject matter, there will remain a distinct authorial presence beyond even a first-person narrator. Student writers should recognize the importance of allowing their own voices to develop in their writing.

LITERARY CREDITS

Chinua Achebe, "Girls at War" from GIRLS AT WAR AND OTHER STORIES by Chinua Achebe, copyright © 1972, 1973 by Chinua Achebe. Used by permission of Doubleday, a division of Random House, Inc., and Harold Ober Associates, Inc.

Marjorie Agosin, "A Visit to the Mothers of the Plaza de Mayo" from THE MOTHERS OF PLAZA DE MAYO: THE STORY OF RENEE EPELBAUM by Marjorie Agosin. Copyright © 1990 by Marjorie Agosin. Reprinted by permission of The Red Sea Press, Inc.

Anna Akhmatova, "Lot's Wife" by Anna Akhmatova from SELECTED POEMS translated by D. M. Thomas. Reprinted by permission of John Johnson Ltd.

Sherman Alexie, "This Is What It Means to Say Phoenix, Arizona" from THE LONE RANGER AND TONTO FISTFIGHT IN HEAVEN by Sherman Alexie. Copyright © 1993 by Sherman Alexie. Used by permission of Grove/Atlantic, Inc. Excerpt from SMOKE SIGNALS by Sherman Alexie, p. 148. Courtesy of Hyperion.

Agha Shahid Ali, "Postcard from Kashmir" by Agha Shahid Ali from THE HALF-INCH HIMALAYAS. Reprinted by permission of Wesleyan University Press.

Maya Angelou, "Still I Rise" from AND STILL I RISE by Maya Angelou. Copyright © 1978 by Maya Angelou. Used by permission of Random House, Inc.

Gloria Anzaldúa, "Horse" and "To Live in the Borderlands Means You" by Gloria Anzaldúa from BORDERLANDS/LA FRONTERA: THE NEW MESTIZA © 1987 by Gloria Anzaldúa. Reprinted by permission of Aunt Lute Books.

Margaret Atwood, "You fit into me" from POWER POLITICS copyright © 1996 by Margaret Atwood. "Game After Supper" from THE CIRCLE GAME copyright © 1998 by Margaret Atwood. Reprinted by permission of Stoddart Publishing Co. Limited.

W. H. Auden, "Musée des Beaux Arts," copyright 1940 and renewed 1968 by W. H. Auden from W. H. AUDEN: COLLECTED POEMS by W. H. Auden. Used by permission of Random House, Inc.

James Baldwin, "Sonny's Blues" by James Baldwin. Copyright © 1965 by James Baldwin. Originally published in PARTISAN REVIEW. Copyright renewed. Collected in GOING TO MEET THE MAN, published by Vintage Books. Reprinted by arrangement with the James Baldwin Estate.

Amiri Baraka, "Preface to a Twenty Volume Suicide Note" by Amiri Baraka. Reprinted by permission of Sterling Lord Literistic, Inc. Copyright © by Amiri Baraka.

Matsuo Bashō, "Blue Heron" by Matsuo Bashō. JAPANESE LINKED POETRY. Princeton, NJ: Princeton University Press, 1979. Translated by Earl Miner.

Gwendolyn Brooks, "The Chicago Defender Sends a Man to Little Rock" and "We Real Cool" by Gwendolyn Brooks from BLACKS. Reprinted by Permission of The Estate of Gwendolyn Brooks.

Frederick Busch, "Ralph the Duck" by Frederick Busch from ABSENT FRIENDS. New York, NY, 1991.

Albert Camus, "The Myth of Sisyphus" from THE MYTH OF SISYPHUS AND OTHER ESSAYS by Albert Camus, translated by Justin O'Brien, copyright © 1955 by Alfred A. Knopf, a division of Random House, Inc. Used by permission of Alfred A. Knopf, a division of Random House, Inc.

Raymond Carver, "Cathedral" from CATHEDRAL by Raymond Carver, copyright © 1983 by Raymond Carver. Used by permission of Alfred A. Knopf, a division of Random House, Inc.

Lorna Dee Cervantes, "The Refugee Ship" by Lorna Dee Cervantes is reprinted with permission from the publisher of A DECADE OF HISPANIC LITERATURE (Houston: Arte Publico Press—University of Houston, 1982). "Uncle's First Rabbit" from EMPLUMADA by Lorna Dee Cervantes. Copyright © 1981. Reprinted by permission of the University of Pittsburgh Press.

Anton Chekhov, "Lady with Lapdog" from THE PORTABLE CHEKHOV by Anton Chekhov, edited by Avrahm Yarmolinsky, copyright © 1947, © 1968 by Viking Penguin, Inc. Renewed © 1975 by Avrahm Yarmolinsky. Used by permission of Viking Penguin, a division of Penguin Putnam, Inc.

Sandra Cisneros, "The Monkey Garden" and "My Name" from THE HOUSE ON MANGO STREET. Copyright © 1984 by Sandra Cisneros. Published by Vintage Books, a division of Random House, Inc., and in hardcover by Alfred A. Knopf in 1994. Reprinted by permission of Susan Bergholz Literary Services, New York. All rights reserved.

Grant Clarke and Harry Akst, from "Am I Blue" by Grant Clarke and Harry Akst. Copyright 1929 (renewed) Warner Bros. Inc. All rights reserved. Used by permission of Warner Bros. Publications U.S., Inc., Miami, FL 33014.

Hart Crane, "Episode of Hands" by Marc Simon, editor, from COMPLETE POEMS OF HART CRANE by Hart Crane, edited by Marc Simon. Copyright 1933, © 1958, 1966 by Liveright Publishing Corporation. Copyright © 1986 by Marc Simon. Used by permission of Liveright Publishing Corporation.

Countee Cullen, "Incident" by Countee Cullen. Reprinted by permission of GRM ASSOCIATES, INC., Agents for the Estate of Ida M. Cullen. From the book COLOR by Countee Cullen. Copyright © 1925 by Harper & Brother; copyright renewed 1953 by Ida M. Cullen.

E. E. Cummings, "somewhere i have never travelled, gladly beyond." Copyright 1931, © 1959, 1991 by the Trustees for the E. E. Cummings Trust. Copyright © 1979 by George James Firmage, from COMPLETE POEMS: 1904–1962 by E. E. Cummings, edited by George J. Firmage. Used by permission of Liveright Publishing Corporation.

Edwidge Danticat, from KRIK? KRAK! by Edwidge Danticat. Soho, NY. Vintage, NY. Reprinted by permission.

Simone De Beauvoir, "Woman as Other" from THE SECOND SEX by Simone De Beauvoir, translated by H. M. Parshley, copyright © 1952 and renewed 1980 by Alfred A. Knopf, Inc. Used by permission of Alfred A. Knopf, a division of Random House, Inc.

Greg Delanty, "Leavetaking" by Greg Delanty from SOUTHWARD. Reprinted by permission of Louisiana State University Press.

Charlotte Delbo, "Prayer to the Living to Forgive Them for Being Alive" by Charlotte Delbo from AUSCHWITZ AND AFTER, pp. 229–231. Reprinted by permission of Yale University Press.

Junot Diaz, "Fiesta 1980" from DROWN by Junot Diaz, copyright © 1996 by Junot Diaz. Used by permission of Putnam Berkley, a division of Penguin Putnam, Inc.

Emily Dickinson, "My Life Had Stood . . ." and "I Heard a Fly Buzz—When I Died" by Emily Dickinson. Reprinted by permission of the publishers and the Trustees of Amherst College from THE POEMS OF EMILY DICKINSON, Thomas H. Johnson, ed., Cambridge, Mass.: The Belknap Press of Harvard University Press. Copyright © 1951, 1955, 1979 by the President and Fellows of Harvard College.

Rita Dove, "Adolescence I," "Adolescence II," "Adolescence III" from THE YELLOW HOUSE ON THE CORNER by Rita Dove. Carnegie Mellon University Press. Copyright © 1980 by Rita Dove. Reprinted by permission of the author.

T. S. Eliot, excerpt from "Burnt Norton" in FOUR QUARTETS by T. S. Eliot, copyright 1936 by Harcourt, Inc., and renewed 1964 by T. S. Eliot, reprinted by permission of the publisher.

David Elkind, from THE HURRIED CHILD by David Elkind. Copyright © 1988, 1981 by David Elkind. Reprinted by permission of Perseus Books Publishers, a member of Perseus Books, L.L.C.

Shusaku Endō, "The War Generation" by Shusaku Endō, translated by Van C. Gessel, from STAINED GLASS ELEGIES, copyright © 1959, 1965, 1969, 1973, 1979 by Shusaku Endō. English translation © 1984 Van C. Gessel. Reprinted by permission of New Directions Publishing Corp.

Louise Erdrich, "Indian Boarding School: The Runaways" from JACKLIGHT by Louise Erdrich, © 1984 by Louise Erdrich. Reprinted by permission of Henry Holt and Company, LLC.

Martin Espada, "The Sign in My Father's Hands" from IMAGINE THE ANGELS OF BREAD by Martin Espada. Copyright © 1996 by Martin Espada. Used by permission of W. W. Norton & Company, Inc.

G. Blakemore Evans, editor, THE RIVERSIDE SHAKESPEARE, Second Edition. Copyright © 1997 by Houghton Mifflin Company. Used with permission.

William Faulkner, "Barn Burning" from COLLECTED STORIES OF WILLIAM FAULKNER by William Faulkner. Copyright © 1950 by Random House, Inc. Used by permission of Random House, Inc.

Lynn C. Nikky Finney, "South Africa: When a Woman Is a Rock" by Nikky Finney. Copyright © 1995. Reprinted by permission of the author.

Dudley Fitts and Robert Fitzgerald, "Oedipus Rex" from SOPHOCLES, THE OEDIPUS CYCLE: AN ENGLISH VERSION by Dudley Fitts and Robert Fitzgerald, copyright © 1949 by Harcourt, Inc., and renewed 1977 by Cornelia Fitts and Robert Fitzgerald, reprinted by permission of the publisher. CAUTION: All rights, including professional, amateur, motion picture, recitation, lecturing, public reading, radio broadcasting, and television are strictly reserved. Inquiries on all rights should be addressed to Harcourt, Inc., Permissions Department, Orlando, FL 32887–6777.

Carolyn Forché, "The Memory of Elena" from THE COUNTRY BETWEEN US by Carolyn Forché. Copyright © 1981 by Carolyn Forché. Reprinted by permission of HarperCollins Publishers, Inc. "The Colonel" from THE COUNTRY BETWEEN US by Carolyn Forché. Copyright © 1981 by Carolyn Forché. Originally appeared in WOMEN'S INTERNATIONAL RESOURCE EXCHANGE. Reprinted by permission of HarperCollins Publishers, Inc. "Ourselves or Nothing" from THE COUNTRY BETWEEN US by Carolyn Forché. Copyright © 1981 by Carolyn Forché. Reprinted by permission of HarperCollins Publishers, Inc.

Robert Frost, "Birches" from THE POETRY OF ROBERT FROST edited by Edward Connery Lathem, © 1969 by Henry Holt & Co., LLC. Reprinted by permission of Henry Holt & Co., LLC.

Athol Fugard, from "MASTER HAROLD" . . . AND THE BOYS by Athol Fugard, copyright © 1982 by Athol Fugard. Used by permission of Alfred A. Knopf, a division of Random House, Inc.

Allen Ginsberg, "America" from COLLECTED POEMS 1947–1980 by Allen Ginsberg. Copyright © 1956, 1959 by Allen Ginsberg. Reprinted by permission of HarperCollins Publishers, Inc.

Nikki Giovanni, "Ego Tripping" from THE SELECTED POEMS OF NIKKI GIOVANNI by Nikki Giovanni. Compilation copyright © 1996 by Nikki Giovanni. Reprinted by permission of HarperCollins Publishers, Inc.

Susan Glaspell, TRIFLES by Susan Glaspell. Reprinted by permission. Copyright © 1951 by Walter H. Baker Co. For all rights contact: Baker's Plays, 100 Chauncy Street, Boston, MA 02111.

Nadine Gordimer, "Amnesty" from JUMP AND OTHER STORIES by Nadine Gordimer. Copyright © 1991 by Felix Licensing, B.V. Reprinted by permission of Farrar, Straus & Giroux, LLC.

Mary Gordon, "The Imagination of Disaster" by Mary Gordon. Copyright © by Mary Gordon. Reprinted by permission of the author.

Susan Griffin, "I Like to Think of Harriet Tubman" from LIKE THE IRIS OF AN EYE by Susan Griffin. Copyright © 1976 by Susan Griffin. Reprinted by permission of the author.

Lorraine Hansberry, from A RAISIN IN THE SUN by Lorraine Hansberry. Copyright © 1958 by Robert Nemiroff, as an unpublished work. Copyright © 1959, 1966, 1984 by Robert Nemiroff. Used by permission of Random House, Inc.

Joy Harjo, "For Anna Mae Aquash Whose Spirit Is Present Here and in the Dappled Stars" by Joy Harjo from IN MAD LOVE AND WAR. Reprinted by permission of Wesleyan University Press.

G. B. Harrison, "Hamlet" from SHAKESPEARE: THE COMPLETE WORKS by G. B. Harrison, copyright 1952 by Harcourt, Inc., and renewed 1980 by G. B. Harrison, reprinted by permission of the publisher.

Robert Hayden, "Those Winter Sundays" by Robert Hayden. Copyright © 1966 by Robert Hayden, from COLLECTED POEMS OF ROBERT HAYDEN by Robert Hayden, edited by Frederick Glaysher. Used by permission of Liveright Publishing Corporation.

Seamus Heaney, "Digging" from DEATH OF A NATURALIST by Seamus Heaney. Reprinted by permission of Faber and Faber.

Liliana Heker, "The Stolen Party" by Liliana Heker, translated by Alberto Manguel, copyright © 1982 by Liliana Heker. Translation copyright © 1985 by Alberto Manguel from OTHER FIRES: SHORT FICTION BY LATIN AMERICAN WOMEN edited by Alberto Manguel. Used by permission of Clarkson N. Potter, a division of Random House, Inc., and Westwood Creative Artists Ltd.

Ernest Hemingway, "Hills Like White Elephants" reprinted with permission of Scribner, a Division of Simon & Schuster, from MEN WITHOUT WOMEN by Ernest Hemingway. Copyright © 1927 by Charles Scribner's Sons. Copyright renewed 1955 by Ernest Hemingway.

Beth Henley, "Am I Blue?" by Beth Henley. Copyright © 1982 by Beth Henley. Reprinted by permission of The Gersh Agency.

Linda Hogan, "Heritage" from CALLING MYSELF HOME by Linda Hogan. Copyright © 1979 by Linda Hogan. Reprinted by permission of the author. Published by Greenfield Review Press.

bell hooks, from BONE BLACK by bell hooks, © 1996 by Gloria Watkins. Reprinted by permission of Henry Holt and Company, LLC.

Langston Hughes, "Let America Be America Again" from THE COLLECTED POEMS OF LANGSTON HUGHES by Langston Hughes, copyright © 1994 by The Estate of Langston Hughes. Used by permission of Alfred A. Knopf, a division of Random House, Inc. "Harlem" from THE COLLECTED POEMS OF LANGSTON HUGHES by Langston Hughes, copyright © 1994 by The Estate of Langston Hughes. Used by permission of Alfred A. Knopf, a division of Random House, Inc.

David Ives, "Sure Thing" from ALL IN THE TIMING by David Ives. Copyright © 1989. Reprinted by permission of the author.

Judith Emlyn Johnson, "Stone Olives" from THE ICE LIZARD POEMS by Judith Emlyn Johnson. Copyright © 1992 by Judith Emlyn Johnson. Reprinted by permission of The Sheep Meadow Press.

James Joyce, "Eveline" from DUBLINERS by James Joyce, copyright © 1916 by B. W. Heubsch. Definitive text copyright © 1967 by the Estate of James Joyce. Used by permission of Viking Penguin, a division of Penguin Putnam, Inc.

Jamaica Kincaid, "Girl" from AT THE BOTTOM OF THE RIVER by Jamaica Kincaid. Copyright © 1983 by Jamaica Kincaid. Reprinted by permission of Farrar, Straus and Giroux, LLC.

Martin Luther King, Jr., "Letter from Birmingham Jail" by Martin Luther King, Jr. Reprinted by arrangement with The Heirs to the Estate of Martin Luther King, Jr., c/o Writers House, Inc., as agent for the proprietor. Copyright © 1963 by Martin Luther King, Jr.; copyright renewed 1991 by Coretta Scott King.

Barbara Kingsolver, "Rose-Johnny" from HOMELAND AND OTHER STORIES by Barbara Kingsolver. Copyright © 1989 by Barbara Kingsolver. Reprinted by permission of HarperCollins Publishers, Inc.

Maxine Hong Kingston, "No Name Woman" from THE WOMAN WARRIOR by Maxine Hong Kingston, copyright © 1975, 1976 by Maxine Hong Kingston. Used by permission of Alfred A. Knopf, a division of Random House, Inc.

Etheridge Knight, "Hard Rock Returns to Prison from Hospital for the Criminal Insane" and "The Idea of Ancestry" from POEMS FROM PRISON by Etheridge Knight. Copyright © 1968 by Etheridge Knight. Reprinted by permission of Broadside Press.

William Severini Kowinski, "Kids in the Mall: Growing Up Controlled" from THE MALLING OF AMERICA by William Severini Kowinski. Copyright © 1985 by William Severini Kowinski. By permission of the author.

Maxine Kumin, "Making the Jam Without You." Copyright © 1970 by Maxine Kumin, from SELECTED POEMS 1960–1990 by Maxine Kumin. Used by permission of W. W. Norton & Company, Inc.

Jhumpa Lahiri, "The Third and Final Continent" from INTERPRETER OF MALADIES by Jhumpa Lahiri. Copyright © 1999 by Jhumpa Lahiri. Reprinted by permission of Houghton Mifflin Company. All rights reserved.

D. H. Lawrence, "Piano" by D. H. Lawrence from THE COMPLETE POEMS OF D. H. LAWRENCE by D. H. Lawrence, edited by V. de Sola Pinto & F. W. Roberts, copyright © 1964, 1971 by Angelo Ravagli and C. M. Weekley, Executors of the Estate of Frieda Lawrence Ravagli. Used by permission of Viking Penguin, a division of Penguin Putnam, Inc. "Tickets, Please" by D. H. Lawrence, copyright 1922 by Thomas Seltzer, Inc., renewal copyright 1950 by Frieda Lawrence, from COMPLETE SHORT STORIES OF D. H. LAWRENCE by D. H. Lawrence. Used by permission of Viking Penguin, a division of Penguin Putnam, Inc.

Li-Young Lee, "Persimmons" © 1986 by Li-Young Lee. Reprinted from ROSE by Li-Young Lee, with the permission of BOA Editions, Ltd.

Lyn Lifshin, "My Mother and the Bed," by Lyn Lifshin. Copyright © by Lyn Lifshin. Reprinted by permission of the author.

Audre Lorde, "The House of Yemanjá" and "Hanging Fire" from THE BLACK UNICORN by Audre Lorde. Copyright © 1978 by Audre Lorde. Used by permission of W. W. Norton & Company, Inc.

Manning Marble, "The Prism of Race" from BEYOND BLACK AND WHITE by Manning Marble. Copyright © 1995. Reprinted by permission of Verso, London.

Gabriel Garcia Marquez, "The Handsomest Drowned Man in the World" from LEAF STORM AND OTHER STORIES by Gabriel Garcia Marquez. Copyright © 1971 by Gabriel Garcia Marquez. Reprinted by permission of HarperCollins Publishers, Inc.

Bobbie Ann Mason, "Shiloh" from SHILOH AND OTHER STORIES by Bobbie Ann Mason. Reprinted by permission of International Creative Management, Inc. Copyright by Bobbie Ann Mason.

Edna St. Vincent Millay, "What lips my lips have kissed, and where, and why" by Edna St. Vincent Millay. From COLLECTED POEMS, HarperCollins. Copyright © 1923, 1951 by Edna St. Vincent Millay and Norma Millay Ellis. All rights reserved. Reprinted by permission of Elizabeth Barnett, literary executor.

Czeslaw Milosz, "American Ignorance of War" from THE CAPTIVE MIND by Czeslaw Milosz, translated by Jane Zielonko, copyright © 1951, 1953 by Czeslaw Milosz. Used by permission of Alfred A. Knopf, a division of Random House, Inc.

Janice Mirikitani, "Suicide Note" excerpted from SHREDDING SILENCE, copyright © 1987 by Janice Mirikitani. Reprinted by permission of Celestial Arts, P.O. Box 7123, Berkeley, CA 94707.

Pat Mora, "Elena" by Pat Mora is reprinted with permission from the publisher of CHANTS (Houston: Arte Publico Press—University of Houston, 1985).

Cherrie Moraga, "Loving in the War Years" from LOVING IN THE WAR YEARS by Cherrie Moraga. Copyright © 1983 by Cherrie Moraga. Reprinted by permission of South End Press.

Alberto Moravia, "La caccia (The Chase)" from UNA COSA E' UNA COSA by Alberto Moravia. Copyright © R.C.S. Libri Spa-Milano Bompiani 1967. Reprinted by permission of Rizzoli Corriere della Sera Libri.

Toni Morrison, "Nobel Prize Speech" by Toni Morrison from Nobel Lecture, The Nobel Foundation, December 7, 1993. Reprinted by permission of The Nobel Foundation.

Huda Naamani, "I Take You an Orange" from OPENING THE GATES: A CENTURY OF ARAB FEMINIST WRITING. Copyright © 1990 by Huda Naamani. Reprinted by permission of Indiana University Press.

Njabulo Ndebele, "Death of a Son" by Njabulo Ndebele. This story originally appeared in TRI-QUARTERLY, publication of Northwestern University. Reprinted by permission.

Pablo Neruda, "Tonight I Can Write" from SELECTED POEMS by Pablo Neruda, translated by W. S. Merwin, Nathaniel Tarn as editor and Jonathan Cape as publisher. Used by permission of The Random House Group Limited. "Sweetness Always" from EXTRAVAGARIA by Pablo Neruda, translated by Alastair Reid. Translation copyright © 1974 by Alastair Reid. Reprinted by permission of Farrar, Straus and Giroux, LLC.

Joyce Carol Oates, "Where Are You Going, Where Have You Been?" by Joyce Carol Oates published in THE WHEEL OF LOVE AND OTHER STORIES in 1970 by Vanguard. Copyright © 1970 by Ontario Review, Inc. Reprinted by permission of John Hawkins & Associates, Inc.

Tim O'Brien, "The Things They Carried" from THE THINGS THEY CARRIED by Tim O'Brien. Copyright © 1990 by Tim O'Brien. Reprinted by permission of Houghton Mifflin Company. All rights reserved.

Flannery O'Connor, "A Good Man Is Hard to Find" from A GOOD MAN IS HARD TO FIND AND OTHER STORIES, copyright 1953 by Flannery O'Connor and renewed 1981 by Regina O'Connor; reprinted by permission of Harcourt, Inc.

Mary Oliver, "Ghosts" from AMERICAN PRIMITIVE by Mary Oliver. Copyright © 1983 by Mary Oliver; first appeared in National Forum. By permission of Little, Brown and Company, Inc.

Tillie Olsen, "I Stand Here Ironing," copyright © 1956, 1957, 1960, 1961 by Tillie Olsen, from TELL ME A RIDDLE by Tillie Olsen, introduction by John Leonard. Used by permission of Dell Publishing, a division of Random House, Inc.

Simon Ortiz, "My Father's Song" by Simon Ortiz. Copyright © by Simon Ortiz. Reprinted by permission of the author.

Wilfred Owen, "Dulce et Decorum Est" by Wilfred Owen from THE COLLECTED POEMS OF WILFRED OWEN, copyright © 1963 by Chatto & Windus, Ltd. Reprinted by permission of New Directions Publishing Corp.

Cynthia Ozick, "The Shawl" from THE SHAWL by Cynthia Ozick, copyright © 1980, 1983 by Cynthia Ozick. Used by permission of Alfred A. Knopf, a division of Random House, Inc.

Octavio Paz, "My Life with the Wave" by Octavio Paz, translated by Eliot Weinberger, from EAGLE OR SUN?, copyright © 1976 by Octavio Paz and Eliot Weinberger. Reprinted by permission of New Directions Publishing Corp.

Marge Piercy, "To have without holding" from THE MOON IS ALWAYS FEMALE by Marge Piercy. Copyright © 1980 by Marge Piercy. Used by permission of Alfred A. Knopf, a division of Random House, Inc.

Luigi Pirandello, "War" by Luigi Pirandello. Reprinted by permission of the Pirandello Estate and Toby Cole, Agent.

Sylvia Plath, "Fever 103" from ARIEL by Sylvia Plath. Copyright © 1963 by Ted Hughes. Reprinted by permission of HarperCollins Publishers, Inc. "Fever 103" originally appeared in *Poetry Magazine*. "Daddy" from ARIEL by Sylvia Plath. Copyright © 1963 by Ted Hughes. Reprinted by permission of HarperCollins Publishers, Inc. "Ariel" from ARIEL by Sylvia Plath. Copyright © 1965 by Ted Hughes. Copyright Renewed. Reprinted by permission of HarperCollins Publishers, Inc.

Plato, "The Allegory of the Cave" and "The Sexes" from THE SYMPOSIUM: THE COMPLETE DIALOGUES OF PLATO, translated by Michael Joyce and edited by Edith Hamilton. Copyright 1961 by Princeton University Press. Copyright renewed 1989. Reprinted by permission of Princeton University Press.

Katherine Anne Porter, "The Jilting of Granny Weatherall" from FLOWERING JUDAS AND OTHER STORIES, copyright © 1930 and renewed 1958 by Katherine Anne Porter, reprinted by permission of Harcourt, Inc.

Adrienne Rich, "Diving to the Wreck" from THE FACT OF A DOORFRAME: Poems Selected and New, 1950–1984 by Adrienne Rich. Copyright © 1984 by Adrienne Rich. Copyright © 1975, 1978 by W. W. Norton & Company, Inc. Copyright © 1981 by Adrienne Rich. Used by permission of W. W. Norton & Company. Poem 3 of "Contradictions: Tracking Poems" from YOUR NATIVE LAND, YOUR LIFE: Poems by Adrienne Rich. Copyright © 1986 by Adrienne Rich. Used by permission of W. W. Norton & Company, Inc.

Maria Rainer Rilke, "Sonnet 1" and "Sonnet 29" by Maria Rainer Rilke from SONNETS TO ORPHEUS, edited/translated by C. F. MacIntyre. Copyright © 1960 C. F. MacIntyre. Used with permission of University of California Press.

Edwin Arlington Robinson, "Eros Turannos" reprinted with the permission of Scribner, a Division of Simon & Schuster, Inc., from COLLECTED POEMS by Edwin Arlington Robinson. Copyright © 1916 by Edwin Arlington Robinson, copyright renewed 1944 by Ruth Nivison.

Theodore Roethke, "My Papa's Waltz" copyright © 1942 by Hearst Magazines, Inc. "The Waking" copyright © 1953 by Theodore Roethke, from COLLECTED POEMS OF THEODORE ROETHKE by Theodore Roethke. Used by permission of Doubleday, a division of Random House, Inc.

Wendy Rose, Three Thousand Dollar Death Song" from LOST COPPER by Wendy Rose. Copyright © 1980 by Wendy Rose. Reprinted by permission.

Liz Rosenberg, "In the End We Are All Light" by Liz Rosenberg, reprinted by permission of the author from her book of poetry, THE FIRE MUSIC.

Edward Said, "Reflections on Exile" by Edward Said as appeared in GRANTA 13, Autumn 1984. Copyright © 1984. Reprinted by permission of The Wylie Agency.

Mary Jo Salter, "Welcome to Hiroshima" from HENRY PURCELL IN JAPAN by Mary Jo Salter, copyright © 1984 by Mary Jo Salter. Used by permission of Alfred A. Knopf, a division of Random House, Inc.

Léopold-Sédar Senghor, "Nuit de Sine," reprinted by permission from NOCTURNES by Léopold-Sédar Senghor, translated by John Reed and Clive Wake, copyright © 1971. Third Press, Okpaku Communications, 222 Forest Avenue, New Rochelle, New York, 10804.

Anne Sexton, "The Moss of His Skin" from TO BEDLAM AND PART WAY BACK. Copyright © 1960 by Anne Sexton, renewed 1988 by Linda G. Sexton. Reprinted by permission of Houghton Mifflin Company. All rights reserved. "Little Girl, My Stringbean, My Lovely Woman" from LIVE OR DIE by Anne Sexton. Copyright © 1966 by Anne Sexton. Reprinted by permission of Houghton Mifflin Company. All rights reserved.

Ntozake Shange, "Sorry" reprinted with the permission of Scribner, a Division of Simon & Schuster, Inc., from FOR COLORED GIRLS WHO HAVE CONSIDERED SUICIDE WHEN THE RAINBOW IS ENUF by Ntozake Shange. Copyright © 1975, 1977 by Ntozake Shange.

Leslie Marmon Silko, "Yellow Woman" by Leslie Marmon Silko. Copyright © 1981. Reprinted by permission of The Wylie Agency.

Anna Deavere Smith, from TWILIGHT: LOS ANGELES 1992 by Anna Deavere Smith, copyright © 1994 by Anna Deavere Smith. Used by permission of Doubleday, a division of Random House, Inc.

William Snodgrass, "Heart's Needle" from HEART'S NEEDLE by W. D. Snodgrass, copyright © 1959 by William Snodgrass. Used by permission of Alfred A. Knopf, a division of Random House, Inc.

Gary Snyder, "The Bath" by Gary Snyder, from TURTLE ISLAND, copyright © 1974 by Gary Snyder. Reprinted by permission of New Directions Publishing Corp.

Cathy Song, "Heaven" from FRAMELESS WINDOWS, SQUARES OF LIGHT: Poems by Cathy Song. Copyright © 1988 by Cathy Song. Used by permission of W. W. Norton & Company, Inc. "Lost Sister" from PICTURE BRIDE by Cathy Song. Copyright © 1983 by and reprinted by permission of Yale University Press.

Gary Soto, "Black Hair" and "Oranges" by Gary Soto from NEW AND SELECTED POEMS by Gary Soto. Copyright © 1995. Reprinted by permission of Chronicle Books, San Francisco.

Wole Soyinka, "Telephone Conversation" by Wole Soyinka. Copyright © 1962, 1990 by Wole Soyinka. Reprinted by permission of Melanie Jackson Agency, L.L.C.

Gloria Steinem, "Ruth's Song" from OUTRAGEOUS ACTS AND EVERYDAY REBELLIONS by Gloria Steinem, © 1983 by Gloria Steinem, 1984 by East Toledo Productions, Inc., 1995 by Gloria Steinem. Reprinted by permission of Henry Holt and Company, LLC.

Wallace Stevens, "The Idea of Order at Key West" from THE COLLECTED POEMS OF WALLACE STEVENS by Wallace Stevens, copyright © 1954 by Wallace Stevens. Used by permission of Alfred A. Knopf, a division of Random House, Inc.

Wislawa Szymborska, "Hatred" from VIEW WITH A GRAIN OF SAND, copyright © 1993 by Wislawa Szymborska, English translation by Stanislaw Baranczak and Clare Cavanagh, copyright © 1995 by Harcourt, Inc., reprinted by permission of the publisher. "Could Have" and "The Century's Decline" from VIEW WITH A GRAIN OF SAND, copyright © 1993 by Wislawa Szymborska, English translation by Stanislaw Baranczak and Clare Cavanagh, copyright © 1995 by Harcourt, Inc., reprinted by permission of the publisher.

Amy Tan, "Scar" from THE JOY LUCK CLUB by Amy Tan, copyright © 1989 by Amy Tan. Used by permission of G. P. Putnam's Sons, a division of Penguin Putnam, Inc.

Dylan Thomas, "Do Not Go Gentle into That Good Night" and "Fern Hill" by Dylan Thomas, from THE POEMS OF DYLAN THOMAS, copyright 1945 by The Trustees for the Copyrights of Dylan Thomas. Reprinted by permission of New Directions Publishing Corp. and David Higham Associates.

Lewis Thomas, "The Medusa and the Snail," copyright © 1977 by Lewis Thomas, from THE MEDUSA AND THE SNAIL by Lewis Thomas. Used by permission of Viking Penguin, a division of Penguin Putnam, Inc.

Lao Tzu, "Weapons at Best (31)" from THE WAY OF LIFE by Lao Tzu, translated by Raymond B. Blakney, copyright © 1955 by Raymond B. Blakney, renewed © 1983 by Charles Philip Blakney. Used by permission of Dutton Signet, a division of Penguin Putnam, Inc.

Luisa Valenzuela, "I'm Your Horse in the Night" from OTHER WEAPONS by Luisa Valenzuela. Copyright © 1988 by Luisa Valenzuela. Reprinted by permission of Ediciones del Norte. "The Verb to Kill" from STRANGE THINGS HAPPEN HERE: TWENTY SIX SHORT STORIES AND A NOVEL by Luisa Valenzuela, copyright © 1975 by Ediciones de la Flor, English translation by Helen Lane, copyright © 1979 by Harcourt, Inc., reprinted by permission of Harcourt, Inc.

Kurt Vonnegut, Jr., "Harrison Bergeron" from WELCOME TO THE MONKEY HOUSE by Kurt Vonnegut, Jr., copyright © 1961 by Kurt Vonnegut, Jr. Used by permission of Dell Publishing, a division of Random House, Inc.

Diane Wakoski, "Wind Secrets" by Diane Wakoski. Copyright © 1988 by Diane Wakoski. Reprinted from EMERALD ICE: SELECTED POEMS 1962–1987 with the permission of Black Sparrow Press.

Derek Walcott, "A Far Cry from Africa" from COLLECTED POEMS: 1948–1984 by Derek Walcott. Copyright © 1986 by Derek Walcott. Reprinted by permission of Farrar, Straus and Giroux, LLC.

Alice Walker, "Am I Blue?" from LIVING BY THE WORD: SELECTED WRITINGS 1973–1987, copyright © 1986 by Alice Walker, reprinted by permission of Harcourt, Inc.

Margaret Walker, "Lineage" from THIS IS MY CENTURY, NEW & COLLECTED POEMS by Margaret Walker. Copyright © by Margaret Walker. Reprinted by permission of the author. Published by the University of Georgia Press, 1989.

Anna Lee Walters, "My Name Is 'I Am Living' " by Anna Lee Walters from "Worldview" in TALKING INDIAN: REFLECTIONS ON SURVIVAL AND WRITING. Copyright © 1992 by Anna Lee Walters. Reprinted by permission of Firebrand Books, Ithaca, New York.

Terry Tempest Williams, "The Wild Card" from AN UNSPOKEN HUNGER by Terry Tempest Williams. Copyright © 1994 by Terry Tempest Williams. Used by permission of Pantheon Books, a division of Random House, Inc.

William Carlos Williams, "The Red Wheelbarrow" by William Carlos Williams, from COLLECTED POEMS: 1909–1939, VOLUME I, copyright 1938 by New Directions Publishing Corp. Reprinted by permission of New Directions Publishing Corp. and Carcanet Press Limited.

Virginia Woolf, "Professions for Women" from THE DEATH OF THE MOTH AND OTHER ESSAYS by Virginia Woolf, copyright 1942 by Harcourt, Inc., and renewed 1970 by Marjorie T. Parsons, executrix, reprinted by permission of the publisher.

James Wright, "A Blessing" from THE BRANCH WILL NOT BREAK by James Wright. Reprinted by permission of Wesleyan University Press.

Wakako Yamauchi, "And the Soul Shall Dance" by Wakako Yamauchi. Borrowed with permission of Darhansoff and Verrill Literary Agency.

W. B. Yeats, "The Second Coming" reprinted with the permission of Scribner, a Division of Simon & Schuster from THE COLLECTED POEMS OF W. B. YEATS, Revised Second Edition edited by Richard J. Finneran. Copyright © 1924 by Macmillan Publishing Company, renewed 1952 by Bertha Georgie Yeats. "Sailing to Byzantium" reprinted with the permission of Scribner, a Division of Simon & Schuster from THE COLLECTED POEMS OF W. B. YEATS,

INDEX OF AUTHORS, TITLES, AND FIRST LINES OF POETRY

First lines of poetry are in italic.

SUBJECT INDEX